# LIVERPOOL DOCKERS

## A History of Rebellion and Betrayal

## Mike Carden

First published in 2022 by Carden Press Ltd, UK.

Paperback edition.

ISBN: 978-1-7396563-0-0

Edited by John Carden

Cover Design and Layout by John Carden

Carden Press
CardenPress@gmail.com

THIS BOOK IS DEDICATED

to the memory of MIKE CARDEN

20.02.1953 – 9.12.2021

*"Without contraries is no progression.*

*Attraction and Repulsion, Reason and Energy,*

*Love and Hate are necessary to Human existence."*

William Blake, The Marriage of Heaven and Hell (1790)

# Contents

# Editor's note

Throughout his life, Mike Carden kept meticulous records in the form of personal diaries, meeting notes, correspondence, and official minutes and documents, and he would catalogue pamphlets, flyers, posters, or anything else he felt held historical significance. This book is the culmination of over twelve years' work and draws upon the author's records, along with the personal archives of his contemporaries, official records, documentary films, and media coverage of the events from the time.

The original manuscript was close to one million words long. Following an initial edit by Matthew McKeown, Mike spent the next two years rewriting the book, and it was significantly consolidated and condensed. As part of this process, Mike read the entire book aloud to his wife Mary over the course of six weeks, making notes and changes as they went along. Mary said: *'it was very powerful to hear Mike reading the book aloud because he was speaking his own words. It brought back memories of the dispute and that time in our lives, and I feel privileged to have shared this experience with him.'* This extensive reworking means that the final product is well written and remarkably readable (in spite of its length), and Mike was rightly very proud of this achievement.

In February 2021, Mike was diagnosed with lung cancer. Whilst initially he responded relatively well to treatment, he had less energy to write and found it especially hard to maintain the concentration required for the complex task of editing a book. Having drafted the final section, Mike needed some support with restructuring and asked me to help. We sat together on the sofa in our Liverpool home and spent the best part of four days working for as long as his energy levels would allow. I am immensely grateful to have had the chance to work with Mike in this way, and to understand a little better his writing process, and to see another side of my father. The confidence with which Mike approached writing brings to mind a talented painter making big, sweeping brush strokes onto an empty canvas: *'Just let me get it down roughly first, John, and then I can see what we need to do next.'*

Mike spoke regularly about the book with his lifelong friend, and fellow shop steward, Tony Nelson. In one such conversation he explained to Tony that *'the book is all inclusive; it includes the voices of everyone who was a part of the dispute from all sides'*, however Tony disagreed: *'That's not true, Mike, because there is one person missing... you.'* Please bear in mind, therefore, that the author has underplayed his own significance in this history, as was always his way. I note this because Mike's personal experience is central to the fact that this history could be written at all. As a young man who left school with no qualifications, it was with the educational support of his trade union that Mike went on to gain a BA, an MA, and an MPhil. He decided early on to put his academic training to the service of his class, and not the betterment of his own standing; I doubt he would have considered doing anything else. He was fiercely intelligent, a critical thinker, and a wonderful writer – these were his gifts and his contribution.

To say that a work published posthumously is the author's "life's work" is cliché, however to some extent it is accurate in this case. The central theme of this book is related to the oligarchic tendencies of organisations as identified by Robert Michels in *Politcal Parties* (1911) and how this played out on the Liverpool docks. Mike wrote about this idea in his Masters degree, and it was the focus of his PhD Thesis. **Liverpool Dockers: A History of Rebellion and Betrayal** is the culmination of a lifetime of thought and reflection on this idea into a form with which Mike was truly happy.

Mike wanted his book to be as up-to-date as possible, and decided to include relevant contemporary events from 2021. By this time Mike had gone into hospital, but we discussed the points he wished to make, and I drafted the relevant paragraphs in keeping with the work we had done together. We reviewed these final additions in hospital, eventually finalising the manuscript together shortly before Mike died on 9 December 2021, aged 68.

## Technical Notes

In completing the final edit of the book, I have made a number of changes to the manuscript which I believe wholeheartedly would be in line with the author's wishes and that I hope gives the work greater coherence. Firstly, I have added two additional 'parts' so that the overall structure is clearer, bringing together the contextual chapters into the *Introduction* and moving the chapters concerning events after the end of the dispute into a separate *Aftermath and Legacy* part. The final chapter was originally much longer and featured a series of sub-sections, which I have separated into shorter chapters that are more in keeping with the rest of the book. I edited chapter titles to improve clarity and to shorten the more extravagant ones. In proofing, I have done my best to remove the vast majority of typos and errors (or at least make them consistent) and I am grateful for the help I received from family and friends in completing this mammoth task.

Mike's family are extremely grateful to Kathy Lewark for a kind donation in honour of her late husband, the civil rights activist and socialist, Jim Lewark. We are touched by the generosity of our dear friends Jack Heyman and Carol Canter, and their determination to see this important history published. We would like to thank Co-Director Mike Morris and the team at Writing on the Wall for their support in making this book possible. We would also like to thank Dave Sinclair and Andrew Testa for permission to use some of their wonderful photographs of the dispute.

John Carden
April 2022

# Foreword by
# Len McCluskey

My lifelong friend and comrade, Mike Carden, has succeeded in producing a unique and detailed history of the Liverpool dockers and the origins of an industrial dispute that began on the waterfront in Liverpool in September 1995 and concluded in the bleak winter of January 1998. He has attempted to allow the record of personal diaries, union minutes, official documents and individual statements of the time to speak for themselves. This approach to labour history has allowed the facts and reality of this bitter dispute to drive a powerful and philosophical narrative that evokes the story of an unofficial working-class struggle that won support from Australia to Japan, from West Coast and East Coast longshoremen in the USA to their Irish comrades in Dublin and Belfast and throughout Europe; but failed to generate support from their own union, and so many other official organisations that claimed to represent the interests of their class.

I had the pleasure to have worked alongside and known so many of the comrades mentioned in this book and in the late 1960s to the 1970s these men and women provided me with a set of trade union principles, a sense of working-class solidarity, that have set the compass and direction of my trade union values. The legacy and struggles of the Liverpool dockers, the numerous unofficial and official strikes I took part in have forged in me an unrelenting belief in supporting workers in struggle along with the fundamental axiom of never crossing a picket line.

'The trade union movement took a long time to gather itself after the defeats inflicted by the Thatcher government. Stripped of their confidence, unions became accommodationist – always looking to compromise rather than fight for the interests of their members – both in the industrial and political arenas. It was no coincidence that the period when this approach was most in vogue coincided with the rise of New Labour. But it was no coincidence, either, that the experience of workers being sold-out while Labour refused to lift a finger triggered a backlash. The historic shift to the left in the trade union movement was a direct result and laid the foundations for the political developments that followed.' (McCluskey:2021 pp.75-76)

Carden exposes the level of betrayal that the Liverpool dockers had to experience whilst they struggled to organise an *unofficial dispute on a local, national and global stage*. This history of Liverpool dock workers is, beyond doubt, a book that all trade unionists and socialists should have on their bookshelves. As Tony Benn said of this extraordinary workers' struggle, 'this dispute will be remembered in the history of the Labour Movement on the same scale and with the same honour as the Tolpuddle Martyrs and the Miners' Strike of 1984/85.' I can think of no better tribute.

Len McCluskey
UNITE General Secretary 2010 – 2021

# Acknowledgements

When I began work on the Liverpool docks in 1970, I had just been expelled from an Irish Christian Brothers school, leaving with no qualifications. It was my union, the Transport and General Workers Union, that offered me a second chance to learn through Jack Jones's Home Study Courses and numerous day-school classes. The T&G showed me another world of learning; one that was anchored in a political reality that I could readily understand. Now confident in my ability to learn, I felt empowered to take up Harold Wilson's Labour government's offer of access to an Open University course. I completed a Bachelor of Arts degree in the 1970s and gained a Masters Degree in Industrial Relations at Warwick University in the '90s before completing a Masters in Philosophy at Liverpool University; all the while still working on the docks. By the time of my dismissal in 1995, I had been on the docks for 25 years, the bulk of which I spent as a shop steward. During this period, I was fortunate enough to be elected to every rank-and-file constitutional committee of the union, including the General Executive Council in 1993, just two years prior to the conflict about which I now write. Like so many workers, I owe everything to my trade union, the Transport & General Workers' Union, for the history that I was able to live through, and the people that I am so proud to have learned so much from.

As a direct participant in this history, I have tried to avoid the use of the first-person singular which has proved difficult and may make the narrative seem a little disjointed at times. I have made use of my own diaries, minutes and documents going back to the 1970s, together with my own studies of the dock industry and the TGWU during the '80s and '90s. I have made extensive use of the magnificent archive created on *LabourNet* by Greg Dropkin and his colleagues, as well as the detailed diaries of dock shop steward, Kevin Robinson. Jack Heyman, the Oakland longshoreman, provided inspiration and guidance throughout the years that I worked on this history. In addition, many shop stewards and lay members were generous with their time, advice, documents and official union minutes. The work of Ken Loach, Jimmy McGovern, Irvine Welsh, Xavier Carniaux and Elisabeth Marliangeas of AMIP Paris, Daniel Sultan Artis Diffusion, Paris, Dave Cotterill, Monica Clua-Losada and Doreen McNally, from the Women of the Waterfront, have, along with the wonderful working-class histories of Harold Hikens, Eric Taplin, Frank Deegan, Bill Hunter and D.F. Wilson, provided an easy map to follow.

The dockers' archive is now kept in the Initiative Factory at the Community Advice Services Association (CASA) on Hope Street in Liverpool, where Tony Nelson and Terry

Teague allowed me access to all documents, audio tapes and video tapes from the dispute. The extraordinary photographs taken by Dave Sinclair from the start of the dispute in 1995 provide a graphic testimony to the iron, granite and soul carved into the faces of the Liverpool dockers and their families who never gave up in their struggle for justice. Andrew Testa has also been very generous in allowing me access to his archive of photographs. Nick Craske's photographs provide a wonderful insight into the men, women and children who took part in this dispute as well.

It would be impossible to name all those who supported and contributed to this history – the list is truly endless – and I apologise in advance if I have failed to respect their contribution to the events that follow. I am grateful to editor, Mathew McKeown, at the Liverpool Editing Company. I thank Mike Morris, at Writing on the Wall, for his advice. Sacked Liverpool dockworker, Ken Forsyth, worked on designs and layout for the book for which I am indebted. Finally, my thanks and gratitude go to Mary Collings, my partner, who took the time to allow me to read the manuscript aloud to her, providing a final opportunity for corrections, clarity and sense. Our sons John and Daniel were extraordinary in pushing this project forward, and John helped me with the editing of the final chapters.

Mike Carden, November 2021

# Author's Preface

The Liverpool dockers' dispute lasted from September 1995 to January 1998. It was a trade union struggle that involved a bitter conflict with local union officials, the leadership of the Transport and General Workers' Union (TWGU), the Trades Union Congress (TUC), the International Transport Workers' Federation (ITF) and Tony Blair's New Labour Party. As the trade union and labour movement sought to disconnect itself from their historic roots the dockers were portrayed as being locked in a form of trade unionism from another century – a class of workers that had long-faded into the mists of the past; like a lost memory of a history without relevance or meaning in modern times – a forgotten civilisation. From the 1980s onwards, the working-class and their communities had become identified as a political liability. They would be abandoned by New Labour and their trade union backers as both organisations evolved structures that diminished democracy and celebrated bureaucratic / managerialist control that continue to this day.

Many of those who took part in this struggle lost everything because they refused to cross a picket line; many would never work again. They upheld the basic trade union principle of solidarity, a principle of unity forged in the revolutionary glow of *new unionism* in the 1880s, which traced its traditions back to the People's Charter of 1838, the oath of the Tolpuddle Martyrs in 1834 and the Peterloo Massacre of 1819. In this book, I attempt to capture the iron and the soul of these exceptional working-class men and women who fought an industrial struggle that was organised on an epic scale and a global stage, only to be betrayed by the *official* trade union movement. In December 1996, after fifteen months in dispute, journalist Decca Aitkenhead, writing in the *Sunday Independent*, recorded one Liverpool docker's thoughts at the time:

> *The roots of the docks are so deep, they go down to the bowels of the Mersey. They don't pull up so easy… It's not a job, it's a part of our life. It's a culture. We made it that way. We were always fighting the conditions… When we were on the docks, we backed the journalists when they went out, we backed the printers, the miners, the seamen. Now there are so-called trade union members driving past that picket on the dock.'* [1]

On Saturday 26 September 2015, in a speech made at the 20th Anniversary of the Liverpool dock dispute, Len McCluskey, general secretary of Unite, and a former Liverpool dock worker himself, apologised for the union's betrayal of the dockers:

*'When the trade unions of the day sought to hide behind anti-trade union legislation as a reason not to act, the Liverpool dockers responded with the most impressive campaign imaginable, gaining support from every corner of the globe. The Liverpool dockers rejected the Thatcher anti-democratic, anti-worker creed. They rejected the onward march of casualisation, and by doing so, they showed the way forward for fighting-back trade unionism. The same spirit now is needed to reject the scourge of zero hours. They were, without doubt, ahead of their time. They were certainly way ahead of the leadership of the trade union movement of that time. So, let me say this, the leadership of the T&G betrayed the Liverpool dock workers. They themselves did not have the courage or the conviction that the dockers had. Had they had that conviction we would have won that struggle. And I stand before you today, as General Secretary of Unite, to apologise for that betrayal. I only wish I'd have been General Secretary then!' [2]*

On 24 September 1997, two years into the struggle, TGWU deputy general secretary, Jack Adams, told dock shop stewards in Transport House, Liverpool: 'I've never seen a dispute run like this in my life, and I am very proud to be part of it.' [3] The history that follows hopes to provide a record, an insight into the pride and dignity of a class and generation of workers that will never exist again. It has not been an easy undertaking given the inherent controversy of the subject and the ongoing effort by many to rewrite this history or erase its relevance. In this regard, I heed the words of the writer Thomas Flanagan, in his reflections on the Irish Rebellion of 1798: 'The menaces which we confronted, sporadic and unpredictable, enfolded themselves within the monotony of our days. But perhaps in this I am deluded by memory, that treacherous spy upon our past.' [4] With this advice in mind I have sought to use only primary sources, citing contemporaneous minutes, records and analysis of events as they happened, to form a chronological account of the working-class families who created this extraordinary history.

For over a century, waterfront confrontations pitted dock labourers against a triumvirate of opposing forces combining port employers, dock unions and the state. Inevitably, it was their establishment narrative that shaped and distorted the image of dock workers and their history. Liverpool dockers were characterised as 'unthinking beasts of burden' who, through their industrial militancy, proved that they sought only permanent 'conflict with the employer class.' At critical times Liverpool dockers were accused of undermining the 'war effort of the government'. [5] To tell the story of the Liverpool dockers it is important to reflect on the profound influence of their heritage whose roots can be traced back over many generations to the foulness of human chaos and the stench of quays and wharves that spoke of the insatiable greed of the capitalist class. Throughout the 1800s, the savage origins of Liverpool's emergent working-class imposed a unique character upon an impoverished mass of hardened labourers, who would themselves shape the construction and human existence of the city over the following two hundred years.

In its hunger for labour, the port's dangerous and unforgiving casual work fell predominantly to Irish immigrants, whose own history and experiences shifted from the barren fields of their homeland to the wretched *industrial poverty* of Liverpool docks. Casual dock work, as local labour historian, Eric Taplin observed, ensured: 'The Liverpool dock labourer was… condemned to a lifestyle that encouraged fecklessness, corruption and brutality.' [6] It would be work grasped by this first flow of Irish immigrants and passed from one generation to the next. According to E. P. Thompson: 'Their generosity and impulsiveness was easily imposed upon; it is literally true that they "would die… before they would be beat".' [7] An observer at Liverpool docks noted the manner in which oats were loaded onto a vessel:

> 'These men (chiefly Irishmen) received the full sacks as they were lowered by the crane off the hitch on their shoulders and carried them across the road. They pursued their heavy task during the working hours of a summer's day at a uniform, unremitting pace, a trot of at least five miles an hour, the distance from the vessel to the storehouse being fully fifty yards…' [8]

Thomas Carden sold his labour to the twice-daily hire for random casual work on Liverpool docks in 1820, after leaving County Sligo passing through the harbour at Ballina, with his young wife, Bridget Swift, on the long march down towards Dublin. They were soon deported back to Ireland for vagrancy under the Poor Laws, but, like so many of their compatriots, they returned to Liverpool's Clarence Dock almost immediately. [9] Edward Rushton, the Liverpool-born poet, radical abolitionist and founder of the Liverpool Blind School on the city centre's Hardman Street in 1791 (which became the Merseyside Trade Union and Unemployed Resource Centre almost two centuries later), wrote to the Home Secretary on 2 April 1849, describing how the exodus from Ireland to Liverpool consisted of: 'paupers, half naked and starving, landed for the most part during the winter, and becoming immediately on landing applicants for parochial relief.' [10] Too poor to ship-out to Canada or New York, or too weak from the ravages of the Irish famine, it was this human cargo, discharged onto the wharf of the Clarence Dock, that became the primary source of labour for the rapidly expanding port economy of Liverpool. [11] In the slum courts and cellars clustered around Liverpool's waterfront, on Kitchen Street, just off Jamaica Street, Thomas Carden's son, John, was born in 1840, and he would go on to join his father on the docks as a casual labourer. My grandfather, also John Carden, was born in 1889, the year of the great labour upheavals, and he, too, followed the well-worn cobbles to the docks, where he was killed on the quayside after being 'accidently knocked down by a sling of timber on 25 May 1933,' aged 44. [12] His son, my father, Felix (Joe) Carden, born in 1922, also withstood the twice-daily hires on the docks until he died aged 52 in 1974.

This Irish legacy flowed through the veins of the majority of men and women who worked on Liverpool docks. Their existence was defined by the omnipresence of the past and a shared history that helped connect and shape each generation of dock labourers with a world view inherited from their ancestors. These 'men of few words', in their frayed shirts and black shiny ties, flat caps, boots and threadbare *Crombie* overcoats, became an indomitable force. They had a quiet dignity about them. The conditions forced upon the first seam of dockers in the late nineteenth and early twentieth century was a ruthless world of misrule, in which: 'the young, strong, single man unencumbered by family ties might survive, but the married man or those with dependents was less fortunate.':

*'Age and declining strength brought increasing fears of future insecurity… These were forbidding prospects. Though dismissed with bravado, the risk of accident was high. There was enough disfigurement, disablement and death to make even the most carefree pause from time to time. Death or disability could lead to the total impoverishment of the family. Not surprisingly, dock labourers secured a reputation for hard living. Petty corruption was widespread. Many foremen exercised a tyranny over the men. Religious discrimination in the selection of men was trivial compared to the bribery of taking a portion of a man's income either directly or in drink or worse… Only the most frugal or thrifty could hope to avoid the clutches of those who lived parasitically upon the poverty and deprivation of dockland.'* [13]

These men and their families came from backgrounds that bred strong sectoral loyalties that would often degenerate into fierce conflicts based upon the most remote connections, from religion to union branch autonomy. [14] These factors imposed either a casual or militantly loyal attitude towards trade union membership in these early days. It was a closed world that could bring out the best and worst in people; one in which those existing beyond the colossal, foreboding walls of the dock estate were outsiders. Frank Deegan's father came to Liverpool from Portlaoise, Ireland, in 1894, aged 17; he took work as a casual dock labourer. Frank was one of 11 children (six daughters and five sons, with three of the boys dying in infancy), and his story epitomises that of so many noble sons and daughters of Liverpool. Writing in the *Irish Post* in 1986, Tony Birtill recorded how the poverty and unemployment of those years on the docks led Frank, along with many others, to join the Communist Party. According to Frank Deegan: 'The docks and Bootle branches of the Communist Party were nearly all Liverpool Irish,' giving a voice to generations of rank-and-file leaders, such as Leo McGree, Joe Byrne, Albert McCabe, Alec McKechnie and so many more. In the docks area, the working-class community was often 75% Irish and they were great rebels.' [15] Frank Deegan fought against fascism when Oswald Mosely and William Joyce held a meeting at the Liverpool Stadium in 1936. The Stadium was a regular meeting place for Liverpool dockers up until the 1970s. The anti-fascists that day were led by another young dock worker, James 'Jack' Larkin Jones, named after James Larkin, the Irish revolutionary who 'roared out of the slums in Combermere Street, Liverpool, in 1876.' [16] Jones would become general secretary of the Transport and General Workers' Union in 1968. [17] These events and experiences forged the solidarity and lifeblood of a trade unionism unique to Liverpool dockers. They had little trust in those not from their world, they rebelled against authority and disliked being told what to do by either the state, employer or union. A far cry from the 'unthinking beasts of burden', long discarded by the Labour Movement and New Labour, these dockers and their families would 'rise like lions.' [18]

This book is a celebration of rank-and-file trade unionism, of the inspirational Liverpool dockers and their families, and all that I have learned from them and all that we can still learn from working-class communities to this day. [19]

# PART ONE:
## Introduction

# 1
# Liverpool and the
# 'Liverpool Way'

*'Almost all of us made the decision to stand up for the principles handed down to us and renewed throughout our own working lives.'* ~ *Jimmy Nolan\**

In February 1996, over fifty rank-and-file dockers representing fifteen countries travelled over oceans and seas, from Ireland, Le Havre, Canada, Australia, Aarhus, Oakland and Gothenburg, to organise direct action in support of Liverpool dock workers. They gathered at Transport House, the headquarters of the Transport and General Workers' Union. This building stood on a hill overlooking the sublime architecture of a gently sloping William Brown Street, not far from the site where the first union hall had been built on Christian Street in the early 20th century. As delegates were greeted by the Liverpool dockers and the Women of the Waterfront on the steps of the union's district office, some gazed to their left, towards St George's Hall, as it rose against a red horizon. Ahead of them the magnificent Central Library, the Liverpool World Museum, the Walker Art Gallery and, immediately in front of them, the County Sessions House which, in 1995, was the home of Liverpool's Labour History Museum. These towering monuments were the cultural gems of the city, and that day some of the visiting dockers, who had never been to Liverpool before, may have thought that the streets facing them were like those of Ancient Rome, Greece or Byzantium. Liverpool was no ordinary harbour town. This part of the city-centre united high art architecture with sweeping granite curves of sublime neoclassical forms that housed the culture of a global port city which would become a UNESCO World Heritage Site in 2004 (withdrawn in 2021).

However, as with Rome and Greece, the original wealth of this great port city, the money that paid for such magnificent architecture, came from Liverpool's trade in slavery

---

\* LabourNet (18 November 1997) http://www.labournet.net/docks2/9711/Robert.htm

that ran from the 15th to the 19th century. Eric Lynch, the trade union activist and creator of Liverpool's Slavery History Tour, tells visitors: 'If you don't know where you came from, you can't know where you are going. This aphorism, pertinent to individuals, is also relevant to cities.' [1] It was where the working-class of this great port city came from, where they set sail from and set sail to, that shaped and determined its history to the present day. According to Ramsay Muir, a local historian, 'It was the slave trade that raised Liverpool from a struggling port to be one of the richest and most prosperous trading centres in the world.' [2] Herman Melville, recorded on his first sailing to the city in 1839, that a local minister informed him: 'The whole city was built up by the blood of the poor Africans.' [3] By the 18th century, Liverpool's maritime history was, in the words of another local historian, Michael Macilwee: 'Split between Greenland whaling ventures, slavery and privateering. None of these enterprises were for the faint-hearted. Any town teeming with fierce privateersmen, inhuman slavers, reckless merchantmen and violent men-of-war's men was bound to produce a tough, ruthless and bloodthirsty populace. Even children were brought up in a culture of grasping violence.' [4]

Liverpool's burgeoning population of human labour understood the power and political significance of the industry that they were to be involved in on the docks and in the building of the city's expansive centre. The pre-eminence and immortality of the new civic buildings that they came to build were intended to be eternal monuments to the great and the good of Victorian capitalism, but they would be captured and occupied by the people; by barefoot children, Liverpool's 'street urchins', trade unionists, revolutionaries and all who would campaign and fight for justice in the future life of this brutal harbour town. [5] The abject poverty of the slum cellars and courts in which these immigrants co-existed rubbed against the wealth and opulence of the *nouveau riche*, who sought to buy legitimacy and respect whilst the working-class sowed the seeds of resentment, rebellion and revolution. This enduring conflict between rich and poor, power and privilege, would always have deep roots in Liverpool and, in the decades to come, whenever the people of the city rose up or reeled through tragedy or celebration, they would gather on the steps of St George's Plateau dwarfed by giant Corinthian columns. Political demonstrations and trade union rallies would take place on the edge of the city, against the backdrop of the black marble water of the River Mersey, where the Port of Liverpool Building, Cunard Building and the Royal Liver Building would eventually provide other epic locations for their incessant rebellions.

Liverpool absorbed a working-class diaspora of poor Irish, Welsh and Scottish immigrants that clustered alongside Britain's oldest African and Afro-Caribbean communities. This force of humanity existed amidst the daily influx of thousands of sailors from faraway lands, carried over seas by an armada of sail and steam. In 1845 alone, some 20,521 ships docked alongside berths thundering with the clash of coal, steel and smoke, while horses' hooves hammered and sparked incessantly upon the cobbled streets of this bustling, intolerant port. [6] Liverpool had, by this time, become the centre of Europe's largest Chinese community, many of whom had sailed with the Alfred Holt & Company (Blue Funnel Line), who had established the first commercial trade with China. As local historian Lynn Bateman noted, 'the first Chinese people to make their home here were sailors who had been forced to work on ships against their will.' [7]

# 1
## LIVERPOOL AND THE 'LIVERPOOL WAY'

Of all the teeming humanity that laboured to carve out an existence on the banks of the Mersey, those of Irish descent remained by far the largest section of the immigrant population. The Great Famine of the 1840s, *An Gorta Mor*, an Irish holocaust in which more than a million perished, fuelled mass migration that saw some two million leave Ireland for America, Canada or beyond between 1845-1849, with most passing through Liverpool on the way. Many arrived at the Clarence Dock in such a pitiful state that they could not go any further. Disorientated, starving and penniless, and in many cases seriously ill, the Irish took shelter where they could in the cellars and courts of the dockland area. There, they fell prey to an industry of thieves and hustlers. Irish historian, John Kelly, says of Liverpool at this time:

> *'In the 1830s and 1840s, the first sea that two out of every three Irish emigrants crossed was the Irish sea, an expanse of grey-blue light embroidered with hundreds of frothy white ship wakes, most leading to and from the mouth of the Mersey, entrance to the great bazaar of the Victorian world economy: Liverpool. The 'bully of the litter' of eighteenth-century English port cities, Liverpool was as clever as she was amoral. Through the American wars and the French wars, through slave revolts and slave suppressions, through the Rights of Man and the Declaration of Independence, Liverpool had grown steadily wealthier on the high-end vices of the white man: African slaves, sugar and tobacco.' [8]*

Liverpool was not a city that produced goods beyond the needs of the shipping industry. Casual employment on the docks, construction sites or canals did not mirror the *security* of factory life and the space, between jobs, was filled with idleness, which in turn was filled with drink, violence and criminality. [9] The men and women who poured daily into the city would be often directed by organised gangs to overcrowded lodging houses. [10] Some alternative to these slum dwellings could be found in the Seamen's Missions, Hardman House, the Sailors' Home in Canning Place, the Liverpool Seamen's Mission in Seaforth or the Stella Maris in Bootle. [11] But it was the desperate filth and overcrowding of court and cellar dwellings that sold a mean floor for Liverpool's exponential immigrant working class. These black airless cesspits ran along the river from Vauxhall Road and Scotland Road, rolling up the hill towards Toxteth and the crossroads of Jamaica Street and Grafton Street, where the West Indies met Dublin; where the oppression of slavery met that of the oppression of the Irish people. [12] The dark slum prisons of overcrowded courts and cellars erected around the harbour were the result of property investments made by the profiteers of slavery. It was they who speculated on the poverty of so many migrant families to turn a profit on their typhus-ridden slums. Businessmen and merchants, such as John Yates & Company and Foster Cunliffe & Sons, were slave traders who invested the fortunes they had made from slavery into the building of these courts and cellars. They had strong reserves of capital following the Abolition of the Slave Trade Act in 1807, and slum courts and cellar dwellings offered a logical transition from the slave boats, allowing for similar cruelty in the matter of providing the minimum amount of dwelling space for the largest number of human beings so as to maximise profits. [13] The same slave traders were to receive over £20 million compensation for their loss of 'business'; this debt to the UK taxpayer was finally paid off in 2015. [14]

Illegal drinking dens and street gambling often provided the only distractions from the daily grind of poverty and hunger. These brightly lit, warm gin palaces became the living rooms of the community as they moved from one street-distraction to the next. One city engineer's plan for Blundell Street recorded that five public houses existed on the street, and with so many drinking establishments in these slum areas, drunkenness, fighting and crime were everyday realities. Thomas Burke, the Irish Nationalist Councillor for the Vauxhall Ward, noted at the time that, 'the curse of drink in Liverpool is one of the results of casual labour.' [15] The wretchedness recorded by contemporary observers survive in the deeds for the old Liverpool Corporation, through the work of I.C. Taylor and Dr William Duncan, as well as in Friedrich Engels's *Condition of the Working Class in England*, written between 1842-1845. [16] Dr Duncan, who was to become Liverpool's first medical officer of health, declared, 'Liverpool is the most unhealthy town in England.' [17] In 1863, Liverpool's second medical officer of health, Dr Trench, attributed the ebb and flow of disease that killed and maimed so many families to:

> *The number of poor especially of Irish and other destitute immigrants promiscuously collected in certain squalid localities; filth and penury pent up in airless dwellings, frequent changes of residence, scattering and resewing thereby the seeds of infectious diseases, the crowding together of many families in single houses… the preponderance of narrow ill-ventilated courts and alleys, the construction and position of middens and cesspools.' [18]*

Dock labourer, Thomas Carden and his descendants, like so many other dock workers and their extended families, spent more than one hundred years in the same courts and cellars that smothered the dockside streets on the south and north side of the city, lodging at 50 and 10 Court 5 on Kitchen Street, before later moving to 14 Prince Alfred Cottages on Upper Frederick Street. All of his male descendants would work on the docks until the 1995 dispute brought an abrupt end to this tradition. [19] On my mother's side, dock labourer, Martin Cloherty and his family left Ireland in the 1800s and took apartments at 23 Dwerryhouse Street, near Kitchen Street, just a few feet from where the stanchions of the future overhead dockland railway would be raised in 1893. These were the life stories of so many port workers, who fought daily struggles to carve out an existence against the futility and chaos of this shambolic city. In the 1900s, some of the courts and cellars had been cleared away when two Cloherty families moved into new two-up two-down houses at 32 and 10 Fisher Street situated between the Devil and Exciseman public house (now known as the Coburg), the Grapes Inn and the battlement architecture of the Robert Cain brewery, built next to the Kardomah Tea factory in 1875. [20] The Cloherty family lived on Fisher Street, a few feet from the south-end docks, until the late 1960s. [21]

The port of Liverpool dominated European emigration routes to the United States of America. What the tides brought in, they then swept out through the vast shipping lanes of the Atlantic Ocean. Magnificent liners set their compass towards the Pier Head. This was the point from which Liverpool looked out at the world and its gaze was returned with imported goods, ideas and a lasting diaspora of cultural influences. In 1828, across the river in Birkenhead, workers at Cammell Laird began building the ships that would power the burgeoning shipping industry, and over the next century Liverpool firmly established itself as a city that traded on the seas, and it was via this passageway to the world that its citizens' lives and attitudes were imported. [22] It was a legacy defined by the ebb and flow of the river that connected Liverpool to many other *edgy port cities* boasting a diverse range of urban contexts, from New York to Marseille and New Orleans. [23] John Lennon would speak of the profound influence that growing up in a port city had on him:

> *'Apart from meeting Yoko, the biggest [influence] of my life was hearing rock 'n' roll. Liverpool was a port where there were many black people and they still have the slave rings on the front of the docks there. But one thing about being a port is that it's usually a bit hipper… The music — the sailors would bring it in. We were hearing old funky blues in Liverpool that people across Britain or Europe had never even heard of because they didn't know about them.' [24]*

Alternative cultures swept through the living and breathing tumult of quaysides that unloaded an array of human cargo and languages onto noisy, dangerous streets, where the sailors all came in. And these cultures bleached the streets with a vibrancy of colour, confidence and attitude that would be imitated and reinvented by the generations that followed, amalgamating this chaotic mix into a single culture, the *Liverpool Way* - a recipe for survival. Once the great sail and steam vessels had been guided through complex shipping lanes and a narrow lock system by the Liverpool pilots, the first human point of contact for ships dropping anchor would always be dock labourers who gathered at the gates or in the pens awaiting the twice daily hire for work. By the end of the nineteenth century, dockers traditionally went to one, or a small group of stands where, according to Taplin:

> *'…regular men would be well known by the putter-on, and the experienced, trusted men would normally secure work. At any given stand the men would be in two groups: the regular men, the casuals, and the fringe element of totally unknown or irregular men, the 'casual casuals' as they were called. It was this latter group who secured work only if the supply of regular men was exhausted… By the 1890s, if not earlier, the system had become more refined at the north end. The large steamship companies issued numbered tallies to their regular and trusted employees… from 1890 the National Union of Dock Labourers (NUDL) was recognised by most of the firms at that end of the docks and union men were taken on before non-union men. A union delegate attended all the stands, the men displaying their union badge or button. Men congregated in two distinct groups, union and non-union men, and the latter would be taken on only when all union members had been employed, although once taken on union badges had to be removed from the lapel. [25]*

In 1890, Edward McHugh, one of the founders of the National Union of Dock Labourers in Liverpool and Birkenhead docks, wanted to impress upon the diverse loyalties of the dockers:

*'...that the wearing of the [union] badge is not only an essential duty to yourselves and your fellow working men but... it is a badge of nobility... the only sign a working man can show that he wishes to better his own condition.' [26]*

Once the bosses' tallies and the trade union badge had done their work for the twice-daily degradation of casual hire to be completed, these dockers climbed aboard to work the steam winches on deck and operate huge quayside cranes with their busy hooks, as holdsmen scurried down into the bowels of ships' hatches to unlock covered cargoes as stevedores prepared other ships for loading. Communicating through screamed orders and hand signals, shouted threats and curses, this was a job in which only the hardest and the strongest survived. Rope-slings and nets bursting with animal hides, bags of sugar, salt, asbestos, limbux and all manner of produce flew back and forth, with no thought of risk or danger. Porters dashed along the quays beneath the smog of steam and smoke, into the sheds and up in the lofts with hand trucks – or later, battery-powered bogies – ready to run the cargo from the stage-end to their allotted stows on open quays or inside covered sheds. And, in the long winter months, if men stood they would always ensure that a block of wood insulated their feet from the cold steel of the ship or the frozen cobbles of the quay. All this human labour was conducted in the shadows of huge vessels, enormous sheds and gigantic silos; a colossal architecture of steel and cement that hung from the skyline above the monumental walls of the dock estate. Walls that kept the eyes of the city away from their cold-hearted endeavours and daily industrial struggles. [27]

These men and women, with their hard Gaelic language and brogue, which evolved to determine an equally hard *Scouse* accent, would shape the perceptions of the social and political world that they not only traded with, but also existed in. These frontiersmen of Liverpool embraced a vast scope of humanity, of new arrivals and seafarers that ebbed and flowed against them, drank and fought in their pubs and made this harbour town their home. Doreen McNally, who was to become one of the founder members of the Women of the Waterfront in 1995, could trace her family back to the earliest memories of the Liverpool docks, and she recalled: 'The docks was the city. It was the lifeblood; it was the pulse – it was everything. In every other house, the dad was a docker. There were thousands of men on the docks. There were always people walking or on bikes, buses full – it was noisy, it was loud and just busy, busy, busy.' [28] Liverpool was the gateway to the British Empire, as 'over 25,000 seamen passed through the city at any one time.' [29] So it was that this rich human canvas rose and fell on the winds and ocean waves that crashed against the city's shores. Tony Lane, a local labour historian, referred to Liverpool as, 'The City of the Sea.' [30]

To survive in these conditions, the people of Liverpool had to develop a collective confidence, resilience and aggression; a *hardness* that empowered them to refuse to be told what to do or when to give up by employers, trade unions or the state. [31] This resolute, close-knit approach could manifest itself as anything from collective opposition to collective defiance, to open rebellion. In August 1911, it would lead to revolt by the working-class of Liverpool on what became known as both 'Bloody Sunday' and 'Red Sunday,' as Winston Churchill directed gunboats to the River Mersey to take aim at the city as a means of putting an end to a general transport strike. A month later, the city was denounced as, 'a nightmare of civilization... The most criminal, the most drunken, the most lawless city in the United

Kingdom.' [32] Merseyside Police displayed their shared militant culture with a strike of their own in 1919 over a number of issues including the fact that they were being paid less than Liverpool dockers. [33] For Jim Allen, the playwright who for many years worked alongside Ken Loach, such events were proof enough of the revolutionary potential in the way Liverpool people articulated their world view. To Allen, this city was 'the battleground of Britain,' leading him to assert that: 'If a revolution was to start anywhere, it would start in Liverpool.' [34]

The immigrants who stayed and made their homes in Liverpool were submerged in the swirling pool of life that was creating a unique city with its own language, its own exceedingly rare accent, *the craic* and all its abundant hospitality. They had a humour and generosity of spirit that were counterbalanced by an all-encompassing brand of sarcasm and cynicism, whose contrary nature was expressed most vociferously in their pubs, in their two cathedrals and football grounds. [35] This future birthplace of *The Beatles* and *Merseybeat* had a need to build two cathedrals alongside the country's first mosque, established in 1887 by a leading member of the 1911 Liverpool strike committee, William Henry 'Abdullah' Quilliam, who converted to Islam during a period of residence in Morocco. [36] Liverpool also built the tallest Chinese Arch outside of mainland China, with the aid of craftsmen from its twin city, Shanghai. The people of Liverpool have always had their paradoxes, but these could be observed, according to one journalist, as connected or epitomised by the plight and actions of its dockers:

> *'Its people are survivors, including the famous dockers. Their wit, wisdom and legend live on. The dockers are as much a part of Liverpool as the Liver Birds, the football teams, the comedians, The Beatles. It has been said that the dockers made great soldiers in World War I and World War II because they were the type of people you wanted in the trenches with you. They were instilled with a sense of duty, loyalty, camaraderie – all qualities passed on from father to son and generation to generation. When industrial strike action was called for, they were usually the first out and the last back. Dockers wives, too, were strong, and despite hardships to their own families they stood by their men.' [37]*

Ken Loach, the acclaimed film director and political activist, described Liverpool as a city: 'full of very articulate, thoughtful people and it's always a joy to be there. I always feel connected because the people make you feel welcome.' [38] Writing in 2012, another observer brought together the broad sweep of social and political upheavals that connect the contradictory and radical ways in which *Scousers* confront the world that they exist in; ways that challenge and reject, oppose and fight the status quo irrespective of the cost, which makes them unpredictable and uncontrollable. From the 1972 Kirkby Rent Strike to the 1981 Toxteth Uprising [39], they have always had a way with rejecting authority. Chris Tobin identified how this *'Liverpool Way'* clashed with conservative and fiscal wisdom regarding how things *should* be:

> *The demands of Sky Sports had no time for such madness (as Robbie Fowler's support for the Liverpool dockers or the Hillsborough Justice Campaign). The Liverpool Way*

*would not just be about football; through the 1970s and '80s it would be a home for the masses of unemployed, people dis-enfranchised through Margaret Thatcher's years in office, a Community Centre, a church to come and pay homage, their very own place of worship, they would kneel and pray toward Gods with feet of clay. The Liverpool Dockers strike would be the longest in British industrial relations history, supported by the Liverpool Way with Robbie Fowler wearing a supporting t-shirt which would be revealed during a goal scoring celebration. Hillsborough and its justice campaign for innocent supporters, innocent children lost to a stadium disaster, would run red hot through the very veins of this club, everyone to a man or woman would fight like they themselves had been a parent to those 96 that perished from that day. The Liverpool Way would make sure they would not be forgotten, they would not allow them to be lied about, they would boycott The Sun whose lies would harm so many The Liverpool Way would be to seek justice and the truth. Hillsborough would be entrenched in the thoughts and minds of every Liverpool fan, and subsequently educating new followers of their responsibility to seek justice. The Liverpool Way would be an honest way, where truth could and would be accepted.' [40]*

The tireless and relentless struggle for justice, led by bereaved families and survivors of the Hillsborough football disaster, whose loved ones went to watch a game of football on 15 April 1989 and never came back, epitomises the intensity of the human spirit and a heightened sense of justice that exists on Merseyside, one that goes beyond the usual social boundaries of endurance and solidarity. These people recognised no limits in a campaign for justice that, for over 32 years, pitted them against a state-managed media, police and political conspiracy to blame Liverpool supporters for causing the events that led to the deaths of 96 men, women and children. In July 2021, Andrew Devine died due to the severe brain damage he sustained in the crush at Hillsborough. The senior coroner of Liverpool ruled that Andrew was legally the 97th victim of the disaster. Writing in *The Spectator* in 2004, Conservative MP and current Prime Minister, Boris Johnson, spoke for the establishment when he commented that people in Liverpool: 'Cannot accept that they might have made any contribution to their misfortunes, but seek rather to blame someone else for it, thereby deepening their sense of shared tribal grievance about the rest of society.' [41] Johnson added: 'Liverpudlians wallow in their victim status,' claiming that this was part of the 'deeply unattractive psyche' of many in the city. [42]

For the people of Merseyside, the struggle of the Hillsborough Campaign was a reminder of the human spirit's epic potential for resistance. By 2016, the Hillsborough families had successfully exposed the lies, betrayals and conspiracies perpetrated by the most powerful in our society. They also uncovered similar abuses against Yorkshire miners in 1984, carried out by the same police force and supported by the same *Sun Newspaper*. In the case of the Orgreave Coking Plant, which stood just seven miles from the Hillsborough stadium on the outskirts of Sheffield, there were brutal attacks on miners and their supporters in June 1984, and the victims had long claimed that they were subjected to state lies, cover-ups and conspiracies, not only at Orgreave, but throughout their year-long strike. [43] Liverpool and London dockers, together with other dock workers across the UK, went on unofficial strike in solidarity with the miners in 1984, refusing to handle ships importing coal to break the strike. [44] Since Hillsborough, the people of Liverpool have effectively boycotted the Murdoch owned *Sun Newspaper*. [45] Five years later, the Liverpool dockers would be fighting for the survival of their industry, defending laws that stopped port employers from using casual labour on the docks.

# 2
# Historical Overview of the Dispute

*'What right have any of us to sell our kids' futures? How could you look yourself in the face shaving each morning if you'd done that!' ~ Jimmy Campbell\**

By the late 1960s, Transport House had stood on the same flat iron of land in Liverpool City Centre since the turn of the previous century. It was the place where Commutation Row met Islington, on a hill that looked down the slope of William Brown Street towards the River Mersey. The original home of the Transport and General Workers' Union had, in all its art-deco functional brutality, been a hub of intense political and trade union activity throughout the 20th century. Thousands of workers and their union leaders passed through its windowless, cavernous basement main hall and its open-plan spaces on the upper floors, filled with solid tables and 'captain's chairs,' that provided meeting rooms for the growing number of shop stewards' committees. [1] They came to argue, they came to debate; they came to kick those chairs and bang those tables, to politicise the workers' struggle in Liverpool and across the world. Importantly, opportunities arose for all those who entered Transport House to be placed alongside men and women of older generations, whose living memories of labour history connected *trade union apprentices* to the tumultuous events of 1889, 1911 and 1967 and towards 1989 and 1995.

A post-war generation of unofficial port workers and seafarers met in one of the top-floor rooms, representing the interests of over 80,000 dockers [2] alongside twice as many port workers and sailors throughout some of the most dynamic periods of trade union and revolutionary activity. It is important to understand that the Liverpool dockers were refused the right to elect shop stewards and have any form of workplace organisation until

---

\* Jimmy Campbell (Sacked Liverpool Docker) in Urban 75:
http://www.urban75.com/Action/dockers.html

*decasualisation* in 1967. Their union, the TGWU, and the port employers refused any negotiation or representation rights to dockers so the dockers organised through their own unofficial committees and structures that ran parallel to those of the union. The air that occupied these vast halls would be *charged with electricity* during these profoundly political moments of industrial and trade union upheavals. Transport House was an ideal place for young trade unionists to learn the ropes of local, national and international activism from their older, more experienced comrades. [3] It was a venue for sharing in the passion and emotional soul that needed to be injected into the working-class politics and trade unionism of Liverpool, influenced as it always would be by an international influx of radicalism and ideas, of socialists and revolutionaries. Communists, Trotskyists, workers' revolutionaries and syndicalists. Young and old served their time alongside socialists from another century and from so many other countries and cities, all fighting the common forces of exploitation, capitalism and trade union bureaucracy. [4]

Syndicalist themes were present in the trade union movement by the end of the 19th century, focused upon a hostility to the concept of unelected full-time trade union leadership declaring that: 'no man was ever good enough, or strong enough, to have such power at his disposal.' [5] The Unofficial Reform Committee of the South Wales Miners Federation in their 1912 pamphlet *The Miners' Next Step*, challenged unelected union positions as fundamentally anti-democratic. [6] Influenced by Tom Mann and James Conolly, J.T. Murphy asserted: 'to be *agin* the officials was as much a part of the nature of the syndicalist-minded workers of that time as to be *agin* the Government was a part of the nature of an Irishman.' [7] Many of the Liverpool dockers and their leaders mirrored this mindset in their antipathy towards Ernest Bevin's unelected army of trade union officials that by the 1970s exerted a powerful influence on rank-and-file trade union democracy and activity. This almost constant source of conflict between members and union was to have a dramatic impact on the history of the Liverpool dockers.

By the 1960s, the dockers' leaders found themselves standing on the shoulders of giants, as they profited from the victories and defeats of those that went before, oblivious to the fact that these gains were about to be dismantled. In 1989, the Conservative government abolished the National Dock Labour Board Scheme, opening the sluice gates of casualisation in every UK port. In Liverpool, the Mersey Docks and Harbour Company was the only port that did not dismiss its Registered Dock labour force, instead privatising everything else and opening the port to the domination of casual dock employers. Six years later, the Liverpool dockers were confronted again by a combination of port employers, a Conservative government and a trade union leadership unwilling to support them. The dockers proclaimed their determination to fight for another principle, that of *refusing to cross a picket line*. As one of the sacked dockers, Andy Dwyer, told film director Ken Loach after a year on the picket line, the sacking of 500 Liverpool dockers in 1995 was: 'A total injustice about good men who gave a life to the dock industry, to be just cast aside by somebody who is motivated by profit.' [8]

Transport House would become the centre of both the official 1989 dock strike and the 'unofficial' dispute of 1995. The original Transport House had been replaced by the current one built on almost the very same site in the early 1970s, only to be abandoned by TGWU General Secretary Bill Morris after the dockers' conflict shuddered to its conclusion in January 1998. It was a curt dismissal of its historical importance for Merseyside's trade unionists and their political organisations. This act was influenced in part by Morris's determination to erase *industrial conflict* as well as the TGWU Region 6 members' adherence to *the Liverpool Way* by shutting down the place where militant trade unionists and their predecessors had met for over a century. Their voices would be silenced, and his cultural vandalism remains a hidden tribute to the significance of these buildings and their architecture in the political and social affairs of the city and beyond. The official reason for the closure of the union's hall, given by the TGWU's General Executive Council, was that it was simply part of a 'much-needed restructuring of Region 6.' [9] This explanation came from a general secretary who, according to his biographer, Geoffrey Goodman: 'had in earlier dealings with his Liverpool members been compelled to expel a group of particularly militant far-left activists across the Merseyside zone. In fact, the whole Merseyside Region had become a perpetual and challenging problem for Morris, and it was always top of his action pad.' [10]

Here was a union leader who conflated union amalgamation with growth, as opposed to any radical transformation of trade union organisation as the basis of recruitment in a modern post-industrial society. Liverpool's TGWU offices were moved from a prime city centre location to a smaller office with no main hall, part of a new-build development in an old dock area that was difficult to access. It was as if the building and the organisation itself were being put out to pasture, hidden from view; hardly the best way to establish a presence in the community and grow the union. [11] The former union building remained symbolically silent for a number of years, rattling with the echoes and spirits of old communists and international socialists until Bill Morris retired. Then, in an effort to recapture the vibrant cultural and political significance of the original Transport House, as well as to make another obvious architectural political statement, the building was reopened by Morris's successor, Liverpool-born Tony Woodley, in 2005. It was to be renamed Jack Jones House, in celebration of the radical Liverpool dock worker and Spanish Civil War veteran, who himself became General Secretary of the TGWU in 1968. [12] However, equally symbolic was the fact that as part of the redevelopment, the iconic meeting hall was lost, to be replaced by more rented offices and a glazed entrance, with automatic doors opening into a space enclosed by more automatic glass doors.

Back in the 1970s, the main meeting hall had been a dynamic space, a key venue for all political and trade union gatherings in Liverpool. [13] Running the entire length of this huge building, the old hall could accommodate almost 500 people, making it an ideal place for the Liverpool dockers sacked in September 1995 to run their campaign from and also hold their weekly mass meetings. Situated on the first floor, large floor-to-ceiling windows ran along one side of the room towards the gable-end of the hall, flooding the room with natural light as open balconies offered a panoramic view of the city's most stunning architecture. It was in this hall that the history of the dispute was written each week for almost two and a half years, while out on the streets, the dockers made use of St George's Hall and the Pier Head for their marches and rallies, following in the traditions of the great revolutionaries and trade unionists of the previous century. Dave Cotterill, an influential and respected supporter of the dockers, attended and recorded these weekly mass meetings:

*'[The protests] became something else; held every week they became the centre-point of the week, creating a bond between the men and the stewards, which has held throughout. Packed to capacity with standing room only, with no restrictions on smoking, they would often go on for two or three hours. Every detail that could be reported was reported, delegations from around the world were cheered to the rooftops, those who went to every corner of Britain and the world reported back. Celebrities who attract audiences of thousands admitted to being proud and humbled to appear on the dockers platforms and normally found themselves on the receiving end of a bit of banter.' [14]*

For socialist and local historian Bill Hunter, the dockers' mass meetings provided the location from which the strategies and intensity of the dispute were forged and shaped:

*'The policy of the dispute leaders towards left political groups and tendencies was impeccable. Their mass meetings were open; their policy was for 'political and industrial' support and solidarity committees from trade unions and socialist organisations including Trotskyist tendencies and those developed from the Communist Party. [15]*

In March 1996, just a few weeks after the international dockers delegates had left Liverpool, Bill Morris walked up William Brown Street towards the top of the hill where Transport House loomed above him. Perhaps he, too, cast a glance behind him at the magnificence of the city's architecture as he entered the union's Liverpool office, or perhaps his thoughts were elsewhere. Perhaps his mind wandered towards Ray Collins, his administration officer, 'who consistently claimed,' according to Morris's biographer that Morris, 'was a man who had exceptional bottle.' [16] Perhaps he was thinking of the not-too-distant future, when both he and his fellow trade union officer would claim the titles afforded to those selected to sit in the House of Lords, becoming Baron Morris of Handsworth in 2006, and Baron Collins of Highbury in 2011, clad in red cloaks edged with ermine. Perhaps he was thinking of his deputy general secretary, Margaret Prosser, who in 2004 would be the first of his highly-paid officials to be elevated to the House of Lords, taking the title Baroness Prosser of Battersea, in the London Borough of Wandsworth.

The grandeur of entitlement and high office was all for the future for these trade union leaders and a far cry from the industrial dispute that he would betray as general secretary of the UK's largest trade union. It was just another day in the life of the Liverpool dockers' dispute; another mass meeting had been called, and the speech that Bill Morris was about to deliver to the sacked dockers might have been made to a hundred thousand trade unionists outside St George's Hall, or at the equally imposing setting of Liverpool's Pier Head. It was a speech that demanded to be captured amidst the immortal backdrop of these heroic streets of Rome, where a jet-black river ran against the edge of the city, appearing to knock it, occasionally, from side to side. It was a speech that he could have made standing alongside Tom Mann or James Larkin, or that other Irish revolutionary, James Connolly. Instead, it would be a speech to be remembered for all the wrong reasons. That afternoon, Bill Morris began his betrayal of the Liverpool dockers' struggle by telling them that they would not be betrayed:

# HISTORICAL OVERVIEW OF THE DISPUTE

*'And I can tell you that I speak on behalf of every single member of the Transport and General Workers Union, and it's not very often the general secretary can make that claim. But I can, with certainty, this morning make that claim. I can, with certainty, bring you the greetings, the commitment of every single one of our members, because as I go around the country, I get from them, to pass onto you, their admiration, their pride, their understanding of your struggle. They no longer see it, colleagues, as your struggle, they see it as their struggle, they see it on the basis that if you do not win, then we all will have lost. That is what they are saying to me, that the Liverpool dockers must win and they've got to be reinstated, because they're fighting a struggle for jobs, and if there's one thing that we need in this country, it is jobs for our children, our grandchildren and our community. And I tell you why we're gonna win this dispute.' [17]*

Someone shouted, 'He's right!', and the room ignited in the warm glow of their leader's words. A hundred cigarettes were lit in unison and the smoke slept under the union hall's low ceiling forming clouds that thickened ominously in this man-made atmosphere, choking everyone within its Woodbine-scented walls. 'God's on our side!' came another shout, [18] and Bill Morris repeated the call, declaring, 'Because we have got something, God's on our side.' [19] Now, his words echoed around the room before being drowned by a tidal wave of cheers and applause, as some men stood up to urge on their leader to even greater expressions of his support for their struggle. Other dockers still did not trust their general secretary, as they observed two of the most powerful union leaders in the world. Bill Morris looked down towards the seated New York dockers' leader, John Bowers, the President of the East Coast International Longshoremen's Association (ILA), and Bowers, in turn, glanced towards Morris, as if to acknowledge their combined global power and influence. [20] Morris re-focussed his gaze upon the people, *his* people, packed into *his* union's hall as a grey and blue haze obscured the view for those standing at the back. Others could be seen leaning forward in their seats, as if to hear more or get closer to the platform. His speech ebbed and flowed on tides of internationalism, the principles of socialist struggle and the guarantee of trade union solidarity, and then he predicted that after six months in dispute:

*'This ain't gonna be no short-term victory. This is gonna be a victory which is gonna change the face – change the face of international stevedoring, because wherever they are, they know about your dispute. They're watching Liverpool, and therefore we're fighting for international solidarity not just for ourselves, but for dockers everywhere. So, I leave you in conclusion to say I am here to reaffirm the Executive Council's commitment and support. I am here to speak on behalf of the union. I am here to say to you that whatever happens, our spirit will never be broken, and our bellies will never be starved, because, comrades, you in Liverpool will never ever walk alone. Good luck, and victory to the Liverpool dockers.' [21]*

The room overflowed in a sea of shouts, whistles and claps, more for the New York dockers' leader than the leader of the TGWU, for this was the theatre of workers' struggle. After six months of dispute, the Liverpool dockers were marching towards a conclusion behind banners held aloft by their general secretary, who'd assured them that they 'would never walk alone,' evoking the song that so many dockers would sing on a Saturday at the start of each Liverpool football game. As they left the meeting hall that afternoon, so too did the cigarette smoke that had mixed with the warm embers of Morris's words and the dark reality that crept behind them. Perhaps nobody truly believed the claims of their union leader as they drifted *alone* from that main hall, filtering onto the cold streets that tumbled down towards the Mersey, a river that knew only too well the stench of misery and betrayal. Bill Morris never walked or marched with the Liverpool dockers and their families. He left them to walk alone.

The Liverpool dockers were not betrayed by one individual but by an organisational culture underpinned by a well-oiled bureaucracy of local and national paid officials who, in turn, were supported by the decisions of the senior lay-member committee of the union, its General Executive Council. Bill Morris simply administered the power of patronage that trickled through every aspect of union life being replicated from the TUC to the ITF to New Labour. The 1980s witnessed the start of the disconnection in workplace trade unionism and Labour party politics that turn its back on traditional labour and their communities. The many good pro-*rank-and-file* trade union officials and office staff within the union would always find themselves diminished or overwhelmed by the dead weight of union bureaucracy and the power it could impose. Democracy and accountability should be at the heart of all life in a trade union. In 1912, the South Wales Miners Federation, in their document, *The Miners Next Step*, provided a highpoint of syndicalist philosophy in its opposition to unelected paid officials of the union:

> 'For a moment let us look at this question from the leaders' standpoint. First, they are "trade unionists by trade" and their profession demands certain privileges… Can we wonder then that leaders are averse to change? Can we wonder that they try and prevent progress? Progress may arrive at such a point that they would not be able to retain their "jobs," or their "jobs" would become so unimportant that from their point of view, they would not be worth retaining. The leader then has an interest - a vested interest - in stopping progress. They have therefore in some things an antagonism of interests with the rank-and-file… Leadership implies power held by the Leader. Without power the leader is inept. The possession of power inevitably leads to corruption. All leaders become corrupt, in spite of their own good intentions… He is compelled in order to maintain his power, to see to it that only those, who are willing to act as his drill sergeants or coercive agents shall enjoy his patronage. In a word, he is compelled to become an autocrat and a foe to democracy.' [22]

It is important to realise that the views expressed in *The Miners Next Step* have been widely referenced throughout the history of the trade union movement and have lain at the heart of the debate on trade union bureaucracy and rank-and-file control since the establishment of new unionism in 1889. Unions by their very existence affirm and reinforce capitalist class society. Writing in 1902 Lenin took up this theme of the limits of trade unionism in his pamphlet *What is to be Done?* He identified what he termed as economism; that the working class will not spontaneously become political simply by fighting economic battles with employers over wages and working hours. Marx considered how trade unions functioned in a 'legislative and administrative' system which meant, 'nothing more than the struggle for economic reform.' [23] The absence of democracy and accountability undermined the Liverpool dockers from 1995 and in the critical years before their dismissal. It would be no surprise when, after some thirteen months in dispute, on 3 February 1997, Dock Company boss, Trevor Furlong, told the Liverpool Daily Post that: 'The union had never supported the action of the Liverpool dockers.' The results of TGWU collusion with the Mersey Docks & Harbour Company were imposed upon the dockers to devastating effect.

Prior to *de-casualisation* in 1967 the old Dock Board never employed any dockers or involved itself directly in cargo handling. After taking over Scruttons Ltd. in the late 1960s they would eventually become the only employer of dock labour in Liverpool by the 1980s. The abolition of the National Dock Labour Board Scheme in 1989 released the Dock Company from any constraints on its control of the port and the land assets that lay before them. Four years on, the 1993 acquisition of the Medway Port would prove to be the final key to unlocking a reason for MDHC to dismiss 500 Liverpool dockers in 1995 replacing them with a 'scab' workforce. In purchasing the Medway Port, MDHC bosses saw first-hand how its manager, Peter Vincent, had imposed rigid contract changes on the Medway dockers, before dismissing them once they took industrial action to defend their previous terms of employment. With a local casual, strike-breaking labour force ready and waiting to take over the day-to-day running of the docks, Vincent and his financial backers made millions by purchasing the sacked dockers' shares at £2.50 per share, and then selling them on to MDHC at £37 per share. He was awarded a directorship on the MDHC board, who employed his Medway strategy in ousting the Liverpool dockers. Vincent's tenure on the board of MDHC would last only one year. [24]

Threats, disciplinaries and dismissals were the human resources model long adopted by the Port Authority in Liverpool, who all the while maintained a close working relation with local TGWU officials. It was a process that began prior to 1989 and continued after the abolition of the Dock Labour Board Scheme. This fatal acquiescence of the union would continue right up until the dispute finally ended in January1998. A local TGWU dock official observed at the time:

> 'We have for too long allowed a totally undisciplined attitude to prevail, which has resulted in the employer being allowed to make the following claims that there are currently men employed at the Seaforth Terminal who refuse to train; who are not fit to do the job. The trade union affirmed that these factors undoubtedly represented a very real threat to these men's jobs.' [25]

Within a month of this statement, the Liverpool dispute began. It could have started at any point during the previous decade. It was all too easy for bosses to manufacture a dispute with the dockers, get men out the gate and dare the remaining dockers to cross their picket lines. It was all so predictable, and the dockers saw it coming before the bosses or the union. In 1996, one year into the dispute, Trevor Furlong, MDHC Chief Executive, told *International Freight Weekly* that they should have sacked the Liverpool dockers in 1989. 'I suppose in hindsight we were too soft in 1989. We should have got rid of the lot of them and recruited, as Mersey Docks had suffered in comparison to other ports, which had de-recognised unions.' [26] Unlike Medway, London and many other UK ports, MDHC did not opt for privatisation or management/employee buyouts straight away, and they continued to recognise the local TGWU. In a press release issued following the purchase of Medway, there was distinct celebratory tone from a company that saw itself as 'going places.' [27] MDHC's press officer, Eric Leatherbarrow, dismissed criticism of the deal because, for him, this was truly a striking example of wealth creation. 'We're not in the business of calming prejudices of individuals against what other individuals may achieve in their lives,' he proclaimed. [28] The chairman of MDHC, Gordon Waddell, commented at the time that, 'It was odd that a company with a government shareholder should be buying a privatised port.' [29]

All of this personal wealth creation among the Medway and Mersey bosses would be paid for by others. The taxpayer footed the bill when the government, which owned 20% of MDHC, stood by while the value of its 'golden share' in the company fell to less than 14%. [30] It was taxpayers' money that floated the company in 1970, after the old Mersey Docks and Harbour Board were driven to bankruptcy due to port bosses and shipowners using their office to make themselves and their shipping lines rich. In March 1974 the reconstruction of the Dock Company's (formerly the Board) finances was finally determined by the High Court and debenture stock debt was written down from £92m to £37m. 'But as partial compensation to debenture holders they were required to issue a unique from of stock consisting of £20m of unsecured loan stock combined with £2m of equity shares. The terms of the loan stock were that it was to be interest free until 1995 but in the meantime was to be progressively redeemed by profits… and, more germane to the present topic, from proceeds of sale of surplus assets. This in effect acted as an incentive for the Dock Company to defer any outright sale of their surplus land assets at least until 1995.' [31] It was taxpayers' money, again, that wrote off £112m in loans and funded up to £200m's worth of redundancies and paid out £37.5m for the regeneration of the dock area in the decade prior to MDHC sacking their dockers. This was also a company that exploited European taxpayers by obtaining £76m of City Challenge funding in addition to some £13.3m in European Regional Development Funds. According to journalist and writer, John Pilger, as if to underline MDHC bosses' personal wealth creation plan, 'Managing Director, Trevor Furlong, took an £87,000 pay rise just before the company sent 329 men to the dole. Furlong's 38% increase brought his earnings to £316,000 a year. He also had a £293,000 share option over the next two years.' [32]

Within a few years of the conclusion of the Liverpool dock dispute, more personal wealth creation opportunities would fall into the laps of these same bosses. In 2000, the baton of control of the company passed from CEO Trevor Furlong to his successor, Peter Jones, then head of the Port of Liverpool division, following Furlong's retirement. Jones was present for the second attempt at a takeover of MDHC by Peel Holdings in 2005, and his eventual departure would see his personal wealth increase through share options worth more than £500,000, as well as a £640,000 payoff based on two years' basic salary. At the time, a company spokesman claimed that the possibility of Jones staying on in the event of a takeover had not even been discussed. [33] He was not wanted by Peel Holdings, despite his 35 years at the top of the Port of Liverpool management team. Two years later, on 1 April 2007, Associated British Ports Holdings Ltd. announced that Peter Jones would become their company's new Chief Executive. [34]

# HISTORICAL OVERVIEW OF THE DISPUTE

When you follow the money, the roots of the dockers' dispute that began in September 1995 quickly become exposed. MDHC bosses had rightly calculated that, whatever the outcome of the dismissal of 500 dockers, neither they nor any other UK port bosses would be prosecuted or held accountable for their actions. Their union and the New Labour Party could be expected to stand on the side-lines. On 15 September 1995, ten days before their dismissal, the influential shipping paper *Lloyd's List* ran a story about the significant improvements that had taken place over recent years at the Port of Liverpool, declaring Liverpool dockers 'the best in Europe.' [35] Just a few months earlier, in May 1995, new contracts were offered to the dockers, as if to reaffirm MDHC's confidence in their labour force. As Mick Cullen, one of the sacked Seaforth shop stewards, commented at the time: 'You don't offer a two-year pay deal to a bad workforce. It's all about bad management.' [36]

Bill Morris would dismiss the Liverpool conflict as unofficial, and yet three official Electoral Reform Society postal ballots were organised for the dockers to take part in, *jointly sponsored* by the employer. On three occasions, the dockers overwhelmingly voted for their struggle for justice to continue. But this was to be a conflict largely ignored by the media and the political left, and to this day, discussion of its significance and relevance is avoided. The Liverpool dockers' dispute was an industrial struggle that involved far too many complex conflicts with powerful individuals in the labour movement, whose leaders were not only bankrolling New Labour, but also the lucrative parliamentary and trade union careers of its ambitious officer corps. The Liverpool dockers' dispute was portrayed as being from another time; one which had been discarded by New Labour in the early 1980s, as it strived to modernise at the dawning of a new age of politics. As such, this 'strike,' as it was so often wrongly referred to, was cast as a relic from a monochrome past, of men once more reduced to unskilled beasts of burden, easily identified by their flat caps and mufflers. They contradicted the New Labour *world view* of modernity in an era designated as marking the end of conflict, as the Blairite soundbites of a 'third way' mirrored the rise of neo-liberalism. Bill Morris embraced this age of compromise and partnership with employers. It was a situation that posed fundamental dilemmas for the left in the decades that followed as they thought they could wave farewell to the working-classes.

In short, the dockers had always presented a celebrated history of working-class struggle against their union, port employers and the state; now it had been transformed into a *toxic history* best forgotten, and so Labour and trade union academics alike avoided the subject like the plague. Others continued to stand by workers in struggle. They knew all too well that the word so often used by the Liverpool dockers and their families in describing their own experience was 'betrayal,' and Tony Benn, speaking within a few days of the dispute ending, proclaimed: 'That the plain blunt truth is that these men and the Women of the Waterfront fought a magnificent fight on the principle that you don't betray people who have been sacked for not crossing a picket line. They were let down by the Labour Movement, they were let down by the labour government after May 1997.' [37] In 1999, Liverpool-born screenwriter and producer Jimmy McGovern made a film, *Dockers: Writing the Wrongs*, and in examining the process of the dockers writing the script of their own struggle, he explained how it was:

*'Becoming extremely complex, as the dockers and Women of the Waterfront began to write down their own story. It needed simplifying. I think the turning point was when we found the structure, and that structure was a series of betrayals. Betrayal by your employer, betrayal by your friends, betrayal by the Labour Party, betrayal by your union.' [38]*

Mark Steel, comedian, writer, political activist and loyal supporter of the Liverpool dockers, writing on the end of the dispute in 1998, concluded that: 'Unions depend on the principle of standing up for one another instead of just for yourself. Five hundred ex-dockers, many of whom were nearing retirement and could have opted for an easy life, sacrificed a tremendous amount for that principle, and will be remembered with great affection by the many people they touched.' [39] *The Liverpool Daily Post* proclaimed the end of the dockers' conflict in January 1998 under the banner headline, *'The dog that's had its day.'* The view expressed here was that:

*'The dispute, while real to those involved, seemed to symbolise something from another era to those glimpsing the drama from afar. It was as though an old yard dog, wearied and weakened by beatings, managed to bare his teeth once again, and in so doing recalled the lost years when he was young and strong; when a snarl and a display of fangs warned strangers to back off... It was, however, appropriate that this final uprising of trade union solidarity should have happened on Merseyside. But the old yard dog does bare his teeth from time to time, it will serve as a reminder that some things can never be forgiven or forgotten.' [40]*

The Liverpool dockers had to go elsewhere *to discover* solidarity; they had to explore and create new lines of support from rank-and-file dockers across the globe, along with trade unionists, politicians, academics, environmentalists, entertainers, filmmakers and journalists. They had to replace the vacuum created by New Labour, the TUC, the ITF and their own union's disinterest. Unsurprisingly, the Liverpool dockers celebrated the solidarity displayed by their comrades from ports across the world, from Canada to France, Ireland to Australia, New Zealand to Portugal, Spain to the USA and beyond. The profound legacy of their internationalism would lead to the creation of a radical rank-and-file international union, the International Dockworkers Council, of which the Liverpool dockers hold the Honorary Presidency for life. By 2017, the IDC had over 100,000 members representing a new generation of dockers, combining a diverse, youthful membership with matching leaders.

Contrary to its portrayal in the media, the Liverpool dockers' dispute was a harbinger of the conflicts that would define the looming new century; it was far more modern than the 'modernisers' of New Labour could possibly comprehend. Unlike their industrial counterparts dock labourers had only small windows of opportunity to strike against their port bosses. Factory work is static, whereas dock work was a constantly moving battleground as ships left or moved around the port to avoid industrial action. As a result, the industrial actions applied by dockers to ships or berths in dispute had no limits – they applied whatever leverage they had to in confrontations against the TGWU and the ports bosses who negotiated directly without any involvement from rank-and-file elected 'unofficial' dock shop stewards.

For 28 months, these workers fought an immense and uniquely imaginative struggle for their reinstatement, utilising the inherent internationalism of their port industry and embracing the potential of the internet to communicate directly with dockers and trade unionists across the world. The Liverpool dockers became ground-breaking students, exponents and advocates of the virtual picket line. [41] With long experience in how to undermine an employer when in struggle the Liverpool dockers always championed radical new forms of leverage. Their campaigns knew no boundaries or borders, and within days of the conflict beginning, the wives and partners of the dockers had formed their own highly influential and radical support group, the Women of the Waterfront. They embraced cutting-edge alliances with environmental groups, anarchists and youth who marched under the banner of 'Reclaim the Streets,' while also embracing the city's marginalised Turkish and Kurdish communities. Everyone and everything connected to the Dock Company, were viewed as potential targets, from politicians to ports and shareholders to customers; basically, any organisation or party that held an interest in Liverpool docks were considered likely points of leverage.

The profoundly modern scope of this dock workers' industrial conflict was referenced again in the film *Dockers*, directed by Bill Anderson, when one of the key characters, played by the actor Crissy Rock, made her first impassioned speech to a local meeting of the National Union of Teachers: 'This is not some *antwacky* [Liverpool slang for 'old-fashioned'] labour force sticking to some antwacky principle. This is the most modern dispute imaginable.' [42] The script for this drama was another modern twist in the conflict, as it was written by a combination of sacked dockers, the Women of the Waterfront and their supporters. Len McCluskey, the General Secretary of UNITE, reflecting upon the modernity of this Liverpool dockers' struggle some twenty-years later declared: 'The same spirit now is needed to reject the scourge of zero hours. The dockers were, without doubt, ahead of their time. They were certainly way ahead of the leadership of the trade union movement of that time.' [43] But still, the tragic deaths of five dockers during the struggle – Jimmy McCumisky, Billy Rooney, Joe Best, Billy Dunn and Kenny Kennedy – had a profound effect upon all involved, for these were men they had worked alongside for many years; ate and drank with, laughed and cried alongside. The stress of their final years in work impacted heavily upon the general health of the dockers. For some, it affected their personal relationships; families split, and without the sense of purpose so often derived from work, the social connections and support offered by comrades, some fell into the abyss of ill health, depression, alcoholism and, subsequently, premature death.

The TGWU maintained that they could not be seen to support the Liverpool dockers, and this was the message that the union delivered to all trade unions both in the UK and around the world. 'Avoid the Liverpool dockers! Don't support them!' came the official war cry of the TGWU, as they attempted to preserve the fabric of a union that they claimed was at risk from its Liverpool members' 'illegal' action. And so, the dockers became outcasts; outside the law and outside their own union, an institution they helped establish when they kick-started New Unionism in 1889. Now, they were pariahs, their exclusion based upon betrayal and deception. [44] Eighteen months into the struggle, Bill Morris used the union's official publication, the *TGWU Record*, to 'set the record straight' on how the dispute had begun, and why the union was powerless to act in solidarity with its Liverpool membership:

*'The MDHC workers were not in direct dispute with their own employer and had broken their contract of employment without first holding an industrial action ballot, the TGWU became vulnerable to legal action for damages by MDHC or any ship owner… the TGWU has an obligation to all its 900,000 members, which must include avoiding action which could render the union unable to operate on behalf of those members.' [45]*

As the conflict reached its conclusion in January 1998, Bill Morris distributed another bulletin to all union TGWU Branches, officers and staff, in which he returned to the subject of why the union did not support the Liverpool dockers: 'Our policy has always been to seek a negotiated settlement, to preserve the fabric of the union, and to relieve hardship among the families of the dismissed men… it cannot lead to any change in the union's determination to preserve its fabric against threats of legal action.' [46] This myth of sequestration was to remain the official position of the TGWU's lay-member Executive Council, union officials and the majority of the union's Broad Left organisation. The International Transport Workers' Federation, together with the Trade Union Congress, ensured that no meaningful industrial or political support would ever be given to the Liverpool dockers as directed by Morris. As a result, no local or national officials of the TGWU, and hardly any officials of UK trade unions, spoke at dockers' mass meetings or public demonstrations. Hardly any, if any at all, marched with the dockers during their 28 months of struggle, and no official contact was ever made by the Trade Union Congress, locally or nationally, to extend the hand of solidarity, nor did any official representative of the ITF appear in support of the dockers.

From the beginning of the dispute the Liverpool dockers had the unsolicited support of their Irish comrades. TGWU officials and members from Belfast to Dublin, including John Freeman, Mick O'Reilly, Eugene McGlone, Howard Burns and Maurice Cunningham and so many others. Despite the ongoing 'Troubles,' neither the Irish TGWU in Dublin or the Belfast union ever had their funds or union buildings sequestrated for being in breach of industrial relations law for their overt public support of the Liverpool dockers. However, the legal position of the TGWU in England, Wales and Scotland pursued the untested illegality of the Liverpool dockers' cause, even though this did not reflect the barristers' advice of their own union's legal department in October 1995. This advice affirmed that the Liverpool dockers were not on strike, but were rather, 'more like a protest group, like Greenpeace.' [47] As such, they were not subject to industrial legislation, but by common law. The policing of the dockers would be governed using the same analysis, as the police themselves declared that they were not dealing with an industrial dispute, but a protest group or a campaign. The dockers did not march out on unofficial strike, they were locked out by their employer. On Wednesday 4 October 1995, four days after their dismissal, the TGWU's legal director, Fergus Whitty, informed the dock shop stewards at Transport House that:

*This is just not a trade dispute, it is about personal contracts and de-recognising the union in the same way as the Tilbury dockers when they had been dismissed in 1989 whilst taking part in the official strike over the abolition of the National Dock Labour*

*Scheme. No question existed about abandoning anyone in this situation. It's irrelevant to sign a personal contract. The law says if you sign a personal contract under duress, it has no legal standing. Personal contracts can be beaten by everyone acting together, by returning to work on a unified basis.' [48]*

Following the advice of their trade union, the dockers attempted to return to work in the first week of their dispute. That Monday, 9 October 1995 they were locked out for a second time, and their return to work was blocked by a phalanx of the Dock Company's own port police and Merseyside Police. In the official biography, *Bill Morris: A Trade Union Miracle*, Geoffrey Goodman stated the: 'dilemma facing Bill Morris and the TGWU leadership was that to come out in full support of the dockers' case would have flouted the new laws which in turn could have led to employers, backed by the Conservative government of the time, enforcing the law at huge financial risk to the entire union.' [49] Goodman uses four terms to describe the nature of the Liverpool dockers situation: 'a dispute, a lock-out, a dismissal and a strike.' This loose and casual use of language was repeated throughout the conflict, creating a fog of confusion that clouded the real source of betrayal. Political commentators on the left often got lost in the default position that the dockers had to be 'on strike,' and these substantive failures of definition also exposed a poor level of understanding in relation to the legal significance of the way in which the dockers' actions were described by those who, essentially, did not support them. Goodman could not avoid the impact of the Liverpool dock conflict on Bill Morris and his leadership from 1995 onwards, writing: 'In many ways the Liverpool docks dispute was the most immediately contentious, difficult and emotionally explosive issue of any Bill Morris had to handle. This was chiefly due to the historic role the dockers had played in the history of the TGWU.' [50] Making use of the union's communications access to over one million members via the *TGWU Record*, in February 1997, Morris referred to the:

*'Unofficial action which has resulted in the employer being able to use Tory legislation to sack the dockers thwarting the union's ability to intervene. The Merseyside Port Shop Stewards assert that there is no difference between the positions of the employer and the TGWU in the Liverpool docks dispute and that there is little hope of a negotiated settlement to the dispute... notwithstanding the fact that the dispute falls foul of the draconian anti-union legislation passed over the last 17 years, a fact many of the TGWU's critics simply ignore.' [51]*

The Trade Union and Labour Relations (Consolidation) Act of 1992 was reasonably succinct regarding the liability of trade unions for any unofficial strike action. The law was again clear on what the union needed to do to avoid any potential financial liabilities:

*'Repudiation is completed by a trade union when the actions of its members are repudiated by the executive, president or general... written notice of the repudiation must be given to the committee or official in question, without delay, and the union must do its best to give individual written notice of the fact and date of repudiation, without delay to every member of the union who the union has reason to believe is taking part, or might*

*otherwise take part, in industrial action as a result of the act, and to the employer of every such member.' [52]*

This legal *command* was never met, and no such statement or record of repudiation was ever produced by the TGWU, its general secretary or the General Executive Council. The Liverpool dock shop stewards had immediately sought legal advice on the status of their dispute and John Hendy QC, Damien Brown and Louise Christian, among others, offered legal advice and guidance to the dockers. Hendy was of the opinion that: 'The dispute was official as from day one because the union had not sought to, under law, repudiate the action.' [53] Christian later helped clarify precisely the detail of Hendy's council:

> *The question is simply whether or not the dispute is regarded by the law as 'official' or 'unofficial.' This is relevant to a number of issues such as payment of unemployment benefit and social security by the State, payment of dispute benefit by the union. On 29th September 1995 a union delegation went to see the MDHC and Torside. Although the union delegation advised the employers that this was not official action, and the employers' representatives accepted this, there appears never to have been anything in writing to this effect.' [54]*

Hendy concluded that, 'there having been no repudiation in the prescribed form, it follows that the industrial action (or rather the acts of organising, encouraging or supporting the industrial action) is deemed by statute to have been official.' [55]

In July 1997, at the TGWU Biennial Delegates Conference, the key lay-member policy-making forum of the TGWU, Bill Morris appealed, 'for unity and a course of action within the law.' [56] This was rejected by a clear and visible majority, despite the general secretary's warning that they faced a straight choice between, 'Unity or oblivion if it supported the Liverpool dockers.' [57] The GEC's policy, and that of the TGWU General Secretary, was overwhelmingly rejected by a majority of 101 votes - 182 for the GEC policy and 283 against - only for the chair of the meeting to rule that the vote had actually supported the GEC policy. Amidst the uproar that followed, it was clear that the union would have to accept that they had been defeated. The following morning, the leadership of the union reluctantly conceded that their policy had been rejected by a majority of two to one. These votes opposed the General Secretary, the GEC and the TGWU's actions in failing to support the Liverpool dockers, but this rejection was ignored both at the conference and after it. It was then ignored by the GEC, whose role, under the rules of the union, was to carry out the decisions of the membership as determined by the BDC. Nevertheless, the magnitude of the Liverpool dockers rank-and-file 'overturning' of the union's leadership at its major decision-making forum has to be seen against the factual reality that: 'TGWU general secretaries could often control the Biennial Delegate Conference and they exercised very considerable patronage powers.' [58]

What follows is the untold story of how the Liverpool dockers developed a uniquely imaginative and fearless industrial action strategy, organised, through necessity, outside of the official trade union movement. This history is a tribute to extraordinary men and women, who daily planned for their reinstatement that exemplified both their character and heritage

# HISTORICAL OVERVIEW OF THE DISPUTE

as dock labourers and trade unionists. It is a history that attempts to capture the iron and the soul of these men and women, their families and their supporters; to provide a record and an insight into the dignity of a class that will never exist again in this form. Many of these men could trace their lineage back directly to the same dockers who fired inspiration into the heart of a new, radical and revolutionary trade unionism in the 1800s, which in turn won rights of representation and gave a voice to all UK workers beyond the narrow parameters of craft unionism. [59] From the end of the nineteenth century dockers redefined a timeless model of workers' organisation; of a period where workers supported workers, right or wrong; of a principle worth fighting for; of the right to refuse to cross a picket line knowing the extreme personal consequences of those actions. Their labour had no value beyond that of the beasts of burden [60] that they had become in order to feed the capitalist economies need to move goods from ship to quay and quay to ship across the globe, for the purpose of trade and profit. These events were being mirrored throughout industrialised Europe and men and women in the UK began organising from port to port amid what Ben Tillett described as the *degradation of humanity*, as they went about their dismal business of searching for casual work and food in London's docklands:

> *'To tramp hour after hour round the dock; to see men picking the rubbish heaps of refuse, the furtive search for any kind of food… this was at times the only means of living and of hope to many. No wonder the contractors called the casuals dock rats… The dock labourer came in for the foulest contempt… the submerged being a term of respect for the casual labourer. All of us who were dock labourers concealed the nature of our occupation from our families as well as our friends.' [61]*

The organisation these dock workers established in 1889 contained limitless scope in its potential, and through port-based industrial action they used their rank-and-file radical trade unionism on the quays and decks of ships to raise their conditions above that of low-paid, casual dock labourers, or 'people of the abyss,' as Jack London and Robert Tressell would describe them. [62] In 1890, Liverpool dockers took part in a similar struggle, involving almost as great a number of strikers as on the London docks in the previous year. This Liverpool strike had all the makings of what the academic, R. Bean, labelled a 'labour war:'

> *'And it resulted in a profound impact upon industrial relations on the Mersey waterfront. However, the events and consequences of this dispute together with the activities of the National Union of Dock Labourers which organised it have so far received less detailed attention than either the dock strike in the metropolis or the London dockers union.' [63]*

Writing in 2015, in a Unite Education publication on the history of the Great Dock Strike of 1889, Len McCluskey reflected on the influence that the dockers had on union organisation in the UK:

> *The Great London Dock Strike of 1889 was the foundation stone on which the modern trade union movement is based. Before 1889 trade union membership was largely the*

*preserve of skilled craftsmen. The dock labourer's achievement, assisted by magnificent international solidarity from Australia, lay in convincing other unskilled workers that improvements in pay and working conditions could be won through trade union activity. Nothing was to ever be the same again. Our great union does, of course, have its own origins in the 1889 Strike… the momentous events of August and September 1889 and a sign of our commitment to an ongoing collective struggle for a better future for all working people. One hundred years later the Liverpool dockers again received financial and physical support from their docker comrades in Australia.' [64]*

The Liverpool dockers could look upon their heritage in the Labour Movement as a magnificent history of struggle that not only raised their own pay and conditions of labour, but often involved taking direct action in support of other workers. In so doing, dock workers in Liverpool set the wage scale for many workers on Merseyside throughout the 1970s. In the spirit of their global profession, they embraced internationalism in offering shelter to Chilean seafarers escaping Pinochet's military dictatorship in the 1980s and refusing to handle South African ships or cargoes in opposition to apartheid, blockading uranium hexafluoride from Namibia being shipped through Liverpool. They struck for the miners, seafarers, steel workers, nurses and so many others, engaging in such noble direct action in defence of trade unionism and justice for the working class. All these actions were undertaken at the risk of losing their own jobs. It was a legacy to be respected and celebrated, but it was quickly forgotten and lost when they, too, needed a display of solidarity from their own trade union, the International Transport Workers' Federation, the Trade Union Congress and the New Labour government that was elected in 1997.

In 1995, the Liverpool dockers were betrayed by the general secretary of the Transport and General Workers' Union, who, along with a group of paid officials, were supported by the decisions of the senior lay-member committee of the union, the General Executive Council. A year into the dispute, on Tuesday 17 September 1996, Bill Morris, in a statement to the GEC, expressed his belief that the Liverpool dockers were saying, 'Thanks, you're doing nothing. You betrayed us.' [65] What follows is an attempt to tell the dockers' side of a story that echoes throughout their proud history and brutal industrial struggles. In the words of James Larkin, the Irish trade unionist: *'We are beaten. We will make no bones about it; but we are not too badly beaten still to fight.'* [66]

# PART TWO:
## The Origins of Betrayal

# 3
# Life on the Docks

*'Dock labour all over the world has a bad name; in the popular estimation, "the scum of the earth" drifts down from trade to trade and from occupation to occupation to form at last the dregs of our industrial system, the loaders and unloaders of ships. There is a certain amount of truth in this estimate... The Liverpool docks have no better, perhaps rather a worse, reputation than the average. It was known that we had there, in the crudest from, the economic and social evils of casual labour and irregular employment...' ~ L.S.Woolf\**

Dockland history seemed destined always to repeat itself. [1] Dock workers captured the public imagination in their 1889 strike, which lasted five weeks, establishing a minimum of four hours work each day for a minimum wage of six pence an hour, the 'dockers' tanner'. Their victory was aided by the financial support they received from other trade unionists, including a £30,000 donation from the Australian Seamen and Wharfies. These same *Wharfies* would come to the aid of the Liverpool dockers over a century later. At the core of constant unrest across Britain's ports, and every waterfront the world over, lay the dockers' abhorrence of casual employment and the pen system that governed it; of bosses hiring only the men they wanted, only when they needed them. Still, men gathered twice daily in anticipation of a few hours' work, an injustice that ran through the veins of everyone who came into contact with it. This base inhumanity, imposed by *the greed of the bosses,* left an indelible mark on those who witnessed. It permeated through dockers' families, crossing generations, flowing through their communities, building a story that could only be told by dockers themselves. In 1889, Ben Tillett, one of the leaders of the Great London Dock Strike and general secretary of the General Workers' Union, recalled his own experience of 'shaping up' for casual work:

> *'[in front of the] grinning caller-on, who walked up and down, protected by stout iron bars, facing a raging and shouting mass; he would pick and choose the slaves with*

---

\* L.S. Woolf – The Economic Journal Vol:24 No.94 (p. 314-319) June 1914 - Oxford University Press *wanton brutality, as one throwing scraps to hungry wolves, to delight in the exhibition of a savage struggle for existence.' [2]*

Over fifty years later, in 1945, Labour MP Lesley Solley addressed the House of Commons during a discussion on the Dock Work Registration of Employment Bill:

*'What about the dockers? They were starving… The dock labourers of London, the poorest, most wretched and worst-paid men in London… they have to suffer under a system of sub-contract which permits them to be driven like slaves, at the bidding of men who are selected from the most brutal of their class, who underpay, overdrive and restrict the numbers necessary to do a fair day's work.' [3]*

On 14 October 1995, Jimmy Davies, secretary to the Merseyside Port Shop Stewards Committee, in an interview in *Socialist Worker*, recollected how Liverpool dockers:

*'Went into the pen each morning and waited like animals. You were hoping that somehow, whether through religion or whatever [some Liverpool dock employers would only recruit protestant or catholic dock labourers], you got a tap on the shoulder. If you didn't, there was no work that day and you had to go home. This humiliating process of queuing up every morning for the 'call' endured in one form or other until the 1960s. Those who did not get picked by the bosses would often go hungry. Conditions and wages for all dockers were appalling.' [4]*

In 1996, Jimmy Nolan, chairman of the Merseyside Port Shop Stewards, said: 'the pen hiring system was a disgrace and an obnoxious way of hiring people, because you're standing in a big hall and someone comes up and taps you on the back to say that you're going to such and such a ship.' [5] Gerry McDonough, a retired docker and trade union activist, remembered how: 'you were all day in the pen, and you all had to fight for work and fight one another to get your book into that fella, and if your face didn't fit, you never got the job, it was as simple as that.' [6] According to Larry Fogarty, another retired Liverpool docker: 'it was hard – it was just a black shed, gaslight, no ventilation or nothing, and when you had a high tide, it used to get flooded…' [7] Billy Jenkins, one of the dock shop stewards sacked in 1995, reflected on the nature of dock work and the bleak inheritance that it passed from one generation to the next:

*'My father was a docker for 42 years, my brothers have been there for 35 and 33 years, and I've been there since 1968. I used to go home thinking I'd had a hard day, and my dad would tell me how much worse things were before. Before 1947, you were given a tally with a number on and you had to beg to get a day or two-days' work. In 1947, the National Dock Labour Scheme introduced the pen system. Workers had to queue in pens and wait to be picked for work. This was actually an improvement on the old system, where you would queue in the street, but you were still fighting one another for work and the boss could still pick and choose. There were filthy cargoes, you could always tell what cargo my dad had been working on because you could smell it in the house,*

# LIFE ON THE DOCKS

*Palm kernels, fish, hooves. If you went on a bus, people would move away. My dad was proud when my two brothers started in 1961, but the younger lads found the conditions intolerable, particularly as there were more jobs to choose from in the early '60s. The dole office used to threaten unemployed people with jobs on the docks. By 1967, the port shop stewards had achieved everything they asked for – the removal of the pens, decasualisation, protective clothing from the company, better bonuses. In 1972, the ten-hour day went, it created 500 new jobs. But in 1989, the National Dock Labour Scheme went. We knew in Liverpool that they took a more subtle approach… They thought that the anti-union laws would stop us defending ourselves.' [8]*

Liverpool dock worker and deputy chair of the Merseyside Port Shop Stewards' Committee, Frank Lannigan, recalled in 1995:

*'My dad got me down the dock 1972; he'd been down the dock since before the war. He came back after the war and went back down there in 1945. He was on those docks 40-odd years till tragically, he got hurt. He nearly lost his legs and he could never go down there again. Seven ton of steel fell on my dad's legs when he was discharging a wagon – 'stowing back,' as we called it. My uncle Ted died on the docks after being down there 50 years. All my uncles were down there, and most of my cousins. By 1981, the conditions by then had improved a hell of a lot. I can go back to the time when my dad was on the dock and he was working to 7 o'clock of a night, and Saturday mornings and Sundays. You had to work those hours if you were lucky enough to get them, to keep the family going – 7 o'clocks and working Sundays when they were really busy – even this would only put a few bob in your pocket to have a drink. The filthy cargoes, the degrading jobs had mostly gone. We still had a lot of dirty jobs, like the bones. The City boats and another line that went out to India, came back with fertilisers, dry bloods, hoofing horn, dried bones, and ground bones. They were filthy cargoes. You could smell yourself, never mind other people smelling you. After the 1967 strike, if you got a good job you could earn a few bob, unlike pre '67. The stewards fought for the piece rates and a higher rate per ton for those commodities. I didn't like going on them, but you know if you got sent; you had to work where you got sent. But those jobs started to dwindle away with the birth of containerisation…' [9]*

The impact of this casual system of employment was never lost on dockworkers, as it shaped the history of close-knit communities that had long been the natural recruitment base for dock work; a ready-made supply of labour that lived in the shadows of those huge dock walls, on the cobbled streets that ran alongside the black river where all the ships came in. It was a job that nobody else wanted, donated from father to son because no other employment options really existed for them outside the docks. A dock labourer was a second-class worker, who would never benefit from being able to purchase or borrow money because they were deemed as not working full-time, and its low pay and casual status stigmatised their existence and *marked them.*

The only real power the dock labourer had was to control the speed at which they worked, or to stop work altogether. From the first ship that ever cast its anchor in London or

Liverpool, the cry from the owners was for speed in loading or discharging their cargoes. The tempo, speed or productivity at a ship's hatch or on the quay would be determined by a number of critical factors, from the nature of the cargo, be it bales of wool, animal hides or steel coils, to the location of the cargo within the ship or the nature of its stow; the stability of the cargo; had it been affected by weather, physical deterioration, movement or infestation? The list went on and was extended regularly by the industrial struggles of the dockers to impose a rate for this work. These factors would be noted in a bonus, or impedance payment book that would record the appropriate rate for each cargo, with payment being based upon weight and space, chronicled in ledgers with a Victorian eye for detail. Every commodity had a price, and the award made at quay or shipside arbitrations were negotiated by appointed full-time union delegates with the boss, never directly involving the men affected as they were excluded from this process because their union refused to recognise their rights to elect shop stewards on the docks until 1967. Prior to this date all dock trade union activity was conducted on an unofficial basis recognised only by the dockers who elected their representatives on the quaysides.

In Liverpool, the clerical record of loading vessels was undertaken by those known as *wharfingers,* and the discharging of vessels was the responsibility of the *counter-off.* In the majority of *registered ports* post 1967 this work was undertaken by *Registered Dock Workers* (RDWs) with the exception of Liverpool docks. In Liverpool *RDWs* had to relinquish their registration books to take staff jobs. While dockers worked on ships or on delivery, they would constantly check with the office in the shed to see what bonus rates were being applied to each cargo. Whenever disagreements occurred, which they often did, the dark, tiny, two-floor brick office, with slanted wooden tables running its length, would be packed with men each arguing their case as to what they should be earning for that day. The following day, the tonnage clerk would record the rates being paid to each gang for each commodity worked. Contrary to the view often held by bosses, union and government, while a ship was running, it was in the interest of the dockers to be as productive as possible, despite all the shouting, arguing and bluster, it was the processing of multiple cargoes and tonnage payments that put money in their pockets and food on their tables.

Aside from the inherent danger and filth, the dock labourer would have to contend with the physical toll of their human labour being unsustainable over long periods. In Liverpool, a system known as the *dockers' welt* (it had a different name in every port, but this system of *spelling* was common to dock work and other forms of human labour), in which a gang of dockers in a hatch, on the deck or on the quay, would allow an agreed number of men to leave the job and come back, normally after an hour, to relieve the men who had been left working. This practice was originally referred to as *ca'canny,* whereby dockers determined the pace at which work would proceed. It seems fitting that the founders of the Liverpool dock workers' trade union organisation, two Irishmen, Edward McHugh and Richard McGhee, the first General Secretary and President of the union (1889-1893), provided the primary analysis of the dock labourers' exploitation. During one strike, the employers had publicly praised the 'blacklegs' (scabs) brought in to break the strike and expressed confidence in their efficiency and productivity. McHugh realised the significance of this, and once the strike had ended, he advised the dockers to work 'like the farm workers' who had been used to replace them, and so pleased their employers. McHugh introduced the tactic of *ca'canny,* working as slowly and as inefficiently as scab labour, which eventually forced the employer to agree to the dockers' demands. This profoundly Marxist analysis of human labour and labour power became a 'distinctive policy of the union,' and was as significant to dockers' work in 1995 as it was in 1889. [10] The union, for its part, reluctantly recognised the inevitability of this system, whereas to the port bosses, it was simply another of many restrictive practices that stood in the way of profit. [11]

In May 1951, the report of a Committee of Inquiry, under the chairmanship of Sir Frederick Leggett C.B., titled *Unofficial Stoppages in the Port of London* (Cmnd, 8256), was published, and for the leaders of the London dockers, it was simply a reaffirmation of the employers' opposition to the dockers' control of human labour, for they still had: 'the outlook of the casual worker… in the continuance of restrictive practices, and in the tradition of the unquestioning solidarity in strike action.' [12] As with all employers, it was about controlling the work process. [13] Any dispute aboard a ship had to be solved as quickly as possible; time was always of the essence, as the next day a ship could be sailing, and with no ship there, or with the dockers being moved to other ships, the workers had to strike when *the iron was hot* - when the ship in dispute was still in the port. Unlike a factory, where a strike could go on for weeks or months, the dockers had to get results there and then, and these harsh realities helped establish unity as a matter of survival. They lived by shared momentary experiences; they could identify with their own fathers and their uncles, who fought in so many dock struggles, through the ceaseless guerrilla stoppages and unofficial strikes that reinforced their physical connection to a rich history that underpinned the beat and the rhythm of dockers' solidarity. The dockers' union would never support their actions, further consolidating the mythology that industrial conflict on the docks was always *unofficial and illegitimate*. But the reality of the dockers' condition could never be ignored forever, and the government conceded that the absence of humane working conditions and even basic amenities had been: 'a constant source of irritation, and there can be no doubt that the general attitude of dock workers to employers and to the community is greatly affected by conditions which are so often primitive and degrading.' [14] In the 1940s, Harry Constable, a London dockers' leader, stated that it was never really in the interest of the docker to be unreasonable or to actively stop the job for no reason: 'He would be out of pocket, possibly losing a long run of work that he would have gained if he had been ready for a fresh ship when he had finished working on the ship in dispute.' [15]

Local labour historian, Eric Taplin, described how between the late 1800s and early 1900s, dock work witnessed some technological advances, but that essentially the loading and unloading of ships:

> '…remained a manual job requiring strength, stamina and skill in the lifting, carrying and stowing of cargo… the waterfront was teeming with men at work, the quays and wharfs choked with an infinite variety of goods in transit. Hand-trolleys, carts and horse-drawn vehicles added to the confusion. Cranes and hydraulic equipment were seen in growing numbers by the end of the century, but the most important tool remained the [dockers'] hook with which the docker manipulated the sacks, boxes, barrels, crates and bundles of goods to be moved.' [16]

The docks were a world of steam, coal and noise; of giant, busy cranes of steel and iron flying back and forth overhead, shadowing gangs of men below who scurried with ropes, hooks and electric bogeys to keep up with the motion of the cranes that lubricated the bonus payments that they all relied upon. Every movement, from ship to quay and quay to ship, carried danger in this world of work – a human choreography of a world in a hurry. Liverpool's port depended on horsepower well into the 20th century. Horses and carts were used to move goods from the docks and into the city for more than 250 years. The Liverpool Retired Carter's Association claimed that at their peak, more than 250,000 horses worked in the city with numerous stables located around Liverpool. Behind the high dock walls existed a reality that was virtually unknown to outsiders. [17] Writing in 1849, the author Herman Melville wondered at the immensity of these structures that isolated the docks from the teeming populace living just feet away: 'In Liverpool, I beheld long China walls of masonry; vast piers of stone; and a succession of granite-rimmed docks, completely enclosed and many of them communicating… The extent and solidity of these structures, seemed equal to what I had read of the Pyramids of Egypt.' [18] Only those who experienced life inside these walls could understand it; only those who experienced it could be trusted, and this often brought with it a narrow, sectarian and combative attitude towards other workers or trades and even fellow dock workers.

Often respected and celebrated dockers' leaders found themselves the victim of the heightened sense of sectoral solidarity and loyalty that dominated dockland relationships as transient conflicts flared intermittently along the line of Liverpool docks. Peter Kerrigan, one of the leaders of the National Amalgamated Stevedores & Dockers Union (NASD), started work on the docks as a coal heaver in 1935, loading coal into ships' bunkers before they went to sea. In 1967, he was stopped from addressing dockers at a mass meeting during the strike that ended casual labour and gave recognition rights to elected rank-and-file shop stewards. Kerrigan had just become an officer of the Blue Union, and he was called to address dockers at a meeting that contained NASD (Blue Union) and TGWU (White Union) members. According to Larry Cavanagh, who would become chairman of the Merseyside Portworkers' Unofficial Committee, Kerrigan was about to speak when dockers' leader, Jackie Lydon, challenged his credentials to represent dockworkers by yelling: 'He's not a docker!' Jimmy Benbow, chairman of the Blue Union, requested that Peter Kerrigan sit down to avoid fuelling the distraction of such arguments that so often erupted at mass meetings. [19] Similarly, Jack Jones, with his working-class credentials as the son of a Liverpool docker, while being a Liverpool dock worker himself, as well as a member of the Liverpool Trades Council, a Spanish Civil War volunteer and General Secretary of the TGWU, would not escape the personal wrath thrown up during times of dockers' conflicts. [20] Dock leaders could be heroes one day and class-enemies the next. In the 1970s, the developing Liverpool dock staff of TGWU Branch 6/567 also experienced conflict with dockworkers, caused by suspicion and mistrust stemming from the fact that they were not registered dockers. Although the majority were sons and brothers of dockers, this mattered little, as did their 1970 branch policy of seeking *registered dock labour status* for the grades they represented on the docks, from storekeepers to timekeepers, to ship and quay foremen; roles performed by registered dockers in other UK ports, such as the Port of London. [21]

# 3

# LIFE ON THE DOCKS

Outsiders labelled the world of the dock worker as unskilled and strike-ridden, dominated by ignorance and communist infiltration. During the Second World War, some government observers saw Liverpool dockers as little more than traitors. 'A considerable proportion of Liverpool dockers are showing very little interest in winning the war or working hard to win it. There is a major emotional conflict from the dockers against the employer class.' [22] Another observer remarked: 'Dockers were unthinking beasts of burden.' [23] Unsurprisingly, given such an unforgiving status in the national psyche, dock labourers expected no quarter to be given by the triumvirate they faced daily – the power of the state, the employer and their official union. For the dockers, every ship, every hatch, every quay, every shed and every cargo were an opportunity to bargain, an opportunity to strike for more pay and better conditions; to raise their heads above the abyss they had been plunged into. [24] An opportunity to stop the job was a chance to enforce permanency at the core of dock work. However, they also knew that the State and the employers would respond with laws and troops to defeat their ambitions. [25]

Liverpool dockers had a history of militant rank-and-file unofficial organisation. It was a history not short of its own contradictions, but one that in turn gave all port cities their own culture of radical and revolutionary organisation that flowed from the river through the streets and their communities. Fearless and fiercely loyal to one another, their industrial experience fostered a unique a sense of their own trade unionism, a trade unionism that had no limits. In 1958, Peter Kerrigan, was to recall: 'Older men on the docks remembered the thirties very well. The humiliation of the stands. The 'muscle feeling.' The scramble for a job. They remember the 'blue eyes' system; the whisper of 'You're staying behind' in the ear of a favoured one. The militant was isolated. The man who refused to overload a sling on the last ship was left standing.' [26] It is not surprising that dockers like Kerrigan and so many others saw the way forward as being welded to the NASD's growth in the north, in opposition to the White Union, the TGWU. Many unofficial dock shop stewards held elected positions on district, regional and national committees within the TGWU. Their own unofficial committees of dockworkers also had structures at national and local level. They exploited their dual existence, their parallel organisation, within and without the TGWU to such a degree that, in essence, they were only as loyal to their union as their union was loyal to them. They fought for everything they called their own, and battles were often against powerful interests within their own union as much as they were with the port employers. These dockers fought governments and prime ministers; theirs was a history of struggle that bred in them a certainty that meant they feared nothing. Reflecting on his experience of the Liverpool dockers, Jimmy McGovern, the Liverpool playwright, was to observe: 'Dockers are not easily impressed. That to me is a real quality.' [27]

The history of the TGWU and the Trade Union Congress depicts battles fought with their membership across Britain's industrial heartlands, leading to bans and proscriptions. These inquisitions victimised workers who were members of the Communist Party, along with anyone who challenged the power of the union's bureaucracy. They would be hauled before their union to account for themselves or face expulsion. Official unions herded trade unionists into the catch-all allegation of being 'fellow-travellers' with the communists. These tactics were used with great effect against trade union activists, especially dockworkers, in every UK port, and this dreadful period of witch-hunts and expulsions only ended in 1969.

The British security services took an active interest in the TGWU throughout this period, recruiting many on the docks and in the union to spy on their behalf. In 2009 it was claimed that Jack Jones, the TGWU's general secretary, was a KGB spy. A London docker, Brian Nicholson, who became TGWU President in the 1980s, was alleged to have been involved with MI5. According to Nicholson: 'MI5 agents flitted around the docks, posing as left-wing activists and do-gooders during the industrial upheavals of the early 1970s, although others were associated with right-wing groups, such as Catholic Action and Moral Rearmament.' [28]

The strikes, conflicts and struggles of the dockers only served to unite them across numerous political divides in opposition to all *bans and proscriptions* imposed by their trade unions and the TUC. For Birkenhead and Liverpool shop steward Larry Cavanagh:

> *The reason for this was that the docks had a strong political leadership (not just members of the Blue Union); there were Trotskyists, Communist Party members and even one or two members of the Labour Party who had a history of fighting. People had their differences with the Communist Party, but they were recognised by the dockers, like the others, as the leaders, and the employers were not pleased about this.' [29]*

Generations of dockers' leaders in Liverpool from Tom Mann to Peter Kerrigan, Leo McGree, Jimmy Benbow, Joe Byrne, Albert McCabe, Alex McKechnie, Frank Deegan, Paddy Doherty, Denis Kelly, Jimmy Symes and Jimmy Nolan – contributed to the fight, inspired and educated by the same ideas, principles and people that would lead the struggles of 1989 and 1995. It is very important to understand that these leaders, along with the dockers themselves, had, through their trade unionism, an influence that went beyond the docks into communities, political parties and international organisations. For example, Paddy Doherty maintained his connection to the Irish liberation movement through various groups, [30] as well as his lifelong friendship with Kevin McNamara, Labour MP and Secretary of State for Northern Ireland. Tim Pat Coogan, the Irish historian, noted how Liverpool-born McNamara had, like Doherty and so many other Liverpool dockers, a deep affinity with their Irish brethren:

> *The resumption of strife in Northern Ireland meant that, as in previous years, trouble in Ireland was replicated in Liverpool... McNamara grew up in a strongly Irish background. Irish music, Irish games were the recreations of his childhood. The Irish were a politically aware community. A joke of McNamara's boyhood was that the Irish in Liverpool grew up trained to do three things: go to mass on Sunday, vote Labour and join the Transport and General Workers' Union.' [31]*

In this world of politics, the dockers functioned with great confidence and political awareness. When Margaret Thatcher's Conservative government abolished the National Dock Labour Board Scheme, the dockers were not surprised. According to Nigel Lawson, writing in his memoirs, Thatcher wanted to watch this moribund organisation 'wither on the vine' [32] but the National Port Employers wanted the government to end the NDLB in 1989. A year chosen specially to ridicule the plans of the trade union movement, and in particular the TGWU, to celebrate the centenary of the London dock strike of 1889 and the birth of New Unionism that brought with it a working-class history that was as unique as it was extraordinary. And yet, it was as if this historical legacy of the dockers was always left unfinished, incomplete. The abolition of the Dock Labour Scheme in 1989 did not end conflict on the docks. Like a strike that never ends, the dockers' history was to repeat itself over the decades of the twentieth century – like storm waves on the Mersey rising in cold fury to crash perpetually in a calm sea only to be reawakened again. In this sense the dockers present seemed always to be a victim of its turbulent past.

# 4
# The Formation of the TGWU

*'As in 1911, it was (so to speak) a soldiers' battle, for it was not the dockers union that called them out. Far from it, the Transport and General Workers Union had assisted, at national level, to devise the new scheme, and its officers genuinely believed it to be a good development for their members. It indicated, perhaps, how far these officials now were from the rank-and-file union member, how out of touch with working-class feelings, that their only answer to the Liverpool dockers was to repeat over and over again that the strikers must go back to work... by appearing side by side with the representatives of the employers when union official and employers' man jointly urged the dockers to go back to work, the union officials clearly demonstrated that they felt themselves to be part of the machinery of the establishment...' ~ Building the Union\**

The seeds of the Transport and General Workers Union were planted by the political struggles of the Liverpool-based National Union of Dock Labourers, led, amongst so many others, by James Sexton, James Larkin and George Milligan together with the London Dock, Wharf, Riverside and General Labourers Union, led by Ben Tillett and Harry Orbell. They were the two major constituent parts of 'one big union' in 1922. [1] The singular pre-eminence of Ernest Bevin was not the original intention of those union leaders involved in early amalgamation discussions. [2] Unsurprisingly, some of the union leaders involved in the original amalgamation process in 1921-22, 'resented the relinquishing of their own union's autonomy, along with their own personal power upon amalgamation.' [3] James Sexton and Ben Tillett looked to the state to provide a fairer framework within which to operate, and, like Bevin, they were scarcely revolutionary once in office. [4]

---

\* Building the Union, edited by Harold Hikens, Toulouse Press, 1973, pp.183-184; also, The Liverpool Transport Strike, William Jones, 1911
(www.roydenhistory.co.uk/mrlhp/students/transportstrike/transportstrike.htm)

In 1923, during the first year of the TGWU's existence, Bevin negotiated a wage reduction for dockers, arguing that it was 'to protect jobs.' [5] This sparked a seven-week unofficial strike involving around 40,000 workers. However, with the union refusing to issue strike relief, the men ended up going back to work without regaining their previous pay levels. As a result, the new union's reputation was damaged from the beginning, and its position in London permanently weakened. This came a year after Bevin had failed to incorporate the Amalgamated Stevedores' Labour Protection League (ASLPL) into the TGWU and, following the 1923 strike, several thousand dockers left the union to form their own section of the ASLPL, which later reconstituted itself as the National Amalgamated Stevedores and Dockers (NASD). [6] Internal divisions within the new union were now formalised by its very own dockers' breakaway union, led by an unofficial committee, the 'Unknown 39,' and one of their leaders, Bert Aylward, would go on to become a prominent member of the NASD. [7] Not only was the split official it was also colour-coded; the NASD becoming known as the Blue Union and the TGWU the White Union, named from the colours of their union membership cards. Bevin moved quickly to secure the foundations of his authority through an elaborate network of a permanent, full-time officer corps appointed at both national and regional levels. Jack Jones would later describe the TGWU as: 'a highly centralised union with authority vested ultimately in the General Secretary… Bevin did not like the idea of any rank-and-file movement… Bevin had the concept of all power to the top.' [8]

According to Geoffrey Goodman, Bill Morris's official biographer, Bevin was to become: 'Britain's most politically influential trade union leader of all time. It was in its own way a foundation stone upon which Bill Morris, eighty-one years later, would take his stand as Ernest Bevin's true heir.' [9] Bevin, along with his successor, Arthur Deakin, instilled in their officer corps a rigid career-based discipline, *enforced through the ultimate power of patronage*. This was to have obvious implications on the nature of rank-and-file activity within the union, forging a culture of bureaucracy and in-built democratic restrictions upon lay-membership power. Not that this stopped rank-and-file organisation, but it did mean that the TGWU's *unelected officer corps* would often act, wittingly or otherwise, as institutional barriers to rank-and-file influence, particularly as it unfolded in the dock industry. In 1931, nine years after the formation of the TGWU, Jack Jones began work on Liverpool's Garston Docks. He very quickly observed: 'in the workplace, the officials were almost an arm of the management,' evidenced by many union officers seemingly developing an aversion towards conflict with port employers. [10] This attitude flowed downstream from the union's leadership, and, according to Jones: 'Arthur Deakin held the view that a union should appease the employer and really be a close friend.' [11] When Jones arrived at the union's London Office in 1963, he was to discover: 'Some of the officers of the union were very much of the Deakin era who took the view that what they said was good for people and that people should not have a say… Many of the officers and branches remained faithful to the traditional right-wing policies of the union.' [12]

When Deakin died in 1955, his replacement, Jock Tiffin, was only in post for six months before his untimely death. He was followed by Frank Cousins, and the right-wing monolith that the TGWU had been since its inception began to falter and change. Jones's election in 1968 would prove to be a major turning point, as he put into practice his firmly held convictions regarding the ability of union members to make decisions on policies. He embarked upon a devolution process aimed at enhancing both the internal democracy of the union and the influence of the rank-and-file membership that had, at least theoretically, been enshrined in the union's original rulebook. [13] The history of the TGWU was set to be transformed, and especially in Liverpool, where Jones's local roots made his acceptance by the dockers, as their very own *Scouse* General Secretary, a relatively easy transition. He was one of them and, as such, he was part of their heritage and legacy, although this did not prevent conflict with him wherever it was deemed necessary. Still, even these incidents were disputes with 'one of their own,' as the dockers' saw it. [14] Nevertheless, support for the officer-led traditions established by Bevin in the TGWU would always exist amongst the paid officials and those aspiring to life-time employment in the union. Ernest Bevin never inspired much deference among the Liverpool dockers, as John Pilger observed for himself at Transport House in 1996, where a bust of the union leader was routinely employed as a coatrack. [15]

The transformation in the internal organisation of the TGWU reflected the contemporary reality of unofficial workplace organisations that had become the central focus of the government's Donovan and Devlin reports in the early 1960s. [16] The power and influence of rank-and-file shop stewards was largely ignored but, by the early 1960s, the 'push from the shop floor' would result in 'wage-drift' as nationally negotiated official agreements would be enhanced by powerful shop stewards' movements on the shop-floor. Ironically, their power was eventually countered by the phenomenal growth of aspirational unelected, paid union officials in the 1970s. [17] As one former General Executive Council member and Dunlop (Liverpool) shop steward, Charlie Parker, observed in 1986:

> *'Union officers then were nothing like they are now. They used to ride around on bikes, use public transport and live in Council houses. A man who took a union officer's job in those days did not have the incentive to take it, no real financial incentive, a union officer wasn't all that well paid. Now it's the easy option to be a union official.' [18]*

The Second World War provided the government and Ernest Bevan, now appointed Minister of Labour and National Service in the wartime coalition government, with the opportunity to reclaim greater control of Britain's ports, especially following the dock strike of 1945. In that year, the incoming Labour government established a committee, under Sir Kenneth Foster KC, to make recommendations on the decasualisation of dock work. Foster's committee made its report in January 1947, proposing that ports should register all dockworkers, along with a reserve pool to meet any fluctuations in labour requirements, and it also suggested equal power sharing between the union and the employers. At the same time, the Unofficial National Portworkers' Defence Committee held a meeting at Canning Town Public Hall, to report on their campaign against the Foster Report, which they believed fell short of the full employment originally promised by Bevin. It was at this meeting that an alternative scheme was discussed, based on the American dock hiring hall system. London dockers' leader, Bert Aylward, argued that if this system were adopted: 'it would place control in the hands of the unions and take away controls from a clique of shipowners who were never seen on the docks.' [19] Both Aylward and Harry Constable held the opinion that dock nationalisation was not the answer, workers' control was. [20]

By 1947, the National Dock Labour Board Scheme was being used to provide more influence and control to port employers, the TGWU and the state. Writing in 1972, D.F. Wilson described how: 'Supreme control was vested in the National Dock Labour Board Scheme, as effectively each port had its own local Dock Labour Board consisting of an equal number of representatives implementing national decisions as well as, amongst other duties, enacting disciplinary procedures for dock workers.' [21] A 1986 Trade Union Congress review of dock labour history reported that prior to 1940, some dockers valued the relative freedom to choose whether or not to try for work on a particular morning, and to accept or reject what work was offered. Dockers were free from the constraints of the rigid working week and, as others noted in describing the casual dock labour system: 'skilled pieceworkers, for example, could often earn enough money in the first part of the week to cover the cost of a three-day rest at the end of the week.' [22] This nature of dock work impacted on how dockers related to trade unionism; they were not going to be shackled or controlled by membership. Understandably, dockers had major trust issues; their response was to fall back on their independent organisation where it always existed, on the ships, quays, sheds, pens and hiring halls of the major ports. This parallel organisational structure, of official and unofficial activity, existed for the dockers until 1995.

# 5

# Internal Conflict and 'Breakaways'

*'For much of its history, the TGWU has been, as one historian wrote, "an encrusted, complacent bureaucracy," which, in containing the anger of its ordinary members at the injustices imposed on their working lives, has served the aims of the British establishment.' ~ John Pilger*[*]

In 1945, the Labour government used the army to force an end to a dock strike involving over 45,000 men. This dispute, which became known as the Dockers Charter Strike, lasted from 24 September to 4 November 1945, ending only after the government deployed more than 21,000 troops to break it. Soldiers were again seen on the docks in 1949, during a solidarity strike with the Canadian Seamen's Union; between July 1945 and October 1951, military intervention was used on no less than 14 occasions. At no point did this extreme response galvanise TGWU officials into action. In fact, the union justified and supported military strikebreaking against their own members [1], as historian Jim Philips wrote: 'The complete refusal of the TGWU to support the dockworkers' struggles and the collaboration of the union in the management of the industry, through the Dock Labour Boards, encouraged, within the ranks of the men, the idea of forming or joining an alternative union.' [2] According to Harry Constable, one of the unofficial London dockers' leaders: 'It was agreed after the 1945 Dockers Charter Strike that leaders of the Unofficial Committees should strive to make contact throughout the ports with other progressive workers... Most of the northern ports were forming committees.' [3]

According to Liverpool labour historian Harold Hikens: 'the presence of unofficial leadership in the main northern ports ensured that any breakaway would immediately be given an organised form.' [4] In June 1948, a strike began on a small ship at the Regents Canal Dock in London, and the union officer, dealing with an arbitration over the discharging of a

---

* John Pilger, They Never Walk Alone. The Guardian, 23rd November 1996

cargo of zinc oxide, failed to convince the dockers to reach an agreement, resulting in 11 TGWU members being suspended for refusing to obey their employer and the union. On 17 June, the local shop stewards' committee responded by moving a resolution, stating:

> *'We, the accredited delegates of shop stewards, recommend to the men on strike that this punishment meted out by the tribunal is a direct attack on all militant workers on the docks. Further, we cannot recommend acceptance of the tribunal's findings, our reply to this attack is that we pursue the issue to the utmost of our ability and report back to our members for their decision.' [5]*

Some 19,000 London dockers withdrew their labour over these suspensions, which they considered a national issue that affected all dockers, and so Constable, along with Bert Saunders, was sent to Merseyside to present their case on behalf of the London Unofficial Portworkers' Committee. A meeting took place on Lord Street, where the Liverpool dockers voted to support the London men who, the following day, addressed a further eight meetings of dockers from Birkenhead to Garston. This unofficial strike took place during May and June, ending only when Clement Atlee, the post-war Labour Prime Minister, declared a State of Emergency on 28 June 1948. Arthur Deakin, the TGWU's sitting general secretary, took this as an opportunity to launch a General Executive Council Inquiry into this unofficial strike. [6] On Friday 9 February 1951, the dockers' distrust towards union officials gained fresh impetus as police raided the White Hart Public House in East London, a popular dockers meeting place, arresting six. Bill Crosby, a Liverpool docker, had been arrested the night before. [7] The dockers were charged at Bow Street Magistrates Court with conspiring to incite fellow port workers to take part in illegal strikes and were remanded on £100 bail until 20 February 1951.

On Tuesday 3 April, TGWU officials appeared in court to give evidence against the seven dockers who had been arrested under Regulation 1305 (Conditions of Employment and National Arbitration Order), which banned strikes and imposed arbitration. They were charged at the Old Bailey with leading an unofficial wage dispute that had started on Merseyside before eventually spreading to London. The Port Workers' Defence Committee formed at this time would eventually become the Unofficial Port Workers' Committee, a body that organised itself on the basis of the 'election of delegates carried out at open air meetings at each of the control points or pens on the docks.' [8] D.F. Wilson, in his classic study of the dockers' organisation during this period, observed:

> *'When the unofficial committees sprang up in London in 1948 and in Liverpool and Manchester in 1950-51, dissatisfaction with the TGWU was at such a pitch that they found a ready audience. Throughout the sporadic publication of bulletins and journals, and the frequent use of mass meetings, the unofficials established better lines of communication than the TGWU. They could claim, dubiously, to be democratically elected at the dock-gate. In their Charters, they had programmes which were militant but not hopelessly unattainable and they could make enormous capital out of identifying the right-wing TGWU with the bosses' interest.' [9]*

# INTERNAL CONFLICT AND 'BREAKAWAYS'

John Magginnis, who started work on the docks in 1951, recalled:

> 'All strikes… at the end of the war and after, were unofficial… Trade union officials, from the highest to the lowest, were hated. We worked in dirty, unhealthy, dangerous conditions. But, if the men had a grievance and sent for the delegate [trade union official] he would walk round the sheds, straight into the office, come out, walk past the men without saying a word and you would find out later from the employer's representative that nothing had changed. The favourite phrase of delegates was: 'My hands are tied, what can I do'.' [10]

In 1952, Harry Constable, Dickens, Jack Dash and other rank-and-file dockers were expelled from the TGWU because of their unofficial activity. Other dockers, such as Danny Brandon, a Revolutionary Communist Party member, one-time secretary of the Birkenhead Portworkers' Committee and former editor of the *Portworkers' Clarion*, were victimised by the employers and the union, often at the cost of their jobs. The calls to break away from the TGWU still focussed on the National Amalgamated Stevedores and Dockers Union (NASD, or Blue Union), which was the long-established dockers' union that challenged the 'centralised, officer-led Bevin union.' [11] The NASD embodied both militant and democratic traditions that, according to Bill Hunter, ensured: 'All major decisions referred back to the rank-and-file for a final decision. This was a constant source of criticism by TGWU officials, employers and government alike; a fact that did not go unnoticed by the dockers.' [12] By 1954, the Blue Union was picking up members in the northern ports, including Hull, Birkenhead and Liverpool, as dissatisfaction with the TGWU reached boiling point. During this period, the Hull dockers' unofficial strike committee put out a leaflet openly attacking the TGWU. [13] For Walter Greendale, the Hull dockers' leader during the mid-1960s, there was 'no love lost between the dockers in Hull and their trade union officials'. [14] According to Constable: 'anger at the officials continually grew as we felt they were treating the union as a sinecure. They were entrenched: each paid officer owed his position to the strength of his loyalty to the men above him.' [15]

In August 1954, many London dockers decided to leave the TGWU and join the Blue Union, and they appealed to dockers on Merseyside to do likewise. Dock labourers in Birkenhead, Liverpool and Manchester soon followed suit, and by 1955, the new union was firmly established, with offices and full-time officials operating in all these towns. Between September 1954 and May 1955, ten thousand dockers left the TGWU and joined the Blue Union, which in some cases amounted to 40% of the local membership. The response of the TGWU was immediate; they used their power to get the Trades Union Congress to suspend the NASD for poaching members under the TUC's Bridlington Agreement. The TGWU also used their immense influence over dock employers to get them to refuse to issue new registration books, needed for work on the docks, to those with Blue Union cards. These actions only succeeded in uniting dockers in both unions, who immediately stopped work and defeated this triumvirate of the TGWU, the TUC and the port employers. [16]

Michael Foot MP attended a meeting of the Birkenhead dockers, and pledged support from Labour's Tribune Group of MPs, who were opposed to the leadership of the TGWU. [17] By October 1954, the NASD's overtime ban had become a full-blown dispute,

[18] and at the centre of this crisis lay a membership challenge to the structure of Britain's largest trade union, as the TGWU District Secretary, P.J. O'Hare, became the subject of another resolution from Birkenhead No.12 Branch, calling for his removal from office within 21 days. [19] Now, with confidence growing, the NASD began issuing membership cards to Birkenhead and Liverpool dockers, and the TGWU Regional secretary in Liverpool, Fred Hughes, informed the Regional Committee that: 'Well-known Communists were among the strike leaders in all the ports affected.' [20]

Liverpool dock shop steward and Communist Party member, Denis Anderson, expressed the view that the development of the Blue Union detracted from the struggle to organise and change the TGWU. The Blue Union activists recognised that the position of the Communist Party regarding the TGWU was to, 'stay inside and democratise it,' using Port Liaison Committees, 'as negotiating bodies between the *white union* and the TUC.' [21] Dockers were proud of their unofficial status and their independence, and especially their liberty to take industrial action whenever it was necessary. As academics, Tony Lane and Ken Roberts, observed:

> *'To go on strike is to deny the existing distribution of power and authority. The striker ceases to respond to managerial command; he/she refuses to do his/her 'work'. A new dimension of living can thus be revealed to the striker; an existence in which 'ordinary' people are able to control events and command the attention of 'them'. The experience of this new reality can transform the striker's perceptions of normal life. What was 'normal' can no longer be regarded as 'natural'. Attitudes towards work and authority become critical as opposed to acquiescent.' [22]*

The deep internal conflicts created by casual employment on the docks were another natural inheritance of later generations along with union membership that was donated from father to son like a family heirloom. Employers' tallies handed out or thrown to dockers at the twice daily hires for work dominated the need for effective union and workplace organisation in Liverpool from the 1900s. [23] The history of this fight for dignity and control in work connected one century to the next and forged the iron resilience that dockers displayed against any organisation, employer or government whenever they experienced injustice or unfairness. Harold Marr, a Liverpool docker who, when he became an official of the TGWU in the 1960s, had only a bicycle as a form of transport, recalled in 1984:

> *'When I was four years of age, I was taken down the docks by my father and he worked for the White Star Line. He was on the docks in 1889, and he said, "I'm going to show you the largest ship in the world," that would be in 1925. We went down to the docks, the Canada Dock, and there, lying in the West Canada Dock, was the Majestic. We captured her from the Germans as restoration after the First World War, and the Majestic finished her days in Southampton as a training ship, and I was always fascinated with ships. I liked the atmosphere and I like the free and easy way of the approach of a docker. By the way, and this is a fact, he's the only man living today, the dock labourer, who could tell a supervisor, "You stupid bloody so and so, go and get stuffed," and not get the sack. Couldn't do it in a factory, but he can! My father was on*

*the docks, all my cousins, Charlie Marr, he was a Ships' Foreman at Raes, Sammy Marr, Billy was a crane driver and Ernie's still on the docks. Runs right through the family, my uncle George was on the docks.' [24]*

These close-knit family ties – Harold Marr was a relative of Len McCluskey – provided almost all of the docks' labour requirement. [25] In 1995, Kevin Robinson, a Liverpool docker and Seaforth Container Terminal shop steward, described his upbringing in a docker family: 'My father worked on the docks, my grandfather worked on the docks and my two uncles worked on the docks; and they knew what fighting was all about. Because it was through their fight then, that we got some decent wages. That was before 1967, when we did away with casualisation.' [26] Even at the height of industrial turmoil, the Liverpool dockers were never explicitly anti-union. Membership was always a contentious subject but eventually joining the TGWU was *more or less* required in order to qualify for the right to undertake work. [27] Sometimes, membership would lapse and be left unrenewed until it became absolutely necessary while some managed to fly under the radar and avoid it altogether. [28] It would not be uncommon for one family member to join the Blue Union despite having relatives in the White Union, and some had dual membership, [29] allowing them to apply for work in any area along the Liverpool and Birkenhead docks. Proof of union membership became extremely important, especially during the 1989 and 1995 disputes, but despite understanding the situation of the NASD and their brother dockers, the leadership of Merseyside's Unofficial Dockers' Committee advised against joining the Blue Union. [30] They argued that it was better to reform the TGWU from the inside, but the Blue Union's growth throughout the 1950s only emboldened them to continue poaching TGWU dockers. [31] Numerous allegations were made against the Blue Union, with family ties, political leanings and trade union affiliations providing the backdrop to a civil war as the situation on the Liverpool docks deteriorated. Frank Deegan believed that some dockers were intimidated into joining the Blue Union, stating that:

*'those of us who strongly opposed the breakaway were treated as if they had black-legged [scabbed] strikes, which is an unforgiveable crime in dockland. The atmosphere was explosive. Whole families were divided; fathers, sons and brothers fighting among themselves over whose union was best.' [32]*

The TGWU fell back on its use of bans and proscriptions against any members that had supported or expressed sympathy towards the NASD. Like the Trade Union Congress, the TGWU leadership had a shameful history of suppressing militancy by expelling those who they decided were communists or 'fellow travellers', such labels were thrown at any Liverpool dockworker caught challenging the authority of union officials. [33] Under the leadership of general secretary Jock Tiffin, the union affirmed that membership of the Unofficial Port Workers' Committee was inconsistent with membership of any constitutional committee of the TGWU. There was no limit to this determination to impose the will of the union's hierarchy, supported by the employer and the state, upon dock labourers, [34] a view shared by the NASD in their own *Port Workers' News*. 'The attitude of the TGWU was now to ensure that the Dock Labour Scheme worked, even if this meant that it worked against the men.' [35]

In answer to press questions about the demands for wage increases by Liverpool dockers, James O'Hare, the then Liverpool docks district secretary commented: 'It is best to say nothing to anybody about the dockers. That is the way they like it. Why? Because their wives would read about it and a lot of dockers don't want their wives to know how much they earn.' [36] O'Hare would be described in the Devlin Report as: 'A dedicated trade unionist, a man of great force of character, upright and honourable in his ways, but rather autocratic in manner and himself a focus of dissention.' [37] Peter Kerrigan recalled:

> '...We were part of a decade and a half of struggle on Merseyside up to 1970 and it built the consciousness of the dockers, both industrially and politically. And it did have a big effect on the TGWU: it shook the bureaucracy and forced them to retreat and give shop stewards in 1967.' [38]

However, without any consultation with TGWU dockers, O'Hare, along with the Employers Association of the Port of Liverpool, set about designing an elaborate local de-casualisation scheme. In a 'New Deal for Merseyside Registered Dock Workers,' the union made use of publicity consultants to ensure that they got their message across. [39] They called branch meetings on the proposals contained within this New Deal, recommending that Liverpool dockers accept its proposals. According to Frank Deegan: 'They were the best-ever attended meetings on Merseyside. The men were determined to show their disgust at this rotten deal. It was rejected unanimously, and every Branch passed votes of no confidence in Brother O'Hare and called for his resignation or dismissal. Unfortunately, this wasn't possible. He had the full support of the powerful General Secretary.' [40] Even allowing for the socio-political context of this period in the union's history (it was the peak of the Cold War and it was also a period of full employment) the TGWU leadership felt at ease punishing its members with bans, proscriptions and blacklists. If these aggressive tactics did not work, they would collaborate openly with the port employers at the dockers' expense. It is important to note here that the Blue Union, to their credit, did not impose any bans or proscriptions on dockers who chose to join the Communist Party. [41] Tony Burke, a dock shop steward, recalled that prior to 1967, the relationship between the Communist Party and the Unofficial Port Workers' Committee was amicable:

> 'Basically. It was a good working relationship insomuch as they encouraged the masses to play a role in the trade union movement – and they helped organise and give a lead to the unorganised section because of the distrust they had to the 'selected officials.' The Party, I would suggest, were the majority and the most vigilant before 1967. Jackie Lydon, Denis Kelly, Paddy Doherty, Frank Deegan… other people followed another political line. Before 1967, there was a proscript on party members, and little between the unofficial movement and the official lay committees of the union made up by constitutionalists and those who often hid behind the trade union ticket as a meal ticket. The proscribed organisations like the Trots and the Communist Party could not hold lay-official jobs within the union. Also, the antagonists, and indeed, individuals, Syndicalists even to a

*point, there was quite a number of them around and encouragement was given by Party members.' [42]*

For Frank Deegan, the true nature and character of the men he worked alongside on the quays and ships of the Liverpool waterfront was that they, 'were proud men, proud of their history.' [43] The unofficial leaders of the dockers in UK ports would not be allowed to speak on behalf of rank-and-file dockers unless they had their confidence and agreement. During the 1967 national dock strike, Colin Ross, a London dock shop steward, recalled how the unofficial committee sent him, along with three others, to Liverpool in November of that year:

*'We were met by the chairman of the Liverpool docks unofficial committee, Denis Kelly, a truly wonderful person who, like many Liverpool dockers, said it as they saw it… Denis Kelly had a way with words… Denis was like a godfather in Liverpool, he was widely respected by his men, even as we walked along the dockside with him, it was as if no one would walk past him without bidding him good morning, he in turn would just nod back. But respect doesn't just appear, it only appears after you have earnt it.' [44]*

Dockers' leaders would be judged by those that went before them as the post-1967, shop stewards transitioned from unofficial to official and took the name of the Merseyside Port Shop Stewards Committee. A new era was about to begin involving another generation of dockers such as Dickie Lewis, Billy O'Hara, Albie Brown, John Hulme, Kenny Kelly, Paddy McKeown, Harry Cunningham, Jimmy Symes, Denis Kelly, Denis Anderson, Paddy Doherty, Frank Conchie, Tony Burke, Tommy Shandley, Larry Kavanagh, Jimmy Nolan, Jimmy Davies, Larry Dowling, Jimmy Thompson, Kevin Robinson, Frank Lannigan, Billy and John Jenkins and so many, many others. As with previous generations of leaders most possessed the innate ability to lead, but this did not stop the worst examples of individuals who abused their roles and became little more than pawns of either the employer or the union. In this sense, no history of the Liverpool dockers could ever portray a faultless industrial or political record of shop steward rank-and-file organisation.

Within a year of the docks being de-casualised in 1967, on Tuesday 23 April 1968, just three days after Enoch Powell had delivered his infamous 'Rivers of Blood' speech, 1,000 London dockers marched from the West India Docks in Poplar to Westminster. They were joined over two days by London dockers from St Katherine's Docks in Wapping and the Royal Group of Docks in Newham. It was not the best of days for rank-and-file dockers as television and press images of their march to Parliament were used to maximum effect in order to discredit the London dockworkers. Communist dockers, like Jack Dash and Michael Fenn did distribute a leaflet at the West Indies Dock the morning after the strike 'attacking those who marched…' [45] This demonstration had in fact been organised by extreme right-wing activists, according to secret intelligence briefings to the prime minister at the time. An MI5 report to Harold Wilson, submitted four days after Powell's inflammatory Birmingham address, detailed how the supposedly spontaneous strike and demonstration was led by Harry Pearman, a supporter of the anti-communist fundamentalist group, Moral Rearmament. [46]

This did nothing to ease the media-led shaming of the participants as Satnam Virdee records in his study, *Racism, Class and the Racialized Outsider*. [47]

Some four years later, the state would again intervene following the actions of London and Liverpool dockworkers. Essentially, this phase of dock history related to the introduction of containerisation and the modernisation of the port transport industry. Encouraged by the ambitions of the Tory government to 'modernise' the dock industry, it would not be long before two haulage firms, Heaton's Transport, based in St Helens, and another firm, Craddocks, decided that they could perform dock work in their own transport depots by stripping and stuffing containers prior to their distribution to the ports for import or export. Heaton's involved the Merseyside Port Shop Stewards directly when both firms took legal action against the TGWU for allowing unofficial action to take place at their depots. These disputes came down to the dockworkers' claim that the work of stuffing and stripping containers, wherever that took place, was their work, and not for the first time, the Liverpool Road Haulage Section (TGWU 6/541) played an active role in supporting the dockers. [48] Eventually, the courts ruled that the TGWU was responsible for the unofficial action and fined it £5,000 for contempt after refusing to show up to court. The union then faced a further fine of £50,000 and the threat of sequestration of assets under the new Industrial Relations Act (1971) if they refused to lift the dockers' boycott. According to Jack Jones:

> *The union was caught between the devil and the deep blue sea. From the dockers there were increasing calls for a national strike; on the other hand, the threat of sequestration posed a challenge to the very existence of the TGWU. Because of its size the TGWU was very vulnerable, but I was still convinced that a collective response by the whole trade union movement could defeat the challenge.'* [49]

In an article, *In Defence of Marxism*, Terry McPartlan argues that:

> *Even Jack Jones, a very sincere genuine left winger, failed to fully understand the potential power of the TGWU and lacked confidence in the members. The T&G leaders were divided over the issue of the fines and eventually the decision to pay was passed by a wafer-thin majority, including Jones. The movement from below was running up against prevarication from the leadership. Despite this the dockers continued to refuse to lift the boycott.'* [50]

Within three years, the London dockers were revisiting their troubled past as more of their shop stewards were imprisoned for trade union activities. The accused were named by private investigators acting on behalf of the Midland Cold Storage Company, they were: Conny Clancy, Tony Merrick, Bernie Steer, Vic Turner and Derek Watkins, and arrest warrants were issued citing contempt of court ahead of their incarceration on 21 July 1972. They became known as the Pentonville Five and were released four days later, following threats of a general strike by the trade union movement, in an incident that crystallised not only the struggle of dockers, but the seemingly unlimited power that would be used repeatedly against them by state, employers and their own trade union. In 1974, the

# INTERNAL CONFLICT AND 'BREAKAWAYS'

Conservative government led by Ted Heath made secret plans to establish a Civil Contingencies Unit, as they sought to scrap the National Dock Labour Board Scheme that guaranteed dockers' jobs and the work that they undertook. In the end, though, they backed off, due to what one commentator observed was a fear: 'Union officials were having difficulty retaining control, in the face of increasing militancy at a local level.' [51]

Under the leadership of P.J. O'Hare, the union embarked upon a major publicity campaign aimed at redressing its historically dismal and disrespected image on the Liverpool waterfront. Changes in working practices were introduced with the establishment of a national 40-hour week and the end of compulsory Saturday morning shifts, suggesting that a faint breeze of change would soon be felt on the quaysides of Britain. [52] The union produced another leaflet to mark the shift, this time without the help or support of the port employers. The banner headline proclaimed, 'It's Good to Belong to the TGWU,' [53] and the date for the implementation of the 40-hour week was declared 'TGWU Victory Day.' [54] Once again, Merseyside's dockers were called to unite under the banner of the country's largest union, but it would take more than a leaflet and a government/employer-sponsored concession to change a generation of dockers' antipathy, open hostility and mistrust of their own trade union.

# 6

# Incorporation and the Struggle for Control

*'They never gave some of our friends a vote, like the Boatmen, and they expect us to vote for them and they don't get a vote, it's just despicable and it just shows you what kind of management are in there. I wouldn't take that money on no account. Every man that you see standing on this road now tells you that they are not going to take the money. That is why they are standing here. People all over the world are backing us and to take that money like that is undermining them, and it's also undermining the younger element of Merseyside who are looking for decent jobs and that's what we are fighting for. We are not just fighting for ourselves we are fighting for the next generation. We want decent standards of living and working conditions and we think this is the only way we can get it.' ~ Marty Size\**

Writing in 1995, Sean Matgamna observed:

> *'Docks strikes were quick and frequent then, in the mid-60s. Dockers fought back; they stood together. Lord Devlin's Commission of Enquiry into conditions in the ports reported that to get a strike going in Liverpool often all that was needed was somebody running down the quays shouting, 'everybody out.' Dockers would stop, to see who was in dispute, who needed support, what it was all about. That was essentially a true picture. It was not only true of Liverpool. And there was nothing senseless or mindless about it.'* [1]

Dockers knew the importance of solidarity as a prerequisite for survival. For the majority of dockers in the close-knit communities of berths and areas, where lives and families touched one another daily, the idea of being part, quite literally, of a gang made unity a natural state of being. It was a hard, physical and mental act to betray your fellow worker, but some men

---

\* Marty Size, sacked Liverpool docker (Radio Merseyside Audio Tape, April 1997)

managed it. The idea of gangs of dockers was fundamental; these men worked in gangs and these gangs generally always sought to be hired together. In some pens, the structure of gangs evolved as the most efficient mix of labour, from foreman to deckhand to match the many and varied port operations. This system suited the labour control officers and ship owners, as they, too, sought to hire labour across the port that met the diverse needs of the port's quays and vessels. [2]

When Liverpool dockers spoke of where they worked, they would refer to their *pens or boxes*. For example, Box 11 South End, Box 10 Kings and Queens Berths, Box 6 Huskisson Dock and Box 3, known as 'the Kremlin' because of its militancy, where men such as Bunny McKechnie and Jimmy McCumisky, whose nickname was 'Ban the Bomb,' could be found. Indeed, the employer, the Local Dock Labour Board and the TGWU were all too aware of such obvious variations in militancy amongst areas of the Liverpool docks. It has been recorded how the Mersey Docks & Harbour Board: 'although it has no standing under the law or even by formal agreement... decided which ships, and accordingly types of dock labour, were to be given priority on its docks, in co-operation with the local TGWU and Dock Labour Board. [3] 'Mustering' [engagement] times were similar in most Liverpool Dock Labour Board areas... even so, variations emerged. Number 1 'pen' (employment point) became that of first choice among most employers, composed as it was of the 'best' gangs, while no. 3 pen – nicknamed 'The Kremlin' - was utilised by employers only as a last resort because of its militant reputation.' [4]

In the opening paragraphs of his 1965 report, Lord Devlin displayed an ignorance of a world in which the only protection from poverty and disadvantage was that offered by your ability to stand up to your bosses alongside your fellow workers. Devlin wished to erase the power of that solidarity when he declared that there was: 'undoubtedly a minority in the docks of men who are well aware of the damage that can be done to the national interest by disruption in the ports. The source of that power is the misconceived loyalty of the docker and that source must be removed.' [5] The Devlin Report, was greeted enthusiastically by government, employers and trade union officials alike. The report focused upon the causes of dissension and inefficiency, concluding that there was: 'An irresponsibility peculiar to the docks which is rooted in the casual system and the excessive loyalty which seems in its intensity to be peculiar to the docks and which although deriving from the casual system, has now become something to be reckoned with on its own.' [6] The spring 1965 edition of the dock workers' rank-and-file journal *Solidarity* asked how Lord Devlin hoped to overcome the dockers working-class loyalty. It provided a unique insight into their world:

> 'The Devlin Committee was horrified to discover that since 1960 of the 421 strikes in the docks, 410 were unofficial... any docker knows... the trade union official just doesn't want to know. The TU official is completely divorced from the everyday issues in the docks, he was not elected by the dockers, but appointed by the union bureaucracy. In their own interests the dockers have no alternative but to turn to their own rank-and-file committees.' [7]

This, almost one hundred per cent record of refusing to officially support strikes on the docks, ensured that the union's dock section was, in financial terms, very low maintenance.

These union members paid their union dues and were, at times, a *cash-cow* for the T&G – more income than expenditure in the form of strike pay. The TGWU's lack of interest in their dock membership was captured in their official submission to the Devlin Inquiry, as the union: 'submitted no written evidence for the first part of the Devlin Inquiry apart from copies of minutes from negotiating meetings. The evidence submitted for the second part of the Inquiry was a letter covering half a sheet of foolscap together with reproductions of a few earlier documents.' [8] Devlin commented on the union's poor representation of its docks membership, asking: 'has the policy of the TGWU inclined too far towards the employers? Put bluntly, has it been less militant than the ordinary rank-and-file dockers would wish it to be? The record suggests it has.' [9] Nevertheless, Devlin opposed casual labour because it encouraged an: 'exaggerated sense of solidarity and loyalty amongst dockers. What the men needed was a sense of loyalty towards one main port employer and not a group of employers.' [10] For Devlin, 'Casual labour produces a casual attitude,' [11] therefore, each docker needed to be assigned an employer who could instil in his workforce a new discipline, a new loyalty. [12] To further this aim for *modernisation* demanded by the impending take-off of containerisation, Devlin wanted to reduce the number of employers licensed to use dock labour, which in Liverpool meant a reduction from 114 employers to 10. Union organisation would also need to be rationalised, [13] and Devlin was prepared to offer permanent employment with an assigned employer, together with the promise of no compulsory redundancies, although, somewhat ironically, a redundancy compensation scheme would be introduced at the same time. [14] The Dock Work (Regulation of Employment) Amendment Order (1967) ensured that all future job losses, predicted as a direct outcome of containerisation, would be on the basis of a voluntary severance scheme, and this method of reducing labour was to be used with devastating effect over the next thirty years.

The impact of containerisation would predictably reduce the need for labour [15] and in Liverpool, companies such as Lamport & Holt, Elmer Dempster Lines, Pacific Steam Navigation Company, Scruttons Ltd., Harrison Line, A.E. Smith Coggins, Raes Ltd, Liverpool Maritime Terminals, Port of Liverpool Stevedoring and West Coast Stevedoring Company would emerge as the main employers until their eventual replacement by the restructured Mersey Docks and Harbour Board from 1972 onwards. [16] Prior to this, MDHB had no involvement in cargo handling. The Unofficial Committee, which led the 1967 strike in opposition to Devlin's proposals, were to form the nucleus of the new, officially recognised TGWU Port Shop Stewards Committee. Larry Cavanagh, a Liverpool docker who was a chairman of the Merseyside Port Workers' Unofficial Committee, recalled:

'Once the shop stewards came on the scene, and with the men's feelings that they had won an enormous victory, there was a whole series of strikes on individual ships and berths, sometimes full-scale strikes for a few days. The men now had an 'award system,' where there was an on-spot assessment by the shop steward and the superintendent of the ship who could immediately grant money for bad or hazardous conditions and so on. The men were getting half a crown, five shillings or even as much as ten shillings an hour extra payment. The men had never known the employers to concede so much and this went on for a number of years.' [17]

What was once illegitimate would now be legitimate, and this transformation took place overnight. [18] By the mid-1970s, directly elected shop stewards on the docks had started to take on roles that were previously the domain of their unelected, full-time union officials, although the TGWU ensured that their activities always took place under the supervision of a paid official. As this transfer of power materialised, some shop stewards soon found themselves experiencing the same suspicion and distrust that they and the dockers had cast upon their union officials prior to 1967. Some embraced their newly acquired status in the eyes of both the port employer and the TGWU, while others rejected it. The growth in the number of shop stewards and their bargaining areas became a national trend, matched by comparative expansions in company industrial relations departments, as a plethora of legislation, covering everything from health and safety to workers on the board [19] followed in the slipstream of Donovan moving shop stewards beyond the workplace and into a complex labyrinth of employer and union-sponsored committee rooms. Workplace shop stewards, convenors, deputy convenors and District, Regional, National and General Executive Committee members all came to dominate the time, nature and status of the democratically elected union member. They were being professionalised, with the ideal shop steward to be forged in the image of both the union and the employer. This potential for the rank-and-file shop stewards' movement to be *incorporated* as little more than another tier of full-time officialdom 'with all the perks' was highlighted to devastating effect by Liverpool-based academic, Tony Lane, writing in 1982 in Marxism Today observed that:

> *'Some stewards had used their position as a stepping-stone to promotion to Charge-Hand and Foreman. A favoured few, usually Convenors and full-time officers, have gone on to become personnel officers and even industrial relations directors. Such routes to progression, to say the very least, induce a mixture of cynicism and resentment amongst the rank-and-file. Other shop stewards have simply used their role as a means to an easy life, an opportunity to get off the job and out of the plant with spurious excuses of union business. In the closed community of the workplace where words seemingly travel faster than the speed of sound and where union rhetoric proclaims altruism, such behaviour must inevitably have unfortunate repercussions for the way trade unionism is evaluated.'*
> *[20]*

Lane's unpopular prognosis did have relevance for an evolving tendency within the culture of UK workplace trade unionism. Almost ten years earlier he had written of the: 'TGWU's purchase of a London Hotel to reduce expenses of shop stewards and other delegates on overnight stays in the Capital. Here we are simply observing the creation of a new working-class elite…' [21] On the docks, shop stewards of all trades were taken out of the workplace and confined to a maze of newly established constitutional committees for the purpose of negotiation or consultation. In the grand offices of the Port of Liverpool building a Joint Consultative Committee and Central Consultative Committee evolved, subject to the persistent collective influence of the local union and employers. Many of these profound changes coincided with the introduction of new blood in the Employers' Association of the Port of Liverpool, such as young men like Bernard Cliff and Peter Jones, who would eventually repudiate consultation, finding their true expression and confidence in a new combative management philosophy that would be underwritten by the Thatcher government at the dawn of the 1980s. Donovan and Devlin would be thrown out of the windows of the Port of Liverpool Building on Liverpool's waterfront, despite Cliff's own personal admiration for the pluralist model offered by both lords. [22] Before the convulsions of Thatcherism, the internal organisation of the official Merseyside Port Shop Stewards Committee was, at times, becoming increasingly pressurised by the management of the MDHC and the local TGWU to fall into line with their mutual world view, in which industrial conflict had ended.

Under the patronage of the local TGWU and the port employers, some shop stewards found their influence and status enhanced, whereas others were noticeably diminished. By the 1970s, many stewards that were expected to present themselves for work were instead going straight to Transport House or the Port of Liverpool Building, until eventually they were provided with full-time credentials to spend their time at meetings representing dockers. The culture of incorporation and bureaucratisation, which had made a limited impact within the unofficial organisation of TGWU dock workers and the Blue Union, was now fully unleashed and, with the passage of time, despite ever-present conflicts, the maintenance of stable bargaining relations and recognition rights for shop stewards became the main thrust of the approach adopted by the local union and the Employers Association. Margaret Thatcher would set new parameters for industrial relations in the UK, with the tactic of incorporation being replaced by one of open confrontation. Now, in heated exchanges during what became almost daily meetings with shop stewards, it was common for port boss Bernard Cliff to demand acceptance of new proposals under threat of imposition, with the automatic response of some shop stewards being to bang tables and threaten strikes.

These were impressive, hyper-formal meetings, where a line of 20-30 shop stewards would flank their chairman and a TGWU official seated in the centre. A similar line of managers and bosses faced them. The official would lead negotiations, but no shop steward could ever be stopped from speaking and tempers often flared, causing lengthy adjournments that could last for hours on end. Physical threats, intimidation and insults could dominate these breaks in negotiations before a line was agreed on to take back to the employer. Divisions existed amongst the dockers, pre-determined by the areas that they represented, and amid these conflicts of interest they had to compromise, concede, or as sometimes happened, just storm out. Such meetings could often deteriorate into physical and verbal confrontations, and on rare occasions, punches were thrown. Grandstanding was not uncommon, allowing shop stewards to tell dockers on the berths how they had 'told' the bosses or the union, or failing that, just walked out banging as many doors as possible behind them. Positions and hierarchies still meant little to the dock shop stewards making the position of the chairman an almost impossible role to fulfil. He was often respected only on the basis of being first among equals when it came to attempting to impose discipline.

But the tide had turned, and the number of employers who made up the Employers Association of the Port of Liverpool, were reducing as the influence of the Dock Company grew. Now very familiar with the personnel and internal politics of the shop stewards and their union officials, the remaining *elite* were confident enough to invite, and even taunt, them into calling a strike. These dares increased throughout the decade until 1979, encouraged by a government that endorsed aggressive anti-union responses to organised labour. No longer bound by the philosophical digest of Donovan's pluralist approach to employer-union relations, the port employers now threatened to close the gates and carry on through whatever means without the dockers if they ever went on strike again. This new generation of employer militants was to be sponsored by Trevor Furlong and the young Bernard Cliff, who, along with an even younger Peter Jones, would lead the employers throughout the 1980s, right up to 1995. Although, they would first have to contest a power struggle for control of the port against James Fitzpatrick, who had held various posts on the old Mersey Docks and Harbour Board since 1951.

Fitzpatrick was of a generation and character that many dockers could deal with, and on the formation of the Mersey Docks and Harbour Company in 1971, he was named managing director, before becoming chairman in 1984. He was a man who was trusted by many of the Liverpool dockers' leaders, and one who cared little for the latest crop of dock bosses. He was what many would have called old school, more than comfortable in the company of the dockers and their leaders, such as Dennis Kelly, to whom he had always shown respect. He led the company in a singularly modern fashion during the late '60s and early '70s, opening an entire air-conditioned floor of the MDHC's head office devoted to rows and rows of huge computer banks, beyond what some of the leading UK industries had at the time. He was part of the group that developed the first trading and business links between Liverpool and Communist China. Supported by his wife, he launched a healthy food campaign publicised on the docks, with huge posters encouraging the workers to look after their hearts and wellbeing by eating less meat and fatty foods and taking more vegetables and exercising. This radical computerisation programme and health initiative began in 1970. Under his leadership, the port employers and the MDHC engaged in a highly sophisticated and innovative public relations strategy, utilising regular bulletins, professionally produced videos made in their own TV studios and their *Port News* tabloid newspaper. Fitzpatrick hired BBC Radio Four *Today* presenter, Brian Redhead, to communicate the company's message to the dockers, directly. However, behind this veneer of sophisticated industrial relations and modern communications lay the application of the force and power preferred by Trevor Furlong and the new elite of acquisitive managers waiting in the wings.

In June 1981, members of TGWU Dock Staff Branch 6/567 had begun a series of one-day strikes. In line with the employers' new strategy for industrial relations, these actions were ignored by both the MDHC and the local TGWU, as strikes were now considered to be 'opportunity areas' in which the port would make greater demands with even greater confidence. At a seminal meeting of shop stewards from all sections involved in the port, Jim Fitzpatrick entered the main boardroom of the Port of Liverpool Building – a wood-panelled former courtroom, surrounded by huge paintings of past directors, smothered in the light of floor-to-ceiling Victorian windows that scanned the Mersey for ships that passed by day and night. He made the following statement:

> *'I am here to spell out some of the points which had arisen as a result of changes in trade in the Port. I am not here to answer questions or to negotiate. Negotiations are dragging on, and unless they achieve success with changes in working practices there will be no increase in pay at all. There is no way we can make an increase unless it is paid for. There is no money.'* [23]

# INCORPORATION AND THE STRUGGLE FOR CONTROL

Not long after this meeting, in June 1981, the MDHC issued another *Port News* bulletin. Once again, they let it be known that they intended to implement changes in working practices with or without an agreement. [24] Writing in the *Guardian* in 2006, Larry Neild said of Fitzpatrick:

> *'[He] had a reputation for a caring approach and integrity, inherited from a father and grandfather who were both lifelong socialists. That day, however, he pulled no punches. The future was perilous unless staff accepted changes in working practices. Some dockers believed there was a pot of gold, he said, but such thoughts were a form of madness. His sermon lasted 10 minutes and the union representatives left the meeting feeling "stunned, shocked and disillusioned."'* [25]

Roger Elgin, for the *Sunday Times* in 1983, was one of the first journalists to observe the transformation that had taken place in the Port of Liverpool over the previous decade under the guidance of Fitzpatrick. The changes were the culmination:

> *'...of the effort Fitzpatrick had put into labour relations in recent years. His strategy has been to put Liverpool's plight and problems across to the dockers as bluntly as possible. One of the main weapons has been the remarkable series of video interviews between Today's Radio 4, Brian Redhead and Fitzpatrick. These interviews were produced by the Mersey Docks and Harbour Company's own studio. The interviews were recorded then shown to the dockers.'* [26]

A *Port News* survival bulletin was issued at the same time that Brian Redhead spoke directly to the dockers with the air of a neutral BBC correspondent. He was paid for his work with the MDHC, the same as the dockers he was addressing. These videos were taken around the docks, and workers were instructed to watch them at specific times and venues. Two years earlier, in May 1981, Fitzpatrick told the Liverpool dockers that the age of unconditional pay offers was over, [27] and these negotiations were to be a major test of the MDHC's resolve. After an agreement was eventually reached, the employer produced a new range of bulletins, titled 'Revival' as opposed to 'Survival.' Revival No.1 proclaimed, 'Now we are on course for recovery and the dockers have turned out to be very co-operative.' [28] By the spring of 1982, talks had already begun with the dockers Local Modernisation Committee, and in July of that year the MDHC decided to speed up the process and apply pressure with another bulletin threatening that there would be no pay increase unless negotiations were brought to a swift conclusion. [29] For the first time, negotiations were moved from the Port of Liverpool Building and the noise of the docks to a Liverpool University campus in Sefton Park, Liverpool.

Irrespective of the purpose of the venue change, within a matter of months a strike was called in relation to the MDHC's determination to reduce labour. Dockers discharging copper from a vessel, the *M.V. Rubens*, withdrew their labour over a dispute on the number of men allocated to the job. Shop stewards attempted to get the men to relent, while the MDHC threatened to take the ship to another berth if the men did not return to work immediately, but the dockers working at the ship refused to concede. As a result, rather than pay the cost of two additional dockers, the *Rubens* was diverted to Garston Docks. Almost immediately, the MDHC published another bulletin, declaring that that they would not be dragged back into the past. [30] This was now a case of the employer attacking the union for failing to control some of its shop stewards, as well as the shop stewards for failing to control dockworkers. The joint union-employer strategy, which incorporated some of the shop stewards and their leaders, was beginning to unravel, and even at this early stage it was, to all intents and purposes, finished. [31] The dispute over this one small ship would prove significant as a key point in the writing of the contemporary Liverpool dock story, contextualising the official national strike in 1989 and the unofficial dispute of 1995 by introducing the key players who evaded control by their union, their employer and the state.

The dispute over the *Rubens* was an example of the employer's determination to drive through an agenda irrespective of the cost, and the preceding seven years would be defined by the impact of employer militancy, as dramatic changes to workplace agreements, including reduced earnings and manning levels, as well as increased hours were ruthlessly imposed. TGWU Dock Staff Branch 6/567 began to produce their own monthly bulletin, *Quay News*, edited by Mike Carden, in an attempt to counter the MDHC's in-house propaganda. Initially, the union side of the Joint Union Consultative Committee agreed to this publication, after being persuaded by another port worker, Paul Laverty, who worked alongside Carden on *Quay News*. However, the JCC soon tired of the bulletin's opposition to the company message and eventually withdrew their reluctant support. Early editions of *Quay News* were printed using Letraset, an electronic typewriter and the 6/567 Branch photocopier, based at the Seaforth Container Trailer Park, until eventually it was handed over to professional printers, S&A Print, on the dock road. Interviewed in 1989, Tony Nelson, a 6/567 Branch shop steward, said:

*'It was really a turning point; the employer had been getting his own way for so long. Their strategy of grinding the workforce into the ground with little co-ordinated opposition had been successful. 'Quay News' provided an alternative, the bosses thought they were talking to the men in their own language but they hadn't got a clue. The men may have read the bulletins and seen the videos but they were taken as a joke. Our bulletin, 'Quay News', knew exactly what the majority of men thought. It always amazed me that whenever the bosses put a Bulletin out they would hang around for months. When we distributed Quay News they went missing in hours. The bosses certainly read them. Some issues were better than others. I remember when we discovered the Finance Director of the MDHC was also a Director of a major port competitor, when we published the story this Director left within weeks. We even knew when to expect a company Bulletin and we prepared one to coincide with this. It was exactly the same lay-out as theirs, it looked like their leaflet but with our words.' [32]*

Despite pockets of unofficial resistance from the dockers, the Dock Company's industrial strategy proved to be successful throughout the early 1980s. [33] By 1983, the MDHC could confidently assure its customers that they had received a dispute promise from the local TGWU Docks and Waterways Section. This gave:

# INCORPORATION AND THE STRUGGLE FOR CONTROL

*'Written assurances to the owners of the Compac Container Group that their ships will not be locked in the Port by secondary action. Jimmy Symes, Full-Time Official of the TGWU described the assurance as unique. Mr. Frank Major, Cargo Operations Director of the MDHC said, "This is a significant breakthrough in our relationship with the TGWU."' [34]*

By the 1980s, shop steward organisation became increasingly silenced and demoralised. Although regular monthly report-back meetings with the dockers still took place, they generally ended in chaotic sectoral arguments. Internal differences of opinion between shop stewards were sparked by those who openly defended the employers' programme as one that would benefit dockers in years to come. The disharmony that emerged only aided the employer's ability to progress further rationalisation programmes achieved by playing one set of shop stewards or workers off against another. Throughout this period, local officials of the TGWU displayed no appetite for opposition or challenge to the actions of the Dock Company. [35] James Fitzpatrick's role in the MDHC would diminish as others challenged for his position. He eventually left the company in 1987 although he remained a fixture in public life until his death in 2006, serving as chairman of Liverpool Health Authority, the Royal Liverpool Hospital Trust and the Eldonians, a Liverpool housing co-operative that provided decent homes for dockers' families and members of the local community. He was also credited with being instrumental in saving the Institute of Irish Studies at Liverpool University and received a CBE in the 1983 Honours. [36] With his departure from the story, events were set in motion that would culminate in the single greatest dispute of them all.

# 7

# The Liverpool Dockers' Fightback! Support the Miners!

*'If any coal is imported by ship into this country it will not be discharged by Registered Dock Workers and any dock worker who loses a day's pay then every dock labourer in this country will immediately withdraw their labour.' ~ Albie Brown\**

In May 1985, Sid Vincent, general secretary of North West National Union of Mineworkers, wrote to Jimmy Symes, the Transport and General Workers' Union's docks official, asking Liverpool dockers not to handle 27,000 tonnes of South African coal, imported by the Banbury Coal Company of Northwich and due to arrive in Liverpool on the *M.V. Sleeping Beauty*. The Liverpool dockers supported this request. A month later, Peter Heathfield, NUM secretary in South Yorkshire, wrote to Labour MP for Walton, Eric Heffer, bringing him up to date on the blockade. On Tuesday 28 August 1984, a national dock strike was called over the use of non-registered dockers to offload coal from the *M.V. Ostia*, a vessel berthed in Hunterston, Scotland. Dockers there had originally struck on 23 August, and in the midst of the miners' strike, it was unthinkable for the National Port Shop Stewards Committee to allow imported coal to be shipped through either registered or unregistered ports. [1] As the *Guardian* reported at the time: 'Depending on your politics the national docks strike is either a blatantly political act in support of the miners or a genuine industrial dispute.' [2] In Liverpool, striking dockers were in no doubt that this was action taken in support of the miners, [3] and officials of the TGWU announced that their dock delegates conference had voted 78 to 11 in favour of an immediate stoppage on Friday 24 August 1984, bringing more than 36,000 dockers to a halt. John Connolly, the TGWU's National Officer for the Docks and Waterways Section, said at the time that the strike was in response to the

---

\* Albie Brown - Liverpool Dock Shop Steward @ MinersStrikeOTD -During the #MinersStrike Liverpool dockers raised funds in #solidarity with striking miners pic.twitter.com/jK1hagHulW

use of scab labour to unload foreign coal at Hunterston. The *M.V. Ostia* was bound for the state steel works at Ravenscraig. According to a *Reuters* report, the ship was eventually unloaded by members of the steelworkers' union. [4]

The strike began on shaky ground with Dover and Felixstowe continuing to work as normal. Heated negotiations took place between the British Steel Corporation and the port employers until the dispute finally came to an ignominious end on 18 September. [5] This national dock strike exposed dockers to the reality that the influence of the National Dock Labour Board Scheme had been substantially reduced over the years, as almost twice as many non-registered dockers now worked across Britain's ports. Weekly collections continued to be held on the docks and in dock union branches, 'adopting' mining pits that they would support directly. In some rare TV footage from the time, dock shop stewards Kenny Kelly, Frank Lannigan, Albert Brown, Larry Cavanagh and Denis Anderson, along with many other dockers, are shown loading lorries and containers of aid for miners in pit areas such as Cannock Chase and Point of Ayr. Larry Cavanagh told an interviewer:

> *This is what's in store for the rest of the working-class if they crush the miners. We know we've got problems on the docks and we know for a fact that we were set up to be taken on by the government and the only reason they're not provoking us at the moment, with the attacks on the National Dock Labour Scheme and so on is that they want to deal with the miners first.'* [6]

Branch 6/567 made a weekly trip to Armthorpe Colliery with food, money and clothes for the miners and their families. Workers at the Heinz factory in Wigan, organised by Ken Brindle amongst others, donated pallets of damaged tinned food that were collected each week by the branch from the plant. Branch 6/567 produced badges featuring a miner's lamp to commemorate the year-long strike. Solidarity with the miners and the actions by UK dockers put pressure on the Thatcher government, although this would only become public knowledge when the 1984 Cabinet Papers were released to the National Archives in January 2014. At the height of the dispute, Thatcher was secretly preparing to declare a state of emergency and deploy military troops, as she feared that Britain would run out of food and subsequently grind to a halt. Alan Travis, Home Affairs editor at the *Guardian*, wrote of the disclosures that:

> *Thatcher asked for contingency plans to be drawn up to use troops to move coal stocks, despite official government policy ruling out the use of service personnel… She gave the backbenchers the impression that she was keenly aware of the importance of reaching a settlement in the docks so that the government could give its full attention to the miners' dispute. She said that, but for the scenes of violence, the dispute in the mines had made little impact in its 19 weeks. By contrast, the effect of the docks strike had been severe and immediate.'* [7]

The Downing Street papers also showed that Norman Tebbit MP, then Thatcher's employment secretary, wrote her a secret and personal letter warning, 'I do not see that time is on our side.' [8] Thatcher's own handwritten notes on possible strategies for the coal and dock disputes were noted on paper, dated 18 July 1984, during a meeting of the special Cabinet Committee on coal that she chaired. Here, she outlined the details of a plan to use 2,800 troops in 13 specialist teams that could unload 1,000 tonnes a day at the docks. This level of intervention would require the declaration of a state of emergency to ensure access to the necessary port equipment. The dangers of this approach were spelt out by Peter Gregson, head of the Cabinet Office Civil Contingencies Unit:

> *The political and economic stake(s) are much higher for the government in the coal dispute than in the docks dispute. Priority should therefore be: end the dock strike as quickly as possible, so that the coal dispute can be played as long as possible. He reminded Thatcher that troops had not been used to break a dock strike since 1950 and could bring more severe picketing and law-and-order problems.'* [9]

That same year of the miners' strike, in June 1984, Brian Redhead officially declared himself an employee of the MDHC, proclaiming through an MDHC bulletin that it would be he, 'not the shop stewards,' who would keep the dockworkers informed. 'The management want more changes the stewards want more money. Both want to do a deal. They are still hard at it. I'll let you know how they get on.' [10] A wage deal was eventually settled for 1984, but then in March 1985, another dispute over redundancies, this time affecting TGWU 6/567 Branch members, began in the port. Workers occupied a ship, the *M.V. Pevril*, and mounted pickets on the dock gates. This action created serious divisions that took some time to heal, if only for the fact that not many dockers could ever remember the need for picket lines once a ship had been stopped in the port. Ian Gronback, the *Liverpool Echo* shipping correspondent, who was also employed by the MDHC to write articles for *Port News*, reported on the incident with the employer's public image very much in mind:

> *'On Thursday morning, with pickets on the gates, the situation looked grim. The dockers were on the horns of a dilemma and only about half reported for work that morning. At midday the dockers were called to a mass meeting at the Liverpool Stadium, when they were told of the union [TGWU] ruling that the picketing was not official. The meeting accepted a recommendation for an immediate return to work and that the dock staff should be urged to end their picketing. Liverpool's 2,000 dockers have not always been given credit for the major contribution they have made in recent years to the new-found stability in industrial relations in the port. They had shown an example to other workers in their readiness to accept flexibility in working practices. The clerical workers' [6/567 TGWU Branch] dispute provided a severe test of the statesmanship of the union's Docks and Waterways District Committee. When the chips were down they recognised the long term interests of the port and for that they deserve full marks.'* [11]

Contrary to Gronback's article the *M.V. Pevril* dispute was an official TGWU strike, the dock staff made a complaint to the union, but this was later withdrawn in an attempt to build bridges with their dock shop steward comrades. For their part, the dock shop stewards' 'statesmanship' and 'full marks' would soon be forgotten by Gronback and the MDHC. [12] By June 1985, the MDHC announced that over 400 dockers had been signing-on, indicating to the company that no work existed for them. [13] News of the need for more redundancies also had to be set against a trading profit of £1.4 million in the first half of 1985. [14] Work for the dockers existed in the port, but it was being done by a growing supply of casual agencies. Final details of the dockers' latest severance scheme were announced in October 1985, which, according to the employer, 'would bring security to the men and the port.' [15] The severance offer would be £25,000 a reduction on the £35,000 that had been available to UK dockers for over a decade. To encourage applications Brian Redhead made use of another bulletin, in which company directors stated that this severance would be the last to be directly funded by the government, and thus '300 jobs must go by March 1986.' [16] Writing on behalf of his MDHC employer, Redhead added, 'nobody has a job for life these days.' [17]

In 1979, the Port of Liverpool employed 5,202 registered dockworkers, and less than six years later, only 1,862 remained. [18] In December 1986, the final severance scheme from March of that year had reconstituted itself as an increased offer of £35,000, and on 29 November 1985, Aintree Container Base announced their decision to close with a loss of 102 jobs. [19] A message to critics of the Port of Liverpool was conveyed by Redhead again: 'Every time I hear somebody being rude about the Port of Liverpool, and far too many people are, I bang them about the head with a few facts. Fact number one, the Port of Liverpool makes a profit. The Port of Liverpool handles ten million tons of cargo a year; the Port of Liverpool is a strike-free port.' [20] Then, in an attack on many of the dock shop stewards, he concluded that, 'Delays to reaching an agreement puzzled employers. It was make your mind up time with employers just waiting to see how much more the shop stewards are planning to throw away.' [21]

In December 1986, a mass meeting of the remaining 1,600 dockers rejected their shop stewards' recommendation to accept the employer's latest set of demands, which also meant that they were rejecting some £300 in backpay. Now, the absence of registered dock workers from the berths they once worked caused increasing resentment, as they saw their traditional roles being performed by non-union labour that was hired and dismissed as required. All their sacrifices, all the promises made by the TGWU and the MDHC about job security, had proved meaningless. Despite the new names on the waterfront docks, the MDHC maintained a controlling interest in almost every one of these new enterprises, using shell companies directly owned or managed by the Port Authority, their senior managers and directors. The MDHC was actively diluting the registered dockworker labour force in the port to further dismantle the last vestiges of the National Dock Labour Board Scheme, the influence of which was now *withering on the vine*. However, despite jobs for registered dockers continuing to diminish by the day, the 1989 national dock strike began to loom over the horizon, while at the same time the Liverpool dockers' fightback was taking shape.

# 8

# The End of the Dock
# Labour Board Scheme

*'For years now the employers in this country have disciplined the workers through the constitutionalists and right-wing leaders of the trade union movement. In practice, the TGWU has become an instrument through which the employers carry out their policies.'* ~ Port Workers' News*

In 1987 Mersey Docks and Harbour Company's profits rose by 80% on the previous year's figure, as shares became: 'The most outstanding on the stock market. Share prices leapt from 31 pence in early 1987 to £2.80p by December 1987 and at their peak they hit £4.60, a rise in the year on share price alone of 803%.' [1] Despite this, the closure, fencing-off or separation of areas where registered dockers once worked continued, and in 1988, another long-established firm, Liverpool Maritime Terminals Ltd, ceased trading. The TGWU and some shop stewards were still determined to convince the dockers not to take industrial action. According to the *Liverpool Echo*, 'It took shop stewards nearly two hours to persuade the men to call off their stoppage.' [2] The efforts of some union officials and shop stewards to end this strike was significant, as it was the first major stoppage in Liverpool for almost five years. [3] Recognising the dangers apparent in a re-emergence of sporadic, unofficial strike activity promoted by rank-and-file dockers, the MDHC returned to the printers, using language that would be regurgitated in 1995 by its managing director, Trevor Furlong, in an attempt to discredit the action as being that of a small group of malcontents and not the majority of dockers: 'We have no intention of being knocked-off course by a small group who want to walk back into history; if those few hands raised in anger really reflect the views of all the men who have brought us so far in the last eight years then something has gone sadly wrong and the Port of Liverpool is in serious trouble.' [4] As it turned out, those few raised hands did reflect the views of the majority of Liverpool's dockers, and their anger now

---

* Port Workers' News (NASD broadsheet, 16 April 1955)

began to spill over into mass meetings. The dock shop stewards had no option but to demand a strike ballot, and Liverpool's 1,300 dockers voted two to one in favour of action. [5] The MDHC moved to diffuse the situation by informing the local press that they, together with the local union, were confident: 'That a satisfactory conclusion could be reached... Liverpool's reputation in recent years as a highly stable port has been achieved through a spirit of commitment and realism in negotiations from both the employer and the union and we expect the same spirit to apply for these talks.' [6] In turn, the *Liverpool Echo's* Ian Gronback noted: 'Shop stewards have so far not commented upon the reason why they decided to ballot for strike action.' [7]

Unofficial action now spread to the Seaforth Container Terminal, marking a rebirth of the movement of dockers standing in opposition to both their union and their employer. The ballot for strike action was now almost five months old, and some shop stewards, as well as the local TGWU, had made no effort to implement the dockworkers' democratic and legal industrial decision. By September 1988, an unofficial overtime ban was imposed at Seaforth Container Terminal, initially involving only a small number of dockworkers, centred on the critical roles of the container straddle and gantry drivers. Mindful of the legal implications of their contracts of employment, the plant drivers simply insisted that they could not work overtime because they had all made arrangements to be with their families at the weekend or after their normal working shift. This infuriated local union officials and the employer, as well as some shop stewards, because overtime was still voluntary, which meant that no disciplinary action could be taken to force the men to work additional hours. It was highly significant to note that the MDHC did not publish one bulletin at this time, nor did they make use of their allies in the local press or hire Brian Redhead to speak on their behalf. Silence was the response to their failure to control the situation, as unofficial action by the dockers, led by their equally unofficial leaders, together with some shop stewards, served to silence the employer and the local union. [8]

On Monday 3 October 1988, *these unofficial dockers' leaders* called their first port-wide strike against the employer, making news that could be no longer covered-up or silenced. Those involved in the unofficial strike action made it their priority to inform their employers and local radio stations that the Port of Liverpool was now involved in an unofficial strike beyond the control of either the MDHC or the TGWU. The following day, the *Liverpool Echo* reported:

> '[The] Port of Liverpool was hit by a one-day token strike when more than 1,000 dockers stopped work in protest at delays in finalizing a new pay agreement, some rank-and-file men, who are insisting there should be no strings, won support for yesterday's stoppage which was against the advice of the union officials and the shop stewards.' [9]

That same day, a request to hold a mass meeting was refused by the Dock Company, but went ahead regardless, and in retribution, the employer took the decision to withdraw the facility of deducting union contributions from the 6/567 Branch dock staff wages for the TGWU, letting it be known that other actions were also to be taken against them. [10] Liverpool dockers, together with the dock staff, were also involved in refusing to handle work normally assigned to a haulage firm, George Davies & Sons, who had made one of their

# THE END OF THE DOCK LABOUR BOARD SCHEME

drivers redundant. In this, the 6/567 Branch were supporting a direct request from 6/541 Branch (road haulage), serving to compound refusals by dockers and clerical workers at Seaforth to handle containers relating to the import of Namibian (South African) uranium hexafluoride from, and to, British Nuclear Fuels. This was not just another act of solidarity, but also a declaration of their support for the official TGWU/Trade Union Congress policy of opposing the apartheid regime of South Africa. [11] On Tuesday 11 October, further unofficial action took place involving both dockers and dock staff, reaffirming their discontent with the port employers and their local union officials. For the *Liverpool Echo*: 'this protest followed what union leaders called a savage blow by the management. The biggest attack on trade unionism, at the port, for over twenty years.' [12] The local union were angry at the withdrawal of the facility by which membership funds were collected direct from wages by the employer and sent directly to the union. Despite the silence from the union and the employer, this wave of unofficial industrial action could no longer be ignored. Another article, this time in *International Freight World*, covered the dispute in much greater detail than the local press:

> *'A wave of industrial unrest has hit Mersey Docks spoiling the Port's long strike-free record. Disputes involving dockers, clerical workers and haulage drivers, all members of the TGWU, have caused disruption and delays. Twice within eight days about 1,000 dockers walked out stopping work on up to seventeen ships. On October 3rd the dockers staged a one-day token strike in protest at delays in finalising a new wage agreement... The dockers walk-out last Tuesday afternoon, October 11th, was less clear cut and there was a full return to work on Wednesday morning. On the same day clerical workers in the port held a stop work meeting to discuss the decision of the Dock Company to withdraw the facility of deducting union subscriptions from pay. No reason was given for the change. Last Monday, October 11th, road transport drivers picketed dock gates causing some disruption as part of a campaign for more work from shipping companies.'* [13]

On 13 October 1988, the *Liverpool Echo* finally reported on the growing evidence that life in the port was not quite as the MDHC, via its own journalists and Brian Redhead and the local union, were saying. The industrial chaos that had been unfolding was not reported on by the paper's usual shipping correspondent, Ian Gronback, but by another journalist, Linda McDermott, leading with the headline, *'First Shots in the Battle of the Docks.'* [14] McDermott outlined a tense and sensitive situation on the docks, which the MDHC 'did not wish to comment on,' [15] until, within a week of the article's publication, they offered their first response through Gronback, who expressed what could only be considered the company's analysis of the situation:

> *The current spate of unofficial action has provoked critical comment. There is a stark realisation on both sides that an early agreement is now vital and that two token strikes by 1,300 dockers in as many weeks, and a ban on overtime must not be allowed to tarnish the port's hard-won industrial relations image. Both sides in the negotiations recognized the dangers and that this weekend the overtime ban was lifted as a prelude to*

*talks. Shop stewards have appealed to the men to leave it to them to achieve the best deal possible and not to support unofficial action because of the potentially damaging effect on port users' confidence; nearly all of the changes sought by the employers demanded a new approach from the labourforce and in the eyes of a militant minority enough was enough. The fact that a ballot for the election of shop stewards is due again this year brought added pressures as prospective candidates decided to show their strength.' [16]*

By the end of the year, unofficial leaders had taken the decision to seek election to become shop stewards. The plan to stand in upcoming elections was leaked to the shop stewards, the TGWU and the MDHC, as part of a strategy that had been devised in the Elm House Pub, where the 'unofficials' met regularly. At a dock shop stewards' meeting on 19 October 1988, it was agreed that they would accept the employer's latest offer. [17] A mass meeting was called for 24 November, but this was suddenly cancelled at the last minute, and for the first time in eight months, the Dock Company produced a new edition of *Port News*, issued on the day that a strike ballot was due to take place. This long-awaited comment from the company was, unsurprisingly, critical of the dockers, but more importantly it also attacked the shop stewards, who were accused of doing a U-turn by balloting for a strike after deciding to recommend the pay deal. [18] The shop stewards were also accused of being weak, in an extraordinary demonstration of dominance and control over both the local union and some of its elected shop stewards. It was not the first time, nor would it be the last, that the MDHC had publicly informed the dockers and their union how they should conduct their affairs, as well as their democratic processes, and now they were telling shop stewards how to deal with hecklers at meetings:

*'Why were the shop stewards swayed by a small group of vociferous men, the same men who made as much noise last year against a new agreement aimed at retaining the Canary Island trade? Where is that trade today? In Southampton. What the shop stewards don't seem to know is how to respond to barracking from a handful of men. The unexpected attack came not even at a port mass meeting but at a stop work meeting involving only MDHC men, it is no use being wise after the event. If the men lose their pay rise and even their jobs they will only have themselves and the shop stewards to blame.' [19]*

This long-awaited news brief had nothing new to add to the same old threats that the dockers were more than accustomed to receiving, but now the MDHC openly attacked those same shop stewards that they had worked so hard to incorporate. Consensus was replaced by open conflict with the Dock Company, who were no doubt aware that within months the Conservative government would announce its intention to abolish the National Dock Labour Board Scheme. Of the 21 shop stewards up for re-election, nine were replaced by those dockers who had led the unofficial movement, and it was this new shop stewards' organisation that would play a major part in the defence of the Dock Labour Scheme in 1989, and ultimately lead the Liverpool dock dispute of 1995. [20] In March 1989, these new shop stewards acted quickly to replace members of the MDHC's Consultative Committees of those shop stewards who had long been seen as cyphers for the company's policies. Within 24 hours, the MDHC closed-down the Joint Union Consultative Committee and Central Committee structures. These committees consisted of influential senior convenors and shop stewards from all departments and unions across the Dock Estate. Neither the official TGWU or the AEU raised any objections with the company. It was as if these two very influential and high-profile committees had never existed. [21]

By March 1989, the MDHC had come to the realisation that its sophisticated public relations and costly videos and bulletins, not to mention Brian Redhead, had all been an expensive waste of time. Their strategy of incorporation had failed, as had their alliance with the TGWU, and philosophies of pluralism were thrown out of the boardroom window along with the compliant local union officials who had enjoyed what one dockworker, Kevin Bilsborrow, later described as, 'a sweetheart agreement' with the company. [22] For newly elected shop steward, Jimmy Davies, who would eventually be elected, secretary to the Merseyside Port Shop Stewards:

> 'The Dock Company had always indicated that they could work with the union, and they still say it today (1996). We ain't got a problem with the TGWU, the people we have a problem with are the elected representatives, and unfortunately, we've got a problem with the TGWU because we can't work with the official.' [23]

The battle lines were drawn between a militant employer and the newly elected, equally militant, shop stewards, as the end of the National Dock Labour Board Scheme loomed. [24] In the past, the Unofficial Port Workers' Committee had established a sophisticated, efficient and effective system of organisation that acted as a counterbalance to the seemingly inherent weakness of their union. It was the same structure that, after the events of 1967 and post-Devlin and Donovan, had seamlessly connected to the brave new world that was to follow the abolition of casual labour and the creation of officially recognised elected shop stewards. [25] The role of the National Dock Labour Board Scheme had afforded a unique level of joint control of the industry through local and national boards, with unions and management working together on all industrial matters including that of dockworkers' discipline. These mutual elements of authority could have their darker side, as 'TGWU officials, sat on the boards that disciplined the dockers trade unionists who 'kicked' against working conditions, who quickly found that they had to fight not only the employers but also their own union representatives. Union officials thus had almost complete power inside the union.' [26] Nevertheless, the 1989 strike would underline a depth of support for the National Dock Labour Board Scheme among dockers, and for the London and Liverpool dockers' leaders, the defence of the scheme, warts and all, was of critical importance. Their experiences convinced them that the benefits of the scheme outweighed the opportunities for the union and the employer to effectively undermine rank-and-file influence, and they regarded its loss as, 'an essential weakening of their position.' [27]

# 9

# The Dockers and the TGWU's Broad Left

*'While we should be pleased about our record as an electoral machine, the question which rightly came to dominate the meeting was can the United Left [formerly 'Broad Left'] be anything more than an electoral machine? ...The most coherent attempt came from many comrades who, however gently, attempted to shift the UL focus towards a rank-and-file-ism. Whether a R&F movement / shop steward movement is possible, the UL cannot possibly undertake such a function... as the UL already runs the bureaucracy and large numbers of UL members are part of the bureaucracy; including of course the GS.'* ~ *Jim Kelly**

On 6 April 1989, the Conservative government declared its intention to abolish the National Dock Labour Board Scheme. The following day, rank-and-file dockers responded with an unofficial national strike, and within a week the Transport and General Workers' Union General Executive Council had voted to provide: 'overwhelming support to use all lawful means to oppose the government's plans for abolition of the Dock Labour Scheme.' [1] Ron Todd, the union's general secretary at the time, recognised the consequences of these unofficial strikes, which the government would declare to be political and, therefore, unlawful, [2] exposing the union to the risk of having its assets sequestrated. The TGWU declared its wish to meet with the National Association of Port Employers to negotiate an agreement, 'to establish national conditions that are no less favourable than the current provisions.' [3] The logic behind this strategy was that if the union was unsuccessful, any subsequent strike would be deemed industrial and not political, and thus lawful. Unsurprisingly, talks with employers over an agreement to replace the NDLBS collapsed, and the docks committee delegates sanctioned the holding of a national ballot on 20 April 1989. [4]

---

* Jim Kelly - Wither the United Left? (3 July 2017) -
https://shirazsocialist.wordpress.com/2017/07/03/unite-the-union-whither-the-united-left/

75

On Saturday 15 April 1989, five days before the ballot was scheduled, 96 Liverpool fans were killed and 766 fans were injured at Hillsborough Stadium, Sheffield. They had gone to watch their team play Nottingham Forest in the semi-final of the FA Cup. On 26 April 2016, following a 30-year campaign for justice that continues to this day, an inquest into the disaster found that the fans had been unlawfully killed. This tragedy touched every person on Merseyside and beyond. In London, the TGWU went ahead with a national ballot that resulted in a three to one vote for strike action, while the National Association of Port Employers (NAPE) took their case to the courts, arguing that the union's actions were political. As a result, the union's decision to strike was placed on hold while the courts deliberated over its legitimacy, and eventually the High Court decided that industrial action would in fact be legal. This was a short-lived victory for the dockers and their union, as the Court of Appeal granted an injunction to prevent the planned strike on 7 June. The following day, registered dockworkers again took unofficial action, and this continued, albeit sporadically, in various ports across the UK, despite a request from Ron Todd to wait until an appeal to the House of Lords had been completed. On 19 June, following continued pressure from the union's national leadership, dockers at the major ports voted to return to work pending the outcome of their appeal.

The legal appeal was successful, but because more than 28 days had elapsed since the ballot, the union was obliged to hold a fresh vote under the terms of labour legislation. Then, on 3 July 1989, the National Dock Labour Board Scheme was formally abolished and new employment contracts were immediately distributed in ports, declaring that long-established operational practices agreed with the union would cease forthwith. On 7 July, the union announced that in a second national ballot, registered dockworkers had once again voted three to one in favour of strike action. [5] The National Docks and Waterways Committee responded by putting intense pressure on their union to call a strike, and on 9 July, Ron Todd supported his union's Docks National Committee. Although this strike was initially solid, it rested on unity between registered and unregistered ports, as the latter were encouraged to offer support based on the central demand to extend the benefits of the NDLBS to all ports. At this time, the TGWU had only 13,000 registered dockers covered by the scheme, all of whom stopped work as soon as the strike was called, but the major non-scheme ports had over 22,000 unregistered dockers in ports such as Felixstowe, Harwich and Newcastle. These ports finally voted to join the strike on 4 July, although they were not prepared to disrupt passenger services and by 16 July, dockers in Dover eventually voted to stop all freight. This support for the strike would not last long as, on the same day, tugmen in Swansea went back to work along with 200 dockers at two oil industry supply bases. In the days that followed dockers at Dover were challenged by lorry drivers, who began to blockade Channel ports in protest at not being able to take their lorries onto the ferries. This led to 300 lorries that had been parked on the M20 moving off in a convoy for Dover to negotiate with the harbour board and, by next day, the dockers' shop stewards had called off the freight ban, 'because of fears of violence in the port.' [6]

The Liverpool dockers and their shop stewards had always held influential positions within the TGWU, on district, regional and national committees, as well as the unofficial bodies that they belonged to, such as the National Port Shop Stewards Committee. A broad left organisation was active and influential in the union, especially in Ireland, Liverpool and

London. On Merseyside activists had created a Merseyside Co-ordinating Committee to receive reports directly from their regional General Executive Member, Stan Pemberton in the 1970s. This was a unique unofficial committee in Region Six, and it was challenged by some who objected to a GEC member having to report to anyone other than a regional secretary or a Regional Committee. Alan Quinn, who succeeded Pemberton, continued this democratic tradition, which only existed in the North West. Mike Carden was the secretary to the MCC for a number of years before he eventually followed Alan Quinn onto union's GEC. Dockers were not overtly involved in the TGWU Regional and National Broad Left as personnel and policy differences had always meant a low level of involvement for them. [7] These differences were to be exposed during the 1989 national strike, when support from both the local and national Broad Left was alarmingly non-existent. Not one meaningful meeting of the Broad Left took place in Liverpool, or nationally for that matter, to discuss tactics or support for the dockworkers. This absence of the Broad Left in a major national industrial dispute would be repeated with the Liverpool dockers in 1995.

It was expected that the traditionalist, male-dominated industrial base of the TGWU, which had always opposed change or modernisation, would be very proactive in their support of the 1989 dock strike, not least because the union's president, Brian Nicholson, was an influential London docker. [8] Writing in the *Financial Times* in April 1989, Charles Leadbetter observed:

> *'Senior Officials in the TGWU were confident that the Executive, on which the Left has a 22 to 17 majority, will back Mr. Todd. They almost unanimously back Mr. Todd, even though they have been consistently hostile to him over the last three years. The right-wing had its fair share of TGWU traditionalists who are much more comfortable with an old-fashioned dockers' strike than the union's plans to recruit amongst women part-time workers in the service sector. Indeed, some of the right are dockers who will almost certainly oppose Mr. Todd. It is conceivable that some on the right would enjoy playing upon the left's dilemma to either lead a potentially disastrous strike or publicly disown it amidst accusations of a sell-out.' [9]*

According to Andrew Murray's book, *The T&G Story: History of the TGWU 1997-2007*, Ron Todd did not just have to deal with a new political and economic environment; there was also pressure from below inside the TGWU as executive elections were very closely fought along political lines, and at one stage, the work of the GEC was brought to a halt after an unprecedented walk-out by the anti-Todd elements. [10] Murray identified an: 'intransigently hostile political environment, contracting membership and bitter divisions over strategy and perspective,' that influenced the union's activities throughout this period. [11] In her study of the Liverpool docks' dispute, Monica Clua-Losada argued that Todd's situation could be better characterised by the patronage often delivered by the union's Broad Left to individual members: 'In particular, the workings of the Broad Left resembled a jellyfish within the organisation. Invisible, quiet and with the ability to sting before victims knew it was there.' [12] But the Broad Left's preoccupation with capturing official positions in the TGWU dominated its activities - the left perceived their role in selecting candidates for every role in the union as critical. The *left* often referred to the principle of *left discipline* and it was normally here that the Broad Left's *discipline* fell apart as many *comrades* ignored those decisions that halted their careers in the union. The union's Regional Secretaries held the provinces for the London-based General Secretary, who they generally owed a debt of gratitude to for their original appointment, but this was not always the case. One London docker, Colin Sparks, believed the: 'General Secretary of the TGWU is like a feudal king, playing-off the sectional interests of the different barons in order to wield for himself supreme power.' [13]

With more of the paying dock section membership employed in the non-scheme ports, the dockers' position was further diminished by the new unionism of impending technological revolution and industrial compromise, as a new power dynamic emerged that had no place for militant cloth-capped dock labourers. This was undoubtedly, the position of the Broad Left as they evaded the striking dockers, not for the first time. Charles Leadbetter, considered that:

> '*The right wing of the TGWU will not want to jeopardize the union by plunging it into a costly strike for the sake of internal union politics. Right-wingers will, this November, start a campaign to regain control of the Executive. They will want to present themselves as logical supporters of Mr. Kinnock in contrast to the left's critical approach to the Party's Policy Review with almost all the 17 right-wing votes, Mr. Todd, would only need the support of four left-wingers to win the Executive. But he would be uneasy winning by relying on the right. It also seems unlikely that the left will suffer a serious split. In the past the left has been united in confronting the political controversy which its industrial decisions have provoked. Many of the left of the Executive feel a strong sense of loyalty to Mr. Todd. Senior left-wingers stress that they will take a realistic approach to the issue. As one said 'the important thing is to win rather than lose. Industrial suicide would make a very doubtful contribution to victory.' [14]*

The industrial reality of a national dock strike became entangled in the even more complex internal politics of the union's bureaucracy, as descriptive divisions of left and right lost their significance in the personal ambitions of many to hold office/gain employment in the union. On Monday 31 July 1989, over 1,000 dockers returned to work at eight ports, in open defiance of union instructions. On Tuesday 1 August, an emergency meeting of the TGWU General Executive Committee changed those instructions, conceding with an air of inevitability that a national strike to replace the National Dock Labour Board Scheme like-for-like was unwinnable. The union's GEC decided by 19 votes to 12 to call off the strike and concentrate on negotiating local agreements, including elements of a national deal, while preserving union recognition. This meeting was picketed by many dockers, mainly from Liverpool; some invaded the Executive Chamber and directly confronted GEC members. Emotionally charged verbal attacks took place in the old Transport House building on Smith Square, London, further clouding what was already a bleak day for the union and its dockers. It was not a good day for anyone. As one observer noted:

> '*The national docks and waterways committee, after a day of tense and sometimes ugly scenes involving more than 200 dockers, many from Liverpool's Region, who lobbied the meeting, did not agree with Mr. Todd. Leaders of dock workers were told by Mr. Todd*

*that he had to take into account the interests of the whole union in the event of a legal*
*challenge to strike action.' [15]*

Most of the remaining striking dockers began to return to work on Wednesday 3 August. Following the abolition of the National Dock Labour Board Scheme, the major ports quickly made use of the government-backed severance scheme that obliterated their registered dockworkers, replacing them overnight with either casual contracts or casual labour. [16] The Liverpool dockers, who together with their London counterparts had been the vanguard of this struggle, would always need more convincing than most before they were prepared to give up. Ron Todd stressed that the decision of the union's GEC was the only one they could have taken in the face of the government's trade union laws and the port employers' unscrupulous tactics. The TGWU had pledged to fight in support of former registered dockworkers as long as they themselves were prepared to battle for local recognition and reinstatement, with Todd stating: 'no one would be thrown to the wolves,' while at the same time acknowledging: 'There was little or no chance of pursuing a legitimate dispute.' [17] Effectively, the union was saying return to work, seek local negotiations and reinstatement and continue the fight. That was exactly what the Liverpool dockers did, and it was this same strategy that would lead to their dismissal six years later, affirming the claim of Michael Meacher, Labour's shadow employment spokesman, that the docks dispute was: 'proof positive that it is becoming impossible, even with overwhelming right on your side, to hold a legal strike in Britain.' [18] The GEC's decision came only four days after dockers' delegates agreed overwhelmingly to continue the strike, with Todd insisting that the union had not: 'necessarily thrown the towel in as dockers still had to retain union recognition on their waterfronts and to win the reinstatement of sacked colleagues.' [19]

Ron Todd was in the line of fire not only from the dockworkers, but also the complex political groupings that dominated the GEC at this time who were all essentially claiming to be part of the broad left, all linked and/or controlled by some who claimed to be Communist Party members. This GEC was widely recognised at the time, especially by delegates such as Ken Brindle, Barry Miller, Dave Irvine, Colin Beresford and Mike Carden from Region Six, as profoundly *not* left-wing in reality. The attacks on Todd came from the 'broad' right-wing majority on the GEC, irrespective of the political labels or badges that they paraded for public consumption. The dock section of the TGWU had more in common with old industrial traditions that had been cast upon the anvil of an extraordinarily militant communist history, and while they could also have conservative tendencies at times, the dockers now found themselves at home within neither faction. On the left, the dockers were seen as part of an industrial history that had long run its course and seen its finest hours, while on the right, where a white, male industrial hegemony should have welcomed them, they shuddered at the thought of industrial action, or any effective confrontation with an employer.

In 1989 casual labour was introduced in all former registered ports except Liverpool. [20] Liverpool docker, Kevin Bilsborrow pointed out at that:

*'Whilst the MDHC said they would never use casual labour, the way they got around*
*that was we started finding small stevedoring companies getting set-up, and these involved*

*MDHC directors and they were 51% owned by the MDHC, and then we found out that our work was getting syphoned-off to companies who employed casual labour; but MDHC don't employ casual labour. They know a man who does, though, and that's how they done it.' [21]*

Writing in his introduction to *The Great Dock Strike 1889*, Ron Todd claimed: 'that if the 1889 dock strike had failed, our movement today would be a pale shadow of its reality.' [22] In one of the Liverpool dockers leaflets issued during the 1989 strike, they responded to their general secretary's words by stating: 'if the 1989 dock strike fails, our movement will not cast a shadow in the future.' [23] The strike in 1989 was effectively led by the Unofficial National Port Shop Stewards' Committee, which focussed on the registered ports of Liverpool, Hull and London dockers, leaning on the long-established rank-and-file connection between dockworkers nationally and across the globe. Walter Cunningham from Hull together with Mickey Fenn, Kevin Hussey, Frank Shilling and Colin Coughlin, alongside so many other London dockers, used their political and trade union experience, as well as their innate intelligence, to help guide the actions of the UNPSSC.

London was the natural hub of this national strike, and the various dockers' leaders met there at every opportunity. Together, they organised the international call for solidarity action among Dutch, French, German and Belgian dockers, and the Liverpool dock shop stewards that were involved would continue in the 1995 dispute. Jimmy Nolan, Frank Conchie, Jimmy Davies, Frank Lannigan, Bobby Morton, Mike Carden and others travelled to the major European ports with leaflets written in French, German and Dutch, calling upon their fellow dockworkers to support their defence of the UK's National Dock Labour Board Scheme. Carden organised the leaflets along with Greg Dropkin, with local community and union activists providing translations. The relevance of this internationalism was based upon the logic of the 1889 dockers' strike, the logic of the global nature of dock work, as similar labour schemes existed, and could potentially be threatened, in almost every organised port across the world. The 'blueprint' for 1889 was used in 1989 and would inform the tactics of the Liverpool dockers' dispute in 1995. Casual labour had always been the natural hire for harbour bosses internationally providing the source of infinite conflict by dock labourers against its use. Equally important was the fact that trade union history, organisation, working practices and even architecture was mirrored from New York to Port-au-Prince to Halifax. In 1989, the NPSSC's efforts to gain support in Europe set the agenda for the dispute. As academic and international ports historian, Peter Waterman observed:

*'Much of the activity came from Liverpool, where unions in general, the T&GWU, and the dockers in particular, had been involved over the years in a range of solidarity activity. Mike Carden, one of the local shop stewards, had been to the Philippines for a conference on free trade zones (Liverpool has had a free port for some years), and to an international trade union school in Spain. He was also responsible for getting local leaflets translated into foreign languages for European distribution. Jimmy Nolan, a long-time leader of the Liverpool dockers and equally long-time Chairman of the NPSSC, was also an old friend of the Co-ordinator. But the activity in 1989 seemed to have been organised by the British directly and without contact with the old network.*

# THE DOCKERS AND THE TGWU'S BROAD LEFT

*Three London dockers went to Zeebrugge in Belgium and to the northern French ports. Three Liverpool men went to Antwerp, Rotterdam and Bremen. In Bremen they were hosted not by the local dockers but by BUKO, an anti-imperialist action group that - like the Liverpool dockers - had been involved in action against importation of Namibian uranium.' [24]*

On Kees Marges, the Docks Secretary of the Dutch Transportworkers Union of the FNV, and later the leader of the ITF, Waterman wrote:

*'Whilst encouraging the Dutch dockers to give force to the ITF recommendations, he also warned against unofficial solidarity activities: In order to ensure that so-called strike tourism does not show its face again (see the experiences with the British miners' and seamen's strike), and that, in this manner, uncoordinated actions take place that could bring both the TGWU and the continental unions in legal difficulties. The TGWU will, in a letter to all shop stewards, urgently request that no visits to European ports be carried out on their own initiative.' [25]*

Of the ITF meeting in London, Waterman wrote: 'Jimmy Nolan made a point of expressing his appreciation to Marges, who reported this to his own members and incorporated a Liverpool leaflet (translated in Liverpool into a somewhat awkward Dutch) into his mailing to the Dutch shop stewards.' [26] Waterman's analysis of the event concluded:

*'The British dock strike of 1989 showed well both the extent and the limits of official trade union internationalism. It implies activity carried out by or through national and international officials. It implies diplomatic caution and legal finesse in avoiding laws against solidarity strikes, and in then specifying particular ports, particular ships, particular cargoes, or even part cargoes, to be boycotted. It implied hostility to direct contact between dockworkers internationally, this only being conceivable with approval from above. The policy is one that the ITF officer responsible for dockworker unions is proud of... Successful strikes are run by unions, not by ad hoc and often unrepresentative groups of shop stewards.' [27]*

It was clear after 1989 that nothing was ever going to be the same again in the dock industry, as every major UK port employer immediately reintroduced casual labour in their ports to replace dismissed ex-registered dockers. Liverpool, however, was the exception to the rule, as the MDHC sought to maintain a facade of opposition to casual labour. Writing to Jimmy Symes, the TGWU docks officer in Liverpool at the time, MDHC's managing director, Trevor Furlong, categorically stated that the company: 'had no intention of using casual or cheap labour systems of work in line with previous undertakings.' [28] Two weeks later, the MDHC Port Operations' Manager, Bernard Cliff, wrote to all Liverpool dockers to complain about, 'Malicious rumours being spread about the company's plans to abandon general cargo. The company is committed to remain in General Cargo and there are very good prospects of attracting new services.' [29] Opposition to casualisation held firm in Liverpool after 1989 until their eventual dismissal. This opposition brought the dock shop stewards into another period of prolonged and open conflict with the MDHC and the leadership of the TGWU at both national and local levels.

# 10

# Foundations of Chaos

*The 1989 dispute was the biggest one because it changed all the dockers' lives. That was the biggest single factor in the situation we are all in now. Everyone says it was when the five Torside men got sacked, it wasn't. Nineteen eighty-nine was the main thing, because that's when everything collapsed. The dockers lost all their rights, everything, and that was what brought Bradley in. It was disgraceful the hours we had to work.' ~ Joe Ladd Jr\**

Liverpool dockers returned to work in a very different port. A world apart from that envisaged by national officers of the T&G and its local officials. The dockers expected that the Dock Company would continue with their aggressive industrial strategy, reducing permanent labour and opening the port to casual agencies. Many of the Merseyside Port Shop Stewards involved in 1989 would go on to lead the 1995 dispute, finding themselves in conflict with the same union officials, government bodies, MDHC bosses and lay-member General Executive Council. The Liverpool dockers on the picket lines in 1989 would stand on the same picket lines, often at the same gates, in 1995, and in archive film footage one of those dockers spoke of the TGWU's withdrawal of support as he left the mass meeting that ended the 1989 strike: 'We are disgusted and the union has thrown the towel in, but we're not going to throw the towel in yet until we get a proper deal.' [1] The meeting, organised by the local TGWU at the Philharmonic Hall, had been called to allow Ron Todd and the regional secretary, Bobby Owens, to tell the Liverpool dockers that the national strike was over and they had to go back to work.

This was a bitter and angry meeting in which the dockers appeared to be considered a threat to the physical safety of the General Secretary. Local union officials had organised a number of officers to act as 'security,' both on the stage of this famous hall and at the entrance, where membership cards were vigorously checked, leaving dockers feeling like they were being treated as the enemy by their own union. It was an acrimonious meeting, where

---

\* Joe Ladd Jr interviewed by D. Cotterill, 13 December 1996

dockers were ordered from the platform to 'shut up,' and when one docker, John Jenkins, was repeatedly refused the right to speak, Bobby Owens asked someone 'to remove that person from the hall.' The meeting did little for the TGWU's reputation, and for many dockers it simply compounded their distrust of local union officials. Joe Ladd, a Liverpool docker who, along with his son, also took part in the 1995 dispute said at the time, 'We've been sold down the river, but it may be a fight for another day.' [2] At the Philharmonic Hall that day was Denis Anderson, an influential dock shop steward, who said that what the union had done was, 'Disgusting, a disgrace.' [3] Another docker told reporters, 'The deal done by the TGWU was not worth a balloon. Not even a burst balloon!' [4]

In the same archive film footage, Ron Todd is shown leaving the hall alongside dock union officials Jack Dempsey and Mike Carr. Dempsey would serve as senior docks officer during the 1995 dispute, replacing Jimmy Symes on his retirement. Mike Carr was a full-time dock official based at the Garston office. He had previously been a dock clerical worker at Harrison Line and 6/567 Branch member who would soon become the Labour MP for Bootle. On 14 June 1990, he made his maiden speech in the House of Commons, and then a month later, on 20 July 1990, he took ill during a constituency meeting and died tragically later that same night. [5] The union officials who walked out of the Philharmonic Hall that day were powerful men who could exercise considerable influence among employers on the docks, politicians in the Commons and the European Parliament, and the national and international trade union movement. The Philharmonic Hall meeting was a display of how not to use such power. The meeting ended a national dock strike, but it did not end the long running dispute the Liverpool dockers had with their employer. Trevor Furlong, the MDHC's managing director, welcomed the union's recommendation to return to work by telling a reporter:

> 'That the Dock Company did not issue idle threats. We are not issuing threats, please get me wrong [sic], we're issuing what we consider to be a fair contract. If men do not want to take that contract that is their decision, but we are not threatening anybody.' [6]

On their return-to-work, former registered dock workers and clerical port workers from TGWU 6/567 Branch were labelled Port Operations Workers (POWs) by the bosses. This attempt at sarcasm was not lost on the two previously separate groups, who all started working together as one unit. For example, someone previously employed as a clerk could now find themselves driving a forklift truck, while an ex-RDW could become a clerk, acting out a managerial mirage that was a nightmare for many workers. [7] A large number of dockers were not physically able to perform some of the more traditional dock work tasks, nor could they meet the new demands of plant / crane driving. Other problems relating to age and health demographics were soon to be highlighted by the employer, as the docks became a world turned upside down with timekeepers and clerical workers being put to work as holdsmen, deckhands and drivers. It was *year zero*, punishment was work and work was punishment. Unlike any other port in the UK post 1989, the local TGWU managed to retain union recognition. However, for the Liverpool dockers new contracts of employment were imposed that introduced drastic changes which, in the words of Trevor Furlong, were 'nonnegotiable.' Shop stewards who attempted to open negotiations on the basis of previously existing agreements were swiftly turned away. [8]

According to Monica Clua-Losada's 2010 study, the deal achieved in Liverpool was still impressive considering the climate at the time and the situation in other ports such as Tilbury [9], and it's true that the MDHC did adopt a very different approach to other UK ports in maintaining just over half of its pre-strike labour force of approximately 600 men. [10] They accepted the continuation of recognition rights with the TGWU, which was understandably seen as a major concession for the union locally and nationally. In July 1996, one year after he had sacked 500 Liverpool dockworkers, *International Freight Weekly* published an interview with Trevor Furlong – who they claimed was regarded as a hawk on the board of directors – in which he revealed the root cause of what was then a nine-month-long dispute: 'I suppose in hindsight we were too soft in 1989. We should have got rid of the lot of them and recruited, but we did not believe it was right.' He denied that the motive was to destroy organised labour but acknowledged that the Dock Company had suffered in comparison to other ports, who had de-recognised the union. [11]

On Tuesday 8 August 1989, the Liverpool dockers became the last strikers to return to work, marching along the dock road to the sound of a lone bagpiper dressed in full Scottish regalia. [12] Upon their return to work, shop stewards would no longer be recognised by the MDHC and some accepted severance payments within hours of being presented with a new contract of employment that had to be signed there and then. The shop stewards brick hut had been padlocked shut, in a very physical display of power, and yet the Dock Company continued to stress their willingness to recognise the TGWU and its local full-time officials. Most importantly of all, the people who really mattered in this de-recognition fiasco, the dockers themselves, maintained their support for their democratically elected shop stewards from 1989 until the end of their dispute in 1998. The employer would meet with de-recognised shop stewards whenever it suited their purpose, and for their part, the stewards would never accept the power of their union or their employer to decide who the dockers could elect as their representatives.

The Port of Liverpool would now be divided into six independent economic units and all work-sharing rotas were to be abolished. Berths were privatised and given over to companies such as Pandoro Ltd and Coastal Containers, who used many of the same dockers that were made redundant prior to 1989. Some of these men were on the former National Dock Labour Board Scheme's Temporary Unattached Register, or what the Liverpool dockers used to call the 'sin bin,' a holding pen for dockers waiting to be assigned another employer under the terms of this national agreement. Unfortunately, the abolition of the scheme put these dockers in the impossible position of being registered under a banner that no longer existed, effectively making them redundant. New cargo handling companies sponsored by the Port Authority took their opportunity to trade in the Port of Liverpool, with Coastal Containers, a newly created MDHC satellite, having the confidence to insist on a no-strike deal that local TGWU officials accepted. Specifically, those dockers employed at Coastal Containers could go on strike by themselves, but they could not go on strike in solidarity with their fellow dockers. The new company claimed a berth at Seaforth Container Terminal, cordoned off by a low channel iron fence that allowed the MDHC to call the area a dedicated berth with an equally dedicated labour force. The first strike to take place in this new terrain was at the Irish ferry service, Pandoro Ltd, which Terry Southers, together with other dockers employed at Coastal Containers, joined. 'The eight men at Coastal who took part in the strike got victimised with a twelve-month probation during which they could be sacked for anything.' [13]

Southers recalled how his father, a merchant seaman, had followed the usual compass that led such men from sea to docks, and in an interview with Dave Cotterill, he discussed his family's heritage on the open seas and the open docks. These men had an affinity with dock work and their fellow dockworkers; of being on the quays and on the river; of being outside in what could be a beautiful environment depending on the season, the work and the weather. These dockers spoke of 'a love for dock work and the docks,' and in answer to Dave Cotterill's question, 'Do you like dock work?' Southers reflected the view of so many when he replied that he 'loved dock work, up to 1989.' [14] Another Liverpool docker who loved the docks was Joe Ladd, having first started working there in 1965:

'... me and John Gibbons [another sacked docker] started together, and from our school you could see the docks and our teacher said, "No problem, you will end up there," and we did. The first time I went below, I was with seven people and they must have been three thousand years between them, seven old men, and talk about people who've called young people they're all whatever, they made me so welcome. They taught me so much and the solidarity then was so much, and its good today with the way we are at this present moment with this dispute, but then solidarity was so good, yet we didn't have the actual solidarity until the 1967 dispute came up, and that's when we really kicked off with the likes of the unofficial strike committee, which stemmed from the likes of the Blue Union, which was Jimmy Benbow, Denis Kelly, Tommy Wright, Gerry Edwards. The way they sorted the '67 dispute, we came back on good wages and never ever looked back since. I was always in the T&G, they were number one for me, but when I went onto the docks I found there was another union, the Blue Union, and to me they were the union on the docks; they were the stevedoring union and they should still be the union today. I was in Box Six, and if you were not fully paid-up members of the T&G, then when an arbitration down for a hatch for dirty cargo, only the fully paid up members would get paid. If there were eight people down the hatch and only two were paid-up, then only two would get paid. The Blue Union came along and said, "No, you're wrong. Everyone's equal, they will all get paid." The Blue Union was on its way out, but they done us a lot of good favours, hell of a lot of good favours, very good. The Dock Company were a good company when they took us out of Smith & Coggins, Scruttons, Freight Conveyors and the Port of Liverpool Stevedores, they were a good company, but all of a sudden the powers to be, whoever came in, it went to a bad company and then this is the dispute we are in now.' [15]

The de-recognition of the shop stewards' organisation in 1989 saw the victimisation of two Liverpool dockers' leaders, Jimmy Nolan and Jimmy Davies. During this period, four attempts were made by the rank-and-file dockers to organise an official strike ballot and three meetings took place with the union's new general secretary, Bill Morris, who was elected in 1992. Morris was told by Nolan that if the local union continued to oppose workplace organisation in the port and openly side with the employer, 'we will all be sacked in Liverpool.' The casual employment that had first eased its way into the Port of Liverpool during the 1980s at the Liverpool Freeport and berths handling scrap metal and other cargoes spread like wildfire across the docks after 1989. Some 300 Liverpool dockers' jobs were lost during the initial period following the dockers' return to work in August of that year.

On Wednesday 27 June 1990, the de-recognised Merseyside Port Shop Stewards met to discuss the growing reality of casual labour in the Port of Liverpool. They agreed upon a policy to fill vacancies in the MDHC and to get the men to stop working double shifts due to serious labour shortages in some areas of the port. Recruitment had always been an aspiration for the dockers, and it was now dominating the agenda of the shop stewards' movement. [16] At a June 1990 meeting with MDHC managers Larry Burrell, Budha Majumba, Mike Gelling, George Edgar and Mervyn Bull, shop stewards rejected the compulsory overtime that had been imposed. [17] Three days later, in the presence of Jimmy Symes, the local TGWU docks officer, those same managers spoke about the largest shipping company, Atlantic Container Line, threatening to leave the port unless compulsory overtime was worked. [18] Pressure was now being exerted on the Seaforth Container Berth dockers to work weekends on the ACL until the ship finished, and with no shop stewards recognised by the MDHC. The Seaforth shop stewards did recognise some of the problems of a five-day shift pattern that did not encompass the weekends and, along with the men on the berth, plans and discussions took place regarding a seven-day coverage that could be acceptable to both the company and dockers on the berth. The management on the berth were involved in these discussions and they saw some merit in the ideas being put across to limit overtime and provide cover for the ACL. But by the end of the month, Jimmy Symes had told the MDHC Shop Stewards Committee that, 'the union's position was clear that the Seaforth Shop Stewards should sign the agreement that the MDHC wanted to impose.' [19]

The now unofficial shop stewards refused to agree, stating that only the men at Seaforth Container Terminal could accept or reject the proposals. At a meeting of the Seaforth Committee, Jimmy Davies and Jimmy Nolan supported the men who were now calling for the overtime ban to continue, [20] and at the TGWU Docks and Waterways District Committee, held 10 September 1990, a discussion took place on the real and expanding problem of casual labour in the Port of Liverpool. As minute No.73 recorded:

> 'In response to questions raised relating to casual and contracted labour, the District Secretary explained the reported difference between casual and contracted labour, and expressed the view that this union has an opportunity to maintain an organised presence in respect of contracted workers, who are members of this union. Furthermore, he advised that with regard to Faber Press, the labour force had since been recruited from the DSS (the Dept. Social Security) and were now seeking trade union recognition. During this discussion, members expressed their opposition to the employment of those dockers who had accepted severance payments being re-employed on the docks. Attention was drawn to the fact that the MDHC had advised that they would not employ men who had accepted severance payments.' [21]

It was this tortuous attempt to justify casual labour and defend the union's wish to recruit anyone who turned up on the docks post-1989 that was to become the real cornerstone of local union inaction in relation to their former registered dock membership. As the use of casual labour increased, the port continued to experience labour shortages, but this did not stop the Dock Company from deciding in October 1990 that it wanted some 180 redundancies in the North Area of the Liverpool docks by January 1991. [22] That same month, the company refused to meet with the de-recognised Seaforth shop stewards, [23] and it would be almost two years before they agreed to recognise any shop stewards; even then, they would only be allowed to function within rigid boundaries and with limited powers. On 16 November 1990, the de-recognised shop stewards met with Trevor Furlong, Bernard Cliff and Larry Burrell of the MDHC, where it was revealed that the company had received over 200 requests for severance pay to leave the industry. Furlong promised the stewards that redundancies would be voluntary, with the caveat: 'if a dramatic loss of trade took place, he would review the situation.' [24]

By January 1991, the Dock Company were rapidly facilitating the growth of new satellite casual agencies at the expense of former registered dockers. Confusion would reign as these companies changed their names on a regular basis undermining the contracts of employment for those dockers involved. For example, dockworkers who had been employed by Liverpool Maritime Terminal – which became West Langton Stevedores, which became Central Stevedoring, which then went into liquidation – were left idle while their traditional work was farmed out to casual agencies. Bernard Cliff informed Jimmy Symes, the union's Docks Officer, that he wanted to form a joint venture company with another new operator called Powell Duffryn, to perform dock work together with other new enterprises such as Eurosal, Sheppards, Seahorn Marine and Pan Ocean. Around this time, an ex-dockworker formed a co-operative with 23 dockers, through which £17,500 was put into a TGWU trust for men who worked at Raes and Knowsley Freight Ltd, which had since changed its name to Nelson Freight. Former registered dockers who were transferred to the newly created Liverpool Cargo Handling would not be given a guarantee that they would be re-employed by MDHC in the event of this joint venture failing, [25] with Bernard Cliff informing Symes:

> '...former RDW's employed by the Joint Venture would be offered jobs. If insufficient volunteers were forthcoming, to fill the required number, the MDHC would have the right to direct former RDW's from the Joint Venture to jobs to be filled within MDHC.' [26]

MDHC also stated in writing that: 'the Joint Venture would not employ former RDW's who had left the industry under the £35,000 redundancy scheme,' [27] but like so much that had gone before, it was a meaningless undertaking. Local TGWU Dock and Waterways officials raised no opposition to the development of these new companies and formally agreed their establishment without the involvement or support of their dock membership. These actions by the union would have obvious implications for rank-and-file dockers terms and conditions of employment on the waterfront. The message was clear, long-term labour shortages would not be solved with direct recruitment by the MDHC, enabling the toxic mix of casual, semi-casual, low-paying, pop-up stevedoring companies to proliferate in the port challenged only by the Liverpool dockers. Liverpool docks was a new *Klondike,* and everyone wanted a share of the spoils of these 'shell companies'.

As a response to these developments in the port, Liverpool dockers in the general cargo area refused to work alongside former dockers who had taken severance payments and were now returning to the docks in droves. They also made it clear that they would not work with the casual and non-union labour that was being hired by the new *shell companies.* Around this time, the government expressed the view that it was wrong for former dockworkers to be in receipt of severance payments, only to continue to work in the same port that had made them redundant. The MDHC continued to abuse and exploit the opportunities provided by the same government's redundancy payments programme to rid itself of registered dockworkers, and then re-employ them in the new casual stevedoring companies. As Turnbull and Woolfson observed: 'The Mersey Docks & Harbour Company, despite its claims to be less hard line, was no less determined than other employers.' [28] In fact, the Dock Company used casual non-union labour during the 1989 dispute and, on one vessel, the *M.V. Falcon* (a ship carrying cement and timber), they openly confirmed that they were determined to utilise casual, non-union labour. The vessel was, according to Peter Turnbull, 'Offloaded over the sea wall on the Wirral by local young men who lacked the essential health and safety equipment, such as adequate footwear rather than trainers.' [29]

Following the upheavals of 1989, and amid the ensuing chaos on the docks, the *unofficial* Merseyside Port Shop Stewards re-elected Jimmy Nolan as their chairman, with Frank Lannigan as his deputy and Jimmy Davies as the secretary / treasurer. An important change in personnel also took place in the management of human resources in the Dock Company. Allan Price was employed to take the lead in human resources and, with no background in the industry, he had no baggage, no historical reference point and no personal links to anyone in the port. On Monday 15 April 1991, Alec Hampton, manager of the Seaforth Container Terminal, received a call from one of the shop stewards regarding the interpretation of their latest contractual change, during which he was advised that there could be an immediate stoppage of work. A meeting had been called for 6pm. According to Allan Price, the shop stewards 'did not seek permission for this meeting... [where] the men refused to work over-time and this decision resulted in ships sailing without containers, and the ACL vessel missed the tide. At least twenty vehicles were left in the queue. These events damaged the image of the company.' [30] On the same day a meeting took place with the TGWU's dock official, Jimmy Symes, as well as Larry Burrell and Allan Price of the MDHC, regarding the calling of this unofficial meeting by the three Seaforth shop stewards at the container base. Jimmy Symes reminded the Dock Company that they had de-recognised the shop stewards after 1989; as a result, they could only turn to the Advisory, Conciliation and Arbitration Service (ACAS) for the use of disciplinary procedures. Furthermore, the company were refusing to discipline the three stewards together, instead wanting to deal with them separately. [31] Price was to inform Jimmy Symes that:

> *Billy Duffy, one of the stewards, was given a final warning. Frank Jones and Mike Carden were brought in at 5.25pm. This was an issue of gross misconduct in terms of loss to customers. It was a serious act of insubordination wilfully refusing management's*

*request not to hold the meeting. We cannot afford to let this happen again. As a result, a final warning will be issued on your records for twelve months.' [32]*

At Seaforth Container Terminal, 350 dockers experienced no real challenge from casual or cheap labour as, supported by the dock company shop stewards, they consistently reiterated their refusal to work with casual labour. This was possible because container ships bound for Liverpool could only dock at the Seaforth Container Berth, making it, as some of the Liverpool dockers had intuitively called it, their *Alamo*. On Friday 19 April 1991, a meeting of the Dock Company stewards agreed to call a ballot for strike action over the victimisation of the three Seaforth shop stewards. Meanwhile, matters were about to become much more complicated on the Liverpool docks, as the foundations of Torside Ltd and, subsequently, the 1995 conflict were being laid. Jimmy Symes called the shop stewards to Transport House for a meeting, where he informed them about 22 dockers from Liverpool Grain Storage following the abolition of the national dock labour scheme. [33] Symes then explained to the stewards that the night before, an advert had been placed in the *Liverpool Echo* for jobs on the docks. This related to a phone call he had received from Bernard Bradley, an ex-Garston docker, who had also been a member of the TGWU's Docks and Waterways District Committee. Having taken severance pay in exchange for his job, Bradley now wanted to form his own stevedoring company, as Symes described it: 'to put permanent labour back on the docks.' [34] He had received a letter from Bradley's new company, Torside Ltd, requesting labour to be supplied to the MDHC at a rate of £160 per week. [35] Ironically, given his own actions, Bradley was offering employment only to those workers who had not taken severance from the Liverpool docks, and Jimmy Symes took this opportunity to reiterate to the shop stewards: 'the Dock Company would not be recruiting labour direct.' [36]

Some stewards thought the deal had already been done once the advert had been placed in the *Liverpool Echo* and that there was no reason to provide legitimacy to a company that already existed. Clearly, both the MDHC and TGWU were keen to get the shop stewards' endorsement as this would be key to establishing the credibility of Torside Ltd. No other company in the port had ever received the open sponsorship of the TGWU/MDHC nor had the shop stewards ever been approached to agree their existence. This was of critical significance in the establishment of Torside Ltd. At 11am on Friday 26 April 1991, the Merseyside Port Shop Stewards met at Transport House, Liverpool City Centre. Outside the room, a group of dockers from Liverpool Grain Storage lobbied the stewards about their situation, as a great deal of anger and confusion existed around this time especially in relation to the Torside advert for dockers' jobs in the previous week's *Liverpool Echo*. The chairman and secretary of the port stewards assured the men that they knew nothing about any recruitment or what the role of the ex-docker Bernard Bradley was in this company, claiming that they had not been involved in any discussions with him or Jimmy Symes. The meeting had to be adjourned until Symes arrived to explain the link between the position of the Ex-LGS dockers and Bradley's new company but, in reality, no connection existed, save for the desire of the stewards to help sort out the issues of the former LGS dockers who were now redundant. Jimmy Symes told the stewards:

*The Dock Company would not employ labour direct and Bradley's company, Torside Ltd, would be used for this purpose. Over one thousand applications had been received since the advert appeared in the Liverpool Echo that previous Thursday 18 April. The union had also been asked to provide a list of applications that would be submitted to Torside, and it was expected that interviews would take place the following Tuesday for sixty to seventy men to be employed.' [37]*

The stewards were also informed by the TGWU docks officer that MDHC wanted their approval to establish Torside Ltd; they wanted the shop stewards to sanction the creation of this labour supply agency, even though Torside would halt, forever, the objectives of the dockers to see MDHC recruit dockworkers directly on the same rate of pay and conditions. This had long been their policy, and now it was disappearing in front of them as the employer was about to succeed in formalising yet another cheap labour supply company, openly sponsored by the Port Employer and local officials of the TGWU. This development would cause major divisions among the dock stewards and the dockers themselves for years to come, and Torside would ultimately be the catalyst for the dismissal of 500 Liverpool dockers. That Friday, many of the shop stewards in the room did not know that in 1989 MDHC bosses had held secret talks with the same full-time TGWU officials over the establishment of Torside Ltd. The local union had full knowledge of this plan long before the elected shop stewards knew anything about it in 1991. [38]

At this Port Shop Stewards meeting much discussion took place regarding the rates of pay and conditions of dockworkers, with some shop stewards asking if anybody in the room thought that Torside dockers would remain on less pay than their MDHC counterparts. A three-month time limit for wage parity to be achieved was then ratified, but it was a heated and passionate meeting that effectively pivoted on the fulcrum of Jimmy Symes trying to convince the stewards to agree to create jobs for young Liverpool people. Other shop stewards argued that the decision to establish Torside had already been taken, demanding to know why the union now wanted the stewards to endorse and legitimise low pay on the docks? Backwards and forwards the arguments went, and as the fog of cigarette smoke got thicker, so too did the vehemence and threats from one steward to another. It was not a positive meeting, and its outcome would spill onto the Dock Estate, causing splits and accusations among dockers that continue to this day. When the vote was eventually taken, six Merseyside Port Shop Stewards voted in favour of sanctioning Torside Ltd and five voted against; a majority of one provided the MDHC and TGWU with the authority they were seeking. [39] Never before had these unofficial and de-recognised shop stewards been asked to endorse any of the myriad casual or cheap labour agencies that operated in the port, not to mention the fact that Torside already existed and was recruiting labour. This begged the question: *why were the MDHC and TGWU so insistent that the dockers representatives, who they did not recognise, had to agree to this venture?*

The stewards held a stop-work meeting in the Alexander Pen, where all dockers from the container, timber and general cargo areas listened to arguments from the stewards as to why they should agree to the introduction of a new labour supply company. This was another highly charged meeting, with the key debate focussing on the rate for the job. Many dockers vehemently opposed the shop stewards and, once again, so close was the vote that it was difficult to really see a majority. You could cut the atmosphere with a knife, as the divisions that would set docker against docker on the issue of Torside were being established right there in the pen. This was a place which also served as an amenity block for the general cargo area dockers, who were at constant risk of redundancy as they saw ships being redirected to other berths that were long in disuse before being resurrected for agency labour. Many felt that Seaforth dockers had the advantage as they had plenty of work, whereas general cargo dockers had no work. At this meeting it was agreed that a recruitment list be drawn up and submitted to the TGWU / Torside Ltd, with promises made that Torside would eventually pay the established rate for the job. This never happened.

For Terry Barrett, one of the Seaforth dockworkers, the Torside initiative was wrong from the start: 'We should never have let Torside start on the docks without proper pay and conditions. It was obvious they would expand their operations and force conditions down elsewhere.' [40] This was a view shared by many dockers, although others did hold a different view. The one thing that all dockers would agree on, however, was the fact that Torside Ltd had been created by the MDHC and local TGWU, and as a *fait accompli*, it was subsequently endorsed by the men. The young Torside dockers were interviewed by MDHC senior managers at their headquarters in 1991 and were trained and given certificates to operate machinery by the MDHC, who also owned all of the facilities used by Torside. [41]

Five years later, when dockers and their partners sat down in the Workers' Educational Association (WEA) writers' workshop, alongside Jimmy McGovern and Irvine Welsh, the divisions over Torside emerged again. In the resulting film, *Dockers*, first shown on Channel 4 TV on Sunday 18 July 1999, as the opening credits begin, the characters of two older dockers, played by Ricky Tomlinson and Ken Stott, are seen walking along the quayside when a gang of six younger Torside dockers walk towards them. The scene actually involved two former Torside dockers who took part in the film, Jimmy Davies Jr and Tony Melia. As both groups of dockers pass each other looking at their pay packets one of the younger dockers, played by Davies Jr, says to the two older dockers:

> *'Hey! Look at fat wallet.' Tomlinson replies, 'Hey, just because you're on £4 an hour and we're on £10 an hour, you think you're gonna be gettin' £10 an hour as well? Ya won't, because we'll be down to £4 an hour like you fellas. That's not if we're out on our ear before that. Ya know what we're doin. We're trainin' you to take our fuckin jobs off us!' Tellingly, the other older docker, played by Ken Stott, tells his fellow docker, 'Hey Macca, you're out of order now, you voted for them to come on the dock.' Macca replies, 'No, I didn't vote for them.' [42]*

The significance of Torside rates of pay and their recruitment could not be overstated. According to Monica Clua-Losada's study, many of the former registered dockers, particularly those who did not stand to gain from the establishment of Torside, viewed this development with resentment, for not only was agency labour now 'agreed' in the port, but some dockers' sons, and primarily those of shop stewards, had managed to get jobs. In fact, many rank-and-file dockers brought up the issue during her interviews. They felt that their sons could have been considered. [43] Initially, Torside was created by recruiting 15 dockers that were nominated by dockers. Those eventually chosen involved shop stewards and union officials' sons, as well as 15 workers picked by Torside bosses themselves. Regardless of one's interpretation of this process, it did follow the century-old tradition of recruiting dockers' sons. In the end, Torside would employ 80 dockers on different terms and conditions to those of the former registered dockers. [44]

Torside Ltd was registered at Companies House on 14 June 1989, coinciding with the abolition of the National Dock Labour Board Scheme. It was registered by two ex-dockers, Bernard Bradley and Thomas Hendrick, who were named as company directors almost two years before their existence was revealed to shop stewards by the TGWU and the MDHC in 1991. They registered another company, Lineside Ltd, in 1994, and both companies kept an office at the Alexandra Dock and Canada Dock in Liverpool. These companies were linked, usually through family members, to other companies in a labyrinth of enterprises that included Montforce Ltd, Alpha Taxi Rentals Ltd, Alpha Cars and Speke Freight Services. The local TGWU, the Dock Commpany, Bradley and Hendrick held discussions ahead of the creation of Torside, to the extent that vacancies for dock labour, or rather the identified need for dock labour, had been agreed prior to the company's official launch. With just £70,000 invested by Bradley and Hendrick from the severance money they received from the docks, there was little room for risk, as the wage bill for just 30 workers would have been at least £10,000 per week, even with moderate employer costs. Only guarantees of work and the financial backing of the MDHC could have made this business plan even faintly viable. Torside was not just another low-pay agency like so many others that littered the port, they were a special case, sponsored by local TGWU officials and the MDHC. Frank Lannigan knew Bernard Bradley, as did many other the dockers, and his analysis of the man is worth reproducing at length:

*The Dock Company had overstretched itself, it had too much work, too little men, and they needed a new workforce. Now they knew they couldn't get casuals in – we wouldn't have stood for casuals. So, they had to form this company. They formed it with Bernard Bradley. They were paying the majority of the wages, because Bernard Bradley used to start crying, 'Frank, I've got 54% down time this year, I've got to go to the bank.' I wanted to know what bank manager, where you've got 80-odd lads on, and if you've got 54% down time in a twelve-month period, it's more than £30,000 wages. Now he only got £35,000 in 1989 himself, but he went back to the bank manager three years on the run. He had no collateral; he never had a stacker truck. All he had was an agency for hiring labour. Which bank manager in them times, because they were bad times then for the economy and everything, and banks had stopped lending people with collateral – they'd cut down and curtailed their amount of borrowing – but this fella found a lovely bank manager that was willing to pay the Torside wage for three years. A load of nonsense.*

*He went out, he's not bankrupt, all his assets, whatever they were, was a phone, that's all he had was a phone and a desk and an office, maybe a typewriter, but all his assets have staved him off of bankruptcy. Who saved him from bankruptcy? That's what I want to know. If he could answer me that, for all the money that he borrowed off the banks, and the union officials used to tell us this, he'd had to go and borrow money off the bank for the men's wages. Yet that man is still solvent, that company Torside is still solvent. No creditor has taken him to court. And let's face it, the banks are the first in. Because if you've borrowed money from a bank, before you've had any wages, your lads' wages, that bank will take what you owe it.*

*Now there's never been nothing in the paper, nothing to my recollection, since this strike begin, or till this dispute began, that any bank has took the owners of Torside to court to retrieve the hundreds of thousands of pounds that he borrowed to pay the men's wages. So, maybe the Dock Company had paid the wages – maybe the Dock Company were paying the wages all along. That's my recollection of it, and almost, I'll go to me grave not doubting a word that I've said over the Torside affair.'* [45]

In the Ken Loach film, *The Flickering Flame* (1996), a few of the dockers and shop stewards reflected on the critical point of the absence of the rate for the job, which was key to the establishment of Torside Ltd. One of those dockers, Kevin Bilsborrow, is quoted as saying:

*'Every working man has got to have good pay and conditions, and if you don't stand up for yourself, and if the trade unions don't back the members and you don't get good pay and conditions – the most important thing in any job is the rate for the job. Once you lose the rate for the job and let agencies take over, you're finished. You all start killin' yerself for work.'* [46]

By giving their support to the establishment of Torside, shop stewards became locked into all future events linked to this company. Jimmy Davies Jr recalled how his father had told him that he did not want him to apply for a job with Torside: 'I don't want you down there,' his father told him. Davies Jr believed that his dad foresaw the coming problems: 'I don't think he wanted me down there anyway, for whatever reasons, but I needed a job.' [47] Joe Ladd's son was in the same position, and he explained in December 1996 that his dad did not want him to go down on the docks:

*'Because he knew this would happen – he could see it coming six or seven years in advance, and a lot of the dockers could, but he said we'll get them down and get them the better wages, but it never happened because they were shafted themselves.'* [48]

The stewards called a mass meeting to again discuss the establishment of Torside Ltd and put their final recommendation to accept its existence. Held on Saturday 11 May 1991, in Transport House, this was another bitter and heated debate. After much argument it was finally agreed that Torside Ltd would officially be recognised, although some of the shop stewards and many dockers voiced their objection. Others promised to limit any potential damage, as 'over three months they would change the wages and conditions of the new dockers to match those of the Dock Company's dock workers.' [49] According to Meyer et al:

*'A supposed agreement equalizing Torside workers' pay and conditions with those of the MDHC dockers was slow to bear fruit. On three occasions, the Torsiders balloted for*

*official strike action, in support of their expectation of equal pay and an equivalent work regime.' [50]*

By this time, it was common to see ships previously manned by MDHC general cargo dockers being diverted to berths where the new labour agencies now operated. It was also common for workers from various different companies to work on the same ship, doing the same job, while all earning different rates of pay. As Bob Ritchie recalled, after the first six months:

*'Everybody became aware why Torside was there – my view was we were there to reduce wages and conditions in the Port. [51]*

Through the combined efforts of the MDHC and local officials of the TGWU, Torside was now established as a union-approved employer, in a move that would have profound implications for dockworkers in the coming years.

# 11
# De-recognising Shop
# Stewards on the Docks

*Jimmy Davies told the Company Stewards that it was now time 'to put up or shut up. If the union are not prepared to fight, we are. We have to mount a campaign', he told the stewards. 'The MDHC are making millions – they don't want us. Other options will be taken up by the company to cut more jobs. We have a right to remain and fight for our jobs.' ~ Mike Carden\**

On 23 May 1991, Jimmy Nolan, chairman of the Merseyside Port Shop Stewards, called upon the union: 'To direct dock workers from ex-LGS and Torside to refuse to work a particular ship. Jack Dempsey, the TGWU docks officer, would not agree to do this, and an immediate mass meeting was held at 0800hrs in the North Area of Liverpool Docks calling for a ballot for strike action to take place.' [1] Later that day, a meeting was held involving MDHC's Trevor Furlong, Jimmy Symes (TGWU docks officer), Jimmy Nolan, Jimmy Davies and Mike Carden. Symes told Furlong that the union were indeed going to organise a ballot of the dockers over the chaos that now existed on the docks, as MDHC were clearly directing ships to casual low-pay agencies at the expense of their own dockworkers, who remained idle. Furlong claimed that he had: 'kept the word of the Dock Company paying the union rate. We have an agreement with the union, over Crombie and Bradley (two ex-dockers turned agency bosses) using recognised union labour.' [2] Jimmy Nolan replied that, 'Liverpool Cargo Handling dockers should be used before any other labour,' [3] to which Furlong responded: 'We do not intend to swamp LCH with casual labour.' [4]

On Monday 22 July 1991, Jimmy Nolan and Jimmy Davies were again formally de-recognised as union convenors. Ironically, the employer had not recognised any democratic union elections since the return to work in 1989 and they were now demanding a reduction in shop stewards across all areas of the company. In response, the unofficial dock shop stewards

---

\* Author's Notes (Company Stewards, 12.6.92)

refused to meet with the management. On Tuesday 27 August 1991, MDHC's Bernard Cliff accepted that new LCH shop stewards could now be elected as convenors, following the intervention of the TGWU's deputy general secretary, Jack Adams. As a result, the employer would agree to recognise nine shop stewards, two of whom could act as convenors; three at Seaforth Container Base, one each at the Grain Terminal, Pandoro, Timber and Belfast berths, as well as two at LCH. [5] It is important to note here that dock stewards had always been organised along company lines, both as unofficial representatives pre-1967 and in an official capacity thereafter until 1989.

On 1 October, Jack Dempsey, Jimmy Davies and a Seaforth shop steward, Mike Carden, met with MDHC's George Edgar and Allan Price. The purpose of the meeting was to discipline Carden but it also allowed Price, the newly appointed personnel manager, the opportunity to define the role of a shop steward as dictated by himself. Carden was issued with a final warning, an act that came right in the middle of wage negotiations at the strategically important Seaforth Container Terminal. [6] The message was clear, and the discipline or de-recognition of shop stewards had long been a tactic used by MDHC up to September 1995; they were no longer prepared to recognise any TGWU shop steward who did not follow the local union official's lead. A month after Carden's disciplinary hearing, on 6 November 1991, a mass meeting took place at Transport House to discuss the continuing struggle against MDHC's goal to use low-paid agency labour wherever and whenever it pleased. The TGWU's docks officer told those assembled that: 'Dockers at LCH were under threat of their employer imposing a new contract worse than the present one whilst also withdrawing all links with the MDHC. Men at LCH and Pandoro had now been taken off pay and a ballot had to take place otherwise strikers would be liable to legal action.' [7]

Another mass meeting would be held the following day, during which the results of last-minute negotiations allowed the stewards to recommend acceptance of a new agreement that honoured a previous deal made in January 1991, providing LCH men guarantees regarding work and wages. [8] It was on the proviso that more than 100 redundancies take place in the General Cargo area. [9] At the next meeting of the Port Shop Stewards, held on Saturday 16 November 1991, it was reported that Torside Ltd wanted to increase its labour force by another 30 men, prompting Jimmy Nolan to remind the stewards that they had not yet been successful in obtaining the standard rate of pay for the first Torside dockers. [10] One of those stewards, Billy Jenkins, believed at the time: 'No one should be allowed in until the thirty-five original men have been paid the rate for the job,' [11] a sentiment echoed by Billy's brother, John Jenkins. Some stewards spoke of the success they had previously achieved in getting the Shore-gang at Pandoro Berth the rate for the job. But the basic need for MDHC to recruit labour to fill vacancies created through excessive use of voluntary redundancy schemes remained at the heart of the matter. As a result of labour shortages, there were dockers working overtime at Seaforth in response to increased port traffic, while at the same time, MDHC persistently diverted ships from berths where former registered dockers were standing idle in the general cargo area. [12] Asked to comment on the situation, Frank Jones, a Seaforth shop steward, stated: 'the union has not backed the stewards, and they must be told we will not allow cheap labour in the port.' [13] Frank Lannigan said that it was the shop stewards' responsibility to fight for the rate for the job for all workers in the port, especially now that they were all part of the union. [14] It was decided that Torside dockworkers should be paid the full rate for the job, and that any further recruitment should be controlled by the dockers themselves. On 25 November 1991, Dempsey, Nolan and Davies met with Bernard Cliff, in a session of such significance that Cliff was compelled to write to a local TGWU docks official:

> 'To put on record one major point which arose at the meeting we had yesterday at which Mr. Nolan and Mr. Davies were present. The point concerned the possible use of Torside Labour in MDHC operations. In response to this point I made it clear that MDHC has not and will not require or use Torside labour at any of its operations; namely the Container, Timber and Grain Terminals and the various Irish Ferry Operations. There can, therefore, be no possibility of Port Operations Workers employed by MDHC being supplemented by Torside Ltd.' [15]

The signed agreement contained in this letter was never implemented, and Torside labour would be used wherever and whenever they were needed. On 23 December, the de-recognition of the two convenors, Jimmy Nolan and Jimmy Davies, was discussed at a stewards' meeting; both men wanted an inquiry and for the TGWU to defend them. [16] Davies was quoted as saying: 'We should build our own movement representing the labour force, and we should not be beholden to the employer for the structures he wants to create for his own benefit.' [17] Terry Teague felt that the stewards should have been devising a formal response to Allan Price, MDHC's employee relations manager, who was heading up the process of transitioning to a wholly casual labour port: 'We reject his proposals, his wage cuts and his threats to close Dublin Ferries. It should be the Company Stewards that progress this, not Jack Dempsey.' [18] By April 1992, the Timber and Container berths were refusing to work any overtime following their refusal to agree terms on a new deal imposed by the employer. Mike Carden, one of the stewards at the Container Terminal, had now been disciplined via a formal letter, whilst at a meeting with company director, Bernard Cliff, to discuss the Atlantic Container Line vessels. Cliff stated that shop stewards, 'Carden, Teague and Morton could face the sack.' [19]

The MDHC now blamed the TGWU official along with the dissenting shop stewards as Price insisted that they were: 'All representatives of the TGWU, whether they be yourself [Dempsey] or lay officials and they speak, so far as we are concerned, as agents of your organisation. If representatives are wilfully choosing to ignore our agreements, in which case we deem them guilty of misconduct, whether they act as an employee or a shop steward.' [20] With this, MDHC were simply emphasising their policy that they would only recognise shop stewards who followed the company line, and that they were holding the union accountable for those who it failed to control. This animosity towards the TGWU would only last a short while. Price was now writing, almost daily, to the secretary of the Docks Regional Trade Group and in a letter, dated 16 April 1992, he complained of:

> 'It seems that the three representatives at the Terminal, Billy Duffy, Frank Jones and Mike Carden, had unilaterally declared that they will not be conducting any business with the management at the Terminal unless you, the District Official, are present. This 'policy' has taken forms which the company cannot tolerate namely; failure to attend

*meetings arranged by management, advising employees instructed to attend a Disciplinary Hearing not to do so etc. We need to deal with this vital issue at the earliest possible time.' [21]*

The tactic of the three shop stewards at Seaforth Containers was as much ironic as it was realistic; ignored both with and without their TGWU official, they knew that by only attending meetings with MDHC in the presence of a union officer, they would make the situation unworkable for an employer so obsessed with TGWU endorsement. Nevertheless, it was the de-recognition of convenors, Nolan and Davies, that continued to dominate the stewards' agenda, as they in turn opposed the action being taken against their two principal leaders by the port's bosses. [22] On 4 April, a stewards' meeting was called at Transport House, where ex-LGS, Torside and Nelson Freight dockers, among others, showed up to lobby their representatives. Objections were raised against the status of the meeting. It was specifically for Port Shop Stewards rather than an open forum, but it eventually went ahead and provided Jack Dempsey with a platform to order the stewards to accept labour from any of the companies now operating in the port.

The meeting was as chaotic and complex as the dockworkers' employment status in the Port of Liverpool, with much of the discussion addressing the pay rate for ex-LGS dockers in comparison with traditional dockers, since the former had clearly been victims of the abolition of the National Dock Labour Board Scheme. As such they should have had some legal redress to their technical employer of last resort, the NDLB. At the same time, one of the new dock companies, Merlin Stevedores Ltd, had announced losses of £800,000 and were seeking to reduce wages and conditions even further than their already low setting. Another new company, Gladhills Ltd, was also claiming that it needed to cut wages further, as the Merlin dockers prepared for strike action on 28 April. The management at LCH wanted their dockers to cross the Merlin picket lines, before a ship due to dock at Merlin's berth was diverted to Euromar, where LCH dockers faced further threats of consequences for refusing to work with Nelson Freight employees. It was around this time that Powell Duffryn Ltd pulled out of the port, [23] to be replaced by Pro-Carbon Ltd, and on 29 April 1992, the Port Stewards met to discuss the unofficial strike at Merlin, where a picket line was in place on two ships at the Huskisson Dock. LCH dockers refused to cross the picket line, and the stewards decided to extend the picket to other areas of the port. LCH dockers were still on strike when the company stewards met on 12 May to revisit the issue, but the compromised position of the local TGWU had been compounded by the two de-recognised convenors reluctantly being forced to seek independent legal advice regarding their case.

At the next stewards' meeting, dock union official, Jack Dempsey, threatened to resign, [24] and amid the subsequent confusion, a special meeting of the Docks and Waterways District Committee and the Port Stewards took place on 6 June 1992, as they tried to fathom a way out of the anarchy that was enveloping all aspects of industrial relations in the port. At this special meeting of the Port Shop Stewards, the TGWU docks officer, paraphrasing Trevor Furlong, reported that, '[Furlong] now wanted to sack Teague, Morton and Carden, as well as Davies and Nolan.' [25] Six days later, MDHC announced that its £35,000 severance scheme would end on 31 July 1992, and that they no longer wished to maintain their stevedoring licence, effectively washing their hands of direct cargo handling and the direct employment of dockers. To add to the ensuing mayhem, Bernard Bradley, the ex-docker boss of Torside, was now threatening to close-down his company. [26]

On 12 June, the TGWU dock official received a phone call from Bernard Cliff, informing him that Dublin Ferries was to close and Pandoro wanted to employ their own labour. At a company stewards meeting held that day the proliferation of casual labour and the arbitrary victimisation and disciplining of shop stewards were discussed again. The reopening of a severance scheme when the port was suffering major labour shortages was unacceptable to the stewards. Jimmy Davies spoke for many when he told the stewards that the time had come: 'to put up or shut up. If the union are not prepared to fight, we are. We have to mount a campaign. The MDHC are making millions – they don't want us. Other options will be taken up by the company to cut more jobs. We have a right to remain and fight for our jobs.' [27] All the union docks officer could offer in reply was, 'The severance is out, and we will get killed in the rush. The boss will select who goes.' [28] By the end of the month, some 74 dockers had applied for the company's redundancy scheme, which was advertised as the final opportunity for dockers to receive £35,000 to leave, and although many believed that the offer would remain until every last one of them was gone, it did in fact turn out to be the last time severance was offered in the port. This left MDHC with a core workforce that was determined to stay in the industry whatever the cost.

By 13 July, the stewards were calling for a mass meeting to recommend strike ballots in the port. Pandoro voted 95% in favour of action, and when the National Union of Seafarers was asked by both the employer and MDHC to provide replacements for the striking dockers, the request was refused. The leader of the National Union of Seafarers (NUS), Liverpool-born Tony Santamara, was, along with Kenny Usher and other comrades, always outstanding in their support for the Liverpool dockers with whom they shared a long trade union history. Men like Jimmy Nolan, Jimmy Davies and Frank Lannigan could often be seen sitting with local seafarers Mattie Banbridge and Tucker Mullen in the Lord Warden pub on London Road, Liverpool, drinking bottles of Guinness, cider and pints of bitter whilst reminiscing about times gone by and lamenting the decimation of their respective industries. At a mass meeting, two Pandoro shop stewards, Terry Teague and Kevin Robinson, outlined the struggle they had endured for some time, and explained why they had now decided to call for the official strike that would begin on 20 July 1992. Within two days of action commencing, Bernard Cliff had written a formal letter to his employees, refusing to acknowledge their legal right to withdraw labour following an official secret ballot:

*'Since Monday 20th July, you have withdrawn your labour from the company in order to pursue strike action. This action means you are in breach of your contract of employment. By this letter, the Company is giving you formal notice that if you do not return to work, i.e. report at your normal place of work before 8a.m. on Friday 24th July, your employment will be terminated as at that time with immediate effect and without further notice. Men whose employment is terminated will be replaced by newly recruited full-time employees.' [29]*

It was during the tumult of July 1992 that MDHC again took the step of de-recognising dock shop stewards while continuing to recognise the TGWU: 'Following a port dispute over job losses, the Dock Company withdrew its recognition of all dock shop stewards, accusing them of being in conflict with both the company and their union, the TGWU.' [30] For Monica Clua-Losada, this was to prove a significant event:

> 'The 1992 dispute has been repeatedly mentioned during my research. In the dockers' minds, it was clear that it became the prelude to the 1995-98 dispute. In 1992, the union also failed to recognise the strike. The union did not feel it had that much to lose from de-recognition, as the MDHC were just de-recognising the shop stewards, not the union. In fact, the company was quite happy maintaining negotiations with the union and its officials. For the union, removing a group of unruly shop stewards did not appear as being such a bad thing after all.' [31]

# 12
# Unemployment – a Liverpool Inheritance

*'One thing I can promise all longshoremen, the Liverpool dockers will not let them down. We will not be bought off. We are not going to let any scabby bastards take our jobs without a fight. With your assistance we can get our victory, and then our victory will be your victory too.' ~ Mick Kilcullen\**

Between 1972 and 1982, Liverpool lost more than 80,000 jobs as its manufacturing sector shrank by 50%. In the 1980s, Peter Hooton, a Liverpool musician, would recall his time as a youth worker on Cantril Farm, one of Liverpool's poorest estates:

> *When Thatcher was in power, we felt that she looked at Liverpool and thought, "Well, they're not really English, are they?" Liverpool had always seen itself as separate from the rest of the country. As a city, it has more in common with Belfast and Glasgow than it does with London. There was the big influx of Irish and, because it's a port, it's always been international. We look to America and Ireland, to New York and Dublin, more than we look to London.' [1]*

As deprivation increased, a Liverpool Labour Council organised a fight back against the impact of Thatcherite economic policies that were devastating inner-city economies. Then, in March 1986, the High Court upheld the district auditor's decision to surcharge and disqualify 47 Labour councillors from holding public office after they failed to set a rate in time, losing the city £106,000 in interest. Councillors argued that they had no option but to challenge the government directly in the face of mass redundancies and long-term unemployment. Derek Hatton, a leading voice among the rebel councillors, recalled: 'We were on the back of the

---

\* Mick Kilcullen 'Confessions of a Sacked Docker' Dispatcher 54, no.6, July/August 1996, 10, http://archive.ilwu.org/wp-content/uploads/2015/04/19960901.pdf

dock industry completely closing, every factory around closing, massive decline… We were borne out of the crisis, we were borne out of these problems… We never lost an election in Liverpool. Every time we stood, we got more votes…' [2] For Tony McQuade, who lost his job at Standard Speke No.2 Plant in 1978, and was later to become a local official of the Transport and General Workers' Union, the period that followed the seismic closures of Tate & Lyle, Plessey, Bryant & May, Meccano, Dunlop and many other factories on Merseyside had a profound impact on many young men and women in the trade union movement:

*'Obviously, in this part of the world in the '60s, with Merseybeat and everything, people got more confident, a bit more cocky, a bit more prepared to stand up for themselves… That was a time also, amazingly when you look back now, when jobs were plentiful, there was 20,000-odd dockers then, Cammell Laird had 10,000-15,000 people working for them and you could almost walk out of one job and into another. So, you had people, ex-seafarers, building workers, all sorts of industries, people from the docks going into car factories because they were well-paid jobs. You had building workers who were used to fighting, dockers who were used to fighting, those sorts of people, people from ship building industries coming into it, they were more inclined to stand up for their rights. An awful lot of people in car factories were younger people, in their 20s and 30s, who were less inclined to listen to what the boss said, if they thought something was wrong, they'd say.' [3]*

On typing out a CV for his brother, Liverpool playwright Jimmy McGovern recalled: 'From 1976 onwards it was this litany, Birds Eye, Fisher Bendix, Leyland, every one of them, reason for leaving: factory closed, factory closed, factory closed.' [4] Liverpool had always been a city that dared to fight, [5] and in 1978, the workers at Standard Triumph took part in a 17-week strike in an attempt to keep the No.2 Plant open. Not only did the No.2 Plant close it was followed by the closure of the No.1 Plant in 1981. [6] Bobby Owens, a shop steward at Standard Triumph, came to symbolise a new generation of trade union activist on Merseyside, and he was later to become the only lay-member to ever be appointed a TGWU Regional secretary. Owens was sacked during the closure of British Leyland's Speke No.2 Car Plant. He was a relative of Tony McQuade and family connections and community roots were, like for so many, in his blood. In their report, *The Failure of Triumph in Speke*, the BBC spoke of how the history and influence of the docks had impacted upon many Liverpool workers and their philosophy of trade unionism:

*'In 1978, there was a perception that industry on Merseyside suffered because of the area's reputation for strikes and poor industrial relations. People talk of the so-called 'Merseyside Disease,' the idea that somehow people here don't work as hard as in other parts of Britain. One British Leyland worker thought the problems were a legacy of Liverpool's dock system. "I think it dates back to our grandfathers and the time when they were on the docks in pens. It's just a thing that they hate management. They don't really hate them, but it dates back to that time when you were picked if your face fitted or if you'd work for less money."' [7]*

# UNEMPLOYMENT – A LIVERPOOL INHERITANCE

Every generation has the potential to change history by making it, and this was a group that came of age during a unique industrial epoch that provided a radical apprenticeship to all. Each of them had the benefit of many experienced trade unionists to learn from; men and women who had served their time, fought in a World War and returned home expecting a land fit for heroes. They had aspirations beyond their past, and they inspired their children to fight for a greater share of an unequal society, creating a generation of Merseysiders that would propel many to some of the most powerful positions in the TGWU, the trade union movement and the political world. Tony Woodley, a shop steward at the Vauxhall car factory would see himself elected to the position of TGWU General Secretary in 2004. From 2007-11, he served as joint-General Secretary of Unite, a new union formed through the merger of TGWU and Amicus, to be succeeded by Len McCluskey, who in 1979, became one of the youngest officials ever appointed in the union. Another notable name is that of Jim Mowatt, who was an Education Officer with the Trade Union Congress in Liverpool as a young man before becoming a National Officer for TGWU and Director of Education for Unite in the 1990s. Eddie Roberts, a young shop steward at Fords, would eventually work alongside Bobby Owens in the local TGWU. They worked together establishing a vibrant Broad Left organisation that, in one brief moment in time, had the potential to transform trade union organisation at every level. Owens and Roberts knew that to exercise real power in the union they needed to have influence in the union's headquarters in London. Woodley, McCluskey and Mowatt first travelled down to London from Liverpool as TGWU national officials, doing what newly appointed Regional secretary, Bobby Owens, described as *'missionary work'* - extending the influence of Liverpool to London. Perhaps Liverpool was a place where trade union barons could become kings, or so the theory went, but the key was always London, the *principality* of the General Secretary. The TGWU Broad Left played a role in the radical alternative organisation being established in Liverpool but it would also play its role in the eventual *witch-hunt* against Owens, Roberts and others in Liverpool, Manchester and Ireland a few years later.

This generation of young trade unionists and political activists had been influenced and educated by men such as Wally Nugent, Jimmy Goulborne and Pat Harkin from RTC 6/541 Branch and Dunlops Convenor, Stan Pemberton the Region 6 GEC member who was to become President of the TGWU under General Secretary, Jack Jones. Lay-members such as Alex Roberts, from Dunlops, who was elected to the GEC also carried some influence, often enhanced by their roles as communist party members. Ford car workers like Frank Banton, Charlie Parker and the young Eddie Roberts joined others from across Merseyside industry and politics such as Marie Jockins, Tommy Jockins, Paula Lace, Marie Harrison, Ian Lowes, Lesley Mahmood, Terry Harrison, Jimmy Wilson, Alec Doswell, John Cook, Paul Astbury and Tony Mulhearn. Men like Peter Kerrigan, Frank Deegan, Denis Anderson, Denis Kelly, Paddy Doherty from the Liverpool dockers, and so many, many more activists ebbed and flowed over these years organising and strengthening the union in industries and communities across Merseyside. So many local political activists and historians such as Roger O'Hara, Bill Hunter, Tony Lane, Ron Noon, Harold Hikens and Eric Taplin worked to develop workers' organisation across Merseyside and to record its history. Many were Communist Party members who were influential amongst groups organising on the Liverpool docks and factories in the City. A new *Militant Tendency* would soon hold power in the Town

Hall and Merseyside County Council would be led by progressives such as Keva Coombes. These workers now held Liverpool. [8]

Many of the most influential activists of the time relied upon the Communist Party's organisational power in the unions to win elected positions in the unions and elsewhere, although some merely used it, and the left in general, as a vehicle for their careers before shedding any semblance of socialism once it no longer served their own personal ambition. This was the febrile environment in which young men like Bobby Owens and Eddie Roberts first experienced trade unionism, with all of its horizons and limitations, through the struggles that they led and supported. Both men were very able and influential from the beginning, with Roberts being one of the youngest elected shop stewards at Fords before he was appointed a full-time TGWU official in 1970, responsible for the dock staff of 6/567 Branch. Following his redundancy from Standard Triumph, Owens, together with a number of other local trade unionists and political activists, began campaigning for the unemployed. People such as Pat Harvey, Martin Cantor, Kevin Coyne, Greg Coyne, Alan Quinn, John Cook, Bob Braddock, Maureen Twomey, Muriel Mayor, Tony Boyle, May Stone, Jimmy Stone, Joe Vickers, Steve Murphy, Chris Mooney, Alan Kelly, Dave Kelly, Carol Austin, Mark Ward and Jim Dempsey (of Kirkby Unemployed Centre), Steve Donnelly (of AC Delco in Kirkby), Jimmy McGoldrick, George Riley and countless other comrades worked to organise the unemployed within the TGWU, building a wider trade union movement that had ambitions beyond the factory as part of a radical philosophy that knew no boundaries. It is important to note that many of the activists named above operated at one level of workplace organisation supported by another tier of activists that permeated down through robust trade union rank-and-file organisations and the communities they existed in. When this structure worked it gave the labour movement a depth of real influence and power that reached its peak in the early 1980s. After Thatcher's de-industrialisation programme, the subsequent impact of neoliberalism and globalisation, these building blocks of solidarity, of working-class organisation began to crumble and fall to be replaced by a new elite whose power base hovered within the union's expanding bureaucracy.

In an era where a worker's trade union membership effectively ended once they were made redundant, the campaign for the unemployed met with much opposition from the TGWU's bureaucracy. After all, what role could the jobless play on the elected committees that represented the great crafts and trades of 20th century industry, since the unemployed could not go on strike? Yet while a person's employment might have ended, their lives in the increasingly disconnected communities of Britain went on, and it was the union/left failure to recognise this that limited their reach among those cut adrift from society, alienated from the very class they were created represent. In 1981, trade union members and political activists from Merseyside joined with their comrades in other major cities to organise the first People's March for Jobs from Liverpool to London, supported by the Merseyside County Association of Trades' Councils. A second People's March for Jobs took place in 1983, with much of the organisation being carried out by the old TGWU 6/612 Branch, which had covered the Standard Car plant. As part of their radical and innovative approach, they created a funding model, the One Fund for All (OFFA), through which local trade unionists joined together to make a monthly donation directly to the Merseyside Trade Union Community and Unemployed Resource Centre project. The Centre, which would become the largest of its kind in Europe, eventually opened on Hardman Street, Liverpool, in November 1983, having used the Liverpool TGWU office as its base since the late '70s. [9]

The unions did play their part in this radical campaign that pushed trade union organisation towards increasingly marginalised communities that were rapidly becoming disenfranchised from both work and society at large. It would not be long before this impending transformation of trade union organisation in the community stuttered to a conclusion in its attempts to organise what Marx called, 'this industrial reserve army.' [10] Many complex reasons exist for this and according to Jean Faniel some fault rested on: 'the absence of any significant organisation of the unemployed at the heart of the unions or the little weight they carry within the union bodies.' [11] Bill Morris would describe one of the key motivators of this community organisation, the late Bobby Owens as, 'A member of the Liverpool-based far-left militant tendency'; [12] it was untrue. The trade union activists who agitated for change in Liverpool were part of a *complex and fluid movement* that engaged in political argument, analysis and alignments that rose and fell on the waves of so many political, social and economic battles. It was this spirit of independence, of not being told what to do, that gave Merseyside trade union activists the scope to see *the whole of the moon*. [13] However, some activists adopted a mindset in which the union was viewed principally as a means of transitioning from low-paid factory work to management or a career in the union: 'Here we are simply observing', what Tony Lane, uncomfortably, for many rank-and-file trade unionists, identified as: 'the creation of a new working class elite which has the opportunity (and too often takes it) of sharing in the expense account syndrome: the franchise of perks and fiddles has been widened. Shop stewards and full-time officers have had other opportunities. Some stewards have used their position as a stepping-stone to promotion.' [14]

Bill Morris's own TGWU career followed the classic pattern of *how to get on in the union*; he joined in 1958 and was elected to shop steward in 1962, and after serving on the TGWU General Executive Council from 1972-73, he was appointed as a full-time official in 1973. From there, he rose to District Officer in 1973 and District Secretary in 1976. He became National Secretary of the Passenger Services Trade Group in 1979 and was elected to the post of deputy general secretary in 1986, working under General Secretary Ron Todd, who he succeeded in 1992 before winning re-election in 1995. This career path was the template for so many lay members to become paid officials of the TGWU. The true nature of power within the union was not lost on Morris or his increasingly influential Central Office manager, Ray Collins, who would be rewarded by the general secretary with a newly created post, Head of Administration. In 1999, Collins was appointed to the position of assistant general secretary without ever having been elected to hold office by the membership; he had the ear of the general secretary for over a decade *until eventually he became his voice*. [15]

Morris had inherited a trade union that, like every other union at the time, was haemorrhaging members amidst an economic and social transformation powered by long-term unemployment and globalisation. His answer was to bring in the 'experts', after convincing the GEC that it had no alternative other than to surrender its constitutional power and control to non-union consultants who would tell them, quite literally, how to run their union. The name Adam Klein was peddled as the only answer to the TGWU's problems, and at a rumoured cost of over £1m, his group of US-based consultants presented the 'Klein Report,' as it became known, to the General Executive Council in 1992. [16] The plan was simple: under the banner soundbite of 'One Union', they would sell off the TGWU's historic Central Office in Smith Square, along with other land assets and buildings, and then remodel the union's archaic trade group structure in order to grow membership through amalgamation. This was opposed by a small minority of the GEC. Morris completed the City of London's takeover of the union by recommending that they appoint Peter Regnier, a finance director at the Rover car plant, to shape the future of the trade union alongside Klein & Co. [17] Morris's decision to hand the reins to private consultants came at a vast cost to its membership through the irretrievable losses of both assets and founding principles. The union now had no policies or visionary leadership to guide it through the 1990s save for unfettered amalgamation with other membership diminished unions. Trade unions appeared unable to transform or remodel their structures to meet the challenges of a new-age that screamed out for a new-unionism. The TGWU would not increase union membership through recruitment and expansion; they would not, initially, seek to involve themselves directly in the post-industrial communities that were once the bedrock of trade unionism and labour working-class politics.

It was Region 6 where an unemployed car factory worker along with other rank-and-file activists from Liverpool had the aspiration to break the *career* mould within the TGWU. Lay members could apply for full-time officer jobs then they could apply for district, regional of national posts. It would take three attempts, due to objections from the union's bureaucracy, for Bobby Owens to eventually be appointed Regional secretary. Such developments only added to the folklore that boasted of the power of the 'Broad Left' in Region 6 as a direct threat to its Central London-based equivalent in Region 1. Monica Clua-Losada, describes the profound influence of Liverpool and Manchester union branches that made up the north-west region of the union at this time:

> *'If anything, Region 6 was the most indomitable region of the TGWU, and one which, in part, was difficult to control for the Broad Left machinery, the Communist Party or the right-wing of the union. In a sense, none of the groupings within the TGWU were able to keep the region tamed.'* [18]

The political infighting amongst each region's Broad Left took-off at the top of the union [19] against a backdrop of family ties, personal politics and naked ambition. These debilitating factors were compounded by the sectarianism of some Broad Left adherents, especially in relation to their obsession with officer appointments, that split the left and Region 1 and Region 6 in particular. Many lost their way in the heady atmospheres in which they now existed. Founding principles seemed lost in a fog, forgotten in exchange for often meaningless political machinations and personal ambition. This sectarianism that was to engulf the union would spill over into the Liverpool docks and it was at this moment that the dockers, local TGWU officials, the MDHC and Bill Morris would all collide.

# 13

# The Local TGWU Alliance
# with the MDHC

*'You asked me the question of how did we do with shop stewards? Well shop stewards themselves were voted in freely by the men on the dockside, in the sheds, and, we did end up with some marvellous forward looking men, I mean, we had some marvellous fellas like Kelly for instance, like my friend Jimmy Nolan who I think the world of. We were doing 100% better than what we ever done, and because we were doing ok people then started to turn on the shop stewards and say, "Well he's in the Communist Party, or he's in this Party, he's doing this, he's doing that." I always couldn't believe that people could turn on men and women whose whole life is surrounded by making life better for the people that they love. I could never see that.' ~ Ted Woods\**

On 20 July 1992, Liverpool docks were shut down by a port-wide strike and, at a mass meeting held two days later, the TGWU docks officer called for an immediate return to work. [1] The Dock Company acted swiftly, telling the dockers in no uncertain terms: 'to return to work by Friday 24 July or to consider themselves sacked.' [2] That same day, Port Operations Director Bernard Cliff wrote to the TGWU docks official, Jack Dempsey, stating the following:

> *The dispute involving MDHC Port Operations Workers, which occurred between Monday and Thursday this week, 20 July to 23 July. On Monday 20 July, the first sailing of the Pandoro service, under their own operational control, took place. The Port Operations Workers who had worked at the service occupied part of the Berth and picketed the working of the vessel. They stood on the ramp of the vessel, stopping all loading and discharging. At approximately 11.30am, Mr Teague, who had been a shop steward at the Pandoro, placed himself between a Tugmaster unit and a trailer. A*

---

\* Ted Woods, Liverpool docker in Bill Hunter Workers' History as Told by Those Who Made It - http://www.billhunterweb.org.uk/interviews/History_as_Told.htm#Ted%20Woods

*policeman asked him to move, he refused, and a scuffle ensued when Mr Teague was removed. By 1pm, the shop stewards in each of the Company's areas had brought the Port Operations Workers out on strike after the dispute started. It concerned so-called issues of casual labour, casual rates. Messrs Carden, Davies and Robinson variously, and at different times, appeared on television and radio articulating and giving support to these causes… I have to advise you therefore that as from 25 July 1992, the Company is suspending its relationship with shop stewards representing Port Operations Workers in its Cargo Handling operations. The Company will deal with all matters through you in the interim.' [3]*

On 31 July 1992, Cliff issued a three-sided A4 letter to all dockers, telling them how wrong they were to strike over Pandoro and confirming its decision to de-recognise the shop stewards. The letter also explained how MDHC: 'closed the door, once and for all, on the era of the Dock Labour Scheme and the dinosaurs who would seek its return.' [4] He then wrote once more to Jack Dempsey, reaffirming this decision:

*'The company is not prepared to give their recognition to individuals whose priority is to undermine the present system of organising the employment of Port Operations Workers and to replace it with a system based on the pre-1989 principles. The company is not prepared to recognise as valid the activities of those who wish to destroy the basis of its commercial and financial viability. In order to avoid any doubt, the following named are the individuals whom the company will not recognise as shop stewards in the future:- Messrs M. Cullen, F. Jones, R. Morton, T. Halsall, T. Teague, K. Robinson, C. McDonald, M. Jones, H. Hollerhead, J. Davies, M. Carden and J. Nolan. The Company also advised you that it is no longer prepared to provide a facility for meetings of the Company Stewards during working hours. The Company is also not prepared to provide the facility for any meeting of the POWs during working hours, although the Company will recognise the TGWU.' [5]*

The TGWU's response was to seek permission from MDHC to hold fresh elections to replace the shop stewards. On Wednesday 11 November, the Port Stewards met the union's three leading local officials, regional secretary Bobby Owens, Divisional Organiser, Eddie Roberts and Docks District Officer Jack Dempsey, in the boardroom of the TGWU Liverpool office. It was a heated exchange, in which the local union officers sought to expound on the chaos that had engulfed the docks for almost a decade. Bobby Owens said the union would make representations to MDHC regarding the recognition of the shop stewards, and Eddie Roberts told the stewards: 'a massive range of issues confront us. It's a whole new environment on the docks and it is a changing scene. We want the stewards to endorse our attempts to sort matters out.' [6] On 14 January 1993, Allan Price, MDHC's employee relations manager, wrote to each individual dockworker employed at the Seaforth Container Terminal with a new contract of employment. Its opening paragraph proclaimed:

*'A new system of working is required at the Container Terminal. This has been discussed at length with your union representatives over several months, and in view of the*

*heavy losses which continue to be experienced, its implementation cannot be delayed. All existing jobs, including your own, are to be eliminated, with new jobs being created which will fit in with the new working system. The accompanying letter gives notice that with effect from 8 April 1993, your existing contract of employment is terminated. The Company is, however, prepared to re-engage you without loss of service on the following terms and conditions.' [7]*

The employer demanded that dockers: 'confirm your acceptance of the above terms and conditions of employment by signing each attached copy of this letter and returning it... at the earliest possible time.' [8] Price wrote again to the Seaforth dockers, three days later, on 17 January 1993, informing them: 'the company had reached a formal agreement with local TGWU officials on new terms and conditions of employment for all employees at the Royal Seaforth Container Terminal.' [9] Individual employees were now required to sign their acceptance of the new terms and conditions or, as the Dock Company insisted:

*'It will be viewed that you do not wish to take up the new contract of employment. Your signed acceptance needs to be returned to the Personnel Department via your immediate supervisor no later than Wednesday 19 January 1993 at 10.00am. If you wish to take up the new contract it is essential that you meet this deadline.' [10]*

By January 1993, Torside dockers were, for the first time ever, being used at Seaforth Container Terminal, even though no agreement existed for this. They were still not being paid the rate for the job. [11] On Wednesday 5 May, a unique meeting took place between the TGWU and MDHC at Transport House, called in an attempt to reach a solution to the labour relations problems in the port. At 9am, the three Seaforth Container Shop Stewards, Frank Jones, Billy Duffy and Mike Carden arrived with Bobby Morton from the Seaforth Timber Terminal. Kevin Robinson, Terry Teague and Herbie Hollerhead were there together with a representative from the Seaforth Grain Terminal, while dockers' leaders Jimmy Davies and Jimmy Nolan refused to attend on the grounds that Billy Jenkins and John Jenkins, dock shop stewards from Liverpool Cargo Handling, had not been invited. Attending on behalf of the union were its three senior local TGWU representatives, Bobby Owens, Eddie Roberts and Jack Dempsey, and at 10am, MDHC's Bernard Cliff, Trevor Furlong and Allan Price entered the room. Owens announced the purpose of the meeting as being: 'informal, with one simple item on the agenda: the re-recognition of the shop stewards employed by the Mersey Docks and Harbour Company.' [12] Dempsey then referred to a letter, dated 24 July and 4 August 1992, listing the 12 non-recognised shop stewards, to which Roberts declared:

*'All reports and discussions had centred on the communications gap. Dempsey cannot represent everyone. Responsible, disciplined shop stewards and the company had been at fault to say the least... the union's democracy is not being allowed to work and the union will ensure the discipline of the stewards.' [13]*

Trevor Furlong's response was to reiterate the point that: 'Other port employers thought the MDHC were foolish to recognise the TGWU. Every port in the UK has made dockers redundant. The MDHC have not. We believe overall that the MDHC is a good employer. We have no complaint against union officials, but traffic is leaving the port and difficult decisions have to be made in the future.' [14] Furlong gave assurances that he would tell the Norse Irish Company that they could not employ their own labour to unload or load their ship, agreeing: 'They cannot do their own stevedoring.' [15] The following week, on 10 May 1993, the business of the TGWU Docks and Waterways District Committee was dominated, as it had been since 1989, with arguments over casual labour in the Port of Liverpool. The minutes at this meeting recorded: 'Torside Ltd had raised the question of bringing people on a part-time basis... He had been trying to arrange a meeting with the company, but management have told employees these changes must go ahead.' [16] In response to Jack Dempsey's report, shop steward Frank Lannigan raised the point that Torside were originally a supplementary workforce, but now they themselves were requesting supplementation. [17] This highlighted the new reality that Torside was growing in both influence and employment potential, an expansion they wanted to facilitate using casual and part-time workers. According to the minutes: 'the Chairman advised that the Company had made it clear that twenty part-timers will be employed by Torside and will be used as they wish... Brother Davies finally moved: 'A Rejection of casual labour or part-time labour.' This was seconded by Brother Maher. All voted in favour. There were no abstentions. The motion was carried unanimously.' [18] The union continued to demonstrate its ambivalence towards the argument against casual labour and, in the words of their own dock official, the fact that Torside wanted to employ casual and part-time labour was not of significance; what mattered was Torside's recognition of the TGWU. [19] A comment made later by John Jenkins captured the mood of the stewards, as he predicted: 'The union will be de-recognised in three years.' [20]

On Saturday 24 July, a mass meeting of over 200 Liverpool dockers received an update on the numerous conflicts that now engulfed almost every working day on the waterfront. Talk of the inevitability of strike action had dominated life in the port since 1989, and it now seemed simply a matter time. The meeting unanimously declared its opposition to casual labour, calling for a ballot ahead of taking official, union-backed strike action. Four days later, the TGWU 6/601 Docks Branch held another vote, only this time it was a vote of: 'No confidence in their Dock Official and other local officers of the union.' [21] In protest against the local TGWU, shop stewards at Seaforth Container Terminal succeeded in getting the majority of their dockers to withdraw from the direct-from-wages payment of union subscriptions, normally deducted at source by MDHC, indicating their anger at the local union's failure to represent them. By switching to monthly cash payment of dues, they forced the union to account for each individual member's fees, a move which TGWU officials were naturally highly critical of. The following resolution was also moved by Mike Carden and seconded by Joe Baxter: 'We the members of TGWU 6/601 Branch have no confidence in our Regional Officers concerning their handling of the recruitment of part-time and casual labour without prior consultation with the Merseyside Port Shop Stewards and Dock Branches.' [22]

In July 1993 celebrations were planned to mark the Battle of the Atlantic, and this was the time chosen by Torside dockers to take unofficial action over their pay by picketing the Canada Dock. After two days of strikes, Jack Dempsey arrived with Danny Maher and

Eddie Roberts, asking the Torside men to withdraw their pickets and attend a meeting in the canteen. According to one Torside shop steward:

> *Jack Dempsey spoke first. He said he wanted us back in work so we could start a negotiation procedure. Jack went down like a lead balloon at that meeting, he got savaged, the men really ripped into him, then Eddie Roberts spoke and it was the same with Eddie. Danny Maher spoke and gave a lot of bullshit to the lads, "You will be the predominant workforce, etc, etc, the port's safe in your hands, let's get back to work and get the stewards and the official in there and start negotiations." The Torside dockers went for it and we returned to work. The talks went on over a six-week period, but looking back in hindsight, we should have stayed out unofficially because we could have got concession after concession. The last thing the Dock Company wanted that week was a picket on a gate when the general public was coming round to look at battleships. [23]*

On Friday 30 July, the Port Shop Stewards met at Transport House at 4pm. They had invited the regional secretary, the Divisional Organiser and the docks official, all of whom failed to attend, and in their absence, the dockers again expressed concerns regarding the union's agreement to allow Torside to recruit casual labour. [24] Legal advice from the union informed the shop stewards that, somehow, the Torside dockers could not hold a ballot for industrial action, but then the same official had also told stewards at Willies Ltd. that there was: 'No need for the dispute over redundancies as the union could apply for 'interim relief,' where the employers would have to continue to pay wages.' [25] The stewards thought this to be fanciful at the time, and that is exactly what it turned out to be. These same dock officials also called off the picket at Willies during the Battle of the Atlantic celebrations and cancelled weekly collections among MDHC dockers for the men on strike, as once again the TGWU sought to 'keep a lid on the situation.' [26] The following Wednesday, Bobby Owens, Eddie Roberts and Jack Dempsey were due to meet the Dock Company again to discuss the shop stewards' de-recognition. The employer offered to agree recognition on the proviso that an 'accreditation document,' jointly sponsored by the company and the union, was signed by each prospective shop steward. This proposal was met with vehement opposition amongst the dockers.

Meanwhile, in London, Bill Morris was determined to dismantle what he identified as the 'militant far-left activists' that made up the powerbase of Region 6 (North West). [27] The TGWU national and regional bureaucracy saw many Region 6 officials as Broad Left Trotskyites, on whom Morris was ready to wage war, specifically targeting Bobby Owens and Eddie Roberts, the two most senior officers in the region together with Tom Hart, the NW Education Officer, Birkenhead-based John Farrell and others. According to Geoffrey Goodman's 2010 biography of Bill Morris, the General Secretary viewed these Merseyside officials as 'plotters,' who were part of:

> *'An extraordinary alliance of opposites both outside and inside the TGWU... The Broad Left campaign against Morris was led by a talented rank-and-file communist member of the General Executive Council, Peter Haggar. He had powerful support from full-time National Officials including the deputy general secretary, Jack Adams, Bobby*

*Owens, the regional secretary in the North-West and a member of the Liverpool-based far-left Militant Tendency, and John Freeman, the Regional secretary in Ireland.' [28]*

In Liverpool, the union's work continued. At a Port Shop Stewards' meeting held at Transport House on 6 August, Eddie Roberts told the stewards that:

*'It was now twelve months since they had been de-recognised. We have managed to keep things together. Our brief was to assist Jack and get stewards back in harness. The Company believed they had the whip hand and the Dock Company are adamant that they will not recognise some of our people, but they still recognise the union. We have a commitment to defend the democracy of our union. If not, we will be involved in a struggle with the Dock Company. The company are saying the union do not carry the membership with them. We have to show discipline. Without this, our bargaining power is nothing.' [29]*

With the disputes involving dock workers at Willies and Torside still rumbling on without resolution, Roberts also addressed the issue of casual labour:

*'We had to recognise some of the realities in the port today. Joint accreditation between the TGWU and the MDHC on how shop stewards should conduct themselves is being drafted now, but we have not finished it yet. People are sounding-off about casual labour in the press and this upsets the Dock Company. You have to have confidence in the union. Furlong is very dismayed again, but we have pulled it back. We can restore recognition, but we will have to sign that we will abide by procedures and this will be signed by the union.' [30]*

Perhaps the most controversial element of this joint TGWU/MDHC accreditation process was that the arrangement would allow elected shop stewards to 'represent the views of their members only within their constituency.' [31] In other words, the concept of a Port Shop Stewards Movement no longer existed, nor did the right of elected shop stewards to meet or combine with other elected shop stewards representing dockers from other stevedoring companies in the Port of Liverpool. The union's officials denied this but as the joint TGWU/MDHC accreditation document stated:

*'You accept that the Terminal within which you are elected is a separate and independent unit. Your authority as a shop steward is limited to representing only your constituent members within your terminal and does not, in any way, extend to any other groups or employees. You have no jurisdiction for involvement in the affairs of any separate companies. You will not arrange, organise, attend or address any meetings of the membership at the Terminal unless the express agreement to do so has been obtained from the Company. This agreement must be obtained by the TGWU District Official, Jack Dempsey, from the Company Employee Relations Manager, Allan Price. No industrial action will be considered until the procedure for resolving grievances is fully exhausted and further that you accept and acknowledge that no industrial action, of any*

*kind, will be taken which does not fully comply with the requirements of the law. You acknowledge management's right to plan, organise and manage its operations. Any breach of these conditions may render you liable to withdrawal of your accreditation by the Company.' [32]*

Later that month, on Saturday 28 August at Seaforth Container Terminal, John Simon, a dock clerical worker and a former 6/567 Branch member, was killed on board an ACL vessel at 15 minutes past midnight. [33] In respect for their comrade, work stopped immediately, and many dockers stayed away from work the following day, with no former TGWU/ACTSS men returning until 24 hours had passed. This refusal to continue working after the accident caused more uproar at MDHC and, one year later, Allan Price was to write to the union with new rules regarding the funerals of dockers killed at work, stating that productivity would not be affected by the death of any docker during working hours. The TGWU did nothing to challenge this edict.

In September 1993, MDHC's plans for the re-recognition of shop stewards began to unfold. It was clear that in order for elected representatives to be recognised, they would have to sign an accreditation document co-produced by the employer and the union, and at a Port Shop Stewards' meeting on 10 September, it was disclosed that the company: 'had agreed not to bar shop stewards, but fresh elections must take place and stewards would have to sign a joint MDHC/TGWU accreditation form.' [34] The union official present would not allow the stewards to have a copy of the accreditation document, stating that only nominees would be shown it and that elections would be conducted through postal ballots. [35] The stewards declared their opposition to this, with Jimmy Nolan and Jimmy Davies condemning the idea of any accreditation as: 'a no-strike clause agreeing to divisions into separate areas with no links whatsoever amongst dockers in the port.' [36] Local TGWU officials acted against the wishes of Branch 6/601 and organised, for the first time in the TGWU's history on the docks, a postal ballot at the Seaforth Container Terminal. Two of the Seaforth shop stewards, Billy Duffy and Mike Carden, refused to sign the accreditation document, which was essentially a contract, and as a result: 'they would have an asterisk placed against their names on the ballot paper, indicating that, if elected, neither the TGWU nor the MDHC would recognise them as shop stewards.' [37] In the Seaforth election, the asterisks against the names of those shop stewards who refused to sign the accreditation document also came with a message written clearly on the ballot paper: 'A vote for this person is a wasted vote.' [38] More than 100 TGWU members boycotted this election, but it did not stop the union from declaring a result, and it was later revealed that MDHC had paid for the postage of the union ballot papers, which were also issued to workers who were not even members of the union; some were not members of any union. [39]

The TGWU allowed itself to be further diminished in the eyes of the Liverpool dockers. Numerous irregularities surrounded the ballot, including the MDHC's declared aim to impose substantial wage cuts and introduce a seven-day compulsory working pattern once the stewards were in place to agree them. In response, over 200 Seaforth Container dockers signed a petition condemning the joint actions of the employer and their local union officials. [40] The MDHC reacted by threatening redundancies unless the new deal was agreed to. At 8am on Thursday 16 September 1993, the union's dock official met with the Seaforth dockers in their inappropriately named 'amenity block,' which was in fact a filthy dump that symbolised the decline in facilities provided for dockworkers throughout the 1970s and '80s. It was in this dismal hall that the TGWU's *unity* with the employer was declared. 'Good news,' Jack Dempsey, told dockers: 'we've got the stewards back! It's nothing I couldn't live with.' [41] He then began to read aloud the various terms and conditions associated with shop steward recognition. The men again voiced their objections to the union proposals and at a TGWU branch meeting a week later, the same dockers rejected the union's deal and demanded a workplace secret ballot. This they organised themselves in the same way as they had always done. [42] Less than two weeks later, at another 8am meeting, the local union official informed the dockers that the workplace ballot they had completed would not be acceptable to the employer.

A boycott was organised on the berth, although many of the dockers were divided on the matter, with some feeling that any shop stewards were better than none. Of 236 eligible voters, 148 decided to take part in the union/employer postal election, in which Mike Carden, the longest-serving elected shop steward at Seaforth, and Billy Duffy were both included on the ballot paper, but with an asterisk against their names and the notation that a vote for either candidate was a wasted vote because of their refusal to sign the accreditation document. They would not be recognised by either the union or the employer. [43] The union official kept the returned postal ballot papers in a plastic John Lewis shopping bag. At the next Port Stewards meeting on 14 October, it was reported that the union had given a deadline for the accreditation to be signed, [44] but by then a sequence of events that would result in the dismissal of 500 dockers, had already been set in motion, in a port on the south-east coast of England.

# 14
# The Acquisition of Medway Ports

*'Our own workers let us down. Our own workers. Fellas working in the grain, working wherever. They let us down. If they would have all come out this port would have just stopped.' ~ Jimmy Hagan*

O n 22 September 1993, MDHC announced its acquisition of Medway Ports Ltd. for a total of £103.7m, including a £65.8m offer for the entire issue of ordinary share capital, as well as the purchase of £15m of Medway Preference shares. MDHC directors forecasted that they would make a pre-tax profit of at least £19m, while Medway was expected to make a profit of £10.7m, with the final dividend set to be £6.15 per share (up £1.15 PPS from 1992). Medway's Chief Executive, Peter Vincent, was to join the board of the MDHC, [1] and in a press release to announce the deal, the company presented the purchase as evidence of a successful port extending its influence over another successful port: 'That the acquisition of Medway represented an important step in the continuing development of Mersey Docks. The Company's proven skills over the past decade… These skills can now be brought to bear to expand Medway's operations and to support revenue and earnings growth.' [2]

The details of how MDHC came to acquire Medway Ports in 1993 informs our understanding of the sequence of events that led to the dismissal of the Liverpool dockers in 1995. As one journalist reported at the time, any potential buyer of Medway Ports could not really raise more profit out of the dockers there because a lot of rationalisation had already taken place: 'it is hard to see what extra could be squeezed out of the operations. Having said that, Medway is a cash cow with good niche markets on the south coast and should benefit from the economic upturn.' [3] The valuation of the Medway Port upon its privatisation was determined by KPMG, a firm with a long history of connections with the Dock Company,

---

* Jimmy Hagan, quoted in Simon Sloane 'We had good days and bad days – Triumph and Tragedy in the Oral History Narratives of the Liverpool Dockers. MA, University of Leiden, August 2019 (p.21)

117

for whom they acted as registrars. [4] Shares in the Medway Port were changing hands at £37.25 following the takeover bid, but this was after Peter Vincent had made a significant profit on shares he acquired at just £2.50 in June 1993. The history of these purchases was exposed by David Hellier in the *Independent*:

> 'On 4 June 1993, Mr. Vincent made two purchases of shares in Medway Ports: one of 20,900 and a second of 30,963. Ten days later he bought a further 53,186. On these two transactions he made more than £3.64m profit. In total, Mr. Vincent is understood to have held 139,000 ordinary shares, valued at around £5m, and a further 206,000 deferred shares, valued at around an extra £7.5m.' [5]

At the time of the takeover, which left the remaining 300 full-time employees with an average shareholding worth £76,000, Vincent was to comment: 'Even our Mrs Mops are going to get £25,000 each.' [6] A few weeks after the shares purchase, Vincent wrote to all employees of Medway Ports, advising them that the board had decided to float the company on the Stock Exchange or sell it to a trade buyer earlier than expected; the letter also stated that the board had decided to accelerate its exit policy in line with the mission statement made in July 1992. [7] Within months, he sold the shares that he acquired from dockers to MDHC, making a substantial profit. The Medway dockers sued MDHC for unfair dismissal, while also considering legal action against KPMG related to advice received on their original share price valuation. Eventually, MDHC agreed to pay each of the 270 Medway dockers a £10,000 settlement fee, although this did not address the share price issue imposed upon the same dockers. All of Medway's top managers resigned from their positions, including the MDHC-bound Vincent, leaving the new owners in the difficult position of having no one at the helm of their latest subsidiary. [8]

The resale price of Medway Ports to MDHC was eight times more than the amount that the UK Treasury had received from the original sale only eighteen months earlier, prompting an investigation into the government's handling of its privatisation [9] that saw the House of Commons Public Accounts Committee report: 'With regard to the sale of the trust ports there was a management buy-out in respect of the trust ports. Once again, this was a strange situation.' [10] The PAC acknowledged that the initial sale of Medway Port for £13.2m upon its privatisation allowed the managing director to profit by £12m in selling the very same shares to MDHC, which was itself still partly government owned. This meant that the taxpayer had indirectly bought back some of the same shares that were sold at a knockdown price whilst at the same time Charterhouse Development more than tripled its outlay by selling its shares for more than £35 million. One Member of Parliament commented in the House that:

> 'Something was drastically wrong somewhere in the way in which the company was evaluated. The reality was that a short time after the company was privatised, half the work force no longer worked for Medway. Under the deal, they were required to sell back their shares at an enforced price. They had to sell their shares back for £2.40, only to see them sell a short time later for £37. One can understand that there is bitterness among those ex-employees. Perhaps we can understand why they sought legal retribution. When

*we asked how the share price could rise from £2.40 to £37 if the government had got the privatisation right, the permanent secretary told us that that reflected the increased profitability. I examined the increased profitability. Profitability had risen 50 per cent., but a 50 per cent increase in profitability does not explain a 15-fold increase in the market value of the shares.' [11]*

Joan Whalley MP, Labour's transport spokeswoman at the time, condemned reports that the sale could net so much for management: 'If this is true, then it is disgraceful. The government must now call a halt to all further port privatisations. The government has sold for a knockdown price a port that it didn't own in the first place, to a consortium which is now selling it on, at over three times the price, to a company (MDHC) which has already been bailed out once by the government and in which, up to two weeks ago, the government was the biggest shareholder.' [12] She would ask the controller and auditor general to launch an investigation into the events surrounding the privatisation of Britain's ports, but such an inquiry never took place. Following the abolition of the Dock Labour Scheme a Management and Employee Buyout (MEBO) of Medway Ports had claimed that it would protect the terms and conditions of employment for its dockers. But within months of privatisation, bosses were already instigating contractual changes that imposed new working conditions and a reduction in wages. Then, in December 1992, events in Sheerness confirmed that these new contracts, 'Replaced a two-shift system with a more flexible roster.' [13] In what would prove to be a carbon copy of the Liverpool dockers situation in 1995, some 300 Medway dockers voted to take industrial action to protect their terms and conditions of employment from the new contract. [14] Management had anticipated this reaction and local scab labour, that would be used in Liverpool in September 1995, was on standby to cross the picket lines. Within days, the dockers were claiming that they had been constructively dismissed, a case which was ultimately accepted by an Employment Tribunal, prompting Medway to put aside £1.13 million for settlement fees, amounting to £3,340 per sacked worker. [15]

The Articles of Association of the MEBO forced Medway dockers to sell their shares, not on the open market, but back to the very same bosses who had just sacked them, [16] and by September 1993, the number of workers employed by Medway Ports had been reduced from approximately 600 to 270, [17] with Peter Vincent himself confirming: 'We have moved from two-shift to three-shift work, giving round-the-clock coverage. We also have complete flexibility; an employee can be driving a fork-lift truck one day and painting a buoy out in the harbour the next.' [18] When asked if he was angry about the course of events, Les Harris, who led the TGWU's opposition to attacks on dockers' terms and conditions, answered:

*'Of course. I am angry and bitter. With me, it's not the share issue. Peter Vincent could have walked away with whatever he wanted as long as he left us with job security, our pension benefits and the rest of it. We were told there would never be a return to casual labour and that the buyout would safeguard our future. In five short months, the whole lot had gone.' [19]*

In their 1999 analysis of these events, Arnold and Cooper exposed many of the extraordinary instances of personal wealth being gifted to UK port bosses following the 1989 abolition of the National Dock Labour Board Scheme by Margaret Thatcher's Conservative government. [20] The subsequent privatisation of Britain's ports also benefited the hidden interests of the financiers and bankers who encouraged, advised and managed the original MEBOs. For example, according to the 1994 Public Accounts Committee Inquiry, Charterhouse Development, the financial backers of the Medway MEBO team, 'Owned something like £15 million in equity preference shares and £1 million in ordinary shares prior to the Medway reorganisation in October 1993. This same company advised Mersey Docks on their acquisition of Medway and Charterhouse Bank which were all subsidiaries. Charterhouse PLC was wholly owned by the Royal Bank of Scotland.' [21] Charterhouse Development reportedly made £30 million from the MDHC takeover, [22] and this exact scenario was played out again and again across various UK ports, such as Tilbury Docks, which was also privatised through a MEBO in 1992 before being resold to Forth Ports in September 1995. [23] At Clydeport, both the CEO and his deputy became millionaires overnight when their port was floated on the Stock Exchange in December 1994, [24] and it is beyond doubt that events at Medway inspired the conspiracy that ended with MDHC dismissing 500 Liverpool dockers.

According to Peter Turnbull's study on the restructuring of UK ports, prior to the long-running dispute at Liverpool, MDHC was the only major container operator not to utilise a supplementary labour pool. Turnbull explains how the Port of Felixstowe established Port of Felixstowe Services (PFS) in 1993, a subsidiary company employing supplementary labour on 12-week contracts, while in London, Tilbury Container Services used contract labour in order to allow them to man at the troughs of demand, rather than the peaks, significantly reducing overtime costs. A similar system was in operation at Southampton Container Terminal, where contract labour was provided by Southampton Cargo Handling Services, a subsidiary of Southampton Cargo Handling. The 80 workers employed by SCHS were all former SCT dockers who had been made redundant in 1993 after the employer threatened to subcontract 'non-core' operations to Drake International; the same company that would be used to devastating effect in replacing the sacked Liverpool dockers in September 1995.

Turnbull also described how the main impetus for cost-cutting in container trades had come from Thamesport, where casual and contract labour was hired from the ranks of ex-registered dockers previously employed in the ports of London and Medway. [25] He also notes that by 1993, Felixstowe sought to cut dockers' pay by 40 per cent on the grounds that the company should pay local labour market rates rather than industry wage rates, resulting in just 50 of 260 Medway workers holding permanent contracts, with additional labour being drawn from five different subcontractors. At the Port of Tilbury, where the dockers had always been comrades of their Liverpool counterparts, attempts were made to force management to maintain a fully permanent labour force in the wake of the NDLBS' abolition, but they, too, lost their jobs after casual labour was reintroduced in the port in 1991. [26]

# 15

# The 'Far-Left Militant Tendency' and the General Secretary Share a Platform!

*'It is very, very hard for everyone but don't you worry about us. We'll be all right, we've no pain left, we've nothing left to lose. You worry about this country when people aren't allowed to refuse to cross a picket line. We'll still be here for as long as it takes to get our jobs back. We've nowhere else to go.' ~ Jimmy Nolan\**

On Saturday 6 November 1993, the Merseyside Port Shop Stewards held yet another crisis meeting at Transport House. Upstairs, in the main hall, hundreds of TGWU members were gathered at a special meeting with the union's General Secretary. On the platform alongside him that morning were Bobby Owens, the regional secretary, and Eddie Roberts, divisional organiser. The purpose of the meeting was to discuss a new piece of government legislation, the Trade Union Reform Act (1993), and its impact upon the union, especially in relation to direct-from-wages union contributions deducted from members' pay by the employer and then transferred to the union. This was obviously a system that unions in the UK did not want to see the end of. [1] Once their own meeting had finished, some of the dock stewards went upstairs to the main hall to hear Morris, who had declined to meet them in private earlier that morning. Within minutes of their arrival, the room erupted into countless angry arguments as dockers and de-recognised stewards took the opportunity to challenge local union officials over the chaos that consumed their place of work.

For Morris, it might well have been confirmation of his long-held views on the 'far-left militant tendency' in Region 6, an area that he was looking to close-down, but to observers, this extraordinary event was indicative of a union that had lost control of its

---

\* Jimmy Nolan, Chairman of the port shop stewards committee – The Independent, 20 September 1997

Liverpool waterfront membership. [2] As far as the dockers and their shop stewards were concerned, Owens and Roberts were Jack Dempsey's senior officers, and so they, too, were held responsible for the TGWU's policies and relationship with MDHC. They had also now taken a prominent role in events on the docks directly intervening with senior directors of the company. Morris, on the other hand, looked at Owens and Roberts and saw ultra-leftist insurgents, operating within the union's Broad Left structure, whereas Dempsey fitted the General Secretary's image of a good trade union official. The irony of this was not lost on the dockers present, and in her study of the Liverpool docks dispute, Monica Clua-Losada noted:

> 'Region Six was the most idiosyncratic region of the TGWU and one which was difficult to control for the Broad Left machinery, the Communist Party or the right-wing of the union. None of the groupings within the TGWU were able to keep the region tamed... [the Broad Left was] a powerful, clandestine, electoral machine with no explicit political programme, minimal democracy and little role in industrial disputes. It was increasingly driven by rivalries between its two main strongholds: Region 1 [London and the South East] and Region 6 [North West]. These centred on disputes over the choice of candidates for mainly full-time paid officer posts and elected posts on influential constitutional committees; especially the GEC. Much was related to the overarching interests of former Communist Party members as opposed to non-communist TGWU activists, especially between Region 1 [London] and Region 6 [the North West].' [3]

John McIlroy, the labour historian and academic, observed: 'By 1993, the Broad Left was fractured by attempts to establish an alternative organisation,' [4] and according to Graham Stevenson, a future Docks and Waterways National Officer, the crucial split between these two regions came to a head in 1993: 'It was no longer possible to work with the Region 6 elements due to their inability to adhere to agreements. The result was that most of Region 6 was effectively expelled from the Left.' [5] In truth, the argument centred upon differences over jobs, careers and sinecures within the TGWU that came to represent the exercise of power and influence in the union. These divisions would affect the Liverpool dockers as they ran the gauntlet of their local union's fractured relationship with the London-based leadership. For their part, the MDHC had no problem with the local union, nor did they recognise the *militant* labels placed upon them by Region 1 officials and Bill Morris, [6] who had travelled to Liverpool seemingly with his mind already made up over the futures of Owens, Roberts and the other officers and activists in Region 6. The General Executive Council had given Morris the authority to do whatever he wanted, and as his biographer was to record years later: 'The whole Merseyside region had become a perpetual and challenging problem for Morris and was always top of his action pad.' [7]

The power struggle between Region 1 and Region 6 eventually led to the suspension of both Roberts and another local official, John Farrell, following false allegations of financial mismanagement when, in late 1993, Morris asked Albert Blyton, the TGWU's legal director, to begin a probe into Merseyside branches. Internal union politics took priority over industrial struggles, and so when these Broad Left splits over power and control erupted, Morris was quick to see to it that Region 6's Farrell, a TGWU recruitment chief and well-respected rank-and-file official, was sacked. Farrell's dismissal caused such resentment among

# THE 'FAR-LEFT MILITANT TENDENCY' AND THE GENERAL SECRETARY SHARE A PLATFORM!

members on Merseyside that an initially unsuccessful campaign for his reinstatement was launched. Additionally, Steve Broadhead, the Automotive District Secretary, was put on a final warning, as was Tom Hart, the capable and influential Region 6 education officer, who would resign rather than tolerate such a charade. Then, in July 1994, Morris sent Roberts a letter outlining allegations and unilaterally suspending him. Eddie Roberts was eventually demoted back to the first job he had held within the organisation some 20 years earlier. Fifteen years after these events, reporter Ben Scofield wrote on the wider personal ambitions of Bill Morris: 'Ahead of Labour's 1997 landslide election victory, Bill Morris was elected joint chair with Tony Blair of the Labour Party Trade Union Liaison Committee and he was widely credited with delivering the unions for Blair, being given a life peerage in 2006.' [8]

In December 2007, the union's personnel and development director, Ray Fletcher, sifted through papers that originally went before Morris's disciplinary panel fourteen years earlier, compelling him to write to the new general secretary, Tony Woodley, advising that the decision to discipline Eddie Roberts was 'unjust.' [9] It was only then that both he and Farrell were vindicated, winning a court case against the unfair dismissal and demotion. In 2008, Roberts stated: 'You work with employers all your life, but you never expect your own to turn on you. Morris and his cohorts knew exactly who to take out of the North West region to denude us and take out our fire power. We had become unfashionable and embarrassing for New Labour.' [10] Former Liverpool car plant worker Woodley, together with another Liverpool-born national officer, Len McCluskey, also experienced the aftershocks of Bill Morris's work on Merseyside. However, Woodley was destined to become Joint-general secretary of Unite, following the amalgamation of TGWU and AMICUS, while McCluskey would go on to succeed him. Woodley would send a written apology to Roberts, stating:

> *The decision to relieve you of your Divisional Officer responsibilities was neither fair nor justified. When the action was taken against you in 1994, you had an unblemished record in the union and were regarded by your peers and lay activists as an officer of the highest principles and integrity. I am happy to put the record straight in relation to your service as both a valued member and an officer whose ability, passion and commitment to our Union was a beacon to those who worked with you.' [11]*

Sitting on the platform of the main hall in Transport House, Liverpool, Bill Morris was focused on his re-election and need to remove or discredit all opposition to his leadership ambitions. With Morris now entrenched in Liverpool his personal interests also extended across the Irish Sea to another TGWU region that did not follow his leadership. A region that shared much more than just hereditary solidarity with their Liverpool comrades. On Tuesday 26 June, Morris suspended both the Irish regional secretary and regional Organiser of the Amalgamated Transport and General Workers' Union; officers who had worked throughout the Troubles, in one of the most difficult and dangerous environments for any trade union officials or members. The two officials in question, Mick O'Reilly and Eugene McGlone, had been leading left-wing comrades in the union, who along with John Freeman, the then regional secretary, would be the first, and only, regions to officially declare support for the Liverpool dockers in September 1995. They were suspended without consultation with either the GEC or the Irish Regional Committee, who were profoundly shocked and disturbed by this turn of events. O'Reilly had only recently been appointed despite opposition from Morris himself, and both he and McGlone had long records of loyal union service, with the latter being chair of the Northern Ireland Trade Union Congress at the time. It was the view of some IRC members that Morris's action was clearly a response to the consistent opposition of the Irish region to the social contract in the Republic of Ireland, not to mention the fact that Freeman was seen as a potential candidate in the upcoming General Secretary election. Other factors that made the timing of Morris's attention on Ireland significant included a meeting of the Irish Congress of Trade Unions, due to take place the following week, where a resolution opposing the social contract was to be presented, with good prospects of obtaining a majority. This resolution was to be presented by O'Reilly and McGlone, but their suspensions now made this impossible. [12]

In 2008, 'Lord' Morris (as he now wished to be known) failed to recognise events in Liverpool and Ireland as a meaningful part of a history that he had since disconnected himself from: 'Reopening the file was an attempt to rewrite history, the process was totally exhausted. Any attempt to rewrite history will not change the facts. I have not got the time to respond to the historical fabrication that's been attempted,' he stated. [13] He made no secret of his desire to leave this world behind: 'What happens in the organisation today is of no interest or consequence to me. I abided by the constitution and in the interests of the members… I'm quite content for people to do what they think they need to do.' [14]

At a TGWU Region 6 Finance and General Purposes Committee held on 22 November 1993, the agenda was dock shop steward accreditation, part-time labour and a letter written by Mike Carden to Bobby Lamb, the local TGWU legal officer. Bobby Owens, Eddie Roberts and Jack Dempsey were all in attendance. Dempsey opened the meeting by objecting to the presence of some of the dockers, such as Kevin Robinson, but he was overruled by Owens, who made it clear he just wanted proceedings to start. Jimmy Nolan provided the committee with a background of industrial issues in the port, reporting that a fax had been sent from 6/601 Branch at Seaforth Container Terminal, bearing the names of 50 workers calling for support of Mike Carden over objections to the imposed postal ballot and non-constitutional nature of the accreditation process imposed by the union and the Dock Company. Not for the first time, the union's dock official offered to resign. [15] Eddie Roberts told the committee: 'only Jack [the dock official] could comment in detail on what happened. We have to organise ourselves when companies split up.' [16] Both Roberts and Owens asserted that the accreditation agreement did not prevent dockers from one area of MDHC supporting those working elsewhere within the company, [17] and on the subject of Seaforth dockers' decision to withdraw from paying their union dues via the employer, Roberts objected claiming that: 'encouraging members to pull out of the check-off system was a disgrace, unprincipled and deplorable. It should be roundly criticised.' [18] It was then left to the docks official to confirm that, 'casual labour would be allowed, and this would affect 80 men at Torside.' [19]

It was at this meeting that the union outlined the Dock Company's demands for radical changes to working conditions and contracts of employment at Seaforth Container Terminal. [20] Roberts was asked to provide both the regional secretary and the influential Regional Finance and General Purposes Committee with a further report on the Shop Stewards' Note of Accreditation. [21] The local union's Legal Officer, Bobby Lamb, was

15

THE 'FAR-LEFT MILITANT TENDENCY' AND THE GENERAL SECRETARY
SHARE A PLATFORM!

assigned to provide assistance in the running of a shop stewards ballot at Seaforth. [22] Roberts then recounted the events of 7 August 1992 that saw shop stewards derecognised following the Pandoro strike: 'This decision was in the aftermath of the ill-fated Pandoro strike which was, the company asserted, the final straw as far as they were concerned. This was not the first derecognition issue, but it was the most serious.' [23] He also recalled a meeting of shop stewards that he, Owens and Dempsey had attended on 21 September 1992, during which, 'emotions, anger and frustrations were much in evidence... They had no confidence or belief that the 12 derecognised shop stewards would work within agreed procedures. Mr Furlong, MDHC managing director, declared: "the door was shut tight" on this matter as far as the company were concerned.' [24] Roberts described his own response to the dispute:

> 'I said it was the right time to rebuild relationships, but the stewards must be re-established and become quickly involved... Although something brand-new to the Port Industry, the principle of laying down the conditions within which recognised shop stewards' function is nothing new. We felt we could agree, in principle, and on 4 August, the final redraft was to be considered. This document had, in the main, been reassembled by Brother Dempsey and myself.' [25]

Eddie Roberts continued to explain:

> 'We had to work extremely hard to retrieve this situation and pull things back together. Eventually, Messrs Cliff and Furlong came around and accepted our determination not to let things go off the rails again. On 6 August 1993 (my 52nd birthday!), Jack Dempsey and myself reported back to the stewards. It was quite a stormy meeting, and we did not feel we were getting any support or credit for our efforts. We felt that the lads had got their heads in the sand and were in danger, if they did not grasp the nettle, of reducing themselves to a protest movement. The meeting was understandably upset over the part-time labour business and other concerns; the stewards would prefer continued derecognition to having to accept stringent constraints. We had to make it clear that this was not an option.' [26]

In discussing the reaction of shop stewards to the accreditation document, Roberts said:

> 'We were concerned about getting on with the job. I had been involved now for 12 months; we did not have the shop stewards functioning to represent our members. The accreditation document was agreed, and it was left for Jack Dempsey to communicate the position to our members and put in hand the arrangement for the election of shop stewards. I have to declare that upon returning from holiday on 28 September, I was dismayed to learn that serious problems had arisen over what should have been an uncomplicated exercise. We still had, and to date still have, stewards who refuse to sign acceptance of the accreditation. The elections had gone badly wrong and Jack Dempsey had been placed in an impossible situation. The F&GP had now to consider a letter of complaint addressed to Bob Lamb from Mike Carden dated 11 October. On that same

*date we met with the Company, where Mr Cliff complained bitterly at what they perceived to be deliberate disruption of the agreed election procedure. I urged the management not to over-dramatise the situation. I also made it clear that nobody who was unprepared to abide by the terms of the accreditation should be eligible to stand for steward.' [27]*

The goal of the union was to get dock shop stewards recognised again, even though other TGWU members employed by MDHC would not be affected by the strictures imposed upon the dockers. On this matter, Roberts acknowledged that:

*'Other MDHC bargaining groups would be naturally apprehensive that they will, by default, have these same terms imposed upon them without consultation. We have assured them that we do not believe this to be so. As for the shop steward election upheaval, it is before the F&GP to determine whether the results stand or whether there is a ballot rerun. Jack [Dempsey], Regional Trade Group Secretary, will no doubt provide a detailed account of the events which occurred prior to and during this ballot. Your committee have before them Brother Carden's letter of complaint. My only hope is that an honourable conclusion is reached, as unless this is the case, possibly irreparable damage will be done to our union in the Port of Liverpool, which I still believe at this juncture can be averted.' [28]*

Brian Dawson, another TGWU official, confirmed in correspondence to Bobby Owens dated 25 May 1993 that:

*'Casual labour is indeed employed at Pandoro on Liverpool Docks. On 7 August 1992, the shop stewards were de-recognised and Bro. Dempsey's view was that the stewards should have resigned and allowed others to replace them. On 10 September 1993, the union's Dock Officer informed the stewards that the company would agree to fresh elections. All stewards would have to sign a TGWU/MDHC accreditation, which would make it illegal for dockers from one area to support dockers from another area, even though they were employed by the same company, but the Dock Company would not accept anyone who did not sign this accreditation. A meeting of the Dock Company stewards on 15 September 1993 decided unanimously not to sign this accreditation. [29]*

On 8 December 1993, Bobby Owens wrote to the secretary of the Regional Docks Trade Group to confirm that:

*'Region 6 F&GP had upheld the agreement negotiated between officers of the TGWU and the MDHC on the question of [shop stewards] accreditation… Bro. Dempsey is removed from any stricture placed upon him by the Docks Trade Group in terms of negotiating for the part-time labour already recruited into the ranks of the TGWU in the Port of Liverpool. In regard to a letter of complaint from Bro. Carden concerning the ballot for shop stewards, the Regional F&GP concluded that there was sufficient controversy surrounding this matter that it called into question the integrity of the ballot*

# THE 'FAR-LEFT MILITANT TENDENCY' AND THE GENERAL SECRETARY SHARE A PLATFORM!

*and was therefore widely discredited. A rerun ballot should be held for the election of shop stewards at the Seaforth Container Terminal. In line with the above, as regional secretary and senior officer of the TGWU in the North West, this is to advise that the Regional Trade Group Secretary, Brother Dempsey, continues to enjoy my full support. This includes an appreciation of the role played by the Divisional Organiser in this regard and, to this end, I have requested that Bro. Roberts make himself available to be in attendance at all meeting of the Docks and Waterways RTGC, until the current issues, as outlined above, are expedited.' [30]*

Ignored by the right and betrayed by the left, in conflict with both their local union and their employer, the Liverpool dockers had no alternative but to continue alone.

# 16

# The Seaforth Container Berth Contract (Fire and Re-hire)

*We discussed picketing Seaforth; there was arguments amongst the lads as to the rights and wrong. Should we put it on the main gate at Seaforth or just on the timber berth, which was our working area, but bearing in mind we had already been sacked, there was no way we were going to gain access to the dock estate to picket the timber berth. So, it was decided the picket would go on the main entrance at Seaforth. So, on Thursday 28 September 1995, the picket line was placed at Seaforth along with the Canada and Huskisson gates. It was then the men from Seaforth refused to cross the picket line. ~ Bob Ritchie\**

On 16 December 1993, the Dock Company's Human Resources Manager, Allan Price, wrote to Jack Dempsey at the Transport and General Workers' Union regarding 'changes in working arrangements at the Seaforth Container Terminal.' [1] Price followed-up with another letter to the TGWU a day later, agreeing with their suggestion that:

> 'A Review Committee be set up to monitor progress. Finally, I would like to express great satisfaction with the way that you and the local representatives have conducted yourselves in what we all knew would be very difficult discussions...' [2]

This was a celebratory letter, but the sense of victory would not last long. Ultimately, these were meetings that only involved the Dock Company and local TGWU officials; the exchange of letters were meaningless in the real world of the dock estate, and that same month, more votes of no confidence in the union and its officers were submitted again by the dockers to their union. [3] Another meeting with Bobby Owens, Eddie Roberts and Jack Dempsey took place with the Seaforth stewards, where it was finally confirmed that stewards

---

\* Bob Ritchie (former Torside shop steward) transcribed from an undated interview conducted by Dave Cotterill

who refused to sign the accreditation would not receive TGWU or employer credentials. [4] At the Seaforth Container Terminal, MDHC wanted to get shop stewards elected in order to legitimise substantial changes to working practices on the berth. At a shop stewards' meeting held Tuesday 14 December 1993, Mick Cullen, one of the new shop stewards at Seaforth, reported on talks with the employer regarding Seaforth's new contract. The stewards were opposed to the fresh terms, and they called for a mass meeting to unite all dockers against the imposition of yet another new contract.

The employer wanted to abolish the three-shift system and weekend overtime in favour of an annualised hours system, under which dockers had to work 117 hours across a three-week period, covering all hours over seven-day periods in blocks of 12-hour shifts, or longer if necessary. To make this a reality, MDHC would utilise its experiences from the Medway Port foretelling the *Covid* 'fire and rehire' tactics of 2021. [5] They issued every Liverpool docker with a 90-day redundancy notice and advertised their jobs in the *Liverpool Echo*. Around 1,800 applications were received from Merseyside's unemployed, but none would ever be interviewed, as the tried and tested process of threats, humiliation and intimidation were used again by the employer with no recorded opposition from the local union. Monica Clua-Losada noted that this contract in 1994 was introduced:

> '…*without any complaints from the union. The change brought in annualised hours, which meant that dockers would not have a normal working week. Rather, their hours of work would be organised according to the number of ships in port at any one time. This meant they had to be available for work, and could be called in at little notice, but also, it meant that they could go for days without work. The impact of this was that dockers could end up 'owing' the employer hours if they had not been called to work sufficient times in any given year.*' [6]

A Seaforth steward described the contract as:

> '*Like a slave contract. You end up owing the employer hours because in a potentially casual industry where you weren't guaranteed five days' work… a situation like annualised hours you were always gonna owe the employer hours, and even the most moderate dockworker was damaged by that. You couldn't avoid it, everyone was affected by it, and I think that had a big impact on – on the militancy of the workforce… you were down to a hardcore of 5-600 workers, who had sort of made the decision that they were staying in the industry, and some felt that the industry owed them something, you know. I felt that way, you know, we all could have left, we all could have sold our jobs, in a sense, and we didn't, so then, to not do that and then being met with constantly low wages, longer shifts, you know, there is 12-hour shift, 16-hour shifts, it was dreadful. It was absolutely dreadful.*' [7]

At 10am on Tuesday 11 January 1994, a meeting of all Seaforth dockers took place at the Dockers' Club in Edinburgh Park, Liverpool. Frank Jones, Joe McKenna and Mick Cullen were now the *accredited* shop stewards at the berth having signed the TGWU/MDHC joint documents. Mike Carden and Billy Duffy refused to sign the accreditation document. Frank

# THE SEAFORTH CONTAINER BERTH CONTRACT (FIRE AND RE-HIRE)

Jones informed those assembled that the paper produced by MDHC, 'was a load of crap!' [8] Mick Cullen spoke of a 20% pay cut for dockers employed at the Groupage Sheds in Seaforth. Jack Dempsey's main contribution on behalf of the TGWU, was that: 'Auditors have said the books and records are correct and the company are losing £2m; these are the facts of life… the company had contingency plans, it was now a multi-national company.' [9] Contributions from the floor made it clear that no matter what the local union thought, the new deal would be rejected, and attention turned to the black metal ballot box that Dempsey had with him, the likes of which had never been seen on the docks before. The dockers voted by a show of hands to reject MDHC's demands, as it was noted that another feature of this union-endorsed 'new deal' was that the dockers would no longer report to work for hire. Instead, they would wait at home, by the phone, where they could be called at any time of the day or night with only two hours' notice to commence work.

Not for the first time, imposed contracts, 90 day redundancy notices, dockers' jobs advertised in the local press to replace them, final warnings and the omnipresent spectre of dismissal were held over the heads of dockworkers as the Dock Company, in partnership with local officials of the TGWU, sought to impose its will. Various disciplinary actions were taken against those that refused to accept the changes as the MDHC took the opportunity to clarify their intention to sack any docker who refused to follow their instructions:

> *The MDHC was now implementing its rescue plan for the Royal Seaforth Container Terminal. The 232 men employed at the loss-making operation have failed to endorse the plan introducing the 21-day work cycle. There is no alternative to this plan. Existing jobs need to be replaced by others which will allow the Terminal to operate successfully. Therefore, in accordance with employment legislation, the current 232 jobs will be terminated. Each employee will receive formal contractual notice within the next few days. At the same time, he will receive a new contract of employment containing the new working arrangements. Each employee will have the opportunity, provided he signs acceptance of the new terms, to remain in employment with the company. Those who do not sign their acceptance of the new contract will cease to be employed by the company. The District Official of the TGWU has received formal 90 days' notice of 232 redundancies. The Company made it clear when consultation began last summer and throughout lengthy discussions since, the major changes were needed if the future of the Terminal was to be secured. The plan has now to be implemented without delay. Each employee must decide quickly whether he wants to be part of the plan.' [10]*

Under the terms of this latest new deal, wages were to be cut by over £6,000 per annum, and yet on 11 January 1994, a TGWU official told a mass meeting of Seaforth Dockers that their three shop stewards, who had signed the joint employer-union accreditation, had 'not missed a trick' in negotiations with the bosses. The disputed elections at the Container Terminal had seen more than 100 dockers denied their right to vote, while at least one non-union member was known to have been handed a ballot paper. Eventually, the Region 6 F&GP concluded that the postal ballot, paid for by MDHC and supported by the TGWU in a letter dated 8 December 1993, was widely discredited, leaving the regional secretary, Bobby Owens, to state: 'There was sufficient controversy surrounding this matter that it called into question the integrity of the ballot.' [11] But it was all too little and too late. Work at Seaforth Container Terminal was now rigidly controlled, to the point that if dockers were not hired to complete their allocated hours within a three-week period, they would owe hours to the employer. Shifts would be 12 hours long, starting and finishing at MDHC's convenience, with disciplinary action taken against anyone who failed to respond to an instruction or an order to attend work. Liverpool dockers were reduced to being prisoners, quite literally, in their own homes. The dockers referred to it as a 'slave contract,' which some recognised as the final step in the re-casualisation of Liverpool's docks, with the men's own homes serving as the new pens and new hiring halls.

On Thursday 13 January 1994, another mass meeting of Seaforth dockers took place in the amenity block, called by the union's dock official and the three newly accredited shop stewards, McKenna, Jones and Cullen. The stewards had met with MDHC management the previous day to inform them that their proposals had been rejected, with the response being that another: 'letter would now be sent by the Dock Company to all dockers at home by post, and they would have to sign this new contract, and if the contract was not signed, then a 90-day notice would be given.' [12] The company made it clear that if Seaforth dockers did not sign yet another new personal contract by 14 January 1994 they would all be dismissed. As the meeting drew to a close, all three shop stewards recommended that the dockers: 'accept the employer's demands because they were going to send out new contracts, and they thought that the majority of men would sign them anyway.' [13] The motion was passed by 105 votes to 101. [14]

Two days after the mass meeting at Seaforth, non-accredited shop stewards met in the local TGWU boardroom. Many of those derecognised were still elected representatives of the most senior official committees of the union from the National Committees of the Docks and Waterways Section, the District Committee, the Regional Committee to the General Executive Council. None of the accredited Seaforth stewards were in attendance, but the chair, Jack Dempsey, hoped to, 'put accreditation to bed.' He wanted elected shop stewards to sign it. [15] Jimmy Davies was blunt in telling Dempsey he: 'wasn't interested in accreditation while the docks were in chaos.' [16] In an even more concerning development regional committee members Bobby Morton and Kevin Robinson were informed that they would no longer be allowed to attend any constitutional meetings of the union until they signed the accreditation form, even though neither was a shop steward at the time. In effect, the MDHC/TGWU shop steward accreditation contract was being extended to the internal constitutional democracy of the union and its rule book.

In relation to the imposition of personal contracts on the docks some of the dockers decided that if they were going to be employed on a 'personal' contract, as opposed to a collective trade union agreement, they were free to negotiate directly with the employer. They were effectively refusing to authorise the TGWU to agree to further amendments to their personal contracts on their behalf. [17] So concerned about this development and challenge to their joint authority the TGWU and the MDHC ensured that this was discussed at the earliest formal opportunity. On 27 January 1994, the first official meeting of the Monitoring Group, established jointly by the local TGWU and MDHC, took place at Seaforth Container Terminal. Present at this meeting were Allan Price, Larry Burrell, Mervyn Bull and George Edgar of MDHC, with Jack Dempsey and two of the accredited Seaforth stewards, Mick

Cullen and Kevin McKenna, representing the dockers. The minutes of these MG meetings reflect the corporate ideal of a close working relationship between the employer and the union, with a TGWU official seeking clarity over the issue of how personal contracts might have affected their position: 'the question they ask, is the contract a personal contract or one negotiated by the union?' Price responded: 'I will make that point clear, maybe by letter.' [18] The problem with both this question and the answer is that a union official should not be having to ask if an employment contract is either a personal or a collective agreement, just as an employer should not be informing its employees or their union of what type of employment contract they have as workers.

Within a month of the new contracts being issued, Seaforth men were working 12-hour shifts, and with some 40 men off sick at the time, threats of discipline for not working fast enough became the norm. Excessive overtime working started when the new contracts were imposed. Meanwhile, the accredited shop stewards were locked in continuous meetings with management. For all the hustle and bustle from this Monitoring Group, that was desperate to show what a success their new arrangement was, not a lot was actually happening in the real world of a working container port. Another meeting took place at Transport House on Saturday 19 February, where it was reported that more than 50 men at Seaforth were on some stage of disciplinary measures. [19] Because of the numbers involved the company were demanding the right to discipline dockers in their own time, before or after their shifts and without pay, so as not to interfere with productivity. So intense were both the workload and the volume of disciplinary correspondence that the terminal manager, Alec Hampton, began writing each letter by hand, as MDHC flagrantly acted outside the parameters of agreed disciplinary policies without any challenge from the TGWU. [20] Two Seaforth dockers, Kevin Bilsborrow and Tony Gardiner, each had £100 deducted from their wages without prior notification or official procedures being started, and on 28 February 1994, Allan Price wrote to inform all Seaforth dockers:

*'This letter is to make all employees aware of the serious developments occurring since the introduction of the new working arrangements about which the management must take action to safeguard ALL jobs at the Terminal… it is vital that everyone works to their new contracts of employment, some it seems are determined not to do so.' [21]*

The letter concluded with a warning: 'those people who signed their new contracts of employment but who are determined not to fulfil them will not be allowed to jeopardise the jobs of everyone else. Please heed this message in which case it will be unnecessary for the Company to take this serious action.' [22] Such unchallenged threats only enhanced the employer's power in the minds of the Seaforth dockers, as the script for their future dismissal was being written. Within three days, Price had sent another letter laced with threats of dismissal, before Keven Bilsborrow, one of the most capable and efficient container straddle carrier drivers, received a final warning on 3 March. Dave Pendleton, a skilled, conscientious and fair-minded clerical worker, a gentleman, was also disciplined over job performance, while another clerical worker, was given the same treatment without any clear reason as to why he was being disciplined. Former clerical worker Maurice Thompson received a three-day suspension, and Tony Delahunty, a container gantry crane driver responsible for a container crane valued at hundreds of thousands of pounds, was disciplined for refusing to report to work for a 12-hour shift at 7am on the same morning he finished a night shift. Repeatedly, Price openly claimed that he had the TGWU's approval to do what he pleased to the men, many of whom were of outstanding calibre, highly skilled and professional in their handling of complex machinery worth millions of pounds. These men were key employees, yet MDHC was doing everything in its power to antagonise, humiliate and crush them.

On Sunday 6 March 1994, another meeting took place at Transport House involving the two Seaforth stewards, Joe McKenna and Mick Cullen, and on the platform with them were Bobby Owens, Eddie Roberts and Jack Dempsey. Tony Delahunty had been sacked from his job at Seaforth two days earlier, and Eddie Roberts observed that, 'The anger of the men was apparent, and it was a horrendous situation.' [23] The official TGWU leaflet for this meeting claimed that, 'We are concerned at the number of disciplines, some we believe because of the men's frustration, but it is not helping us in our negotiations on your behalf, giving management weapons to use against us.'[24] The following Wednesday, MDHC wrote to remind all Seaforth employees that as per the terms of the New Deal, 'Pre-authorisation of sick pay has ceased; employees will need to convince the company of their eligibility for sick pay before it will be authorised.' [25] In reflecting on this period of strife, Cullen was later to recall that, through the press, MDHC were claiming that they wanted to get rid of:

> 'A hardcore of 50 or 60 men, not because they were union militants, but because they could not or would not physically drive heavy plant; men who worked on the ship, that's who they wanted to get rid of. Jack Dempsey sat beside me and he knew, when the late Bernard Cliff turned around and said, "These men are no good to me, they won't train up." That's what this was all about. Not because of any militancy. The Dock Company wanted men to drive heavy plant and there were lads there who could not drive heavy machinery, many couldn't drive cars. It was all about flexibility and profit.' [26]

On 11 March, Mike Carden attended another disciplinary meeting with Price, Burrell and Edgar of MDHC. Jack Dempsey acted as Carden's union representative throughout a hearing that lasted over six hours, with management asserting that the defendant had: 'Made it clear he did not wish to stay with the company and work within the rules. We cannot avoid the serious nature of events, but the procedure was about avoiding dismissal.' [27] Carden was issued with a final warning for an indefinite period, along with a 10-day suspension and a transfer to the Timber Berth to work as a forklift truck driver. [28] On 19 May, Eddie Roberts responded to a letter from a dockworker, Geoff Liddy, expressing criticism of the ballot at Seaforth and the imposition of accreditation which Liddy complained was undemocratic. [29] Two days later an article in the *Liverpool Echo* reported that:

> '1,800 hopefuls applied for jobs advertised by the Mersey Docks Company and all were turned down. Port bosses backtracked after receiving an avalanche of replies for a dozen positions starting at £18,800 a year. But bosses said the decision did not reflect badly on local job hunters. Every applicant received a reply, and many were told they would remain on file. Letters flooded in when the recruiting campaign for gantry drivers and straddle carrier drivers was mounted.' [30]

On 4 July 1994, Tony Gardiner, a container straddle carrier driver at Seaforth, was presented with another hand-written letter from berth manager, Alec Hampton, [31] and four days later, he was sacked for refusing to work past midnight. The decision was met with an immediate stoppage, and despite the stewards' request that they return to work until an appeal could be launched, the dockers refused. Gardiner himself asked the men to continue working until the appeal process had been enacted. For Liverpool dockers like Micky Tighe, a container gantry crane driver, these events were the genesis of the 1995 dispute: 'I was working 12-hour shifts, four and a half hours in bed, back to do another 12 hours in the gantry; just unbelievable, just asking too much, all engineered; bringing up for the big smack, for casual labour; cheap labour. We're the last port in the country to have a bit of organised labour left. You've got men standing here with 40 years' service.' [32] Another Seaforth docker, Ritchie Gerrard, said of this time:

> *They should have got the lawyers working on it because it goes back to 1989, the breaking of our system, you know registered dockworkers and then the employers can do what they want. The union's finished now in Liverpool. It's not broken as an organisation; our local officials are broken. The main fella that signed this deal and said it's a good deal before we started all the trouble, he's just disappeared off the scene, an employer's lackey.' [33]*

Cathy Dwyer, a founder member of Women of the Waterfront, spoke of how her husband's wages and conditions had been diminished by MDHC since 1989:

> *We could have nipped it in the bud when we saw what it was doing to the men, the stress on them. Men in their 50s who never worked nights in their life. Suddenly, they get told to work 12-hour shifts on nights. The body cannot take it. But rather than admitting that they were having stress problems, they'd probably go off with a bad back. These are tough men – how can they admit they can't cope? It's a stigma that they didn't want.' [34]*

With the new contract imposed, working conditions were transformed overnight, and within days the system was shown to be as incompetent, inefficient, unproductive and unworkable as the previous arrangements. Eventually, some former shop stewards saw the chaos as it unfolded and relented in their objections to signing the accreditation document. As Frank Lannigan recalled:

> *'After 1989 there was an assault on the rank-and-file organisation, based on the imposition of six different contracts for workers in six defined areas of the port. Management attempted to curtail the role of the stewards on the shop floor, and if we undertook activities they didn't like, they would derecognise us. This eventually occurred in 1991-2, and the result was that a number of inexperienced men became shop stewards and the management and the union steamrollered them. There was a major attack on our conditions and a deterioration in our working lives. Faced with this situation, we decided*

*to accept the 'accreditation process,' so we could get in and represent our members and gradually repel the assault, but the sackings of 1995 stopped that process.' [35]*

Terry Teague and Kevin Robinson, two of the original derecognised shop stewards, decided to accept the accreditation so that they could directly challenge MDHC bosses at Seaforth, and in an election held in May 1994, Mick Cullen received 176 votes, Terry Teague 152 votes and Kevin Robinson 138 votes. The new rules stipulated that, once elected, incoming shop stewards were required to attend a *signing ceremony* at MDHC's head office, witnessed by representatives from both the employer and the union. [36] On the evening of Thursday 2 June 1994, an open meeting of Seaforth dockers took place at Transport House, with Teague telling those assembled that:

*'Under the present working agreements that operate, weekend time is precious for family and social commitments. But there is also a need to set-up meetings between the stewards and the membership so that reports back can be given, workers grievances can be voiced and future policy, in the form of clear mandates, can be given. Hopefully, this type of meeting will become a regular set-up every four or six weeks. On a personal note, can I thank everyone for their support in the stewards' elections, especially the scrutineers whose work enabled such a good turnout. I would also like to give a special mention to Mike Carden, who did more than anyone else in achieving the re-ballot at Seaforth, so that all the workforce would be allowed to have a say in who should represent them.' [37]*

Teague then proceeded to identify the main aims of the Seaforth shop stewards as being the rebuilding of confidence in the stewards' movement, the branch structure, the constitutional committees and, more than anything else, the official side of the union: 'For too long now we have had to argue more with our own union officials before we could even attempt to take on the employer. We need to be on the same side to achieve anything. Most importantly, the workforce themselves need to have a confidence in themselves.' [38] Less than a month after being elected, the shop stewards at Seaforth were derecognised once again, with Allan Price writing to Bobby Owens, Eddie Roberts and Jack Dempsey, asking them to impose the terms of the employer-union agreement on their members. [39]

*'At last week's monitoring committee meeting we spent the best part of 2 hours discussing the issues of rostered days off. At no time during that meeting did you, as District Official, deny that there was a collective responsibility on Container Terminal employees to work these when necessary.' [40]*

In the letter, Price said that he had spoken to Teague: 'on the previous day and he informed me that he was "not happy" with the Company Bulletin and that it was the shop stewards' intention to publish their own... I reminded him that you had agreed otherwise at the recent meeting and this was a view contrary to the official union position.' [41] Price then pointed out that the shop stewards had published their own bulletin, 'on T&G headed note paper, a position quite contrary to that agreed by yourself. The result of employees accepting the views expressed in this 'unofficial' bulletin can only be detrimental to employees, either through the loss of customers or through them involving themselves in disciplinary action.' [42] The letter contained the customary threats of punishment for being 'let down' by the TGWU, describing the stewards' bulletin as: 'totally irresponsible in this respect, it contains a view contrary to the official Union position and it is quite outside not only the terms recently agreed in the accreditation, but also, it is entirely outside the long accepted principles that the Company and the Union have a joint responsibility for ensuring that customers' requirements are met.'[43] Price concluded: 'This letter is to inform you that with immediate effect their accreditation is suspended as are all facilities and we will no longer acknowledge any authority for them to operate as representatives. We have, therefore, reverted to the situation where we recognise **you only** [original emphasis] as having authority to discuss issues on behalf of employees based at the Container Terminal.' [44] Copies of the letter were sent to both Teague and Robinson. The union accepted this position without argument.

# 17

# The Bullying and
# Intimidation Continues

*'From any political perspective, the sheer determination of the people involved must command a measure of respect. The strikers say they are no longer fighting just for the lost jobs. They believe they are battling to save the country's employment culture. Their problem is that no-one appears to be listening, certainly not in the national media. One journalist working for a local news agency summed up the lack of interest. "Striking Scousers just aren't sexy," he said.' ~ The Herald\**

The enforced implementation of the annualised hours rota system at Seaforth Container Terminal led to the shop stewards making another official complaint of: 'alleged interference by regional officials against the wishes of the membership, in disputes and other matters.' [1] Region 6 representatives attending the Docks and Waterways National Committee meeting in October 1994 raised these issues with the General Secretary, three months after a resolution had been sent to the union's central office stating that the Liverpool dockers were: 'Completely opposed to Full-Time Officers negotiating on our behalf without being asked… A Region 6 delegate said the request was for a delegation meeting with the General Secretary about the interference of the Regional secretary in Trade Group matters.' [2] According to Monica Clua-Losada's paper on the 'Retreat of the Union' in 2010, it was a fact that the problems between the local shop stewards and their full-time official had already been made known to Bill Morris in 1994. In a faxed response to Morris from the Merseyside Port Shop Stewards, dated 9 April 1997, the stewards captured the concerns of the dockers during this period, highlighting the profound breakdown in the relationship between shop stewards and their local full-time officials:

---

\* The Herald - Deadlock at the Docks, 10 March 1997

139

*'Between 1989 and 1995 the Liverpool Dockers, through their Docks and Waterways Regional Trade Group, requested on four occasions, an official ballot relating to job losses, privatisation and casualisation. These requests were refused by the local union for various reasons; ongoing negotiations, companies no longer trading, the illegality of holding ballots amongst different companies albeit direct subsidiaries of Mersey Docks etc.'* [3]

On 13 September 1994, the Dock Company were again writing to the docks officer to remind him of what they had jointly agreed for the Seaforth Container Terminal, where the company: 'requires cover for <u>all</u> operational requirements and the union has agreed that this should be provided. The individual employee will have a contractual responsibility to participate in providing this cover. This obligation will be communicated to each individual as part of their contract of employment in the form of a letter sent to each individual.' [4] Within a matter of days, Price wrote yet again to each individual Seaforth docker, reiterating that MDHC had an agreement with the union to cover all work on the terminal as required. [5] Price's letter opened with the threat that: 'If the offer is not accepted then each employee will have their current contract terminated and they will be issued with another personal contract which is likely to be different from this.' [6] The new personal contracts had to be signed and returned within seven days. [7] This endless cycle of de-recognition, disciplinary action, enforcement of union official agreements; the constant imposition of new personal contracts running alongside the threat of instant dismissal; consistently undermined the position of the Liverpool dockers to defend themselves against the force of their local union and their employer. The local TGWU did not oppose the imposition of personal contracts upon the Liverpool dockers. Price wrote again to Jack Dempsey, the TGWU docks official, on 17 November 1994, to address the subject of dockers attending the funerals of comrades killed at work:

> *Those who leave work without having received permission will be regarded as in breach of their contract of employment and subject to disciplinary action. Surely, this matter can be dealt with reasonably and with responsibility and dignity by both of us.'* [8]

This edict, which essentially prevented dockers from paying their final respects to comrades killed at work, came a year after John Simon was killed at the Seaforth Container Terminal. The following day, another letter from Price landed on Dempsey's desk, explaining that: 'A surplus of employees had developed within the Cargo Operations Department, and that the Company wished to deal with this position urgently,' [9] with the personnel manager referring to an 'optimum establishment' of labour at the Norse Irish and the Container Terminal, along with details of a voluntary severance scheme. The following Monday, a third letter arrived bearing the subject line 'Container Terminal,' in which the word 'optimum' was prevalent once more, only this time it was linked to the concept of an 'optimum skill mix required by the management at the Terminal,' in order to, 'Satisfy the needs of our customers and properly deal with problems which continue to affect the operation of the roster.' [10] Here, Price was declaring the need for MDHC to get rid of more dockers on a severance scheme paying a maximum of £20,000, when those same dockers could have accepted £35,000 at any time during the preceding 15 years.

Price's next letter to Dempsey arrived on 23 December 1994, as he wrote to dispute Carden's right to seek re-election to the TGWU General Executive Council, arguing: 'Mr Carden's previous disciplinary record and the fact that he is presently on an indefinite Final Warning for conduct relating to time-off issues prohibits him from being given the sort of privileges associated with this type of office.' [11] Once again the MDHC was confident in its domination of the local union to again extend their sphere of influence into the very heart of the union's democratic structure. It was also at this time that the MDHC appointed three new berth superintendents at Seaforth.

Before the 1970s, the job of a berth superintendent had, particularly in general cargo, been the sole preserve of former seafarers holding a 'Mates Ticket,' which distinguished a returning Merchant Navy Officer as possessing skills and expertise that were typically in high demand on the docks. As was the case with so many posts, the qualification requirements diminished over time, but it remained a position reserved for only the most capable, intelligent and experienced individuals. That was until the unexpected appointments of three former 6/567 Branch members at Seaforth; one the son of a dock worker and another being the son of a dock shop steward. These were appointments that shocked many on the berth because of the three individuals involved. It was only once the Liverpool dockers were dismissed in 1995 that the true purpose of these appointments became self-evident. None of the three men had any relevant knowledge beyond the most basic level of receiving and delivering containers, but it was they who would head up a small group tasked with training and directing the strike-breaking labour force recruited to replace the sacked dockers, crossing their former 6/567 Branch comrades' picket line each and every day throughout the dispute.

After the tumult of 1994, the new year began with MDHC's Bernard Cliff, acting in the capacity of Operations Director, issuing a summary note of a meeting between management and the Seaforth shop stewards that took place on Tuesday 3 January. The notice recorded various shipping companies' threats to pull out of the port, and MDHC's own complaints about failures to attend for rostered work by large numbers of port operations workers on 27 December and 2 January. [12] A total of five threats were made to all men on the berth, including:

> 'Any failure to work as required by the Agreement will be dealt with. If any strike action takes place the company will not be chasing to bring men back nor does it intend to allow its terminal to stand idle. In the event that any of our current customers leave, redundancies on Redundancy Payment Act terms will take place to balance numbers employed with work that remains. There is no need for any of the dark side described here to come about. You know what you have to win or lose. The choice is yours!' [13]

For an employer to talk openly about unleashing 'the dark side' in communicating with its employees is quite extraordinary, and Terry Teague, one of the shop stewards in attendance at the meeting with Cliff, was later to write: 'All the problems stem from the present deal. The workforce wish now to terminate the deal after twelve months and we wish to renegotiate new terms and conditions.' [14] Not allowed to meet during working hours a meeting of the TGWU Branch 6/601 was organised for Saturday 7 January 1995, providing an opportunity to express how the 'Seaforth Deal' was affecting lives and earnings. Outstanding disciplines were also high on the list of concerns, with Kevin Bilsborrow urging the stewards to: 'do something; have a ballot in the Dockers Club to all stop work.' Some suggested meeting with Andrew Weir and ABC Shipping Lines to explain why they were experiencing problems, while Jimmy Russell put forward getting rid of rota days and Tony Nelson recommended that the men be entitled to an eleven-hour break in between each shift. Ultimately, the overall consensus among Seaforth dockers was in line with Frank Lannigan's desire to 'cancel the deal' altogether. [15]

On 18 January 1995, two of the three Seaforth shop stewards, Terry Teague and Kevin Robinson, took the decision to respond directly to Cliff's threats in an open letter to all Seaforth workers, written on TGWU Docks and Waterways-headed paper:

> *The meeting started with Mr. Cliff waving a letter from two shipping companies. Cliff was clearly upset over the decision by the Seaforth workforce to spend time [like the majority of MDHC employees] with their families over the Christmas/New Year bank holidays. He then launched into an attack on our 'productivity and performance' levels, which he said had fallen dramatically since August 1994. He then demanded to know what we as shop stewards were going to do about it. We made it quite clear that, unfortunately, we had no formal contact with the shipping companies and therefore no way of channelling the real frustrations and grievances of the workforce to them. We stressed that a settlement of the overdue wage claim, a reduction in the number of 12-hour shifts and changes of shift allied to a more humane and acceptable agreement.' [16]*

The dockers' refusal to work overtime hit MDHC hard. With their joint employer-union deal at Seaforth beginning to unravel, it became clear that the working practices they had imposed were not working. From its inception, this initiative had been doomed to fail, but that did not stop the Dock Company from publishing what could only be read as an unwillingness to acknowledge the reality of a situation that they themselves had created, and it was only later that the dockers learned how the proposed annual roster system had been produced using computer software designed for the police. [17] In defence of the new contract and casual system of hire that now haunted and confined the Seaforth dockers in their homes or at work, MDHC explained that:

> *'In early 1994 a Flexible Manning System (FMS) was introduced to the Royal Seaforth Container Terminal to cover ship and park operations. The objective was to better match the normal supply of labour with uncertain demand. The key benefit was to be a reduction in overtime payments.' [18]*

It was the employer's view that dockers at Seaforth were dissatisfied with the new system because wages had been reduced. [19] Portia Travel Ltd, a subsidiary of MDHC, would be appointed to review why the project at Seaforth was collapsing. The local TGWU took part in this charade without objection. [20]

# THE BULLYING AND INTIMIDATION CONTINUES

*The computer system is not used to hold historical information on actual hours worked and is not used to optimise future labour allocation. Either it is incapable of doing so or the operators have had insufficient training. Furthermore, there appear to be a number of clear deficiencies. As a result, the computer is little used. The system of labour allocation is largely manual and necessarily very costly. A properly specified system would substantially reduce the costs of implementing the FMS and may obviate the need for Labour Officers.' [21]*

In their own words the Dock Company admitted that their decision to use a computer system that replaced the job of labour control officers was a disaster. Now they wanted to scrap the computer system and replace it with labour control officers. [22] On 21 January 1995, a meeting of recognised and derecognised shop stewards took place before another mass meeting of dockers, with Billy Jenkins giving a report on a meeting that he and Jimmy Nolan had with MDHC's Trevor Furlong. Jenkins and Nolan had also met with Bill Morris and Jack Adams of the TGWU to discuss the situation at Liverpool Cargo Handling, where Furlong had given dockers one week to either end their strike or watch LCH go into liquidation. The union's position was that the men should return to work, and then a ballot could take place, despite Jack Dempsey informing the mass meeting that Furlong had confirmed to him that LCH would be going into liquidation no matter what, as they, along with Pandoro and Seaforth, were losing £2m. [23] MDHC's Cliff, Burrell and Price met with the union and the shop stewards Cullen, Teague, Robinson and Nolan on 6 February, and here it was reported that 124 dockers at Seaforth were now on discipline, with 70 of those on a final written warning. Cliff spoke about shipping lines being unhappy with the service at Seaforth. Cullen identified the practical problems at the Terminal, citing everything from potholes to quay design, while Nolan pushed for a return to: 'eight-hour shifts and an amnesty on the disciplining of dockers.' [24] Cliff's response was to complain about the shortage of skills and poor fitness of many dockers, saying that he wanted younger clerical workers to train as carrier drivers, which could possibly reduce the number of 12-hour shifts, albeit they could never be done away with altogether. The union asked for the problems brought up by Cliff to be put in writing, as according to Terry Teague's written record, the meeting's agenda was split between two items:

*'Mass disciplines and stoppage of men's money. But before Jack [Dempsey] could fully explain our agenda, Mr. Cliff cut him short and launched into a tirade on the workforce, accusing us for all the problems currently happening at the Terminal. His [Cliff's] belief, as it has [been] in the past, is that there is a concerted and organised action to undermine the present working agreement which has led to performance levels on both ship and landside operations reaching an all-time low. He directly told the stewards that the Terminal was now well and truly fucked-up.' [25]*

At a mass meeting held on Wednesday 8 February 1995, the dockers' anger and frustration was apparent. There, Micky Tighe made it clear: 'the management should resign,' as Tony Nelson pointed out how: 'the new deal was not working, and that they were handling ships faster twelve months ago,' [26] Billy Jenkins expressed the men's desire to: 'go back to three 8-hour shift patterns,' and George Johnson suggested: 'two midweek rota days off each week.' Frank Lannigan demanded that the stewards' accreditation be: 'removed – and get a solid agreement for Seaforth.' [27] Nevertheless, the TGWU saw fit to tell Cliff that their: 'members accepted that there was a need to service the customers, and to this end, the meeting agreed to carry out this function by working in a manner in which the customer and yourselves would see the resultant substantial improvement in productivity.' [28] It would be another two months before MDHC finally admitted: 'it intended to operate as closely to an eight-hour rotating shift pattern as it is possible.' [29] They still continued to blame the dockers for the New Deal's inherent unworkability.

February 1995 also saw new problems developing for one of the former dock shop stewards, Mike Carden, who had the Broad Left's support for his candidacy for Region 6's Territorial Representative on the General Executive Council. Additionally, Carden enjoyed the support of Region 6's other GEC member, Ken Brindle, as well as full-time TGWU officials such as John Farrell. However, just a day after nominations for the GEC had closed, Carden received a phone call from Bobby Owens's secretary, informing him that his nomination could not be accepted because his membership card was not paid up to date. If this ruling had gone unchallenged, Carden's candidacy, under the rules of the union, would have ended there and then. It would have been the easiest of decisions for Jack Dempsey to simply agree with his regional secretary and declare Carden's nomination void due to lapsed membership. To Jack Dempsey's credit when he met with Carden at Transport House on Thursday 2 February 1995, he would confirm that he was in fact in compliance with election protocols. [30] Dempsey then telephoned the union's Salford office and spoke to Margaret Casey, the TGWU's regional finance officer, who accepted his verification of Carden's membership card.

The difficulties did not end there as once the election was underway, Carden was forced to contact Owens's office and the Electoral Reform Society to ask why Dock Branch 6/603 and the Torside dockers had still not received their GEC ballot papers. [31] On 16 February, Dempsey contacted Carden by phone to tell him that MDHC's Allan Price had written to Bill Morris informing him that the company would not authorise time off for Carden to attend GEC meetings, and to express their belief that he was not a suitable candidate for such a post. [32] Morris then forwarded this letter to Bobby Owens, and on Wednesday 22 February 1995, Andy Murphy of the Electoral Reform Society, contacted Carden to let him know that neither he nor Tony Nelson, another dock shop steward, were on the voting register. Eventually, they both received ballot papers. [33] In the end, Carden was successfully elected to the GEC, [34] but this did nothing to halt the slide towards the 'dark side' for the Liverpool dockers, as MDHC's bullying and intimidation continued unabated into the spring, ratified as usual by senior local officials of the TGWU.

# 18

# Torside Ltd and the March
# of the Yellow Cranes

*'You know what would have been at the back of Colin's mind? The same that was at the back of all our minds, "This is going to blow!" Because Seaforth was a time bomb! And the men reacted in different ways. Some men thought: right we'll work it at present because it's going to explode; I think that was the feeling. But they all wanted to fight. They were all waiting for the explosion because everybody knew it was just round the corner... That's why if people say it's because of Torside or wherever, I go, "No! Seaforth was ready to blow!" And if it hadn't been Torside it would have been something else.' ~ Doreen McNally\**

At the Seaforth Timber Terminal, another dispute was unfolding between the travelling Torside dockers and a set of huge yellow mobile cranes that followed them along the horizon and came with their own workers. Meanwhile, on the Container berth, the Dock Company threatened that if the dockers continued to refuse to work overtime, they would also be replaced by Torside dockers. As Bob Ritchie, a Torside shop steward, recalled: 'We wouldn't have gone in there without an agreement, everywhere we went there had to be an agreement.' [1] In addition to hiring these state-of-the-art mobile yellow cranes to discharge ships, MDHC also set-up another satellite company, comprised of roughly five men, whose purpose was to drive the new machinery around the port. This represented yet another threat to traditional dock labour, and it was agreed during a meeting at Transport House that the Liverpool dockers would not work alongside these cranes as they were not being driven by dock workers. [2]

As a Liverpool docker and MDHC shareholder, who always attended Annual General Meetings, John Ferns maintained a keen interest in the history and management of the Port of Liverpool. At the 1995 AGM, held on 11 April at the Merseyside Maritime

---

\* Bill Hunter. Workers History As Told by Those Who Made It. Merseyside Dockers, and Women of the Waterfront. Available: http://www.billhunterweb.org.uk/interviews/History_as_Told.htm

Museum, he was aware of rumours circulating that the company were considering relinquishing all stevedoring activities. In answer to a direct question from Ferns, MDHC stated that they: 'had absolutely no intention of withdrawing from stevedoring,' [3] but evidence to the contrary would come to light as quickly as Saturday 1 July. During a meeting of the Seaforth dockers at the Dockers' Club in Edinburgh Park the three Seaforth shop stewards, Mick Cullen, Terry Teague and Kevin Robinson, gave the men an update on wages and shift patterns at the Container Terminal. By this point, Robinson had already had his accreditation withdrawn by the employer, setting the tone for another angry meeting in which the men refused, unanimously, to change shifts at short notice or work longer than eight hours on nights. The dockers also decided that all future talks with MDHC must involve all three shop stewards, including Robinson. [4] Then, on Tuesday 3 July, Joe McKenzie, a Liverpool docker and chairman of the Container Terminal's Transport and General Workers' Union 6/601 Branch, wrote to the Labour Party:

> 'To bring your attention to the plight of the dock worker, not only in Liverpool, but in other ports throughout the country since the abolition of the National Dock Labour Board. We have seen a return to the bad old days of casual and part time labour, we have also seen a fall in safety standards and a dramatic rise in accidents and death in the industry.' [5]

On Friday 7 July, Kevin Robinson met with Bobby Owens, the TGWU's Regional secretary, Bobby Lamb, its local legal officer, full-time official Dave McCall and Danny Maher, the General Executive Council representative for Docks and Waterways. Owens was due to meet MDHC's Trevor Furlong to discuss the Liverpool dockers submitting a request for an official strike ballot. [6] By 10 July, Mick Cullen had decided to resign as a shop steward, and the following Saturday another mass meeting of the Seaforth dockers took place, during which Terry Teague gave a report on a meeting with MDHC's Bernard Cliff and Allan Price. Cliff did accept some of the blame for the problems at Seaforth. '50 to 60 men at the Terminal were untrainable – they could be let go to recruit about 30 replacements on 70% pay to start with. Personal contracts and derecognition could be solved.' [7] Jimmy Nolan spoke again of the need to organise an official ballot, while Tony Nelson read out the remits to the TGWU Docks District Committee from 28 July 1994, 24 October 1994 and 13 March 1995 criticising the union. It was also agreed that a delegation should travel to meet General Secretary, Bill Morris, with a view to advancing calls for an official strike ballot. [8] A week earlier, the local docks officer had written to all Liverpool dock branches explaining that he was:

> 'Writing to them today to explain the very serious situation in the Port of Liverpool at this moment in time, which carries a very realistic threat to people's jobs... The MDHC have advised members at Seaforth Container Terminal by letter that they will be dismissing people who take part in any unofficial action.' [9]

According to Monica Clua-Losada: 'The regional union official knew that he had lost credibility amongst the dockers. But in a final attempt to try and appease them, he sent the following letter two months before the 1995-1998 dispute started, warning that the dockers' jobs were at risk.' [10] By the end of July, dozens of Seaforth Container Terminal dockers had landed on the conveyor belt of MDHC disciplinary procedures. It was later reported to the Employment and Education Committee on 17 July 1996 that at this time, '172 Seaforth Container Terminal dockers, out of 220 dockers working there, were on some form of company discipline.' [11] Torside dockers were now being subjected to threats of redundancies and replacement by casuals, as well as mass disciplines that the union again failed to challenge. In an interview with Dave Cotterill, Ritchie recalled:

> 'That Jack Dempsey agreed we had reached a crisis of confidence position, and that the employer believed that the union no longer has any control over its members, and they were therefore questioning why they should recognise the union. [12]

The young Torside dockers referred to themselves as the *Torside Tigers,* and on their yellow coats they had the image of a tiger's head, a reference to their view that they worked like wild beasts. Something that the young Montreal dockers' leader, Michel Murray, would later see as wildly amusing. Nevertheless, competition from zero-hour casual workers was too great an obstacle for even the most dedicated labour force, and in another recorded interview with Dave Cotterill, dated October 1996, a young *Torside Tiger,* Steve Southers, son of Liverpool docker, Terry Southers, provided a unique insight into the nature of dock work that had been inherited by the young Torside men, explaining how his:

> '…grandfather, father and uncle had been dockers, and it seemed like a good job opportunity once Torside Ltd started recruiting, but the company was, like, family-based. I didn't really know the family. It was run by the Bradleys. They had sons and cousins, in-laws, all working for them. You had to watch every step because news would filter back.' [13]

According to the son of another Liverpool docker employed at Torside, Joe Ladd Jr:

> 'The Torside dockers were angry, but there was nothing we could do; we had no sort of protection from the union. The union weren't protecting us. So, we couldn't protect ourselves from them bringing in these twelve-hour shifts, an hour's notice if you had to work two or three or four hours extra when people had to pick their kids up after work. It was disgraceful the way we were treated.' [14]

As soon as wage negotiations were due to start, the Torside bosses disclosed that the company was not able to withstand the competitive pressures of the casual workforces that now dominated the general cargo areas of both Liverpool and Birkenhead docks, and it was decided that 20 dockers had to be made redundant. They selected the 20 candidates using a points system based on skills, attitude, quality of work, performance, versatility, attendance, timekeeping and discipline, with all of those chosen just happening to be either dockers' sons or those who had caused grievances in some way. This method of sacking workers was unacceptable to the dockers but went unchallenged by the union. The shop stewards at the time were Steve Morris and Tony Melia, who organised an official union ballot in which the majority voted to take action; only five voted against. The bosses responded by withdrawing the redundancies, and the next day some 30 Torside dockers were sent to the Canada Dock to work with non-union casuals from a company called Seaboard. The Torside dockers contacted the TGWU, who claimed that the Seaboard men were all union members, and when it was pointed out that this was definitely not the case, they were simply told, 'Just do it – just work with them.' The Torside dockers rejected the TGWU's advice to work alongside non-union labour. On 28 July 1995, the TGWU dock officer wrote again to all dock branches, providing members with an update in which the headings of each paragraph proclaimed the union's sentiments towards the dockers exactly one month before their dismissal:

> 'MDHC Seaforth Container Terminal, the company are drawing up their plans, as a result of the last industrial action... Torside are adamant that to maintain jobs, they need to cut their costs and labour by 20 men, this is a very serious situation and if allowed to continue could result in further job losses... I see this as being a very clear symptom of why we have some of the problems we now face in the port. Put quite simply the employers do not trust us.' [15]

After a lengthy, convoluted explanation of the employer's difficulties, the TGWU then got to the point, and to ensure that each docker got the message, it was all written in capital letters, as the local docks official declared:

> 'It is my responsibility as Regional Trade Group Secretary for the Docks and Waterways Group, to inform you that we now face the very real prospect of needless job losses in the Port of Liverpool. We have for too long allowed a totally undisciplined attitude to prevail which has resulted in the employer being allowed to make the following claims that there are currently men employed at the Seaforth Terminal who: refuse to train; who are not fit to do the job... these factors undoubtedly represent a very real threat to these men's jobs. I have no doubt you will understand my very deep concerns, as a priority we must build an effective workplace organisation built on democratically elected and accredited shop stewards throughout the port. The security of your job and livelihood is of paramount importance, therefore we cannot afford to ignore the reality of the current situation. I would urge you to support our union in our efforts to secure for you the just rewards that discipline and organised labour can achieve.' [16]

Within one month everyone who received this letter had been dismissed. On 18 August 1995, Jack Dempsey wrote, in response to a letter from Charlie McNally, one of the Seaforth dockers:

> The letters you refer to were not threatening letters but information bulletins and an appeal for the lay-membership to re-organise and giving the reasons why. With reference to the questions appertaining to Seaforth, these matters are being dealt with by the Shop Stewards and myself and there have, and will continue to be, meetings of the members to discuss their problems. I do not keep copies of contracts for distribution. You should ask

*Mr. Hampton, the RSCT Manager. I will advise him to require a copy. Your reference as to what this union has done for you over the last six years at LCH and the MDHC. I would suggest that your current wages and conditions would compare with any in the UK and that is down to the fact that we as a union, i.e. you, me and other members who are the one body the union have worked at maintaining standards, not always winning, but most certain not always losing and I would further suggest that the majority of your colleagues do not share the view you expressed. We will continue to strive for the best conditions and wages for all our members and I am confident you will be prominent in any struggle, as you have in the past.' [17]*

The Liverpool dockers produced their own angry and personal response to their union's continued capitulation to the Dock Company, as a leaflet titled *The Liverpool Docker* was quickly circulated. This leaflet described a different world and a different version of events, in a bitter attack on the local TGWU and its relationship with MDHC management. [18] Writing in the *Guardian* on 30 August 1995, the newspaper's shipping correspondent, David Osler, reflected on the impact of deregulation on dockers' pay and conditions post-1989, despite Norman Fowler, Margaret Thatcher's employment secretary, promising that there would be no return to: 'scenes depicted in Hollywood's *On the Waterfront*. Casual working has gone for good. Modern cargo handling systems require a permanent skilled workforce.' [19] The abolition of the National Dock Labour Board Scheme meant that every UK port was opened up to casual labour agencies, as Osler recounted how:

*'Colin Coughlin, one of the Tilbury dockers' shop stewards, and comrade to the Liverpool dockers, still leaflets the dock gates in 1995. The men in there are living in fear. Anyone contesting a dismissal is told not to bother filling in an application for an industrial tribunal because management will write out a cheque for the maximum possible compensation then and there. That's how arrogant they are.' [20]*

This, according to Osler, was the situation for dockers nationwide, at a time when, 'The Mersey Docks and Harbour Company takes on young non-union casuals with just two-days' guaranteed pay a week. [21] On 7 August 1995, Jack Dempsey, wrote to TGWU members employed by Torside Ltd. co-signed by the two shop stewards, Tony Melia and Steve Morris:

*'You are being balloted as a result of the Company's decision to declare twenty redundancies. We are opposed to these redundancies and in particular the Company's decision to insist that those made redundant must be all full-timers. This gives a number of major difficulties for example, when the part-timers were introduced, they were to supplement the full-timers! How do the part-timers get made up to full-time if the full-timers are being made redundant? The selection process only applying to full-timers means the process is flawed, 'Last in, first out', policy not applying? The points application to eight specific points without them having a rating means it applies on a subjective basis and not a factual position. Because of the foregoing we are asking you to support a 'Yes' ballot for 'strike action' and 'action short of strike'.' [22]*

Although it accepts the need to oppose redundancies by taking strike action, the letter was a strange mix of conflicting ideals, not least in its reference to 'last in, first out' as a trade union principle, and the union's argument that the part-timers should have been sacked before the full-timers, which legitimised the employer's points system. The following day, Tuesday 8 August 1995, the sudden and tragic death of Bobby Owens, the TGWU's Liverpool-born Regional secretary, was announced at the Sefton Geographical Committee. Bobby Owens was a charismatic and forceful trade unionist, who was the only lay-member ever to be appointed by the TGWU's General Executive Council to the post of regional secretary. His influence and leadership substantially transformed trade unionism, workers' organisation and the radical development of the unemployed on Merseyside and beyond. [23]

On 16 August 1995, an official strike ballot took place among Torside dockers. Torside had only been trading for three years, and yet this was the third time that the TGWU had given its support for official strike action over the treatment of its workers, to which bosses responded by writing to 60 of their dockers on 1 September, promising that their jobs would be safe if they signed a disclaimer and called off their action. The young dockers ignored this offer, which would have seen 20 of their comrades sacked. The ballot was returned with a 100% vote in favour of a strike that would begin at midnight on Friday 8 September. The day before this deadline, Jack Dempsey met the Torside dockers at the Seaforth Timber Terminal, where according to Tony Melia, the TGWU docks official: 'Tried to persuade the workforce to call off their strike action on the basis that it would change nothing,' suggesting: 'In a battle, you always lose a few troops along the way,' [24] before advising them to accept the compulsory redundancies demanded by the company. [25] However, the *Torside Tigers* were unmoved by the union's threats, reiterating their intention to engage in an official strike against their employer. [26]

At a meeting of the Port Shop Stewards on Tuesday 5 September, the TGWU informed the stewards that they would not enforce the ballot for action against the redundancy situation facing the Torside dockers. The union said Torside was said to be losing £79,000 a year, and it was claimed that a strike would put them into liquidation. At this meeting, the TGWU official again repeated the call for a no-strike clause, together with the acceptance of at least 20 redundancies. [27] At another meeting attended by all union representatives in Transport House on Thursday 7 September, those assembled were informed, 'That Torside Ltd was to seek voluntary liquidation the following day and would therefore cease trading in the port. All 80 dockers would effectively be made redundant.' [28] Then, at 10am on Friday 8 September 1995, Torside Ltd withdrew the 20 redundancy notices, as for the first time in what felt like decades, it was the employer who backed down. There was, however, still a sense of foreboding in the air, with Tony Melia writing at the time: 'although this was a victory, we still felt that there would be repercussions…' [29]

# PART THREE:
## The 1995 Dispute

# 19
# Monday 25<sup>th</sup> September 1995: The Dispute Begins

*'They should have got the lawyers working on it because it goes back to 1989, the breaking of our system, you know, registered dockworkers and then the employers can do what they want. The union's finished now in Liverpool. It's not broken as an organisation; our local officials are broken. The main fella that signed this deal and said it's a good deal before we started all the trouble, he's just disappeared off the scene, an employer's lackey.' ~ Richard Gerrard\**

On the morning of Monday 25 September 1995, a meeting of the Region 6 Docks and Waterways Trade Group Committee was taking place at Transport House, Liverpool. The union's dock official reported on problems at Torside Ltd, before a resolution from 6/603 Branch called for him to be removed from all negotiating responsibilities. The branch also confirmed the dock workers' view that if Torside did go into liquidation, the dockers there should be re-employed by the Mersey Dock and Harbour Company. [1] Jimmy Nolan, chairman of the Docks & Waterways Committee, reiterated to port representatives that the Torside dockers would not be allowed to lose their jobs. [2] This meeting was followed by a celebration for the Labour MP, Eddie Loyden, a former port worker, who was going to be presented with the TGWU's prestigious Gold Badge Award. The ceremony would be attended by some of the most influential union officers, members of National and Regional Committee, Members of Parliament, the General Executive Council and countless shop stewards from the docks. While the food and drink flowed in the union building that afternoon something else was unfolding on the docks.

A small vessel berthed at Canada Dock, *M.V. Sygna*, was about to set in motion a chain of events that would trigger a conflict lasting two years and four months when 500

---

\* Richard Gerrard (foreman) speaking in an interview for the Dockers' Charter, 20 November 1995. Available: http://www.labournet.net/docks2/9511/gerrard.htm

Liverpool dockers were sacked for refusing to cross a picket line. It became a conflict that would have extraordinary consequences for so many good men and women and their families. It began over an innocuous argument regarding two hours' overtime at the ship. In Liverpool's city centre, Transport House was quite literally heaving with the *great and the good of the political and trade union world*. It was a *who's who* of men and women who held power in the TGWU. Some of those celebrating Eddie Loyden's achievements had been in attendance at a General Executive Council meeting the week before. Essentially, everyone capable of resolving a minor dispute was present in the union's Liverpool office that afternoon.

Dock Company management were present across numerous berths and companies in the port, and it was two of their supervisors who insisted that dockers on the *Sygna* had to work overtime. Normally, dockers would be given two hours' warning and then work in two-hour blocks, as per the employer's agreement with the union, but that afternoon they were given just half an hour's notice and told that they would only be required to work one hour. Some of the men claimed that this notice was too short, and that they had already made arrangements for the evening, one young docker said that he needed to collect his children. Jimmy Nolan was later to say: 'it was two MDHC supervisors who asked the Torside dockers to work overtime,' the men asked if: '...they were on the correct rate of overtime?' The supervisors said: "No." It was engineered by the MDHC.' Nolan also stated that this original refusal to pay the full overtime rate was, 'not Torside's, but MDHC's.' [3] The five dockers who refused to work overtime that afternoon were sacked, along with a further 24 who stopped work in solidarity. [4] In a radio interview given in 1997, Peter Jones, MDHC's Port Operations director, refuted the claim that the company had any involvement at the beginning of the dispute: 'That can be established by talking to the managers at Torside. There was absolutely no involvement from Mersey Docks and Harbour Company when the dismissals at that company took place.' [5] Kevin Robinson, a Seaforth shop steward, contradicted Jones's statement:

> *The fact that came to light was that the supervisors on that particular Torside operation were Mersey Docks and Harbour Company personnel, and they were the superintendents that told the men to work...'* [6]

According to journalist and writer, John Pilger, the trap had been set:

> *Because the overtime dispute was not theirs, the dockers' refusal to cross the Torside picket line was illegal under Margaret Thatcher's anti-trade union laws. Mersey Docks and Harbour Company claimed that it was 'entirely independent' of Torside. This meant that the dockers could be sacked for 'secondary' picketing. But to those who knew the life of the port, there was no doubt that Torside was merely a device set up to enable the principal company to disassociate itself from labour practices that echoed the discredited past.'* [7]

In another record of these events, it was stated that the Torside dockers were being paid almost by the hour, with little or no notice provided for overtime working, [8] and in a later report into the dock dispute, dated 11 November 1996, Dave McCall, the TGWU Regional secretary, described the dispute as occurring after: 'the five dockers left the ship to go into the dock canteen on that Monday evening, 25 September 1995, they were met by Bernard Bradley, the Managing Director of Torside, who sacked them.' The other dockers on the vessel were also sacked when they refused to return to work. In evidence given to the Education and Employment Select Committee on 21 May 1996, Bernard Bradley recalled that:

> 'He received a telephone call at about 3.20pm from Bob Jones, of Liverpool Cargo Handling, an MDHC Supervisor, who told me that five Torside men had walked off the ship, gone to the canteen and the work on the ship had stopped. I was very disappointed. I complained they had not used set procedures... In my mind, I dismissed them at that point. About three weeks earlier, a similar situation had arisen which was settled by the steward contacting me and the men were paid. On this occasion, it appeared to me that these five men specifically wanted a dispute.' [9]

Shortly after the dispute began one of the young Torside shop stewards, Tony Melia, telephoned Mike Carden, TGWU General Executive Council member and a derecognised dock shop steward. Carden was at home at the time, following an accident at the Seaforth Timber Terminal, where he had been working alongside the Torside dockers for some time. As their GEC representative he advised them earlier on their official strike ballot in August that was opposed by the local union dock official. That evening, he urged Tony Melia to tell the men to return to work and not to strike. He also asked Melia to speak to Jimmy Davies Jr and get him to contact his father for further advice. Later that evening, Jimmy Davies Sr told his son to get the men back on the ship, and some years later, he reflected on that conversation with his son, during which he stressed the importance of 'negotiation rather than picketing.' [10] For his part, Tony Melia was to recall that:

> 'It was probably me who rang Mike Carden, as I presume Jimmy would have spoken to his dad. There was no choice to go back to work, as we were all sacked. When I asked Bernard Bradley to reinstate the men on the day, his words were akin to, "You're all sacked, and if I'm made to take you back, I'm spewing it." I think I remember the men turning up for work the next day but being refused entry.' [11]

According to Jack Dempsey, at around 6pm on the day of the dispute, he picked up a phone call from Tony Melia, who wanted to speak to Jimmy Davies Sr, only for the line to be redirected to Dempsey's office. Melia was reluctant to speak to the docks' official, but he did tell him that five dockers had been sacked, and how they had been supported by another 20 men, who were then sacked. [12] Breaking away from the celebrations that evening at Transport House, Dempsey told Melia that he would meet him at 8.30am the following morning, in the office of Bernard Bradley. 'I was due to be there in any case,' he said, [13] having previously arranged to meet with the Torside boss to discuss another docker's dismissal, Steve Southers. [14] That same evening, Jimmy Nolan attempted to try and 'keep the lid' on events as they unfolded at the Canada Dock. He was well aware that if a dispute did take place, it would eventually involve every docker employed in the port. Nolan later told the Education and Employment Committee:

> 'I stated very clearly, "Bernard, why are you dismissing young people? If you have got a problem with MDHC with regard to the financial side of your operation, don't be taking it out on the young people of Torside. If we can assist you in trying to get the Mersey Docks and Harbour Company to fund more, we will do that, because we are rather disturbed that the Torside labour is still in receipt of no pension benefits or sick pay." Bernard Bradley assured me after approximately two hours' discussion with him that he would be reinstating that labour force.' [15]

The following day, shop stewards met at Transport House to discuss the *Sygna* incident. Jimmy Nolan chaired the meeting and representatives from all areas of the Port of Liverpool attended, as did Jack Dempsey. It was put to the dock official that the disciplinary measures against the first five sacked Torside men must be rescinded, even if it meant using MDHC to put pressure on Bradley. Dempsey agreed. [16] According to one group of academics writing in 2002, this critical moment demonstrated weakness on the part of the stewards and the unbridled militancy from the young Torside dockers:

> 'The Torsiders found themselves in conflict over strategy not just with their paid officials. There was also disagreement between them and the main body of shop stewards representing the MDHC dockers. The stewards' committee suggested they 'keep a lid' on the dispute, while seeking a negotiated resolution, but the young Torsiders argued that this would achieve little and that their action should be spread to the whole body of Liverpool dockers.' [17]

In evidence to the Commons Select Committee the Torside boss, Bernard Bradley, claimed that when Jack Dempsey met him on the docks the following morning, he offered to reinstate the Torside dockers, [18] only for Dempsey to reject the proposal. In his book, *Hidden Agendas*, John Pilger wrote of Bradley's actions: 'having passed the offer to a regional official of the TGWU, Jack Dempsey, he heard nothing. The Torside dockers were never told about the offer. Had they been told, Mersey Docks would never have had a pretext to get rid of the main workforce.' [19] One of the sacked dockers, Kevin Bilsborrow, later commented that Dempsey:

> '...had everyone's number in his Filofax that he carries and there, lo and behold, in front of him were 500 dockworkers, and he had the secret buttoned-up that he had the five Torside lads reinstated and he never told a mass meeting. We had another mass meeting, he never told that mass meeting. Why did he not inform, at least the labour force, that he had the five Torside lads reinstated and that really there was no need for the dispute? So, it is gross negligence on behalf of the TGWU officer.' [20]

In 1996, Tony Melia recalled that the night the Torside dockers were sacked, 25 men moved from the ship to the canteen area to wait for Bradley, with five going inside and the rest staying outside to smoke and talk between themselves:

> 'When Mr Bradley arrived at the Canada [Dock], he just walked straight into the canteen and the five men sitting down. He just said, "The five of you are sacked. Go on, I don't want you anymore." So, they were all just gobsmacked. So, when the eighteen outside said, "what's goin' on?" they said, "He never even asked us what's wrong, he just sacked us," and they said, "Well, we're not goin' back to work because you've been sacked for nothing." So, one of them actually run over to Mr Bradley before he got in his car and said, "What's happening?" and he said, "Them men are sacked, and if you don't get back to work, you're sacked as well." [21]

Melia initially made contact with Jack Dempsey on the evening of Monday 25 September, at approximately 7.20pm. During this telephone conversation, the TGWU officer told him: 'Oh, I knew this was going to happen – return to casual labour. I will get in touch with Bernard Bradley to set-up a meeting.' [22] Jimmy Nolan later claimed that when he contacted Bradley directly, he was assured that the sacked dockers would be reinstated, [23] and according to Bradley's own testimony to the Commons Select Committee:

> 'He telephoned Jack Dempsey of the TGWU that evening, Monday 25 September, at approximately 7.30pm, and told him what had happened. I agreed to meet him at 9.30am the following morning to deal with the five men who had been dismissed by way of appeal, which was normal procedure... That was where it was left. I did not expect what happened the following morning... I stayed at the office until approximately 9.30am, when Jack Dempsey arrived. At that point, I conceded to Jack Dempsey that to stop the strike the five men could be reinstated, and Jack Dempsey said that he would go out to the men and see what he could do. Dempsey returned, I think, about 2.00pm that afternoon. He said he was unable to proceed with the appeal for the five men.' [24]

Bradley also claimed that he faxed a letter to Dempsey at Transport House to confirm that he had offered to reinstate the men, [25] but the TGWU claimed at the time that 'there was no such fax.' [26] On the evening of the dispute, at around 9.30pm, Dempsey telephoned Bradley to warn him: 'the issue might escalate into a full stoppage of the Docks, unless he agreed to take back all the lads... He was reluctantly prepared to deal with the five through the disciplinary procedure, and on this basis, he would reconsider reinstating the five if everybody else was back in work at 8.00am the following morning.' [27] Dempsey was due to meet the dockers at 6.30am the next day.[28] That Monday evening he claimed he had telephoned Melia's house but got no answer; he then phoned Steve Morris, the other Torside shop steward, and left a message with his father. Dempsey asked his own son, also a Torside docker, to speak to the shop stewards at the 6.30am meeting, giving him his mobile phone so that he could contact him directly. [29]

Within a week of the dispute starting, according to Dave McCall, the TGWU Regional secretary, Dempsey began writing his report for the next Trade Group meeting as early as 6 October 1995. He wished for it to be stated clearly in writing that he had attempted to intervene, 'and had been told by the employer that if they returned to work on 25 September [Monday] or by 26 September [Tuesday], he [Bradley, the Torside boss] would have accepted them all back.' [30] Dempsey's report was presented to the Regional Committee on Tuesday 17 October 1995, and a copy was also submitted to the Region 6 Docks and Waterways Trade Group Committee on Monday 6 November 1995. Despite having written on events that were still reasonably recent, Dempsey would later deny that he was ever offered any re-instatement option, after Danny Maher, the National Docks and Waterways Section General Executive Council member and leader of the Liverpool Tug Boatmen, challenged the docks official's account of the first 24 hours of the dispute. [31] Dempsey claimed that the minutes of this Regional Committee were incorrect, [32] despite having previously confirmed them as, 'being a true and correct record' of the meeting:

> *Jack Dempsey confirmed that he had visited the picket line on Tuesday 26 September 1995, following discussions with the company [Torside], and advised the men that they would be taken back if they returned to work. Following a further conversation with Mr. Bradley [Torside Ltd. Managing Director] that evening, Mr. Bradley agreed to reinstate all the men if they returned to work on Wednesday 27 September 1995 at 8.00am.'* [33]

Following further queries of the report, the minutes were to record that: 'Bro. Dempsey stated that his understanding of the matter was by Tuesday afternoon, Mr. B. Bradley would have taken all the [Torside] men back into work.' [34]

# 20
# Tuesday 26<sup>th</sup> September 1995: Day Two

*'We believe in the value of negotiation, not confrontation. We have worked successfully for 15 years with the T&G in Liverpool in improving efficiency and modernising working practices. The men in the dispute want a return to the old jobs-for-life culture before dock regulation in 1989 and that is not on.' ~ MDHC\**

In a letter addressed to Bill Morris, on 10 October 1995, Tony Melia stated that the day after the Torside dispute began: 'our steward met Mr. Bradley and asked for the immediate reinstatement of the eighteen men...' [1] On Tuesday the Torside shop stewards were in a meeting with dockers when their boss, Bernard Bradley, burst into the room and sacked them all on the spot. Among the five dockers originally sacked were Jimmy Davies Jr, the son of the Port Shop Stewards secretary, as well as three young relatives of shop stewards Billy and John Jenkins, the sons of the TGWU docks official, the former Regional secretary, the docks District Officer, the Torside managing director and numerous other dock shop stewards' relatives. However, despite this plethora of close family connections, the TGWU dock official found it impossible to relay messages to their very *influential fathers*, telling them that if their sons returned to work, they would be reinstated. In fact, on the morning of Tuesday 26 September 1995, Bradley had allocated work to his dockers. [2] According to Jack Dempsey's version of events, he arrived at Bernard Bradley's office at around 8.20am to find:

> *'All of the lads who had turned up for work that morning had gone home. None of the shop stewards were present. Bradley and his son, James, were present and prepared to continue with the meeting about the previous day's incident in the absence of the shop stewards. I tried to persuade him to take everyone back on the basis that we could sort out any problems within the procedures. He made it clear that our members were already*

---

* MDHC spokesperson, speaking to The Financial Times (21 May 1996)

*out of procedure and that the incident on Monday afternoon could easily have been sorted out without a stoppage. He was not prepared even to consider taking back the five who had originally stopped work. However, he would take back all the others if they returned to work.' [3]*

The union official said that he returned to his own office and tried to contact the shop stewards without success. As the Torside shop stewards conveyed the reinstatement message to their members at 8am, they advised that the matter could be negotiated, and that the 60 remaining Torside dockers should go back to work while talks proceeded. However, before any decision could be made, the meeting was interrupted by Bradley and his personnel manager, who appeared at the canteen door at 8.10am and proceeded to walk from table to table, writing down workers' names and sacking them for not having commenced work that morning. [4] That same day, Jack Dempsey was called to a dispute at Heysham Docks, in addition to having a scheduled meeting of the Sefton Geographical District Committee to attend, [5] and when he contacted Bradley for an update, he was told that nobody had turned up for work and there were now pickets on the Huskisson and Canada gates. [6] According to Professor David Meyer's account: 'Faced with their sudden and unexpected sackings, the Torsiders responded by immediately setting up a picket line at their usual dock entrance. They displayed TGWU strike placards, left behind from a previous dispute.' [7]

Dempsey would inform the TGWU Regional Committee that at approximately 1.45pm on Tuesday 25 September, he went to the picket line at Huskisson Dock and received abuse, even though he advised the men that they would be taken back if they returned to work. [8] He had objected to there being official TGWU picket posters attached to the fence, instructing that they be taken down. [9] According to Bob Ritchie, a Torside shop steward, Dempsey also visited the picket at Canada Dock that same afternoon but gave no advice regarding reinstatement. One Torside docker recalled how: 'The official's car screeched to a halt, he jumped out, pushed Torside docker, Tony Fallon, out the way to get at this poster we had up on the gate, it stated *TGWU picket line*. On the top was the word 'official,' but we had bent the 'official' over so it couldn't be seen.' [10] Dempsey asked Jimmy Davies Jr where he could find the shop stewards before going to the Canada gate and speaking to Bob Ritchie, they told him that they were at Mike Carden's house. Dempsey said that he then told Ritchie: 'Bradley had offered to reinstate everybody except the original five, but I was confident that if there was a full return from the rest, I might be able to get the rest also. Bob said that without the five being included, there was no way that there would be a return to work.' [11]

In another statement that Dempsey gave to John Hendy QC in 2005, he claimed that he was told by Ritchie, 'Jack, this is all being done behind your back, lad.' [12] Carden would confirm that the two Torside shop stewards, Tony Melia and Steve Morris, did in fact visit his house for assistance with drawing up a leaflet for the strike, and to collect TGWU picket line posters that were left over from the 1989 strike. Both Torside stewards were concerned by the fact that they were just standing at the dock gates with no information to give to anyone about their dispute, and so the leaflets that were typed out told how they had had an official ballot to protect 80 jobs two weeks before:

*'We are on strike to regain our jobs. We call upon all trade unionists in the Port to refuse to work with casual labour and to respect our picket lines. We only seek permanent employment on fair rates of pay and conditions.'* [13]

Melia later confirmed that he and Morris arrived at Carden's house and, 'drafted a leaflet up together to be printed up at the Picket [the Unemployed Centre on Hardman Street, Liverpool].' He did not recall personally receiving any posters but did say: 'some must have been on display at the Huskisson Dock and Canada Dock gates, as Dempsey tore them down when he passed.' [14] More importantly, Melia emphasised the view that the Torside dockers still had a legal mandate to withdraw their labour as they had, only a fortnight before, balloted successfully for official industrial action which, it could be argued, was still active when the Torside dockers walked off the *Sygna*: 'We had already balloted to go on strike and won over our pay deal, so arguably it was not unofficial, although we were now at the gates as we had been sacked. We were all in limbo as to our official position.' [15] At 2pm that afternoon, Dempsey joined two shop stewards, Terry Teague and Frank Lannigan, at a meeting with MDHC's Bernard Cliff and Allan Price. [16]

According to John Hendy's submissions, after Frank Lannigan expressed concerns regarding the Torside situation and the risk of Dock Company employees becoming involved, Cliff stated plainly that Torside was an independent company, and that if the MDHC dockers allowed themselves to be 'dragged in' to the dispute, they were in danger of 'dismissing themselves.' [17] At the close of the meeting the dock official informed Teague that he would be speaking with Torside management again to try and resolve the matter, [18] and Teague observed that at no time during the course of the MDHC meeting did Dempsey mention that a reinstatement offer had been made by Bernard Bradley. [19] At 4pm, Dempsey attended a meeting with TGWU members at Heysham Docks and, later that day, a meeting of the Shop Stewards Committee took place to discuss the Torside problem. [20] Dempsey insisted he had again unsuccessfully attempted to contact Tony Melia and Steve Morris by telephone that Tuesday night, [21] while dockers such as Joe Ladd Jr, one of the Torsiders working at MDHC's Timber Terminal at the time, said that he did not even hear about the dispute until earlier that morning. He recalled that the Torside shop stewards told him and other Torside dockers:

*'...to picket the Canada gate first, and then they moved to the Huskisson gate and that brought the Nelson Freight lads out. My dad was at the Norse Irish and I didn't think there was a picket line there, but one of the lads said there was a picket line set up and those lads came out. ...I believe that if it wasn't the dispute at Torside that started, it would have started on Seaforth anyway, as they were having their own problems.'* [22]

It is important to remember that many of the Merseyside Port Shop Stewards had, since their return to work following the national dock strike in 1989, been derecognised and / or disciplined for their trade union activities by either the MDHC or the TGWU. As a group, they had lost the right to call meetings during working periods, and now met, and called mass meetings of dockers, at Transport House at weekends. Their policy was to ignore the actions of MDHC and the TGWU in relation to recognition, and on that Tuesday some of them met, under the chairmanship of Jimmy Nolan, with Jack Dempsey at Transport House, and again later that afternoon at a local pub, Nina's Bar (previously known as Bloods). The meeting in the pub was practical in the sense that it was the nearest place to the Torside main picket line, allowing for as many of the stewards to attend as possible. Some of the derecognised shop stewards recalled that the consensus among those at Nina's was that the priority should be getting the Torside dockers back to work, with the belief being that they could arrange a compromise with Bradley that involved the original five sacked dockers going through some form of disciplinary procedure as a condition of reinstatement. [23]

The Port Shop Stewards recognised the potential implications that a dispute could have for the rest of the port. A full-blown strike over two hours' overtime did not carry the same principled resonance as many of the other issues that had dominated the last decade on the docks, but this did not change the fact that the Torside dockers had every right to fight for their jobs. However, despite the sackings, almost half of them were still manning ships on various berths across the port. Ultimately, the sacked dockers could not be stopped from picketing any berth that they were assigned work on, and the Merseyside Port Shop Stewards would make no attempt to challenge them.

# 21
# Wednesday 27<sup>th</sup> September 1995: Day Three

*'...the real cause of trouble was the TGWU's long-term inability to put down solid organisational roots in the docks. History always counted for much in the closed world of the docks, and history was always working against the TGWU.' ~ J. Philips\**

At 6.30am on Wednesday 27 September 1995, Jack Dempsey received a phone call from his son, who was employed as a dockworker at Torside Ltd. The union official was told that the planned Torside dockers meeting had not taken place, and that those who turned up had simply been given copies of a picket duty roster. [1] Dempsey then telephoned Bernard Bradley, the Torside managing director, at 8am to let him know: 'he had not been able to speak to the shop stewards to pass on the reinstatement offer, but he would meet them very shortly. Bradley said that he wasn't interested, and in any case, reinstatement was no longer on the table.' [2] The dock official recalled that some of the Torside dockers met him at Transport House within the hour, and he was asked to establish whether or not Bradley was prepared to talk. [3] Steve Morris, Tony Melia, Bob Ritchie, Tony Farrell, Joe Morris and Steve Southers were all present and yet the union official would later claim: 'he could not contact the shop stewards, and had he been able to, then he could have got everybody back in work.' [4] The Torside dockers made it clear that they would be available to meet Bradley any time, day or night. [5] Dempsey then asked those present:

> *'...for the authority to negotiate on their behalf. The delegation asked whether the company was still trading. I replied that it was. They asked whether the company was prepared to talk, if we contacted them, they might consider it. At that point, I was still*

---

\* J. Philips, The Great Alliance: Economic Recovery and the Problems of Power 1945- 1951. Pluto Press, 1966 (p.133) *hopeful, if I could get the cooperation of the shop stewards, we might get some resolution from the employer. At the end of the meeting, I asked whether I had authority to speak for them. They replied that they'd have to go back to the lads and seek their permission for the negotiations.' [6]*

Jack Dempsey tried to contact Bradley, who was in Bristol for a funeral, and so he spoke to his son, James, instead: 'We were prepared to talk to the company at any time... Bro. Maher was also present. The meeting ended and I returned to the picket line, no mention yet again that any men would be reinstated. The next contact I had with Bro. Dempsey was on Thursday 28th September 1995 at a mass meeting at the Dockers' Club, yet again, no mention of reinstatement.' [7] This account was corroborated by another Torside docker, Joe Morris, who stated, 'There was never any mention of the five men returning to work, or any meetings arranged,' [8] and Steve Morris said the Torside delegation then went back to the docks. [9] While this follow-up meeting was taking place, the Torside dockers had already placed a picket line at Seaforth Container Terminal where, according to Terry Teague (one of the Seaforth shop stewards): 'the Torside pickets did not immediately ask for support from their fellow dockworkers.' [10] Torside pickets did not arrive at Seaforth until Wednesday 27 September, and even then, there was no request for involvement. At the Container Terminal gates, they distributed literature and made Teague and other Seaforth dockers aware of the circumstances surrounding their dispute placing official picket notices on adjacent walls. [11]

At this time the Huskisson picket did not have any effect because the Nelson Freight dockers were already at work; later that evening the Torside dockers discussed plans to picket Seaforth. As one of the Torside men recalled: 'There was arguments amongst them as to the rights and wrongs; should we put it on the main gate at Seaforth or just on the Timber berth, which was their working area. But bearing in mind we had already been sacked, there was no way we were going to gain access to the dock estate to picket the Timber berth, so it was decided the picket would go on the main entrance at Seaforth.' [12] The following morning, a picket line was placed at Seaforth that the MDHC dockers refused to cross. Of that Wednesday afternoon, Dave Sinclair, who was to become the trusted photographer of the dockers' struggle from the start, recalled how he:

*'...was phoned by the Socialist Worker; they told me something had kicked off on the docks and could I get a picture. After driving around a bit, I eventually found about five dockers somewhere around the Gladstone gate, I asked what was going on and could I take a picture. They told me, I think it was Tony Melia, that it was really sensitive, a meeting was going on right then in Lu Lu's [Nina's Bar, and also known as Bloods] Bar on the Dock Road and they would really rather I didn't take a picture. They said if the problem wasn't sorted there'd be a proper picket at Seaforth the next morning. I was there the next morning. It was really unprofessional of me to not get a picture that afternoon, but it was like a group of mates asking, and they had their reasons, so out of respect I agreed.' [13]*

The same derecognised and recognised stewards who had met with the Torside dockers on the Tuesday reconvened the following day, to receive updates and discuss the situation. The outcome of this meeting was an agreement to support the striking dockers in establishing a picket line for their fellow Torside employees at Seaforth Timber Terminal who were still working on the docks. There was, however, the issue of gaining access to the Timber Terminal, situated on the westside of the docks, without crossing the picket at the main dock entrance, which was also the way into the Seaforth Container Terminal. As Bob Ritchie explained:

*'It was lashing down with rain. We were taking secondary action, but the port police allowed us to stand there and insisted we had yellow coats on because it was dark at that particular time in the morning. Although some men crossed, the bulk of the men went to see their own stewards to ask what to do.' There was a few heated exchanges – "You shouldn't be picketing here, you should be at the timber berth!" – but when we gave them the argument that we couldn't get through the gate, they were alright about it. At 11am, we adjourned to Transport House and Dempsey was invited to speak, but he refused to.'* [14]

In Dave McCall's official report as Regional secretary, it was recorded that Jack Dempsey confirmed that the Torside dockers wanted him to organise a meeting with the employer. [15] At around 4.30pm, Dempsey picked up Bobby Lamb, the TGWU legal officer, on the way to another scheduled meeting at Heysham Dock:

*'We arrived at Heysham at 6.00pm. After the meeting, we were driving back to Liverpool. Bob Lamb phoned Dave Glassey [ACAS] who had tried to contact Bernard Bradley but was also unable to speak to him… My son, Mike [a Torside docker], told me that the Torside lads were going to picket the Seaforth gate on the following morning, Thursday 28 September.'* [16]

As he drove back to Liverpool from Heysham, Dempsey was aware that a meeting was taking place on the Dock Road involving some of the shop stewards, and it was there that the decision was made to support the Torside picket line on the Seaforth gate the following morning. [17] According to Tony Melia: 'We made it clear through the media that we intended to picket the Seaforth Container Terminal. On Thursday 28 September, still no approach was made to us by our union official. On the Thursday, we did set up picket lines at Seaforth and were welcomed by the police.' [18] During negotiations with MDHC, accusations that the shop stewards had allowed Torside dockers to picket the Seaforth Container Terminal were firmly denied. At one point during these talks, MDHC's Bernard Cliff proceeded to catalogue events as he saw them, charging that there had been:

*'An organised refusal to work [during] days off at Christmas and bank holidays, as well as refusing to allow Torside men to replace them on lower rates of pay. Then, on Wednesday 26 September 1995, the stewards invited people from Torside to come to picket Seaforth.'* [19]

Frank Lannigan and Jimmy Davies vehemently objected to Cliff's accusations, informing the managing director that, 'no meeting took place to organise pickets at Seaforth.' [20] It is inconceivable that these young dockers would have established a picket line against their own fathers and relatives without at least having a conversation about it first. The Torside dockers had never worked at the Seaforth Container Terminal, but if a picket was set up there, it was the duty of the shop stewards on the berth to stand alongside them when it started, not just to offer support, but also to explain the situation to their members. Like everyone else on the docks, the Seaforth men believed that the dispute would be resolved within a couple of days, not realising that the situation was already spiralling out of control.

# 22
# Thursday 28<sup>th</sup> September 1995: Day Four

*'There is no reason why we can't set the National Audit Office onto the MDHC. Let's have professionals look at how they have been spending public money; let's make them account for the way they have spent the money to some of the most vicious accountants in the country.' ~ Marie Eagle MP\**

That morning black clouds unleashed an unremitting rainstorm on the Torside dockers as they established their picket line at the Seaforth Container Terminal gates. It was before 7am on Thursday 28 September 1995. [1] They were joined by the three Seaforth shop stewards, Terry Teague, Kevin Robinson and Frank Lannigan, as well as a number of the Merseyside Port Shop Stewards, including Jimmy Nolan, Jimmy Davies, Bobby Morton and Herbie Hollerhead. The Seaforth stewards were there to ensure that they made up part of the six pickets allowed by industrial legislation to attempt to stop vehicles and explain to dockers and other port workers why they should not cross the picket line. Jack Dempsey, the Transport and General Workers' Union dock official, would later claim:

> *'He got a phone call from one of the dockers, to let him know that there was a picket at Seaforth. He said that some of the lads were going across the picket and others were refusing to cross. I then got a call from Bernard Cliff. He was extremely concerned about the situation and wanted to make contact with Jack Adams to arrange an urgent meeting.' [2]*

---

\* Marie Eagle MP, speaking to a fringe meeting during the 1997 Labour Party Conference (via BBC Radio Merseyside audio tapes, Ref: Docks April 1997)

This ease of contact that the union official describes is interesting, considering the difficulties he supposedly faced in trying to communicate with dockers over the preceding three days. Reflecting on the first day of picketing, one of the Seaforth shop stewards recalled:

> '...the MDHC, were part-owners of Torside Ltd. They also told me... their dispute was official. Finally, they asked that I did not cross their official picket line. My view was that I believed that the dismissed men were wrongly dismissed and that if the trade union was backing it officially, then I had no problem in supporting the Torside dismissed members of my union.' [3]

According to union official Dempsey's account of that Thursday morning:

> 'I went into the office at Transport House, Liverpool, and met dockers' leader, Jimmy Nolan, in the canteen about 9am. I asked Jimmy what was happening. He said that the lads had all refused to cross the picket line, and that there was a mass meeting at the Dockers' Club at 11am. I asked who was speaking at the meeting, and Jimmy replied that since the meeting wasn't being held in our building, it was fuck-all to do with me. I said, "So, I am not invited to the meeting?" Jimmy said, "No, it is unofficial."' [4]

The committee that met with the men at the Dockers' Club included Bobby Morton, Frank Lannigan, Herbie Hollerhead, Jimmy Davies, Jimmy Nolan, Kevin Robinson and Terry Teague. Notes taken by Robinson recorded that Tony Melia, a Torside shop steward, gave a report, while Tony Russell, representing the Nelson Freight men, who had now been sacked for originally refusing to cross the Torside picket line, clarified the dockers' position there. Lannigan brought everyone up to date with what was said during Tuesday's meeting with Bernard Cliff, [5] and Terry Teague confirmed that:

> 'Jack Dempsey was in attendance. Once the meeting had started, it was addressed by members of the joint shop stewards and the Torside stewards. I addressed the meeting in my capacity as shop steward. My contribution was based on my belief that the TGWU was supporting the dismissed membership and it was an official dispute. At no time before, during or after that meeting did Mr Dempsey make me aware of any reinstatement offer regarding the original dismissed Torside membership. Similarly, Mr Dempsey did not participate in the meeting and at no time offered any advice or instructions regarding the conduct of the meeting. I can firmly state that if I had known of a reinstatement offer being made on Tuesday 26 September 1995, then events of Thursday 28 September 1995 would have been different.' [6]

Jimmy Nolan, speaking as chairman of the port stewards, offered all dockers the opportunity to be part of their emergency committee, demonstrating a genuine belief in rank-and-file democracy and accountability shared by the majority of Port Shop Stewards. By this time, most of the stewards had been barred from holding elected office by the Dock Company and the TGWU. Local labour historian, Eric Taplin, was conscious of the significance of the need to provide a clear definition for the structure that Nolan and the stewards were now establishing. Taplin studied the development of the Merseyside Port Shop Stewards over many years, and it was he who eventually came to label them, from this point, the *'Disputes Committee.'* [7] Dempsey refused the invitation to speak at the meeting, [8] although he did have a conversation with Jack Adams, the TGWU deputy general secretary, later that same day, of which he said:

> *'I think I painted the whole picture for him, including the discussions with Bradley. I recall telling Jack I could possibly have had the lads back on the previous morning… Jack wasn't very happy about meeting the company, but he agreed to meet the lads later on. During the afternoon, I also made contact with the national secretary, John Connolly. I had been trying to reach him since Tuesday, but he hadn't been in his office. I filled him in on the details.' [9]*

Another meeting took place at Transport House at 2pm, where it was reported that Jimmy Nolan and Danny Maher spoke with Jack Adams, Jack Dempsey and Bobby Lamb, the local TGWU legal officer, ahead of a 4pm appointment that the three union officials had with the MDHC. [10] Dempsey recalled: 'Jimmy Nolan wasn't very happy about me being there… he asked whether Torside was even still trading. I phoned James Bradley, who confirmed that the company had ceased trading.' [11] Adams urged the dockers to return to work as soon as possible, and to resolve the dispute inside the gates, 'making it very clear that they were going into a strike which they would lose. One of the stewards asked, "What would you do?" Adams replied: "If I was in your position, I'd get back to work as soon as possible." [12] Dempsey would later state for the record: 'Torside members took the decision to picket the Seaforth Gate, and the majority of MDHC employees refused to cross the picket line,' [13] but according to Terry Teague:

> *'Torside pickets did not ask for support until Thursday 28 September, and the decision of the MDHC men to get involved was taken at the meeting in the Dockers' Club that day. I would estimate a group of twenty-plus people were there. At the end of a three-hour meeting, everybody agreed that Jack Dempsey should continue discussions with Bernard Bradley and the MDHC.' [14]*

That evening, letters were sent out by Dock Company through hired couriers, instructing dockers to return to work by 7am the next day, otherwise it would be taken that they were 'dismissing themselves.' [15] TGWU officials arrived to meet MDHC bosses at their new head office in Maritime House, situated just inside the gates of the Seaforth Container Terminal. There, Adams, Lamb and Dempsey were received by company directors, Bernard Cliff, Bill Hogg, Ken Wharton, and Allan Price, MDHC's personnel manager. Adams insisted that he alone would speak on the TGWU's behalf, [16] with Dempsey recalling how: 'Jack Adams raised the Torside issue at least once, but Bernard Cliff simply insisted that they had nothing to do with Torside. Bernard Cliff did ask me at the end of the meeting whether I had got anywhere with Torside. I told him, "Nothing that will make any difference at this stage."' [17] It was during this meeting that Cliff told those present that if MDHC dockers did not return to work by seven o'clock the following morning, they would be sacked. At this critical moment in the early days of the dispute this meeting provided Jack Dempsey with an opportunity to inform the Port Authority and TGWU officials that there had indeed, been an offer by Torside, '…to take back all the workers.' [18] Of this meeting Dempsey recalled: 'We were advised by the Dock Company that Torside had ceased trading.' [19] Different versions of the events of this day continue to exist, with one official record noting that at midday, Adams and Dempsey met representatives of the dockers' Dispute Committee, where they repeated Cliff's threat that, 'if the other dockers came out, they would be dismissed.' [20] Dempsey was also made aware of the courier letters that had been sent to employees' homes, advising them that if they should decide to meet the return-to-work deadline, they would be required to sign yet more new personal contracts. In this letter to dockers on behalf of the Dock Company, Price made it clear:

> 'As a result of your participation in unofficial industrial action you have failed to report to work and as a result you are in breach of your contract of employment. Unless you report for work at 7.00am on Friday 29th September 1995, regardless of your normal working shift, your contract of employment will be terminated with effect from that date and time. Your action will have disqualified you from any entitlement to contractual notice.' [21]

That night, Neptune Security, a company owned by MDHC, along with other motorcycle couriers and taxi services, hand-delivered the company's ultimatum to its dockers. The speed with which the letters were both written and distributed is indicative of either an exercise in extreme organisational efficiency, or the implementation of a pre-existing plan to dismiss 400 MDHC dockworkers within an extremely narrow timeframe. All other MDHC employees would remain immune from such actions, as their collective agreements were ringfenced, and, according to one source, it had also been made clear that the company, 'were not blaming the Union for the dispute, and it would not be the MDHC's intention to take legal action against this union.' [22] For Pauline Bradley and Professor Chris Knight of the London Dockers Support Group, the Liverpool dockers:

> 'Were got rid of so quickly that within twenty-four hours their jobs were being advertised in the local press. It was the end of the bloodline. Men like Jimmy Campbell, whose father was killed on the docks, had almost forty years' service. "When my husband received his P45 after twenty-eight years' working in the port," said Pat Dooley, "it was like someone had died in our house."' [23]

Few dockers doubted that they had walked into a trap, not least because the overtime dispute was not theirs, and they knew that their refusal to cross the Torside picket line was illegal under Margaret Thatcher's anti-trade union laws. John Pilger was to later write: 'the Mersey Docks and Harbour Company claimed that it was entirely independent of Torside.' [24] The latest new personal contract to be imposed upon the dockers also contained the company's declaration that it intended to use casual labour:

*'None of the terms and conditions of employment in this contract are determined via collective agreement with any Trade Union. Your shift rota covers 7 days a week 365 days a year... If circumstances prevent the Company from obtaining full cover internally, then contract labour will be used to give full capacity.'* [25]

The same tactic had been used in March 1994, when MDHC imposed new contracts on 350 dockers at Seaforth Container Terminal, but the September 1995 contracts also came with a substantial reduction in pay. On 28 September 1995 approximately 120 dockers did not receive a contract, including all shop stewards and known union activists. Dockers who were offered a new contract were ordered to sign and return them by 12 noon on Monday 2 October 1995. [26] Any dockers who happened to be on holiday or sick leave were sacked automatically. The men who stood on the picket line that morning knew that some of their comrades had already been sacked, while others still had a job to lose. This made it impossible for any docker to accept the new contract, and within one week, on Friday 6 October, they were all issued P45 redundancy notices. This was the start of one of the longest-running industrial disputes in British labour history. An MDHC spokesperson gave a terse statement: 'The striking men are in breach of their contracts, and they have therefore terminated them.' [27]

Ten days earlier *Lloyd's List*, the influential shipping paper, had run a story on the significant improvements that had taken place in recent years across the Port of Liverpool: 'This was reflected in record tonnages and record performances, marking a leap forward for the Port of Liverpool with cargo volumes and customer confidence at a premium. It was the most profitable port in the UK.' [28] In evidence to the High Court in 2002, Terry Teague reaffirmed that had he known of the reinstatement offer made to the union on Monday 25 September:

*'... the events of Thursday 28 September would have been very different. By this I mean we would have had both the time and the opportunity, as shop stewards, to discuss a settlement with the Torside employer. There would not have been a need for the Torside membership to evolve their picketing activities to the Seaforth Container Terminal.'* [29]

At the start of the dispute, some of the Torside dockers were certain that it would be over in just a few short weeks, believing that once the rest of the Liverpool dockers joined them, 'that would be the end of it.' [30]

# 23

# The 'Official Record' of the First Four Days

*'What are unions for? Why do people form them? They do it because they know that the strength of the many will protect the few. That is the fundamental principle of trade unionism. Lose that, as the TGWU has done, and there is no reason to join or remain in a trade union. The Mersey Docks dispute should have been won.'*
~ *Jimmy McGovern**

The significance of the first four days of the Liverpool dockers' conflict was not lost on the Transport and General Workers' Union or the legal profession. It seemed fitting, given the extraordinary amount of public financial investment in both the old Mersey Docks and Harbour Board and the reconstituted Mersey Docks and Harbour Company during the 1970s and '80s, that formal discussions over the Liverpool dock dispute would eventually take place in the House of Commons. [1] It was in front of the Select Committee that Bernard Bradley, the managing director of Torside Ltd. disclosed that he had presented Jack Dempsey, the union dock officer, with an offer to remove the dismissal notices that were served to the Torside dockers on that fateful Monday evening in September 1995. Bradley also stated that he was never approached by the TGWU in search of a settlement in those critical opening days of the conflict. 'We requested to come here today,' Bernard Bradley told Mr Ernie Ross MP, the chairman of the Select Committee, 'because since the dispute started, we have kept quiet, although we have been in touch with the official side of the union all the time. We have not gone to the press, or anyone else for that matter. A lot of what I have read in the press and heard is contradictory to what in fact took place. If we are looking for an end to this dispute, I think we have got to look back at the inauguration of Torside, because I feel that is why we are here.' [2]

---

* When you're a Liverpool docker, it never rains but it pours. The Observer Review, 1 February 1998. Available: http://www.labournet.net/docks2/9802/Mcgovern.htm

Bradley went on to describe how he had been a TGWU shop steward, a member of the union's District Committee and a convenor at Ford Liverpool, adding that his father was a Liverpool docker and his brother was a national officer of the union. In short, he and his family were from a trade union background. He then explained that he owned and ran a building firm in Liverpool, before setting-up Torside in response to the city's unemployment problem:

> 'So, I went down to the union office and said to the officials down there, "Why have we not got people from Liverpool doing this building? Why do people have to come from Manchester to do the work?" Neither the trade union side, nor anybody else, nor the Mersey Docks and Harbour Company, was requesting me to come down because with the ending of the Dock Bill [Dock Labour Scheme in 1989], the future, as they saw it, was in a state of flux and change. They had near enough maintained the status quo at the MDHC, while outside everyone had gone for casualisation. In those terms, I was agreeing that I had worked there, but the intention behind Torside being formed was to stop any further casualization.' [3]

Speaking on Dempsey's actions, Bradley stated that the union's dock officer:

> 'Had not spoken to the men on the site that day when he came to my office… He told me that he had been chased by the men. It was a strike, yet there had been no demands made to me… he returned sometime later to inform me that there would be no appeal on behalf of the five men who were dismissed, despite the fact that I had offered to reinstate them.' [4]

Directly arising from this Commons Select Committee was the allegation that a TGWU official had failed to communicate an offer of reinstatement to the Torside dockers made by Bernard Bradley. [5] In submissions to the Commons Select Committee it was also revealed that no one from the TGWU or MDHC had attempted to contact Bradley since the dispute had begun. [6] Almost a year later Bill Morris directed Dave McCall, Region 6's Regional secretary, to conduct an investigation into Dempsey's actions, leading to a report that was completed in November 1996. To lay the blame for such cataclysmic events at the feet of one local union official would be far too simplistic. [7] Queen's Council for the Liverpool dockers, John Hendy QC, considered that there was crucial controversy within Bradley's testimony:

> 'Mr Dempsey says that the offer to reinstate all the Torside employees was made by telephone at 22.30 and not before, though he says that in the morning, Mr Bradley had indicated that he would accept all the others back who had stopped work, but he would not take the five he had dismissed.' [8]

In 2002, Judge Coningsby QC, heard the repeated claim that Dempsey failed to convey Bradley's reinstatement offer to the Torside dockers on Tuesday 26 September:

# THE 'OFFICIAL RECORD' OF THE FIRST FOUR DAYS

*'... despite innumerable opportunities to convey that offer to the Torside workforce in general, or workers in particular or to shop stewards, Mr Dempsey elected to keep the offer to himself. An early offer had been put on the table to resolve the whole affair, and the only reason it had not been resolved was that, for reasons best known to himself, Mr Dempsey chose to conceal the offer. Had it been known that in fact an effectively sensible offer had been put on the table to resolve the whole dispute, they would not have struck, particularly knowing that to do so could cost them their jobs. But, ignorant of the offer, they did strike, and they did lose their jobs wholly needlessly.' [9]*

The TGWU's response to these allegations was that on the morning in question: 'the union's officer tried to communicate the offer but could not. Later, he was to claim that he did not regard it as a genuine offer, and therefore he did not think it necessary to communicate it.' [10] According to Geoffrey Goodman's official biography of Bill Morris he was: 'trapped in an impossible deadlock between his members, the law and the government's refusal to get involved.' [11] At a special meeting of the Region 6 Finance and General Purposes Committee on 13 August 1996, it was agreed that Dave McCall, the union's Regional secretary, would conduct a formal enquiry into various matters relating to the dispute. The use of 'enquiry' as opposed to 'inquiry' was telling, with the key focus being to *ask*, 'If the servicing official believed, on 25-27 September 1995, that any offer had been made which suggested that a return to work at Torside might be achieved.' [12] The subsequent 22-page report concluded that no offer was made to Dempsey, despite the official record of minutes held by the union recording Dempsey as speaking of: 'This offer of reinstatement for the Torside dockers.' McCall dismissed this evidence on the grounds that the vagueness of such minutes: 'has helped create some of the concerns under investigation,' [13] and, in reference to another meeting's minutes, he concluded:

*I asked Jack Dempsey about the section of the minutes which record, "Brother Dempsey stated that his understanding of the matter was by Tuesday afternoon, Mr B. Bradley would have taken all the men back into work." I accept Jack Dempsey's assertion that, once again, this statement is inaccurate. I do not believe that the offer made to Jack Dempsey on Tuesday night, 26 September 1995, was any more genuine than the offer made to Jim Nolan on the previous night. I conclude that Jack Dempsey conducted himself properly throughout these events.' [14]*

On Wednesday 13 November 1996, the TGWU Region 6 Finance and General Purposes Committee rejected McCall's report. Jimmy Davies referred to a previous report submitted by Jack Dempsey, in which the Torside members denied any knowledge: 'that their jobs had been on offer, as if this was so, then 500 men would not be on strike,' [15] to which Dempsey responded by claiming, 'Because the men did not return to work at 8am on Wednesday, the offer was withdrawn.' [16] These ignored minutes contradicted McCall's report by outlining Dempsey's explanation under further questioning that:

*'...all dismissals would be rescinded, and all the Torside men reinstated (paras. 4&2). Jack Dempsey repeated again this offer in para 3, p.3, where he clearly states his*

*understanding of the matter was that by the afternoon of Tuesday 26 September 1995, Bernard Bradley, the Torside Managing Director, was prepared to take back all the dismissed men. On 18 December, at the TGWU RD&W Trade Group Meeting, Minute 255, the union's officer reiterates that the offer of reinstatement was given as per his reports of 6 October 1995 and 6 November 1995.' [17]*

This was the official record of the first four days of the Liverpool dock dispute.

# 24
# In for the Long Haul

*'I fear for the future of my children and all who will have to live with the insecurity of casual labour, low pay and poor working conditions to make ever greater profits for companies and their shareholders. I am confident that this dispute will be won; the rats, weasels and snakes will find a damp, dark place to hide (may I suggest the hold of an ACL ship), the dockers will go back to work and the employers and the government will have to rethink their attitudes towards their workforce. Onward to victory; don't quit; remember your heritage; keep the faith; may the Force be with you!'* ~ Jean Fox\*

Monday 2 October 1995 marked the official start of unemployment for the sacked Liverpool dockers, and it was also the day that the Port Shop Stewards delivered an update on their situation to Bill Morris, who was attending the Trade Union Conference in Brighton. The following day, Bernard Bradley, managing director of Torside Ltd, sent formal letters of dismissal to all of his dockworkers. On Thursday 4 October, the shop stewards met with Fergus Whitty, TGWU Legal Services Director, and Jack Adams, TGWU deputy general secretary. Whitty was to explain to the dockers' Dispute Committee:

*'This is just not a trade dispute; it is about personal contracts and derecognising the union in the same way as the Tilbury dockers. We had won all the legal arguments then, but dockers did not get their jobs back. No question existed about abandoning anyone in this situation. It's irrelevant to sign a personal contract. The law says, if you sign a personal contract under duress, it has no legal standing. Personal contracts can be beaten by everyone acting together. We must not say don't sign contracts. You must return to work on a unified basis. Torside have a good claim for unfair dismissal, but we must not have another Tilbury situation. Everyone must return to work so that we can ballot the whole of the workforce, including Torside.'* [1]

---

\* Jean Fox, member of Women of the Waterfront (reprinted in LabourNet, October 1997)

Whitty urged the dockers to sign and return declaration forms confirming the following disclaimer: 'I have been forced to sign the attached document under duress, as I have been threatened with dismissal if this is not signed. As such, this contract has no force in law. I wish to make it clear that I wish my union, the Transport and General Workers' Union, to negotiate for me on my terms and conditions.' [2] This advice was based on the union's experiences in the wake of the dismissal of the London dockers in 1989. This fog of unreality was soon lifted when it was pointed out that Whitty's advice contradicted that given to Seaforth stewards who had wanted to reject numerous personal work contracts in the past, only to be told that there was no room for disclaimers in circumstances of contract imposition. It also went against independent legal advice that was offered to the Liverpool dockers by local solicitors at Edwards, Abraham and Doherty, and the stewards knew that the Mersey Docks and Harbour Company would never allow a return to work. This was proven to be the case when, on Thursday 5 October, MDHC dockers began receiving another courier-delivered letter from their former employer, stating that:

> 'It has been reported on the local radio that you intend to return to work on Monday 9 October 1995. The letter which you received from me dated 28 September 1995 terminated your employment with effect from that date. There is, therefore, no longer any work or job available to you. If you were to arrive at work on Monday, then you would not be allowed to start work nor be in receipt of any payment for any time spent in the vicinity of the dock estate. Please find enclosed, however, a form which you should complete and return to the company immediately. This will enable us to give full consideration to your request for employment.' [3]

The following morning, Friday 6 October, the Dock Company placed full-page adverts in both the *Liverpool Echo* and *Daily Post* under the banner headline, 'Port of Liverpool: Pickets – The Facts. Forget the rhetoric of the picket line militants. These are the facts.' [4]:

> The MDHC had no dispute with its port workers until they refused to come into work. They 'chose' not to cross a picket line which had been set up at the dock gates of the Port of Liverpool without reference to the union and without a ballot. Faced with the absence of 300 men over an unofficial dispute, Mersey Docks had no alternative but to terminate the contracts those men had broken, so that services in the port could be reconstructed. But that action was only taken after Mersey Docks had given each man a chance to return to work on the pay and conditions of their existing contracts. They said, 'No.' Twenty-four hours later, nearly 200 of them were offered their old jobs back under new contracts but at the same rates of pay and on the same terms and conditions. A bold but limited number signed new contracts.' [5]

That same day, another meeting was held at the Dockers' Club, in which care workers employed by Liverpool City Council were invited to speak about their own strike action over redundancies aimed at cost-cutting and, ironically, a move towards casualisation. Among the guest speakers were Eileen Peoples and Caryn Mathews, who would be involved in providing welfare rights advice to the dockers and their families from that day until the conclusion of the dispute in 1998. This meeting had been called in order to recommend an end to the dispute and a return to work based on the TGWU's legal advice, not that the committee thought that this had any merit as they knew that it was unrealistic and would be rejected by the employer. They felt they had to 'go through the motions' to prove how improbable the union's recommendation was and also to ensure clarity at the start of their dispute. This recommendation was not met with much enthusiasm by the dockers in attendance, especially since MDHC's newspaper advert included an indication that they intended to recruit 'scabs' from previous job applications made when their jobs were advertised in the press. The company stated:

> 'Now they have all decided to end their unofficial action and return to work. But they have no jobs to return to. Each man has been notified that his employment has been terminated after he failed to report for work. Fewer jobs will now be available in the Company for dockside workers. It will select from the 1,000 applicants who responded to advertisements in the Daily Post and Echo; and if any of the men who have lost their jobs as a result of the unofficial action want to be considered, they too are invited to apply.' [6]

In any industrial dispute, a desire to return to work is normally viewed as a positive development from the employer's perspective, but this was not the case with MDHC, who had given their 420 dockers' jobs away within seven days of sacking them. MDHC also took the opportunity to inform the people of Liverpool that they were issuing another final warning to their former employees, many of whom had over 30 years' loyal service to their names. The company demanded that dockers should stay at home and wait:

> '...for a response from Mersey Docks. There is no point in them returning to the Port where they no longer have a job. New recruits will be given permanent contracts of employment. The Mersey Docks and Harbour Company has never employed and has no intention of employing casual labour. The eighty Torside men who went on strike in support of more overtime pay, and to force a struggling company to close, must face the consequences of their actions. That is why necessary steps are now being taken to return areas of the port hit by this unofficial, wild cat action back to full and efficient operation.'
> [7]

By this time, the shop stewards had already agreed to recommend a return to work on Monday 9 October, [8] as an editorial comment in Lloyd's List recorded: 'Mass sackings with employers acting in a muscular fashion, is a reminder of a bad old past.' [9] The Liverpool dockers heeded the advice of their union and attempted to report for work the following Monday, hoping to finally establish that they were not, and indeed could not be, involved in an unofficial strike because they no longer had an employer to strike against. On that dark, freezing cold morning, more than 200 dockers were met at the locked gates by city and port police officers with clear instructions from MDHC's press officer, Eric Leatherbarrow, demanding: 'I want anyone who steps on this property arrested for trespass... I don't know what they're doing here – they don't work here.' [10] At the Seaforth gates, Kevin Robinson, an elected, accredited and now derecognised shop steward formerly employed by MDHC, told one of the Port Police (also employed by MDHC) that unlike him, he had lost his job, 'but lads here want to go to work. I've worked 28 years for the Dock Company.' [11] Andy Dwyer, a member of the Dispute Committee, explained to news reporters present how the dockers had explored every possible avenue through their union, and that they were quite willing to go back to work, but had been, 'turned away, heavy-handedly, by the Merseyside Police.' [12] Brian Roberts, another sacked dockworker, was quoted as saying that dockers over the years had become, 'more flexible, but the Dock Company have become harsher and this has been tailor-made for them, in fact probably even orchestrated.' [13] This prompted Bernard Cliff, MDHC's port operations manager, to deny allegations that the dispute was:

> '...a ruse by management, then we would have created the dispute; we were not involved. On Thursday morning, the week before last, we were in a position not of our making, no input from us at all, where we had very few dockers in at work and customers to service. But we now have to react to that problem and shape the port and its operations so that our customers do not have this problem again.' [14]

In an interview with BBC Radio Merseyside's Paul Grant, Cliff claimed that the dockers were twice offered the opportunity to return to their posts, and that on both occasions this was turned down, resulting in a shift towards reorganising the port and recruiting a new labour force. Grant, surmising that this process would require a lot of time and energy, asked why the company didn't simply allow the men to return to work, to which Cliff responded by insisting: 'We didn't start this stoppage, strike, picket – we were faced with the position that all men refused to come into work over an issue that was nothing to do with MDHC... The port is open – every terminal, every operation in the port is still working.' [15] The following day, Tuesday 10 October, Fergus Whitty wrote to Dave McCall, the TGWU Regional secretary, stating that the union could not give support to unofficial strike action: [16]

> 'In order to give support in any dispute, there has to be a return to work which results in the acceptance into employment by the employer, and then the union can consider a lawful ballot on industrial action. This must be on the basis of a genuine dispute with the employer over an issue which is separate from any part of the unofficial dispute. I advanced the example of the threat of Union derecognition at the port as evidenced by the content of the personal contract documents issued by the employers.' [17]

Then, on Wednesday 18 October, Whitty repudiated the unofficial action being taken by Danny Maher's Tugboat members at Cory Towage Ltd, in support of the dismissed Liverpool dockers. On 12 December 1995, Bill Morris would write to Maher in relation to this and other unofficial strikes, confirming that, 'I have today repudiated the above action in accordance with Section 21 of the Trade Union and Labour Relations (Consolidation) Act 1992.' [18] Following demands made by Alsop Wilkinson, solicitors acting on behalf of Cory Towage Ltd. Fergus Whitty also wrote to Bill Bowley, MDHC's director of legal services, on 22 November 1995, informing him that:

*'I can confirm that the actions presently being taken by your former employees do not have the support of this union. I can state unequivocally that any action which they have taken or may continue to take, is not official T&G action. As the union has advised your colleagues on numerous occasions, it is the policy of this union to act lawfully at all times and the union would wish to disassociate itself from any unlawful action that has taken place. You should be aware, however, that your dismissed employees remain members of this union to whom we continue to owe legal and moral obligations. It is the role of unions to give lawful assistance to members who have lost their jobs and this we shall continue to do. I should also point out that you are incorrect in your understanding that it is automatically unconstitutional for unemployed workers to hold office within our union. Should you be able to advise me of any specific unlawful act for which you think this union may be responsible, I would be most grateful to hear from you further in order that I might take appropriate action.'* [19]

One week prior to Whitty's repudiation of Maher and the tugboat men, on Wednesday 11 October, the Port Shop Stewards met with local MPs Angela Eagle, Joe Benton, Bob Parry and Eddie Loyden, following discussions held between the parliamentarians and Bernard Cliff. The MPs saw the situation as one in which the employer had simply taken the opportunity to selectively employ, as they clearly had a list of dockers who they would not accept back. Bob Parry MP saw a long, hard and bloody battle ahead: 'I am of the opinion that this was a set up,' [20] while Joe Benton MP told the stewards that the dockers had the full support of Sefton Council, as he stated that the meeting with Cliff had made it clear that MDHC were: 'inflexible; no consideration was given to their appeal for reinstatement. My conclusion is that this has been orchestrated by the company. I am totally appalled at the thought that everyone should reapply for their jobs.' [21] Benton also informed the stewards that he had asked Trevor Furlong, MDHC's managing director, what would become of those who were not to be offered a job, with 'No comment' being the only reply. [22] That same day, the dockers made it clear that they would welcome action by other unions to support them. [23] A day later, Jimmy Davies was surprised to observe that, in line with local MPs, the *Liverpool Echo* had expressed an element of sympathy for the dockers: 'We have been just amazed at the Liverpool Echo. It's never supported us, and now it has editorials two nights running criticising the company's attitude.' [24] This was followed by Doug Chadwick, a local road haulier, writing to the paper to complain that it did not help for them to sow division: 'The company should be left to sort out the situation without outside interference.' [25]

Monday 16 October saw the first dockers' march take place in Liverpool, culminating in a rally at St George's Hall. The following day, the Port Shop Stewards, or rather the Dispute Committee, took out a full-page notice in the *Daily Post*, presenting the public with the dockers' side of the story and exposing the true nature of what local business promoters, the Merseyside Partnership, had been celebrating as 'a strike-free world,' where workers did what they were told and never challenged the bosses' authority. The Merseyside Partnership sought to attract investment by perpetuating the idea that strikes were a thing of the past, going so far as to launch an advert depicting two players from Liverpool Football Club, Ian Rush and Robbie Fowler, as the 'last two strikers on Merseyside.' [26] However, this nationwide campaign, displayed prominently in high-value sites, such as London's Euston railway station, had to be quickly reconsidered in light of the Liverpool docks dispute hitting national headlines. On Wednesday 18 October, Eddie Loyden MP secured an early day motion in the House of Commons to discuss the dispute and condemn the actions of MDHC. [27] Liverpool Labour MPs outlined the sequence of events to Parliament, recognising the significance of this dispute not only to Liverpool dockers, but also the port and the city in general. [28] Loyden affirmed the support of his fellow MPs Angela Eagle, Joe Benton and Bob Parry, who shared his concerns that MDHC's actions exposed their intention to move towards employing casual labour. [29] Loyden was of the opinion that the company set out to create a disturbance that would cause the men to finally go through the gate, providing an opportunity to get rid of them and recruit externally, [30] and he warned the Commons that:

*'We are returning to the dark days of threatened casualisation. I believe that that is a serious threat. I believe that people are entitled to work with dignity under conditions that are human... At one time, the dockers were the butt of the jokes of some poor comedians, but they themselves have a sense of humour that no one can match and they are men, in that sense, who are proud to be dockers. They are proud of the work they do and proud of the port in which they work, and so are their families and friends and their communities.' [31]*

This comment about the renowned sense of humour Liverpool dockers had was an apt political statement by their local MP. Liverpool dockers' humour was not defined by jokes it was more their authenticity and ability to comprehend reality. It was a sarcasm and realism that defined other people and situations within which they would weave a tale or tell a story. Nicknames had a profound ability to sum up the character, faults and idiosyncrasies of most men. It was a very special Liverpool talent, street wise and so full of perception, one liners and tall tales. They were very funny men and women. Loyden then read out a letter from the wife of a sacked docker:

*'I am speaking as the wife of a man who has worked on the now booming and highly profitable Liverpool Docks for 28 years, through good times and bad. He has constantly refused severance pay because he wants to work. I do not work, I look after my elderly parents; our children are still in the education system on inadequate grants that we have to subsidise. We are totally dependent on my husband's income and I stand firmly beside him whatever the outcome.*

*I am not political. The only organisations I am a paid-up member of are Amnesty International and the Christmas Hamper Club. On Thursday, when the letter threatening dismissal arrived, I put it in the folder with the others. On Friday when he was sacked, I felt perversely relieved, because over the last 3–4 years, we have lived constantly under this threat. I have stood by and watched as MDHC have, in my opinion, used and totally abused a loyal, hardworking, cooperative workforce, which is acknowledged as the best in the country. I have watched my husband being bullied by threats and borne the knock-on effects this has on family and social life. "It might be*

*OK," I said. "You will know your rota in advance. It will only be changed occasionally. We can plan our lives around it."*

*How wrong I was. We have phone calls practically on a daily basis, altering his shift… We get calls on his day off, asking him to work or to change the next day's shift. Bank Holidays, you are expected to work 12 hours. But for your day in lieu, you get seven hours' pay. We have had a call when he has been in bed less than four hours after a 12-hour night shift; he was back at work, driving a straddler. The Minister will be well aware of that docking implement… I wondered how human beings could treat their fellow men in such a cruel and insensitive way, without any apparent thought for the social and economic consequences. Well, Mr Furlong and Mr Cliff, when you climb into your beds tonight, spare a thought for me, Doreen McNally, human being, wife and mother; red hair, blue eyes, flesh and blood, and as much right to shelter and nourish my family as you have yours.' [32]*

Bob Parry, Merseyside's Member of Parliament for Riverside appealed to his fellow MPs for direct intervention, while speaking frankly of his disgust at dockers with up to 35 years' service being thrown on the scrapheap without redundancy pay, while those under 55 were having their pensions frozen: 'That is inhuman, and it is a disgrace that the company can treat workers in that manner.' [33] Jonathan Evans, the Conservative parliamentary Under-Secretary of State for Trade and Industry, responded by stating that he was brought up in the mining town of Tredegar, South Wales, and thus understood the resonance of picket lines. However, in spite of this, Evans believed that:

*'A large number of Mersey Docks and Harbour Company employees refused to cross the picket line, and work at Seaforth's Container and Timber terminals stopped. After three days, the company held that the men had dismissed themselves…' [34]*

Evans added that he had provided legal advice to the TGWU in the past, and that he was of the view that the action of the Liverpool dockers was unofficial. [35] In responding to the statements from Labour MPs, he said that it had always been the law, even under legislation passed by the last Labour government, that workers who break their contracts of employment can be dismissed and may not be able to claim for unfair dismissal:

*'The law does not provide for immunity from court proceedings for anyone who takes industrial action against an employer who is not a party to the trade dispute to which the action relates. The law also requires a union to hold a properly conducted ballot of its members before organising industrial action. It must provide notice of the ballot and details of the result to the employer. It must give seven days' notice of industrial action to the employer and describe those whom it intends should take part. If there is a failure to do that, the union will not be protected from the possibility of legal action for inducing breaches of contract.' [36]*

In closing, Evans lauded MDHC as one of the most significant contributors to the region's economy, citing a Liverpool University study, *The Employment Impact of the Port of Liverpool in the 1990s.* [37]

Meanwhile, back in Liverpool, the dockers' main focus was the picket line. The organisation of pickets was left to Tony Nelson, Kevin Robinson and Larry Riley, among others, while demonstrations were the responsibility of Bobby Morton and his team. All London activities were a result of the extraordinary work of Micky Tighe and Nick Silvano, and the picket centre was the Elm House Pub, just off the Dock Road run by Ritchie Gerrard, one of the sacked dockers, and his wife, Margaret. The Elm House became a central hub for food, rest and communication for all dockers and their supporters, and the generosity of the staff there, whether before, during or after the dispute, can never be overstated. One of those staff members, Mary, helped provide toast, tea and coffee from first light, while dockers Tony Delahunty, 'Little Davy' and Kenny Denis prepared food on a daily basis from September 1995 to January 1998. The reality of the dispute was quickly beginning to hit home for many of the dockers and their families, they could perhaps see the long haul ahead. They would be joined by two Liverpool Boatmen, Bobby Hagan and Peter Wharton, who refused to cross the picket line and supported the dockers until the dispute finally came to an end. It was an act of solidarity, requiring huge personal and family sacrifice, which would never be forgotten by the dockers and their families.

# 25

# The 'Scabs'

*'One old fella once told me "You have got to be prepared to defend something you have won off the employer because, given half the chance, he would take it back". He then told me, "Always remember son if you don't fight you have already lost; if you do fight you have a chance to win!"' ~ George Langan\**

Mersey Docks and Harbour Company's *first 'final offer'* was made on Wednesday 18 October 1995, but it was only applicable to former MDHC and Coastal Containers dockers, and not those previously employed by Torside Ltd. Additionally, the company had taken the opportunity to introduce its new strike-breaking labour agency, Drake Port Services Ltd, who were on-site within days of the start of the dispute. They took 150 jobs leaving few, if any, openings for the sacked MDHC dockers to return to. The new hire was a collection of casual, non-union men and women, whose actions amounted to a declaration of their willingness to do anything that was demanded of them. The majority left their homes in Kent, travelling more than 250 miles coast-to-coast from south east to north west, which was itself another indication of their commitment to strike-breaking, as the link between MDHC's Medway and Liverpool port served its purpose. Arriving in Liverpool without knowing where they would be living or what pay and conditions they could expect, the DPS workers must have been the most rapidly deployed replacement labour force in industrial history. Unquestionably, theirs was a situation devoid of dignity, representative of a world in which those who are prepared to offer their labour for the lowest possible price are most prized, especially if they're willing to cross a picket line. Saundrey and Turnbull described the anti-union significance of this southern-based employment agency:

> *This replacement labour force was recruited and trained to work alongside the handful of dockers who had returned to work, and the labour supplied was DPDS. On the general*

---

\* George Langan (Sacked Liverpool Docker), written note re-tweeted by Alex Nunns (@alexnunns) 9 November 2020. Available: https://twitter.com/alexnunns/status/1325861480479170561

*cargo berth, contract labour was initially supplied by Kent United Stevedores (KUS), a cooperative set up by Sheerness dockers, which has since been undercut by another Kent-based labour agency which employs local Liverpool labour. The dockers who set up KUS were themselves dismissed when they too refused new contracts of employment imposed by Medway Ports in February 1992. The dismissals were subsequently declared to have been unfair by an Industrial Tribunal.' [1]*

Drake International had operated security and bailiff services while also training a replacement dock labour force in Tilbury, Southampton and other ports. DPS were now being used to ship scabs in Liverpool. [2] According to the minutes of the 1993 Docks and Waterways National Committee meeting, Drake Port Services Ltd. had established itself as:

*'...a reliable strike-breaking port employment agency based in Kent. In 1993, Southampton dockers had also faced the threat of Drake's. Management had been preparing a plan since Christmas on how to run the berth with a greatly reduced labour force, changed working practices and the use of sub-contract labour... they had engaged... Drake International, to secretly recruit and train a number of people at Tilbury and Barking to drive the cranes and straddle carriers at Southampton Container Terminal.' [3]*

MDHC management claimed that they needed a reserve workforce to act as an insurance against potentially prolonged dispute negotiations. Liverpool dockers expressed concern that a TGWU-recognised employment agency, Drakes, already used at Southampton Container Terminal, would undermine their reinstatement as Drakes established itself in the port of Liverpool. [4]

Two years later, MDHC would praise its low-paid, casual agency labour in its 1997 annual report, claiming the Seaforth Container Terminal team as one of the best of its kind in Britain. Les Hedder, DPS' Liverpool-based operations manager, was quoted as stating that his dockers were, 'highly qualified, highly motivated and well-trained.' [5] According to their own advertising campaigns, DPS had a reputation for providing a professional workforce trained to the most exacting standards. In Liverpool, they worked closely with MDHC's established management team and 24 other port workers, before launching a recruitment campaign in October 1995 that saw 150 employees, including 18 women, added to the Seaforth Container roster, with selection based entirely on suitability for vacant positions. [6] However, the image of a content and professional workforce was very much contradicted by the employer's imposition of the Port Operatives Agreement in 1996 under which manning scales did not apply. [7] This contract asserted that:

*'All men are required to book on thirty minutes prior to their ordered start time. Mealtimes could be brought forward or deferred... no man will work more than five hours before a meal break is granted, staff as a group have an obligation to undertake necessary overtime. Zero hours to be reviewed after two pay periods/8 weeks, and on absence caused through sickness this would be monitored monthly, and if found to be*

*abused will be renegotiated to include waiting days for which no payment will be made.'*
*[8]*

In an updated contract of service, to commence 8 May 1996, the casual and draconian nature of MDHC terms and conditions for Drake's *scab* labourforce, both before and after September 1995, were clarified as follows:

> 'The worker is not entitled to secure payment from the contractor for holidays or absence due to sickness. There is no obligation on the contractor to provide the worker with a guaranteed number of working hours in any day or week. The worker acknowledges that the nature of the contractors' business may mean that there will be periods when no work is available. The worker agrees that if his employment is terminated by the contractor the worker will not approach any of the contractors' clients in the attempt to obtain work. If this should happen then the worker agrees to pay the contractor six month's salary.' [9]

The first offer made by the Dock Company to the sacked Liverpool dockworkers meant that they had to apply for work via Drake Port Services, with no guarantee that they would be recruited. [10] The company offered the Liverpool dockers a chance to establish a co-operative that would receive a lump sum ex gratia payment of £10,000 but had no exclusivity rights when it came to work allocation. [11] On 20 October 1995, this offer was presented to the Merseyside Port Shop Stewards by Jack Adams, the union's deputy general secretary, and Dave McCall, who had recently been appointed by the General Executive Council to the position of regional secretary. This offer would be rejected by the dockers. At a local TGWU Geographical Committee meeting, the reading of minutes from the previous session seemed to lack urgency in describing how Jack Dempsey advised that he was attempting to facilitate a conciliation process through the Advisory, Conciliation and Arbitration Service to resolve the matter. [12] Minute 40 recorded that a general discussion took place on ballots, as well as what was now being euphemistically referred to as 'the dock problem.' [13]

There were, however, much more pressing matters on the mind of Bill Morris, the TGWU's General Secretary, whose main concern was protecting his position from any challenges in an election that was not expected to take place for at least another year. According to Geoffrey Goodman's 2002 biography of Morris:

> 'All routine assumptions had been based upon Morris's re-election campaign being launched towards the end of 1995. In fact, shortly after the union's BDC in July of that year. Of course, this would have accommodated those who were planning to use the BDC as a major launching pad for disrupting the Morris leadership.' [14]

Those close to Morris knew where their priorities lay, and they came up with what Goodman described as a 'brilliant move' to counter any plots to replace the General Secretary. This 'one year early' campaign strategy was the brainchild of Ray Collins and his allies, [15] designed to outmanoeuvre potential rivals on all sides:

*'The Broad Left campaign against Morris within the union was led by a talented and impressive rank-and-file Communist member of the GEC, Peter Haggar. He had powerful support from full-time National Officials, including the union's deputy general secretary, Jack Adams, Bobby Owens, the Regional secretary in the North West and a member of the Liverpool-based far left Militant Tendency, and John Freeman, the Regional secretary in Ireland. This led an extremely powerful group with a single objective, to remove Bill Morris from leadership of the union by denouncing his policies and forcing a vote of confidence at the BDC.' [16]*

While Region 6 and the Broad Left had supported Morris in 1991, this time around some, controversially, backed the Blairite supporter, Jack Dromey. [17] This was essentially born out of a belief that any candidate other than Morris would do. Some members thought Dromey was the only credible alternative to Morris, whom the former accused of being so out of touch that he was a threat to Labour's chances ahead of the 1997 General Election. [18] Another obstacle facing Morris was his failure to seek the advice of senior TGWU officials, who could have helped guide him through the complexities of a dock dispute that was outside his personal sphere of knowledge and experience. As Tilley et al note:

*'The TGWU refused to declare the Liverpool dispute official, fearing that this would put it at risk of the sequestration of its funds, and, as the campaign drew on, threaten a 'New Labour' victory. Under Bill Morris, the TGWU and its Executive refused to call for the support of the ITF or to field widely for advice on legal and tactical challenges, preferring instead to simply focus on a negotiated settlement with redundancy packages. There were, however, alternatives to such closure to innovation. The TGWU had undergone a series of internal changes since its heyday under the legendary Liverpudlian, Jack Jones, its creatively militant tradition and cadres had not been defeated. And while Morris himself had little experience with ports, there were many at Transport House who did. Inside the TGWU were senior officers with intimate knowledge of the Liverpool region and strong ties of trust with the Liverpool Dockers; and some were also highly informed about the MDHC, and its expanding and vulnerable business interests and networks. But the new leadership denied these officers' postings in the region or in the union's docks section. When they tried to approach Morris with suggestions, they were barked back into their non-Liverpool posts and non-port affairs... the union's National Officers based in London with any birth or employment links to Liverpool, such as Len McCluskey, Tony Woodley and Jim Mowatt.' [19]*

Liverpool docker and former General Secretary, Jack Jones, now based in the union's new London office, was leader of the TGWU's Retired Members Association and the National Pensioners' Association. Despite his legendary role in the dock industry and Liverpool docks specifically, his advice was never sought by Morris: 'The elderly Jones sat there, in his cupboard, during this long dispute, heart-broken and concerned that victories are denied to leaders who do not build trust with the membership and who do not see the membership and its communities as a resource.' [20] Bill Morris appeared more comfortable in placing the union's future in the hands of an inner circle that looked exclusively to private sector financiers and American consultants. In the eyes of this alliance, it would seem that the Liverpool dockers and their families, along with their inventive community supporters and environmentalists, were viewed as militant troublemakers.

At the shop stewards' meeting on 20 October 1995, Jack Adams warned them that they needed to be mindful of potential personal claims being brought against unofficial leaders. [21] But the dockers' committee were more concerned about one key element of the MDHC's latest offer which was the formal admission that they had been replaced by Drake Port Services. DPS would be supplemented by other casual labour agencies such as PDP Services Ltd, based at Canada Dock. A copy of their contract was sent to MDHC's Liverpool Freeport manager, Frank Robotham, confirming that PDP would provide MDHC, with casual labour on demand. At the same time, MDHC was also hiring labour through another start-up agency, PNT Ltd., who on 31 July 1996 wrote to Walter Scott, MDHC's Seaforth Timber Terminal manager, confirming the terms of a labour supply agreement. [22] In an interview on BBC's *Newsnight*, aired 23 October 1995, Bernard Cliff, MDHC's port operations manager, admitted that the company had hired casual workers from both DPS and PDP, justifying the decision on the grounds that he did not know how long the dispute would last. [23]

On Friday 27 October 1995, Liverpool dockers, along with their families and supporters, marched through Bootle, Litherland and Seaforth to raise awareness and rally local support. On Sunday 29 October, a group of dockers' wives and children attempted to deliver a petition to MDHC's managing director, Trevor Furlong, whose door was not opened to them. One of those dockers' wives, Val King, was quoted as saying: 'I feel that the dock employers are very evil men, interested in their own power, how much they can make and lining their own pockets.' [24] Another, Marie Curran, told reporters: 'We want an end to the dispute. The whole family came up with this idea. We're a family unit. We work together, we play together and we want to stay together. We're also worried about the toxic waste on the docks. We're worried about our future, our health, our livelihood; not just our generation, but the next generation.' [25] During a later visit to the Furlong residence, on 18 November, the families of sacked dockers arrived carrying a surprise birthday cake for the managing director. It was Collette Melia who handed over the gift, which Doreen McNally described as a good-natured form of protest: 'If he did not want the cake, we asked him to give it to a worthy cause such as a local children's group.' [26]

On Tuesday 31 October, the dockers' leaders met with David Cockburn QC, and it was here that Cockburn stated that the Liverpool dockers had clearly been dismissed and could therefore not be considered to be on strike, 'as you would require an employer to be on strike against.' [27] As such, the dockers were similar to 'a protest group such as Greenpeace,' and would be subject to common law rather than employment law. This came shortly after the local Department of Health and Social Security had arrived at the same conclusion, thus entitling the sacked dockers to claim unemployment benefits and validating a point that was constantly reiterated by the dockers and their representatives throughout the dispute. In an interview given to BBC Radio Merseyside in 1997, Mike Carden stated: 'Very early on in this dispute, we took Queen's Council advice, and the Barrister's advice was quite clear that this dispute is not an illegal strike. The law is quite straightforward. Bill Morris and the union have hidden behind the law and said that they can't act to support the dockers for fear of sequestration. There has been no sequestration in two years.' [28]

On Thursday 2 November 1995, Michael Meacher MP, Labour's shadow employment secretary, issued a statement backing the Liverpool dockers: 'The actions of the port employers were in a direct line from the worst abuses of casual labour in the 19th Century, and they confirm the fears Labour expressed when the Dock Labour scheme was abolished in 1989.' Meacher also wrote to the president of the Board of Trade, Ian Lang MP, demanding that the Conservative government use its 13.8% shareholding in MDHC to pressure bosses to reinstate the sacked men. [29] The following day, two Merseyside firefighters used a fire engine to help the dockers hoist a 30ft banner up a lamppost outside Seaforth dock. The banner read simply: 'Support the dockers.' Fire chiefs ordered it to be taken down immediately following complaints from MDHC. The two firefighters, who raised the banner, were both based at a station in Kirkdale where it was eventually agreed that they would not be formally disciplined for their unauthorised action. The Fire Brigade Union were also in dispute with their employers at the time. [30] This all happened just days before the dockers again offered to go back to work in an effort to kickstart talks and end their dispute, but according to the *Liverpool Echo*:

> *The dismissed workers said they were prepared to service ships and give their wages to charity if it means negotiations with management at Mersey Docks could get off the ground. The dramatic development came amid allegations from the men that a split has emerged among dock bosses, who were being pressurised by customers to resolve the dispute. But a dock spokesman said, 'There is no split whatsoever. Management is entirely united on this issue."* [31]

In response, Jimmy Davies, one of the dockers' leaders, told assembled reporters at a press conference:

> *We are fully aware that the port is not functioning. We have spoken with all the major shipping companies and offered to service their vessels in the port using traditional dockworkers. Payment for this work would be given directly to the Roy Castle Cancer Appeal Fund. By this action, we would hope for a window of opportunity in which a negotiated settlement would be achieved in a very short space of time.'* [32]

Davies also went on to state that many of MDHC's customers were concerned about the situation and had made their views known to management calling on Trevor Furlong to intervene directly. This claim was supported by the Belgium-based ABC Container Line, who had warned MDHC to get their act together or risk losing business to another port. On Thursday 2 November, out on the picket line, one of the sacked dockers, Dennis Halsall, was knocked down by a scab's car, leaving him hospitalised for two days while his grief-stricken wife and three children worried at home. In a letter submitted to the *Liverpool Echo*, Mrs Halsall said, 'I had the most awful experience of driving along to find him lying in the road being treated by paramedics.' [33] While Dennis, who had 23 years' service to his name before being summarily dismissed, lay injured in hospital, Furlong was busy receiving an honorary fellowship from John Moores University: 'in recognition of the contribution he has made to the life and development of Liverpool and Merseyside.' The Liverpool dockers requested that the university withdraw the honour, which John Moores himself must have felt some embarrassment over, having expressed personal sympathy for the sacked men. [34] It was also during this month that Terry Teague, a shop steward, spoke on the topic of trade union solidarity, providing a unique insight into the thoughts of the dockers' leaders at the time:

> *The main message going out to the movement is we are now looking to the big unions and workplaces on Merseyside for a 24-hour stoppage. The main problem as we see it now is that the MDHC is digging in. Any compromises put forward have been totally rebuffed by the Dock Company. It's straightforward for them, either victory or defeat. There's no middle ground at all… what we have decided is we have to step up the action.' [35]*

This increased action included a six-point plan to step up mass picketing, with calls for a nationwide stoppage on Monday 6 November aimed at increasing political pressure and, in particular, the blocking of City Council-approved grants and planning permission for MDHC. The dockers wanted to extend the role of support groups, especially those run by the women, whose first formal meeting had been held on 1 November 1995. A leaflet was produced, titled *Mass Picket: Seaforth Main Gate, Every Friday at 6am*, explaining that, 'Liverpool dockers call on all trade unionists and supporters to join a regular 6am mass picket of the Seaforth Gate, beginning Friday 6 February and every Friday.' The plan was to let it to be known that the dockers continued to uphold the principle of honouring a picket line and that their spirit remained unbroken, in a declaration of intent that concluded with the statement that they, 'know many thousands of workers recognise that we are fighting for all trade unionists. We hope you will take your place by our sides in this fight. An Injury to one is an Injury to All!' [36]

Further mass rallies and demonstrations, as well as the calling for an International Port Workers' Conference, were also agreed to, although the emphasis was still very much on the call for big unions and workplaces on Merseyside to join in the proposed 24-hour stoppage. Dave Cotterill recorded that Jimmy Nolan, the leader of the Liverpool dockers, had followed this up by speaking at the Trade Union and Unemployed Resource Centre AGM, where he appealed for solidarity from the labour movement. [37] The delegates in attendance each promised to go back to their respective branches and drum up support for the dockers in any way they could, but these positive responses did not prevent criticism of the methods employed by dockers' leaders in an editorial comment published in the November 1995 *Socialist Worker* newspaper:

> *'Some weaknesses in the way the fight is being conducted are making it harder to mobilise the solidarity that can secure a quick victory. Strike leaders are reluctant to call and fight for mass pickets and publicise them in advance. This misses the point of why mass pickets and protests are vital. And it needs dozens of dockers fanning out across the country, day after day, to visit other workers and argue for solidarity. Dockers leaders are*

*badly mistaken to make excuses for T&G leaders who shamefully refuse to back the fight. It is not a case of working on the officials to act. Even without them dockers should get directly to other workers and argue for solidarity with the strike.'* [38]

At the first Friday mass meeting, plans were made for the following day's demonstration, which would begin at the city centre's Roman Catholic Cathedral. Speakers were to include sacked Tilbury dockworkers and union leaders from the giant Vauxhall and Ford car plants on Merseyside, while the Fire Brigades Union would be present to promote their own dispute over job cuts scheduled for New Year's Eve. FBU members refused to agree new contracts undermining their current wages and conditions of employment; they too were being considered as sacking themselves, much like the Liverpool dockers. In discussing the firefighters' situation during an interview with *Newsline*, Neil Thompson, a Merseyside FBU leader, explained:

*'The firemen's strikes this week have been 100% solid. Our members are totally committed and are resolved to winning this dispute. We are refusing to sign the new contracts and the Fire Authority will consider that we have sacked ourselves on January 1st. If it means breaking the anti-trade union laws, then we will have to do it'.* [39]

Jimmy Campbell, one of the sacked dockers, told *Newsline* that he and his comrades were not going to: 'lose this fight, because if we do, the docks will die. All that we have fought for will be lost. My father was killed on the docks in 1941 and left five kids, and I have been on the docks for 29 years. We have to keep the pickets solid. The TGWU are like Pontius Pilate, sitting back and washing their hands of the whole affair.' [40] On Monday 6 November, Merseyside Police had to cordon-off Seaforth Container Terminal due to a mass picket, with more than 400 demonstrators gathering at the main gate before 7am, forcing traffic to be diverted and stopping lorries from entering the port. [41] According to one eyewitness report:

*'That Monday at about 6.30am, the announcement went up, "We're marching on the gates." The police were caught completely by surprise; one solitary policeman stretched out his arms and said, "You can't come down here." Within a minute, the gates were slammed shut and stayed that way until 9am, causing massive traffic jams. A police inspector walked down, beckoned to a steward to come forward. A solitary docker marched regimental style to meet him. Halfway he stopped, stood to attention and saluted. The inspector saluted back to howls of laughter. In the evening, the pickets were back, though this time faced by 120 police with side-handle batons and videoing the pickets.'* [42]

At 6am on Thursday 9 November, more than 100 dockers marched on Canada Dock to occupy this working berth. The pickets forced their way inside the gates and ran to the quayside, providing cover for those who set about scaling a 100ft-high crane to unfurl banners as part of a demonstration that marked a change in tactics. Meanwhile, down on the quay, dockers and their supporters organised a sit-in that lasted almost two hours before at least 10 police vans carrying more than 100 officers arrived, creating a scene that also saw police horses deployed for the first time since the dispute began, as a further 150 protestors were contained at the dock gates. The ship in question was the French-registered *M.V. Bouguenais*, and the scabs working her were part of a 30-strong team from outside of Merseyside, who were living in portable cabins on Seaforth Dock.

The action prompted a major police operation as, according to Marty Size, a Liverpool docker, 'The horses came in to move us. I said to the policeman, "I'm not moving. My old feller worked on these docks for 45 years. I've been here 22 years. I've a daughter at university studying. I have to subsidise her and I'm fighting for my livelihood now. I don't think I should be moved.' [43] No arrests were made, although *The Financial Times* reported that several incidents of criminal damage were to be investigated, as was an alleged assault on a police officer. [44] Mr John McCormack, chief of the Port Police, stated that his office was taking these allegations very seriously, and that he expected charges to follow. [45]

The protest included many of the dockers' wives, who chanted, cheered and blew whistles throughout a peaceful demonstration that ended without a single arrest. Eric Leatherbarrow, MDHC's communications manager, was forced into making a statement regarding rumours that strike-breakers were now sleeping on the docks, as he claimed to have no knowledge of such living arrangements describing the notion as 'far-fetched.' [46] However, being acutely aware that any accusations against MDHC would be challenged, the Dispute Committee knew better than to make unfounded allegations, and they waited until they were in possession of evidence from the photographer Dave Sinclair, who had entered the dock estate and taken photographs of the cabins, before leaking the story. Leatherbarrow's denial contradicted correspondence from the Health and Safety Executive's principal inspector of factories, who had written to Jimmy Campbell to confirm, 'That temporary employees are living in temporary accommodation provided at the Timber Terminal. Beer has been allowed in the accommodation for consumption after a shift.' [48] The inspector's letter was proof that 22 scabs were being sold beer while living on the dock estate in temporary quayside huts, flagrantly contravening dock by-laws. As a result, Leatherbarrow was forced to admit that he had misled the public, while attempting to avoid the real issue of the sale of alcohol by issuing the brief statement: 'The huts have now been removed.' [49] After a follow-up visit by the port health manager and a port health officer, the head of Liverpool's Environmental Health Services found that:

> 'The contractors PDP had used accommodation on the dock provided by two portacabins in which were some eleven divan beds each; it was stated alcohol had been sold to staff. The port health inspector told the council environmental committee there was no planning permission for living accommodation and no alcohol license. He went on to say he would be contacting the police... the scabs were being transported to work along the river by motor launch... the scabs were moved to a hotel in Runcorn, later some would be moved to the Solna Hotel...' [50]

On Monday 20 November, more than 1200 demonstrators turned up at the Liverpool Irish Centre in support of the dockers, and the following Sunday, Bob Ritchie of the Torside shop stewards was in Scotland to meet with James Kelman, Alistair Grey, Tom Leonard and Bernard MacLaverty, who subsequently called for the dockers' struggle to be covered in the pages of *Scotland on Sunday*. The next day, 25 members of the Merseyside Dockers Support Group led by Ron Brown, former Labour MP for Leith, and members of Scottish Militant Labour, including Tommy Sheridan, former leader of the anti-poll tax movement and spokesperson for Scottish Militant Labour, carried out protest action at the offices of Drake International, owners of DPS. This action was over their supplying of strike-breaking casual labour to MDHC, forcing the company to agree to a meeting with the Liverpool dockers. [51] Meanwhile, back on the Liverpool docks, MDHC erected a huge wall of containers to shield the scabs as they worked in the port, creating a 20ft-high structure around the perimeter fence of Royal Seaforth Dock that the sacked dockers quickly named 'the Iron Curtain.' When asked about this new addition to the dock estate, Eric Leatherbarrow said, 'The containers were not brought in specifically to conceal the dockworkers. They are normally stored at Seaforth and frequently stored on top of each other at the same time to hinder the blatant intimidation of port workers.' [52] In one of the first editions of the dockers' newspaper, *The Dockers Charter*, the Liverpool dockers made clear their need for the support of the entire labour movement in the UK.

> *We cannot allow this tragedy to unfold. Our port is the historic lifeblood of our community, and it symbolises the regeneration of our great city. We cannot allow the scars of casual labour, inhumane working environments and the absence of democratic rights of representation to destroy the dignity of our waterfront. We ask the Merseyside community to support our just cause to right a wrong. We ask workers everywhere to support us.'*
> [53]

On Wednesday 13 November, the recently formed Women of the Waterfront organised one of their first public events involving Liverpool dockers' supporter and reader in Anthropology at the University of East London, Dr Chris Knight. Together with his sister, Liz Knight, of the London Support Group of the Liverpool Dockers, and Camilla Power from the Department of Anthropology at University College London, they took part in an event at the Unemployed Centre in Liverpool (MTUURC) on the subject of 'Women and the Origins of Human Morality.' [54]

# 26
# Women of the Waterfront!

*'And next week, when the ITF meets in Stuttgart in Germany, rest assured with what the ITF has done so far, and there may be some who feel that more could have been done and more can always be done in any situation, but rest assured, between the three of us on this platform, we give you a guarantee this morning, that your dispute, and these issues for which you are fighting, which are issues which are germane to every single docker anywhere on this planet, because it is the same forces that are at work which are seeking to bring casual workers in, seeking to ensure that management manage with impunity; for workers' rights, trampling on workers' rights, it is Liverpool today, it is Copenhagen tomorrow, it's Antwerp the other day, and it is the United States in any single day.'* ~ *Bill Morris\**

From the very earliest beginnings of the dispute, the wives and partners of the Liverpool dockworkers were militant in their support. In an interview with Bill Hunter, Doreen McNally admitted that, at first, the women:

> *'...didn't know how to form a committee, so there was Bobby Morton and Kevin Robinson in the room with us, and they said you need this and you need that. You need a chair, you need a secretary; you need this, you need that.'* [1]

Sylvia Pye, a member of the Women Against Pit Closures, formed during the 1984 miners' strike, told the dockers' wives and partners that when they started their support group, 'we muddled our way through, and eventually it all fell into place.' [2] At the first meeting of the Women of the Waterfront (WOW) at Transport House, Kevin Robinson and Bobby Morton were the only shop stewards present, and they provided an update on the dispute while answering any questions. At this meeting it was agreed that Doreen McNally would be the chair of the new committee. Irene Campbell volunteered to act as secretary, initially on a temporary basis due to family commitments, although she would end up remaining in the

---

\* Bill Morris, speaking at a Liverpool dockworkers' mass meeting (14 March 1996)

195

position for the duration of the dispute. She quickly proved herself to be an excellent organiser. Sue Mitchell, who owned a car, offered to help with any running around that needed to be done, and she, along with many other women, could be found on the picket line morning, noon and night, in addition to being part of countless national and international delegations. Another founder member of the group, Collette Melia, was unsure about how the other women would receive her, since her husband was a Torside shop steward, but according to Doreen McNally, 'she needn't have worried. We all knew who the enemy was, and it wasn't the wives of the Torside dockers.' [3] Ann Morris, a talented networker, was named deputy chair. It was she, in tandem with Doreen, Irene, Collette and Sue, who formed the committee alongside the meticulous Joan Bennett (treasurer), Val Bibby (vice-treasurer) and Cathy Dwyer. [4] Members of the Women of the Waterfront included Doris Kays, Janey Jewel, Glenys Johnston, Pat Dooley, Margaret Ferns, Sylvia Tighe, Rose Kilcullen, Winne and Denise, Pat Walker, Tina Duffy, Cathy Kelly, Jackie Wharton, Frances Stanton, Lily Lowe, Elsie Jones, Jeanette Fox, Marie Curran, Mary Gilchrist, Lesley Mahmood, Dot Langan, Teresa Ledden, Margaret Roach, Margaret Lloyd, Cathy Wilson, Mary Pendleton, Anne Farrell, Mary Bilsborrow, Margaret Brady, Celia Ralph, Carol Reardon, Margaret McCall, Ann Bannister, Ann Monahan, Trish Barrett and Marie Eustace amongst many, many others.

Women were not exempt from the Mersey Docks and Harbour Company's acts of retribution, either. Cathy Kelly, a MDHC employee, suffered considerable victimisation and great personal risk as a result of her direct support for the dockers, while Eileen Devaney took it upon herself to allow the dockers access to the Container Terminal, as well as numerous Liverpool City Council meetings. Although they were very well-organised, the women kept their meetings informal, only choosing a name after Sally Ryan commented that, 'they needed their own identity.' [5] The others agreed, and so in homage to the classic Elia Kazan film, *On the Waterfront* (1954), they became the Women of the Waterfront. They also adopted the colours of the suffragette movement: purple to symbolise dignity, white for purity and green for hope. According to Doreen McNally:

> *There were discussions of our own badges and it was agreed to adopt the colours of the suffragettes, then a banner was needed and David Jacques, a local artist from Kirkby Unemployed Centre, offered to make it, but he wanted an input from the women, so a number of the women discussed it with him, and the final plan was brought to the meeting for everyone to agree. He did a fabulous job, and the women were very proud marching behind it, at every demonstration both in this country and abroad.' [6]*

Mike Carden would describe the Women of the Waterfront: 'like a hurricane of fresh air blowing through the union,' [7] as they wrote to shareholders, organised and attended welfare rights courses, and discreetly provided information to those families that were too embarrassed to seek advice regarding the financial losses and debts they were incurring. After speaking at the first dockers' rally, Doreen McNally began to receive telephone calls from the media, and when she asked one of the stewards what he thought she should do, he told her: 'Speak to them. Just tell them the truth.' [8] This encouraged her to seek advice from Sue Hesk, both a neighbour and friend, who happened to work as a press officer at Liverpool City Council, and Sue was more than happy to offer her expertise, coaching the women and stewards to answer questions in a way that made it difficult to twist their words through strategic editing. With so much new information to digest on top of having homes to run, picket lines to organise and delegations to attend, it was an extremely stressful period, but the injustice of their situation kept these women together; kept them as motivated and single-minded as their partners, whose working-class blood and heritage they shared. For Cathy Dwyer, there was no doubt whatsoever that theirs was a righteous cause:

> *'I think my husband done the right thing, yes, I've no doubt about it. My husband can walk around with his head in the air now, in support of other men, that's what trade unionism is all about. If more people were to support each other in this world instead of fighting against each other, we wouldn't be in this position. And even though there's half of these men walking around now without a penny in their pockets, they can hold their head up high and I think that is more important than having a big bank book. You know, your respect in life, you earn it, you can't buy it. And it's a material world now, people starting with, "Oh, me mortgage. I've got to pay the mortgage," and all this. Unfortunately, that's the way life is, but I admire him for what he done because I think it took guts and courage not to go in them gates. That's how I feel anyway.' [9]*

*Words of Liverpool*, a film by Daniel Sultan (Artis Diffusion, Paris), is an insightful study of the Liverpool dock dispute in 1996, compiled with wonderful interviews of a living working-class history. In this film, Rosie Dwyer (Cathy's mother-in-law) spoke with some passion about her docker son, Andy:

> *'I am the mother of a docker son that has been sacked for, more or less, nothing. He's been on the docks for nearly 30 years, and he had never caused any trouble and has always been a very good son.' [10]*

On 21 November 1995, some 50 women turned up at Transport House for a Women of the Waterfront meeting; the movement having grown to such a degree that they now had a creche set up downstairs. With Christmas on the horizon, the women had been out shaking collection buckets at the football stadiums, speaking at public meetings, writing to TV stations, planning a kids' party and delivering birthday cake – in the shape of the ACL ship, diverted from Liverpool – to Trevor Furlong, MDHC's managing director. Recounting the trip to Furlong's house, Colette Melia said:

> *'After everybody left, we said let's see what happens here with these bobbies. I was hiding behind a tree for 15 minutes, shivering. I just ran towards this copper, who nearly died. "Where are you going with the cake?" Well, I've been asked to remove it from the property. So, I said, "There's nothing offensive about this cake. It's a symbol of peace, we'd like the man to see it," and he said, "I'm really sorry, would you like your cake back?" So, I said, "Yeah, I would like it back." I took the cards out of their envelopes and put them back through Trevor's door at 4am in the morning. He saw them, he saw peace letters, he saw, "Your birthday's going to be better than mine in December, Trevor."' [11]*

That evening at Transport House, Doreen McNally was in the chair when another committee member, Linda Shaw, read out a letter addressing the wives, partners, sisters and daughters of the sacked dockers, copies of which they planned to give to every man at the next mass meeting. The letter read:

> *'Our men, and probably yours, were happy for us to remain away from the action while they, with the help of the stewards, fought for reinstatement. They were too proud to ask for help. However, we saw the need to face facts, that we must all play our part to end this awful situation. Some of us have managed to go outside of Merseyside and have been amazed and humbled to find the esteem in which Liverpool dockers are held. We firmly believe that we'll win this fight because morality and human decency are on our side. Victory will come all the sooner if you demonstrate that you are too.'* [12]

Speaking to the academic Peter Kennedy in October 1997, Doreen detailed the WOW's relationship with the Merseyside Port Shop Stewards, with whom they would meet once a week, and how Kevin Robinson, acting as a liaison between the two groups, often attended the women's committee meetings. She recalled: 'Sometimes, we'll know things before the men's weekly mass meeting on Fridays. For example, last week a women's support group in Holland phoned us up at our Wednesday night meeting to inform us that dockers in Amsterdam had been sacked, and we were able to pass this information on through Kevin to the stewards, who were still unaware of this.' [13] In an interview with local trade unionist and labour historian, Bill Hunter, the WOW outlined the complex and deep-seated causes of the dispute, and the effect it had had on them and their families. Sue explained to Hunter that her husband, Colin Mitchell, had worked on the docks since 1964, starting with the Caledonian Stevedoring Company in Birkenhead as a rigger and storekeeper, before moving over to the Liverpool side once they were married in 1976, eventually taking a job as a counter-off. He worked on the Timber berth for some 15 years until, in 1990, he and 60 others were forced to move to the Container base as a result of new enforced contracts, which included fluctuating shift patterns. Speaking on the changes to her husband's work-life balance following the abolition of the National Dock Labour Board Scheme, Sue said:

> *We were used to having him at home of a night; he only worked nights very, very rarely. I think I can count on one hand the times he worked nights. He did work, sometimes, weekends for overtime. But suddenly he was out of the house at all different hours... I gradually saw a deterioration in him as a man. He just became like a robot. He was working long hours for weeks on end. We did not see one another. The children no longer saw him. He used to get telephone calls at home. They used to ring up and sometimes we had visitors, and we might have been sitting in the garden and the phone would go and he would be saying, "I'm not in! I'm not in!" It got to the point when you couldn't live normally for fear of the phone going because you knew they either wanted him in or... they'd ring up and say, "You're not required." So, as soon as he reached a point where they needed to pay him overtime, they would say that, "We don't want to see you for four or five days." So, all the time they were kicking him; taking every ounce of energy from*

*him and then either saying, "You're not required," or "We want you more because the ships are in."' [14]*

She then spoke of how unhappy he became, so much so that he decided to train on the huge container straddle carriers. 'Don't you think that it's a bit dangerous now, because you're not getting any younger?' she'd ask. 'No', he'd say. 'If I'm going to earn a decent living, that's what I have to do,' as he went from rigger and storekeeper to counter-off, and then finally to straddle carrier driver, returning from work caked in oil so thick that he could not scrub it off of his skin, which he blamed on the poor quality, often dangerous machines that gave off heavy fumes and constantly broke down. He would later tell his wife that one day, when he was really exhausted, he had been up eight straddle carriers, each requiring a 60-ft climb to reach the driver's cab, and that all the bosses had said to him was, 'Keep going, keep going. It's blowing smoke in but keep going.' [15]

In the same interview with Bill Hunter, Doreen McNally recalled her own furious reaction to hearing about the Torside dockers from her husband, Liverpool docker Charlie McNally, and how she wrote a letter to Jack Dempsey, the Transport and General Workers' Union's dock official, informing him that she had no confidence in his ability to represent the men. A copy of the letter was sent to Bill Morris, and although she received a reply from the TGWU General Secretary, there was no response from Dempsey, who had failed to challenge the arrival of cheap, casual labour on the docks:

> *'When Torside came in, they were on a lesser rate than the dockers, so what they used to do was, any ships where you could make money, they'd cop the job. They could make a lot of tonnage on that. They'd put the Torside on it where they weren't getting paid tonnage. And that was the type of thing they started to do. Initially, the LCH men were giving the Torside the overtime, but then they decided, "Well no, we can't give them the overtime; we've got to do our own overtime because they're not having to pay them." There was a lot going on at Liverpool Cargo Handling, which complicates the dispute.' [15]*

The men were soon physically and mentally worn out by the new work schedule. [16] By this time, many of the women knew that such a chaotic situation could not continue much longer:

> *'Seaforth was a timebomb! And the men reacted in different ways. Some men thought, "Right, we'll work it at present because it's going to explode." I think that was the feeling, but they all wanted to fight. They were all waiting for the explosion because everybody knew it was just around the corner. Seaforth was a timebomb! That's why if people say it's because of Torside or wherever, I go, "No! Seaforth was ready to blow!" And if it hadn't been Torside, it would have been something else.' [17]*

Within a few days of the dispute beginning, Transport House became the central hub of a fresh approach to trade unionism. Steve Murphy and Dave Kelly, socialists and labour activists who were also employed as the building's caretakers, soon established themselves as key supporters in the dockers' dispute, proving themselves invaluable in meeting virtually all of the campaign's practical needs, while TGWU officers Mickey Dunne, Tony McQuade,

Tommy Kirwin and Colin Carr did their part alongside the administrative and finance staff, such as Geraldine Durning, Donna Bernard, Chris Yates, Joe Vickers, Alan Kelly, Carol Austin, Maureen Banford, Linda Harkin, Carol Bennett, Joe D'Arcy, Mark Holt, Lilly Philips and Chris Weston. Along with so many others, they donated a great deal of time and energy in support of the Liverpool dockers, in addition to fulfilling their own duties in a union building that at times could be quite manic, with shop stewards, dockers, Women of the Waterfront and support group activists all requesting help and assistance with everything from providing stationery supplies and printing leaflets, to fielding phone calls and sending faxes. Geraldine and her team worked tirelessly to organise, manage and account for the complex dockers' welfare fund, to ensure that those hit hardest by the struggle did not go without. The building was reaffirming its magnificent history as a centre of rank-and-file trade unionism, at a time when, according to Dave Cotterill, many TGWU officials, both locally and nationally, were seeking to avoid the dockers and their dispute:

> *The union building was a white elephant. Though there was tremendous support and solidarity from most of the office staff, the officers with one or two exceptions were noticed only by their absence. One of the officers who stood out in his practical, moral and physical support for the dockers was Mickey Dunn. But many had no involvement, not even to the extent of simply asking the dockers how they were getting on.' [18]*

Transport House was the engine room of the campaign, but it was the picket lines that remained the key battleground for dockers and their leaders, serving as a physical declaration that these were their docks by utilising tactics that enabled them to hit port users at any time of the day or night. On 20 November 1995, Micky Tighe, a gantry driver at Seaforth, spoke for many dockworkers when he gave an interview to the dockers own newspaper, the *Dockers' Charter*, describing the importance of closing dock gates and applying pressure on the port that would limit or halt its ability to function:

> *They reckon about 80 men are in there. There's men who took the £35,000 [and] come back, some of them... There's lads going in and out, and a couple of lads have gone back in. They know in their heart and soul that they're wrong. Every day we appeal to them... Allan Price, the MDHC human resource manager, wrote to my home about loyalty. This man has only been in the company for three years. My father and myself have got 73 years... and he's telling me about loyalty.' [19]*

Another of the Seaforth gantry drivers, Ritchie Gerrard, writing in the same edition of the *Dockers Charter* newspaper, spoke of the conspiracy surrounding MDHC's acquisition of Medway Ports:

> *So, they had a clear access to other non-union labour willing to break a dispute in another port. It's most of the problem, because they've brought scab workers from them ports – Medway dockers doing two weeks up here and two weeks back home – and they're living inside the dock in portacabins. But last week, an ACL ship turned around. They call the ACL the "jewel in the crown," it's the biggest ship to come here.*

*Twice a week they come. We got in touch with our brothers on the east coast ports in the States, and they said, "If it's loaded in Liverpool, we'll boycott it," and the Dock Company put out, "Oh, we didn't have enough scabs to do it," but the reason was that ACL now are scared of east coast dockers.' [20]*

With Christmas 1995 fast approaching, the Women of the Waterfront and their children picketed Trevor Furlong's house again, this time singing, 'New York, New York, it's a wonderful town,' in celebration of direct action being taken by the Newark longshoremen against the *M.V. Atlantic Companion.* [21] Doreen's husband, Charlie McNally, was the brother of John McNally, one of the lead members of Liverpool pop group, the *Searchers*, who rose to fame alongside the Beatles in the 1960s, and it was not long before they agreed to perform a fundraising concert for the dockers at the Grafton Rooms, just outside Liverpool City Centre. The gig was advertised as 'Grab a Docker Night,' in reference to the Grafton's reputation as a place where older singles could meet on what was known locally as 'Grab a Granny Night.' This wonderful event took place Friday 9 February 1997.

Around the same time, another support group was being formed in London, where more than 100 people attended a meeting of Workers' International at Conway Hall. This support group would be the most influential throughout the dispute, providing diverse and innovative leverage for the Liverpool dockers, from Reclaim the Streets to musicians, comedians, film makers and writers. The meeting was chaired by Mickie Fenn, a former London docker and activist, and a great friend of the Liverpool dockers. Tony Santamera, a Liverpool seafarer and another comrade of the Liverpool dockers, was leader of the Rail and Maritime Transport Union; he declared:

*'We must challenge these laws. Just because the dispute is illegal does not mean to say it cannot be won or should not be supported. The only chance of getting rid of these laws is to get a Labour government. Blair will have to do more than he wants to.' [22]*

Also present were Frankie Shilling, another sacked London Docker and secretary of the TGWU London Docks branch, and Bob Tennant, secretary of the Greater London Association of Trades Union Councils, while Jimmy Nolan and Jimmy Davies spoke on behalf of the Liverpool dockers. Alongside them stood Nick Silvano and Micky Tighe, who were to spend much of their time in London acting as delegates to the London Support Group, liaising directly with their fellow dockers in Liverpool. They were to do an exceptional job of raising both funds and awareness in the capital throughout the dispute. Eventually, this newly formed support group would attract many activists and supporters, including Dot Gibson, Bronwen Handyside, Jackie Vance, Steve Ballard and Nick Bailey (both Workers' International), Liz Knight (ex-SWP and Campaign for Human Rights in Turkey), Bob Towers (ASLEF Official and Workers' Press), Roger Gow (London Docker post-NDLBS), Hassan Irwa (Iranian comrade), Liz Leicester (Camden Unison and Workers' Press), Tony Nicoliades (CWU and Labour Party), Francis K Krause, Rod Finlayson (TGWU steward at Ford Dagenham and Communist Party member), Chris Knight (Labour Briefing, NATFHE and professor of Anthropology), Kevin Hemsley (Campaign Against the Arms Trade), Kevin Hargreaves (Labour Party), Giorgi Giandomenici (Pay Day Men's Network, linked to Wages for Housework Campaign), Tekin Kartal, Cemal Gizli and Keenan Erkan (all Turkish / Kurdish comrades), Dave Chanter and Cristina Roe (Labour Party), Ed Hall (Unison and fantastic banner maker), Joseph Odusanya (Nigerian activist), Peter Gates (building worker / activist), Andrew Young (Workers' Power), Kim Hendry (Labour Party, would go on to join TUC Academy), Alan Thornett and Roland Rance (both Socialist Outlook), Brian Casey (CWU), Massimo de Angelis (NATFHE), Les Lavidow (AUT), Nick Craske, Owen James and Chris Knight. Representatives at these dockers' meetings also included the Hillingdon Hospital workers, Magnet Strikers, Reclaim the Streets, Homeless Campaigners and Incapacity Benefit campaigners. Comedian, Lee Hurst, helped organise the *Dirty Three and a Half Dozen* show at London Palladium in support of the Liverpool dockers. He was the son of a London docker and a close friend of London dockers' leader Mickie Fenn. [23] Support groups such as these became the foundation upon which the Liverpool dockers' campaign for reinstatement was built, often sustaining areas of the dispute that were beyond the reach or influence of the shop stewards.

Back in Liverpool, the dockers' wives and partners presence on the picket line made them a prominent feature of the media's coverage both nationally and globally. Recalling her feelings at the time, Cathy Dwyer said:

> *I felt embarrassed when I first went down, me on the picket line! The first morning, I stood a mile across the road thinking I'd love to go, but I didn't. The next day, I went a little bit nearer, and now I am down by the fire and at the gates. The men make you feel welcome.'* [24]

Asked by the *Dockers' Charter* if she believed that some dockers might have felt ashamed or embarrassed by their situation, Cathy answered, 'The men do feel this, as they're dignified men. If they had no dignity, they'd be on the other side of that gate.' [25] Irene Campbell, wife of sacked docker Jimmy Campbell, said:

> *'A lot of the men don't go back and tell their wives. I know for a fact, Cathy and myself, I had a word with Jimmy at 6 o'clock, he said, "You're not going this morning." I said, "I am going this morning," and she said the same, and so we're all boxing with our husbands before going in the morning, and we don't want to be.'* [26]

Another woman suggested that the stewards take this up with the men. Bobby Morton replied, saying that:

> *'…we are entering fresh territory with this dispute. It's an intimidating atmosphere when you're down there first thing in the morning, the lights are flashing, the police horses and a lot of the men they're actually worried about their partners going down and getting involved. Now we'll follow this up at the mass meeting tomorrow, telling them to back off.'* [26]

When the women had their first meeting at Transport House, most just wanted to know what was happening, with Doreen McNally commenting some years later that they: 'had never been involved before, and they were frightened because they knew this was serious.' [27] In joining delegations abroad and speaking through translators, or speaking to union officials and activists, they were sometimes made to feel out of their depth by the men in control, but they never gave up, eventually establishing themselves as an authority on all matters pertaining to the dispute. They spoke openly and passionately about the hardships faced by their families, leveraging an acute sense of injustice to galvanise their revolutionary spirit again and again, with the children present at each meeting serving as a reminder of what they were fighting for. At the conclusion of one such meeting, they voiced their frustration at being left to talk only among themselves, and so Doreen requested that they be allotted time to speak at the next rally, to which Jimmy Nolan said, 'Why not. Tell them yes.' [28]

Young Joanne Bennett was the first child of a docker to stand on the platform at St George's plateau and, as Doreen McNally recalled, she was, 'All blonde plaits and ribbons, and made a confident and moving contribution. We were all very proud.' [29] The next rally was to be held at the Pier Head, and it was agreed that one of the dockers' children should speak, with a very young Neil Fox chosen to represent his parents and peers. Neil talked about the wonderful friendships that he and the other dockers' children had made during the dispute, as they were introduced to the Turkish community, children from the London Support Group and other dockers' supporters and families from around the world. After he had finished speaking, someone said to Neil that he must be very proud to share a platform with Arthur Scargill, at which he turned to Doreen and asked: 'Who's Arthur Scargill?' [30] As the dispute wore on and the campaign stretched further afield, more delegations were sent out across Europe. In Germany, Theresa Ledden and Dot Langan met with young activists who sought to engage them, possibly for the first time in their lives, in conversation about Karl Marx. [31] On the matter of involving children in the dispute, Doreen recalled an interview that Theresa Ledden gave to a German newspaper:

> 'On their return, a German journalist came to do an interview with Theresa. Her daughter, Camille, came in from school and said we are doing the history of Germany in school. She got her school bag and, much to Theresa's embarrassment, pulled out a gas mask to show him. Young Graham Mitchell kept everyone up to date on how the Dock Company shares were doing; he would come in from school and instead of putting children's TV on, Graham would check the stock market. He would arrive at the picket and inform all the pickets how dock shares were down two points. "That's £2 million pounds wiped off," he would proclaim. [32]

At one point during the dispute, Sue Mitchell was regularly followed home from the picket line by a policeman, who would tail her car and then hang around near her home, in what was a very blatant attempt at intimidation. An official complaint was made to Merseyside Police, and Sue went, along with Anne Morris, to meet with the Chief Constable, who told her: 'You are a very attractive woman. Maybe that's why he follows you.' [33] This was not the first or last instance of patronising or offensive behaviour being directed at the women. Meanwhile, bills were piling up at dockers' homes, with one of the children telling his mum to sell his bike to pay the electricity bill, further compounding the stress that was building up, as some families began to fear that they would lose their homes. The men started to look ill, tired and worn-out, while some were clearly depressed, and though the women did their level best to help one another out, some came from families where the children suffered from chronic health problems and there were also elderly parents to care for. Others were attempting to support children studying at university, as all the while their men were being arrested and banned from the picket lines, gaining criminal records in the process whilst also attending compulsory interviews at unemployment centres across Merseyside.

Another responsibility the women had was the acquiring and distribution of food donations, the dockers were entitled to EEC food aid which they received on a regular basis. Meetings of the Women of the Waterfront normally took place every Wednesday from 7-9pm, although they generally tended to go on much longer. At one Wednesday meeting, Kevin Robinson was addressing the group when he noticed that Rosie Dwyer, Andy Dwyer's mother, was there. His mother was great friends with Rosie, they were both from the South-End and had known each other for over 50 years. Such links and memories occurred regularly within these communities of dockworkers. As the work of the WOW developed it also provided a platform for other women engaged in struggle across the world. They met with representatives from the Women from Srebrenica and that left a very lasting impression on so many of them. Doreen McNally was to recall how: 'These women were so courageous. Their poverty was absolute – not even able to get sanitary products. The women organised people and brought in what they could, toiletries and underwear. The faces of these women were haunted. They were hoping all their males were imprisoned in a mine, but they acknowledged they were maybe dead.' [34] The dispute heightened the women's sense of empathy, as others' distress became their own. Speaking in January 1996, Frances Jones spoke for many of her fellow WOW members when she told the *Dockers' Charter* how the preceding months had made her more politically aware:

> *'Some people say the dockers are just militants, but now the women are involved it's made people aware that there is a problem, which needs to be sorted. The women were just as adamant as the men about refusing the £25,000. People say they can't understand that, but this dispute is about jobs, not money.' [35]*

It wasn't long before the WOW gained international acclaim for their efforts, with a Non-Government Organisation based in Geneva inviting Doreen McNally to speak at a human rights conference in London, which she attended along with Sylvia Tighe. After Doreen had spoken, she was approached by Silas Cerqueira, a Portuguese academic and human rights activist, who asked her to send him as much information as possible regarding both the dockers' struggle and the WOW group, beginning a process that would see them receive an invitation to be presented with a peace award from Colonel Muammar Gaddafi in Libya. Sue Mitchell was to accompany Doreen McNally to collect the award in Tripoli, and Sue Hesk recommended that they announce this beforehand, rather than let the media find out for themselves. [36] Nevertheless, Doreen's husband, Charlie McNally, was contacted by the *Daily Mail* to see if he supported this meeting with the Libyan president. He told the reporter how proud he was of his wife: 'Since the day I was sacked, she has campaigned tirelessly for us to get our jobs back, and to be honoured this way on an international level is just amazing. Now all the dockers are benefiting from the effort she's put into our campaign.' [37] Kevin

Robinson agreed, stating that he had, 'no qualms about accepting money from Gaddafi. We are very honoured and proud to be considered for this.' [38] The press attacks would continue for some time, but this did not deter the women from continuing their solidarity work with and for the Liverpool dockers.

Christmas parties and trips to London for the children to stay with the families of Turkish textile workers all needed to be organised, as did a separate children's trip to Colomendy. All the while, the women were learning from their experiences and growing in confidence. In October 1997, Peter Kennedy published an interview with them in *Journal Critique*. [39] For Doreen McNally, the solidarity that defined the WOW was born out of MDHC's intrusion into their family lives from 1989 onwards. Their husbands were under pressure, and their children were rarely seeing their fathers, so even though many of the women had never met before, they each had the same score to settle. Reflecting on her personal road to activism, for Sue Mitchell: 'Working-class women have been more politicised in Liverpool, mainly because they have always had to work hard and fight for any gains. It was a while before my husband could earn enough to enable me to even think about giving up work. My husband had to do seven years' training as a rigger and that was hard. We were married about five years before he had a decent wage.' [40] Joan Bennett described how she became involved with WOW because she was:

> '...so angry and disgusted at what they had done to my husband. After almost a quarter
> of a century of hard work, we could lose everything. When the P45 came through the
> door, it was a horrible feeling. The employers seemed to think they could get away with
> anything.' [41]

Another docker's wife, Pat Walker, said that she: 'wanted to know what was going on and to be involved. My children have all been with me as well, on the marches and the picket lines, and they recognise how important the dispute is to all our lives.' [42]

One docker whose wife was an active member of WOW put it this way: 'When the women get up to speak, they don't gloss over things the way some other people do,' [43] and like so many of those women who spoke-up in support of their partners and husbands, Val Bibby and Marie Eustace did an enormous amount of campaigning throughout the dispute, and in the winter of 1997, they both spoke at the University of Ottawa during delegation work in Canada. In discussing the experiences of the dockers and their families, Val and Marie couched their struggle within the context of global privatisation and downsizing, [44] as part of a campaign that saw them doing everything from dancing on the steps of St George's Hall to confronting government ministers and the TGWU's General Secretary. They were fearless, and in this sense they were the true leaders of a movement; it is hard to imagine how this dispute would have lasted beyond that first winter of 1995 without the strength and determination of these Women of the Waterfront.

# 27

# The International Campaign

*'The International Dockworkers Council (IDC), strongly condemns the massacre that is taking place against the Palestinian people at the hands of Israel and makes an urgent call for peace and dialogue, respecting international agreements and laws governing the area once and for all. We cannot stand idly by without raising our voices in the face of such atrocities against civilians and children.' ~ IDC\**

In some of their early delegation work, Liverpool dockers and the Women of the Waterfront travelled throughout the country as part of their campaign for reinstatement. In Bristol, Herbie Hollerhead and Terry Southers were unsuccessful in attempting to contact local Transport and General Workers' Union officials, so they took it upon themselves to visit their offices, where they managed to meet a handful of dock shop stewards. Bristol had always been a well-organised port, and they promised money and support for the Liverpool demonstration on 2 December 1995. In South Wales, Tony Russell and Joe Harrison spoke to nine UNISON branches as well as the Regional Committee. Russell and Harrison also went to Tower Colliery where the miners made a donation of £500 and laid the groundwork for the creation of the impressive South Wales Dockers' Support Group. A new, grassroots-driven form of activism was quickly taking shape, which, as Dave Cotterill observed, created a demand for public speakers:

> *Jimmy Nolan had to appeal to rank-and-file dockers to come forward to be trained as speakers and ambassadors for their struggle. This was a completely different situation to 1989, or for that matter any previous disputes, at least in living memory. Formerly, the disputes had been very much in the hands of the shop stewards and leading activists; the men for the best part often played a largely passive role. This type of direct involvement*

---

\* IDC declaration of policy on Palestine, 18 May 2021

207

*was to transform the outlook of a very wide layer of the men and later on their partners.'*
[1]

On 1 December 1995, the Dispute Committee wrote to Prime Minister John Major on behalf of the 500 sacked Liverpool dockworkers, accusing his government of gross negligence, informing him that they were: '…currently seeking legal advice as to your personal responsibility in law, with particular emphasis on the use of taxpayers' money and those undertakings established under law covering the abolition of the National Dock Labour scheme in 1989.' [2] The next day, more than 15,000 trade unionists marched through Liverpool City Centre, culminating in a rally at St George's Hall, where Jimmy Davies gave a speech asserting that: 'Our people in this dispute, whether official or unofficial, should be supported by our leadership and they are not doing it.' [3] This was one of the first public declarations that the dockers were not seeing the expected level of solidarity through direct action from the TGWU along with various national trade unions. Tony Benn, MP for Chesterfield, and Ritchie Venton of Scottish Militant Labour, received huge support from the crowd when they backed the call of the shop stewards for a united 24-hour general strike on Merseyside. A few days later, Bobby Morton told *The Financial Times* that if the dockers' dispute led to sequestration, he hoped it would: 'wake up the whole trade union movement after years of sleep.' [4]

Down in Southampton, Liverpool dockers and their supporters, including Mark Rossiter and Derek Wainwright from Torside, occupied the offices of Drake International, and on Wednesday 6 December, 200 dockers occupied the Liverpool office of the Andrew Weir Shipping Company until its manager, Chris Wardle, agreed to look into the possibility of meeting with dockers' representatives. [5] That same day, the Dispute Committee met at Transport House ahead of informing a mass meeting of their plans to hold an international conference in February 1996. The TGWU in Gibraltar had already been in touch, and Jimmy Knapp, General Secretary of the National Union of Rail, Maritime and Transport Workers' (RMT), also lent his support, as did Tony Santamara, General Secretary of the National Union of Seafarers. A close friend of Jimmy Nolan, Jimmy Davies and Frank Lannigan, Santamara had been involved with the dockers all his life, but there still remained the immediate need to convince the tugboats to stop bringing ships into the port. [6]

By October 1995, the Liverpool dockers had settled on a routine that was to continue unchanged until the dispute's conclusion in January 1998, holding a mass meeting at 11am every Friday at Transport House, with additional meetings being called whenever necessary. These assemblies kept to a fairly rigid pattern, with everyone sitting in the same place each time, maintaining a sense of continuity, consistency and tradition that the dockers' leaders recognised as being important to all involved. Jimmy Nolan would open every meeting by outlining the day's agenda, followed by Jimmy Davies providing items of correspondence pertaining to financial support and any other welfare matters. Mike Carden, speaking in his capacity as a General Executive Council member, delivered a general update that covered many elements of the dispute, particularly the contributions of TGWU officials at both local and national levels. Terry Teague and Bobby Morton were responsible for international reports, with Teague often reading out from copious notes, while Tony Nelson and Kevin Robinson gave instructions for upcoming pickets. There would usually be guest speakers to close the more formal proceedings before the floor was opened up to anyone wishing to address the room.

Very early on in the dispute, Tony Nelson told the stewards that they needed to, 'deliver something new to the dockers every week,' [7] meaning that in order to sustain a long, drawn-out battle, the Committee had to present a new strategy, a new success or a new picketing idea that would inspire the belief that victory was possible through consistently damaging the economic base of the port of Liverpool. This hypothesis formed the basis of an approach designed to maintain the solidarity and momentum of the dispute amongst the dockers, the Women of the Waterfront and the many political and trade union activists supporting their campaign. No limits were placed upon the dockers use of any *lever* that had to potential to damage the Dock Company. No organisation is ever perfect but through regular open meetings the Dispute Committee were able to encourage transparency, discipline and diligence that saw dockers attend pickets and other actions as reliably as they had always attended work. The 6am picket at Seaforth Container Terminal took place almost every day although more strategic demonstrations took place whenever opportunities arose. The stewards recognised the importance of being visible at these dawn pickets, which they would leave at around 9am to reconvene for endless meetings and planning sessions at Transport House. There, the Committee would occupy the impressive third-floor boardroom – the only space big enough for them – while one of the TGWU officials, Mickey Dunne, allowed them use of his very small office as an international communication hub, which was where the fax machine, phone line and computer would be located in the weeks ahead.

At a meeting on Thursday 7 December, Jimmy Nolan relayed news from Mike Carden that the GEC, whose meeting he was attending in London, had confirmed their support for the Liverpool dockers. Decisions by the TGWU's most senior lay-member committee would normally become policy, essentially directing the General Secretary. Terry Teague reported on letters of invitation being sent across Europe and North America, together with information about Canmar Shipping taking legal action against Canadian dockers for striking in solidarity with their Liverpool comrades. The following morning, the stewards heard that Bob Ritchie and Jimmy Davies Jr had been invited to speak in front of Swedish dockers, and that East Ham Town Hall in London had been booked for a support meeting. [8] These developments failed to alter the fact that tugboats were still bringing ships into the Port of Liverpool. At the mass meeting held later that day, Davies told the men about the Canmar Shipping Lines situation in Montreal, where the *Syndicat des débardeurs du Port de Montréal*, under the leadership of a new President, Michel Murray, were unmoved by CSL's threats. Tony Nelson then gave a report on pickets and shipping in the port, while Kevin Robinson discussed pickets and policing. It was explained that all calls made to the Port Police were now being diverted to the office of Mersey Docks and Harbour Company (MDHC)'s public relations manager, Eric Leatherbarrow. Robinson also announced that contact had been made with dockers in Australia followed by Tony Melia informing the meeting that Billy Bragg would be holding a fundraising concert at the Irish Centre in Liverpool on 22 December. [9]

The ongoing issue of the tugboats was addressed when the stewards met with Danny Maher, the Tugboat men's leader, on Saturday 9 December, as a request was made for the Seaforth Container Terminal's largest vessel, an Atlantic Container Line ship, to be blocked from entering the port. Maher understood how valuable ACL's custom was to MDHC, and he agreed to raise the matter with his members. Tony Nelson then informed Maher that a picket would be set up at the Bramley Moore gate at 8am the following day, and more than 100 demonstrators turned up while Nelson, along with Terry Teague, Kevin Bilsborrow and Kevin Robinson, met with one of Maher's tugboat men, Steve Atkinson, aboard his vessel. At this meeting it was revealed that the last ACL vessel to enter port had arrived with its own team of dockers on board, ready to discharge the cargo at the Seaforth Container Terminal. [10] On Monday 11 December, Nelson, Robinson, Jimmy Nolan and Herbie Hollerhead attended a national tugboat men's meeting, during which Maher asked his members to attend a meeting at Transport House later that same morning. The situation was clear: if the tugs refused to cross the dockers' picket lines, they could not gain access to their boats, and the dockers would stand by them and ensure their reinstatement if they, too, were dismissed by their employer. Of all the many different types of worker in the port, the tugboat men were unquestionably the most indispensable, as without them larger vessels could not enter the river or navigate the narrow lock system leading to the complex maze of berths at Liverpool. At 1.15pm, Danny Maher told the stewards that the tugboat men would be going home until 5pm the following day, ahead of holding a mass meeting of all union members on Thursday 14 December. The following morning, the shop stewards decided to commission union badges to be sold in support of the Hardship Fund, which would include a limited set bearing the message, 'One of 500 dockers sacked in 1995,' to be presented to each sacked docker. [11]

As talks with the tugboat men continued, Bill Morris let it be known that the dockers were not to meet with Maher and his members at Transport House, out of fear that any secondary action could result in legal issues for the TGWU. Subsequently, the next meeting would take place at the Bramley Moore pub, opposite the gate where the tugs usually docked, [12] and on Monday 18 December, the tugboat men put further pressure on MDHC by walking out in support of the sacked dockers. The tug crews had initially stopped work after a mass picket by the dockers, before deciding at a mass meeting of their own that this would continue for 24 hours. Another meeting to discuss further action was set for that coming Thursday. This came at a time when multiple shipowners were imploring MDHC bosses to reach a settlement after dockers in both the United States and Australia threatened to blockade any vessels unloaded by scabs in Liverpool. Lloyd's List added to these critical voices by warning that 'the port of Liverpool could be killed off for good by a prolonged dispute.' [13]

The dockers had known from the outset that success of their campaign hinged upon the support of international ports, as they did not expect any direct action from their UK counterparts. They utilised contacts they had with rank-and-file dockers, some of whom were members of the International Transport Workers' Federation; faxing out invites across Europe, Australia, the US and Canada for an international conference to be held between Saturday 17 and Friday 23 February 1996. These invitations asked for their attendance and co-operation in seeking to 'mobilise maximum international support for our dispute, and other disputes with international repercussions.' [14] In Australia, dockworkers had already begun action in Sydney following the arrival of a delegation from Liverpool, leading to Robert Coombes (Seamen's union) and Jim Donovan, the joint branch secretaries of the Australian Maritime Union, writing to inform the Dispute Committee that they could be:

*'Assured of the continued support of our members and other members of Australian unions... The Australian dockers wanted to convince the ABC Line of their intentions to continue to support their Liverpool comrades, stating that, "The next vessel may rust at the berth." Your struggle has been an inspiration to our members.' [15]*

When Terry Teague and Kevin Robinson were invited to Sydney on 25 November 1995, Donovan and his colleague Barry Robson were assigned to escort them to all meetings of the Australian *wharfies*, as well as 'stop work' meetings, trade councils and meetings with politicians. Donovan also took the dockers to meet the CEO of ABC Lines, where they presented their case and asked that ABC not send ships to the Port of Liverpool. The following week, an ABC vessel was due into Sydney from Liverpool, but the dockers there refused to discharge it, in a display of action that was described by *Lloyd's List* as an extension of 'an exceedingly long-range picket line.' [16] Back in Liverpool, another mass meeting took place on Friday 8 December, where it was explained that rumours of the sacked dockers being offered employment by Drake International was unrealistic for a number of reasons, both in principle and in practice. Pensions, for example, would be a critical factor in any future employment negotiations and, with that in mind, a meeting of the Former Registered Dock Workers' Pension Fund had been arranged for later that same week. Jimmy Nolan then announced the Dispute Committee's intention to force a vote to remove MDHC's Bernard Cliff from the board of the National Dock Labour Board pension trustees. Other matters for discussion included a delegation leaving for Baltimore and Maryland the following day. Kevin Robinson clarified the policing situation on the picket lines and Tony Nelson spoke about MDHC's declaration that an increased number of ships would soon be docking at the Seaforth Container Terminal. It was also reported that Bill Morris was willing to meet with MDHC bosses the following Tuesday, 19 December 1995. [17]

On the night of Wednesday 13 December, a number of dockers and shop stewards attended a support meeting at the House of Commons, where Jimmy Davies stated: 'The solidarity given to us has taught us an important lesson... about working conditions and struggles in other countries. Now we want to know more. We want to build on the solidarity actions our dispute has opened up.' [18] Meanwhile, Bobby Morton, Tony Nelson and Kevin Bilsborrow had left for America to picket the docks in Baltimore where ACL's *Atlantic Companion* was due to arrive. Under US law, the International Longshoremen's Association on the East Coast were unable to organise a solidarity strike in support of the Liverpool dockers, but if a picket line was set up, each individual worker had the right to decide whether or not to cross it. [19] This first Liverpool picket on US soil took place amidst a winter blizzard, with Bobby Morton writing in a journal that he kept:

*'On Friday 15 December at 6.00am, we put up a picket line at the Baltimore Dock gate which met with limited success. Some dockers decided not to cross and major disruption was caused to the discharging operation... ACL directors knew of our decision and offered the Baltimore dockers four times their normal rate of pay to unload the containers. They refused. The ship sailed that evening.' [20]*

After Baltimore, the delegation travelled to Norfolk, Virginia, where they were met by port officials who, backed by an attorney and a massive police presence, advised them that, under Virginia state law, a picket could only be set up at a venue assigned by the port officials and state representatives. The Liverpool dockers refused to budge, [21] telling a local ILA official that they were prepared to go to jail if it meant that the ship would not be worked. No action was taken against them directly. [22] On Monday 18 December, they arrived in Newark, New Jersey, erecting a picket line that the longshoreman there refused to cross. That evening, they were served with papers by Louis Pachman, an attorney acting on behalf of the port, instructing them to appear at the New Jersey State Court the following afternoon. [23] At 6am the next day, as Bobby Morton prepared to resume the picket line, he was followed by both Pachman and the head of the New York Shipping Association, Jimmy Melia. Later that morning, an ILA official named Al Sernadas arrived at the picket and introduced himself to the Liverpool dockers. They explained to him that they had no money or knowledge of the US legal system. Sernadas advised them to contact the American Civil Liberties Union, whose legal director agreed to defend them in court, arguing that under the First Amendment they were allowed freedom of expression on a public highway, which was where the picket had been set up. The three dockers then became the subject of negotiations between ACL and the ILA, who had been asked to act as intermediaries on their behalf in a three-way telephone conference with the Dispute Committee back in Liverpool. ACL offered to issue a public statement compelling MDHC to sit down with the TGWU and attempt to find an immediate solution, adding that, if the matter was not resolved by 15 January 1996, the company would begin discharging and loading its vessels at another UK port. [24] During the course of the afternoon, Bernard Cliff telephoned the executive vice-president of ACL, Conrad Dezago, criticising the statement and asking him to reconsider. This sparked a heated exchange between the two directors that, according to the Liverpool delegation, ended with Dezago telling Cliff: 'I ain't taking any more shit out of you. Get it sorted or we leave permanently!' [25]

It is important to note here that this first visit to meet the US longshoremen was a physically demanding and intimidating experience, as the delegation was tasked with convincing hundreds of longshoremen to respect a picket line for a dispute taking place some 3,000 miles across the North Atlantic Ocean. They did not travel as the welcome guests of any union and when talking to other dock workers across the globe the question was often asked why other workers in the port of Liverpool, and especially the tugs, continued to work. Without doubt, the Liverpool pickets found such questions very difficult to answer. Now, on the East Coast of America, Liverpool dockers soon found themselves at the centre of a serious civil action suit in New York City, where the New York Shipping Association, including Maher Terminals, Atlantic Containers and others, all sought an injunction in the Superior Court of New Jersey against the three men. But they did win the support of the International Longshoremen's Association (ILA), the dockers' union there. Eventually, they would be represented by a combination of the American Civil Liberties Union (ACLU), the New York dockers and John Bowers, the president of the ILA. [26]

With the Liverpool dockers' international campaign gathering speed, the ILA donated generously to the Hardship Fund, while branches on the west coast pledged active support. Canada's Halifax Longshoremen's Association (Local 269) and the Montreal dockers both confirmed that they would boycott all ships bound for Liverpool. The Quebec Labour Federation also pledged its support, and Australian dockers in Sydney also donated a large sum of money to the Hardship Fund, with the promise of more to follow. *Lloyd's List* commiserated with Tsvi Rosenfeld, owner of ABC shipping lines, saying that the company was, 'a victim of what can only be described as exceedingly long-range secondary picketing from Australian unions acting in sympathy with sacked Liverpool dockers.' [27] New Zealand dockers added their names to the growing list of those pledging support and financial aid, and dockers in Rotterdam requested a delegation visit. A letter arrived from union representatives at the Spanish ports of Tenerife, Lanzarote and Las Palmas, stating that, 'We stand with you in your fight; this is ours and every worker's fight,' at a time when Spanish dockers were also engaged in a series of one-day strikes against casual labour. Dockers in Sweden decided to boycott ships bound for Liverpool and an invitation arrived from Genoa, Italy, for a delegation to meet with both union officials and the directors of an Italian shipping company. Additionally, messages of support came through from dockers in France and Germany, as well as the International Department of the All Japan Dockworkers' Union (Zenkowan). [28] The Liverpool dockers had maintained an active trade union presence throughout Europe, most recently during their official strike in 1989, but this particular campaign would have an extraordinary impact on trade unionism globally, resulting in the establishment of a new rank-and-file international dockers' organisation, the International Dockworkers Council, on 27 June 2000. [29]

Back on the Liverpool picket line, Richie Gerrard, a gantry crane driver at Seaforth Container Terminal, gave his opinion on international trade unionism: 'Well, internationalism is about the only thing we can hope for now, because we don't seem to be getting much hope off our own people. Financial support, but no strike support. They say if it was official, no problem, we'd all be out with you, but with it being unofficial...' [30] At the Seaforth gate, another docker said of the situation in general, 'We've got plenty of firewood and we're getting a 12-foot Christmas tree with lights. We're digging in. We're here for the duration. We've got nothing else to lose. If it's gonna be Christmas next year, we're still here. We're hanging in.' [31] However, for all the solidarity amongst the dockers, the goodwill and much-appreciated generosity, even at its earliest stages, the International Transport Workers' Federation (ITF) and the TGWU were actively restricting the involvement of international unions that might have been contemplating direct action in support of the Liverpool dockers.

The Australians were among the first to declare their support for the Liverpool dispute via their trade unions, and their experiences were, with a few exceptions, similar to other unions that stood alongside the Liverpool dockers. These were usually non-ITF unions and indicative of what was happening across the globe, as various obstacles and threats were used to undermine their efforts to stand alongside their Liverpool comrades. The *official* international trade union movement was a complex entity, deeply factional and split along *communist and non-communist lines* in the past. The Liverpool dispute had come to the attention of Australian dockers through a faxed circular, *Lockout Never Cross a Picket Line*, forwarded to Jim Donovan by the Socialist Party of Australia. The Waterside Workers' Federation and the Seamen's Union of Australia had merged in 1993, becoming the Maritime Union of Australia, and prior to this merger, the WWF had been affiliated with the ITF, whereas the Seamen's Union (SUA) were linked to the World Federation of Trade Unions. At the time, the

Waterside Workers' Federation (WWF) enjoyed a close relationship with the ITF, with its then national secretary, John Coombs, also acting as deputy president of the ITF's Dockers' Section while awaiting the retirement of the sitting president, John Bowers. Once the amalgamation had eventually taken place, both sections retained their separate international affiliations, which meant that any MUA members offering support to the Liverpool dockers would be doing so in direct opposition to the policies of the ITF.

Jim Donovan, the elder and more established of the two joint branch secretaries, gave his support for action to be taken on behalf of the Liverpool dockers, as both the WWF and SUA had a long history of international activism dating back to the 1889 London Dockers' Strike, to which they donated $56,000. This brought about pressure at John Coombs's end, but despite the wishes of the ITF, where he was actively pursuing higher office, he was willing to match Donovan's generosity, never attempting to, or even suggesting that they should, end or tone down their vocal support. After returning from the first international conference held in support of the Liverpool dockers, Donovan was set to attend the recently formed MUA's inaugural National Conference, which was to act as the supreme decision-making body of the new union, with delegates travelling from all over Australia to represent many transnational organisations, including the president of the ITF, David Cockcroft. During the conference, Coombs asked Donovan to take their international guests out to lunch at a local Chinese restaurant, which according to Donovan, was the only time that Coombs, noting Cockcroft's presence, ever requested that he not discuss the Liverpool dockers issue. [32] Unfortunately, however, another guest asked Cockcroft why he and the ITF were not supporting the Liverpool dockers, to which he responded by saying: 'they are being led by a bunch of Marxists.' [33] Upon hearing this, both Donovan and Dave Morgan, the New Zealand Seamen's secretary and staunch supporter of the Liverpool dockers, took the ITF president to task, asking that he name the Marxists. Cockcroft took a moment to think before finally singling out Jimmy Nolan, and Donovan replied with, 'That's one, and Jimmy parted company, to my knowledge, with the Communist Party of Britain many years ago.' [34]

As far as Donovan was concerned, Cockcroft was telling the rest of his organisation's affiliates, 'not about the magnificent struggle of the Liverpool dockers; he was telling lies.' [35] Thus, it was a great relief when Paddy Crumlin was elected to the presidency of the ITF in 2010, having been a senior Seamen's Union (SUA) official since 1987. [36] Following the publication of Len Mcluskey's autobiography, Always Red, in early September 2021 [37] David Cockroft was to write:

> 'Although Len and I have never been close politically, I can personally confirm the accuracy of the only reference in the book to the ITF when he says that Bill Morris, "stopped the ITF from galvanizing solidarity action" for dockworkers… this was one of several occasions on which he threatened, without any action, to disaffiliate from the ITF.' [38]

Kees Marges, head of the Dockers Section of the ITF in 1995, affirmed Cockcroft's recollections. In the same WhatsApp group another contributor states: 'The way I heard it.

Likely from you two [Marges and Cockcroft] is that Morris explicitly told the ITF not to lift a finger to support the Liverpool dockers… All of this under the threat of disaffiliation.' [39]

Initial contact with the Australian *wharfies* was made by the Liverpool dockers in October 1995 with Kevin Robinson and Terry Teague, who Donovan described as:

> '…*terriers, never having a spare moment to themselves, visiting many ports, explaining the true position of the dockers and raising much needed funds. The delegation was a credit to all the Liverpool Dockers.' [40]*

Robinson would visit Sydney again, this time with Terry Southers and Tony Russell, hitting as many ports as possible in a campaign of rank-and-file internationalism. This same strategy was employed in other countries, too, sending a primary delegation to establish relationships and gain access for a secondary group to build upon, creating a global network that came together for the first international conference of its kind in Liverpool in February 1996, which Donovan, along with his loyal, well-respected secretary and office manager, Ina Heidtman, travelled to attend. In discussing Heidtman's contribution, Donovan said: 'Her support was second to none, and she was made most welcome by the Women of the Waterfront in Liverpool as the only female international delegate.' [41] Also representing Australia was Phil Toby, secretary of the rank-and-file Container Terminal Australia Line committee, a company owned by P&O Ports as part of a global conglomerate that was opposed to organised labour. The Liverpool Conference allowed delegates to see just how well-organised the Dispute Committee was, and to understand that events on Merseyside were symptomatic of a worldwide attack on waterfront trade unionism. This message resonated with every delegate in attendance, not least the Australians, whose MUA members would themselves be sacked and locked out by Patrick's Stevedoring in 1998, putting 1500 people out of work. It was Donovan's view that they were fighting, as one, against the threat of globalisation, and that the need for unity and comradeship was greater now than ever before. The formation of the International Dockworkers' Council (IDC) was a direct result of this first international conference, demonstrating to Donovan that: 'Internationalism was the cornerstone of the Liverpool dockers' dispute, and, yes, it will be part of the future for others, and so by the very nature of that dispute we have learned so much.' [42] The dockers' campaign had indeed gone international and as the decades passed it would never be forgotten.

# 28

# The TGWU Condemns MDHC
# (for the First and Last Time)

*'Liverpool people are very like Newcastle people, very friendly; pretty much up front in a different way than the way the Geordies are, obviously very humorous and all. But the thing about the dockers is that they seem to be in a different league, you know their generosity and the way they support each other and help each other and so on. You know, you get this business like at the mass meetings where they say, "Well, Mrs Burns has sent in a fiver. I move that we send her £20 back."' ~ Dave Cotterill\**

The December 1995 session of the Transport and General Workers' Union's General Executive Council voted to: 'Condemn the behaviour of the Mersey Docks and Harbour Company in sacking its 500 dockers, and pledge to take steps to relieve the hardship caused to families,' [1] with Bill Morris, adding:

> *The dispute is an example of unfair Tory laws being used to sack skilled and long-serving employees. The T&G fully shares the sense of outrage felt throughout the community in Merseyside. The General Executive Council's resolution condemned the company's refusal to continue to work towards a negotiated settlement to this dispute and demanded immediate negotiations.' [2]*

This was a significant development for the dockers, as they now had the official backing of their union, but when the Dispute Committee gathered on Friday 15 December, ahead of the weekly mass meeting due to be held later that morning, the limits of Morris's support quickly became apparent. Danny Maher, who along with Mike Carden had attended the GEC session, addressed the stewards explaining that their resolution to picket the tugboats, passed two days before, was opposed by Morris. The General Secretary had informed them that if

---

\* Dave Cotterill, audio tape (October 1996)

the tugboat men refused to cross a picket line, it would be classed as secondary action, leaving the committee, Maher and the TGWU liable to face legal action. Maher requested that the tugs not be picketed before a scheduled meeting between the TGWU and MDHC. Jimmy Nolan responded by declaring that the tugs, as well as others in the port, must stop servicing *scabs* doing the sacked dockers' work, a situation that he described as 'indefensible.' He then said that the tugs should have already taken unofficial action, believing that it would have resulted in the dockers' immediate reinstatement. Nolan recognised that seeking international support was pointless as long as Liverpool tugs were bringing ships into port. Drake International had now been given a three-month contract to hire scabs on MDHC's behalf. Carden described the blow that was dealt to the dockers when the Liverpool tugboat men opted to carry on working throughout the dispute, rather than striking in solidarity with the dockers:

*'We had tugboat men from Liverpool bringing ships in each day to the Port of Liverpool, so that was a big problem for us. That's what workers in other countries couldn't really understand.'* [3]

News of the GEC's support was well-received by the dockers at the mass meeting, who knew that those elected rank-and-file delegates had the power to direct union policy - if they used it. Jimmy Davies reported on a recent parliamentary debate on the dispute, as well as the Former Registered Dock Workers' Pension Fund meeting that had taken place the day before. The dockers' representatives who attended this meeting had attempted to remove MDHC's Bernard Cliff as a trustee of the pension fund. John Connelly, the TGWU's National Docks Officer, had also been in attendance at the Pension Fund meeting, and Davies had taken the opportunity to brief him on the dispute ahead of the union's meeting with MDHC the following week. Davies concluded by adding that despite the GEC's approval, no money had come through from the union for the Dockers' Hardship Fund. Billy Jenkins reported that a mass picket had been called at the Norse Irish berth at 6.30am on the following Sunday, while Monday's picket would take place at the Alexander Dock and on Tuesday they would be at Seaforth. Jimmy Nolan read out a letter of support from Italian and French workers, and Kevin Robinson spoke about police tactics on the picket lines. Tony Melia gave an update on Billy Bragg's promise of a fundraising concert. Mike Carden then announced the Dispute Committee's decision to call for a public inquiry into MDHC's financial activities, and the occupation of the Glasgow offices of Clydesdale Bank, a major MDHC shareholder, involving Liverpool docker Tony Gardiner. From the floor, Mick Cullen stated that he had inside information regarding the state of affairs on the docks, which he described as, 'a disaster.' [4] Later that night, MDHC held their annual Christmas dinner at the Liverpool Medical Institute on the corner of Hope Street, details of which were passed to the dockers by post office members of the Communication Workers' Union. The Women of the Waterfront and their children were very prominent during the picket outside this function, lobbying MDHC managers and their wives as they entered the building. Emotions ran high, with many of the WOW, as well as several dockers, making their way into the hall where their former bosses were set to enjoy food and drinks paid for by the same company that three months earlier had sacked 500 men. After ending their demonstration at 9.15pm, the dockers and the WOW reconvened at Transport House to have a Christmas drink of their own with the local union staff. [5]

On Monday 18 December, the dockers heard a report from two Torside shop stewards on delegation duty in Sweden. Bob Ritchie and Jimmy Davies Jr informed them that the leaders there, Björn Borg and Peter Shaw, had stated their commitment to supporting the Liverpool dockers. Sweden was a key location for Atlantic Container Line ships, but according to Ritchie, the International Transport Workers' Federation (ITF) had warned Swedish dockers to 'take a step back,' providing the first real indication of the ITF's reluctance to support the Liverpool dockers' struggle. The delegation also met with members of the Anarcho-Syndicalist trade union, the Central Organisation of the Workers of Sweden (SAC). [6] Tony Russell then reported on his meeting with Jimmy Knapp, General Secretary of the Rail Maritime Union, who pledged his union's support to the Liverpool dockers. Herbie Hollerhead and Terry Sutton telephoned from Spain to give an update on blockades of Liverpool-bound ships, such as the *M.V. Churruca*. Bobby Morton telephoned from the US, as the internationalist strategy of the Liverpool dockers was clearly beginning to take shape.

Hardship among dockers and their families was beginning to have an impact, as welfare rights advisor Peter Clee set to work with Kevin Robinson and the Citizens Advice Bureau to examine the most extreme cases. The Docks and Waterways Trade Group also met that day and it was made clear by some representatives there that the TGWU's dock official, Jack Dempsey, should not attend the planned negotiations with MDHC. A point that was reiterated by Danny Maher when he spoke to Bill Morris at the GEC. [7] The following morning, a mass picket took place at Seaforth Container Terminal that brought together supporters from Manchester, Bolton, Scotland and Newcastle, among others, with many bringing along Christmas gifts for the dockers' families. Press coverage of the picket line was viewed as positive, as it informed the public that the port was effectively closed for almost two hours until the Operational Support Group from Merseyside police arrived and forcefully broke-up the demonstrators. The next day, Wednesday 20 December, Jack Adams and Dave McCall reported back to the Dispute Committee following their negotiations with MDHC, revealing that Trevor Furlong, MDHC's Chief Executive, had held talks with Bill Morris over the legal implications of the tugboat men's potential involvement in the dispute. Furlong had told the union: 'MDHC was a working port, with Drake Port Services providing the labour. Only 40 jobs would be available for the sacked dockers.' [8] The union wanted their members back on the docks as employees of MDHC, who themselves demanded no escalation from the tugs and the removal of US pickets. Jack Adams informed the stewards that pension and severance payments would be included as part of an 'honourable settlement,' but that all 500 men had to be reinstated first. [9]

The following morning, a special mass meeting was called to report on negotiations and to hear directly from both Bill Morris and his administration officer, Ray Collins. Jimmy Nolan opened the meeting by introducing Mike Williams, National Officer of the New Zealand Seafarers' Union, who offered fraternal greetings together with a contribution to the Hardship Fund. Jimmy Davies then gave an update on developments in the US, and Herbie Hollerhead also reported that the Spanish delegation had bumped into an old comrade from the Tenerife tomato trade days, Francisco 'Paco' Ramos Vargos, who would again play a major role in supporting the Liverpool dockers right up until his tragic death in a dock accident some years later. [10] While the meeting was in progress, Bill Morris entered the packed hall to a standing ovation, marking the first of only two mass meetings he would attend throughout the two-and-a-half-year dispute. The General Secretary thanked everyone for the warm reception and spoke about 'how proud [he was] that the dockers are making their mark. Other workers are watching this dispute, especially as talks are about to start with the Dock Company,' [11] adding that they had now entered into 'exploratory talks to clarify the jobs and pension situation and ensure that the union supported the families of the dockers. The fabric of the union must stay intact while we seek justice for our members. This was the position of the December GEC.' [12] He also told the dockers that ACL, the Port of Liverpool's largest client: 'are seeking an injunction against the TGWU, and under the law I should not be at this meeting.' [13]

The meeting closed at 12.30pm, and the dockers were informed that the afternoon picket would be held at the Huskisson Dock. [14] At that week's usual Friday mass meeting, guest speaker, Ken Stewart MEP, talked about the solidarity that they should expect from the Labour Movement, as all of the various 'factions' that were offering support were thanked, including Militant Labour, the Socialist Workers' Party, the Communist Party, church leaders, members of parliament, welfare rights workers and local TGWU staff. In declaring that the dockers' struggle was everyone's struggle, Jimmy Nolan invoked the memory of Joe Hill, [15] while Jimmy Davies explained that, although the US pickets had now finished, solidarity work with the International Longshoremen's Association would continue. It was acknowledged that the Liverpool dockers and their families had received magnificent support and genuine kindness from all over the world in December 1995, which did go some way towards relieving the hardship that many were being exposed to.

On Friday 22 December, a fundraising event was held at the Irish Centre, featuring local band Wig Wam, [16] while South Wales colliery workers raised thousands of pounds to buy sacks of toys and games for the dockers' children. [17] These miners formed a co-operative to buy the colliery, and had mined almost one million tons of coal, with Miriam Kamish of the South Wales dockers' support group confirming that the miners had been paying a levy on their wages to support the dockers, reciprocating support given by the Liverpool dockers to their historic strike in 1984. [18] Donations were flooding into Transport House, where special hampers, including turkeys donated by a local firm, were put together and distributed by the WOW, but the need to constantly raise awareness and seek publicity for the dispute could not be put on hold for Christmas. Writing in Issue No.2 of the *Dockers' Charter*, Chris Mooney, an organiser at Kirkby Unemployed Centre, described the 'really big struggle' that was still ahead:

> *The MDHC had treated the dockers in a despicable manner. It has angered every worker in Liverpool. It's also a shock to see them being treated like this and it's frightening because, somehow, we thought; at least the dockers are still there... What the dockers are doing is fighting for everybody, and we must ensure that everybody knows that we can fight back — that we can have our own independent representation. Most people realise that there will be a fight when Labour is elected because the Blair government will continue with Tory policies. All the more reason why the TGWU should officially*

*support the dockers, and their members would welcome that. The time to prepare the fight is now.' [19]*

At the local Unity Theatre, pantomime tickets were donated to the dockers' children, as efforts to provide some sense of normality at home would very briefly take precedence over the fight for solidarity in the workplace.

# 29

# Out on the Picket Lines ('Who's this ILWU fuck?')

*'We're not going to lose this fight, because if we do the docks will die. All that we have fought for will be lost. My father was killed on the docks in 1941 and left five kids, and I have been on the docks for 29 years. We have to keep the pickets solid. The TGWU are like Pontius Pilate, sitting back and washing their hands of the whole affair.' ~ Jimmy Campbell*[*]

From the very start of the dispute, the majority of the Liverpool dockers understood the critical importance of their presence on the picket lines, both to stop traffic moving in and out of the port and to show the world that they were prepared to fight to get their jobs back. The organisation of the pickets followed the same pattern seen in almost every other aspect of this conflict; they were planned by the stewards and, most importantly, executed by the men, the Women of the Waterfront and their supporters. Some of the dockers, such as Larry Riley, John Farrell, Gerry Daley, John Brough and Ronnie Fawcett, along with so many others, would be up and on the picket lines before 5am, each and every day. They accepted responsibility for putting up the banners and lighting the braziers, and no matter the weather, they were there, relentless in their determination to defend their industrial legacy. Other dockers, such as Ronnie Bibby, who drove the picket-supply van, dealt with transporting firewood, food and whatever else was needed, enabling the dockers to efficiently manage and distribute picket resources throughout the dispute seven days a week. Ronnie was also the main driver for international delegates whenever they arrived at Manchester airport.

The dockers relied greatly on their practical philosophy that had always been a key component of dock work; they were very capable people. A new language was developed to ensure that jobs were done, as opposed to half done or not done at all. If a question was asked about anything from feeding pickets to welfare issues, the answer was expected to be

---

[*] Jimmy Campbell, quoted in Newsline, 'Smash Anti-Union Laws', 4 November 1995

223

instant, and that answer was always *'done!'*, with longer explanations dismissed as tantamount to admitting that a job had not been completed. Many dockers now treated picketing as their new line of work, to be approached with the same conscientious commitment that they, like their fathers before them, had displayed on the docks. Some would stand on the picket lines even if they were sick, while others sought permission before taking a necessary leave of absence, only taking time off after arranging cover with their comrades. Picketing could be a soul-destroying task at times, and it was not long before rotas were replaced by targeted demonstrations, but some still saw it was their duty to maintain a permanent presence. Thankfully, the Elm House pub was on hand to offer dockers a chance to relax, grab a bite to eat and have a few drinks, as well as share information, opinions, concerns, ideas and criticisms with their comrades.

The dockers were creatures of habit, and their experience of working in gangs fostered a sense of comfort in one another's company, making it easy for the picket captains to know who would be at certain gates at a given time, since they would invariably be with the same lads they had always worked with. Everyone knew their role and they were capable of organising among themselves. The main pickets at the Seaforth and Alex Gates existed with the same distinctive, competitive behaviour that had been displayed on the docks since the nineteenth century when sectionalism, loyalty to the gang, berth or union branch, mattered more sometimes than unity or collective action. A point highlighted by local labour historian, Eric Taplin, in his study of the Dockers' Union 1889-1922 as being a constant challenge to organizing one big union for the Liverpool dockers. Competition amongst the pickets extended to the permanent pickets as to who had the best food, best drink and best pubs, and whose picket was more militant than the others. Dockers like John Turner, John Barr, Sid Grace, Eddie Mathews, John Deaves, Frank O'Neill, Roy Hayes, John Turner, Ken Forsyth, Bobby Hollier, Denis Connolly, Tommy Byrne, Peter Cain, John Lowe, John McMahon, Bobby Ambrose, Jimmy Hagan, Joe Best, Lenny Sarath, Billy Lomas, Mick Kilcullen, John Ryan, Eddie Ledden, Tommy Farrell, Robert Skelton, Bobby Rankin, Tommy Williams and Peter Atkinson regularly entered into this competitive *banter* with dockers along the picket lines of the Dock Road. Dockers were particularly adept at disseminating information to those on the ground, and this informal communication system operated throughout the dispute. Tommy Farrell sadly died at the start of 2020, and at his funeral his coffin was draped in the Irish flag. Tragically, Tommy's son, Tony Farrell, one of the Torside dockers, passed away just a few years earlier.

At Seaforth, someone kindly donated a caravan and eventually another one was given allowing dockers to ease the burden somewhat by having constant access to tea, coffee and biscuits, while for those manning the early morning picket, there would be toast, bacon, egg or sausage sandwiches made on an open fire. It would not be too long before the caravans became the target for legal challenges by the Dock Company and sabotage by the scabs. These basic facilities provided a physical point of contact whilst maintaining a constant public presence, as those who braved the elements to fight for the cause became not only the heart and soul, but also the true face of the dispute. It was Dave Cotterill who made the suggestion that the dockers buy whistles and foghorns to make as much noise as possible during pickets and demonstrations, which proved to be a great idea that really enlivened the atmosphere. Although the Dispute Committee were realistic in their expectations of what could be achieved through picketing, especially in a port with multiple access points and two police forces patrolling, there were days where they could rightly feel that they had achieved their aims by blocking traffic and forcing temporary work stoppages on the dock estate.

Being a former timekeeper, picket captain Tony Nelson knew virtually all of the dockers' names, work numbers and gang ties; this kind of in-depth knowledge was vital in making the process of co-ordinating delegations, demonstrations and flying pickets as streamlined as possible. The dockers of 1995 also had the benefit of a pre-existing set of routines and tactics to lean on, carried over from the 1989 Dock Labour Board Scheme strike, even down to little details like the stuffing of a daily newspaper into the wire mesh fence at the Alex gate every morning for as long as the strike lasted. Most picket lines had their own makeshift huts and shelters, what dockers called a *'caboose'*, that often needed to be rebuilt after a team of police officers or scabs had smashed them up. [1] George Preston was a docker for 23 years until he was sacked, and the sight of him riding his bicycle while carrying tools and timber to repair the damaged shelters made him one of the enduring characters that Jimmy McGovern wrote about in an article published in the *Observer* in October 1997. George later found himself immortalised in an iconic image captured by the photographer Andrew Testa. [2] Such men and women, as were found on those picket lines, could have built canals in the desert, and yet they accepted their situation with unfaltering dignity, humility and humour, recognising it as an inevitable consequence of the decision to stand by their principles. Having refused to cross a picket line, their job for the next two and half years was to try and stop others crossing the same picket line to do their work.

Christmas 1995 was as short as it was bleak. Pickets restarted at Canada Dock on Wednesday 3 January 1996. Despite the heavy physical presence of the Operational Support Group (OSG), the lines proved successful, with the evening picket at Huskisson Dock seeing a massive hold-up of wagons while the police waited on reinforcements. After several hours, the police decided to escort each wagon into the dock, using their horses to break through the picket lines, creating a surreal visual and a very long queue that gave dockers an opportunity to cut some wagons' air lines, causing further delays as repairs were made to damaged vehicles. This small victory was particularly satisfying after trouble had broken out at the earlier Canada Dock picket, where police had been waiting with what seemed like a plan to incite violence and justify heavy-handed actions against the pickets. A van displaying the name 'Medway Ports' arrived carrying a team of scabs, which unsurprisingly resulted in police throwing punches at men and women alike. [3] Four dockers were arrested and then released later that afternoon, and the next day the pickets were back at the Canada gate as normal, with the ever-present OSG ready to protect the scabs that were bussed into work for a general cargo vessel on the berth. From that point on, the Dispute Committee advised that all picket lines should aim to have at least one camera on hand to record events as well as acts of police brutality. It was around this time that the WOW also discovered that 40-50 scabs were being put-up at the Tree Tops Lodge, Warrington. Along with their children they began to picket this hotel every Thursday evening, while down on the dock the pickets' focus was shifting from Seaforth towards the General Cargo area.

Away from the picket lines, the first serious media coverage of the dispute featured the WOW's delivery of a petition totalling 100,000 signatures to Downing Street on Tuesday 9 January. Liverpool MPs Bob Parry and Eddie Loyden joined the delegation in presenting the petition to John Major, the Conservative Prime Minister, condemning MDHC as, 'a callous, uncaring and bad employer.' [4] A similar delegation was led by Paul Foot, involving Geof Liddy, Tommy Lloyd, Brian Dooley and Terry Barrett. There were still regular obstacles to overcome with the union, as they stopped access to the fax machine that the committee used to communicate with supporters worldwide. This was done because of the potential threat of sequestration, and within days the dockers got their own fax machine. A supporter of the dockers, Dave Graham, in one of the first of his regular 'blogs', recorded his thoughts on the complex difficulties facing the dockers in their use of picketing as a tactic in their struggle:

> *The dockers had attempted to picket various different gates, but since they are already 'dismissed' they cannot be sued for secondary action, although it is almost certain that some law will be found under the Criminal Justice Act to try and prevent this. Certainly, some stewards fully expect to be locked up before long. The only thing that appears to be holding back the authorities is a fear of creating 'martyrs.' It is important to realise that this is not a mass picket to stop the dock. The stewards are quite clear about this, rejecting the mass picket as a tactic of the past. It is also of course quite impractical. The dockers have called the docks a 'colander' because there are so many entrances.' [5]*

Bob Ritchie took charge of organising the picket of MDHC's Medway Ports in Kent, the home of Drake International, as they called upon their fellow workers to act in solidarity. As Greg Dropkin, reporting for LabourNet, wrote at the time:

> *Fireworks lit the Kent sky before dawn, as 100 sacked Liverpool dockers marched behind their banner then stood their ground in front of the gates of the Port of Sheerness this morning. Two coachloads had travelled through the night from Liverpool. Blowing their whistles and leafleting the traffic, the dockers turned back several lorries while two huge car transporters remained inside the port, refusing to cross the picket line.' [6]*

Ritchie stated that it was heartening to see that there were still good trade unionists in Britain, prepared to respect picket lines and turn back, as the Liverpool dockers once again breached anti-trade union laws that banned secondary picketing, with Mark Crichton declaring: 'We will continue to defy these laws.' [7] According to Crichton, the most supportive reactions to the Medway picket lines came from the car transporters who, 'wouldn't cross.' [8] In reflecting on MDHC's purchase of Medway Ports in 1993, which resulted in more than 300 dockers losing their jobs, Dave Cotterill wrote:

> *'Kent United Contractors, a labour supply agency, was set up by redundant dockers from Sheerness... the majority of the people who work for this company are also members of this union [TGWU], and the boss himself is a branch secretary... he and the rest of these members who are being used as scab labour should be expelled from this union. This very same company had supplied scab labour to the Port of Liverpool during the first weeks of the dispute?' [9]*

# OUT ON THE PICKET LINES ('WHO'S THIS ILWU FUCK?')

On 7 April 2003, during an anti-war demonstration in California, an Oakland City Police officer, M. Powell, was heard exclaiming, 'Who is this ILWU fuck?' [10] as Jack Heyman, International Longshore and Warehouse Union's Local 10 business agent, was being violently thrown to the ground and arrested, while nine other ILWU Local 10 members lay bleeding and bruised after being shot at by police. Seven years earlier, that same 'ILWU fuck' made his way across the Atlantic Ocean to support the Liverpool dockers and stand on their picket line. His involvement would transform the international profile of the dockers.

On the night of Thursday 11 January 1996, Jimmy Nolan and Mike Carden travelled to London to meet Heyman, who was due to land at Heathrow Airport the next morning, with the plan being to get him up to Liverpool in time for the Friday mass meeting. The Dispute Committee believed that Heyman was perhaps the most important visitor to Liverpool since the dispute began, although, while he would certainly not disappoint, the dockers had initially thought him to be the ILWU's president, a mistake resulting from the US style of assigning elected union officer titles in their union. [11] Heyman had recently been nominated for the role of International Transport Workers' Federation Inspector, which was the reason for his visit to the UK, and while Nolan and Carden did not know what he looked like, Jack said he would wear his Stetson hat so that he would be easily recognised. Between his attire and his broad West Coast accent, Heyman was a hit with the dockers and an instant media draw, having raced back to Liverpool just in time to offer fraternal greetings and promises of both direct action and financial support to a packed mass meeting. A lifelong political activist, he was well read, articulate and an exceptional orator. It was thanks to his work that the ILWU became great allies of the sacked dockers. [12] For the dockers and their families Jack Heyman might well have been the 'Hollywood docker' or the US president himself, as he arrived in the wake of rank-and-file members of the East Coast International Longshoremen's Association refusing to cross a picket line set up by Liverpool dockers in Newark, New Jersey and other US ports. Heyman received a standing ovation following his introduction at Transport House, where he told the dockers that they, along with their supporters, were responsible for 'reigniting trade unionism all over the world.' [13]

Now, the impending loss of Atlantic Container Line loomed as a potentially devastating blow to MDHC. At that Saturday's demonstration the Lord Mayor of Liverpool, Mike Black, a former MDHC employee, used the platform to condemn the dismissal of the 500 dockers. Peter Skinley, the local Fire Brigade's Union leader, led the speakers after Jimmy Nolan, Jimmy Davies and Mike Carden had given their weekly updates. They were followed by a tired and jet-lagged ILWU longshoreman, Jack Heyman. He thanked the crowd for supporting the Liverpool dockers: 'It's heartening to see the militancy here. Liverpool is showing that the class struggle is alive and well. Longshoreman back home will be inspired.' [14] Heyman's visit injected fresh impetus and a sense of belief, as he spoke at length on the importance of developing international support, all the while acknowledging inherent weaknesses in the makeup of organisations such as the ITF. He also identified the potential impact of real action taking place on ports along the US West Coast, furnishing the Dispute Committee with new insights and forms of analysis that broadened their understanding of how an international strategy could be underpinned through direct action. Jack Heyman won the crowd over and at the end of his speech he began the chant, 'Dockers in – scabs out!' giving rise to what would become the chant for the dockers and their supporters. It was during this rally that photographer Dave Sinclair captured the iconic image of Heyman and the two Jimmies, Nolan and Davies, in front of the dockers' banner, which became one of the most celebrated pictures of the entire dispute. [15]

The BBC's *Newsnight* team was in attendance at the rally, interviewing demonstrators and providing media coverage that raised not just awareness, but also the morale of dockers on the picket lines. At the conclusion of the event, Heyman gave an interview to LabourNet, telling his compatriot, fellow American, Greg Dropkin:

> *'I have not seen this kind of militancy for years. I'd have to think back to some of the militant miners' strikes in West Virginia… the support they're getting is astounding to say the least, because there hasn't been this sort of international campaign in a long time… the employers have been pushing casualisation everywhere. So, to the extent that the Liverpool dockers are successful in combatting the employer here, it will have a ripple effect around the world. That's why solidarity is exploding internationally.' [16]*

The following Monday, the Dispute Committee again debated the importance of picketing the Liverpool tugboats and developing greater international support. The next day, a picket line was set-up at Birkenhead Docks for the first time, while more than 1,000 demonstrators picketed Bootle Town Hall, where a public inquiry into the closure of Dock Road as part of MDHC's redevelopment scheme was taking place. Inside the hall, dockers and their supporters mingled with senior representatives of MDHC, as they informed the inquiry of the employment opportunities that lay ahead if the Dock Company was granted planning permission. The ITF was due to convene on Wednesday 17 January 1996, and, as a delegate Jack Heyman convinced Jimmy Nolan that he should attend this meeting and speak directly to the delegates. The stewards did not agree that their chairman should travel to London and request support from an organisation which, they expected, would refuse to sanction any serious action. For some, it seemed a waste of time, and the fear was that a direct call for support before an international campaign had really been established would weaken the Liverpool dockers' position. Several members of the Dispute Committee preferred to build up towards gaining official ITF support on their own terms, beginning with the international conference due to be held in Liverpool the following month. It was felt that failure to obtain support at the ITF conference would bolster MDHC. Nolan disagreed with this analysis, making it clear that he wished to pursue all options, and he was to be proven right after returning to Liverpool with two official letters of support. Heyman was already showing himself to be an invaluable source of advice and guidance at a time when Bill Morris and the TGWU had still not really committed to backing the dispute long-term.

Delegates from various docker and seafarers' unions had interrupted the ITF conference's agenda to pass a resolution in support of the Liverpool dockers, with Ray Familathe of the Los Angeles ILWU explaining how: 'We got wind of the Liverpool situation on the very day we were demonstrating against non-union labour.' [17] Dave Morgan, an ITF delegate from New Zealand, said that he hoped the resolution would be passed, while Germany's Ali Memon agreed, adding that dockers and seafarers must unite: 'The Mersey Docks and Harbour Company had asked a German company to supply tugboats, but the German crews had refused to sail them in solidarity with the Liverpool men. We must support the Liverpool dockers.' This left the ITF secretary, David Cockcroft, with little choice but to concede: 'Many of our affiliates are completely behind the Liverpool dockers' strike. We will take the matter back to our respective unions and do our very best to ensure the maximum solidarity.' [18] The ITF's dockers' secretary, Kees Margees, told his fellow delegates: 'We cannot sit in our chairs because of anti-trade union legislation. I am convinced we must step up our campaign against non-union labour.' [19] Jimmy Nolan told the conference: 'This is an historic occasion. Thank you for your support; this is the meaning of internationalism. I can assure you that we will not accept casualisation, and once reinstated, we will give every support to international struggles.' [20]

Within a week of the conference, these expressions of support from the ITF had already begun to sour, and the Liverpool dockers were angered by what they saw was an attempt to undermine their calls for action via a statement issued in the final week of January 1996:

> 'Notwithstanding the mood of many of our affiliates, we wish to stress the need for an effective co-ordination in order to prevent any damage to the case of the Liverpool dockers. Effective co-ordination requires the ITF's affiliates to wait for a request from the ITF before supportive actions are organised. Do not start any action against any vessel known to be loading or discharging cargoes to and from the Port of Liverpool without contacting the ITF secretariat!' [21]

Put simply, the Liverpool dockers believed that this statement did not correspond with calls for the stepping up of solidarity action that were expressed by the majority of more than 100 international delegates in attendance at the ITF conference in London. [22] According to Jack Heyman's account of the ITF's response to Nolan's presence:

> 'The unfolding events were more dramatic. Cockcroft, after being asked if the Liverpool dockers could address us, replied that if they were invited, they'd act like a bunch of Liverpool hooligans and wreck ITF's new headquarters. The delegates were persistent, so Cockcroft acquiesced and allowed the Liverpool 'scousers' to speak at a special session in the evening at the 'end of business.' Of course, he expected no one to show after a long day of seminars, but it was a full house with only Jimmy Nolan representing the dockers. Inspectors heard Nolan lay out the plight of the Liverpool lads… Feigning support for the motion, Kees Marges rose to the deck to congratulate the delegates but had only one proviso: we had to wait for approval from the ITF after checking with its official affiliate the TGWU. Of course, Morris supported the motion like a rope supports a hanged man, and the ITF approval from the TGWU never came.' [23]

Twenty-seven years later Marges, and other leaders of the ITF, affirmed that Bill Morris had warned them not to get involved in the Liverpool dockers' dispute. [24] The ITF relied upon the financial contributions of its affiliated trade unions, and the TGWU was its largest UK contributor. However, like the ITF, the TGWU could not control all of its members, and some began to pledge alliance to their docker comrades. Can-Mar Shipping, now the biggest client at Seaforth Container Terminal, announced that if the situation inside the port did not improve, they would also pull out of Liverpool. Then, on 15 January, the Israeli dockers' union, having received Frank Lannigan and Kevin Robinson as delegates, contacted MDHC with the following message, signed by Mati Ayache, an Ashdod Dockers' Union representative:

> *'After meeting my comrades from the port of Liverpool, I was disgusted to hear what is happening to my fellow stevedores in Liverpool... I say that we in the port of Ashdod are not prepared to stand by and watch our 500 fellow trade unionists and their families be treated in the way that they have been treated for the last fifteen weeks.'* [25]

The following Tuesday evening, Jimmy Davies and Mike Carden were called to a secret meeting with a former employer on the docks, Muhammad Iqbal, who had been the Managing Director of Streeds Ltd. Iqbal had been involved in a series of controversial industrial disputes with the TGWU and the dockers in the past. As one of the first employers to set-up in the Free Port Area, he felt that promises made by MDHC had not been fulfilled, and that this had caused his business to fold. Both Davies and Carden hoped to obtain some useful information from this clandestine meeting at Liverpool's Adelphi Hotel, where various documents were presented as evidence of his many grievances against MDHC. But it soon became clear that much of the information was already known and the two stewards left with little more than a claim from Iqbal that he was going to sue MDHC and expose their 'internal financial corruption' once and for all.

On Wednesday 17 January, John Bowers, the president of the International Longshoreman's Association, telephoned Jimmy Nolan to inform him that he had spoken to ACL's Conrad De Zago, who had faxed MDHC's Trevor Furlong two days earlier to reiterate his intention to leave the Port of Liverpool if the dispute was not brought to a swift conclusion. Nicholas Frayling, Canon of Liverpool, had also written to Deputy Prime Minister Michael Heseltine, expressing his concern over the dismissal of the dockers and the impact that it was having on the viability of the port, as MDHC's share price continued to drop. That same week, a delegation from the Dispute Committee met with Jack Adams to discuss the union's lack of financial support for the dockers' Hardship Fund, at a time when the Regional Finance and General Purposes Committee had given £2,500 from its strike contingency fund. A further meeting was scheduled to take place with both the TGWU and MDHC the following Wednesday, at the offices of the Advisory, Conciliation and Arbitration Service in London, but Adams was not happy with either the venue or the attitude of the General Secretary, who did not like the idea of there being too many shop stewards in attendance. For their part, the position of the Dispute Committee was that all shop stewards should be present during any negotiations involving MDHC.

Meanwhile, it had been revealed that Torside Ltd were still trading in the Port of Liverpool, and MDHC continued to insist that their contract with Drake International was a long-term agreement, making it obvious that they were not open to reinstating their sacked dockers. Adams was of the opinion that this was little more than a bluff and that growing pressure would soon compel them to enter into meaningful negotiations. Eventually, Bill Morris accepted that all stewards could be present at the ACAS meeting, although some would have to wait outside while a smaller delegation handled negotiations. The TGWU also agreed to donate £30,000 to the Hardship Fund, while the Dispute Committee discussed at great length the implications of calling on shipping companies to leave the port. In the case of ACL, the union had expressed the view that such a move would be self-destructive, as the number of jobs available would be reduced if reinstatement was achieved, but the stewards believed that their campaign needed to be fought on multiple fronts to be successful, and that any action which could possibly force MDHC's hand should be considered. Finally, on Thursday 18 January, the Dispute Committee issued a statement calling on ACL to carry out their threat and leave the port, which MDHC's Bernard Cliff decried as being tantamount to sabotage, during a local radio appearance the next day.

On the international front, contact was made with the Port of Genoa, whose dockers were experiencing similar problems with privatisation and casualisation. They invited a delegation to go and explain the Liverpool situation to the workforce, with Tony Russell and Terry Teague being chosen to make up the delegation while work continued ahead of February's international conference. The Dispute Committee had agreed to explore the possibility of hiring a private venue, fearing that the TGWU would try to halt plans to hold such an event at Transport House. Representatives from Australia, Canada, Italy, Israel, Denmark, Germany, Spain and the Canary Islands had already accepted invitations, and Liverpool Town Hall, St George's Hall and the Moat House Hotel were all being considered as potential options. A letter was sent to Harry Rimmer, leader of the Labour City Council, seeking his support for the use of the Town Hall, and Pat Harvey of the Trade Union and Unemployed Resource Centre was again called upon to use her influence to obtain permission for its use, amid increasing pressure from the Liverpool Chamber of Commerce and local business to deny the dockers' request. In Issue No.4 of the *Dockers' Charter* Jimmy Davies declared that: 'The dockers would not sell their jobs in 1989; we are not going to sell them now, and the International Conference of Port Workers will step-up the campaign for reinstatement.' [26]

At the weekly mass meeting held Friday 19 January, morale was high as the dockers, their families and supporters received news of the letter from Israel and the decision of dockers in Salerno to refuse to handle ships from Liverpool. Jimmy Nolan took great pride in reporting on the support promised by the ITF, as well as the cheque received for the Hardship Fund from the TGWU. Bob Parry MP addressed the dockers, telling them about a meeting he had with Neil Kinnock in Strasbourg, France, where Kinnock promised to write to employers and shipowners regarding the dockers. That same day, Prime Minister John Major gave a quote to the *Liverpool Echo* in support of MDHC on the eve of ACL's decision to leave the port. [27] Bill Morris now declared that only four shop stewards would be allowed to meet with ACAS and MDHC, while insisting that Danny Maher, the GEC member for the Docks and Waterways Section, also be in attendance. Morris also expressed concern over how payments were being made to the dockers via the Hardship Fund, even though it had already been agreed that beneficiaries would sign for all payments received from the TGWU office in Liverpool and the fund would be managed externally by local community leaders.

As pressure on MDHC built, financiers Brewin Dolphin Bell Lawrie Ltd recommended that shareholders sell their interests in the company on a weekend of mixed press coverage for the dockers, with a negative *Sunday Times* article being balanced out by fairly positive pieces appearing in the *Sunday Independent*, the *Financial Times* and, somewhat surprisingly, the *Daily Express*. As Dave Cotterill noted:

> *'Picking up on some of the regular spoiler articles in the Liverpool Daily Post and Liverpool Echo, often containing allegations of violence against pickets and scabs from dockers shooting at cars and heavy haulage vehicles as they crossed the picket lines, fire-bombing scabs' cars in driveways', political extremism and communists, The Sunday Times claimed that "members of Militant, the far-left organisation, banned by Labour, and the SWP had swollen the picket lines."'* [28]

As the dispute rolled into January 1996 attempts were made in some sections of the press to insinuate that the far-left was attempting to hijack the dispute. According to Dave Cotterill, the Times ran an article about one supporter of the dockers, Lesley Mahmood, stating that she was: 'a Militant member and former council colleague of Derek Hatton, who has been one of the most prominent figures on the picket line.' [29] The *Daily Express*, ran an exposé on the burgeoning world of the flying picket, which would apparently become the norm in Britain under a New Labour government: 'What one senses more than anything else is an unbreakable confidence among the Liverpool pickets that things will work out all right, even when right is overwhelmingly on the boss's side.' For Cotterill: 'These sporadic attacks were not to be sustained and were more of an exception than the rule. In general, the policy of the media and official society was to draw a blanket of silence over the whole affair.' [30] Bill Morris would later return to allegations that the Liverpool dockers had become a 'political party' aligned with 'environmentalists and anarchists.'

# 30

# The First Ballot – a 90.3%
# Rejection of MDHC's First
# and Final Offer

*The TUC managed to donate one sentence to the Liverpool dock dispute in its online history: 'The dismissal of the remaining few hundred unionised Merseyside dockers during an* unofficial dispute in 1995 *led to the biggest (but eventually unsuccessful) strike support campaign of the 1990s'. ~ TUC\**

At a Friday mass meeting held 19 January 1996, Frank Lannigan and Kevin Robinson reported back after their delegation work in Israel. It was at this meeting that Steve Alcock's widow expressed her thanks to all of those who had attended the funeral of her husband, who was a much-respected T&G comrade and a supporter of the Liverpool dockers. Jimmy Nolan then spoke about the International Transport Workers' Federation campaign, and Mike Carden discussed a forthcoming parliamentary sub-committee session. Bob Parry MP was there to tell the dockers about his meeting with Neil Kinnock. On Wednesday 24 January, the long-awaited meeting between the TGWU and MDHC took place at the ACAS offices in London. Excluded from the meeting, most of the shop stewards waited at the new TGWU's head office on Palace Street, as talks rumbled on from 2pm – 10.30pm. Radio City in Liverpool contacted the stewards just after midnight to find out what, if anything, had been agreed and the story at this time was that Drake International would leave the port, Torside Ltd would carry on trading and Nelson Freight dockers would be paid off with £1,000 severance. This left 40 jobs available to the sacked MDHC dockers, with the rest to be made redundant with a £25,000 pay-off, all of which would be voted on in a secret ballot organised through the Electoral Reform Society.

---

\* 'The Union Makes Us Strong – TUC History Online', available:
http://www.unionhistory.info/timeline/1960_2000_7.php

The offer from MDHC was disclosed to the dockers at their meeting on Friday 26 January. The key point for the stewards being that Drakes would stay in the port. The employers' offer was costed at £8m and the company insisting upon a secret ballot on condition that no victimisation of workers in the port would take place once it had been accepted. Jack Adams reminded the stewards of the need to hold an official ballot, which was not a point of contention with the real issue for the dockers being that the terms of the offer were unacceptable. The idea of dockers applying to Drake International for employment was viewed as an insult. Perhaps the most interesting aspect of the offer was the fact that a dispute labelled as an 'unofficial strike' by both the TGWU and MDHC should require an official legal ballot. At the meeting, Jimmy Davies concluded his Docks and Waterways National Committee report emphasising the absence of any concrete action from Danny Maher and the Liverpool tugboat men. At the mass meeting held later that day, two of the city's church leaders requested an opportunity to address the dockers, and this was granted in light of the extraordinary role that Bishop David Sheppard and Archbishop Derek Worlock had each played in their respective working-class communities. The industrial chaplain, Randell Moll, told the dockers that their struggle was: 'a fight for justice for all,' and that the MDHC were 'only interested in profit and gain.' [1] On the matter of MDHC's recent offer, Canon Frayling prefaced his comments by acknowledging that it was ultimately for the workers themselves to decide, before admitting that he did feel as though the dispute continuing would only mean increased suffering for all those affected, telling the men: 'if you ask for jam today, you may get bread tomorrow.' [2] The absence of a representative from the Catholic Church was a source of some wry humour among the assembled dockers. Father Michael de Felice of Bootle would always be their spiritual leader, especially since he had recently been appointed their 'banker' for the Hardship Fund.

After weeks of braving snow and ice on the picket lines, this meeting to discuss MDHC's 'final offer' turned out to be a stormy two-and-a-half-hour affair, as the dockers disregarded pleas from the union and local church leaders in unanimously rejecting their former employer's terms. The shop stewards, who had called for such a response, were correct in predicting that the result of the ballot would reflect the mood at the mass meeting, as speaker after speaker stood to remind everyone that they had not been fighting for money, but for jobs. Doreen McNally, representing the Women of the Waterfront, said at the time: 'The whole world's eyes are on these men. Every working man and woman in this country is affected, because they all face short-term contracts and loss of rights. The dockers' wives are one hundred per cent behind their husbands in continuing this fight for jobs and rights.' [3] Jimmy Nolan then reiterated that the only way for the dispute to be resolved was by reinstating all sacked dockers, [4] citing the fact that international secondary action had so far cost the Dock Company an estimated £4m, in addition to a £3.3m loss for Euro-link. Still, even in the face of serious revenue drops, MDHC maintained its passion for threatening a labour force that no longer worked for them, warning that their offer was conditional upon their largest customer, Atlantic Container Lines, agreeing to stay in the port. This obvious attempt at forcing the dockers to call off their US-based action only emboldened them to revisit the international ports that had supported them so significantly, despite it becoming increasingly apparent that the ITF was now actively undermining those efforts. [5]

# THE FIRST BALLOT – A 90.3% REJECTION OF MDHC'S FIRST AND FINAL OFFER

The next mass meeting began with a minute's silence for the brother of docker John Brittles, before Jimmy Davies made a impassioned plea for dockers to turn down the severance money and fight for their jobs. Jack Adams, the union's deputy general secretary, and Dave McCall, the regional secretary, presented a detailed report of negotiations with MDHC. Adams informed the dockers that the company had no legal responsibility to the sacked dockers, only a moral one, and he also explained that following threats of sequestration, the only recommendation that Bill Morris was willing to make was that the offer be put to a ballot. This prompted Eddie Loyden MP to declare that the abolition of the National Dock Labour Board Scheme in 1989 had led to the dismissals of 1995, as he called upon the next Labour government to repeal Margaret Thatcher's anti-trade union laws. Finally, the offer was put to the dockers and was unanimously rejected, but it was also agreed that a postal ballot should go ahead with their full participation. The Liverpool dockers were confident in their solidarity, knowing that whether it was a show of hands or a secret ballot, the results would be the same. Morris, on the other hand, seemed to fear that the ballot would go against the view he had held from the very start of the dispute, as the TGWU enclosed a document with the ballot papers that clearly stated, 'the Union's Executive Officers accept the Proposals are not the best deal desirable but, in the circumstances, they clearly represent the best deal possible.' [6]

On Monday 29 January, that day's picket succeeded in closing three gates and causing large queues that left MDHC's Trevor Furlong stuck in his car for an hour and a half. The attitude of the company's hired security had hardened, and they had taken to clearing any braziers and huts at the various gates along the docks, while at Seaforth they had threatened random arrests if the line did not clear. One inspector informed the pickets that they were demonstrators, not strikers, and that this entitled both Merseyside Police and MDHC's own police force to control the lines as they saw fit. In Transport House the stewards now discovered that MDHC's offer only applied to their 329 former employees. Questions soon arose over whether or not this ballot would change the unofficial status of the dispute, with neither the TGWU nor MDHC appearing to realise that they were both now acting jointly as though it was an officially recognised *strike*. If the employer was not in fact colluding with the union, it means that the TGWU exposed itself to all manner of litigation by representing their members in what they had consistently referred to as an unofficial strike, yet no legal action would ever be taken by MDHC throughout the dispute. When the stewards met again at Transport House, they attempted to clarify exactly who was being allowed to take part in the ballot, as by their calculations there should have been 329 from MDHC, 80 from Torside, 11 from Nelson Freight, 6 from Excel and two boatmen, totalling 428 eligible voters, with approximately 72 dockers who had crossed the picket line since September 1995 ineligible to vote. There was talk of the historical significance of this vote, and how it was a case of the greater the majority in rejecting this offer the greater the potential of forcing real solidarity action through the TGWU and ITF. At least that was the theory.

Support continued to develop outside of the UK as New Zealand seafarers and dockers issued an invitation for a delegation to visit their ports in February, while arrangements were already made for delegations to Belgium, Greece and France. ABC Containerline ships were still being boycotted in Australia, and this, according to the company's owner, Tsvi Rosenfeld, was bankrupting them. Rosenfeld would appear on BBC's

*Newsnight* to express sympathy for the dockers – his fee was donated to the Hardship Fund. [7] Liverpool Town Hall was confirmed as the venue for the inaugural International Conference of Port Workers, with Pat Harvey using her connections and influence to convince local councillors that they should support the dockers' cause. On Monday 29 January, John Bowers of the International Longshoremen's Association telephoned to inform the dockers that David Cockcroft (ITF) and John Connolly (TGWU) had asked the ILA not to do anything to encourage ACL to pull out of Liverpool without their joint permission.

The following day, a mass meeting was called to discuss the men's rejection of MDHC's offer the previous week, and it was explained that the MDHC and the TGWU planned to hold three separate ballots and declare three separate results; the dockers recognised this as a deliberately divisive and undemocratic process. At the same meeting Jimmy Davies announced that Liverpool-born footballer, Steve McManaman, had donated £500 to the Hardship Fund. Tony Nelson then reported that the WOW had succeeded in closing the Seaforth gate the day before. It was also announced that Peel Holdings, owner of Manchester Docks and future owner of MDHC, had sold their 8.3 % share in MDHC for £31.2m, which were acquired by Prudential and Mercury Asset Management.

The next Friday's mass meeting was more subdued, as the dockers waited for the ballot to be counted ahead of a result being declared the following Thursday. A minute's silence was held for Peter Turnbull's 10-year-old son, who had tragically passed away. Peter was a labour historian, an academic and a respected friend and comrade of the Liverpool dockers. The following day, the 10th dockers' rally took place with great success, as more than 12,000 people from all over the UK and beyond lined the streets of Liverpool, although some stewards felt that with more organisational work, they could have drawn an even larger turnout. There was also some disappointment that Arthur Scargill did not make the rally, but Mike Grindley, sacked for speaking out in defence of trade unionism at Government Communication Headquarters (GCHQ) gave a speech on the repression that was facing workers at Wapping, P&O Dover, Silentnight, Tilbury, Timex and Arrowsmiths. [8] Eddie Loyden MP, himself a former port worker, closed the meeting by saying that what he saw from the Liverpool dockers was: 'The best example of working-class leadership in the last 16 years. Liverpool workers are involved in a struggle on behalf of British and international working-class movements, and the only political and industrial leadership is coming from the Liverpool dockers.' [9] That week, heavy snow had made picketing difficult, and on one picket line some 60 demonstrators were confronted by 70 police officers. Plans for the International Conference of Port Workers continued especially in relation to the general logistics of hosting such an event from delegates accommodation to the matter of sourcing translators. Unlike the TGWU, the dockers had the requisite organising and networking skills to get the job done without the need for expensive private consultants. [10]

At 10am on Thursday 8 February, the much-anticipated postal ballot result was faxed through by the Electoral Reform Society, confirming 50 votes for and 271 against MDHC's offer, giving an 84% majority in favour of rejecting their settlement package. This was a vindication of the dockers confidence in their struggle and their solidarity. It was a resounding rejection of the Company's offer and the union's support for it. The aim of the alliance between the Dock Company and the TGWU had been that by conducting separate ballots they could manipulate the MDHC employees into abandoning the other dockers, but

# 30

# THE FIRST BALLOT – A 90.3% REJECTION OF MDHC'S FIRST AND FINAL OFFER

when adjusted to include results from the Torside and Nelson Freight ballots (56 against, six in favour and 14 abstentions), the final result was a resounding 90.3 % against the company's offer. It was also discovered that 16 men who had crossed the picket line and were working in the port, had also been sent ballot papers. In an interview with *Newsline*, Torside's Bob Ritchie described the vote as: 'an overwhelming result, even though people who are working in the docks received ballot papers.' [11] Ian Spencer, another sacked Torside docker, commented to a newspaper reporter that he was always confident in the resolve of his comrades, adding: 'We think it's a disgrace that men working received ballot papers. They turned their backs on the dispute from day one.' [12] The *North West Business Insider* seemed to understand this vision of solidarity better than the dockers own union, as they analysed MDHC's role as both catalyst and antagonist in this dispute:

> *'The dispute between the MDHC and its dockers is threatening to untangle the delicate industrial stability that has been created in the country over the past five years. It began innocuously enough but has now escalated well beyond the boundaries of Merseyside, thanks, it can be said, to a combination of poor management and appalling industrial relations. The MDHC management has clearly attempted to use the dispute as an excuse to bring in changes to manning levels that they did not have the courage to impose. The refusal of the MDHC dockers to cross a picket line may have been misguided, but it was not enough to warrant the sacking of an entire workforce. The docks, particularly in Liverpool, have a justified reputation for militancy, but in this instance, it is the managers who are returning to the bad old ways. The company deserves better.' [13]*

The mass meeting on Friday 9 February was a celebration of the ballot result, although some dockers wanted to know the identities of the 56 who voted for MDHC's offer; they also questioned how the TGWU could justify representing roughly 60 of the Kent-based scabs that, it was revealed, were working in the Port of Liverpool. [14] A report was heard from the delegation that had returned from Le Havre, France, with pledges of support from the CGT union. Derek Reardon and Brian Roberts visited this huge influential port after being informed that French union officials had sent out an invitation, only to discover upon arrival that no communication between the local union and the dockers had really taken place. Obviously, there was a considerable language barrier to overcome, but common ground was eventually reached, in keeping with the prevailing theme of the international delegations that the life of a dockworker was the same the world over, right down to architecture. 'The pens are the same, the work is the same; we are the same,' [15] Reardon remarked, before relaying a message from their French comrades: 'Courage! Courage!' which, he explained, translates into English as 'courage,' sending the hall into uproarious laughter. [16] The Le Havre dockers that he and Roberts met would go on to play a remarkable role in supporting the Liverpool dockers taking direct action against ships that used MDHC's ports. They were also to be founder members of the International Dockworkers Council.

All dockers were given a *'One of 500 sacked Liverpool dockers'* badge in time for the conference, comprised of two colours, red and blue for the two Merseyside football teams, under the joined hands symbol of trade union solidarity. It was very a limited print run, with only a few spares produced in case some were lost, although a 'Support the dockers' badge was also released for sale to the public on a much larger scale. [17] Terry Southers planned for the arrival of dockers attending the International Conference of Port Workers on a huge chart that he hung up on the wall of the boardroom at Transport House. Visitors were expected from everywhere across Europe and North America – when the Canadian delegation arrived at Manchester Airport, by pure chance they came across Peter Jones, a MDHC director, and took great delight in confronting him about his role in the dismissal of the Liverpool dockers. It was a time of renewed optimism, as after four months out on the picket lines, the dockers had rejected, by 90.3%, a 'final' offer from the Dock Company that had been supported by their union. This was an achievement in the face of immense pressure from an employer and a union that united to manufacture an entirely different result.

# 31

# The First International Conference of Port Workers; the Dispute Goes Digital

*'On Sunday 28 December 1997, the dockers were informed that Billy Rooney, one of the sacked Liverpool dockers, had died in hospital. The brother of Terry Southers, one of the Port Shop Stewards, had died also at the weekend. The situation amongst the dockers was at an all-time low.' ~ Kevin Robinson\**

O n Monday 12 February 1996, the Dispute Committee received confirmation that the group of 47 formerly elected Liverpool city councillors, who had been banned from holding office after refusing to implement cuts to local services imposed by the Thatcher government between 1983-1987, would support the dockers' struggle. The ex-councillors had decided to release money from their 'fighting fund' to help finance the upcoming International Conference of Port Workers, which Tony Mulhearn, the former deputy leader of Liverpool City Council, saw as a potential key turning point in the dispute and a vindication of the dockers' solidarity in rejecting the Mersey Docks and Harbour Company's severance package:

> *'It was a magnificent vote of the Liverpool dockworkers to reject that offer. They are fighting for jobs for the future and for conditions to be built up. Our fathers and their fathers before them established these conditions. This vote is a tremendous inspiration. They are not bluffing; they are serious to win this battle. Every one of the 47 victimised councillors is proud. There is no doubt that the history of this struggle will be told in the future... When the 47 councillors took their unanimous decision to make this financial contribution... We have all been involved in redundancy; cash on the table is a big*

---

\* Kevin Robinson (from notes on the mass meeting held 19 December 1997) *factor. Every May Day we hear leaders talking about internationalism, but this conference is internationalism.' [1]*

For the Dispute Committee, the importance of securing Liverpool Town Hall as the venue for the conference could not be overstated, as it raised the profile of both the event and the dispute. There was also the satisfaction of knowing that local employers objected to its use for such purposes, since the Grade 1-listed building, built in 1754 and then rebuilt in 1802, was originally the property of Liverpool's slave traders and the rest of the city's self-proclaimed great and good. For those attending the workers' conference, perhaps the most important aspect of the building's history was the fact it was the centre of the 1775 Liverpool Seamen's Revolt. [2] Eric Leatherbarrow, MDHC's press officer, told Radio Merseyside that allowing the dockers to use the Town Hall would bring the city into disrepute and undermine attempts to generate business in the area. This view was shared by the Liverpool Chamber of Commerce. Paul Foot, writing in *The Guardian*, expressed an alternative view: 'The most inspiring feature of this dispute has been its internationalism, or as one of the international delegates said, 'When I shook the hand of a Liverpool docker, I was shaking the hand of a docker who would shake the world.' [3]

Dave Cotterill and Pat Harvey played major roles in organising the conference, an unexpectedly key element was the setting-up of a computer that delegates could use to update those following the event across the world. This conference was, quite possibly, the first ever rank-and-file international trade union e-conference, at a time when global connectivity was very much in its infancy. Fifty-three delegates attended from fifteen countries and the event would be remembered for its sophisticated display of grassroots organisation, achieved less than two months after the idea for an international conference was originally floated by Jimmy Nolan to Mike Carden in Peppers, the pub facing Transport House. The Liverpool dockers had always been extremely capable and practical people, and they arranged every aspect of the event between themselves and their dedicated supporters, from Terry Southers and Andy Dwyer meticulously planning the transport rota and booking accommodation for delegates, to scheduling mealtimes around the packed itinerary. The conference, like the dispute, was the product of rigid organisation and unerring attention to detail, from folders containing all documents and agendas right down to each delegation's respective table flags (the only correction needed was for the Montreal dockers, who wanted the Quebecois flag). These were to be five momentous days, marking an organisational accomplishment that any official trade union or business with unlimited access to efficient bureaucrats and highly paid consultants would have been proud of. This was an international conference organised by dock labourers and their supporters – a working-class conference.

It was around this time that John Bowers, the president of the International Longshoremen's Association, sent word that he wanted a small Liverpool delegation to travel to the United States again and meet with New York dockers. The effects of Atlantic Container Line's reduced traffic through Liverpool was, along with its threat to pull out altogether, impacting upon other users in the port, especially Coastal Containers, a subsidiary of MDHC. It would also impact upon other ports that serviced these shipping lines throughout the world. John Bowers's friend, Henry 'Whitey' Disley, president of the Marine Firemen's Union in San Francisco and uncle to Peter Wharton, one of the two boatmen who

# THE FIRST INTERNATIONAL CONFERENCE OF PORT WORKERS; THE DISPUTE GOES DIGITAL

were sacked for supporting the Liverpool dockers, also had a hand in winning the support of this hugely influential trade union. [4] As was often the case throughout the dockers' long history, connections with their US-based supporters ran through Ireland, where ACL relied heavily on trans-shipments being loaded onto vessels bound for American ports via Coastal Containers. Just a few weeks before MDHC sacked its labour force in September 1995, the company was the subject of an Office of Fair Trading investigation into claims that they were attempting to monopolise Irish Sea traffic. At the time, these complaints centred on container-handling facilities in Ellesmere Port, where Irish Ferries had recently launched a thrice-weekly service to Dublin, and a Swansea-based firm, Dragon Shipping Line, claimed that they were effectively being blocked by royalty payments that MDHC had secured for any containers loaded or discharged there. This had been the case since 1992, when MDHC had bought cranes stationed at Ellesmere Dock and moved them to Seaforth Container Terminal, demonstrating how the company, 'Once seen as the sick man of the UK ports sector, was now seen as a dynamic operator capable of dominating the growing Irish Sea trade.' [5]

Having dropped a lawsuit against the Merseyside Port Shop Stewards in US Courts, the Dock Company were now threatening to sue the ILA over Bowers' actions regarding ACL, with Chicago based law firm, Mayer Brown and Platt writing to demand that he formally disassociate his union from disrupting or diverting ACL shipping bound for or coming from Liverpool. The law firm warned: 'if this demand is not met, we will institute a suit for damages… running into millions.' [6] Bobby Morton and Tony Nelson, two members of the original US delegation, attended a meeting of the Transportation Trades Department of the American Federation of Labor and Congress of Industrial Organizations (AFL-CIO) in February 1996, where on behalf of the Liverpool dockworkers, the International Longshore and Warehouse Union submitted Resolution No. 996(f), the preamble being: 'The AFL-CIO will support and assist any industrial actions by the International Longshore and Warehouse Union, the International Longshoremen's Association, and the International Transport Workers' Federation to protest at ports where vessels are known to be loading / discharging cargoes to and from the port of Liverpool; and unequivocally condemns the unjust firing of 500 Liverpool dockworkers.' [7]

Back in Liverpool, the inaugural International Conference of Port Workers began on Saturday 17 February. Bernard Cliff, MDHC's port operations manager, was invited to speak at the event, but the offer was declined with the statement: 'The company has invited the overseas delegates to talks in our quiet offices. At the conference, they will be told only what the leaders of this unofficial action want them to hear, not the case put by the company, the TGWU or the thousands of union members who don't acknowledge the pickets' claim.' [8] Jimmy Nolan opened the conference by explaining that the Liverpool dockers had addressed some 2,500 meetings in the UK since their dispute began the previous September. [9] The central theme of this conference was not simply the discussion of the Liverpool docks dispute; it was also the examination of employee contracts in the various international ports represented; the role of international solidarity in opposing casual labour and the privatisation of ports across the globe. The role of women in the struggle was also on the agenda, along with a tour of the picket lines, and a labour lawyer spoke on UK trade union laws. The importance of international communications with particular emphasis on the internet was accepted as vital to the international struggle of the Liverpool dock workers. Each delegate attended at least one mass meeting, where they saw first-hand the ambition to challenge the leadership of the TGWU and the ITF as well as the port employers. Mike Carden was dealing with the standing orders of the conference and he explained to delegates that, the Liverpool dockers wanted: 'to build an international organisation.' [10] On Thursday 22 February, MDHC published a full-page condemnation of the conference in the *Liverpool Echo*. [11]

John Bolger, of the Amalgamated and General Workers' Union of Ireland, put things into context when he said: 'The Liverpool fight is the fight of the working class against the Tory governments of the world,' [12] while Australia's Jim Donovan said he was: 'amazed to find such a conference as this taking place.' [13] Donovan asserted that the trade union movement in Australia had its roots established by the Tolpuddle Martyrs and that unions, once again, were under attack. Michel Murray, from Quebec, Canada, pointed out that a conference of this kind had not been held since 1947, in Detroit: 'Fifty years is too long to wait. This is a sort of beginning of dockers' solidarity around the world.' [14] Murray later predicted that the conference would deliver a message to MDHC and all the shipping companies to, 'Reinstate the sacked dockers because international dockers are going to take action, and don't do this again because international dockers will act again!' [15] Canadian dock worker, Pat Riley, echoed the sentiments of his compatriot when he talked of how the plight of the Liverpool dockers reflected those faced by dockers all over the world, citing the example of 150 oil refinery workers in St John's, who had been locked out for 22 months after mounting picket lines in response to 50 dockers being fired with no reasons given. Riley viewed the conference as a timely reminder of the need to replace the corporate world of Thatcher, Reagan and Muldoon, which would require bringing many workers who didn't formally belong to the trade union movement into the fold. Ole Muller, from Copenhagen, Denmark, recalled how: 'Nine years ago we had faced the same situation as that in Liverpool,' before adding, 'We are greatly interested in the conference because it could be us next time.' [16] A representative of the Le Havre dockers, Philippe Gaudillo, said that his delegation, which also included Charles Thieullen, were all, 'very happy to be at the conference. It is necessary to build a structure in Europe and the world to fight against world capitalism.' [17] From Greece, Nick Georgiou, a docker from the port of Pireaus, said: 'What is happening in Liverpool is being brought about throughout Europe by privatisation. Greek dockers have the will to take a full part in this international initiative that had been launched,' [18] to which seafarer Savas Tsiboglou agreed: 'Thousands of Greek dockers face the sack as privatisation gets under way. Society is being driven back to medieval conditions of work. It is necessary for the movement to impose its logic and politics, a logic and politics in direct opposition to that of capital.' [19] Gerry Quigley, a TGWU shop steward from Derry, Ireland, informed the assembly that:

> *'The dockers of Derry were victorious in a protracted dispute lasting 13 months, when the employer wanted to sack every docker or de-unionise the port, despite no support from the union. I personally still have a fine of £200,000 hanging over my head for blockading the port, boarding the vessels and staying inside the hold of a ship. The law is there to be obeyed, but we have a greater obligation to the working class.' [20]*

# THE FIRST INTERNATIONAL CONFERENCE OF PORT WORKERS; THE DISPUTE GOES DIGITAL

Gianni Dozza of Genoa, Italy, believed that the conference was extremely important because it had reached dockers all over the world, convincing him that if everyone pulled together, positive results would follow, while Bilbao, Spain's Francisco Mellado stated that he had, 'not been in an international conference for a long time, but there must be a conference like this every year. Privatisation is coming to Spain, and so we face the same problems as in Liverpool. The only difference between us is language. We are all workers.' [21] Mellado's fellow Spaniard, Francisco Ramos Vargos, had been a docker for 26 years, and as a veteran of the Tenerife disputes of the 1980s, he had experienced the sort of problems that Liverpool was attempting to overcome. It was his belief that the dockers could not win while fighting alone; they had to unite with others. [22] Jorg Wessels, from Hamburg, Germany, told the conference that many of his comrades had been, 'shocked when the British dockers' National Dock Labour Scheme was abolished,' not least because it had been held up as an example for German dockers in how it protected wages and conditions. [23] From New Zealand, Terry Ryan recounted how his country's 1991 Employment Contract contained some of the most repressive legislation in the world, through which trade union influence had effectively been removed, prompting him to declare, 'We have to win.' [24] Ryan's seafarer countryman, Pat Lumber, was saddened to say that he now represented only 1,500 members, as opposed to 3,000-4,000 prior to containerisation, while Antonio Mariano spoke of how dockers in Portugal had seen the national labour force fall from 10,000 to 1,000. Mariano told his fellow delegates, 'We have to use this Liverpool fight to unite. This is a great City; you don't deserve what is happening here. We will try to help as much as we can.' [25] Jack Heyman, of the International Longshoremen and Warehousemen's Union, San Francisco Local 10 said:

*'There is now the beginning of the process of the development of workers who know that class struggle can win for the working class. This is just the beginning; there is class consciousness among the delegates. This is where we must begin. There must be an open and frank discussion. It is important to connect the conference discussion to a programme based on action. Words are not enough. There have been conferences before – great platitudes – but platitudes are insufficient to deal with the power of the employers and the state which backs them.' [26]*

Arturo De Rosa, from Salerno, then invited all present to be united to confront and resolve the problem, 'with the same hard-headedness of those who perpetuate this problem,' [27] and Sweden's Peter Shaw reported that, 'My union had very good relations with the Unofficial Port Shop Stewards Committee in Britain, but after the 1989 strike the phone stopped ringing. Now I can see that the Mersey Shop Stewards are still alive.' [28] Björn Borg, a member of the same union as Shaw, followed-up by announcing that the Swedish dockers were already taking action in support of Liverpool, which was enough for Michel Murray to observe how it was clear that all present were in agreement and should, 'get on with our business.' [29] Terry Teague spoke on behalf of the Liverpool dockers, informing the conference that their dispute had entered its 22nd week, and explaining how, 'In the early days, many people, including many friends, thought that it would go like many others over the last 20 years, but after a well-organised and historical campaign, we are still here! We believe that we are on the verge of victory.' [30] He acknowledged that the greatest support they had received had come from their international comrades, and that this had encouraged the sacked Liverpool dockers to believe that they could win. Over the course of the following days, the delegates moved swiftly to finalise a number of key objectives:

- To carry out every type of direct and indirect action against all vessels and companies which continue to do business with the employers of the 500 dockers sacked in Liverpool.

- To provide the Liverpool dockers with material aid and call upon other port workers' unions to do the same; to set up an international steering committee to meet no later than August 1996 to decide on the venue and frequency of future international conferences, and to coordinate actions, first for the Liverpool dispute, and then on any attack affecting dockers.

- To campaign to ensure that the rights of all workers are defended and continually upgraded, and therefore to declare that all laws that take away the right to strike run contrary to basic democratic freedoms.

- To take solidarity action, if required, in defence of New Zealand dockers facing the introduction of non-union casual labour and the West Coast (US) dockers confronted with possible strike action to defend their contract.

- To support the Trans-Tasman Accord, linking the struggles of Australian and New Zealand dockers and seafarers.

- To declare a 'Hot Cargo' edict for all Irvine Oil Limited products if called upon to do so by the Canadian Labour Congress, in support of the 150 sacked Irvine workers locked out for 22 months.

- To call for the immediate release of the jailed Sataur-100 trade unionists – bus workers in Mexico City, Mexico – victimised for their struggle against privatisation.

- To endorse the use of the International Communication Network to provide information on issues and struggles of all maritime workers.

- To send letters expressing international support to the dockers of North Quay, Drogheda, taking a strike ballot against their sacking, and to write to the Argentinian president to protest the imprisonment of trade unionists and left activists.

The International Conference of Port Workers helped to forge genuine solidarity and friendship among the delegates, including the Women of the Waterfront, who played a prominent role in the daily organisation. Speaking to *LabourNet*, Jim Donovan's secretary and office manager, Ina Heidtman, said at the time that she:

> '...*felt a great pride and emotion when I read the stories of your women and their role; of their first hesitant steps to the picket line, with their desire to be an integral part of the struggle, not merely bystanders, but right amongst the action of the struggle. They have certainly proved that by their action early last week, when deep in snow, they closed the Freeport Gates. This was the act of courageous and dedicated women.*' [31]

Heidtman also spoke of her experience during the successful waterfront strike against a coalition of shipowners and the Menzies Conservative Australian government, which had taken place 40 years ago that week:

> *'It also brings back memories of the role of the Dockers' Women's Committee in Australia, who took part in the great historic struggles of the waterfront in 1954 and 1956. They, too, were hesitant about the picket line, but once there, they were a force to be reckoned with. They were not only defending their husbands, their way of life, but the union and labour movement as a whole. They were active on all committees, speaking at factory gates, on publicity committees, organising welfare just as WOW are now doing! The power, the tenacity and dedication of women to a cause. It is reflected in all their endeavours, from the home to the factory floor, to the picket line.' [32]*

She had attended the conference along with Phil Toby, vice-president of the Maritime Union of Australia, who told the *Workers' Press* that his union was 'right behind these dockers; we've raised finance for this dispute. It was a master stroke to involve dockers across the world.' [33] Translations for the conference were facilitated by a number of supporters, led initially by Greg Dropkin and Chris Bailey, who worked to ensure that *LabourNet* was at the heart of this event, reporting and recording for a global audience. It may have not been known to the dock stewards, at the time, but this was perhaps the UK's first industrial dispute to have its own website, at a time not too far removed from the days where hand-cranked mimeograph machines (stencil duplicators) were state-of-the-art technology for trade unionists publishing their own leaflets. Within days of the Liverpool dockers being sacked, there were comrades on hand to provide unique advice and guidance on the need for them to make full use of the information, communication and digital technology (ICDT) revolution that was unleashing its phenomenal potential at the time. Greg Coyne helped to set up and co-ordinate the trade union movement's first European electronic mailing list, Union-D, through which subscribers could contact one another cheaply and quickly. Union-D had initially been created in 1994, but the idea really came alive in 1995, pioneering the global march towards *the cyber picket*. [34]

From his base at the Merseyside Trade Union Centre, Greg Coyne began posting information such as the Dispute Committee's address to Union-D, asking subscribers to advise on ways to conduct community campaigns or simply send messages of support, as well as donations and information on the Port of Liverpool and its international connections. He also asked the emergent global community to assist in contacting European Union MEPs to report on the activities of MDHC, which had been a beneficiary of substantial EU grants. This information was also passed to other trade union electronic networks, including Canada's *Labor-L* and US-based *LaborNet*, as the stewards found themselves being able to communicate with comrades in Australia instantaneously. It became the responsibility of Chris Bailey, based in Cambridge, to forward new information to *GreenNet*, which was a member of an international organisation called the Association for Progressive Communications. Another APC affiliate, the American site *LaborNet*, had itself been working to develop a trade union computer network, comprising of workers in auto, rail, public sector and maritime industries, and when the Liverpool dockers' dispute was presented to *GreenNet*, they agreed to launch a UK *LabourNet* by providing a free web space and address. This act of generosity was later extended to include all strikes and lockouts, with the Hillingdon Hospital strikers also joining the network. The Liverpool docks dispute had gone viral, with these links to prominent trade union websites making the story accessible to anyone with an internet connection. In 1996, news presented on a computer screen could feel impersonal, static and remote, but *LabourNet* was quick to utilise photographs to humanise the dockers as real, living people, not just characters in a story from a distant cyberspace. Thanks to some technical ingenuity, pictures of Jack Heyman visiting with the dockers were projected onto a screen at a support event for the dispute in San Francisco and at the suggestion of one of *LabourNet's* readers, the site began supplying images to various labour movement publications. The next step was to put the whole of the *Dockers' Charter* library online.

The issues raised in Liverpool were being echoed in places like Ireland, where the Dunnes Stores' workers were fighting against zero-hour contracts, and at Packard Electric, a subsidiary of the giant multinational General Motors, which had decided to close its Tallaght plant at the cost of 800 jobs. Here, the great advancements made in terms of international solidarity became important lessons for all workers, with Jimmy Nolan writing in the May 1996 edition of the *Dockers' Charter*:

> *'We have confirmed that globalisation of capitalism necessitates the global international solidarity of the working class. Throughout the world, workers are exploited by the same companies and face casualisation and anti-trade union laws. It is imperative that the international working class continues to recognise that we are the producers of all products and all wealth.'* [35]

The Liverpool dockers' battle with MDHC was playing a crucial role in the development of a global online communications network for rank-and-file trade unionists, and it should be remembered that this was a time when many journalists reporting on the dispute did not know what a worldwide web address even was, or what on earth the dockers were using this technology for. Initially, the dockers had used letters, fax machines and telephones to contact international supporters, which was a problem for someone like Jack Heyman, for example, who constantly complained about receiving faxes – 'Endless faxes! – in the dead of night and early hours of the morning, but by January 1996, the international campaign had moved online with tremendous success. According to Carter and Clegg (2003):

> *'It was the creative use of trade union communication channels by the Liverpool dockers [that] highlighted the inability of unions to control their internal communications in this case. This was due to two factors: the dockers' determination to keep the control of the dispute within their own organisational frameworks [particularly the shop stewards' committee and the Friday mass meetings], together with the development of instant communication in the form of fax and email, which happened alongside the dispute.'* [36]

However, for all that was achieved through the online campaign, it was truly the human element of the International Conference of Port Workers that won the hearts and minds of the global trade union and socialist movements. Speaking as the lone female delegate, Ina Heidtman said of the conference, 'As you say in Liverpool, "Absolutely brilliant!" And I know that you're going to win this victory, and when we go home, we're going to make sure that it continues until it is resolved in your favour. Thank you, comrades.' [37] Jim Donovan added, 'These people don't know what they've started. Because what they have started, we're going to finish. The lads from Australia will make sure that before the day is over, whether it be this day, tomorrow or the next day, there is a victory not only for the Liverpool workers, but also all dockers and seafarers the world over.' [38] Jack Heyman, meanwhile, had a message for Bernard Cliff himself: 'For the time being, you can load these containers with scabs, but they're not going to be unloaded in the other ports around the world. And only for the time being, because we're going to come back here in bigger and bigger and bigger numbers until we win this strike.' [39]

During a delegates' tour of the picket lines, Michel Murray spoke of how he, 'Saw in the eyes of the Liverpool dockers, the young ones and the older ones, in the eyes of their families, the children, that the victory is gonna be soon.' [40] The dockers' own video film, *One for All*, shows how the megaphone suddenly stopped working at this point, with Kevin Robinson telling the crowd, 'It's a police one; you've got to beat it up first,' [41] drawing groans before Murray continued: 'We already started what we call Operation Liverpool. We don't have the right to blockade a ship in our country, but we do have the right to fuck it up!' [42] Irish docker, Gerry Quigley, said: 'We talk about *when* you win your strike. Victory to the Liverpool dockers. Victory to the working class.' [43] Ciro Oriljo, from the port workers co-operative in Salerno, was a cross between football fan and film star, and through an interpreter he claimed to be, 'A man of very few words, which is unusual for an Italian,' [44] to which the Women of the Waterfront shouted back: 'All action, eh?' [45] Unfazed, Ciro continued: 'Before now, it was maybe only Liverpool football that was known around the world. Now it's the Liverpool dockers that are known around the world.' [46] Terry Ryan told the conference that the New Zealand waterfront workers had a saying: 'United we bargain, divided we beg,' before adding, 'From what I've seen here, you won't be doing any begging. It's gonna be a complete victory. It mightn't be tomorrow, but it will come because the momentum is gathering all over the world. Stick in there and power to your arm.' [47] Then, Nico Georgiou announced to wild applause: 'Solidarity with the Liverpool dockers is put into action, and tomorrow we close the port of Piraeus. We phoned all the mass media and it will have a big support from other unions as well in Greece. If need be, we will spread our support even further. We want you to win, and we believe you are going to win. We are with you'. [48] Winding up the demonstration, Kevin Robinson declared: 'If capitalism and big business has no boundaries, then trade unionism and struggle and solidarity worldwide can have no boundaries. United, we will win.' [49]

Back at Liverpool's historic Town Hall, a guest speaker at the conference, sacked miner Billy Pye, thanked the Liverpool dockers for their direct action in support of the mining communities during their 1984-85 strike, and argued in favour of strike action in support of the dockers. He spoke of three types of trade unionists: 'those who are convinced that the class struggle is over, and that the interests of workers and the owners of industry are the same; those who offer nothing more than verbal support; and those whose path begins and ends with simple universal principles, namely that you never cross a strikers' picket line, no matter what the law says; you give solidarity when it is requested and you demand solidarity when you need it, no matter what the laws says. 'I know that this conference is discussing the anti-trade union laws,' Pye concluded. 'No matter in what country, they have the same driving factor: the crisis and collapse of the world economic system. They are one of the attempts to offset this crisis.' [50] Another guest speaker was the London docker Mickey Fenn, whose connection with the Liverpool dockers was decades-long and with them he worked to set up the National Port Shop Stewards Committee in 1967, of which Fenn had been secretary until the National Dock Labour Board Scheme was abolished in 1989. [51] Fenn recalled how:

> 'The trade union movement was powerful, but one after the other they were defeated: the miners, printers, seafarers and then it was our turn. We would have preferred the union to take action officially, but they said this was impossible because of the laws and possible sequestration.' [52]

Fenn stated that the plan to defeat the unions was co-ordinated by the government and the employers, [53] and he then introduced Damien Brown, one of the barristers who represented the sacked London dockers at their industrial tribunal. Brown spoke at length on the proliferation of anti-trade union legislation. This was followed by Doreen McNally, chair of the Women of the Waterfront, telling the conference all about:

> 'The Dock Company's aim to return to the cheap labour of Victorian times. The men were constantly threatened with dismissal if they didn't agree to sign various contracts, accepting disgraceful working conditions... The Mersey Docks and Harbour Company intruded in our family lives; the men were quizzed about their whereabouts, as if they were accountable 24 hours a day.' [54]

Doreen explained that this unprecedented level of intrusion was a major strategic error, because it brought out the women's instinct to fight to protect their family. When the men refused to cross the picket line, 'their partners were right there with them ecstatic that finally, after six years of being held to ransom, they were making a stand for justice,' she said. [55] Alan Fox, a Liverpool docker's young son, sent delegates a letter that summed up the feelings of so many who experienced the extraordinary international solidarity present in Liverpool that week:

> 'Thank you for coming to Liverpool to support our dads. I hope you have all enjoyed yourselves. Please help our dads to win this dispute. They did nothing wrong and were sacked. When they get their jobs back, we are having a big party and you can all come. Love from Alan Fox XXXXX.' [56]

The conference decided, among other matters, to establish an alternative international dockworkers' organisation, the International Dockers' Committee. Resolution 1, submitted by Port of St John (New Brunswick, Canada), Port of Le Havre (France) and Port of Montreal (Quebec, Canada), stated:

# THE FIRST INTERNATIONAL CONFERENCE OF PORT WORKERS; THE DISPUTE GOES DIGITAL

*'These initiatives are but the first phase of efforts to support their fellow dockers sacked in Liverpool. Actions carried out within the framework of both phases will not cease until the 500 sacked dockers are reinstated in their jobs.' [57]*

Resolution 2, also submitted by Port of St John (New Brunswick, Canada), Port of Le Havre (France) and Port of Montreal (Quebec, Canada) stated that in order to give proper support to the Liverpool dockers' struggle, all delegations present at this International Conference would make the commitment to provide them, in as far as their mandates allow:

*'With material aid, and also to do their best to convince the dockers' and port workers' unions not present here to help provide such aid. In order to ensure coordination, information, prevention, action and management of actions related to the dispute… in the event of any attack affecting dockers.' [58]*

The delegations submitted the following proposal that an International Commission be created, the composition and mandate of which was to be settled as soon as possible. [59] This first international conference also recognised the importance of the global internet communication systems that had been set in place by *LabourNet*, [60] and Jim Donovan seemed to speak for everybody when he said:

*'On behalf of all our members I want to say that this is one of the most remarkable weeks of my life. This will go down as one of the greatest weeks of my life… When your delegates turned up in Australia, I asked myself why? We've sent messages of support, we've sent money. What else do they want? Those two magnificent ambassadors of yours never left a stone unturned. From an ordinary dispute, it became a worldwide political dispute. It has become the starting stone of what we must do, coming back and fighting back. Humour is your weapon and you know how to fight. There is dignity up there [pointing to the shop stewards on the platform], and that's why we will win.' [61]*

On 22 February 1996, MDHC placed adverts attacking the conference and the dockers' campaign in both the *Liverpool Echo* and *Daily Post*, [62] before all of the attending delegates addressed the mass meeting held the following day, which concluded with Jimmy Nolan calling Mike Carden's sons, John and Daniel to speak, followed by the now traditional chant of 'Dockers in, scabs out!' Atlantic Container Lines had just lost a contract with Jaguar as a result of the damage being done to cars being unloaded in the Port of Liverpool, which led to Merseyside Police making two visits to Transport House to discuss the conduct of the pickets, promising to deal with the demonstrators respectfully in exchange for being informed about them beforehand; a request that was rejected by the Dispute Committee. Another mass meeting was called on Monday 26 February, after news broke that ACL would pull out of Liverpool on 1 March, citing loss of custom due to the ongoing actions of the sacked dockers. ILA president John Bowers said that he was: 'highly impressed with the organisation of the dockers,' and that he, 'hoped to be in Liverpool for March.' [63] In response, MDHC attempted to recover some of its losses by suing the East Coast Longshoremen's union, filing a lawsuit in a Brooklyn, New York state court. [64] A spokesperson for ACL stated that the company had stopped using Liverpool because of threats made against its ships in US ports, insisting that there was, 'no problem in Liverpool at all.' [65] The two immediate problems that had undoubtedly forced ACL's hand were the declaration made by Swedish dockers that they intended to delay every ACL ship by 12 hours, and the decision of the Liverpool tugboat men to not cross a regular Saturday picket line. It is believed that docking without being guided by a tugboat would invalidate a ship's insurance, creating panic when one large vessel nearly ran aground on a sandbank. Meanwhile, the refusal of US longshoremen to cross a Liverpool dockers' picket of ACL in Newark, New Jersey represented an independent act of conscience on the part of those involved, after the company had tried to sue the Dispute Committee and their chairman, Jimmy Nolan, in a US court.

The Liverpool dockers' slogan had become, 'The world is our picket line!' It seemed as though its attacks on the ILA were ill-judged at best, as Bobby Morton reported that John Bowers had told him by telephone that he had been trying to contact Bill Morris all day. 'The evening before, John Bowers had been having lunch with President Bill Clinton, and it was suggested that the ILA had provided support and protection for President Clinton during his election' [66] Within a couple of days, Morris was the one trying to contact Bowers following conversations between MDHC and ACL, as the realisation dawned that they had made a very powerful enemy. [67]

# 32

# Bill Morris Makes *That* Speech

*'Jimmy Davies drew the analogy that the Saturday morning letters sent out by the union were just like the redundancy notices sent out by the Dock Company. It was a disgrace that Torside had been ignored and not given the right to vote.' ~ Dispute Committee meeting notes*

By 28 February 1996, picketing was largely based on Tony Nelson's system of hitting gates at all hours of the day and night, concentrating on berths where ships were docked. Most of the picket rosters needed to be confirmed ahead of time, but there would also be a designated 'on-call' team ready to act at a moment's notice. A popular target was the Canada Dock where reports indicated that more than 100 strike-breakers were working, and it was there that a sailor was killed in a tragic accident when a container dropped onto the deck of a ship. That evening, John Bowers telephoned Jimmy Davies to say that he had received a fax from the Liverpool Chamber of Commerce, asking the International Longshoremen's Association not to press for Atlantic Container Lines to leave the city's port. Bowers did not trust the TGWU's national docks officer, John Connolly, or the General Secretary Bill Morris, who he felt were backtracking on their promise of support for the Liverpool dockers. The TGWU leadership was actively attempting to undermine the ILA's efforts to get ACL to pull out of Liverpool. On Thursday 29 February, the stewards faxed a letter to Morris, expressing concern that the TGWU was asking the ILA not to support the sacked dockers. That same day, Morris replied with the following message: 'We are calling for face-to-face talks with the Dock Company. The first thing is for the 500 dockers to be reinstated, then we can talk about severance deals.' [1]

The phone calls from Bowers and the fax exchange with Morris also coincided with Mersey Docks and Harbour Company taking out yet another full-page advertisement in the *Liverpool Echo*, in which business leaders again condemned the dockers' international campaign. Meanwhile, the Dispute Committee was in Salford for a meeting with Jack Adams.

---

* Dispute Committee, author's meeting notes, 19 October 1997

Jimmy Nolan spoke of the dockers' wish to directly involve other Liverpool port workers, most notably the tugboat men. [2] Adams claimed that the TGWU was supporting the dockers despite potential legal implications. However, it had recently been discovered that Drake International had approached the union with a view to having their strike-breaking workforce join the TGWU. Adams flatly denied this, [3] as he reaffirmed that there was no chance of the dockers being betrayed. This was a position that Adams would maintain throughout the dispute. Bernard Cliff, MDHC's port operations manager, had told the union he did not have a problem with 80% of the men. [4]

An inquiry into MDHC's plans to close Regent Road as part of their expansion programme heard from Kevin Robinson, who ridiculed evidence provided by lecturers from Liverpool University Economics department that the project would create thousands of jobs in the port. These latest recruits to the MDHC's decision to dismiss 500 Liverpool dock workers were Professor Patrick Minford and Professor Peter Stoney. They would be presented as 'independent academic observers' employed to justify the arguments to use public money to fund the MDHC's business ventures. They would be joined by the Liverpool Chamber of Commerce, shipowners, freight-forwarding companies and the chartered shipbrokers, in demanding that the sacked dockworkers accept the last redundancy offer so that the port could 'move on'. Minford and Stoney were portrayed as neutral observers with: 'no axe to grind,' despite Minford's long history of lamenting the economic cost of workers' rights, not to mention the fact that MDHC were paying for the privilege of his expertise. A close adviser to Margaret Thatcher long before she became the British prime minister, Minford presumed to speak in the name of reason, but he was merely an advocate of what was referred to as the 'rational expectations' school of economics. [5] He held senior positions within the Adam Smith Institute, the Institute of Directors and the Centre for Policy Studies, with the CPS having been founded by Thatcher and Sir Keith Joseph in 1974, as a response to PM Edward Heath's U-turn in the face of working-class resistance to proposed anti-trade union legislation. [6] It was while working for the CPS during the 1980s that Nicholas Ridley drew up his plan to defeat the miners' strike; Minford and Stoney's position was one which championed a low-wage economy based on individual short-term contracts and the withdrawal of welfare benefits. For a number of years, Professor Stoney was employed to present academic arguments that justified MDHC's continuing receipt of lucrative European Union grants, and in 1992, he was hired to produce a report in which he estimated that the Port of Liverpool generated between 49,000-105,000 jobs on Merseyside. Here, Stoney hypothesised that once the government and EU grant aid was received, the subsequent increase in trade would lead to the creation of between 9,000-23,000 jobs locally, and another 29,000-76,000 across Britain. 26 years have now passed since the docks dispute began in 1995, and none of Minford and Stoney's projections, in terms of job creation have ever materialised, despite the two academics telling a parliamentary Select Committee that the Liverpool dockers were destroying the Merseyside economy and threatening the livelihood of thousands of workers. In a statement which included the claim: 'the dockers are only holding out so they can force the company into granting them yet bigger payments.' [7] It was not surprising that the International Conference of Port Workers attracted a large number of overseas delegates because they too were facing the same free market threats of privatisation, casualisation and anti-trade union legislation. [8]

In an interview with BBC Radio Merseyside, Jimmy Nolan was asked to comment on MDHC's latest round of newspaper adverts, and his reply was to point to the fact that the company remained unwilling to defend its position in a public debate. Around the same time Bill Morris issued a press release calling for further negotiations, and on Friday 1 March, Jimmy Nolan, Mike Carden and Bob Parry MP met with Bishop David Shepherd at his house in Woolton, Liverpool. This turned out to be quite an extraordinary experience, during which the bishop warmed to Nolan, a communist trade union leader, who asked that church leaders do all that they could to put pressure on MDHC to reinstate the sacked dockers. Sheppard offered to act as a mediator in future negotiations, which was welcomed by Nolan. The bishop then leaned over and asked Nolan if he smoked, and when Nolan answered that he did, Sheppard took great delight in showing the visitors his stunning gardens, where they were free to smoke cigarettes while they talked to a man who was not only a bishop, but also a friend of the working-class and a famous cricketer!

The next day, the dockers mounted a picket at Norse Irish that closed the gate from 7am until around 9.30am when police arrived with reinforcements to break the line. More successful pickets were held throughout the week and on the following Monday they were able to close three gates. In the same week the stewards met to agree that MDHC would no longer be permitted to determine who could or could not represent the dockers in negotiations. It was decided by the stewards that they should nominate representatives to participate in the talks as a way of forcing both Morris and MDHC to accept that their elected positions provided them with a constitutional right to attend. After being derecognised in 1989 the stewards were confronted with a company/union shop stewards accreditation process which served to remove their democratic right to participate in influential rank-and-file bodies, such as the General Executive Council and the National/Regional Committees of the TGWU. Both the union and the Dock Company were effectively stopping dock shop stewards from sitting on the union's constitutional committees to which they had been elected. MDHC bosses continued to insist that the Dispute Committee was 'self-appointed' and thus had no democratic mandate to represent the dockers. It was the bosses who had no democratic authority. It was with reluctance that both the union and the Dock Comapny eventually met with a negotiating team consisting of Jimmy Nolan, Jimmy Davies, Frank Lannigan, Bobby Morton and Mike Carden.

On Friday 8 March, Jack Adams met with the TGWU members who were still working in the Port of Liverpool, including pilots, lock gatemen and dockers who had crossed the picket line. They all wanted to know what would happen to them if shipping companies kept pulling out of the port; there was no discussion about how they could support their former colleagues. [9] Adams and Dave McCall had recently met with Bernard Cliff to discuss the practicalities of any further negotiations, and it was made clear that MDHC would only accept the presence of three members of the Dispute Committee. This was rejected by the dockers. It was Cliff's view that these talks needed to be conducted with acknowledgement of the fact that any docker over the age of 50 would not be considered for re-employment, with the added caveat that all pickets and international campaigns must cease beforehand. For his part, Adams would not accept Jimmy Nolan's assertion that the only issue to be discussed was reinstatement, as the union wished to negotiate on a broader agenda; a position quietly shared by many on the Dispute Committee, who were also keen to avoid a split with their chairman. Discussions went ahead at the Lord Daresbury Hotel, Warrington, on Wednesday 6 March 1996, with the five representatives of the sacked dockers; Adams, McCall, John Connolly and Jack Dempsey representing the TGWU; and Cliff, Price and Peter Jones attending on behalf of MDHC. [10] It was the first time that the stewards had come face-to-face with their former employer since their dismissal some six months earlier, and it was made abundantly clear over the course of the four-and-a-half-hour meeting that the bosses preferred the company of the TGWU officials over the dockers.

From across the Atlantic, John Bowers had again warned MDHC that ACL would pull out of the port if the company declined to meet the dockers and with their annual general meeting just a few short weeks away, the company opened talks that focussed on reinstatement, voluntary severance, pensions and the future employment of the men brought in to replace the Liverpool dockers. Cliff attempted to apply pressure by citing Rule 10e of the former Registered Dock Workers' Pension Scheme, which stated that sacked dockers would lose their pension entitlement after six months out of work, marking 28 March as a de facto deadline for a settlement to be reached. On the matter of casualisation, Cliff made the revealing comment that before the dispute broke out, MDHC had never employed casual labour, adding that while they would be willing to employ *some* of the sacked dockers in peripheral areas, the men recruited by Drake International and PDP would continue to operate Seaforth Container Terminal. From the dockers' standpoint, their demands were clear and uncomplicated: full reinstatement, including pension entitlement, for all sacked workers and voluntary severance for those who wished it, plus permanent employment without sub-contractor involvement; Drake and PDP to be removed from the port of Liverpool.

Ahead of this meeting, Jack Adams stated that his analysis of the ballot result was that the dockers wanted jobs rather than money, while reiterating that the solution was still reinstatement, severance for those who were ready to volunteer for early retirement and an end to casual labour. [11] Cliff challenged the narrative that MDHC had conspired to dismiss 500 dockers, and after a short exchange of opinions, the meeting adjourned at 10.55am and resumed at 1.25pm, at which time Adams once again repeated the dockers' unchanging demands. [12] Cliff replied by stating that casual labour was not an issue, [13] and within six minutes of resuming the meeting, another adjournment was called. At the next restart, Cliff outlined MDHC's position more precisely:

> 'We have to say, Torside can only be dealt with by the Torside owners… Nelson Freight, we have a 50% responsibility for them, so let's put them to one side… If we accept the removal of Drake, then less than 200 jobs are available, but Seaforth containers are now handling more than this time last year. It is more efficient, and the customers at Seaforth are very happy with the service.' [14]

Cliff then informed the stewards: 'Reinstatement and severance is not practical because the jobs are not there. Unfair dismissal claims would have to be dropped, and this involves almost 100 sacked dockers.' [15] After 35 minutes of discussion, Adams and Connolly told Cliff and his colleagues that the stewards needed time to reflect on what had been said. This was done because the stewards knew that Cliff had an offer to make, which was obviously going to amount to little more than a cash payment for the vast majority of dockers. Cliff expressed his disappointment that the meeting had come to an end before he had a chance to put a new severance figure on the table, and the following day, the Dispute Committee met for an update from the stewards who had been chosen to represent them. [16]

Around this time some stewards were feeling that the campaign was beginning to drift. Organisation was becoming lax in several key areas, as faxes seemed to be going missing, leaflets were not being circulated and nothing was really being done to organise meaningful demonstrations, creating a sense that the unity between the stewards themselves was starting to fracture. That week's Saturday demonstration took place at Norse Irish, and dockers Kenny Weston and Joe King were arrested after the police moved in on the picket line. The following Monday, three gates were picketed, but despite a good turnout, police were again ready and waiting to restrict access for the dockers and their supporters. Morale continued to deteriorate, and this was soon being reflected openly among the dockers committee as they all realised the full impact of the cost of travelling to and from pickets together with the general financial hardship affecting all dockers' families. Fatigue was beginning to set in. Many of the dockers were fearless and they seemed to believe that they could get away with anything on the picket lines, and the stewards were becoming genuinely concerned about the personal safety of the dockers. One docker, Joe Spray, was hit by a minibus carrying scabs into the port, but despite sustaining a broken leg and other superficial injuries, he joined his comrades on the picket line after three days in Fazakerley Hospital. The incident was seen by 10 eyewitnesses, and Merseyside Police opened an investigation that Labour MP Bob Parry pledged to ensure was carried out in good faith.

In an effort to strengthen Tony Nelson's leadership as head of the picket captains the Dispute Committee agreed that everyone should maintain discipline and only move-off once he gave the signal, and that only he and the designated picket captains should liaise with the police. Even more concerning was the fact that some stewards on the Dispute Committee were no longer bothering to attend pickets, preferring the warmth and comfort of Transport House. This was not acceptable, and when Tony Nelson was personally threatened by a senior police inspector, it was agreed that in order to encourage better attendance on the pickets, hardship payments would be reduced for those dockers who turned up fewer than five days a week. Jimmy Nolan believed that it would be a disastrous decision not to pay all dockers the same at each weekly mass meeting, as it risked causing divisions among the men, but the majority of stewards felt that it was fair and monitoring of daily attendances at each picket gate was introduced. The stewards agreed to call upon all workplaces on Merseyside to take part in a day's stoppage on 1 May 1996. Dot Gibson had organised a support meeting at Conway Hall, London, and she was also trying to initiate a debate with MDHC's two academic advocates, professors Peter Stoney and Patrick Minford, at Liverpool University.

John Bowers and Sammy Gleason of the ILA were due to arrive in Liverpool on 13 March. [17] Morale within the dockers' committee began to improve. At some point over the previous weekend, Bill Morris had received confirmation from Bernard Cliff that MDHC was not prepared to budge on any of the issues raised by the sacked dockers, prompting the TGWU General Secretary to indicate that he wished to meet with John Bowers. The Dispute Committee, always suspicious of Morris's motives, knew that the day before Bowers and Gleason arrived in Liverpool, the American National Labour Relations Board had withdrawn a lawsuit against the ILA that it had filed on MDHC's behalf just two weeks earlier. The stewards acknowledged that Morris could not be stopped from addressing the same mass meeting that had been scheduled specifically for the ILA delegates for that coming Wednesday. In due course Morris was clapped and cheered as he entered the main hall to give his now famous speech; a speech that was to define his relationship with both the Liverpool dockers and trade unionism. Some said it was a speech directed at John Bowers, who sat impassively on the same platform having already identified Morris as: 'the biggest problem for the dockers.' Others believed that Morris was only there because Bowers was known as one of the world's most influential trade union leaders, not least within the ITF. The two American trade union leaders had a waterfront pedigree that Morris could only dream of, but on that day, the general secretary was embraced by the dockers and their families. They were to hear a powerful speech, rich in working-class imagery, of soaring visions of struggle and a dignity that rose up before them. These were the last words that Morris would utter in solidarity with the Liverpool dockers. Words to be forgotten no sooner than they had left his lips. Full of meaningless promises that were never to be enacted. Nobody ever found out who wrote this speech; nobody ever asked or cared. It went as follows:

'Thanks, Jimmy, and good morning, sisters and brothers. Can I say first of all that I'm here this morning, not just pleased to be with you, not just delighted to see the spirit the solidarity and the commitment, but proud to be with you and proud to be part and parcel of an experience which we did not seek, but an experience which I think will become part of the history and the struggles of the working class and our movement for justice. It's one of those situations which passes in time, but when you look back you have to justify where you were and what contribution you made. It's one of those situations where, as you age, and your grandchildren says [sic] to you, "Where were you at the great moment?" you either stand up with pride and said, "I was there," or you hung your head in shame, without an answer. [At this point, the Liverpool dockers cheered and some shouted, 'Hear! Hear!']

And I tell you this, when my grandchildren says to me, in 15, 20, 25 years from now, "Where were you when the Liverpool dockworkers was fighting for their jobs, their community, their dignity and their pride?" I want to be able to say, "I was there marching with them, side by side." [Cheers and applause]. I'm here this morning,' Morris continued, 'I'm here this morning full of that pride, and feel almost privileged to be part of this history in its making... I can tell you this morning that I speak on behalf of every single member of the Transport and General Workers' Union... as I go around the country, I get from them, to pass onto you, their admiration, their pride, their understanding of your struggle. They no longer see it, colleagues, as your struggle; they see it as their struggle. They see it on the basis that if you do not win, then we all will have lost... And this morning I'm here to thank you on behalf of the Transport and General Workers' Union, every single member of our union, you fight for them.

This company is beginning to understand that every single day that goes by marks – makes a further step – in your victory. What is it, they said? That you were no longer their responsibility? They wouldn't sit down and talk with you? The great victory, as far as I'm concerned, is to force them to recognise that it's not the bureaucracy that's *gonna lead the working class and the dockers to victory, it is the leadership which you elect; it's the Jimmy Nolans and the Davies and the Cardens and all the other leadership that you elect, that will in fact lead this dispute to victory, and they better understand that, because nothing less than a recognition of that is going to bring about the sort of solution that is required. ['Hear! Hear!']*

*I saw it. The way I saw it was like standing on a window ledge with a great big drop; that's how it looked at one stage. But, with our courage, with our determination and with the justice in the case, in the demands, we have worked our way forward off that window ledge into the safety, and now we're setting the agenda, we're calling the shots and we're making the demands, and that's why we're gonna win this dispute [applause] …We say that the people support us because they have a duty to support us. We know how great it is, we hope that we never have to be called on to repay it, but I say to John [Bowers] and his colleagues, if we have to repay it, rest assured, comrades, we will [applause].*

*And, next week, when the ITF meets in Stuttgart in Germany, rest assured with what the ITF has done so far… your dispute, and these issues for which you are fighting, which are issues which are germane to every single docker anywhere on this planet, because it is the same forces that are at work which are seeking to bring casual workers in, seeking to ensure that management manage with impunity for workers' rights, trampling on workers' rights. It is Liverpool today, it is Copenhagen tomorrow, it's Antwerp the other day, and it is the United States in any single day, and unless we put that mark down, unless we make a stand now, and unless we deliver on behalf of dockers everywhere, on behalf of British workers everywhere, then it seems to me that we will only be saying it's a short-term victory. This ain't gonna be no short-term victory. This is gonna be a victory which is gonna change the face – change the face of international stevedoring because wherever they are, they know about your dispute, they're watching Liverpool, and therefore we're fighting international solidarity not just for ourselves, but for dockers everywhere.*

*So, I leave you in conclusion to say I am here to reaffirm the Executive Council's commitment and support. I am here to speak on behalf of the union. I am here to say to you that whatever happens, our spirit will never be broken, and our bellies will never be starved, because, comrades, you in Liverpool will never ever walk alone. Good luck, and victory to the Liverpool dockers!' [cheering, applause, whistles.] [18]*

Jimmy Nolan thanked Bill Morris, and then said to the dockers: 'It gives me great pleasure to introduce the next speaker, the president of the International Longshoremen's Association of the East Coast of North America, John Bowers.' [19] Bowers received a standing ovation. They knew all about the trade union and political power he held in his hands together with the financial muscle that this man controlled. They were aware of his New York waterfront credentials. John Bowers stood and waited for the room to fall silent, so that he could speak personally, a conversation, one docker to another:

*'Good morning, mates. I know you've been sacked. It happened to me, too. I had Local 333 and the employers gave a contract there was no way they could deliver. So, they hit the bricks and were replaced by scabs… People lost their homes…'* [20]

The dockers applauded and cheered, and one of them shouted, 'Can I join your union?' [21] Once the laughter had subsided, Bowers continued:

*'Your battle is important to us because Nolan called me, and we spoke, and I asked what the beef was. He told me that everybody's sacked. I never heard that; we get displaced, it's like a replacement, and I went to the Atlantic Container Line and I said they have a problem down there, which I didn't know until Nolan got me, and I said that I don't want you crossing their picket line because you've got ships here, and my people are gonna be very upset. And the first ship he didn't, if you remember. And then he came back. I didn't talk to him for a while, but he crossed the line, and he came and tried to talk, and I hung up the phone. I said, "You went through their picket line," and he sent the head of New York Shipping down to me and he said, "John, the man wants to work it out." So, I sat down with him. He said, "I'll never do that again, John. I won't listen to any more bullshit [more laughter]. You were right, I was wrong, and what can I do to help?'* [22]

With the audience hanging on his every word, this speech filled the hall with an expectation that their conflict was over; it was being won that very day. This was the way that it was meant to be, with two of the most powerful trade union leaders in world industry pledging infinite support against the injustice imposed upon good men and women, as Bowers recounted his talks with ACL bosses. [23] He then confided in the dockers in a way that only those within this global family could really comprehend. It was a tale of family, of dockers' sons, daughters, fathers and mothers, involved in the same struggles in ports across the world; a tale of a shared industrial history; of the union, *the book and the hook*; of casual labour and the twice-daily hire; of tallies and brutality; of men and work; of machinery and giant cranes; of huge, brutal architecture and waterfronts that were identical in every port, and familiar to every docker no matter their country of origin. The men and women gathered in Transport House that day knew one another like family, and they knew that both Bowers and Tommy Gleason shared their history, as did the TGWU. It was a history, like all dock histories, that took off at the end of the 19th century, with the same bans and proscriptions that UK dockers experienced in the post-war era.

The history of the ILA collided with McCarthyism. It went back to the Kennedys and their alleged links to the Mafia, and in so many ways it mirrored the global history of all dockers. This was a history of the New York dockers, along with the power of the waterfront to attract theft, smuggling and crime on a grand scale. New York dockers were known and respected by their Liverpool comrades throughout their parallel journeys within which major strikes against government and employer actions, casualisation and containerisation took place concurrently on both sides of the Atlantic. [24] The ILA had long been the subject of persistent media criticism for alleged connections to organised crime, but the incoming Bowers was considered to be, 'industry savvy, as well as an intelligent union leader.' [25] He was another New York Irishman, like Gleason before him, who came up through ILA Local 824 on Manhattan's West Side docks. Gleason Sr had maintained an iron grip on the docks on both the Atlantic and Gulf coasts, only to see it prised open by containerisation, and when this son and grandson of longshoremen died at the age of 92, with him passed this final unique generation of trade unionists. Men such as the Reuther brothers of the automobile industry and Jimmy Hoffa of the Teamsters Union, who developed their organisational and political manoeuvring skills during the bitter industrial conflicts of the 1920s and '30s, which saw them hailed proudly as 'Just a Gang of Rebels.' [26]

Back in the packed and stifling main hall of Transport House, Liverpool, this shared history and heritage was there for all to see, as the successor to Tommy Gleason Sr told his own personal story while his mentor's son sat listening at his side. [27] Bowers explained to the Liverpool dockers: 'ACL is gonna leave any time you people say. They don't like working with strike-breakers. Believe it or not, there are some employers like that – very few, very few. You gotta win this because, like, I'm in negotiations, it can happen to me. It already happened to me…You gotta win, and I, this is like when I came from the West Side. I was born two blocks from the piers; this is the kind of meeting we used to have. We don't have many meetings like this, you don't see them anywhere. The fact that you're here fighting for your jobs, I know you're gonna win and you have my support. Thank you.' [28] When John Bowers finished speaking, the hall erupted with cheers, applause and whistles. The president of the ILA then turned and looked towards his attorney, Tommy Gleason, before telling the dockers, 'Tommy said I didn't say anything to get us sued!' [29]

Once again, the dockers cheered their East Coast waterfront brothers, and Jimmy Nolan stood and offered Bowers a warm handshake. 'Thanks very much, John,' Nolan, the leader of the Liverpool dockers said. [30] Tommy Gleason stepped forward to tell the dockers, 'Well, first of all, I would like to say that it's with pride that John and I are here. John and I, I guess to give a little history, and get off the track a little…' [31] He paused for a moment to listen as Bowers said something to him, and then continued: 'Yeah, well, indirectly, John and I started about the same time. I worked on the docks, too.' [32] He went on to explain that the problem they faced was a concerted effort by the steamship companies to break down trade unionism. He used Rotterdam, Netherlands as an example: 'God, they got nobody working, strictly automated. If you see when they load a ship, it's three men: crane operator, checker and a relief man, and the problem is they're trying to do the same to us in the United States.' [33] Clearly enjoying the fact that he knew he had everyone's ear, Gleason added:

> '…if you remember, they came down and served you and I had them going into court, and so the next thing was let's get the American Civil Liberties for them [again, laughter filled the hall]. 'So, the problem was, and then the man head of ACL, that's when he came to John and said, "Hey, this wasn't me. I made a mistake, letting them come in, the industry come in and try to take over and break you down to get at me and get at Liverpool… they wanna take on the dockworkers all over the world that were the strong people. And the theory is to break that down, you break down everybody else.' [34]

When Gleason finished speaking, the hall erupted in a tumult of cheering and clapping and as the dockers left the meeting, they knew they had heard powerful union leaders speak of solidarity and action, of global trade and the shared history of the dockers as a class of workers united by the parallel history of international dock work. Later that afternoon, Andy Dwyer organised a meal at a small Italian restaurant, the *Casa Italia*, where he knew the owner, and the two ILA leaders were hosted as the guests of honour. Bill Morris was also in attendance.

At the mass meeting on Friday 15 March, it seemed fitting that Jimmy Davies took time to reflect on the significance of Bowers and Gleason's visit. The dockers attending these meetings each and every Friday expected honesty from their Dispute Committee, as they believed that they had just as much of a right to know about anything that could affect them and their cause, and for their part, the stewards acknowledged this expectation and sought to divulge as much information as possible. This had been a week where two of the world's most influential trade union leaders, Bill Morris and John Bowers, had walked into Transport House and pledged their support. Jimmy Davies now told the dockers that he thought Wednesday's meeting was:

> *'One of the best meetings we've had since the start of the dispute… We had a discussion about it after, among the shop stewards. I've always been proud to represent dockworkers and I've been a shop steward since 1968, and I've had people ask me, "Who are you a shop steward for?" I've said, with pride, "For dockworkers." And one of the proudest moments of my life representing dockworkers was on Wednesday. We had the president of one of the most important unions, or the most important union in the world, on the platform and the impression you made on him was nothing short of staggering. He couldn't believe that 500 men, who have been in dispute for six months, could have the morale and the spirit that you had. As Jimmy Nolan said, we did take them for something to eat afterwards, and I'm telling you, lads, we'll win this dispute because that man and his members are going to support you to the hilt because of the position you adopted on Wednesday. John Bowers was so impressed with you that it was all he talked about all afternoon. He said, "I've been to a lot of meetings. I haven't been to a meeting like this, on the East Side, for many, many a year. It brought back fond memories because many meetings I've been to there has always been a criticism or some sort of the criticism of the platform. I never sensed or heard any criticism towards you Liverpool stewards. You'll win that dispute, not only because you've got the support of us, you've got the support of other people throughout the world. You'll win because you've got the solidarity of the men behind you and you've got the solidarity of the men supporting each other."' [35]*

Davies expressed his thanks to the men and women who had been there to welcome the American delegates, and thunderous applause broke-out once again. It was then explained that the Dispute Committee had been issued with an injunction from the United States National Labour Relations Court, in response to the picketing of East Coast docks. 'They intend to bring Jimmy Nolan to America over this, so we'll be paying his fare and getting him out there as soon as possible,' [36] The hall erupted in howls of laughter. But dockers are hard to impress. One of the Liverpool dockers, Billy Johnson, would later observe of his general secretary: 'I believe he's on £60,000 [salary per year]. He's not in touch with the working class.' [37]

# 33

# Economic Distortions

*'We do have a meeting tomorrow [Saturday 16 March 1996] where we've called on all the Merseyside shop stewards in every workplace to come in here, try and fill the hall, because we're trying to pull together every dispute that's going on in Merseyside, and there's many of them. We've got certain ideas. One of the things we are looking for is a day of action, where we can possibly bring the whole of Liverpool to a halt.' ~ Bobby Morton**

Patrick Minford, the Mersey Docks and Harbour Company's Thatcherite economist, had been invited to speak at the Liverpool Chamber of Commerce on Wednesday 20 March, and so a picket and a print run of leaflets were arranged. Minford had already been challenged, along with Peter Stoney, his University of Liverpool colleague, to a public debate over their analysis that MDHC was a major contributor to the city's economy. As pickets stood leafleting opposite Moorfields Station in the city centre, a taxi driver presented them with the professor's bag, which had been left in his cab by mistake, and inside they found details of the previous month's International Conference of Port Workers. [1] Minford and Stoney vehemently opposed the dockers, and this had led to them clashing with other senior lecturers at the university, 16 of whom described comments made by the pair as: 'Objectionable and unpalatable.' [2] On the day before Minford was due to address officials at the Chamber of Commerce, Jimmy Nolan called for talks with local business leaders, including Freight Forwarders and the Liverpool Shipowners and Users' Association, stating: 'Despite our differences, we may be able to conclude this most damaging of periods for our local economy and the people of Merseyside.' [3]

March 1996 also saw the release of *Dockers' Charter #5* that included articles by the WOW together with updates on the dispute by various contributors. A general discussion took place among the stewards that the dispute had reached a plateau. ACL was still active in Liverpool, and this was having a substantial impact on the morale of the men, especially since

---

* Bobby Morton, speaking at the weekly mass meeting, 15 March 1996 (Jane Kennedy, Tape 6)

it was rumoured that new trade was about to enter the port. The prevailing view seemed to be that the dispute was drifting aimlessly again, with a lack of local support being compounded by the fact that the international campaign was largely being ignored and denied by the shipping companies. The stewards called on John Bowers, Michel Murray and the Spanish dockers to redouble their efforts – this was a difficult *demand* to make given the harsh reality that the tugboat men were continuing to service ships as normal, and that no other section of the country's working-class were willing to take solidarity action. Additionally, the financial pressure was becoming so intense that the stewards acknowledged the need to begin fresh talks with both MDHC and the union. A small number of MDHC shares were bought by the committee, entitling holders to attend the forthcoming AGM at the company's new headquarters at Maritime House on Seaforth Dock. [4]

The Dispute Committee felt as though the Dock Company bosses were digging in, while at the same time picketing was becoming increasingly difficult in the face of worsening police violence. To this, Jimmy Nolan responded by accusing the stewards of being too pessimistic, as he made it clear that he did not want the men hearing such defeatist talk. He told them: 'It's going to be a protracted war. International support is developing, and everything possible is being done.' [5] The delegates who had attended the International Conference of Port Workers had since returned home to call their own mass meetings in order to implement boycotts of trade with Liverpool and donations to the Hardship Fund were being recorded at Transport House. Meanwhile, Kevin Robinson and Terry Southers were on their way to Lisbon, where various issues, including the Liverpool dispute, had provoked an overtime ban that would eventually extend to other ports, such as Leixoes, and cover all conventional cargo. Robinson and Southers were also expected in Bilbao, Spain, where five port unions had agreed to consider united action against the *M.V. Churruca* (Andrew Weir Line), which ran a weekly service to Liverpool. An invitation arrived from Denmark's Ole Moller, asking that a delegation visit Aarhus docks and reporting that a financial appeal had already been circulated in Copenhagen, while in Canada, mass meetings had been organised with a view to taking industrial action in Montreal and potential 'pressure tactics' were being discussed in the port of St John. In Australia and New Zealand, crippling debts had led to ABC ships being impounded, with frequent holdups in Liverpool being partly blamed for the line's financial crisis. Terry Ryan reported that the *M.V. Cornelius Verolme* was held for three days in Auckland, New Zealand. The Australian Labour Party's loss in a national election led to immediate attacks on both the Maritime Union of Australia and the mineworkers' union.

In the United States, John Bowers addressed a mass meeting of the East Coast International Longshoremen's Association on 13 March, and in San Francisco, the West Coast branches wrote to ask what action would be appropriate regarding OOCL and Hapag Lloyd shipping companies. Reporting from Sweden, Björn Borg announced that following a National Committee discussion, Gothenburg dockers were ready to take action against ACL, after the Women of the Waterfront's Colette Melia and Mary Pendleton had travelled to Stockholm as guests of SAC, the syndicalist union, on International Women's Day. By this point, the WOW's influence over the direction of the dispute was growing, as according to Cathy Dwyer:

*'What we want is the jobs back for our families and for future generations, and we will not accept that our husbands and partners work under those inhuman conditions again… WOW should now get in touch with the wives and partners of workers in other companies, like Ford and Vauxhall, and get them involved. Nothing can stop us now.'*
[6]

In a draft article for the *Dockers' Charter* written in 1998, Mary Pendleton spoke of the wonderful work that she and her husband, Dave, did in creating various posters and banners:

*'We started doing banners for the dispute by accident really. David used to do writing on boards. He used to look at the picket line and see no one had a placard, so he got some boards and some paint out of the shed and painted 'Scab Port' on them. There were no walls to write on at Seaforth, and you had to do something. Then, we started doing something on tarpaulin. We did a second WOW banner, because the first one was too heavy… In September 1996, on the first anniversary march, we hired a truck and made a boat; it was called 'Dignity.' We put up the wooden framework and put paper around the sides, and painted portholes and sea. We did a big sail down the middle. We did a banner for UNISON, for the hospitals and they paid us for that and we put the money in the dockers' fund. We made one for the Socialist Party as well, but we didn't take any money because of the help they gave us during the dispute.'* [7]

Sadly, Mary died in April 2015 a few years after her husband, Dave Pendleton. Mary's husband had been a conscientious, hardworking dockworker his entire life, and despite battling serious illness he used his artistic talent to paint in support of his fellow dockers throughout the dispute. He also recorded a video diary of the picket lines, which he attended on a daily basis.

In Greece, the Piraeus dockers maintained their support by following a 24-hour general strike with coverage of the Liverpool dispute in their mass-circulation union newspaper, while Irish dockers announced plans to organise an all-Ireland conference, with Jimmy Nolan invited to chair the meeting. Russian dockers had also written to pledge solidarity, asking the Liverpool dockers for more information on the Latvian and Baltic shipping lines. An offer for a free holiday for 100 Liverpool dockers' children and their mums arrived from a firm in Poland, whose plans to move into Liverpool Freeport were cancelled due to the dispute. Less promisingly, the International Transport Workers' Federation was due to meet in Stuttgart, Germany, where Bill Morris was expected to provide an update on the Liverpool dispute, and it was obvious that he would not be calling for any direct action. On Thursday 21 March, several stewards worked with the WOW to decide on a suitable format for a new pamphlet, and it was agreed that the two parties would meet every Thursday thereafter. The WOW also planned to visit Liverpool's Aintree Racecourse, home of the Grand National, where MDHC had hired a corporate hospitality tent.

At a mass meeting on Friday 22 March, Jimmy Nolan reported that a proposed injunction against the Dispute Committee and the ILA would not be successful, and the following day, at what proved to be one of the largest demonstrations that the dockers held, Lola Onibiyo, appealed for support in a campaign against her father and brother's deportation. Lola, along with her sister, Toro, spoke about their father, Abdul, a member of UNISON who, despite living in Britain since 1963, was deported back to Nigeria by the UK Home Office in October 1995. After this he disappeared without a trace, his family and friends feared that he had been detained by the brutal military regime, the sisters wished to express their gratitude for the support they had received from MPs such as Bernie Grant and Jeremy Corbyn and Rodney Bickerstaffe, the UNISON General Secretary, in persuading the government of Guyana to agree to offer their brother, Ade, temporary asylum. Arthur Scargill, president of the National Union of Mineworkers, then took to the platform to condemn both the Trades Union Congress and Labour Party leaders, who he claimed: 'should pledge to renationalise the docks,' [8] after which Jimmy Nolan remarked optimistically, 'We had resilience then, we are resilient now and we will have resilience in the future, until such time as we are reinstated.' [9] Another speaker that day was WOW's Pat Dooley, who in an interview with Dave Cotterill would reflect on how her husband had lost his job: 'When my husband received his dismissal notice after 28 years working at the port, it was as though someone had died in our house. Our immediate thoughts were that we would end up on the streets, but after six months we are still fighting.' [10] Pat told Dave that it had been her first time addressing a rally, before explaining how despite the hardship that her family had suffered, her involvement in the dispute had left her with some wonderful memories of kindness and solidarity that a scab would never experience. 'The family unit must be incorporated into trade union life,' she added. [11]

The dockers received a morale boost on Thursday 28 March, as a frontpage headline in the *Liverpool Echo* revealed that a huge wage increase had been awarded to Trevor Furlong, MDHC's managing director, on the same day that a meeting of the Dockers' Pension Fund trustees was taking place in London. This meeting had been called to clarify whether or not MDHC's threats against the dockers' pensions were truly actionable, since no precedent existed. Employers' representatives from other ports did not like the Liverpool bosses cavalier attitude, with some feeling the treatment of the Liverpool dockers was unacceptable. Jimmy Nolan and Jimmy Davies, two elected members of the Pension Fund board of trustees, cited Rule 10(E), relating to 'exceptional circumstances' in an effort to preserve the sacked dockers' pension entitlement. Most of those present were in favour of this interpretation, and the Tilbury representative agreed that the Liverpool dockers' case was indeed a special circumstance. Cliff declined to comment during the meeting, perhaps realising that he did not enjoy the support of his fellow employers, plus there was the contradiction of him needing the dockers' pension entitlements to be protected in order to form a viable financial settlement to the Liverpool dispute. Essentially, the dockers' pension entitlements had to be protected under the rules of the fund, due to the situation that they found themselves in following their dismissal.

Elsewhere, the campaign to call on all British workers to strike in support of the dockers was gaining momentum, leaflets were produced and all TGWU branch Secretaries were contacted directly. On the international front, the Dispute Committee again asked John Bowers to pressure ACL into carrying out their threat to withdraw from Liverpool, only to be told that on each of his three previous attempts, the shipping line had responded by claiming that MDHC had assured them that talks with the dockers were ongoing. Then, at the Friday mass meeting held 29 March, discussion centred on the International Communist Party issuing a pamphlet attacking the 'Stalinist leadership' of the Dispute Committee. Here, the ICP charged that:

*'...the stewards were not building an international movement of the working class but touting the labour of the Liverpool dockers around the boardrooms of the world, while building links with other union bureaucrats equally eager to establish such relations with big business on a global scale. The dockers' banner expressed this corporatist perspective very succinctly. It carries the slogan, 'Liverpool dockers: the Best in Europe.'* [12]

According to the ICP:

*'...the fundamental lesson of this experience is that genuine internationalism cannot be organised by the existing trade unions. The role of the stewards throughout has been to direct that action into bureaucratic channels, effectively stifling it and using it not to strengthen the working class, but to build relations with transnational companies.'* [13]

Writing in response to these allegations, Dave Graham, who wrote regular commentaries on the Liverpool docks dispute, stated that the accused shop stewards:

*'...had no option but to go through the existing union channels, such as they were, to get the solidarity they needed. No-one who knows anything of the history of this particular section of workers can be in any doubt that they fully expect the TGWU and its officials to try to sabotage the dispute, but since the union fears sequestration of its funds and assets above all else, the union has limited its efforts to behind-the-scenes manoeuvring in international organisations such as the ITF.'* [14]

A meeting was arranged involving a team of representatives made up of Nolan, Davies, Lannigan, Carden and Morton, who met with Jack Adams and Dave McCall in Manchester on 1 April 1996. Bernard Cliff had indicated to Bill Morris that he was not too keen on reopening dialogue, but the Dispute Committee was adamant that the last meeting had been adjourned to allow time to clarify the pension position, which had now been achieved. At the Manchester meeting, Adams outlined what he felt was MDHC's position following conversations with Cliff, stressing that the company would only deal with their own 329 former dockers, and that they felt the dockers had conceded nothing during past negotiations. Adams then expressed concern that MDHC likely wanted nothing more than to issue a joint statement saying that talks had broken down again, and he agreed that Drake International, PDP and any other casual labour had to be removed from the port, before adding that 'the fit,' as he put it, 'was negotiable'. He was convinced that Cliff was looking to pre-empt an impasse before negotiations started, in an effort to expose the dockers as being unwilling to consider all options that would include a voluntary severance scheme for those dockers who wanted to retire, and a reinstatement clause for those who wanted to return to the docks.

The following day, the four shop stewards joined Adams, McCall and John Connolly, the TGWU National Docks and Waterways Officer, and local union official Jack Dempsey, in a meeting with Cliff, Peter Jones and Allan Price of MDHC at the Lord Daresbury Hotel,

Warrington. Before proceedings had even formally begun, Adams repeated his view that Cliff was more interested in what was going to happen once the talks broke down, although the port operations manager appeared concerned about who was going to report back to the dockers, Adams or the stewards. Adams spoke first, outlining the situation as the dockers saw it:

> *'We adjourned the last meeting to clarify certain points. We are committed, today, to try and reach a settlement. We are concerned about the damage to the port and its people. Whatever the problem, from experience, we can achieve a solution. The postal ballot clearly indicated this was about jobs, not money; jobs are at the core of reaching any accommodation. We do not reject the January package out of hand. You said that even if Drake's left, enough jobs would not exist in the port, but we have to see if we can get that fit.' [15]*

Cliff's response was brusque, for here was a man seemingly not too bothered about finding a solution: 'Our objective is stability, efficiency and quality of service, which we cannot achieve without Drake Port Services.' [16] Adams asked, 'Are you saying that the sacked dockers cannot give this service?' [17] Cliff replied, 'Because of the problems we had in 1995 training people, we gave everyone at Seaforth Container Terminal a medical. One hundred and seventy-two men were identified as not being medically capable for driving plant.' [18] Adams then asked if this situation was not also engineered, as Cliff was effectively saying that these people, 'were unfit to be dockers,' and Cliff proceeded to catalogue events as he saw them, stating that there had been an organised refusal to work during days off and bank holidays over Christmas, as well as a refusal to allow Torside men to replace them on lower rates of pay. 'Then,' he added, 'on Wednesday 26 September, the stewards invited people from Torside to come to picket Seaforth.' [19] Lannigan and Davies both objected to this claim, insisting that no meeting took place to organise pickets at Seaforth. Cliff did not accept this, as he began to itemise the situation in the Port of Liverpool as it now stood, with Drake International being the main labour provider. [20] After an adjournment, Cliff reiterated that no work was available in the Container berth, but he wanted to know how many dockers actually wanted to return to work. Talks resumed on a voluntary severance scheme, removal of Drake International and the reinstatement of all dockers who wanted to go back to work. Then, after another adjournment, which lasted almost an hour, Cliff spoke of a transitional period of two-to-three weeks, in which they would divest of Drake's services and reinstate a number of dockers, and that they would not accept any responsibility for Torside, before going on to say: 'The mould was smashed on September 28. It will never be the same. Reinstatement will be chaotic and impracticable, but we want to find jobs for those with appropriate skills, although no more than 200 jobs currently exist. We all know a large number want to leave, and we need to identify this number.' [21]

Adams asked if MDHC intended to get rid of Drake International, and Cliff answered that he needed to: 'guarantee service, productivity and efficiency. Two hundred jobs? It's a problem. Ten jobs? No problem.' [22] Peter Jones then repeated once again that they needed to know just how many dockers would be prepared to take severance, as the talks effectively broke down. By their own statements, MDHC were admitting that they did in fact engineer the sacking of the dockers, and when negotiations resumed 20 minutes later, Adams informed Cliff: 'We have tried to address our fundamental differences, and the transitional period was a genuine movement to resolve our differences. No formula for reinstatement and your refusal to divest yourselves of Drakes is regrettable, but that is where we are. You have a casual contract in place. You have not moved in negotiations and all you have done is replace a loyal labour force.' [23] There was another brief break, after which Cliff reiterated his position: 'We made an offer of 40 jobs and £25,000. We remain prepared to negotiate on an open agenda, but we need to know the facts of who wishes to leave and stay. We are happy to meet in intensive sessions to arrive at a conclusion.' [24] Adams rejected this as a propaganda point, saying that: 'We do not want talks to break down, and yet we have received no room for jobs in the port.' [25]

On Thursday 4 April, the Dispute Committee received a report on these talks, from which they concluded that while they could not refuse to continue negotiations, little hope existed unless they started affecting trade in the port. John Bowers and the ILA were still being threatened with legal action regarding their stance on ACL. Mike Carden had attended a meeting with the TGWU's Irish Regional secretary, John Freeman, who pledged his full support to the dockers. A women's march had been organised for the coming Wednesday, but morale was at a very low ebb following the failed negotiations and the ILA's inability to convince ACL to pull out of Liverpool. There was, however, good news in the form of Japanese dockers donating £6,000 to the Hardship Fund, as well as word from Portugal that a boycott of all Andrew Weir vessels had been agreed. Support was also developing in the Netherlands, even if in Belgium support was much less promising, and prior to the Easter school holidays, the *Liverpool Echo* ran an editorial calling on the dockers to end their dispute and accept MDHC's offer.

With the ten shares that Jimmy Davies bought at Midland Bank, dockers and shop stewards were able to attend MDHC's AGM on Thursday 11 April, but despite having the opportunity to challenge the company's annual report findings, as well as the election of Trevor Furlong and Bernard Cliff to the board of directors, it was a largely futile endeavour, since a small number of majority shareholders could easily block any motions from the floor. Hired security marched back and forth along the rows of seats occupied by the dockers, as though expecting some violent outburst, and on the BBC's local evening news, Jimmy Nolan told reporters: 'The profitability of MDHC does not refer to the Port of Liverpool.' [26] Indeed, MDHC had many interests outside of Liverpool, yet they were claiming that productivity was up 50% and tonnage exceeded 30 million for the first time ever in the port's history, with the company's chairman, Gordon Waddell, later clarifying that on profits: 'It is very difficult to be precise about that, but in those figures are legal fees and everything else.' [27]

That same day, a scab's car drove through the Canada Dock picket line at 30mph, hitting Jimmy Davies and Kevin Bilsborrow from behind. Fortunately, neither man was seriously injured, although Davies was taken to hospital as a precaution. This came after Bilsborrow had been threatened by a police inspector at another picket, who told him: 'We're going to have you.' Eventually, Bilsborrow was arrested, charged with causing a breach of the peace, dragged before the magistrate and fined £50, in addition to being bound over to keep the peace for six months. [28] At the next Friday mass meeting, a minute's silence was observed for Eddie Lundon, a leading dock shop steward who had died earlier in the week, and the general atmosphere in the hall was very subdued. Bowers had again spoken to De Zago from ACL, who was raising concerns about Cast Shipping Line picking up their work if they pulled out of Liverpool, prompting the Dispute Committee to contact Michel Murray in Canada, to ask if he could put similar pressure on Cast, Can-Mar and Morline, while on the US West Coast, Tony Nelson and Bobby Morton were busy drumming up support among the ILWU, who occupied the Cast offices on Thursday 11 April. Back in Liverpool, the plan was to picket the tugboat men, as the fundamental contradiction of seeking international solidarity while simultaneously being unable to gain local support was seen the be undermining the campaign. ACL and Cast were the keys to the port's continued profitability; losing them would severely weaken MDHC's position. Incidentally, it is interesting to note that no one from ACL attended MDHC's hospitality tent during the 1996 Grand National, which the WOW picketed.

On Tuesday 16 April, Jimmy Davies had a telephone conversation with John Bowers, who assured him that ACL would pull out in two weeks, although they were still not happy at the prospect of Cast stepping in and profiting from the opportunities this would create. The ever-worsening morale amongst the dockers was reflected in subdued picketing, while some dockers were becoming increasingly antagonistic towards the tugboat men. The WOW march held Wednesday 17 April was another great success overall, but the safety of the children had been compromised by the behaviour of Merseyside Police. By the end of the week, coverage had appeared in the *Liverpool Echo* regarding the wish of the Education and Employment Sub-Committee to hold an inquiry into the Liverpool docks dispute, and the Scottish TUC declared its support for Jack Adams's call for financial aid. Meanwhile, international action in Portugal, Spain and Sweden was having a direct impact on vessels trading with Liverpool, boosting the mood at the Friday mass meeting as confirmation of ACL's withdrawal appeared imminent. That afternoon, the stewards met with local MPs Eddie O'Hara, Bob Parry and Eddie Loyden to discuss the form and structure of the Department of Education and Employment inquiry, and they were told it was imperative that they make a full written presentation detailing evidence of the main issues behind the dismissal. Whilst the MPs agreed that such an inquiry was very important, they cautioned that it could also be used to vindicate the employer.

Additionally, Patrick Minford and Peter Stoney continued in their attempts to subvert the dockers' message through bogus academic arguments that justified MDHC's behaviour. Minford wrote to John Bowers, asking him to withdraw support for what he described as a small group of dockworkers who were wrecking the Merseyside economy, together with the interests of his employers. [29] He also sought to legitimise his ongoing interference in the dispute by publishing a letter in the local press as a full-page piece titled, *The Docks Dispute and the Voices of Reason*. Here, Minford claimed to have no axe to grind with the dockers, and no interest in anything other than the people, jobs and business in the area. This led to 15 of Liverpool University's social scientists disassociating themselves from Minford and Storey, forming a group headed by Professor Chris Jones and Robert Moore, who wrote to the same papers that published the letter to explain that: 'Minford is an advocate of the managerial style and incessant drive for profits at all costs which lies at the basis of the dock dispute. Mr Stoney's involvement is more direct; he is an economic advisor to the Dock Company.' [30]

On Monday 23 April, John Bowers, Tommy Gleason and Al Cynadez had a conference call with Jimmy Davies ahead of a meeting with ACL. The ILA men were clear that it was of paramount importance that Cast would not be able to snap up any trade left behind by ACL, with Bowers stressing that ILA members in Montreal would not support a picket of Cast or Can-Mar vessels. The Dispute Committee were more than concerned at these developments, and contact was immediately made with Pat Riley, the ILA's representative in New Brunswick, Canada, who had been trying to arrange a meeting with Cast that week to discuss ACL's withdrawal from Liverpool. Such was the importance attached to the proposed withdrawal of ACL, it was decided that Jimmy Davies and Mike Carden would be dispatched to attend the meeting between Riley and Cast in Montreal. Representatives from the major Canadian ports also attended, including Michel Murray and Theo Baudin from the Debardeurs and the ILA's David Nooss. Riley told Cast that he wanted to establish a picket, but the management was adamant that this was purely a Liverpool issue and some of the union representatives shared their opinion that ACL would end up taking legal action against Bowers and the ILA. Meanwhile, on the picket line in Liverpool, a scab fired a gun from inside the dock, and two others threatened demonstrators with a lump hammer and an iron bar. All three men were arrested.

# 34
# May Day 1996

*'We did this to drive home to all concerned that the working class is prepared to use whatever means are necessary to achieve the reinstatement of the Liverpool dockers.'* ~ Robert Irminger*

For May Day 1996 Liverpool City Council workers were preparing to stop work and, with the backing of their employer, join the picket lines in support of the sacked dockers. Lol Duffy, a spokesman for UNISON, described the planned action as 'a show of solidarity.' [1] Labour leader Joe Devaney and the Wirral Trade Union Council called on its 18,000 members to join the strike. [2] Mike Carden and Billy Jenkins travelled to a workers' rally in Belfast standing alongside the Irish Dockers' Support Group. Carden gave a speech alongside Rodney Bickerstaffe, the UNISON General Secretary, and the Amalgamated Transport and General Workers' Union leader, John Freeman, before meeting with local union officials Howard Burns and Eugene McGlone, lay member Maurice Cunningham and the Socialist Party's Peter Hadden. The two dockers told their Irish comrades that they were: 'eternally grateful for the solidarity given by John Freeman and Michael O'Reilly of the ATGWU,' [3] as they were the first TGWU/ATGWU full-time officials to come out in support of the Liverpool dockers, taking part in many demonstrations and meetings from the start of the dispute in September 1995 irrespective of anti-union legislation. No legal action would ever be taken against these Irish trade unionists.

In Dublin, a meeting of 200 local union members and activists collected funds for the dockers' Hardship Fund during a march that culminated at the Post Office on O'Connell Street. In Derry, Liverpool docker Fred Roberts and the Women of the Waterfront's Doreen McNally addressed a gathering of trade unionists, with Doreen expressing her admiration for Multiplex 5, a group of women who had recently won a dispute against a multi-national cinema group. The women had gone on to write a play about their struggle, which they performed at the Derry Theatre as a way of raising money for the Liverpool dockers.

---

* Robert Irminger, a member of the Inland Boatmen's Union (LabourNet, September 1997)

Roberts, along with Geoff Liddy, also attended the Irish TUC conference in Newcastle, Co. Down. On the international front, 'May Day in Denmark was a good experience,' Herbie Hollerhead said, upon the conclusion of a delegation that started with him and Terry Southers meeting dockers' leaders in Norway. On arrival, they immediately received a donation for the Hardship Fund, with Southers recalling that, 'this was followed by great support from transport, oil and metalworkers' unions.' [4] In Germany, docker Jorg Wessels, arranged for the two stewards to meet port workers in Hamburg and Bremerhaven, and they also met Rolf Fritsch and Uwe Sehroder, president and vice-chairman of the influential ÖTV union, who offered financial support and a letter of solidarity condemning the actions of the Mersey Docks and Harbour Company. While speaking to dockers in the gigantic German ports, Southers realised that many of the workers there had not yet grasped the fact that what had already happened in Britain was about to happen to them: 'Thousands of German workers have already been out on the streets demonstrating against the government's attacks on welfare benefits,' he explained. 'Thousands more will follow as they realise that the so-called 'German miracle' is over. No wonder there were so many interesting questions at the public meeting in Bremerhaven, and those present set up a support group for the Liverpool dockers.' [5]

A letter of support had arrived from the Iranian Refugee Workers' Association, [6] whilst at the same time, Billy Jenkins and Kevin Robinson had visited Turkey, and both were present in London for the launch of *Emek Partisi* (Labour Party), where they committed themselves to the struggle of the Turkish and Kurdish workers and community groups. They each became founder members of the Campaign for Human Rights, launched by a Liverpool dockers' delegation to Turkey in July 1996, campaigning in Parliament and across the world for a judicial investigation into the death of Metin Goktepe, a Turkish journalist who died in police custody on 8 January 1996. Eventually, some 48 police officers were charged with his murder. [7] Speaking on behalf of the Dispute Committee, Robinson suggested: 'just as the bosses know no boundaries, nor should we. All we have is our labour and solidarity as a class. When we organise together with the necessary discipline and commitment, we are unstoppable,' [8] before Jenkins added that: 'as workers, we have one language, and understand each other perfectly.' [9] This was a time when thousands of Turkish and Kurdish workers were fleeing across Europe to escape persecution and torture, and when Levent Tusel, the *Emek Partisi* General Secretary, touched down in Cologne, he was greeted by a 12,000-strong crowd, supplemented by a further 2,000 in London and another 45,000 supporters in cities across Turkey. The London launch included a night of Kurdish, Turkish and English music, dance, theatre and conversation, following an afternoon of political discussion. A visit to Liverpool further strengthened links that endure to this day. Tekin Kartal, chair of *Day-Mer*, and the rest of the comrades from the Turkish and Kurdish Community Centre were a source of extraordinary friendship and solidarity for the Liverpool dockers even going so far as to make new winter coats for the WOW, to keep them warm on the picket lines. Later in the year, the Turkish newspaper *Emek Gunluk* published one of many articles supporting the Liverpool dockers' struggle. [10]

On Monday 2 May, Mike Carden was interviewed by Radio Merseyside on the subject of the dockers' call for all local workers to support their dispute with a city-wide May Day stoppage. The interviewer seemed to be more interested in the views of Peter Stoney, the

Liverpool University Economics lecturer and consultant to MDHC. Forty minutes later Stoney, along with Peter Cluskey, an MDHC clerical worker whose brother was a sacked docker, arrived at the studio, with the latter stating that he worked for: 'a good employer, and people like Carden would set up a peace camp, *a la* Greenham Common, if allowed to.' [11] Later that evening, Cluskey was quoted in a full-page advert in the *Liverpool Echo*. Meanwhile, at the Liverpool dockers' own May Day rally, the investigative journalist, political campaigner, author and long-time member of the Socialist Workers' Party, Paul Foot, delighted the crowd by quoting Percy Bysshe Shelley: 'Rise like lions after slumber, in unvanquishable number! Shake your chains to earth like dew. Which in sleep has fallen on you: We are many – they are few!' [12] Foot would later describe the rally as his, 'best May Day... marching with sacked dockers and their supporters, who flocked with their flags and banners to support them in their selfless stand. Liverpool is the last of the big ports to have some semblance of decent working conditions, all other major ports have been casualised.' [13]

That May Day thousands marched through the streets of Liverpool in support of the sacked dockers, including the actor Margi Clarke, who addressed the people from the balcony of the Town Hall, before Jimmy Nolan declared: 'This tremendous support was a tribute to the solidarity of Merseyside workers who want justice for the sacked men.' [14] Fikret Suljic, the Bosnian miner's president, was there to confirm support for the Liverpool dockers, concluding that, 'Serbs, Muslims, Croats – we are all miners.' [15] Another full-page advertisement appeared in the *Liverpool Echo*, this time criticising the stewards for attempting to drum up international support instead of encouraging the dockers to accept the Company's final offer. [16] Staff at the local TGWU office were threatened with disciplinary action if they took part in the May Day stoppage whilst hardly any other workplaces in Liverpool took strike action. It is not surprising that there was a strong feeling among the 7,000 marchers that the dispute needed to be made official. Steve Donnelly, representing the Amalgamated Engineering and Electrical Union (AEEU), told the crowd: 'Our members are out in force today – 50 of us have taken the day off to support the dockers. This is the biggest struggle since the miners' strike,' [17] while Ray Bazeley of AEEU Rolls Royce added, 'This fight is our fight. It is time the TGWU gave their support to it. It is really vitally important to win the fight against casual labour.' [18] For his part, Mick Murphy, a shop steward from TGWU 6/532 Branch (Kirkby), stated plainly that his members had come: 'especially, to support the dockers. All employers would like to do what the MDHC has done,' [19] and UNISON's Jeff Bowe agreed that the aim had to be to get as many people out to support the dockers as possible, in order to 'keep this dispute strong.' [20]

The 1996 May Day rally turned out to be by far the best-attended that Liverpool had seen in years, with Local Authority workers in both Liverpool and Sefton defying their own union officials at UNISON by advocating for strike action. The absence of national union leaders on the march spoke for itself but did not prevent large contingents of trade unionists from turning up anyway. Other workers from a wide variety of Merseyside workplaces booked the day off to attend the rally, and UNISON's Ralph Parkinson and Nigel Flanagan, from the Liverpool and Sefton branches respectively, both pledged to continue to support the dockers in spite of legal threats from MDHC. [21] Rodney Bickerstaffe had repudiated any such action from his officials, stating that anyone being dismissed will have no right to complain of unfair dismissal. [22] According to Dave Cotterill, a spokesperson for Wirral

TUC, Alec McFadden, in trying to sidestep the trade union legislation said, 'We are not asking people to go on strike. Just take the day off.' [23] Toni Byrne, Liverpool UNISON branch secretary, pointed out that the employers have the right to dismiss employees even if it is an official dispute. 'If hundreds of us strike in support of the dockers on May Day no-one will face dismissal or disciplinary action... Our national and regional officers' fear of the anti-union laws is greater than their fear of the dockers being defeated.' [24]

At the Friday mass meeting held 3 May, dockers heard the sad news that Mike Black, the Liverpool Lord Mayor, had passed-away. Cllr Black had worked for MDHC for many years and had used the platform of his office to support the dockers. He also gave the welcome address at the inaugural International Conference of Port Workers earlier in the year, having argued in favour of the Town Hall being used to host the event, ignoring opposition from influential businessmen and academics. This meeting also heard the announcement that representatives of the International Communist Party were no longer to be granted access to mass meetings, on the grounds that they condemned everything that the Dispute Committee did. On a more positive note, the atmosphere on the picket lines had improved, as had the number of supporters, banners and placards. There was also very little cargo moving around the Port of Liverpool. A series of meetings were due to take place in London the following week and a small delegation was set to meet with Jack Adams on Monday 6 May, ahead of a Commons inquiry scheduled the next day. All these activities raised morale on the picket lines.

# 35
# Casual Labour and Negotiations Begin Again

*'To look in the faces of that hungry crowd is to see a sight that must be ever remembered. Some are smiling to the foreman to coax him into remembrance of them; others with their protruding eyes, eager to snatch at the hoped-for pass. For weeks many have gone there, and gone through the same struggle, the same cries; and have gone away, after all, without the work they had screamed for.' ~ Henry Mayhew\**

O n Monday 20 May 1996, Frank Lannigan and Mike Carden met with Jack Adams at the Transport and General Worker's Union's London head office, where the deputy general secretary explained to the two stewards how important it was that the dockers sought conciliation, not arbitration, in their meeting with the Advisory, Conciliation and Arbitration Service. The primary purpose of Lannigan and Carden's visit to the capital was to pick up a copy of the written submissions made by the Mersey Docks and Harbour Company and Torside Ltd to the Commons select committee, and that afternoon they sat on a bench on the banks of the Thames and quickly scanned the contents of a heavy brown envelope. It was at this point that both men realised for the first time that Bernard Bradley had reaffirmed how he told Jack Dempsey, the TGWU's docks official, that he was prepared to withdraw the dismissals of the Torside dockers back in September 1995. The following day the Employment Committee met at 4pm. The Dock Company was represented by Gordon Waddell (chairman), Trevor Furlong (managing director) and Bernard Cliff (port operations manager), in what *The Financial Times* referred to as the longest-running unofficial dispute in Britain. Speaking to the newspaper, the directors insisted that the government's involvement was entirely unnecessary, as the company had never had a problem with the TGWU:

---

\* Henry Mayhew, 'London Labour and the London Poor', Wordsworth Classics (1987 Ed.) p. 387

*'We believe in the value of negotiation, not confrontation. We have worked successfully for 15 years with the T&G in Liverpool, in improving efficiency and modernising working practices. The men in the dispute want a return to the old jobs-for-life culture before dock regulation in 1989, and that is not on.' [1]*

In their written submission to the Education and Employment Committee on 17 July 1996, MDHC thought it was worth restating their view that the Dispute Committee, or more specifically, the Merseyside Port Shop Stewards, was unofficial, and that the dockers' leaders *were self-appointed and had no democratic mandate:*

*'Unofficial elements have controlled events throughout. The status of the Merseyside Port Shop Stewards is further evidence of the unofficial character of the conduct of this dispute. This body is an unofficial, unaccountable, self-appointed group that has no standing within the constitutional structure of the union. Moreover, the name chosen by this self-proclaimed group is misleading. They do not represent all ports on Merseyside. They do not cover all dockers in the port, let alone all other grades of port shop workers. Furthermore, few of their members can claim recognition as properly accredited shop stewards.' [2]*

This statement was false. In reality, the Dispute Committee members held every official, elected constitutional position within the TGWU, from the General Executive Council and the National Docks and Waterways Committee to the Regional Committee and District Committee, which contrasted sharply with the non-existent democratic processes observed by MDHC or the TGWU's full-time officer corps, who had all been appointed rather than elected. Throughout the rich history of the Liverpool dockers, being accepted and recognised as a workers' representative was no small achievement, considering the hard nature of both the men and the environment in which they toiled. Add into this cauldron the toxic mix of competing political allegiances, and it becomes clear that the role of the shop steward demanded extraordinary intellect, skill and resilience. Some of the stewards failed to meet those challenges, but the majority did. Dockers' leader Jimmy Nolan, had what it took, and now he was telling a parliamentary committee that the Liverpool docks dispute was a result of the failure to deliver guarantees given by Norman Fowler, the Employment Secretary, during the Commons debate over the abolition of the National Dock Labour Board Scheme in 1989. Hansard's record of the bill going through Parliament at that time confirmed Fowler's promise: 'there would be no return to casual, part-time labour; there would be no erosion of pay and conditions and definitely no erosion of pension benefits.' [3] Nolan informed the sub-committee that dockworkers had seen a reduction in their pension rights since 1989. Referring to the use of scab labour in the Port of Liverpool, Nolan said:

*'The National Dock Labour Scheme which protected dockers' jobs, wages and conditions was abolished in 1989, with guarantees that there would be no return to casual, part-time labour, but immediately upon abolition, casualisation of port work commenced.' [4]*

Here, MDHC were not only in breach of employment contracts, but also political legislation. Nolan continued: 'I am not accusing the government of conspiring with the MDHC, but I am accusing them of negligence.' [5] The Dispute Committee had submitted a 25-page report with 63 supporting documents, clearly demonstrating that casualisation was at the heart of the dispute. Answering a question on casualisation, Mike Carden, who had compiled the report to the inquiry, said: 'I don't think there is any problem with the definition of casual labour. It is simply labour that is employed from time to time when work is available, and the individual is only paid for that.' [6] At the time, Torside Ltd was employing 20-30 casuals, who were being paid only 20 hours per week:

> *Practically all dock work in Birkenhead is casual. When there is no ship in, there are no dockworkers... The problem is that the Dock Company has total control over everything that happens in the port. They have shares in so many companies, such as Stanton Grove and Birkenhead Stevedores, [and] both employ casual labour. The directors of Birkenhead Stevedores are also senior management, former management or even directors of MDHC. [7]*

According to evidence presented by the dockers, MDHC used Drake Port Services and PDP Services Ltd. to replace its sacked dockers, and in the initial weeks of the dispute, Drake imported casual labour from the Medway port. [8] Jimmy Davies and Terry Teague referred to a list of companies that were fully owned, part owned or contracted by MDHC, demonstrating that the process of replacing dockers had started long before their dismissal in 1995. [9] In an exclusive *LabourNet* report, Greg Dropkin disclosed evidence collected from inside the Port of Liverpool, with papers revealing the web of employment agencies supplying scab labour behind the picket lines and exposing how accident rates were shooting up to the point where MDHC was facing prosecution by the Health and Safety Executive. [10] Dropkin named Sontrade, Country Wide, Man & Machine and Workforce as MDHC's casual labour suppliers, [11] and, when asked how many times their services had been used, or if any specific training had been given to their staff, Country Wide refused to comment. Peter Main, a director of Man & Machine, offered a terse, 'No comment whatsoever,' when pressed on allegations of unsafe working conditions, while Sontrade's Graham Robertson claimed that it was company policy not to discuss business matters with journalists. [12] PNT, a Warrington-based employment agency, opened a Liverpool office on 6 August 1996, providing casual labour to no fewer than five companies operating on both sides of the Mersey, including Sontrade, and an agency based in Canada Dock. PDP Services Ltd, placed an advert for dock work in the local newspaper in April 1996 [13] and they also sent a model contract to Frank Robotham, MDHC's Liverpool Freeport manager, which set conditions for a clearly casual service. [14] Invoices showed that PNT had been billing MDHC directly for labour supplied since 1995. [15] This increase in casualisation coincided with a dramatic rise in accidents and injuries, although many of these went unrecorded; a claim disputed by MDHC spokesman Eric Leatherbarrow. [16]

On Wednesday 22 May 1996, Jimmy Nolan, Bobby Morton, Jimmy Davies, Frank Lannigan and Mike Carden joined the TGWU's Jack Adams, Dave McCall and Jack Dempsey for a meeting with MDHC and the Advisory, Conciliation and Arbitration Service in

Manchester. During the afternoon session, MDHC informed ACAS that a severance scheme would be offered to the 900 ancillary workers who continued to work in the port, but this figure was challenged by the dockers, whose calculations had it nearer to 300 (the TGWU did not have accurate membership records of ancillary workers). The following day, Norse Irish sacked its casuals, employing a new hire of labour on £3.50 per hour. [17] At the Friday mass meeting, dockers welcomed detailed reports from the Commons select committee and ACAS meetings. John Bowers had, along with his West Coast counterpart Brian McWilliam, written to the International Transport Workers' Federation, calling on them to maximise their support for the Liverpool dockers. On Tuesday 29 May, the stewards met with Adams and Dave McCall, where it was said that Cliff was uncomfortable with the term 'reinstatement,' preferring to define the offer as 're-employment' on an interim basis, paying a lump sum rather than a wage. Dempsey, as the TGWU's docks officer, had been speaking to Bernard Bradley, managing director of Torside Ltd, who was also willing to discuss re-employment. For Adams, two options appeared: either a postal ballot or further negotiations. [18] However, his view that this was effectively an offer of jobs for all dockers was dismissed by the Dispute Committee, who decided that negotiations should continue. They were aware that the TGWU's General Executive Council was due to meet the following week, and their view was that the union was negotiating itself into a position where it would repeat its performance of 1989 by using the GEC to call an end to the dispute. On 31 May, the dockers issued a press release, *Towards a New Future for the Port of Liverpool and the People of Merseyside*, which stated that:

> *'In the interests of the port and the people of Merseyside, all casual contract non-union labour must cease… All sacked Liverpool dockworkers to be reinstated by the Port Authority, MDHC… A recruitment process to establish a balanced labour force be instituted, offering real employment opportunities to the young unemployed of Merseyside.'* [19]

The GEC met in London on Monday 3 June, where Jack Adams informed the delegates that another meeting with ACAS was due to take place the following day, with MDHC exploring the possibility of the interim re-employment of 329 former employees, along with pension protection and an offer of 120 permanent jobs. Adams then declared that the dockers, 'should reach agreement, or we will lose the dispute. The offer will be conditional on a postal ballot and time limited for a week.' [20] The next morning, the same negotiators faced one another at ACAS, and Bernard Cliff opened the meeting by reiterating what he referred to as the 'final position' in stating that:

> *'We can't agree to reinstatement, but we will agree to re-employ people, and this would allow severance to be activated in line with their pension entitlements. Re-employment would be for three weeks, and each individual would have to sign a contract whether he wishes to take severance or consider a job.'* [21]

Adams pointed out that these were not the original terms, but simply a limited contract, a 'fixed term contract', with which the dockers would be sacked again. Cliff responded by repeating the offer and adding that, 'If we do not agree today then the offer will be withdrawn and we will restructure the business.' [22] Adams then told MDHC that he had no intention of negotiating on the basis of the paper he had just seen, to which Cliff cited the potential legal ramifications of reinstatement, while claiming that opportunities may yet exist for Torside workers under Bernard Bradley's son, who had taken over the company. Within five minutes of meeting face to face, both sides had left the room, and Adams was now adamant that Cliff was, 'simply seeking a device to sack the dockers for a second and final time with a payment of £25,000 for 329 dockers,' [23] The negotiations broke down once more.

On Wednesday 5 June, the GEC received a report from John Connolly, the union's National Docks and Waterways Secretary, on the Commons Education and Employment sub-committee. Connolly also outlined the offer made by MDHC during the recent ACAS meeting, which he stated would, 'resolve all matters relating to current docks dispute on the basis of a postal ballot.' [24] Jack Adams stated that, in his view, the offer was, 'providing the opportunity for compulsory redundancy, making it unacceptable. It is re-employment, and not reinstatement.' [25] Once again, no real debate took place among members of the GEC; no emotional speeches calling for support for the sacked dockers and their families; no suggestions how the TGWU lay-membership could win this dispute by taking solidarity action. Instead, it was left to the senior officials to deal with the matter however they saw fit, and by Friday, pressure was building for another ballot on the latest offer from MDHC, with local church leaders joining press and union voices in explaining why they supported the idea of a ballot. This backed the stewards into a corner from where they could not refuse to ballot, as this would, ironically, be perceived as an indication of them being undemocratic or fearing the true depth of solidarity among the men. What angered them the most was the fact that such a so-called test of democracy would only be acknowledged by MDHC and the TGWU if it came in the form of a vote to accept the employer's demands, with any rejection resulting in the offer being withdrawn altogether. So much for choice; so much for democracy. The following day, news was received that the Communication Workers Union had decided to support the dockers with a week of solidarity action, which was a truly huge contribution, but this much-needed boost was quickly undermined at that week's Friday mass meeting, where Jack Adams spoke of MDHC's belief that they could collapse the strike, as he stated that: 'it is the responsibility of the union to report back accurately on the basis that this is the final offer of the company.' [26]

From the floor, it was raised that the stewards should ask how many dockers would want to accept severance, while two men indicated their lack of belief in the dispute and another brought up Torside as, 'the first mistake, bringing cheap labour into the port,' before making the accusation that: 'The platform doesn't want a postal ballot because they're frightened of it. What do we do if it's rejected? ACL are still in the port!' [27] For the next 10 minutes or so, the meeting seemed out of control as arguments erupted, until speakers from both the floor and the platform eased tempers and Jimmy Nolan spoke forcibly about the need for a 24-hour national trade union strike, telling the meeting that, 'Enough is enough. Our demands on reinstatement have not changed.' [28] The stewards then recommended a rejection of the offer with no ballot, which only one docker voted against, [29] and then later that afternoon, they met with Adams and McCall to discuss their next move and consider the implications of what had happened at the mass meeting. Adams felt that without a ballot, the dispute would collapse, but the stewards argued that this would split the dockers and the dispute would collapse anyway. The point, at least for some on the Dispute Committee, was that neither the company nor the union would accept the decision of the ballot, so why have it in the first place? MDHC's formal offer did not include the Torside men and gave no guarantees of re-employment, and the feeling among the vast majority of dockers was captured in a *Newsline* article in which John Cowley, one of the sacked dockers, was quoted as saying that, 'We have had a ballot and don't want another. Their deal is not on.' [30] Pat Bennett agreed, wondering aloud, 'What kind of trade union leader would recommend 250 job losses? What they should be negotiating is our reinstatement, nothing less.' [31]

The next morning, Tony Nelson and Tony Weadon met with Danny Maher, leader of the tugboat men, at the Bramley Moore pub on Dock Road. Maher agreed to honour the dockers' picket and ensure that seven out of eight tugs would refuse to go to sea, leaving an Atlantic Container Line vessel and a Cast ship stranded in the river. The ACL ended up entering the locks without tugboat assistance while the Cast ship was only delayed by 12 hours. At the time, England was hosting a major international football tournament, Euro '96, and Liverpool's Anfield stadium had been chosen as one of the venues, necessitating a considerable police presence within the city. This left the bulk of the responsibility for policing the docks dispute to the Operational Support Group, and according to one observer, that Saturday morning they came blazing down Dock Road with lights flashing and sirens blurring, driving straight at the picket line and stopping inches from a baby's pram. It had been expected that the OSG would step up their intimidation tactics while left to their own devices. As far back as 1981, Margaret Simey, chair of the Police Committee of the Merseyside County Council, had described the OSG as: 'trained thugs' and 'overt racists.' [32] This was long before accusations against them led to no fewer than four local MPs demanding a public inquiry into the policing of the Liverpool docks dispute. [33] According to the tugboat men, Bernard Cliff had gone 'berserk' over the action they had taken in support of the dockers, and with a Euro '96 match due to kick-off at 3pm, it was considered to be a good time to organise a mass picket.

That same weekend, Jimmy Nolan and Bobby Morton attended a meeting of the International Labour Organisation, while in Gothenburg, the *M.V. Atlantic Concert* was delayed by fourteen hours on Saturday 8 June, following a decision by Svenska Hamnararforbundet, the Swedish dockworkers' union, to delay every ACL vessel coming into the port until the sacked Liverpool dockers were reinstated. Shipping companies calculate delivery times to the minute, expecting ports to turn their vessels around in the shortest possible time and the cost of the Swedish dockers' action would have run into the millions. Bob Ritchie told *LabourNet* that, 'support in Sweden is excellent,' [34] as he and Jimmy Davies Jr expressed their gratitude to a number of Swedish comrades, such as Björn Borg, Peter Shaw, Jan Annerback, Kenny Karllson and Bosse Johanson, who together with Lars Hammerburg and Sharoach Razavi of the Antwerp Syndicalist Movement organised action against ACL. [35]

On Monday 10 June, it was reported that the local TGWU road haulage branch, 6/541, would be making another contribution to the dockers' Hardship Fund. Tommy Kirwin, Tony Woodhouse and Dave Williams from the branch were in regular contact with the dockers, but they were worried that information on the dockers' dispute sent between their respective TGWU offices, were not getting through. These concerns reflected the TGWU's policy of ignoring the international solidarity efforts that the dockers organised across the globe, limiting any trade union action within the TGWU, the TUC and the ITF. Bill Morris extended his dismal understanding of trade union solidarity by reassuring the leader of New Labour, Tony Blair: 'We ask no favours from Labour, and we will give none in return. The anti-union laws were unjust, but they are a fact of life which the union must accept. We will not put union funds at risk.' [36] UNISON's Rodney Bickerstaffe was another trade union General Secretary who repudiated the actions of the Liverpool and Sefton council workers who had voted in solidarity with the dockers. [37]

At the Region 6 Finance and General Purposes Committee held 11 June 1996, several complaints from Docks and Waterways branches were heard in regard to incidents at the start of the docks dispute. These resolutions were mostly about Jack Dempsey's past statement that five Torside men had been reinstated, but Dave McCall, the Regional secretary, responded by saying that Jack Adams had advised him not to investigate Dempsey at this time. He did offer assurances that there was, 'No question of these issues being brushed under the carpet. Bobby Owens, the TGWU's Regional secretary, did so much work, and the matter was constantly raised at the Regional Committee.' [38] Adams argued that the dispute would collapse if Dempsey's actions became common knowledge, as people would simply walk away, while Vauxhall shop steward, Mick Whitley, speaking as the committee's chairman, reminded those present that, 'members had delegated powers to call an inquiry.' [39] It was eventually decided that they would, 'instigate an investigation into the unproven allegations made against Bro Dempsey.' [40]

At a Dispute Committee meeting held 12 June 1996, a discussion took place regarding the growing number of labour agencies hiring casuals on MDHC's behalf. The incestuous nature of casualisation in the port of Liverpool involved a former manager of Torside, named Carmichael, sending Nelson Freight casuals to work the Seaforth Timber Berth. Frank Bradley, Bernard Bradley's son, took over Laird's Cargo Handling, another new casual labour company, and began offering casual work to ex-Nelson Freight dockers. [41] Meanwhile, PDP Services Ltd was working with Frank Robotham, the Liverpool Freeport manager, to provide casual, or what are now known as zero-hour contracts, [42] creating a chaotic mess that was adequately highlighted when it was discovered that Jack Dempsey had written a letter to Allan Price, MDHC's personnel manager, regarding Seaboard Ltd, a company created by John Miller, a MDHC safety officer. In this letter, Dempsey lodged a pay claim for five strike-breaking casuals, asking for wages comparable to those of the dockers they were replacing, 'recognising that the Dock Company is a caring company that should consider his request.' [43] The dockers now had a record of all the new companies that had been set up by people with clear links to MDHC: Mersey Bulk Services, owned by Graham Chadwick and Tommy Muirhead; Liverpool Freeport Warehousing Ltd, owned by James Stewart and Ken Wharton (MDHC director); Birkenhead Stevedoring, SGM and Stanton Grove Ltd; Merlin Stevedores, Seaboard, Birkenhead Bulk Handling and Freeport Warehousing; Birkenhead Stevedores, owned by Ken Wharton, Bernard McCusker (MDHC managers); Nelson Stevedoring, Liverpool Cargo Handling and Euromar, owned by Bernard McCusker. [44] It was as though the Dock Company had told their managers to take full advantage of the *Klondike* economy that had emerged on Liverpool docks, and all they needed to do was stake their claim to make some serious money. A new era of *cronyism* had been born.

On Friday 14 June, it was reported that John Bowers planned to make time to visit the Liverpool dockers again at some point during a trip to the UK at the end of the month. Meanwhile, concerns were raised over the lack of action against Cast in Montreal, with the shop stewards resolving to contact Pat Riley of ILA Canada to arrange picketing. The Liverpool tugboat men had asked to be picketed again at 10pm the following night in order to stop them moving an ACL vessel, adding to what was a fairly good atmosphere at the weekly mass meeting. Nigel Flannigan, a UNISON representative and Socialist Workers' Party supporter, also spoke at the meeting despite a request by senior TGWU local official, Paul Flaherty, that supporters of Militant Tendency and the SWP be barred from attending meetings at Transport House. Björn Borg, the committed Swedish dockers' leader, was present at the meeting, along with other delegates from an International Conference in London, as dockers demanded to know why ACL had still not pulled out of Liverpool. From the floor, one docker expressed his doubts about the success of the international campaign, as well as his concern that the mass meetings were becoming increasingly stage-managed, with some people being stopped from speaking. [45]

The Saturday picket of the tugs had been organised for 6pm and it proved to be successful. Andy and Cathy Dwyer had visited the Bakers' Union and the GMB while the Society of Telecommunications Executives donated £1,000 to the dispute and, at the UNISON conference in Bournemouth, there was talk of a potentially huge donation, but it was dependent on Jimmy Nolan being there to speak on Thursday 20 June. Two Liverpool delegates were requested for the Genoa Dockers' Conference on 27-28 June, and on Monday 17, Jack Adams told Mike Carden that Bill Morris wanted to recommend that the GEC call on the Liverpool dockers to hold a postal ballot on *MDHC's second* final offer. Adams admitted that he, 'thought he'd got Morris off the idea,' [46] all the while citing rumours that 168 dockers had contacted MDHC directly to request severance payment. This was a turning point as Morris now had the GEC actively discussing and acting on what they had previously declared an unofficial strike. [47]

On the 19 June, the GEC met in a special session in Eastbourne to discuss a presentation made by a private financial consultant, Peter Regnier, on the future of the TGWU's central office in London, with Morris seemingly determined to sell the historic Smith Square building. The reasons given were as follows:

*'Lack of disabled access, unattractive reception, closed atmosphere, no car parking facilities, expensive to run, difficult to use new technology in the building. It would cost £4.9 million to 'gut the interior;' £1.25m to fit-out basement and other floors. £2.1m for fees all unrecoverable along with a total capital cost over £8m.' [48]*

This was unnecessary and unacceptable for a small minority of GEC members providing yet another example of the union's leadership operating out of its depth in the London money and property markets. According to Morris and Regnier, the sale value of Smith Square was £11.6m, despite them both also claiming that it was, 'a prime site... no real problems for sale of £12m.' [49] At the same meeting, Danny Maher revealed to Carden that Adams had been ordered by Morris to give a report on the docks 'strike,' as if to create a sense of illegality around the dispute in the minds of the GEC members. Carden relayed the message to Jimmy Davies back in Liverpool, and at 1.07pm, Adams gave his report on the re-named 'unofficial strike', telling the GEC that:

> *'I told them it was a final offer and not part of a series of offers. Every member received a paper and signed for them with their Hardship Fund. A unanimous vote rejected a postal ballot... the company have confirmed it is the final offer, and they will now restructure the company.' [50]*

Danny Maher responded by telling the GEC: 'the port is suffering, and ship owners are questioning using the port. Social problems are being created when they see the conduct of women and children on the picket lines. It is having an impact upon workers in the port.' [51] Bill Morris replied that, 'nobody is attempting to impose a ballot from the GEC. When a union is involved in such negotiations, the GEC cannot be excluded from the decision-making process. We have to have regard for 900 people still working in the Port of Liverpool. At what point can we expect the suffering of our people in the community to continue? The GEC has a responsibility overall.' [52] It was obvious during this meeting that some GEC members opposed the sale of the office, as well as the use of expensive financial consultants, and yet this 'left-dominated GEC' eventually agreed to the sale, and financial consultants continued to drive the TGWU's own restructuring process throughout this period. The GEC had no discernible position on the Liverpool dockers other than what was put forward by Bill Morris, viewing the dispute as nothing more than an unofficial and illegal strike that just happened to last for two and a half years. However, Liverpool dockers had a different perspective, and they were demanding official backing from their union. In an interview given to *Newsline*, Peter Barrett, a sacked Liverpool docker, stated that, 'We are a thorn in the side of the TGWU leaders. They never come up with plans to save jobs; they always give a million and one reasons why they can't do anything. We should get down to TGWU headquarters and lobby it to get official backing for the dispute.' [53] Paul Kinneally, one of Barrett's former colleagues, was very much in agreement, adding that:

> *'This final offer is worse than the first one. What Jack Adams said at the mass meeting about brokering a deal was a disgrace. He should be fighting to give us official union backing. The union should be saying "Enough is enough," because now it's time to kick the Tories out.' [54]*

# 36

# The Cunard Line and the Leaving of Liverpool?

*Atlantic Container Line, which had had a ship unable to unload in the Port of New York and New Jersey since Monday because local dockworkers were unwilling to cross the Liverpool workers' picket line, pledged [on] Thursday to abandon Liverpool if fired union dockworkers there were not hired back. "It looks like we're going back to work here in New Jersey", said a jubilant Al Cernadas, executive director of the International Longshoremen's Association and president of ILA Local 1235 in Newark, N.J. If Mersey Docks [Liverpool's operator] does not reach an agreement [by 15 January], then ACL will pull out of Liverpool permanently. "How they fix it [the labour dispute], that's up to them [Mersey Docks]" said Olav Rakkenes, chairman and chief executive of ACL.\**

New York dockers succeeded in convincing the Atlantic Container Line to pull-out of Liverpool. On the morning of Friday 21 June 1996, Jimmy Nolan and Mike Carden met again with Bishop David Shepherd at his house in Woolton, Liverpool, together with various other church Leaders. Nolan expressed his concern that Bishop Shepherd had contacted John Bowers of the International Longshoremen's Association to say that if Atlantic Container Line left Liverpool, 'it would not be a good thing'. In addition, the church leaders also appealed to dockers to reconsider the Company's redundancy offer. Bishop Shepherd had even gone so far as to send a fax to Bowers, asking about his intentions regarding the dispute, but still Nolan recognised that the local churchmen were genuine in their concern for the Liverpool dockers; he just disagreed with them. At the mass meeting held later that morning, many speakers affirmed their support for the dockers, with Joe Benton MP stating emphatically that there was no altering the injustice of what had taken place, and declaring, 'I am here to assure you of our support and that of other MPs.' [1] The headlines in the *Liverpool Echo* spoke of how, '£43m had been written-off MDHC shares,' [2] as the company

---

\* Journal of Commerce, 21 December 1995

287

attempted to recover some of those losses by suing John Bowers the president of the ILA. They were seeking millions of dollars in damages from any unions or individuals who supported the dockers, but these lawsuits failed, and the Dock Company did not pursue the Transport and General Workers' Union or the Liverpool dockers through the British courts. [3] An MDHC spokesperson would later claim that ACL had stopped using Liverpool because of threats to its ships in US ports, as the company had experienced, 'no problem in Liverpool at all.' [4]

The ILA's action on the United States East Coast was unquestionably critical and compounded by dual action taken by the Swedish dockers led by Björn Borg. Their boycott delayed every ACL ship by 12 hours whilst at the same time Irish Transhipments were also being affected. The decision of the Liverpool tugs not to cross a regular Saturday picket mounted by the dockers and the Women of the Waterfront added to the problems for ACL. The US longshoremen's refusal to cross a Liverpool picket of an ACL ship in Newark, New Jersey in late 1995 was claimed, by the ILA's legal advisors, to be an act of individual conscience by those longshoremen involved. Earlier, MDHC had moved to sue Jimmy Nolan and the Dispute Committee through US courts, but the case was dropped after they were advised that a British company trying to sue its own workforce in a foreign country did not stand much chance of winning, and an agent of the US National Labour Board confirmed there was no claim in the charges that an American union was in any way aligned with the Liverpool shop stewards. [5] Writing at the time, Greg Dropkin confirmed that ACL's decision to leave the Port of Liverpool was a direct result of the nine-month docks dispute, as MDHC shares fell 49 pence in the first hour of trading after news broke that ACL would now: 'call at Thamesport, an East Coast Medway port on the Isle of Grain.' [6] Andrew Weir Shipping was another likely casualty of the Liverpool docks' dispute, as its vessels were already suffering a near-total boycott of Liverpool trade in Portugal, in addition to go-slows in Italy and Greece. In mid-April 1996, a spokesperson for Andrew Weir told *International Freight Weekly* that it would consider leaving Liverpool. An internal company memo warned that in view of escalating damage to containers left in the care of MDHC, any such problems were to be recorded and management notified immediately. [7]

Billy Jenkins and Terry Teague had been to meet with Irish comrades, and, as usual, it was a successful trip, with support in both Belfast and Dublin having been recognised as critical from the outset of the dispute. On Friday 21 June, ACL was finally diverted from Liverpool to Thamesport and port operations manager Bernard Cliff issued a statement insisting: 'the company could survive this.' [8] Almost a month earlier, on Monday 27 May, a bank holiday, Jack Adams had spoken to Cliff, who offered to 'broker a deal,' but Adams did not wish to pursue negotiations; a decision that he would later regret, seeing it as a missed opportunity. [9] The dockers' focus switched to ensuring that John Bower's ILA action would not be undermined by ACL cargo simply being transferred to Cast or Can-Mar vessels. The view had been expressed by some that MDHC could have contrived to have ACL leave in order to justify further downsizing of their workforce and a bitter twist of irony was to hang over an ancillary workers' meeting held at Transport House on Monday 24 June. This meeting was called to consider redundancies demanded by the Dock Company. [10]

Bernard Cliff told BBC Radio Merseyside that the company had the resources to deal with the loss of ACL, and Terry Malone, chairman of the Liverpool Shipowners and Port

Users' Association, confirmed his solidarity by calling on other employers to: 'hold the line and keep faith with the Dock Company.' [11] Cliff later informed the *Liverpool Echo* that the impact of ACL leaving Liverpool could cost many hundreds of jobs, possibly a thousand, not just at MDHC but also in supporting industries, such as haulage firms and shipping agents. However, the employment implications of ACL's departure would depend on how long the shipping line stayed away, and there was no evidence that this was anything more than a temporary arrangement, especially since Thamesport could not conceivably rival Liverpool in terms of size or location, with the port's own managing director, Robin MacLeod, admitting: 'ACL has had good service in Liverpool and has been a very major customer there. They would be silly to rush away, but if it becomes impossible, they may have no choice.' [12] Furthermore, the port authority at Thamesport, Medway Ports Limited, was owned by MDHC, suggesting that they and ACL were not finished with each other just yet.

Professor Patrick Minford, the Liverpool University economist, was called upon again by MDHC in the wake of the ACL story, condemning the iniquity of unemployed dockers standing on picket lines for over nine months while receiving unemployment benefit. [13] No longer ruminating on the scandal of unofficial strike action destroying the port, the sacked dockers were now a group of idle, unemployed scroungers funded by the state. Speaking at a Merseyside Business Prospect dinner party, Professor Minford argued that:

> *'Benefits are only extended to people on the basis that they are searching for work. Sitting on a picket line and going around the world drumming up support for what in this country is an illegal dispute is not looking for work. How much succour is Merseyside going to give a guerrilla band that is trying to destroy what prospects the region has for economic growth. The dock has enormous scope for revival, but this is being hit on the head by the dispute.'* [14]

Meanwhile, the international pressure on the Port of Liverpool increased with the arrival of an International Transport Workers' Federation inspector, whose mandate was to prevent shipping lines using seafarers to perform dock work as crews on the North Irish ferry service between Liverpool and Belfast had been observed lashing and unlashing containers. Brian Allen, acting on behalf of the ITF, immediately obtained a promise from Wagenborg, the company's Dutch owners, that they would instruct crews not to perform dockers' duties. Over the next week, the ITF inspector was to target all shipping arrivals in the port, including the *M.V. Churruca* (Andrew Weir) and the *M.V. Can-Mar Flory*. Internal industrial chaos was now flowing inside the dock gates, spreading uncertainty and unrest among ancillary workers, Drake International casuals and numerous other agency labour suppliers. Eric Leatherbarrow, MDHC's press officer, had told the *Liverpool Daily Post* that ACL pulling out would result in compulsory redundancies affecting ancillary workers in the port. [15] At Seaforth Container Terminal, graffiti scrawled on a container straddle carrier by scabs read, 'No two-tier wage system at Seaforth – We pulled you bastards out the Shit.' [16] An interview given in June to BBC Radio Merseyside by Bernard Cliff clarified the company's position:

> *'Mersey Docks will cope with this, and action will be taken immediately to neutralise any financial impact this may have on the company... They are the ones who have lost*

*the work, they have driven work away, which is going to affect hundreds, literally hundreds of other jobs… The men have now lost the offer of £8m and 100 jobs.'* [17]

Cliff then accused the dockers of being totally intransigent from start to finish and of finding reasons why progress could not be made. He had tried to negotiate, he said, but the campaign had been going on for nine months and MDHC's business was working very successfully. 'Our customers have been enjoying an excellent service… The ACL has gone, and we have to work on the basis that the ACL has gone for good.' [18] Speaking on behalf of the dockers, Bobby Morton said of ACL's decision to pull out of the Port of Liverpool, 'There is no mood of elation on the picket line. We think it is a very bad day for the port and the port users.' [19] Jimmy Davies told the BBC that the dockers would do everything in their power to affect some action against Cast and Can-Mar. [20] *Lloyd's List* published their analysis of ACL's departure from Liverpool:

> *'Felixstowe and at least one other UK container port admitted they are attempting to take ACL's business away from Liverpool… ACL withdrew from Liverpool in June, after being hit by the dispute… Other UK ports clearly believe they can provide the facilities ACL requires and that the company is still open to moving from Liverpool… Felixstowe managing director Derek Harrington said, 'We have been in contact with ACL, as we have with all potential customers.'* [21]

# 37

# The Dispute Rolls on

*'The rally showed solidarity, with the people of Liverpool seeing that they all support us, and show the Labour government that we're here to stay and to show the employers that we are not moving; we've got nowhere to go.'*
~ *M Curran**

On Friday 28 June 1996, Jack Heyman of Local 10 International Longshore and Warehouse Union, arrived in Liverpool as news was coming in that Canada Maritime were leaving the port. At the weekly mass meeting, Heyman told the dockers that they were like the Harry Bridges 1934 strikers on the West Coast of America. [1] The following day, after Nolan had spoken to more than 300 delegates at an end-of-business session of the International Transport Workers' Federation, delegates called for an international day of action in support of the Liverpool Dockers. He was due to meet with John Bowers of the East Coast International Longshoremen's Association in London. [2] ITF leaders David Cockcroft and Kees Marges opposed any action, but Canadian dockers in Vancouver had already started boycotting Liverpool cargo from a Gear-Bulk vessel without the support of their union's officers. Bowers added that action needed to be taken by the Canadian dockers against Cast Shipping Line. It was in London that the stewards' decided upon the need for picketing to take place in Canada immediately. Jack Heyman telephoned Michel Murray, the young and charismatic Montreal dockers' leader, to ask for his support. For the ITF, Cockcroft and Marges set about quoting Bill Morris to justify their inaction. John Bowers had invited the dockers to Commonwealth House, so that they could confront Morris directly. Morris told them: 'no one in Liverpool is starving, and I don't want to fall into a pattern of giving money on a regular basis for legal reasons.' [3] Around this time the French Confederation Generale du Travail (CGT) made a large financial contribution to the Liverpool dockers' Hardship Fund as did the French Workers' Party. In Liverpool it had now

---

* M Curran, speaking to BBC Radio Merseyside on 27 September 1997 (Audio Tape Ref: Docks April 1997)

been confirmed that Liverpool Cargo Handling and Nelson Stevedoring were to cease trading. [4]

On Saturday 29 June, thousands of dockers and their supporters marched through Liverpool City Centre to demand reinstatement, braving 40mph winds that saw marchers struggling to keep their banners aloft as they arrived at St George's Plateau for a rally featuring the dancing Turkish workers from J.J. Fast Foods in London. Jimmy Davies informed the crowd that the international solidarity campaign was bearing fruit, announcing that he had received a fax that very morning stating that the Can-Mar shipping line was pulling out of Liverpool. He went on to express his disappointed that local church leaders were trying to push the dockers into accepting a cash settlement without consideration for the Torside workers, arguing: 'if we were to let these lads down now, we might as well have crossed the picket line on the first day.' [5] Many of the speakers emphasised the need for both the TGWU and the Labour Party to fight for workers' rights, with Tony Benn MP declaring: 'You have right on your side and are standing in solidarity with other workers across the country that have seen their jobs destroyed.' [6] Benn reminded the people that all throughout history, rights had been won as a result of struggle, and that the dockers' struggle had inspired many. Nevertheless, Tony Benn told the crowds that he would like to see, 'every member of the Shadow Cabinet on the platform with the Liverpool dockers. What we need in this country is a return of self-confidence for the people, and this is what you have achieved in Liverpool.' [7]

At the TGWU Regional Finance & General Purposes Committee a decision was made to call Jack Dempsey, the Docks and Waterways district officer, before a committee on 13 August 1996 to explain his actions in failing to report Bernard Bradley's reinstatement offer in September 1995. This coincided with the passing of further resolutions condemning the union's officer at a meeting of the Regional Docks and Waterways Committee on Monday 1 July 1996. Michel Murray returned Jack Heyman's telephone call, he also spoke to Jimmy Davies. Murray requested that a Liverpool delegation be sent to Montreal as soon as possible, as his dockers would not cross their picket line and numerous Cast vessels would therefore be locked in the port. The ILA had more than 120 dock checkers working in Montreal, with most of those being of Irish descent, but the Liverpool delegates would have to avoid creating splits between the Montreal Union, Syndicat des Debardeurs (SCFP), and the ILA. [8]

At the next Friday mass meeting, Jimmy Davies gave a detailed report on finances, telling the dockers and their supporters that the Communication Workers Union had donated £35,000 to the Hardship Fund. The Graphical Paper & Media Union and Manufacturing, Science and Finance had also made donations, and two of their respective leaders, Ray Williams and Sue Tallon, also addressed this meeting. John Ireland, secretary of the Liverpool CWU branch, spoke after attending an all-night picket line for a one-day Post Office workers' strike, and further donations were gained following Jimmy Nolan's speech at a UNISON conference and a successful delegation to France. Steve Donnelly of AC-Delco brought news from the plant in Kirkby and a report from his charity cycle ride from Land's End to John O'Groats. Liverpool dockers Derek Wainwright and Mark Rossiter, described as 'both senselessly sacked dockers' in the booklet published for Donnelly's fundraiser, were thanked for taking part. Steve Donnelly's life was tragically cut short in 2005 and in a tribute letter published in the *Liverpool Echo*, he was described as:

> *'A true son of Kirkby. He had a real love of people and his aim in life was helping others... Steve led marches, raised morale and led such a successful campaign that he ensured Delco stayed alive and in Kirkby. Steve died at the tragically young age of 48. He was a giant – just ask his workmates. Ask the dockworkers of Liverpool and their families, ask the people of Kirkby.'* [9]

A world away from Steve Donnelly and the working-class Kirkby industrial estate he grew up in, the Port Users' Committee (PUC) decided to meet at the Liverpool Maritime Museum on Friday 5 July, where they voiced their objection to, 'the wilful campaign to discredit the Port of Liverpool led by the former dock workers.' [10] While launching a campaign to promote the UK port at a crisis meeting attended by over 40 shipping lines, agents, freight forwarders, hauliers and local chambers of commerce, the PUC discussed Atlantic Container Line's withdrawal. Here, Terry Malone said that he would be addressing a further meeting on Monday to establish an action plan, before going on to blame the dockers who he claimed had not only, 'got the men sacked, but had managed to get a £25,000 severance payment and commuted pension agreement taken off the negotiating table.' [11]

Back at Transport House, Jack Adams informed the stewards that the port's ancillary workers wanted to meet the TGWU that coming Thursday. It was also explained that Paterson and Brewer, solicitors acting on behalf of the union, would come to Liverpool for one week to interview more than 120 dockworkers ahead of unfair dismissal cases due to be held on 30 September 1996, almost one year to the day since the dispute started. The Dispute Committee decided to oppose this development, as they considered it a means to further undermine the dockers' struggle, despite the union's claims that it was simply pursuing, 'a mechanism that needed to be set in motion.' As one of the stewards said at the time: 'If we had proper legal advice a year ago, we would not be in the mess we are in now.' [12] Dave Cotterill reflected the thoughts of some dockers who felt that the dispute had been a conspiracy from the start. Herby Hollerhead, a Norse Irish Ferries shop steward, echoed these sentiments when he commented that, 'We cannot prove that it was a set-up, but the length of time that the docks have been closed down shows that the management were well prepared for the dispute.'[13] It was Cotterill's view that: 'The realisation was there that this was part of the Dock Company's strategy, that once the scabs were 'up to speed' and trained then ships would be brought back to Liverpool.' [14]

On Wednesday 10 July, Jimmy Nolan and Mike Carden went to Parliament to speak with David Alton, the local Liberal MP and Lord Nolan, who wanted to act as conciliators in the dispute. It was here that Jack Adams told Nolan and Carden: 'Dempsey called in the Health and Safety Executive because Mersey Docks had "fucked him over," and that scabs were working 20-hour shifts.' [15] The world had indeed been turned upside down as Dock Company shares continued to fall, and on Thursday 11 July, Dave McCall joined Dempsey in addressing another meeting of ancillary dockworkers at Transport House. This was a follow-on from a similar meeting held 24 June at which McCall claimed that he had raised a number of points regarding, 'how to support the sacked dockers.' [16] Dempsey informed the meeting that he was unable to negotiate on their behalf, but that he had told Allan Price, MDHC's Personnel Manager, how he: 'did not agree that the ACL leaving the port was a cause for redundancies among ancillary workers in the port.' Dempsey also spoke of the 800 ancillary workers in the port not being represented properly because he, 'would not cross a picket line to discuss 80 redundancies.' [17] The irony was painful, although in this dispute it seemed that irony flowed from the employers and the union like the Mersey, ever onwards towards the sea.

 *Newsline* published interviews with sacked dockers around this time. Kevin Jones made the argument: 'If the TGWU made our dispute official, we could expect other TGWU members to join our dispute.' [18] Another docker, Alan Haig, added that, 'We are not only fighting for our jobs back, but for the future as well,' [19] while John McCabe felt as though: 'the TGWU does not want to know about this dispute. They should never have entered into negotiations about money; the dispute is about our reinstatement'. [20] This point was reiterated by Brian Dooley, who said that: 'Our struggle is about reinstatement and an end to casualisation, poor pay and bad working conditions.' [21] A 'Summer Festival' was held at the Dockers' Club in Edinburgh Park on Sunday 14 July, with local bands, cultural stalls, prizes, a barbecue, bouncy castles, kids' treats and face-painting. In the programme for the event, messages of support from a wide range of groups and local companies were printed. Torside shop steward Tony Melia's Dock Band was among the musical acts, as was Reverb, a group of 12-year-olds including John Carden, Doug Arnold, and Stuart Barker; other groups such as Jonti, Poke, Hoodwink and Jackaray also played and a splendid time was guaranteed for all! [22]

 The following Wednesday, Jimmy Nolan and Mike Carden were at Dublin's Liberty Hall to meet with the Rail Maritime Transport Union and the Services, Industrial, Professional and Technical Union, for the purpose of developing a strategy to protect wages and conditions in the port. A week later, the Dispute Committee aired concerns about the safety of two comrades, Tony Gardiner and Billy Jenkins, who were both in Turkey, while Kevin Robinson, Terry Teague, Terry Southers and Tony Nelson had arrived in Montreal and successfully occupied a container gantry for over four hours. According to Greg Dropkin's report, the Liverpool delegates were poised 200ft above a container terminal, paralysing the *M.V. Cast Bear* for five hours on Monday 15 July, as Montreal longshoremen refused to board the ship. [23] Nelson was in contact with *LabourNet* via mobile phone throughout the trip, describing how negotiations had taken place between dockers' union leader Michel Murray and Kevin Doherty, the latter being a Cast Shipping representative based at the terminal. [24] The Liverpool men did eventually meet Cast's management, conveying their intentions to pursue the company worldwide before being taken into police custody for questioning, although it was unclear whether any charges had been filed. A Canadian Broadcasting Corporation eyewitness radio report indicated widespread support from the Montreal longshoremen for the arrested men, [25] and according to an article in the *Montreal Gazette*:

> '*while perched atop the cranes yesterday, the men dropped bilingual pamphlets explaining their plea for help. They accused Cast of being determined to support scab labour and the strikebreaking tactics of Mersey Docks. The workers spoke yesterday with Cast vice-*

*president Kevin Doherty. Doherty told them he would pass on their concerns to the company's president.' [26]*

Terry Southers would later explain how the delegation had tried to meet with Cast officials for several months before resorting to occupation tactics, [27] while Kevin Robinson defended the initial decision not to cross the picket line of the 80 young Torside dockers, who had been unjustly fired: 'Those boys are the sons and brothers of the older dockers. They need our support.' [28] The four men ended their protest shortly before noon following the intervention of Michel Murray, and they were escorted from the bottom of the 45m-high cranes to the Cast terminal office by a throng of around 75 local dockworkers. It was Murray who drove them to the office at Cite du Havre, with an escort of both Port of Montreal and Montreal Urban Community police cruisers, but despite the disruption, they all escaped criminal charges. [29] These exploits were recounted at the next Friday mass meeting, as was *Newsline's* criticism of the dockers' failure to attend a demonstration in support of the Hillingdon Hospital strike. This had been a mistake on the part of the Dispute Committee, and they did attempt to explain their absence. [30] A week later, on Thursday 18 July, Trevor Furlong, MDHC's Chief Executive, confirmed what the Liverpool dockers had known all along when he was quoted as saying: 'I suppose in hindsight we were too soft in 1989. We should have got rid of the lot of them and recruited, but we did not believe it was right.' [31] Another MDHC spokesperson: 'denied that the company's intention was to destroy organised labour, while acknowledging that it had suffered in comparison to other ports that had derecognised unions in 1989.' [32]

# 38
# Splits and Sectarian
# Interests

*'One of the reasons is that dockers like me are from families that have a history of the dock. I've not just a father who was on the dock; I had three uncles on the dock. So I've understood some things since I was a young lad when I went on the dock myself. I understood that they fought for decent conditions within the dock industry, and I understood the atrocities that were going on with the hiring system. My father died prematurely because of conditions on the dock. He had an accident when [a] heel block hit him on the head and he never went back to work.' ~ Micky Tighe\**

On Saturday 20 July 1996, a Dockers' National Support Group meeting was held at Transport House, Liverpool, for the purpose of bringing together all support groups to report on, discuss and review the dispute. The Scottish Support Group, covering a number of unions, were organising collections and direct action; they wanted the stewards to write to Clydesdale Bank in regard to their shares in MDHC and they expressed concern that there appeared to be a news boycott that necessitated the printing of more leaflets. The Scottish and Welsh Trades Union Congresses were working together in support of the dockers, and the Edinburgh Support Group wanted to ensure that action by other UK support groups was co-ordinated more efficiently. Phil Turner of the Rotherham and Sheffield Socialist Workers Party spoke of the need to improvise news bulletins, [1] while the Civil and Public Services Association's Dave Owens suggested organising regional collections and criticised block job adverts for scabs at employment agencies. [2]

Mariam Kamish, representing the South-East Wales Dockers' Support Group, welcomed the opportunity to support the Liverpool dockers, explaining that although Tower Colliery was the only coal mine left in Wales, the great traditions of working-class solidarity

---

\* Liverpool docker Micky Tighe in 'Workers' history as told by those who made it' – Bill Hunter. Available: http://www.billhunterweb.org.uk/interviews/History_as_Told.htm#Micky%20Tighe

still existed. The Dispute Committee recognised the need to organise structured collections in Wales, especially where large workplaces were sited, [3] and Dave Sherry of the Glasgow Support Group wanted to lobby the TUC and demand a dockers' speaker at the Scottish Transport and General Workers' Union conference scheduled for October 1996. [4] A delegate from Manchester brought up the need to go directly to the rank-and-file, while Jeremy Drinkle of the Cardiff Support Group and Socialist Caucus called for, 'a one-day General Strike, stopping scab ships using Cardiff and occupying a gantry, with the TUC and Labour Party needing to launch a national newspaper.' [5] The Manchester Socialist Alliance's Chris Jones complained that there was, 'no coordination between Manchester Support Groups,' [6] and the Liverpool Turkish Support Group addressed the marginalising of working-class movements by bureaucrats in the Labour Movement. [7] A UNISON representative from Sheffield requested official levy sheets to raise money in factories, while their Haringey counterpart wished to forge links with environmental groups. Another UNISON speaker, this time from South London, argued: 'Face to face contact with workers is required. Factory levies needed to be more aggressive, demanding support with a determined role of leadership. Nobody should have political franchise of the dockers, but we need to coordinate local conferences to establish proper support.' [8]

Representatives of the Midlands TGWU agreed that the union should make the dispute official, citing how it had not even circulated details among the membership. Dot Gibson suggested that the *Dockers' Charter* become the bulletin for all support groups, while speaking at length on the need to, 'overcome sectarianism.' [9] She then asked why the SWP did not attend London Dockers Support Group meetings, to which Nigel Flannigan, a member of both the SWP and UNISON, answered that he had been organising collections, before adding his opinion that, 'the stewards were blocking solidarity support and need to organise factory gate collections. Dockers need to be let off the leash. A need exists to nominate co-ordinators in individual areas and additional pressure needs to be stepped up.' [10] Many of the contributions were now merely repeats of claims made by competing political groups, each seeking to place their particular ideology above the rest. Finally, Doreen McNally spoke on behalf of the Women of the Waterfront, and film director, Anne Marie Sweeney, reported on various videos she had completed covering the dispute. [11]

At this time, Dave Graham had been writing updates and analyses of the Liverpool docks dispute for some time, and his contemporaneous reports – what would now be referred to as a *blog* – provided useful insights into the tension that lay beneath a thin, brittle veneer of unity and solidarity among the various political groups connected to the dispute. The divisions that existed between so many of the dockers' supporters often exposed the open sectarianism that expressed itself during the life and subsequent conclusion of the dispute, inspiring Graham to record how he had, 'lived with this dispute on my doorstep for nearly two years now.' [12] Reflecting on his internet reports, Graham would later write:

> '...according to tradition, such reports are supposed to serve the 'party line' and be part of a fully worked out 'world outlook'. Well, I regret to say [that] I have no such world outlook other than to tell the truth as I see it, and to do all in my power to aid the struggle of a group of workers, their partners and supporters whom I have gradually come to know over all these months.' [13]

Graham understood the shop steward's appreciation of the work that Greg Dropkin and Chris Bailey had done in using new technology to promote the dispute, and he knew that the dockers themselves were now able to navigate the internet, perhaps enabling the left to at last be able to 'subvert' new technology and to use it to their advantage.' [14] He also wanted to thank other online activists for turning the internet into a communication tool of the working class, praising Steve Wright (*Autopsy List*, Melbourne, Australia) and Curtis Price (*Collective Action Notes*, Baltimore, USA), as well as Brian Ashton, chair of the Liverpool Dockers' Support Group, who allowed him to endlessly pick his brains on all the many issues that the dispute had raised. [15] Graham attended the Liverpool Dockers' Support Group meeting, which in his opinion was where autonomous bodies and the dockers themselves had made it perfectly clear from the beginning that they were not in a position to impose conditions on other organisations. Yet, according to Graham, it was odd that speaker after speaker seemed anxious to demonstrate that they were willing, and indeed eager, to submit to the dockers' non-existent direction, as he observed that perhaps this was an indication of the: 'weight of bourgeois society on people, an indication of how far we still have to go.' [16]

Graham's analysis informed many of the contradictions now being thrown-up regarding an industrial dispute that had been considered a throwback to another age, as he argued that one of the reasons why people believed in the importance of the dockers' dispute was because it has attempted to look forward to a 'new movement' that was fighting to be brought into existence: 'We only have to look at how seriously the state takes the dockers' relationship with Reclaim the Streets and others to see that they recognise this as a real threat. The role of the left has been to continuously attempt to pull the dockers away from this course, rather than help in pushing out...' [17] On the critical debate over solidarity and direct action with the Liverpool dockers, Graham considered how, 'despite the damage being done to the port, it is more important that the dockers are not defeated than the Port of Liverpool survives as a viable business.' [18] He understood the contradictions of the dockers' situation, especially in relation to how political groups and fellow trade unionists related to the shop stewards committee. [19] On these divisions and sectarian interests that emerged during the course of the dispute, his view was that:

> '*As ever, the Left have limited themselves to tail ending the dispute or even worse doing their routine of passing resolutions, calling for support and so on. So far, they have had little practical influence except for one incident, which is interesting. A group called the International Communist Party, a Trotskyist organisation, but with an unorthodox and 'ultra-left' view of unions and shop stewards, produced a leaflet calling into question the role of the dock stewards in this dispute. For their pains, they managed to get themselves ejected from a supporters meeting. Now they might be formally correct in their view of unions and shop stewards, but of course, even for unorthodox Trotskyists, the crisis for the working class is one of revolutionary leadership, not the working class' own view of itself and its struggle. In any case, the practical effect of their intervention has been in a small way to solidify the dockers around their existing leadership – whom the ICP blamed for preventing effective solidarity action.' [20]*

Here, Graham believed that there was a lesson for us all. There is a process going on here that we must learn to relate to; a questioning of everything as the old certainties crumble in the face of a new reality for everyone from avowed Stalinists, like Jimmy Nolan, or long-time Labour Party supporters. [21] In pursuing this line of thought, he raises the idea that: 'if by some miracle a whole new shop stewards' committee was elected, it would almost certainly represent the same mixture of views and conception of struggle as its predecessor.' [22] However, writing in 2002, academic, David Meyer, contradicted Graham's analysis by arguing that somehow the Liverpool dockers, and specifically the shop stewards, did not seek the support of other UK workers as part of their solidarity campaign:

> *The stewards did not issue a call to other workers for practical as well as financial support. A militant former Tilbury docker visited Liverpool during this second week, urging a mass occupation of the Liverpool docks and a spread of the dispute to other major local workplaces, to pressurize the port employers to negotiate. But his advice was ignored... Any other tactics, of course, would have posed the question of breaking the law: secondary action, secondary boycotts, and mass pickets were all potentially illegal. The TGWU officials would have strenuously opposed any such moves. Yet these forms of action, along with independence of union officialdom and defiance of anti-union laws were all part of militant dockers' historical repertoire of contention and indeed were part of the personal traditions of many leading stewards. But now, they believed, these things could no longer be done, even though they had, themselves, struck illegally on September 28th.'* [23]

For the SWP, Michael Lavalette and Jane Kennedy, writing at the time of the dispute, argued:

> '*...although leading a militant campaign for reinstatement and utilising a range of 'traditional' trade union methods of struggle, the strike committee reflects some of the elements of trade union 'new realism' and share the view, not held by all of their trade union supporters, that the law has effectively shackled trade unionists in Britain from providing secondary action. The acceptance of this idea has had an important effect on the way the strike committee has run the dispute, on what they have thought it possible to achieve and on the demands they have made on other workers.*' [24]

Lavalette and Kennedy consistently refer to the dock dispute as a 'strike'. This ignored the consistent analysis of the dockers, that they had been dismissed. They were not on unofficial strike and as such they were not shackled to any section of current industrial relations law. Lavalette and Kennedy's analysis had been criticised by numerous observers and activists involved in the Liverpool dispute, including Greg Dropkin, Bill Hunter, Mike Carden, Hugh Rodwell and Peter Waterman. [25] For Rodwell, writing from Sweden at the time:

> *Bill Hunter, Greg Dropkin and Mike Carden have demolished the factual basis of many of Michael Lavalette's assertions. An important reason underlying his errors and omissions is his failure to grasp the character of what Bill Hunter calls 'a living movement.' Basically, no political force can legislate for or bring mobilization by*

*proclamation. Mobilization is what happens when people can't put up with their situation any longer and organize to fight for a change… Hunter pointedly asks why the SWP hasn't thrown the weight of its membership behind the actually existing mobilization of the Liverpool dockers… There are signs of fresh mobilization around the world, and the example of Liverpool is giving hope and inspiration in these struggles.'*
*[26]*

Bill Hunter noted that the dockers and their supporters had earned the right to ask for support during the course of their struggle, whether in the form of trade union action, solidarity demonstrations or direct protests:

*'One of the many refreshing things about this dockers' struggle had been its openness to all socialist tendencies and its welcoming of an industrial and political front of support… The SWP is the biggest of the revolutionary socialist groups; it is said to have 7,000 members. That could be a force in helping the needed response to the dockers strike, organised to assist the aims of the strike, in full integration in the dockers' support groups, and in full consultation with the dockers committee who are in the firing line.'*
*[27]*

At the time, Carden addressed how Lavalette and Kennedy's *Solidarity on the Waterfront* sought to reaffirm an ill-informed, poorly researched analysis of the Liverpool docks dispute:

*'To assert that the Liverpool dockers had one 'dominant strategy' i.e. internationalism, as the 'force to deliver the victory' in their struggle is simply not true. Similarly, his view that Liverpool dockers 'argue that British workers cannot and will not fight' is insulting both to the dockers and the working class of our country …the thought that Liverpool dockers' leaders like Jimmy Nolan and Jimmy Davies, who had stood up to Chilean and South African dictators, blockaded uranium from Namibia; in 1972 they struck and forced a Tory government to release five London dockers imprisoned in Pentonville jail and they organised a strike for the miners in 1984 that lasted for two weeks, the list could go on, that these men would be fearful of the leadership of the TGWU or be reluctant to call upon other workers to support their current struggle in 1995 was hardly imaginable. [28]*

The dockers wanted every worker in the UK to strike in support of their dispute, as well as those of the Magnet and the Hillingdon workers.

*'The Liverpool dockers failed in this objective of achieving mass direct action in the UK. Debate and discussion on the Liverpool dock dispute is vital and so is criticism but the ill-informed and poorly researched views expressed by Michael Lavalette contributed nothing to the struggle of the Liverpool dockers. Perhaps the most informative aspect of Michael Lavalette's personal views is that he had never taken the opportunity to raise them directly with the dockers themselves.' [29]*

In reviewing Lavalette and Kennedy's work, Greg Dropkin observed:

*'On its own, [the international] strategy has not brought enough pressure on MDHC. His alternative is a strategy of 'blacking and mass pickets' by the 'organised labour movement in Britain.' Well for a start, Lavalette might agree there is a lot of historical evidence that mass pickets alone don't guarantee victory either. The failure to win the vote for industrial solidarity to halt postal deliveries to Grunwick in 1977 and the failure, in general, to block supplies to power stations in 1984 were decisive obstacles not offset by the determined mass pickets at Grunwick and Nottinghamshire, which the British State knew how to contain. Nor did mass picketing win at Timex.' [30]*

Dropkin argued that the dockers convened meetings with local shop stewards in other industries, from which no action was forthcoming, and so they turned to the international arena because it seemed a more likely source of industrial action that could actually have a direct impact on Liverpool trade. On the subject of seeking solidarity at home as well as abroad, Dropkin recalled that:

*'On the first anniversary of the Lockout, in front of a mass audience including plenty of industrial workers and SWP members whose placards asked, 'Which side is Tony Blair on?' Secretary-Treasurer Jimmy Davies declared the dockers were now demanding the physical support of the entire trade union movement. Both he and Doreen McNally [Women of the Waterfront] were explicit: we want industrial action… The organised labour movement did not, by and large, turn up. Neither did the SWP, who are perfectly capable of ordering their 7,000 members to mass pickets anywhere in mainland Britain… But it was mainly dockers and their latest supporters, anarchists and environmentalists… Morris denounced the anarchists. The dockers defended them.' [31]*

On 9 July 2015, Bill Hunter died at the age of 92. He was a socialist, a writer, a campaigner and a comrade of extraordinary intellect. Jerry Spencer of the Liverpool Anarchist Federation remembered Bill as, 'a kind, intelligent and passionate person, with real fire where it counted, and an indomitable spirit coupled with wisdom and an intellect that illuminated everything he turned it upon.' [32] Martin and Celia Ralph wrote at the time of Bill Hunter's death:

*When Bill was 90 years old, he very much wanted to mark the occasion in celebration of his life as a Trotskyist. Even as his memory faded, his deep conviction for the struggle, his humour, his spirit and his faith in the working class never wavered. Bill was a great writer, speaker, propagandist and agitator, and our memories of the many battles that he waged, that we know about, come flooding back at this moment. [33]*

# 39

# Atlantic Container Line Returns and the death of Mickey Fenn

*'It was not the last chance, they're crucified; they're dying on their feet, that's what happening with them. They're dying on their feet and they're panicking. I'll just put my X's for now. I'm 61 years of age and there's my paper... We'll beat these... Europe's with us, the ITF's with us. Why have they said this at the last minute? Morris, God blimey, he's a disgrace him.' ~ Jimmy Campbell\**

The morning picket line on Monday 22 July 1996 was well attended, but a new sense of drift now hung in the air as rumours of Atlantic Container Line (ACL)'s pending return to the Port of Liverpool spread from one docker to the next, and from one picket line to another. [1] That day's Dispute Committee meeting was billed as one where they had to 'do something,' with the prevailing view being that the dispute had stalled through inaction and a lack of focus. Billy Jenkins and Tony Gardiner had returned from Turkey with a desire to organise support meetings to oppose the oppression that was taking place there, and 10 dockers had gone to a 'Marxism Week' amid feelings, amongst some stewards, that they were entering a period in which people were turning up from nowhere to be looked after distracting from what was supposed to be the *organisational hub* of an industrial dispute. No political party was going to reinstate the sacked dockers, and some felt they should be arranging the blockading of ships rather than chasing political philosophies and ideologies. Several committee members were blunt and brutal in their criticisms, calling for direct action that concentrated on hitting UK ports like Glasgow and Cardiff, and a move away from politicising the dispute. It was now nine weeks since the Transport and General Workers' Union had last put money into the Hardship Fund, and such delays were starting to worsen the despair among many of the dockers' families. Birkenhead Docks were booming and there was a need to organise pickets there, along with planned pickets of Coastal Lines in Cardiff

---

\* Jimmy Campbell, sacked dockworker, speaking to Radio Merseyside (audio tape, April 1997)

303

and Dublin, and international action against Cast in the ports of Zeebrugge, Lisbon and Le Havre.

John Bowers, president of the East Coast International Longshoremen's Association, spoke to Jimmy Nolan about legal action from ACL, who now wanted to return to Liverpool, while Francisco 'Paco' Ramos, a leader of the Spanish dockers, advised the stewards to begin targeting Cast's European business. A man of immense dignity and intellect, Paco would be tragically killed in a workplace accident on the Tenerife Docks in July 1999, after which Greg Dropkin wrote a touching tribute to a man who 'sang Arias.' [2] By 24 July, the Liverpool dockers were mounting pickets against ACL's imminent return, delaying the *M.V. Atlantic Conveyor* by three hours when the tugboat men refused to cross the dockers' lines, and causing the ship to eventually enter the port in high winds without assistance. Two other ships, the *M.V. Cast Bear* and the *M.V. Orimulsion* were both delayed by 12 hours, only 10 days after the *M.V. Cast Bear* had been held up for five hours by the Liverpool dockers' occupation of a crane in Montreal. Occupation again became a pressing topic among the stewards and the men and women on the picket lines; it was the very same discussions that had taken place when the dockers were still working. Confrontation with the Mersey Docks and Harbour Company was fully expected after 1989, and as the attacks on the dockers evolved, it became clear that it would only end in open conflict. By 1993, MDHC bosses were engaging in a process by which they were openly humiliating their employees while the local TGWU did nothing, so it is no surprise that some rank-and-file dockworkers arrived at the conclusion that when confrontation finally came they should not walk out of the gates and give MDHC the opportunity to lock them out. Occupation was the preferred tactic of the majority of dockers; it was always the plan, but it was arguably the case that the reality of the events of September 1995 caused these plans to unravel.

On Thursday 25 July, the dockers heard that Ken Loach, the acclaimed film director and political activist, had agreed to make a film about the dispute. Using his own production company, Parallax Films, Loach would begin filming in September 1996 and be finished by October, having secured funding from the BBC and ARTE a French European Culture TV company. AMIP, a small, independent left-wing film company based in Paris, was instrumental in bringing together the financial investment that enabled the film to be made with Xavier Carniaux and Elisabeth Marliangeas working tirelessly to ensure that everything possible was done to promote the dockers' struggle and support the Hardship Fund. They were admirers of Ken Loach's work as were the French generally. On Friday 26 July, Loach visited Transport House to explain to the Dispute Committee how the film, which would be part of the BBC's *Modern Times* series, would approach the dispute, but while the importance of his interest was not lost on the majority of the stewards, some failed to realise the cultural significance of Loach's contributions to the art of cinema and socialism.

At the following day's Dispute Committee meeting, it was reported that Graham Stevenson had been appointed to replace John Connolly as the TGWU's Docks and Waterways National Officer. Ernesto Arrelano, one of Jimmy Nolan's old comrades, was there to speak on behalf of Aid for Chile. They had acquired a fire engine that needed to be shipped through Liverpool, and Arrelano addressed the moral dilemma of having to cross the picket line because they could not use any other port. The stewards' acknowledged that allowances should be made and it was agreed that Aid for Chile would move its shipment through Liverpool. Elsewhere, the *M.V. Atlantic Conveyor* was due in Gothenburg on Monday 29 July, but it would be delayed for at least 12 hours, possibly longer due to a national overtime ban in Sweden. [3] However, at the mass meeting held later that morning, the sense of disappointment was tangible. The men knew that ACL was returning, as Thamesport lacked the required roll-on / roll-off facility for larger vessels and that two ships had almost run aground there. The following day, 'the picket line was very sombre, and the challenge facing all the stewards was how they could raise the profile of the campaign in the absence of anything happening.' [4] This depressing mood was compounded when, on Sunday 28 July, Mickey Fenn, the legendary London dockers' leader, passed away. Fenn's funeral was to be held in London on 5 August, celebrating the life of a sacked Tilbury docker who had been a socialist and a fighter right up until the end, travelling and campaigning for the Liverpool dockers' cause. He had helped lead the successful bid to free the Pentonville Five in 1972 and had been a member of the unofficial National Port Shop Stewards' Committee for many years. Above all else, he was a comrade and a friend to the Liverpool dockers. That same week, Eddie O'Hara MP called in to see the stewards as he was conscious that an impasse had been reached and he wanted to find out if he could do anything to move the dispute along.

On 1 August, the ITF's Kees Marges telephoned to offer support for a Liverpool delegation to Zeebrugge, however Bob Baete, the Belgian dockers' leader, was on holiday at the time, so they would have to wait before organising travel to Antwerp. Meanwhile, tugboats were out on the River Mersey, 'waiting for ships, maintaining radio silence,' [5] which made organising pickets on the docks more difficult, as the dockers were not receiving intelligence regarding vessels arrivals. Michel Murray, the Montreal dockers' leader, telephoned Jimmy Davies to let him know that his members had lost a day's pay as a result of their action against Cast, and that this had caused a major problem for him but the potential for solidarity action was being discussed in Le Havre, France. It was during this period that reports circulated of Trevor Furlong, the MDHC managing director, having his house *firebombed*, leading to allegations of intimidation against the dockers. The increasing economic and emotional strain on dockers and families was not helped by the sense that the dispute was, once again, flatlining. There were fewer delegations going out on fundraising campaigns, and the TGWU was late with its Hardship Fund payment again. Evidence, from the Citizens Advice Bureau, confirmed that more than 150 dockers and their families were facing repossessions due to unpaid rent. The shop stewards did not want Bill Morris to know just how perilous the dockers' personal financial situation had become, for fear that he would pass such information on to MDHC and embolden them to sit back and wait for the dispute to collapse in on itself. [6] Jimmy Nolan, Kevin Robinson and Mike Carden arranged to meet Dave Martin, the Electrical, Electronic, Telecommunications and Plumbing Union docks' ancillary convenor, and a local Liberal Democrat councillor, at Bootle Town Hall on Monday 1 August in the hope of convincing him to withdraw any council support for the Dock Company. Martin was prepared to raise the issue at the next meeting of Sefton Bootle Council, where many of the leaders had found themselves in conflict with MDHC and its directors over the years, for reasons ranging from coal dust affecting Bootle families to the port and its land being run as the company's private fiefdom. Company boss Trevor Furlong was greatly disliked by local residents and politicians in the area surrounding the docks for the damage done to their environment over many years.

When the Dispute Committee met at 5pm on 1 August, Colin Coughlin, a London dock shop steward, telephoned Jimmy Davies to let him know that the TGWU National Finance and General Purposes committee (F&GP) was about to call for fresh negotiations with MDHC. Davies then spoke to Jack Adams, who denied any knowledge of the F&GP's plans, [7] before adding that the memo sent by the Dispute Committee on 26 July, regarding the absence of Hardship Fund payment, was being used as 'an excuse to intervene directly.' [8] The union were calling for fresh talks to find an end to the dispute, with the union's F&GP agreeing that the General Secretary should write to MDHC seeking a resumption of negotiations. This led to Bill Morris issuing the following statement: 'This dispute has done great harm to the dockers, their families, the community of Liverpool and the company. In the light of ACL's decision to return to the port, it is time to make a fresh start in negotiations without any pre-conditions on either side.' [9] This was exactly what the stewards' feared. Yet again the TGWU's intervention only served to undermine the dockers' position by reminding MDHC of their dominance, and it was believed that Morris's choice of words was informed by discussions with the ITF, whose General Secretary, David Cockcroft, was unhappy that the Liverpool dockers picketed a recent celebration to mark the organisation's centenary. The ITF had done little in real terms to facilitate international support for the sacked dockers, and so the stewards were ready to hold a second International Conference of Port Workers at the end of August. [10] Jack Dempsey now reported that MDHC had received around 140 severance applications from its ancillary workers, and that the union now wanted a ballot over a Drake International scab who was working 55 hours per week between two jobs. [11] Bernard Cliff, for MDHC, was said to be furious over Dempsey's call for a strike ballot, and it was alleged that Bill Morris told his officer: 'We are going to lose everything – we *need* to negotiate.' [12] Jack Adams assured Jimmy Nolan that he would accept the steward's guidance on negotiations without pre-conditions. [13] Barry Robson of the Australian Maritime Union arrived in Liverpool with his wife, Kate. The two Australians sat in on a Dispute Committee meeting that evening, and the following morning they were standing on the Seaforth picket at 6am.

At the next weekly mass meeting, Jimmy Davies gave a short eulogy for Micky Fenn, whose death was marked by a notice placed in the *Liverpool Echo* that read: 'Michael Fenn, socialist and sacked Tilbury docker, anti-racist activist. Died suddenly on 28 July. He leaves a beloved and loving family. Wife, lover and best friend Denise, and children, Michael, Daniel, Jessica, Patrick and Shaun. He will live forever in our hearts.' [14] Jimmy Nolan then opened the meeting in his customary manner, welcoming everyone present, and Caryn Mathews, who had worked tirelessly with the families of the Liverpool dockers through the Citizens Advice Bureau, asked for support in developing evidence and records to indicate the scope of hardship being experienced by the dockers and their families. It was reported that the TGWU's Hardship Fund payment had arrived – the first in over ten weeks – and the atmosphere was generally positive following news that talks with MDHC would soon reopen. [15] The meeting also heard how dockers in Gothenburg had again blocked an ACL vessel for 17 hours, and the MUA's Barry Robson became so emotional while addressing the room that his wife had to take over. One of the stewards, Tony Russell, gave a report from the

# ATLANTIC CONTAINER LINE RETURNS AND THE DEATH OF MICKEY FENN

Cardiff Dockers' Support Group's occupation of a Coastal gantry. Irene Campbell, Women of the Waterfront secretary, concluded by adding to the emotion shown by Barry Robson with a report on the children's holiday in Colchester that had been organised by the Turkish Textile Workers. It was reiterated that the campaign would not be hijacked by anyone, including the TGWU. [16]

News of talks resuming between the TGWU and MDHC made headlines in the *Liverpool Daily Post*, [17] and on Monday 5 August, a Dispute Committee delegation including Jimmy Nolan, Jimmy Davies, Frank Lannigan, Mike Carden, Billy Jenkins and Bobby Morton attended Micky Fenn's funeral in London. The family, Colin Coughlin, Kevin Hussey and the London dockers organised the day with their typical generosity and kindness, in what was a real expression of working-class dignity and a fitting celebration of the life of an extraordinary comrade. More than 300 people were in attendance, walking behind the banners of the London and Merseyside dockworkers, while the coffin was draped in a 1972 strike banner bearing the slogan, 'Arise Ye Workers!' Micky Fenn's wife, Denise and her family requested that instead of flowers, people send donations to the Liverpool dockers, and during the service, an extract from PB Shelley's *Masque of Anarchy* was read out, with Kevin Hussey, Elisabeth Lutzeir and Richard Smith standing as the main speakers. The wake that followed was extraordinary, with an abundance of love, music, socialism, solidarity and alcohol!

The following day, Tony Nelson, Andy Dwyer, Bob Ritchie, Tony Russell and Terry Southers travelled to London to join this delegation headed by Jimmy Nolan for a meeting with Jack Adams. [18] The feeling amongst these men and their supporters was that the TGWU's public statements on seeking negotiations for no apparent reason could not have come at a worse time. The mood among the stewards was sombre as they waited for Adams in the union's temporary central office on Palace Street, [19] and when the deputy general secretary arrived, he brought news that Eddie O'Hara MP (Knowsley South) and two other local MPs had met with Trevor Furlong to discuss talks. According to Adams, Bill Morris had told a pre-meeting of executive officers at the F&GP that he had received, 'disturbing reports from David Cockcroft of the ITF.' [20] Adams said that he did not know what Morris meant by this, and Nolan made it clear that he would not endorse statements made by the F&GP. [21] Adams gave assurances that he would not go against the committee's wishes to leave ancillary port jobs out of any negotiations, and Nolan outlined how the dockers' campaign would continue, with an invitation from Japanese dockers potentially allowing for a boycott of Canadian Pacific, Cast's majority shareholders. In the meeting with Adams, Jimmy Davies spoke well and with some authority in defence of the dockers, stating plainly: 'We have nowhere to go, and the dispute will not be sold-out.' [22] For his part, Adams had told Morris two months into the dispute that, 'this is a dispute that may be sold-out, but not quietly.' [23]

At 7am on Wednesday 7 August, dockers picketed the offices of the *Liverpool Echo* and *Daily Post*, while Terry Teague made arrangements for a delegation to Belgium with Bob Baete in Antwerp, where both Cast and ACL ships would be targeted. Teague was joined in Antwerp by Mike Carden and several international comrades, as well as Ken Loach and his film crew, who were on hand to record Bob Baete speaking about the organisation and training of professional dockworkers, emphasising how this kind of work was not suitable for casual employees. During a meeting at the Belgian union's Antwerp headquarters, Canadian dockers' leader, Michel Murray, spoke of the importance of a victory for the Liverpool dockers, which would be a victory for all dockers: 'If they lose, then probably the company will try to do the same thing everywhere.' [24] Also in attendance was Ole Muller, the wonderful dockers' leader from Arhuus, Denmark, who told Baete that: 'If we succeed in Liverpool, then I can look at the future much more bright, but if Liverpool dockers were to be defeated, I know every time somebody speaks of international solidarity, people will say: "Look at Liverpool; what happened?"' [25] Baete admitted that it was difficult for them: 'to attack the shipping companies here in Antwerp and have the chance that they disappear day by day to Rotterdam. I have to be honest today that people say we have to support the shop stewards of Liverpool or the decisions of the TGWU. That's very principled.' [26] To this, Michel Murray, spoke in English rather than French:

> *The TGWU want the scabs to continue to work in the Port of Liverpool, that is the big problem; that is the big fucking problem. You have 500 families that suffer since one year, and they do sweet fuck-all about that. They still have their big chair. TGWU Bill Morris, I didn't – I never saw him, but he has a big chair and everything is good for him. ITF, everything is good; I do sticker, I put the sticker; I do my job. Why ITF are keeping away from the Liverpool struggle? Politics. And I'm not here to speak about politics, I'm here to speak about 500 families who are out since a year – since last year. And you were in struggle since the last year probably? You know what it is to be in struggle for a month, two months; for three months, for six months; for one year! One year. I was in struggle for three weeks last year, and after three weeks my dockers said, "Good thing that we signed." One year out!' [27]*

Baete answered by promising, 'I will strongly support your action, and I will give you my word that tonight we will delay the most important ships in Zeebrugge and Hamburg.' [28] Back in Liverpool a feeling hopelessness pervaded the atmosphere of the Friday morning meetings. [29] It seemed as though fewer dockers and supporters were attending, and inside information from the docks was that ACL's move away from Liverpool was never intended to be permanent. Andy Dwyer and Tony Nelson had taken Ken Loach into the dock estate, and they were at least able to offer some crumbs of comfort by reporting that nothing much seemed to be happening there. [30] Loach's subsequent documentary, *The Flickering Flame* (1996), focussed on the sacked Liverpool dockers and also, 'referenced back to his 1968 film, *The Big Flame.* This was a story set on the Liverpool docks in the 1960s, written by the late Jim Allen.' Loach later recalled that Allen had said, 'Liverpool is the battleground of Britain. If a revolution is to start anywhere, it will start in Liverpool. The city is full of very articulate, thoughtful people and it's always a joy to be there. I always feel connected because the people make you feel welcome.' [31] In addition to its UK distribution, the film was also set to be broadcast on French TV station ARTE on 20 May 1997.

# 40
# Reclaim the Streets

*'I had only been in Sweden for a few hours, but I soon found that the same attacks were being carried out on the people of Sweden as are being carried out here. The unemployed are being taken off benefits by a similar scheme to the JSA, simply to make the unemployment figures look good. They have a sickness insurance scheme, benefits on this are being reduced and being made harder to claim. The Health Service is also under attack... the trip to Sweden will leave a lasting impression on me.' ~ Brian Dooley\**

By August 1996, Coastal Containers were down to one sailing per day in the Port of Liverpool, and Bob Ritchie, a Torside shop steward, had secured an agreement for Scottish tugboats to blockade all Andrew Weir vessels. Meanwhile, in Gothenburg, Sweden, another 14-hour blockade delayed an Atlantic Container Line ship, and at the mass meeting held on Friday 9 August 1996, Terry Barrett, a sacked Seaforth dockworker, criticised the lack of support through industrial action that the dispute had received. [1] A mass picket started at 6am on Monday 12 August was very successful, with only a couple of dockers being arrested, and staff at NEI Ltd, who were responsible for servicing the container straddle carriers and cranes at Seaforth Container Terminal, revealed that Mersey Docks and Harbour Company was: 'suffering as a result of the action.' [2] Later that morning, a delegation led by Tony Nelson met with Reclaim the Streets (RTS), an environmental direct-action group, to plan demonstrations in support of the dockers under the banner, 'Right to Strike – The Right to Party.' Initial plans were made for an event to be held on 28 September, where a coalition of environmental groups, trade unions and political groups would come together in marking the one-year anniversary of the dispute. It was a radical plan that would integrate the dockers within a section of the working class that understood how the political and trade union landscape had been transformed over the past 30 years creating a new alliance between working-class communities, the unemployed, environmental groups and anarchists. It was Chris Knight who, along with the London Support Group, helped develop the dockers' links

---

\* Brian Dooley, sacked Liverpool docker, LabourNet, November 1996.

309

to Reclaim the Streets, with Knight later reflecting that, 'it was true to say that the dispute would not have lasted into its second year without their input.' [3] This view of the influence of Reclaim the Streets on workers' solidarity was shared by Bob Crow, leader of the National Union of Rail, Maritime and Transport Workers, as well as many others.

In preparation for the anniversary demonstrations, 'RTS activists went to Liverpool to survey some buildings that could be used as a base for them and their supporters. They decided upon the old Customs House, near the docks, complete with electricity supply, cells and toilet drugs detector,' and they were greatly amused to discover that, 'someone's job must've been to examine people's shit for drugs, which came through a glass-topped table thing from a toilet. Anyway, the venue was appropriate with lots of floor space, carpets, several levels, etc.' [4] According to Knight the solidarity between RTS and trade union struggles was not a seamless blending of ideas, but the former was looking for a cause to define their next major action. Knight recalled some support for the idea of taking up banners for the dockers, but also quite a lot of opposition, as there were some who believed that RTS should remain fundamentally an anti-car, environmentally conscious movement:

> *"What are we doing supporting the dockers? I thought they imported cars? What on earth have we got in common?" I just said, "Well, why don't we invite some dockers down and let them explain?" Using the Day-Mer community centre's fax machine, I outlined this plan and checked that the dockers (by now good friends of my sister) would themselves welcome RTS support in Liverpool. They sent back a fax: "Chris, go for it!" So, at the next meeting in that bus garage, Micky Tighe and Nick Silvano from Liverpool came down to explain to Reclaim the Streets why they should support their year-old dispute.' [5]*

At the same time, Nick Silvano and Micky Tighe had been meeting with the London Support Group and RTS about occupying London Transport HQ in support of the tube workers, and a giant banner proclaiming, 'Don't Squeeze the Tube,' was unfurled. A couple of days later, the demonstrators got a letter from the London Region RMT, signed by Bob Crow, whose father had been a London docker. His involvement with the Liverpool dockers would continue up until his untimely death on 11 March 2014. His official letter of thanks stated that: 'Reclaim the Streets achieved for the tube workers in one day more than the TUC has done in a decade,' and for Chris Knight, this was a beautiful gesture of acknowledgement. [6] However, RTS' involvement in trade unionism remained complex and fraught, with not only political contradictions but also logistical challenges. Much of their activity centred on London or at the Newbury bypass, with Knight recalling how they had:

> *'...the police, saying they wouldn't give permission to use Hyde Park or Trafalgar Square on September 28th... and I was thinking, "Well, how about going up to Liverpool? ...It would give us all a completely different image, signalling that we're not just London-based, we're not just middle class. We'd be branching out into a big industrial dispute up in the North West, which has lasted almost a year. We would get a lift, adding a completely different dimension to Reclaim the Streets." I remember coming home that night and confiding: "Something really big has happened today. Now I've got*

*Reclaim the Streets and Justice and the whole wonderful bandwagon to go up to Liverpool on the 28th.'" [7]*

In an article for *Do or Die*, environmentalists considered the strategy of linking up with the dockers and the wider trade union movement, connecting classical strands of the environment struggle, anarcho-syndicalism, Marxism and workers' alienation and ennui:

> *'Reclaim the Streets had taken what, for some, was a surprising and yet predictable route. Surprising in that there was no obvious link between 'anti-car activists' and 'sacked dockers,' and yet predictable in that there was an obvious affinity between them and the radical ecology movement. Both the dockers and radical ecologists argued for some form of social change, although so far in this country for wholly different reasons, and perhaps even with vastly different goals. RTS suggested that it was time we recognised the common social forces against which we are fighting... We're saying that the power that attacks those who work, through union legislation and casualisation, is the same power that is attacking the planet with over-production and consumption of resources; the power that produces cars by 4 million a year is the same power that decides to attack workers through the disempowerment of the unions, reducing work to slavery. That this power is capital. As long as economies run on the basis of profit for business, social and ecological exploitation will occur... 'Why Reclaim the Streets and the dockers?' is even asked shows that there is a common perception that ecology does not include social issues. The belief that the environment is nothing to do with how society runs, that it is something remote and 'out there,' somewhere to drive to for the day, something that just happens to be suffering because of the way we live. That we work in repetitive, meaningless jobs and that this is organised for the sake of profit is taken for granted and remains somehow unconnected. This separation and presentation of the ecological crisis as unconnected to other forms of exploitation only serves the interests of business and state and needs to be overcome if society is to survive. Indeed, it is precisely the industrialisation process itself that has separated us from ourselves, each other and the earth.' [8]*

Years later, Sue Mitchell would reflect on her admiration for the environmentalists and social campaigners who supported the Liverpool dockers' struggle so magnificently. On the matter of the Criminal Justice Act, RTS were determined to raise awareness of their campaign of opposition, even printing statements in the *Dockers' Charter*, [9] and their involvement formed an extraordinarily relevant and meaningful connection that Sue captured in telling Peter Kennedy about how they had opened her eyes to the reality of trade unions and the Labour Party:

> *'Put it this way, I've now got little time for trade unions, while I've got total respect – total respect – for environmental and Reclaim the Street activists, etc. I get told by women, brilliant women, in the T&G that you can only fight from within the union, but I say to them it is only when you get rid of the bureaucrats that the union can be what it should be... I admire them [environmentalists] because they're totally committed to causes. When I saw them fighting alongside wealthy people out to protect their homes at*

*the new Manchester Airport construction site… I know my own experience has changed my views, and I'll always support them.' [10]*

After a poor turnout at a Norse Irish picket Police Commander Finnigan gave demonstrators a one-minute warning to clear the gates, as the policing got as heavy–handed as ever. The men sat down to block the gate, and Terry Teague, Tony Nelson, Phil McInally, Nat Gibbons and Pat Harvey were all arrested, and although Granada TV and the BBC both ran stories on the escalating violence, Merseyside Police were happily providing media outlets with details of arrests and charges in order to discredit and demoralise the dockers. On Friday 16 August, a community march to Seaforth, led by the Women of the Waterfront, was followed by a mass meeting where Brian Dooley spoke from the floor, suggesting that the dockers occupy cranes at the Grain Terminal, and that more men needed to do collections with UNISON members at least once a month. Mick Cullen spoke about the previous Monday's mass picket, which had involved supporters from all over the country, before questioning why local trade unionists had not attended in any great numbers. He also asked why Princess Anne was speaking at the Trade Union Congress when the Liverpool dockers had not even received an invite. [11] During a 19 August meeting of the WOW, final arrangements were made ahead of a trip to Colomendy, Wales for some 35 dockers' children, as MDHC again declared its willingness to seek a conclusion to the dispute by calling for yet another ballot. In this mutual world of compromise and shared social and political vision, Gordon Waddell, MDHC's Chairman, went on BBC Radio Merseyside to state that because of the damage being done to the port, both parties needed to seek a settlement. This was basically just another joint effort between the company and the TGWU to undermine the dockers' position, after Trevor Furlong, MDHC's Managing Director, was quoted as saying that, 'we are seen as a bad employer, and that is not good for Merseyside. Some men have 30 years' service. We have to be compassionate and seek a settlement.' [12]

However, behind these public calls for diplomacy lay the assertion that the dispute was having little real effect. As Jimmy Nolan stood at the Seaforth picket line for an interview with BBC Radio Merseyside's Caroline Adams, who informed him that MDHC had just announced losses of £2.9m and a 17.1% reduction in profits. [13] Trevor Furlong was still claiming that the port was booming, with volumes of containers increasing at the port, a declaration that gained national coverage on BBC News, where it was said: 'normal port operations at both Liverpool and Medway continued to grow.' [14] Nolan explained to BBC Radio 4 that ongoing international action against shipping lines using the port was the main cause of MDHC's financial problems, as it was decided that the campaign would begin to target Shell Oil deliveries to Tranmere Oil Depot, along with ACL and Canadian Pacific Line. At this, MDHC replied with a press release expressing their unity with the TGWU in opposition to the unofficial dockers' leaders, stating their, 'deep regret that the dispute has not been resolved in spite of repeated efforts by the company and Transport and General Workers' Union officials. The unofficial leaders of the dismissed workers remain intransigent and continue to press their original demands which are wholly unacceptable.' [15] A week later, Gordon Waddell issued a two-page statement, released on Wednesday 21 August, in which he blamed the company's financial issues on Eurolink Ferries, a MDHC subsidiary said to have lost £4.5m in addition to a further £2.5m predicted losses for the rest of the financial year. Another subsidiary, Coastal Container Line, recorded an 18.8% loss that was ascribed to over-capacity on the Irish Sea. Waddell also claimed that the dockers' voluntary severance scheme was responsible for a further £945,000 loss, but no figure was placed on the four-week withdrawal of ACL, which was blamed on a combination of industrial action in Sweden and pressure from rank-and-file US longshoremen, with the shipping line still not having declared a permanent return to Liverpool amid rumours of a switch to Felixstowe. [16]

On Tuesday 13 August, at a meeting of the TGWU's Region 6 Finance and General Purposes Committee in Salford, plans were put in place for Jimmy Nolan to present the Liverpool dockers' case against their union-appointed dock official. A report was given regarding a disciplinary hearing held the previous day, which seemed to centre on the official receiving a fax from Bernard Bradley, Managing Director of Torside Ltd, saying that he would reinstate the dockers whose dismissal had triggered the dispute. The union official denied the existence of such a fax, claiming that he had informed Gerry Flaherty, the TGWU's Merseyside District officer, of its existence before withdrawing that statement. He also claimed that he was not present at any meetings that might have taken place with Bradley on Thursday 28 September 1995, and while Dave McCall, as Regional secretary, offered to take ownership of any inquiry into his official, the fear was that this was floated as a means of sidestepping the F&GP, among whom the dockers had a chance of support from the rank-and-file delegates. [17] The dockers were unhappy at the prospect of McCall's involvement, [18] who on Wednesday 14 August 1996 joined Jack Adams in the boardroom at Transport House. He reported on a meeting they had attended with MDHC's Trevor Furlong and Bernard Cliff. Adams told the Committee that he wanted to keep everything above board and open, as he explained that Cliff had seemed very relaxed [19] and was willing to reopen negotiations based on the last offer with added pre-conditions, while stressing the need for trust between all parties. [20] McCall added that the talks with MDHC had lasted 30 minutes and were not very detailed, although this was time enough for Furlong to state that in a meeting with Sefton Council, Jimmy Nolan and Mike Carden had expressed their joint lack of faith in the TGWU's officers. [21] McCall and Adams had themselves spoken with Sefton Council leaders, who told them that the two stewards did not criticise any union officials. Adams had also met with local MPs in London, as the question for the Dispute Committee became: should they wait for a meeting with the TGWU executive officers on 29 August, or go directly to MDHC on their own? Adams acknowledged that the stewards were free to meet MDHC without pre-conditions, while stating his opinion that the international campaign was: 'an irritant, not a knockout punch. We have to negotiate a victory,' [22] as he suggested that this was their last chance to negotiate before Cliff left the country until 24 August.

Out on the picket lines, four men and women were arrested at Brocklebank Dock on Wednesday 21 August, after which Bobby Morton told the local press: 'the police were very heavy-handed. They have accused us of changing tactics by moving from Seaforth to the Brocklebank. The number of police was staggering. We held a sit-down protest in response to the arrests.' [23] On hearing Morton's comments, the superintendent at Crosby Police Station claimed that their main concern was ensuring that people were able to protest peacefully while everybody went about their business. [24] At Friday's mass meeting, the atmosphere had notably improved following news that MDHC shares had dropped 17p, with the *Liverpool*

*Daily Post* running an article suggesting the company was on the verge of being taken over. This was a welcome boost at a time when the Hardship Fund was struggling to pay the men and their families, despite a huge contribution from Jim Donovan, leader of the Australian dockers. Vauxhall car workers had also made a substantial donation to the dockers' Hardship Fund. Terry Teague was busy organising the second International Conference of Port Workers and he had to speak with Nick Stamp in Rotterdam, who was refusing to attend because David Cockcroft of the International Transport Federation had been told by Bill Morris: 'the Liverpool dockers are trying to create an alternative to the ITF.' Apparently, Morris had also informed Cockcroft that if the dockers did not accept the expected offer from MDHC, he would: 'pull the TGWU out of the dispute.' [25] Elsewhere, Bob Ritchie had broken his ankle while trying to occupy a roof crane at the Port of Greenock.

On Thursday 29 August, the stewards travelled to the TGWU's head office to meet with Bill Morris, Jack Adams and John Connolly. As they were entering the building, Frank Lannigan told Mike Carden that a senior MDHC employee had seen Danny Maher at a football match the previous weekend, where he told the leader of the tugboat men that the company's finance figures had been creatively accounted for by some £8m [26]; Lannigan's information was usually accurate. Morris opened the afternoon meeting by stating that he had received the steward's request for a meeting with the F&GP, which he said could not be done, although the executive officers would see the dockers if necessary. Morris then asked Nolan to speak. He raised the unacceptability of talks with MDHC being held without pre-conditions, citing how statements made by the union could be misinterpreted by the media, the employers and the ITF. Nolan argued that there being 'no pre-conditions' indicated a move away from the dockers' primary claim for reinstatement, especially since Waddell had already stated in MDHC's annual financial report that the dockers' demands were wholly unacceptable, which was itself a pre-condition. As far as Nolan was concerned, victory would come only when the dockers diminished MDHC's financial power. [27] This was one reason for the continued emphasis on the level of international support that the dockers needed to put pressure on the company's finances. [28] Nolan then asked to speak at forthcoming ITF and TGWU conferences. Finally, after exactly one hour, the General Secretary felt motivated to speak:

> *'Discussion is important. We have arrived at a point where we have to be honest with one another. The [F&GP] have to be guardians of everyone's interests. We have the common objective to secure people's employment and a settlement. We may disagree on strategy, and there are fundamental principles we cannot depart from.' [29]*

Morris then outlined the position he had held from the very start of the dispute:

> *'The dispute is not official; this places a mountain of constraints. Recognising the gravity of the situation, the executive officers have given a greater latitude than any other dispute in the history of the union. We may in time be happy to have turned a blind eye, a whole face, to certain things in this dispute. To maintain it and allow a thousand, a million flowers to bloom. But some time we have to settle this problem... We don't need Cockcroft; we are the union and the members will decide... The [F&GP] can still send*

*signals to the employers that you are not standing alone. I met Cockcroft and Jimmy Knapp, and Cockcroft mentioned the concerns of direct approaches to dockers globally; the calling of a steering committee, this has never happened before. We have to work through structures; I am getting concerned about this… There will be no veto on talks.'* [30]

Adams spoke again of the 'irritant' that was the dockers' international action, while espousing his view that 'pure attrition' would not win the day; there would have to be a negotiated settlement. [31] John Connolly, the docks National Officer, mentioned the ITF's confusion over rank-and-file interference with international union business, [32] to which Nolan replied with what, according to some of those present, was a brilliant exposition on the philosophy of the dockers' struggle, [33] giving a history of dockers' struggles past and present. The meeting ended soon after, and for Bill Morris, Nolan's appeal to trade union heritage and socialist principles might well have been a glimpse into an unknown realm that was completely alien to him and David Cockcroft of the ITF. Cockcroft had written to Morris on the problems the Liverpool dockers were causing with their international campaign: 'Concrete examples of difficulties which has been reported to us by ITF dockworkers' unions during the course of the Liverpool dispute, which has sometimes made it difficult for them to maximise support for the Liverpool dockers.' [34] According to Cockcroft, the substance of these difficulties stemmed from left-wing political parties involving themselves directly with the dockers' unions in Sweden, Belgium, Germany and the Netherlands. [35]

The following day, Friday 30 August, delegates from all over the world began arriving in Liverpool for the second International Port Workers' Conference, to be welcomed by the dockers and the WOW as they entered Transport House for meetings and debates that went on late into the evening. Ken Loach had started filming. [36] The atmosphere at the mass meeting held that day was lifted by the presence of the international delegates, as well as the fact that further talks appeared to be on the horizon in the wake of MDHC's profits falling by 17%, representing a £3-4.5m loss on their investment in Dutch Ferries for an accumulated loss of £13m, including £1m spent on severance payments on the docks and a £10m drop in share value. [37] At the mass meeting Björn Borg of the Swedish Dockworkers' Union spoke of how pleased he was to be back in Liverpool, and to see: 'what good spirits you are in after 11 months of struggle; that is very heart-warming. I can tell you what we have done in Sweden; we have a blockade of all goods coming to Liverpool, and in Gothenburg they have been running a 12-hour delay on all ACL vessels.' [38] At the same meeting, Terry Barrett spoke for many of the rank-and-file dockers when he told the international comrades that:

*'I hope I don't offend anybody, because I don't mean to. The speeches have been fantastic, but Jim Donovan [the Australian dockers' leader] made the one true statement: if the law is bad, you fight it. We have done nothing wrong in our dispute. We refused to cross a picket line and I am proud of that. It's nothing great, it is nothing exceptional; it's just an honesty that we refused to do in a fellow worker. So, what I would like of the delegates — and please don't be upset about what I am going to say — we want action, we*

*don't want promises. Delegates, go away and do the business, and make it so that nobody will ever pick on us again.'* [39]

To this, Michel Murray, leader of the Montreal dockers, replied:

*'For sure, we are not here for tourism. We didn't take the plane for seven hours, or like Jimmy [Donovan], the plane for 20 hours, to take tourism in Liverpool. We are here to first rebuild the solidarity and to continue the fight for the Liverpool victory; not for us, for you. And after that, if you win, every place in the world is going to win, that's the fact.'* [40]

# 41

# The Second International Conference of Port Workers and the ITF

*'Dockworkers at the Port of Liverpool stopped work today at 4.00pm in solidarity with the Black Lives Matter movement. Huge props to John Lynch and other Unite activists who have been working tirelessly for years to rebuild the Liverpool dockers into the fighting force that they always were before their union was crushed in the 1990s.' ~ K. Fox-Hodess\**

On Saturday 31 August 1996, 100 sacked Liverpool dockers began legal proceedings in pursuit of a claim for unfair dismissal at an industrial tribunal. [1] On the same day, the second International Conference of Port Workers opened at the Merseyside Trade Union, Community and Unemployed Resource Centre on Hardman Street, Liverpool, with introductory speeches made by Jimmy Nolan and Jimmy Davies. The main hall was filled with delegates, dockers, the Women of the Waterfront and other family members and supporters, creating public forums for addressing issues relating to many of the most influential ports in the world. The International Transport Workers' Federation (ITF) had made efforts to prevent some delegates from attending. Terry Teague opened proceedings with one of his typically meticulous reports on how international solidarity had evolved over the course of the 11-month dispute, while Bobby Morton provided an update on the Mersey Docks and Harbour Company's financial plight and Mike Carden detailed how right-wing organisations had abolished the National Dock Labour Board Scheme in 1989:

> '...it was about eradicating – doing away with – the culture of dockworkers; the culture
> that we all share in this room. They wanted to abolish this culture and introduce a new

---

\* K. Fox-Hodess, 'Life Cycle of Containerships', 9.6.2020

317

*culture to dock work that accepted the authority of the employers; a culture that accepted*
*you do this and you do this for this amount of pay, you do it for this amount of hours…*
*and when you have finished that, you will do something else, and when we don't need you*
*on Monday, you go home and get no pay…' [2]*

With Michel Murray on hand to translate, Patrick Minot of Le Havre dockers considered: 'the main thing of this kind of action is to tell our enemy, because we all have the same enemy, to do something to tell to them, to this fucking bastard, that we are never going to stand for this again,' [3] drawing laughter across the hall that prompted Murray to jokingly insist that it was a 'real translation.' [4] Gerrard Luggi, a Toulon-based political activist and dockers' supporter, arrived carrying bottles of French wine bearing the label, 'Support the Liverpool dockers!' [5] Doreen McNally, of the WOW, spoke of the history of the Liverpool dockers and their families, and local MPs George Howarth and Eddie Loyden voiced their support for the campaign. On day two, the issue of the ITF's call to boycott the conference was debated, as the Danish dockers shared this concern about joining a breakaway rank-and-file organisation. For the Liverpool and London dockers, there was no real contradiction here, and Norman Parks, one of the international delegates, suggested the use of the word 'alliance,' [6] as delegates agreed to call an International Day of Action for 30 September 1996, details of which would be presented to the ITF. [7] This was essentially the formation of an independent, international rank-and-file dockworkers' organisation – an ITF in exile – and it would eventually take the name of the International Dockworkers' Council. Richard Flint, for the ITF, issued a press statement in response to the second International Conference of Port Workers, in which he denied allegations that they were undermining support for the Liverpool dockers:

> *The ITF did not attempt to sabotage the international conference. I have ITF General Secretary David Cockcroft's complete assurance that not a single fax was sent to anyone discouraging or commenting in any way upon this meeting. The same goes for Dockers' Secretary, Kees Marges. ITF affiliates are autonomous organisations who are perfectly free to establish any bilateral contacts they wish… the ITF has not, nor will ever attempt to detract affiliates from supporting this dispute.' [8]*

On Monday 2 September, it was back to picket duty as normal, albeit with a later start time of 10am to allow any delegates still in the city to join the lines. At midday, the Dispute Committee met with their international comrades to discuss support and tactics in greater and more practical detail, and later that evening, Michel Murray, Patrick Minot, Phillipe Gaudillo and a group of Italian dockers ate at a small French restaurant on Lark Lane, Liverpool, with several of the stewards. It was at such informal meetings that the finer details of business were often settled, as comrades were able to speak frankly in exchanging critical views and ideas on what needed to be done. The ITF agreed that Jimmy Nolan would address their London meeting on Thursday 5 September, but despite his appeals for solidarity, the European Regional Committee voted to unite behind an ITF resolution supporting Bill Morris and the TGWU. [9] Fears grew that Morris was gathering momentum ahead of forcing an end to the dispute with a meeting of the General Executive Council just a fortnight away. Nolan left the meeting to speak with Kees Marges about the ITF's support for the TGWU's leadership as its communications secretary Richard Flint confirmed support for the Liverpool dockers in a press release that contradicted the organisation's well-established position:

> *The ITF and its member union had the greatest sympathy for the aims of the Liverpool strikers, namely reinstatement of dismissed workers and no casualisation of permanent employment.' [10]*

According to Greg Dropkin, the ITF issued a circular that was much less supportive of the Liverpool dockers and clearly fearful of a 'parallel organisation' being formed. [11] On the eve of the inaugural conference, Marges also confirmed that he wrote to an ITF inspector explaining that the TGWU had not requested the ITF to initiate or organise supportive actions by affiliated dockworker or seafarer unions; an instruction that was again confirmed 'very strongly' in a discussion between David Cockcroft and a representative of the TGWU. The ITF also acknowledged that participation in Liverpool meetings by any ITF inspectors, such as Jack Heyman, would represent 'a violation of this agreement.' [12] The labour historian Peter Waterman added to the debate on the ITF's role in the Liverpool docks dispute, after reading with interest Flint's response to Chris Bailey and the *Union-D List*, dated Monday 9 September 1996. Waterman was particularly well placed to comment on the matter, having studied international rank-and-file dockworkers' organisation and actions over a number of decades, including the depth and sophistication of their unofficial trade unionism. It was during the process of redrafting a manuscript containing a chapter on the informal European dockworker network of the 1980s and its role in the 1989 docks strike that Waterman wrote:

> *The unofficial internationalism of the shop stewards was made by the National Port Shop Stewards' Committee of the T&GWU in the UK. Much of the activity came from Liverpool, where unions in general, the T&GWU, and the dockers in particular, have been involved over the years in a range of solidarity activity.' [13]*

Waterman recounted that: 'Mike Carden, one of the Liverpool shop stewards, has been to the Philippines for a conference on free trade zones in 1984 and to an international trade union school in Spain. Liverpool has had a free port for some years. He was also responsible for getting local leaflets translated into foreign languages for European distribution.' [14] He also describes Jimmy Nolan as a long-time leader of the Liverpool dockers, and equally long-time chairman of the National Port Shop Stewards' Committee, as well as an old friend of the *coordinadora* of Spanish dockworkers, unaffiliated to any national or international organisation. The 1989 official strike over the abolition of the National Dock Labour Board Scheme had been organised by the Liverpool dockers directly, without contact with the 'old network,' as three London dockers went to Zeebrugge and the northern French ports, while three Liverpool men headed to Antwerp, Rotterdam and Bremen. In Bremen, they were hosted not by the local dockers, but by BUKO, an anti-imperialist action group that, like the Liverpool dockers, had been involved in action against importation of Namibian uranium. [15]

Waterman considers the ITF's role in events of 1989, which had received official backing from the TGWU, and concludes that little had changed between that strike and the dispute of 1995. At the 1989 ITF meeting in London, Jimmy Nolan made a point of expressing his appreciation to Marges, who reported this to his members and agreed to incorporate a Liverpool leaflet (hastily translated into a somewhat awkward Dutch in Liverpool) into his mailing schedule for Dutch shop stewards. In comparing the events that followed the September 1995 dispute with his study of the 1989 international solidarity campaign, Waterman writes:

> 'The British dock strike of 1989 shows well both the extent and the limits of official trade union internationalism. It implies activity carried out by or through national and international officials... It implies hostility to direct contact between dockworkers internationally, this only being conceivable with approval from above. The policy is one that the ITF officer responsible for dockworker unions is proud of.' [16]

The second International Conference of Port Workers was staged without the support of the TGWU or the ITF, and neither organisation sent a single representative.

# 42

# The Dispute Continues
# (Without the TUC)

*'Liverpool dockers have a long record of struggle. The sort of things they have struggled for are a decent living wage, regular work, the right to belong to a trade union. This has been going on for well over 100 years. The first dock strike that brought this port to a stop was as long ago as 1879. So, this dispute is part of a very long tradition… The extraordinary thing about this dispute is the lack of media coverage, because in the past when there was a strike or any dispute, it hit the headlines; certainly locally and often nationally… Now there is a whole new attitude to disputes… perhaps the most extraordinary thing is that people internationally know about this strike. Port workers throughout the world have supported this strike, while many people in this country don't even know there is a dispute in Liverpool.' ~ Eric Taplin\**

At a mass meeting held on Friday 6 September 1996, a minute's silence was held following the death of Ken Stewart, the local European MEP who had been a great supporter of the Liverpool dockers. Jimmy Nolan welcomed everyone to the meeting and then spoke of the importance of lobbying the Trade Union Congress that coming Monday. A successful city centre picket of Argos, led by Brian Ashton and other supporters, was celebrated by the dockers as this was a high-profile retailer that shipped a great deal of cargo through the Port of Liverpool. The regular mass meeting then went through its usual agenda of report-backs and discussion. Morale amongst the dockers that Friday was upbeat. Following this, another meeting took place between the stewards and representatives of Reclaim the Streets, despite Nolan's concerns about RTS' plans to occupy Seaforth Docks. Nolan was worried about the safety of the young RTS activists. [1]

Writing in the *Guardian*, journalist Stuart Millar documented the dockers' lobby of the TUC, vividly describing the impact of the dispute through the eyes of one docker's family; Sue Mitchell, a leader of the Women of the Waterfront, along with her son, Graeme, and

---

\* Eric Taplin, in an interview with Radio Merseyside (April 1997)

dockworker husband, Colin, who were part of the Liverpool delegation early that Monday morning. In an article titled, *Smart New Unionism Faced with Protests by Betrayed Dockers*, Millar remarked:

> 'They could have been like any other Merseyside family enjoying a late summer day trip up the coast in Blackpool. But instead of buckets and spades, the Mitchells, Colin, Sue and their son, Graeme, brought placards… The Mitchells and other families went [by train] to Blackpool to let the union movement know they were still fighting… It was a symbol of industrial struggle strangely incongruous with the smartly-dressed, mobile-phoned new unionism taking place inside… As the TUC President, Margaret Prosser, opened the conference, they unfurled a banner from the gilded balconies surrounding the conference floor. It earned them the first standing ovation of Congress, but to the dockers, the applause from the platform at least, sounded hollow.' [2]

The president of the TUC was Margaret Prosser, a TGWU National Officer. Despite holding these two powerful positions in the British labour movement she would never use her influence to support the Liverpool dockers. She went on to become deputy general secretary of the union in 1998 and was named Baroness Prosser in 2004. Stuart Millar recorded how the TUC and the TGWU had been, 'unable to offer official, substantial support' - but despite the inaction of the trade unions, Sue Mitchell was still proud that her husband refused to cross a picket line: 'We're not just doing it for their jobs, but for the future of Graeme and the other children, who will need jobs when they grow up.' [3] On the same train, Doreen McNally said: 'they should be supporting us, that is what trade unionism is all about.' [4] Also on the train that day was Kenny Kelly, a recently retired dock shop steward who sadly died in 2014, travelling in support of his comrades and, as always, standing alongside his old shop steward friends John Hulme and Denis Anderson. [5] Sadly, Denis Anderson, died in 2017. In Blackpool, Billy Jenkins spoke of the media black-out of the dispute, and the cry outside the conference hall was, as usual: 'TUC, get off your knees, support the Liverpool dockers!' [6] Nobody expressed surprise at a year-long dispute not being first and foremost on a trade union agenda.

From the balcony of the impressive Blackpool Winter Gardens, the dockers were able to shout, 'we're still here!' which earned them a standing ovation at the start from many of the TUC delegates. [7] Doreen McNally asked Bill Morris if one of the WOW could address congress: 'You do not know how the women feel or experience their struggle.' [8] After being confronted by the women, all Morris could do was to assure them that he would be at the meeting scheduled to discuss the European Union later that evening, and it was there that Irene Campbell told the Labour MP Peter Hain that, 'a lot of European money has been ploughed into MDHC. I understand that EU money is about creating jobs. I would like someone to explain to me how the MDHC can get loads of EU funding and sack 500 men. So, has anyone got any answers for me please?' [9] Hain replied by saying that he regarded the behaviour of MDHC as totally unacceptable, adding that he hoped: 'a Labour government would seek to rein in such employers.' [10] This did not happen. The meeting was then cut short by its chairman, but Doreen McNally managed to have her moment with Hain, as she accused the Labour Party of simply standing by and failing to support the working class, while pointing out that Tony Blair, 'said he would not alter the trade union legislation; he said it in Hong Kong.' [11]

At 5pm, Bill Morris, Jack Adams, Dave McCall and George Henderson of the TGWU met with a large group of Liverpool dockers and Women of the Waterfront. There was a heated exchange of views, with Morris declaring: 'The union's position has not changed.' [12] Doreen McNally replied: 'We are the union, and we have a right to support.' [13] Irene Campbell explained how the women were, 'the economists, running our families – other unions are doing more,' [15] before ordering the General Secretary to, 'sort it out!' [16] Jimmy Nolan was scheduled to address the TGWU's 'Broad Left' delegates on Sunday night, and when the week-long TUC event had finally ended, one of the stewards was heard to exclaim, 'Just had four days at the Trades Union Congress, God help us all.' [17] In a special TUC-themed edition of the *Dockers' Charter*, printed in September 1996, the banner headline was *Help Us Win This Fight*, above an article that began with: 'an appeal to all unions affiliated to the TUC: Do not leave 500 sacked Liverpool dockers in isolation. It is time to stand up, pick up the cudgels and fight back! Help us win this fight.' [18]

Around the same time, the International Communist Party (ICP) issued another leaflet attacking the shop stewards. [19] Dave Graham commented on the ICP's insistence that the existing leadership of the stewards, and especially the arch-Stalinist Jimmy Nolan, should resign in order to allow the dispute to be led, 'properly by the rank-and-file.' [20] The ICP believed that the trade unions had become organs of the capitalist class and they accused the former dock shop stewards of being part of the union's bureaucracy [21]:

> 'They have portrayed themselves as 'rank-and-filers', with the best interests of the dockers at heart, but who are also loyal to the union. In fact, their loyalty is solely to the union bureaucracy of which they themselves are a part. Their proof for this assertion, for that is all it is, is a direct quote from Mike Carden, "Look at this platform," he told a dockers mass meeting in Transport House, "Jimmy Davies is on the National Executive of the TGWU Docks and Waterways Committee. Bobby Morton is responsible for 130,000 TGWU members in the North West. Jimmy Nolan is the Chair of the TGWU National Port Shop Stewards Committee. Terry Teague is an elected shop steward for more than 20 years. I sit on the union's General Council. I'm a big cheese." The ICP claimed that the stewards will do nothing that will endanger their own career in the union.' [22]

Graham acknowledged that he was not present when Mike Carden spoke the above words, but was assured by those who were there that, 'it fits the character of the man that I know, that this speech was intended to be wholly ironic.' In Graham's view, the TGWU leadership, and by that he meant the real bureaucracy of, 'full-time paid officials, not the lay jobs mentioned above, have made it clear that it intends to strip Nolan, Morton, Carden and all the others of any and every position they hold in the union.' [23]

Two years later, further observations came from the other end of the same spectrum, as Ann Douglas, writing in The *Guardian*, gave a review of the Channel 4 play *Dockers*, which she criticised for perpetuating the notion that:

*'...somehow all working-class struggle is doomed to betrayal by trade union leaders, which ultimately serves only to undermine those organisations at a time when they need all the strength and unity that they can get. The fact is that the Mersey dockers were not betrayed by the T&G, they were victims of anti-union laws and anti-trade union bosses. The roots of the dockers' dispute go back to the neo-liberal economic policies pursued by the reactionary governments around the world on behalf of transnational capital, out to secure bigger profits at the expense of wages and conditions. The election of the Tories in 1979, the defeat of the Miners' strike in 1984/85 and the failure of the entire labour movement to oppose effectively the imposition of anti-trade union laws were all staging posts to a dispute that was, nonetheless, heroic. If the 1995-98 Liverpool dockers' dispute holds any lessons, it is that if the working class is to take on the might of the state, it must do so united.' [24]*

On Saturday 14 September, a meeting of the TGWU Broad Left took place at the Merseyside Trade Union Community and Unemployed Resource Centre, with discussions focussing on what the union's rulebook stated in regard to the Finance and General Purposes' power over the General Executive Council. The need for rank-and-file members to be able to challenge the power of the F&GP was raised, and the following day a meeting of the National Broad Left was held at the London Merchant Navy building, with 20 TGWU members in attendance. London docker Colin Coughlin moved that the GEC suspend its standing orders until a day could be set aside to address how the union could support the Liverpool dispute, while Jimmy Nolan explained the importance of holding negotiations without pre-conditions, citing that the dispute was about reinstatement, although this in itself was a pre-condition. Nolan spoke about the supposed legal constraints on the union that did not exist in reality, but this did nothing to convince the National Broad Left to directly alter the position of the TGWU on the dispute through its GEC. [25]

On Monday 16 September, the GEC met in full session, and managed to complete a whole day's business without mentioning its sacked Liverpool membership, who had been in dispute for a year. The following day, John Connolly, who was set to retire as National Docks and Waterways Officer, gave his final report, and Danny Maher, leader of the Liverpool tugboat men and an elected docks and waterways representative, raised the Jack Dempsey inquiry, which Bill Morris dismissed as a matter for the Region 6 committee. Carden provided an update on the dispute and called upon the union to influence the International Transport Workers' Federation to support the dockers, adding that the TGWU's Hardship Fund contribution needed to be regularised, urging Morris to lend his support. [26] Ken Brindle, Carden's fellow Region 6 Territorial Representative, spoke in support of the dockers' position on talks without pre-conditions, and Barry Miller, also of Region 6, told the committee that the inquiry into Dempsey will conclude that he was, as an officer of the TGWU, offered the reinstatement of the original Torside dockers, and that his subsequent inaction could end up costing the union a lot of money. [27]

Jack Adams argued: 'it is sterile to go back before the 28 September 1995. The dockers were sacked for being in breach of contract. My view is that it is a breach of legislation, but we have a contract with our members. We were clearly warned that they would be sacked. We have to be very, very honest with our members. It was an imaginative campaign. It was no pre-conditions on the Dock Company. This restriction on ancillary jobs prevents a settlement.' [28] Morris followed this by quoting from a letter sent by the Dispute Committee to the F&GP: 'Thanks, you're doing nothing; you betrayed us,' before adding: 'I'll defend the F&GP's decision to seek negotiations; it is right now and then. The last offer made by the Dock Company was acceptable. The point is wanting to negotiate without pre-conditions. If I phoned the MDHC, they would agree to a meeting. Without a ballot, the union throws caution to the wind.' [29] The meeting concluded with Connolly reading from a letter in which the ITF supported the TGWU's desire to reach a negotiated settlement, while condemning the brutal sacking of the Liverpool dockers. [30]

At a Dispute Committee meeting on Wednesday 25 September, a message from Bob Baete in Belgium reported that Cast and ACL would experience delays in Zeebrugge and Antwerp the following week, adding that the last three ACL vessels they had worked had been carrying increased cargo loads. It was also hoped that the Liverpool tugboats would take action the following Monday. [31] In the Manchester office of the TGWU, Docks District resolutions on their local official were not included in Regional, F&GP or Trade Group minutes. The official position was that these matters were now sub-judice, and that as both an officer and a member of the union, Jack Dempsey was entitled to protection under the Officers' Representation Scheme. [32] McCall's subsequent, *Private and Confidential Report: Docks Dispute*, would be rejected by the Region 6 F&GP on Wednesday 13 November 1996 and the following day McCall wrote to Bill Morris confirming his conclusion that the docks officer had: 'conducted himself properly throughout these events. I have made it clear that I would only release my report on advice from yourself, as general secretary. Indeed, I have ensured that all copies of my report, presented to the Finance and General Purposes Committee have been returned to me, so that they should not be in general circulation.' [33] The dispute would continue without either the TGWU or the TUC, but while this came as little surprise to the Liverpool dockers, it might have seemed odd to anyone who came across Bill Morris's bold vision for a future Labour government in September 1996:

> *The next Labour government has a duty to rescue the British people from the despair which is now rife in the country. The right of people at work to join an independent union and have it recognised should be established without delay. We demand nothing less from the Labour government. It must remove lock, stock and barrel the anti-union laws which have allowed the sacking of the Liverpool dockers without any regards whatsoever. We are adamant that there must be the reinstatement of our members employed by the Mersey Docks and Harbour Company.' [34]*

# 43

# The First Anniversary
# of the Dispute

*'The strategy that was adopted was correct, but there were certain things that weren't adopted that should have gone along with it. Maybe our attitude to the T&G was wrong. I think we should have faced up to the fact that Morris and the Executive were our enemies and we needed to confront them much earlier on in the dispute, which we never did, because of the money that they were putting into the fund or whatever reasons, but I think that was a mistake. Maybe we should have occupied Transport House in London as some of the lads suggested; we should have definitely taken more direct action to confront Morris... It was winnable at certain points. Right at the beginning, I think the Torside lads should have been invited to come in and occupy the gantries, and we should have stayed inside the port. I mean, it was no secret, we'd known for a long time that the Dock Company were out to get us, and a lot of the lads had said there was no way we could fight a dispute outside the gate; that we had to fight it from inside. But once the picket was set up, it just had a momentum, a life of its own... We should have tried an occupation then as well.' ~ Frank Carberry**

At the mass meeting on Friday 27 September, Jimmy Nolan told dockers: 'that two representatives of the MDHC were actually in breach of employment... Since then, what we have said on many occasions is that we want a barrister to come forward to pursue the legal side of our problem.' [1] In answer to another question on support from other workers in the UK, Nolan stated:

*'I would not be in opposition to whatever the dockers decided, but tomorrow at the demonstration, it will be proved beyond any doubt that we have consistently advocated international support, and at the rally tomorrow there will be thousands upon thousands of people that will participate in it, and you will find that the British working class itself is beginning to consolidate behind us. But unfortunately... we are still isolated, and the*

---

* Frank Carberry, speaking in an interview with Greg Dropkin (LabourNet, 17 February 1998)

*reason we're isolated is because, in our opinion, the trade union leaders are no longer in opposition to anti-trade union laws or privatisation… as human beings, they should make it very clear that they're going to address the brothers and sisters who they represent in the various factories, and what they should be saying is that they want to see some sort of action because if everyone stayed off work in our country, not just in support of ourselves, but in opposition to political legislation… We would hope that the brothers and sisters and the various organisations at the rally accept the call that we are going to make, and we would hope that they go back and actually advocate that there should be a stoppage of all working-class people in opposition to political legislation in support of our reinstatement.' [2]*

It was announced that the musician Billy Bragg would perform a sell-out gig to help the sacked Liverpool dockers, and he, like so many other artists supporting the campaign, donated time, money and art in ways that would never be forgotten by the dockers and their families. [3] Saturday 28 September 1996 marked the first anniversary of the dispute, which triggered a 24-hour tugboat strike in Liverpool from midnight on Sunday 29. Global industrial action was expected to follow the tugboat stoppage, and early reports indicated a 24-hour blockade on all Atlantic Container Line vessels and containers in Sweden, with the *Reuters European Business Report* detailing how, 'Thousands of demonstrators brought the northern English city of Liverpool to a standstill on Saturday in support of 329 dockers who were sacked exactly a year ago after refusing to cross a picket line.' [4] Police reports estimated that around 10,000 people marched in support of the sacked dockers [5], and according to Reuters:

*'The company said the dispute had cost it nearly five million pounds… The dispute does not have official backing from the Transport and General Workers' Union. The dockers were joined on their rally by groups campaigning, amongst other things, for animal rights and against new roads.' [6]*

In an article printed in the *Morning Star*, it was reported that the Liverpool dockers also extended an invitation to John Major, asking the prime minister to address the anniversary rally, and to perhaps expand on the Conservatives' recent advertising campaign aimed at attracting trade unionists to the party. [7] John Davie and Bronwen Handyside of the *Workers' Press*, described how this demonstration displayed the breadth of solidarity existing across the political, trade union and social movement:

*'The many union and labour movement organisations represented by their banners included the Hillingdon strikers, Camden UNISON, the Irish Seaman's Union, the electricians' union, EPIU, the rail-workers' unions, RMT and ASLEF; the printworkers' union, GPMU, Haringey and Leeds Trades Councils, British Aerospace and Rolls Royce Shop Stewards' Committee, and over 200 Turkish workers from the north-east London Textile branch of the TGWU and the Day-Mer Workers' Centre. In pride of place was the Women of the Waterfront banner and they had a lorry decorated as a ship, named 'Dignity,' the seafarers being the dockers' singing children*

*with multi-coloured balloons. Then came the Merseyside dockers' own banner and behind that the banner of the London Royal Group of docks with the words made famous in the 1972 jailing of striking dockers in Pentonville, 'Arise Ye Workers.' In that delegation were dockers sacked in 1989 for the 'crime' of defending the National Dock Labour Scheme, and among them, Denise Fenn, wife of Mickie, ex-secretary of the Unofficial Port Shop Stewards' Committee, who died suddenly on 28 July that year at the age of 58. Never before has an industrial dispute inspired support from so many individuals and groups, not traditionally associated with the organised working class.' [8]*

The article reminded those prepared to listen and take note that times were changing, and that the Liverpool dockers were at the forefront of a radical new approach to trade unionism. According to Davie and Handyside, the dispute had brought together trade unionists and socialist groups, including the *McLibel Campaign*, ecological groups such as Eco-Trip and Earth First, Reclaim the Streets, Workers Aid for Bosnia, the Animal Liberation Front and young people associated with the Job Seekers' Allowance Campaign. The writers described how colourful union banners were rivalled by gaudy and imaginative creations proclaiming that the future was going to be won for humanity, although the standard 'Scabs out! Dockers in!' chants kept the happy, carnivalesque atmosphere tethered to goals of realistic, achievable aims. The beat of the drums and dancing of the Turkish and Kurdish youth created a flamboyant, noisy backdrop, dictating the mood as they were joined by RTS drummers at the head of the march as it swept down Castle Street and James Street. The banners of the Haringey Trades Council and Rolls Royce Shop Stewards bounced up and down to the staccato rhythm, but for Alexis Richter, an Anthropology student at the University of East London and member of the Radical Anthropology Group, the most impressive attendee was a 35-ft scarlet, fire-breathing dragon, which came into its own when the march ran into a sinister line of police in full riot gear that were snapping pictures of the demonstrators as they protected the hamburgers and chips inside the McDonald's restaurant that they were posted in front of.' [9]

In *Another World is Possible*, Pauline Bradley and Chris Knight wrote of the extraordinary atmosphere of solidarity and community that permeated through all of the dockers' demonstrations, and here they describe:

*'...older members of the march shouting rude words at the coppers, the dragon sashayed up and smothered them in a huge snort of smoke. The bewildered officers did not know whether or how they should kill it, and all those who saw the incident laughed their socks off. The dragon was St George, and slew the police, the real monster. The idea behind the dragon is creating solidarity through dance, and through partying. The dragon itself is a symbol of power, and of female solidarity. If everybody joins the dragon, they become the dragon, but only if we all get together... It seems like the dockers are the last bastion of trade union solidarity. No wonder the government hates them... My idea of the trade unions was of the big union barons, but now I see all kinds of people coming together, uniting against the multi-national corporations. Alexis Richter was in fact the creator of the fabulous smoking dragon that had now become a regular guest at all Liverpool dockers' demonstrations. He was also the lead person inside it during the incident outside*

*McDonald's, when the Operational Support Division were made to look ridiculous as they recoiled from the dragon's breath actually produced by a fire extinguisher. On the march, before Pauline Bradley reached the incident, a Turkish comrade said to her: "The police have been on their radio saying there's a dragon here; there could be some trouble!"'* [10]

Another observer who understood the significance of these rallies was Dave Cotterill, who wrote in the 28 September 1996 edition of *Workers' Press*:

*'So, the dockers entered their second year of dispute fighting the company, the shipowners, the local press and, behind the scenes, the government. Their efforts in twelve months had produced nineteen union community marches and rallies, two national support group conferences. They had addressed nearly 6,000 meetings throughout Britain, all of which was carried out in the teeth of a virtual media boycott and with Blair... instructing members of the PLP not to support the dockers. More sinisterly this anniversary march was also accompanied by overhead helicopters from the Merseyside Police and massive detachments of police and the infamous OSD, the Darth Vaders of policing.* [11]

The direct involvement of environmentalists would elevate the dockers' dispute beyond the limits of trade unionism. These young men and women did not fear the police or the courts, and they were present as the march culminated in a rally on the steps of St George's Hall, where Jimmy Nolan insisted that any future Labour government must abolish all anti-trade union laws: 'We are the producers of the wealth; that wealth should be distributed among the nation's people. We must oppose the capitalist system and pursue the goals of our mothers and fathers. That is socialism.' [12] Arthur Scargill, leader of the National Union of Mineworkers, welcomed the new dockers' allies before informing the rally that Bill Morris should initiate industrial action by the TGWU membership each and every Wednesday until the dispute was settled, and that the rest of the trade union movement should follow suit. Andrea Needham, one of four women recently acquitted after disabling a British Aerospace Hawk trainer aircraft due for sale to the Indonesian government, was cheered as she declared that the Maritime Union of Australia was now boycotting trade with Indonesia in protest at the imprisonment of two trade unionists there. Jimmy Davies supported Scargill's call and backed it up by, 'demanding the physical support of the entire trade union movement.' [13] From across the Atlantic, Scott MacNeil, formerly of the *Detroit News*, illustrated how globalisation affected workers rights everywhere by empowering employers to recruit scab workforces without any serious opposition from the unions or intervention by the Clinton administration. Back in Detroit, paramilitary police were guarding property on behalf of big business, a role that had fallen to the Operational Support Group in Liverpool, who were ready to demonstrate just how brutally effective they could be.

The rally ended in an exuberant party mood. [14] The website *One Eye on the Road* also reported on this day in September 1996, where 200 environmental activists and anarchists took up the invitation to help mark the first anniversary of the sacking of 500 dockers for refusing to cross a picket line. Saturday's march was followed by a free party that livened up a rainy night in the old Customs House, which became a squatters' graffiti-coloured residence for the weekend. Sunday was a day for planning and workshops for a mass action at Seaforth Container Terminal on Monday 30 September. Greg Dropkin reported on this for *LabourNet*:

> *'The day that Labour Party delegates were allowed into their own conference only after being vetted by Lancashire Police [by agreement with Blair], the Merseyside cops set out in full riot gear to intimidate all those who turned up in support of the dockers. Four dock shop stewards were among the 42 arrested. The police had their complete modern arsenal on display: CS gas, dogs, horses, Darth Vader riot squads. Dockers and their wives, well used to being pushed around by the police over the last year, were taken aback by the violence of the riot squad who were deployed several times when pickets tried to block the road. Armoured robocops punched, kicked and kneed the pickets with real hatred in their eyes. Maybe the police violence arose from their discovery of a large group of Reclaim the Streets activists on the roof of the administration building and on two gantries. The sight of the flag and the Women of the Waterfront banner 'Sack the bosses, not the workers!' fluttering from the roof of the Mersey Docks and Harbour Company building inspired singing and chanting from the dockers and their supporters throughout the morning but acts of conscious thuggery from the assembled police as the pickets attempted to make their way home.' [15]*

Monday's picket began with 15 activists carrying a 'Sack the Bosses, Not the Workers' banner, as they danced on the roof of MDHC's offices, which was also known by the dockers as 'the Rat House'. Anarchist flags flew above the docks. Striking tugboat men closed the port, and pounding drums encouraged pickets to swarm across the street and make incursions into the docks, where crane gantries were occupied and used to hoist a delighted docker up onto the Rat House roof, before a nine-hour stand-off eventually saw everyone come down without arrests being made. This led to Merseyside Police imploring MDHC to finally resolve the dispute as they could not afford to go on policing it at the level it demanded. Several coachloads of trade unionists had been stopped and turned around before reaching Liverpool. The Operational Support Group, in full body-armour, arrested 24 demonstrators including two shop stewards. That night, a party was held at the dockers' main pickets' pub, the Elm House, as a newly-forged solidarity between workers and the direct-action movement was born. [16] Kevin Robinson defended the dockers' unity with environmentalists when he told the *Liverpool Daily Post*: 'the rooftop protest was to raise the profile of the dispute. I was in radio contact, acting as a go-between between those on the roof and the authorities. We're pleased with the excellent help we've had today, [but] not with the overkill by the police.' [17] The police referred to the young environmentalists they had brutalised that day as 'scum' and 'yobs,' [18] Greg Dropkin, celebrated the dockers' radical links forged with various community groups and environmentalists, and he spoke for all dockers and the Women of the Waterfront when he reported on Monday's events:

> *'Peaceful occupations began at dawn when dockers and supporters passed through the fence by the Kellogg's Grain Terminal, where shop steward Jimmy Davies was immediately arrested… the black clad OSD, who operated without identification*

*numbers, began arresting protestors for unknown offences as comrades were handcuffed and thrown into vans that swerved dangerously alongside demonstrators provoking road blockades throughout the day. Motorways leading into Liverpool were blocked by police as seven coachloads of supporters were prevented from reaching the port. Tony Nelson, Mike Carden and Terry Teague were snatched by the OSD and taken to Cheapside Police Station in the City Centre.' [19]*

Monday's clashes coincided with the opening of the Labour Party Conference in Blackpool, and as a result news from the dockers' picket lines were widely reported on national and local TV and radio. [20] At the TUC, the chasm between trade union bureaucrats rank-and-file trade union activists, the community, young people, environmentalists and political campaigners was visible. Those who associated themselves with Morris's leadership of the UK's largest union all shared his vision. It was a vision of the role of a trade union movement separated from society, from radical youth, ecology movements and abandoned working-class communities. Bill Morris was dismayed by the images of solidarity and anarchism; he told *The Financial Times*:

> *'We deplore the violence and unlawful action that has taken place. The dockers must disassociate themselves from those who have become involved in the dispute. The union is very concerned that people who are not dockers and were not employed by the Mersey Docks and Harbour Company are embroiled. The union believed the dockers had a 'just case,' but it 'could only be resolved through negotiations.' [21]*

# 44

# The TGWU Condemns Solidarity as the ITF and ILWU Clash

*Mr Jimmy Symes, the union's docks district secretary in Liverpool, said: "Nothing has changed at all. With the lads going back to work tomorrow, we have a firm base on which to go to the employers." ~ The Herald\**

On Wednesday 2 October 1996, Bill Morris declared his view on the solidarity shown by others to the Liverpool dockers. After one year in struggle, Morris issued a statement condemning the violence of the Liverpool campaign, while in another world, John Pilger captured the significance of the same moment of solidarity involving what the press had labelled 'eco-warriors'. In a *Guardian* article published a month after the demonstration, Pilger quoted Jimmy Davies, who described how the dockers saw their: 'banners fluttering over the occupied docks, we didn't see the TGWU, whose officers should have been there. Now we know who our friends are, and we welcome the young people's support and idealism.' [1] Morris, who was in Blackpool for New Labour's party conference, espoused another view of trade union solidarity that deplored: 'the violence and unlawful action that had taken place.' [2] In reality, the violence belonged exclusively to Merseyside Police and the Operational Support Division, who seemed to focus their attacks on people half their size and either twice or half their age. It was moving to see dockers shielding their young supporters and leading them to safehouses or guarding them from the police until their buses and trains had left. Earlier, at the start of this September rally, 11-year-old Neil Fox made a speech that expressed more iron and soul, more understanding of his father's struggle, than the General Secretary of Britain's largest trade union. Young Neil thanked all those who supported his father and the other dockworkers, 'I always thought my dad was brave [because] he drove a gantry crane. He was so high up in the air, working that massive machine. He sometimes

---

\* 'Liverpool Vote Ends the Dock Strike', The Herald, 8 August 1989 worked 15 hours a day. Our families will not give in; we have been through too much. Thank you for coming to Liverpool.' [3]

Bob Baete, National Secretary of BTB, the Belgian dockers' union, wrote to Bill Morris on 4 October, following a meeting with delegates from Liverpool, Aarhus, Stockholm and Quebec on 23 September. Baete informed his UK counterpart: 'I promised the delegation [that I would] organise some actions in Belgium against Atlantic Container Line and Cast Companies. The trouble is that I [have exceeded] the decision of the ITF's European Regional Dockers' Meeting of the 5 September 1996 [to] only undertake actions on request of the TGWU… to support as much as possible our affiliate, the TGWU.' [4] On the 9 October, Morris replied to Baete, declining to take the opportunity to seek or support solidarity action from the BTB for the Liverpool dockers:

*'We have… limited our activities to relieving hardship for their families… We have sought further meetings with the MDHC and will advise the ITF of any progress in this regard.' [5]*

A verbatim copy of the letter was sent in reply to correspondence from Brian McWilliams, president of the International Longshore and Warehouse Union. [6] McWilliams ignored the requests to do nothing in support of the Liverpool campaign, declaring in a letter to MDHC that as far as his union was concerned: 'We fully support the dockworkers and will take appropriate action to help settle this dispute.' [7] Dock shop stewards led by Jimmy Nolan were present at the Labour Party Conference, where Frank Lannigan was an official delegate, and it was here that Bill Morris told him and Nolan to: 'drop the anarchists, or the union will drop you.' [8] At a Dispute Committee meeting the following day, Nelson relayed Morris's warning over their links with Reclaim the Streets and all other Dockers Support Groups, as well as his disgust at seeing an 'anarchist flag' flying above the Mersey Docks and Harbour Company's offices. [9] The General Secretary had openly threatened that the union would abandon the dockers if they did not cut ties with non-TGWU groups and individuals, and he had also ordered local MPs to, 'Stay out of the docks dispute.' [10] For their part, the stewards thought that the sight of the black flag of anarchy flying over MDHC's offices was magnificent. Encouragingly, dockers' leaders across multiple continents were ignoring the 'worldview' of the TGWU, its leadership and its lay-member General Executive Council.

In Aarhus, Ollie Muller organised support at four Danish ports, while in Sydney, Australian National Line vessels were hit with go-slows and other actions, and ZIM Australia was held up for 24 hours. Bernard Cliff, MDHC's port operations manager, had recently travelled to Israel to discuss the situation with his fellow port owners, and in Montreal, rail workers had conducted a four-day work-to-rule on the freightliner system, disrupting 80% of all container traffic passing through the port. The Montreal dockworkers had met the president of the Canadian Labour Congress, who agreed to circulate a letter of support for the Liverpool dispute among all affiliates, and in France, the magnificent Le Havre dockers held up a OOCL vessel for 16 hours, targeting their slot-sharing scheme with Cast and Can-Mar, which shipped containers through Liverpool. On 1 October, the ÖTV congress agreed to monthly financial donations, publicity and industrial pressure in German ports against MDHC and all shipping lines using the Port of Liverpool. On 3 October, a special Spanish delegates' meeting arranged for all ports represented by *La Coordinadora*, UGT, and CCOO to hold a one-hour solidarity strike on 28 October. Meanwhile, in the ports of Gothenburg, Helsingborg and Stockholm, a 24-hour blockade was successfully imposed on all ACL containers transported by road, rail or sea. In Cyprus, a Liverpool delegation was invited to Nicosia by the Pancyprian Transport, Port Seamen and General Workers Trade Union. Responding to the solidarity shown by the Liverpool dockers' international comrades, Jimmy Nolan concluded that these actions were: 'having a big effect on the financial base of the Mersey Docks and Harbour Company, as the share value continues to fall to an all-time low. On behalf of the Liverpool dock workers and their families, may we once again thank you all.' [11]

Lord David Alton, a local Liberal politician, voiced his support for the sacked dockers on Radio Merseyside, as he called for an intermediary, such as Lord Nolan or Jack Jones, to intercede in the dispute. [12] The following Monday, as share prices rose across the FT Index, MDHC's dropped another 7p. [13] Despite Morris's open opposition, the stewards remained proud of its developing allegiance with not only Reclaim the Streets, but also the numerous environmental groups and political activists who now rallied to their support. Dot Gibson began the process of arranging a meeting in London with RTS to discuss handing over the *Workers' Press* to them, while in Liverpool, Kevin Robinson was organising formal complaints against the police's heavy-handed treatment of young, peaceful demonstrators. Lord Alton and Bob Parry, a local Labour MP, had asked Bernhard Ryding, president of ACL, and Frank Halliwell, President of Cast Europe, to act as intermediaries as part of a combined academic and industrial panel to resolve the dispute. Eric Leatherbarrow, MDHC's communications manager, rejected any such intervention, as he told the *Liverpool Echo*: 'No matter how well-intended, ill-informed and ill-advised intervention can only prolong and hinder the practical efforts being made to resolve the dispute.' [14]

Elsewhere, the International Transport Workers' Federation and the International Longshore and Warehouse Union clashed in a major debate on *LabourNet* involving ITF inspector and ILWU Local 10 longshoreman, Jack Heyman. This online debate became a unique primary source for comprehending the machinations and sophistry that had been employed by the ITF and the TGWU, as they did everything in their power not to be involved in any actions that supported the Liverpool dockers. It is a truly extraordinary insight. Interestingly, Heyman referred to the dispute as a strike, as he produced an open letter to the ITF communications director titled, *ITF betrayal of the Liverpool Dockers' Strike*. [15] In this lengthy analysis of the issues that separated the ITF from the Liverpool dockers, Heyman opened by stating that he had been:

> '...*following with interest the internet correspondence with Chris Bailey, Greg Dropkin, Kevin Brandstatter and Peter Waterman over the question of the relationship of the ITF to the Liverpool dockers' strike. Being simultaneously an ITF Inspector and supporter of the Liverpool dockers, I felt myself conflicted and ultimately resigned my ITF post effective from October 1st 1996... Some of your statements are blatantly untrue. Other errors are distortions and omissions.' [16]*

The ITF believed, 'the dockers couldn't win.' Heyman was then taken off the ITF payroll which he saw as a political decision and nothing to do with finances. [17] He would later state that he had copies of two faxes that proved his recollection of events. [18] This was followed by the ITF resisting requests to offer the Liverpool dockers a forum at their own conference in London, although eventually an evening slot was given to Jimmy Nolan, who according to Heyman: 'gave a cogent presentation on the history of the dockers' struggle. It was one of the most well-attended and well-received of all the week's sessions, though one could hardly tell from General Secretary Cockcroft sitting on the *dais enveloped in feigned ennui*. The standing-room-only audience gave Nolan a thunderous ovation.' [19] Recalling Nolan's speech, Heyman noted that the reaction of Thulani Dlimani, of the South African TGWU, was 'most impassioned,' as he 'remembered well the Liverpool dockers' solidarity actions during the bloody anti-apartheid struggle,' while Norm Pickles, an ITF inspector from Australia, suggested a resolution that passed unanimously, and was acknowledged in a glowing letter the following day, January 19, from Marges to the Liverpool dockers, 'calling upon their unions throughout the world to organize financial and moral support, and where possible to organize industrial action including boycott actions.' This was also accurately quoted in another inspector's statement that: 'The trade union movement in the UK has lost many battles, [but] this needs to be won.' [20]

'The ITF was supporting the Liverpool dockers, or so we inspectors were led to believe,' Heyman later noted that immediately following the London conference on 23 January, a subsequent circular by Marges halted any support for the Liverpool dockers with the instruction that: 'ITF affiliates must await the signal of the ITF before organizing any solidarity action.' [21] In expressing his view on how this affected the Liverpool dispute, Heyman said:

> *The militant leadership of the Liverpool dockers uses class struggle tactics which challenge capitalist property 'rights,' such as the occupying of container cranes, and seeks to build picket lines that stop scabs. For this, they have been ostracised in Rupert Murdoch's Sunday Times and other of the capitalist press as being 'self-avowed' communists hellbent on violence, not different than the news media's red-baiting of Harry Bridges and other leaders of the 1934 West Coast Longshore Strike that launched our union. Against all odds, against an anti-labour government, anti-labour laws, anti-labour news media, a predatory employer, Mersey Docks and Harbour Company, and a class-collaborating union bureaucracy, the Liverpool dockers have succeeded in inspiring real international labour solidarity, like no other struggle in recent maritime history. [22]*

The ILWU longshoreman then went on to consider the irony of the whole affair as the ITF celebrated its centenary year, having been launched in 1896, when British seamen sailing into strikebound ports in the Netherlands joined with striking Dutch dockers without first requesting official union authorisation or checking to verify that it was legal, or filling out forms before taking action; they just did it. That is how the ITF was born, and as far as Heyman was concerned:

'Now, British dockers are slandered as 'strike tourists' by you, Kees Marges, the Dutch ITF dockers secretary, and ITF General Secretary Cockcroft for not getting prior approval before going to Holland to seek dockers strike support, both in 1989, when British dockers unions were being wiped out, and now when the last union port appeals for help. Shame!... Many dockers are the sons and grandsons of dockers. Their roots reach deep into the class struggles of Britain and Ireland. In sharp contrast, only a scant few in the ITF leadership have ever worked in maritime. Tourist?!' [23]

# 45
# Negotiations Begin Again

*'And the three of us, sitting together here now, we never had sons on the picket line, or brothers or uncles, we were just friends… it was their sons on the picket line.' ~ Billy Johnson**

MDHC was under no pressure to concede anything of value during negotiations; they could place any offer they liked in front of the dockers, safe in the knowledge that the union would endorse it. In the three *official ballots* that were held over the course of two and a half years, the union's involvement always pointed towards agreeing to whatever MDHC put on the table, reflecting the message that cascaded down from Bill Morris with the full support of the majority of the General Executive Council. [1] The situation was understood by the dockers who, on Friday 4 October 1996, crowded into what was possibly their 70th mass meeting since September 1995. The atmosphere in the hall was one of expectation after a long wait for negotiations with MDHC to begin again. By Thursday 10 October, confidence was high among the dockers, as the actions of Reclaim the Streets (RTS) had shown MDHC what they were capable of.

The organisation of the dockers had evolved immeasurably over the course of the dispute, considering that in the first few weeks, all faxes, press releases and general communication duties had been taken care of by one or two former shop stewards. Now, an internal division of labour was producing individuals for all roles, with everyone making equal contributions, and although some of these roles were more high-profile than others, it was extremely rare that this ever led to petty jealousies. [2] 'After one year it was extraordinary to examine the role of the shop stewards who had literally spent that year living in each other's pockets. No real animosity existed. No anger, no real distrust. Forced together in a unique unity of purpose, these men had acted with dignity, aware of the responsibilities that rested on their shoulders.' [3] Still, the organising of workers required a balancing of many complex factors, and so it was never a case of everything resting solely upon one individual leader or

---

* Billy Johnson, Liverpool docker, in an interview with Greg Dropkin 17 February 1998

339

group of leaders; the scope for leadership flowed from the picket lines to the Women of the Waterfront, reinforced by weekly mass meetings and support groups. The humour and grounded outlooks of men like Tony Russell, Andy Dwyer, Kevin Bilsborrow and Tony Gardiner, among others, influenced and determined the day-to-day atmosphere in the boardroom at Transport House, while Greg Dropkin and Dave Cotterill worked to provide support and encouragement in developing a critical and intellectual analysis of the dispute. These two experienced and respected activists became a political alternative and sounding board for ideas, while dockers such as Ronnie Bibby and so many others worked tirelessly to service the practical needs of the picket lines, acting as the moral measure, compass and judge for the Dispute Committee.

A large turn-out of pickets gathered for the 11 October demonstrations, with roughly 170 people at the Seaforth picket alone. At the mass meeting that day, Jimmy Nolan was able to report that support for the campaign was growing, not falling, unlike share-prices in MDHC, which were down to 335p. Jimmy Davies then reported on problems facing Peter Clee and the Wallasey Unemployed Centre, who had spent so much time in Liverpool advising the dockers and their families that his own welfare rights work was suffering. The following Thursday, Davies would meet with Peter Clee and Martin Cantor, from the Merseyside Trade Union and Unemployed Resource Centre, to discuss this problem, with the plan being for more Liverpool dockers to receive their benefits and welfare advice in Wallasey. [4] This was followed by the weekly finance update bringing news of donations from John Sheridan's Liverpool Council branch, the National Union of Journalists, NATFE, Vauxhall and Jimmy Kelly and the shop stewards at Waterford Crystal in Ireland. [5] Concluding, Davies expressed his confidence that MDHC was hurting, as he reassured the men that:

> 'Something's going to happen in our favour, and when we get around the table, lads, we will work to get the best possible deal to get you back into work, and get the best possible deal for those lads who want to leave the industry, because we recognise that there are lads who have now reached an age when they can say, "I think I've done my stint..." Keep your spirits, keep your courage. We've done it for twelve months; a little bit longer and we're there. Victory to the Liverpool dockers!' [6]

Terry Teague followed Davies with a detailed report on international solidarity action, Tony Nelson and Terry Southers were campaigning for support in Cyprus and the French dockers had been working on the organisation of the next international conference. Teague reported that they were:

> 'Organising the international conference that will be taking place at the end of the month. That's a big burden on our shop stewards' committee, but to think that another organisation, another major port, who are now going to organise and set up the next major international dockworkers' conference, and the sole issue there is going to be increased international support for the fight of the Liverpool dockworkers...' [7]

Sacked docker Brian Roberts also spoke, giving a report on a rally that some Liverpool dockers had attended the previous Saturday in solidarity with sacked Hillingdon workers; Roberts thanked Tommy Lloyd and Brian Dooley for all of their hard work in organising the delegation. Elsewhere, concerns had again been raised about police brutality on the picket lines, and the Dispute Committee asked that dockers start taking photographs whenever the police approached them on the picket lines: 'We've also got some dockers with video cameras, and that's a sort of protection policy for ourselves,' Kevin Robinson explained. [8] He had been in London the day before for a meeting with Michael Schwartz, a solicitor acting on behalf of the young Reclaim the Streets activists who had been attacked by police during the anniversary demonstrations. According to Robinson:

> 'Michael Mansfield QC called, and we've asked for a public inquiry into the actions of the police, not just after last weekend but over the 12 months... People come up to support us for whatever reason; wherever they come from, we have to protect them.' [9]

From the very start of the dispute, Marty Size, Dave Pendleton, Billy Jenkins and Neil Sharp realised the importance of recording events on the picket line. In 1996, taking a photograph actually required possession of a camera, and to make a video you either had to be a filmmaker or own the fairly basic, but very expensive, video cameras that were available at the time. Of course, this was before smartphones, and photographs had to be professionally developed at a cost, but the men and women on the picket lines still managed to capture some of the most memorable images to come out of the dispute. That weekend, Jimmy Nolan and Mike Carden went to Dublin to celebrate the 60th anniversary of the Spanish Civil War with Irish comrades, they joined Jack Jones and Jack Adams who were the main speakers there. Elsewhere, Terry Southers and Tony Russell had been campaigning in Newcastle where great support had been shown for the Liverpool dockers. On Tuesday 15 October 1996, the dispute entered its 13th month, leaving men who had worked their entire lives, some with as many as 42 years on the docks, to navigate a new world of unemployment and poverty. [10] At a Dispute Committee meeting on Wednesday 16 October, the outcome of the previous day's Regional Committee report on the Jack Dempsey inquiry was top of the agenda, leading to a heated discussion over the regional secretary's refusal to set any terms of reference. One steward felt as though the stewards now had no choice but to decide:

> 'Either to cut the union away from us or work within the constitutional machinery of the union. This is at the core of our dilemma. People want to nail colours to the mast that we had to follow the bureaucrats. If we want to sack an official of the union, we won't sack him by telling him to fuck off; we have to use the rulebook. As bad as the union is, we have to recognise that we are representing 500 families. It is likely that Morris will get a meeting with the MDHC and sell us out with an indemnity clause against any form of legal action. [11]

Some years after the dispute ended, in 2004, the potential for legal action against the TGWU was still an issue, with the *Liverpool Echo* reporting that:

*'300 dockers are bringing a multi-million-pound lawsuit against their union after one of the city's most bitter industrial disputes. In a joint action, the dockers are suing the TGWU, claiming it failed to communicate an offer which could have ended the two-year dispute within days... Now they want compensation for lost earnings, which could cost the union millions.' [12]*

The dockers' lawyer, Anthony Marriott of Lees Lloyd Whitley, was quoted as saying: 'It has taken six months to gather all the information,' adding that if both sides were satisfied that all possible evidence had been disclosed, they would then get a date for the civil action in Liverpool High Court. According to solicitors, the main claim was for breach of the obligation owed to members by the TGWU, as an employee of the union failed to pass on vital information to members involved in a trade dispute. The claim was that on 26 and / or 27 September 1995, an offer was made to the TGWU that would have changed the course of the dispute. Witnesses would be called in time, including local union officials, whilst a TGWU spokesperson said at the time: 'We can confirm that a claim has been lodged against the union. We are defending the action vigorously.' [13] A settlement would be reached later with the union.

In October the 47 Labour Councillors, who had refused to impose a budget for Liverpool set by Margaret Thatcher's Conservative government in the 1980s, had generously agreed to donate £11,000 that was still left in their campaign funds to the dockers' welfare fund. By Friday 18 October 1996, Jimmy Nolan had spoken to Jack Adams about reopening negotiations, as MDHC's Bernard Cliff had again repeated that no jobs were on offer, as they had, according to him, been conceded to other non-union and casual workers in the port. [14] Adams had responded by reminding Cliff that reinstatement was paramount, Cliff replied by saying that he would speak to Trevor Furlong, the company's managing director. On Monday 21 October, Trevor Furlong wrote to International Transport Workers' Federation (ITF) affiliates explaining again that the cause of the dispute was unofficial action led by unofficial leaders, claiming that the conflict had no support among UK docks and related industries. [15] More importantly, he wanted to say that: 'the union wishes to negotiate, the company wishes to negotiate, but the unofficial leaders do not.' [16] On the same day Furlong wrote another letter, citing wholly different causes for the conflict, to Lew Adams, the General Secretary of the Associated Society of Locomotive Engineers and Firemen:

*'The dispute with MDHC was not about casual labour or low pay, MDHC has not, does not and will not employ casual labour. Neither is it true that MDHC locked out its employees.' [17]*

Furlong appealed to Adams to support a proposed directive that would give the TGWU, what he interestingly referred to as 'total authority,' respectfully suggesting that ASLEF and its members put pressure on the dockers to hand their appointed TGWU officials a mandate to negotiate on their behalf, 'and to put the resulting proposals to the test by a secret ballot.' [18] These letters from Furlong coincided with the stewards writing to Bill Morris to express their:

# NEGOTIATIONS BEGIN AGAIN

'...*sadness in relation to serious problems with both the perceived position of the ITF and the TGWU. We have attempted to clarify our position, but this understandably, under the circumstances, does not contain the authority of the union's official statements... we urgently request that you clarify our union's liaison with the ITF and the need to uphold all forms of supportive action by this organisation. Whilst we await negotiations, we cannot allow our campaign to collapse. This would be madness. Clear leadership must be given by the TGWU to the ITF and its affiliates.*' [19]

# 46

# The Paris Conference and
# the creation of the IDC

*'[The ballot was] just another tactic to split us. It's going outside of the boundaries of the T&G rules about doing everything democratically, and I don't think it's a fair thing that the MDHC are saying. I think they are running scared now, and they are just trying to split the ranks, and I just think we will just stay solid… That is why they are standing here. People all over the world are backing us, and to take that money like that is undermining them, and it's also undermining the younger element of Merseyside who are looking for decent jobs, and that's what we ae fighting for. We are not just fighting for ourselves, we are fighting for the next generation. We want decent standards of living and working conditions, and we think this is the only way we can get it.' ~ Marty Size\**

On Saturday 26 October 1996, dockers from 18 ports across 10 different countries met in Montreuil, on the outskirts of Paris, to co-ordinate further international solidarity action in support of the Liverpool dock dispute. This Dockers' Steering Committee, a follow-up to August's International Conference of Port Workers, was hosted by the Le Havre dockers and included representatives from Denmark, Germany, USA, Canada, UK, Spain, the Netherlands and Italy. Jimmy Nolan, Terry Teague, Bobby Morton and Mike Carden were there to represent the Liverpool dockers, as Patrick Minot welcomed delegates to what was now formally named the International Dockworkers' Committee (IDC). Apologies were received from Australia and New Zealand, whose maritime unions remained committed to the Liverpool campaign. A separate Liverpool delegation travelled to Cyprus, where support was expected in the ports of Limassol and Larnaca, at the same time that the International Transport Workers' Federation were repeating allegations that that the Liverpool dockers were attacking both them and the Transport and General Workers' Union. Over the course

---

\* Marty Size, in an interview with BBC Radio Merseyside (audio tape from Dockers' Archive, dated April 1997)

345

of that weekend, 35 ports in Spain were poised to strike for one hour, and the Spanish delegates at the IDC reported that the shipping line Ellerman had demanded to know what Liverpool's problem had to do with Spain, only to be told by the Spanish dockers that, 'It could happen to us.' [1] The delegates recognised that all unions now involved in solidarity action would be affected by the eventual outcome reached with or without the Mersey Docks and Harbour Company, and it was in the interests of these international shop stewards to defeat the Liverpool-based employer and establish the force and unity of this new international dockers' movement.

The Paris conference would organise approaches to other European ports, with a particular focus on Belgium, the Netherlands and Germany, seeking industrial action against shipping lines sailing directly to Liverpool. A fund, to be administered by the Le Havre dockers, would finance the visits to these European ports, with the Montreal dockers pledging $5 per man, per week to Liverpool, in addition to a substantial donation to their Hardship Fund. This unofficial committee also wrote to Bill Morris requesting a meeting to clarify his union's attitude towards international solidarity, and they also hoped to arrange similar talks with Morris's ITF counterpart, David Cockcroft. Doreen McNally and Sue Mitchell of the Women of the Waterfront were already in Paris a few days before the IDC as guests of the French Workers' Party, attending a conference organised by the *Parti des Travailleurs* that focussed on opposition to privatisation and deregulation, as well as ways to defend the public sector. McNally told delegates at the conference: 'It's true that after 13 months, the struggle is very hard, but we don't have any choice, and we do not have the right to refuse to fight. We are the guardians of the future. If we don't resist, there won't be a future in this society for our children.' [2]

On the other side of Paris at the IDC, Terry Teague gave a detailed summary of the unofficial international action that had taken place since the dispute began in September 1995, reporting that on Wednesday 23 October 1996, Jimmy Gleason of the International Longshoremen's Association and John Coombes from the Australian dockers had met in London to discuss solutions to the Liverpool dispute. [3] Patrick Minot wanted to force all employers and their unions to take this evolving rank-and-file movement of dockers seriously, declaring his belief that, 'this is a serious organisation.' [4] The Le Havre dockers also wanted Bob Baete of the Belgian BTB union to join the movement, [5] and Eusebio Penalver spoke of the Spanish CCOO union's wish to ensure that the attacks on Liverpool dockers would not set a precedent for attacking dock labour in other ports. Canada's Michel Murray wanted the IDC delegates to meet with Bill Morris and ask him precisely what his position was, [6] while the French would meet with Baete and then send a letter to the ITF, expressing their views on internationalism. [7] Jack Heyman spoke about his experiences of the ITF, voicing his own critique of its role in the Liverpool dispute. He agreed that a letter needed to be sent to the ITF requesting that they actually undertake the actions already contained in their own resolutions, as part of a plan of action to, 'let MDHC know that we are not going away.' [8] Minot then spoke with some authority on the substantial influence and experience of the French and Montreal dockers, declaring with his usual passion and intellect that the IDC came about organically because, 'we exist as a committee.' [9]

On the second day of conference the ILWU made a substantial donation to the dockers' Hardship Fund, and letters were written for both the ITF and Bill Morris by French secretaries and clerks who organised the practical elements of the conference. A new organisation was emerging, although in truth, as Minot philosophically stated in his welcoming address, 'it already existed'. Criticism of union bureaucracies continued to be raised throughout the day, with many of the delegates having long ago concluded that they were being failed by their official unions. [10] Minot modestly declined the office of secretary of this new organisation, which Sweden's Björn Borg was eventually harangued into accepting, and it was agreed that Theo Baudin, the retired Montreal dockers' leader, Phillipe Gaudillo and Michel Murray would ensure that this radical alternative organisation would truly exist. Terry Teague then spoke of the importance of creating an international sub-committee to bring this IDC idea to life, [11] as the position of the ITF was now being openly condemned by all delegates. Jack Heyman raised the plight of the Black Panther, Mumia Abu-Jamal, on death row in Pennsylvania, explaining how the ILWU, along with other trade unions and leftists like Angela Davis, had defended America's most prominent political prisoner, who had been framed by a racist justice system. Now the delegates were demanding his freedom, as Heyman argued: 'any international dockworkers' organisation worth its salt must also address important social struggles, as well as economic issues.' [12] The IDC was born, and Philippe Gaudillo was to write to Bill Morris, more to announce their existence than anything else. This historic letter, sent from International Dockworkers' Committee, Le Havre, 28 October 1996, to Bill Morris, General Secretary of the TGWU, stated that:

*The only purpose and objective of this international committee is to create a movement of solidarity in the dockers' profession, which is now internationally threatened.' [13]*

Within a day of the IDC forming, 4,000 dockers throughout Spain, including the Basque Country, the Canary Isles and the Balearic Isles had paralysed ports for one hour in solidarity with Liverpool, and as a warning shot to their own employers and government. Called jointly by the *Coordinadora, Union General de Trabajadores* and *Comisiones Obreras*, the stoppage took place the morning after the Paris conference. The Spanish unions demanded the reinstatement of the sacked Liverpool men, and sought a negotiating framework to guarantee that workers in Spain would not experience the same fate as their Liverpool comrades. [14] In Bilbao, the strike received 95% approval, while in Algeciras, 1,000 dockers stopped work, affecting two container vessels, and in Cadiz, seven boats were affected. In Tarragona, where all 210 dockers supported the strike, Eusebio Penalver, national delegate of the *Coordinadora* international section, advocated a boycott of all shipping companies using the Port of Liverpool, to show total opposition to the attitude of MDHC. [15]

On Wednesday 30 October some of the stewards waited in the TGWU's London head office for a meeting with Bill Morris. [16] Following on from the IDC conference in Paris, the dockers' position was clear: Morris had to tell the ITF that they should enact their own policies in support of the Liverpool campaign. Carden's opinion was that the dockers needed to challenge Morris to come out openly in favour of their cause, as after 13 months, MDHC had not taken any legal action against the TGWU. [17] Nolan maintained that their demands were as simple as 500 dockers sacked, 500 dockers reinstated, in what could be considered a display of strong, militant leadership. His politics were forged in the Communist

Party and sometimes his personal views would collide with others'; he could be unpredictable. Above all else, Jimmy Nolan had integrity. He was well read, intelligent and an experienced trade union leader, who as a young trade unionist on the docks had learned so much from men such as respected dockers' leader Denis Kelly. Nolan's political knowledge covered a huge swathe of working-class history and experience, but like most people, he could be contradictory and difficult.

Nolan spoke to the ILA's Tommy Gleason in London the week before. The ILA had convinced Atlantic Container Line to pull out of Liverpool, but had since agreed on its return, and Gleason would be key to forcing them to leave again by petitioning its boss, Conrad De Zago, who really did sympathise with the dispute. When Nolan, Frank Lannigan, Terry Teague and Bobby Morton travelled to New York City to meet with the ILA, Gleason was very well informed about MDHC, the TGWU and the ITF, and he explained that the priority was to get as many Liverpool dockers back to work as possible, before asking Nolan directly how many of the men were likely to reduce the job creation aspect of negotiations by seeking early retirement. Nolan responded by suggesting the attorney did not, 'fully understand the position,' [18] unsurprisingly, a man as powerful as Gleason did not take too kindly to such a remark, especially since he and Bowers were both New York longshoremen, the direct descendants of the same characters who inspired Elia Kazan's film *On the Waterfront*, which carried the tag line, 'The man lived by the jungle law of the docks!' [19] Nolan invoked memories of 1967, as he so often did, and then told Gleason that he did not know exactly how many Liverpool men would retire, estimating that perhaps as many 60 would be interested. This was a very low estimate. [20] At that point, Gleason placed both of his hands on the table and said that he had a phone call to make, [21] a gesture which signified that the meeting had ended. Nolan walked away feeling as though it had been a good meeting; the ILA had enough power and financial muscle to impose itself upon both Bill Morris and the ITF. By this stage in the dispute the stewards were considering if it was now time to dump Bill Morris before he dumped them. [22]

MDHC were expected to reopen negotiations, although not to reconsider some element of reinstatement, but rather to collapse the dispute with the TGWU's support. Recognising the age profile of the dockers who had been dismissed, technically any settlement would have to involve the reinstatement of every sacked docker in order to legally facilitate potential voluntary severance or pension schemes for those who wished to leave the industry. This could only be achieved once the dockers were returned to employment even if it was a 'legal technicality'. Therefore, it was a legitimate and lawful claim for Nolan and the committee to seek full reinstatement, a reasonable estimate had at least 200 dockers wanting to retire with dignity. These conflicting factors needed to be thrown back to Morris, and he needed to be challenged on why he and his General Executive Council could not support the Liverpool campaign. Once this question had been answered, the dockers could move forward, so in this sense, Nolan's stubbornness was no more unreasonable than the position of the TGWU and the MDHC.

As the stewards awaited their meeting with Morris, Nolan did not want to create any pretext for storming out and then proceeding to plot the collapse of the dispute. The atmosphere was tense, although Jimmy Nolan appeared unfazed by the moment, declining to actively promote or encourage discussion among the stewards before Morris's arrival. He remained silent. With no formal time having been arranged, the stewards sat waiting for about 45 minutes until, at 3pm, Morris entered the room flanked by Adams, Graham Stevenson, the new National Secretary for the TGWU's Dock and Waterways section of the TGWU, and Dave McCall, Regional secretary for Region 6. Morris introduced Stevenson and then he began his opening statement by claiming that the GEC held a four-hour debate on the dispute in September, where a call was made for reopening talks without pre-conditions. Morris asked for an honest assessment of where they stood, as a year in dispute was a long time, and MDHC had now restructured its business. In his opinion, some of the Committee's demands were not achievable, and so: 'the sooner they realised this, the better.' With that said, he then moved on to voicing his real concerns about the dockers and their trade union struggle:

> *'In Blackpool, I expressed concern about outside political groupings having an impact upon solving the dispute. We support some of their issues, we accept that on rallies and demonstrations they will turn up. They cannot have an active role in our industrial dispute; you choose between the T&G and these groups. They cannot be allowed to run this dispute; they are not accountable.'* [23]

Adams added that since the GEC last discussed the matter, he had met with MDHC on two separate occasions, in addition to telephone conversations, and that it was clear that the company was: 'hardening its position with no apparent offer on the table. The longer it goes on, the harder it gets.' [24] Nolan repeated his belief that political legislation had prevented the TGWU from properly supporting the campaign, and so for him, internationalism was the only way to victory. He then informed Morris that the dockers had addressed over 6,000 meetings, and that internationalism had reduced MDHC's financial base. [25] Nolan then lapsed into history – 1967, the National Dock Labour Board Scheme and the National Port Employers' Association – before turning back to Morris and saying that, 'the ITF say they will implement their proposals when they get an instruction from the TGWU. There should be an open statement to the ITF, or secretly, whatever. The Mersey Docks will negotiate. Trade unions progress because they break the law. You don't have to speak as the General Secretary, you can speak as Bill Morris. We have suggestions from legal people that trade union laws are not relevant when workers have been dismissed.' [26]

Here we had an *unofficial strike*, according to the TGWU, with all its attendant legal risks, in which the union was insisting on leading negotiations and representing its sacked members on an unofficial strike, yet neither the union nor MDHC had any issue with this breach of industrial law; if they had, they would have done something about it. Kevin Bilsborrow and Billy Jenkins both spoke in defence of the international support, as well as the contribution made by Reclaim the Streets, both of which stood in stark contrast to the lack of visible support from their own union. [27] To this, Morris responded by again telling the stewards that their demands were not achievable:

> *'I'll not kid the Executive. Jimmy, your history is interesting, but it is not real life. International support is an aid, not the main thing. It will not bring the MDHC to its knees. The ITF say you go above people's heads. There are three phrases to this dispute:*

*"Thank you; you've done nothing; you've betrayed us." The GEC can intervene directly in negotiations. Reclaim the Streets have no role in our dispute. You cannot divorce the name of the TGWU away from this dispute.' [28]*

Morris concluded by saying: 'you can't make Niagra Falls go up.' [29] Adams followed by stressing that there were no jobs on the table, and no money in the pension funds, adding that: 'I think you will lose a battle of attrition. You will not collapse the Dock Company through its share price.' [30] Graham Stevenson suggested that they agree to seek a just settlement acceptable to the members. [31]

Back in Liverpool supporters of the dispute had produced a video, *Port in a Storm*, which was a film compilation of four short programmes. *Snow on the Waterfront* featured the Women of the Waterfront picketing through the previous February's snow and ice, showing how and why they were so important to the dispute; *The Tide is High* was shot during a mass picket for the inaugural International Conference of Port Workers in February 1996; *The Dockers' Club* celebrated the unique encounter between international delegates and Liverpool dockers and their families in an evening of songs, speeches, plenty of alcohol and plenty of laughter; and *Reclaim the Future* covered the one-year anniversary demonstration and mass picket in September 1996, where RTS and various environmentalists occupied the roof of MDHC's headquarters, while police waded into dockers on the ground. The video was produced on behalf of the Dispute Committee, with labour donated by Anne-Marie Sweeney (director) and Greg Dropkin of Conscious Cinema. [32]

At the weekly mass meeting held on 1 November, dockers accepted the idea of restarting negotiations. Reports on the meeting with Morris informed the men and their supporters that talks could begin as early as Wednesday, and it was announced that the pension fund had a surplus of £37.7m, which was increasingly at risk the longer the dispute lasted. Mike Williams, leader of the New Zealand Seafarers, was there to speak about how the dispute was affecting port workers and seafarers globally, and Kevin Coyne, secretary of the Merseyside Trade Union Community and Unemployed Resource Centre, reiterated his support while bringing everyone up to date with how unemployed workers were campaigning nationally on their behalf. He also reported on the impact of Job Seekers' Allowance on unemployed families, and Babs Hennessy of the Citizens Advice Bureau asked again for evidence of police violence on the picket lines, as well as violence against her. Richie Venton, representing Militant, had travelled south to talk about the Scottish Support Group, and after a positive meeting the stewards regrouped in the afternoon, with Jimmy Nolan relaxed and clear in his analysis of the present circumstances. [33]

A scab, who had fired two shots at a picket line, was granted a two-year conditional discharge by the appropriately named Judge Ian Trigger on 5 November 1996, although readers glancing at the *Liverpool Daily Post* headline, *Docker Who Fired Gun Walks Free from Court*, could have been forgiven for presuming that one of the sacked Liverpool dockers had somehow managed to evade justice. [34] It was also during November 1996 that WOW's Irene Campbell joined docker Brian Dooley in Gothenburg, Sweden, at the invitation of local dockworkers. At the time, Irene wrote that they had received fantastic support and solidarity from the Swedish workers, which was something that puts some people to shame. [35] Women in Gothenburg were interested in getting together themselves so as to be prepared for the cuts that were already taking place in Sweden, as many of the anti-trade union laws that had been passed in the UK seemed to be on the horizon in Sweden. [36] Recalling the trip, Brian Dooley wrote that:

> *'I had only been in Sweden for a few hours, but I soon found that the same attacks were being carried out on the people of Sweden as are being carried out in Liverpool. The unemployed are being taken off benefits by a similar scheme to the JSA, simply to make the unemployment figures look good.' [37]*

He later confirmed that, as was the case for so many of his fellow dockers, the delegation work that they undertook during the dispute left lasting impressions and lasting friendships.

# 47
# Negotiations Re-open

*'It's just not good enough to turn up at the dockers and talk about your own dispute, when they've been out for two years and the labour movement locally has failed to deliver tangible solidarity action.' ~ Steve Higginson\**

I n November 1996, the dockers' campaign seemed to be flatlining again, with the wait for negotiations to re-open dragging on. On Tuesday 5, the *Liverpool Daily Post* ran an article on Bill Morris ordering the Dispute Committee to 'listen' to him. [1] The TGWU had issued a joint statement alongside the Dock Company. Tommy Gleason of the International Longshoremen's Association and Robert Coombes of the Australian Maritime Union wanted to apply pressure to Atlantic Container Line, but they were still asking how many jobs the Liverpool dockers actually wanted, or rather needed, with 250 being the number they had in mind. If Gleason and Coombes could get confirmation on that figure, they would instruct ACL and ZIM to put pressure on MDHC to concede as many jobs as possible. Although this represented a move away from total reinstatement, Nolan telephoned Gleason and told him that this would be acceptable. [2]

Jack Adams confirmed that negotiations would take place on Thursday 7 November at the union's Manchester office. The General Executive Council was due to meet and discuss the future of Transport House London that coming Friday in Eastbourne which would give Morris the opportunity to seek their endorsement for a deal. [3] The TGWU's Finance and General Purposes committee had first called for talks without pre-conditions on 22 August, it was now early November. On the morning of 7 November, following a pre-meeting with Adams and Dave McCall at Transport House Salford, the delegation left for the Advisory, Conciliation and Arbitration Service (ACAS)'s Manchester offices to meet MDHC's Trevor Furlong, Bernard Cliff, Peter Jones and Allan Price. Cliff opened the meeting by saying that: 'Contact has been made with the union, we last met in June, that was

---

\* Steve Higginson, secretary of the Merseyside Communication Workers' Union (LabourNet, 10 October 1997). Available: http://www.labournet.net/docks2/9710/post.htm

the last offer. No offer is on the table. We are starting from a blank piece of paper. People's minds carry with them the last offer. We need to build up from a blank sheet of paper.' [4] Adams replied that he would still argue for some measure of reinstatement, a severance mechanism, a maximum number of jobs and the restoration of pensions rights. [5] Cliff responded by stating that the port of Liverpool and its company structure had altered fundamentally following the dismissal of the dockers, with MDHC now acting more like a 'landlord.' [6] This was a phrase that the port operations manager would regularly return to throughout these discussions, as he explained that, 'Canada Dock is casual, with labour paid when we use it, but the work continues to decline and if they [other dock companies] employ casuals that is their business.' [7] Furlong, speaking as both managing director and chief operating officer, stated firmly to the lead negotiators, Adams and Nolan: 'Let's get down to business. Berths were appropriated to ship owners, and the MDHC is now solely the landowner.' [8] Cliff interjected here, pointing out that he did not want, 'to be involved in the business of general cargo,' [9] to which Furlong added that, 'the person who controls the Timber berth now is out in Canada winning new contracts. The MDHC will also do this.' [10] Cliff then rebuked Nolan directly because he was:

> 'Trying to reinvent the Dock Labour Scheme… When the offer was turned down in June, we had to make policy decisions.' [11]

During another adjournment, Chris Grise of ACAS was called into the room and Adams explained the dockers' position to him. Grise then left to conduct similar talks with MDHC, returning 25 minutes later to inform the stewards that, 'Cliff has not closed down talks,' [12] but Adams dismissed this as simply: 'a propaganda position for when talks do break down,' [13] and after another 40 minutes, Furlong, Cliff, Jones, Price and the two ACAS Officers, acting strictly as observers, re-entered the room. In the distance, fireworks could be heard exploding in the cold dark winter streets of Manchester as Adams again reiterated that jobs were the key to successful negotiations, while Cliff answered that he was looking for something to consider. [14] Adams demanded to know if any jobs were available, as that was where any 'clean sheet of paper' would need to begin, [15] but Cliff merely repeated much of what he had said earlier adding that: 'Drakes are not our employees,' [16] and it was at this point, after only two minutes back in the room, that the meeting ended with all sides agreeing to meet the following Wednesday.

The next day, the delegation reported back to the rest of their committee and despite the awful weather conditions that morning's picket line was well attended. Jimmy Nolan made an unusually long, philosophical speech that outlined the simplicity of the struggle: 'We cannot concede because there is nothing to concede. We must fight and continually develop our campaign.' [17] According to one steward on the platform that afternoon: 'It was a swansong speech. He was enjoying himself, analysing the contradictions of capitalism in a very grandfatherly way. He spoke of the contribution of all the stewards. It is the principle of reinstatement. You cannot have severance before jobs. We have to have jobs first. It was a great speech.' [18] From the French Workers' Party, Jean Pierre Barrois addressed the mass meeting. Discussions then took place regarding advice received from John Hendy QC, dated 5 November 1996, stating that in his view, 'the dispute was official as from day one; the union had not sought, under law, to repudiate the action.' [19] The stewards wanted to ask Louise Christian, one of John Hendy's colleagues, to clarify precisely the detail of Hendy's counsel and she responded by saying that:

> 'The question is simply whether or not the dispute is regarded by the law as 'official' or 'unofficial.' This is relevant to a number of issues such as payment of unemployment benefit and social security by the State, payment of dispute benefit by the union... Although the union delegation advised the employers that this was not official action, and the employers' representatives accepted this, there appears never to have been anything in writing to this effect.' [20]

In Hendy's view, authorisation or endorsement of the tortious act by a person including a shop steward, is subject to the defence of repudiation by the principal executive committee, president or general secretary. There had been no repudiation in the prescribed form, so it followed that the industrial action, or rather the acts of organising, encouraging or supporting the industrial action, is deemed by statute to have been official. Even if the union wished to do so (presumably unthinkable), repudiation is no longer an option since the period, 'as soon as reasonably practicable after coming to the knowledge of the executive committee, president or general secretary', had long passed. The employer was in breach of contract by insisting on a lower rate of overtime pay, and Torside might have been a shell company controlled by MDHC. The fact that no ballot was conducted before the outset of the industrial action or thereafter means that by Section 226 of the TULR Act (1992), the TGWU was denied immunity for legal proceedings in respect of tortious acts. This immunity would not have been necessary had the act been repudiated, while the absence of a ballot had no other relevance to the 'officialness' of the dispute because the action was official and not repudiated. It was, and continued to be, the acts of the officials (shop stewards) in encouraging and organising the industrial action that made the industrial action official. [21]

On 4 November 1996, MDHC had issued a six-page press release on the Port of Liverpool, titled *Brief on the Current Situation.* [22] This document outlined the company's position on the dispute, and it was laid out in the same chronological detail that the dockers had used to great effect in their own leaflets at the time; the company copied it. MDHC claimed that on 28 September 1995, when Torside dockers, 'established an unofficial picket line at the gates of Liverpool Docks they were demanding that the MDHC should take them onto its books, even though they had no work for them and no link with Torside. Within a day the Dock Company offered new contracts offering 200 of the men their jobs back on 29.09.95.' [23] The document then worked its way towards the involvement of Drake International and, 'the mindless militant claim of all back or none back, including the 80 Torside men.' Perhaps the most significant section came on page six under the headline, *Major Incidents of Unofficial Industrial Action by MDHC Port Workers from April 1994*, which recorded how between April and August 1994, there were numerous unofficial actions and, 'a continuous overtime ban':

> '...which resulted every week in the Container Terminal being unable to service all its customers. On 18 May 1994, a one-day strike took place when the first of three mobile

*quayside cranes was introduced. From 8-12 July 1994, a four-day strike occurred when a port worker, who repeatedly walked off the job before the end of his shift, was sacked following numerous disciplines including a final warning. The four-day strike throughout the port resulted in Mersey Docks reinstating the man. On 18 November 1994, following the death of a port worker in an accident at work, the whole of Seaforth Container Terminal left work late morning 'to attend the funeral' and did not return for the rest of the day. From 27 December 1994-2 January 1995, all the port workers failed to report for work. The Company then spent three months disciplining every single man. On 6 July 1995, port workers at Royal Seaforth Container Terminal went on unofficial strike for five days, claiming they were unhappy with the shift pattern which was introduced in January 1994. Throughout the 12-month period up to the start of the current dispute, more than 600 disciplinary actions were taken against 300 of the Company's port workers.' [24]*

In admitting to such chaos unfolding under their management, MDHC unwittingly raised serious questions about how and why they had allowed matters to get so out of hand. At the heart of these events lay the inaction of the local TGWU. The inquiry into one docks' official was due to be finalised by Wednesday 13 November, and there was talk of the TGWU erecting a 'ring of steel' around him. But he was not to blame. He acted with the authority of many senior local and national officials of the TGWU.

On Tuesday 12 November, the 10am picket line was deemed a success. At 12.30 the stewards received a phone call from Carlton TV, who were planning to record an interview in London featuring John Pilger, the journalist, writer and filmmaker, and Bernard Cliff. However, the day before Cliff had been involved in a serious car accident on his way to Runcorn Station to catch a train to London. According to a spokesperson for Warrington Hospital NHS Trust, the 45-year-old port operations manager, who had been acting as MDHC's chief negotiator, was said to be in a stable condition in intensive care. The ACAS talks that had adjourned on 7 November were due to resume on 13 November but following the accident these were now provisionally postponed until 21 November. [25] Bernard Cliff was the youngest-ever chairman of the Employers' Association of the Port of Liverpool, and the Dispute Committee expressed their sympathy and concern for both him and his family. On Wednesday 13 November, the front page of the *Liverpool Daily Post* was devoted to Cliff's accident and its potential implications for the docks dispute. He was seen as a 'firm but fair' negotiator, but he was now hospitalised, and many of the stewards had known him for over 20 years, having daily meetings with him as the primary and lead negotiator, firstly for the EAPL, and then as a senior director of MDHC. [26]

# 48

# More Negotiations

*'In late 1954, at a mass meeting at Birkenhead, across the River Mersey from Liverpool, a resolution was passed declaring that the men had `no further confidence in the officials and policy or the undemocratic structure of the TGWU.' ~ David Critchley\**

On Tuesday 12 November 1996, the TGWU's Regional Finance and General Purposes Committee voted to reject the report submitted by Dave McCall, the regional secretary, who had concluded his investigation into the actions of *his* Liverpool dock official. McCall had produced a 23-page report and the committee believed that the case against the official had to go to the GEC, whereas McCall argued that it should first go to Bill Morris. [1] Alan English, a former Liverpool dockworker turned full-time TGWU official, had represented Dempsey using a defence that amounted to little more than asking: 'Who do you believe? Him [an officer of the union] or Bradley [the Torside boss], whose submission was full of inaccuracies?' [2] Phil McNulty, another full-time TGWU officer, was also there to represent Jack Dempsey and they all claimed that a report written by the officer, dated 6 October 1995, was not factual: 'The minutes were vague, and Dempsey was saying that he did not mean what he said about the Torside men being reinstated.' [3] McCall had accused Jimmy Nolan of being wrong in claiming that on the night of the dismissals, Bradley had told him that the Torside dockers would be reinstated, [4] with the argument being that this did not qualify as a genuine offer. [5] However, two days after the dispute began, Dempsey told TGWU officers Bobby Lamb and Jack Adams that he: 'could have got the men reinstated,' [6] while McNulty was claiming that:

> *Full-time officials have to walk on eggshells in such situations, knowing the legal and financial implications for the union from possible challenges by employers... It is therefore*

---

* David Critchley, 'Working Practices and Malpractices in the Ports of Liverpool, London and New York 1945-1973' (Phd. Thesis), Liverpool John Moores University, October 2003, p.150

*preposterous to imply that Jack Dempsey, as an experienced full-time officer, would have wilfully withheld a critical piece of information [about Bradley's offer] from his colleagues. We should conclude, rather, that the 'offer' was not genuine, or that Jack Dempsey certainly had not seen it as critical.' [7]*

McCall's report concluded that the official had in fact conducted himself appropriately, while recommending a formal repudiation of Bernard Bradley's statement to the Commons Select Committee. [8] Tony Nelson said at the time that the dockers were locked into the system, and it was likely that the December GEC would delay any conclusion on McCall's report until the March GEC, if not later. [9] Jack Dempsey would be promoted to TGWU Regional Trade Group Secretary by McCall in April 1998, as the possibility of taking legal action against an officer of the union was raised again by some on the Dispute Committee. [10] Jimmy Nolan and Frank Lannigan were against the idea of taking legal action, but others felt they had every right to seek redress as a result of the TGWU's failure to represent them. This matter would continue to be a controversial topic among the Liverpool dockers and the wider national and international labour movement in the months and years ahead. [11] The GEC was due to meet on 2 December 1996, and the stewards wanted the Region 6 committee to instruct Dave McCall to ensure that all documents relating to the inquiry were sent to London in time for them to be added to the agenda, or else the dockers would begin legal action against the TGWU. This reflected the majority view of the stewards although Jimmy Nolan made it clear that he would not be party to taking the union to court; [12] later he would eventually approve of pursuing legal action *against corruption.* [13] Some four years later, on 24 August 2001, a meeting took place at the Silvestrian Social Club in Vauxhall, Liverpool, involving dockers and legal representatives from Lees Lloyd Whiteley solicitors, and in a letter from the law firm to the dockers, dated 10 September 2001, it was suggested that a fighting fund was required in order to protect the positions of all parties participating in court action against the TGWU, at a cost of £20 per person. [14]

On the picket line Tony Nelson reported on three planned days of action and the possibility of another occupation effort on the docks, with Reclaim the Streets. At this time some of the stewards were concerned about tactics on the picket line, as they did not want to see actions that would end with pickets and supporters being beaten and arrested by riot police. Once the occupiers were in place, the stewards wanted negotiators to speak on their behalf, roles for which Joe Benton MP, Eddie Loyden MP and Father Michael de Felice volunteered. The estimates were that 50-60 dockers would occupy areas of the docks, along with their supporters, and on Monday 18 November, the Port Police and Merseyside Police ran a joint exercise to prepare themselves for the next phase of direct action. The views on occupation as opposed to organising a conflict from outside the dock gates had been long established in the minds of many of the dockers before September 1995. In a series of interviews conducted by Greg Dropkin in the immediate aftermath of the dispute, Brian Dooley reflected on this question of occupation that although the Torside men had the right to place a picket line at Seaforth, he thought that:

*'We could have approached it from a different way, and the way I would have thought would have asked the Torside lads to hold back from putting up a picket line, for us to*

*go into work as normal, and when we got there, for the drivers to get into their straddle carriers and carry containers, and block off all the entrances and exits to the docks, especially Seaforth, and occupy the place so that no work could get carried on whether the ships came in or not, and no scabs because they'd have been in there with us.' [15]*

The stewards met with Jack Adams at the Unemployed Centre's Flying Picket bar to discuss Bernard Cliff's absence and the potential impact it may have on negotiations. It seemed like Nolan did not wish to discuss anything or have any action taking place while negotiations were on the table. [16] Adams was there to attend a TGWU Broad Left meeting to address the need for unity in light of major splits between Region 1 and two other regions, Region 6 and Region 3 (Northern Ireland). In truth, the future of the Broad Left did not matter much to the dockers at this point, as its *Left-wing GEC* members continued to allow Morris to ignore the dispute and make false claims about it being both unofficial and illegal. At the mass meeting held Friday 15 November, the atmosphere was upbeat [17] following a Hardship Fund donation from Japanese seafarers, and discussions about the need to picket the Argos store in Liverpool City Centre the following morning. Brian Ashton would lead the demonstration as chair of the Liverpool Dockers' Support Group, and it was often these high-profile actions that kept the dispute in the public eye. Mike Morris, a Citizens Advice Bureau advisor, pledged further support from the Militant Tendency. He also wanted to organise more youth support for the campaign, and to lead the struggle against the Job Seeker's Allowance in favour of the real jobs that the dockers and their families were fighting for. The dockers' already knew one of their young supporters, Joe McLaughlin, who they had nicknamed 'the Youth of Liverpool,' and whenever that phrase was mentioned, he immediately came to mind. [18]

On Tuesday 19 November, Jimmy Nolan and Billy Jenkins returned from Germany, where they had met with the Turkish EMEK Party. The struggle of the Turkish workers, and the work of Jenkins, Tony Gardiner and Kevin Robinson in partnership with so many outstanding Turkish and Kurdish comrades, was truly extraordinary. The stewards agreed to write a letter to the Turkish Embassy in London to condemn the suppression of workers' rights in Turkey, and they also had the issue raised in the House of Commons in November 1996. [19] On the picket line Robinson and Nelson had met with Merseyside Police, who were complaining about the pickets being a drain on their resources. This only served to compliment the leadership of the pickets and the tactic of randomly choosing the time of pickets, not only for maximum impact on the docks, but also in regard to drawing on police resources at times where they had other priorities, such as during well-attended football matches at Goodison Park or Anfield. [20] The police wanted to do a deal with Tony Nelson that involved sanctioning the closure of two identified gates at agreed times, but no agreement was ever reached over the course of the two-and-a-half-year dispute.

When the Liverpool dockers were sacked for refusing to cross a picket line, the city lost one of its few remaining shields against environmental pollution and hazardous cargoes. The dockers had always reported health and safety violations and refused to unload cargoes that would compromise the environment. In 1989, a battle with waste disposal company Rechem followed their attempts to import consignments of the contaminated remains of a fire at a chemical storage facility at *St Basila le Grande*, as the ship carrying the waste, the *M.V.*

*Nadezhda Obukova*, was turned away from Liverpool after protests from Greenpeace and local residents. Without the Liverpool dockers, the scab labour that now worked in the port would handle any cargo and according to one report: 'This may have gone some way to explain why the Mersey Docks Company provoked the dispute in the first place. They needed a docile workforce if Liverpool was to submit to its planned role as a dumping ground for toxic waste. If the dockers were beaten, Liverpool would become the dumping ground for waste from all over the world.' [21] In 1994 alone, an estimated 13,500 tonnes of hazardous waste imports, mainly solvents from the Irish pharmaceutical industry, passed through the Port of Liverpool, with Greenpeace's Simon Reddy declaring that, 'This dockside represents the floodgates for genetic pollution. Cargill wanted to bring it in without telling anyone, and then mix it in our food without giving people any choice. It's underhanded, devious and wrong. The public does not benefit from this genetic engineering. We can't risk releasing it into the environment.' [22]

Talks with MDHC were due to resume on Thursday 21 November, after Trevor Furlong wrote to Jack Adams to express the company's wish to reach a settlement. Adams suspected that this was more of a PR stunt than a genuine reflection of the company's desire to negotiate, not least because Bernard Cliff's absence raised doubts as to the legitimacy of the talks. [23] Earlier that morning, Jimmy Nolan had made a comment about the stewards not being able to understand the complexities of the struggle and although he seemed generally more relaxed, the animosity he felt towards the MDHC directors was palpable. Adams asked the Dispute Committee for a copy of John Hendy's latest legal counsel, as Cory Towage Ltd. had recently threatened the TGWU with litigation after industrial action by the tugboat men that had subsequently been repudiated by the union. [24] The meeting went ahead at the same ACAS office in Manchester where the last round of negotiations had taken place. Adams seemed brusque towards the stewards; he claimed that Bill Morris was furious that the dockers were seeking independent legal advice. Morris's growing disdain for the dockers increased with the publication of the legal advice from John Hendy QC on the *official status* of the dockers' dispute, the release of the Ken Loach film and a *Guardian* article by John Pilger. [25]

The talks began just before 3pm, this was two hours later than scheduled because Trevor Furlong and Peter Jones were unable to leave the docks due to the picket lines at the Seaforth gate. Peter Jones replaced Cliff as lead negotiator and he began by reiterating MDHC's position. [26] Both Adams and Graham Stevenson referred to the GEC's decision on free and unfettered negotiations, and when talks resumed at 4.30pm, Adams told MDHC that the TGWU could not accept the position of giving up its right to defend members at tribunals if a full and final settlement was not reached. [27] Jones agreed that Adams had identified a number of issues that had not been covered before, as they had, 'only dealt with the headline issues,' [28] and so another adjournment was called, this time lasting over an hour, after which Jones informed the TGWU's negotiators that:

> *'We do not have vacancies at Seaforth Container Terminal, as this belongs to Drakes…*
> *We need to construct a situation that makes it look like a conventional redundancy*
> *situation; this may mean more than one week.' [29]*

Jones appeared content that he had covered all the key issues, and Adams asked for confirmation that MDHC would not obstruct any development in General Cargo. [30] Jones replied saying that they could nudge shipowners in their direction under such circumstances, but that they could not provide guarantees. [31] Adams confirmed that the TGWU had no problem with a full and final settlement but repeated that they could not take away an individual's right to pursue tribunals because, 'you have casualised labour on the docks.' [32] Jones countered by stating: 'the security of Drakes' labour force is secure,' [33] and for the shop stewards, the situation was clear: MDHC was offering nothing; 319 dockers would get either £25,000 severance or the possibility of one of 41 ancillary jobs. [34] Adams told the directors that the dockers would not end the dispute through a severance scheme, to which Jones replied that it would be absurd to spend £8m to recreate a loss-making entity at General Cargo. He argued that employment at Drakes was permanent, solid and safe, not casual, before repeating that it was not an option to get rid of them at a time when productivity at the Seaforth Container Terminal was up by 40%. Trevor Furlong sought to have the final word by firing a direct question at Nolan: 'What have you got to put up?' [35] with the response from Nolan being that the managing director should: 'Rid himself of Drakes and negotiate a contract to compete with them.' [36]

At the weekly mass meeting held the following day a full report on the negotiations was given. Tony Nelson gave a report on the picket line after Kevin Robinson talked about his discussions with the police, and this strengthened the belief that picketing was having an effect, especially the tactic of 'hitting' three gates at a time. Mike Morris was there as a guest speaker to discuss organising another demonstration in Liverpool City Centre, to which Nelson added that past attendances at these events had been 'shameful,' as he appealed for as many dockers as possible to participate: 'We want everybody – *everybody!* – to turn up at these pickets at the weekend in town.' [37] Harry Hunter and Jimmy Davies Jr provided feedback on their recent delegation with the Danish dockers, and there was also an update from the Women of the Waterfront, who along with the dockers' children had picketed Trevor Furlong's house on Wednesday 20 October. This was followed by Harry Hunter and Frank Carberry relaying messages from the Manchester Dockers' Support Group, as they had been the key coordinators of much of the campaign work done there, and it was revealed that the Dispute Committee had agreed to write to Bill Morris and seek a meeting with Jack Adams, Graham Stevenson and the International Transport Workers' Federation president, David Cockcroft. After much debate, MDHC's latest offer was rejected by a show of hands to conclude a very good-humoured meeting. [38] A few days earlier, Bill Morris wrote to Mr D. Statham, branch president of GMB Holborn, to say:

> *I am grateful to you for your advice on how to run my union. In this regard, I wish you to know that I stand by every word of my reported comments in the Financial Times… I was referring to the involvement of a number of political groups whose actions on Monday 30 September were totally unacceptable, and which will not be tolerated by this union in this or any other dispute.' [39]*

# 49

# The Human Cost of the Docks' Dispute

*'To all those political groups who have supported us magnificently or not over the last 17 months, the working class throughout this country, and in this city in particular, [that we called upon] to support us: We believe that if there was a general strike in this city, that if all businesses shut down for a day, a week or a month, then the Mersey Docks and Harbour Company would be forced immediately to reinstate the sacked dockers... The reality is that it hasn't happened. A resolution is not a revolution. People have got to understand the reality that we are confronted with.' ~ Mike Carden\**

The Liverpool docks dispute was a conflict fought in an industry that, like so many others, had been forced into meltdown by the policies of Margaret Thatcher's Conservative government. It took a severe toll on the dockers' families, some of whom could trace their connections to the Port of Liverpool back as far as the revolutionary trade unionism of the late 19th century. A trade unionism that gave rise to the Trade Union Congress in 1868, the International Transport Workers' Federation in 1896 and the British Labour Party in 1900. UK Dockworkers would be forced back to the iniquities of a casual labour system in 1989, a system that had haunted the docks since the times when sail was the only form of movement between the continents and the Liverpool dockers dispute in 1995 would be the last stand for one of the most influential sections of the UK's industrial working class. Len McCluskey, the UNITE General Secretary and former Liverpool dockworker, would later compare casual labour on the docks to the contemporary abolition of employment rights and a living wage in 2014, referring to an:

---

* Mike Carden, speaking at a dockers' mass meeting, Friday 31 January 1997 (D. Cotterill, Audio Recording)

363

*'Increasingly insecure economic climate, with growing numbers of people on short-term or zero-hours contracts. It seems pretty clear to me that we are being taken back to what it was like on the docks, when men would gather first thing in the morning and the bosses would walk around and tap people on the shoulder and hand them a brass tally, meaning they had a day's work... We are heading back there again under this government with zero-hours contracts, and it is no way to treat people or to give them a sense of dignity, a sense of belonging to a decent, respectful society.' [1]*

The Liverpool dispute in 1995 was a trade union struggle fought in a most imaginative and radical manner and Tony Benn MP would pull together many of the strands of the dockers' history when he said: 'This dispute will be remembered in the history of the labour movement on the same scale and with the same honour as the Tolpuddle Martyrs and the miners' strike of 1984-85.' [2] Despite Benn's analysis, the dispute has been largely forgotten and undocumented by a movement and a *Left* that refused to recognise the reality of its impact. The Liverpool docks dispute represented an uncomfortable history, a history to be avoided and, beyond some academic studies, not one book has been dedicated to it. Nevertheless, the primary source records of the dispute provide evidence of a unique history captured in real time; a history of struggling workers that shames those who stayed silent or failed to show genuine leadership when it was really needed. A wonderful archive exists of the granite images of these extraordinary men and women, preserving their power and physical strength, as well as their limitless humour and decency. Photographs taken by dockers such as Neil Sharp, Marty Size, Tony Tyrell, Billy Jenkins, Kevin Robinson and Dave Pendleton, together with those produced by professional photographers Andrew Testa, Nick Craske and Dave Sinclair, often in black and white, succeed in creating an air of timelessness about their subjects; a sense that these pictures could have been taken in another century or in any port in the world. Above all else, they provide an insight into the dignity of the working-class; but this moral campaign was waged at a high price for the dockers' families, many of whom lost almost everything they had.

From the first week of the dispute, the Bootle Citizens Advice Bureau was involved in supporting dockers' families, all the while keeping records of the scale of their financial hardships. Caryn Mathews and Helen Booth, who worked directly with the dockers and their families, were to produce a report titled *Employment Rights – In the Dock: A Bureau Experience of a Modern Labour Dispute*, published as a CAB booklet in February 1997. In it, the authors drew from two main sources:

*'Firstly, the experience of the advice workers and agencies involved in both the outreach sessions and the referral scheme for dockworkers. Secondly, the comments of the dockworkers themselves. These were collected by a survey designed by advice workers and completed by the dockers. 300 surveys were given out and 72% returned completed.' [3]*

The survey was the work of Sean Roberts, Sharon Fryer and Tommie Reeves of the CAB, along with Peter Clee at Wallasey Unemployed Centre. Its findings showed that the unique problem faced by many dockers was that they had been continuously employed for over 30 years and consequently had no experience or practical understanding of the benefits system.

# THE HUMAN COST OF THE DOCKS' DISPUTE

Several of them still referred to the National Assistance Board, which by that time had been abolished some two decades earlier. Of the 94% that used the advice service (initially offered at Transport House Liverpool) in October 1995, the vast majority were confident that the dispute would not last too long, and so advice was always given from both short and long-term perspectives. By the summer of 1996, advice workers were still coming across dockworkers who had not claimed the contribution-based benefits that they were entitled to because they had been managing on savings, their expectation being that they would soon be reinstated. [4] Due to the critical importance of the dockers' employment status (i.e. were they sacked or on strike?) none of them received payments from the state until the issue was finally resolved on 16 December 1995, following a successful test case that went in their favour. This led to all benefits being paid in full, as the Employment Service concluded that the Liverpool dockers were not involved in a trade dispute but had been dismissed. [5] Obviously, this fact was relevant to their legal status of *not being on strike, either officially or unofficially*.

The CAB report also uncovered the fact that many of the dockers' wives had not been in formal work for some time because their partners had been employed on a reasonable wage. As a result, they had not previously considered themselves eligible for benefits. The majority of these women had been receiving treatment for various health conditions for several years but had not viewed this as relevant to making claims, with some not only entitled to Disability Premium and Income Support, but also Incapacity and / or Disability Living Allowance. [6] Additionally, the report highlighted a wide range of other benefits that the dockers were unaware of and could have applied for in the past. Many found it impossible to claim on insurance policies that should have become active as a result of their being made redundant. Insurers refused to pay out for pre-existing conditions or to policy holders not in gainful employment immediately prior to claiming. Some 40% of sacked dockers disclosed a rise in priority and secondary debt since their dismissal. [7] The work of the CAB and the unemployed resource centres in Kirby, Liverpool and Wallasey was extraordinary, they dealt directly with the financial plight of the dockers. Their work also brought to light the physical and mental scars that the dispute was beginning to inflict upon an increasing number of Liverpool families. In a letter submitted to the *Liverpool Echo*, just one month after the dispute had started, Alison Davies, herself the daughter of a dockworker, stated that:

> *'I am devastated at what has happened in the docks dispute, as both my father and brother have lost their jobs. My father has worked on the docks all his life, and my brother wanted to follow him. As the MDHC were not recruiting, he went to work for the ill-fated Torside. Both of them work long hours. My dad had a serious accident earlier this year and was lucky not to have lost his foot, but he could not wait to get back to work. My brother also had an accident while in work resulting in hospitalisation. These sort of people, not the MDHC, have made the docks what they are today – a great profit-making company, and I cannot believe that they have been treated in such an appalling way. Is this the thanks they get after the way they have worked over the last few years?' [8]*

Two years later, Jan Brett would speak about the tragic loss of her father, Jimmy McCumiskey, who was one of the largely unheralded heroes of the dispute before passing away from a sudden heart attack in January 1998. He was just 59 years old. He left behind two daughters, Jan and her sister Marie, and according to his wife Ann: 'Jimmy worried and worried and worried. It's such a shame he had to die after having two years of stress, and without doubt the stress contributed to his death. He was a changed man.' [9] Jimmy McCumiskey had worked on the docks for over 33 years, and like the majority of his colleagues, he had expected the dispute to be settled quickly, but as weeks became months he began to, 'worry about money and future employment hopes,' [10] with Jan recalling how her dad: 'was never a shirker; he'd worked all his life to provide for us, and we never wanted for anything. He loved Christmas because he loved giving. He was really upset last year because he felt that he couldn't buy us what he wanted to.' [11] Marie was heavily pregnant when her father died, and her husband, Jimmy Brett, thought it important to stress that: 'Jimmy McCumiskey did not just go along with the dispute, he totally believed in fighting for jobs and against casualisation. He couldn't understand why some people didn't understand their case, and why some were calling them scroungers.' [12] These sentiments were echoed by Joanne Glover, daughter of sacked docker John Glover, who said:

*'I'm proud of my dad for standing by what he believes in, and we have always supported him 100%, but it has had an effect on the whole family. My dad has always had a job; he doesn't know what to do. It's like someone has taken a piece of his life away.' [13]*

In January 1998, dockworker Steve Smith reflected on surviving his third Christmas struggling on benefits and like many of his comrades being close to breaking point: 'It's gone on too long. We have lost our jobs and our livelihoods, and some of the men feel almost suicidal.' [14] Steve Smith admitted that he had: 'hit rock bottom on New Year's Eve, going to bed at 9pm despairing about his future.' [15] Perhaps at the root of this despair lay the belief, amongst the majority of dock workers, that their dispute could have been won from the very start. This was a view I held and still hold to this day. As the dispute spluttered towards its conclusion, I suffered a breakdown in my physical and mental health linked to my disbelief that a dispute that could have been won so easily was strangled at its conception, suffocated by trade union bureaucrats aided and abetted by influential lay members.

That December, in 1997, seven French dockers from Le Havre arrived at Transport House Liverpool in a huge lorry filled with presents for the dockers' children. From the Wirral, donations of Turkeys had been sent across the Mersey, in addition to gift vouchers and boundless generosity from supporters across the world. However, despite this much-appreciated show of solidarity, one of the Women of the Waterfront admitted to wishing that Christmas could be, 'postponed until things have been sorted out.' [16] Terry Barrett said: 'You know, I used to love Christmas – highlight of the year – but I just don't want this one. Fed up! We're proud, standing up for what we believe in. We've made a stand because this isn't about money, it's about something more. A fight against intimidation and for a secure job, not casualised like so much in Britain.' [17] With the dispute having been rumbling on for over two years, it was quickly becoming a story that journalist Peter Hetherington described as one of: 'Misery, family stresses, mounting debt and, worse, the threat of housing repossessions. The question of personal circumstances, apart from the modest demands of children, rarely crops up.' [18] Teresa Ledden, whose husband Eddie was a second-generation docker with 27 years of continuous service to his name, recalled telling her youngest son:

> *'Father Christmas hasn't any room on his sledge, and he understands. With three other children aged 17, 18 and 20 – one a student, another an apprentice and the third on Youth Training – matters have gone from bad to worse. It was like a bereavement when Eddie was out of a job. He loved the docks and the ships. It was in his blood.' [19]*

Marie Eustace, whose husband Tommy was a docker with 30 years' service, admitted that their family had: 'debts hanging around our necks,' with their only source of income being her part-time job in a care home for the elderly. She added: 'I try to do a lot of extra hours, and we've sort of changed places. If anything, the dispute has brought us together. We're just managing to keep our heads above water.' [20] It was around this time that Kevin Bilsborrow, a member of the Dispute Committee, who had followed his father and grandfather onto the docks, stated: 'The finances are not good. We have some toys from France. Turkeys, yes, we have been promised, but we've got to stick together... you feel sorry for the kids. They deserve better.' [21] In December 1997, Billy Bragg had performed another fundraising concert in London that earned a large sum of money for the dockers' Hardship Fund, while his son donated a Christmas card. [22] The rejection of MDHC's second 'final offer' was welcomed by the Liverpool dockers. For them, another attempt at buying-out the dispute had failed. Billy Barrett was: 'made up with the result,' while Tommy Byrne, who had been on the docks since 1973, was prepared to continue until he got his job back. [23] Pat Dooley and her husband were active in the dispute from the start, with Brian, who had spent 28 years on the docks before being dismissed, regularly undertaking important delegation work, while Pat was a founder member of the Women of the Waterfront. Speaking in 1997, she recalled that: 'The reason why I went down the picket line with him was because I knew in my heart of hearts it was the right thing to do, to stand by him.' [24] Brian explained how: 'We're closer as a family now I'm at home when the family are home. In some ways, we're a lot happier. I feel that I'm fighting for my family, and my family are behind me.' [25] He then recalled the time that he volunteered for a delegation to Aberdeen as a way of both representing the cause and visiting his daughter, who was studying at university:

> *'A very nice couple of SWP members put me up for the duration, I had told them about my daughter being at University. A short while after my visit, I got a letter from them saying they were going on holiday to Spain for two weeks, and my family could have use of their house if we wished. I jumped at the chance, and when we arrived, they had already left beer and wine for us and said to help ourselves to food in the freezer. We didn't, because they had done enough. I tended the garden in their absence, and as it was Autumn, I planted lots of spring bulbs but never told them. By the following April, I got a phone call from the lady, who was surprised and delighted at the newly blooming daffodils in her garden. That was the start of a friendship which still exists over 20 years later.' [26]*

In an article in the *Observer*, Jimmy McGovern captured with raw honesty the humanity of the Liverpool dockers. He recalled how the pickets insisted that he meet others on the picket line and being introduced to: 'Nice Tony and Geoffrey Boycott', whose real name was Tony Morton:

> *'I expected two people, but they're one and the same man. Nice Tony is called Nice Tony because he's, well, nice. And he's called Geoffrey Boycott because first, he's the image of the man, and second, this is the first time he's been out in 42 years. This is Nice Tony: 'Forty-two years and they sack me. I was staff (a member of the original TGWU 6/567 Dock Staff Branch). I'd been in the office 30-odd years. When the new contracts came out, they sent me out to lash down cargo. I was 56 years old, and I didn't have a bloody clue.' This sounds like a moan, but he is laughing as he tells it, and everyone around him is doubled-up too.' [27]*

Tony Morton sadly died in June 2012. McGovern was also introduced to another docker, Billy 'Kipper' Lynch, also on the picket line that morning:

> *'I'm a timekeeper. I started on the docks in 1965. There were 92 timekeepers then. I loved it. I just had this gift for columns of figures. By the end, there were only two of us left. I had 28 years in when the new contracts came out. They finished my timekeeping job and I had to work outside. I accepted it. It was a job. I knew we had to be flexible. When they sacked me, I had 30 years in.' [28]*

McGovern then met other characters such as Frank O'Neil, Davey Hughes and Eddie Ainscough, who he noted had 95 years of service between them. [29] In a magnificent picture of docker George Preston, which accompanied the article, photographer Andrew Testa captured an extraordinary image of determination. A classic portrait of not only a worker, but an emblem of the essence of being working-class. This was a class of people in transition, guided by an intangible human spirit to fight injustice no matter the price, and in his flat cap and dirty, well-worn yellow high-visibility winter coat, an unshaven George Preston faces the camera with his bicycle cutting horizontally across the frame, bisecting the picture into two halves. He had decided that it was his new job to repair the huts that provided some shelter to the pickets along Dock Road, hence the wood that he has carefully and neatly tied to the frame of his rusty old bike, as string trails randomly from his only form of transport. He has one hand on the seat and the other on the handlebars, his feet are spread apart, and if you look closely, you can see a handsaw tied to the crossbar. All of these assorted bits and pieces appear as one with the bike; they are part of it. The scene is set against a weather-beaten but solid brick wall, a relic from another century, and it is just about possible to make out the '1 One of 500 sacked Liverpool dockers' badge pinned to his coat like a medal, alongside the clenched fist and dockers' hook symbol of the International Longshore and Warehouse Union. In the newspaper, the caption beneath this sublime image read: 'George Preston was a docker for 23 years until he was sacked. He uses the saw he carries on his bicycle to help rebuild shelters that have been damaged or destroyed by 'scab' workers.' [30] It is one of the most beautiful and iconic images of the dispute, and an extraordinary, wonderful record of the man it portrays, a sacked Liverpool docker. Another man of few words, a dignified man, a man named George Preston.

The effect that the dispute had on the children of the Liverpool dockers should not be underestimated. They were forced to suffer the chaos of family emotions that such a protracted period of strife can inflict. At the second anniversary rally, held on 27 September 1997, Joanne Bennett's gave an account of her personal experiences of the dispute to thousands of people, who had travelled to Liverpool City Centre in support of men like her father. *LabourNet* published her speech:

> *'My name is Joanne Bennett, and I'm here to talk about the docks dispute. When my dad got sacked, I found it very hard to understand the situation, as it was difficult time for my dad. But as time went on, my mum joined up with a group of other wives, and they became involved with the Women of the Waterfront... But now two years have gone by, and I fully understand the dispute, which makes me more determined to believe that my dad will get his job back, and all the other dockers. And in the end, they will all be able to march through the dock gates proudly...'* [31]

Joanne was 14 years old at the time of the rally, where Simon Melia, son of Torside shop steward Tony Melia, also addressed the crowd:

> *'When the dock dispute first broke out, our family was distraught. My dad had lost his job and things were looking very bleak. At the time I was only 12, and I didn't fully understand, but what made things so much better for me, my brother, and sister was meeting with other children whose dads or granddads had been sacked. We all seemed to have the same sort of problems. At first, going to the picket line was an adventure, but as I've grown older, I have realised what the picket line and the dispute is all about. It's not just about the men fighting for their jobs in this generation, but for the younger people of the next.'* [32]

Recalling her own son's speech at the really, Jeanette Fox wrote about how she found herself thinking:

> *'Was that my son shaking hands with Arthur Scargill? Was that really him standing at the microphone talking to thousands of people? His voice echoed around the plaza, clear and full of confidence, with my heart beating frantically and tears filling my eyes. I felt so proud. His nan stood beside me, two days away from her 80th birthday and with tears running down her face, and said, "As long as God spares me, I'll never forget this day." Her husband worked on the docks and fought for the rights that are being eroded now. It is a moment I will treasure for the rest of my life; say with pride that was Neil, that was my son, did you see him?'* [33]

The conflict irreversibly altered the lives of those involved in it. The police made regular arrests on the picket lines, and although this never led to long periods of imprisonment, it could still be a shockingly brutal experience, especially for the younger 'out-of-town' supporters. Kevin Robinson worked with Michael Schwarz of Bindman & Partners solicitors to support demonstrators that were the victims of police brutality, and according to Schwarz: 'Kevin took over the burden of collating defence evidence himself.' [34] Some of the Reclaim the Streets campaigners had participated in efforts to stop the building of the Newbury bypass in the early 1990s, and one of them, who gave his address as the Newbury Diggers' Community, came in for particularly rough treatment, as he was facing charges of, 'assault occasioning actual bodily harm on a police officer and possession of a blade instrument.' [35] He pleaded not guilty to the charges, and in a statement made at the time, the young environmentalist explained how he, like virtually every other campaigner, carried a camping knife, and that he had bought his at a camping store in Newbury, as during his time there he had, 'lived in the woods or in trees. I tend to have only a few possessions: a rucksack, a drum and bedding. It is unremarkable to have a knife in the culture I live in, among squatters, travellers and protesters.' [36] He also gave a detailed account of his experiences when he, along with his fellow RTS members, decided to support the Liverpool dockers on the weekend of 28 September 1996. He had travelled with the advance party, the 'raver organisation,' and on the Saturday he joined the march through Liverpool City Centre before attending Sunday workshops by the Liverpool School of Samba, the Sarajevo McDonald's and the blagging food workshop. [37] The following morning, one of the protesters, Rouri Martin, was arrested within three hours of joining the Liverpool dockers on the picket line for what he described as merely: 'talking to the police assertively, but reasonably. I was trying to get inside their heads. I was saying things like, "How do you feel helping dockers out of their work? How do you feel about their families?" [38] Later, when he left the picket line for lunch, he was arrested after what became a violent struggle:

> 'With the Operational Support Group hitting me, I was getting battered in the police van by six OSD officers. I had blood coming out of my face. I was locked in a police cell van along with many other pickets who had been arrested at the same time. I was handcuffed and transferred to another police van, where I was assaulted for a second time… it was slow and methodical. They would hit me, wait, laugh, insult me. Then they started saying things like, "You're messing with the big boys now. We're Liverpool Police. We're vicious. We're nasty. We hurt people. We're not fluffy like the Berkshire police." I remember a number of threats… one officer held me behind the head, pressed his face right up to me and shouted at me, "You don't want arresting, you want fucking exterminating." I was very scared. There were times when I really did think that they were going to kill me.' [39]

Due to the fact that this young man had an Irish name, he was also accused of being a member of the Irish Republican Army, and he was one of around 30 RTS activists to be victimised by Merseyside Police. Kieran Dunne from the Liverpool UNISON Branch was also arrested, and he appeared in court alongside three other campaign supporters in April 1997. In July, at the Alexandra Dock gate, docker Steve Stanton: 'had his head banged against the pavement' in the process of an arrest that took place with 20 officers in attendance. Stanton was taken to Fazakerley Hospital by ambulance, and his fellow dockers Kenny Weston and Herbie Hollerhead made an official complaint about the actions of at least five other police officers that day. [40] Micky Tighe was also on picket duty and he later recalled how:

> 'The Port Police wanted to push Kenny Weston and manhandle him… Once they had caught Kenny, we were shouting for his release, that he had done nothing. This was when Stevie Stanton was kicked from behind by one of the Merseyside Police. We thought some were OSD because some of them had no numbers visible. I pointed out that he had stopped breathing and his face was going bluey purple. That is when the police got off him and took his handcuffs off; they seemed to be in a state of shock when they saw what they had done. Stevie was unconscious for about ten seconds. I and another picket took charge and resuscitated him.' [41]

These events were typical of the experiences faced by the dockers and their supporters, as they were regularly arrested and would subsequently carry criminal records for many years. Mick Cullen was arrested in June 1997, and July saw Kenny Weston, Gary Halsall, Chris Langan and Kevin Bilsborrow suffer the same fate. In the summer of 1997 the following dockers found themselves being charged with anything from obstruction to threatening behaviour: Chris Clynch, Tony Nelson, Colin Mitchell, Ian Brittles, Ray Walklett, John Gibbons, George Chapman, Peter Cain, Terry Teague, Billy Langley, Derek Nolan, Tony Farrell, John King, Jeff Jones, Frank Byrne, Phil McNally, John Maguire, John Ferns, Mike Carden, Stan Philips, Peter Kilhane, Eddie Ledden, John Jenkins, Jimmy Davies, Fred Roberts, Nat Gibbons, Terry Southers, Tony Russell, Bob Ritchie, Andy Owens, Kevin Flynn and Bernie Gleaves. Babs Hennessy, one of the dockers' advice workers and a UNISON activist, and Pat Harvey from the Trade Union and Unemployed Resource Centre were also arrested around this time. [42] Sammy Hopkins would later offer some insight into the strength of feeling that fuelled the dockers' courage to fight on against the unassailable force of the state, as he told the *Dockers' Charter* about working on the docks for 37 years:

> 'And at the age of 59, I am now not in the industry. My father and brother died in the industry. My brother was 55 and my father was 58. My family has 116 years' service altogether on the docks. No man should have his livelihood taken away because he supported his fellow worker in struggle. That's all our fight was for. That's what my father and brother fought for. There was no backbone, especially from the T&G. Bill Morris said that the anti-union laws Thatcher laid down were laws that could not be challenged, but no one even tried to challenge them.' [43]

Dave and Mary Pendleton were regulars on the picket lines, catering for meetings, contributing to discussions, video recording daily events and creating magnificent banners, placards and paintings. Dave expressed the commonly shared view that the Liverpool dockers: 'had no support from the union and this pseudo-Labour government. What I hate is letting the MDHC get away with it.' [44] The Pendletons were facilitators of a solidarity that lay at the heart of this most bitter of disputes. Malkait Bilku of the striking Hillingdon Hospital workers echoed this sentiment, as she acknowledged the vital roles of unity and comradeship in maintaining the traditional ideals of trade unionism: 'We thank the sacked

Liverpool dockers for their tremendous moral and practical support. We owe you so much. You have taught us so much, and together we have made a lasting alliance in struggle.' [45] In a lengthy analysis published by Greg Dropkin on *LabourNet*, Jean Fox of the Women of the Waterfront, observed that:

> *'Our lives have been absolutely and utterly transformed by the actions of the MDHC. We never asked to be sacked. We voted within a week to return to work and Cliff said a few months after that, "I had to get scabs in because we didn't know when they were coming back." …It must be the fact that the dockers have shown that the working class can still stand straight and tall and fight back against tyrannical employers.' [46]*

Pat Dooley was one of the WOW members interviewed by Ken Loach for *the Flickering Flame*, where she explained that: 'What really touched you as well is that people came with parcels for you from the Harvest Festival. You find out who your friends are, and that's the real thing none of us will tell you, but we had to put out an insurance policy or something like that.' [47] In the same scene, Val Bibby said that she had: 'something like 300 years of dock heritage in my family, from my father, grandfather, uncles… and to see that one man can just sack 500 men…' [48] At this point, she was stopped by a swell of tears in what was one of the most powerful scenes of the entire film, leaving Sue Mitchell to finish her friend's statement:

> *'Seeing the strain and the stress, and you say to yourself, what can we do? When is it going to end? When are that Dock Company going to say, "God, look what we have done to these people? And they have given half of their lives to this firm." It's just the injustice of it, and it is not just happening here, it's happening everywhere. What's going to be at the end of it? A casual job with low pay, ill health [and] no future for their children. That's what it is all about.' [49]*

These were the most poignant moments of a scene that depicts just one aspect of the human cost of the Liverpool dock dispute, before sacked docker Micky Tighe spoke for many of his comrades as he succinctly summarised the genesis of what was now a two-year conflict:

> *'Some people say we should have crossed the picket line, but I wouldn't know how. We have always prided ourselves that we didn't even need to put up picket lines. The company engineered this strike. They knew that under the law they could have had the Torside lads' picket removed. They knew how they would react. Some of the lads on that picket line are our sons.' [50]*

# 50
# John Pilger Writes and Bill Morris Responds

*'They haven't got their jobs back because other trade unions haven't supported them, and their own union has been led by donkeys... What's the point in a national union? You have a union to defend your job, defend your wages and to defend your conditions. If your union can't do that, then what's the point in it? TGWU members have crossed the picket line... The dispute wasn't illegal... Unjust labour laws should have no respect.' ~ Ken Loach\**

O n Saturday 23 November 1996, John Pilger published an article in the *Guardian* that would raise the profile of the Liverpool dispute to an unprecedented level. Among other aspects of the dockers' struggle, Pilger exposed the role of the union with particular focus on the failed leadership of Bill Morris. Under the title, *They Never Walk Alone*, Pilger considered the role of the TGWU some 14 months into the dispute, writing how:

> *'Five months after the dockers were sacked, TGWU general secretary Bill Morris, who has refused to make the dispute official, came to Liverpool and made an emotional speech. 'I am proud to be with you,' he told the men and their families. 'Your struggle is so important that our grandchildren will ask, "Where were you at the great moment?" and you will either stand up with pride and say, "I was there," or you'll hang your head in shame, without an answer. There can be no turning back and no backsliding until victory is won.' He pledged that the union would 'keep going... until we get this company to understand that a negotiated settlement which gives people their jobs back is the only way.' He added, 'God is on our side.' The dockers cheered him.*
>
> *I have tried repeatedly to elicit a comment from Morris, or from anyone at TGWU headquarters. It has been an instructive, if farcical, exercise... I was passed to*

\* Ken Loach on Roger Phillips, BBC Radio Merseyside (Tuesday 28 January 1998) *a press officer, who said, 'Bill Morris cannot legally speak to you.' I asked him for the names of the lawyers advising Morris not to speak. 'They don't want to be bothered by journalists...' I then phoned the Trades Union Congress. As it happened, John Monks, the general secretary, had made a ringing speech in Liverpool that weekend about moral values. 'You cannot have a moral society,' he had said, 'when people feel they can be treated like dirt by their employers.' I asked to speak to Monks. 'What's it about?' said a TUC press officer. 'The Liverpool dockers.'... 'Sorry, John never comments on disputes, and that one is far too sensitive for him to be involved in.' [1]*

In the February / March 1997 issue of the *TGWU Record*, the official publication of Britain's largest union sought to *set the record straight*, in an article that summarised the thinking of the union's leader. It was a view endorsed by the majority of the lay members on the TGWU's main decision-making body, the General Executive Council.

*'Because the MDHC workers were not in direct dispute with their own employer and had broken their contract of employment without first holding an industrial action ballot, the TGWU became vulnerable to legal action for damages by MDHC or any shipowner... the leadership of the union has an obligation to preserve the fabric of the TGWU and not engage in activities for which it has no immunity or legal protection.' [2]*

Morris wanted to inform the membership that:

*'Everyone would wish to be able to give full support to any group of members unjustly dismissed, as the Liverpool dockers had been. However, the TGWU has an obligation to all its 900,000 members, which must include avoiding action which could render the union unable to operate on behalf of those members.' [3]*

He then went on to defend himself and the TGWU against those who supported the Liverpool dockers:

*'Pilger seeks to make much of my reluctance to be interviewed by him, a reluctance more than justified by the anti-TGWU bile which suffuses from his article. He would have been more honest had he referred to his own aggressive refusal to submit written questions when this was offered by the union's press officer, possibly because unambiguous answers which could not be twisted may not have suited his pre-determined thesis...' [4]*

Morris concluded by reiterating his overall strategy for supporting the dockers:

*'Our survival owes nothing to the advice of John Pilger and the like. If John Pilger's article serves any purpose, it is only in reminding us that ultra-left politics so often end up in the same place as the policies of the right, attacking the organisations of the labour movement.' [5]*

# JOHN PILGER WRITES AND BILL MORRIS RESPONDS

In solidarity with his TGWU counterpart, David Cockcroft, of the International Transport Workers' Federation also penned an article for the *TGWU Record*, stating that:

> '*In the Saturday weekend supplement there was an article by John Pilger about the Liverpool dockers' strike... The ITF, like our affiliate the TGWU, has strongly supported the Liverpool dockers' demands for reinstatement from the beginning and, within the bounds of what is legally and practically possible, we continue to do so...*' [6]

The dockers used their newspaper, the *Dockers' Charter*, to set the record straight regarding arguments presented by Morris and the TGWU leadership. This lengthy article acted as a summary of the dockers' position to date. The union had done little more than provide financial support to the Hardship Fund and pursue negotiations with the port authority, with Hardship Fund donations standing at £500,000 at the time of writing. This was the equivalent of £15 per week to each docker and his family, amounting to a fraction of official strike pay. The union had helped in developing proposals for dockers to set up a labour supply company, but unfortunately, they, in partnership with MDHC, had chosen KPMG to develop the business plan. KPMG were MDHC's registrars and had been involved in the valuation of the Medway dockers' shares, a matter which resulted in the TGWU challenging the two companies in court. The remainder of the *Dockers' Charter* made reference to John Pilger's article and highlighted the tenacity with which Morris attacked those who the dockers considered to be respected comrades. [7]

On Saturday 23 November a 'Resistance Fayre' was held at Transport House Liverpool. It was probably the first and last time that such an event had been organised in a TGWU building, as it was essentially a Reclaim the Streets event. As the flyers circulated explained: 'We hope you will take the opportunity to participate in the workshops and launches which we are running throughout the afternoon.' [8] The festivities were opened by Jimmy Nolan. There were numerous workshops on international solidarity run by Terry Teague, plus a workshop on juggling, the launch of Young Socialist Resistance by its national organiser Jude Ritchie, a percussion workshop by local band Zeb, a global warming launch and a final workshop, *Why Women Need Socialism*, organised by 'militant' women. [9]

The following day, a meeting took place at Haigh Hall, a Students' Union building in Liverpool, where the topic of discussion between the dockers and RTS was the occupation of the Grain Terminal. Two vans were going to be hired, with a solid blue one to act as a decoy at the Pandoro gate, and another, curtain-sided van, which would drive into the Grain Terminal at 6am, when the scabs were due to start work. The weather was forecast to be atrocious after a weekend of heavy rain, and the plan was to use picket lines as both protection and cover for the occupiers. [10] A mass picket had been advertised for 10am while demonstrators were asked to arrive four hours earlier. At 6.30am, the curtain-sided van approached the Alexander Dock gate carrying ten Reclaim the Streets activists and ten dockers, along with all the ropes, food and clothes required for an occupation. However, the van stalled at the gate, leaving those inside with no choice but to get out and carry as much gear as they could manage without drawing too much attention to themselves. Meanwhile, some 350 pickets tried to act as a decoy for the occupation confronting police officers, dogs, horses and the Operational Support Division. Overhead a police helicopter circled at an estimated cost of £1,000 an hour. Some of the dockers who stayed at the Seaforth gate in order to split police resources were arrested, including Brian Dooley, John Delaney, Neil Sharpe and Keith Walker. [11] After some struggles and confusion, six demonstrators were able to access the Grain Terminal and climb two of the enormous cranes there. *LabourNet* reported that following, 'negotiations with the harbour master and port police at Mersey Docks, Greenpeace agreed to lift their four-hour blockade of the lockgates. By the next morning, the continuing occupation had delayed, for almost a day, the off-loading of genetically engineered soybeans imported through Liverpool Docks by the grain multinational Cargill.' [12]

This occupation was effectively led by Greenpeace and their various animal rights affiliates acting on information provided by the dockers and the Reclaim the Future alliance. The Polish registered *Orleta Lwowskie*, en route from New Orleans with 56,000 tonnes of soybeans, including the highly controversial genetically engineered Roundup Ready soybeans, designed by Monsanto for use only with their own herbicide. At Gladstone Dock, a banner reading, 'Floodgate to genetic pollution,' was hung across the ship's path, while other activists chained themselves to the lock gates and ladders. Simon Reddy of Greenpeace said at the time:

> *This dockside represents the floodgates for genetic pollution. Cargill wanted to bring it in without telling anyone, and then mix it in our food without giving people any choice. It's underhanded, devious and wrong. The public does not benefit from this genetic engineering. We can't risk releasing it into the environment.' [13]*

On Wednesday 27 November, Nick Silvano, Micky Tighe, Billy Jenkins, Kevin Robinson and Kevin Hargreaves from the London Support Group met with MPs Tony Benn, Jeremy Corbyn, Lynne Jones, Eddie Loyden, Denis Skinner and Lord Monkswell, at the House of Commons. There, they discussed support for the dockers' campaign, although Jenkins and Robinson also wanted the Turkish situation to be addressed via an early day motion. The march and demonstration planned for London on 14 December was also a key point of their discussions along with the speakers to include Jack Jones, the former General Secretary of the TGWU and Jeremy Corbyn MP. [14] On 29 November, Joe Benton MP, Robinson, Nelson and Teague met with Superintendent Steve Finnigan and Doug McGarvey at Crosby Road Police Station, and the dockers made it clear that their issue was with MDHC, and not the police. Benton declared his total support for the dockers, while expressing concern about the cost of policing and what he considered to be a change of tactics, [15] prompting a lengthy discussion on picketing and the legal obligations that it placed upon the police. Finnigan acknowledged that the dockers were not on strike, and so picketing was not strictly the correct legal term, which meant that any future marches would have to be deemed *processions*. [16]

This meeting took place just two days after the OSD had waded into a peaceful picket line and arrested five dockers, and much of the excessive violence that unfolded was captured by a Dutch film crew. It was clear that the police were simply furious over how successful the pickets had been, and how recent demonstrations, such as those involving RTS, had really stretched their resources. John Delaney, a 61-year-old dockworker, had been kicked by the OSD for no reason, but the police response was that the 5pm picket, which caused massive disruption to traffic in and around the docks, was a watershed for them; they were going to clamp down harder than ever. The two officers stated plainly their intention to make mass arrests, while requesting that Robinson no longer be sent to represent the dockers in future talks, as the police found him 'too abrasive,' but this was flatly rejected by the Dispute Committee. By this time, Merseyside Police had taken to waiting outside Transport House and the dockers' van, driven throughout the dispute by Ronnie Bibby, had been impounded. Bibby undertook extraordinary responsibilities throughout the dispute, and despite coming under tremendous pressure from the police, he never complained, was never late, never let anyone down and was totally committed to the principle of natural justice in all matters, including the dispute. He was typical of so many dockers who quietly led the campaign by continuing to go about their business no matter what. On the picket lines, the braziers were taken away by the police, who were able to hide behind the Criminal Justice Act while harassing protestors with impunity. [17] But there came a point where enough was enough, and Kevin Bilsborrow used a mass meeting to call on dockers and their supporters to, 'get on the picket line and realise the need for civil disobedience.' [18]

The impact of John Pilger's article was substantial in raising the spirits of the dockers and drawing national attention to their struggle. Much like Ken Loach, Jimmy McGovern and many other artists and writers, Pilger gave a voice to the dockers and created a public record of their struggle. On Tuesday 26 November, Mike Carden travelled to London to meet with Ken Loach to clarify some of the practical questions that the director had, as his film was now at the final editing stage. This provided Carden with a wonderful, once-in-a-lifetime opportunity to watch as a truly great film director cut and spliced endless strips of film, most of which hung from the ceiling above. Meanwhile, plans were being finalised ahead of the London demonstration on 14 December, with the Dispute Committee hoping to get as many dockers down to the capital as possible, as rumours were circulating that Bill Morris was going to attend in support of the Liverpool cause. This would never happen. 30,000 leaflets were produced declaring:

> '15 Months on Strike! March with the 500 Sacked Liverpool Dockers! The Liverpool dockers invite all who oppose this government to resist casualisation and make this day a celebration of all our struggles. Assemble 12 noon at Speakers' Corner, Hyde Park. Wear Something Red – Bring your Banners.' [19]

The leaflet carried the names of numerous supporters, from Jeremy Corbyn and Ken Livingstone to Rory Bremner; the Jewish Socialist Movement to the Day-Mer Turkish and Kurdish Community Centre. [20] Bobby Morton, Terry Southers and Kevin Bilsborrow were to co-ordinate the organisation of the demonstration, together with the London Support Group. [21] Plans were also being made on the US West Coast by Jack Heyman, the International Longshore and Warehouse Union Local 10 agent, and Brian McWilliam, the union's president, to involve John Bowers, the East Coast International Longshoremen's Association's president, as well as Michel Murray, the leader of the Montreal dockworkers. The support of the Canadian ports of Halifax and Vancouver was considered critical, and Jimmy Davies would try to contact both Murray and Pat Riley directly. Elsewhere, on the 4

December, dockworkers in Veracruz, Mexico, had called a one-day stoppage in support of the Liverpool dispute and the Mexican dockers' leader made arrangements to visit Liverpool. Tragic news from Australia described how four miners were killed on the day that their government abolished compensation schemes for miners killed or injured in work, which led to a strike. In the UK, the National Tugboat Association offered to make a donation to the Liverpool dockers, but this was refused by the Dispute Committee. [22]

At Friday's mass meeting, the atmosphere remained upbeat. [23] Jimmy Davies gave his finance report. Björn Borg made another generous donation to the Hardship Fund on behalf of the Swedish dockworkers' union. Davies informed the men that the police authority had complained that policing the picket lines was costing £7,000 a day in overtime payments, and Jeremy Corbyn MP also addressed the meeting, along with the musician and socialist, Billy Bragg. On Sunday 30 November, the sad news of Bernard Cliff's passing was shared with the dockers. [24] Some of the stewards wished to attend his funeral and pay respect to a man who they had known and worked alongside for over 20 years, others cautioned that this could have been perceived as inappropriate. On 5 December, *LabourNet* conducted a series of interviews with Liverpool dockers, which provided some insight into to their feelings at this time. Unfortunately, the interviewees were not properly identified, going only by their first names, as one docker, Jimmy, told Greg Dropkin:

> *'I'm 60 years of age, and I can get a pension and that, but all I want out of there is the scabs, that's the first thing. My father actually got killed on the docks; my brother was down there, my grandfather and everything, so I'm one of them that won't give in. But there are lads that will give in, I've got to say that.' [25]*

Another docker, referred to as Steve, said that:

> *'We've had a talk many a day down on the Alex gate, and we have our Dr Doom's among us. People get disheartened, saying, "Oh well, we've been down these docks 14 months now, and what's the outcome?" None of us know the outcome, but we know that we've got nowhere else to go… But the likes of me, Jimmy and the lads who are sitting around here now, we're resilient; we've just got to buck those up that are getting disheartened.' [26]*

The Alex gate was a hub of activity during the dispute, with many of those who manned it in 1989 being there once again in 1995. Men like Ray Karlson, Richie Donohue, (Sadly Richie passed away 10 August 2017) Billy Barrett, Peter Wharton, Phil Cawley, George Carter, Gordon O'Keefe, Mick Kilcullen, 'Snowy' Joe Best, 'World Cup Willy' and so many others. Some of the lads from the 1989 pickets, such as Eddie Lundon, had sadly passed away, while at the Norse Irish gate, dockers like Nat Givens, Stevie Stanton, John Jackson, Terry Markey, Joe Ladd, John Ferns, Eddie Ledden, Tony Seasmen, Mark Crichton, Tony Tyrell, Terry Woods and John McCabe braved everything from adverse weather to police intimidation to fight for their past, present and future. The picket line was their forum and their parliament, where John Delaney, Danny Sweeney, Dave Pendleton, Steve Aldersley, John Simmelker, Tony Morton, Geoff Bayley, John Deaves, Ronnie Shaw, Freddy Portis, Billy

Hope, Larry Riley, Alan Loy, Joe McMullen, Gerry Roache, George Riley, Stan Philips, Peter Wharton, Kenny Forsyth, John Craven (John sadly passed away 31 October 2016) Stevie Booth, John Jackson, Tommy Duffy, John Cowley, Jimmy Campbell, Dave Hughes, Billy Walker, John McCabe, Tommy Christy, Jimmy Singleton, Peter Stroud, Billy Williams, Ronnie Fawcett and Peter Dempsey united, along with hundreds of comrades; with the Women of the Waterfront; with their wives and partners, as they made their presence felt. The picket lines were the heartbeat of the campaign, and the stewards listened intently to its rhythms as it planned and plotted a way forward. One docker, interviewed on the picket line, spoke of the unprecedented length of the struggle:

> *'As it's gone on for nearly 15 months now, I'm actually getting stronger, not weaker… I want to see the scabs out of the port, I want to see the men back that want to go back and I want to see the union back in there, calling the shots. And let's have decent conditions. That's what I want.' [27]*

Another docker spoke of the ever-reducing wages and worsening conditions of employment that the men suffered before their dismissal:

> *'It's just a gut feeling that they are starting to crumble a little bit inside those dock gates. I think there is a bit of turmoil going on now, it's actually getting to them, and I feel that we're on the turning point and we've just got to stay where we are and "hold the line," and I think we'll get the result.' [28]*

One anonymous docker shared his belief that: 'It's the commitment of the men that is going to make us win. They might moan and groan down on the picket line, and it's only natural after 14 or 15 months, but you hear them here at the meeting, and if there's anything that comes out, they're very supportive of what the shop stewards say, so the men's commitment is still there and that's what's going to win it for us.' [29] Over the course of the interviews, *LabourNet* raised the question of the lack of support from other UK workers who could, in theory, have taken solidarity action, to which one docker replied that he would tell those people:

> *'…it's gonna be a victory for everybody. Because the conditions that they did actually impose upon us when we were in them gates are beginning to creep into other industries… We want physical support. We want people now to have the guts to come out and say, "What's happened to those Liverpool dockers is wrong," and any other workers that's been sacked as well. And get on board and say, "Well OK, we send containers to there. They're not going there." Drivers to have the balls to do what the French drivers done and say, "No, we're not going across a picket line." We want to get back to the days when workers supported workers, and that's the only way that workers are gonna win things.' [30]*

Another docker repeated the call for rank-and-file strike action, despite many on the left claiming that solidarity was never something that the stewards actively pursued: 'We should be striving for a national day of action. We should start with that foot in the door, a couple of hours [of] stop work, and then maybe a national day of action in all unions, and all industries. I mean, without sounding rebellious, that's what we need.' [31] As one of his comrades commented:

> 'Fear, economic fear. They're frightened because they know there's someone there to take their job… If everyone in that port had supported us, that strike wouldn't have lasted a couple of weeks. We are very confident that we'll get a result…' [32]

Jimmy, a docker with over 30 years' experience working in the port, made his feelings crystal clear: 'All I want is the lads who want to go back, to go back, because the likes of me, I don't want to go back. It suits me to retire. But the lads who want to go back, they've got to go back. If we split, that's it. Even the kids, they've got to go back.' [33] A docker referred to as Brian considered what an agreement could look like: 'The settlement of this dispute has got to involve everybody. Otherwise, we've been taking this action for 15 months for nothing. So, there's no way that a deal can be sorted without Torside, Nelson Freight and all the other parts. It's got to involve everybody.' [34] On a personal note, another docker added:

> 'I've been on the docks since the day I left school, and I've never been unemployed in my life until this dispute started, and we're talking 28 years. And I've enjoyed working on the docks, I've learnt a lot off a lot of fellas, I've learned to develop a lot of friendships with the people down there, and I don't think that I should be torn away from those docks over this dispute and the way we were set up. I know there's a living for me down on them docks, and I want to go back to it.' [35]

# 51

# The December 1996
# General Executive Council

*'We are not just fighting for ourselves, we are fighting for the next generation. We want decent standards of living and working conditions, and we think this is the only way we can get it.' ~ Marty Size\**

As the Broad Left meeting held before the union's General Executive Council gathered in London on Sunday 1 December 1996, a delegate from Region 1 spoke on behalf of the Liverpool dockers, explaining how, on average, £13 a week had been given to each docker over the course of their 14 month dispute. If the dockers had been receiving official strike pay for this period, the figure would be £700,000 short overall, and so he suggested that they needed to push the GEC to support a Christmas bonus for the dispute's Hardship Fund. [1] However, the main priority was still that the union should instruct the International Transport Workers' Federation to take part in a Day of World Action planned for 9 December. [2] When the GEC met the following day, they instead focussed on an inquiry into the Liverpool dock official and the need for the union to avoid any legal risks in supporting the dockers' campaign. During the Docks and Waterways Report, Carden raised the issue of police violence against the Liverpool dockers and their supporters at the anniversary demonstration on the 28 September 1996. Bill Morris responded by suggesting that: 'inviting Reclaim the Streets to be active participants was not productive; they are not going to take over the dispute. This will not give credit to the dockers. I did not say people caused violence, the actions they took will provoke a response.' [3]

In Barnsley, Jimmy Nolan accompanied Arthur Scargill to a meeting of the Socialist Labour Party to appeal for physical and financial support for the dockers' campaign, and on Tuesday 3 December, Bill Morris replied to a letter from Nolan (dated 29 November 1996),

---

\* Marty Size, sacked Liverpool docker, in an interview with Radio Merseyside (audio tape, April 1997)

in which he asked the General Secretary to attend a forthcoming dockers' rally. Morris's answer was as follows:

> *'As general secretary, I am, together with the General Executive Council, confining our activities to working for a negotiated settlement and to relieve the hardship being endured by the dockers and their families. To promote any other activity may leave the union vulnerable.'* [4]

In a second letter dated that same day, Morris refused Nolan's request for a meeting with both himself and the ITF leadership:

> *'I have explained to you on numerous occasions that it is not legally permissible for either the union or myself to promote action abroad for which we are constrained, by law, from supporting at home. Both myself and the GEC are obliged to operate within the framework of the law, by BDC policy and the rules of the union... the ITF... will continue to support the dockers' cause within the bounds of what is legally and practically possible.'* [5]

The views expressed in these letters explain the paralysis that cascaded down from Morris through his *cyphers* on the GEC and the union's *Broad Left* organisation. It flowed through every region of the TGWU to impose inactivity in response to the dock dispute. This disconnect extended to every other union, not just in the UK, but also throughout the international trade union movement. At the Tuesday morning session of the GEC, numerous documents pertaining to the Liverpool docks dispute were circulated. [6] Ken Brindle, Carden's fellow Territorial Representative for Region 6, raised an issue in response to Dave McCall's inquiry into Jack Dempsey, calling for the remits from the region to be disclosed to the GEC. Morris wanted the remits to be restricted to Region 6, not to be discussed at GEC level. Danny Maher, the GEC representative for Docks and Waterways, and leader of the Liverpool Tugboat men, echoed Ken Brindle's concerns, while stating that other issues will come out because relations on the docks had been worsening since 1989. [7] At this point in the meeting Morris informed the GEC:

> *'Dave McCall, had undertaken a detailed investigation that had been rejected by the Regional Committee. The GEC is the final arbiter, and we are acting totally within the constitution.'* [8]

Pat Oliver, another council member, informed the GEC that Region 2 had held an inquiry that was reported to the GEC and he expressed the opinion that if the GEC involve themselves in this case, 'we will regret it.' More importantly, he wanted to make it clear that the majority of the GEC should, regardless of their political leanings, be inclined to support their General Secretary because: 'this is about an employee of the union and based upon the *prima facie* evidence there is no case to answer.' [9] Morris then outlined the terms of the debate in case any members were unsure as to the decision that they were expected to take:

# THE DECEMBER 1996 GENERAL EXECUTIVE COUNCIL

*'The issue before the Council was not an inquiry into the dock strike; it is about the conduct of an officer... It's down to believing Bradley [the Torside Boss] or Dave McCall... I support this report and we seek endorsement for this.' [10]*

Carden and Maher each made lengthy contributions about the need for the matter to be dealt with by the GEC, citing the fact that McCall's report had been rejected at regional level, making it necessary for the GEC to examine the veracity of its findings. To this, Morris replied that he knew all along about the problems on the docks before the dockers were dismissed:

*'We are in the middle of a bitter and protracted dispute. Fourteen months on, it is not surprising that we have no clear ending in sight. It's a very messy dispute, and the whole problem on the docks had been discussed with me well before the dispute began... The GEC must endorse the report and leave the residual issues to himself and the executive officer of the union to look into the relationships with the officer.' [11]*

A vote was taken, and the elected lay-member representatives of the most senior committee of the union voted to support their general secretary by what could only be described as a crushing majority. The GEC voted 18 to 8 in favour of doing nothing beyond declaring their wish to end the conflict at any cost, again reiterating their long-held position that the Liverpool dockworkers were not to be supported. On 10 December, the Dispute Committee would respond to this decision in a letter addressed to Morris, in which Jimmy Nolan, as chairman, expressed his:

*'Total disbelief that a committee of our union, least of all the primary committee, our GEC, could reach a decision on serious allegations made against an officer of the union without even knowing the basis of those complaints... The GEC acted outside of the rules of our union. As a result of this, I inform you that we intend to prosecute the valid and genuine complaints of TGWU members through the rulebook of our union, the certification officer and the legal process. Such actions have been imposed by the disgraceful manner in which the constitution of our union has been abused to silence the concerns of the membership.' [12]*

The day after the vote in favour of McCall's report was another anti-climax, as it became obvious that as far as 18 GEC members were concerned, the dispute was over and all power to act had been, as usual, placed in the hands of the General Secretary. Perhaps the Liverpool docks dispute was over as soon as it had begun in the minds of those 18 members, for whom it must have been a meaningless distraction when Jack Adams gave an update on negotiations with the Mersey Docks and Harbour Company. [13] Adams disclosed that talks were being conducted through the Advisory, Conciliation and Arbitration Service, before confirming that he had upheld the original demands of Morris and the GEC for free and unfettered negotiations. [14] It was reported that the Dispute Committee had moved away from total reinstatement to maximising jobs, and that MDHC had:

*'Put us in a worse position… as the union cannot accept the clause that accepts the company's right to dismiss the dockers. They have withdrawn the [proposed] interim period because they believe the number of dockers they want to retain is so small.' [15]*

Finally, Adams stated that MDHC were adamant that Torside dockers would not be taken back, [16] and after the previous day's GEC vote, it made sense that the employer would not be in any rush to arrange meetings with a group of workers whose own union did not support them. Adams was followed by Graham Stevenson who said he was frustrated by MDHC's unwillingness to negotiate, and after repeating much of what Adams had already said, added that the Dock Company had again mentioned their customers' happiness with the work of Drake International. [17] Stevenson told the GEC: 'The union faces difficulty if illicit action is taken by the ITF. Colleagues in the ITF have been told that we are negotiating. The ITF are saying they are being told by the TGWU not to do anything. That's not true. We need to have a joint meeting with the ITF.' [18] Morris eventually intervened by imploring: 'Let us not attack each other or the ITF. They are doing more than I expected. They negotiated as a secretariat, so they, the ITF, do not have immunity.' [19] One of the Region 1 (London) GEC members was the London docker Colin Coughlin, a close comrade of Jimmy Nolan and the Liverpool stewards for many decades; he spoke of Dave McCall's inquiry into the dock official, the presumed illegality of the dispute and the fact that the real hardship experienced by the dockers was having a great impact, which necessitated the donation of a large sum to see them through the winter. [20] In direct response to Coughlin's contribution, Morris argued that:

*'What has been moved by Colin has not been agreed as executive officers on this remit. Magnet workers sacked since August 1996 – they are suffering; they have not got the tradition etc of the dockers. We have to look after all our members on strike. I have heard a lot about the union doing nothing. I have a list of hardship funds. We have repudiated the action in court when we have been challenged. They can take us on. We will recognise Christmas again for all members. All regions have been instructed to raise the financial support…' [21]*

On Friday following the GEC, Morris issued a press release to say that a new offer was to be made by MDHC, which, not for the first time, was reported by local radio and press without the Dispute Committee first being informed. Meanwhile, 200 miles away from the TGWU's London offices, on Tuesday 3 December, Jimmy Campbell and Joe 'Snowy' White were arrested on a picket line in Liverpool. On Sunday the 8 December, Decca Aitkenhead wrote a centre-feature in the *Independent on Sunday* titled, *Thirty Years That Shook the World*. This was a major retrospective of Ken Loach's work with the dockers, from *The Big Flame* (1967) to *The Flickering Flame* 30 years later. In an interview for the piece, Loach observed how: 'The fundamental pattern never changes. You start with the struggle against the employer, and then the union leadership who don't support you, and you end up fighting with the police.' [22] The underlying theme was that both films essentially told the same story, and for the dockers, it cemented the acclaimed filmmaker's status as a genuine comrade. Speaking about Loach, one of the former shop stewards was quoted as saying:

# THE DECEMBER 1996 GENERAL EXECUTIVE COUNCIL

*'He's going to help us, you see. He's going to send a message to other workers that if you get off your knees and fight, you can change things. The roots of the docks are so deep, they go down to the bowels of the Mersey. They don't pull up so easy, and this isn't my job to sell. I'm just a custodian of it, I've got two sons, and if, when they say to me, "What did you do about it?" I'm not able to say that we fought and we won, what is left? McDonald's jobs? Forget the money. It's not a job, it's a part of our life. It's a culture. We made it that way. We were always fighting the conditions, but we were happy. If you were in trouble, I was there with you. When we were on the docks, we backed the journalists when they went out, we backed the printers, the miners, the seamen. Now there are so-called trade union members driving past that picket on the dock. The boys have got to win this one. We fought for our sons and grandsons. They're fighting for theirs. If they don't win, everything we ever won is wiped out.' [23]*

Towards the end of *The Big Flame*, one of the key characters says of the 1967 strike: 'We've got to shift it from the industrial to the political. The Mersey dockers will have lit a bonfire that will be seen by the workers for miles.' [24] Ken Loach still believed that the bonfire could be rekindled in 1996. At the shop stewards' meeting held on Monday 9 December, a discussion took place on the invitation extended by Jean-Pierre Barrois to the Women of the Waterfront's Doreen McNally and Sue Mitchell, asking them to visit France and Germany. They had previously travelled to Paris and taken part in a march through the city from the Bastille, attended by coachloads of demonstrators from all across France. They returned with a large Hardship Fund donation arranged by Barrois. Sue and Doreen attended scores of meetings together during their delegation work, winning support from the French railway union, the CGT and many others. [25] In the wake of Dave McCall's report on the Liverpool dock official being rejected by the Region 6 Finance & General Purposes Committee the dockers were angry that it was accepted by the GEC without a shred of supporting evidence, documentation or information. This happened at the same time as Morris wrote a letter to the *Guardian*, effectively 'dumping' the Torside dockers. For the dockers there was no point in appealing the GEC's decision, some felt as though the only correct course of action was to seek legal advice. Jimmy Nolan wanted to complain about the TGWU to the trade union certification officer, in addition to exploring legal options, although he was still reluctant to pursue litigation against the union. [26] It was agreed that John Hendy QC and Louise Christian would be asked to advise on the matter.

The next meeting with Dock Company was scheduled to take place on Monday and some stewards felt that unless they could come up with some new ideas, an offer would be placed on the table and the union would push for another ballot. The situation had deteriorated greatly since the GEC voted so unanimously in support of Morris and MDHC. Carden suggested that they formally propose a dockers' co-operative as a means of getting ahead of whatever their opponents were planning. [27] Jimmy Nolan was due to travel to London on Wednesday 12 December, and Jack Adams would be heading up to Liverpool for a meeting with the stewards a day later. It was expected that Adams would not come bearing good news, which only added to the growing belief that they needed to take the initiative and lead the impending negotiations. [28] The deputy general secretary promised Nolan that he had had nothing to do with Morris's letter to the *Guardian*, and Nolan said that he would not be opposed to Adams's previously floated idea of a labour co-operative. [29] At a Dispute Committee meeting held that same day, Earl Gillman, a delegate from the American Social Workers' Union, sat in on the discussion. This was not unusual, as hardly a day passed without a visitor spending time among the stewards, and on this occasion, this American comrade spoke about his father, who was a checker on New York docks, and referenced his contacts in Mexico, Chile and on the US West Coast. After he had finished Terry Teague voiced his concern that Morris planned to force any Dock Company deal to go to another ballot. [30] Nolan replied by reassuring the group that they would simply walk out if such a thing was to happen. Carden again raised the co-operative idea, even if it was only to buy more time: 'If we go along this line, we have to make a public announcement well before Monday's talks. Cliff wanted us to be imaginative. He expressed doubts about how long Drakes would be in the port. This would be popular and imaginative.' [31] Frank Lannigan was not too keen on the idea, feeling it was 'pie in the sky,' especially since it meant competing with Drake International. [32] Jimmy Davies shared Laningan's scepticism, stating that he was: 'very unhappy about co-ops. If men talk about co-ops only for Torside, we will be casting Torside adrift. A Torside co-op would not last six months, and the Dock Company would starve us of ships, like they did in the Canada and Birkenhead berths.' [33]

A major debate was unfolding, centred around an expectation Monday's talks would focus solely on a ballot for MDHC dockworkers and a co-op for Torside. Tony Nelson believed that it would be tantamount to attempting to dump Torside, prompting Terry Teague to state emphatically that no steward would allow that to happen. [34] Carden reiterated that it was a co-operative for all dockers not just Torside. Jimmy Nolan was sure that MDHC would never accept a co-op anyway, as it would hand control of the port to the dockers, while reiterating that: 'Torside will never be part of any sell-out.' [35] By Friday 13 December, there was growing concern about the fact that the TGWU had not sent any financial support, which meant that hardship payments could not be issued that week, despite 6/541 Branch, comprised of local transport drivers, donating another huge sum. It had also recently been discovered that the dockers' pension fund had a £35m surplus, and everyone was aware that, 'obviously, the employers would want to get their hands on that surplus.' [36] At the mass meeting held later that day, Jimmy Davies informed the dockers about a book titled *Solidarity on the Waterfront*, which had recently been published. [37] Billy Jenkins and Tony Russell provided feedback on their meeting with Italian dockers in Genoa and Swiss workers in Zurich, with the room descending into laughter after Billy revealed that the Italian dockers came to them with two work permits, and how he'd told them, in his usual understated way, that they had better keep hold of them, 'as we may well need them.' [38] Russell then added to the sense of levity by demonstrating his amazing command of the Italian language, getting particularly positive reactions with the over-the-top accent and inflections that he used while pronouncing the names of the people they met. The pair had also been invited down to Naples, to speak with shipbuilders who themselves had been on strike for two years in response to the introduction of casual labour. Like the Liverpool dockers, they had been dismissed after going on strike, and they had since occupied their shipyard. [39] Collette Melia then delivered a report from the WOW, covering the work that they had been doing via meetings and delegations, before Jimmy Davies's financial report listed the latest support from across the globe, with donations arriving from Ford Dagenham, Waterford Crystal, the Fire Brigades' Union, Rolls Royce workers and the New Zealand Seafarers and Wharfies. This was followed by Earl Gillman speaking on the importance of international support.

Attention then turned to the following day's London demonstration, with seven coaches set to leave Liverpool at 7am. The event would feature speakers such as Jimmy Nolan, Irene Campbell, the Hillingdon workers, Magnet Southern, Glaziers in Scotland, John Pilger, Tony Benn MP and Jeremy Corbyn MP. Bill Morris had again refused to address a public meeting of trade unionists. The London Support Group (LSG) had only one month to organise the demonstration, for which they took out an advert in the *Guardian* and contacted as many MPs, trades unions and high-profiled names as possible. Meanwhile, according to Chris Knight, he, along with two other members of the LSG, Kevin and Jackie, had the unenviable task of negotiating a route with the police, with Oxford Street and Charing Cross Road being their preference, and going from Hyde Park to Red Lion Square, via Piccadilly Circus and Shaftesbury Avenue, an acceptable second choice. They would end up going with option two, marching right through the heart of London, on a route that no demonstration had ever taken before. The LSG worked tirelessly to organise mailing and fly-posting campaigns to raise awareness ahead of the demonstration, and Knight was later to note that:

> *This was probably the most enjoyable demo and rally I have ever been on. The Dragon, puffing smoke and dancing in the street, with the dockers' children surrounding it, led the march. I'll not forget seeing amazed tourists' faces as the demo went around corners, and Mike Carden's nine-year-old son [Dan] at the front with a megaphone shouting, "I'd rather be a picket than a scab!"' [40]*

Both the demonstration and the subsequent rally at Conway Hall were a tremendous success. When John Pilger spoke, he was greeted with cries of, 'Pilger! Pilger! Pilger!' [41] after his article, *Today's Marching Orders*, was printed to coincide with the demonstration in that morning's *Guardian*. John Pilger implored readers to support the dockers' campaign by joining the march:

> *The Liverpool dockers march through London today. After 14 months, the dockers' dispute is now longer than the miners' strike of 1984… Bill Morris, the general secretary, told the TUC conference in September that he would 'die for the dockers.' Dockers' wives, who were prevented from speaking, replied, 'Don't die, just support us.' …the ITF may be shedding its caution as key members privately favour an unprecedented shutdown of major world ports that would express, according to one of them, 'an international labour solidarity like no other struggle in recent maritime history.' [42]*

Pilger had always been impressed by the Liverpool dockers' internationalism, and he referred to an open letter that the ITF received from one of its American inspectors, Jack Heyman, in which it was declared that a victory for the dockers: 'would offer an alternative to the defeatist strategy of the British trade union establishment that has so far lost every port save

Liverpool, much to the dismay of maritime workers around the globe... This aristocracy of labour, while bemoaning draconian Thatcherite anti-labour laws which their darling Tony Blair has vowed to uphold if elected!' Heyman, who resigned from the ITF in October, reminded the international union that it was, 'launched in 1896, when British seamen sailing into strikebound ports in Holland joined striking Dutch dockers. They didn't fax their union for official authorisation or check to verify if it was legal. They just did it.' [43] Pilger noted:

> 'It is too early to judge if the dockers' campaign signals the beginning of a wider resistance to the anti-union onslaughts of the 1980s and the obedience of the union bureaucracies...
> By their action, the dockers bring into sharp focus the iniquities of casual and part-time working which today impoverish not only the docks but the service industries, manufacturing, even the professions and the media. They also demonstrate that a small number of unofficial, isolated workers can ignite an internationalism that is said to have died with the so-called end of history. [44]

On 19 December, Bill Morris wrote to the *Guardian's* editor, Alan Rusbridger, refuting the main thrust of Pilger's article. [45] Morris's letter of complaint was sent the day after *The Flickering Flame*, Ken Loach's film on the docks dispute, was shown on BBC television at 9pm prime time. Unlike the TGWU's 1996 General Executive Council meeting, Loach's work would have a dramatic impact on the Liverpool dockers' campaign.

# 52

# Negotiations Resume

*The IDC was founded after the 500 Liverpool dockers were sacked in the 90s. The IDC motto is: "You will never walk alone again". Dock workers at the Port of Liverpool wanted to show our solidarity [with Black Lives Matter]. In recent years we have built up powerful workplace organisation and the membership have taken unofficial action when necessary.' ~ John Lynch\**

On the afternoon of Monday 16 December, the dockers negotiating committee met with Jack Adams and Graham Stevenson at the Salford offices of ACAS. Adams and Bill Morris had been speaking with the Dock Company's Peter Jones and Trevor Furlong, who claimed they would accept a one-month or three-month interim period of fixed-term reinstatement. MDHC was in the process of finding out if their proposed £25,000 redundancy lump sum would be subject to income tax. This would not be the case in the event of full reinstatement. They would not include the Torside dockers in any settlement, but they were prepared to assist them in creating a co-operative labour supply company if enough supplementary cash could be raised. [1] Jimmy Nolan attacked Morris for attempting to create separation among the dockers, repeatedly telling Adams that: 'We will not isolate Torside from ourselves.' [2] MDHC based the projected cost of ending the dispute at £8m to dismiss their 329 dockers, plus £1m to dismiss 41 ancillary workers and a further £2m to cover a one-month interim period of employment. [3] At 2.40pm, Trevor Furlong, Peter Jones and Allan Price joined the meeting; with the loss of Bernard Cliff, Jones was now the company's lead negotiator.

Adams sought to clarify the basis of this offer of 're-employment,' particularly in relation to individuals that were pursuing tribunals, as well as the situation with Torside and various other small companies involved in the dispute, such as Liverpool Cargo Handling. [4]

---

\* Liverpool Dockers BLM solidarity, reported in: 'Anti-Racism and Re-Building Union Strength' by Raymond Morell, Conter, 17 June 2020, available: https://www.conter.co.uk/blog/2020/6/17/anti-racism-and-re-building-union-strength

Jones replied that these companies were not the concern of the Dock Company. [5] Adams again raised the co-operative issue, to which Furlong said that MDHC would: 'help with administration and advising customers to use the co-operative. If price and productivity are right, no reason exists as to why it should not be a success.' [6] Nolan clarified that the pension was: 'simply a question of dockers re-joining the scheme, which should not be a problem.' [7] At 3pm, an adjournment was called, and a lengthy discussion took place among the stewards and TGWU officers. The stewards wanted to:

> '...explore the possibility of getting rid of Drakes. The economics are £8m plus £2m etc. We should examine the labour supply company covering the whole of the port. Morris will want a postal ballot, and this offer gives nothing more to Torside but the sack, and for MDHC dockers, the sack after three months of re-employment, which was purely a mechanism for dismissal again as the dockers would not be physically re-employed on the docks.' [8]

Adams appeared reluctant to challenge MDHC over Drake International, while Nolan did not seem to want to pursue negotiations further, as the conversation turned to tactics, and the question of whether or not they should walk away rather than allow Morris to demand a postal ballot on the offer. Adams saw this as little more than posturing as MDHC would clearly not concede on Drakes. Upon reconvening, the company kept their options open in relation to how many jobs could evolve following a settlement, [9] and within five minutes another adjournment was called. Talks restarted 40 minutes later, with Jones producing a new paper demanding a ballot, adding that the offer would be permanently withdrawn if this was rejected. The stewards assessed the detail of the fresh offer, if only as a token gesture, as Jones warned that a ballot had to be held by the end of the month. There was another adjournment when Furlong received a phone call from Brian Wilson, MDHC's pension fund manager, informing him that Tony Nelson was no longer a trustee of the Weekly Staff Pension Fund, [10] having been removed from office without any prior discussion, following a decision made by *working* Dock Company employees sitting on the Board of Trustees.

Once the meeting had resumed, Adams argued for the 12-week redundancy period to be made applicable to all dockworkers employed but, during the next adjournment, he told the stewards that he was, 'not prepared to recommend this paper. Morris will recommend a postal ballot.' [11] At 8pm, MDHC submitted a third document for the stewards to examine, which led to an exasperated Adams advising that: 'We are wasting breath and time on Torside; he ain't gonna take this on. Morris is meeting national officers in a hotel in London now.' [12] Adams then asked Jimmy Nolan if he intended to report back to the membership, to which Nolan answered: 'Everything will be reported back, and I am positive the men will reject this.' [13]

Adams reminded the stewards that everything they had been offered was conditional on a postal ballot, but Nolan was adamant that, 'We will have no more postal ballots,' [14] despite Adams repeating that this would result in the offer being withdrawn. [15] Nolan was unmoved, stating that he knew: 'exactly what this was all about, and the mechanics of a ballot will go beyond two weeks. If this is rejected, what is Bill going to do? He will obviously go for a secret postal ballot.' [16] Adams challenged this line of argument insisting that, 'I don't think, for one minute, Bill will organise a ballot above your heads. If the men say: "Fuck off," he will say he has exhausted every avenue.' [17] At this point, Nolan declared that as chairman of the dockers he would ultimately act upon whatever the majority of stewards decided. [18] Adams outlined how the paper would be reported back to the dockers, stressing that Torside and Nelson Freight remained a problem. Furlong added that he would still like everything to be completed by 31 December: 'because that is important to us.' [19] The following day, the *Liverpool Daily Post* printed MDHC's final offer on its front page, as the Dispute Committee rejected the employer's proposals. According to one steward, 'The deal had been cut before the meeting. It was a surgical exercise to buy-out the dispute.' [20]

# 53

# The 20<sup>th</sup> December Mass Meeting and the Third Offer

*'In the 1990s Jeremy Corbyn came to Liverpool to speak up for the 500 dockers who refused to cross a picket line. Today I got to show him and his wife Laura our exhibition of Dave Sinclair's photographs from the 1995–97 Liverpool dockers' dispute, which is on display in my constituency office thanks to the brilliant Dead Pigeon Gallery. Thank you Jeremy for your solidarity.' ~ Dan Carden MP\**

On Friday the 20 December 1996, the atmosphere amongst the stewards was tense. [1] Jimmy Nolan wanted to hold two votes; one to reject a postal ballot and another to reject the offer. That day's mass meeting was bound to be a stormy affair, with the men ready to take full advantage of two key Transport and General Workers' Union officials, Jack Adams and Dave McCall, scheduled to be in attendance. Nolan, in his usual way, stressed the need for a disciplined debate. The report from the early morning picket line was that while the men were divided, the majority were in favour of rejecting the latest offer from the company. [2] Jimmy Davies opened the meeting with his weekly financial report, reading out the various Hardship Fund donations received from individuals and unions, and then concluding with his own analysis of the campaign, in what was described as, 'an excellent and moving speech, centred upon a dignified settlement for all dockers. He received a standing ovation.' [3] Bobby Morton then gave a detailed report on the negotiations with MDHC, [4] reiterating that there could be no acceptance of any negotiated settlement that did not involve every single man that refused to cross the picket line.

Nolan then invited Dave McCall to speak; he wished to make it clear that on the matter of speaking to Bernard Bradley: 'We wanted to leave no stone unturned. Bernard

\* Dan Carden MP, post to Facebook page, available: https://hi-in.facebook.com/DanCardenMP/posts/in-the-1990s-jeremy-corbyn-came-to-liverpool-to-speak-up-for-the-500-dockers-who/1584903208365770/

Bradley is no longer involved in the docks, James Bradley, his son, is now in charge, but nothing has developed from Torside.' [5] One of the dockers, Jimmy Campbell, took the opportunity to ask about the pension fund surplus, and whether or not it could be seized by MDHC and used to finance a severance deal. [6] Kevin Bilsborrow, who despite being a member of the Dispute Committee always sat with the men, made an extraordinarily emotional and political speech; one that stripped away all complexities of language and laid bare a message that was easy to comprehend. He spoke with a brutal integrity and clarity; his words made all the more impactful by the fact that he rarely spoke at mass meetings, as he told his fellow dockworkers:

> '...you will never ever get anything off this Dock Company because we're gonna have to fight for it, no matter how hard it is and how soul-destroying, but you're gonna have to fight for it because they are the dirtiest, low-down scum that's every walked the face of this earth, or crawled on the face of this earth. You know the way they treated the men in this hall. I look around me, [and] I regard myself as the head of the family, you know for the people I'm responsible for, and there is no way I'm gonna help them grow up by signing-on for the Jobs Seeker's Allowance, 'cause that's what I'm on now. How am I gonna help my kids when I'm receiving £45 a week, because that's what we all do? I know there's grandads in 'ere who support their grandkids, I know it. The lads and daughters have got no jobs, they've got kids and they support their grandkids through education... And the people my heart goes out to are the older men. I think the most fantastic people; I'm proud to be with them. I'm just asking them as a fellow docker, I want my job back. I'm asking the older lads to stick by us. I'm in no two minds, boys, you'll live forever when we win this dispute; you'll live forever! Davies was right when he said, "We are an inch away from victory." If we win this, we will live forever.' [7]

It was a formidable speech, as evidenced by the applause it elicited, and while many dockers did take the opportunity to attack the TGWU in the presence of two of its senior officials, Terry Barrett made a forceful argument that ended with a message for Jack Adams to deliver to Bill Morris: 'Is he a trade unionist anymore, or is he a bureaucrat?' [8] After this contribution, in addition to other questions about Bradley and Torside, McCall once again stepped up to the microphone:

> 'At this stage, I know that he [Bradley] has ceased trading. I know he is going into the estate [on the docks], but there is no trading going on through Torside.' [9]

From the floor, Frank Carberry spoke about the two Gig Boatmen and the sacrifices that they and everyone else had made, as he stressed the importance of not selling anyone out. [10] Sitting near to Carberry was Marty Size, who stood up to tell the men that after Thursday's picket line, he was asked to go and do collections locally but he was somewhat hesitant to do it because of all the offers and talk of severance money, as he wondered if people would now be less interested in the dockers' cause:

*'After that programme last night [referring to Ken Loach's Flickering Flame], they were amazed. One half didn't know nothing about it, and they were amazed at that programme. My sister said to me at the beginning of this strike, "I don't know what you're goin' down there for; you wanna take the money and get out of it." Now, after she's seen all of these programmes and read all the comments by Pilger and everybody, she's saying to me now, "You've been out this long, you wanna stick at it and get everything you've asked for."' [11]*

Jimmy Nolan then asked Jack Adams to respond. Adams spoke softly and slowly in his strong, matter-of-fact Birmingham accent. Nobody doubted his sincerity as he told the dockers:

*'I've been involved in this dispute right from day one. I've not moved an inch from the wishes of the leadership of this dispute. I've tried to broker three deals; each one of them has got worse in terms of jobs. Your leadership have known every single phone call I have had, and this has been reflected back to the stewards, and I've been proud to be associated with this dispute… If you're asking me whether our union will get off the fence and defy the law, and instruct our affiliated international ITF and so on, then I don't believe we will. That's the truth of the matter, and I've got no intention of trying to mislead you on that.' [11]*

Adams concluded that this dispute had always been a struggle of power; of who would exercise the most influence: 'You'll take the decision. We'll report back to our General Secretary and the GEC, because they control us and don't expect us, who spend our lives in the movement, to start ignoring them. So, I'm sorry we've not been able to produce what you're all looking for on this occasion, but I just say that I hope the movement responds to you for Christmas, and at least we have a Christmas that you can still be proud of.' [12] This prompted Jimmy Davies to remind the dockers that:

*'The union has put a big amount of money into us this week, in order that we can facilitate what we can do for you today. So, they have been very generous in regard to what we have had off them before. We appreciate it, Jack. We have been critical of the union, but I do believe personally that the union are still behind us, and they are still supporting us in whatever way they can do it, and that amount of money has shown that to me to be perfectly honest. I was quite pleased when we got that message about that money coming in, because we wanted to make that Christmas the best as we could for you, and it's only through the efforts of the union that we are capable of doing that.' [13]*

Nolan thanked both officials for the support they had given to the campaign, before recommending that the dockers reject MDHC's latest offer, with only 15 voting to accept, and six being in favour of a postal ballot.

The Christmas holiday was a short one for the Liverpool dockers, and they were back on the picket lines at 6am on Monday 30 December. Transport House opened for the stewards and when they returned from the line Tony Nelson informed his fellow stewards that the police wanted to know why the dockers were not balloting. Malcolm Thornton, a local Conservative MP, had been voicing the complaints of local residents who were unhappy about the noise caused by the demonstrators on the Dock Road, while total policing costs were now estimated at around £2m. [14] On the Day of World Action scheduled for 20 January 1997 Japanese dockers in 50 ports were planning to support the Liverpool dockers, while in the US, the fact that it was also Martin Luther King Day guaranteed action. But inside the International Longshore and Warehouse Union, some 'locals' (union branches) were looking to challenge the leadership of their president, Brian McWilliam. According to Jack Heyman, attacks against McWilliam were believed to be more political than issue-based: 'Brian was an internationalist, which is why he approved of me going to Liverpool in the first place. He was the last socialist president of the ILWU.' [15] In Sweden and Denmark dockers joined the day of action although in Cyprus, Spain, Belgium, the Netherlands and Germany arrangements were yet to made. Italian dockers in Genoa had written to Bill Morris, condemning MDHC's latest offer and calling on the TGWU to embrace international support, at a time when the threat of deregulation and privatisation loomed in both Belgium and Japan. Michel Murray, leader of the Montreal dockers, was organising support as a letter, co-signed by Kees Marges and David Cockcroft, of the International Transport Workers' Federation, told their affiliates that:

> *The ITF wishes to reconfirm its support for the striking Liverpool dockworkers. Though the striking dockers' trade union, the UK ITF-affiliated TGWU has not been able to make the dispute official due to British anti-trade union legislation, the position of the ITF remains... It encourages its affiliated organisations to undertake all possible legal trade union strategies to put pressure on the Mersey Docks and Harbour Company, and on shipping firms carrying cargoes that have been loaded by strike-breakers in Liverpool.'* [16]

Elsewhere, Jimmy Nolan wanted to call a National Support Group meeting to try and spark a much-needed boost in support, and debate took place among the Dispute Committee about what was to be done if Morris sent out ballot papers again. Nolan now seemed more comfortable with the idea of openly opposing the TGWU, and it was decided that since the dockers had already rejected a ballot, the stewards would ask that any voting papers be brought to Transport House. However, there was also talk that the wife of a sacked dockworker was attempting to form a pressure group in support of a ballot, and that she and her supporters were threatening to boycott the picket lines if the stewards blocked Morris's efforts. Terry Teague acknowledged that: 'We cannot simply ignore a ballot. Some dockers will send them in, and if the union accepts a simple majority, of those voting, then this will be damaging.' [17]

The dockers' leaders were conscious of the need to sustain unity throughout their struggle, and they had already resolved to wait for Morris to act first. The General Secretary had recently written to the dockers confirming that Jack Adams had informed him of their rejection of MDHC's offer stating that he would be contacting the employer with regard to the impracticability of their 31 December deadline for a ballot. Put simply, the TGWU could not organise a ballot over the Christmas period (Morris's letter to MDHC was dated 23

December). This meeting of the stewards came one week after they had been delighted to be able to sanction increased hardship payments to the dockers' families as Jimmy Davies suggested that the men receive another payment before Christmas. The financial response to the dockers' struggle had been extraordinary, owing much to the impact of Ken Loach's film and John Pilger's article in the *Guardian*. [18] At 5pm on 31 December, Bill Morris gave an exclusive interview to BBC Radio Merseyside, in which he announced: 'An agreement exists for a postal ballot, and I am appealing for an extension of the Mersey Docks' deadline. Certain points need clarifying, and the ballot should involve all dockers.' [19] The fact that he would make such a statement on New Year's Eve displayed a lack of empathy that caused one steward to remark that, 'We now need to open up our conflict with the union, that has existed since September 1995.' [20] Morris had also been busy seeking legal advice concerning Ken Loach's film, *The Flickering Flame*. [21]

On 2 January 1997, the first 10am picket line of the new year was well supported. That day Jimmy Nolan tried to get in touch with Morris to express his concern about his Radio Merseyside interview. At Friday's mass meeting, Jimmy Davies reported that the wife of Lew Lloyd, a former TGWU dock official, had joined the actor Ricky Tomlinson, along with many others, in making personal donations to the Hardship Fund. Terry Teague gave an update on the international campaign ahead of the Day of World Action. Mike Carden provided his usual summary on events to date, which on this occasion included comments on the impending postal ballot, its rules and the inherent problems of simply thinking you could ignore the imposition of a postal ballot. The reality was that the dockers could not stop a postal ballot being *posted through their doors* by Morris and the Dock Company. Carden reminded the dockers that the ballot held in June 1996 had rejected MDHC's offer by 84%, and that while the company had spent millions attempting to defeat them, no litigation had been brought against the TGWU, the dockers or their leadership. In effect, there was no good reason for Morris to do nothing beyond declaring, 'I support the Liverpool dockers. Ours is a fight for justice.' [22]

From the floor, Tony Delahunty appealed for unity when it came time to cast their votes on the latest offer, while Terry Wood suggested that the men return their ballot papers to the stewards unopened. Mick Cullen then reiterated the fact that they had been sacked to make way for the total casualisation of the Port of Liverpool. [23] Frank Lannigan articulated the dilemma now facing the Dispute Committee: 'We can't simply ask men to bring ballot papers in and then refuse to vote. The Electoral Reform Society will simply declare a result on the ballot papers cast. Yes, we can have a ballot if Morris makes the dispute official when the paper is rejected.' [24] Nolan eventually got hold of Jack Adams, who insisted that he should speak to the General Secretary himself about the postal ballot being impracticable. [25] Officially, Morris was on holiday until the 8 January, but this did not prevent him from writing to all GEC members condemning the Liverpool dockers for threatening legal action over the outcome of the disciplinary inquiry into their local dock official. [26] On the 6 January, the *Liverpool Echo* ran a story on the TGWU wishing to impose a ballot, which several shop stewards fully expected to see finalised at that Thursday's national F&GP meeting. Later that same night, Bobby Morton was on Radio Merseyside with local Labour MP Peter Kilfoyle, discussing the issue of a secret postal ballot. [27] After the interview, Jack Adams telephoned Morton and informed him that, 'Morris will dump the dockers at the [F&GP].' [28]

In the wake of Morris's public statement, picket numbers were beginning to dwindle, with falling numbers from both Torside and, more alarmingly, Dock Company dockers. The shop stewards became so concerned that they again floated the idea of incentivising picket attendance by adding bonus payments to hardship entitlements, but Jimmy Davies pointed out that: 'We could not sustain this.' [29] On Wednesday the 8 January, Morris met with Adams and McCall, where surprisingly he agreed not to call a postal ballot. [30] Elsewhere, plans were being made for a dockers' National Support Group meeting as news came through that ILWU Local 13, which covered some 2,000 dockers in Los Angeles, California – the third largest port in the world – was expected to participate in the Day of World Action. [31] On the 10 January, Nolan briefed the stewards following a conversation about the ITF with Graham Stevenson. Stevenson had mentioned the previously proposed formation of a labour supply company, which Nolan remained open to exploring, and at the weekly mass meeting held later that morning, Peter Hendrickson of the Alaska ILWU offered fraternal greetings, while Jimmy Davies reported that financial support was continuing to grow in response to *The Flickering Flame*. Staff at Ken Loach's production company, Parallax Pictures, were the latest to make a large donation to the Hardship Fund, but this was not enough to lift a particularly subdued atmosphere amongst many dockers and their families. [32]

The following day, Saturday 11 January, more than 50 delegates from various dockers' support groups attended a mass meeting at Transport House, Liverpool, as Terry Teague gave a detailed breakdown of confirmed international support in the run-up to the Day of World action planned for 20 January. He also called on industrial workers across the UK to boycott cargo from Liverpool. [33] An open discussion took place covering all aspects of the dispute, from how Morris could potentially impose a ballot to the failure to generate meaningful solidarity in their own city. Guest speaker Jane Lofthouse, of the Communication Workers Union, talked about her union's annual conference, to be held the following week, which would provide opportunities for boycotting postal services and organising a mass picket of the docks. Ken Brindle, the GEC representative for Region 6, then informed the dockers that a special meeting of the GEC had been called for 20 January. UNISON's Nigel Flannigan spoke of the:

> *'Change in the nature of the dispute. Practical action and support for the dockers is needed, and the dockers should attend plant meetings. A whole range of services from electricity, telephone, gas and water should be stopped. A virtual picket should be mounted against the MDHC… the need is for the dockers to picket other workplaces in the area.' [34]*

John Cooper, from Vauxhall Motors, asked what Bill Morris was doing about the situation, to which Jimmy Nolan responded at great length. Tony Woodhouse from the 6/541 Road Haulage Branch, himself a future president of the TGWU, asked how the union could, 'impose an official union-employer ballot on an unofficial strike?' [35] This encouraged Ken Brindle to say: 'We should run the union, but the lay membership are weak.' [36] *LabourNet's* Greg Dropkin wanted to look at services provided to MDHC by other, non-docker trade union members. Mike Carden then explained how Morris and the GEC were the largest obstacles facing the dockers. Peter Moore, a convenor at Ford, spoke of a meeting where his employers had outlined their future plans for job losses. The session concluded with Ritchie Hunter, son of local socialist and historian Bill Hunter, talking about the need to make it clear that the problems faced by the Liverpool dockers today would soon be – and in some cases already were being – shared by workers worldwide, reinforcing the notion that this had always been an international dispute. [37] TGWU shop stewards were particularly keen to examine the handling of the dispute by their own union, and they were also concerned by the extraordinarily divisive prospect of their leadership forcing another official ballot in an unofficial dispute. They were urged to put their views in writing to Bill Morris, before the meeting concluded with a unanimous vote being taken:

> 'To confirm our determination to impose a physical boycott upon any raw materials or products shipped through the Port of Liverpool to our workplaces, and on services supplied to the Mersey Docks and Harbour Company...' [38]

Sadly, little direct action emanated from this resolution.

# 54
# A Day of World Action

*'If I had not become a professor, my next choice probably would have been to become a dock worker or warehouse worker in order to be a member of the most radical union in the country: the ILWU. You represent the potential and power of the labor movement. Hopefully, this action will influence other unions to stand up and say no to racism. And yes to abolishing the police as we know them.' ~ Angela Davis\**

On Monday the 13 January 1997, Jimmy Nolan and Bobby Morton attended a meeting of the International Transport Workers' Federation in London. Cockcroft and Marges reaffirmed their support for the Liverpool dockers by endorsing the forthcoming Day of World Action. The ITF cited information printed in *Lloyd's List* regarding the extent of global solidarity action that the Liverpool dockers had inspired [1] as these senior officials of the ITF listed the various issues that existed between themselves and non-ITF affiliated unions. Cockcroft and Marges wanted to push the international action scheduled for the 20 January beyond the proposed 24-hour period. [2] The Liverpool dockers' believed that this dramatic change of position stemmed from the creation of a mass movement involving powerful and influential North American unions, the International Longshore and Warehouse Union and the International Longshoremen's Association, as well as Japanese dockworkers. Mersey Docks were still pursuing damages against ILA President John Bowers through the US courts. [3]

Elsewhere, Volkswagen-Audi were facing a possible industrial dispute with haulage drivers in the UK after awarding a contract to ECM, the only car delivery firm still crossing dockers' picket lines in Liverpool. TGWU drivers who had respected the picket lines were set to see job losses once the contract began on the 16 February, and they were now appealing to VW-Audi trade unionists to raise the matter with their management in Germany. Many

---

\* Angela Davis, 'The whole world is watching Oakland: The Juneteenth protest and port shutdown' by Amanda Bartlett, 19 June 2020, available: https://www.sfgate.com/news/slideshow/Oakland-Juneteenth-Protest-204147.php

delivery firms had rearranged contracts in order to steer clear of Liverpool since September 1995 and Axial drivers had respected dockers' picket lines in Sheerness following MDHC purchase of Medway Ports. In October 1996, the Axial men were told that their refusal to cross picket lines was putting them in danger of losing the VW-Audi contract, and by December, much of their work had been switched to ECM. It was expected that the links forged between the TGWU car transporter section and IG Metall workers would continue, as further meetings were arranged, and if a satisfactory settlement of the problems faced by car transporters in Sheerness was not reached this would lead to another official strike from which the Liverpool dockers would instigate solidarity action on behalf of their fellow TGWU members. [4]

The seeds of unity between the dockers and their German comrades had already been sown in the spring of 1996, when Blue Monday, a Germany political group, invited the Liverpool dockers to travel to Germany and attend the ÖTV congress held the previous October. [5] When Herbie Hollerhead and Terry Southers visited Germany in August 1996, their main base of support came from IG Medien. This was a general union for media workers, whose membership donated money and arranged meeting venues. The dockers did manage to visit the Works Council at *Eurokai* (Euro Quay), which had strong links to the ÖTV leadership. The head of the organisation eventually promised to take limited action against Cast and Can-Mar, but then in front of a large mass meeting, he also said that 'outsiders' were trying to push for action that may have harmful effects on the Hamburg dockers. When the Day of World Action happened on 20 January, Blue Monday leafletted union branches and organised a gate meeting of 50 people outside *Eurokai*, where a banner reading 'Support the Liverpool Dockers; Stop the ships going to Liverpool' hung from the bridge while Blue Monday picketed the workforce. Five days later ACL's *Atlantic Conveyor* was held up for two hours in Bremerhaven after the ÖTV called 60 dockers into the canteen to discuss the Liverpool dispute, having already issued a port bulletin. Many solidarity messages for the dockers, along with damning letters to MDHC, were sent out through ÖTV branches and Social Democratic Party structures, and while Blue Monday did not claim credit for the Bremerhaven stoppage, they did point out that the ITF had a base in nearby Bremen, and it was likely that at the very least, their rank-and-file efforts were instrumental in helping to awaken the ÖTV in the run up to their congress. [6]

In the Belgian port of Antwerp, dockers had already started to answer the latest call to action by imposing a seven-hour boycott on ACL's *Atlantic Compass*, reflecting the ITF's recent change of position. Liverpool dockers had made four trips to Antwerp and it had been a film location for *The Flickering Flame*. This represented the first instance of industrial solidarity by Belgian dockers and their union, the BTB, since September 1995; it did help that Bob Baete, the leader of the BTB, was a great admirer of Ken Loach's work. Antwerp had held its own strike against privatisation on the 9 December 1996, and further demonstrations were planned across Belgium, beginning with a picket outside the British Embassy in Brussels, to coincide with the Day of World Action. Dutch dockers in Rotterdam were also expected to take industrial action the following week, while in Montreal, the *Syndicat des Debardeurs* held a mass meeting of longshoremen, and dockworkers in the Canadian Port of St John implemented a stoppage. In New Zealand, the Port of Auckland would be reduced to a skeleton crew, as workers exercised their right to a 'picnic day,' and on Sydney Harbour, the

Maritime Union of Australia was targeting ZIM, who also faced action by the Federation of Transport, Petrol and Agricultural Workers in Cyprus.

Writing in the *San Francisco Chronicle* on Thursday 16 January 1997, Ilana De Bare covered the West Coast longshoremen's action in support of the Liverpool dockers. 'Members of the International Longshoremen and Warehouse Union planned to halt work for the day at the biggest West Coast ports, including Seattle, Portland, Oakland, San Francisco, Los Angeles and Long Beach.' [7] Meanwhile, George Romero, president of ILWU Local 10, which represented more than 850 Bay Area longshoremen, declared: 'The Liverpool fight is part of a worldwide trend of [port] privatisation that has also happened in Mexico and New Zealand. We think the Liverpool workers are getting very bad treatment, and we are going to do everything we can to support them.' [8] Shipping industry officials said that the work stoppage would delay the loading and unloading of as many as 50 ships up and down the West Coast, with officials at the Port of Oakland, which handled an average of five ships a day, estimating that it could cost shipowners an extra $3,000 or $4,000 in docking and crew costs for each hour their vessels sat idle. 'Our members will have to employ additional longshoremen to work extra shifts [on Tuesday] to complete the loading as planned. Plus, we anticipate some delays in shipping because of this,' said Terry Lane, vice president of the Pacific Maritime Association, a group of 100 shipping firms that hired longshoremen to load and unload their goods. Lane also stated that shippers in the Los Angeles area had asked an arbitrator to rule on the legality of the planned work stoppage: 'This type of coordinated effort up and down the coast is very unusual. The last time was 1985, when the issue was the discipline of some longshoremen in Seattle. This is the first one I can recall that seems to come out of an international issue.' [9] Jack Heyman, steward for ILWU Local 10 said: 'The reason why Liverpool has struck a chord with longshoreman around the world is that we are all facing the same threat. They're trying to privatise the docks, casualise the workforce and break the unions.' [10]

With the support of the ITF many unions would target Liverpool trading vessels on the Day of World Action, while others planned to raise awareness through public demonstrations. The list of participants was impressive, reaching countries as far as Australia and Japan, while in Belgium, the *Belgische Transportarbeidersbond* and the Christian Transport and Diamond Workers' Union both publicly expressed their sympathy, having already instigated a stoppage on the Atlantic Container Line's *Atlantic Compass* ahead of action over a wage dispute planned for the following week. In Cyprus, the Federation of Transport, Petroleum and Agricultural Workers declared their solidarity with the Liverpool dockers and in Denmark, meetings were to be organised by the general workers' union (SiD) in Aarhus, Copenhagen and Odense. In France, the *Force Ouvriere* and *Federation de l'Equipement, des Transports et des Services* declared their support for the Day of World Action, using a press statement to appeal for support from all French workers. This led to an OOCL vessel being delayed in Le Havre on the evening of the 19 January, before those same dockers attended a rally in Paris that attracted some 1500 supporters. In Marseille, a demonstration in support of the Liverpool cause took place outside the British Consulate, while in Italy, a rally and stop-work meeting was organised by the Genoa dockworkers' section of FILT-CGIL. In the Netherlands, the *Vervoersbond FNV* transport workers' union showed their solidarity by dedicating the week of the 20-25 January to demonstrations.

Across the Atlantic, support was being organised by the Canadian International Longshoremen's Association in the port of St John, and further actions in other Canadian ports were also under consideration. In the US, actions were arranged in most West Coast ports by the ILWU. CNN San Francisco ran videotape of the previous February's international mass picket of Seaforth as part of a news item on the Day of World Action. In Liverpool, eight dockers and seven environmentalists occupied three cranes at the Seaforth Grain Terminal for 27 hours, delaying the *M.V. Lake Erie* by a total of 35 hours. Upon their eventual descent from the cranes, most of the activists were arrested and charged with aggravated trespass, with trials being set for mid-February. Elsewhere, the ILA was organising a major demonstration outside the British Embassy in Washington, DC, as unconfirmed rumours emerged of possible action against Liverpool trading vessels in New York and across several German ports. [11] On Sunday the 19 January, the Dispute Committee contacted Michel Murray, the Montreal dockers' leader, after 1,000 dockers had met in the city that Saturday and agreed to support the Day of World Action, resulting in the respective offices of both Cast and Can-Mar being occupied. The managing director of Can-Mar responded by fleeing his office, while at three container terminals, health and safety rules were strictly applied by the *Syndicat des Debardeurs*, revealing how all manner of equipment was in need of maintenance, which meant delays for Cast's *Elk* and Can-Mar's *Spirit*. By this time, the Montreal longshoremen had established their own French-English website, which linked up with the *Liverpool Lockout* site to provide up-to-date reports on the action.

In Australia, the *M.V. Zim Australia* was diverted from Sydney Harbour in the same week that the *Zim Sydney* faced disruptions in Sydney and Melbourne. The Israeli-owned Zim Line shipped to Liverpool, and the company's Australian offices had written to their counterparts across the world regarding the boycott. In New Zealand, seafarers picketed the three major container terminals in Auckland, Wellington and Lyttelton, while on the US West Coast, all Oregon ports, including Portland, shut for 24 hours, and Los Angeles, Long Beach, San Francisco, Oakland, Tacoma, Seattle and Dutch Harbour (Alaska) all stopped for eight hours. In LA alone, over 100 cranes were stopped with 32 ships in the harbour and another 16 due later that day. In Mexico, the *Associated Press* reported that 125 unemployed transport workers from the transport union Ruta 100 and the Proletarian Movement (MPI) were marching to the British Embassy in Mexico City in support of the Liverpool dockers. 'We are here because they supported us,' explained one of the Mexican workers, before adding, 'This is happening because of neoliberalism.' In Brazil, the three national Brazilian dockworker organisations, representing more than 70,000 members, wrote to Brazilian and foreign shipping companies to request that they persuade MDHC to reinstate their dockers, in addition to informing all 145 affiliated unions to brief each of their members on the Liverpool dispute, and calling for a national meeting to discuss effective boycott action against Liverpool cargo. Back on the US East Coast, *Lloyd's List* quoted ILA members in New Jersey, Baltimore and Hampton Roads (the ports served by ACL vessels calling at Liverpool), who all stated their intention to, 'honour the request for a boycott.' John Bowers, the ILA president, confirmed that this action did indeed take place, while in Boston, the Industrial Workers of the World leafleted the ILA's hiring hall. In New York City, the Workers' Solidarity Alliance joined with Blackout Books to picket the British consulate.

# A DAY OF WORLD ACTION

In Norway, the *Sandnes* dockworkers' union was to accept requests from the ITF and Norwegian Transport Workers' Union for direct action and material support, and in Russia, the Russian Trade Union of Dockers of the Sea watched the Port of St Petersburg for vessels and cargoes of companies calling at Liverpool, while *Solidarnost* of Kaliningrad sent a solidarity message. In Spain, Portugal, Austria, Algeria, Mauritania, Kenya, Zimbabwe, Pakistan, India, Bangladesh, Hong Kong, unions informed their membership, wrote to MDHC and the British government, or sent money and solidarity. In his summary of events, Greg Dropkin described how in 105 ports across 27 countries, dockers, seafarers, and other workers took part in meetings and demonstrations at British embassies and consulates, while stoppages ranging from 30 minutes to two, eight or even twenty-four hours were carried out. The Dispute Committee had arranged for their own mass picket to begin at 6am outside Seaforth Container Terminal, in what according to the event leaflet was, 'a rejection of casual labour, anti-union legislation, fighting for real employment and trade union principles.' [12] During this period, the Liverpool stewards received 220 faxes of support, as the various forms of action were widely reported across myriad media platforms outside Britain. [13] John Payne, one of the Liverpool dockworkers who helped to co-ordinate international solidarity throughout the dispute, would later describe his satisfaction at the remarkable show of unity displayed during the Day of World Action: 'We had a message from the Jordanian mineworkers and from people like that. I think it is tremendous.' [14] Payne was assisted by Mark and Liam LIoyd, sons of dockworker Tommy LIoyd, in organising this and other aspects of the dispute.

# 55
# Nolan Meets Morris

*'We have to recognise some of the realities in the port today. Joint 'accreditation' between the TGWU and the MDHC on how shop stewards should conduct themselves is being drafted now, but we have not finished it yet. People are sounding off about casual labour in the press, and this upsets the Dock Company. You have to have confidence in the union. Furlong is very dismayed again, but we have pulled it back. We can restore recognition, but we will have to sign that we will abide by procedures, and this will be signed by the union.' ~ Eddie Roberts**

News from the picket line that day was good. Information from inside the docks confirmed what the dockers knew all along: that the scabs were being forced to work on a 'call-out' system, which meant getting shifts only as and when required. Some of the men from Drake International were said to be doing 20 hours on-call at a time as the atmosphere on the docks was said to be dreadful and often violent. These men and women had no sense of community or solidarity, they were strike-breakers. This chaotic and dysfunctional labour force was now divided into three groups: those original scabs who refused to support their brother dockers at Torside, the Drake scabs and the recent additions to the mix, what local labour historian Eric Taplin would have identified as 'casual casuals.' [1] New faces replaced old faces that had had enough, before they too were replaced by other newcomers to the culture of labour exploitation that reigned in the port. In another port city, the International Longshore and Warehouse Union's delegate, Jack Heyman, was organising global support to enable the Liverpool dockers to rid their port of the very labour practices that Jack London fought in Oakland in 1903. London's infamous description resonated as clearly at the end of the 20th century as it had at its beginning: 'The modern Strikebreaker sells his birthright, his country, his wife, his children, and his fellow men for an unfilled promise from his employer, trust or corporation… A Strikebreaker is a traitor to himself, a

---

\* Eddie Roberts, speaking at a Port Shop Stewards' meeting at Transport House Liverpool (6 August 1993)

traitor to his God, a traitor to his country, a traitor to his family and a traitor to his class. There is nothing lower than a Strikebreaker.' [2]

Inside the Dock Company, rumours emerged that directors were resigning under constant pressure from shareholders, as well as threats of hostile takeovers from companies keen to cash in on this 'wounded and degraded' company. On Wednesday 15 January 1997 the stewards were due to meet Bill Morris in London. Their chairman, Jimmy Nolan, appealed to the stewards to be disciplined and allow him to speak to Morris without interruption. He would explain why they were rejecting his proposal for postal ballots. He reminded the stewards of the problems that Southampton dockers faced upon forming a co-operative; they had been forced to leave the Dockers' Pension Scheme and were still fighting to be readmitted. Bernard Cliff had begun threatening the pension fund after only six months in dispute, as its £40m surplus was being used to protect pensions in the absence of sacked dockers' contributions. [3] They would also pursue the idea of a co-operative acting as a labour supply agency if Graham Stevenson, the TGWU's National Docks Officer, raised the matter in London. [4] This initiative was now being seen as more acceptable by many of the stewards, even if it was predominantly viewed as a means of calling the bluff of the union and MDHC, who after 15 months continued to demand that the dockers simply accept an offer that was made to them in 1995.

Another argument which divided the stewards ahead of their trip to London was over the practicality of boycotting a postal ballot if Morris did decide to impose one again. Billy Jenkins argued: 'We should just oppose the ballot, and if Stevenson mentions labour supply, we respond without opposition.' [5] At the heart of this disagreement among the stewards lay the constant fear that, deliberately or otherwise, some in the group would prefer to avoid open debate on the basis that it was easier to simply oppose anything other than total reinstatement. If Morris carried out his threat to go over the stewards' heads, a postal ballot would be sent to all MDHC dockers, some of whom would cast their votes regardless of calls for a boycott. The Electoral Reform Society would then count the ballots submitted and declare the result. However, the majority of Liverpool dockers understood the political subtext of the situation and would act accordingly. [6] Jimmy Nolan chaired the meeting well. Jimmy Davies was still not in favour of the labour supply agency proposal, and it was vital that some element of consensus on the matter was reached with the Morris meeting only a day away. Pressure was on to make decisions and Nolan's own scepticism was based on the fact that a co-operative was effectively a mechanism to collapse the dispute and cut Torside dockers adrift from any final settlement; this would never be acceptable to the stewards. At this meeting it was agreed that picket allowances would be raised from £12 to £20 per week. Other items on the agenda that day included Reclaim the Streets' plan to occupy Medway Ports' dockside cranes that coming Monday. [7]

At 1pm the following day, Bill Morris, Jack Adams, Graham Stevenson and Dave McCall met the dockers' negotiating team in London. Nolan opened the meeting by referring to Morris's stated wish for an 'honest and open debate,' before proceeding to provide him with a summary of the dispute, which concluded with the previous week's mass meeting that both Adams and McCall had attended. At this meeting, the dockers had rejected the employer's offer and the idea of a postal ballot. Nolan then told Morris: 'We welcome dialogue with you, but the media distort everything we say; your statements on New Year's

Eve created doubt for our members. I am speaking to you as a trade unionist. The Liverpool Echo and Post try to create divisions between us. We have every intention of remaining in dispute until we are reinstated. We will continue to negotiate as long as it takes.' [8] He also explained some of the issues relating to the pension fund, expressing his view that Stevenson should now replace the retired John Connolly as the TGWU trustee for the Dockers' Pension Scheme. [9] Morris appeared unimpressed and impatient, telling Nolan bluntly that, 'I am not sure what there is to respond to. I have heard it all before. No response is appropriate.' [10] Nolan then asked for more effort from the union, calling for the open support of the General Secretary, his deputy and the GEC, arguing calmly and clearly: 'The GEC should say that they are in opposition to MDHC and political legislation.' [11] Here, a long, pregnant pause filled the room, before Morris, as if emphasising his disinterest in the subject of the Liverpool dockers, signalled to Jack Adams to respond. Adams spoke of how negotiations had only got worse in terms of jobs, to the point that the situation was now money up and jobs down, especially since the business restructure meant that MDHC was no longer an industrial employer. 'Whatever you think about the package,' Adams said, 'the pensions are protected. You can mobilise support in both determined and creative ways, but you are dealing with a bad employer. You can't collapse them… After 15 months, you have not collapsed them, and they are prepared to sit it out. It's a war of attrition.' Adams added that he had been grovelling in private and in public for a solution based on the labour cooperative idea, but now he was, 'not prepared to do it anymore.' [12]

Throughout these exchanges, Morris remained silent. Nolan stressed that the labour co-operative could only exist once Drake International had left the port, before concluding with an acceptance that, 'our campaign continues. If you can't support us officially, we have to do it unofficially.' [13] At this point, stewards revisited the issue of Morris's New Year's Eve statement undermining the dockers' campaign, declaring that, 'if you've got something to say, spit it out. If it's over the way we have conducted ourselves, then say it.' [14] Morris finally disclosed what was really on his mind:

> 'I have never known a dispute like this with time, money and resources. I defended the union against a similar attack by Pilger in the Guardian, and I will continue to defend the union against Pilger and Loach. Our union has been seriously damaged by their intervention and others… we live in the real world. Our position in terms of support is total, but we have responsibilities to defend the good name of the union.' [15]

Nolan replied: 'If the dispute is unofficial then leave us alone. The dockers are opposed to a postal ballot,' at which point Carden asked: 'Are you going to impose a ballot?' [16] Morris answered, 'No,' and then Frank Lannigan outlined in detail how MDHC had exploited General Cargo to the present day, explaining that, 'a co-op in General Cargo would be a farce. Men are working in Birkenhead on £3 per hour. MDHC own most of the companies there, with their senior personnel in charge.' [17] Nolan attempted to speak again, but Morris interrupted, and despite what he had just said, his determination to impose a ballot was clear: 'I can't see the employer getting rid of Drakes. It is an illegal dispute,' [18] he said, before telling Nolan: 'We have a totally different view, Jim.' [19] The meeting came to an abrupt end, and the stewards returned to Liverpool.

Elsewhere, news broke of a possible 1300 job losses at Ford Liverpool, due to the manufacturing of the new Ford Escort being moved to another plant, possibly in Germany or Spain. Tony Woodley, the TGWU's National Officer for auto workers, was at Ford Liverpool that day, as the dockers considered the potential implications of another group of Liverpool workers in dispute with their employer. Judging by their own experiences, the former dock shop stewards feared that the Ford workers would fall victim to Bill Morris's deeply conservative worldview of trade unionism. But, for the Liverpool dockers, Jimmy Nolan still believed that Morris would not impose a ballot, [20] perhaps because the union had since been in touch with the *Liverpool Echo* to inform them of their intention to seek another meeting with MDHC. Whatever the case, the position of the stewards remained unchanged: Drake International had to leave the Port of Liverpool, and the stewards would reserve the right to examine the potential for a co-op to cover all work on the docks.

# 56

# The Dockers Call for
# Support from All Workers

*'The dockers' union in Aarhus strongly wants to express its concern that a decent solution can be achieved, due to the fact that the TGWU is in a key position to assure a just settlement of the Liverpool struggle. We want to urge you to use your position to obtain a victory for the Liverpool dockers. Don't forget that you said, "You'll never ever walk alone." The Liverpool struggle is the struggle of all true trade unionists, and also a struggle for the future if trade unions want to be representing the working people.' ~ Ole Moller\**

On Saturday 18 January 1997, Jimmy Nolan opened another National Support Group meeting at Transport House Liverpool, involving representatives from various trade union groups and political parties, who had received invitations proclaiming: 'the heroic struggles of the Hillingdon workers, Magnet workers, Glacier, communication workers, railway workers and environmental groups who had all raised the potential of unifying the struggles against privatisation, casualisation, Job Seekers Allowance and the Criminal Justice Act. We hope that all our comrades may be able to attend to play their rightful role in developing victory for our struggles.' [1]

The meeting heard from Bernie Kilrie of Glacier who described the strategy that he and his fellow workers had utilised in November 1996, during which more than 100 people took part in a workplace occupation in response to being sacked and replaced by non-union labour. Their union, the Amalgamated Engineering and Electrical Union, had repudiated their action only for all those sacked to eventually be reinstated. Lyn Fawcett, representing Magnet workers who were dismissed after calling an unofficial strike, explained that their dispute was now into its fifth month, and a scab labour force had been brought in. On behalf of the Hillingdon Hospital workers, Wally Kennedy spoke about their extraordinary 16-month dispute, for which UNISON had recently decided to withdraw its support after the

---

\* Ole Moller, Danish dockworker

411

contractor, Pall Mall, offered a redundancy package to the predominantly female workforce. UNISON told the women to take the money, and then refused to meet them when they demonstrated outside their offices, as more than 30 police officers were deployed to protect the union from its own members. The Hillingdon Hospital workers would be on strike for five years, in a dispute that shared the same defining characteristic as the others mentioned above: they did not have the unequivocal support of their trade union, reflecting an age of a new unionism; of collaboration with the bosses, as promoted by Tony Blair's New Labour party. [2]

Billy Webster, from Derry, gave a summary of the financial support that been received from Ireland since the very beginning of the docks dispute. John Bohanna, from the local Ford plant, delivered an update on redundancies while it was reported that both Kodak and Gallagher were also set to close their plants. Irene Campbell then talked about the Women of the Waterfront's latest actions, and Bob Ritchie outlined the work being done by various support groups whilst highlighting that, 'speaking tours need to be increased.' [3] The idea of a 'virtual picket' of the Mersey Docks and Harbour Company was floated once again, although little progress had been made on a plan to attempt a shutdown of MDHC's communication systems. Computer hackers with the skills to implement what the dockers knew would be an extremely powerful weapon never materialised. The stewards had previously considered cutting the GPO cables under MDHC's offices, but access to the central underground junction was on the other side of the Seaforth Dock fence. Brian Ashton again highlighted the importance of boycotting Argos, who were shipping the bulk of their stock through the Port of Liverpool, and he planned to speak with some of their workers in Stafford, while a mass picket had been scheduled at the Magnet plant in Darlington on 14 February. Nigel Flannigan considered the difference that Ken Loach's film was making to workplace collections, [4] whilst Bob Towers, of the London Support Group, handed over a substantial cheque for the Hardship Fund. The Manchester Support Group reported that it was meeting every two weeks under the direction of numerous local shop stewards, and the Welsh Support Group's Mariam Kamish called for more support for the dockers' families. The meeting concluded with the suggestion that despite some magnificent displays of solidarity between these parallel industrial struggles, there was still much more to be done. [5]

In Liverpool, hundreds of pickets lined the Seaforth gates where several dockers had chained themselves to cranes in an attempt to stop ships being worked. Chris Knight and his sister Liz joined the pickets that day, with Chris beating out a rhythm on his trusty drum in the early morning winter darkness. Meanwhile, around 100 taxis drove slowly up and down the line, causing traffic chaos that lasted for hours, and at around 6am, Reclaim the Streets activists joined several dockers in occupying cranes at the Liverpool Grain Terminal, enduring one of the coldest nights of the year in order to maintain their positions until 10am the following day. Eight Liverpool dockers and five RTS activists were subsequently arrested and spent the night in Liverpool City Centre's Cheapside Police Station, [6] before being released on bail ahead of February court hearings. Among the occupiers were Jimmy Davies Jr, Tony Farrell, Terry Southers, Steve Robinson, Billy Jenkins, Steve Aldersley, Andrew Godfrey, Oliver Herbert and an environmentalist who gave his name as Merlin Mathews - address: 'the Oak, the Tree'. Two dockers' supporters, Catherine Sawyer and Denise Bishop, were also charged with aggravated trespass, and afterwards it was agreed that picket captains should carry mobile phones, especially during occupation attempts. John McDonald, the Grain Terminal manager, later claimed that the Day of World Action cost MDHC £20,000 per hour, and on Thursday 24 January, Tony Nelson, one of the picket captains, reported that it had been, 'a great boost to the morale of all the dockers,' [7] as evidenced by George Johnson, a sacked Liverpool docker on the picket line that day, beaming at how, 'the Port of Belgium and Rotterdam, and all major ports, came to a standstill. The action could carry on for the rest of the week.' [8]

While the Day of World Action was going on, Mike Carden attended a special session of the TGWU's General Executive Council at the Trades Union Congress in London. According to Bill Morris, the meeting had been called to consider the organisation's financial situation, and it was reported that its income was, at the time, £60m with an overall surplus of £4.1m. The fundamental issue confronting the union, as well as every other UK trade union, was that membership levels were in a perpetual downward spiral. Instead of addressing the fundamental reasons why this was happening, the solution put forward by private sector consultants, the General Secretary and the GEC was to amalgamate with other unions. Morris and his administration officer, Ray Collins, saw joining with other (equally moribund) trade unions as the future, perhaps because it was less of a challenge than pursuing a more sustainable alternative, such as mounting a recruitment campaign that would feel relevant to traditionally disparate and hard to organise sectors, like hotels and catering.

Some GEC members argued for a recruitment drive among the growing army of unemployed former and prospective new members, which would involve providing much-needed services to their increasingly disconnected communities; no longer the thriving hubs of working-class life and culture that they had once been. Such a radical vision of modern trade unionism did not fit the post-war paralysis of the role of unions in an ever-changing industrial, political and social environment. Morris and his expensive American business consultants, who merely wished to sell off the union's assets as a means of covering the loss of membership dues, condemned the TGWU to a dismal process of managed decline that would prioritise maintaining a growing salaried industrial officer corps and its diminishing Victorian trade group structure. The closure of so many *dark, satanic mills* that threw millions of trade union members out onto the cobblestones of a rapidly evolving scandal of generational unemployment appeared to pass unnoticed in the TGWU under the leadership of Bill Morris. [9] Ironically, despite its financial situation, the TGWU saw fit to spend over £1 million having this analysis confirmed by various City of London and American consultants, underlining the limits of this union's ability and ambition to protect and grow the fundamental principles of trade unionism that the Liverpool dockers were fighting to defend.

It was around this time that reports were circulating in USA ports that Bill Morris had been telling the ILWU that the Liverpool dockers' opposition towards him was racially motivated. [10] Tony Nelson was in Oakland around this time and was due to speak at a meeting in the hiring hall of ILWU Local 10 in Oakland. Just before he spoke, Tony was informed by one of the longshoremen of the rumours that Morris had spread and that he could expect some of the dockers there to raise the issue; the issue was never raised. During his first election campaign to become General Secretary Morris was supported by the union's left-wing, who celebrated the opportunity to be the first UK trade union to elect a black trade union leader. The right-wing in the TGWU stood firmly behind his main opponent, regional secretary, George Wright. During a 1991 radio interview, held shortly before the election, Wright vociferously denounced, 'those elements in the [election] campaign who had raised racialist questions about Bill Morris's suitability,' before adding, 'I know who's played the race card. It's been played by Bill's supporters in the desperate hope of whipping up some kind of anger about it. Racism is evil, it's repugnant. I want no part of it. I don't seek to exploit it and I seek no advantage from it. I am with Bill on that.' [11]

Years later, Geoffrey Goodman, Morris's official biographer, would claim that at the TGWU's Biennial Delegates Conference in July 1997, the Liverpool dockers had, 'invaded the conference at Brighton to harangue and barrack the union's leadership. Some of them were admitted to the conference and sat in the gallery chanting racial slogans at Bill Morris.' [12] It was extraordinary that it took thirteen years for this allegation to ever come to light. None of these alleged racist slogans were captured by the live official TGWU recording of the conference, or any of the numerous television, radio and newspaper journalists in attendance. The Dispute Committee sent the ILWU's Jack Heyman a copy of Greg Dropkin's film made for Liverpool based *Open Eye*, which covered the dockers' boycott of Namibian uranium hexafluoride during the 1980s. [13] Liverpool dockers had also boycotted South African cargoes for decades in opposition to apartheid, and according to journalist John Pilger, the Liverpool dockers had not only:

> 'Stopped the import of uranium hexafluoride from South African-occupied Namibia. The following year, when the waste disposal company Rechem won a contract to dispose of 3,000 tonnes of highly toxic chemical waste from Canada, the dockers refused to unload it, forcing the ship to return to Montreal… There is big money in toxic waste. Rechem is owned by a company called Shanks & McEwan, whose non-executive chairman is Gordon Waddell – who happens also to be chairman of Mersey Docks and Harbour Company. In the first year of the dispute, the amount of waste passing through Liverpool increased by more than a third, to 19,500 tonnes.' [14]

In a *Big Issue* article titled *Danger on the Dockside*, Ally Fogg celebrated the role of the Liverpool dockers in the struggles against apartheid and the import and export of environmentally dangerous cargoes, while pointing out that, 'since the sacking of the Liverpool dockers, the number of toxic waste consignments travelling through the port have doubled asking the question: 'Is the health of Merseyside at risk?' [15] Fogg argued that the dockers and their specific form of radical trade unionism, underpinned by direct action, acted as gatekeepers against racists, dictators and toxic cargoes, going as far back as their blocking of imports from Augusto Pinochet's Chile in the 1970s. Jimmy Symes, in his role as elected chairman of the Merseyside Docks Shop Stewards' Committee addressed the Chile Solidarity Campaign's trade-union conference in 1975: 'The torch of socialism, once having been ignited, will never die. But it is the responsibility of us, as a labour movement, as socialists, as internationalists, to support the people of Chile in their struggle.' [16] The class feeling which had animated Liverpool dockers in their mass strikes for improved pay and an end to casual conditions was also evidenced in the repeated actions that they, along with other working-class communities, took in solidarity with the Chilean people. Fogg's article also demonstrated exactly why the

# THE DOCKERS CALL FOR SUPPORT FROM ALL WORKERS

Liverpool dockers had every right to combine and unite with environmentalists and other social action groups, quoting from Greg Dropkin's reports on their principled stances:

> *'A natural by-product of derecognising unions and employment rights is to reduce the control that workers have over the work they do, and in the absence of these rights, employers will take every opportunity to exploit their workers or the environment for the sake of a quick profit.'* [17]

In London, Bill Morris was due to meet with Jack Adams and Graham Stevenson on Friday 24 January, and on that morning, Jimmy Nolan spoke on Radio Merseyside an hour before he opened a press conference at the Liverpool Town Hall. [18] There was a good turnout as the dockers' chairman expanded on the idea of a 'not for profit' labour supply company to provide labour to the whole of the Port of Liverpool. Terry Teague then briefed the media on international support from Japan, Australia and Canada. [19] The general response to the labour supply company proposal seemed to be positive in light of the latest impasse in talks between the TGWU and MDHC. [20] It was a decisive attempt to break that impasse with both their union and their employer. For some shop stewards this proposal was a genuine opportunity for workers to own and control their labour, regardless of how some of the dockers' trade union supporters and political allies disliked the idea.

News broke that Bill Morris was set to call a press conference to declare that the dockers should vote on MDHC's most recent offer through a postal ballot, [21] which led to Frank Lannigan getting into a heated conversation with Morris, who had accused the stewards of 'moving the goalposts' by suggesting a labour supply agency that was not restricted to Torside. This latest public statement from Morris, as with his comments on New Year's Eve, undermined the dockers again with his persistent declarations about the union's only objective being to seek an end to the dispute based solely upon any offer the company made. Following the dockers' news conference, that evening on the BBC's television news programme *Look North*, Terry Malone of the Port Users' Committee went back on his previously positive reaction to the dockers' labour supply company proposal. Appearing on the same news programme, Mike Carden could only presume that Malone had been, 'whipped into line by the Dock Company.' [22] On Saturday 25 January, Malone would tell the *Liverpool Daily Post* without any hint of irony that he gave, 'a cautious welcome to the sacked dockers' offer to set up a labour agency,' while stressing that other agencies' recruits should not suffer under the new offer: 'I'm sure that I speak for all our association members when I say that I would not sanction the wholesale dismissal of workers engaged by other companies, such as Drakes or anybody else.' [23]

Elsewhere, Bill Hunter and Greg Dropkin strongly opposed any potential labour supply company, as they felt it meant that, 'the struggle was being betrayed,' a view shared by the ILWU's Jack Heyman. [24] Many of the stewards understood such arguments in the context of the dispute; they did not agree to the general opposition towards co-operatives by some on the left, who appeared to consider co-ops as a failed model in comparison capitalist control of industry. It was as though these critics were suggesting that workers could not function without capitalist employers, yet they supposedly wanted those same workers to own the means of distribution and exchange. It was along these lines that both Carden and Teague argued in favour of a labour supply company, although they acknowledged that more details were needed. Clearly, such a plan had its risks, but then so did every other strategy employed by the dockers over the course of their long campaign. After two years in dispute, the stewards could not hope to sustain such a lengthy struggle by simply regurgitating the same ideas, over and over again. This was a conflict that had developed a life of its own, that ebbed and flowed like the Mersey itself; it was a struggle that could not exist within the rigid confines of rhetoric, political semantics or sectarianism.

The dockers and their supporters remembered 6 October 1995, when the stewards had recommended a return to work within a week of the dispute beginning. Here, the accusation had been that the Dispute Committee was meekly following orders from their TGWU bureaucrat bosses; that they were selling out the men. In some sense this was true, but only to the extent that the action was taken at a time when every shop steward involved knew that the dockers would not be allowed back through the gates, [25] and it was only through this action that the lockout could be exposed, along with the fact that the dispute over Torside was part of a conspiracy to rid MDHC of more than 100 dockers who they had previously identified as either unfit for work or untrainable. Throughout the entirety of the dispute, the stewards worked to prevent Morris from collapsing their campaign in one way or another, and in obvious collaboration with the employer. As Tony Nelson observed, Morris supported a workers' co-operative, but only for Torside, while Jimmy Nolan was convinced that MDHC would not get rid of Drake International. It was also around this time that sacked docker Mick Cullen announced his intention to stand for election as MP for Wirral, as a representative of the Socialist Labour Party. [26]

At a rally at GCHQ in Cheltenham on Saturday 25 January, Labour Party MP Peter Hain stated that a Labour government would reinstate the Liverpool dockworkers. At the Region 6 meeting of the Finance and General Purposes Committee (F&GP) held on Wednesday 29 January, Dave McCall addressed the issue of the local TGWU docks officer. [27] He repeated a recommendation that had already been unanimously rejected by the committee, who wished to send related remits from branches back to the GEC. [28] McCall relayed Morris's message that while branches did in fact have the right to send remits to the GEC, decisions on disciplinary matters remained the preserve of the individual regions, prompting Pat Harvey, a delegate from the Trade Union and Unemployed Resource Centre, to challenge a disciplinary policy that clearly did not exist. [29] Mike Carden then stated that GEC members had not properly examined McCall's report before asking, 'are officers employed for life?' [30] Peter Dunnico, an elected member of the F&GP, answered: 'Officers do have a procedure, including BDC Appeals. Allegations should be considered, of course. This is a right, and the line officer has to deal with the matter first and the GEC has responsibility to protect the rules of this union.' [31] He also declared his belief that the GEC had not acted unconstitutionally which was a view shared by the regional secretary. [32] Ken Brindle then referred to McCall's report as not being a full regional inquiry, while others expressed the view that the local docks' officer's disciplinary status would have no bearing on the outcome of the dispute. Terry Abbott, another Region 6 delegate, argued vehemently that it was, 'a matter of justice, not of administrators over the membership.' [33] At this point, Dunnico predicted: 'the opinion of the GEC will be that this matter has already been dealt with.' [34]

# 57

# A Proposal to Supply Dock Labour in the Port of Liverpool

*'Religious leaders have condemned the company; the Liverpool Echo, which I have never known to praise or support any striker, let alone dockers, at any time in its history, has made rousing comments about the way in which the company has handled the situation. Further support has been provided by the local community. Recently, even the head of ...Radio City said, at a dinner for businessmen no less, that the company was acting like the mill owners of the 19th century. That shows the depth of feeling in Liverpool about the way in which the company has treated its dockers. These are decent men, who stayed in the docks rather than taking £35,000 and walking away. They wanted to continue to work in the docks, and they had a right to do so.' ~ Eddie Loyden MP\**

O n Monday 27 January 1997, the *Liverpool Echo* reported that a 'peace bid for a workers' co-operative' had been launched at a dockers' press conference, where it was stated: 'We are not discouraged by the Dock Company's initial response to our plans. We believe it is something positive, which could herald the end of the dispute.' [1] However, Eric Leatherbarrow, the Dock Company communications manager, was less enthusiastic stating: 'The linking of a workers' co-operative to the dismissal of the Drake workforce is unacceptable.' [2] That Thursday, Kevin Coyne, the secretary of the Merseyside Trade Union and Unemployed Resource Centre, joined Mike Carden, Bobby Morton and Terry Teague at a meeting with Peter Fell, an assistant to Ken Livingstone MP, to discuss the economic feasibility of the dockers' co-operative. Meanwhile, Liverpool City Council had put together an influential team of advisors to consider every opportunity, from European Social Fund investment to the Urban Fund for Regeneration, as possible means of raising support for the

\* Eddie Loyden MP, Early Day Motion 1484, House of Commons Hansard, 25 October 1995 vol 264 cc1119-26, available: https://api.parliament.uk/historic-hansard/commons/1995/oct/25/mersey-docks-and-harbour-company#column_1120

initiative. [3] At the weekly mass meeting held on Friday 31 January, Jimmy Davies informed the dockers that following discussions with Jack Adams and Graham Stevenson, it appeared as though the Transport and General Workers' Union was open to introducing their proposal for a port-wide co-operative at the next round of negotiations. Stevenson had said to Davies that he would explain to the Bill Morris that he did not, 'see any value, personally, in a postal ballot; no value whatsoever, as all it would create was probably bad feeling between the union and the membership.' [4] Stevenson was also aware of the shop stewards' certainty that a postal ballot would result in a rejection of any offer made by MDHC, and he reaffirmed his previous observation in telling the stewards that: 'the option for the dockers to pack up and walk away does not exist; you can't walk away from the dispute. You have to win it.' [5] Reporting on this conversation with Stevenson, Davies said that the national docks officer had:

> '…also picked up on what had been said about the co-operative, and he said as far as he is concerned, he believed it was worth pursuing. People have got other ideas about that. The MDHC have got different ideas about it because they are absolutely terrified of the fact that we could have control of the labour supply in this port.' [6]

On the same day, the Socialist Workers Party produced a leaflet condemning the idea of a dockers' co-operative, and with Frank Lannigan chairing the meeting, Jimmy Davies expressed his disappointment with this development:

> 'We would have thought that an organisation like the SWP, who'd been involved in our dispute since day one, would have possibly had the courtesy to come along if they wanted to discuss something over co-operatives and sit down with the stewards and discuss it… we would expect them to come along and have a meeting with you to identify what your position over a co-operative is, as opposed to putting a leaflet out, which I don't think serves any useful purpose at all. It's divisive; very divisive.' [7]

Mike Carden then explained the need for the dockers to consistently 'capture the imagination' of workers and the media, in order to preserve the struggle for as long as it needed to last. The co-operative initiative: '…isn't a stunt. It is part of a tactical effort to carry on the support, whether that be in this room, support nationally or internationally.' [8] He addressed the criticism that somehow the stewards had not sought industrial support for direct action, either in Liverpool or nationally:

> 'For 17 months, for those who haven't heard, to all those political groups who have supported us magnificently or not, over the last 17 months we have called upon the working-class throughout this country, and in this city in particular, to support us. We believe that if there was a general strike in this city – that if all businesses shut down for a day, a week or a month – then the Mersey Docks and Harbour Company would be forced immediately to reinstate the sacked dockers; there is no question about that. The reality is that it hasn't happened. A resolution is not a revolution. People have got to understand the reality that we are confronted with.' [9]

# A PROPOSAL TO SUPPLY DOCK LABOUR IN THE PORT OF LIVERPOOL

Jimmy Davies explained the importance of all dockers remaining in compliance with the union's membership rules, while the stewards would ensure that the next six months were covered with the union at Transport House. [10] Frank Lannigan then put the Dispute Committee's recommendation bluntly and succinctly to the men: 'The dispute continues until 500 men are back in those gates.' [11] Jimmy Nolan was not in attendance at this meeting, as he was in Dublin to meet with Ireland's president, Mary Robinson, at a celebration of the life of Irish revolutionary James Larkin. Elsewhere, on Monday 3 February, MDHC managing director Trevor Furlong was quoted in the *Liverpool Daily Post* as saying that, 'the union had never supported the action of the Liverpool dockers,' [12] providing further evidence that the employer and the TGWU were united in their opposition to the dockers' campaign for re-instatement. [13] This came after MDHC's Eric Leatherbarrow informed journalist John Pilger: 'The company is delighted with its good relationship with the union,' before boasting that they ran: 'the only unionised port in the country. We show the TGWU far more respect than the [sacked] men.' [14] The following day, Furlong gave an interview to the *Liverpool Daily Post*, during which he stated:

> 'There are some very good chaps out there, and I feel sorry for them... The union have never supported this action...' [15]

That week, more arguments took place concerning the proposed dockers' co-operative. The TGWU had now published a four-page document titled *Job Rescue Package: A Proposal to Supply Dock Labour in the Port of Liverpool: February 1997*, which simply asked if MDHC 'is supportive of the Job Recovery Package.' [16] It was hardly a *tour de force* of socialist intent or ambition, and the structure and form presented was certainly not supported by the stewards. That same day, Carden attended another meeting at the MTUURC with Kevin Coyne and Mike O'Neil, to discuss in detail how a co-operative could be established. This included pursuing available grants and exploring the type of structure that would best suit the dockers' organisation, as well as the development of a comprehensive business plan. It was agreed that a feasibility study would be undertaken. [17] Greg Dropkin had already published his concerns regarding the labour supply proposals online, and the ILWU's Jack Heyman was also very unhappy with the idea, with Dropkin writing: 'Beyond the tactical questions, the labour supply proposals are fraught with dangers should they ever come to pass. Readers with experience of joint union-management co-operatives may wish to respond directly to the stewards or via *LabourNet*.' [18]

On Tuesday 4 February, Graham Stevenson arrived in Liverpool, and that afternoon told the stewards that he was supportive of the co-op proposal, but that Bill Morris was not. He was focussed solely on forcing a ballot. Thus, it was important to clarify what the dockers' negotiating position was going to be in order to offset any damage that Morris could do. [19] The conversation centred on the details of employee ownership ventures and employee common ownership schemes, as well as the need to raise capital to get the project up and running. The potential for failure of such co-operatives were openly discussed, with the conclusion being that unless the stewards could offer a viable alternative, Morris would impose the ballot that he believed would finally sink the morale of the dockers and collapse the dispute. The proposal needed a costed business plan, based on a minimum amount of expected work in the port before trading began. At 6.30pm, Jack Adams and Dave McCall joined the meeting, at which point Stevenson declared that the co-operative represented a concrete proposal supported by the TGWU despite MDHC's rejection of it. Stevenson had his laptop with him, and so he immediately began altering the paper he had originally produced. Not many of the stewards had ever seen a laptop before, and so this was a very impressive scene: a TGWU officer who was young enough to operate at the cutting edge of technology. It was agreed that the financial base of the co-operative needed to see investment from the dockers themselves, to show a financial commitment, as a new document began taking shape titled, *A Proposal to Supply Dock Labour in the Port of Liverpool*. Much of it had already been written by Carden, with the support of Kevin Coyne and others at the MTUURC, and it would be much longer and more detailed than the four pages offered by the TGWU and KPMG. Unlike their union, the Dispute Committee had the freedom and ability to do whatever was necessary without need for expensive consultants. [20] On the matter of costings, Jack Adams said that the TGWU had based their projections on Felixstowe Docks, as he told the stewards:

> *'After the March GEC, Morris will push for a ballot; he will impose it. I am cautious about these proposals. If we can sell the introduction of this to the MDHC, it will be a victory. They will not take Drakes out as a precondition, so it's a labour supply with Drakes still present, but you are challenging them publicly. I do not want a publicity stunt.'* [21]

Jimmy Nolan replied: 'If Morris wants to impose a ballot, then so be it.' [22] Adams believed that the General Secretary still wanted one last contact with MDHC but Jack Adams conceded: 'This initiative has superseded this process. It's not a delaying tactic or a bullshit exercise. It has to be a serious option. I'm not going grovelling again.' [23] The following day, the Dispute Committee met. Their stance on Drake International was that it had to be removed from the port, [24] making the argument that this could be done quite easily as MDHC was not the employer and Drakes was merely a contract labour agency. Adams and Stevenson sat in on the stewards' discussion, where it was decided that they would, 'rewrite the paper with Drakes out and dockers in.' [25] While Stevenson was willing to accept this, he stressed that, 'Drakes out is a demand that creates problems.' [26] A few days earlier, on the 31 January, Morris had a letter published in the *Tribune* stating his intention to hold a ballot, which coincided with another rise in MDHC's continually improving share price. This had emboldened the company to such a degree that they openly declared that Drake International was there to stay, [27] and Adams was of the opinion that: 'the co-op was my idea over Torside, but I am not prepared to play games over a co-op or enter into a charade. This serious proposition could well offload the push for a ballot from Morris and the GEC. It will buy time prior to a general election.' [28] This was also the outcome that the stewards wanted from their 'co-operative proposals'.

Out on the picket lines, a police horse died of a heart attack while being led from its box, creating a deeply upsetting scene for those present, and the police officers were obviously very distressed themselves. A number of dockers tried to help treat the horse, whose name was Justus II, and on the 14 February the *Liverpool Echo* published a letter from its rider, thanking the dockers for their empathy and assistance. [29] At the next Friday mass meeting, Jimmy Nolan outlined further details relating to the labour supply company, noting that while MDHC would not release Drakes from their contract, 'neither will we compete with them.' [30] In answer to a number of questions on the proposed labour supply, it was clarified that it would cover the whole of the Port of Liverpool, including Birkenhead, and the overall atmosphere was positive, with only three dockers voting against the dispute continuing. [31] On Saturday the 8 February, the Socialist Party organised a fundraising event, 'Stand Up for the Dockers,' at the MTUURC's Flying Picket bar, featuring, among others, Neil Anthony, Francis Galbraith and Rob Heeney. [32] The following Monday, Jack Adams, Graham Stevenson and Dave McCall introduced the idea of what they referred to as 'a hiring company' to the stewards, which seemed to indicate that the dockers' initiative, 'had been hijacked by the union, as the principal point that separated them centred upon the dockers providing labour for the whole of the port, and this meant Drakes out.' [33]

The stewards' original proposals, which had been shown to local journalists two weeks earlier, were now to be relaunched by the TGWU, only this time they ignored the issue of Drake International; the main stumbling block for MDHC. The three union officials joined Jimmy Nolan and Randall Moll, a local church spokesman, to present the media with the latest version of *A Proposal to Supply Dock Labour in the Port of Liverpool*. This five-page document, drafted by Stevenson and Adams, and broadly backed by the stewards, began with an initial statement of principle and questions for MDHC's consideration, inviting the company to talk with the union: 'to realistically assess their mutual interest, and that of the whole community of Merseyside, in achieving a negotiated settlement.' [34] The TGWU explained that the dockers' repeated call for reinstatement was no longer to be interpreted as reinstatement for all dockers, as some may wish to retire from the industry, and then argued that MDHC should welcome such an initiative, given their insistence on the outsourcing all dock labour:

> 'The TGWU, the shop stewards and its members seek a job for those who wish it and a voluntary retirement package for those who wish it. We believe the only way to achieve this is by a two-fold strategy that establishes a new labour supplier which has the consensus support of the Merseyside community... The new supplier is variously described as a labour supply device, company, employee share ownership plan, cooperative, or consortium which could adequately provide permanent work.' [35]

For his part, Graham Stevenson believed that there were, 'no obstacles to resolving the dispute, provided Mersey Docks accept the open, pragmatic and flexible proposals aimed at providing a reasonable number of decent dockers' jobs with reasonable pay and reasonable conditions.' [36] Regarding Drake International, Stevenson cited the proposed 'minimum standards agreement' and described the agency as, 'MDHC's problem, not ours.' Asked whether the Drake workforce had to go, the union's officer replied that, 'We haven't said that at all,' [37] before describing as purely 'hypothetical' the question of whether or not the proposed co-operative could work alongside Drake, insisting that MDHC must first reply to the union's questions before any detailed negotiations could begin. Jack Adams then declared that while the union retained the option of holding a secret ballot, the final offer tabled by MDHC in December 1996 did not provide sufficient jobs to justify re-balloting, pointing to the fact that the dockers had rejected a similar offer by a five-to-one majority in February 1996. 'We must overcome the jobs issue,' the deputy general secretary stated, 'and until then, there is no point in an imposed ballot.' [38] Greg Dropkin reported that Randall Moll had stressed that he could not replace the dockers or union leaders in negotiations with MDHC and would only concern himself with the hardship suffered by families, whose prospects he felt would be improved by what was presented in the TGWU proposal, which had 'more potential than ever' to resolve the dispute. It should, however, be noted that Moll had previously urged the dockers to vote in favour of MDHC's February 1996 offer.

The shop stewards would later disclose to the rank-and-file that the co-operative proposals were aimed at drawing on the West Coast US workers' experience of hiring halls and achieving international parity on pay and conditions, with all contract labour being removed from the port, as they had no intention of establishing an agency if it meant competing with casual contractors. Replying to a question on the continuity of pensions, Jimmy Nolan explained that MDHC would be offered a 51% share in the labour supply company and that should they decline, pensions would be transferred to the new company, although this idea of a joint ownership concept, cited in *Morning Star* articles on 25 January and 10 February, was later denied by other stewards, and it remained absent from the TGWU's official document. [39] A copy of the proposal was sent to John Bowers, president of the International Longshoremen's Association, who encouraged Atlantic Container Line's Conrad Dezago to use his influence to push MDHC towards accepting it. Bowers also told Jimmy Davies that: 'Mersey Docks' injunction, lodged against me last year after rank-and-file ILA men honoured a Liverpool picket, has now been lifted.' [40] Meanwhile, as the relationship between the Dispute Committee, the TGWU and Jack Adams appeared to be deteriorating, Dave McCall telephoned the stewards at 5pm on Wednesday 12 February to tell them that Ken Loach would not be welcome at Transport House, Liverpool the next day, when he was due to speak to the dockers about a special screening of his film, *Carla's Song*, at the Odeon Cinema in Liverpool City Centre arranged in aid of the Hardship Fund. [41] That Friday, the Dispute Committee decided to send a letter to all GEC members and Regional Secretaries, inviting them to the next dockers' demonstration. Two dates were suggested, and it was thought that following a march and a rally, a meeting could be held inside St George's Hall to discuss the detail of the dockers' struggle.

# 58
# Support for the Conflict

*John Cowley, one of the sacked dockers said, 'I've always wanted to write, but it's not something you tell other dockers" ~ John Bohanna\**

On Tuesday 11 February 1997, John Linden and Jeremy Hawthorne attended Sefton Magistrates' Court to represent all Liverpool dockers and Reclaim the Streets activists that were arrested over the course of the Day of World Action on the 20 January. Jimmy Davies, Tony Farrell, Terry Southers, Tony Russell, Billy Jenkins, Merlin Mathews and others were charged with various offences. The following day, Dave McCall confirmed the union's decision to ban Ken Loach from entering Transport House Liverpool. [1] On Thursday 13 February, a provisional second draft of the People's Charter for Social Justice, which would be launched jointly by the dockers and the Women of the Waterfront, was completed, calling for, 'the immediate reinstatement of the Liverpool dockers, the Magnet workers and the Hillingdon workers, together with other identified rights, from the right to join a trade union to the right of workers to organise internationally.' [2] Friday's mass meeting was much smaller than usual, as more than 50 dockers were away supporting the Magnet workers' picket line, and another group had travelled to Milford Haven to join in with environmental protests in response to a major oil spillage on the docks there. Cathy Dwyer, wife of a sacked dockworker and member of the WOW, announced plans for a Valentine's night out, and sacked docker Dave Pendleton unveiled a poster for a delegation to India. Pendleton, who had worked on the docks for 28 years before being dismissed, received a round of applause for his artwork, and he would later lament how the campaign had seen no support: 'from the union and this pseudo-Labour government. For every week the scabs are in there, there is less chance of us going back.' [3] The previous week, only three dockworkers had voted against fighting on, [4] and at this mass meeting Dave Cotterill appealed to the men and

---

\* John Bohanna, reviewing Dockers: Five Minutes' Experience Is Worth Fifty Years of Reading (26 July 1999)

women to keep all documents from either the TGWU or the Mersey Docks and Harbour Company, going back to before the dispute began, as they looked towards building the archive of the dispute and the history of the Liverpool dockers. [5]

On Saturday 15 February, dockers travelled to Darlington to support the miners at Armthorpe Colliery, as they had done throughout 1984, only this time they were supporting the sacked workers at Magnet Kitchens. The following Monday, Liverpool docker Mick Kilcullen was arrested on the picket line by the Operational Support Group, having apparently said something to an officer that led to a thumbs-down gesture, after which Kilculllen was sprayed in the face with CS gas. [6] He then spent the night in a cell, without being allowed to contact either a doctor, his family or a solicitor, and upon his release he was admitted to hospital. At a court hearing on the 16 March, the police would claim that he had shouted, 'Let's take the gate!' despite the fact that he was away from the picket line at the time of his arrest, while Sharon Kinney, a supporter of the dockers, said in a television interview at the time that she, too, had been sprayed with the same substance. According to Kilcullen, four officers held him down while another sprayed him directly in the face, and both he and Sharon Kinney were very angry about the way they had been treated. On Wednesday 26 February, solicitor John Linden met with potential witnesses of the attack on Kilcullen, including Billy Johnson, Joe Quinn, Peter Wharton and Kevin Robinson, among others. [7]

Meanwhile, Jimmy Nolan was in London, trying to arrange a meeting with MPs, and Mike Carden had been in Germany for a meeting with Jorg Wessels, Lars Stubbe and Olof Christianson from the ÖTV union. On Thursday 20 February, the *Liverpool Daily Post* published an article about 'drug and alcohol tests' imposed on the Drake International strike-breakers. At the following day's Dispute Committee meeting, members of the TGWU's General Executive Council were in attendance to discuss their position on the dockers' campaign, with Ritchie James, Barry Miller, Dave Irvine, Colin Beresford, Martin Mayer and Ken Brindle being among the handful who had openly supported the dispute from the beginning. Bill Morris had sent a letter to all GEC members instructing them not to 'attend the Liverpool dockers meeting because the dispute is illegal.' [8] It was reported that the Labour MPs Tony Benn and Jeremy Corbyn had agreed to be the main speakers at the next march and rally scheduled for the 22 March, and Jimmy Nolan announced that despite planned changes to pension legislation, due to come into effect in April, the dockers' pension fund had a declared surplus of some £40m; the benefits of which would only be felt if reinstatement was achieved.

At the mass meeting held later that morning, Jimmy Nolan told the men that Bill Morris had again been invited to address them, but not only had he declined he had also ordered all GEC members not to attend any meetings of the Liverpool dockers. From the floor, Terry Barrett asked why the TGWU leadership did not want to support the campaign, and Tony Deveraux followed up by asking why *all* members of the union were not supporting them. Geoff Liddy then explained how despite Magnet workers being on official strike, the TGWU was not seeking to challenge the laws used to dismiss them. Sacked docker Mick Thompson commented that while they were in work, they had been unable to get their union to organise official ballots, but once they were sacked the union and the employer had no problem promoting ballots. Frank Carberry remarked that the company had never refused to meet either the stewards or the TGWU throughout this so-called unofficial strike, and Neil

Caddock pointed out that MDHC's profits had risen recently. Tony Deveraux then stated that, 'the mass meetings are like a maternity ward now – one last push!' [9]

This was also the day that comedian Lee Hurst appealed to people to stop playing the National Lottery, and instead send the money to help sacked Liverpool dockers. Hurst was one of 42 comedians involved in the planning of a benefit show for the dockers at the London Palladium, along with Jo Brand, Steve Coogan, Mark Lamarr, Eddie Izzard, Alice Nutter, Sean Hughes and dozens of others, whose aim was to raise up to £30,000 per week in support of the Hardship Fund. Hurst, whose father and grandfather had both been London dockers, told journalists: 'We are asking people to pledge one pound a week to the dockers from their bank accounts. You may spend a pound a week on the Lottery, which you have no chance of winning, but this way you will get some self-respect.' [10] He explained how he had heard about the dispute at the funeral of his friend, the former London docker Mickey Fenn. Other comedians and celebrities had been moved to help the dockers after reading John Pilger's *Guardian* article, leading to the organisation of the Palladium show, *Dirty Three and a Half Dozen*, on Sunday 16 March. This was one of many comedy fundraisers to take place in aid of the dockers that year. Rob Newman, who was involved in a sell-out benefit concert at the Hackney Empire on Saturday 22 February 1997, was quoted as saying: 'Tony Blair thinks strikes are part of the past, and that any association with workers in a dispute might be damaging to his election prospects.' [11] Tickets for these events were raffled and the proceeds were donated to the Hardship Fund. [12]

At the same meeting Jimmy Nolan expressed his respect for the work of the Japanese dockers, before providing an update on the latest round of talks with the union. Mike Carden then gave some general feedback from the GEC, and Jimmy Davies Jr talked about his delegation work in India for the fourth annual Congress of Trade Unions in Calcutta. Jimmy Davies Sr broke the news that UNISON had dropped their support for the Hillingdon Hospital workers, making it imperative that the Liverpool dockers support their comrades with financial aid, for which Joe Ladd suggested that they organise regular collections at the gates. Jimmy Campbell asked what the up-to-date position was regarding TGWU branch resolutions condemning the actions of the local dock official. Billy Johnson asked what would happen if dockers completed and returned any ballot papers that the union sent out. The answer was quite obvious; the Electoral Reform Society would only count and declare a result based on the number of ballot papers returned. [13] Representing the Women of the Waterfront, Doreen McNally spoke of a benefit night planned for the 14 March at the Liverpool Irish Centre, and she also called on dockers to boycott the *Daily Mirror* in response to its lack of support for the dockers' campaign. Nolan did not think that this would be a good idea and Doreen would later explain: 'We rang the *Mirror* on a daily basis. Piers Morgan was the editor; he wouldn't speak to us, and we rarely got past reception. I informed the men of this, but I didn't ask them not to buy it, as Jimmy Nolan said not to as a lot of the men read the *Mirror*. John Pilger put a microphone on my telephone and recorded a conversation with them. At the pier head rally, Arthur Scargill was speaking, and John Pilger said I should ask them to boycott it, [because] it would be interesting to see what happened. Jimmy said not, as they couldn't buy the *Sun*.' [14]

On Thursday 27 February, Kevin Robinson, Mike Carden, Rob Newman and Ken Loach appeared on Roy Greenslade's Granada TV programme, *Britain Talks Back*. Greenslade wanted to know why the Liverpool docks dispute had gone largely under-reported in the British media, and Loach suggested that it was because it was about: 'work, the right to work and the right to really contribute to the society you live in. This is not on anyone's political agenda. It's not part of New Labour or the Tories' agenda; it doesn't fit anybody's agenda.' [15] Greenslade then drew comparisons with Wapping, and the 'fathers and sons and unions,' [16] but for Loach, the dockers' struggle identified two conflicting priorities in society, putting it ahead of its time: 'The myth at the heart of contemporary politics is that we all share the same interests. We don't, and that is the fraud at the heart of all political debate.' [17] Newman agreed, adding that this issue was, 'at the heart of everything that's happening. The real political issues are not discussed. It's the same as Magnet and Hillingdon; the media debate has just got so shallow.' [18] Greenslade kept referring to the dispute as a 'strike' until he was corrected by Robinson, and he eventually accepted that it was in fact, 'not a strike, but a lockout.' [19]

On the same show, David Madel, the Conservative MP for Bedfordshire South-West, talked about improvements in industrial relations on the back of, 'freely agreed three- and two-year wage deals,' [20] while the *Guardian's* Seamus Milne accused the Tory government of being involved in the dispute through its links with MDHC. Here, it is interesting to note that this discussion focussed on the increase in casualised work and low wages, which, according to Milne, 'puts more and more pressure on those workers in full-time jobs.' [21] Loach then lamented the Labour Party's failure to represent 'ordinary people,' and the fact that there was, 'no political voice for this huge amount of unrest and dissatisfaction. Nobody speaks for them because the Labour Party is now the party of business; because it is business that drives down employment conditions.' [22] Greenslade referred to, 'the new global economy,' arguing, 'we have to take reductions in jobs and wages, but in the long-run it will all work out well for us,' [23] before an agitated Ken Loach described for him a situation that was much less simplistic:

> *'The system is failing. It is the crisis of capitalism, because the system has no equilibrium; it cannot match people's needs. We have massive wealth and massive poverty; people starving and dying of starvation in Third World countries, and people bloated and overfed in other countries. People like the women in Hillingdon and the Liverpool dockers, when they stand up and say they will not take it anymore, they are the heroes for tomorrow.' [24]*

Ken Loach accused Greenslade of being editor of the newspaper that made false allegations against Arthur Scargill, the miners' leader. Greenslade replied by saying that he was not 'in a position to apologise, as the matter is still in the courts.' [25]

On the docks the Mersey River Pilots were set to launch a series of strikes over pay and safety; the significance of this being that their action would stop ships entering the Port of Liverpool. The 50 or so pilots were angry that their employer, MDHC, had reduced their earnings from £30,339 to £24,000 per annum over the course of several years, and they were also concerned about ships carrying dangerous cargoes using the port. The pilots issued a six-page report to local MPs, stating that they, 'were totally disenchanted and demoralised by the way we have been treated,' as in addition to reductions in pay, the number of pilots employed had fallen from 137 to 50. [26] On Tuesday 18 February, Jack Adams told the dockers that Bill Morris planned to push for a ballot at the GEC, while he and Graham Stevenson had agreed to meet MDHC's Peter Jones and Allan Price at Manchester Airport that coming Thursday. Jimmy Nolan now wanted to explore the concept of a labour supply company despite the degree of criticism it had already evoked. Kevin Bilsborrow spoke in favour of pursuing legal action against local TGWU officials; liability had arisen from their failure to inform the dockers at Torside that they had been *reinstated*. Further questions were asked about how the union could justify labelling the dispute as an illegal strike while simultaneously organising official ballots. [27] At this point, the Dispute Committee's primary concern was stopping Morris from holding a third ballot, with Jimmy Davies urging his fellow stewards to find ways of, 'neutering or boycotting the ballot. The lads are fed-up to the back teeth. It's hard, lads are getting sickened by it, and we need a quick end to a victory.' [28] Another significant hurdle to overcome was the role played by TGWU Regional Secretaries for London, the Midlands and Scotland, Barry Camfield, Jim Hunt and Jim Elsby, who were all keen supporters of Morris. They had been accused of spreading rumours about the Liverpool dockers, that they were *anti-union* and had been flying *first class* on their delegation trips. This came as no surprise to the dockers as they continued to contact Labour MPs to raise support for the labour agency initiative as a means of forestalling Morris's efforts to impose a ballot. [29]

When Jack Adams and Graham Stevenson met with Peter Jones and Allan Price, the TGWU officials were unhappy that MDHC had not waited to speak to them before declaring that: 'Drakes retention is not a principal to stay forever and a day. If the business developed, we would be quite happy to state publicly that Drakes would leave, and the labour supply would replace them.' [30] Canada Dock was offered as a potential base for the new company, but Adams needed to know volumes, revenue and expected turnover from this berth before accepting it as a viable option, although he did report: 'it looks like a goer; the union should fund the business plan.' [31] Thus, the concept of a dockers' co-operative began to develop into a civic partnership involving the Labour Party, Liverpool City Council and the Trades Union Congress, but this was not welcomed by Jimmy Nolan, as the stewards' chairman did not believe that the initiative addressed the problem of competing with casual agencies, and he was still very much of the opinion that, 'the issue was reinstatement.' [32] Stevenson responded by pointing out that, 'the Dock Company will not reinstate everyone,' [33] at which point Nolan became angry, making it clear that he did not want the discussion to continue, [34] before accusing Carden of being *out of order* in saying that some sacked dockworkers would take voluntary severance. [35] Stevenson then interjected to argue that it would be, 'dishonest to go back to the position of full reinstatement by the MDHC,' [36] as the entire debate now centred on Drake International; '...timing is key. If Drakes leave, MDHC will class it as a total victory for the dockers. The minimum standard approach is good, but the Port Users are a bunch of cowboys who don't represent anyone.' [37] Jimmy Davies responded by acknowledging that, 'for the purpose of negotiations with MDHC, we agreed to work around the problem of Drakes, which could be set aside. But the Dock Company are not saying that Drakes would be pulled out at this time.' [38] Terry Southers added: 'At Coastal Containers, MDHC have had to employ another company, and some of the men there are ex-Liverpool dockers who took the £35,000 severance years ago.' [39] This explained why Terry Teague felt strongly that the labour agency: 'should start at Seaforth Containers and work itself into the rest of the port from there.' [40]

Ultimately, the stewards needed concrete assurances that Drake International would leave before any settlement could be reached, with Terry Teague stating: 'No steward has ever said they would accept Drakes staying in the port.' [41] Adams then reminded them that the idea of a co-operative was raised a year ago, as a means of dealing with the Torside situation: 'They [MDHC] offered Torside and Drakes out at one stage, and they offered us 20 to 50 jobs at the Container berth, but we refused to discuss ancillary jobs. They engineered this dispute. They walked you into it. 'We no longer want to be the employer of labour, said the MDHC. We can't get them out of that.' [42] Adams repeated his firm belief that Morris would impose a ballot on the latest offer at the March GEC, [43] before he and Stevenson left to allow the Dispute Committee to establish their position. The meeting closed and then restarted an hour later, as the stewards again debated the challenging practicalities of a co-operative trying to untangle its many contradictions. It was pointed out that an estimated 75% of the container straddle carrier drivers did not want to go back on the docks, which meant that they, 'would struggle to man Seaforth containers,' [44] and since the agency idea was, on some level at least, a device to buy time prior to a general election while delaying Morris's ballot, Nolan was sticking to the stance that Drake International had to go before negotiations could proceed. Stevenson opposed this idea, earning him Nolan's distrust; [45] a feeling that was only strengthened when, on Monday 24 February, booklets promoting the co-operative arrived at Transport House, to be described by one steward as, 'stupid; an outrage. They will not be distributed.' [46]

That same morning, at 7.30am, MDHC announced annual profits of £29.7m for 1996, representing a £2m drop on the previous year, in addition to declaring a £10 million 'special charge' as the cost of paying off the dockers, with City of London insiders fearing that the company's reputation had been irreparably damaged. [47] On the morning picket line, Bobby Morton and Irene Campbell were interviewed for BBC Two's *Business World*, as was Liverpool University economist and staunch MDHC supporter Professor Peter Stoney. [48] The night before, Jimmy Nolan had been speaking about 'treachery' as he telephoned Jack Adams and, 'went on about his obsession over pensions.' [49] As far as many of the stewards were concerned, their position was clear. Even if Stevenson and Adams still supported the labour agency, Bill Morris could continue to ignore them and push for a ballot. Regardless, the Dispute Committee did not fear a ballot, and they certainly did not fear Bill Morris, although they were disappointed to learn that one of the dockers had been disclosing details of weekly picket rotas, times and locations to Merseyside Police.

# 59
# All Docks and Dockers Are the Same – Nearing A Conclusion?

*'Bobby Owens, the regional secretary in the North-West and a member of the Liverpool-based far-left Militant Tendency, and John Freeman, the regional secretary in Ireland; they led an extremely powerful group, with a single objective to remove Bill Morris... It was one of a series of bitter feuds within the Liverpool branches of the union, in a region that had continuously brought problems to Bill Morris from the moment he became general secretary. At one stage in his earlier dealings with his Liverpool members, he had been compelled to expel a group of particularly militant far-left activists across the Merseyside zone following evidence of financial corruption. In fact, the whole Merseyside region had become a perpetual and challenging problem for Morris, and it was always at the top of his action pad.' ~ Geoffrey Goodman\**

O n Wednesday 26 February 1997, Japanese dockworker Akinonbu Itou arrived in Liverpool and met with members of the Dispute Committee, to whom he spoke passionately about deregulation. In Japan, 50 ports had held 'stop work' meetings on the 20 January, the Day of World Action, and a 24-hour national strike was planned for the 12 March. Itoh was the assistant General Secretary of the influential All Japan Dockworkers' Union (*Zenkowan*), and when he addressed a mass meeting of Liverpool dockers at Transport House, he told the men and their supporters:

> *'I would like to express our admiration towards the consistent unity you Liverpool dockers have maintained throughout your struggle of over a year and five months. I greatly sympathise with you, for your hardships standing on the picket line day and night in the freezing weather...' [1]*

---

\* Geoffrey Goodman, 'Bill Morris: A Trade Union Miracle', 2010 (pp.136-141)

Itoh went on to explain how the Japanese dock labour scheme operated, describing the attacks it had suffered in 1989, as he called on his Liverpool comrades: 'Let us join our hands to establish a system that provides stable employment and living conditions for dockers,' [2] for which he received a standing ovation. *Zenkowan* was one of the world's most influential dockers' unions, and its links to the US West Coast longshoremen served to emphasise the significance of Itoh's presence that day. He was also in regular contact with Jim Donovan, the Australian dockers' leader, who was himself in the process of organising another Liverpool delegation to raise money for the Hardship Fund. Other guest speakers that day included Denise Lonlet and Jean-Pierre Barrois from France. A discussion then took place on the potential ballot that Morris wanted to impose. The Dispute Committee had agreed to send confirmation of their refusal to accept an imposed ballot to Bill Morris via fax. At the mass meeting two dockers voted against this course of action. Kevin Bilsborrow insisted that, 'If we get ballot papers, we will return them unopened.' [3] Tony Deveraux, who had opposed the plan to fax Morris, reiterated the fact that: 'they [the Electoral Reform Society] will count however many ballots are sent in.' [4] The following day, the stewards discussed how Bilsborrow's suggestion, that they collect dockworkers' ballot papers, could potentially create problems by feeding into the idea that the dockers were anti-democratic. [5] In reality, if the ERS sent out ballot papers to the Liverpool dockers, they would have to be completed.

Jack Adams, Dave McCall and Graham Stevenson travelled to Birmingham to meet with the Dock Company's Peter Jones and Allan Price. It was around this time that *LabourNet's* Greg Dropkin published an analysis of the dispute in an article titled, *Nearing the End Game?* [6] in which he discussed:

> '...this week's decision by the union's General Executive Council to refrain from imposing a postal ballot for the moment. A three-week delay is expected, during which time the labour supply plan will be examined by all parties. The gulf between MDHC's desire to retain the services of Drake International and the dockers' demand for 'scabs out, dockers in' will be confronted, and the intentions of the TGWU itself in the run-up to a general election may be revealed... One mass meeting after another has been taken up with debate on the absurdity of imposing an official ballot on an unofficial dispute of men who had already voted to reject an equivalent offer in February last year, by an 84% majority. On two occasions, General Executive Council members were invited to attend the mass meetings to judge for themselves the conduct of the dispute and the mood of the men... it seemed likely that Morris would heed the continuing pressure from Mersey Docks' Trevor Furlong and simply impose his will on the dockers.' [7]

Graham Stevenson telephoned Frank Lannigan on the evening of Friday 28 February to let him know that MDHC had made a number of concessions, although issues still existed with Drake. The company had recently written to Bill Morris asking when a ballot was going to take place. [8] Two days later, on Sunday 2 March, Frank Lannigan, Jimmy Nolan and Mike Carden petitioned a meeting of the TGWU *Broad Left* to allow the dockers to negotiate without the imposition of a ballot, and after hearing Nolan speak, the members spent only 25 minutes considering the proposal. [9] Clearly, the *Broad Left* had other important matters to discuss. For example, John Aitken, a prominent *left-wing* GEC member, objected to Steve Riley, the committee's chair, handpicking candidates for union positions. This led to an endless argument that perfectly encapsulated the TGWU's culture of prioritising career and position over *rank-and-file* trade unionism. It was not the practice of picking candidates for full-time posts that bothered Aitken, but rather the fact that *one faction's* preferred people were not being chosen. Andy Holmes, a leading member of the GEC, questioned why the Liverpool dockworkers had been permitted to address the meeting, before wondering aloud why GEC members had been invited to attend one of their mass meetings. [10] Although it was alarming to hear such comments from a member of the union's most senior elected body, it was neither rare nor unusual, and it was certainly not a minority viewpoint. On the other side of London, the rock band, Dodgy, were joined by a variety of special guests for an acoustic set at the Mean Fiddler, as part of the *Rock for the Docks* fundraising initiative. [11]

At the GEC on Monday 3 March, Jack Adams gave a positive report on meetings with church leaders and members of parliament, along with the press conference for the proposed dockers' labour supply agency. [12] That night, Danny Maher arrived in London ahead of the Tuesday session. Adams and Graham Stevenson brought him up to speed on Bill Morris's wish to end the docks dispute by forcing a ballot. As the GEC representative for Docks and Waterways, Maher shared his constituents' belief that it would be very difficult for Morris to sell out the Liverpool dockers in this way. The following day, Steve Riley told Mike Carden that he had heard from Ray Collins, the TGWU's head of administration, that Morris did not plan to push for a ballot after all. [13] Nevertheless, in that month's edition of the union's journal, *The Record*, Morris wrote an article seeking to 'set the record straight' on the Liverpool docks dispute. [14] Back in the council chamber, Stevenson announced that MDHC's latest offer had been rejected by the dockers in a show of hands, citing the fundamental issue of the absence of real dock jobs. He then explained how the proposed dockers' co-operative was a response to the company's refusal to employ labour directly. The removal of Drake International, in his opinion, was an unachievable negotiating objective. Nevertheless, the TGWU was committed to developing a business plan within three weeks. [15] Adams added, 'MDHC will not keep an £8m offer on the table forever, and Bill Morris has apparently received a letter from the secretary of the trustees of the RDW Pension Fund, asking for indemnity in case the wrong advice was given.' [16] Maher then identified the ways in which MDHC was suffering as a result of international solidarity action. He informed the GEC about the planned river pilots' strike which would stop all shipping in the port of Liverpool. This threat of strike action would be averted at the last minute following the regional secretary's intervention, after the pilots expressed their dissatisfaction with the efforts of their own appointed union official; the pilots had overwhelmingly adopted a position of no confidence in Dempsey. [17]

In Liverpool, Frank Lannigan reported on the previous weekend's meeting with the Broad Left in London, where he and Jimmy Nolan had also spoken with Graham Stevenson regarding allegations made by some GEC members about 'slush funds and first-class travel,' in what was an obvious attempt at discrediting the dockers' campaign while justifying the TGWU's inaction. [18] The following week, on the 11 March, it became clear that the union was working to a three-week deadline for settling every aspect of the labour supply agency proposal. The night before, the *Liverpool Echo* had printed a statement by Eric Leatherbarrow,

MDHC's press officer, in which it was declared: 'Drakes are here to stay.' [19] The stewards began to suspect that the union and the company were planning to hit them with a ballot on a co-operative without any guarantees that they would not be competing against other agencies. [20] Nonetheless, regardless of the concerns or criticisms of stewards, dockers and political supporters, the labour supply initiative was successful in buying time, and there was every chance that Leatherbarrow's statement was designed to calm the fears of the scabs still working on the docks. [21] It was reported that a large Hardship Fund donation had been received after the fundraising show at the Hackney Empire. Elsewhere, publication of the *Dockers' Charter* had been delayed because of internal political problems faced by Dot Gibson, as objections were raised to her about the Women of the Waterfront's calls for the abolition of the British monarchy, amongst other matters. [22]

On Thursday morning, Jimmy Davies was told by Graham Stevenson that the GEC had agreed that the TGWU and MDHC would jointly fund the business plan for a dockers' labour supply agency. [23] Later that same day, in an interview with Radio Merseyside, Morris claimed, 'An end to the docks dispute is in sight. Labour supply proposals, being drawn up by MDHC and the TGWU through Peat Marwick [KPMG], will be completed within two or three weeks, and this will create more jobs than were previously on offer. Then, a secret postal ballot will take place.' [24] The dockers held a discussion on Morris and Stevenson's statements, with the majority of stewards opposing any joint union-company business plan. The proposed co-operative had nothing to do with the Dock Company. [25] By Friday 14 March, a copy of the labour supply proposals had finally been issued to all dockers, as the *Liverpool Echo* reported:

> *Bill Morris saw this as an end to the dispute, as he believed the proposed Mersey dockers' cooperative would create enough jobs for sacked men who want one. The others would then vote to accept £28,000 as settlement and leave… Morris said, 'Within two or three weeks, we will have something public to say about the feasibility. We're confident we will create more jobs than are on the table. Through that mechanism, we will have a secret ballot and resolve the dispute."* [26]

That evening, a 'Rock the Dock' benefit night took place at the Irish Centre in Liverpool, where Neil Thompson of the Fire Brigades Union presented the dockers with a statuette in recognition of their struggle. Two days later, the London Palladium show organised by Lee Hurst marked the first time that a strike benefit had ever been broadcast on national television. According to Stuart Cosgrove, the commissioning editor for Channel Four, 'the dockers' dispute has been ignored by the mainstream media.' [27] Musician Elvis Costello said, 'If you rely on the papers, it's like there has been an embargo on the story,' [28] while Primal Scream's Bobby Gillespie agreed that, 'There has been a conspiracy of silence in the British media, and a lot of people don't know anything about it at all.' [29] It was Jimmy Davies Jr and Tony Melia who were responsible, along with others from the London Support Group involving Micky Tighe and Nick Silvano, for galvanising support among musicians and comedians. Another show, *What's Up, Dockers?* was scheduled for Liverpool's Royal Court Theatre, featuring Eddie Izzard, Jo Brand, Rob Newman, Sean Hughes, Jeff Green, Ronni Ancona, Neville Raven, Milton Jones, Alistair McGowan, Alan Davies and Steve

Coogan. As part of the televised broadcast, Julian Clary interviewed numerous people connected to the campaign, asking why the dispute had hitherto been, 'one of Britain's best kept secrets.' [30] Clary spoke with Val Bibby and Sue Mitchell at their homes, before interviewing three generations of dockworker Andy Dwyer's family: his mother Rosie, his wife Cathy and their young daughter. After asking Cathy what a scab was, the programme ended with a wonderful scene where Clary asked Rosie Dwyer for three words on her family's struggle, and Rosie answered by proclaiming, 'We will win!' [31]

At the weekly mass meeting held on Friday 14 March, Herbie Hollerhead and Tony Gardiner returned from Denmark with a large donation for the Hardship Fund. Dave Cotterill updated the meeting on the dockers' writing group and Brian Ashton, chair of the Dockers' Support Group, reported on the Argos picket. There was also a thank you from 11-year-old Daniel Carden, who had collected £74 for Comic Relief with the dockers' help, and then Jimmy Nolan spoke at great length on the Registered Dockworkers' Pension Scheme, before announcing that Graham Stevenson would be told on Monday that 'the labour supply is only acceptable once Drakes have been removed.' [32] The following day, Jimmy Nolan and Mike Carden attended an extraordinary anti-Maastricht meeting in Paris alongside some 300 delegates. [33] On Monday 17 March, the Dispute Committee heard that the TGWU was paying KPMG £25,000 to draw up a business plan for the proposed labour supply company. [34] This came as a shock to the stewards, as much of the work had already been done by Carden and community business experts, and neither the MDHC or the involvement of KPMG were necessary; it was never discussed beforehand and would never have been accepted. On 4 April, Nolan would write to Bill Morris explaining that the stewards had serious concerns over the inclusion of both MDHC and KPMG in the planning process, as the stewards did not accept their business plan, or the projections put forward in a document presented on Monday 24 March. There was also the critical matter of an obvious conflict of interest arising from KPMG's ties with MDHC:

> 'KPMG are the MDHC registrars, and they had been involved with the MDHC for many years. In a joint project with the MDHC, KPMG have acquired over 60% residency of the new prestigious office building on the Dock Estate. KPMG were involved in the acquisition of the Medway Ports in 1993… following this involvement, a representative of KPMG was appointed to work for MDHC. The TGWU were due to take KPMG to court in 1996 on behalf of our members employed at Medway. We do not feel that KPMG are a fit or proper organisation. Other business advisors in which we have confidence should be appointed.' [35]

Jerry Spencer, a Community, Business and Economic Development officer at Liverpool City Council, would become the key advisor to the dockers 'to support the establishment of a labour supply co-operative serving docks and port operations around Merseyside.' [36]

# 60

# Robbie Fowler and the Liverpool Dockers

*'This hasn't been the only time the dockers' T-shirt has courted controversy. As recently as 2019, Tory MP's Damien Collins and Andrew Bridgen, the now (thankfully) disgraced (racist) historian Dr. David Starkey and the right-wing rag, The Daily Mail were up in arms over Samantha Morton's appearance on the BBC's magazine programme the One Show in which she wore the T-shirt and discussed the negative impact the government's austerity programme has had on working-class families.' ~ Mark Cunliffe\**

On the night of Thursday 20 March 1997, Liverpool Football Club played a UEFA Cup Winners' Cup match against SK Brann Bergen of Norway. Liverpool cruised to a 3-0 victory in a game that would have gone largely unnoticed were it not for Toxteth-born Robbie Fowler celebrating the first of two goals by lifting his shirt to reveal a 'Support the Sacked Liverpool Dockers' t-shirt. The solidarity shown for the dockers by Robbie Fowler would make the front and back pages of every UK newspaper. Seven days later, in Geneva, Switzerland, Fowler was fined 2,000 Swiss francs for this demonstration of solidarity, as UEFA regulations prohibited players from displaying political logos during matches. This ruling came two days after Fowler made headlines again, receiving praise for his sense of fair play when, having been awarded a penalty, he argued that he had not actually been fouled by Arsenal goalkeeper David Seaman, prompting Sepp Blatter, the General Secretary of FIFA, to say of him: 'your reaction in the penalty incident did you great honour. It is the kind of reaction which helps maintain the dignity of the game.' [1] Fowler's teammate Stig Inge Bjørnebye had provided the assist for the infamous goal against Brann, and he took it upon himself to quietly, and without any publicity, visit the dockers' picket line:

\* Mark Cunliffe, 'Remembering Robbie Fowler's Support for the Mersey Dockers', The Penny University, 27 March 2021. https://ayewellhmm.wordpress.com/2021/03/27/remembering-robbie-fowlers-support-for-the-mersey-dockers/

*'I remember the directors driving through the gates and they were quite aggressively jeered. It was a small visit; I took them by surprise after training one day. I was curious about the strike and the reasons behind it, so I went there and stopped for a bit. We were very privileged to play professional football, and you had a situation where people are out of a job. I was the one asking questions, because they were there every day. We had a good conversation. I remember it as a positive experience for me and for them.' [2]*

Tony Nelson was one of the sacked dockers who spoke with Bjørnebye that day, and would later recall:

*'The thing we all liked was that there was nothing to Stig Inge's visit. He just tagged himself to the end of the picket line of about 200 people. He never spoke to anyone beforehand or announced he was coming. People started recognising him straightaway, but he was a quiet man, very understated. He just wanted to offer his support, not as a footballer particularly; just as a human being.' [3]*

Writing in 2012, Chris Tobin brought together a broad spectrum of factors that connected the ways in which *Scousers* responded to the world around them, in what he described as the 'Liverpool Way.' It was an outlook that challenged, rejected, opposed and fought the status quo, irrespective of the cost. Incidentally, Chris Tobin also noted how this 'Liverpool Way' always seemed to come into conflict with conservative fiscal policies:

*'...this 'Liverpool Way' did not really meet the demands of Sky Sports, that has no time for such madness [as Robbie Fowler's support for the Liverpool dockers or the Hillsborough Justice Campaign]. The Liverpool Way would not just be about football; through the 1970s and '80s it would be a home for the masses of unemployed; people disenfranchised through Margaret Thatcher's years in office; a community centre; a church to come and pay homage; their very own place of worship; they would kneel and pray toward gods with feet of clay...*

*The Liverpool dockers' strike would be the longest in British industrial relations history, supported by the Liverpool Way, with Robbie Fowler wearing a supporting T-shirt which would be revealed during a goal scoring celebration. Hillsborough and its justice campaign for innocent supporters – innocent children lost to a stadium disaster – would run red hot through the very veins of this club; everyone to a man or woman would fight like they themselves had been a parent to those 96 that perished from that day. The Liverpool Way would make sure they would not be forgotten; they would not allow them to be lied about; they would boycott the Sun, whose lies would harm so many; the Liverpool Way would be to seek justice and the truth. Hillsborough would be entrenched in the thoughts and minds of every Liverpool fan, and subsequently educating new followers of their responsibility to seek justice. The Liverpool Way would be an honest way, where truth could and would be accepted.' [4]*

On 16 May 1997, the Major League Soccer Players' Association's John Kerr wrote directly to Robbie Fowler:

> 'Your show of support came to my attention through the English newspapers and from Whitey Disley, who is the president of the Marine Firemen's Union in San Francisco, California. Whitey is a Liverpudlian who recently met with some of the wives of dockers who visited the United States to enlist the help of American labor on behalf of the dockers. In speaking with Whitey, we agreed that I should write U.E.F.A. to express our outrage at the fine that was levied on you... on behalf of myself and the Major League Soccer Players' Association, we wish to applaud you for your stand. Also, Robbie, if you will, please pass on my best regards to Jason McAteer.' [5]

Speaking at the time, sacked dockers Billy Barrett and Marty Size were to say: 'We were on the picket line, and a mate of ours called Berno said he had been out the night before with Robbie Fowler and his dad.' [6] Fowler's father had been a Liverpool docker, and Marty Size, who was also a St John's ambulanceman for every game at Liverpool FC's stadium, recalled that the family seemed interested in the t-shirts printed in support of the dockers' campaign. Marty Size was coming up the tunnel with a stretcher at the next Liverpool home game, he happened to ask, 'Robbie, have you got our T-Shirt on under there?' to which Fowler laughed and answered, 'No, we haven't got them yet. And by the way, we'll need them for this European game.' Robbie Fowler was given his '500 Liverpool Dockers Sacked Since 1995' t-shirt. In a wonderful YouTube clip Marty Size and Billy Barrett recounted how during the Brann game, the dockers were waiting excitedly for Fowler to score and display their t-shirt, [7] only for Barrett to interrupt and, with the kind of ironic sarcasm typical of Liverpool, point out that, 'I hoped he wouldn't score; I wanted him not to score. I'm an Evertonian, but I love the lad!' [8] Recounting the moment where Fowler finally lifted up his shirt, Size recalled how, 'Everyone says, "What's he showing?" so I was telling everyone, "He's got one of our T-Shirts on," so we were made up.' [9] By the next Liverpool game, the dockers' T-Shirts had sold out, with Barrett saying, 'That lifted us up; it gave us a buzz,' [10] while for Marty Size:

> 'It was talked about all over Merseyside and all over the world. At our mass meeting the following Friday, we were all talking about it, like, and they were saying what a terrible thing it was that he was being fined by UEFA, and one of the dockers shouted out, "Let's have a whip around for him!" Later on, Fowler was putting in for all sorts of money, wanting £40,000 a week or so, thinking that we'd turn on him, but we said we were made up for him, so they [the press] had no story then. They wanted a story like, "Dockers turn on their hero," [but] we said good luck to him.' [11]

It was Tony Melia, a young Torside shop steward, whose idea it was to design and sell a T-Shirt, and he would later recall how:

> 'When Robbie Fowler, or God, as he was known in Liverpool, raised his shirt, it was superb. I just thought it would be an eye-catching way of putting the message across,

*particularly to young people… I saw someone wearing a Calvin Klein, or CK, T-shirt, and I thought we could fit the word dockers around it. We designed and printed them in September 1996, when we had been in dispute for a year. The T-shirts had the desired effect, because you had to take a second look before you realised what it said. The words '500 Liverpool dockers sacked since September 1995' were emblazoned across the front, with the 'CK' in 'dockers' used as the logo.' [12]*

On Monday the 24 March, representatives of Calvin Klein threatened legal action against the Liverpool dockers' use of their emblem. In 2000, Naomi Klein would mention the dockers' flagrant trademark violation in her book, *No Logo*:

*There was yet another twist in this branded tale. The shirt Fowler revealed didn't bear just any political slogan, it was also an ad bust: in a not-so-subtle subversion of a ubiquitous brand, the letters 'c' and 'k' in the word 'dockers' had been enlarged and designed to look like Calvin Klein's logo: doCKers. When photographs of the T-shirt were splashed all over British newspapers, the designer threatened to sue for trademark violation.' [13]*

On Friday 21 March the comedian Mark Steel travelled, as he so often did, from London to attend the mass meeting at Transport House Liverpool. It was a good meeting, with Jimmy Nolan attacking labour leaders such as Bill Morris for their failure to show support for the dockers. Danish dockers Peter Shaw and Ole Muller also addressed the men. The following day, a demonstration took place in the city centre, and then on Sunday 23 March, the International Dockers' Committee met. Nolan opened the session, before Peter Shaw voiced his concerns about the potential dockers' labour co-operative, as well as the proposed location for the next international dockers' conference, which he believed should take place in Liverpool rather than Montreal. Elsewhere, Atlantic Container Line had threatened to pull out of Gothenburg if Swedish dockworkers continued to take action against them, and the company was also claiming that solidarity action taken by Danish dockworkers was illegal. The International Longshore and Warehouse Union representative then presented the Liverpool dockers with a framed collage of photographs, [14] as the attending delegates moved that:

*This steering group of the International Dockers' Committee supports the Liverpool dockers' initiative of obtaining reinstatement through the mechanism of a labour supply company. However, this objective may only be achieved following the removal of Drake International and other strike-breaking casual labour in the Port of Liverpool…' [15]*

That morning, after the usual picket duties had been completed, the Dispute Committee met to discuss a new document on the labour supply agency, which was to be presented to KPMG later in the day. In what was a stormy meeting, Jimmy Nolan attacked his fellow stewards, warning them that 'indiscipline will destroy us.' [16] Then, at around 1.45pm, KPMG asked the stewards for a copy of an agenda prior to a meeting that was due to begin in 45 minutes' time, and at 2.30pm, Mike Owens and Angela Kershaw, two of the young management consultants hired by the TGWU and MDHC, arrived at Transport House. Mike Carden and Tony Nelson greeted the impeccably dressed KPMG representatives, who stepped out of the lift looking like Mulder and Scully from the television series *The X-Files* and, according to Nelson, 'Looking for the crime scene, amongst these alien Scousers.' [17]

As Owens and Kershaw entered the boardroom to discuss the details of what was now *their* labour supply initiative, it was as if two continents had collided. This was not their world; they looked and dressed like two young city financiers from London, probably because that was exactly what they were. The pair set about establishing their authority and control over this *rag tag and bobtail* of unemployed dock labourers, asking where the demand was for another labour supply company in the Port of Liverpool, how many jobs were expected and what type of company would it be. They then informed the stewards that they had liaised with the Dock Company to find out how the port worked, [18] before questioning if the shop stewards were being realistic in believing that they could go into business for themselves: 'What skills; what management abilities do you have?' [19] It was as though they had been sent to convince the stewards that the whole thing was a bad idea and following little more than a minute's worth of introductory observations, they went quiet. Nolan opened up on the various issues of co-operatives and his understanding of how a labour supply company would work. [20] But Owens and Kershaw had difficulty understanding his broad Scouse-Irish accent, and within ten minutes an adjournment was called. During the break, Nolan told the stewards, 'Now we know the plot has unfolded,' [21] as the stewards prepared to unveil a detailed, costed business plan and then get the consultants out of the building as quickly as possible, which was exactly what happened. [22]

The following day it was disclosed that Calvin Klein would not sue the Liverpool dockers, as Jimmy Nolan called a Dispute Committee meeting to address discipline and the campaign in general, stating: 'This is long overdue; things are getting out of hand.' [23] He had already spoken to Jack Adams about the TGWU going to KPMG and MDHC behind the stewards' backs, and Adams had acknowledged that this should not have happened. Nolan seemed to be satisfied by Adams's response, but it did not stop him from itemising indiscipline during stewards' meetings: 'People walking out to get phones, take messages, etc; fax information, delegations, meetings, political intrigues; indeed, all the information that is now not getting through to all the stewards. Political egos, personal egos, etc; publicity seeking, trips abroad, etc… are all getting out of hand.' [24] It was decided that all correspondence and faxes must go to the secretary, Jimmy Davies, because a system had developed in which information, and therefore knowledge, was being used as a means of obtaining power within the group, to the point where discussions could take place over many hours without all of the stewards receiving all of the information. Sometimes, information would seep out during the course of a meeting, often via the reading out of documents that some stewards had not yet seen, but this was only part of a far larger malaise. After all, more than 3,000 faxes had been received since the dispute started, and so communication chains were always going to be strained, but certain individuals were abdicating their specific responsibilities in relation to the recording of faxes that were deemed critical to the international campaign. [25] Additionally, Tony Nelson spoke up about the fact that out of those who comprised the Dispute Committee: 'only four attended the picket line', adding that, 'the mass meetings every Friday go on far too long, turning our struggle into a circus. The men understand everything. We need to get back to basics!' [26]

It was undeniable that some mass meetings had descended into political rallies, due to some stewards feeling as though they had the individual power to act however they saw fit. The stewards needed to work more closely with the Women of the Waterfront, providing them with information and allowing direct access to meetings. Jimmy Nolan then expressed the view that: 'The reason why the union exonerated their officials of any responsibility or liability in the dispute was because they were terrified that 500 dockers would take them to court.' [27] Everyone was aware that individual legal action could be taken against the union by anyone at any time, it was never a discussion to be entered into lightly by the dockers, as the idea of taking the TGWU to court ran contrary to their core beliefs. Nolan himself was particularly opposed to this course of action, and he always encouraged the other stewards to speak out against it in front of the men. It was also Nolan's call to embrace all political groups that wished to support the dockers, but some were asking for much-needed financial aid. The notion that potential Hardship Fund money could be used to fund third-party activism was contentious to say the least and not appropriate. [28]

Debate among the stewards over the degree to which their dispute should be politicised proved to be exceptionally timely, as on 25 March, they received Bill Morris's reply to a letter sent to him by sacked docker Mick Kilcullen some 10 days earlier. In his letter Morris made clear his belief that the dockers were no longer in dispute and had instead become a political movement:

> *'I note the comments you have to make and fully accept that your principles promoted your actions, despite the warning from the deputy general secretary that such action would result in dismissal. I trust that, in turn, you will accept that, as general secretary, I am responsible for the whole of the union, and, given the anti-union laws and our own conference decisions, I must not jeopardise the fabric of the union in the interests of one section of its members. I must refute the notion that the TGWU has done nothing to support the dockers at Liverpool. From the outset, both myself and other senior officers of the union have done all that we could to seek the best possible settlement through negotiations… However, as you know, the dockers have moved on, and they are no longer running an industrial dispute but a political movement. This was made clear to me by Jimmy Nolan during the Labour Party Conference at Blackpool.' [29]*

Around this time, a document came to light directly linking PDP and PNT, two casual labour supply companies, with the Dock Company, which the Dispute Committee wanted to bring to the attention of local MP Joe Benton. [30] That same week, on Wednesday 26 March, letters of appreciation were sent out to a number of workers who had refused to cross the dockworkers' picket lines, including Jim Morgan (P&O driver), Robert Taylor and his two drivers from Dublin Street, and also Peter and Henry McConnell. At the Friday mass meeting, comedian Rob Newman appeared as a guest speaker once again, and the BBC were permitted to film in the main hall of Transport House. It was reported that the cost of policing picket lines now stood at an estimated £3m, and that MDHC insisted that Merseyside Police begin breaking up demonstrations because they were diverting investment away from the port. [31] On Tuesday 1 April, it was confirmed that Jack Adams would be in Liverpool the following day, and a meeting was arranged with Joe Benton MP, as Tony Blair, the leader of the New Labour Party, announced that he would give workers the right to take employers to industrial tribunals. With a general election on the horizon, the dockers were developing links with MPs Margaret Beckett and Ian McCartney, in an attempt at assuaging fears that Labour's internal politics would ultimately distract from the principle aim of reinstatement. The stewards were wary of becoming embroiled in what one of them claimed to be: 'the political machinations of attacking the New Labour Party. Gesture politics may be good for the ego, but it's useless if we are trying to achieve reinstatement.' [32]

The Citizens Advice Bureau had produced a report using all of the data and information collated over the 19 months of the dispute. Eric Leatherbarrow, MDHC's press officer, contacted Caryn Mathews at the CAB and threatened to complain about her to the Charity Commission; a complaint that was backed up by the Advisory, Conciliation and Arbitration Service, who argued that the CAB had no right to involve itself in an industrial dispute. [33] On Wednesday 2 April, a mass picket of Norse Irish took place at 4.30pm, during which demonstrators were allowed through the dock gates by a combined force of Merseyside Police, Port of Liverpool Police, private security guards and Special Branch officers, in what the front page of the *Liverpool Daily Post* alleged to be a violent protest aimed at blocking trade in Belfast. According to those in attendance, it was a clear set-up, [34] with the *Liverpool Echo* reporting that the police appeared to have been in contact with a BBC film crew beforehand:

> *The four-strong crew was from Sue Lawley's Here and Now programme, who were tipped off about a picket at the Norse Irish ferry terminal in Bootle last night. Around one hundred protesters, including sacked dockers' wives and children, broke through security and tried to board a ferry. The purpose of the picket was to give support to men who have regularly manned the dock gate around the clock, in very difficult conditions. One or two protesters went through the gate, and others followed. It was impromptu.'*
> *[35]*

The following day, Jack Adams arrived at Transport House Liverpool, and although he did not wish to speak to the Dispute Committee as a group, he did have a conversation with Jimmy Nolan and Frank Lannigan. [36] By this point, KPMG had informed Graham Stevenson that, by their estimation, some 60-70 jobs were available for the proposed labour supply company. [37] It was also revealed that MDHC's contract with Drake International still had 18 months left to run, although a get-out clause existed. [38] However, as far as some stewards were concerned, the fact that Adams did not meet with them represented a turning point where: 'the confidence of the stewards had been undermined.' [39] This coincided with the stewards' response to Bill Morris's article in *The Record*. They wanted their views published in the same TGWU newspaper which the union refused. On Friday 4 April, Mike Carden approached Nolan with the suggestion that the dockers should 'consider calling a ballot themselves,' [40] in effect calling Morris's bluff over a ballot that was, he argued, virtually inevitable: 'We are now simply waiting for Morris to decide when his time is right to force a ballot. It's a very dangerous move, but we must recognise that a ballot will take place sooner rather than later.' [41]

This was a time when everyone involved in the dispute appeared physically tired and a sense of finality hung in the air. Ole Muller invited Micky Tighe and his wife Sylvia to join Tony Gardiner and Herbie Hollorhead on a delegation to Denmark. In London, Tony Nelson and Bobby Morton were on their way to meet representatives of the ILWU and the International Longshoremen's Association, as well as dockers' leaders from Japan and Montreal, where Michel Murray was again calling for direct action against MDHC. Much criticism was now being aimed at the dockers by various political groups opposing the internationalist aspect of the campaign, which they dismissed as, 'a diversion away from local action.' [42] The comedian Lee Hurst was a guest speaker at the weekly mass meeting held Friday 4 April, where he talked about the life and struggles of his friend, the deceased London dockers' leader Mickey Fenn. This meeting also marked the return of Tony Russell, Terry Southers and Kevin Robinson following a fundraising delegation to Australia. 'The International Transport Workers' Federation, of which the Maritime Union of Australia was a member, had raised thousands of dollars to keep the Liverpudlians fighting,' was the message from their Aussie comrades, whose wharfies had been duly warned: 'legislation introduced into the Federal Parliament last year would have the same impact on the Australian waterfront as the Thatcher law.' [43] Other guest speakers that day included Emma Ward, who was raising awareness about the imminent closure of the cystic fibrosis unit at Liverpool's Alder Hey Children's Hospital. [44]

For all the doom and gloom surrounding the board room, there was cause for celebration when, on Monday 7 April, all of those who had been arrested for occupying dockyard cranes saw their cases thrown out of court on the grounds that multiple policing failures had been committed. The following Friday, US news station CNN attended the dockers' weekly mass meeting, along with representatives from the East Japan Railway Workers' Union. Sacked docker Mick Kilcullen had an article published in *The Socialist* detailing the dockers' struggle. On Saturday 12 April, the Dispute Committee again discussed Bill Morris's article in *The Record*, as well as the role of KPMG as not only MDHC's Registrars, but now also as the dockers' business consultants. Jimmy Davies expressed his concern that the Hardship Fund was running very low, before a lengthy discussion took place regarding the expectation that Morris would inevitably impose a ballot. There was also the matter of the impending general election, due to take place within a matter of weeks, but the reality was that even if a Labour government was elected, it would mean little for the dockers' prospects. On 22 April, in the United States House of Representatives, Congressman Ron Dellums challenged the silence of Tony Blair, the leader of Britain's New Labour Party, on the Liverpool dock dispute. 'It has come to my attention,' Congressman Dellums began:

> 'I was surprised to discover that Liverpool is the only port with a union workforce in England, a country with a proud trade union tradition that many in the United States sought to emulate. It seems incredible to me that 500 dockers were fired for honouring a picket line in light of this tradition. On January 20 of this year, longshoremen on the West Coast of America, including the port of Oakland, which I represent, engaged in a solidarity action... I would ask that you use your influence to remedy this situation, as

*the British government owns 14% of the shares of the Mersey Docks and Harbour Company.' [45]*

Unlike Robbie Fowler, Tony Blair remained deaf to all appeals to aid the Liverpool dockers, but the fight would continue to be fought regardless.

# 61

# A March for Social Justice – Respect to the Chartists!

*'Chartism was a working-class movement, which emerged in 1836 and was most active between 1838 and 1848. The aim of the Chartists was to gain political rights and influence for the working classes. Chartism got its name from the People's Charter, that listed the six main aims of the movement.' ~ National Archives*

By April 1997, real concerns were being voiced by some on the Dispute Committee regarding Reclaim the Streets' plans for an upcoming London demonstration, which the police were already billing as another poll tax riot in the making. This would prove to be a self-fulfilling prophecy, as the occasion was marred by violent clashes between the police and Liverpool dockers' supporters, in what the BBC reported as a riot that:

> '...erupted in violence, mounted police and officers wearing riot gear had to be brought in after missile-throwing protestors tried to climb the gates of Downing Street. At the Social Justice March in London, protestors threw missiles at police. An orange smoke bomb was hurled in Downing Street, and distress flares were let off. The crowd was dispersed by mounted police and three protestors were arrested. Four police officers were taken to hospital.' [1]

Two demonstrators were arrested for attempted murder, only to later be released without charge. The following day, Sunday 13 April 1997, Mike Carden gave what he himself would later describe as: 'a terrible interview to the *Liverpool Daily Post*, who distorted everything.' [2] Carden claimed that the interviewer kept repeating her assertion that the Liverpool dockers could not be seen to support groups whose members had been charged with attempted

---

* The National Archives, Power, Politics and Protest: the growth of political rights in Britain in the 19th century, available: https://www.nationalarchives.gov.uk/education/politics/g7/

murder. It was not known at this time that all these charges had been dropped. But this did not detract from the damage done by the story upon its publication on Monday 14 April. The newspaper presented the article as though the dockers were denouncing RTS. [3] A press statement issued by the stewards read:

> 'Prior to our celebration in London, press coverage in the capital appeared intent on provoking a climate of violence in which a 'poll-tax-type' riot was to be expected. The police embarked upon arrests on the Friday afternoon for 'incitement to cause affray' when supporters distributed a free broadsheet. Such suppression of free speech only served to heighten tension prior to Saturday's demonstration. On Saturday, others were arrested for 'attempted murder,' although both sets of charges were dropped much later the following day, but the damage of this false charge by the police had already been done. The presence of over 1,000 riot police on the march destroyed the peaceful carnival atmosphere that had previously been planned jointly with the Metropolitan Police. Even the horses were dressed in riot gear before the march had even set off, as they waited their time in the London side streets. [4]

Writing on the behaviour of some groups during the demonstration, *SchNEWS*, a direct-action news sheet, felt compelled to:

> '...speak its mind after the disgraceful scenes on the March for Social Justice last Saturday. A minority of extremist troublemakers who provoked ugly confrontations, first outside Downing Street and then in Trafalgar Square. This spoiled an otherwise brilliant day, and it is clear that these troublemakers did not care at all for the march or the issues involved and wanted to claim it for their own extremist agenda. We can now reveal that they had been planning the trouble for weeks beforehand and would stop at nothing to make sure that violence erupted. It seems the only reason they turned up was to start a riot. They had come equipped with a whole variety of weapons, including sticks, shields and mobile phones to communicate with each other; some even having their own vehicles in which to spread confusion and fear. SchNEWS strongly condemns these individuals.' [5]

Whole sections of the capital were sealed off by riot police, who refused to allow marchers the right to leave the area. An atmosphere of fear and intimidation prevailed, as hundreds of demonstrators were 'kettled' into key areas around London as police violence against peaceful demonstrators went unreported. The sacked Liverpool dockers had always welcomed RTS' support, ensuring a mutual respect that was only strengthened after this incident, and the dockers also expressed their gratitude to the London Support Group for organising a very successful demonstration of more than 20,000 people demanding social justice. [6] The march had again united anti-roads environmentalists with sacked Liverpool dockworkers, as they assembled at South London's Kennington Park before heading down Lambeth Road and passing the Houses of Parliament, with leaflets handed out in the park instructing participants to follow the brightly-coloured RTS flags and thunderous tribal drums. Unfortunately, the carnival atmosphere was swiftly ruined following confrontations between protestors and police near Whitehall. [7] According to Pauline Bradley and Chris Knight of the London Support Group: 'The first March for Social Justice, on April 12 1997, took a great deal of organising; getting unions to sponsor it, booking the route, getting the publicity out, getting people to raise it at their union and political meetings, etc.' [8] The LSG provided extraordinary support for the Liverpool dockers, whose dispute inspired them to create a *People's Charter for Social Justice*.

> *'Because the dockers' fight touched so many people and embraced so many causes, the London Support Group decided to devise a Peoples' Charter for Social Justice. The idea was in the spirit of the original Chartists, naming several minimum demands. Much time was spent on this, and the idea was to get groups of homeless people or women or anti-racist groups, and such like, to write their demands in it...' [9]*

For the comedian and writer Russell Brand, the March for Social Justice represented his first taste of political protest:

> *'I think by accident, I was too high to truly engage in activism, it was the Liverpool Dockers protest in 1997. I was lured from a humid underground carriage into a furore of ricocheting protesters and mounted coppers. To me, that day, adolescent and in perpetual internal revolution, the spectacle of a horse galloping up Charring Cross could only have been trumped by the presence of a marauding dinosaur piddling up Nelson's Column. It was exciting. Afterwards, I learned about the circumstances of the protest and the poor treatment of the unions, but my interest was initially piqued by the chaos.' [10]*

Brand would revisit the protest in 2014, recalling: 'There were police horses galloping up Charing Cross Road, people ripping up pavements. I didn't think [he puts on a posh voice] "About time, too – the Liverpool dockers are finally being heard here." I thought, "Fuckin' hell, this is brilliant." The internal mayhem I'm feeling is spilling out everywhere. I loved it, and I felt very connected to activism; particularly activism that seems like there's a stasis around it – earnestly sincere, but a monolith equal to the establishment.' [11] According to the London Support Group:

> *There were dockers and WOW [Women of the Waterfront] dressed as Chartists leading the march, two dockers in kilts playing bagpipes, a long banner at the front with 'March for Social Justice' on it, and all the pendants with the demands as mentioned above. People from all over the world came along... The press coverage of the demo focused on the few incidents of violence; some stone-throwing at the end when the majority of people had left. This was a shame because, for most people, the day was peaceful and enjoyable. Jack Straw made a statement in the press condemning 'the violence.' [12]*

In their article *Hate Riot Frenzy in Mob Rampage*, Mark Sully and Christopher Fenot wrote:

*'The police, attempting to manage the media coverage of the day, announced at a press conference they called on Friday afternoon that the event would be violent. This was then reported as fact by a number of papers, with one having the headline: 'anti-road militants spent weeks planning their bloody breakaway from London protest march.' A spokesperson for Reclaim the Streets responded to this by saying, 'The idea that a group who have carefully built-up links with the dockers, including going to Liverpool to support their picket, would then organise a riot on a march they've called is sheer fantasy.' In addition to this, many papers, using a police press release, reported that three people from the demonstration had been arrested for attempted murder; but what most then failed to say was that they were released without charge six hours later. In an insidious attempt to sow division, it was also alleged that dockers and their supporters left early in disgust at the behaviour of Reclaim the Streets members, who had hijacked their event. In fact, they left to catch coaches due to depart back to Liverpool.' [13]*

According to Sully and Fenot, the media created a 'virtual riot' where a few bottles thrown, often in response to police charges, were then reported as a full-scale riot. The authors suggested that the media had perhaps reduced real life to a vacuous spectacle in an effort to sell more papers. They went on to say: 'Or do they, as part of the dominant structure, see any dissent as a threat and therefore use their power to misinform the public, and to divide and misrepresent movements of opposition? The strength of the common bond between striking workers and radical greens has not been diminished by hostile and lazy media coverage.' [14] Speaking on behalf of the dockers, Billy Jenkins reiterated this view stating: 'It was a marvellous day, organised jointly between the Liverpool dockers, Reclaim the Streets and other environmental groups, and if anyone hijacked the march it was the police. The only way forward is to get together more and more. Speaking for the dockers, we can't wait to organise our next joint action. No amount of disinformation can wipe out the memories of the 20,000 people, who will remember the joy and festivity of the day long after the police-hyped media spectacle is forgotten.' [15]

On Monday 14 April, Tony Nelson telephoned from the United States to inform his fellow stewards that John Samson, an International Transport Workers' Federation inspector, who was a good friend of John Bowers, the International Longshoremen's Association president, was going to tell the ITF that they had to send delegates to the Montreal dockers' caucus. Nelson and Bobby Morton also met with International Longshore and Warehouse Union executives. On Friday 18 April, plans for yet another May Day rally were finalised, one day after the National Docks and Waterways Committee had met and objected to the way in which Jack Dempsey, the union's docks officer, had been declared innocent of any wrongdoing during the outbreak of the Liverpool docks dispute. Across the Atlantic, Nelson and Morton were made honorary members of the ILWU at the organisations 30th International Convention. The two stewards were delighted with the backing they had received from the ILWU, and they appealed to all other dockers' unions across the world to follow suit, making the case that, 'International solidarity in the fight against casual labour and privatisation is a question of survival.' [16] Details of the ILWU International Convention were reported in a lengthy article published on *LabourNet*, praising the Americans' ability to recognise that despite facing incredible economic hardship, massive political opposition and a conspiracy of silence within the British press, the Liverpool dockworkers' fight for reinstatement remained a cause that must be supported:

> '...it is clearly imperative that this trend toward privatisation and casualisation be stopped once and for all now in Liverpool. It is further imperative that all dockworkers' unions do everything possible in a coordinated effort to aid the Liverpool dockworkers in their ongoing struggle to regain their jobs...' [17]

As the ILWU discussed the dockers' struggle at their convention, the March for Social Justice paid respect to the Chartists, this heroic working-class movement that first met on Kennington Common in 1848. The Liverpool dockers could only wonder if their own campaign would end in the kind of success that had immortalised their pioneering forebears. [18]

# 62

# The Liverpool Dockers Fail to Call for UK Solidarity Action?

*'Every week, the platform has reported the ups and downs of struggle. These men and women have gone through their disappointments and their hopes; and every week, they carried the same resolution demanding reinstatement for everybody... After eighteen months locked out, they continued to reiterate their resolution for full reinstatement, and in opposition to the TGWU leadership – that this reinstatement of the 500 and the removal of Drake International and the scabs, was the only basis for negotiation.' ~ Bill Hunter\**

Political analysis of the Liverpool docks dispute continued without respite. Following the publication of a book on the dispute by academics Jane Kennedy and Michael Lavalette, another debate was chronicled online by the team at *LabourNet*. Lavalette stated:

> *'I have just recently joined the labor-l [email message board list] and received a letter sent three weeks ago by Chris Bailey, on globalisation and the Liverpool docks dispute, which included an attack on the Socialist Workers Party in Britain. Bailey argued that the SWP had been critical of those arguing for the dockers' international strategy...' [1]*

Lavalette argued that there was considerable debate among the dockers regarding strategy and tactics, and that it was not the case, 'as Bailey seems to suggest, that it is merely the Socialist Workers Party on the 'outside' who disagree with the dominant international focus of the campaign. Within the dispute, there are a number of tactics being advocated: some stress the need for unity with community leaders; others stress the possibilities of local trade union solidarity, while the dominant strategy of the stewards is to look to the international dock

---

\*Bill Hunter, 'Globalisation, labour internationalism and the Liverpool docks dispute' message exchange took place initially on the Labor-L list, available on LabourNet:
http://www.labournet.net/docks2/9704/GLOBAL.HTM

labour force to deliver the victory for the dockers.' [2] *LabourNet's* Greg Dropkin observed that while the writers noted that the unionised workforce in Britain had consistently raised money and support for the dockers, they neglected to mention the fact that the dockers and the Women of the Waterfront had toured the country in order to make it possible. Lavalette was of the view that, 'the dock stewards have been unwilling to try and move beyond this, to argue and win more active support.' [3] Meyer, Robnett and Whittier, writing in 2002, claimed:

> '...the pickets were few and made no significant effort to turn back transport. They were 'token.' Throughout the whole course of the dispute, the dockers were somewhat reluctant to use mass pickets. The stewards did not issue a call to other workers for practical as well as financial support. Fatalism in the dockers' case meant not that they would refuse to fight on, but only that they believed they must fight alone. So far as Britain was concerned, all they could demand of other workers was financial aid and occasional token demonstrations of support.' [4]

The reality was that during the early weeks of the dispute, the dockers repeatedly appealed for support from their fellow Transport and General Workers' Union members still working in the Port of Liverpool. They also called for support from the working-class in general, both in their own city and across the UK. Local support groups were created and thousands of meetings and delegations were undertaken to raise support for their struggle. All these actions took place in addition to campaigning for support from dockers across the globe along with the international working-class. Evidence of this multi-faceted approach to industrial action, or leverage, is well documented. The Liverpool dockers struck in support of so many other workers – from the miners to the nurses; from opposition to Pinochet and apartheid to blockades of South African trade and illegal Namibian uranium hexafluoride. It makes sense that the same dockers would expect some level of return direct action from workers they had supported over many years, with a history of solidarity and direct action that put them on picket lines fighting for other Liverpool workers in Stanley Racing, Cater-Cups, ASDA, Moat House Hotel and A1 Feeds, as they helped those workers fight for union recognition. John Farrell, a TGWU organiser, worked with other officials and members to organise effective occupations of ASDA and the Moat House Hotel to impose union recognition on these companies. During the 1979 closure of Dunlops in Liverpool, dockers took part in 'civil disobedience' activities such as blocking the dock road. In 1995 the Liverpool dockers forged new alliances with environmental groups, anarchists, Turkish, Kurdish and numerous other community groups across the UK. No limits existed to their strategies to hurt their employer. The dockers had always been a politicised workforce, boasting a living tradition of radical trade unionism and action in their communities. Theirs was an unrivalled legacy of solidarity, unique to this section of the working-class in its ferocity and consistency. At key moments in labour history, it seemed as though the UK's dockers would forever be locked in conflict with their employers, their union and the government, and it would be ridiculous to suggest that any workers who would refuse to cross a picket line, and be sacked for sticking to that fundamental principle, would then fail to recognise their right to call upon their fellow trade unionists for support.

# THE LIVERPOOL DOCKERS FAIL TO CALL FOR UK SOLIDARITY ACTION?

The Dispute Committee convened meetings with shop stewards from other industries including those still working in the Port of Liverpool. But for all the sympathy this garnered, no action was forthcoming. They then turned to the national arena: no action was forthcoming. The docks had been internationalised since the first ship set sail and so the dockers were always part of a global industrial working-class. On the first anniversary of the dispute, at a rally attended by thousands of workers as well as SWP members, whose placards asked: 'Which side is Tony Blair on?' Jimmy Davies announced that the Liverpool dockers were, 'calling for the physical support of the entire trade union movement.' [5] When the Liverpool dockers declared that the world was their picket line, they included the rest of the UK; something which the WOW's Doreen McNally stated explicitly at every opportunity. It was the dockers and their supporters, trade unionists, political activists, anarchists and environmentalists who faced the onslaught of Merseyside Police's brutal Operational Support Group; the same young, idealistic activists who Bill Morris denounced while dockers were arrested in the act of protecting them. Writing in the *Dockers' Charter* sometime after the anniversary demonstration, Jimmy Nolan addressed the issue of his own union not supporting the dockers: 'It is over eighteen months since we were sacked for refusing to cross the picket line, and our union will not support us for fear of breaking the law and having its funds sequestrated!' [6] In another issue of the *Dockers' Charter*, under the headline *A Fight for All*, Nolan wrote that the purpose of the dockers' fight was to secure regular employment, and to safeguard the conditions and rights that their forefathers won, such as the right to collective organisation: 'Our fight is therefore the fight of millions of men and women throughout Britain facing uncertainty of employment, both day-to-day and long-term. Everywhere, employers are introducing casual labour and individual contracts. They want to cut their costs through flexible labour. They wanted workers at their beck and call, to be brought to work or discarded at their will. Nearly half the labour in Britain today is casual and part-time. In education, in services, in industry, in banking and other clerical work there is a rash of individual short-term contracts.' [7]

Presented in this light, the dispute became a conflict that all workers could, or should, have understood and related to. The Tories' secondary picket legislation had been used by the TGWU, the Trades Union Congress and other unions as a reason not to endorse solidarity action with the Liverpool dockers, and yet the Liverpool dockers were not on strike; they had been sacked by their employer, so how could they, as unemployed, possibly go on strike? Considering the absurdity of these circumstances, it is difficult to comprehend how trade union leaders continued to claim that the dispute was illegal. If meaningful legal action had ever been brought against the TGWU, perhaps the officials in charge of the UK's largest trade union might have done something to defend their buildings and cars; their infrastructure; 'The fabric of the union,' as Bill Morris very tellingly puts it. The TGWU had nothing to fear from the Dock Company, who had openly and publicly declared on many occasions their intention not to pursue legal action against the union.

To create the image of an army of working-class trade union comrades that were just waiting for the call from the Liverpool dockers' leadership is disingenuous at best. This was a dispute that lasted two years and four months, providing ample opportunity for solidarity action and, as sacked docker Harry Hunter told *Green Left Weekly* in May 1997, 'If everyone came out in support of the dockers, the bosses could not do anything. The problem for the miners, in their 1984 battle with the Thatcher government, was that they were isolated.' [8] In 1984, dockers in the UK went on strike for the miners. In a book review for the April 1997 *Dockers' Charter*, Bill Hunter wrote that *Solidarity on the Waterfront* provided readers with an important glimpse into the method of sectarianism, which he felt had to be overcome if the SWP was to take part in rebuilding working-class consciousness and confidence. [9] Dot Gibson, writing in 1998, noted: 'early on in the dispute, the Socialist Workers Party members in Liverpool University had the stewards support, they were very helpful with material, only to find that the final product was critical of them and was simply a vehicle to advertise the SWP.' [10] In the same paper, Gibson recalls that Jimmy Nolan had also told her that dockers had held meetings with members of the Socialist Workers Party ahead of publishing their book, and that the stewards had no idea what they were saying. 'If there are criticisms of me,' Gibson records Nolan as saying, 'then I want to be able to answer these!' [11] The dockers' own criticism of *Solidarity on the Waterfront* was not aimed at the SWP itself, but at the analysis of the dispute, particularly the notion that internationalism was used as a mechanism to, 'avoid direct confrontation with the TGWU leadership.' The Dispute Committee, despite all their efforts and calls for support, had failed to organise mass direct action across the UK, and in his open response to Lavalette and Kennedy, Carden asked if the two academics:

> *'...could please tell us their secret formula for instigating a general strike both locally and nationally? Debate and discussion on the Liverpool dock dispute is vital and so is criticism. The ill-informed and poorly researched views expressed by Michael Lavalette contributed nothing to the struggle of the Liverpool dockers.' [12]*

In publishing his critique on *LabourNet*, Carden sought to challenge Lavalette and Kennedy's argument that the dockers' international campaign:

> *'...reflected the politics dominant within the dispute; at heart it is a position which argues that British workers cannot and will not fight... Thus, the international campaign has not been launched from a position of strength; it reflects the stewards' pessimism at what it is possible to achieve at home... We shouldn't forget that the Tory laws were designed to prevent 'traditional' forms of working-class activity and action. The irony is that they are providing a cover behind which Bill Morris and the trade union leadership are hiding, and the forthcoming 'New' Labour Government will not repeal.' [13]*

A number of Liverpool dockers' supporters voiced their disagreement with Lavalette and Kennedy. One of those supporters, Bill Hunter, author of *They Knew Why They Fought: Unofficial Struggle and Leadership on the docks, 1945-1989*, [14] wrote of the two academics' perspective:

> *The comments and conclusions in the book which criticise the running of the struggle were, in effect, grafted on to the research and interviews they did. I think we have the same method of ignoring concrete reality in Michael Lavalette's letter. The real importance of this strike, the real lessons of its evolution and its place in the history of*

62

THE LIVERPOOL DOCKERS FAIL TO CALL FOR UK SOLIDARITY ACTION?

*trade union struggle and dockers' struggle are missed. Instead of discussing a living movement there are dead assertions.'* [15]

Hunter's critique leans towards the view that the conclusions drawn in *Solidarity on the Waterfront* had likely been reached before any research-based historical context had been fitted around them. As the writers themselves confirmed to the *Socialist Review* in January 1997, it was their *belief* that political differences between the stewards were what informed their decisions on how to take the dispute forward:

> *'The politics of the senior stewards, who are well respected and have won their spurs in hard times, carry a lot of weight. There are disagreements, but these are suppressed in a display of unity, not expressed in real debate to dockers and supporters. So, the strategy that has emerged is coloured by the experiences of the 1980s and 'new realism' that Tory anti-union laws can't be broken for fear of funds being sequestrated, and that the wider trade union movement cannot be seriously called on for solidarity because workers have been too beaten down by the Tories.'* [16]

By contrast, Bill Hunter referred to the tenacity and strength of the dockers:

> *'Week after week, they reiterated that they had to be treated as a body; they would not hand over hostages, neither the Torside workers nor militant trade unionists, in a bargain with the Mersey Docks and Harbour Company. That was contrary to the policy of union leaders. Every week, the platform has reported the ups and downs of struggle. These men and women have gone through their disappointments and their hopes; and every week, they have carried the same resolution demanding reinstatement for everybody.'* [17]

Greg Dropkin and Hugh Rodwell, whilst accepting some of the issues raised by Lavalette and Kennedy's against the dock shop stewards, rejected their view on the international campaign and its relation to local industrial action:

> *'One aspect of this argument has been the union's attitude to international solidarity action. Bill Hunter, Greg Dropkin and Mike Carden argued the factual basis of many of Michael Lavalette's assertions, as an important reason underlying his errors and omissions was his failure to grasp the character of what Bill Hunter calls 'a living movement.' Basically, no political force can legislate for or bring 'mobilisation' by proclamation. Mobilisation is what happens when people can't put up with their situation any longer and organise to fight for a change. Policies develop in relation to a given mobilisation, great or small, local or worldwide. Also, they can weaken or boost mobilisation. But they can't create it.'* [18]

Hugh Rodwell considered that:

*'Looking for support in the real-world means going through organisations, and this discussion has given examples of the confrontations this has led to nationally with the T&G and TUC, and internationally with the ITF. But the rank-and-file has been reached, both in Britain and abroad, and the effects of this have already been seen. There are signs of fresh mobilisation around the world, and the example of Liverpool is giving hope and inspiration in these struggles.' [19]*

In concluding, Bill Hunter wrote that, 'for many of the Liverpool dockers and the shop stewards, this only shows how you can exist in the middle of a conflict and not know what is going on.' [20] Hunter's analysis was supported by the fact that on the day when Jane Kennedy presented Jimmy Nolan with a copy of the then unpublished *Solidarity on the Waterfront*, offering him an opportunity to appraise the final draft, he was happy just to thank her for taking the time to write it; simply trusting that she and Lavalette would have produced a realistic commentary on the dispute, especially since they had been given unlimited access to the stewards and the dockers.

# 63

# Rock the Dock:
# An Occupation?

*'I don't think we're the last gasp of a dying era. I think we are the beginning of a new one. We are showing a greedy nation that there are other values.' ~ Cathy Dwyer**

In London, at the annual Brit Awards, held on 24 February 1997, the author Irvine Welsh wore a 'Support the Liverpool Dockers' T-Shirt as he went up on stage to receive an award from the musician Damon Albarn for the soundtrack to the movie *Trainspotting*. Live on television, in front of millions of viewers, Welsh dedicated the award to: 'Everyone in Leith and Muirehouse, and the Liverpool dockers. At the end of the day, it's like all inspirations for fighting for their rights, getting off their knees; that's where art comes from; that's where music comes from. Everything else is just fucking nonsense.' [1] There was more support from the world of music when, on Sunday 20 April, Noel Gallagher, from Oasis, played a set for the dockers at London's Mean Fiddler, and in a television interview, Tony Melia said that Jimmy Davies, the dockers' secretary, recognised that this was the modern equivalent of John Lennon representing a cause. [2] Davies's son, Jimmy Davies Jr, said after the concert: 'Noel Gallagher, the biggest pop star in Britain, if not the world, is supporting us, so it is a major, major boost for us.' [3] The Beautiful South were another band to perform a series of fundraising gigs on behalf of the dockers, and at London's Sound Republic, some of the biggest names in British music would join forces to draw attention to the ongoing plight of the sacked dockworkers, in what was billed as the first 'Rock the Dock' concert. Gallagher and the Who's Pete Townshend were the main artists at an event, which drew celebrity support from actors such as David Thewlis (*Seven Years in Tibet*) and Dexter Fletcher (*Lock, Stock and Two Smoking Barrels*), as well as the singer Bob Geldof.

---

* Cathy Dwyer, quoted in Dave Cotterill, 'Official History of the Liverpool Dock Dispute', 1995 (p.105)

Rock the Dock became an extremely high-profile aspect of the dockers' campaign, as musicians helped raise awareness for a cause that they felt had been wholly ignored by the majority of the British national press, with Oasis, Primal Scream, Dodgy, Cast and Paul Weller all featuring on a Rock The Dock CD, a Creation Records compilation put together in support of the Hardship Fund. The CD was released on 20 July 1997. Tracks on the album included: Don't Look Back in Anger (Oasis), Come Together (Primal Scream), Found You (Dodgy), For So Long (Cast), Setting Sun (the Chemical Brothers), One By One (Chumbawamba), Cast Out in the '70s (Gene), Always the Star (60ft Dolls), Lazarus (the Boo Radleys), So You Want to Be a Dancer (Paul Weller), Foxy Folk Faced (Ocean Colour Scene) and Never Cross a Picket Line (Billy Bragg). Matthew Priest, the drummer for Dodgy, regularly appeared with the band and at every opportunity he was seen wearing his dockers t-shirt. The proceeds from the album were put towards easing the financial struggle that many dockers' families were enduring. [4] Alan McGee, founder of Creation Records, told the *New Musical Express* that:

> '*We've been going to do this for about six months, just trying to get the bands together and firm the tracks up. Ultimately, we're more than just a record label. It's not our job to support these families, but our libertarian attitude means we've got to help people when we can help them. There's still work to be done. I wish that in a perfect world, there wasn't this whole casualisation of labour but there is, and these people have been sidelined by society. They've been shafted, and people have suffered really badly. They shouldn't be forgotten.*' [5]

McGee's support for the Liverpool dockers was extraordinary. Ian Broudie of the Lightning Seeds was another great supporter, and his album covers and inlays often contained references to 'Justice for the 96' and 'Support the Liverpool Dockers.' On 14 March 1997, Broudie was the guest host of *Top of the Pops*, and later that year, the Lightning Seeds headlined the Hillsborough Justice Concert at Liverpool's Anfield Stadium. He also wrote an original song for the dockers. On Monday 21 April 1997, the morning picket was scheduled for 11am, and the London Support Group intended to lobby Tony Blair, the New Labour Party leader, at a press conference in the capital. At the Scottish Trades Union Congress, Bill Morris ignored Liverpool dockers. His deputy, Jack Adams, was to tell the dockers that the Dock Company were due to meet with Graham Stevenson and business consultants KPMG to discuss the proposed dockers' labour supply company. By Thursday the 24 April 1997, it was expected that KPMG would make a statement on the labour supply company, but the following day, Stevenson sent a fax explaining that the meeting with the business consultants would remain confidential. That month a number of stewards attended MDHC's annual general meeting to directly challenge company directors over the dispute, while Jimmy Davies and Mike Carden joined workers from Hillingdon Hospital and Magnet at Ken Loach's studio in London, for a short piece to be shown on BBC's *Newsnight*. At that Friday's mass meeting, a letter from an American congressmen calling on Tony Blair to reinstate the Liverpool dockworkers was read out to the men. [6] Guest speakers that day included Dave Williams of the TGWU 6/541 Branch Road Hauliers, who reported on problems at

Sheerness, as Liverpool dockers had previously played a role in supporting his branch members. A representative of the Workers Revolutionary Party also gave a speech.

At this time, the dockers wanted to send Jimmy Nolan and Jimmy Davies to speak to John Bowers. In Amsterdam, employers were looking to sack 400 dockers and put a further 300 on casual contracts. Elsewhere, Mike Carden and Bob Ritchie addressed a meeting of the Socialist Party later that night in Dublin, and on Monday 28 April, Jack Adams told Jimmy Nolan that the TGWU had legally committed themselves to secrecy over the labour supply company discussions. [7] No fewer than 16 local labour agencies submitted confidential information to KPMG, whose final report was due to be completed by the 7 May. Bill Morris planned to go before the union's Finance and General Purposes committee with a recommendation that they agree to whatever KPMG suggested, [8] as it became increasingly obvious that he felt more comfortable with expensive consultants than his own union members. When KPMG produced their report, they would say that it was not debateable, and it was expected that Morris would use their business plan as an excuse to impose a ballot on the basis that nothing else could be achieved. [9] Much discussion took place among the stewards about how the labour co-operative was now being used to collapse the dispute, prompting Terry Teague to float the idea of occupying Seaforth Container Terminal: [10] 'We must stop the ships; we must occupy the five gantries at Seaforth, and when we do, we will need protection.' [11] Jimmy Nolan supported this idea: 'It's an occupation. Principle agreed, secrecy is vital and there needs to be a diversion.' [12]

The stewards met at Transport House at 9.30am on May Day, with Jimmy Davies again warning that the Hardship Fund was struggling, although a donation following the Channel 4 London Palladium show would soon bring a much-needed boost. [13] Frank Lannigan said that he would get the matter onto the agenda for the following week's meeting of TGWU national officers. [14] The May Day demonstration in Liverpool started at noon and saw a successful turnout, and thanks to *LabourNet*, the dockers discovered that in Zurich, Andrea Stauffacher, a leading member of the revolutionary collective *Aufbau*, had been arrested along with 130 other protestors. All of those arrested were interrogated and faced charges of participating in an illegal demonstration, but only Stauffacher remained in custody because, according to the authorities, she was part of Zurich's hardcore *autonome* scene, and so she was to be charged with destruction of property and rioting. Stauffacher had long suffered repression for her political orientation: the 47-year-old social worker had been convicted of riot charges in the past, and in 1994 she lost her job after being sentenced to a month in prison. [15] Billy Jenkins would write to her:

> '...*be assured that our thoughts and actions are with you. I have informed the shop stewards of the details of your arrest, and this will be relayed to our next mass meeting on Friday. If we can do anything to assist you, practically, please let us know.*' [16]

In the weeks ahead, events such as an International Dockworkers' Committee conference, the KPMG report on the labour supply company, the election of a Labour government, the occupation of Seaforth and a meeting with John Bowers and the Miami International Transport Workers' Conference were set to take place. [17] A number of dockers and stewards began to report back from various solidarity and fundraising delegations and the common theme among these reports was news of increased casualisation. The prevailing narrative was always one of solidarity and working-class unity; of a sense that despite the physical distances between them, these workers were united as one. At the weekly mass meeting held on Friday 2 May, Jimmy Nolan reported that Joe Benton MP was going to arrange a meeting with Labour MP Ian McCartney, to try and get the minister of state at the Department of Trade and Industry to use the government's 14% shareholding to exert influence over MDHC. This would never happen. Kim Hendry, a young journalist involved with the London Support Group, spoke about the importance of the dispute, and it was also reported that both Nolan and Jimmy Davies would soon meet with John Bowers. [18] On Tuesday 6 May, the Dispute Committee received a report from Terry Barrett and Peter Huxley, whose delegation to Berlin had not been very well organised. In a discussion about broadening support in Belfast, it was suggested that the Irish TGWU would work with Peter Hadden, the Liverpool dockers' comrade in the Irish Socialist Party, to liaise with other political groups in Ireland on the dockers' behalf. [19] Additionally, the need to occupy Irish docks was addressed, as was the possibility of linking up with the Montupet dispute

Out on the Liverpool picket lines, MDHC ordered the picket caravans to be removed by the Port Police and scabs; the caravans were placed inside Shed No.1 at Seaforth Container Terminal. Dave Martin, a Sefton councillor and port worker, and Joe Benton MP promised to help the dockers to retrieve the stolen property. According to TD Williams, MDHC's director of estates, the presence of the caravans was a threat to the integrity of the port's security. [20] John Linden of Linden Kenna Solicitors was asked to represent the dockers in a subsequent legal case regarding the caravans. Linden would contradict Williams's claims by arguing that:

> 'The whole thrust of your public pronouncements from the beginning of this dispute has been the presence of the pickets and, presumably by necessary influence, the caravan has had no such effect. On that basis, we believe that your notice is of no effect and your proposed action unlawful.' [21]

A month later, vandals would break into a replacement caravan that had been donated by a member of the public. [22] Ken Loach's film played to two packed houses on Wednesday 7 May to the dismay of Bill Morris and his supporters. The following day, Jimmy Davies telephoned from the US and told his partner that the meeting with John Bowers and Tommy Gleason, the ILA president and his attorney, had not yet taken place. A meeting with the ILA leadership did take place, with Bowers expressing concern that Michel Murray, the Montreal Dockers' leader, had not co-ordinated their action against Cast Line when Atlantic Container Line pulled out of Liverpool. [23] Gleason added that he believed the Dispute Committee had set its sights too high, as there was no way that all 500 dockers would ever be reinstated. [24] Understandably, Bowers stated that if Murray took action following the next IDC conference, the ILA would hit 'hot' cargo bound for Liverpool. [25] Another ILA representative, Al Sinardez, met with Nolan and Davies whose request to Sinardez was for direct action to follow the IDC conference. [26] The fact remained that it was Bowers and the ILA who had managed to get ACL to pull out of Liverpool for one month. In Canada, Michel Murray received a letter from David Cockcroft, the ITF president, stating that neither

Bowers nor his Australian counterpart, Robert Coombes, would support the upcoming conference to be held in Montreal, as the IDC was now considered as having been established in opposition to the ITF. Just one month later, in welcoming delegates to the ITF's own conference in Miami, Bowers asked that: 'time used in speeches be restricted in order to concentrate on actions,' as he explained that dockworkers throughout the world were under attack from the common policies of privatisation and deregulation, making special note of the need to do more to resolve the Liverpool dispute. [27]

At a Dispute Committee meeting held on 8 May 1997, the stewards discussed the possibility of asking John Bowers if he could encourage US President Bill Clinton to contact Tony Blair and convince him to intervene in the dispute. [28] On Monday 12 May, Frank Lannigan spoke to Graham Stevenson, who told him that the KPMG report would be delayed by another two weeks. Jack Dempsey expressed his concern that port users were being dishonest in providing information on the business potential in the Port of Liverpool. Meanwhile, plans to occupy the Seaforth Container Terminal were progressing but other events would knock all the shop stewards' plans off-course.

# 64

# The Death of Billy Dunne

*'They should have got the lawyers working on it because it goes back to 1989, the breaking of our system. You know, registered dockworkers, and then the employers can do what they want. The union's finished now in Liverpool. It's not broken as an organisation; our local officials are broken. The main fella that signed this deal and said it's a good deal before we started all the trouble. He's just disappeared off the scene, an employer's lackey.' ~ Ritchie Gerrard\**

At the weekly mass meeting held on Friday 9 May 1997, Jimmy Davies informed the men of a benefit night at the Phoenix pub, before stressing the need for as many dockers as possible to attend the picket line at Hillingdon Hospital the following week. Doreen McNally, Jimmy Nolan and Mike Carden were in Paris with film director Ken Loach to promote *The Flickering Flame*. Jeff Liddy had been on delegation work in Manchester, where he had his motorcycle stolen, while Terry Southers, Herbie Hollerhead, Kevin Bilsborrow, Micky Tighe and Tony Gardiner had all been on delegation work in Norway and Denmark. Peter Huxley and Terry Barrett gave a report from Germany, and guest speaker Jeff McClay, from Montupet, the former Delorean plant in Belfast, gave an update on the dispute that was happening there. It was also reported that dockers' children would be going on a holiday to County Durham on the 24 May, thanks to supporters from the Woodcraft Folk organisation. [1] The next day, the North-West Labour History Group held a meeting on the subject of *'the Struggles of the Liverpool Dockers, Yesterday and Today'*, featuring presentations by Eric Taplin, Doreen McNally, Jimmy Nolan and Kevin Robinson. This provided a great opportunity for Taplin to share some of his extraordinary knowledge of the history of Liverpool docks. [2] On Monday 12 May, Frank Lannigan chaired a Dispute Committee meeting, where everyone present was united in expressing their concerns over KPMG and various other obstacles to the development of a business plan for the dockers' labour supply company. The following day, Jimmy Davies gave feedback from his meetings with John Bowers and the leadership of

---

\* Ritchie Gerrard, the Dockers' Charter, 20 November 1995

the International Longshore Association while also explaining the differences of opinion between the ILA and Michel Murray's Montreal dockers. [3] On Wednesday 14 May, several stewards met with the campaign group of Labour MPs, where the need to 'get into government ministers' was made clear. [4]

One day after the meeting with Labour MPs, the dockers were notified of an increase to their pension entitlements, as they received a year-for-year pension calculation. [5] At the same meeting Graham Stevenson, the docks national officer, let Jimmy Davies know that the KPMG business plan would not include jobs at the Seaforth Container or Timber terminals. At the following day's Dispute Committee meeting, Terry Teague and Andy Dwyer reported on a speech given by the Fire Brigade Union's General Secretary, Ken Cameron, who told a gathering in Bridlington that, 'General Secretaries should be pulling Bill Morris.' [6] They had also spoken with union delegates from the Nigerian Campaign for Independent Unionism and the Japanese Railway Workers Union, who would later attend that week's mass meeting. At this mass meeting Helen Milne, of the Citizens Advice Bureau, was thanked for her tremendous, selfless work with the dockers and their families, ahead of her promotion to a national position. Jimmy Davies then repeated his US report for the men, as he confirmed that the ILA would support any decisions that resulted from the IDC conference in Montreal. It was around this time that Eric Leatherbarrow, the Dock Company's press officer, gave an interview to BBC Radio Wales, in which he claimed that:

> 'There are no scabs in this port. I'm talking about, first of all, the men who worked for the MDHC and would not listen to the leaders of this dispute. It's about 80 dockers, 60 to 80 men, who had been coming in throughout this situation… We recognise that a lot of men out there who have given a lot of service to the company were misled, and were actually trapped outside by the picket line as much as the people inside have been intimidated by that picket line.' [7]

On Monday 20 May, a number of stewards sat down to learn how to use the new Macintosh computer that had been donated to the dockers' campaign by Liverpool John Moores University. This was a result of a lot of hard work by Dave Cotterill, as well as a reflection of the commitment of Chris Bailey and Greg Dropkin in their use of information and communication technology, which had become one of the driving forces behind the dispute. [8] At the following day's Dispute Committee meeting, a discussion took place regarding the number of fronts that the stewards' time and energies were being spread across, with issues ranging from KPMG, Montreal and John Bowers, and the supposedly unofficial and illegal nature of the dispute. Ritchie Gerrard, a sacked gantry driver at Seaforth Container Terminal, talked about the how the TGWU and the press continued to insist on referring to the dispute as an unofficial strike, as he told the *Dockers' Charter*: 'The law says that you can be dismissed for being on an official strike, so what's the difference?' [9] Perhaps, as some dockers argued, they should have focussed on the official status of the dispute when Bill Morris imposed an official secret ballot in January 1996 on what he called an *unofficial strike*. [10] There was good news in regard to picket line caravans, as following support from the chief executive of Sefton Council, it was decided that they would be allowed to remain in place outside the Dock Estate.

# THE DEATH OF BILLY DUNNE

On Tuesday the 20 May, Liverpool docker Billy Dunne passed away at just 60 years of age. A letter written by Billy's wife, Maureen, was published in the June edition of the *Dockers' Charter*, after it had previously been read out at the mass meeting held on 23 May. 'Dear Lads,' Maureen began:

*'I want you to listen to what I have to say. Willy loved you all very much. He should be with you here today, not in a box. Those 'fat cats' of the MDHC killed him, just as much as if they had put a gun to his head. He loved the docks for 35 years of his life, it was all he knew, and being sacked broke his heart. Don't let the bosses of Mersey Docks win. This has been written from my heart. I will be rooting for you all to win the dispute and be reinstated.'* [11]

That same month, the television programme *Here and Now* did a feature on Mersey Docks and Harbour Company bosses and the Liverpool dockers, during which director Peter Jones claimed: 'People who just want to do a normal daily job have been subjected to abuse and harassment, and we owe a great debt to our employees who have worked on in those circumstances.' [12] The programme showed the dockers attempting to occupy the Norse Irish berth, with accompanying comments from Philip Shepard, manager of Norse Irish Line, who said that he had: 'very little sympathy for the dockers, or the ex-dockers, hurling abuse at the workforce here.' [13] The presenter, Anastasia Cook, then talked about how the dispute had been largely ignored, as footage showed the dockers gathering at 5am to set up a picket line, preparing tea and sandwiches for their supporters. [14] Ronnie Bibby and his son, Alan, a Torside docker, were interviewed at their home, with Alan saying: 'If my dad had crossed the picket line that day, he would not be sitting there today with me, and vice versa.' [15] Ronnie then spoke of how his own father had also been a docker, as had his wife's father, before it was put it to him that if low wages and long hours were a reality for so many UK workers, what gave the Liverpool dockers the right to expect anything different. Alan answered that the dockers also experienced low pay: 'We have had enough of this. We want to provide for our families.' [16] The next scene featured Jones responding to the reporter saying that many dockers believed that MDHC had welcomed the dispute as an opportunity to introduced cheap, casual labour:

*'The MDHC dockers who refused to come to work [in September 1995] had no dispute with their employer. They had no ballot for industrial action; they had not attempted to resolve any grievance they might have had through their union officials. They simply withdrew their labour.'* [17]

This was followed by docker's wife Rose Kilcullen speaking about her: 'pride for her husband and the other dockers,' adding that her life had changed, 'from day one of the dispute. Everything's gone.' [18] Peter Jones, for the Dock Company, then stated his desire to: 'put the episode behind us, but resolution can't involve turning the clock back and re-employing the people who have been dismissed.' [19]

At the next stewards' meeting, it was reported that a two-hour telephone conversation had taken place with an MDHC manager, in which it was claimed that there had been, 'a high turnover of staff on the docks, with managers terrorising scabs while Drakes dominated the docks, much to the annoyance now of the MDHC.' [20] As the dispute was approaching the end of its second year, some of the scabs were now entitled to employment rights, and Les Hedder, one of the new 'bosses' on the docks, was already making demands of the Dock Company, knowing that they would always concede for fear of the scabs going out on strike. [21] On Wednesday 21 May, Jimmy Nolan returned from a short illness in time to hear that campaign finances were weak again, with only enough cash in the Hardship Fund to last another two weeks. Dot Gibson was at the meeting to speak about issues relating to the London Support Group, as an argument developed over political groups and certain individuals organising conferences and demonstrations, over topics such as Maastrict, without even consulting the dockers. However, Kevin Robinson was keen to steer the discussion back towards the practical matter of getting the Hardship Fund recognised as a registered charity, so that money arising from various projects, most notably the Ken Loach film, could be classed as charitable donations, separate from any political agenda. [22] To achieve this, Ian Dodwell, of Linden Kenna Solicitors, guided the stewards through the application process, [23] with Loach, Canon Nicholas Frayling and the Women of the Waterfront's Irene Campbell named as potential trustees. They would later be joined by Alan Bleasdale, the acclaimed Liverpool-born playwright, who in August 1998 wrote the following message: 'This is just to confirm that I would be delighted to be a trustee of the charity to be formed for the distribution of funds to the families of the sacked Liverpool dockers. Please do not hesitate to contact me if you require any further proof or information. The best of luck and best wishes. Alan Bleasdale.' [24]

On Friday 23 May, at 7.30am, the dockers closed off the road outside Norse Irish and held a minute's silence for their deceased comrade Billy Dunne, and at the mass meeting held later that morning, the men stood with their supporters to pay respect to the life of a Liverpool docker. [25] The following day, the dockers took part in a march from Myrtle Parade to St George's Hall. [26] This British leg of what was a Europe-wide march had been organised several months in advance with Liverpool dockworkers. They provided shelter, food and drink for demonstrators as they passed through the city. A request was also made for rank-and-file dockers to take part in the march and subsequent rally at St George's Plateau, which was made successful thanks in large part to the attendance of the Liverpool dockers and the WOW, who came out in force to support the march against unemployment, poverty and social exclusion. [27] On Tuesday 27 May, the morning picket began at 10.30am, and then at 2pm the WOW set up their own line at the Seaforth Container Terminal gate. They closed down traffic for over an hour and a half, before returning at 5pm to close the gates for another hour, with one of the women, Elsie Jones, who had been slightly injured when a car knocked into her. The next day saw a good turnout for a picket that involved representatives of the East Japan Railway Workers' Union, on what was also the day of Billy Dunne's funeral. [28] The following day there were 5pm pickets at both the Seaforth and Alexandra gates. That week's Friday mass meeting was chaired by Jimmy Davies, who updated the dockers on their pension scheme, while explaining that everyone needed to be reinstated before they could claim their entitlements, and that a pensions advisor, Martin Hartrop, had agreed to travel to Liverpool and answer any queries that the men might have had about the scheme.

# 65

# Internationalism and
# the Second IDC

*'At the Scottish TUC's Women's Conference, Margaret Prosser, a TGWU national official, claimed the TGWU would not pursue a public inquiry into the MDHC.' ~ Author's Notes\**

The internationalism of the Liverpool docks dispute was made all the more extraordinary for the fact that it was unofficial in nature and rank-and-file in its organisation. Nothing like it had ever been attempted on such a scale. It was a highly sophisticated and effective organisational strategy, operating from within an industry renowned for its often hard, physical, sectoral and confrontational trade unionism. All dock workers had a long history of fighting bosses, union bureaucrats and governments, either individually or all at once, and it was this same strength of intellect and political competence that provided the bedrock of their campaign. They knew what they were doing, and they had the confidence to do it on a global scale. Bill Hunter described this process:

> *The dockers and the Women of the Waterfront succeeded in building links internationally in the context of a world where dockers, and workers generally, are facing the same fundamental attacks, and there is more and more prospect of a joint fight beyond frontiers. We are told that the dockers did not seek to move the rank-and-file abroad. However, the policy of the dockers' emissaries going abroad to ports, of which, sometimes, they had no knowledge at all, was the one that produced the connections with the rank-and-file and the actions that took place. That policy was simply to argue for support for the strike wherever they could. They searched for militant supporters and, of course, in the real world, they had to go through the unions to get at the rank-and-file.'*
> [1]

---

\* Author's Notes, Wednesday 19 November 1997

Writer and trade union activist Alexander Cockburn, together with the Industrial Workers of the World, also understood and respected the actions of the dockers, as they recorded the concrete international solidarity of workers who were taking direct action in support of the Liverpool dockers and facing serious legal attacks for their trouble. Cockburn reported on the growing list of prominent endorsers of picket action across the US, which included: Dolores Huerta of the United Farmworkers; Jesse Jackson; the Bay Area International Longshore and Warehouse Union; retired veterans of past ILWU battles; Tony Mazzocchi, the national organiser of the Labour Party; and Jerry Brown and Ignacio De La Fuente, the two leading candidates in the Oakland, California mayoral race. Jack Heyman celebrated the work of Cockburn, who died in 2012, praising him as a strong supporter of rank-and-file longshoremen. In addition to covering the Liverpool docks dispute in the pages of his online magazine, *Counter-Punch*, Cockburn also participated in support rallies on the US West Coast, aiding in the struggle to revive international workers' solidarity. He was not one of those so-called 'left' journalists, cruising along on easy platitudes in praise of the labour movement, [2] nor was he afraid to criticize the trade union bureaucracy whenever it undermined the class struggle. [3]

For Greg Dropkin, another American journalist and socialist activist, who had been based in Liverpool since the 1970s, it was troubling enough that the TGWU did not welcome international action. This was a stance that they justified by hiding behind Thatcherite anti-union legislation, but even worse was how the union had colluded with the ITF to repeatedly push its fellow affiliates away from responding to the Liverpool dockers' direct appeals throughout 1995 and 1996. According to Dropkin, the ITF's eventual endorsement of solidarity action came only after an extensive debate on the subject had broken out in September 1996, culminating in the resignation of an ITF inspector, Jack Heyman, who had himself been a prominent figure in the organisation of action taken by his own union, the ILWU. This debate began in Liverpool on 30 August 1996, as the Dispute Committee told a mass meeting about their recent four-hour encounter with the TGWU leadership, which had begun with a strong complaint about the ITF. Heyman's resignation letter to the ITF attacked both the TGWU and ITF, [4] and in Dropkin's view:

> 'Even though the dockers' historical record in support of every other dispute going gave them the moral right to demand local action, it was simply impossible to unleash when the lockout began. But now, the dockers have an enormous domestic credibility won through 18 months of struggle.' [5]

The Women of the Waterfront were often at the vanguard of the global campaign, and they joined a delegation, including docker's son Mike Dooley, to Amsterdam for a march where Rotterdam dockworkers and their wives invited the WOW to an emergency meeting on threats to dock labour pools. After attending the meeting, Irene Campbell explained how she began to fully understand the pressure and injustice that had been wrought upon the Liverpool dockers, as she recalled that the atmosphere got quite emotional when several of the wives became distraught: 'They were in tears listening to our account.' [6] Like their Liverpool counterparts, the Rotterdam women were well organised, and their secretary,

Halinka Augustin, told the WOW: 'We are right behind you.' [7] The meeting was also notable for Jimmy Campbell's performance, with people gathering around to hear him speak and willing him to keep going. It was indicative of a growing appetite for standing up and fighting alongside workers from all walks of life the world over; unfortunately, further demonstrations in Amsterdam were prohibited due to a scheduled visit by Tony Blair. [8]

With the Second International Conference of Port Workers on the horizon, the various rank-and-file delegations were galvanised into co-ordinating as much support as possible. The primary goal being direct action against the two largest shipping lines in the Port of Liverpool, Atlantic Container Line and Cast. On Sunday 25 May 1997, the conference took place at Montreal's *Hotel du Parc*, as dozens of trade unionists from around the world converged to attend meetings and discuss strategies. 'It was a very impressive conference,' wrote Mike Carden, 'When one examines the quality of the delegates, the detailed work that has gone into the preparation of numerous documents, etc, it is a tribute to rank-and-filism. The ITF and Morris have every right to fear this movement of dockers for dockers.' [9] Michel Murray, the leader of the Montreal dockers, opened the event by remarking on the increasing number of attacks on workers' rights globally, while pointing to Quebec's anti-scab law as an example for the rest of the world to follow. [10] The Canadian Union of Public Employees sent a delegate who gave a sweeping overview of trade union history, politics and its impact upon the economy, and then Murray introduced all of those responsible for organising the conference, noting that: 'The first conference in Liverpool was a historic event.' [11] The delegates then set about developing direct action plans in support of the Liverpool dockers and their families, discussing deregulation, privatisation and the casualisation of dock work, as Murray reaffirmed the dockers objective to establish a new international dockworkers' organisation. [12] Jimmy Nolan led the conference's second session, during which he spoke about globalisation, the Thatcher government and unofficial and illegal action. [13] Unfortunately, much like during a 1989 conference in Germany, the interpreters struggled with Nolan's thick Irish-Scouse accent, which again had to be translated into English and then other languages needed by delegates; but everyone present understood his message. As usual Jimmy Nolan spoke with passion, conviction and an abundance of authenticity.

The Russian Union of Dockworkers invited delegates to their country, so that others could witness for themselves the conditions that they were working under, while Denmark's Ole Muller talked about how the Liverpool struggle had raised the collective consciousness of dockworkers to such a degree that they now fully understood the growing threats of casualisation and diminishing terms and conditions of employment. Sweden's Kenny Kaarlson made reference to port employers examining the situation in Liverpool ahead of rolling out casualisation across the globe, such as in the Netherlands, where 1,400 full-time dockers were in danger of losing their jobs. Port workers in France and Italy were also under threat. In Portugal, the number of employed dockworkers had plummeted from 10,000 in 1980 to just 750 by 1995, while delegates from Spain, New Zealand, South Africa, Japan and Ireland all recounted similar tales of attacks on unionisation, pay and conditions. [14] US docker and ILWU member Norman Parks spoke of the importance of events such as the International Conference of Port Workers, singling out Michel Murray for his role in its organisation, before adding: 'it is a pity that dockworkers' representatives from Mexico, Chile and Brazil are not here.' [15] For their part, the Liverpool dockers, as with so many other international dockers present at the conference, had plenty of experience organising strikes, international boycotts and international solidarity. [16] As far as they were concerned, their dispute was very much winnable, and with their history of solidarity action, they felt that they had every right to expect national and international support. Above all, they had the credibility to command a platform alongside their comrades. [17]

Terry Teague gave the opening address of the Monday session on behalf of the Liverpool dockers, listing the key moments of the Liverpool dispute from its beginning in September 1995 and providing a history of Liverpool dockers' solidarity. Teague had been responsible for co-ordinating international action in support of the dispute, and Greg Dropkin's film was shown to the delegates as an official record of their global direct action. This led into a discussion about the role of the ITF, with many delegates declaring their loyalty to the organisation, while at the same time expressing a belief that it should have had a presence at the conference, as the aim was to bring dockers together, not to oppose the ITF. [18] Some delegates claimed they had the authority to send fraternal greetings from the ITF, [19] and the New Zealand delegate, Terry Ryan, moved a resolution regarding relations with the ITF and the need to avoid conflict with it. [20] This was supported by Japan's Nakamura, who called for further action to be taken. He would personally inform the ITF of the 24-hour international day of action that was planned. The principle of this resolution was adopted unanimously, with Michel Murray suggesting that the action take place in June or July. Norman Parks then opened up a debate by saying that the ILWU supported a shutdown last time around, and would do the same again, but that it was up to the delegates to state firmly what action they planned to take. [21] Pat Riley, from the International Longshoremen's Association in the Port of St John, argued in favour of opening a dialogue with Tony Blair, the UK's new prime minister, while stressing the importance of continuing to work with the ITF: 'We may be rebels,' he said, 'but we are not renegades.' [22] Some delegates asked what action would be undertaken in the UK, to which Jimmy Nolan responded by explaining: 'The legislation of the Tory government is still in existence under New Labour, which limits the opportunities for direct action.' [23] Björn Borg of the Swedish Dockworkers' Union lamented the difficulties involved in executing a 24-hour strike action. The previous Day of World Action, on 20 January 1997, had turned out to be a week of continuous action. [24] Nakamura spoke again of the need for the dockers to be flexible in their approach. [25] It was at this point that Murray suggested an adjournment until the following day, although Tom Dufresne from the ILWU wanted to continue examining what action the unions were taking in the UK. [26]

On Tuesday 27 May, Jimmy Nolan, Terry Teague and Mike Carden called for a month of activity against the Dock Company, while Michel Murray asked for a private session with some of the delegates, as he firmly believed that the international movement could not allow the Liverpool dockers to be defeated. Murray insisted on showing Ken Loach's film, *The Flickering Flame*, the end of which brought tears to Nolan's eyes. It was the first time he was able to watch the film all the way through. Ken Loach's film had a stunning impact on every delegate. [27] Murray and the Montreal Conference Organising Committee wanted to follow this screening of the film with two resolutions, and that morning he moved for a 24-hour strike in support of the Liverpool campaign, along with continuous action that would not cease until the Liverpool dockworkers had been reinstated. [28] Another resolution called for relations with the ITF to be formalised at the organisation's Miami conference, to be held 9 and 10 June. [29] In the June issue of the *ILWU Dispatcher*, Heyman reported on the agreements reached at the International Conference of Port Workers. [30]

Heyman's lengthy and detailed report explained how a Canadian delegate had spoken frankly, saying: 'I do not pretend to have power I do not have. If dockers can support action, then good, but on the West Coast of British Columbia, employers will issue writs of $9 million, and 3,300 dockers could be fined this amount. We would be throwing good money after bad. It's a bad idea. British Colombia ship some cargo to Liverpool, what good would it do? Is the effect worth it? We've done it and it's failed. If we give enough warning, the injunctions will be served.' [31] This delegate felt that it would be more advantageous for the conference to lobby the ITF and get them to exert their political influence on the Blair government in the UK, which Terry Ryan agreed with, adding that they should also put pressure on the TGWU. The Spanish representatives informed the conference that although there were strike restrictions in Spain, they would support any decisions reached by the conference. It would fall to the Spanish, French, Italian and Portuguese dockworkers to co-ordinate the agreed action. The Spanish delegate also pointed out that changes to the industry were not to be blamed on technology, as the recent Loach film had reminded him of Barcelona in 1980, where 180 dockers were sacked. This brought him to the conclusion: 'It's not Liverpool's problem, it's *our* problem.' [32] Ireland's Jack Smith declared: 'We are all members of the TGWU, and our union caused this problem.' [33]

Canadian George Bryan agreed with his compatriot, Pat Riley, regarding the need to lobby the UK's Labour government: 'We cannot close Halifax, it's premature. We have to take it back to our Locals [branches]. The ultimate decision is to be taken by dockers.' [34] The Portuguese delegate then explained that in his country: 'We have 700 dockers with 300 casuals, and the employers want all dockers to be casual.' [35] Michel Murray invoked the memory of previous union leaders by demanding to know: 'What would they make of this conference? Repetition! It is like a psychologists' convention. We are dockers, let's get on with it. The ITF conference would be discussing the agenda of the World Bank, nothing of the dockers of Liverpool. Twenty-one months in dispute!' [36] The Danish representative revealed that Copenhagen would lose 300 dock jobs in August 1997, promising that he would not stand by and let it happen after watching *The Flickering Flame*, while Dutch delegates called for a leaflet campaign. [37] By 3.30pm, it was unanimously decided that these dockers would support a 24-hour strike, along with other supplementary actions. The prevailing reality at the conference was that the situation in the Port of Liverpool was being recreated by port employers worldwide. Murray again spoke of the need to organise an international committee of dockers for dockers, before Jimmy Nolan closed by expressing his confidence that the third International Dockers' Conference, or IDC, as it was now being referred to, would take place in Liverpool after the dockers there had been reinstated. The Spanish dockers were also keen to host an international conference. Later on and in private, Michel Murray, the Montreal dockers' leader, gave a cheque for the Liverpool dockers' Hardship Fund to Jimmy Nolan.

A rank-and-file international movement had been born from almost the beginning of the Liverpool dockers' struggle. The delegates who attended the historic international dockers' conference in Montreal were: Jimmy Nolan, Terry Teague, Mike Carden, (Liverpool); Jean-Louis Affagard, Michel Hardy, Philippe Silliau (France); Gerry Quigley, Jack Smith, John Doherty, Kevin Penders, Patsy Stone (Ireland's ATGWU); Gianni Dozza (Italy); Akinobu Itoh, Yoshi Nori Nakamura (Japan); Harry Kappelhof, Ron Wiechels, Tony Koningh (Holland); Terry Ryan (New Zealand); Antonio Mariano (Portugal); Vadim Ivanov, Vladamir Vasillev (Russia); Marvin Mfundsi (South Africa); Michel Murray, Alain Desrochers, Theodore Beaudin (Quebec); Albert Batten, Doug Sigurdson, Fred Nice, George Briand, James Orr, John Pepe, Martin Campbell, Pat Riley, Rick Robinson, Rick Rondpre, Terry Breen, Tom Vaudry (Canada); Ole Muller (Denmark); Eusebio Penalver, Garcia Gonzalez Julian (Spain), Björn Borg (Sweden); Jack Heyman, Larry Hansen, Lynn Hummel, Norman Parks and Peter Hendrickson (USA). [38] Even if some of these delegates were locked into their support for the ITF and disagreed at the time with some of the outcomes of the conference, they were taking part in an internationalism that differed from that of the ITF and, in this, the reality of the 2nd International Dockworkers' Conference was established.

On Monday 2 June, Jimmy Nolan telephoned Kees Marges, to ask him to allow Liverpool dockers to attend the ITF's Miami Conference. Two days later, the Dispute Committee sent a formal request for permission to address the conference, which was due to begin on the 9 June. [38] It was Nolan's belief that they would need the backing of all ITF delegates who attended the International Conference of Port Workers in Montreal in order for David Cockcroft, the ITF General Secretary, to grant this request. Thus, all ITF Dockers' Section affiliates were asked to call on Cockcroft to reconsider his initial decision to not allocate time for the Liverpool dockers to speak. [39] The ITF responded:

> *'After consulting with the Transport and General Workers' Union about this, I have to inform you that they take the view that the position of the Liverpool dockers can adequately be represented by the union's delegates at the Miami meeting, and that we are therefore not in a position to extend an invitation to you to attend.' [40]*

Bill Morris had written to request that his own members be excluded from an international trade union organisation:

> *'The T&G will be represented at this conference by the National Secretary, Graham Stevenson, and a member of our Executive Council from the Docks and Waterways Trade Group. We therefore feel that the issue of the Liverpool Docks will be adequately communicated to those attending Conference. Any deviation from the elected delegations attending conference would indicate an acceptance by the ITF of unofficial groups to constitutional conferences. If this were the case, needless to say, the T&G would object to ITF business being conducted in this way.' [41]*

# 66

# General Executive Council
# Meeting, June 1997

*'But whatever the rules may say, the running of the TGWU is securely in the hands of the full-time officials, who make up a bureaucracy both willing and able to ride roughshod over the wishes of even a highly organised and militant section like the dockers, as during the 1972 docks strike. To understand the nature of this bureaucracy and its power, we must look at the union's history.' ~ C. Sparks\**

On Monday 2 June 1997, Danny Maher, leader of the tugboatmen, had a conversation with Mike Carden while they were both attending a meeting of the union's General Executive Council in London. Maher told Carden that *Document 58*, on the Liverpool dispute, which was due to be presented to the GEC members, had been written in such a way as to position the Liverpool dockers in opposition to their own union. Later that night, Maher revealed to Carden that Jack Adams and Graham Stevenson would be meeting representatives of the Dock Company the following day, with the intention of reporting back to the GEC on Wednesday. [1] Adams and Stevenson were joined by Dave McCall at the meeting which took place in Manchester. Carden contacted his fellow shop stewards and made it clear that Morris was about to get his own way regarding an enforced ballot, and floated the idea of sending a delegation to lobby GEC members. [2] Terry Teague and Tony Nelson did not see the point in travelling to London to bawl and shout at GEC members, instead reasoning: 'If we accept that they are going to impose a ballot, let's discuss it and plan our own way forward.' [3] Jimmy Nolan recognised that the GEC did not represent TGWU members, and that the KPMG report on a potential dockers' labour supply initiative would not result in full reinstatement. That same day, Nolan received a phone call from Martin Hartrop of the Registered Dockworkers' Pension Fund, who wanted to meet with Nolan on Friday. Frank Lannigan telephoned Danny Maher at the GEC, who informed him how Jack

---

\* C. Sparks, 'The Bureaucracy in the TGWU', International Socialism 1st Series, No.95, February 1977.

Adams had told the previous day's session: 'I cannot talk the Dock Company into getting rid of Drakes.' [4] Meanwhile, picket captain Tony Nelson repeated the call for stewards to start attending the picket line every day, explaining that morale was low amongst the dockers: 'Very low indeed.' [5]

The GEC deferred to UK law and their interpretation remained that the Liverpool dockers were involved in an unofficial, illegal strike. [6] Jack Adams had always said that the Liverpool dispute, 'could never be sold out,' but he also noted that they had, 'never delivered the knockout punch to the MDHC,' and while this might have been true, it was a lot to expect when, as the dockers put it, 'those in your corner are constantly throwing in the towel.' Bill Morris had actively undermined internationalism at every turn, with some of the Liverpool dockers recalling how during their 1980s blockade of Namibian uranium, Morris had attempted to intervene and stop this action, as the union had a substantial membership base at British Nuclear Fuels. It was as though Morris took issue with the very concept of internationalism, and the International Transport Workers' Federation did nothing to dilute his insipid understanding of the matter. [7] ITF leaders David Cockcroft and Kees Marges were happy to blame Morris for their inactivity, [8] although Cockcroft did appeal to unions to be more militant in fulfilling their international responsibilities: 'We will never organise real global solidarity with our present resources, our present working methods, or with the present attitude to international work, which we encounter amongst many of our affiliated unions.' [9] Still, this statement, made on 1 June 1997, rang hollow having come one day after Cockcroft had informed Jimmy Nolan that the Liverpool dockers would not be welcome at the ITF's forthcoming conference in Miami.

For its part, the GEC was hardly making demands of fellow trade unionists in support of a Liverpool docks dispute that had been running for almost two years. This was indicative of the distance between the rank-and-file GEC members who, according to the TGWU's rulebook, controlled the union, and the Liverpool docks membership that they were elected to represent. Patronage and personal interest created this huge gulf between the GEC members and their constituents. At the Monday session dock business had been discussed, with Danny Maher stating his support for the Liverpool campaign, but despite this position receiving the backing of London dockworker Colin Coughlin, Morris was able to use his majority on the GEC to undermining any attempt to support the Liverpool dockers.

It was decided that all resolutions on Ireland, Europe and the Liverpool docks dispute would be dealt with on the basis of an 'executive statement' that would be placed before the union's Biennial Delegates Conference. The significance of this was that it allowed Morris to prevent any open discussion or debate on items protected under such a statement, utilising a popular tactic for avoiding controversial issues at the BDC such as Northern Ireland. Carden held out hope that the debate would be reopened when Adams and Stevenson reported back on their meeting with the Dock Company during the Wednesday session, only for Adams to inform him that the latest KPMG proposals identified only 30 jobs for a labour supply company. A lengthy discussion took place between Carden, Maher and Adams that was, according to Carden, 'almost a post-mortem,' [10] as Adams admitted that: 'Morris does not understand damaging an employer.' [11]

At midday, Morris read out Document 68, which he believed was going to bring an end to the Liverpool docks dispute. Adams denied any knowledge of items in the document which were attributed to him and he asked that these references to him telling the dockers that they would be sacked because they were in breach of contract be removed. [12] Danny Maher wanted references to him, as Docks and Waterways representative, stating that he no longer worked with the ITF changed to, 'continues to work with the ITF in support of the Liverpool dockworkers.' [13] Carden then argued for one hour in opposition to Document 68, calling on the GEC to: 'instruct the ITF to support the dockers; call for a public inquiry into the docks dispute and issue a public statement in support of Magnet workers and the Liverpool dockers.' [14] This was followed by GEC members speaking either for or against Document 68. Their contributions illustrated the General Secretary's influence over individual members, reinforced by compliant Regional Secretaries and other salaried officers of the union. This power of patronage filtered throughout the structure of the TGWU and appeared limitless in its influence to halt democracy.

Lay members who wished to have a career in the union understood the importance of following the lead of senior officials, perpetuating a system handed down to subsequent generations of TGWU members by the first General Secretary, Ernest Bevin. Members of the GEC feared that their elected positions would be at risk if they opposed the bureaucracy, but there were some, such as Steve Riley from Ford Dagenham, who at least wanted to amend, or water down Morris's statement. Barry Cooper called for the document to be rejected and replaced by an updated version from Jack Adams. Ken Brindle, Martin Mayer and Danny Maher all spoke out against Document 68. Adams then gave a dispassionate report on his meetings with KPMG in regard to the dockers' labour supply company, emphasising how, 'it would only create 30 jobs.' [15] Graham Stevenson claimed: 'the Liverpool stewards had refused to co-operate with representatives of KPMG.' Stevenson's statement was wholly inaccurate as the dockers had nothing to gain from refusing to engage with the union/MDHC appointment of KPMG to examine the viability of a dockers' co-operative. [16] Clearly, the purpose of Stevenson's claim was to discredit the dockers and their labour supply initiative, which the stewards had put forward as a means of ending the dispute. Discussion over Document 68 went on for an hour and a half, in what was far from the most memorable moment in the GEC's history. At 1.30pm, Morris responded to the outcome of this short debate by saying that:

> 'I have no disagreement about objectives. Why a statement? It is an industrial dispute. Others are as well, and the statement [Document 68] is about unity. Not everyone at the BDC will speak in favour of the dockers. I have received letters critical of the dockers and how it has been conducted. It is no accident that no amendments exist on the [BDC] agenda. We create this to maintain unity.' [17]

Bill Morris then proceeded to speak of the need: 'to work through the union. Official channels have been bypassed. We will work through those issues where we can work together.' [18] That was his work for the day done, and as the chairman called for a vote, 19 members supported Document 68 while only nine opposed it. The night before, Jack Adams had spoken to Len McCluskey, then a TGWU National Officer, telling him that Stevenson had become far too close and comfortable with MDHC and how the KPMG study had produced only 30 jobs and what a complete farce it all was. [19]

# 67

# The Interview That Established the Dockers as a 'Political Movement'

*'…unions should stick to bread [and] butter issues. The union is run as a business now and isn't lay member led. But the members at the Port of Liverpool thought it was important to show our respect and show our solidarity with our American sisters and brothers.' ~ John Lynch*

B ill Morris was happy to announce the considerable financial contribution to a dispute that he continued to describe as 'unofficial,' which according to his own logic should have exposed the TGWU to sequestration for financially supporting an illegal strike. [1] Similarly, if the dispute was unofficial, why had the stewards been allowed open access to the union's Liverpool office, and why was the union organising a third official ballot? How could the TGWU, along with Mersey Docks, justify sponsoring the examination of a business proposal by KPMG at a cost of £50,000? Why did MDHC not once criticise the TGWU, instead welcoming their involvement? Never did this company pursue legal action against an illegal strike. In reality, the fabric of the union was not, at any time, under threat for the duration of this two-and-a-half-year dispute. Neither had any of the Dispute Committee members ever been subjected to personal injunctions or threatened with having their funds sequestrated. Why did the police never imprison any arrested pickets, irrespective of charges, for only a limited period of time?

According to Morris, the Liverpool dockers were now a 'political party,' which he stated as though it was irrefutable evidence that the dockers deserved to be rejected by their union. [2] The basis for Morris's comment was an obscure interview given by Mike Carden and Terry Teague to *Journal Critique*, an independent scholarly paper founded in 1973, with

---

* John Lynch (Liverpool Dockers' leader) quoted in 'Anti-racism and re-building union strength' by Raymond Morell, Conter, 17 June 2020, available: https://www.conter.co.uk/blog/2020/6/17/anti-racism-and-re-building-union-strength

the purpose of analysing contemporary society through a Marxist critical lens. *Journal Critique* was not a mainstream publication by any stretch of the imagination, yet Morris and his personal secretary, Ray Collins, had somehow availed themselves of this philosophical treatise offered by two Liverpool dockworkers on 10 October 1997. From Carden and Teague's perspective, the interview was simply an opportunity for two trade unionists to take a momentary step back from the dispute and reflect. In his introduction, the interviewer, Peter Kennedy, set the tone by establishing that it was now over two years since the dockers had been dismissed by MDHC for defending minimum conditions of work and the collective principle of not crossing a picket line. In the ensuing period, the sacked dockers, their families and support groups had mounted a national and international campaign that was simultaneously for reinstatement and against the global tide of casualisation. It was Kennedy's opinion that the dockers' strategy was unique in the way it combined old and new collectivist movements, such as rank-and-file trade unionists, women, unemployment support groups, environmentalists, socialists and anarchists: 'to produce the embryo of new forms of class struggle, which hold out the possibility of transcending the traditional boundaries between public / private, industrial / political and national / international.' [3]

Kennedy's writing spoke of a profound disenchantment with established politics and a deep-seated resentment towards official trade unionism, both of which he identified as key features of the Liverpool docks dispute. It was true that the most commonly held perception among dockers and the Women of the Waterfront was that New Labour could no longer cling to the pretence of representing workers, and that trade union officials had become the *non-conflictual agents* of big business. It was this acute awareness of the reality of their situation that provoked the dockers into innovative actions, such as their international campaign, which culminated in the establishment of the International Dockworkers' Committee. It was also the reason why they came to stand side by side with Reclaim the Streets and various other political and environmental activists, as they recognised the need to adopt a much broader approach in the fight against global capitalism. Effectively, the dockers became the centre point of a network of social groups that were brought together by a common enemy, creating new forms of class struggle after acknowledging that the traditional vehicles for opposition had revealed themselves to be part of the problem. The politicising ramifications of this are clearly discernible in the interviews that Kennedy conducted with the two stewards, [4] as he asked Teague to summarise the two-stage industrial action that the Liverpool dockers had adopted since September 1995. Teague replied by explaining:

*'The success of the two-stage action, which was decided at the International Dockworkers' Conference in Montreal last May, is crucial to us right now'* [5]

Teague explained that the second stage of the struggle came about because delegates in Montreal believed that the formation of the IDC was potentially the beginning of an international rank-and-file movement, able to coordinate continuous action in order to achieve victory for the Liverpool dockers. It would also trigger a general fightback through a rolling boycott of ships and ports harbouring scab cargo from and to MDHC. Teague described the role of the International Transport Workers' Federation, which he considered to be a bureaucracy that had gone the way of its affiliated unions, being more concerned with

# THE INTERVIEW THAT ESTABLISHED THE DOCKERS AS A 'POLITICAL MOVEMENT'

maintaining what they termed 'the fabric of their own organisation' and the laws of the land than protecting ordinary members, [6] as he reflected on his role in the dockers' international campaign. [7] Asked if there had been any commitment to maintaining rank-and-file international links beyond this particular dispute, Teague answered by saying that this was what they hoped for:

> 'When the dockers first established the International Dockworkers' movement at the conference held in Liverpool Town Hall, which Mike Carden had a leading role in, it was an historic event because many of the big union bureaucracies never wanted us to meet. In fact, the ITF actually instructed people not to attend... What we have established, particularly with the workers on the west coast of America, is something that will last beyond this dispute.' [8]

Kennedy then asked about the criticism levelled at the Dispute Committee by those political groups that accused them of placing too much emphasis on the international campaign, failing to seriously challenge the TGWU's attempts at limiting the dispute and backing off from building real alliances with other UK workers. To this, Carden replied:

> 'Taking the issue of the failure to build alliances with workers in this country: we met with workers in this country, we met with Vauxhall workers and we met with Ford workers and with council workers in this city... Now, we didn't have to be told this, but it was clear that their own working conditions were under attack, too. As Jimmy Nolan puts it, people are gripped by 'economic fear.' People have put forward fancy analyses about whether we should have done this or done that in Britain. Now, no doubt we have made mistakes in a dispute which has run for over two years, but to assume somehow that there is a kind of tap to be turned on and from which will flow this localised workers' action, at first in Liverpool and then nationally, is simplistic... We have tried but have not been successful so far in winning the active support we seek.' [9]

Asked about the possibility of setting up pickets at other ports and in other industries across the UK, Carden explained that while they were open to such ideas, it was difficult to put up a picket line at another factory or office block because:

> 'Physically it's not difficult, but it's dealing with all the individual politics of the shop stewards' structures. For example, some stewards are tied into the union bureaucracy, others are more or less militant; we'd have to be aware of this. The complications would be enormous, and again it assumes that there is this latent worker power just waiting to be released. I'm not saying there is no latent support there, but it is not quite as simple as that.' [10]

Teague added that the dockers would not accept that they neglected trying to build support within this country, as they had established a network of support groups created by a campaign aimed at unemployed and employed alike, men and women from all over the country:

*'Every major city now has a Liverpool dockers' support group, similar to what the miners had. Again, as with the international movement, if the dockers won this dispute those support groups would stay in place, as something to build on for the future. The London and Glasgow support groups have been magnificent. In addition to this, Belfast and Cardiff dockworkers are building to take industrial action.' [11]*

Kennedy observed that even those in full support of the international campaign would argue that a strategy was needed to make a decisive push to establish a picket line presence in the UK, particularly at other ports. Linked to this was something that had been uppermost in the minds of the shop stewards, namely that all workers were under the same threat of casualisation, flexibility and rationalisation, giving them a clear reason for supporting the Liverpool dockers, who Kennedy believed would have, 'the moral authority and leadership necessary to win the active support of other workers in Britain.' [12] Carden replied by stating that he agreed:

*'Now, while I don't see the dockers as some sort of vanguard – after all, other workers have been in disputes more difficult than we could ever contemplate – nevertheless, at this moment in time, it is true that we have managed to capture the imagination of those workers willing to fight... Personally, I can't understand why workers in whatever industry, and why any shop stewards worth their salt, are not sitting in their workplace and saying, "Well, apart from financial support, how else can we directly support these dockers?" because financial support is not enough.' [13]*

The conversation then switched to the topic of anti-trade union laws and ideological attacks, not just from business and the state, but from the TGWU, telling them that direct action is useless, and that they should flow with the logic of markets and globalisation by accepting *'flexploitation.'* [14] Kennedy then asked if in the face of such circumstances workers needed active leadership: 'given the fact that confidence about the ability to change things runs so deep? I'm thinking in particular of the kind of active leadership you revealed internationally, by establishing the international dockworkers' organisation and setting up picket lines, in this case giving the phrase 'flying picket' a whole new meaning!' Carden commented that in his opinion: 'given the realities we have to deal with, it would be wrong for us to set up picket lines at other plants in Britain. Supposing we did set up a picket line, there's a real possibility that workers will just walk straight past it, and you know what the headline in the Echo would be: "Dockers make appeal to other workers to support their struggle for reinstatement, and those workers have rejected them!"' [15]

Kennedy again pursued the issue of the shop stewards' relationship with those who claimed that it had failed to seriously challenge the TGWU. [16] Kennedy remarked upon the fact that both Carden and Teague had mentioned the need to reclaim the trade unions and the Labour Party, before pointing out that some people argued that these institutions were simply moribund; unable to represent workers' aspirations and, in the case of the unions, little more than business enterprises. As an example, he referenced a Trades Union Congress bid: 'to take up part share ownership of some of the utilities recently privatised, and recently the site of employment rationalisations and work intensifications. What is your response to this?' [17] Teague answered:

> 'They were my thoughts at the recent demonstration in Birkenhead for Tulip workers, at which the union spoke... Jimmy Nolan spoke at the meeting and he actually touched on this issue. On reflection, if it was one thing that you could have passed on to those workers who were standing there, it would be that, "You organise from your rank-and-file, and once you've done this you take the fight out to other workers directly. Don't, in other words leave it to your leaders, whether union bureaucrats or politicians." ...not once during the whole of this dispute has an officer of the T&G bothered to show up on a picket line! Nowadays, it is the furthest thing from their thoughts to go down to a picket line and show solidarity.' [18]

Carden added that: 'The trade unions have adopted a role over the past 18 years of effectively seeing themselves as the employers!' Teague said, 'In the past, most people going for a job in the union would have to have a CV depicting evidence of their active involvement in struggles. Nowadays, they are a different breed. You've got to draw the conclusion that it is a modern-day betrayal.' [19] Kennedy wanted to know if this betrayal had been a permanent feature of unions and the Labour Party, something Carden had suggested earlier:

> 'There is a difference between the past betrayals and the times we live in now. In the past, at least they spoke the language of class struggle and provided a sense of 'us and them.' Modern unions and the Labour Party speak the language of the market; the language of the capitalist!... The whole ethos of the unions has changed; they no longer see their role as representing the industrial working class. The TUC and John Monks, an organisation we wrote off from day one of our dispute, now talk with pride about representing what they term the white-collar middle classes, whatever that may mean. In reality, these organisations no longer represent anyone apart from themselves.' [20]

Kennedy asked if the stewards believed the union's role had become one of out-managing management itself, 'by saying to employers, "We can secure that flexibility deal... We can deliver the flexible wage agreement", etc?' [21] Teague agreed that this was clearly the case. [22] Carden was also in agreement, adding that it was a very contradictory position for them to adopt, because once they had delivered the goods, the bosses no longer need them: 'Take our own case. In 1993, the union went along with MDHC's calls for new working practices, and two years later they don't need the union anymore! The same can be said for the ongoing Tulip workers. Once unions negotiate these contracts, there is no need for them, because from then on, if workers don't abide by the contracts they're simply sacked!' [23] According to Teague, this was confirmed by the recent closure at Spillers, where unions had approached management with a deal through which they (the union) could save the company £2 million through flexibility and longer working hours: 'They gave them the lot, and they still closed the plant. In answer to your question about the role of trade unions, it could actually be that they have come to the end of their time and we're just seeing their death throes. To me, they have just become middlemen for the employer, not the worker.' [24] In Carden's view:

*'In this context, the idea of building new organisations, I think, is one of the many issues that this and other struggles are highlighting right now. If an organisation no longer represents workers, that's telling us we need something else. The problem we then have is convincing others… We've had discussions here about why unions no longer represent us, and there are still differences between us. The discussions suddenly made me think about the issue in the reverse; the question why doesn't the union represent us became, for me, the question, "Why are my views no longer represented in these meetings?"' [25]*

Carden held the view that labour was unable to go back to the old compromise, and he questioned whether or not the sacked dockworkers should even want to go back, as he did not believe in a political solution centred on, 'the right to work at all costs,' adding that, 'I don't want to see my kids struggling for crap jobs. I think we're actually going through a revolutionary period, one where we should be saying, "Fuck you and your jobs, and yer slave labour." If wage labour's slave labour, then freedom from wage labour is total freedom!' He did, of course, also see the obvious issue of how workers were supposed to live in the absence of work. 'But then, that is the challenge. It's a revolutionary challenge,' he said. 'The dilemma for socialists is to recognise this. Now maybe I'm being a bit unfair because I don't know their full perspective, but how many socialists within the political groups that have supported us have or would build a political strategy out of the refusal of wage work? I haven't come across any, but I know that's what the Reclaim the Streets Activists consistently argue, and I find that a breath of fresh air!' [26]

In Kennedy's opinion: 'Reclaim the Streets activists, apart from the international aspect, have been one of the defining characteristics of this dispute, as have been the role of other social movements in your struggle; I'm thinking also of women's movements, environmentalists. Do you think new forms of class struggle are beginning to take shape?' [27] Here, Teague suggested that the dockers had surprised themselves with their ability to organise, especially internationally: 'You kept hearing for years and years about workers going international, but I began to think it was a pipe dream. I think we've made great strides towards this objective in our struggle. But things like the women's movement and support groups were products of earlier struggles, like the miners' dispute, so in that sense it is not new.' [28] Carden added that, on reflection, there was a fundamental movement beginning to occur that went beyond disparate groupings, with the Liverpool docks dispute and others like it highlighting a turning point. He wished to avoid reducing it to a working-class movement, as RTS activists approached social problems from a different angle, preferring to define themselves as *apolitical*, 'but they are very well organised and politically aware, and dockers have a lot of respect for these people; and during the dispute they have built up a strong relationship. One of the successes to come out of this dispute is the relationships the dockers have built up, both here and internationally.' [29]

Carden felt that the dockers and the environmentalists found a common ideology: 'by refuting the idea that there is a little box we can fit people into, but what binds us together is a sense of injustice, against scab labour, environmental damage, casualisation of labour, etc.' [30] Teague then added that it was quite unique to the Liverpool dispute to have other social movements involved so closely, which he believed stemmed from the fact that they had to make diverse links in order to keep the campaign alive. He also pointed to the London Support Group as a key factor, as it was through them that the Dispute Committee made a connection with RTS activists, before concluding that, 'the unity in this sense is based, as Mike says, on a shared sense of social justice.' [31] Asked what the dockers meant by the concept of 'social justice,' Carden explained:

> *'It's a period of fundamental transition we're living through right now... We've got all this technological knowhow, e.g. factories that could operate without labour; we should be living the life of the ancient Greeks. Instead, it's bizarre; we have all this technology, but with people either with no work or people working anywhere up to 80 hours a week! ...when we unite with people like Reclaim the Streets, we have to take on board what they are saying, too, which is, "Get a life. Who wants to spend their days working on the production line like that famous poster of Charlie Chaplin depicting modern times?" I think that is a concept that the labour movement have got to examine and take on board. As I say, we're going through a transition. Nobody is going to invent the wheel again; Ford will never again require on Merseyside, or anywhere else, 10,000 people. We need to mobilise on different ground. If we don't, we as a labour movement will have to do what unions and New Labour is now doing: rationalising work amongst ourselves in the interest of the bosses!' [32]*

At that point, Kennedy brought to a close this most revealing interview with two former dock shop stewards, which would so upset the leadership of the TGWU as, in their and Bill Morris's view, it established the Liverpool dockers as a 'political movement.'

# 68

# LabourNet's Exclusive Report into Casual Labour on Liverpool Docks

*'At the beginning of the twentieth century not only were the vast amount of cargo handling operations at Britain's ports undertaken by both casual employers and casual employees, but it was also considered both natural and essential that this should be the case.' ~ M.P. Jackson\**

In an exclusive report for *LabourNet* in June 1997, Greg Dropkin set the record straight on the use of casual labour in the port. Leaked documents revealed a complex web of employment agencies supplying *scab labour* behind the picket lines, with the accident rate escalating and the Dock Company facing prosecution by the Health and Safety Executive. It was also exposed that on 11 March 1997, a man had been recruited for a day's work, and eventually paid £55 by the employment agency Country Wide, for what he was told was a packing job, but which turned out to involve heaving 60kg sacks of cocoa beans onto pallets in the hold of the *M.V. Rison* at Langton Dock. As he dragged the sacks, a crane lowered a steel plate into the hold and then lifted out the pallets, and from time to time a crane hook or one of the sacks would drop, and: 'Lads fell down the piles of cocoa sacks. There was no supervision. The normal shift was 12 hours.' [1] Dropkin's research showed evidence of workers being denied training or safety equipment, while on the vessel, a team of Customs officers scoured the ship looking for drugs among the cocoa sacks. Shocked at the behaviour of the agency labour and their lack of attention to health and safety procedures, the Customs team approached the supervisor on deck with their concerns, but he simply shrugged his shoulders. In a written complaint to their own management, the officers noted that hardly any of the workers they had seen were wearing hard hats, reflective jackets, or safety boots

---

\* M.P. Jackson, The Decasualisation of Dock Labour – University of Sterling, January 1972, Social Policy Administration, pp.19-33. (https://onlinelibrary.wiley.com/doi/abs/10.1111/j.1467-9515.1972.tb00579.x)

(some wore trainers). In addition, there was no sign of standard manual handling training. The letter also referenced horseplay between workers, with one man dangling above the hold while having his hand stamped on intentionally by a colleague, as another used his hook to scale a ladder and climb out of the hatch. [2]

The West Langton Dock was being operated by Sontrade, a shipping and forwarding agency 63.75% owned by *SONAE Investimentos*, the holding company for Portugal's largest banking, retail and industrial conglomerate. Work formerly carried out by Liverpool dockers employed by MDHC was now subcontracted to such agencies, identified by a scab as the Kirkby-based Man & Machine, Country Wide and Workforce. [3] Country Wide told Dropkin that they had supplied labour for one day before it was withdrawn, 'as soon as we realised there was strike action.' When asked if any training had been provided and if this was the only occasion on which they had supplied labour to the port, the agency declined to comment further. Man & Machine director, Peter Main, offered a terse, 'No comment whatsoever,' declining to hear the allegations, while Sontrade's Graham Robertson explained that it was company policy not to discuss its business with journalists. [4] However, a recovered sheaf of soaking-wet, partly-charred papers shed light on Sontrade and the web of contractors operating in the port since September 1995. One such agency, Warrington-based PNT, opened a Liverpool office on 6 August, offering a '24-hour, seven-day service' supplying 'contract labour when required' to no less than five companies, including Sontrade. PNT operated on both sides of the Mersey, usually on the basis of zero-hour contracts, and a handwritten note from Sontrade confirmed that on 29 / 30 July 1996, they employed one person to work 20.5 hours on the North Alexandra Dock, via yet another company, Henry Bath Ltd, who were invoiced by PNT at a rate of £6.95 per hour. [5] Dropkin, an experienced investigative journalist and filmmaker with the Open Eye Gallery who worked closely with the dockers during the 1980s Namibian uranium blockade, exposed the detailed truth behind this growth in casual agencies supplying labour to the port. [6]

The Liverpool Freeport had long been a source of conflict for the Liverpool dockers, who had effectively been excluded from this huge area of the traditional Dock Estate which was fenced off after being granted 'free zone' status by the UK government in 1984. This provided the Dock Company with a tax-free haven of some 11 acres. Liverpool's free trade zone differed little from those found across the world, such as in the Philippines, where transnational companies were able to produce goods or store cargo for Western markets without the expense of employment or tax legislation. The claim at the time was that a free trade zone would create tens of thousands of jobs in Liverpool, [7] but after three years in operation, the estimated number of jobs created was closer to 100. [8] Despite tonnages rising by almost 400%, up to 265,000 tonnes worth around £57 million, many of the jobs created, if not all of them, were traditional dockers' roles, with labour being farmed out to the same companies that were now supplying scab labour to MDHC. This did not prohibit the TGWU from recruiting members there. On 31 July 1996, PNT director James Morgan wrote to Walter Scott, specifying labour supply terms and confirming the hire of a gang of men, [9] to the Dock Company at a cost of £1049.40 for 11 general operatives working 12-hour shifts at £7.95 per hour. [10] Scott was the operations manager at the Royal Seaforth Forest Products Terminal, where a major accident involving a PNT employee precipitated a joint investigation

# LABOURNET'S EXCLUSIVE REPORT INTO CASUAL LABOUR ON LIVERPOOL DOCKS

by the Health & Safety Executive and MDHC, with the HSE concluding that on 20 August 1996:

> *'Unloading and moving copper cathode cargo [was] being conducted under the control of Mersey Docks and Harbour Company, during which operation a bundle of copper cathodes fell, causing injury to Perry Birch, who suffered serious leg injuries caused through an unsafe system of intermediate quayside storage of copper cathodes.'* [11]

A PNT spokesman, Evaton Binns, declined to discuss the incident, stating only that all company employees were covered by an insurance scheme, and that he had been given legal advice cautioning against providing any information regarding his employer's size or origin. [12] PNT was not registered with Companies House, and their Liverpool and Warrington registered phonelines appeared to be either disconnected or non-existent. MDHC claimed that the company had left the Port of Liverpool, 'sometime last year.' With casual labourer Birch still laid-up in hospital with a broken leg, an almost identical incident took place on 27 September 1996, just as the sacked dockers were entering their second year in dispute. On this occasion, Albert Knowles, an employee of Drake Port Services, the key agency for supplying labour to Seaforth Container Terminal, was knocked down by a stacker truck as it picked up a bundle of copper cathodes. Knowles suffered a broken ankle, and further HSE proceedings against MDHC, under the Docks Regulations Act (1988) and the Health and Safety at Work Act (1974), were scheduled at Sefton Magistrates' Court for 15 April 1997. By law, MDHC was responsible for the health and safety of its subcontracted employees, but just a few days before the hearing was due to take place, it was postponed until 7 May, and then again until 9 July at the request of the company's solicitors. Meanwhile, the Department of Environment replied to a written enquiry from Joe Benton, in which the MP for Bootle pointed out that the number of accidents recorded by HSE as occurring at the Royal Seaforth Container Terminal and Royal Seaforth Forest Products Terminal stood at one for 1995-96, whereas by 1996-97 this had risen to eight. [13] This prompted MDHC's press officer, Eric Leatherbarrow, to claim:

> *'...MDHC has never had casual labour, does not employ casual labour and do not deal with subcontractors employing casual labour. PNT was employed on a temporary basis to enable the Dock Company to keep open jobs to offer to the dismissed port workers...'*
> [14]

The casual worker interviewed by Greg Dropkin resigned after only one day on the dock, having already seen enough. He told Dropkin how, as he was going past the picket line in a taxi, he heard the dockers shouting, 'Scabs! Scabs!'. [15] Outside the gates, the Liverpool dockers continued to picket those working inside, and on Thursday 5 June 1997, at around 2.30pm, MDHC's port police arrested John King, Tony Farrell, Frank Nolan and Franny O'Brien at the Gladstone Dock for 'obstruction and resisting arrest.' Meanwhile, at almost the exact same time, Jimmy Campbell was hit by a red Rover car at the Alexandra Dock, in what was just another day for the men and women fighting for their jobs. At the following day's weekly mass meeting, the stewards announced that dockers' families would continue to receive welfare payments from the Hardship Fund, although no set amount could be guaranteed. Critchley Labels and Magnet Kitchens were other disputes taking place at the same time, and those workers were also struggling to feed their families. Morale was low, and the report from the General Executive Council was dismal as it was again confirmed that neither they nor Morris would support the dockers' campaign. [16] Jimmy Davies briefly expanded on the financial situation, explaining that while it was extremely difficult for everyone, they had no option but to persevere. He also expressed his concern over the GEC tearing up its statement on resolutions to the BDC, before guest speakers from the Australian Construction Workers' Union, the Tacoma International Longshore and Warehouse Union and a group of Danish workers addressed the dockers. After the meeting, Terry Teague telephoned Michel Murray in Canada to discuss the International Transport Workers' Federation's forthcoming conference in Miami.

On Monday 9 June, morale continued to spiral downwards as the options available to the dockers, after almost 21 months in dispute, appeared to be dwindling, with only the BDC, the ITF and Parliament offering some hope for a conclusion, some hope for a victory. Writing in June 1997, GEC member Mike Carden observed that wherever the dockers went and whatever they did, 'all roads led to Bill Morris and his view that their struggle was unofficial, everyone recognises this.' [17] It was also around this time that an organisation promoting the Gaddafi Peace Award wanted to make a presentation to Doreen McNally, one of the leaders of the Women of the Waterfront. This was a matter that the press and media used as another major critique of the dockers, who portrayed it as the dockers accepting money from the Libyan dictator, Colonel Gaddafi. However, journalist John Pilger defended the dockers, writing that:

> 'I don't see why the Liverpool dockers, who get minimal support from their union, who get no support from the Labour government, who get minimal support from other unions in this country, should not get support from every quarter they can get. This is a life and death struggle for them, why shouldn't they get it? This country's human rights record is pretty appalling at the moment, too. Colonel Gaddafi's regime is odious, but Colonel Gaddafi's regime is also the west's bogey man, never forget that.' [18]

Eleven years later, in June 2008 and then again in April 2009, Gaddafi transitioned from enemy to international diplomat in the eyes of the UK press, as Tony Blair, the New Labour prime minister, was twice flown to Libya on a private jet. Film footage was shown of Blair hugging this previously reviled dictator. [19]

On Tuesday 10 June, Liverpool dockers Joe Ladd, Terry Woods, Tony Tyrell and Jimmy Campbell travelled to Amsterdam for a Euro March due to be held on the coming Saturday, an event also attended by two representatives of the WOW. The march involved some 60,000 people, lasting approximately three hours, and concluded with supporters chanting 'dockers in scabs out!' [20] The following Tuesday night, the WOW organised a demonstration outside the house of Trevor Furlong, MDHC's managing director. Around 30 women and 15 dockers' children were present as Furlong looked on from his bedroom window. Later that evening, Herbie Hollorhead and Kevin Bilsborrow returned from a delegation to Dublin, where they had spoken with dockers from the Marine Ports, Coastal

# LABOURNET'S EXCLUSIVE REPORT INTO CASUAL LABOUR ON LIVERPOOL DOCKS

and Drogheda. [21] The following day, dockers Christy Clinch, Billy Langley, Chris Langan, Tony Nelson and Kevin Bilsborrow were arrested on the picket line, resulting in Bilsborrow and Nelson being banned from attending future pickets. In an effort to smash the daily demonstrations, three separate police forces had converged to snatch the five men at Gladstone Dock: MDHC's Port Police, Merseyside Police and the Operational Support Division, or the 'Riot Squad,' as they were known to the dockers and their supporters. The three dockers, one of whom was a 53-year-old with a heart condition, were released after an hour, while the two stewards were held in custody and charged with various offences, with the picket line ban being included as a condition of their bail. MDHC had recently appointed a new chief superintendent of their Port Police, Ray Walker, and these arrests were seen as his attempt to stamp his authority on the dispute. However, in the wake of nine arrests over a two-week period, picketing intensified and morale began to improve among the dockers, although the spirits of the shop stewards had fallen to an all-time low. [22] At a WOW meeting held at Transport House on the evening of Wednesday 18 June, much discussion took place regarding a writers' workshop, and the opportunities that such an initiative could present, as Dave Cotterill set about gathering information ahead of establishing a workshop to record the history of the dispute. [23] Elsewhere, a *Rock the Dock* concert was scheduled for 20 June at Liverpool's Royal Court Theatre, and Colette Melia, Irene Campbell and Mike Dooley reported back on their delegation to Amsterdam for the Euro March.

On Friday 20 June, Kevin Robinson met with John Linden, one of the dockers' solicitors, who had been providing support in dealing with pickets and arrests by the police. Discussions with Linden often covered a wide range of issues, from picket line caravans and complaints about police brutality, to bail restrictions, affecting many of the dockers and their supporters preventing them from standing on the picket line. At this meeting, the list of those facing some level of prosecution for picket line activities included: Tony Farrell, John Maguire, John Ferns, Tony Nelson, Terry Teague, Phil McInally, John Campbell, Babs Henessy, Pat Harvey, Kevin Robinson, Jeff Jones, Frank Byrne, Bobby Evans, Mike Carden, Stan Phillips, Peter Killane, Eddie Ledden, Fred Roberts, John Jenkins, Kevin Bilsborrow and Nat Gibbons. [24] It was noted that despite the hundreds of arrests that took place throughout the Liverpool dock dispute, police policy was always to ensure that, in most cases at least, no one was ever imprisoned for longer than a few hours. It seemed as though the authorities were determined to avoid another Pentonville Five situation, where the imprisoning of five London dockers in July 1972 led to the Trades Union Congress calling for a General Strike. [25] A few days after the meeting with Linden, on Monday 23 June, the locks and windows of a picket caravan at Seaforth were broken, and an appointment was made with Inspector Steve Gittens at Crosby Road Police Station.

# 69
# The ITF

*'Oh, definitely; that's one part of it I wouldn't change. Me and Jimmy, a few weeks into the picket, we went for a cup of tea. First time I've ever had a cup of tea in a pub. Me and Jimmy went up to the Elm House for a cup of tea, and when we come, as we come back, we were the next six to come back to picket the gate. And as we were there, Jimmy Roach and Tony King come out the gate, two scabs, and it was the day Drake International moved into the port. And we'd just heard it on the radio in the car, and as I say, Jimmy Roach went like that, "Billy, you's are gone. You're finished," and I just said to Jimmy Roach, "When I go out for a pint tonight, Jimmy, I'll be able to hold my head up high. You won't be able to." And that's still the same. I wouldn't change, no; no regrets whatsoever about not crossing the picket line.' ~ Billy Johnson**

The Liverpool dockers wanted resolutions from the International Dockworkers' Committee's Montreal Conference, held 9 and 10 June 1997, to be formally put to the International Transport Workers' Federation (ITF). The International Longshore and Warehouse Union (ILWU) began applying pressure on the ITF to bring the resolutions before a Steering Group meeting in France, although for the Dispute Committee, the main aim was to persuade the ITF's next international conference to adopt the two-stage plan of industrial action agreed upon by the IDC in Montreal. The official delegates at the Miami Conference, who had also been present in Montreal, were Norman Parks and Tom Dufresne (ILWU), Antonio Mariano (National Federation of Port Workers' Unions, Portugal) and Vladimir Vasiliev (Dockers' Union of Russia). Also in attendance, albeit without official credentials, were Michel Murray, Philippe Gaudillot and Daniel Ahern (*Syndicat des Debardeurs*, Canada) as well as Julian Gonzalez (*Coordinadora*, Spain). Jimmy Nolan and Terry Teague were there to represent the Liverpool dockers.

It was in Miami that the two Liverpool stewards, along with other non-ITF affiliates led by Michel Murray together with the Spanish and French dockers, became the subject of constitutional challenges to their presence. There were reports that John Bowers, president of

---

* Billy Johnson, Liverpool Docker, interviewed by Greg Dropkin, 17 February 1998.

491

the International Longshoremen's Association (ILA) was unhappy that David Cockcroft, the ITF General Secretary, had allowed non-affiliates to be invited, and the Spanish CGT union objected to the attendance of the CCOO, an organisation that represented around 80% of all Spanish dockworkers. Still, Bowers made the Liverpool delegation very welcome, and was clear that he wanted the ILA to take further direct action in support of their campaign. Graham Stevenson, the Transport and General Workers' Union's National Docks Officer, would receive applause for his update on the Liverpool docks' dispute, while Danny Maher, the TGWU's General Executive Council representative, made an appeal to allow Nolan and Teague to address the conference. This request was turned down although they would be permitted to speak at a special meeting to be held after the official business had been concluded.

The main item on the first day of conference, as Michel Murray had predicted, left the Liverpool contingent wondering if they were at the right meeting, as they sat through a two-hour presentation by an advisor to the United Nations and World Bank, addressing port reforms, the need for labour to start co-operating with capital and the virtues of privatisation. This was unsurprising for an official union conference being held in yet another exotic location such as Miami! [1] Approximately 120 official delegates from 50 countries were present in Miami, including allies from the ILA, ILWU, Australia, New Zealand, Japan, Sri Lanka, India, Russia, Portugal, South Africa, Bermuda and Belgium, as well as less friendly officials from the big European ports in Germany (ÖTV), Holland (FNV), Denmark (SID) and Sweden (Transport Workers). The conference was hosted by the ILA and chaired by its president, John Bowers. A palpable anti-IDC sentiment made it obvious that convincing the ITF to adopt the Montreal resolutions was not going to be easy. Bill Morris had insisted that his ITF counterpart, David Cockcroft, allow only Graham Stevenson and Danny Maher to speak on the Liverpool dispute. The Liverpool stewards even had difficulty gaining observer status for the Montreal and Spanish *Coordinadora* delegation. However, the ILA's objection to Montreal's presence was eventually cleared up following a conversation between Cockcroft and Bowers, although dockers' leader Julian Gonzalez (of *Coordinadora*) was ultimately removed from the building.

In his welcoming address, Bowers asked that time set aside for speeches be restricted in order to concentrate on specific actions, as he explained that dockworkers across the world were under attack from privatisation and deregulation, and he made special note of the need to do more to resolve the Liverpool dispute. Citing New Zealand, where the port industry had gone through extraordinary changes, he argued that every job lost within the dock industry created 10 jobs outside, [2] before Bob Baete, head of the BTB Port Section in Belgium, gave a report on European matters, detailing how employers throughout the continent were on the offensive against dock labour schemes. The Dutch ports of Rotterdam and Amsterdam had both been threatened with job losses and casualisation, while delegates from Asia and Africa reported major issues of their own. The ITF had helped more ports become unionised, but the biggest threat to this progress was coming from privatisation, according to Thulani Dlamini from the South African TGWU, mirroring reports from ports in Nigeria. The Australian and New Zealand delegates then described fresh attacks on the rights of trade unionists through anti-union industrial legislation, with Western Australia bracing itself for a third wave of new laws, which they firmly believed could be countered by a united front of dockworkers, seafarers, miners and construction workers. From the US East coast, the ILA's Tommy Gleason spoke of future threats from the development of 'mega terminals' that would cause some smaller ports to disappear, while others would be reduced to seeing only coastal traffic. He also warned:

> 'Of new super-vessels currently coming on stream, which can carry up to 12,000 containers. They will be owned by one of the big five shipping consortiums, but containers will be placed on board by other shippers using slot-sharing schemes. Because of the uncertain future for East Coast dockworkers, the ILA has just concluded a five-year contract with employers to safeguard the pay, conditions and jobs of our members.' [3]

Glen Ramiskey, of the West Coast ILWU, then talked briefly about concluding a three-year contract for his union's members, as he stated that 30% of the income flowing into the international union was put towards organising for the future. The ILWU had a proud record of offering solidarity to longshoremen in struggle the world over and Ramiskey made special mention of what they had done to support the Liverpool dispute, before adding that, 'we actually need to be doing a lot more'. [4] The ILWU had its own industrial problems, however, as employers at a coal terminal in Los Angeles sought to use non-union labour, while in Hawaii the union was being refused access to a steel terminal. From the chair, John Bowers informed delegates of the special relationship and bond that his ILA had formed with the ILWU, allowing both coasts to work in unison to defend and advance the welfare of all longshoremen. [5] A number of other delegates also made reference to the Liverpool dispute, including Bob Baete, Vladimir Vasiliev, Thulani Dlamini, Bala Tampo (CMU, Sri Lanka), John Coombes (MUA, Australia) and Trevor Hanson (WWU, New Zealand).

It seemed as though the situation in Liverpool and other UK ports was just the tip of the privatisation iceberg, but with Jimmy Nolan and Terry Teague denied permission to formally address the conference, it was left to Graham Stevenson to speak on their behalf. The roots of the problem went back to 1989, Stevenson explained, when the national dock strike collapsed and all but two UK ports derecognised the TGWU. He then named Associated British Ports, owners of 22 non-union UK ports, while lamenting how TGWU port membership was presently as low as 5,000, having already previously fallen from 80,000 to 10,000 between 1979 and 1989. Of the current membership, 1,000 worked at Felixstowe, [6] and according to Stevenson: 'despite all those setbacks in 1989, Liverpool had resisted, maintaining a strong union presence, good representation and fighting to maintain all pre-1989 agreements.' [7] He then added that the TGWU had: 'only admiration for the way the Liverpool dockworkers had supported the young Torside workers. There was certainly no question about the union fully supporting the Liverpool struggle,' [8] before going on to say that he believed:

> 'The Liverpool dockworkers are the cream of the working-class, and in Jim Nolan, who is also the constitutional chairman of the TGWU Docks and Waterways National Committee, they couldn't have a better leader. The TGWU has never shirked its responsibility to the Liverpool dockworkers in trying to negotiate a just and long-term

*solution to the dispute, and with finances to alleviate the hardship the members are suffering. I have had a good liaison with the shop stewards' movement.' [9]*

Stevenson claimed that he fully understood the stewards' mistrust regarding the latest round of negotiations, where a confidentiality clause had prevented them from being involved in tripartite talks between the union, MDHC and their appointed business consultants, KPMG. But he wanted to take the opportunity: 'to nail the myth that the shop stewards had refused to negotiate, and likewise the myth espoused by some European delegates that the Liverpool dockworkers are happy to be classed as "strike tourists."' [10] He then outlined the status of negotiations to date, [11] informing delegates of the dockers' initiative to create a labour co-operative, with two of the main clauses in this proposal seeking to establish 'minimum standards' in the Port of Liverpool, together with trade union recognition. Stevenson stated his belief that this was an excellent idea, which could not only end the Liverpool dispute, but also serve as the foundation for reorganising the entire UK port industry. He then, incorrectly, told ITF delegates that KPMG had, 'no links with Mersey Docks, and are a totally independent company,' [12] before announcing that their report, which had been based on conversations with 16 companies operating within the Port of Liverpool, was now in the hands of Bill Morris. Stevenson stressed that the report was not a business plan.

Despite what Stevenson told the ITF the union would ignore the Liverpool dockers' leadership and would publish the consultants' report without any input from the Dispute Committee in the KPMG/TGWU paper *Towards a Labour Supply in the Port of Liverpool.* [13] Stevenson accepted that these proposals fell short of the sacked dockers' aspirations, and that Drake International would be left in key areas of the port, such as Seaforth Container Terminal. He maintained that this process represented the only means of achieving a conclusion to the dispute, [14] presumably based on the fact that the dockers' rejection of the KPMG report would put the union's leadership in a position where they would simply impose another ballot. [15] In concluding, Stevenson predicted that a victory for the Liverpool dockworkers would act as the blueprint for reconstructing all British ports: 'Now is the moment where we should consider the future and not the past, and that the next ITF meeting I attend will be one where the Liverpool dockworkers have returned to their port, and the rebuilding process for all UK ports will be firmly in place.' [16]

Danny Maher followed Stevenson's speech by explaining that the co-operative proposal would leave the Liverpool dockers with nothing more than redundant berths to work, which he believed made the scheme unviable, before adding that: 'it needs more than words from the ITF. It's time for actions, and the actions should be co-ordinated international actions.' [17] Maher then requested that delegates stay behind at the end of the session to hear from Jimmy Nolan and Terry Teague, but some official delegates walked out. Speaking outside the normal business of the conference, the two Liverpool stewards dismissed Stevenson's version of events as giving:

*'No solution to the present conflict, as it failed to provide long-term full reinstatement, the core issue of the 21-month dispute. The proposal did not deal with the removal of scabs from the port, and in fact leaves the most viable working areas – the Container Terminal, the Timber Terminal and the Grain Terminal – in the hands of strike-*

*breakers. Both spoke on the need to adopt the action plan agreed in Montreal, i.e. an international day of action of up to 24-hour stoppages, and more importantly, a second phase of ongoing industrial actions against the ships and shipping companies that still use the Port of Liverpool...' [18]*

All of those who stayed behind to hear Nolan and Teague gave their support to the Liverpool dockworkers, with the ILA stating that urgent action was needed, and that it should be co-ordinated to include all ports trading with Liverpool. Finally, the mission of Michel Murray's Montreal delegation would be to compel the ITF to adopt the main resolutions of the IDC conference, although this would only be possible if they were to be put forward under the penultimate item of business, namely 'Motions.' The ITF was already planning to adopt a resolution brought forward from the European Dockers' Regional Committee's London meeting on 5 September 1996, which expressed, 'its full support for the attempts of the TGWU to reach a final negotiated solution to the dispute, and is prepared to take appropriate action in support of the TGWU's attempts,' [20] but this was thought to be meaningless as it merely gave the ITF's backing to the TGWU officials, rather than the dockers that had been running the reinstatement campaign since September 1995. The ILWU delegation leader, Glen Ramiskey, told the ITF conference: 'time has moved on since 5 September 1996. The Liverpool dockworkers cannot continue their struggle forever, and there is now an urgent need to achieve a just and long-term settlement to their courageous fight.' [20] Ramiskey recognised the legal restraints preventing the TGWU from suggesting that international actions be intensified, but he was more than prepared to add his own voice to those calling on ITF affiliates to support the demand for a two-staged industrial action plan. [21] Thulani Dlamini fully endorsed Ramiskey's statements by supporting a Day of World Action not just for the Liverpool dispute, but for all dockworkers who found themselves under attack. John Bowers then closed the meeting, and during informal talks between him, Jimmy Nolan, Terry Teague, Jim Coombes and Glen Ramiskey, it was agreed that their new action plan would be put to the ITF Steering Committee, whose next meeting had not yet been arranged. Finally, upon hearing a report back from Miami, the Liverpool dockers now had a fixed date for actions to commence, with further discussions due to take place in France on 21 June, involving the European delegates who had attended the IDC Montreal conference. [22]

# 70

# Preamble to the 1997 Biennial Delegates Conference

*'Who is it speaks of defeat? I tell you, a cause like ours is greater than defeat can know it. It is the power of powers.' ~ Francis Adams**

Bill Morris had written to the dock shop stewards to let them know that they would not be allocated a stall at the union's forthcoming Biennial Delegates Conference (BDC), despite allowing the private sector and big business interests to purchase as many units as they wanted. For the Liverpool stewards, it would be a risk to turn up at the BDC to seek rank-and-file support for their long-running dispute and not get it. But they reasoned that this was the trade union equivalent of *their Parliament*, and so it was their right to challenge and influence policy at the union's primary lay-member body. It represented their first real opportunity to overturn the decision of the TGWU's General Executive Council through the only other rank-and-file decision-making forum left available to them. If the BDC accepted resolutions supporting the Liverpool campaign both the GEC and its General Secretary would be forced to follow this policy mandate. Thus, the pressure on the dockers to successfully convince the BDC to alter the TGWU's course was immense, and on Tuesday 17 June 1997, the stewards met to discuss their strategy. It was also here that Tony Nelson delivered a forceful critique of Graham Stevenson's role as National Docks Officer, which Jimmy Nolan took exception to. Jimmy was prone to pushing back against negativity towards the union, and he told the stewards that he was 'fed up' with some of them because of it. Nolan believed the members were the union! [1] Not for the first time, a heated argument

---

* Defeat (poem), by Francis W. L. Adams. This quote was attributed to James Larkin in a letter sent by the dockers to supporters on 28 January 1998. (https://www.greenleft.org.au/content/liverpool-dockers-draw-lessons-defeat)

broke out in the boardroom of Transport House, with the point being made that the dispute was led by the *collective* and not by any particular individual.

Two days later, the TGWU Broad Left met to discuss the BDC resolutions and to establish their position on the Liverpool dispute. It had already been reported that a GEC statement would cover union organisation, Ireland, the docks and Europe. The 'left-wing faction' of the TGWU had itself previously proclaimed its intention to oppose any forms of direct action in support of the sacked dockers. This had been their policy since September 1995, and their majority share of GEC seats would ensure that Morris's *power through patronage* would not be challenged there. On Saturday 21 June, 'Liverpool Lives! *A Celebration of Working-Class Culture in Merseyside* was held at Transport House, followed by a fundraiser at the Merseyside Trade Union, Community and Unemployed Resource Centre, featuring a number of workshops organised by Brian Ashton, chair of the Dockers' Support Group, and Mike Morris, secretary of the DSG. Jimmy Nolan, Jimmy Davies and Mike Carden delivered the welcome address, and Rogan Taylor started the workshops with *Football: a working-class sport*, followed by the Women of the Waterfront and the Miners' Wives Support Group. This event also included a series of presentations and discussions including, *A History of Liverpool Docks* by Eric Taplin, *Tate and Liars*, Ron Noon, *Racialised Barriers to Working-Class Solidarity*, Ibrahim Thompson, *A City That Dared to Fight*, Tony Mulhearn and *A History of the Irish in Liverpool* by Liam Greenslade. The Hillsborough Justice Campaign led a workshop on their long running campaign. [2]

On Monday 23 June, Jimmy Nolan and Frank Lannigan attended the Rail Maritime and Transport Workers Union (RMT) Conference in Yarmouth and the recent sense of conflict and bad faith among the stewards was amplified in their absence, as the stress and strain of two years in dispute were beginning to take their toll. That night, Carden received a phone call from Steve Riley, chair of the TGWU Broad Left, who spoke of: 'how disgraceful the GEC's statement was on the docks resolutions due to go to the BDC.' [3] However, this outburst did nothing to change the fact that he himself had voted in favour of the statement, although following a heated argument Riley did go on to say that Nolan and Danny Maher, the GEC representative for Docks and Waterways, were both: 'working hard to agree a fresh statement on the BDC.' [4] The Broad Left was seeking a compromise with the dockers ahead of a potential open confrontation at the BDC. Jimmy Nolan would deny that he had engaged in any discussions without first informing stewards. Riley telephoned Jimmy Davies to repeat an offer for Nolan to make a speech at the BDC, which was essentially meaningless as it required an acceptance of the GEC's statement on the docks first. In other words, the dockers would be supporting the TGWU's strategy for resolving the dispute, and any resolutions criticising Bill Morris's handling of the situation would be withdrawn. [5]

The following day the stewards wanted to discuss Steve Riley's statements, as well as the news that Merseyside Police wanted to meet Terry Teague and Tony Nelson in relation to what they saw as the escalation of picket line actions, following the latest scab attack on a dockers' picket caravan. Elsewhere, a 'Festival of Dockers' was held in France, organised by Michel Murray and various other trade unionists, where resolutions agreed at the Montreal meeting of the International Dockworkers' Committee were discussed. The festival was a testament to the work of Ken Loach, whose films were highly respected in France, as his documentary on the Liverpool docks dispute had inspired much-needed support for the campaign from French workers. Murray was to also visit dockers in Italy, South Africa, Australia, Japan and the US, as he gathered ideas for what specific actions should be taken within a timeframe of three to four weeks. On Tuesday 24 June, Terry Teague and Kevin Robinson met with the Chief Superintendent and Chief Inspector based at Crosby Police Station, where it was agreed that clear warnings would be given by senior officers before any future arrests were made. Previously, Teague had been handcuffed and marched through the picket line to the Port Police HQ, to be held for two hours. However, the very next day, dockers Mick Cullen and Colin Mitchell, along with Ian Brittles from Nelson Freight, were arrested when Teague was identified as standing near them. All were charged with obstructing a public highway, with the typical bail conditions forbidding their presence within 25 feet of Mersey Docks and Harbour Company property, taking the total of recent arrests up to 13 dockers, three of whom were stewards. At this point, the Dispute Committee was reconsidering its policy of liaising with police, but there was positive news in that picket line morale remained high, with gates at Seaforth, Alexandra and Gladstone docks successfully blockaded for 45 minutes on the morning of Thursday 26 June. News emerged that scab workers had met again with Dave McCall, the TGWU Regional secretary, and Jack Dempsey, the local docks officer. It was alleged that the two officials were exploring the possibility of recruiting scab labour into the union membership once the dispute was finally *collapsed by them*. [6]

Jimmy Nolan and Frank Lannigan had returned to Liverpool for a meeting at Transport House, where Jimmy Davies and Mike Carden reported on their respective conversations with Steve Riley regarding the GEC's statement on the Liverpool dispute. Nolan dismissed any involvement in what Riley had described. He spoke of the need for Liverpool dockworkers and their families to have the opportunity to address the BDC. Tony Nelson added that Danny Maher had expressed his concerns about the implications of the GEC statement. [7] The following day, the Dispute Committee received a letter from Bill Morris asking for a meeting on Friday 4 July and although they were not happy about it, the stewards felt that they could not refuse to meet him at such a critical time in the dispute. They did, however, request that the meeting be postponed until the Saturday or Sunday before the BDC. A week later, the Irish Congress of Trade Unions was due to meet in Belfast, and the stewards were hoping that John Freeman, the influential Northern Irish TGWU Regional secretary, would be able to secure them an invitation. Carden telephoned Freeman, who was, as expected, joining other Irish comrades in opposing the GEC statement. Nothing about the dispute was more settled than the solidarity of the Irish ATGWU and the Irish TGWU.

At that week's Friday mass meeting it was agreed that Jimmy Nolan would be the only steward to address the dockers, as guest speaker Sheila Coleman reported on the fight to keep the Liverpool Irish Centre open. She accused both the receivers and Merseyside Police of a racist campaign to close the city's only Irish community setting following a number of aggressive police raids culminating in armed officers surrounding the premises and threatening to shoot a member of staff. [8] The mood at the meeting was a sombre one, as Jimmy Nolan spoke of his rejection of a postal ballot, and his preference for a show of hands, while Neil Caddick, one of the sacked dockers, wanted it to be reaffirmed that, 'only the dockers can make the decisions on this dispute.' [9] Tony Weedon called for dockers to be 'disciplined' at the BDC. [10] Terry Barrett then asked what the TGWU's position would be if yet another ballot, the third, rejected MDHC's offer? Nolan reminded the dockers again, that 'pensions will only be protected if we get reinstated.' [11]

On Saturday 28 June, a North West Region 6 meeting of BDC delegates discussed resolutions and procedures. Dot Gibson had been working to ensure that the latest *Dockers' Charter* would be out in time for the BDC, producing an edition that was, 'exciting because some of the documents they were producing were quite excellent.' [12] An example of the quality of analysis and content being produced by the dockers, such as *LabourNet*, the *Dockers' Charter* etc. was the publication of a lengthy document, *The Case for the Reinstatement of the Sacked Liverpool Dockers: the need for a Public Inquiry into the Mersey Docks and Harbour Company: Merseyside Port Shop Stewards' Committee, 1 July 1997*, published on *LabourNet*, which noted that:

> *'After years of financial mismanagement and abuse, the Mersey Docks and Harbour Board was rescued from financial collapse in 1970 by the government [the taxpayer], who effectively took a controlling interest of 21 per cent and appointed three senior directors to ensure that no more financial improprieties took place. Between 1971 and 1989, millions of pounds of taxpayers' money were invested in the 'reconstituted' Mersey Docks and Harbour Company (MDHC). The status of the MDHC was that of a semi-nationalised company, and from this time the government's investment with taxpayers' money was always referred to as the 'golden share.' [13]*

This document, like so much of the contemporaneous source material, was produced by Mike Carden, Terry Teague, Dot Gibson and Greg Dropkin, who between them wrote almost all correspondence and documentation produced throughout the *living history* of this dispute. As the dispute progressed the support groups across the country began to produce outstanding documents and pamphlets. For example, the booklet, *Never Cross a Picket Line*, was produced for the first international conference by Mike Morris, Ernie Nattress, Kenny Kelly, Dave Sinclair, Alan Hardman and Ed, Tony, John and Sarah who typed, collated and printed the booklet. Unlike their union, the dockers rank-and-file organisation had no need of unaccountable leaders with autocratic power, or expensive consultancy firms to do work that they should have been doing themselves. The latest BDC document produced by the dockers drew together previously disparate strands of financial information about the Dock Company's business model, which had largely been either ignored or covered up in the past, for example: In 1987, MDHC shares had leapt from 31p to 280p, peaking at 460p an annual rise of 800 per cent and the company was subsequently the subject of a Department of Trade and Industry inquiry into a director accused of insider trading, resulting in the resignation of the deputy chairman. Also, following the abolition of the National Dock Labour Board Scheme in 1989, all UK ports were privatised and their dockers dismissed with severance pay, at what the government projected to be a cost of £20m. The real cost stood at £151m in 1989 alone. By 1992, the cost had risen to £200m, as all UK dock employers made use of the government severance money to illegally dismiss and then re-employ many of their dockers as casuals. Unsurprisingly, MDHC made full use of this underhanded practice, both before and after they had dismissed 500 dockers from the Port of Liverpool, as exposed by the Public Accounts Committee in 1990. The PAC eventually concluded that the government's estimate, used to justify casualisation in UK ports, had been understated by a staggering 470 per cent, but no one ever faced charges for this privatisation swindle, [14] and so *The Case for the Reinstatement of the Sacked Liverpool Dockers* sought to remind TGWU members of the scale of misappropriation that MDHC had been engaged in over the preceding decade and back to the 1970s.

In 1989, the Thatcher government wrote off over £112m in loans and repayable grants attached to MDHC within weeks of its announcement of the abolition of the NDLBS. But taxpayer funding did not end with the company's privatisation. Merseyside was officially one of Europe's poorest regions, and as a response to this, the European Union promised £630m of new investment, including over £300m from the private sector. An overall grant of £1.5bn was the largest amount received by any one city in the bloc, intended to help with unemployment, poverty, industrial decline and a shrinking population. However, as the initiative reached its halfway point, only £40 million had been properly utilised, with another £70 million spent on soft training programmes that seemingly brought few sustainable benefits. The dockers' document referred to a self-proclaimed major survey commissioned by MDHC under the title, *The Employment Impact of the Port of Liverpool in the 1990s*, in which Peter Stoney, a Liverpool-based economist, claimed that the port contributed between 49,000-105,000 jobs to the Merseyside economy, amounting to 19.5 per cent of the region's employment. Across the UK Stoney claimed that between 125,000-311,000 jobs relied on the port of Liverpool. The proposed 1992-98 capital expenditure programme would generate an additional 4,500 jobs during construction and 3,000 jobs thereafter. This development programme would supposedly then lead to the creation of another 9,000-23,000 jobs on Merseyside, plus 29,000-76,000 jobs nationwide. Stoney believed, not surprisingly, that the decline in direct dock labour from 7,000 dockers in 1976 to just 600 in 1992 had been compensated for by growth elsewhere.

The Dock Company had also benefited directly from European Regional Development Funds of £2.6m for the Sefton Maritime Zone Development, £362,000 for an aggregate conveyor at Seaforth Dock and £2.6m for work on the Langton Dock river entrance. Stoney's imaginary calculations were used to justify MDHC's benefiting from millions of pounds of European and City Challenge money, despite clear evidence that it was merely being funnelled into a private company. Trevor Furlong, MDHC's Managing Director, put his weight behind Stoney's estimates by claiming academic impartiality on the grounds that the data was collected by the Macroeconomic Research Unit at the University of Liverpool. But the truth was that Stoney's study had been paid for by MDHC, with work being undertaken by Liverpool Macroeconomic Research Ltd, a private company whose only directors were Professor Minford and his wife. For his part, Minford, a former monetarist guru to Margaret Thatcher, had contributed immensely to MDHC's model of exploiting planning permission laws whilst accessing publicly funded grants.

In October 1992, more taxpayers' cash arrived through Sefton Borough Council's City Challenge bid, amounting to £37.5 million, with Ken Wharton, MDHC's Marketing Director, who coincidentally was also a member of Bootle City Challenge Board, welcoming, 'this great news… that will benefit the whole community.' By this time, MDHC had received over £13.3 million in EU grants, and then in the financial year 1994-95, the company gratefully accepted further City Challenge donations to pay for the closure of Regent Road at a cost of £325,000, development of the Freeport at £75m, expansion of the Pandoro Irish berth with £390,000 and the filling in of Hornby Dock at a cost to the taxpayer of £250,000. Not one of these astronomical investments created either the jobs or the evidence of employment that Peter Stoney's report promised. [15] *The Case for the Reinstatement* document itemised MDHC's unique history of public funding – from bankruptcy and allegations of corruption in 1970 to profits and casualisation in 1995. In 1993, MDHC acquired the Medway Ports for £103.7m, 18 months after they could have bought the same portfolio for less than £14 million. Worse still, the purchase was preceded by Medway directors sacking more than 300 long-serving dockers, before reclaiming their former employees shares at £2.30 following a report by KPMG; the same registrars hired by MDHC and the TGWU to examine the business potential of a dockers' labour co-operative in the Port of Liverpool. The Medway share value stood at £38 at the time of its sale to MDHC, with Peter Vincent, Medway's Chief Executive, rumoured to have made an overnight profit of £12 million on the shares that he reclaimed from the sacked dockers. In 1993, Vincent became a director of MDHC, only to suddenly resign three months later. The government's shareholding was reduced from 21% to 14 % upon MDHC's purchase of Medway, prompting the company's chairman, Gordon Waddell, to agree: 'it is odd that a company with a government shareholding should be buying a privatised port'. [16]

The Dock Company was able to utilise the Medway blueprint again in 1995, this time in the Port of Liverpool. Unfortunately, and as is usual in these all-too-common circumstances, no questions had ever been asked about the 'odd' behaviour that Waddell referred to; not the TGWU, the national media or the *Liverpool Echo*, as the company continued to enjoy immunity from the kind of scrutiny that their use of public money should have attracted. The Medway purchase also introduced MDHC bosses to Drake International, the supplier of strike-breaking casual labour, registered offshore in the Bahamas, whose job-creating potential for Merseyside was limited by the fact that, 'Drake International does not trade. The consolidated accounts for the group's subsidiaries show that the company is insolvent, the result of repeated losses now totalling £8,343,704. Presumably, the poor financial picture is a convenient fiction connected with the company's offshore status.' [17] MDHC's claim of a 50 per cent improvement under Drake being typical of how employers always praised casual, zero-hour or scab labour dating back to the nineteenth century. [18] The company began a policy of privatising profits made from public investments in the early 1980s, having previously declared losses in order to avoid repayment clauses on government loans, which saw profits rise 1,000 per cent between 1986-95. In 1993, profits increased from £15.2m to £20.9m, before 1994 they showed a leap to £33.6m. Following the dismissal of 500 dockers, profits fell by over £2m, with half-yearly profits dropping to £13.9m in August 1996. That year, EuroLink lost £4.5 million, Coastal Containers saw profits fall by over 18 per cent and MDHC wasted £1m on severance pay for 41 employees as part of a proposal that was ultimately rejected by the sacked dockers.

MDHC would later admit that their dismissal of the Liverpool dockers was costing over £1m a year, resulting in a further £10m being set aside to eventually pay the men off; causing a fall in share value estimated to be more than £70m. There was also the cost of policing to take into consideration, which stood at almost £2m in 1997. Eric Leatherbarrow, MDHC's communications director, made the extraordinary claim that the company was not responsible for this because, 'the police just happened to be at the docks.' [19] These tumbling share prices did nothing to inspire a change of direction by MDHC directors, who in 1996 cashed in share options purchased at a reduced price of £4.37. Between 1993-95, Managing Director, Trevor Furlong's wages almost doubled to £316,000; three times that of the British Prime Minister. The dockers knew that their international boycott was having an impact, with the port in a state of financial and trading stagnation as losses grew. This did not stop MDHC bosses accumulating more shares as they continued to increase their personal wealth. Similar money-making opportunities would arise when the company was finally sold to Peel Holdings, all while the human fortunes of the Liverpool dockers continued to decline. Local MPs Joe Benton and Maria Eagle added their voices to the dockers' calls for a fresh public inquiry into MDHC's financial dealings, only for the lies, damned lies and economists' misrepresentations to triumph. Far away from the ever-increasing salaries and personal wealth of corporate bosses, the port's finances collapsed alongside that of the Liverpool dockers.

At the morning picket on Wednesday 2 July 1997, Liverpool docker Steve Stanton was knocked unconscious by a policeman and taken to Fazakerley Hospital, while another dockworker, Kenny Weston, was arrested that same day. In response, the Dispute Committee intended to make further formal complaints about Merseyside Police, who appeared to be acting under instruction from MDHC's private Port Police force. [20] Eyewitnesses stated that Stanton, a former employee at the Norse Irish berth, was rushed from the scene by ambulance after having his head banged against the pavement while being handcuffed. Sgt Farrell of the Port Police directed the Merseyside Police officers to make arrests, despite the fact that the picket line had already withdrawn. Shop steward Herbie Hollerhead contacted the superintendent to lodge a formal complaint about an assault that was witnessed by dockworkers John Jackson, Billy Rooney and Mickey Tighe. [21] On 10 July, Ray Walklett was again arrested at the Alexandra Dock for breaking his bail conditions, and on 16 July, Bruce Allen, an executive member of the Canadian Autoworkers Local 199, and chairman of its Human Rights Committee, wrote to Merseyside Police:

> *'Merseyside Police should publicly acknowledge that there was no excuse for his brutality and apologize to Mr Stanton and his counterparts and offer him compensation that he will deem appropriate.'* [22]

The Liverpool dockers consistently condemned acts of violence by the Merseyside Police, and particularly members of the Operational Support Division (OSD), who acted aggressively whenever peaceful picketing has been taking place.

Elsewhere, two 6/541 Branch members from the TGWU's Road Haulage section organised a sponsored walk across Wales, which despite being called off after 14 miles due to bad weather, still managed to raise £800 for the dockers' Hardship Fund. This was just one example of the support shown by the branch led by Tommy Kirwin, Tony Woodhouse and Dave Williams. Meanwhile, considerable pressure was being put on the dock branches to withdraw motions supporting the dockers at the BDC, as the stewards discussed how the GEC statement to the conference would actually rule out dock motions 418 to 426; they sought to find a way to draw, 'a very clear line. The motions on the docks stand and should be debated.' [23] The key to this issue might have been that the TGWU Broad Left was concerned that a vote to back the dockers at the BDC would challenge their own power and influence over the GEC, a power that was dependent upon the patronage of the union's General Secretary. But whatever the reasoning, it was obvious that they did not want resolutions supporting the Liverpool campaign being either debated or supported. Later that night, Jimmy Nolan and some shop stewards met with Steve Riley at a London hotel, to consider how to prevent the TGWU from ignoring their dispute by blocking public discussion on it via a GEC statement. [24] Support for the Liverpool dockers began arriving in the form of direct messages to Bill Morris. For example, the Irish Port Workers Liaison Group wrote to their TGWU comrades:

> '*At a meeting held in Dublin on Friday 4 July, the Irish Port Workers Liaison Group came out in full support of the Liverpool dockers, and fully supported their fight to retain their jobs within the Port of Liverpool... The Group were of the opinion that the Brighton Conference should encourage and welcome the plan agreed in Montreal for industrial action to be taken against the shipping lines continuing to call in Liverpool, and that the unions should use their influence in conjunction with the ITF to help in developing the coordination of all of the global supportive actions against Mersey Docks... The Irish Port Workers Liaison Group is also requesting, on behalf of the Liverpool dockers, that all unions use whatever influence possible on the Labour government to conclude a parliamentary inquiry into the Mersey Docks' behaviour and its use of public funds.' [25]*

Another letter, from Donald R. Holzman, secretary treasurer of the International Longshore and Warehouse Union Local 40, began: 'Dear Brother Morris...'

> *I am writing to urge you and your conference to consider the current worldwide support for the Liverpool dockers... You may remember that we had a problem in the United States with the air traffic controllers when they went on strike. They struck in violation of federal law. They were replaced with scabs and most of them lost their jobs. The entire labor community was slow to react, and there is a general consensus that we should have called a general strike of all labor at that time. After that incident, unions have been under direct attack in this country. Strikers cannot be fired, but they can be legally 'replaced.' This country has used its military and economic power to provide for capital to be used to control sovereign nations.' [26]*

Terry Ryan, Assistant General Secretary of the New Zealand Waterfront Workers Union, wrote that: 'all workers in Britain must be proud of the way the dockers have stood up for their principles, the principles of workers worldwide. Also, the magnificent support given by their wives and families. Brother Morris, as one of the most influential leaders of the trade union movement, we would sincerely urge you and the TGWU to make a strong case to the newly-elected British Labour government to resolve the Liverpool dispute.' [27] Denmark's Ole Moller wrote: 'on behalf of the Liverpool dockers' situation, the Dockers' union in Aarhus strongly wants to express its concern, that a decent solution can be achieved... we want to urge you to use your position to obtain a victory for the Liverpool dockers. Don't forget that you said: "You never ever walk alone." The Liverpool struggle is the struggle of all true trade unionists, and also a struggle for the future if trade unions want to be representing the working people.' [28]

On Friday 4 July, two days before the BDC, a delegation comprising of Jimmy Nolan, Frank Lannigan, Jimmy Davies Jr, Mike Carden, Bobby Morton, Terry Southers and Bob Ritchie met Bill Morris, Dave McCall, Jack Adams, Graham Stevenson, Ray Collins and Andy Smith, the chair of the GEC and the union's President at the Stakis Hotel in Brighton. Morris apologised for his late appearance, explaining that he had to prepare for the BDC while attending to other problems, such as the 20,000 members working at British Airways. He then reminded the dockers that they had asked for the meeting, as the clearly busy and impatient General Secretary urged them to begin. Nolan started by expressing dissatisfaction at the length of time it was taking for KPMG to report back on the dockers' labour co-operative business proposal, as well as the absence of joint negotiations with MDHC. Morris replied that: 'We have been quite insistent when negotiations take place; we have always attempted to have representatives of dockers there. No negotiations with KPMG were needed, as it was the GEC that undertook this report and it will go to the GEC. It is their business. KPMG were commissioned by the GEC and the Executive Officers.' [29] Morris finished by turning to Nolan and saying brusquely, 'Next item,' [30] at which point the dockers' chairman reflected on Tory legislation that gave employers the right to sack workers: 'Our economic theory is different to yours. You say negotiations, but MDHC have not given any indications that they will negotiate on reinstatement.' This was followed by Nolan outlining the role of internationalism in the dispute, and how Morris needed to, 'recognise the political economy of the last eighteen years. You must use the ITF and Parliament to instigate an inquiry.' [31]

Morris appeared unimpressed, as he responded by reiterating that the officers of the union acted upon policies laid down by the GEC: 'I will not challenge your views today; we all must accept the policies of the GEC. We must work for a negotiated settlement, whilst maintaining the fabric of the union and helping with financial hardship.' [32] Nolan did not accept this opinion, telling Morris that, 'It is only a cosmetic exercise by the MDHC; they do not want to reinstate us. It is inhumane for you to maintain your strategies; they are out of order, and you must adopt our strategy.' [33] He then compared BA workers to the Liverpool dockers, arguing that they were both, 'victims of bad employers. We must move forward to damage the economic base of the company. Your policy has failed.' [34] However, Morris simply repeated what he had said earlier: 'On a personal basis, I have no policy or strategy. I have no authority to work outside of the GEC policy. We are all bound by this policy.' [35] Effectively, the General Secretary was reducing his role to that of a mere custodian of the *TGWU Rule Book*; nothing more than *a cypher* for the GEC. While this was both technically and legally correct from a constitutional standpoint, of how the union worked within the pages of its rulebook, all power rested with the General Secretary.

Jimmy Nolan continued: 'The GEC has been negligent, and they must understand that after 22 months this policy had failed. When do the GEC meet?' [36] Morris answered, 'I will not call a special GEC meeting, but I will convey your thoughts to them.' [37] Nolan then challenged Morris over his allegations that the Liverpool dockworkers were a political organisation, as trade unionism and politics were indivisible: 'We don't blam Tory laws, but dockers in the past had protected civil liberties by refusing to ha

other workers. We must have a joint approach to Labour's senior MPs to explain the conspiracy of Fowler [Tory Minister for Employment] and Finney [the leader of the National Association of Port Employers in 1989] etc, and the abuse of European money by the MDHC.' [38] Morris replied that, 'this has been done. The Labour government will not involve itself with industrial disputes. This is a matter for ACAS.' [39] This prompted Frank Lannigan to retort that the 1996 inquiry could still be revisited. [40] Morris flatly ignored him, turning back towards Nolan and, looking quite annoyed, asking again, 'Anything else, Jim?' [41] Undeterred, Nolan continued to speak of internationalism, the rationalisation of the docks and the impact of containerisation, the globalisation of capital, the ITF and the forthcoming Day of World Action. He then called on Morris to organise a special meeting of the GEC to instigate action by the ITF and the Labour Party, which had long been proposed by the Dispute Committee. After raising the numerous motions to the BDC regarding the repeal of anti-union legislation, Nolan then asked, 'would it not be possible to await the outcome of these motions opposed to anti-union labour laws before we finalise our business?' [42] Morris's only response to this was to say that the standing orders for the BDC had already been finalised, before repeating his previous question, 'Anything else?' [43] A long, silent pause then filled the room, to be ended by Morris reiterating how it was the TGWU's wish to maximise the number of jobs available in the port, evidenced by the GEC authorising the KPMG feasibility study, which would be scrutinised by the Unity Trust Bank. Stevenson added that KPMG's report was a cautious study, with an initial 28 jobs plus the possibility of 50 more. He then explained that port users were nervous about these proposals, [44] before proceeding to tell the dockers everything they already knew about the docks' wildly fluctuating labour demands: 'This is why casual labour abounds, together with a need for annualised hours,' perhaps forgetting, or not knowing, that this was what had caused the dispute in the first place. [45] The National Docks Officer concluded by acknowledging that none of this was included in MDHC's final offer.

Nolan told the TGWU officials that this was unacceptable, and then, with his usual passion and force, he argued against the labour co-operative idea before again asking Morris, 'to withdraw the GEC statement on the docks.' [46] But the General Secretary continued to hide behind the union's bureaucratic mechanisms, telling the stewards that, 'it is not my right. The GEC is responsible for its statement and it is wrong for me to debate the GEC statement.' [47] Jack Adams finally brought the conversation to a close by asking Nolan, in front of Morris, 'Do you think this union will go illegal?' [48] The following afternoon, the Broad Left met to discuss the BDC agenda, with Bobby Morton, Mike Carden and Len McCluskey all urging a rejection of the GEC statement. At the end of the meeting, an angry Jimmy Nolan spoke in defence of having an open debate at the BDC, not least because the BA dispute was due to begin the very next day, which as an official, endorsed strike would probably still end up with the same fate as the Liverpool dockers if the union failed to really fight the BA employers. However, it was unfortunately becoming more and more obvious that the union's leadership was feeling increasingly comfortable about openly opposing the dockers' campaign, and it had been relayed to the stewards that the very influential Scottish TGWU delegates and officials had been supporting the line that the dockers were now a political movement, having been heard to claim that: 'the dockers leaders are all Trotskyists, out to destabilise the union.' [49]

# 71

# The 1997 Biennial Delegates Conference

*'But don't let it collapse… get a dignified settlement. You have done a wonderful job. I have never seen a dispute run like this in my life, and I am very proud to be part of it.' ~ Jack Adams\**

As midnight struck on Sunday 6 July 1997, four coaches departed a bleak rain-soaked Liverpool for Brighton, where they would arrive at around 5am and then return once the initial vote on the docks dispute had been taken at the Biennial Delegates Conference (BDC). They travelled south knowing full well that, as always, they were in a fight to secure representation from their union officials, but even after two years of being undermined at every turn, they did not foresee the open betrayal of democracy that was to be undertaken by the TGWU leadership. Starved of sleep, they gathered outside the conference centre with placards, leaflets and the specially prepared edition of the *Dockers' Charter*, on which Dot Gibson and her team had worked, determined to get it published in time. Dot had been travelling between Liverpool and London on an almost weekly basis in order to ensure that the very tight printing deadlines for the dockers' newspaper were always met. [1] Andy Smith, chairman of the TGWU's General Executive Council, began the opening day's business of the 75th anniversary of the formation of the UK's largest industrial trade union. It should have been a celebration, but events got off to a faltering, nervous start, with the gallery filled by Liverpool dockers, their wives and their supporters, all of whom were keen to make their presence felt. The conference's Standing Orders Committee, those lay-members responsible for the structure of each day's business, were set to impose an official GEC statement on the dock dispute, thus avoiding any opportunity for debate. This was seemingly the preferred strategy chosen by Bill Morris and his right-hand man, Ray Collins. A tactic previously

---

\* Jack Adams, Dispute Committee meeting at Transport House Liverpool, 24 September 1997.

employed on other contentious issues, such as Northern Ireland, at earlier Biennial Delegates Conferences. Its purpose was simply to prevent open discussion on such matters.

The first debate was dominated by a discussion on composite resolutions covering 'outsourcing and casualisation,' which gave every delegate called to the rostrum an opportunity to declare their support for the Liverpool dockers, who represented both a contemporary and an historic symbol of opposition to these twin enemies of organised labour. Teresa McKay, from the Agricultural Workers, was the first to reference the Liverpool dispute, speaking with great passion as she reminded the conference that many of those workers crossing the dockers' picket lines were TGWU members. She also mentioned the previous year's Chelmsford bus workers' dispute, and how the union had undermined their struggle. She then asked delegates if they were going to support British Airways workers, whose strike was due to start the next day, and finished with the message: 'enough is enough. It is time for the union to support its members!' [2] The next speaker, John Sheridan of Region Six, focussed on the consequences of casual labour, or 'the lump,' as it was known in the building industry in Liverpool, comparing it to the situation that the Liverpool dockers were now facing. Bobby Morton, an official BDC delegate, reminded every other delegate that the Tolpuddle Martyrs, the Suffragettes and Nelson Mandela had: 'all been forced to break the law to achieve their just demands.' [3] In response to these preliminary speeches, Bill Morris listed the campaigns that the union was supporting: 'You cannot have a zero-hour contract; an injustice is an injustice from day one. We want protection for every worker. Fairness in the workplace can only be achieved with fair and just laws, so our task is to persuade government to abolish the anti-trade union laws.' [4] He then went on to explain why he and the GEC opposed Composite 13, which called for the union to act in breach of existing laws, since the TGWU was categorically not a law-breaking union:

> *The applause [from the dockers] for this motion failed to understand what it actually said, because it states that the TGWU and the wider trade union movement should consider any steps necessary, including industrial action outside legal restriction; to support by any means those who defy the law. I have to tell you that not only is that against the policies of this union as decided by this conference, it is against the rules of this union. We are not a law-breaking union, we are a law-abiding union by constitution and by right. However unpopular that may be, we are a law-abiding union; we are a law-abiding union!' [5]*

Following shouts of 'Whose side are you on?' from the dockers and their supporters, Morris replied, 'I am on the side of the TGWU and its 900,000 members,' before loudly repeating, 'Let me say to Bobby Morton... let me say to Bobby Morton':

> *Bobby, your comparison with which laws to obey and which laws not to obey is wrong. Please don't compare the immorality of apartheid with the thuggery of one or two employers in this country. Mandela did not have access to a democratic process – the black people in South Africa did not have a vote – there is a distinction. The TGWU would be brought to its knees by sequestration... our GEC deemed it to be morally wrong to squander all the resources of this union, that supports all our members, in one*

*single cause of going down the road on non-compliance. Make no mistake, this union is not afraid to stand up for its members against bullying employers. We will defend our members at Magnet, BA and the dockers. I sign over 200 authorisations for workers to take action. Defend your union; vote against Composite 13!' [6]*

Region 6's Dave Irvine, speaking as a mover of one of the composite motions supporting the Liverpool dockers, returned to the rostrum and addressed Morris directly: 'How on earth, general secretary, can we support the right to take solidarity action, the right to effective picketing, the right to freedom of association, and then cut loose 500 Liverpool people for 22 months? Whatever these dockers want, this conference should deliver, and the TGWU should deliver!' [7] At this, the conference chairman turned to the GEC's *explanatory statement* on the Liverpool dispute, saying that if the statement was agreed, motions 418-426 supporting the dockers would not be taken and no debate would be allowed. However, if the statement was defeated, the motions would be put to the conference and open debate would take place. Using the *TGWU Rule Book*, Morris and the GEC were seeking to remove branch / regional motions from the agenda and replace them with one GEC statement endorsing their strategy for and handling of the Liverpool dispute. This statement also condemned all media coverage criticising the union's performance. Jack Adams, who had been leading negotiations with MDHC, introduced the controversial statement as a product of the GEC's responsibility: 'to preserve the fabric of the union and operate within the constraints of the law,' [8] before providing details of his dealings with the employer and then claiming: 'the dockers had demanded the TUC call a general strike.' [9] A strategy that had never been formally endorsed by the Dispute Committee, as was made abundantly clear by the gallery and various official speakers, with Jimmy Davies shouting out: 'Don't mislead conference!' [10] Adams continued, recommending the GEC statement: 'because I believe our union and our GEC has supported our Liverpool dockers.' [11] Adams explained:

*The union supported that dispute within the limitations; we did issue repudiations. Legal redress is not time-limited; about 16 or 17 companies have a claim, and so too do the customers. On 23 December 1996, I had delivered a £2m lawsuit, delivered by hand by ACL in the state of New Jersey. I have to tell you, comrades, that most of the unions that I am associated with would have buckled under that type of threat. Your union didn't.' [12]*

One of the dockers shouted something about the miners not buckling under threats of sequestration, and while Adams agreed, he also added that:

*'...there are not many of them left now. We fought along with the miners and we will continue to fight along with the dockers... I've heard calls for the TUC to call a general strike. Well, I'm a member of the TUC General Council, and if you believe the TUC will call a general strike in breach of law, then you are considering the reality to be outside of our own experience. We are in a war of attrition with an employer who I believe engineered the dispute... don't divide this great union's conference on this issue and don't split our struggle in support of our dockers, and support the statement.' [13]*

Adams followed this speech by immediately moving the GEC statement on the dock dispute, before Jimmy Nolan, another official BDC delegate, made his way to the rostrum. Nolan carried with him nothing but a rolled-up copy of the GEC statement and the motions in support of the Liverpool dockers. Speaking without notes he delivered an address that perfectly encapsulated his trade union philosophy:

> 'Over 18 years of Conservative rule, we in Liverpool, we have been in opposition to anti-union legislation, and I can look around this conference at all the industries represented and say that we in Liverpool have always supported any given struggle that you have put forward to us, and do you know how we done that? We used to get up to the members, when we had 16,000 men, and we used to say that the TGWU cannot officially support us if we support these other British working-class people, who are in dispute because of the anti-union labour laws, but we did say to the labour force that we want to know whether we have civil liberties, and when we expressed those principles of civil liberties, we supported every man and woman who came for support from the Liverpool dockworkers.
>
> It's not a question of me and Bobby Morton coming to this rostrum to try and slag the TGWU. In the last few weeks, we have been trying to resolve this question of the General Executive statement, but unfortunately, the senior officers, the general secretary and the GEC, have made it very clear that they wished to put forward this statement. Now, the statement itself is divisive because if you were in struggle and, on the eve of a BDC, the GEC came forward and said that because we don't like these resolutions, and because we don't like what happened in the Guardian, we are going to insert them in a blanket statement based on your struggle. I should imagine that, as delegates to this conference, you would be in opposition to this statement. Even at this late hour, this statement should be withdrawn, but it is not going to be withdrawn for one simple reason, because of the ideology of the GEC, and that ideology, whether they like it or not, whether they are consciously aware or unconsciously aware, that is going to create very serious problems. This statement should be opposed, and we should have a framework similar to the composite motions that you have already agreed upon here today. If we were offered the same type of principle contained in the BA struggle, then we would be satisfied with that. So, that's what we require. We are asking you to be in opposition to this statement.' [14]

At this point, Nolan was asked by the chair to finish speaking, but Nolan asked for more time and continued regardless:

> 'If you have a Labour government in power, surely it's right, based upon the historical principles of Labour, that we in Liverpool, and that we as dismissed port workers, have the right to say that we must have the right to representative democracy. I listen to some of the comments of the GEC that there is no hope; it is wrong for this struggle to continue; we have suffered too much pain. This pain has to be removed, and we have to be reinstated... we got dismissed because we refused to cross a picket line. Now if we were wrong to refuse to cross a picket line, and you vote wrongly here, then you must say to us

*that anybody who is dismissed by an employer because they are in breach of an employment contract, you must cross a picket, then we are in a very bad, bad way. You can't cross a picket line, and we know that the MDHC utilised political legislation to dismiss us, and it is only by political methods that we will resolve this, and it's got to be the Labour government, and particularly the prime minister, to reflect back on trade union and Labour history, and he will know that we were right not to cross that picket line.' [15]*

Nolan was again asked to conclude, but still he persevered:

*'You can see how they can control the platform. They come up here when they address the conference, take as long as they want, very relaxed; so this is an abuse of power. Ideological forces, stemming from the GEC, to make you decide on a statement to support the statement, not understanding the damage you are going to do to us in the Port of Liverpool. We have been isolated for 22 months. You, the British people, in a physical sense, have done nothing to support the Liverpool dockers. Now, that's not a criticism, because we know that economic fear is rife in this country. We went international 25 months ago; this concept of internationalism goes back many, many years. I welcome all the composite motions, the ILO convention, the question of freedom of association, because every man and woman will have the right to stand up to employers without the fear of being replaced by fuckin' scabs! This statement must be withdrawn, or you have to vote against it.' [16]*

Nolan went on to reference further international actions scheduled for the weeks ahead, before turning to the TGWU executives sitting behind him on the platform and, pointing his finger accusingly, saying with anger in his voice:

*'This is not trade unionism. I would say to you, General Secretary, that you and the GEC are completely out of order to put that statement forward, as what's happening here is that you are going to have splits and divisions here, and I say to you, I have been involved for 35 years with regard to struggle on Liverpool docks, and like you, I come from a good family of trade unionists and politicians, and those 500 men and their wives and families come from the same traditions, and so what we say to you is this, and it's not much to ask for by the way, that this bleeding statement be opposed.' [17]*

Once this act of defiance had been committed, Nolan argued, the members could then:

*'Turn around to the general secretary and the GEC and instruct them that they must work with the representatives of the 500 men… we should be reinstated because [of] the courageous thing we did; because we refused to cross a picket line, and I am so proud that we refused to cross a picket line. How proud I am that you raised your voice at a conference; that we are not fodder; that we are going to be re-instated.' [18]*

The majority of delegates gave Jimmy Nolan a standing ovation, as the dockers, along with their wives and partners, shouted their support from the balcony that encircled the hall. Other official union delegates sat impassively, awaiting instruction, while the chair, Andy Smith, sitting only a few feet away from Nolan, waited for the tumult of applause, cheers and shouting to subside before saying in his broad Scottish accent: 'I've actually shown tolerance to Jim Nolan and the role he has played in this dispute. Can I assure the conference that I am on here to uphold the standing orders report that was passed here this morning, so any speaker who comes to the rostrum will have to abide by what this conference has agreed, and I hope you agree with that.' [19] He then called Bobby Morton to the rostrum, who announced straightaway that he would be speaking against the GEC statement:

> 'The fabric of the union is the membership. It's not the money, it's not the buildings, it's nothing else. Reject the statement. The flagship is flying the white flag. If you accept this, and if you do, I'm warning you, you are sending the BA workers to a fate worse than death.' [20]

Many speakers pointed to the illegality of the dispute, defending the GEC as elected lay-members and prioritising the union's funds by arguing that rejecting the GEC statement would condone the illegal action of the dockers; unlawful action that, according to one speaker, was nothing more than, 'immoral, irresponsible and ineffectual.' [21] Attending her fourth BDC, Penny Iverson spoke on the subject of preserving the fabric of the union, explaining how she considered the campaign led by the dockers and the Women of the Waterfront to be inspirational:

> 'Despite the inaction of the leaders of our union, an injury to one is an injury to all. The Liverpool dockers' dispute is not unofficial anyway. They are showing us how to preserve the fabric of a working-class union against vicious bosses. What is a union? Is it the cash? No. Is it the buildings? No! A union is the members, and the will to organise and fight, and if you have that, the money will follow, and if you don't, you lose the money anyway. You lose your money because you lose your membership, because they will see you won't fight for them. Don't accept this statement.' [22]

Another delegate, Tom White, a car worker from Region 5, made an extraordinary speech in support of the Liverpool dockers, quoting former general secretary Ron Todd, in asserting that the TGWU would not exist were it not for the historic struggle of dockworkers of 1889:

> 'We owe the dockers every reason why we are here today. All of us who don't work on the docks, who have never worked on the docks, let me remind you in the 1950s and '60s, when we were fighting for recognition in the automotive industry in Oxford, it was the dockers that blocked the cars and made it possible for our recognition, so I am not apologising for supporting the Liverpool dockers. We wouldn't be here. I can't understand why a man who has led a dispute for 22 months; why can't he be involved in drawing up the statement. It's the delegates who make the policies. Reject this statement.' [23]

The next speaker, from Region 3 in Ireland, urged standing by the dockers and rejecting the motion, while Gerry Guigley, a docker from Region 3 and attendee of the first International Conference of Port Workers in Liverpool, said: 'If the dockers are breaking the law, then I'm a law-breaker, too.' [24] A tugboatman from Region 8 referred to past support that his members had received from the Liverpool dockers. Dave Williams, of the Region 6 RTC, labelled many of the statements made against the Liverpool dockers as untrue, before recalling how: 'The Liverpool dockers gave support recently in Sheerness, against a haulage company that had won a contract in Sheerness because they crossed the picket lines in Liverpool. This was this haulier's reward, but we went to IG Metall in Germany with the dockers, and we won their support and we won the dispute at Sheerness.' [25] Teresa McKay then declared it a scandal that compositing motions were being suppressed in favour of the official GEC statement, before insisting: 'We owe it to the dockers to stand shoulder to shoulder with them. If it is an illegal dispute, why are the union negotiating with the bosses? We don't want to go back to 1889.' [26] This was followed by Joe Elba of Region 1 reminding Bill Morris that, 'Mandela was in prison, and people still fought apartheid; they broke the laws at the time. Their actions were illegal.' [27] Region 6's Dave Quayle said: 'Jimmy Nolan has offered to contribute to a framework for the union to work together, even at this late stage. I am proud to support the Liverpool dockers.' [28] Ken Jones, Quayle's colleague in Region Six, added: 'If we could not get agreement from the dockers on a composite motion, then it was a disgrace that the GEC just produced a statement to undermine numerous branch resolutions supporting the dockers.' The final speaker, representing Region 8, warned of: 'the anarchy and chaos if we support an illegal dispute.' [29] Bill Morris, as General Secretary had the right to respond to the discussion:

> *My friend Jimmy wanted us to reject the GEC statement; this was the only basis for unity. We all want unity. We all want a settlement to this dispute… Colleagues, we cannot find unity in a group of motions that condemns the union on one hand, and on the other hand congratulates Ken Loach on his attack on our union. We cannot find unity on that basis. We have to find unity on the basis of a set of clear objectives based not on Fleet Street principles, but on our principles, our traditions and our values. That is the only way we can find unity. …The real villains in this are the MDHC, and if there is any enemy to be found, then we need to look no further than the anti-union laws under which this union has been forced to operate in line with the policies of this BDC. The real enemies are the capitalist press, who continue to attack our union.*
>
> *But you know, it is not just the so-called capitalist press. From the very safety of the newspaper columns and the television studios, we have seen the Pilgers and the Loaches launching attack after attack on our union… it gave us no pleasure to repudiate actions taken by sections of our membership when we were faced with writs in this dispute. We had a writ served from America for £2m, and it was an indication of how vulnerable this union is… I do not want to read in the capitalist press tomorrow that the TGWU divides on support for the Liverpool dockers. I want the headlines to say that the T&G unites around the Liverpool dockers, [and] the Magnet workers, so that we can send a message to the BA employers and all employers who are attacking our*

*members. You can choose the path of unity, or you can risk this union's oblivion. I urge you to exercise tolerance. I urge you to give support to the dockers. I urge you to give support to this statement, and I urge you to give support to your union. Support the GEC statement.' [30]*

Once Morris had finished, Andy Smith immediately moved the GEC Statement and called for all those in favour, drawing approval from less than a third of the room, while a clear majority raised their hands in opposition. At this, the hall erupted in cries of support and applause, not only for the Liverpool dockers, but also for the rank-and-file members who had asserted their authority at the BDC over the power of the General Executive Council. However, this jubilation quickly gave way to outrage and uproar when a clearly unsettled Smith declared that the GEC statement had been carried, announcing: 'We now stand adjourned until tomorrow morning.' [31] A speaker from the floor made a sudden grab for the microphone, as Morris and Collins stood behind Smith, with Jack Adams being the only executive who appeared to acknowledge the fact that the conference had voted overwhelmingly in rejection of the statement. The delegate in possession of the microphone cried out: 'The vote was lost by the Executive Council! The dockers won this vote! We want the tellers on the platform!' [32] and once again the hall heaved in a wave of anger. Tim Lyle was the first TGWU National Officer to leave the platform, while some delegates on the floor began exiting the hall in solidarity with the union's bureaucracy. The official video recording of the conference faded to a test card at this point; a symbolic declaration that open trade union democracy had been brought to an abrupt halt. Off screen, Smith could be heard issuing an order to clear the hall and close business for the day, and then after several minutes of uncertainty, he announced that due to the closeness of the vote, a card ballot would be taken first thing the next morning. [33]

The dockers decided to stay another night in Brighton in order to lobby the BDC again, as the WOW made frantic arrangements to find hotel floors to sleep on. None of them had a change of clothes, but they were determined to do whatever it took to protect the integrity of their campaign. In the final edited release of the BDC live stream coverage, the result of the vote taken on Monday 7 July was displayed: 182 for the GEC statement and 283 against, giving a majority victory of 101 votes in favour of the Liverpool dockers. [34] On Monday evening the General Secretary, Ray Collins, Regional Secretaries and the Broad Left, spent the night working to ensure their delegates into invalidating this decision by voting in support of the GEC statement for a second time to overturn the original conference decision. [35] The following day, the tables were turned, as the TGWU leadership realised that they could not realistically call for a second vote; they had wasted their time warning delegates that they would have no future in the union if they went against the diktat of their general secretary and *his regional barons*. To roars of approval, the platform declared that the GEC statement had indeed been rejected, with regional results accurately reflecting the union's established right-left divide, as Welsh, Scottish and Midlands delegates all opposed the Liverpool dockworkers.

Orchestrating events alongside Morris on the platform that day were Ray Collins, the TGWU National Administration Officer, and Margaret Prosser, the National Organiser, for whom the whims of the rank-and-file did not seem so important. In 2004, Prosser would be named Baroness Prosser of Battersea, in the London Borough of Wandsworth, two years before the General Secretary was clothed in ermine as Baron Morris of Handsworth, in the County of West Midlands. They were to be joined by Collins in 2011, as he became Baron Collins of Highbury, in the London Borough of Islington. In Morris's authorised biography, *A Trade Union Miracle*, the author recalled the 1997 BDC as an occasion where the union's primary decision-making body had: 'exploded violently when a large group of Liverpool dockers invaded the conference at Brighton to harangue and barrack the union's leadership. Some of them were admitted to the conference and sat in the gallery chanting racial slogans at Bill Morris.' [36] The TGWU's own official video recording did not show any invasion or pick up a single racist slogan, nor did the national press mention anything of the sort. Furthermore, not one person in attendance made a complaint about the dockers' behaviour, either during or after the conference, and that is because Goodman's version of events was both slanderous and false. This was not a good day for trade union democracy or the TGWU's bureaucracy.

On Monday 14 July 1997, the Dispute Committee called a mass meeting of Liverpool dockers, to report back on the outcome of the union's Biennial Delegates Conference. The dockers were informed that the BDC had rejected the GEC statement by a vote of 2-1. It was later confirmed that Jack Adams and Dave McCall had spoken to Jimmy Nolan the day after the vote, where it was said that Morris was 'bitter' about the rejection of the statement. [37] Adams had explained that any potential government inquiry would take a long time to arrange, even with the likely backing of MPs Ian McCartney and Margaret Beckett. However, according to Adams, such an approach to politicians was, 'for the union to do, and this would be done on a private basis with no publicity.' [38] On the matter of petitioning the ITF to exert its considerable influence, the deputy general secretary suggested that the TGWU should, 'stand-down Stevenson, to get him to travel around Europe to drum up support for ITF involvement in the international day of action.' [39] This did not seem such a great idea to the stewards as they were well aware that Morris was due to make a speech at an ITF meeting in Vancouver, Canada, which was unlikely to feature resolutions in support of his dock membership in Liverpool. Terry Teague reiterated the need for urgency in regard to a Labour Party inquiry, noting that Parliament was due to go into recess, and so local MP Joe Benton, a committed supporter of the Liverpool dockworkers and a member of the Commons Employment and Education subcommittee, would need to be contacted. Jack Adams had been critical of a special BDC edition of the *Dockers' Charter*, and in particular an article written by Mike Carden, where it was stated that the dockers: 'had no employer since September 1995, they could not be on unofficial strike, and therefore the union has no restriction on supporting the campaign.' Adams argued that the dockers had broken their contract of employment.

Discussion at the mass meeting then shifted to the National Docks and Waterways Committee, which was set to move a resolution condemning Andy Smith, the chair of the BDC, along with Ray Collins, the union's Administration Officer, who had been responsible for the initial 'mis-counted' vote: 'when he leaned across to Andy Smith and told him the GEC Statement had been carried when clearly it had not.' [40] Bobby Morton added that while he and Jimmy Nolan were speaking on motions relating to the rejected GEC statement, he had overheard one of the union's officers referring to the two stewards as 'Scouse Trots.'

[41] Micky Tighe, who had been working closely with the London Support Group, reported that John Prescott MP had said during a meeting in Durham that he would use whatever influence he had to convince Bill Morris of the need to openly support the Liverpool dockers. In more positive news from New Zealand, a businessman donated £10,000 to the Hardship Fund, and Brian McWilliams was re-elected president of the International Longshore and Warehouse Union. In Liverpool, John Monks, speaking as General Secretary of the Trades Union Congress, told a local radio station that he was, 'going to intervene for the benefit of the dockers, and to restore the port to normal working.' [42] Of course this did not happen.

Picketing continued as always. The Dispute Committee had met with representatives of the Communication Workers Union, as over 1,000 jobs were being threatened by the proposed closure of Royal Mail's Liverpool sorting office. The CWU planned to call a Day of Resistance on 2 August, where the dockers would be joined by trade unionists from Critchley Labels, as well as activists from Reclaim the Streets, standing in solidarity with postal workers. There was also to be a demonstration outside of the offices of Liverpool City Council on Wednesday 16 July, in response to one of their members of staff, Kieran Dunn, being disciplined for actions taken in support of the docks dispute, with the employer looking to utilise police picket line footage as evidence against him. Meanwhile, tensions among the stewards increased as various factions began to openly oppose or ignore one another, often at the behest of external political sponsors who would take stewards out of Transport House to make their own separate plans. But this was also happening with the dockers themselves. The routine of the mass meetings also seemed to have changed, with the normal structure of stewards speaking as holders of roles within either the Dispute Committee or the TGWU appearing to collapse, while some stewards failed to attend important strategy meetings and picket line demonstrations. [43]

On Friday 18 July, it was reported that sacked dock worker Geoff Jones had been arrested on the picket line, as Merseyside Police once again stepped up the violence, threats, intimidation and arrests. At the weekly mass meeting held that same day, Steve Donnelly from AC Delco donated £1,500 to the Hardship Fund and Kieran Dunn thanked the dockers for their support during his disciplinary hearing at work. Lars Stubbs, visiting from the Hamburg Dockers Support Group, also addressed the dockers, as did Tekin Kartal of the Turkish Community Group. [44] The following day, the dockers supported the Merseyside Cuba Solidarity Campaign by filling an aid container for Cuban workers outside St George's Hall, at an event organised by Fr Geoff Bottoms and retired dock shop steward Denis Anderson together with many others. On Monday 21 July, it was reported that Zim Line had left the Port of Liverpool and that overall trade had declined by more than 20 vessels per month. The stewards tried to contact David Osler, the shipping correspondent at *Lloyd's List*, in an attempt to find out just how much of an impact the international campaign was having on global shipping lines. However, even with the news about Zim Line and the successful challenging of Bill Morris at the BDC, the joke at the time was that the stewards might as well have brought a deck of playing cards to Transport House, as there seemed to be little else happening. Morton and Carden attended a meeting of the local TGWU Regional Committee, where it was stated that the union had still not repudiated evidence given by Bernard Bradley, the former Managing Director of Torside, during the 1996 parliamentary inquiry. Dockers' delegation work still continued as Jim and Irene Campbell travelled to Wales to speak at Bangor Rugby Club. The 23 July meeting of the Women of the Waterfront received confirmation that photographer Andrew Testa would soon begin documenting the dispute, while a young French comrade, Zoe Choupaut, explained how she had been sending postcards demanding Prime Minister Tony Blair reinstate the dockers. The WOW had themselves agreed to write a letter to Cherie Blair, appealing to her Liverpool roots in requesting support for the campaign, as elsewhere, Jimmy Nolan decided that the stewards would return to Parliament the following Wednesday to meet with Joe Benton MP, after a letter was received from Ian McCartney MP, the new employment minister, stating that the Labour government would not intervene in their struggle. The following month, McCartney would send his reply to a letter from Bill Morris:

*'I have, as you asked, considered the resolution passed by the TGWU's Biennial Delegate Conference in July, which called on the government to intervene in order to secure the reinstatement of the dismissed dockworkers. Disputes are a matter for the parties concerned; only they can resolve their differences. It is not for the government to intervene, nor would it have the locus to bring about the reinstatement of dismissed workers even if it did so.'* [45]

At the mass meeting held that Friday, Jimmy Davies remarked that, 'despite our own spies, we have spies on the docks,' where it was known that 12 floating plant men were due to be made redundant, and that the TGWU had balloted ahead of proposed industrial action on 20 July. [46] Jimmy Nolan called for unity and discipline amongst the shop stewards as he suggested re-establishing the practice of meeting every morning, asking that they: 'should not undermine each other and work together.' [47] By the following morning, the atmosphere among the stewards had improved. Joe Benton MP informed the dockers that, as a result of McCartney's letter to Bill Morris, their scheduled meeting at Parliament could end up being a waste of time. Meanwhile, Fr Michael de Felice had written to Ray Collins regarding the need for the TGWU to make more regular payments to the dockers' Hardship Fund. The next day, Jimmy Nolan gave an update to a meeting of more than 50 National Support Group delegates at Transport House, where various other disputes were discussed in addition to the docks, including those of the workers at Magnet, British Aerospace, Pall Mall, Hillingdon Hospital and Royal Mail.

On Wednesday 30 July, Tony Blair was due to hold a garden party at Number 10 for those entertainers and celebrities who had supported New Labour's election campaign, and guests such as musician Noel Gallagher and comedian Eddie Izzard promised to wear their 'Support the Liverpool dockers' t-shirts and bring the dispute to Blair directly. That same day, 17 dockers' representatives met with MPs Joe Benton MP and Eddie Loyden in Room 13 of the House of Commons, with Eddie O'Hara MP sending his apologies, and George Howarth and Carol Jones being among a group of MPs due to join the meeting later on, along with Graham Stevenson, the TGWU's National Docks Official. The main thrust of this meeting was to ask the MPs to reopen the Education and Employment Subcommittee inquiry into MDHC's conduct in the lead up to the dispute, following the Department of Trade and Industry saying that they wanted to, 'get it into the select committee.' [48] Once again, Jimmy

Nolan returned to his core concept of *representative democracy*, a term he always used in relation to the union, Parliament and its members. It was, he told MPs: 'TGWU-BDC policy to call on a Labour government to get involved,' [49] as he informed them that the joint TGWU/MDHC feasibility study for a dockers' labour co-operative was costing £50,000 for the private consultancy fees of KPMG. The dockers themselves had not been included in this process. [50] Further reference was made to Ian McCartney's written confirmation that the government, 'could not get involved, nor would it use its shareholding in the Dock Company,' [51] to which Billy Jenkins argued that the government must get involved because, 'it affects the whole of Merseyside.' [52] Joe Benton promised to ensure that a full report of the meeting would be sent to all Labour MPs, as well as the DTI, while Jimmy Davies reiterated the fact that this was now official TGWU policy, following the BDC, and so there was no reason for the MPs in attendance not to support what the dockers were asking. Nolan again stressed the need for the government to get involved, [53] and Benton agreed to contact the DTI with a view to them reopening the inquiry. In the meantime, a group of local MPs led by Maria Eagle would meet with MDHC directly.

Bill Morris eventually wrote to the shop stewards stating that he would discuss the dispute at the September GEC meeting, while the ITF's David Cockcroft was due to meet the ILWU to help plan the next Day of World Action. [54] Back in Liverpool, Kevin O'Hagan from HM Revenue and Customs told the stewards that a *big sting operation* was due to take place in the dock estate, and he also confirmed that nuclear waste was once again being shipped through the Port of Liverpool. [55] At the Dispute Committee meeting held on Thursday 31 July, it was reported that Mike Carden had asked the TGWU to produce copies of the letters of repudiation regarding Bernard Bradley's evidence to the Commons inquiry, which never materialised. [56] Brian Ashton, of the Liverpool Dockers' Support Group, had written to Steve Bell, the *Guardian* cartoonist, asking for his support and on Friday 1 August 1997 Bell dedicated his cartoon championing the Liverpool dockers in which Brian Ashton was thanked. The cartoon was titled, *The World Turned Upside Down* and featured Tony Blair in a dinner suit flanked by two fat cats whilst William Hague, the Tory leader, is shown lifting his shirt revealing a support the Liverpool dockers T-Shirt. Bell would send the original drawing to the dockers sometime later, but unfortunately it went missing. Like all public expressions of support, Bell's cartoon meant so much to the dockers, reminding them that their struggle was not totally invisible, and at that morning's weekly mass meeting, another gesture of support arrived in the form of a donation by 87-year-old Mary Loxton, who had been writing to Jimmy Davies since the start of the dispute in September 1995. She became the oldest supporter to address a mass meeting of the dockers. [57] After getting off the train at Liverpool Lime St. station, Mary Loxton told the taxi driver to, 'take me to the picket line,' where she hoped to be arrested along with the dockers. Although Mary did not get her wish for a run-in with the law, she did stand in front of hundreds of dockers and recall how:

*'Seventy-six years earlier, I was 10 when the miners came out in Durham. We were starving; the Salvation Army came around with soup. I had a big jug and told them I was going to feed the whole street. A policeman hit me, but the miners took care of it and he could never go back on the beat around there again. When I was 13 and a half, I ran away to London. I had no schooling, but I taught myself to read. After working as a*

*cleaner in nursing homes, I became a hotel floor waitress, bringing breakfast in bed to the guests. Sexual abuse was common, and pregnant chambermaids were sent to the workhouse. One day, sensing trouble, I took a colleague with me to the room where a naked man was ready for action. We threw the tray of food at him, snatched the £5 note he'd placed by the bed and ran off. We thought we'd get the sack. Instead, we had the time of our lives for a fortnight on that fiver.' [58]*

Mary had the dockers in stitches before rousing them to cheers with the confession, 'Comrades, if I ever do meet Maggie Thatcher... I wish I were younger, but I'm not down yet. You're just like our miners used to be.' [59] When she told the mass meeting, 'You'll win,' the men gave her a standing ovation, and she announced that a month later, at what would be her first Labour Party Conference, she intended to take the dockers' campaign to government ministers. A *Big Issue* seller also spoke at this mass meeting offering support to the dockers. That coming weekend, the band Dodgy sponsored a double-feature of Alan Bleasdale's *George's Last Ride* and Ken Loach's film on the Liverpool dockers at the National Film Theatre. On Wednesday 6 August at 11.30am, the picket line closed the three main gates. However, the following morning, MDHC released its half-yearly figures, which made for grim reading for the dockers. Profits had increased by 60% to £22m, although share prices had fallen to 368p, as Peter Jones, the Port Operations Director, went on local radio saying that the dispute: 'has to end. It is a sad event, and our previous offer is still on the table.' Striking a conciliatory tone, Jones stated that he was waiting for either the TGWU or the dockers to put a new postal ballot on the table. Around this time a TUC conference and another GEC meeting loomed on the horizon. [60]

At a Dispute Committee meeting, Terry Teague reported back on talks held over the organisation of the Day of World Action. Montreal's Michel Murray had expressed a preference for 8 September, as had dockers' leaders in Australia and Japan. Elsewhere, Albert Batton, from the International Longshoremen's Association Checkers' Union, met with John Bowers, the ILA president, resulting in the news that both the ILA and ITF would support the international action, although the ITF did not want to go public on this. Michel Murray was perceived as the *de facto* leader of the International Dockworkers' Committee and so the Liverpool stewards accepted his choice of date. [61] In the meantime, the stewards had a full weekend to consider the impact of MDHC's financial report, which included the statement that their offer would have a 'sell-by date.' As the next meetings of the TUC, the GEC and the Finance and General Purposes Committee drew nearer, the stewards had to face the reality that the cornerstone of their strategy, to undermine MDHC's financial position, now appeared to be failing; Tony Nelson described this as being the equivalent of, 'the employer's day of action.' [62]

Maintaining morale among the men was always seen as vital, and so it was a great disappointment when Nelson, as picket line captain, reported that more than 80 dockers had failed to turn up at the most recent mass meeting. Like all dock timekeepers, he could instantly recall each and every man's name and number and consequently he was always conscious of dockers' attendance at picket lines and mass meetings. It was also apparent that the number of Torside dockers in attendance at mass meetings was diminishing by the week. This was a matter of concern to the stewards and the dockers. Kevin Bilsborrow predicted that the deadline for accepting MDHC's offer would be published once the Day of World Action was formally announced. Discussion shifted to information provided by *Lloyd's List's* David Osler regarding MDHC's financial structure, with Teague suggesting that they purchase the full details from Companies House. Jimmy Nolan, on the other hand, was of the opinion that not too much could be gained from arguing against MDHC's published financial figures: 'This is simply capital using its power to undermine our struggle. We need to develop a meeting with politicians in Liverpool next week.' [63] Jimmy Davies added that it was, 'depressing, but the men must understand that any pay-off is linked also to their pension benefit [and] that will only flow from our reinstatement.' [64]

On Wednesday 13 August, it was reported that the Floating Plant had voted 46 to 17 in favour of strike action, which was good news for the Liverpool dockers, and at that evening's weekly meeting of the WOW, the TGWU's County Armagh branch was thanked for their generous Hardship Fund donation. Plans for the dockers' children to have a short holiday in Wales were also finalised, and the women continued to collect toiletries and other supplies for those suffering in the Bosnian War. [65] The following day, Terry Teague, Kevin Robinson and Tony Nelson met with officers at Crosby Road Police Station in relation to a number of issues, including the recent arrests of some 42 pickets. For the Liverpool dockers, in the wake of their unprecedented success at the union's BDC, in defeating the GEC Statement, little seemed to have changed. No response came from the GEC, they felt no compulsion to reconsider their policy statement on the Liverpool dock dispute despite its rejection by the union's primary democratic forum. It was as if nothing had happened.

# 72

# International Solidarity

*'You know, when we talk about the union, they talk about recruitment drives. What could have been the biggest recruitment drive? If we'd have won the dispute; if Bill Morris would've backed us and he could have gone to people and said, "Listen, get in my union; look what I've done for them dockers." I mean, if a young lad now, 18 say, goes to Transport House and sees me here and says, "Are you in the union? Are you a docker? How'd you get sacked?" I'll say, "Because Bill Morris never backed me."' ~ Billy Johnson\**

On 14 August 1997, *Lloyd's List* ran a story about South African dockers boycotting Capespan produce bound for Medway Port, a subsidiary of the Mersey Docks and Harbour Company. Marvin Mfundisi, the Vice President of the South African Transport and General Workers' Union, told *Lloyd's* that 10,000 dockworkers would be involved, and that he would also be seeking to bring other port unions on board, while threatening direct action against Outspan if Capespan, its marketing arm, did not do something about the 20-year contract it had signed with Sheerness: 'We might take action against Outspan if there is no development in favour of our Liverpool brothers.' [1] In response, Outspan's Managing Director, John Stanbury, said that Maputo (Mozambique) could pick up extra business thanks to the boycott, while Louis Kriel, Stanbury's counterpart at Capespan, argued: 'We have never used Liverpool, and we do not see why South African ports should be brought into this when it is not being supported in British ports.' [2] MDHC declined to comment on the matter. On 18 August, the dockers wrote to the Trades Union Congress via the TGWU, after John Monks, the TUC general secretary, decreed that the Liverpool dockers could not attend the forthcoming TUC conference without their union's permission. An additional letter was sent to Bill Morris informing him that: 'having spoken to the TUC, we have been informed than an official request needs to be made from our union for a stall and speaker facilities. We therefore seek your support in requesting that the Liverpool dockers be given the opportunity to both have a stall and address Conference.' [3] Morris replied:

---

\* Billy Johnson, in an interview with Greg Dropkin (17 February 1998).

521

*'...my understanding of Congress procedures is that the General Purposes Committee would only consider appeals during Conference proceedings for national disputes sanctioned by an affiliated union or group of unions... In these circumstances the T&G cannot associate itself with any move that did not fully conform to these principles...' [4]*

The dockers' weekly mass meeting followed a 6am picket on Friday 22 August, which began with Jimmy Davies informing the dockers' of the death of Dot Gibson's husband, Jeff Pilling; as well as Bernie Gleves's wife and Freddie Fullalove's mother. A minute's silence followed. The mass meetings had become, amongst so many other things, a gathering of one huge family, with all the attendant heartaches. Davies announced that it was both Brian Boswell and Billy Johnson's birthday, before reminding everyone that coaches had been organised for the Magnet workers' demonstration in Darlington the following day. On 28 August, Brian McWilliams, President of the ILWU, wrote to David Cockcroft, the ITF General Secretary, to let him know that he was planning to shut down all ports along the US West Coast on Monday 8 September, and to hold stop-work meetings on privatisation issues, 'including our beef at LAXT' and also to highlight the struggle of the Liverpool dockers. McWilliams wanted the ITF to disseminate this information to its affiliates, and to keep the ILWU in the loop regarding plans for the next Day of World Action. [5] The following day, Jimmy Nolan, Bobby Morton, Herbie Hollerhead and Mike Carden attended Jeff Pilling's funeral in London. Meanwhile, Donald Holzman, Secretary-Treasurer and business agent at ILWU Local 40 (Portland, Oregon), was writing to John Monks on the nature of trade unionism. In this letter, Holzman reminded Monks that:

*'As trade unionists, the International Longshore and Warehouse Union has strong beliefs about what it is to belong to a Union. I can tell you that my nearly thirty years of learning what that means is engrained into my soul. There is only one voice for the working class in this world, and that is the voice of the trade unionist.' [6]*

Holzman went on to consider how the issues affecting the Liverpool dockers were critical to the survival of all maritime unions the world over, hence the ongoing international support for the campaign. A recent meeting of ILWU presidents in San Francisco voted unanimously in favour of backing the Liverpool dockers, and Holzman stressed that their motto, 'An injury to one is an injury to all,' applied to *all* workers. [7]

Back in Liverpool, the dispute was still being held together by a number of connected strands, for example, it would cost £11m for MDHC to bring an end to the dispute at a time when traffic in the port had diminished by 23%. The South African boycott was making the news and there were impending investigations into smuggling and the handling of nuclear waste on the docks. Also, the Parliamentary inquiry could reopen at any time, as could inquiries into European Union funding as Maria Eagle MP and both the National Audit Office and the Public Accounts Committee were becoming increasingly interested in the company's financial practices. Finally, there was the impending Floating Plant strike ballot which would severely disrupt the port's ability to work normally. [8] These events provided hope that the dockers could still win, as they continued to appeal for action from workers in their own city. It was around this time that a group of Indian trade union leaders asked John Monks what the labour movement was doing to support the Liverpool dockers. At the following Friday's mass meeting, Jimmy Nolan acknowledged, for the first time, that the dispute could not go on forever: 'Two years is long enough. We call again upon other trade unionists to strike with us.' [9]

Support for the Liverpool dockers fluctuated in relation to events and actions as they were covered in the local and national media. This obviously affected the morale of the dockers whose campaign depended upon the sense that their struggle was having some impact upon the Dock Company. Plans to release a fundraising music CD featuring some of the biggest names in British rock music at the time raised the media profile of the dispute. Dodgy, Manic Street Preachers, Cast, Space, the Lovers and Billy Bragg all donated their time and art to this project. By contrast, on Tuesday 2 September, the dockers were facing serious criticism in the press regarding a human rights award from the government of Libya for the work of the Women of the Waterfront. In Dublin, Kevin Bilsborrow and Terry Teague tried to organise solidarity demonstrations for the 8 September Day of World Action, only for the Services Industrial Professional and Technical Union to, once again, fail to attend. The flow of events, both positive and negative deeply affected the morale of everyone involved in the dispute, from the picket lines to Transport House. It was now beginning to seem as though Dispute Committee meetings were no longer necessary, as fewer and fewer were taking place and no new analyses or ideas were flowing as they had done previously. The dispute had fallen into a state of atrophy, with even the Day of World Action appearing to be collapsing.

Jimmy Nolan was due to attend the Liverpool Cargo Handling industrial tribunal, while Tony Nelson had a meeting scheduled with Reclaim the Streets. Then, as if to confirm the lack of resolve now permeating through the stewards, an anonymous letter appeared at Transport House, stating that some 120 dockers wanted a ballot on MDHC's offer. [10] At the following Friday's weekly mass meeting, Jimmy Davies impressed upon the men the need to reopen negotiations and seek a resolution to the dispute. Jimmy Nolan wanted to discuss the possibility of meeting Bill Morris at the Brighton TUC while Tony Nelson argued that the stewards should remain in Liverpool, visible to the rank-and-file, especially during that coming Monday's Day of World Action. Terry Teague agreed with Nelson's assessment, adding: 'We need all the stewards to attend shop stewards' meetings, in order for us to discuss, analyse and lead the dispute as opposed to wasting time with the TUC.' [11] Teague then reported that while some German, Belgian, French, Spanish and Italian dockers may not be taking solidarity action, comrades in Le Havre, Sweden, Denmark, Australia, Canada and India had confirmed their participation. Irish dockers in Dublin and Drogheda would also be striking, although a meeting to raise support from local trade unionists had to be cancelled due to the stewards failing to get it organised in time. [12] Thus, the sense that the dispute was drifting towards collapse was palpable not only among the stewards, but also the rank-and-file dockers and their families. Two guest speakers from Kurdistan addressed the meeting, with Hassan Shalan of the Liverpool Kurdish Support Centre translating, and when, the now ritualised weekly vote was taken, and just two dockers raised their hands against the continuation of the strike, many in the room knew that in truth, the extent of the divide was much greater.

Journalist Robert Taylor had published a piece in *The Financial Times* on the proposed dockers' labour supply company, which included information that the stewards had no knowledge of. [13] Under the headline, *US Ports Face Day of Disruption Over the UK Docks Dispute*, Taylor combined with Christopher Parkes in Los Angeles to write:

> *'Ports on the US West Coast and trading centres worldwide are threatened with disruption next week by action in support of Liverpool dockworkers involved in one of Britain's longest-running industrial disputes… The creation of a labour cooperative [has been] proposed in a feasibility study by KPMG… The report said the cooperative's financial position would be, 'fragile, even on the basis of an optimistic assumption about market penetration,' and warned it would 'require adequate financial backing until a sustainable break-even or profit position is reached."* [14]

On Monday 8 September, Ken Loach's documentary on the Liverpool docks dispute aired on Australian television, and this had a dramatic impact on the level of direct solidarity action seen in Australia's ports. At the TUC conference in Brighton, Maria Eagle MP spoke in support of the dockers at a fringe meeting before later stating her position in writing and communicating her concerns to the Public Accounts Committee. That morning, the Dispute Committee issued a press release titled *Worldwide Dockers Solidarity*, as news rolled in that the Maritime Union of Australia would defy government threats to send in troops to disperse any attempts at strike action, with all major ports set to stop for five hours on both the daytime and evening shifts. The ILWU was expected to shut every port along the west coast of North America, from Mexico to Alaska, for eight hours, despite the Pacific Maritime Association's opposition to action in Los Angeles and Long Beach. Hapag Lloyd ships bound to and from Thamesport were due to be delayed, while a 24-hour shutdown was planned in the Danish port of Aarhus, in addition to stoppages on all Liverpool and Sheerness vessels especially those owned by Atlantic Container Line or Cast in the Swedish ports of Gothenburg, Stockholm, Malmo and Helsingborg. In describing the day's events, international coordinator Terry Teague declared:

> *The action is exceeding all expectations and proves that Liverpool has become a symbol for all dockers who are determined to resist the threats of casual labour, mass sackings and the deregulation of our industry. The Port of Liverpool is stagnating…'* [15]

Steve Zeltzer, of the International Committee for the Victory of the Liverpool Dockers and the Labor Video Project, published an article linking the struggle of the Bay Area Rapid Transit (BART) workers to that of the Liverpool dockers:

> *'Minutes before a scheduled West Coast longshore work stoppage in solidarity with the fired Liverpool dockers, unionists gathered in front of the San Francisco British Consulate to demand that the Blair government rehire the fired dockers. They were joined in the rally by striking BART unionists… Bob Blanchet, an international representative of the International Brotherhood of Teamsters… called for support for their possible strike as well as giving greetings to the Liverpool dockers.'* [16]

According to Zeltzer, Jack Heyman pointed out that under the Tory government, US trade unionists had been permitted to meet with the British consulate, but that this was no longer the case under Tony Blair's Labour government. Following the rally, the demonstrators marched along Market Street during rush hour, chanting in support of the Liverpool dockers and the BART strikers. [17] As part of the tactic of lobbying British consulates across the world, Terry Southers reported that a Liverpool delegation had visited the British Embassy in Tokyo, where they were given a sympathetic reception but were also told that they needed to understand how difficult it would be for the government to solve their dispute. [18] The delegation also lobbied the offices of Orient Overseas Container Line (OOCL) and Sanko shipping, demanding a worldwide boycott of Liverpool and Sheerness that would include slot-sharing schemes with Cast, Can-Mar and ACL. OOCL denied any connection to the Port of Liverpool. During a conference held on 4-5 September, *Zenkoku Kowan* (Japanese National Federation of Dock Unions) passed a number of resolutions supporting the Liverpool dockers, as a delegation of Spanish trade unionists was received by Christopher Ingham, Consul for Economic Affairs, at the British Embassy in Madrid. The Spanish delegation was led by Marcelino Camacho, president and general secretary of the CCOO (Workers' Commissions) and historical leader of the Spanish trade union movement, who was joined by Josi Miguel Villa, general secretary of the UGT's Service Federation; Xabier Arrizabalo, a professor at the University of *Alacala de Henares* in Madrid and CCOO trade unionist; and Francisco Lucena, a member of the CCOO Executive. [19]

The events surrounding this Day of World Action were recorded by Terry Teague and Greg Dropkin, as well as others involved with *LabourNet*. In Vancouver, ILWU Locals participated in the West Coast stoppages. In the Netherlands, a stop-work meeting was held in Amsterdam, ahead of joint action against MDHC and casualisation in general which included a strike by 250 Rotterdam workers in support of their Amsterdam colleagues. In Gothenburg, an ACL vessel was diverted for two days, as dockers refused to handle any feeder ship cargo, and Portugal saw stop-work meetings in Lisbon, Setubal and Sines. Antonio Mariano, president of the Portuguese dockworkers, was quoted as saying that Lisbon and Setubal would be paralysed for several hours, in addition to confirmed reports of action taking place at Leixoes and Aveiro. In South Africa, Liverpool docker Mark Crichton addressed a meeting of 60 Cape Town port stewards on 6 September, where action was also being taken against Australian trade. The local branch secretary declared that: 'these people supported us during the apartheid era. Now they need help, and we have the chance to repay them.' [20] The Centre for Indian Trade Unions called on all waterfront unions to mark the Day of World Action by wearing badges, holding meetings and passing a resolution in support of the Liverpool dockers, in a country where *Lloyd's List* was reporting that a major dispute over working conditions and practices loomed large. Back on the US West Coast, ILWU spokesman Steve Stallone told the Seattle press that, 'Until demands to reinstate the Liverpool workers are met, we will continue taking job actions such as this.' [21]

Across the Atlantic, in Derry, a go-slow and an overtime ban were implemented by ATGWU (TGWU Region 3) members. An overtime ban was also utilised in Belfast, as all ATGWU dockers and maintenance workers took action against MDHC-owned Coastal Containers, affecting three ships. In Drogheda, there was a complete closure of the port from

5pm Monday until 8am Tuesday. On Wednesday 10 September, French dockers took eight hours of action against OOCL in Le Havre. Further action was promised against all ships docking at MDHC-connected ports. Jack Heyman wrote to Kees Marges at the ITF on September 22 to address recent reports and circulars written about the Liverpool dockers' dispute:

> *'Surely, you are aware that it is no easy task to organize port workers around the world to take industrial action simultaneously. Yet, on September 8th, the Liverpool dockers were able to organize dockworkers to shut down over 100 ports worldwide. ...if the TGWU leadership has failed through its legalistic approach to defend dockers' jobs, why not give the Liverpool dockers' efforts a chance? What better banner to organize international solidarity than, 'Never cross a picket line,' for which the 500 dockers were sacked?'* [22]

In the July/August issue of *the Dispatcher*, the ILWU's newspaper, an article was published summarising the Liverpool docks dispute. In his open letter to Marges, Heyman spoke of how the rank-and-file Liverpool dockers had given the ITF 'a big shot in the arm' at the TGWU's Biennial Delegates Conference, where they had rejected a resolution endorsing the union leadership's handling of the dispute. Despite this, Heyman argued, the ITF continued to rationalise its policy of non-support towards the Liverpool campaign on the basis that Bill Morris had not asked for their help. According to Heyman, this failure to act brought into question the organisation's credibility, especially since the ITF's own Miami Conference had passed a resolution in support of the Liverpool dockers, which was amended by Glen Ramiskey, the ILWU's delegate in Miami, before being published in a previous edition of *the Dispatcher*. [23] Heyman signed off with his customary, 'For real international solidarity! Victory to the Liverpool dockers! Jack Heyman, ILWU Local 10,' [24] and Marges's reply was as follows:

> *'You and I know that I did not try to stop you from going to Liverpool... I explained my and ITF's position and our conversation was friendly. You must have a specific reason for giving a different impression of our conversation. There is no need to add to existing information on ITF's position as everybody involved in this matter is aware of the reason. There are no new arguments. I will continue to organise international solidarity for port workers when and where I can.'* [25]

In the spirit of direct debate, Heyman was to put pen to paper once more:

> *'Bill Morris adamantly stated that he did not want ITF affiliates taking supportive action. And now Morris's disastrous course has been repudiated by a card vote of the delegates at the TGWU Conference in July 1997. How many more votes need be taken... President McWilliams explained that he was taking me off the ITF payroll and placing me on the ILWU's in order not to confuse the different positions of our organizations... Stop the twin plagues of privatization and casualization!'* [26]

The Dispute Committee would soon enter into this dialogue with the ITF, publishing an article under the headline *It's Never Too Late*:

> *The TGWU general secretary and the leaders of the ITF owe their very existence to men and women who broke the unjust laws of their mother countries to establish the freedom of trade union organisation. They still go through the motions of saluting the Tolpuddle Martyrs, but they make sure they do not draw any lessons from their struggle. The very principles of trade unionism naturally oppose the forces of injustice, reaction and fascism.'*
> [27]

The stewards' analysis noted that the global action taken in support of their campaign was a reflection of the global nature of the problems they were facing. The Dispute Committee openly rejected the leadership of Bill Morris and his failure to recognise the irrelevance of UK labour laws to the Liverpool dockers, for whom two years in dispute was two years too long. This was the reason why they were demanding that the ITF take action based upon the countless democratic decisions made within their organisation and that of the TGWU. The inaction of the ITF and the TGWU sent out signals of defeatism and fear that gave employers the green light to act against organised labour, but the overriding message of the dockers was that it was not too late for the ITF to intervene. [28] Björn Borg of the Swedish Dockworkers' Union reported that on 9 September:

> *The Swedish Dockworkers' Union, representing 1600 dockers in 20 different ports, had decided to go through with on the Day of Action [on] 8 September 1997. All ships and goods to and from the ports of Liverpool and Sheerness were not to be handled, as well as a blockade of all ships and containers owned by ACL and Cast companies.'*
> [29]

Regardless of what was happening in their own country, the evidence clearly showed that the Liverpool dockers retained the loyal support of their comrades across the world.

# 73

# The Dockers Call for Support amidst the fall-out from the BDC

*'We dared to fight against the anti-trade union laws of the Conservative government. But now there was a Labour government. For years these leaders have been telling the workers that we cannot act against the Tory anti-trade union laws. Wait for a Labour government and then we will get representative democracy. With this cry ringing in their ears, thousands of workers were left to fight alone and were victimised.' ~ Jimmy Davies\**

Information from inside the Port of Liverpool indicated that no vessels were handled from the evening of Thursday 4 September 1997 until the following Monday, when a half-empty Atlantic Container Line ship arrived. At the Port of Sheerness, 10 members of the London Support Group held a demonstration on 8 September, where they handed out leaflets along with copies of the latest *Dockers' Charter* to all workers going in and out of the gates. Sheerness dockers had been called into work early that day, but the LSG got a positive response from transport workers, who were themselves members of the TGWU. At one point, a shop steward came out to meet the pickets and make a donation to the Hardship Fund, before agreeing to call a drivers' meeting and discuss options for further support. In West London, thirty Reclaim the Streets (RTS) activists picketed the house of Gordon Waddell, MDHC's Chairman, with banners proclaiming, 'Injustice is not anonymous; it has a name and address' and 'Victory to the dockers!' There were no arrests, although police did move the group across the road, where a sympathetic neighbour brought out cups of tea. Waddell refused to comment, and RTS eventually moved on to Charles House on Regent St, the offices of Drake International. Thirteen protesters managed to enter the building and occupy an office for over 30 minutes, much to the amazement of staff who insisted that the company was offering long-term as well as casual employment. RTS engaged Drake

---

\* Jimmy Davies quoted in Mukul (1998). Liverpool Dockers; Making and Un-Making of a Struggle - Economic and Political Weekly. 33 (26): 1612–1614.

management in a debate over the Liverpool dispute and attempted to hang banners from the windows before dispersing when police arrived and threatened arrests.

Elsewhere, at the Trades Union Congress in Brighton, BBC Radio 4 interviewed Ken Cameron, the Fire Brigades' Union General Secretary, in what was a stark example of the contrast between British trade unionism and the solidarity shown on the international stage. BBC Radio Merseyside provided extensive live reports throughout the Day of World Action, which included an interview with Björn Borg in Sweden, while an article in the *Liverpool Echo* quoted Jim Donovan, the Australian Maritime Union leader, as well as Peter Jones, MDHC's port operations manager, who dismissed claims of widespread international action as 'fantasy.' [1] On Wednesday 10 September, Cathy Wilson, Lesley Mahmood, Herbie Hollerhead along with Micky and Sylvia Tighe reported back from delegation work as Doreen McNally and Sue Mitchell returned from Libya the following day: 'with a magnificent human rights award and a donation to the dockers' welfare fund. These awards were made to a number of women for their human rights activities.' But their story would not end here. [2] On Friday 12 September, the funeral of Harry Burke, a former shop steward and influential leader of the old TGWU 6/567 Branch, took place. Jimmy Nolan did not attend that day's weekly mass meeting, with Frank Lannigan taking his place as chair. Jimmy Davies reported that Phil Cauley, Mick Thompson and Billy Rooney were still sick, before reading out a letter of support from Maria Eagle MP. Mike Carden reiterated Davies's point from a previous mass meeting about how: 'two years is indeed long enough.' [3] The following morning, Terry Teague opened a Dispute Committee meeting by saying that, 'despite all the international actions, the feeling among the men is to seek a conclusion,' [4] and it was this sentiment that drove the general direction of this meeting. It was not to be an occasion for summoning up the blood, but while Jimmy Nolan appeared to want the session to end as quickly as possible, a decision was eventually taken to issue a statement seeking direct negotiations with MDHC. [5]

On Monday 15 September, the TGWU's General Executive Council met in London, where Bill Morris submitted a report that referred to the Biennial Delegates Conference as a success, and in the debate that followed, Carden challenged the veracity of the general secretary's claims, as well as the role of administrative officer Ray Collins during the BDC vote. Carden was trying to make this the first General Secretary's Report to be rejected by a GEC, but Morris fought back by accusing Carden of not honouring the collective responsibility of GEC members. Carden accused the paid union officers and elected GEC members of not accepting the BDC's decision on the Liverpool dispute; it was their duty to enact the will of the lay membership. Predictably, Morris disagreed:

*'Responsibility starts and ends with GEC members. I saw GEC members briefing delegates to the BDC. The union was rocked to its foundations by events in Region 6, and some of the behaviour on the balcony [a reference to Liverpool dockworkers and their wives], with intimidation, racist comments and language used at the rostrum with no acceptance of procedure of debate... Everyone has to accept standards and the values of collective responsibility.' [6]*

Carden argued: 'This has little to do with collective responsibility, or roles and responsibilities of GEC members. The GEC had reached a decision on the docks dispute in the form of a statement; a statement going to the BDC. The members overwhelmingly rejected this statement, even though the chairman of the union and its administrative officer, Ray Collins, tried to alter the vote, to claim that the majority of over 100 votes cast against the union did not exist.' [7] The following day, Graham Stevenson addressed the GEC on KPMG and the proposed dockers' labour co-operative. [8] Carden had attempted to respond to the KPMG report by mentioning that the general secretary had received a press release from the Dispute Committee calling for fresh negotiations, only for Morris to interject with a terse: 'Oh yeah, it's not addressed to me personally. You'd be surprised at what I get to do with the docks,' [9] making no effort to conceal his apathy towards a struggle that had now been destroying lives for two years. At the end of the session, Carden telephoned Jimmy Davies back in Liverpool, telling him that Morris wanted the dockers to wither away and become so desperate that they would: 'beg him to impose a ballot to end the dispute.' [10]

This was a GEC where the TGWU's *faux Communist, Blairite Broad Left* did the bidding of Morris to ensure that their *imposed* candidates were appointed to important full-time positions in the union. This is what they did best – like any good career service. However, they did not always get their own way despite the power they could wield through regional barons and others they had placed on the payroll. But the Broad Left could be challenged. They failed to secure the critically important post of Irish regional secretary for their chosen candidate. Region 6 backed Mick O'Reilly, who had supported the Liverpool dockers throughout their dispute, and he was selected by the GEC to succeed the outgoing John Freeman by 18 votes to 12. Another great Irish comrade of the Liverpool dockers, Eugene McGlone, proved vital to O'Reilly's appointment. He was also a serious candidate for the post of regional secretary and if he had stood then he would have taken votes away from O'Rielly. It was left to Carden, Ken Brindle and others to speak with Eugene and explain the need for only one candidate to stand. This process was made more difficult by the fact that both O'Rielly and McGlone were very close comrades. In his personal selflessness Eugene McGlone agreed to withdraw his application for the post. The eventual and unexpected appointment of Mick O'Rielly to the post of regional secretary represented a profound political setback for the 'left majority' that typically controlled GEC policy. This disparate group of *leftwingers* wholeheartedly embraced the shallow, image-obsessed politics of the 1990s, epitomising Blair's 'third way' of meaningless soundbites that stood for nothing beyond opposing the Labour Party's traditional values.

Ultimately, New Labour's *third way* would create a major disconnect between the party and its working-class heartlands paving the way for uniting ambitious trade union 'managers' to become the preferred candidates for highly-paid senior positions within the TGWU. This patronage would permeate down to regional nominees for prospective MPs who fitted the post-political era of Blairism. This anti-democratic/de-industrialisation of trade unionism and Labour politics would establish itself into the structure of their organisations for over twenty years until the shock of *Tory red walls and Corbynism erupted* against the class that brought them into existence. The steady non-politics devoid of conflict had now re-inflicted itself upon New Labour and *managerial trade unionism*. But the *flame of working-class rebellion* could never be totally obliterated and in the 1990s *old Labour* showed that it was ready to fight on. This working-class spirit was made tangible in the form of a raw political speech from O'Reilly to members of the GEC.

Despite not having the backing of the *left majority* of GEC members O'Reilly was able to convince the majority to support his nomination by winning them over as he rekindled memories of what it once was, 'to be a trade unionist; to be a socialist; to be Irish!' [11] Carden recalled how O'Rielly entered the chamber of the GEC with rolled-up papers in his hand, and instead of sitting quietly reading from pre-prepared prompt cards in the new-style of presentation much favoured by modernisers in New Labour, O'Reilly, stood bolt upright and delivered a rabble rousing speech that James Larkin himself would have been proud to make. Waving his hands in the air and speaking as if he were addressing a crowd of 20,000 trade unionists O'Reilly's powerful physical presence dominated the chamber. Carden turned to his comrades on the Executive Council, Ken Brindle and Barry Cooper, and exclaimed: 'Oh my god he's brought a bag of chips in with him,' referring to the rolls of paper he clasped in one hand. Two decades later, in his book *From Lucifer to Lazarus*, O'Reilly would recount the day that he was chosen to replace John Freeman the outgoing Irish regional secretary, describing how his predecessor was delighted by his appointment, while wondering if this was simply a case of him being: 'delighted that Bill Morris had been defeated, because him and Morris didn't get on.' [12] Shortly after his appointment, O'Reilly recalled how he travelled: 'over to a huge demonstration in Liverpool. There were twenty thousand people there, but no other regional secretary or National Official of the TGWU were to be seen.' [13]

Elsewhere in London, 2K performed a one-off show titled *1997 (What the Fuck's Going On?)* at the Barbican Arts Centre on 17 September 1997. This fundraiser for the dockers featured Acid Brass, the Liverpool dockers, the Viking Society and Bill Drummond's creative associates Mark Manning and Gimpo. The evening began with a screening of *This Brick*, a short 35mm film of a brick made from the ashes of the K Foundation's £1m bonfire, and then following an introduction by Tony Wilson, founder of Factory Records, Drummond and James Cauty appeared as pyjama-clad, wheelchair-bound pensioners, with horns fixed prominently to their foreheads, mimicking the KLF's promotional videos. They were supported variously by opera singer Sally Bradshaw joining a male choir in a rendition of Que Sera, Sera, and the Viking Society dressing as lifeboatmen while the Liverpool dockers chanted, 'Fuck the millennium! We want it now!' [14] On ITV's *The Line*, Paul Foot said that the Liverpool dockers were: 'principled trade unionists. The employers had planned everything bar the response of the dockers'. In an interview for local BBC television, sacked dockworker George Langhan talked about how the dockers were right to have refused to cross a picket line. There was also an informed assessment of the dispute by Ross Wynne-Jones, who published an article in the *Sunday Independent* titled, *No going back at Liverpool docks – Pickets fight on despite two years of TUC and Labour Indifference*, in which the journalist described the course of events as being like:

> '...from 1979, but this was last week. The Liverpool dockers have been standing here every day for two years... Then they stand accusingly on the pavement, watching the men who now do their jobs passing through the gates to work, reminding the MDHC control tower that they haven't gone away. ...There is the militant history of trade unionism in the area... There is the backdrop of dock life, rooted in the days when the waterfront

# THE DOCKERS CALL FOR SUPPORT AMIDST THE FALL-OUT FROM THE BDC

*employed thousands of men who spent a lifetime there, as did their fathers. But, more than that, there is the power of culture, which on Merseyside transforms a picket into a barrier it is almost genetically impossible to cross. The men were sacked because they chose not to break a local sacred rule: in Liverpool you never cross a picket line.' [15]*

These sentiments were echoed by Anne-Marie Sweeney, whose thoughtful piece in the *New Internationalist* contained an interview with sacked docker Jimmy Campbell:

*'What right have any of us to sell our kids' futures? ...If he had I'd have never forgiven him,' his wife, Irene Campbell, confirmed. 'Now look at him: a man, 60 years old, a grandfather, never been in trouble with the law. And he's been bodily removed to a police cell, charged as a criminal, not once but several times, for a gesture, or something he's shouted. The job's gone, the money's gone, the chances are, like so many others, he'll get a criminal record. Well, let me tell you, I'm proud of him!" [16]*

Back in Liverpool, at a Dispute Committee meeting held on Tuesday 23 September 1997, Jimmy Nolan reported that Jack Adams would be in Liverpool the following day, but this news was overshadowed by Mike Carden's feedback from the GEC, and his conclusion that Morris, 'wants to punish us. He is not interested in any way to help us.' [17] Tony Nelson believed that the stewards needed to make use of the fact that Adams was in Liverpool, and that they should accept Ian McCartney MP's offer to use the Advisory, Conciliation and Arbitration Service (ACAS) as part of a Labour government initiative. [18] Terry Teague agreed with Nelson, citing Jack Heyman's letter exposing Kees Marges, dockers' secretary of the ITF, for claiming that the Day of World Action took place for reasons not related to the Liverpool dispute. [19] Bobby Morton did not see ACAS as anything new, as the Tory government had also pushed that line, and he was certain that a ballot would soon be put forward anyway: 'We can't show any weakness whatsoever. I'd stonewall it. Once we are in with ACAS, there is no way out.' [20] Teague acknowledged: 'we do have spies among us,' before adding, 'we often are too open and honest at our mass meetings,' [21] referring to the fact that anyone who wanted to, could easily find out the dockers' business. Jimmy Davies was another who did not like the idea of ACAS, while Andy Dwyer preferred direct negotiations with MDHC and Tony Russell wanted more international action. Nelson then made the point that many of the men on the picket line just wanted direct negotiations with the Dock Company, and so it was agreed that they would pursue this outcome through Jack Adams. [22]

A week later, Jimmy Nolan and Herbie Hollerhead attended the Labour Party Conference in Brighton, while a delegation travelled to Medway Ports for an RTS demonstration against the environmental damage being inflicted upon the UK's south-east coast. It also provided an opportunity for the dockers to meet their Ford and Vauxhall counterparts to discuss organising direct solidarity action. [23] Elsewhere, at a Trade Union Liaison meeting, the Communications Workers Union confirmed that their members were refusing to cross picket lines in the Port of Liverpool. Steve Higginson, the CWU Assistant Indoor Secretary at Royal Mail's Copperas Hill site in Liverpool, told Greg Dropkin about the unique relationship between local postal workers and the Liverpool dockers. The indoor

CWU membership at Copperas Hill consisted of more than 800 postal men and women, plus catering staff and other allied grades, but in June 1997, the employer revealed plans to shut down the site. In an interview for *LabourNet*, Higginson explained that it was:

> *'Just not good enough to turn up at the dockers' and talk about your own dispute, when they've been out for two years and the labour movement locally has failed to deliver tangible solidarity action. …Our longstanding branch policy is that we never ever cross picket lines. One of the reasons behind that is that postal workers, not just on Merseyside, but wherever there is a dispute, live in those communities. A lot of them feel uneasy about being told to cross the picket line. There is also the aspect of health and safety. Once the disputes are over, they still have to continue delivering mail when those on strike are back at work.' [24]*

For Higginson, the Liverpool docks dispute was the defining industrial struggle of its era, not only in the UK, but also Europe and beyond, because if it failed it would embolden other employers to begin attacking their employees' pay and conditions. In addition to the proposed closure of Copperas Hill, the first half of 1997 had also seen similar situations of *official* trade union weakness being exploited at Spillers', Premier Brands and Tulip, among various other Merseyside factories. This, Higginson argued, was a result of employers being able to say: 'Look, it's a city that have allowed their own dockworkers to be dismissed and stay dismissed for nearly two years without anything being done. And that is why it is of paramount importance that this dispute is brought to a head. And only then will the other disputes that have broken out throughout the country – only then will they be resolved.' [25]

On Wednesday 24 September Jimmy McGovern was in Transport House to speak to the stewards about a newspaper article that he had been asked to write on the dispute. That same day, Jack Adams and Graham Stevenson, arrived at noon for a meeting in which Adams described as: 'a war of attrition [following the BDC]. No real political traction exists to support the dockers effectively. The worker co-op was pretty much desperation, [and] with that rejected we are in a worst position than before. I haven't spoken to [Peter] Jones [MDHC port operations director], but he rang up this morning so he must want a meeting.' [26] To this, Jimmy Nolan replied: 'We are prepared to negotiate, but not to move from the principle of reinstatement. If Jones is not prepared to negotiate, then perhaps we will send a letter to Ian McCartney MP, telling him that this is the company's position. Morris should come out more clearly in our support.' [27] Stevenson then went through a number of possible scenarios, from continuing the struggle to the stewards choosing to 'call it a day,' adding: 'Two years is two years too long, and unlike the miners, you can't go back, although ways may exist to make its end more dignified. You can try tweaking the offer, looking for improvements.' [28] Stevenson also expressed the view that Bill Morris could yet go over the shop steward's heads and simply impose a ballot, [29] before explaining that: 'Associated British Ports shares are lower than MDHC's shares. The latter has by now decided to live with the dispute, but the longer it goes on, the more difficult it will be to resolve under normal industrial ways. It may need a political input.' [30] Here, Nolan reiterated the need to: 'get other trade unionists to support us. The TGWU should send letters to all branches, seeking their support. The general secretary should raise his voice,' [31] at which point Adams said:

> *'I cannot mislead you. The Labour Party won't get close to the trade unions. Look at the BA dispute; they say it's an industrial dispute and nothing to do with the government. The worst thing would be to just sit it out. Ride out your anniversary, but don't let it collapse; get a dignified settlement. You have done a wonderful job, and I have never seen a dispute run like this in my life. I am very proud to be part of it.' [32]*

When Kevin Bilsborrow asked: 'Why has the TGWU not been sued yet?' [33] the response from the union officials was that any company can sue up to six years after a perceived offence, but that the longer the dispute went on, the weaker MDHC's case for economic redress became. [34] After further discussion, the consensus was that the key problem was Morris, and in particular the fact that he had been quoted as saying: 'It is immoral and unprincipled to ask the ITF to support the dockers.' [35] On Thursday 25 September the stewards met with Jim Donovan and John Coombs of the Australian dockers' union, New Zealand Seafarer Mick Williams and representatives of the Japanese railway workers. At the following day's weekly mass meeting, Björn Borg, the Swedish dockers' leader, arrived to rapturous applause from the Liverpool dockers and their supporters, as the mood in the room was transformed to one of high expectation. Elsewhere, interviews with Jimmy Nolan, Cathy Dwyer and Mike Carden were published in *l'Humanite*, the influential French Communist Party newspaper, [36] and on 26 September, the stewards issued a press release received from within the Port of Liverpool. Attached to this document was a newsletter circulated by employees of Drake International, which revealed the dreadful working conditions imposed upon them by MDHC bosses, asking the question: 'Does the management realise that we too have families and home lives? Perhaps they don't care! Perhaps they look upon a transient workforce as a distinct advantage!' [37] This only reinforced what the stewards had been saying all along that there had been a build-up of dissent and resentment on the docks for a number of years, predominantly caused by extreme changes to working conditions that went unchallenged by local TGWU officials. Between the 'New Deal' at Seaforth Container Terminal, nonstop attacks on terms and conditions in other areas of the port, the increasing use of casual labour, men's jobs being advertised in the local press and the imposition of extraordinary levels of disciplinary action, it should have come as no surprise that a general sense of rebellion had been fomented among the dockworkers prior to their dismissal in 1995. [38] Now the scabs, brought in to replace the dockers were ready to revolt. The scabs' newsletter, *The Dart: the Newsletter of Drakes' Workforce*, served to demonstrate that all workers, no matter their starting point, will invariably organise against an employer in order to protect their own interests, with or without trade union backing. The Drake employees complained:

> *'Here we are, nearly two years after the old workforce walked out of the gate, and still we are having to put up with practices such as sixteen-hour shifts… with the threat of the sack if workers do not comply… The new workforce came into Seaforth full of enthusiasm and looked upon the venture as a fresh start, for them as well as the main*

*employer… it is ironical that a Drake's employee has to work alongside an employee that does the same job, but receives a bonus for their efforts… the employees are not allowed any real representation, it can be looked upon as a means to display the current feelings of the workforce.' [39]*

It was a piece that could have been written by any one of the dockworkers sacked by the Dock Company in 1995, repeating many of the same demands for basic rights following the abolition of the National Dock Labour Board Scheme in 1989. Speaking via its own circular, *Port News*, MDHC assured the Drake scabs that: 'Considerable progress was achieved in the first half of 1997,' [40] while boasting about how, 'profits are up 59%, with record cargoes and forecast of future growth as the dispute has no material effect. The offer [to the sacked dockers] is still open, subject to secret ballot, but it will not be on the table forever.' [41] Trevor Furlong, Managing Director and Chief Executive, warned that: 'The offer does have a sell-by date.' [42] John Pilger again reflected on the Liverpool dockers' situation in a letter published in the September 1997 edition of the *Big Issue*:

*'The burning issues the dockers have so tenaciously and courageously sought to bring before the British public; issues such as the stripping of public utilities for huge profit; the collaboration of the trade union hierarchies; the right to set up a picket line, or take virtually any effective industrial action, without the courts enforcing corrupt laws that run counter to the universal declaration of human rights; and above all, the right to security of work. The dockers' struggle represents the struggle of almost a majority of British people, as part-timing and what Blair calls 'flexibility' roll back the gains of a century.' [43]*

# 74
# Tension and Pressure
# Continue to Mount

*'The contrast between the rank-and-file and FTOs [Full Time Officers] can become sharply evident during strike activity. Thus, the basic necessities of workers' lives can often depend on the outcome of struggles with employers, whereas union officials are one step removed. If workers begin to take on the employers independently of the official leadership through militant forms of strike action, then the FTOs function as mediator can be called into question. The more militant and broader the struggle, the more dramatic such a divide between officials and the rank-and-file can become.' ~ Ralph Darlington and Martin Upchurch\**

The mass demonstration held in Liverpool on Saturday 27 September 1997 was considered a great success, with Jimmy Nolan using his opening speech to call on Bill Morris to resign. In addition to welcoming all who had come out to support the campaign that afternoon, the dockers' leader also voiced his frustration at the lack of support they had received from the UK trade union movement as a whole:

> *'Fraternal greetings to all organisations: the trade unions, the unemployed, all the support groups, Reclaim the Streets and the Green Party, and may we condemn all the leaders of all unions in this country and we say to you that after two years, the general secretary of the TGWU should resign, and we also say that the TUC general secretary should resign, because none of these generals have had the audacity to organise any army in this country to confront employers and political legislation. We must say to a Labour government and demand representative democracy. The working class must organise opposition. We have had enough after two years.' [1]*

---

\* A Reappraisal of the Rank-and-File versus Bureaucracy Debate, Ralph Darlington and Martin Upchurch (p.4). Available: https://core.ac.uk/download/pdf/17052047.pdf

Jimmy Davies was the next speaker, and he repeated Nolan's call, thanking those in attendance for their support, and for the international solidarity shown by comrades across the world, before condemning the TGWU members who continued to work ships in the Port of Liverpool:

> 'Our deputy general secretary also told us that our general secretary, Bill Morris, was not supporting our dispute; was actively working behind the scenes to undermine our dispute, telling the ITF that on moral grounds he could not ask them to support the Liverpool dockers because the TGWU did not support them. We say that's a disgrace, and don't underestimate the power of the Liverpool dockers. We also call upon workers from our own city to put their heads above the parapet. It's alright giving us your financial aid. If we would have been in the same position, we would have been out on strike with you because we've done it before.' [2]

Mike Carden followed Davies, and he continued the theme of calling for Morris's resignation:

> 'After two years, we need to reflect how we can win this struggle against the MDHC. You don't need to be a rocket scientist to understand how we can win this struggle; it's dead easy. The leadership of the trade union movement, the TUC, the ITF and the General Secretary of the TGWU, all need to act like trade unionists. They need to realise they are paid £100,000 or more a year to represent good, honest working-class people; to represent the unemployed, the dispossessed, the Green Party, Reclaim the Streets; that's their job, and if they choose not to do their job then, as Jimmy Nolan and Jimmy Davies have said, and I will continue to say at the GEC – and I can see my career ending in tears – but, Bill Morris, you are absolutely useless as a general secretary. The working class needs leadership.' [3]

Nolan then took the microphone and, laughing loudly, said: 'Perhaps we will all have to resign now.' [4] Delays in getting the loudspeakers working at the start of the rally meant that several comrades from Hillingdon Hospital and Magnet were unable to address the crowd, which led to accusations that the dockers were, in effect, silencing other workers in struggle; a criticism voiced mainly by the *News Line* group. [5] Marie Curran, a member of the WOW, was quoted as saying that the rally showed: 'solidarity with the people of Liverpool, seeing that they all support us and showing the Labour government that we're here to stay, and to show the employers that we are not moving; we've got nowhere to go.' [6] The rally had followed a march along the customary route for dockers' demonstrations, going from Myrtle Street Parade to St George's Plateau, where more than 7,000 supporters stood alongside the Liverpool dockers and their families. The list of marchers that day included John Pilger, Björn Borg, Jim Donovan, Mike Williams, Eddie Loyden MP, Bob Parry MP, the San Francisco poet, Jack Hirshman, John Hendy QC, Arnie Williams, Tony Mulhearn and local historian, Ron Noon. Not one TGWU official, local or national, ever made a request to speak from the platform of a dockers' demonstration or mass meeting.

The following day, another major demonstration took place at the Labour Party Conference in Brighton, and then the day after that, the Liverpool dockers picketed Medway docks, where Kent police entered the Port of Sheerness seeking to evict those who had occupied several cranes. Outside the gates, 70 dockers and several hundred supporters picketed in the face of a massive police presence, including special tactical units, as TGWU transport drivers, employed by Axial, refused to bring imported cars through the picket line. Drivers from a second firm, Walons, also refused to enter the port, although ECM employees had no issue crossing the picket line, living up to their reputation for coming into conflict with their Axial counterparts over similar issues in the past. Sheerness was targeted on the second anniversary of the Liverpool docks dispute because the port was 100% owned by the Mersey Docks and Harbour Company, and the deputy manager of the fruit terminal there acknowledged that actions taken against exports to Sheerness in South Africa were 'very disturbing.' Elsewhere, Reclaim the Streets (RTS) occupied the buildings of the Department for Trade and Industry in London, with an activist known as Purple telling BBC Radio Merseyside:

> *'We measure the success of such actions by the amount of interest they get from the media, which means that we raise awareness throughout the country about the dockers, and it would also be nice if other companies that still use the docks in Liverpool would actually pull out and not use those docks anymore, as happened a year ago after similar actions against another company in Liverpool.' [7]*

As two helicopters circled overhead to support a massive police presence on the ground, all traffic was blocked off and all eyes were on pro-dockers banners being unfurled from the roof of the DTI in London. According to reports, the occupation ended with 27 arrests, leading to BBC Radio Merseyside accusing RTS of dragging the dispute into a state of chaos, a charge that Jimmy Davies refuted:

> *'The demonstration in Liverpool on Saturday had over 7,000 people, [and] on that demonstration there was no trouble. We're very well organised, as our two-year dispute has shown. We are not in the ball game of stopping people from taking action in support of Liverpool dockers. There are actions taking place all over the world, not just in this country, so we're not going to tell them to stop. It appears that other people are not taking notice of us. RTS have taken up our fight because they have seen injustices done to the dockers as injustices have been done to them, so they have taken up our cause and they believe they are supporting us.' [8]*

RTS had originally intended to join the picket at Sheerness but were intercepted by police at London Victoria Station as one shop steward explained to the press that the dockers had planned demonstrations around Britain to coincide with the Labour Party Conference: 'The dispute has gone on far too long, and we're actually calling on the Labour government to intervene directly in the dispute as they control 14% of the shares in the MDHC.' [9] A double-decker bus was booked to take dockers, WOW and several stewards to lobby the Labour conference, where MPs Tony Benn and Maria Eagle spoke at a fringe meeting on the need for a public inquiry into MDHC. The story made headline news on BBC Radio Merseyside, with Ronnie Draper, speaking on behalf of the Bakers' Union explaining that:

'Casual labour is the wrong thing in any type of industry, particularly in our industry. It's something we can relate to, and I think it's time somebody stood up against casual labour. I think these guys have been absolutely terrific.' [10]

That week's Friday mass meeting had a lengthy agenda, and Jimmy Davies opened by informing the men that Keith O'Carroll's father had passed away, while 15-year-old Lee Quigley was seriously ill. The birthdays of Frank O'Neil, Billy Jenkins and Colin Mitchell were also reported, and there was news that the Socialist Labour Party had organised a benefit for the dockers at the Unemployed Centre in Liverpool. The Scottish Support Group was picketing supermarket chain Sainsbury's, MDHC's largest shareholder at the time, and Dave Cotterill was organising a course on globalisation. The WOW was thanked for putting on a wonderful fundraising event the previous Friday, and then Tony Nelson provided feedback on recent demonstrations in London, Brighton and Hillingdon. Special thanks were given to all Reclaim the Streets activists for their continued support and their extraordinary solidarity action at the Department of Trade and Industry in London, where the total number of arrests was eventually revealed to be 43. After Terry Teague's update on international action, Jimmy Nolan spoke of the need for political direct action before Mike Carden gave his regular general overview of the dispute, always beginning with the signature line, 'I'll be brief,' to jeers from dockers that knew that he would be anything but. He informed the dockers about matters arising from the latest meeting of the General Executive Council and the actions of the general secretary.

At the mass meeting, Doreen McNally's speech at Brighton Town Hall was hailed as one of the best of many made over the course of the dispute. Young Joanne Bennett had made an appearance on children's television to talk about her father's dismissal and the dockers' campaign for reinstatement. The meeting ended with a question-and-answer session with Maurice Thompson asking how many Merseyside MPs had attended the stewards' most recent Commons meeting and George Johnson wondering aloud: 'Why can't we get rid of Bill Morris? [11] Later that day, the stewards' met with representatives of the Cuban Solidarity Group, and reports from a delegation in South Africa mentioned that dockers there were looking to create a dock labour board scheme based on the principles established in the UK prior to 1989. Jimmy McGovern was again a regular visitor at Transport House, as he put the final touches on an article for that Sunday's *Observer*. At the Labour Party Conference, Bill Morris and his administrative officer Ray Collins breached the policy of the Biennial Delegates Conference by withdrawing two resolutions on the Liverpool docks dispute. Meanwhile, Maria Eagle and the Socialist Group of MPs agreed to meet with the Dispute Committee. On Sunday 5 October, McGovern's *Observer* article appeared alongside photographs by Andrew Testa. According to one of the stewards, the piece was, 'absolutely brilliant; tight and to the point,' [12] as the support of high-profile, critically-acclaimed artists such as McGovern and Ken Loach continued to increase the campaign's visibility and reach.

The TGWU's National Finance and General Purposes committee were due to meet on Thursday 9 October, at a time when Bill Morris was experiencing a number of challenges to his leadership, following the GEC rejecting his choice for a new Irish regional secretary; the BDC voting overwhelmingly against his policy on the Liverpool docks dispute and open calls for his resignation at the most recent dockers' rally. In the end, this would prove to be merely a momentary stirring, rather than a sign that victory was in sight for the Liverpool dockers, but some of the stewards were reinvigorated by these events and by Jimmy McGovern's article in particular. That same week, Liverpool MP Joe Benton informed the stewards that local MPs would be meeting with MDHC's Trevor Furlong on Friday 10 October. At a stewards' meeting held on Monday 6 October, Tony Nelson stated that having previously decided to seek negotiations, some stewards: 'seemed to be talking about the campaign continuing without recognising that we are running out of time. We need a mechanism to get talks going again.' Nelson made reference to one docker, Danny Sweeney, who, at 64 years of age, like so many other dockers, had been standing on a picket for over two years. He reminded the others that they had a duty to represent the best interests of the men and their families, especially those who had given so much of their lives to the dock industry over the course of 30-40 years. [13]

There were, however, some stewards who believed that Morris's recent struggles provided justification for persevering, citing McGovern's article as evidence that the *tide was turning*. Another factor to consider was Jack Adams's warning that: 'during the Tanks and Drums dispute, the GEC invoked a policy of calling a Special GEC when a dispute lasts for two years,' [14] suggesting that the time where the General Secretary would finally make his move was upon them. The stewards then discussed the possibility of using TGWU rules to accuse Morris of bringing the union into disrepute. It was then reported that Tony Melia was to attend a meeting of the Prison Officers' Association, who had been supportive of the dockers' campaign since it started. In the *Daily Mirror*, sacked dockworker David Byrne had his letter published in which he thanked journalist Brian Reade for his article on the dispute.

Unfortunately, the apparent state of euphoria that followed the GEC, the BDC and a general revival of some positive press coverage did not last long. On Tuesday 7 October, the Dispute Committee was back in the *pre-General Executive Council habit* of not bothering to meet. Once again, nothing much seemed to be happening and another period of lethargy hung heavily in the hard, stale atmosphere of the TGWU boardroom. Stewards just seemed to be hanging around Transport House until news filtered through that one of the dockers on the picket line had been diagnosed with bowel cancer. This was obviously an upsetting moment for everyone, but Tony Nelson, who had filled the role of picket captain from the outset of the dispute, felt the pain of it more acutely than anyone. Nelson had consistently referred to picket line morale as being the only true barometer for measuring how the dispute was going, believing strongly that the former shop stewards were obligated to deliver some new hope in the campaign for reinstatement each and every day. That was the challenge he had set for himself and the rest of the stewards, but all that was happening now was that the men and their families were getting older: 'Men are now reaching 61-64 years of age and are losing money on their pensions.' [15] Nelson then took the opportunity to again remind his fellow stewards that some of them consistently failed to turn up to the picket lines, instead spending their time in the warmth and comfort of the union's offices, which had not gone unnoticed by the rank-and-file. He also repeated his concerns about the ever-diminishing attendance of Torside dockers at the Friday mass meetings. This was easy to track since the men generally sat in the same places each week, usually reflecting the areas they had worked in on the docks. The Torsiders were conspicuous by their absence as the orange chairs at the front of the hall, to the left of the raised platform became increasingly empty.

Later that same evening, the actor Tony Booth, father of Tony Blair's wife Cherie, was scheduled to appear in a play at the Liverpool Everyman Theatre, where Jimmy Davies presented him with a dockers' t-shirt while posing for a photograph that would be printed in the *Daily Mail*. The stewards had been pressing for the Labour government to get involved in their dispute, and the article noted that Booth asked for two more t-shirts, 'to send to his grandsons, and he told the dockers he was planning to do a benefit for the dockers himself,' [16] before wondering whether or not Tony Blair's children, '13-year-old Euan and 11-year-old Nicholas would wear the controversial T-Shirts.' Davies was quoted as saying: 'Tony [Booth] was great to us. The public are slowly becoming aware of our cause, and support from people like him will do us the world of good.' [17] Elsewhere, local MPs Joe Benton, Maria Eagle, Eddie O'Hara, Bob Waring and Clare Tansey met with the Dock Company on Friday 10 October. The Labour Party's position on the Liverpool docks dispute remained simply to involve the Advisory, Conciliation and Arbitration Service, whilst Joe Benton wanted to: 'threaten the MDHC with a Department of Trade and Industry inquiry.' [18] Speaking to the Dispute Committee meeting on Wednesday 8 October, Benton emphasised the dilemma that any improved offer by MDHC would create, as there would be intense pressure to put it to a secret ballot. A great deal of discussion then took place on the question of negotiations and ballots, until it was agreed that the purpose of the Friday meeting was not to restart negotiations, but to begin, 'the process for negotiations with the shop stewards.' [19] The stewards were not opposed to postal ballots as they could not stop this process, but they also knew that declaring an intention to seek negotiations without any tangible power or leverage over the employer was an admission of weakness. This was exactly the approach taken by the union since the dispute began in 1995 and the dockers were fully aware of how it had emboldened the Dock Company to treat them with open contempt.

At the mass meeting held on Friday 10 October, it was announced that the writer Irvine Welsh had made a generous contribution to the Hardship Fund and that Jimmy McGovern was planning to donate his fee for the *Observer* article as well. The generosity of these writers and political activists was seemingly endless as another artist, Lee Hurst, celebrated winning an award for his hit television series *They Think It's All Over* by donating his fee once again. Workers at the Spillers factory, who were themselves facing closure, also made a donation, while Mrs Burns sent a gratefully received £5. Meanwhile, the rock band Cast organised a fundraising concert for the dockers at the Royal Court and the Norwegian Transport Union donated a huge sum, all of which combined, along with the blockade of the *Neptune Jade* on the West Coast of America, to have a significant impact on the morale of the dockers and their families. It was also reported that the dockers would not be voting for Danny Maher as the GEC representative for the Docks and Waterways section. He was the leader of the tugboat section and the dockers decided that Jimmy Nolan should replace him. On a personal level, this was extremely difficult for Nolan and many other stewards, as Maher had been a close comrade for many years. Frank Lannigan had already spoken to shop stewards at Ford, who agreed to support Nolan's candidacy. [20] Jimmy Davies delivered a speech on how all the recent developments could yet bring victory to the Liverpool dockers.

On Monday 13 October, Joe Benton MP reported back to the stewards following the previous Friday's meeting with MDHC. According to Benton, much of the one hour and ten minutes was spent recapping the history of the dispute, before the MPs reaffirmed that they were not there to negotiate, but to bring, 'a sense of justice to the dockers and the port. A blight is on the port, affecting any expansion.' [21] For their part, MDHC directors acknowledged the truth of this assessment, as Benton stated that: 'no real objection exists to a ballot, but something has to be there embracing all the dismissed dockers.' [22] Trevor Furlong had apparently informed the MPs that Torside no longer existed and that their last offer would need to be revisited due to the amount of time that had passed since it was last rejected by the dockers. Benton described how the directors seemed, 'better disposed to the MPs this time. They were no longer adamant, but more prepared to listen.' [23] Marie Eagle MP was still keen to pursue the matter of examining the Dock Company's use of European Union and UK government grants and speaking as a member of the Public Accounts Committee, she told a fringe meeting at the 1997 Labour Party Conference: 'There is no reason why we can't set the National Audit Office onto the MDHC. Let's have professionals look at how they have been spending public money. Let's make them account for the way they have spent the money [on] some of the most vicious accountants in the country.' [24] Furlong and his Port Operations director, Peter Jones, were said to want to examine an 'all-inclusive offer' that could be grounds for a new ballot. Jimmy Davies, Terry Teague, Mike Carden and Tony Nelson spoke of the reality that a new offer would inevitably have to be put to a postal ballot, arguing that you could not have one without the other. Nonetheless, some stewards continued to label any talk of accepting a postal ballot as a betrayal, while others were more confident in the rank-and-file dockers' commitment to solidarity. [25]

On Thursday 16 October, Terry Teague gave feedback to the stewards following a successful meeting with dockers in Dublin, while Mariam Kamish reported that a demonstration had been organised for Friday 31 October in Cardiff. Elsewhere, Peter Jones replied as vigorously to dockers in Belfast as he had done with their Liverpool counterparts in the past, warning them that they, too, would be sacked if they took action in support of the Liverpool dockers. MDHC brought out its tried and tested tactic of advertising its dockers' jobs in the local press, safe in the knowledge that this would not be met by any real opposition from the TGWU. Tony Nelson reported that police brutality on the picket line had worsened again, amid rumours that the cost of policing the dispute had now reached £2.6m. The stewards were doubtful that this figure was accurate, however, since costs in the first year alone were said to have been £2m. [26] The following day, a meeting of the Manchester Support Group was held, as the tension and pressure continued to mount on the Liverpool dockers.

# 75

# The Third Official Ballot

*'The 'eco-warriors' who came together under the banner of 'Reclaim the Streets' to support the dockers struggle brought with them new ideas, new ways of doing things and an almost naive curiosity about the dispute.'* ~ *Reclaiming the Future**

On the morning of Saturday 18 October 1997, without notice, ballot papers dropped onto the doormats of the sacked Liverpool dockworkers. The third *official* trade union ballot in this *unofficial* dispute. The TGWU had instructed the Electoral Reform Society to send out ballot papers, despite this action not being authorised by the union's General Executive Council, indicating that Bill Morris was operating outside the rules of the organisation under Rule 6 (3) and Rule 16 (13) of its constitution. In response, Carden telephoned John Hendy QC, who advised: 'that no legality could be attached to the ballot', which was in effect little more than an opinion poll, although he still recommended that the dockers' campaign for a 'No' vote as opposed to, 'chasing law courts who would not be sympathetic.' [1] The union allowed the Liverpool dockers just two working days to make a decision that would define the rest of their lives, barely a week after local members of parliament had met with Dock Company directors Trevor Furlong and Peter Jones, where there had been no mention of a ballot, leading the stewards to believe that the company and the union were conspiring to mislead not only the dockers, but also MPs. In the past, MDHC bosses had sought to ingratiate themselves with local MPs, usually for grant support, information, planning permissions, etc, whereas now they were treating them with the same arrogant, disrespectful contempt that they usually reserved for their employees. It was soon uncovered that the Torside dockers and the two Liverpool boatmen would be denied a vote, despite being in dispute since September 1995, as only former MDHC and Liverpool Stevedoring dockers would be issued with ballot papers. [2] Writing for LabourNet the following day, Greg Dropkin reported:

---

* Libcom.org, Subversion#20. Avaiable: https://libcom.org/history/reclaiming-future

545

*The TGWU general secretary, Bill Morris, has imposed a secret ballot... the ballot closes on Wednesday 22 October. The move comes in response to a letter from Mersey Docks chief executive, Trevor Furlong, dated 13 October, which declared that the current offer would be withdrawn if not accepted in a postal ballot.'* [3]

The union's talks with the Dock Company had not been made public; they were said to have included an insistence that an improved offer, which covered Torside and all other sacked men, be made in order to bring an end to the dispute. But the company's subsequent offer was little different than the first it had made in October 1995. Greg Dropkin speculated that: 'should the dockers vote to reject the offer, it will be hard to see how the TGWU, or the government, could hold back the tide of solidarity action.' [4] Bill Morris's own position had recently come under attack in a powerful article by Jimmy McGovern published in the *Observer*, which resulted in him defending his handling of the dispute in a letter to the same newspaper on 12 October. Morris was clearly angry with the Liverpool dockers, especially after their open calls for him to resign. Moreover, the persistent criticisms from McGovern, Ken Loach and John Pilger had, without doubt, bruised his ego. In *T&G Policy on Liverpool Docks*, Morris expanded upon his initial response to McGovern's piece in the *Observer*, arguing that the newspaper had limited his space to reply by publishing, 'an edited version of a letter sent by Bill Morris.' [5] What followed was the unedited version of Morris's thoughts on the situation in Liverpool:

*'...we have negotiated with the MDHC with the result that the company's offer on jobs and redundancy payments has twice been improved. The offer now includes £28,000 redundancy per head, protected pension rights, 40 jobs back immediately and the creation of a union-sponsored cooperative to provide further employment... Mr McGovern also makes an unfounded attack on a hardworking T&G officer... This allegation has Mr McGovern licking his lips at the prospect of the Liverpool dockers suing the T&G at the end of this dispute. No doubt much of the establishment would relish the prospect... the T&G will continue to campaign for the fairer employment laws, which will not allow workers in future to be treated as the Liverpool dockers have been treated.'* [6]

On Sunday 12 October, the stewards met to discuss the implications of these sudden developments, and it was agreed that a mass meeting would be called for the following day. Terry Teague opened the discussion by stating that they had: 'no option to boycott or oppose this ballot. We have to be very clear we can win this ballot and open up new areas of our political and trade union campaign. The reason for the ballot is because they, the MDHC and the union, are under pressure.' [7] Billy Jenkins saw no reason to panic, believing that they simply needed, 'a good, clear rejection.' [8] Jimmy Davies then compared the Saturday morning letters sent out by the union to: 'the redundancy notices sent out by the Dock Company in September 1995. It is a disgrace that Torside have been ignored and not given the right to vote.' [9] Tony Nelson added: 'the pension rights of workers have still not been clarified, with 200 of 327 dockers unsure of their entitlements and 47 former dock clerical workers, ACTSS 6/567 Branch members, who have no idea what their pensions rights are.'

[10] The ballot openly discriminated against many of the dockworkers who had been involved in the dispute in different ways, with the position of Excel dockers being quite unique, as sacked docker Mick Cullen would explain to BBC Radio Merseyside's Roger Philips. Excel was a casual agency, but prior to its abolition in 1989, the National Dock Labour Board Scheme ensured: 'if a dock company went bust then the Port Authority, the Dock Company, would have to take the dockers on. While they were waiting to be redeployed to the MDHC, the scheme was abolished. Those lads were treated abysmally, and that was why Excel was set up.' [11]

The following day a Regional Committee meeting took place where lengthy reports on the docks dispute were heard, with the overall conclusion being that the general secretary had, without consultation or discussion, imposed a secret ballot on the Liverpool dockers. Both Mike Carden and Kenny Brindle agreed that this represented an attack on the primacy of the GEC which, despite being dominated by Morris and the *TGWU Broad Left's* appointees, had been wholly ignored by him on this occasion: 'McCall admitted that Morris did contact him at the weekend, to tell him that he had a personal responsibility to launch the ballot. McCall could not comment on the GEC policy, but he [Morris] had ultimate power. He applauded the decision of dockers to participate in the ballot, and [agreed that] it was wrong for two dead dockers' wives and families to receive ballot papers.' [12] In addition to those ballot papers, the former MDHC and Liverpool Stevedoring dockers also received a letter from the desk of the General Secretary. [13]

With the ballot papers Morris enclosed a copy of a detailed statement, dated 13 October 1997, sent to the TGWU by Trevor Furlong of MDHC reinforcing the notion that the union and the employer were united in their strategy to, once again, effect a conclusion to the dispute. The Dock Company leaflet, attached to the ballot paper, stated that it was nine months since they had:

> '...tabled an improved, final offer... [and] difficulties have now arisen. In particular, the continuing restructuring of the Company's activities in Liverpool have eliminated some of the opportunities for providing jobs as part of a settlement package. In the meantime, any impact of the dispute on the Company's business has ceased, though it remains a matter of concern both to the Company and Merseyside as a whole... If the Company does not receive formal confirmation by the union of acceptance of its offer by that date, the offer will be irrevocably withdrawn and the matter ended.' [14]

Just in case this correspondence from Furlong failed to have the desired effect on the Liverpool dockers, a further two-sided leaflet titled *MDHC Final Offer – It's Time to Decide – The Decision is Yours* was also included. [15] Here, the precise details of the offer were spelled out: 'the Company will either re-employ or make severance payments to the 327 dismissed port operatives previously employed by MDHC and Coastal. Is the Package on offer new? Yes.' [16] Most notably, in the section outlining potential jobs, MDHC indicated a willingness to work with a dockers' labour co-operative. [17] On the ballot paper, the question was simply, 'Do you accept the Company's offer?' [18] By 17 October the Dock Company was announcing the promotions of several middle managers to the board of directors, no doubt as a reward for their unwavering loyalty throughout the dispute, with Frank Robothom and

Bill Hogg among those chosen for promotion. The company seemed to be on a charm offensive at this time, as Furlong announced: 'the group has achieved dramatic progress in recent years, and expansion of the executive management puts in place a structure to take the MDHC into an even stronger future.' [19]

On Sunday 19 October, comedian Lee Hurst put on a fundraising performance for the dockers at Liverpool's Empire theatre, one day before the *Liverpool Daily Post* ran an article titled *Docks Ultimatum: Take It or Leave It.*' [20] The dockers had until Friday 24 October to accept the latest final offer, with Peter Jones, MDHC's port operations director, telling the *Post* that the time had come to settle the conflict once and for all. One steward told the newspaper: 'We are meeting the men tomorrow at midday to ask them what they want to do. It is their decision.' [21] Meanwhile, a *Liverpool Echo* editorial piece told its readers that:

> *'Whichever way a secret ballot goes, the result would persuade all in the North West of the strength of feeling now remaining after such a bitter 25 months. If the dockers were to vote to reject the final offer, it would demonstrate that there was a foolhardy – but genuine – determination to fight on. We feel that would be mistaken… Every time it is mentioned, outsiders have their outdated prejudices reinforced. If it is not settled this week, goodness knows what will happen. Far better, surely, for the dockers to take advantage of the ballot and act for the good of themselves and of Merseyside. Or do they want to kick their own union in the teeth too?' [22]*

At the mass meeting, Jimmy Davies announced the death of Liverpool docker John Lee, as well as the sad loss of Irene Campbell's mother, with the customary minute's silence being observed. Jimmy Nolan clarified the details of the enforced ballot, and there was much criticism from the floor aimed at the TGWU over its exclusion of the Torside and Excel dockers, as well as the two boatmen, from the vote. Ultimately, it was agreed that they would acknowledge the ballot and reject it. Joe Ladd questioned the legitimacy of a vote where: 'not every docker involved is being given a ballot paper,' [23] and Terry Barrett noted: 'We are supporting future jobs in the port, and the MDHC are suffering.' [24] Micky Tighe called for: 'a total rejection. We are classed as working-class heroes… we must fight for all those who have supported us all around the world,' [25] while Mick Cullen believed that: 'more people than Morris knew about this ballot.' [26] Jimmy Campbell then reminded everyone that he was now 61 years of age, before pleading: 'Don't give in! We're two weeks away from victory,' [27] and Eddie Ledden called on his fellow dockers not to, 'leave it [the port] to the scabs!' [28] Terry Woods declared: 'We have won the dispute,' [29] singling out, 'the two brave boatmen who have supported us since September 1995.' [30] Marty Size asked the men to, 'think of the old dockers – vote no!' [31] George Johnson brought up the Colombian trade unionist who had talked to them about, 'putting their lives on the line.' [32] Eventually, MDHC's offer was rejected by a show of hands, with only four votes in favour, [33] and on Tuesday 21 October, the following resolution was passed unanimously by the elected representatives of Region 6:

> *'On Saturday 18 October 1997, ballot papers issued by the ERS were sent to the houses of 329 sacked Liverpool dockers. The ballot… this 'action' was invoked by our*

*general secretary without the authority of the General Executive Council. Throughout the Liverpool docks dispute, the general secretary has consistently stated that the union's policy relating to this dispute rests solely with the GEC. Indeed, the GEC decided that no actions be taken by either the general secretary or the F&GP without the authority of the GEC… the action of the general secretary, who has clearly failed to obtain the authority of the GEC in this matter under Rule 6 (13) and Rule 16 (3). Furthermore, that this Region Six Committee calls for an emergency meeting of the GEC to be called immediately to discuss this action of the General Secretary and all other matters relating to the Liverpool docks dispute.' [34]*

As details of the *official trade union ballot* came to light it transpired that, based upon the employer and unions' definition, twelve eligible dockers did not receive ballot papers. This was a significant breach of the Trade Union and Labour Relations (Consolidation) Act 1992. On Tuesday 21 October, the *Liverpool Echo* wrongly claimed that the stewards were intent on boycotting the ballot. This third ballot would follow the same failed process as the others. It would be a partnership – a *joint enterprise* – involving the Dock Company and the TGWU, including supporting documents from both parties each affirming the Liverpool dockers absence of choice in this *"democratic ballot"*. In *Animal Farm* George Orwell captured this dual betrayal and the powerlessness of its victims: 'Between pigs and human beings there was not, and there need not be, any clash of interests whatever. Their struggles and difficulties were one,' he wrote. [35] Just like the pigs and the humans, it was made perfectly clear by the union and the bosses that they held dominion over their victims. Both parties falsely described the dockers as being involved in an *unofficial, illegal strike,* now they were busy organising a *third official legal ballot.* When dockers opened their ballot papers they looked from the bosses' paper to the union paper, and from the union paper to the bosses' paper, 'but already it was impossible to say which was which.' [36] The betrayal of the Liverpool dockers was now almost complete.

# 76

# Another Official Ballot – Another Rejection!

*'To be honest, I still don't know how I feel about it; different things going through my head all the time. As Mick said, on that particular day everyone was devastated, but obviously we had to follow our stewards' recommendation. I did follow it myself. It was hard, and I keep trying to think what else we could have done. I do blame Bill Morris; everything comes back to Bill Morris every time. We go back to last May when the Labour government got in. We thought, we hoped, that they would help us, but obviously we were all elated when they got in, but they've done nothing for us. We were let down by them.' ~ Billy Johnson\**

On Friday 24 October 1997, a Drake International employee walked into Transport House Liverpool to collect 150 Transport and General Workers' Union membership application forms. In another part of the building, Jean Fox, a Women of the Waterfront, activist and wife of sacked docker Tommy Fox, was busy writing an article for *LabourNet*, in which she described exactly how she and others felt about the Mersey Docks and Harbour Company's latest offer to its former dockworkers. In an article titled *The Rats, the Weasels, the Snakes! How can they do it to us?* Jean proclaimed her disgust at those who should have been representing her husband and his colleagues, exemplifying the soul and the intellect that drove the WOW to become the radical and fearless organisation it was. She wrote a political treatise that so many politicians and trade union leaders would struggle to articulate with such clarity and political awareness. It began: 'I have just finished reading the MDHC offer and the secret ballot forms. What a nerve; the TGWU should be ashamed of themselves. Just what does Bill Morris think he is doing? This offer was rejected months ago by the men at their meeting. They have consistently made the point that this was no improvement on the original offer which was so overwhelmingly rejected.' [1] She went on to say:

---

\* Liverpool docker Billy Johnson, in an interview with Greg Dropkin (17 February 1998)

*'How strange that the ballot forms arrived on a Saturday morning. A day earlier, and it could have been discussed at the weekly meeting. Why the secrecy? Why the limited time to reply? Assuming that first-class post takes two days, then the early postal time on Monday morning must be caught. Whose strategy was it? As both the T&G and the MDHC had worked hand in hand to destroy the dockers from day one... Nobody that I talk to is looking forward to another winter on the picket line (except the children, who build snow pickets and play snowballs), but if it has to be, then so be it! Our coats may be thinner, but our skins are thicker! Daily abuse from scabs and police alike run off like raindrops now. Nothing can be said to us, or of us, that hasn't been said before. In sacking the Liverpool dockers, the MDHC have opened up a can of worms. They cannot put the lid back on and are living the consequences of their actions.' [2]*

There was also confusion as to why such a heavy police presence was required, with uniformed officers, motorcycle units, horses and the Operational Support Division all routinely visible during picket line demonstrations, and this strange distribution of public resources led Jean to quip, 'I don't have to worry about my house being burgled while I'm on the picket line, as there is nothing left worth stealing.' [3] Jean also outlined some of the WOW's key political concerns:

*'After 18 years of Tory rule, we were all rather downtrodden. Constant attacks on workers' rights had whittled away at confidence and self-image, legislation decreased union power, wages and conditions of work; health and safety was not always implemented. At last, people are beginning to stand up and say, "Enough is enough." The fight against casualisation, low pay and bad employers has started. Many workers in health, education, airlines, post and factories up and down the land are demanding a better deal. They see the struggle by the dockers, and see that though hard times must be endured, they can be overcome... It seems obvious that New Labour is hardly distinguishable from the previous government. Well, we know that there are some MPs who support our cause and we thank them, but we must rely on ordinary people who understand our fight because they are living with the realities of life as it is today.' [4]*

Jean Fox suggested that workers should organise in new, innovative ways, as evidenced by the tremendous international support and solidarity that the Liverpool dockers' campaign had garnered, arguing that if the globalisation of industry was simply now a fact of life, global organisation of labour must follow. She wrote of her fears for her children's future in a world of casual work, and the low pay and poor conditions that they inevitably bring about, but at the same time she expressed confidence that: 'this dispute will be won; the rats, weasels and snakes will find a damp, dark place to hide (may I suggest the hold of an ACL ship), the dockers will go back to work and the employers and the government will have to rethink their attitudes towards their workforce. Onwards to victory. Don't quit. Remember your heritage. Keep the Faith. May the Force be with you!' [5]

Liverpool docker Jimmy Campbell told BBC Radio Merseyside news that despite the threats of the Dock Company and the union, enclosed with the ballot paper: 'It is not the last chance. They're crucified; they're dying on their feet, that's what's happening with them.

They're dying on the feet and they're panicking. I'll just put my X's for no. I'm 61 years of age and there's my paper. We'll beat these. Europe's with us, the ITFs with us. Why have they said this at the last minute? Morris, God blimey, he's a disgrace him!' [6] It was a secret ballot that had been kept *secret* until the envelopes began landing on the dockers' doormats. A complaint was going to be made that the union, in this action, had acted outside its own rules. On the same radio programme, Carden accused Bill Morris of: 'acting in cohort with the Dock Company, simply to send ballot papers to just 327 dockers and not every sacked dockworker. It's a bit of a funny ballot when the union and the Company are only prepared to accept a yes vote. We think that is a bit of an Albanian ballot. It is not democracy as we understand it.' [7] The late Eric Taplin, a highly respected labour historian who wrote several books on the history of the Liverpool dockers, was also interviewed, explaining that:

> *'Liverpool dockers have a long record of struggle. The sort of things they have struggled for are a decent living wage, regular work, the right to belong to a trade union. This has been going on for well over a hundred years. The first dock strike that brought this port to a stop was as long ago as 1879. So, this dispute is part of a very long tradition... Relations between the workers and the employers on the docks, not only in Liverpool but nationally, has been very poor indeed... The extraordinary thing about this dispute is the lack of media coverage, because in the past when there was a strike or any dispute, it hit the headlines, certainly locally and often nationally... while many people in this country don't even know there is a dispute in Liverpool.' [8]*

Sacked docker and picket line stalwart Marty Size described the ballot as:

> *'Just another tactic to split us... People all over the world are backing us, and to take that money like that is undermining them, and it's also undermining the younger element of Merseyside who are looking for decent jobs, and that's what we are fighting for. We are not just fighting for ourselves; we are fighting for the next generation. We want decent standards of living and working conditions, and we think this is the only way we can get it.' [9]*

On Thursday 23 October, Andrew Murphy from the Electoral Reform Society wrote directly to Bill Morris, informing him of the result of the ballot:

> *'Our report of voting for the above ballot, which closed on Wednesday 22 October 1997, is as follows: members formerly employed by MDHC and Coastal Line; number of papers issues, 329; number of duplicate ballot papers distributed, 11; number of ballot papers returned, 316; number of spoilt papers, 6. Thus, the total number of valid papers to be counted, 310; rate of participation, 91%. Result: the question put to the membership was as follows: Do you accept the company's offer? Yes, 31%; No, 69%.'* [10]

Later that day, Jack Adams telephoned Jimmy Nolan to ask him if he had heard the result. When Nolan told him he said this was: 'tremendous' and offered his congratulations. [11]

This was in contrast to reports that Bill Morris: 'very much regretted the decision of the dockers.' [12] Andrew Murray, the TGWU press officer, stated: 'We regret that there is no negotiated settlement to the long-running dispute,' [13] before telling journalist Aviva Freudmann that: 'The Transport and General Workers' Union at Mersey Docks has supported the fired workers with money and negotiating assistance, but has not backed them in their campaign against Liverpool cargo.' [14] Elsewhere, Kees Marges of the ITF again repeated that: 'Our affiliates [the TGWU] have not asked us to do anything regarding the campaign of the former Liverpool dockers.' [15] Nolan responded by seeking an urgent meeting with the ITF: '...to implement policies that the Asia-Pacific ITF Conference adopted, to boycott any ships that call at Liverpool.' [16] Unsurprisingly, and not for the first time in this dispute, MDHC found themselves standing in solidarity with the TGWU and the ITF, as a statement by port operations director Peter Jones confirmed that:

> '...the offer is good until 5pm Monday. After that, the offer will be withdrawn and there will be no further negotiations. The company believes the workers rejected the offer because they were misinformed by the shop stewards' group, particularly regarding their continued eligibility for pension payments. The shop stewards group incorrectly told the men that if they rejected the offer, the company would be forced to make a better offer.' [17]

Jones confirmed: 'there's no possibility of further negotiations taking place.' [18] Various TGWU regions now called upon the General Executive Council to fight the dispute with the intention of winning, and to launch a campaign of industrial action that would see them immediately invoke action by the International Transport Workers' Federation in support of the sacked Liverpool dockers. [19] However, when the GEC met in early December 1997, its chair, Andy Smith, joined Bill Morris in ruling any discussion on the dispute to be 'out of order'. According to one report: 'The attitude of the leadership of the TGWU, in refusing to make this important dispute official, and in manoeuvring to make life as difficult as possible for the strikers, is in stark contrast to the sort of international solidarity being shown for the dockers' struggle among port workers throughout the world.' [20] In Liverpool, the funeral cortege of Liverpool docker John Lee drove slowly along the third, bleak winter's picket line, as *LabourNet's* Greg Dropkin reported how:

> '...both sides of the dock road fell silent and men doffed their caps as a funeral cortege passed. Inside the hearse lay the body of a former dock worker, John Lee, who had supported the men in dispute.' [21]

Jimmy Nolan told the BBC: 'The dockers' decision was a resounding no! A 70% rejection of the MDHC's proposals. So, after two years, I would think that that's a glorious and courageous statement for us to be making.' [22] The Dispute Committee called on: 'the Labour government to intervene and make it very clear to the Dock Company that if they don't reinstate us, they are going to remove the 14% share value that they have.' [23] In a separate interview, Mike Carden was blunt in stating: 'the only result these people are prepared to accept is the result that gives them the decision that they want. We've challenged the democracy of the ballot; it's not a democratic ballot. Two people who are currently working in the port received ballot papers; 12 dockers had not received ballot papers and two ballot papers went out to the homes of deceased dockworkers.' [24] Friday's mass meeting began with spontaneous applause and cheering among the men and their supporters, as the Dock Company scrambled to send out forms for individual dockers to sign if they wished to break ranks and accept the offer. [25]

Speaking to *Channel 4 News* on the day that the result was declared, Liverpool docker Billy Barrett declared, 'Great! Made up with it. They always said they insist on a ballot; we've given them a ballot.' [26] Fellow docker Tommy Byrne said during an interview at the Elm House pub that he was not bothered about those dockers who had voted to accept the offer. The following day, Ian McCartney MP, the minister for Trade and Industry, refuted comments made by Morris about the TGWU writing to request government intervention in the dispute. Speaking at a Manchester meeting of the North West Trades Union Congress on Saturday 25 October, McCartney stated that no such communication had reached his office, contradicting Morris's claim at the September 1997 GEC that he had already written to the government in compliance with the vote taken at the TGWU Biennial Delegates Conference two months prior. [27] It was also around this time that the dockers produced another leaflet, *Time to Organise? Liverpool Docks Dispute Update*, [28] with the intention of informing their supporters of the result of the recent ballot:

> *'Clearly, the union has failed to reach a negotiated settlement. In over two years, the fabric of the union remains intact and unchallenged. The GEC has sanctioned payments of £630,000 to the dockers' Hardship Fund equivalent, over two years of approximately £13 per week per family… The primary function of any trade union is to defend its members. How can we possible encourage recruitment against a climate of fear and intimidation in the workplace fuelled by an absence of human rights underwritten by a Labour government? The Liverpool dockers have been loyal members of our union for many decades; they fought to create this union and were the authors of its great history, along with other groups who fought for justice against all odds. The dockers' struggle is part of this historic inheritance. Do not allow the dockers to be betrayed.' [29]*

Fr Michael, the dockers' 'banker', was also interviewed by BBC Radio Merseyside at his church, St Joan of Arc in Bootle. He remarked upon the generosity of workers from across the world. [30] Speaking on behalf of MDHC, Peter Jones told the same news programme that:

> *The problem with negotiations with the shop stewards is that from the outset their demand from day one has been that the company should take on 80 people employed by Torside Ltd, an independent company who we have no jobs for… We have large investment plans for the port, and we want to get on with those plans and generate employment for the region. What we don't want to do is to leave those men who want to take the settlement without an option'. [31]*

On Monday 27 October, BBC Radio Merseyside dedicated another live phone-in show to the dispute, during which a sacked docker formerly employed on the Norse Irish terminal got into an argument with presenter Roger Phillips, who had read out a statement from Bill Morris lamenting the fact that a negotiated settlement was no longer possible: 'Well, Roger, a few years ago you were on the picket line, and you didn't want your colleagues to cross, did you?' [32] Phillips replied: 'That was different. We weren't out over money; it was a matter of principle,' [33] at which point the docker asked, 'And what do you think this is? Aren't there any principles when it comes to dockers? We're not out for money!' [34] On the same programme Peter Jones read out the following prepared statement from MDHC: 'In good faith, the company will stand by its offer of payment of up to £28,000 to all of the individuals who accept it by 5pm on Monday 27 October [that same day].' [35] Jones was then asked by the presenter, Roger Phillips, 'What if the dockers took the £28,000 on Monday, and then just rejoined the picket lines?' [36] to which Jones responded: 'I think we have a bit more faith in our former employees than that.' [37] The port operations director claimed that MDHC had been inundated with severance applications from dockers wishing to walk away from the dispute, which he cited as the reason why he was, 'sending this money offer to dockers; because I am concerned for the 97 dockers who voted for this offer.' [38] In Ireland, John Freeman, the TGWU regional secretary, wrote to Bill Morris to tell him that:

> *'At the recent statutory meeting of the Irish Regional Committee, a lengthy debate ensued regarding the long-running dispute involving the Liverpool dockers, who were sacked for refusing to cross the picket line... and in that respect the following remit was unanimously agreed. I would, therefore, ask you to bring this remit to the attention of the General Executive Council. That the Irish Regional Committee calls upon the GEC to immediately invoke the unqualified support of the ITF in support of our sacked Liverpool dockers.' [39]*

Whilst Freeman was writing to Morris in London, Greg Dropkin was publishing a report on a Liverpool delegation to Dublin, where dockers picketed Coastal Containers:

> *The Irish dockers refused to cross the picket line. Mick O'Rielly, Maurice Cunnigham, Tom O'Connor, Sean Finnigan and all the Belfast and ITGWU members provided magnificent support again for this action... Dublin handles more Liverpool ships than any other port in the world, including frequent services on Coastal Container Line, which is 100% owned by Mersey Docks and Harbour Company, and also serves Belfast, Greenock and Cardiff. [40]*

At the Irish Ferries berth, dockers refused all work on the *M.V. Coastal Bay*, a Coastal Container vessel. The men were all members of the Service Industrial Professional and Technical Union, and *Lloyd's List* quoted Enda Connellan, the Dublin Port Company's chief executive officer, as saying: 'I regret any disruption caused to my customers. Why do people think that what they cannot do at home, they can go to another country and do?' [41] Mick Corcoran, branch secretary for the deep-sea dockers' section of the Marine Port and General Workers' Union, declared that: 'Today's action is very effective. There's a vessel full of Japanese cars which is now delayed. Our employers would love to impose the cheap labour system currently operating on Coastal and Pandoro (P&O) trade in Liverpool. What's happening there is a threat to all dockworkers, including ourselves.' [42] Speaking for the Irish TGWU, Michael O'Reilly, the incoming regional secretary and long-time supporter of the Liverpool dockers, said that his members were: 'trying to show their solidarity and continue a long association with the Liverpool dispute. We are seeking the support of our colleagues from other unions in the Port of Dublin.' [43] It was common for delegations to produce dedicated leaflets for each of their picket visits, and the Dublin version, *Liverpool Fights On! 220–97 Rejection*, praised Irish comrades for their ongoing support and noted that: 'Dublin is a key port trading with Liverpool, far outweighing any other single port worldwide. We believe that you hold the key to our dispute.' [44] Michael O'Reilly would later explain how the Liverpool dockers were able to circumvent laws surrounding unauthorised disruption in the Irish ports:

> *They came over to Drogheda to stop a boat being loaded there for Liverpool. They slept on the floor of the ATGWU office in Drogheda, and then came up to Dublin the next morning. I told them that if you sit down on the road for no more than 15 minutes, and then walk for another 15 minutes, you're not breaking the law. Don't ask me where I got that idea from. We went from the Four Courts down to the docks, sitting down on the road every once in a while. It caused chaos, and we managed to disrupt the loading of the boat. [45]*

According to Terry Teague's Irish report: 'We must have walked about eight miles that day – Coastal docks are a very big complex – with Mick O'Reilly, Tom O'Connor, Mick Concorran and so many others on the picket line all day. Lilly Bolger laid on all the food.' [46] On the way back from Ireland, the bus broke down just outside Holyhead, and so by the time the delegation made it home, they had been without sleep for almost two days. It would be worth it, though, as the ATGWU agreed to ask Bill Morris to formally request international support for the Liverpool campaign, a month after members in Belfast had imposed five-hour delays on three Coastal Container ships in solidarity with the sacked Liverpool dockers. [47]

By Thursday 26 October, the Dockworkers' Pension Committee had met, but they were forced to wait and see if MDHC submitted pension applications in response to the severance requests that they were claiming to have received. Peter Jones would send a fax, dated 29 October, stating that individual settlements offering re-employment on the basis of a fixed-term three-month contract had been accepted by 35 dockers. Thus, MDHC was seeking the trustees' approval before commuting those 35 pensions under Clause 7B2, which allowed for early retirement, but this request would not be until the committee's next meeting. One of the key issues to consider was that the dockers had lost two years' pension contributions while in dispute, and as it would cost some £3,600 per head to fill this gap, it was in MDHC's own interest to ensure that any pay-outs were officially endorsed by the pension trustees. This situation also created a dilemma for the Dispute Committee, as they had to decide whether or not they should continue making Hardship Fund and picket attendance payments to the 35 men who had effectively left the dispute. [48] Meanwhile, with Jimmy Nolan down in London, Frank Lannigan was in the chair again for the weekly mass meeting held on Friday 31 October. Lannigan was well-respected for his blunt honestly, and he did not cover-up the news that those who had applied for severance would be temporarily re-employed by

November. Jimmy Davies, a trustee of the pension fund, then clarified the situation regarding pension rights [49] before announcing that the stewards planned to meet Labour MPs with a view to calling for further talks with Bill Morris. [50]

On 5 November, the stewards travelled to London for a meeting with MPs, where a leaflet detailing the amount of public money that had been ploughed into MDHC over the course of the preceding 25 years was distributed. [51] Jimmy Nolan provided MPs with some historical background to the dispute, including the Torside situation, but he did not really take up the points made by Tony Benn regarding the financial cost to the taxpayer, and in truth, the stewards spoke for far too long, failing to properly utilise their time with such influential figures as Benn, John McDonnell and Lord Sefton. [52] The following day's feedback on the meeting was soul-destroying for the dockers, as the fact that only one Lord and two MPs, neither of whom were from Merseyside turned up for the meeting. [53] There was, however, more positive news in the form of John Hendy QC agreeing to submit a formal complaint to the Court of Human Rights and the International Labour Organisation, while Gerry Sutcliffe, MP for St Helens, put forward plans to co-ordinate support among his fellow trade unionist MPs. [54] Morale among the Dispute Committee had plummeted again. [55]

A delegation from the Swedish Transport Workers Union arrived alongside three comrades from South Africa, who were colleagues of Dot Gibson. Mike Carden and Ken Brindle, the two Region 6 GEC representatives, had together concluded that they should ask Broad Left members to boycott the meeting normally held before each GEC. Jimmy Nolan dismissed this as a dreadful idea, but others defended it as a means of displaying their anger at the lack of support they had received from the Broad Left and the GEC. Nolan then threatened to resign if the boycott went ahead, arguing that if he was allowed to address the Broad Left personally, he would be able to convince them to back the campaign. [56] It was at this time that Carden received a letter of complaint from Bill Morris, seeking clarification on a report that he had described the general secretary as being 'utterly useless' at a recent demonstration. [57] The Friday mass meeting held on 7 November began with Steve Donnelly giving an update on support from AC Delco. Lesley Mahmood, a comrade and supporter of the Liverpool dockers reported that she was standing in the Liverpool City Council elections. Dave Sinclair was to display his photographs of the dispute at the Unemployed Centre. Additionally, the Le Havre dockers were organising a delivery of Christmas presents for dockers' children, while plans were made to attend a TGWU recruitment conference in Birmingham the following day. The Dispute Committee had met again with local MPs earlier in the week, where Maria Eagle had declared her intention to keep going back to the Public Accounts Committee demanding an inquiry into MDHC, [58] together with advice from Tony Benn MP to keep putting down early day motions in Parliament to raise awareness of the dispute. On the legal front, John Hendy QC was still pursuing intervention via the International Labour Organisation, while at the next GEC, Bill Morris faced further challenges to the imposition of his ballot, as well as calls to finally make the Liverpool docks dispute official. It was also reported that a rally against redundancies would be taking place at Liverpool's Walton Hospital, before speeches on behalf of the WOW were followed by questions from the floor. One of the dockers, Neil Caddick, called on his fellow dockers to do their part on the picket lines, especially now that the Operational Support Division was escalating its intimidation tactics, with Brian Dooley suggesting that they increase the number of cameras at demonstrations. [59] Three days later, in a report for *LabourNet*, Greg Dropkin described how:

> *'Sixty hospital cleaners, catering workers and their supporters from the Liverpool sacked dockers lobbied the Aintree Trust Health Authority (Fazakerley Hospital) meeting on 10 November. Domestic and meal delivery staff at Liverpool's Walton Hospital were fighting to ensure that their jobs were protected when the site closed, and all facilities transferred to Fazakerley Hospital...' [60]*

One of the Health Authority panel members, Dr Robin Walker, asked why the Fazakerley contractors, RCO, were against keeping on the Walton workforce, and was told, 'The problem is that they would inherit their present wages and conditions.' [61] Fifty Unison members employed as cleaners through the contractor Initial also faced the dole queue, along with several dining room staff. Sylvia Tighe, a cleaner with 20 years' service at Walton Hospital, and whose husband was a sacked dockworker, was cheered as she addressed the dockers' weekly mass meeting a few days after the demonstration: 'I went into the Health Authority with two Unison stewards and our branch secretary... These are our jobs and we want them. We all have families to feed, just as you have. We work for £3.69 an hour, which is disgusting! Now you are trying to tell us we are too expensive.' [62] At the same meeting, Mick Cullen gave feedback following his trip to meet with the CGT union in France, where Ken Loach's *The Flickering Flame* was shown to rapturous applause. There were guest speakers from the Fire Brigades Union, as well as trade unionists from Sweden and South Africa, on a day where the mounting pressure on the dockers resulted in a subdued atmosphere. [63] Elsewhere, the WOW had sent a delegation to Canada, inspiring solidarity action by dockworkers in Halifax, St John, Montreal and Vancouver, which was endorsed by unions such as the CAW, CUPE and the Alberta Teachers' Association, creating what would become known as the Liverpool Dockers' Solidarity Network; an ambitious new facet of this historic campaign for justice. The group had organised a two-week speaking tour across Canada, with Val Bibby and Marie Eustace drumming up support for targeted action against Canadian Pacific, whose subsidiary firms had continued to have vessels sent to the Port of Liverpool throughout the dispute.

On Monday 17 November, the Liverpool dockers agreed to lobby the next GEC meeting, and the following day, Terry Teague and Fred Roberts reported back after delegation work in Belfast, where MDHC had started a major expansion operation. Irish Regional secretary John Freeman had once again offered his support for any potential picket line activity on Belfast docks, while advising that Sinn Fein would need to be approached ahead of time. Freeman was said to be confident that a resolution challenging the failure of the GEC to support the Liverpool dockers could still be successful.

Across the Irish Sea in Cardiff, more successful pickets were to be held later in the week, with Associated British Ports seeking a meeting with Cardiff police after 120 demonstrators closed the port for almost two hours on the morning of Tuesday 18 November. This led to hundreds of wagons being backed up several miles to the motorway, in a protest that included 70 sacked Liverpool dockers, and despite complaints from management that the flying picket was illegal, police officers maintained only a low-key presence, insisting that their sole priority was to avoid violence and ensure the safe flow of motorway traffic. Rob Gravestock, the ABP port manager, described the action as, 'a huge inconvenience for thousands caught up in the traffic chaos, including vehicles arriving to the port. This is the second time this month we have been affected, and the police must make contingency plans as protesters have said they will return.' [64] In response, Mariam Kamish, secretary of the Welsh Dockers' Support Group, stated that, 'Our aim is to make clear that if the Mersey Docks and Harbour Company want to get back to normal work, then they're going to have to accept the locked-out Liverpool dockers back to work as well.' [65]

The dockers had travelled overnight for the rendezvous with their Welsh supporters, where they were to target Coastal Container Line, a subsidiary of MDHC, which had five sailings per week linking Cardiff to Dublin and Belfast, although Gravestock insisted that, 'While some deliveries were delayed, there were no delays to ships,' [66] before confirming that a regular Coastal vessel, *M.V. Pellworm*, was docked in port, along with the *M.V. Kaaksburg*, *M.V. Bettina* and *M.V. Petro Severn*. For their part, Coastal's Cardiff office declined to comment, but their Dublin operations director, John Forrester, claimed that the company had no vessels in Cardiff during the picket, and that the *M.V. Pellworm* would not be arriving until later that evening. This came just one month after the *M.V. Coastal Bay* had been delayed eight hours by flying pickets in Dublin, with Bobby Morton explaining, 'local hauliers in Liverpool are upset at Coastal's inability to guarantee delivery schedules.' [67]

In Liverpool, Inspector Gittens of Merseyside Police informed Terry Teague, Tony Nelson and Kevin Robinson that policing of the pickets was going to be even more aggressive than before. [68] However, this line was contradicted by Inspector Garry Watson at Huyton Police Station, who wrote to the *Liverpool Echo* to let the public know that as far as he was concerned, the Liverpool dockers were still part of the local community and should be treated as such:

> *'Last Friday morning, I was the senior officer in charge of 'C' Group at E2 Area, Prescot / Huyton and Halewood [areas of Liverpool], who were grieving for a colleague, Police Constable Shevlin. He was buried later in the day. It was the role of E District to police the docks that day, which would obviously disrupt the attendance of officers at the very emotional police funeral. Consequently, I approached the striking dockers at each of the four gates and asked for their help and cooperation by calling a truce for the day, allowing officers to attend the funeral. The striking dockers at every gate expressed sympathy for the young officer and promised to abide by a gentlemen's agreement by leaving the dock gates clean for the whole day. The police must always remain impartial in any dispute, and this letter has nothing to do with the rights and the wrongs of the dispute. However, I could not let such an incident pass without giving my grateful thanks to those striking dockers for their assistance and cooperation.' [69]*

A few stewards were sat in the small office at Transport House Liverpool that doubled as the Dispute Committee's international communication hub, waiting for feedback to arrive by fax, telephone or email. It was again the case that information was not flowing freely between the stewards as the campaign became increasingly reliant on the single computer located in the smallest room in Transport House. Some stewards nicknamed it *Hal* in reference to Stanley

Kubrick's *2001: A Space Odyssey.* This was because the majority of communications no longer appeared to flow freely from the computer room to the Board room limiting access to vital information that was needed by all the stewards to continue to manage the dispute effectively. [70] Across the border, at the Scottish TUC's Women's Conference, Margaret Prosser, a TGWU national officer, stated that her union would not pursue a public inquiry into MDHC. [71] This was yet another example of how, for some senior officials of the TGWU, power and patronage had become their *raison d'etre* of trade unionism; she would later become Lady Prosser. It was also around this time that Sefton Borough Council discussed a resolution to support the Liverpool dockers. The community of Sefton, some of whom were among the poorest on Merseyside, had always suffered far more than they had benefitted from the Dock Company's activities, which brought everything from pollution to promised employment opportunities that never materialised. The SBC's leader, Dave Martin, was himself a port worker, and both he and the Conservative Les Byron began speaking out against MDHC, labelling them the *worst employers in Liverpool.* [72]

# 77
# The Neptune Jade Picket

*When Neptune Jade set sail from England dock workers in Vancouver, Yokohama and Kobe all refused to let the ship dock and unload its cargo. The ship eventually sailed to Taiwan where it was dismantled and sold. Neptune Jade stands as a significant event in the struggle of the dock workers and has become a model of their international solidarity... A symbolic connection between workers in Liverpool and Taiwan was created, echoing the dockers' phrase 'The world is our picket line'.' ~ Chen Chieh-Jen\**

The 1996 *Medway Ports Handbook* made extensive reference to Thamesport, and in its *Overview* section, the General Manager emphasised that a significant increase in commercial traffic had brought: 'more responsibility for the company's role as port authority... with a rise in vessel calls at Medway and Thamesport which had put an extra workload on the Medway pilots.' It is important to note here that the *Containers* section of the document was entirely concerned with Thamesport, and in particular the Hapag-Lloyd service. It confirmed that the *M.V. Neptune Jade* was a legitimate target for the worldwide solidarity action being taken on behalf of the Liverpool dockers. [1] On 18 November 1997, the dockers wrote again to Brian McWilliams, President of the ILWU, who had been supporting the Liverpool dockers since September 1995. Brian McWilliams originally supported Jack Heyman against the ITF when they objected to him going to the first international conference called by the Liverpool dockers. Without his backing it would have been difficult to win the ILWU's international solidarity that meant so much to the global campaign for the Liverpool dockers re-instatement. The letter from the Liverpool dockers reiterated how they had initially found themselves *locked out* after being confronted by a picket line of young dockworkers. Many of them their own sons, putting them in the position of having to decide whether or not to cross. The letter acknowledged the fact that each man knew the risks involved when:

---

\* Chen Chieh-Jen, Liverpool Biennial (2006). Available:
https://www.biennial.com/2006/exhibition/artists/chen-chieh-jen

*'Almost all of us made the decision to stand up for the principles handed down to us and renewed throughout our own working lives …we are now part of a worldwide movement against the casualisation and deregulation of our industry. Without this international movement, we cannot survive.' [2]*

The letter recognised that through the picketing of the *Neptune Jade*, they would be able to damage one of the key shipping lines keeping MDHC in business. By respecting the Liverpool picket lines, ILWU members would be upholding the industrial principles that all dockers shared, whilst at the same time challenging the US judicial system to drop charges against picket-captain Robert Irminger. [3] Writing in the November 1997 edition of the *ILWU Dispatcher*, Steve Stallone and Tom Price reported that ILWU Local 10 were to describe the subsequent repercussions following the boycott of the *Neptune Jade* as being no different than a retrial of the McCarthyite era. [4]

*'The authorities wanted US West Coast longshoremen to identify the person or persons who first communicated to them the idea of holding a demonstration at a North California port with any connections to dockworkers in Liverpool, along with the person who first communicated the idea of holding a demonstration over the cargo, or any portion thereof, on the vessel Neptune Jade. Every person who was a member of, or in any way affiliated with, the Committee for Victory to the Liverpool Dockers had to be named, along with every person who assisted in preparing or distributing any handbill that was distributed at Yusen Terminals.' [5]*

This was a very serious situation for the US dockers, workers and community activists who had been supporting the Liverpool dockers. On the 18 November, Robert Irminger, the Port of Oakland picket captain, was tried on a charge of contempt of court, after the employers had obtained an injunction limiting the number of pickets, only for an even larger group to turn up for the ongoing leafleting sessions, which continued to persuade truckers and ILWU longshoremen not to cross the picket lines. Although freedom of speech is enshrined in the US Constitution, the judge was considering her verdict, suggesting that Irminger could have been jailed. Additionally, lawyers hired by the dock and shipping industries were also seeking damages running into the millions, all while putting Irminger and Jack Heyman, an ILWU Local 10 executive member, through a special interrogatory routine. The Labour Studies Group at Oakland's Laney College was also being sued, amid demands that its co-ordinator, Albert Lannon, supply membership lists, minutes of meetings and names of everyone he knew who attended any of the demonstrations. [6] Perhaps the most important aspect of the *Neptune Jade* picket was that it saw co-ordinated action across three countries: the US, Canada and Japan. Having found nowhere to unload the ship on the US West Coast, the shipowners decided to sail to Vancouver, where she was met by another picket, and then, much to their surprise, they found themselves to be similarly unwelcome in Yokohama. It was only once the ship reached the non-unionised port of Kaohsiung, Taiwan that she was finally worked, but not before the Liverpool dockers' website had been inundated with a thousand hits from shipowners and maritime companies around the globe, clearly concerned about the potential of this newfound workers' internationalism. [7]

The employers' response to this campaign reflected the legal constraints used to nullify the UK trade union movement, as US longshoremen were charged with violating the Taft-Hartley Act, which outlawed sympathy strikes. Eventually, charges brought by the Pacific Maritime Association (PMA) were dropped against everyone except Robert Irminger. In support of Irminger the ILWU's rank-and-file activists organised a rally that shut down the Port of Oakland for four hours. Steve Stallone, who played a key role in co-ordinating the *Neptune Jade* boycott, then came up with the idea of storing all relevant documents demanded by the PMA in the offices of the *ILWU Dispatcher*, and citing freedom of the press as grounds for refusing to turn them over. [8] Robert Remar, the ILWU's lead attorney, viewed the *Neptune Jade* case as significant in that it set a precedent for such actions to be defended in court, serving as the model for union members in Long Beach to follow during a 1998 solidarity strike for Australian wharfies. In another major article in the ILWU's newspaper, *ILWU Wins Another Round in the Neptune Jade Case*, Steve Stallone described how the union had been successful in opposing the PMA's attempts at forcing them to turn informant on supporters of the Liverpool dockers, following an Alameda County Superior Court judge's ruling that the PMA could not subpoena any documents the union held concerning the planning and organising of the events that took place in September 1997. [9]

These documents were to remain in the possession of the *ILWU Dispatcher*. [10] Raymond Lynch, representing the PMA, petitioned the court to release the evidence in order that his client could identify all participants in the demonstrations, particularly the leaders, labelling the *Dispatcher's* claim of journalistic privilege a sham because it was not a public newspaper, and positing that such a ruling, 'opens journalistic privilege into a wide superhighway.' [11] Another ILWU attorney, An Le, responded by citing a US Supreme Court decision in favour of the principle that a journalist's confidentiality must be protected, or else reporters would be measurably deterred from publishing sensitive information, 'all to the detriment of the free flow of information protected by the First Amendment.' [12] Le also pointed out the absurdity of the PMA's position by simply pointing out that Jerry Brown, the Oakland Mayor-elect, had visited the picket line and made various public statements on its purpose without any attempt being made to subpoena him. [13] Following the hearing, Brian McWilliams addressed supporters who had packed the courtroom: 'It's nice the PMA realised [that] the Dispatcher is not the New York Times or the Wall Street Journal; those papers would never tell working people's stories. They are driven by their advertisers and business interests. If anyone's journalistic integrity and privilege should be questioned, it's theirs.' [14]

The PMA also took the ILWU to federal court on 11 August 1997, one day before the hearing on the document subpoena; it was clear that the PMA still intended to prosecute Robert Irminger and Jack Heyman. [15] At a hearing on 10 March, Alameda County Superior Court's Judge, Henry Needham Jr, had thrown out complaints against both Heyman and the Labour Party, citing First Amendment rights to free speech and assembly, but he did allow the PMA to continue pursuing Irminger as part of its ongoing quest to find someone to hold responsible for its losses. The Pacific Maritime Association subpoenaed all documents possessed by the ILWU Local branches 10 and 34 that, 'related or referred to the action supporting the Liverpool dockers.' [16] Meanwhile, ahead of the 1998 Bay Area Guinness Fleadh, Alice Nutter of the band Chumbawamba told Steve Zeltzer why they supported the Liverpool dockers, explaining the meaning behind their song, *Timebomb*, based on the *Neptune Jade* incident and dedicated to the defendants in the subsequent court cases:

> '...*everything that's happening at the moment is completely global. It's not just individuals being attacked. The reason they're attacking unions and trying to outlaw them and outlaw picketing is because they want to reduce everybody to the same low economic level. They want everybody to accept slave wages, and they can't do it until they knock the unions out... You know, the Liverpool dockers gave us an enormous surge in terms of how much effort they put in and how much work they put in. You thought, "Well, I should be doing something as well." You know that we got stuff out of the dockers' struggle as well.'* [17]

It would not be until November 1998 that all actions against the *Neptune Jade* pickets were dropped by the Pacific Maritime Association, some nine months after the conclusion of the Liverpool docks dispute, with Jack Heyman saying at the time:

> '...*the lesson that we have taken to heart from Liverpool's struggle is that by organising, international maritime workers can defend themselves against attacks of the global shipowners. The Neptune Jade victory is a shining example of that.'* [18]

As part of the settlement brokered by Brian McWilliams, Heyman agreed to drop his countersuit against the PMA. The occasion was marked by a victory party held on 4 December 1998, followed by a Billy Bragg concert at San Francisco's Maritime Hall the following evening, with all proceeds going to the Liverpool dockers and their families. [19]

# 78

# The TGWU's new
# London Office

*'Devastated. You know the day we took the vote, I feel as though we got sacked that day. Not two and a half years ago, actually that day, because in the last two and a half years, although you haven't been working, you've been in contact with your workmates. You've gone through the routine of getting up in the morning, going to the picket line once or twice a day; different times, like you're doing shifts sort of thing. Once that vote was taken, the picket line stopped and that was when it really hit you that your job has finished. Who to blame? You could go through a list of people, can't you, but I think if you was to put the result of the dispute in a nutshell, I think we finished up only a phone call away from winning it, and I think the phone call we waited two and a half years for never came, and the phone call was from Bill Morris to the ITF. He never had the guts to do it, and the Australians proved that it could be done, but he never had the guts or the balls for it.' ~ Mick Kilcullen\**

The London Support Group were busy organising a benefit night to be held on Saturday 22 November at the London Irish Centre, featuring the Irish band *Folk in Hell*. In Liverpool, Peter Clee joined a team of Citizens Advice Bureau advisors in delivering around-the-clock assistance on matters of financial hardship to sacked dockers and their families, with Clee saying that he found it:

> *'Impossible, as an advice worker for 13 or 14 years, not to be moved by the dignity and commitment of the men and women in this dispute. It's really hard not to be touched, because they understood totally the consequences of what they were involved in, and there were people who would have lost their homes if the dispute continued. We may see the first repossessions around or just after Christmas.' [1]*

---

\* Mick Kilcullen, interviewed by Greg Dropkin (17 February 1998)

On Friday 21 November, the weekly mass meeting heard the usual reports and plans for future pickets, occupations, demonstrations and delegations, but the lobbying of the union's next General Executive Council meeting in London was the key talking point. With a third winter on the way, food and clothing donations had started to arrive at Transport House, and Kevin Bilsborrow was put in charge of taking receipt and organising aid packages, along with the Women of the Waterfront. On Tuesday 25 November, Mike Carden attended a meeting in London with Mark Steel, Ken Loach, John Pilger, Paul Foot and Rob Newman. Carden would later reflect on how fortunate he felt to be representing the dockers in the company of such influential and gifted comrades, especially the open and frank discussion that could easily have taken place in the Elm House pub in Liverpool. The conversation focussed on the practical needs of the struggling dockers, and the following day, news came through that Jeremy Corbyn, Paul Foot, John Pilger, Mark Steel and Rob Newman had combined to donate £10,000 to the Dockers' Hardship Fund.

Dockers who had applied for severance had still not received a penny from the Dock Company, nor were they being paid out of the Hardship Fund having been judged no longer part of the dispute. It had recently come to light that a number of those who had left the dispute some time ago had since found work, with rumours circulating that some of them were attending picket lines for an hour or so – just long enough to claim their Hardship Fund money – on their way to their new jobs. [2] Regardless of the distrust and division that seemed to be building by the day, the stewards' priority was how to maintain some measure of organisational discipline ahead of the GEC.

At the mass meeting that week, Mark Steel injected some sharp political humour and much-needed laughter at a time when the men were becoming increasingly despondent. [3] On Sunday 30 November, a London meeting of the GEC's Broad Left agreed to oppose any effort by Bill Morris to collapse the docks dispute, while in Liverpool a leaflet was drawn up to explain why the dockers and their supporters were picketing the GEC. The demonstration would start on Monday 1 December at Palace Street, the TGWU's new temporary headquarters following the sale of the historic Smith Square building. Delegates arriving at Palace Street were greeted by a peaceful crowd of more than 70 dockers, most of whom had been there since 5.30am after travelling overnight, alongside members of the Graphical, Print and Media Union, as well as various supporters from Cardiff and London. The demonstrators carried placards reading: 'Democracy Is Not Disloyalty,' 'Strategy for Recruitment? Support the Membership!' 'Fabric of the Union Is Secure; the Dockers Are Not' and 'Instruct the ITF to Boycott Liverpool.' When Morris arrived in his chauffeur-driven Jaguar, he entered the building through the back entrance, missing his chance to receive a leaflet stating:

> '...after two years and three months of struggle by the dockers and their supporters, failed. A new strategy has to be implemented by the GEC that recognises that Mersey Docks will only negotiate under pressure from the whole of the labour movement.' [4]

A second leaflet was also distributed, featuring what were referred to as 'model resolutions' to be adopted by TGWU branches and other trade unionists. These had previously been sent to all dockers' Support Groups and TGWU members on the 10 November 1997, making the case that the GEC should reject calls to impose specific decisions upon the future of the dispute. It was considered vital that every TGWU branch sent resolutions directly to the GEC, citing Rule 10 (e) in calling on the union to recognise the fact that 70% of balloted dockers rejected MDHC's latest offer, and to implement the Biennial Delegates Conference's policy on seeking direct government intervention in the docks dispute, in addition to instructing the ITF to endorse boycotts of shipping lines trading in the ports of Liverpool and Medway. [5] This leaflet revisited the theme of the dispute having been incorrectly labelled an 'illegal strike', while arguing that MDHC's economic base needed to be undermined before the employer would pursue a negotiated settlement in good faith. The dockers also wanted the GEC to consider International Labour Organisation conventions relating to freedom of association and the rights of trade union members locked in dispute, asking for a united front comprising of the TGWU, the ITF, the Trades Union Congress and the New Labour government. [6] As the day wore on, the dockers received word that Bill Morris had moved all of his files in his office to the Buckingham Palace Hotel, for fear that the TGWU would be occupied by its own members. [7]

As the Executive session began, a majority of GEC members were expected to back a key motion from Region 3 (Ireland) on the Liverpool dockers. According to advance documents received by GEC members, Morris had already decreed that branch resolutions were not going to be heard, although he did agree to meet a delegation of dockers. The dispute was on the agenda for the general secretary's report at 2pm, but it took two hours for the discussion *to roll around to it,* and even then, Andy Smith, the meeting's chair and president of the TGWU, ruled immediately that the remit from Region 3 was, 'outside the rules of the union (Rule 2, Clause 3), following legal advice that the remit would result in a legal challenge.' [8] He also announced that there would be no debate on the relevant motions, ignoring numerous resolutions demanding that the union fight the dispute as though it wanted to win. Region 3 had unanimously agreed to forward a motion calling for, 'the General Executive Council to immediately invoke the unqualified support of the International Transport Workers' Federation in support of our sacked Liverpool dockers,' [9] with John Freeman, the Irish regional secretary, having personally written to Bill Morris on 27 October. Region 6 (North West) forwarded a motion, passed unanimously on 21 October, following the TGWU/MDHC unilaterally imposed ballot, which condemned Morris for: 'having clearly failed to obtain the authority of the General Executive Council to do this.' [10]

These motions were passed just one month after the GEC had agreed that no action concerning the dispute would be taken by either the General Secretary or the Finance and General Purposes Committee without their express authority. The dockers' 70% rejection of MDHC's offer had allowed them to hope that the TGWU leadership would respect their democratic decision to continue the struggle, only for Morris to declare again that no motions on the docks dispute would be debated. Instead, he presented five pages of legal advice supporting the claim that discussing the motions would place the union in breach of employment legislation that had been introduced by the Conservatives and kept intact by the Labour government. GEC members Colin Beresford, Dave Irvine, Barry Miller and Ken Brindle all voiced their support for the dockers, describing the union's failure to deliver solidarity action as a 'disgrace'.

During the British Airways dispute, the ITF had responded to a TGWU request for industrial action by its affiliates. When BA threatened to attack the ITF through the UK courts, the organisation indicated that it would respond by moving its headquarters to Dublin, at which point BA dropped the case. However, with the TGWU refusing to act, Carden wondered, 'how can we ask the ITF to fight our battles for us?' [11] This only prompted Morris to demand that Andy Smith confirm the agenda set by himself and his administration officer, Ray Collins. Smith dutifully complied, angrily stating that: 'This is my ruling, and no debate will be allowed,' [12] before adding that in the case of: 'solidarity actions of the ITF or unions internationally, any call for secondary action is potentially illegal.' [13] At this GEC Morris appeared to be reading from a sheet of detailed scripted notes. Once Smith had finished, Danny Maher, the Docks and Waterways representative, implored his fellow GEC members to vote in support of the Liverpool dockers, with Brindle, Miller, Irvine and Colin Coughlin all joining him in challenging the chair. Carden denounced the leadership's wilful suppression of open debate as:

> 'An absolute disgrace, and pure bureaucratic arrogance. Why don't you rule on BDC resolutions that were carried in favour of the Liverpool dockers? The union is using the position of the chair of the GEC to undermine supporters of the Liverpool dockers on the GEC, who would need a clear two-thirds majority under rule to reject or defeat his ruling.' [14]

Upon seeing some of his staunchest supporters begin to question his wish to strangle discussion of the Liverpool docks dispute, Morris realised that his policies were now facing rejection by the GEC, and therefore, speaking as though he was an observer, a cog in a machine rather than the General Secretary of the country's largest trade union, he repeated that his: 'responsibility is to uphold the constitution,' before asking: 'How did these resolutions get through the system out of rule?' [15] A vote on Smith's ruling was taken, with only seven GEC members backing Carden's challenge, and both Morris and Ray Collins made no effort to hide their sense of relief. [16] Other resolutions relating to the Liverpool docks dispute would be brought before the GEC that day, from various branches up and down the UK and Ireland, but Smith refused to accept any of them and at 5.15pm, Morris began his report on the Liverpool situation, referring to a request for Jack Adams and Graham Stevenson to meet the dockers. Morris claimed that no consensus was reached at this meeting, however and, as the dockers refused to budge on their demand for full reinstatement, he took the decision:

> '...to go to ballot, as I did in February 1996. I knew this decision would be unpopular, and I wrote to every member of the GEC. The dockers had rejected the offer, but the company kept the offer open; but the reality is where is our policy at BDC? As key elements of our position were enshrined in that GEC statement, where next?' [17]

Adams then repeated much of what Morris had said, before Stevenson talked about KPMG's feasibility study into the proposed dockers' labour co-operative, which he claimed Jimmy Nolan had rejected. This was untrue. Stevenson then shared the news that: 'Sixty-two Liverpool dockers left the dispute today. Having signed their COT-3, they would be re-employed and applications will be made to their pension fund.' [18] In other words, the dispute was collapsing. Stevenson went on to say that he: 'spoke to the company on Thursday, and no further negotiations will take place. The stewards have misjudged the situation; they have grown to feel that there is no such thing as a final offer. This is the real world, and we want to move forward with the other 800 TGWU members on the docks in Liverpool.' [19] He then added that MDHC's financial position and share price had been unaffected by the dispute and he dismissed the dockers' internationalism by claiming that the Liverpool campaign consisted of unions taking action over their own issues without hurting MDHC. [20] Stevenson had initially been seen as a *breath of fresh air* by some dock shop stewards when he first became involved in their dispute, but the more he spoke in support of his general secretary's position, the staler the air around him became. [21] Pleased with how the tide had turned in his favour, Morris then spoke of not wanting to raise 'false hopes about the dockers mounting one last push', [22] before producing a writ for £181,000 in damages on behalf of a number of Liverpool dockers, concerning incorrect advice provided by their union:

> *'We have been elected to protect the fabric of the union; the ability of this union to function. More time and effort have been spent on this dispute than any other, and the union is imploding upon itself. At the BDC, I challenged the chairman. These resolutions should not have got past first base. Why is it necessary for the general secretary to send out a bulletin? Pilger attacked this union, and McGovern viciously attacked our union. Remits on the internet and further attacks on the union were made by Carden and Teague. We have got to get a grip on this alternative structure being built by the dockers. No element of compromise exists. At one time, we could have achieved victory.' [23]*

As Morris talked, one could just about discern the shadow of the Tolpuddle Martyrs out in the cold grey mists of labour history, quitting their hidden assemblies for fear that someone would decide to sequestrate the tree where they once convened their meetings. By the time Bill Morris had finished speaking, it was 8pm. The overwhelming view among the GEC, most of whom had never supported the Liverpool dockers, was that the dispute had now finished. Meanwhile, on BBC Radio Merseyside, Roger Philips was devoting an hour of his show to the scabs working in the Port of Liverpool, whilst describing how well MDHC was now performing. [24] Before leaving the TGWU's Palace Street offices, Mike Carden had an emotional conversation with Jack Adams, with the Liverpool steward requesting support in seeking a dignified conclusion to the dispute.

The following day, Carden gave his feedback to the stewards, telling his fellow dockers that he saw no reason why they could not force a change in GEC policy, as they had done with the BDC in July. The reality was that they had failed, and this became clear as he worked through a report that began with Sunday's Broad Left meeting, where support for challenging the GEC's position was not forthcoming. The union was dismantling the dispute giving legal advice to the dockers who wished to accept MDHC's severance payment. Stevenson was now confident enough to ditch the dockers by claiming that the stewards were no longer operating in the 'real world.' [25] The National Docks officer had also dismissed the dockers' international campaign by playing down the ITF's influence on the basis that, 'the American West Coast does not trade with Liverpool as with other ports.' [26] When Ray Collins had entered into the debate, Carden questioned the chair as to why an unelected official was allowed to address the GEC, only for Andy Smith to again rule him out of order. When he mentioned the need to involve Ian McCartney MP, Morris interrupted, stating that McCartney was, 'only a junior minister,' and that meeting with him would be, 'a waste of time.' [27] Morris also stated that John Hendy QC's legal advice, 'will not be used at all,' [28] at which point Carden concluded his report by admitting his belief that, 'the dispute is over. The GEC has ended it, but we should end this with dignity. This task should not be left to the union and the MDHC.' [29]

There were some stewards who considered the outcome of the GEC as another setback, with Jimmy Nolan declaring: 'We need to meet Ian McCartney MP and ACAS. We need to take legal advice,' [30] Bobby Morton referred to: 'business as usual. It is defeatist and negative to say that the dispute is over.' [31] Jimmy Davies was deeply concerned at the news that some 62 dockers had reportedly signed COT-3 forms, but Morton said that Dave McCall, the Regional secretary, had told him that none of the men had asked the union for advice on claiming severance, before suggesting that, 'We must sit tight for this week.' [32] Nolan then made the argument that, 'Positive things have come from the GEC, such as the meeting with McCartney, Beckett and Prescott,' [33] but many of the other stewards did not – or rather could not – share their optimism. It was now obvious that as far as the TGWU was concerned, the Liverpool dockers were on their own. At 12.45pm, Greg Dropkin walked into the room to inform the stewards that Morris had just issued a four-page letter to other unions, officially dropping the Liverpool docks dispute. [34]

At the weekly mass meeting held Friday 5 December, an official union delegation of 27 Japanese dock and railway workers cheered as the Liverpool dockers vowed to fight on, with or without the support of the TGWU. That week, the venerable Nakazato Chujin, a 71-year-old representative of the Central Joint Committee in Support of Railway Workers' Struggle, entered MDHC's headquarters to discuss a matter of great concern, following his attendance at a picket demonstration where, by pure chance, seven vans filled with Operational Support Division officers arrived at the same time as the Japanese trade unionists at the Seaforth gates, leading to whatever plans the OSD had being immediately revised.

Over coffee and biscuits, Eric Leatherbarrow, MDHC's press officer, explained to the Japanese union leader that the picket line was illegal because the TGWU had now approved settlement terms, before claiming that the recent ballot rejection was a result of voter intimidation, which meant that any lingering issues were not the company's concern. After listening politely until Leatherbarrow had finished, Nakazato then told him that he represented 1.5m workers, and that there was great support for the sacked Liverpool dockers in Japan. [35] When he returned to the picket line, Nakazato said to the dockers, 'Mersey Docks let us in because your struggle is affecting them through international support. Have confidence and keep fighting,' [36] a sentiment shared by the All Japan Dock Workers' Union (Zenkowan) Vice President, Mizukami Kenji, who at the mass meeting described how, 'Globalisation and deregulation mean that dockworkers must unite all over the world and act with fighting solidarity!' [37] The Japanese delegation also met with the mayor of Liverpool, warning her that economic growth depended on resolving the dispute fairly, and asking the City Council to use its influence to put pressure on the Dock Company.

# 79
# And in the End

*'I think after the two-year milestone had been passed, people then couldn't see an end to it, and they visualised themselves here in another 12 months' time; and they visualised situations where some fellas were saying, "Well, once it goes past a certain date, I'm away. I'm gonna, you know..." So, two things. The stewards kept us together during those — well, the two and a half years really, they kept us together, and the resilience of the men, and it's very admirable to think that a body of men can sort of stick out for that long. Admittedly, the support from the people, you know, around the world and the country was amazing.' ~ Brian Dooley\**

As the stewards' meeting came to an end, on Wednesday 3 December 1997, they had reached an understanding on the need for some level of secrecy that went against what the majority of them believed. They had always valued the need for openness and transparency in their struggle but confidentiality was now an absolute necessity, as they would still need to negotiate terms with both the Dock Company and the TGWU. [1] To all intents and purposes, the dispute continued. At this point, the aim was to keep the Liverpool dockers united until a dignified settlement could be reached, and meetings with Joe Benton MP and Jack Adams were arranged in the hope that they would act as honest brokers during talks between the dockers, the union and the employer. An increasing number of stewards had already come to accept that the dispute had ended. [2]

On Monday 8 December, the stewards met again to discuss the difficult task of continuing the struggle until a deal was officially made, [3] in the hope that they would not lose more men and see the campaign collapse beneath them altogether. [4] Solidarity remained key to achieving the best possible outcome, with Jimmy Davies telling his fellow stewards: 'It has to be a cash settlement for everyone,' and that, 'Jack Adams is the only one we can trust.' [5] Financially, the dockers were in worse shape than ever, and the stewards feared that they would no longer be able to make subsistence payments as there was barely anything left in the Hardship Fund. Bob Ritchie, a former Torside shop steward, said at the

---

\* Brian Dooley, in an interview with Greg Dropkin (9 February 1998)

time, 'We must be prepared to reach a settlement for everybody. A jobs package is not a necessity for Torside,' [6] while Bobby Morton did not entirely agree with the narrative that the stewards were ending the dispute, preferring to phrase it as, 'we can't win it.' [7] Kevin Robinson spoke of the need for the stewards, 'to be disciplined, everything gets out, the men are weary, and we need to explain this to Adams.' [8] Herbie Hollerhead felt optimistic about their chances of gaining both 'jobs and a financial settlement.' [9] For Terry Southers, the most important issue was that: 'with so much debt among the dockers, a financial settlement is necessary to settle these debts.' [10] Jimmy Nolan was reluctant to accept talk of a settlement, instead arguing that: 'we need to use Jack Adams and Parliament to seek any conclusion.' [11]

On Tuesday 9 December, Jack Adams arrived in Liverpool to discuss recent developments with the shop stewards. He was clearly moved by the fact that the *dispute was stumbling towards an end* as Jimmy Nolan began the meeting by telling him that they were: 'seeking a financial settlement for all concerned. Employment may be sought for Torside and Nelson Freight if possible.' [12] To date, some 64 dockers had applied for severance, and while Nolan explained that the stewards did not oppose this, he did talk at length about the pension issues for those dockworkers over the age of 50, whose pension rights were not guaranteed, and would thus require additional funding separate from the redundancy payoff. [13] In reality, the dispute was still ongoing, so approaches continued to be made to Ian McCartney MP, demanding that he pursue a public inquiry into MDHC whilst Joe Benton MP confirmed that he would be meeting with MDHC directors that coming Friday. He did express the view that McCartney would not be able to influence events on the dockers' behalf because: 'others on the frontbench of the Labour government, as with the leaders of the TGWU, have no enthusiasm for involvement other than to urge a settlement.' [14] For their part, MDHC bosses were not prepared to negotiate outside of their previous offer, with Adams saying that he would: 'explore all opportunities, but it will be difficult. Getting the original offer back on the table will be a grovelling job, [and] Torside will not enter into the equation. I have always said that pensions are not guaranteed until finalised by the trustees.' [15] Adams then implored the stewards not to allow MDHC to: 'collapse the dispute; that would be a tragedy. McCartney will say go to ACAS, but this formal approach may lead to Margaret Beckett's involvement at the DTI.' [16] Nolan revealed that Benton had written to Prime Minister Tony Blair about the Liverpool dockers' situation, but Adams stated plainly that he did not see, 'any beams of light. We don't want it to crumble after the way you have run this dispute.' [17]

When MPs Joe Benton and Maria Eagle met with MDHC directors Trevor Furlong and Peter Jones on Friday 12 December, they made a last-ditch attempt at resolving the matter of pensions, past service and an increase in severance pay, only for the bosses to insist that it was up to the pension fund trustees to protect pension rights, as they claimed: 'the stewards have given the wrong advice on the two-year absence from making pension contributions, and in no way would we look at this. The present offer is not even budgeted for.' [18] In effect, they were washing their hands of the dispute completely, [19] but the fact remained that guarantees on pension rights had been documented in a TGWU press statement on 18 October 1997, as well as in MDHC's well-publicised final offer, and Benton was both concerned and disgusted by the attitude of Furlong and Jones, who were flagrantly provocative in making a settlement very difficult, if not impossible. [20] Meanwhile, at the opposite end of the spectrum, working-class Turkish and Kurdish comrades arrived at Transport House in Liverpool on Wednesday 17 December, with parcels of food that they had collected for the dockers and their families. Once again, the author Irvine Welsh, intervened on behalf of the dockers expressing his dismay over the media blackout of the dockers' struggle. [21] By now, it was becoming increasingly difficult for the stewards to hide the fact that they were actively seeking an end to their conflict; in reality they could not simply end the dispute themselves without some form of negotiated settlement. Chris Knight of the London Dockers' Support Group later recalled how:

*When I arrived in Liverpool, I took the presents to a room at Transport House... The following day, I was introduced to the docker who got the bike for his grandchild; he was "made up," as they say in Liverpool! I met Kim Hendry from the LDSG whilst there, and both of us stayed at Mike Carden's place. We spent a night in the Lord Warden pub with some dockers and WOW, having a laugh and doing the karaoke. Although we had a laugh as usual, something felt different; there seemed to be an atmosphere between some of the men. My comrade Kevin Hargreaves later told me, 'They're preparing for defeat.'* [22]

At the weekly mass meeting held on Friday 19 December, the theme was very much *business as usual*, with negotiations still taking place at various levels. That morning, the pickets had been out at 6am, and it was reported that Carlton TV was speaking with dockers Marty Size and Billy Barrett about filming a documentary on the dispute. The message to all speakers was to keep it brief, as Jimmy Davies touched on delegation trips and the extraordinary recent donations, which included new clothes, fruit baskets and even Christmas turkeys. There was also a huge Hardship Fund donation from TGWU Branch 6/541 (Road Haulage Section), led by Tommy Kirwin and Tony Woodhouse. Guest speaker Dave Williams, also of 6/541, talked about the two Henry Forsyth drivers who had not worked for two years after refusing to cross the Liverpool dockers' picket lines in September 1995. Mike Williams, representing the New Zealand Seafarers, donated a further £10,000, despite the fact that dockers in both his own country and nearby Australia were under attack from the port bosses. AC Delco's Steve Donnelly and Sumi from the Japan Railway Workers' Union were also on hand to address the men, along with a *Newsline* journalist who had been following the dispute from the start. [23] The union made a substantial Hardship Fund contribution compensating for months of non-payment, although it was still a drop in the ocean compared to what the dockers would have received had they been put on official strike or dispute pay. The meeting passed without reference to the attempts, in the background, to negotiate a conclusion to the dockers' struggle. No one on the platform that day was comfortable with this situation. On Sunday 28 December, the Dispute Committee was informed that sacked docker Billy Rooney had died in hospital, during a week that also saw the passing of Terry Southers's brother. The atmosphere among the dockers fell to an all-time low. It had become clear that the Dock Company had no intention of keeping their promises in regard to the pension rights of the 67 dockers who had applied for severance.

The TGWU appointed Lyn Gibson as their legal advisor as they launched into a series of industrial tribunal cases. As far as they were concerned the dispute was over. And it was now the union's job to collapse the dispute by encouraging as many dockers as possible to apply for whatever severance payment they could negotiate. At the same time, many dockers were absenting themselves from the picket lines and mass meetings. After more than two years, the TGWU was finally becoming an active player in the Liverpool docks dispute, going so far as to ask Fr Michael, the Hardship Fund trustee, the 'dockers' banker,' for information on how donations were being spent. [24] Elsewhere, on Tuesday 30 December, staff at Transport House Liverpool opened the building to allow the stewards to meet and discuss the 40 industrial tribunal claims that had now been filed by union-appointed solicitors, as the action moved from cold, harsh picket lines to plush offices and boardrooms. It was this abandoning of the visible side of the campaign, most notably the absence of many Torside dockers, that led Tony Nelson, as picket captain, to speak openly about: 'the need to recognise the end of the dispute.' [25] It was decided that a meeting involving John Hendy QC, Ian McCartney MP and the Advisory, Conciliation and Arbitration Service would be the best way to bring the dispute to a negotiated conclusion. Unfortunately, such a meeting never materialised, and because the stewards had no trust in their trade union, Jimmy Nolan and Mike Carden arranged to speak with Manchester barrister Stella Massey, who advised them not to be too hasty in finalising any industrial tribunal cases. [26] Jack Southers was buried on Friday 2 January 1998, and Billy Rooney's funeral took place on Wednesday 7, just days before the *Catholic Pictorial* ran an article titled, *Dockers' Hardship Fund Only Pays £15-a-Week*, [27] which opened with the statement that the dockers had recently faced:

> *Their third Christmas without settlement. Fr Michael de Felice, secretary of the Liverpool Dockers' Family Hardship Fund, described the situation as, 'winter-bleak. The more it goes on, the more bleak the situation becomes.'...Fr Michael praised the dockers' supporters for their continuing efforts.' [28]*

In the same article, Kevin Robinson was quoted as saying: 'Obviously, it's very hard and families are feeling it, but morale is still high, and people have been very kind with donations. The children have not gone short this Christmas.' [29] On Monday 5 January, Jack Adams told Jimmy Nolan that while he did not know when Ian McCartney, Labour's Minister for Employment, was due to meet ACAS, he was able to confirm that the TGWU had activated over 60 industrial tribunal cases, dismantling the dispute while men, women and children still stood on picket lines. On the international front, Terry Teague reported on a New York picket line organised by Jack Heyman and the US Labor Party, which was said to have more than 100 supporters, including Brian McWilliam, president of the International Longshore and Warehouse Union, as well as Canadian dockers in Vancouver and Montreal. Even at this late stage, these actions served the purpose of trying to persuade John Bowers, leader of the influential International Longshoremen's Association, to intervene directly in negotiations with MDHC. [30] By Thursday 8 January, Jack Dempsey, the local dock official, was busy organising industrial tribunals alongside TGWU solicitors. They were giving advice to dockers as if nothing had happened during the previous two years. With a £14,000 limit on any successful claims for unfair dismissal, this amounted to little more than an exercise in ridding the union and the employer of potentially costly injunctions against both the union and the company. This push by the union for industrial tribunals would free the Dock Company and the union of any further legal responsibility for their members and employees.

The Dock Company's share price had risen to £5 following the announcement of their Twelve Quays Project, which if nothing else provided another location for the dockers to picket. Later that day, the death of sacked docker Jimmy McCumisky was reported, causing further distress at the loss of yet another comrade. Bill Morris had written to all Trades Union Congress affiliates and union branches to confirm that he was now openly withdrawing from the Liverpool docks dispute. [31] It was now common knowledge that Morris wanted to pursue an inquiry into both Fr Michael's management of the Dockers' Hardship Fund and the accounts of 6/567 Branch. This Branch was well financed, but the reason for this was simply that it was a very active and organised branch, which not only collected union dues, but also branch dues; each member paid a monthly contribution, honouring a tradition that dated back to the 1970s. [32] Nothing came of these further attempts to discredit the dockers. On Wednesday 14 January, Jimmy McCumisky's funeral saw his daughter urge the Liverpool dockers to, 'keep on fighting', and at the Women of the Waterfront's weekly meeting held later that evening, it was announced that Dot Gibson's father had sadly passed away. In more positive news, young Neil Fox and his brother had decided to do a sponsored swim for the charity One to One. [33] Elsewhere, Terry Teague gave an interview to Greg Dropkin for *LabourNet*, to be published under the title, *The General Secretary's View and Ours*. Teague spoke about the January 1998 *TGWU Bulletin*, circulated among all branch secretaries, officers and staff, in which Morris stated:

> *The Executive considered the position of the Liverpool docks dispute in the light of much misplaced criticism in recent weeks. Our policy has always been to seek a negotiated settlement, to preserve the fabric of the union… Motions on this issue contrary to BDC policy and to rule were submitted. Regrettably, the chair's decision to rule these out of order was challenged by members of the council. However, the chair's ruling was overwhelmingly upheld.' [34]*

This remarkable rewriting of history by the union's general secretary ran contrary to the live recorded video of what actually took place at the conference. Morris wanted to ignore the decisions of his BDC he also was in denial in relation to the dockers' three rejections of the union/employer *final offer*. Tony Blair had once described the UK's industrial legislation as: 'the most oppressive in the Western world,' before promising that a Labour government would restore a level playing field for workers and employers alike. Terry Teague summarised the shift in mentality that would be required before the working people of Britain could hope to reverse the relentless march of corporate globalism:

> *'Sooner or later, if the trade union movement is not to die out, a lead must be given to show that workers in this country can still achieve better pay and conditions and can still have a say within their industry by directly challenging their employers. Taking action in support of our dispute would also challenge the legislation, and without such challenges I do not believe the laws will actually be repealed. If we can make a breakthrough and win*

*a victory, not only against the employer, but against the system which is so heavily loaded against trade unionists, this will benefit everyone who wants to stand up for themselves.'* [35]

# 80
# The End of the Liverpool Dock Dispute

*'It's just we feel there was such a wrong done by us, by the company, and that should be put right and that's why we stayed together for such a long time. We felt it's been such a bad injustice… when we never turned in on the Friday morning and we were all told we would be sacked, I was one of the 200 men who received another chance to go back to work, having another contract sent out to me on the Saturday morning, saying if I was to report into work by 12 noon on the Monday I would still have a job in the container terminal, but my principles and what I've been brought up as, you know me family, I could never go into a job and leave men outside them gates that I've worked with alongside for many many years, I just couldn't do it.' ~ George Johnston\**

On Thursday 15 January 1998, Frank Lannigan expressed his concern that for a settlement to be reached: 'The money has to be back on the table, together with guarantees on the men's pensions.' [1] The only union official they trusted was Jack Adams. Jimmy Nolan had spoken to Adams about the importance of him contacting the Dock Company directly before final negotiations could commence. Tony Nelson suggested that they ask Len McCluskey to speak to Adams on their behalf. By Monday 19 January, Adams had explained to Nolan that Peter Jones, MDHC's Port Operations Director, was going to be unavailable for a month and so he would instead be meeting with Trevor Furlong, the Dock Company's Chief Executive, with a view to having a package on the table by the end of the week.

On Friday 16 January, after another freezing-cold 6am picket, the dockers' weekly mass meeting opened with Jimmy Davies asking for a minute's silence to mark the passing of Jimmy McCumisky, before he again talked about the campaign having, 'gone on for far too

---

\* George Johnston, Liverpool Docker, interviewed by Bill Hunter. Available: http://www.billhunterweb.org.uk/interviews/History_as_Told.htm#George%20Johnston

long. We need to end it.' [2] Doreen McNally spoke on behalf of the Women of the Waterfront and guest speaker Jean-Pierre Barrois reaffirmed the support of the French unions. Julie Barnett from the Canadian Public Sector Union, who had looked after Val Bibby and Maria Eustace during their delegation, praised the Liverpool dockers for going: 'beyond this country to lead by example for all workers. The Women of the Waterfront were very impressive, and we need global links to fight back.' [3] It was also reported that Dave Temple had contacted the stewards about arranging another delegation to Bosnia. [4] Dave Cotterill gave feedback on Channel 4's production of a Jimmy McGovern play, as well as news regarding education courses and a book of photographs to be released by Dave Sinclair. Considering the growing pressure to bring the dispute to a close, morale at this meeting was surprisingly high. [5]

The following day, a meeting of Dockers' Support Groups took place, where Jimmy Nolan responded to MDHC's announcement that the dispute was over by calling for mass actions in both the UK and across Europe. [6] In attendance at the DSG meeting were Chris Knight, Greg Dropkin, Mariam Kamish, Peter Lawrence, Cath Bann, Linda Moulsdale, Paul and Audrey Smith, Caryn Mathews, Steve Higginson, Celia and Martin Ralph, Brian Ashton, Rod Finlayson, Jackie Vance, Arif Bektas, Robert Etchells, Julie Barnett, Glen Voris and Jim Dye; a total of 25 delegates. Steve Higginson, representing the Communications Workers Union, made a speech about: 'the need to achieve something locally in terms of action from other workers,' [7] but the most emotive contribution came from Mariam Kamish, who was clearly upset after a fourth docker had died before his time and she was scathing about TGWU officials attending a scab's funeral and Bill Morris's attempts at dismantling the dispute. [8] Elsewhere, another London demonstration was being organised for 11 April.

On Tuesday 20 January, the stewards' met to discuss the Jack Adams meeting and the latest Bill Morris circular, as they agreed to continue to act on the assumption that the dispute was far from over. It could not end without an agreed settlement with the Dock Company. The stewards did not have the option to surrender and, if they did, they would become the victims of whatever outcome the TGWU and the company manufactured. A mass picket was still planned for 6 February, followed by another Day of World Action on 1 May. Jimmy Nolan also wanted a demonstration in London on 17 April, where they would join with those who were being attacked by the Labour government, such as single parents and the disabled. In Liverpool, dockers were now being actively encouraged by the local TGWU to meet with the Advisory, Conciliation and Arbitration Service and sign COT-3 forms to effectively leave the dispute. Andy Dwyer stressed the need to: 'avoid ACAS and stick with Jack Adams and our own negotiating team.' [9]

Jimmy Davies and Frank Lannigan met with Adams on Wednesday 21 January, where they were informed that Morris had urged him to go over the heads of the Committee and tell the dockers directly that they had no choice but to accept whatever was offered. Trevor Furlong indicated that the cost of the settlement could not exceed £8m, the figure that had been quoted to MDHC shareholders. Thus, Adams needed to know if the stewards simply wanted the original offer to be put back on the table, as Furlong had made it clear that he did not trust them not to use these latest talks as a device to continue the dispute. Davies answered that Torside and the pension situation remained a sticking point, and Adams asked if it would be possible to organise a mass meeting on Tuesday 27 for him to address the men as one. At the next day's meeting the stewards heard that the original deal was no longer on the table, and that MDHC's board would need to meet before another offer could be made. [10] Jimmy Davies believed: 'more meetings would be needed before the men could accept that it is over. It needs to be an honourable ending.' [11] Carden agreed, stating: 'We asked Jack Adams to get involved, and he has, and we need some time. We will also have to look after our people when this dispute is over,' [12] making reference to employment, training, education support and advice. Terry Southers argued that: 'Morris has gone public saying the dispute is over, and there will be chaos at the final mass meeting. Some men want to go back into the docks.' [13] Tony Nelson backed the call to: 'take Adams's advice. If Morris and co. take-over, we're finished.' [14] By this time, Davies had spoken to Martin Hartrop, manager of the dockers' pension scheme, who said: 'the Dock Company are completely wrong to deduct pension money from men who have left; that's very vindictive.' [15]

A mass meeting was held on Thursday 22 January 1998 with all the dockers, the WOW and supporters. Jimmy Nolan briefly summarised the recent meetings with Jack Adams, and it was agreed that the dockers would reconvene once a definitive offer had been received. This came after Adams had spoken to Nolan and Jimmy Davies in private, to be followed by Nolan telling the rest of the stewards: 'everything has to be confidential; the men cannot be told. If we can commit ourselves to a recommendation, then we can settle it tomorrow. Morris is trying to do Adams in, and Furlong would do the same, so it's a very delicate situation.' [16] It was a very difficult position for the stewards as they could not consider ending the dispute without an agreed settlement as this would just leave the union and the Dock Company to carve-up whatever conclusion suited them. Adams was comfortable with the need for the stewards not to be declaring an end to the dispute without an agreement. 'But conditions have been placed upon him, and if the company finds out that any [aspect] of the offer has been leaked, it will be withdrawn.' [17] Jack Adams had contacted Chris Grice of ACAS to get talks going again. Furlong was prepared to meet Adams and McCall, but the employer and Bill Morris remained united in not trusting the stewards.

Morris stood in sharp contrast to his deputy, a former British Leyland shop steward who both understood and respected Nolan and Davies, two men with whom he shared strong bonds of past Communist Party membership. The respect was mutual, with the two being genuinely grateful to have a comrade on their side. [18] Adams was sincere in wanting to see the dispute end with dignity, having told Furlong how: 'The dockers will haunt you until they die if you do not reach a settlement.' [19] The remainder of the day was spent discussing whether or not money could be saved by not accepting the original 40 jobs that had been reluctantly offered in the past, as it had now been accepted that MDHC had restructured the docks to such an extent that: 'dockers will not work on the docks again, but if a labour supply was created, some men may wish to return or join a register for future work.' [20] The stewards were all resigned to the fact that they would never return to work on the docks, and after a lengthy, emotionally draining and at times stormy debate, Nolan asked them what their decision was.

It was 3.15pm, on Thursday 22 January 1998, over two years and four months since their conflict began. The shop stewards agreed to: 'accept full responsibility and recommend to a mass meeting on Monday 26 January to effectively end the dispute.' [2] Frank Lannigan and Mike Carden brought up the need to raise as much money as possible to solve the issue of Torside, Nelson Freight and the boatmen, to which Adams suggested that an appeal could be made to all TGWU branches. Terry Teague and Tony Nelson discussed the practicalities of building up a fund. [22] Adams asked the stewards if they wanted him to attend the mass meeting, and it was Davies who reminded him that: 'At the union's BDC, I told you that this dispute would not be sold out in Brighton. We will take responsibility for all our actions.' [23] Adams responded by praising the dockers as 'unique,' before telling a heart-breaking story about a car plant worker who hanged himself after seven weeks on strike. He told the stewards: 'You need to end it with dignity. These men deserve better.' [24] Nolan said that he wanted Adams to stand alongside him on the platform when he broke the news to the men, who he was confident would react with dignity. Finally, in his own extraordinary way, the leader of the Liverpool dockers evoked James Larkin as he told the stewards: 'You haven't lost, you've won,' [25] such was his belief that whenever workers stood united against employers, victory was theirs regardless of the outcome.

The following day, MDHC's offer stood at £28,000 severance. Torside, Nelson Freight and Excel dockers would be entitled to make a joint application to be included in this settlement, but the pension situation had yet to be clarified. The stewards estimated that in order to cover all workers involved in the dispute, a further £350,000 needed to be found. It was agreed that Carden and Frank Lannigan would contact Morris to find out if the TGWU could find a way to make up the difference and settle this dispute once and for all. Later that afternoon, Jack Adams confirmed that the latest figures were £28,000 plus £60,000 and 20 jobs for Torside, but only £2,000 for Nelson Freight. This left 69 Torside, Nelson Freight and Excel dockworkers needing to be assimilated into the deal before it could be considered acceptable, with Peter Jones set to meet Graham Stevenson, the TGWU's National Docks Official, in London the following Wednesday to address these outstanding issues. [26] The stewards understood their responsibility to bring a suitable proposal before the dockers and their families, [27] as discussions shifted to matters of future employment, fundraising for non-MDHC dockers not fully covered by any financial settlement and the securing of pension entitlements. It had already been suggested that they ask ex-MDHC dockers to donate something to help their Torside and Nelson Freight comrades as nothing ever came of their request for financial assistance from Bill Morris. Eventually, the mass meeting to break the news to the men was scheduled for the following Monday. It was agreed that only Nolan, Davies and Carden, would speak, at this closed meeting for the dockers and the WOW. There would be no admittance for supporters or members of the press. [28]

As the men gathered at Transport House on the morning of Monday 26 January, it was clear that they had some idea of what was about to come. Earlier that morning, Carden had spoken to Ray Collins, the TGWU administration officer, to ask again if the union were prepared to donate £350,000 required to construct a financial settlement for all Liverpool dockers. Collins wanted Jack Adams to confirm this request before taking it to Morris. [29] No payment was made. It had been well established that the Dispute Committee would prioritise confidentiality so as not to compromise any potential settlement, but there were fears that certain individuals would adopt a populIST position as a way *to out-militant the militants*. Kevin Bilsborrow witnessed this first-hand when he overheard one of this fellow stewards telling a docker how he was: 'not in favour of pulling the plug on the dispute.' [30]

# THE END OF THE LIVERPOOL DOCK DISPUTE

Jack Adams and Dave McCall arrived at Transport House following a meeting with MDHC's Trevor Furlong and Chris Grice of ACAS, where according to Adams:

> 'Furlong seemed nervous at attending the meeting, but ACAS was an escape mechanism if necessary. Furlong has agreed to put some of the offer back on the table, but he insisted it was not an offer; it was an agreement which upon acceptance today would cease all activity. Picketing would cease today, with all Tribunals subject to a COT-3 compromise agreement.' [31]

On the idea of a new labour supply company, Adams said Furlong was keen on this or other options because: 'he wants competition against Drakes,' [32] and there would be no problems with the pension fund, which MDHC controlled anyway. Ever cautious, Adams continually repeated Furlong's statement: 'this is not an offer; it is an agreement, and the restoration of the original offer of £28,000 severance, as opposed to the current offer of £25,000, is subject to agreement today.' [33] Mention was made of the need for MDHC to inform the City that a declared deficit of £8m would result from costs associated with ending the dispute, as Adams again emphasised the company's: 'need to change the accounts that have already been posted by the company with the City. These changes have to be notified by 18 February,' [34] adding that MDHC was expanding rapidly and had agreed a new contract with Jaguar. [35] Within an hour of the TGWU officials' arrival, they were joining the stewards on the platform as Jimmy Nolan opened the meeting and Jimmy Davies brought the dockers and the WOW up to date by explaining:

> 'The stewards cannot take the dispute any further. The GEC refuses to accept resolutions supporting the Liverpool dockers, and international support is dwindling. The dispute had been subjected to political exclusion by the Labour Party. Morris had sent out to all branches that the dispute is over and the MDHC are bleeding us dry; about 80 men have left.' [36]

Davies spoke with emotion when he recounted the deaths of four dockers, and when he told the men: 'we cannot carry on the dispute without the support of the union,' [37] the cry from the floor was, 'We never had the support of the union!' [38] Nolan then endorsed the right of individuals to voice their opinions at this meeting, before informing those present that he wanted to:

> 'Congratulate Jack Adams; he's been isolated by the union. If we could have met Ian McCartney MP, we could have proved that the Torside men were sacked by MDHC bosses. The government were also not prepared to use their 14% share in the MDHC. We understood the economic fear of the big organisations, but there was no excuse after two and a half years, but there were too many forces against us.' [39]

Chairman, Jimmy Nolan, went on to advise the dockers: 'if you think that the platform is wrong, that is your right, but it would be wrong on this occasion to reject the shop stewards' recommendation.' [40] He said what everyone in the hall was thinking when he told the dockers that the majority of them: 'won't be employed again in this city.' [41] He then outlined the key points of MDHC's offer, before Carden expressed his view:

> 'This is not a defeat. The turning point was the October ballot with a 70% rejection. Then, the dispute went into a tailspin. Some people in the union have helped us behind the scenes. This is not a defeat. You have nothing to be ashamed of. We have exhausted every avenue to defeat the Dock Company, and you have earned the respect of everyone. You have defended the principles of the trade union movement.' [42]

Jack Adams rose to address the men whom he had represented since September 1995, and he began by telling them that he was not there as an 'apologist,' before stating honestly that he had:

> 'Never run away from members; this is a ruthless employer. We could have got jobs at the beginning, but you won two magnificent ballot victories. The shop stewards asked to get the offer back on the table, but 70-odd dockers have now applied for a COT-3. I'm prepared to grovel up to 18 February [when MDHC would inform the City stock market of any eventual cost to the company following a settlement with their former employers], but I will go on if necessary. You have fought with flair and principle, but if we write if off today, where do we go?' [43]

Again, Adams talked about the difficulties of: 'grovelling to get the company to reinstate the package while they are being so vindictive.' [44] Liverpool docker, Eddie Ledden began by praising the stewards, but wanting their recommendation to be rejected.' [45] Micky Tighe argued that: 'We haven't exhausted all avenues, and the social justice rally in London will soon start a fightback against the government.' [46] Brian Dooley then talked about solidarity action across Europe, and a letter received from Jack Heyman: 'about going to prison. It doesn't look like the dispute is over. It's not over here in Liverpool.' [47] Mick Cullen acknowledged:

> 'It is easy to tell the meeting what they want to hear. We were defeated by the rank-and-file. The big battalions in this city have not supported us, but the internationalism has been fantastic. If the recommendation to accept the MDHC's offer is rejected, it will be a drip, drip effect of people leaving the dispute. We could be left with nothing. We took guidance from the shop stewards. Do you think they wanted to say it this morning?' [48]

Joe Ladd stated plainly: 'I am not a professional t-shirt seller or a militant shop steward. I am not going against the stewards, but I will vote against them.' [49] Jimmy Campbell asked: 'What will happen about Jack Dempsey?' [50] This was followed by Mick Thompson asking, 'Why have the vote today with no mention of Excel workers, and why isn't Graham Stevenson here?' [51] Tony Weedon also raised the case of the Excel dockers, to which Jimmy Nolan answered that they would be included alongside Torside and Nelson Freight as part of any settlement. Bobby Moss believed that the stewards should have waited until they had a firm agreement on pensions, [52] and Tony Gardiner made the case: 'We have people dying on the picket line, so if the recommendation is rejected, we need to be prepared to do a lot more.' [53] Ladd then spoke up again, asking if this was a unanimous decision among the stewards, [54] before attacks were launched against Jack Dempsey, with Jack Adams repeatedly asked what the TGWU intended to do about him. Adams admitted: 'Dempsey did not tell the Torside men that they had been reinstated.' [55] Frank Kenny asked: 'If the dispute is over, will the TGWU now recruit Drakes?' [56] Terry Barrett spoke of: 'tremendous pressure on the men today to vote,' [57] before Weedon asked Adams directly, 'What is your position on the Excel dockers' situation?' [58] Jimmy Nolan then took the opportunity to announce: 'If the recommendation is accepted today, the next mass meeting will be next Friday'. [59] Jimmy Davies requested that no one give statements to the press or television. Finally, at 1.45pm, the Dispute Committee's resolution was put to a vote and accepted by a majority, although a significant number of dockers, estimated to be around 80, voted against. [60]

At 2.15pm, Dave McCall telephoned Trevor Furlong to inform him of the outcome of the vote, and Jack Adams asked Graham Stevenson to arrange an urgent meeting between the trustees of the dockers' pension fund and MDHC's Peter Jones, while it would also be necessary to have ACAS organise the signing of COT-3 forms, which needed to be done before 5 February. As for the stewards, they were left with the unenviable task of letting their international comrades know about the decision, and later that same day, Jimmy Nolan sent out the following message to all of the supporters of the Liverpool dockers:

> 'At a mass meeting today, the Liverpool dockers decided to call an end to their long-running dispute on a recommendation from their shop stewards. The decision to end the dispute was taken after hearing about a number of very important and significant developments which made it more or less impossible to continue. We ask the comrades to appreciate the difficulty that confronts us at this stage, and to understand that all the relevant details of the final settlement will follow in due course. Thanks for all your magnificent and wonderful support.' [61]

In the United States, two days after the vote was cast, the Liverpool Dockers Victory Defence Committee made their response public: 'In a stunning, short statement issued Monday January 26 1998, Jim Nolan, chairman of the Merseyside Port Shop Stewards, notified longshore workers and supporters around the world that the Liverpool dockworkers decided to call an end to their long-running dispute.' [62] The article went on to report that after nearly two and a half years of waging a militant fight against not only MDHC, but also international shipping conglomerates, the UK government and even their own union leaders, the Liverpool dockers, perceiving dwindling national and international support, had decided to end their campaign for full reinstatement. [63] The California-based support group then made the argument that:

> 'Although our brothers in Liverpool have been defeated in a valiant effort through no fault of their own, they have awakened workers around the world and taught us all a critical lesson: united action through international labor solidarity is the only way to challenge the power of international capital. If we absorb this lesson, it will be a victory

*for the Liverpool dockers; their shining contribution to the international workers' struggle embellished forever in the pages of labor history. The Liverpool dockers concluded their January 28 letter to supporters by quoting the great Irish trade unionist, James Larkin: 'Who is it speaks of defeat? I tell you, a cause like ours is greater than defeat can know it. It is the power of powers.'' [64]*

Jimmy Nolan would later reflect: 'the political and economic structures of our society are utilised in the interest of multi-national corporations. The passing of political legislation, which oppresses the nation's people, bears witness to this fact. This type of legislation is in abundance. However, the legislation which oppresses the people, and in particular the labour and trade union movement, could be summarised as deregulation – trade union laws. What is obnoxious is that in the pretence of democracy, governments use our parliamentary system to oppress the majority of people,' adding that within this context he had, 'the positive conviction that the nation's people should revisit the legacy which previous generations passed to us. Over time, they recognised through struggle that changes within the political and economic framework must be made in the interest of all.' [65] On the evening of the stewards' recommendation being accepted, Roger Phillips's phone-in show on BBC Radio Merseyside was dominated by the dispute, with a sacked docker's wife explaining how her husband:

> *Worked all the shifts the Dock Company wanted, and his family never saw him from one week to the next. We had no social life, but that means nothing to the Dock Company; all the company wanted was to get them men out and get their scabs in... The stewards have left them high and dry, as they did in 1989, and the stewards are the ones to blame here, as well as everybody else. Nobody has backed us... The Port of Liverpool was the only port that did not pay their dockers off. A docker is a qualified man; you've got to know how to load a ship and how to unload a ship. It's a highly skilled and dangerous job, and they wanted to get union men out of the docks in 1989. Not one of those men will get their jobs back. Why suddenly call a meeting to end the strike? They must have known something.' [66]*

Roger Phillips made the argument that the dispute had started because MDHC: 'wanted to get rid of 40-50 men who they felt were not helping the Dock Company to move forward into the 21st century,' [67] only for another caller to inform Phillips that he remembered things differently:

> *Before the sacking match began, people were on to you saying they were getting harassed, coming off night work, going to bed, getting woken up within an hour to go back to work. They were issued with bleepers; people were being disciplined for not being at home when the phone rang. Every docker apparently was getting this...' [68]*

A Labour Party member then called in and said that he was:

'...not a rabid right-winger, but we have to live in the real world. The dispute began because the Dock Company wanted to get rid of some men, perhaps the ringleaders of this strike. I think those ringleaders knew exactly what this situation was, and I think they knew that when they chose to take the action, I think they knew what the law was; I think they knew what the attitude would be of the official trade union involved, and also the views of politicians who may otherwise have had some sympathy. My own feeling is that this is an example of the industrial relations of the past, and if Liverpool is to move forward, we have got to move forward with a modern-looking city moving into the 21st century. I am afraid this sort of activity that we have seen over the last two and a half years does no good to promote that whatsoever. Liverpool must forget and bury the language of class struggle... the leaders of that strike did know exactly what they were doing. Unfortunately, for people with certain political views, the great class struggle, the headlines on the extreme left-wing rags, are that all the lives of the people involved are nothing. It's exactly the same as Scargill and the miners all over again'. [69]*

Phillips insisted that he still remembered all the calls that he used to get on his programme: 'well before the dispute began about the way the dockers were treated, and the Dock Company were not treating them in a very nice fashion to say the least.' [70] The following night, his guest was Canon Nick Frayling, the rector of Liverpool, who described:

'...a deep sense of sadness that the struggle will be seen by many former dockers to have come to nothing. I don't see it like that. It had to come to an end, [and] the fact that they themselves and their leaders have initiated the end of it, I think, is a principled and dignified position. This struggle was perceived as a very real principled struggle by people, many of whose families have worked in the Port of Liverpool for many generations and have bitter memories of the bad old days of the pen and all the rest of it and have been desperate that such conditions shall not come again... There was a real principle behind this dispute.' [71]

Ken Loach was also interviewed. He had not yet spoken to the stewards, but he had:

'Enormous respect; their struggle gave hope to many people around the world, and they've made a mark which won't be lost. The employer and the government, as a shareholder in this company, has refused to acknowledge their basic trade union demand which they made, and they haven't got their jobs back because other trade unions haven't supported them, and their own union has been led by donkeys. What's the point in a national union? You have a union to defend your job, defend your wages and to defend your conditions. If your union can't do that, then what's the point in it? TGWU members have crossed the picket line. The dispute wasn't illegal. Unjust labour laws should have no respect.' [72]

Phillips asked Loach if he agreed that he and the dockers were: 'living in the '60s past,' unable to recognise that industrial relations and employment conditions had changed over the preceding decades, to which Loach replied:

*'If you think the expectation of secure jobs, sick pay, expectations of a proper shift pattern... do you think it is right to be rung up and told when to work, and if you don't work you don't get paid? Is trying to protect that living in the past? Just think, you are a man of middle age faced with not working again, yet you stay for two and a half years and you won't be bought off, because what is at stake is the right for your children to work; an extraordinary principled stand to take.' [73]*

In a moment of unique predictive analysis of future labour conditions, a caller identified as Terry from Widnes talked about the opening of a new sludge plant in his local area, with the promise of 40 new jobs, despite opposition from environmental groups. However, once the plant was built, the bosses outsourced recruitment to an employment agency, and Terry explained: 'they were not regular jobs. In fact, they've been kidded; it's North West Water. They've got an agency, and if you don't like it, you're out, just like the dockers. It's all one con-trick, all these agencies. You pay the lowest wage, exactly what the dockers fought against.' [74] Tony Benn MP told Roger Phillips:

*'The plain blunt truth is that these men and the Women of the Waterfront fought a magnificent fight, on the principle that you don't betray people who have been sacked by crossing a picket line. They were let down by the labour movement; they were let down by the Labour government after May.' [75]*

That week, the shop stewards resolved to maintain their public silence, having collectively agreed that this was not the time to analyse the campaign, and when they met on Wednesday 28 January, they heard feedback from the previous day's meeting between Jimmy Nolan, Jimmy Davies, Tony Nelson and the TGWU's Graham Stevenson, where a joint union-employer solution to the pension situation was discussed. Nolan and Davies had then joined Stevenson at a meeting with MDHC's Peter Jones in Birmingham, and when the two stewards were offered a lift back to Liverpool by Jones, he told them that he was: 'very keen on the idea of a labour supply company, as we [MDHC] are being screwed by Drakes.' [76] Later that evening, the WOW held their weekly meeting amid an atmosphere of great sadness and disappointment. Caryn Mathews of the Citizens Advice Bureau was on hand to offer information on everything from sick pay and income support to the challenges of means-tested benefits, and Dot Gibson thanked the members for flowers received for her father's funeral, before reporting on the next March for Social Justice and speaking at length about the magnificent courage they had all shown. Mike Carden was also in attendance to report on the most recent GEC meeting and to personally thank the women for their outstanding support, as he proclaimed that, 'this committee must stay.' [77] Guest speaker Cathy Wilson thanked the WOW for all of their support and activism in relation to a wide range of social and political campaigns, and Lesley Mahmood asked the members to, 'keep together. You must write down how you feel now or put it on a tape.' [78] According to Kevin Robinson's notes: 'It was a very, very emotional meeting'. [79]

The stewards met again on Thursday 29 January, against a backdrop of employers such as Merchant Ferries moving to the Canada Dock, and the announcement that the

Twelve Quays Development would be run by Pandoro and Norse Irish. This would create new opportunities for dock labour jobs, and Jimmy Davies told his fellow stewards: 'we could only supply the men.' [80] John Farrell, a former full-time TGWU official who had been dismissed by Bill Morris just a few years earlier, was set to represent many of the sacked Liverpool dockers in their struggle for legal redress against both MDHC and the TGWU. [81] On Friday 30 January, the dockers held another closed mass meeting at which they were addressed by Chris Grice from ACAS, who explained the purpose of the COT-3 document, which would entitle each of them to a final settlement covering the two-and-a-half-year dispute, as well as a new contract of employment lasting three months, during which time they would not be expected to attend work. The signing of the COT3 forms would stop the dockers taking part in any future industrial tribunal cases. [82]

Peter Clee informed the men that he and his team would be providing welfare rights advice at Transport House, asking for patience at the end of a speech that earned him a standing ovation, and Mickey Tighe passed on a message from the London Support Group. Joe Benton MP was there to talk about the need to develop the labour supply company idea as a way of creating employment opportunities for as many dockers as possible. Mark Evans, a dockworker from Melbourne, Australia, spoke of similar issues to those that caused the Liverpool dispute arising across Australian ports, with strikes being manufactured as an excuse to introduce scab labour. [83] From the floor, John Fearns shared his opinion that: 'it was disgraceful the way the dispute ended,' [84] sparking another debate about who and what was responsible for this as tensions rose with the confirmation of what the Liverpool dockers had known all along: that they had been made redundant in September 1995, that they had never been on strike, and that no legal restrictions had ever existed to prevent the TGWU from supporting their victimised members. Despite all the arguments and bitter conflicts that now erupted as the dispute hurtled towards a conclusion the stewards still maintained a press silence refusing to speak to any media outlets until they had completed the end of the dispute for all dockers. The stewards knew that as the end was now in sight this exposed everyone involved to some form of retribution or betrayal, with the settling of old scores being targeted by both the left and the right.

# PART FOUR:
## The aftermath of the dispute and legacy of the Liverpool Dockers

# 81
# Settling Old Scores

*'They done everything legally, had a secret ballot, they done everything by the book. So, what's Bill Morris's answer to their situation? Now, the reason I'm pointing this out is, supposing we would have done everything by the book, I don't think it would have made any difference. We'd still be sacked, Bill Morris would still refuse to back us, but I'd just like to make that point about the Magnet workers, because they done everything by the book.' ~ Pat Bennett\**

On Wednesday 28 January 1998, *Newsline*, the Workers Revolutionary Party newspaper, declared:

> *The dockers have been betrayed by Morris and local leaders. After 28 months of the most heroic struggle, the Liverpool dockers have been betrayed into defeat by the Morris leadership of the TGWU, aided and abetted at local level by Jimmy Nolan and the leadership of the Liverpool docks shop stewards' committee. From day one, the shop stewards' leaders – Stalinists, Scargillites and left reformists – had worked for some type of compromise settlement, and had even allowed the TGWU leaders, who did not support them, to negotiate for them.'* [1]

The article concluded by suggesting that it was the dockers' own leaders who failed to respond to, and indeed ran away from, the working-class call to be mobilised by their cause:

> *The reality is that Nolan, Davies and Carden's leadership of the shop stewards, right at the point where tens of thousands of trade unionists were there to be mobilised to take action against Morris's leadership to win the struggle, ran away.'* [2]

---

\* Pat Bennett, in an interview with Greg Dropkin (17 February 1998)

Writing in his diary on the day that the dispute's conclusion was announced, Tony Benn MP recorded how:

> *'I heard the Liverpool dockers had ended their dispute today. A nice woman called Sally from Radio Merseyside rang me and said, 'I can't get any of the Liverpool dockers to say anything on the radio because they are so upset and so distressed. Will you say something?' So, tomorrow morning I will say something on Radio Merseyside. But that is a classic struggle, betrayed by the Transport and General Workers' Union, by the labour movement when the Tories were in office, and doubly betrayed when we came into power and applied the same Tory legislation against our people, who were sacked for not crossing a picket line. Apparently, Blair told trade union leaders at a meeting at Number 10 that marches by trade unions were as out of date as Orange Order marches.'* [3]

In the Thursday 29 January edition of the *Liverpool Daily Post*, a banner headline declared, *The Dog That's Had Its Day*:

> *'The dispute, while real to those involved, seemed to symbolise something from another era to those glimpsing the drama from afar. It was as though an old yard dog, wearied and weakened by beatings, managed to bare his teeth once again, and in so doing recalled the lost years when he was young and strong; when a snarl and a display of fangs warned strangers to back off. The dispute at Seaforth has only just finished, but its images belong in the archives. It's over. Our region has moved forward. The PR men and women with their Thames Valley accents, the computer technicians; those fresh skills replace whole departments of people, and the university-educated managers are the new monarchs of the office and factory. There is no place now for employees who don't recognise that. Experience doesn't match youth in a world which advances with such alarming haste. It was, however, appropriate that this final uprising of trade union solidarity should have happened on Merseyside. But if the old yard dog does bare his teeth from time to time, it will serve as a reminder that some things can never be forgiven or forgotten.'* [4]

Elsewhere, John Hendy QC prepared to present the dockers' case to the International Labour Organisation, for consideration by the ILO's Committee of Experts. Hendy's application described how:

> *'Britain's laws on trade unions are the worst in Western Europe. The Labour Prime Minister at the time, Tony Blair, refused to change anti-trade union laws introduced by Conservative governments between 1979 and 1997. He boasted that, 'the changes that we do propose would leave British law the most restrictive on trade unions in the western world.'* [5]

The key point of Hendy's submission was that the Liverpool dockers did not have enough time to reflect on MDHC's actions, as they were sacked on the spot. [6] Another contradiction between UK law and UN conventions related to the issue of secondary action, with any action taken by British workers not directly affected by an industrial dispute being treated as illegal. [7] Unfortunately, however, these legal arguments were being made far too late in the day. From day one, the dispute carried all the hallmarks of an official strike, as the Dock Company met regularly with TGWU officials and the union ensured that money was paid to the dockers, not to mention the fact that three official ballots were organised via the Electoral Reform Society. The dispute was also discussed regularly by various TGWU committees, all of which lent weight to Hendy's case. On Thursday 29 January, Bill Morris wrote the following reply to a letter published in the *Guardian* by the journalist John Pilger:

> '*Why does Mr Pilger always reserve his venom for workers' own organisations, rather than bad employers or unjust laws? Indeed, it is John Pilger and others like him, with their message of false hope to the dockers and their families, who did more than anyone to prolong the agony. For the record, the docks dispute on Merseyside has probably been the most expensive in the union's history... That the dockers' solidarity and resilience did not succeed in securing their just demand for reinstatement is down to the most repressive anti-union laws in the western world, not the T&G. These are the facts. The view that victory could have been achieved if only the T&G had been prepared to ignore the law and put the entire union at risk is a fantasy, disproved by the history of the last 20 years.*' [8]

Three days after Morris's response to Pilger, on Sunday 1 February, Jimmy McGovern published an article in the *Guardian* under the title, *When You're a Liverpool Docker, It Never Rains But It Pours.* McGovern discussed the possibility of a different world, an alternative to the status quo that exuded confidence and, above all, was an incisive summary of the dockers' struggle, drawing upon his own working-class *Scouse* upbringing to articulate the dockers' heritage and the *Liverpool way*, explaining how:

> '*Many of the dockers were not young... the men consistently rejected the Mersey Docks' offer: not because it didn't suit the majority, but because it didn't suit them all. These were men of the highest principle. You would have expected Bill Morris... to applaud such principle. He didn't... Morris consistently argued that the dispute was illegal. There is strong evidence that he was wrong, but let's suppose he was right. Would that have mattered? If a law is bad, that is a very good reason for breaking it. And a law that allows a company to ruin the lives of hundreds of loyal, long-serving workers is surely a bad law. So, I doubt if even Bill Morris ever questioned the morality of supporting the dockers. It was more the wisdom of it... above all, they are angry that a union to which they have been loyal all their working lives could so callously betray them.*' [9]

In an equally radical and challenging article, Fr Michel de Felice, the Liverpool dockers' Hardship Fund 'banker', wrote in the *Catholic Pictorial* under the banner headline, *Dockers: They Can't Live On Fresh Air*:

> '*I can't praise the women and their families enough. It came right out of the blue. The men are very sad. They are feeling low, £28,000 a man sounds a lot, but not when you*

*work it out. Many will have to pay it back. They're on loan schemes, so they've got to repay it. Six families I know of have had their homes repossessed, it is very harsh. However, it wasn't about money. The issue was deeper than the dispute. The debate was all about workers' rights and conditions. I know the business community are pleased.'* [10]

Fr Michael's closing sentence displayed more political awareness than many paid TGWU officials could muster during the two-and-a-half-year dispute, and the following week, Mrs Joan Grocott, the wife of a sacked Liverpool docker, expressed her family's deep gratitude to Fr Michael and the *Catholic Pictorial* for its coverage of the dispute. [11] On February 3, Mark Steel voiced his opinion on the TGWU's role in the dispute, in an article titled, *Yellow Pages, Yellow Wages – In our Union*:

> *'I am just old enough to remember the days when union leaders appeared on television with their waistcoat buttons done up wrong and gravy down their tie. 'With regards to the offer, we can only reconfirm that we are appalled at the level-ness of unfairment contained within this offer,' they would say. The modern union leader is well dressed, an expert in camera technique, writes grammatically perfect letters to the broadsheets, and makes even less sense than before... Early on in the dispute, Morris made a speech to the dockers which won him a standing ovation, in which he told of how he'd be proud to tell his grandchildren of his role in the dispute. Well, that's going to lead to some pretty confused grandchildren. 'Mummy', they'll say, 'this afternoon Grandad put us on his knee and said, "Are you sitting comfortably? Well, let me tell you about my proudest battle. Two and a half years it went on, and in all that time not once did I spread an ounce of false hope."'* [12]

A busy and proactive Bill Morris felt the need to write yet another letter to the *Guardian*, in what had to be his most prolific period of activity since September 1995:

> *'I do not wish to strain your readers' patience by responding to personal abuse from the glitterati of the Socialist Workers Party over the Liverpool docks strike... I was not prepared to sacrifice the interests of every T&G member and their families and see our organisation smashed up to no avail.'* [13]

*LabourNet's* Greg Dropkin added his voice to the public debate that Morris had sparked, writing that:

> *'Reading the latest letter to the Guardian signed by Bill Morris, I cannot tell whether he wrote it. Whoever did so is either incompetent or a liar. Their contempt for the truth indicates an equal contempt for their readers. In its first point, Morris's letter states, 'There was no support for solidarity action whatsoever within the T&G.'* [14]

Dropkin went on to reflect how Morris blamed the UK's *anti-trade union laws* for stopping the TGWU from supporting the Liverpool dockers. However, those same laws did not force the

TGWU to dissuade other trade unions from taking industrial solidarity action during the 1997 British Airways dispute. The TGWU appealed to the ITF for support. The ITF responded by threatening international action against BA and when BA attempted to use UK laws against the union, the ITF simply indicated that it would move its headquarters to a more 'union-friendly' country, causing BA to drop their action. By contrast, Morris and his supporters on the GEC opposed every attempt by the Liverpool dockers to persuade the ITF and its affiliates to join the extensive actions against shipping companies trading with MDHC. Furthermore, at the December 1997 GEC, delegates were prevented from considering a motion from Region 3 (Ireland), calling on the TGWU to instruct the ITF to give full support to the Liverpool dockers. Morris made the claim that the law prevented the GEC from discussing the motion, and for Dropkin it was this, 'utter lack of democracy within the union which was one key factor in the defeat of the Liverpool dockers.' [15]

Not content with merely forcing a conclusion to the dispute, the TGWU leadership continued to undermine the Liverpool dockers' attempts at building a new future for themselves. An article in the April 1999 *Trade Union Review, the voice of the TGWU Broad Left*, made various allegations aimed at discrediting both the stewards and their ongoing campaign for justice:

> '...*the far-left grouping, which slipped off the Broad Left within the TGWU, is slipping in terms of its influence. In practice, the group was beginning to fragment, and one of the very negative aspects of this failed power struggle was the way in which the Liverpool dockers were drawn into the fight for dominance within the union by this grouping. About a year after the end of the [Liverpool] dispute, there are rumours a substantial surplus remains in the fund. Some money has, apparently, been put into the production of a play which depicts their struggle as having been scuppered by right-wing bureaucrats within the union's national office, with specific reference to Bill Morris.' [16]*

According to Graham Stevenson, TGWU Docks and Waterways National Official, the article represented nothing more than the opinion of its author, Jimmy Barnes, who Stevenson believed to be a trade unionist and Communist Party member like himself, before devoting his energies to the *Trade Union Review* in his later years. According to Stevenson, the *Trade Union Review*:

> '...*ended up as his [Barnes'] personal publication that attracted intense hostility, regular retractions and the occasional lawyer's letter and libel case. The Trade Union Review specialised in scandalous disclosure, gossip and rumour, quite often with a tenuous hold on actuality. It was almost single-handedly written by Jimmy... Trade Union Review began to hold most favoured status amongst the leadership of the T&G during the final years of the General Secretary, Bill Morris... Large numbers of the journal appeared in some of the union's offices and were sent free to individuals.' [17]*

At the dispute's conclusion, Mike Carden decided that he would resign from the GEC, and in early 1999, the *Trade Union Review*, which was still seen by some activists in the TGWU as a Broad Left pamphlet, published an article attacking him for his role in both the Liverpool dock dispute and on the GEC. It was a deeply personal attack by Barnes, who Carden contacted by telephone after receiving a copy through the post from an anonymous source. After a heated exchange, it was agreed that Barnes would print a response from Carden, and thus in *A Reply to Jimmy Barnes*, Carden was to write that:

> '*My decision to resign from the TGWU General Executive Council had been taken and reported to rank-and-file members in Region 6 as early as January 1998, when the Liverpool dockers' dispute concluded. I was requested to serve out my term of office and possibly reconsider my position in 1999. One major problem appears to be the view that such elected positions are for life; you join the club and hang on in there, which in many instances is the easiest option of all. I have always felt that this position negates genuine democracy and restricts opportunity. I sat on the TGWU GEC for five years, and it is interesting to note that neither you nor your coterie of powerful patrons in the TGWU chose to raise these matters with myself, face to face, so as to speak as part of the democratic process of debate.*' *[18]*

All this settling of old scores was to be expected, however, as Bill Morris finally roused himself into action and the TGWU Broad Left pondered the utility of its own *left-wing ideological wastelands* that did not include supporting workers in struggle.

# 82
# Part of the Union?
# Scab Labour?

*'I think the unions now, if there's any dispute going on, if you do go into dispute, they're not there to win it as far as I'm concerned. All they're there for is to broker you a deal, to get you some money, because they don't go out to win a dispute. They say, "Our hands are tied," and this, that and the other. A load of rubbish. It's a load of rubbish. They don't want these laws repealing. There's no way they want the laws repealing, because they're having an easy ride. While them laws are not repealed, all's they say is, "Our hands are tied, boys. What can we do?" A load of rubbish. They don't want the laws to be changed. They'll give a load of rhetoric out that they do, but deep down, I think every man in this dispute, or I think most people in the union, recognise that they don't want the laws repealing because they're having an easy ride of it. It suits them.' ~ Eddie Ledden\**

Within a few days of the Liverpool docks dispute starting, the Dock Company had recruited 'scab' labour to replace their former registered dockworkers. They inherited both the action plan and the casual labour agency, Drake International, from their take-over of Medway Ports. As a result, they were able to implement an *instantaneous strike-breaking programme*. By the end of the dispute, the relationship between the TGWU and the Drake Port Distribution Services (DPDS) workforce continued; representing men and women who had committed themselves to crossing picket lines for two and a half years. Ironically, when one dispute finished another began, as the hard winds of change *blew-back* against the strike-breakers; they responded by attempting to join a trade union. They launched their own workers' bulletin, *The Dart*, which on 1 February 1998 reported contact with local TGWU officials being made before the dockers' campaign had ended. The *Drake scabs* were increasingly disenchanted with the TGWU's reluctance to recruit them. [1] With emotions still raw [2], not every sacked docker was prepared to recognise the right of *all* workers to join

---

\* Eddie Ledden, in an interview with Greg Dropkin (17 February 1998)

a union, and few were sympathetic to the cause of strike-breakers threatening to strike while bemoaning a lack of union support. [3] The *Drake scabs* published the following lament in their newsletter:

> *'Well, it's all over! The strike that is, although one would be forgiven for failing to notice this very important fact… the MDHC, together with Drakes, have failed to credit this occasion with the importance that it deserves. At the time of writing, there has been no official statement from either of them. This is true to form and fits in with their usual strategy of providing minimal information to their employees… In what way will our working conditions change now that the dispute is over and management has a free hand? Will we see more casual labour at Seaforth Container Terminal? This has, unfortunately, been the case in other areas of the dock complex… evidence shows that these casual workers are not provided with the correct safety apparel, unlike the 'showpiece' container terminal. Casual workers are a cheap, undisciplined form of labour and they take away the benefits that we might otherwise receive if they were not used.' [4]*

Drake International was failing to retain workers after putting significant time and money into training them, which the *Dart* described as: 'unknown in the past, when workers were queuing up to get into the place! Are the current management happy with a transient workforce?', they asked. [5] The scabs were seeking recognition; not in the traditional trade unionist sense, but in response to the fact that they had been discarded by MDHC, a company they had supported and stood alongside for over two years:

> *'Mr Jack Dempsey of the TGWU has recently paid us a visit. This was not to talk with employees of DPDS, but to talk with the MDHC workers who have managed to hold onto their jobs throughout this dispute. Mr Dempsey was asked by Drakes employees, when would he be able to represent the main body of the workforce? His reply was that he will get around to it in a couple of weeks… The majority of the workers are now free to join a trade union and will do so at the first opportunity. [6]*

The scabs made it clear that this was not a return to militancy and they acknowledged that the bosses also had to: 'face the dilemma of how to keep two sets of workers operating in the same place doing the same job, at the same time, under different pay and conditions.' These were the same circumstances that had led to the 1995 docks dispute. It would be almost 22 years before the DPDS contract ended and a new workforce came together that had the confidence and unity to organise strike action against the new port authority. [7] In a simple twist of fate they would be represented by TGWU sacked dockers, Terry Teague and Tony Nelson. The engine behind this change in attitude was UNITE the Union, which leveraged the influence of the International Dockworkers' Council that was formed during the dockers struggle. All of this was for the future, though, and back in 1998, at the end of the Liverpool docks dispute, Bill Morris appeared to be sabotaging efforts to secure a dignified and effective final settlement. [8]

On Monday 2 February 1998 a business plan outlining how a dockers-run labour supply company would operate, based on 227 sacked dockers registering their interest in returning to the port was presented by Mike Carden. [9] Concerns were expressed about rates of pay, fall-back pay and appropriate conditions of employment, during a lengthy discussion that ended with the decision that weekly Hardship Fund payments would now have to cease. [10] Graham Stevenson told the stewards that Morris had sent him a letter stating that the dockers had: 'rejected the labour supply company, so he would not aid or support it.' [11] This was also the day that Morris contacted Dave McCall, the TGWU Regional secretary, to tell him that he wanted the stewards out of Transport House by the end of the week. Within days of Morris's ruling, Charlie Hughes, a friend of Tony Gardiner, offered rooms free of charge at his Rodney Street offices, before the dockers were eventually provided with a much larger space, again free of charge, by trade unionist and community leader George Knibb at the North Liverpool Regeneration Company. In addition to furnishing the stewards with a place to work from, the NLRC also gave them advice and guidance on community projects for the sacked dockers and their families.

Now the stewards found themselves occupied with building a support programme for all sacked dockers and their families. Dave Cotterill explained the potential of education courses through the Workers' Education Association, as well as work he had been doing with Liverpool John Moores University, while his partner, Caryn Mathews, along with Peter Clee and others from the Citizens Advice Bureau, continued to offer welfare advice. Cotterill began urging the stewards to collate, copyright and archive the bundles of documents, papers, files and photographs that had been accumulated since 1995; to preserve a history that could only be put into writing by the dockers themselves. He pitched the idea of a book of poems and pictures, with all proceeds to be split between the Hardship Fund and various post-dispute initiatives, having already invited some dockers to a writers' workshop supported by the author Irvine Welsh, playwright Jimmy McGovern and Channel 4. There was also news that European Objective One money could be made available to fund a multimedia course for 12 dockers at LJMU, with the possibility of further funding from the Trades Union Congress and the WEA, potentially bringing as many as 30 dockers into some form of paid training or employment. [12] Any literary or media endeavours would be complemented by a huge archive of pictures taken by local photographer Dave Sinclair, whose predominantly black and white record of the dispute featured many of the most iconic images of a *working-class struggle* that could have been from another century. In addition to Sinclair's collection, dockers such as Marty Size, Billy Jenkins, Kevin Robinson and Dave Pendleton had managed to capture some wonderful moments on video and audio tape, supplementing a wealth of both professional and amateur photography. [13]

On Thursday 5 February Nolan and Davies attended a London meeting of the Registered Dockworkers' Pension Fund, where it was confirmed that some 265 Liverpool dockers would now be in receipt of their pension benefits. There was, however, the issue of the other trustees, who were unhappy at the £1m cost of allowing members to re-join the fund without having contributed to it for over two years. As part of their settlement all former Dock Company sacked dockers would be effectively *re-employed* by MDHC on a fixed term contract to last three months. During this time, they would not be allowed anywhere near the docks - it was a paper transaction. [14] Carden reported that Ken Brindle had contacted him from a meeting of the National Finance and General Purposes Committee, where Morris had declared that a request for assistance on behalf of the young Torside dockers was to be rejected. At the weekly mass meeting held Friday 6 February, Jimmy Nolan encouraged the men to consolidate their TGWU membership by seeking election to constitutional committees and playing an active role in union life. Jimmy Davies warned that Bill Morris planned to restructure dock branches in order to pave the way for Drake scabs to be recruited and diminish the Liverpool dockers' traditional powerbase. [15] Jimmy Davies then announced the passing of four comrades: Joe Clark, Matty Hailwood, Jimmy O'Connor and Tommy Jackson. A minute's silence was observed, after which came a full report on the pension fund meeting, as well as an update on the labour supply company. The stewards had informed the Dock Company that they would not work with *scabs* and would require dedicated berths. One suggestion was that Merchant Ferries, situated at the Canada Dock, would become the dockers' main berth, and Peter Jones, of the MDHC, was expected to respond to this idea within a week. [16] Comedian Mark Steel was also in attendance as a guest speaker, addressing the men with his customary humour and passion, as he considered Morris's pessimistic attitude towards the principles of trade unionism:

> *Morris is full of gloom and doom, and yet the rich are richer today than 20 years ago. The lesson from the union was, "Why bother?" If Morris would have made it official and run a national levy – UNISON did it in Liverpool – the employers would look and say, "If we sack workers, we will we have a two-and-a-half-year struggle on our hands." The Liverpool dockers have inspired lots of workers, the same as the miners.'*
> *[17]*

Steel then told a joke about Kirk Douglas's comedian son: 'One evening, he was getting heckled, and he told the hecklers to shut up. "Don't you know who I am?" he asked his audience. "I'm Kirk Douglas's son." One of the hecklers stood up and said, "No you're not. I'm Kirk Douglas's son!" Everyone remembers Spartacus; no one remembers the traitors like Morris.' [18] Doreen McNally picked up where Steel left off, but her speech finished on a positive note, with everyone in the hall singing Happy Birthday to her. [19] The following day, a national meeting of Dockers' Support Groups took place at Transport House Liverpool, and it was there that Nolan and Davies outlined the main reasons for ending the dispute, citing: the General Executive Council's decision not to support the Liverpool dockers in December 1997, dwindling international support, the Labour government's refusal to intervene, the extraordinary ballot decision, MDHC's use of personal contracts to split the dockers, the TGWU's work to get dockers in dispute to leave the campaign and take a severance payment, the lack of UK solidarity action, increasing financial hardship, rising mortality among dockers and the ongoing pension issue. [20] They also discussed their intention to get men back on the docks via the labour supply company, before concluding that, 'We fought as long as we could.' [21]

One delegate asked about the Liverpool dockers' relationship with Bill Morris prior to the dispute, [22] and Ken Brindle replied: 'Morris's power exists because he is allowed to get away with it.' [23] The Manchester Support Group then talked about, 'the failure of the dockers to occupy the docks at the start of the dispute,' [24] and Greg Dropkin spoke of the need to discuss: 'the fundamental strategic errors made by the dockers,' adding that, 'the internet history has already been written.' [25] Dropkin also raised concerns over the absence of support from other UK industrial workers, while Martin Ralph expected the dispute to continue in one way or another. Richie Venton looked forward to, 'a revival of the labour movement, led by the dockers.' [26] Celia Ralph brought up, 'the need to organise a fightback,' [27] and Fr Michael de Felice championed, 'the principle of never crossing a picket line,' before bemoaning, 'the opposition of the government, union and media,' and praising the dockers for fighting, 'a brilliant fight. Strike-breakers complained of violence, but I think it was orchestrated.' [28] John Bohanna, from Ford Liverpool, asked about allegations against TGWU officials, Bill Hunter highlighted, 'the working-class and internationalist lessons of the docks dispute. We have to look to the history of our class,' [29] and Lesley Mahmood highlighted: 'the restrictions imposed upon the dockers by the union's leadership.' [30]

Mariam Kamish of the South Wales Support Group praised, 'the determination of dockers, a marvellous new start to our struggle. These are heroes; ordinary people inspired and inspiring others.' [31] Teresa McKay described the need to develop: 'an open Broad Left in the TGWU. Union officials should not earn more than the workers' average pay.' [32] Dave Cotterill again emphasised the need for the dockers to record the history of the dispute in their own words [33] and Dot Gibson reminded the meeting of: 'the influence of the March for Social Justice, and the need to keep this organisation going for other struggles. These organisations should develop into a new rank-and-file movement.' [34] Doreen McNally responded to a question raised about the 800 other workers in the port by explaining how various men and women had crossed picket lines in order to continue working in the Port of Liverpool, [35] whilst Malkait Biku, speaking on behalf of the Hillingdon Hospital workers, wished to: 'thank the Liverpool dockers for their support.' [36] John Hendy QC explained that the International Labour Organization would challenge both the TGWU and the Labour government on the principles of freedom of association, before Jimmy Nolan closed the meeting by thanking all supporters for their magnificent solidarity. [37]

Unsurprisingly, post-mortems on the Liverpool docks dispute came thick and fast, and in an article titled *Hard Lessons from the Liverpool Docks Lockout*, Chris Marsden succinctly articulated one political group's analysis:

> *There are crucial lessons to be learned from the bitter end of the long-running industrial dispute on Liverpool's Mersey docks. The dispute joins a long list of defeated workers' struggles over the last two decades. Yet the middle-class left in Britain and internationally, who hailed Liverpool as the rebirth of 'fighting trade unions,' are incapable of explaining why this has happened. The Socialist Party [formerly the Militant Tendency] claim that nothing else could have been done, and that the lesson is that, 'the union needs reclaiming' for the working class. The Socialist Workers Party describe Liverpool as, 'symbolic of the collective solidarity inside the working-class movement,' that will convince the employers that they cannot, 'get away with this sort of behaviour.' This verdict is entirely justified. It was the TGWU which strangled the Liverpool dockers' struggle… Those leading the dispute never sought industrial support from any other section of workers in Britain. Instead, the Mersey Stewards organised an international campaign under the auspices of the ITF, aimed at winning backing from trade union bureaucrats in other countries… the vast majority of workers who stand outside the official labour movement remained unaware of the Liverpool action, even when*

*unions in their country nominally backed it. Organised workers were themselves reluctant to take solidarity action, having become justifiably sceptical towards the possibility of mounting militant struggles through the trade unions... So long as the dockers' dispute was confined to a trade union perspective, its defeat was inevitable. In their efforts to boost the credentials of the trade unions, the middle-class left share responsibility for this debacle.'* [38]

According to Paul Davies and Debbie Delange, writing in the *Militant*:

*'No action was organized to back the Liverpool dockers at other ports in the United Kingdom, however, and the fight took place when there wasn't a broader rise in sustained union struggles.'* [39]

Davies and Delange also pointed to the critical fact that around 80 dockers had individually accepted MDHC's severance offer in December 1997, following the GEC's refusal to discuss offering further backing to the campaign. Doreen McNally published her recollections of the dispute's second year in the *Dockers' Charter*: 'We had to learn a lot and to learn fast,' she wrote, describing how WOW members would speak alongside dockers' delegates at meetings and rallies in the UK and across the world. 'Everyone is still in shock,' Val Bibby said. 'We have four generations of history on the dock. We don't intend to leave our heritage to scabs.' [40]

# 83

# The Initiative Factory
# and the CASA

*The Casa would not exist without Ken Loach and Jimmy McGovern. We are totally appalled at the expulsion of Ken Loach from the Labour Party - "maybe if we tell the truth about the past, we can tell the truth about the present." (Ken Loach)' ~ The CASA**

In February 1998, the former Liverpool dock shop stewards were actively seeking the capital to fund redundancy packages for Torside, Nelson Freight and Ex-LGS dockers. There was just £5,000 remaining in Fr Michael's Hardship Fund but, by this point, Bill Morris had sent out an international circular telling trade unionists to *stop* supporting the Liverpool dockers. [1] Dave Cotterill had written to formally offer 12 training places paying £135 per week and Jimmy Nolan believed that the first chances to earn some sort of wage should go to the Torside and Nelson Freight men. Turnbull at the University of Cardiff had asked Jimmy to write an article for *Capital and Class*, while the TGWU was demanding payment for all faxes sent and phone calls made from Transport House. The dockers were still waiting for the TGWU-MDHC jointly sponsored report on the potential sustainability of a proposed labour supply company. [2]

At a mass meeting held on Friday 13 February, a minute's silence was observed following the death of Tommy Jackson, and although numerous reports were given, nothing of any real substance could be finalised without a response from either the union or the Dock Company. It was announced that a list of all sacked dockers would be placed on a computer file, so that any potential employment opportunities could be made with consideration of age, address, skill profiles and preferences for education, retraining or employment. Dave Cotterill was on hand to discuss the potential for more education and training courses, and Chris

* The CASA Twitter (@CasaLiverpool) on 26 July 2021.
Available: https://twitter.com/CasaLiverpool/status/1419758262635876354

Mooney from Kirkby Unemployed Centre explained the details of a one-to-one scheme aimed at supporting deprived families. Micky Tighe gave a report about the 1998 Brit Awards, where the band Chumbawamba had dedicated their performance to the Liverpool dockers, before launching into their hit song, *Tubthumping*, which included the shout-along chorus: 'I get knocked down, But I get up again, You ain't ever gonna keep me down.' [3] It was a song that resonated with the dockers, especially when the band used the alternative lyrics: 'New Labour sold out the dockers, Just like they'll sell out the rest of us.' [4] The protest was completed by vocalist Danbert Nobacon, who in an act of 'drench warfare,' poured a bucket of icy water over Deputy Prime Minister John Prescott declaring: 'This is for the Liverpool dockers!' [5]

As the mass meeting continued there were also questions from the floor regarding the labour supply company, while John Ferns asked: 'What money is being raised for the Hillingdon workers?' [6] Some stewards expressed concern regarding Greg Dropkin's recent interviews with dockers as the dispute ended which sought a final analysis at a time when emotions were still running high. The stewards had insisted upon a collective discipline to focus solely on securing a fair deal for all dockers who took part in this extraordinary dispute. Greg Dropkin wrote:

> *During February, dockers reflected on the entire dispute and the period after 1989. I joined a few of these conversations. They represent the personal views of ten dockers... Whilst everyone interviewed attacks Bill Morris, the men expressed differing views on aspects of the dispute... Escalating the action at home would have been a gamble. But if that strategy had ended in defeat, it would at least have left no doubt that the dockers lost because the rest of us failed to take our best chance in decades.' [7]*

The interviews conducted by Greg Dropkin caused some rifts among the stewards, but with the passage of time they have become a valuable primary source in the history of the dockers' struggle. In 2002, the MDHC's staff pension fund deficit increased more than 10-fold over the course of six months. The company blamed stock market turmoil for the growing shortfall whilst new accounting laws revealed a deficit of only £800,000 at the end of 2001, which somehow increased to £11m on assets of £153m months later. By the end of June 2002, MDHC's pre-tax profits were down 6.8%, and Jones would comment that: 'A sluggish manufacturing sector and costs associated with the previous year's share buy-back are also a factor in the profit dip.' [8] Dave Cotterill's dockers' writing group continued to meet at the Merseyside Trade Union, Community and Unemployed Resource Centre, with the support of Jimmy McGovern, Irvine Welsh and the WEA. In recalling how he became involved with the writing group McGovern would later say: 'I'm no good on picket lines; I just get frightened. The film offered the dockers the chance to tell a story that they felt had been widely ignored.' [9] Carden and Cotterill were keen to develop a dockers-run arts and industrial co-operative, with the aim of creating training, education and employment opportunities, an idea which eventually became the Initiative Factory (IF) formed under the rules of the Liverpool Dockers' Community Trust. [10] This project carried philosophical and practical ambitions for all workers, operating in partnership with the local community to reduce youth and long-term unemployment through innovative, high-quality training that would fully embrace the potential of information technology. This new organisation would seek to develop positive and practical links with local universities and colleges. Some of the stewards wanted to facilitate access to further, continuing and lifelong education and to establish a physical *hub* in the centre of Liverpool for those excluded from such opportunities. [11]

On Thursday 19 February, a benefit night for both the dockers and the Save Free Education Campaign took place at Club Resistance in Liverpool. That same day a meeting took place in Transport House involving Irvine Welsh, Jimmy McGovern and the deputy head of Channel 4 Drama to discuss the work of the writers' workshop. As they began to explore elements of the drama the meeting deteriorated into an inquest regarding how the dispute started. [12] The view of the stewards was that it was far too early to be discussing such matters as feelings were running high and it was easy for some to *look for people to blame*. [13] The stress and the shock of how this dispute ended, as it shuddered towards its conclusion, affected everyone deeply. Eventually, the focus of the meeting switched to Irvine Welsh and Jimmy McGovern, whose film *Dockers*, written by a group consisting of dockers, wives and supporters, would go on to be televised on Channel 4. The writing team was coached through the process and had their scripts edited by these two acclaimed writers, whose credits included *Cracker*, *Hillsborough* and *Trainspotting*. It would become part of a project that was essentially a joint production by Parallax Pictures, Channel 4 and what became known as the dockers' Initiative Factory. For over 14 months, the writing group met every week, with McGovern and Welsh both attending regularly, and it quickly seemed inevitable that McGovern would act as their inspirational leader, as he explained sometime later: 'This was the dockers' story, and to be able to work alongside them in telling it was a dream for me. It was the most rewarding 14 months of my working life. My mam died during this time, and the dockers attended her funeral, and I was so pleased that they did. These were good, working-class men steeped in the culture of Merseyside.' [14] In addition to the writing group, the film also employed some 200 sacked dockers as extras and technicians, many of whom were keen to pursue careers within a production company formed under the auspices of the Dockers' Initiative Factory. One of the writing group members, dockers' supporter Mike Morris, went on to setup Writing on the Wall, which has become a highly successful literary and publishing agency based in Toxteth, Liverpool. Produced by Sally Hibbin and directed by Bill Anderson, the *Dockers* final script was completed on the 10 March 1999, [15] and sacked docker and writing group member John Cowley said at the time: 'I have always wanted to write, but it's not something you tell other dockers.' [16]

As part of a dockers' training proposal, Ken Loach's company, Parallax Pictures, agreed to employ four dockers on the production team for *Dockers*: Mark Crichton (cameraman), Jimmy Holmes (grip), Derek Reardon (art and design) and Nick Silvano (driver). The film starred Ken Stott and Ricky Tomlinson as two men on opposite sides of the Liverpool docks dispute, with Tomlinson, a former cast member on *Brookside* who was jailed for conspiracy following the construction workers' strike in 1972, playing a *scab* who goes back to work on the docks under the terms of a non-union contract. [17] Ken Stott played the central role of a sacked Liverpool docker. The film focussed heavily on what the dockers saw as the betrayal of their cause by the TGWU and the Labour Party. Essentially, the story labelled him a traitor to the dockers, after a scene re-enacting the infamous speech where he told a mass meeting that he was 'marching side by side in solidarity' with them.

Morris is also depicted as refusing to support what he claimed was an illegal dispute, in addition to manipulating the vote at the union's Biennial Delegate Conference in order to defeat a motion supporting the dockers' campaign. Morris declined to comment on the film after first seeing it on Thursday 1 July 1999, but TGWU insiders were quoted as calling it 'an insult.' [18]

Dockers premiered on Channel 4 at 10pm on Sunday 11 July, pulling in a respectable two million viewers, during an unprecedented evening of television that saw the film preceded by a 60-minute documentary about its creation titled, *Dockers: Writing the Wrongs*. [19] After an emotional private screening in London on Thursday 1 July, Jimmy Nolan once again accused Morris of betrayal: 'You expect it from your employers, but not from your own union. This scoundrel, who calls himself a general secretary, should hang his head in shame after seeing this. We still believe in the union, but not in Bill Morris.' [20] However, blame for the collapse of the dispute could not be attributed to Morris alone, as the TGWU rulebook defines the power of the union's membership over the general secretary. 'The general secretary shall be under the control of and act in accordance with the directions of the Executive Council.' Writing in the *Guardian*, Fiachra Gibbons quoted the character playing the part of Nolan and the speech he made at a TGWU BDC conference. In the drama Nolan is depicted as telling the union's leadership that: 'Hundreds of dockers can go rot, so you can keep your offices, your chauffeur-driven cars and your mobile phones.' [21] In reality, Jimmy Nolan did not say this at the BDC. In another scene, Morris is shown arriving in a chauffeur-driven Jaguar to give a private address to the dockers, during which he pledged solidarity and claimed: 'When my grandchildren ask me what I did to support the Liverpool dockers, I want to say I stood with them every step of the way,' [22] using direct quotes from his March 1996 speech made during a mass meeting in Liverpool. Jimmy McGovern agreed with Nolan about how: 'There is nothing wrong with the T&G itself, but there is something badly wrong with its leadership. It's a disgrace.' [23] By way of response, an unnamed TGWU source accused the dockers of:

> *Trying to rewrite history. The strike was unofficial. They exposed the union to possible sequestration if we had been sued by the employers under the Tories' anti-union laws. The general secretary had to take account of the whole union. The actions the dockers took threatened its survival. We have seen the film and it is a very good drama indeed. There are lots of great things in it, but as a reflection of the reality of the situation it fails. Jimmy McGovern said the union refused to let Parallax Pictures, who made Dockers, shoot on union premises, and threw the former strikers out of the T&G building in Liverpool when actor Robert Carlyle came to offer his support at one of their script sessions. The film had Crissy Rock, whose Pat was loosely based on the experiences of the Mitchell family – Colin Mitchell and his wife, Sue. They helped write many of the scenes themselves.' [24]*

John Bohanna, from Fords in Liverpool, wrote a detailed review of the film, describing how the writing group had grasped this unique opportunity to present their story to the nation in their own words. According to Bohanna, the script was 'quite impressive', [25] and he was satisfied that the dramatised version of events gave an accurate record of the dispute's key recurring themes:

> 'Dockers shows the international solidarity of port workers... Stories of family stress, division and death; the involvement of dockworkers' wives and partners are all interwoven into the performance... the general secretary speaks of solidarity and standing firm, and then refuses to mount any serious attack on the forces which had initiated the dismissals, or on the vengeful ruling class which had instigated the anti-union laws in Britain. All of this was underlined by the blatant manoeuvre at the T&G's Biennial Delegates Conference, where the chair declares an executive motion carried after it was decisively defeated on the floor.' [26]

Bohanna identified the significance of the abolition of the National Dock Labour Board Scheme in 1989, which laid the foundations for the dockers' dismissal six years later, although he correctly notes that industrial relations prior to '89 could not have been worse. This reality is explored in Bill Hunter's *They Knew Why They Fought*, a history of unofficial struggles and leadership on the Liverpool docks from 1945-1989, which details how: 'on the one side in the post-war period, there is a sorry tale of leaders whose policies revolve only around their own bureaucratic interests, and who are far removed from the feelings, aspirations and traditions of trade union membership. On the other side, there is a magnificent story of workers' will to fight and workers' solidarity. Will the leadership never change?' [27] The political nature of the conditions that led to the dockers' dismissal was also touched on by Jimmy McGovern at the start of *Writing the Wrongs*, as he observed that the dispute was:

> '...very modern; casualisation is everywhere, and those with jobs are being worked harder and harder and harder. Dockers conveyed the unity of the men meeting regularly, but the breaking of new ground and democracy, even in terms of rank-and-file organisation, of openly welcoming anybody who offered support or solidarity and debate, was not shown. The dockworkers rank-and-file leadership wiped out the stifling, strangulating sectarianism, which has plagued almost every crevice of the left and often carried the means of defeat into workers' organisations. Equally, activists on Merseyside and nationally were invited to attend meetings with an open forum debate for suggestions or advice on winning the dispute. That sort of action was important to record.' [28]

Both the dramatization and the documentary would be added to the list of authentic primary sources telling the real story of the Liverpool docks dispute, demonstrating extraordinary working-class honesty, humour and humanity, but it would be another 20 years before the dockers regained enough influence within the union to start righting at least some of the wrongs.

The boardroom where the shop stewards held their meetings throughout the Liverpool docks dispute was situated on the top floor of Transport House. It was the most practical place for the union to put them, although at times the needs of a sprawling, nonstop campaign would have them occupying almost the entire building. Micky Dunn, a respected full-time union official, gave up his small office, which became the dockers' communications room, and the Women of the Waterfront were also granted access to their own office. But it was in the boardroom that discussions began on the transition from running an industrial struggle to the development of education, training and job-creation projects. Given the history they all shared in that room it was probably a good psychological move when they were told they had to leave the union building shortly after the dispute officially ended. They now had new problems to solve.

The shop stewards were aware of what had happened to the steel and the mining communities after their industries had *padlocked the gates*, and they were determined not to abandon the men and women who had given so much to a noble fight for work and dignity in the face of encroaching casualisation. Keele University and Liverpool John Moores University (LJMU) were known to offer long-established access courses that would benefit some dockers, and LJMU had previously contacted the stewards about the possibility of leasing them 12 computers for a proposed multimedia course, which according to Dave Cotterill could lead to a European Social Fund grant to cover minimum wage costs for at least one year. [29] Eventually, in February 2001, the work of the dockers' new organisation, the IF (Initiative Factory), would result in it being registered as an accredited learning centre by the Department for Education and Employment, [30] with LJMU's Prof Peter Fowler a keen supporter as the dockers searched for a building to serve as their centre of operations. On 19 June 1998, Fowler wrote to Liverpool City Council's Land Management Committee to promote the IF's wish to have: 'a city centre building, bringing an initiative focussing on the new technologies for the unemployed and excluded working-class communities of the region, with new models of learning through the involvement of John Moores University.' [31] These potential opportunities confirmed, for some stewards, that they were right not to leave the dockers at the mercy of the Jobcentre. Already, the rank-and-file structure that was being created included the potential for a charitable trust, a trading arm, the labour supply company and links or partnerships with the Merseyside Trade Union, Community and Unemployed Resource Centre; LJMU and the Workers' Education Authority (WEA). [32]

At the TGWU's Region 6 Finance and General Purposes Committee meeting, it was reported that docks official Jack Dempsey had requested early retirement, as two lorry driver members of Branch 6/541 Road Haulage Section were still struggling to find work after respecting the Liverpool dockers' picket lines for over two years. [33] The following day, the WEA's Greg Coyne joined Dave Cotterill at a stewards' meeting to discuss what Jimmy Nolan introduced as the combination of a labour supply company and education programmes to support the sacked dockers. [34] Coyne outlined funding opportunities for employment through ADAPT (European Social Fund), before confirming that the WEA would provide education courses for a multimedia-based project, while Liverpool City Council's (LCC) Community, Business and Economic Development (CBED) Department would provide additional support, especially in relation to a community-based labour cooperative. Jerry Spencer from LCC's CBED office would work directly alongside the dockers to this end. Further funding from ESF and ERDF could be used to finance the building of a dedicated site, with the Merseyside Special Investment Fund also an option for raising necessary capital. [35] One idea put forward by Kevin Bilsborrow was the setting up of a forklift driver training school with another docker, Kenny Weston, to run alongside the labour supply company, in line with a business plan to offer accredited Construction Industry Training Board (CITB) courses. By March 1998, 50 Liverpool dockers were due to start a computer course that would last for a number of months, and others were booked onto a global multimedia course due to begin in October, with the key element being that all of these exciting projects would pay participants a living wage. [36]

On Wednesday 25 February 1998, Jimmy Nolan and Jimmy Davies met with Peter Jones, MDHC's Port Operations Director, at the Port of Liverpool Building. In their report back to the stewards, Davies and Nolan described the talks with Jones as 'constructive', [37] with Davies identifying the main talking point as the labour supply company being based in a specific area with exclusive work, premises, costings and equipment supported by the MDHC. [38] Both Nolan and Davies were satisfied with the level of detail that Jones had provided, which they saw as a positive indication of at least some level of transparency as if he did want the labour supply company to come in as competition for Drake International. Jones also confirmed: 'some of these companies are linked to the MDHC, either directly or through their managers and directors, who started them in the aftermath of the abolition of the National Dock Labour Scheme in 1989, and after the docks dispute had begun in 1995.' [39] The irony here was that Jones, one of the main architects of Liverpool docks' casualisation, was now looking to offer that same work back to the very dockers his strategy had ousted. By August 1998 Jones was proclaiming how the end of the dispute had resulted in the departure of the last of the former NDLBS-registered dockers, and that the port now had an entirely different workforce with a very different attitude to work. [40] That afternoon, several stewards met Dave McCall together with Dave Eva and Alan Manning from the North West Trade Union Congress, to discuss possible support for developing business plans for their various proposed projects, with the Unity Trust Bank and the Co-operative Group in Manchester also keen to support the Liverpool dockers. Two days later, the stewards met with their council-appointed business advisor, Jerry Spencer, to discuss the structure, ethos and philosophy of their new company. Spencer helped design the aims and objectives, articles of association, general rules, working arrangements, procedures and contracts of employment, working closely with Mike Carden to support the transition from employees to potential *social employers*. The agreement was that LCC would release funding for every job created, and the Training and Enterprise Council would supply funds for training through the Single Regeneration Budget. [41]

Carden attended a London meeting of the TGWU's General Executive Council on the 2 March, where a lengthy discussion took place following the recent Biennial Delegates Conference, which had seen the chair challenged over a vote on the right of members to force the GEC to debate resolutions. Graham Stevenson told the meeting that the Liverpool docks dispute would not be over until the question of the dockers' pensions was resolved. Danny Maher gave a detailed report on behalf of the National Docks and Waterways Committee. Maher criticised the general secretary directly, before calling on the union to provide financial support to those dockers excluded from the settlement figures agreed with MDHC, and then repeating the argument that the TGWU's own legal officer, Fergus Whitty, had initially advised the dockers that they *were locked out, and therefore not on unofficial strike.* This verdict contradicted the TGWU's official position that the dispute was an illegal strike that would leave the union exposed to legal action if it was seen to support it. Bill Morris responded by speaking about: 'the dignity of the dockers, but it was not a lockout.

Nevertheless, I will examine the hardship of the Liverpool dockers now that the dispute had ended.' [42]

That same day, the dockers held a mass meeting in Transport House, where a minute's silence was observed following the passing of Ray Bromollow; he was a dock timekeeper. A report was then given on the pension situation, after Sandy Morrison, the chair of trustees, conveyed the decision to readmit the Liverpool dockers into the fund with continuity of service covering the previous 28 months. [43] This was a busy mass meeting, with many contributions from the floor, as well as feedback from Nolan and Davies following talks with the Dock Company. Dave Cotterill and Mike Morris gave an update on possible opportunities for training, employment and creative writing courses. [44] It was announced that on Tuesday 10 March, Billy Jenkins, Tony Gardiner, Kevin Robinson and Lis Knight would attend the House of Commons for a discussion on Kurdish and Turkish human rights in the wake of the death of Metin Goktepe, the Turkish photojournalist who was tortured and brutally murdered in police custody in Istanbul on 8 January 1996. Jenkins, Gardiner and Robinson had been instrumental in forming alliances between the dockers and their Turkish and Kurdish comrades, who in turn had supported the dockers throughout their dispute. The gruesome details of Turkey's human rights abuses had been harrowing, and MPs Ken Livingston and Jeremy Corbyn took it upon themselves to become actively involved in this campaign for justice. [45] Meanwhile, back in Liverpool, LJMU's Professor Peter Fell asked the dockers to work with him directly in developing interactive histories, documentaries and films dedicated to the dispute. [46]

As the dockers various 'not for profit' business plans began to take shape, [47] it was agreed that Jimmy Nolan would become the first company director, with Jimmy Davies as secretary and Kevin Bilsborrow managing the plant training programme. On Thursday 12 March, Nolan and Davies attended another pension fund meeting, during which MDHC refused to cover any shortfalls in pension contributions that had resulted from their dismissal of the Liverpool dockers. The pension fund trustees did not accept this, and it also came to light that the first 41 Liverpool dockers to have applied to leave the dispute in October 1997 were to have £3,000 deducted from their severance payment in order to cover the pension fund deficit. The following morning's mass meeting was addressed by the Advisory, Conciliation and Arbitration Service, who had asked to attend because Peter Jones had demanded that they alter the COT-3 compromise agreement, which was the legal basis upon which the employment rights of the Liverpool dockers had been formally ended: 'so that the severance payment could be reduced from £25,000 to £22,000.' [48] ACAS refused, [49] at which point some dockers called for the men to 'get back on the gates,' such was their anger at MDHC continuing to 'bleed them dry'. [50] Billy Johnson, Ritchie Gerrard, Eddie Ledden, Jimmy Campbell and George Johnson were among those who protested vehemently in opposition to this 'trick' by their former employer.

Kevin Bilsborrow gave a report on the plan to set up the forklift training school, asking for volunteers to train as instructors, and Dave Cotterill talked about tutor training courses and preparatory degree courses being organised by LJMU. [51] Unfortunately, there was more tragic news the following day, as docker Joe 'Snowy' Best, had passed away. Snowy was one of the great characters of the docks, himself a product of his industry; a concept that is so difficult – impossible, almost – to explain to those without experience of industries where labour is replenished by generations of the same families. The communities that sprung up around this type of work, from coal to ship building, provided a much-needed support network for many workers and their families. Men such as *Snowy* were dockers first and foremost, it was the only life they knew and like their fathers before them they rarely escaped from their role.

On Monday 16 March, Nolan and Davies met again with Peter Jones to discuss costings for the labour supply company. Jones thought it unbelievable that the dockers had not yet seen KPMG's feasibility report on the project, [52] and he was interested in hearing details of the dockers' business plan and proposed management structure. In the weeks that followed, Jerry Spencer would join several former shop stewards' meetings to discuss KPMG's queries, with MDHC using the consultant firm as an excuse for keeping dialogue open. According to one steward speaking at the time: 'it may be that Jones is protecting his back from those directors who do not want to use the dockers co-op. Hopefully, these detailed questions are good news.' [53] Members of the Hillsborough Support Group met with the WOW at Transport House, [54] and on Thursday the 19 March, a dockers' mass meeting focussed on the pension fund issue, as the reality seemed to be that the men would have to lose £3,000 from their severance payments in order to make up the deficit in their pension contributions. Jimmy Davies, who had been a pension fund trustee for many years, spoke candidly about the pressure they were all under as a result of the Dock Company's failure to accept responsibility in this matter, leaving them with only hours to make a decision before a 5pm deadline imposed by the company. At this meeting it was also agreed that Mike Carden and Tony Melia would work together to set up the training and educational Trust for all dockers. [55] That same day hundreds of dockers left to attend the funeral of Joe Best at St Dominic's Church in Liverpool. [56]

The following day, Carden, Melia and several other stewards joined Dave McCall at a formal meeting with a representative of the Training and Enterprise Council and Business Link, as a lengthy and detailed list of objectives for the dockers' work and training programmes began to take shape. [57] It was expected that all of these proposed developments would be brought together under one roof, eventually becoming, what Carden called, the Initiative Factory. [58] On Tuesday 12 May, Jimmy Davies, Frank Lannigan and Kevin Bilsborrow would meet with Garston Stevedores, who were using a casual agency called Advance Agency. After this meeting the stewards discussed the wages and conditions being offered by these agencies, which they all agreed were unacceptable. [59] This proved to be a challenging period, as some stewards grappled with the potential responsibilities of running various not-for-profit business enterprises and training programmes as opposed to running a dispute or being union shop stewards on the docks. Some of the dockers' supporters considered it a *sell-out* for the stewards to be looking at creating and shaping their own futures, as it seemed to be the case that for some on the left, having control over opportunities for learning, and employment was the preserve of the *capitalist class*. [60] Some stewards failed to grasp that their lives had changed forever. Some wished to drift back to the comfort of the traditional role of *employees under the control of an employer*. Change was difficult. According to one steward this *tendency* was: 'causing frustration and holding back individuals from getting on with their work.' [61]

By Thursday 26 March, a postal strike had broken out in Liverpool, which created a problem for ACAS as they sought to get COT-3 forms out to the dockers for them to sign, since some dockers saw the act of circumventing postal picket lines as essentially an exercise in strike breaking. At a mass meeting held the following day, dockers were informed of the numerous opportunities that could emerge for employment and training over the coming months. [62] One docker, Sammy Hopkins, expressed concern regarding the pension fund situation which by now had become a major problem in settling the Liverpool docks dispute. [63] Dave Cotterill informed the dockers about a CD-ROM history project at LJMU, which would offer a small wage to any dockers wishing to take part in it. This digital history of the docks and Liverpool was based upon an idea originally put forward by Chris Carlsson and his team at the Shaping San Francisco History Project called *Excavating the City's Lost History*. [64] Elsewhere, Dot Gibson, a London Support Group activist and respected comrade, had written a paper, *To All Members of the Faction*, reporting on a meeting with the stewards:

> *The stewards had just had a debate, and there were great concerns about the Dockers' Charter. In particular, Jimmy Davies was worried about finance for it… it is necessary to say that the London Support Group is dominated by a myriad of sectarian political groups… Mike Carden, as the link-man to the Dockers' Charter, wondered whether there was grounds for the paper now that the dispute was over.'* [65]

Dot wanted the *Dockers' Charter* to continue beyond the conclusion of the dispute, and there was certainly no doubting its value and the extraordinary contribution it had made to the dockers' campaign. On her list of proposed topics for the *Dockers' Charter*, Dot included the Hillsborough Justice Campaign, 'because the Labour government has refused to reopen the inquiry into the death of 96 people at a football match in Sheffield. We should report the fact that the families say they will continue their campaign for justice.' [66] Here, Dot was displaying both her political intuition and her support for all who sought justice. [67]

Barely one month after the end of the Liverpool docks dispute, at a time when the stewards were still trying to negotiate a final settlement, it was reported that the Labour government had sold its 14% shareholding in MDHC, in what would be one of the first of many acts of privatisation by the Blair administration. The little-publicised move was announced at 7.30am on Monday 30 March 1998, and the auction was concluded a mere four hours later, with the news immediately boosting the company's shares up from 565p to 576.5p. Gordon Waddell, MDHC's Chairman, had seen the value of his share options rise by £184,324 since the close of the dispute, while fellow directors Peter Jones and Ken Wharton were better off by £65,576 and £68,911 respectively. ABN Amro Rothschild, the merchant bank whose directors included former Conservative cabinet ministers Lord Wakeham and Norman Lamont, acted as advisors and received undisclosed fees, while three other City firms – Charterhouse Tilney, Merrill Lynch and SBC Warburg Dillon Read – acted as joint lead managers of the sale, for which the government itself netted £70m. The only losers from the deal were the Liverpool dockers. [68] The stewards had campaigned in vain to convince New Labour to use its influence as a major stakeholder to push for their reinstatement, and they only heard about the sale once they were contacted for comment by *Tribune*, a Labour Party newspaper. For one docker: 'there was a sense of absolute disbelief. All the way through the dispute, we were asking the government to use the shareholding to intervene. Maybe this was one of the reasons they decided not to.' [69]

At a mass meeting held on Friday 17 April, dockers were asked to attend the picket lines of Aintree Hospital domestic workers the following Monday morning. Meanwhile, a glossy business plan for the labour supply company had been produced, and 14 dockers had yet to complete their COT-3 forms, with Freddy Roberts again voicing his opposition to the diminishing terms of the dockers' final settlement. A lengthy report was given on the Australian wharfies' strike in response to 1400 redundancies being imposed by Patrick Stevedores, describing how legal action was being threatened by employers. Brian McWilliam, president of the International Longshore and Warehouse Union, had been arrested after his members refused to work any ships handled by scab labour. The International Transport Workers' Federation was attempting to co-ordinate solidarity action in support of the wharfies as, unsurprisingly, the end of the Liverpool dispute was taken as a green light for port bosses across the world to deregulate and attack dockers' working conditions. [70] Elsewhere that month, on Thursday 2 April, 22 dockers attended a Business course at LJMU. At a stewards' meeting on 9 April discussions on the growing need to allocate roles and responsibilities as part of the development of the co-op and the training centre was explained. This was a frantic period of endless meetings with various official bodies and organisations. On Tuesday 20 April, a delegation of dockers attended a meeting of Bootle Maritime City Challenge to hear what ESF and ERDF funding opportunities could be available to them, as the emotional and political chains of the dispute continued to drag the stewards in every direction.

Bobby Morton informed another steward that he intended to apply for a job as a union official. Bobby Morton initially took a position with the Unemployed Centre's 'One Fund for All' before taking up a post as a full-time official with the TGWU. At a meeting on 29 April 1998, a discussion also took place on Bobby Morton. He was not present at the time, and it was decided by the stewards that: 'As a result of his application for a paid official's job with the TGWU, he could no longer be a member of their committee.' [71] At the mass meeting on Friday 1 May 1998, Jimmy Davies gave a report back on Bobby Morton's decision; Morton would eventually become a National Official of the TGWU/UNITE representing workers at national and international level.

On May 5, Jimmy Nolan and Herbie Hollerhead joined Irvine Welsh and Dave Cotterill at a meeting with Noam Chomsky in London. Chomsky, an American linguist, philosopher, cognitive scientist, historian, social critic, labour and civil rights campaigner, was keen to show his solidarity with the global nature of the Liverpool docks dispute. Cotterill had been trying to arrange such a gathering for a long time. Over the course of some interesting correspondence with Cotterill, Chomsky said he had been, 'following as best I can (not easy from here) the struggle of the Liverpool dockers. Would very much like to help… I don't use the web myself but can find someone who can do it for me.' [72] Dave Cotterill recalled how: 'At the time, I was trying to get him up to Liverpool. Took until 2005 to get him there! I was there with Jimmy and Herbie, and also Irvine Welsh. We met in the hotel close to the university where he gave the talk, which I went along to. Irvine was made up. I took the photos.' [73] Twenty years later, Chomsky would tell Jack Heyman:

*'Names don't ring a bell, but maybe my bad memory. I once spent several days in Liverpool for talks and discussions at the invitation of the dockers, and spent most of the time with them; wonderful people. Met quite a few, some at their hall, several on a long drive from Oxford, where they picked me up (surprising some of the locals), to Liverpool. They also set up a talk, and I stayed in touch with some for several years. Hope to get back there some day; the real way to keep in touch. Don't recall problems understanding, though I often have them. Could hardly understand a word on the streets in Glasgow, or in parts of Eastern Kentucky for that matter.' [74]*

On 29 May, Prof Peter Fowler confirmed another proposal for the dockers to develop employment opportunities by creating a number of 'intermediate labour market' jobs, which would involve working in information, communication and digital technology. An ESF-funded education course, christened *Akademie* by Dave Cotterill, who was acting as a liaison between the ESF and LJMU, was also being finalised and would eventually pay 15 dockers and various unemployed local young people £650 a month until February 2000. Dave Williams, a local filmmaker and ICDT expert, would run this Digital Technology course alongside ex-dockworker Ken Forsyth, a ships' planner and a very talented and artistic man, who knew how to utilise new technology to produce extraordinary artwork and music. Forsyth was ahead of his time in terms of computer knowledge and design skills, but while all of this was extremely exciting, getting as many former dockers as possible back to work or into training remained the priority for the majority of the former dock shop stewards. [75] Transneeds was the name given to the forklift training centre, and the labour supply company was registered as Liverpool Dockers and Stevedores Company Ltd.

As for the Initiative Factory, the central hub of all the dockers' plans, it was to comprise a bar and a bistro, film and stage production, a multimedia centre and a credit union, and its potential for job creation made it the main focus of many stewards, who had decided that simply sitting back and doing nothing once the dispute had ended was not feasible. Two city centre buildings stood out as ideal locations for the IF; one just off Hardman Street and another on nearby Hope Street, which had formally been known as the Casablanca Club, or 'Casa,' a famous late-night drinking, eating and dancing club.

Recent local elections had placed the Liberals in charge of Liverpool City Council, and so Jimmy Davies, Andy Dwyer and Mike Carden opened negotiations with leading councillors, such as Flo Clucas, who were keen to support the transformation of the unoccupied bar into a community centre. Eventually, the Initiative Factory or *IF*, named after the Lyndsey Anderson film, would indeed find its home at the Casa, where a philosophy was established based on a quote chosen by Mike Carden from Jean-Paul Sartre's *Being and Nothingness*: 'Society demands that he limit himself to his function... There are indeed many precautions to imprison a man in what he is, as if we lived in perpetual fear that he might escape from it; that he might break away and suddenly elude his condition.' [76] The IF also had all the elements of what Tony Melia described as, 'Andy Warhol's Factory Records,' becoming a hub of fresh ideas, proposals and projects that combined politics with the arts, and the refurbishment of the Casa provided some dockers with paid work. [77] Brian Pepper gave structural reports on the building, and Tommy Reason and Ray Stokes, two local builders and talented artists in their own right, drew-up development plans that included options to redesign both the basement and ground floor. Reason and Stokes were long-time supporters of the dockers' campaign, and would, interestingly enough, contribute towards the actual construction of Liverpool's iconic Super Lamb Banana. [78]

It wasn't long before the IF had compiled a list of potential theatre, film and music projects, and on Friday 27 February 1999, less than a year after its original conception, it joined with the Blue Sky Theatre Company to produce *The River of Dreams*, a play by Francis Duffy, which was performed for four nights at Liverpool's Unity Theatre. The IF also collaborated with Paris-based independent production company AMIP to create a one-hour documentary on the work of Ken Loach, with the same two producers, Xavier Carniaux and Elisabeth Marliangeas, who were instrumental in securing funding for Loach's documentary on the docks dispute, *The Flickering Flame*. This project raised donations for the Hardship Fund after its showing at the *Festival Cinema du Reel* in Paris. [79]

In Liverpool, a creative group led by Sol Papadopoulos, Peter Fowler, Wendy Lilly, Dave Williams, Ken Forsyth, Terry Teague, Tony Nelson, Dave Cotterill and Mike Carden continued to work on various film ideas under the IF co-producer banner, including a series of short films on speech and language, a film celebrating Liverpool, a series on work, unemployment and the role of work in a society where it was increasingly hard to find; a short film on Gambia Terrace, its architecture, its history and its past tenants; and a series of short films on Liverpool's parks and gardens. There were also plans for documentaries dedicated to *The Big Issue*, and Chumbawamba and a Bob Dylan fan club, among so many other ideas that would find their way onto the drawing board at the Liverpool dockers' Initiative Factory. On Wednesday 18 August 1999, discussions took place about the IF branching off into becoming a producer in its own right as it now had enough equipment to no longer rely on collaborators. The following day, interviews for Arts Fusion, a diverse European Social Fund music project, were held at Tithebarn House. Jimmy Davies Jr was appointed a joint manager of this project, alongside another person with links to local black musicians, making the younger Davies one of the first sacked dockers to earn a steady wage, as part of an initiative that also provided employment to 10 young Liverpool residents. In reflecting on this period some years later, one steward wrote:

> *'So, when it all ended it was a massive shock to your system. One day, you're part of this big global movement; the next day, you've called it off. Some people agreed, others disagreed, and you're left trying to pick up the pieces. But there was one thing we always said, and that was for all the good people that supported us – and they came from all walks of life. It wasn't just industrial workers, it was the musicians, the comedians who set-up down in London; it was the church. Everyone from within society helped us at some point, so we said we needed to leave something, a lasting memorial to everything that was achieved during that dispute, So, we said, "Look, we need to be doing something. We need to set up something which is tangible, which is always going to be there, and it will reflect on the two and a half years of struggle."' [80]*

# 84
# The CASA

*'We set on an idea of having a building; the idea of the building was that it would be run on socialist ideas. It would be run for the benefit of people, a not-for-profit organisation, and it would be an open house, no barriers for anything, an open house. So, it's easy putting that down on paper; it's actually being able to find, in a city like Liverpool, that type of property. And not just finding it, but to upkeep it.' ~ Terry Teague\**

In December 2000, the *Guardian* ran an article, *Fresh Start – Sacked Dockers Open Nightclub*, [1] which was not exactly the headline that those working hard to refurbish the Casa wanted to see, although the story and the photograph did frame the project in a positive light, quoting one docker who explained how:

> *'It was just a shell of a building; it had been derelict for many years, and all our money had gone on the building. So, we moved in and you got the shock of your life. You think, "Well, that's all problems solved," and then you move in and you couldn't even switch the light on... Sticking with our aims and objectives, sticking with our principles, to me it's the most radical trade union in the country, and that's the RMT. We had Bob Crow come down to open that; he's a regular visitor here, so it keeps us tied in with what's going on in the trade union movement; the problems the workers are facing today. And then the hub of the organisation was upstairs here; what we run from here is general welfare guidance and advice – the Casa Advice and Guidance Service. That will cover everything: benefits advice, lone parent advice, debt advice, computer maintenance.' [2]*

In March 2000, all dockworkers past and present received the news that they now had a base of operations in Liverpool City Centre, [3] thanks to money generated by, amongst so many others, Ken Loach, Jimmy McGovern and Irvine Welsh via the documentaries and dramas

---

* 'What's this place? Stories from radical social centres in the UK and Ireland' (blog), available: https://socialcentrestories.wordpress.com/2008/04/29/the-casa-liverpool/

that they wrote and produced in partnership with the dockers. By Tuesday 14 March 2000, the Initiative Factory Committee had replaced the concept of the Merseyside Port Shop Stewards Committee, even though some shop stewards did have difficulty adapting to these changes. The IFC was now focussing mainly on renovating the Casa, managing finances, establishing training and education courses along with employment opportunities. [4] It was a bitterly difficult period for many of the former shop stewards, faced with a sudden transition from an unofficial trade union movement to a community-based social enterprise. Volunteers continued to work on renovating the building in Hope Street and, despite many setbacks, the centre opened on 16 December 2000. [5]

By 2004, the Initiative Factory had established itself as a hub of community and political activity, offering welfare rights advice alongside community and trade union-based support networks. On 16 June, BBH Solicitors opened an office providing legal services and Bob Crow, general secretary of the National Union of Rail, Maritime and Transport Workers (RMT), also kept an office on site. [6] Together with Crow, Jimmy Nolan became involved in the establishment of a new political party, the Trade Unionist and Socialist Coalition (TUSC). [7] Sadly, 2004 was also the year that the Merseyside Trade Union, Community and Unemployed Resource Centre was forced to close. [8] One key individual who made the CASA a successful social enterprise was Jacquie Richardson who exercised a level of professional control over the bar and the centre that ensured its popularity. Former dock worker Geoff Liddy and then John Deaves managed the financial business of the centre, supported by accountant James Hargreaves. Other dockers managed the day-to-day affairs of the CASA included Tony Nelson, Terry Teague and Andy Dwyer. The community volunteers included Terry Craven, Anthony Thompson, Terry Pettit and many, many others. The CASA would become a city centre community and trade union resource with one of the best bars in Liverpool, a hub/initiator for the arts, theatre and dance all delivered from its impressive four-storey Georgian townhouse in one of the *great historic streets of Liverpool*, Hope Street. As a community enterprise the CASA would always struggle financially. In 2015, Tony Nelson, Terry Pettit and Brian Reade, amongst others, were instrumental in organising a benefit comedy evening held at the Philharmonic Hall in Liverpool. Support was given by John Bishop, Mark Steel, Chris Kearns, The Farm, John Power and Ricky Tomlinson. [9] The CASA would also provide a home for a permanent exhibition of Spanish Civil War photographs and records on its ground floor.

By this time the TGWU had become UNITE the union, via amalgamation with Amicus in 2007. Under new leadership this union, at national level, would support the Liverpool dockers' wish to re-create their own Community Branch NW 567, taking its number from the old Dock Staff Branch 6/567. [10] This Branch would grow to be one of the largest community Branches in UNITE with its base not in Liverpool's newly modernised Transport House, but in the dockers' centre, the CASA, the Community Advice Service Association. It was a trade union branch that attempted to reconfigure the rigid confines of a trade group structure locked in the distant *industrial memory* of the union. At its core was a diverse membership that united solicitors, disabled groups, community advice workers and health workers with the homeless and the unemployed. The role of the CASA was to support rank-and-file community activists, trade unionists, and political groups who now met regularly in the building.

As the austerity of the Conservative government began to hit hard on the poor, Universal Credit started to roll-out across the country; this created an even bigger crisis for those least able to defend themselves, including men such as Stephen Smith. Stephen, articulate and working-class, had a number of serious health issues, yet he was consistently refused benefits and told to *get a job*. He received support from advice workers at the CASA but tragically died in 2019; he weighed just six-stone. Stephen's case became synonymous with a brutal benefits system and Tory austerity. [11] The former Liverpool dockers' work at the CASA would again continue to bring them into conflict with local trade union officials. Steve Higginson, from the CWU, was the 567 Branch Secretary and in this role he would be involved in arguments with local UNITE officials over many issues, including the transfer of CASA branch members to other Unite community/industrial branches. Eventually, the Community Branch that met in the CASA was directed to meet in Transport House. Unsurprisingly, this rift between the officials in Transport House and the dockers would continue.

In Liverpool, a strong tradition of community organisation has always existed. It simply followed the lead of successful radical movements throughout the world who, *embedded* within communities, could *be seen and seen to be* active. During the 1980s, community activists and *not for profit* organisations in Liverpool reclaimed closed schools, council buildings and factories from which to deliver practical and desperately needed social support from Kirkby to Vauxhall, and Everton to the North Liverpool Regeneration Company. Even this work would never be enough to sustain the ever-increasing levels of poverty in working class communities, but it did have an impact. Unions recognized the need to develop services that reflected the daily realities of so many communities and UNITE nationally proclaimed its *community activism* as part of a radical *new* trade union agenda: 'to organise people to strive for a society that places equality, dignity and respect above all else. But our union recognises that we can only achieve this if we bring people together from all walks of life. Even now in the 21st century, too many people in our country are being pushed to the margins of society. They deserve to be heard; they too deserve the support to organise collectively.' [12]

A new generation of community-based organisers within the union challenged the traditional role of full-time officials as they transferred their experiences from working-class estates and social justice campaigns to the trade union movement. This transition exposed the inherent structural problems and conflicts of interest between many industrial full-time officials of the union who were more comfortable dealing with management than the complex, demanding needs of abandoned communities. [13] The dominant culture of *officialdom* actively reduced the impact of this new tier of *community organisers* now employed by the union. To make matters worse, Transport House in Liverpool closed in March 2020 and remains so at the time of writing in November 2021. Here we have a state of the art and recently refurbished building in the heart of the city centre, capable of delivering a vast array of essential community services from welfare rights advice and support to food bank distribution, sat empty and idle and full-time officers were no longer based there: this union building was closed. The workplaces of union members however, such as food workers, bus drivers, dockers, were open.

Running parallel to this refusal, or will, to ignore the realities of post-industrial decline and poverty in the UK, new narratives became popular and, in an effort to explain over five decades of abandoned post-industrial communities, some on *the left* sought to reclaim and re-define people as being somehow still actively connected to their industrial heritage. A new definition was used to locate them firmly in this *pantheon of the left* – they were now to be labelled and re-packaged by Owen Jones, as the *white working class*. [14] Where this placed non-white inhabitants of Sunderland, Bolsover, Workington, and Doncaster, for example, can only be pondered upon. No longer the pig's *bladder on a stick* voter of so many Labour constituencies in the past century, these communities were given a voice in 2016 and it was a voice of rejection: demanding Brexit and an end to immigration. Given another opportunity to speak, they rejected a century of Labour representation and these so-called *red wall seats* were lost to the Tories in the election of December 2019.

# 85

# A Return to Organised Labour

*'Today, the capitalists may, laugh and hand on peerages to their puppets. Tomorrow, when the chain is broken, the whole caboodle of tricksters will fall to pieces. Let us not be deflected by the tricksters from the fight against the main enemy. Capitalism must go!' ~ Harry Constable\**

By all accounts, Simon Jones was a brighter-than-average university student. He was also a committed environmentalist, an implacable opponent of racism, a charming, gentle and caring young man, a free spirit. One of the issues that concerned him most deeply, however, was safety at work, which he might have learned about as a member of *Justice*, a Brighton-based direct-action group that had campaigned in support of the Liverpool dockers. Almost one year after leaving university, Simon was sent to work at Shoreham Port by an employment agency, which, as a Jobseekers' Allowance claimant, he was in no position to refuse. Barely two hours after his arrival at the docks, on 24 April 1998, he was dead. As is the case with most dock work, the job that he was doing for Dutch-owned Euromin Ltd was a hazardous one, that required him to attach bags of cobblestones to hooks that had been welded to the inside of the open grab. He had no experience of this work, and so he was unaware that the conventional method involved attaching a hook to the crane; other employees at Euromin knew enough to claim that the company was reluctant to change the crane from grab to hook and then back again, due to the fact that such a safety measure would cost time and money. Both the crane driver and the company's General Manager, James Martell, were arrested at the time, only to be released without charge. Emma Aynsley, Simon's girlfriend, helped launch a campaign to bring those responsible for his death to justice: 'I'm astonished that there weren't better safety precautions, and that an inexperienced person could be employed to undertake a job that was clearly dangerous.' [1]

---

\* Bill Hunter 'Harry Constable – In His Own Words' (2017, p.217). Living History Library.

Remembering her son, Simon's mother recalled: 'When beggars asked him for money, he invariably gave it to them, even though he had little himself. But his seriousness about politics never obscured his wacky sense of humour. He was exceptionally well-loved.' [2] Campaigners put pressure on the Crown Prosecution Service to take action against Euromin and Martell. The CPS initially determined that there was insufficient evidence for a charge of manslaughter, however they eventually reconsidered their inaction following an impassioned Commons speech on 3 March 1999 by George Galloway, the Labour MP for Glasgow Kelvin. He told his fellow MPs how Martell had 'laughed out loud' upon hearing that he could face prosecution. According to Galloway: 'Martell's contempt for the laws of health and safety in this country, his greed and hunger for profit, and his negligence and carelessness slaughtered a young man just as clearly as if he had pushed him off the dock with his own hands.' [3] As Simon's family awaited the CPS's final decision, the alternative option of pursuing private prosecution remained both expensive and difficult, leaving them to hope for an inquest verdict of unlawful killing that would put pressure on government prosecutors to reopen the case for a third time. Ultimately, on 29 November 2001, James Martell and Euromin were acquitted on manslaughter charges. [4]

---

MDHC acted in concert with the union for the entire duration of the dispute, as they had always done before. At no time did the MDHC seek to utilise anti-union legislation against the TGWU. [5] In his book *Liverpool – The Hurricane Port*, Andrew Lees wrote that, in a sense, the history of the Liverpool dockers ended in January 1998:

> *The two-and-a-half-year Liverpool dock strike proved to be the death of a way of thinking. These traditionalists had battled for a way of life as well as a livelihood, determined that their city should remain a cargo handling giant... The white working-class had become an inconvenient relic and the docks were now cenotaphs.' [6]*

Writing in 1997, one Liverpool docker spoke of how his experiences had guided his own approach to trade unionism and political theory, as he informed Reclaim the Streets: 'our stand is simple and straightforward. We sell our labour-power and we uphold our right to withdraw our labour power, otherwise we're slaves.' [7] This was not a section of the working-class ready to fade into obscurity or become *an inconvenient relic*.

Peter Hadden, who organised support for the Liverpool dockers struggle in Belfast and Dublin from 1995, observed how: 'from its most embryonic stages, the Liverpool dockers' trade union philosophy was driven by their political and class-based experiences for, at the end of the nineteenth century, class lines were being clearly drawn. The iron chains that linked Ireland with Liverpool were forged during this time.' [8] This element of *Larkinism*, together with the roles played by other giants of trade unionism, such as Irish revolutionary James Connolly and the English syndicalist Tom Mann, flowed into the complex web of influences and experiences that comprised the template for the organisation of Liverpool's dock labourers, many of whom carried with them a shared Irish heritage. These deep connections and well-woven stories of their own history were still evident in 1996, as Larkin's grandson addressed a mass meeting of the Liverpool dockers, drawing grumblings from another Irishman, Jimmy Nolan, when the former dedicated a prayer to the dockers' struggle.

In Liverpool, the ramifications of the 28-month docks dispute continued to be felt, with employees of Drake Port Services Ltd. looking to organise a strike of their own, and so the question begged to be asked, *who would break a strike by strike-breakers?* They had issued their own bulletin in February 1998, *The Dart*, to publicise their plight and seek solidarity for their cause, ironically repeating the same complaints that had led to the dismissal of 500 former registered dockworkers, whom they replaced in September 1995. [9] Nothing became of this flirtation with trade union principles because in April 2001 DPS scabs were again being recruited to break a docks dispute. As TGWU members, the Liverpool boatmen threatened the Dock Company with a strike about their pay and conditions. The company was determined to halt any displays of opposition to its will: 'To keep the port going, they and their partners, Drake Port Services, informed their employees that they may be retrained as boat-handlers to cover for any strike action.' [10] The scabs soon reverted to their natural role as strike-breakers. [11] As one *Drake employee* remarked at the time: 'It's a powder keg situation. If the lads are retrained to do this work, they will have to cross the lines, and we have seen before just what trouble that can cause.' [12] In a perfect example of what was never said by any local TGWU official during the Liverpool docks dispute, docks officer, Colin Carr, stated: 'Our advice to members is, don't cross picket lines. Bringing Drake into the frame would just inflame the situation.' [13] On Thursday 5 April 2001, Allan Price, MDHC's personnel manager, was back on Roger Phillips's BBC Radio Merseyside programme, defending the employer's attack on their employees, the boatmen. [14]

A month later, the port was on the verge of a strike involving the remnants of 400 MDHC (non-dockworker) employees who had continued to work throughout the 1995-98 dispute. According to Barry Turnbull, business correspondent at both the *Liverpool Echo* and *Daily Post*:

> *The remaining [port] workers, including mooring staff, river pilots and dredger men, face the final fatal blow following the abolition of the jobs-for-life National Dock Labour Scheme twelve years ago. MDHC seized on the looming legislation to try to coerce boatmen into changing hours and working practices.' [15]*

Local dock official Carr stated: 'We are fighting this tooth and nail at the moment. It was clear that Mersey Docks was trying to jump the gun on the legislation in the dispute earlier this year and made no secret of that. In fact, it was part of their opening gambit. MDHC will seek to have the work done more cheaply, and as a union we will find ourselves having to resist redundancies, reorganisation and so on.' [16] Dock Company boss Price went on to explain the reason for shedding more labour was that: 'it is clear that more shipping lines are seeking to handle their own vessels in the port.' [17] The tide was starting to turn: not for the principles of trade unionism or democracy, but because the TGWU conceded union recognition to, again, protect the *fabric of the union* against legislative fines due to be imposed upon them. On 13 July 2001, the *Daily Post* confirmed:

*'Workers accused of breaking the Mersey docks dispute are to be allowed to join the Transport and General Workers' Union. Union officials, the day before, had backed down in the face of a £3m compensation claim on behalf of 47 men who were denied membership of the union… an employment tribunal in Liverpool in June concluded that the men who work for stevedore firm Drake Port Services had been unlawfully excluded from the T&GWU.'* [18]

Frank Skelly, a Drake employee, who was part of the original tribunal case, explained that this was what he and his colleagues had wanted all along, as he told the *Daily Post*: 'Anyone employed at the docks needs the protection of a trade union, which is why we have fought so hard for membership.' [19] Many of the scabs maintained that they had not 'stolen' the jobs of the sacked dockers because they had been told that they would never be allowed back on to the docks, which in effect meant that it was simply a case of filling vacancies. [20] Skelly intended to organise a strike against the Dock Company, under the assumption that TGWU membership would ensure the kind of union backing that was absent in 1995-98: 'This is going to open a whole can of worms, to ensure the working practices at this firm are going to be fully exposed,' he said. [21] In addition to their demands for union representation, the scabs were still prepared to pursue compensation claims against the TGWU for sums ranging between £5,000 and £63,000 per claimant, following the Industrial Tribunal's judgement that the TGWU was in breach of the Trade Union and Labour Relations Act (1992) by excluding workers from membership without a justifiable reason. This led to the TGWU confirming its offer of membership to those *scabs* wishing to initiate a pay and bonus dispute that was simmering at Drakes. [22] As part of its ongoing coverage of the situation, the *Daily Post* published a letter submitted by Terry Teague:

*'Whilst accepting that it is nearly six years since the Liverpool dock dispute started, the actions of the strike-breakers should never be forgotten or forgiven, for the way they helped undermine a just and courageous campaign for workers' rights. The article, which mentioned that the bad working practices within the port are going to be fully exposed because the strike-breakers now belong to the TGWU, only further justifies the grounds that lay behind the 28-month Liverpool dockworkers' dispute.'* [23]

Uncertainty surrounding the future of the port began escalating as rumours of takeovers and potential mergers circulated in the city. In 2004 the MDHC received a bid from an anonymous private equity group; the news caused shares in the company to rise by almost 10% to 933.5p. It was rumoured that the Dock Company themselves were making this bid to keep control of the port's undoubted value and potential to make some people very rich. In a statement issued to the Stock Exchange on 10 November 2004, the company confirmed that a preliminary bid had been received, but the statement was made purposefully vague, neglecting to state whether or not the buyer intended to retain the existing management team. A report by Dow Schofield Watts considered:

*'One possibility is that existing management, led by chief executive Peter Jones, has been spooked into making a bid in response to Manchester-based Peel Holdings buying a*

*substantial stake in the ports group. Last week, Peel, which owns and operates Liverpool*
*John Lennon Airport, acquired a 9.25% stake in MDHC. Peel already owns*
*Clydeport, near Glasgow, and Manchester Ship Canal and its associated docks. At its*
*current share price, MDHC is worth £716m.' [24]*

This report highlighted how MDHC shares had outperformed the UK transport sector by 16% that year, having become the second-largest ports group in the country after Associated British Ports, posting half-year pre-tax profits of £28.7m. James Dow observed that MDHC assets were extremely attractive to private equity groups, largely due to the fact that: 'a lot of debt can be raised on the back of them.' [25] What seemed strange at this time was that most private equity groups would be expected to undertake a human resources-led due diligence examination of any company it had an interest in purchasing. This would involve a detailed study of potential employee risks, including factors such as employment terms and agreements, individual contracts, collective bargaining agreements and both retention and severance agreements, as well as compensation and stock options for executives. [26] However, none of these basic risk assessments took place prior to acquisition. From the outset of the dispute, MDHC directors Trevor Furlong, Bernard Cliff and Peter Jones had all spoken of the need to protect the interests of '900 other port workers' along with the requirement to keep the company afloat, and these statements were regularly echoed by Bill Morris. [27] These acute concerns for the company's future and their labourforce appeared to fade into insignificance once the dispute was brought to a close in January 1998 and the potential for bosses to make some real money emerged as expected.

Peel Holdings already owned significant shares in MDHC, despite having previously sold 8.3% to Prudential and Mercury Asset Management for £31.2 million in 1996, leaving them with a 25% holding in assets in the ports of Liverpool, Heysham and the Medway towns of Sheerness and Chatham. [28] According to a *Manchester Evening News* report in June 2005, James Whittaker of Peel Holdings had: 'watched Mersey Docks like a hawk for at least the last year and has moved now because of the bid from the venture capitalist. I can't see him failing now. He waited until he had taken Peel private last year before doing this, because it's easier to do a deal like this when you are not listed.' [29] When Peel made their move, they offered £10 for each Liverpool and Medway share, but MDHC had already declared that full-year profits had been hit by charges of £7m relating to advisor fees and executive incentive plans, in addition to £3.5m in fees paid during the private equity group's approach. They wanted more money. Warnings emerged that further costs would be expected to be split between their investment banking advisor ABN Amro, along with their lawyers, Linklaters, and accountants, Price Waterhouse and Cooper arising from the Peel bid. The Dock Company then declared that it would be making a £3.5m provision for share-based incentive schemes, some £2.6m of which was earmarked for directors, led by the newly promoted Peter Jones, who replaced retired former Chief Executive officer Trevor Furlong. Based on two years' basic salary, Jones could expect a £640,000 payoff to supplement share options, worth in excess of £500,000, with a company spokesperson stating at the time that the prospect of Jones staying on post-takeover had not even been discussed. [30]

Later that month, the Port of Liverpool, along with its extraordinary land assets, was bought for £771m by Peel Holdings opening opportunities to transform the port, its estates and its balance sheets. As part of the deal, Peel agreed to pay £18.7m into MDHC's pension scheme, with the first £9.8m deposited within 10 days of a formal agreement being reached, followed by another £8.9m by 31 January 2006. According to press reports, a new era was about to dawn in the history of Liverpool, once the world's greatest seaport: 'The Mersey Docks and Harbour Company disappeared as a publicly listed company at midnight, with ownership switching to Peel Holdings, owners of Liverpool John Lennon Airport, the Manchester Ship Canal and the Trafford Centre. Peel assumed ownership of the MDHC, and with it a vast estate of docklands and real estate spanning some 2,000 acres.' [31] Finance commentators described this as a 'painless takeover.' [32] Peter Kilfoyle, former MP for Liverpool Walton, claimed in 2013, that Peel Holdings had received millions in EU and UK public money, while expressing his concern about the influence that the group was having over local planning:

> 'We have to ask ourselves if putting public money into organisations like Peel, who operate through a web of companies that funnel a lot of money offshore, is actually in the national interest… Where does the investment go?' [33]

By the time of the sale, MDHC claimed it used only 400 DPS *strike-breakers* in Liverpool, all of whom would report for work as normal to facilitate any takeover. [34] Meanwhile, hundreds of miles from Liverpool, Associated British Ports Holdings Ltd (ABP) announced that Peter Jones would be leaving the Dock Company and joining ABP as CEO on 1 April 2007. Ten years after the end of the Liverpool dispute, the basic Marxist philosophy of workers selling their *labour power* revisited the city's docklands, flowing in from the sea like mists from a distant shore, as the moral authority of the Liverpool dockworker was rekindled in a brave new wave of industrial action. On Friday 17 October 2014, Unite declared that the scab labour brought in to break the 1995-98 docks dispute would be removed from the Port of Liverpool. Drake Port Services had finally lost the contract it had held since September 1995. On Thursday 16 October 2014, DPS employees called a mass meeting to ask UNITE to represent their interests following their dismissal, even going so far as to request that sacked Liverpool dock worker, Terry Teague, speak on their behalf. This did not take place as the contract to provide dock labour to Peel Ports transferred to a new labour agency, Blue Arrow Ltd. These new dockers would fight to regain the rights once held by those who had gone before them, reigniting the *Big Flame* of over 150 years of struggle, as they realised that, like all workers, all they owned was their ability to sell their labour; a commodity rendered worthless without the authority to withdraw it. [35]

In 2012, Teague and Tony Nelson's continued involvement on the docks became formalised through a limited funding arrangement with the International Transport Workers' Federation (ITF). This allowed them to influence labour developments in the port of Liverpool through, what Peel Ports management would affirm some years later, their 'knowledge and experience' and their 'strong relationship' with a new generation of dockers. [36] It is interesting to note that these former dock shop stewards could enjoy a strong working relationship with a global company such as Peel Ports and yet not achieve the same relationship with the fairly rudimentary management of the Dock Company and local officials of the TGWU.

By June 2015, news broke that around 200 dockers employed by Blue Arrow were to be balloted ahead of potential strike action after months of negotiations over pay and conditions had reached an impasse. The dockers had already rejected a proposed 2% pay rise and were now demanding that Blue Arrow's two-tier sickness pay system be scrapped, with one of their number contacting the *Liverpool Echo* to warn that a walkout would bring the port to a standstill. [37] Unite explained that Blue Arrow were refusing to budge, despite employees suffering below-inflation pay increases and pay freezes during the preceding five years, and the agency responded by stating that discussions would continue 'amicably until we find a mutual resolution.' [38] Blue Arrow claimed that the rejected pay offer was in line with what had been accepted across the board at Peel Ports, including other sections represented by Unite. But these dockers were not employed by Peel; they were rejecting terms and conditions offered by Blue Arrow, their employer. Peel Ports recognised this critical detail stating that: 'We support Blue Arrow and Unite in their efforts to seek a mutually amicable resolution to the discussions they have been having since February.' [39] Peel Ports declined to comment on claims that any strike action would bring the port to a standstill. [40]

It was at this point that the remarkable story of the Liverpool dockers turned full circle. Sacked Liverpool dockers Tony Nelson and Terry Teague, twenty years after they were dismissed, were back on the docks representing dock workers. Terry Teague was to inform the *Liverpool Echo*: 'We have been back down at the docks organising, as part of UNITE, for the last three years. It's a big change. The head of UNITE, Len McCluskey, is a former Liverpool docker and the union has a spine. Today's young dockers were at school at the time of the dispute, and the union wants to be there to help them… The pay and terms and conditions of the 300 workers at the port of Liverpool should be protected now that Blue Arrow have won the contract to supply labour to the thriving port.' [41]

Now a new beginning was unfolding on the Liverpool docks. On Friday 13 January 2017 at Seaforth Container Terminal, John Lynch, the *new leader* of the Liverpool dockers, called for a mass demonstration against the numerous grievances they had with Blue Arrow, as well as the dreadful conditions that existed in the port following over three decades of de-investment. Conditions and services for road hauliers at the port were also non-existent. But events were moving quickly as Peel Ports attempted to rectify the years of bad management and under-investment in the port of the Liverpool by both the Dock Company and Drake Port Services. Not for the first time, Peel Ports intervened directly. On 8 January 2018, John Lynch announced that Blue Arrow had, like Drakes Ltd. before them, lost the contract to supply labour to Peel Ports. Lynch was active within the International Dockworkers' Council and had strong links with other union-organised ports in the UK. The IDC expressed its solidarity with the Liverpool dockers, as well as its willingness to take direct action in support of their cause, as the *new* port authority agreed to hire all 328 Blue Arrow dockworkers directly, bringing about a return of the pre-September 1995 employment situation. Terry Teague emailed various comrades to inform them of this extraordinary development: 'Peel Ports have made a business decision to take the 328 Blue Arrow Seaforth workforce in-house, so that they will now be employed directly by the port authority, Peel Ports.' [42] On 11 January, Mark Whitworth, CEO of Peel Ports, confirmed the news:

*'...all Container Division colleagues [dockers] together under the Peel Ports Group umbrella is a logical next step. This change will help us to create a safer, more inclusive and more rewarding working environment for all. It is excellent news for our staff, which is why we've had such a positive reaction from UNITE.' [43]*

Len McCluskey, the general secretary of UNITE, welcomed the return of permanent dock labour as a victory for the Liverpool dockers:

*'It is testament to the hard work and perseverance of UNITE members and their shop stewards. It marks a significant break with casual work practices at the Port of Liverpool, and gives the dockworkers involved the security of direct employment. As a former Liverpool dockworker, I know that this agreement will not only bring stability to the lives of dockworkers and their families, but stability to the Port of Liverpool, enabling it to grow and be a source of decent jobs for local community.' [44]*

John Lynch, the Liverpool dockers' leader, echoed McCluskey's sentiments, stating that:

*'This is a massive achievement and can only help all workers at the Port of Liverpool. This couldn't have been achieved without the help and tremendous work that Terry Teague, Tony Nelson and Bobby Morton have done, along with the members and the support from the IDC. Terry Teague, Tony Nelson and Bobby Morton were the original Liverpool dockers that were sacked in 1995, and [they] have been key and instrumental figures that have supported and helped to achieve this deal. It means that we will no longer be working for an agency and working directly for the port authority.' [45]*

In these celebratory emails of 2018, the local union still wanted to challenge the role played by sacked Liverpool dockers in these developments. The regional secretary felt it necessary to correct the official press release of 28 November 2018 issued by Alex Flynn, Head of Media and Campaigns at Unite. E-mailing Flynn directly on the same day, the local Unite official stated:

*'There is a small but very important correction to be made to the press release Alex. It may be pointless now but Terry Teague is not an officer of Unite and he should not have put this out in his name. Kenny Rowe is the officer for the Docks in the North West.' [46]*

Terry Teague and Tony Nelson's role on the docks ended in July 2021. By September 2019, twenty-four years after 500 Liverpool dockers had been sacked by the Mersey Docks & Harbour Company, the Mediterranean Shipping Company's (MSC) entered into a joint-venture agreement with Peel Ports to develop the container facility at the port of Liverpool, in an effort to attract greater volumes of the transatlantic trade. [47] Peel Ports had negotiated a further transfer of around 600 dockworkers to the Mediterranean Shipping Company, bringing the expected number of permanently employed dockworkers up to an estimated 1,000 men and women, all benefitting from equal terms and conditions. However, these increases in employment at the port would be delayed because of the unfolding Covid 19 global pandemic in March 2020.

By August 2021 four new container cranes entered the port as part of the next phase of a £400 million investment creating at least another 240 jobs in the port. [48] In October 2021, a group of dock workers on zero-hour contracts struck after a row over their employer, Staff Force, failing to pay them. 'Because we're zero hours, we have no power, we've got no trade union, no real rights with the company. So we did the only thing we could which was to stand up together, so that's what we've done.' [49] This emphasis upon the need for trade unions to organise workers who are on casual, zero-hours contracts and fire and re-hire contracts etc. rests within the concept of direct action - of *union power against employer power*. It seems popular amongst senior officials and regional secretaries of Unite in 2021 to threaten employers with negative posts on facebook, twitter and other platforms. Hardly a transformational route for radical working-class politics but, still, it is oppositional and publicises union struggles. Unite Northwest asked members in October to: 'Send a message to Interim Chief Executive at East Lancashire Hospitals NHS Trust, Martin Hodgson, demanding he meet with Unite and settle this unnecessary dispute as soon as possible.' [50] Unite politics sent a similar email to members on 'fire and rehire', supporting a strike at the Weetabix Factory.

Internationally, the dockers' legacy would build upon their naturally globalized industry. Australian *Wharfies* supported the Great London Dock Strike of 1889 and these unofficial/official links continued in the 1989 national strike against the abolition of the Dock Labour Board Scheme and the 1995 *Liverpool lock-out*. The Unofficial National Port Shop Stewards' Movement often met with their international comrades, such as the Tenerife dockers over problems relating to the trade in tomato fruit from this island. Unofficial international links always existed and Ken Loach's film, *The Flickering Flame,* would capture the mood of many delegates – especially those from the US, Australia, Sweden, Denmark and France – who shared their Liverpool comrades' distrust of the *official* International Transport Workers' Federation. These rumblings of discontent would eventually lead to the establishment of the International Dockworkers' Council, whose first chairman, Patrick Minot, signed a letter declaring that: 'The only purpose and objective of this international committee is to create a movement of solidarity in the dockers' profession, which is now internationally threatened. It is clear, that the first action of the international committee is to see the reinstatement of the Liverpool dockers in their jobs with dignity.' [51]

Four years later, on 18 April 2000, the IDC would have its first official meeting. Conferences were taking place in Liverpool, Montreal, Antwerp and Paris, [52] before the Spanish *Coordinadora* hosted the inaugural IDC Constitutional Conference in Tenerife, which saw delegates from the US, Canada, France, Sweden, Cyprus and Denmark attend this landmark event. [53] The first International Dockers' Council meeting took place at a time when the rank-and-file international movement, that came to the aid of the Liverpool dock workers, had been re-awakened. On 25 October 2000, Terry Teague, the former Liverpool dock shop steward who became IDC Secretary, responded to the EU's flexibility plans for European ports. [54] In September 2001, an IDC statement on European port action was issued by its European Zone, following a meeting in Marseille, France, arguing in favour of a resolution to: 'fight against the Directive in an action as large as possible.' [55] The

International Dockers' Council would become one of the defining legacies of the Liverpool dock dispute and by 2018 they had recruited over 100,000 members, making it a growing force in global trade unionism, and especially in many African ports. [56]

# 86
# The Dismantling of Democracy

*'Who says organisation, says oligarchy!' ~ Robert Michels*

The Liverpool docks' dispute, after two years and four months, should have been an inspiration to workers wishing to fight back against casual labour, imposed contracts of employment, zero-hours contracts, fire and re-hire, anti-trade union laws and corporate greed. [1] Writing at the end of the dispute Jim Dye, chair of the Public and Commercial Services Union, wanted to know if the outcome could have been different, and in an article titled, *Defeated, But Still Fighting: The Liverpool Docks Dispute – Some Lessons for Socialists,* Dye wrote that the fight of the dockers should not be viewed as being over. 'We need to take it into our unions and also the rotten heart of the Labour Party, and attempt to weaken the bureaucrats in both organisations, exposing their dirty role to the working class as a whole. When the class struggle intensifies again, the lessons of the dockers should not be forgotten... What was key to the dispute was the need to deal effectively with the union bureaucrats. The Broad Left (BL) within the TGWU was a complete failure when it came to mounting any kind of fightback against the leadership of Morris & Co. A small grouping with a secretive nature, the BL could not even mobilise its own members to support the dockers.' [2] The solution for this writer was the launch of: 'a rank-and-file based left grouping, that combines the best elements of the old BL with an open democratic structure... Whilst the winning of union positions was essential, this could only be successfully achieved by placing the rank-and-file at the centre of activity and outlook in order to make any newly-elected left leadership accountable.' [3]

---

* R. Michels, 'Political Parties: A Sociological Study of the Oligarchial Tendencies of Modern Democracy', 1911.

Dye singled out Jimmy Nolan, a Socialist Labour Party member who retained the political outlook of the old Communist Party in relation to the unions, while at the same time describing him as: 'a genuinely nice person who, perhaps strangely, had no apparent sectarian poison within him.' These personality traits may explain why, in Dye's opinion, Nolan received little criticism from large sections of the left: 'Of course, as others have said, we could do with more Stalinists like Nolan in the unions, because at least he led the dispute well in many respects, but on the question of seriously addressing the issue of the union bureaucracy, Nolan had no answers.' [4] His analysis concluded by referring to Nolan's frequently made point about the inherent victory for workers rests within the struggle itself – the act of rebellion:

> 'Even though the dockers had been defeated, they had also been in many ways liberated… as Marx explained, consciousness is changed in struggle… if the dispute has proved only one thing, it is that ordinary people are more than capable of extraordinary achievements.' [5]

In this regard Dye was partly correct in his critique of the *absent role of the Broad Left* but to speak of its reform escapes the essential reality that the left in the TGWU was as much an integral part the union's staggering bureaucracy as the managerial class of its paid officials. Thus, the union was not driven by the *principles of working-class solidarity*, but by the personal ambitions of its paid officials. The TGWU's inbuilt bureaucracy dated back to before its formation in 1922 and marked the *fault lines* that would ultimately undermine democratic accountability. The union's seamless alignment with the ports' employers and the state against the dockers has been well documented in official government reports, inquiries and labour history studies since 1897 and before. [6] Dock labourers were never opposed to the principles of trade unionism; they were opposed to the union's bureaucracy who saw rank-and-file organisation, in the union and on the waterfront, as a threat to the unelected power of paid officials. The failure of the TGWU to support the Liverpool dockers was not the responsibility of one union official or one general secretary – as a democratic organisation, *it was the responsibility of the membership*. It was the *bureaucratic architecture* of the union, the complex network of patronage, entitlement and career, that incorporated rank-and-file activists at the cost of democratic control. Indeed, the structure of unions, such as the TGWU, was that they were officer-controlled as opposed to rank-and-file led; a situation the TGWU *Broad Left* never questioned or challenged. It is not surprising that UK dockers did not engage wholeheartedly with the TGWU *Broad Left*.

Opposition to the power of unelected paid officials has been a consistent theme of internal conflict since the formation of general unions at the end of the nineteenth century. By 1911, the Tonypandy miners Unofficial Reform Committee's pamphlet - the *Miners Next Step* - identified an immutable critique of trade union bureaucracy. These critiques and alternative union structures were pursued by Sydney and Beatrice Webb and established by Noah Ablett, Bill Heywood, James Connelly, Daniel de Leon, and Tom Mann. Robert Michels first developed his 'Iron law of oligarchy' in a study of trade union democracy in 1911. [7] Examining the absence of democracy in the TGWU in 1952, Joseph Goldstein concluded that: 'It becomes difficult to avoid the conclusion that the Transport and General

Workers Union is an oligarchy at every level of its structure, failing to elicit the active participation of its members.' [8]

In 2020, an investigation into sexual harassment in the General Municipal and Boilermakers Union (GMB) uncovered how the power of the union's full-time officer corps overwhelmed their sense of any accountability to membership democracy:

> '…while the Central Executive Council (CEC) formally leads the GMB, in practice it is the Senior Management Team (SMT) who largely run the union. The members of the SMT are the National president, the General Secretary; all nine regional secretaries; the legal director; the director of external relations and training; the finance director (vii) the human resources director and the IT director. This means that the Regional Secretaries [all men] are always in the majority on the SMT… the lay structure formally dominates under the Rules… the real power in the GMB rests with the regional secretaries and the general secretary… it was put to me that 'nothing happens' [at the CEC] without the regional secretary whispering in the ear of their delegate.' [9]

This process of officer control and *unaccountable power* exposed in the GMB was compounded when the union's general secretary, Tim Roache, decided to take a lie-detector test rather than initiate an independent investigation into member allegations of discrimination. The union's National President, Barbara Plant, was apparently: 'unaware of the allegations or the subsequent lie-detector test'. [10] Roache was reportedly given a £500,000 retirement bonus by the union to supplement his annual salary of over £130,000. Such examples of trade union oligarchy indicate the dysfunctionality of an organisational structure operating beyond democratic accountability and the normal experiences and hardships of trade union members and the working class generally. These tendencies are replicated in all UK trade unions to varying degrees. John Pilger highlighted the role of *insipid hierarchy* in the TGWU: 'The dockers did not climb down, they were let down, and forced to end their remarkable two-year struggle because the Transport and General Workers' Union virtually guaranteed its failure. Had this rich and powerful organisation launched a national campaign, the battle could have been won there and then.' [11] This led Bill Morris to repeat his claim that Pilger had a vendetta against the union:

> John Pilger and others like him, with their message of false hope, who did more than anyone to prolong the agony… the dockers' solidarity and resilience did not succeed… The view that victory could have been achieved if only the T&G had been prepared to ignore the law and put the entire union at risk is a fantasy.' [12]

On the subject of the TGWU's role in the dispute, an article published in *Workers' Liberty* argued that:

> 'Morris was right that the anti-union laws were a major factor in his understanding of the TGWU's role in the conflict, and this analysis reflected what happened at the 1997 Labour Party conference. When… [there was] a resolution on the agenda calling for repeal of the anti-union laws, Bill Morris argued against the idea. When it was suggested

*that the Labour government should abolish all the anti-union laws introduced by the Tories, the TGWU argued against it…' [13]*

Rather than challenge the real power structures of the union, the *Broad Left* merely perpetuates the anti-democratic outcome of *unelected and elected elites, expansive systems of managerialism and lucrative career progression* that simply enhance this dominant culture until it degenerates to the state exposed within the GMB in 2020. Under the weight of these top-heavy layers of bureaucracy, democracy is always the first victim. In the GMB's general secretary election of 2019, only 50,571 ballot papers were returned after 595,441 ballot papers had been issued, a turnout of only 8.5%. In the Unite 2013 general secretary election, 15% of members voted and in 2017 only 12% of Unite took part in the same election. In elections for the Unite General Executive Council, only 7.6% of members voted with a third of the positions being unopposed. [14] The continuing decline of democratic involvement as exposed by such low turnout in union elections reflects a much deeper malaise for *the Labour Movement.* This has allowed a *paid bureaucracy* of full-time officials who are employed for life and unaccountable to the democratic wishes or rights of TGWU members.

Len McCluskey retired from office on Thursday 26 August 2021. Of the ten general secretaries who followed Bevin's leadership of the TGWU, six had previously held the post of assistant general secretary, two had been national organisers, while Bill Morris and Tony Woodley had held the post of deputy general secretary. From this narrow male gene pool, the democracy that the TGWU proclaimed ensured that the *crown did not tumble* far beyond the desk of the incumbent general secretary, just like the early Roman kings. But the *keepers of this ancient tradition, the hiders of the fault line,* all seemed to fall apart in unison by April 2021. Steve Turner and Howard Beckett, who both held the posts of assistant general secretary, appeared the likely heirs to McCluskey's crown. The *Broad Left*, now re-branded the *United Left*, claimed their usual influence in these matters and selected Turner as their candidate. In response to this move, Beckett and the *Progressive United Left Scotland* laid siege to each region's powerbase in an attempt to impose the candidate of their choice for general secretary early in 2021. [15] More importantly, the door was finally closed on any lay-member wishing to seek election for the post of leader of their union. The threshold to join the ballot was increased from 50 branch nominations to around 150. This gave even more power to union officials who had sole discretion to bar branches or establish newly-created branches. The main purpose was to stop the nomination of the *Labour Right's* nominee, Gerard Coyne; it failed. The former Midlands regional secretary, who in the 2017 general secretary election received 53,544 (41.3%) as opposed to McCluskey's winning declaration of 59,067 votes (45.5%), would be a serious candidate in the 2021 election. As if matters for the union's elite could not deteriorate any further another left candidate, Sharon Graham, an Executive Officer of the union, declared her intention to stand – potentially splitting the left vote in three. She did not seek the endorsement of any left faction or the regional barons of the union.

During the election Sharon Graham gave an interview to Iain Dale of LBC Radio. As a young parliamentary researcher for Thatcher's Tory party, Dale worked on the abolition of the Dock Labour Scheme in 1989 feeding the Sun newspaper and Tory politicians with all the necessary histrionics to justify the return to casual labour on the docks. He is still obviously very proud of the role he played, writing regularly on how *he defeated the dockers and crossed their picket lines.* [16] Graham told Dale: 'The structures in Unite are 100 years old. They were set up effectively in all our heritage unions when they were domestic employers. We are now dealing with multi-national employers – we need to have a root and branch restructuring of how we do our business.' [17] On 18 June 2021, Howard Beckett withdrew his nomination and on Thursday 26 August Sharon Graham was elected general secretary of Unite with 46,696 votes (37.7%) whilst Steve Turner received 41,833 votes (33.8%), and Gerard Coyne received 35,334 votes (28.5%). Only 10% of Unite members took part in this election.

The *fault lines,* hidden behind rule-book references to democracy and written into the union's constitution in 1922 by Ernest Bevin, ensured that democratic processes could be, and were, ignored by its governing elite whenever necessary. This could only take place in the context of an ever-reducing influence of democratic involvement and control exercised by trade union members. Organised labour's response to Thatcher's economic and social policies in the 1980s would result in the decimation of the trade union movement's industrial heartlands and traditional communities. Conflict would be replaced by managerialism – as labour entered a new period of history, a third way epitomised by the New Labour Party. This meant centralised control at the expense of democratic involvement and accountability, repositioning the labour movement in partnership with capitalism and dismissing its historical roots. This dismissal of internal democratic structures is mirrored in each of the main labour organisations: New Labour, the Trades Union Congress, and the International Transport Workers' Federation. Over 25 years later, the general secretary of the ITF, David Cockroft, confirmed that Bill Morris stopped the ITF from galvanizing solidarity action for dockworkers: 'this was one of several occasions on which he threatened, without any action, to disaffiliate from the ITF.' [18] Here we have four distinct democratic organisations, each with their own rules and procedures, all being jettisoned on the basis of one individual's proclamation: do nothing to support the Liverpool Dockers! In effect, the Labour Movement was following instructions from the New Labour Party to disengage from the working class.

During his time as Labour leader, Ed Miliband sought to resurrect the party as 'a *movement* with a mass membership actively involved in community politics', [19] and established a new system for selecting any future party leader. This system replaced the electoral college with One Member One Vote and widened participation to include *registered supporters*. It was also intended 'to stop a candidate who could not command the Parliamentary Labour Party (PLP) reaching the ballot.' [20] Having gained the necessary nominations from the PLP, Corbyn's campaign was helped by 'a surge in new members and supporters who paid £3 to take part in the vote, leading to a near-tripling of those eligible to about 550,000 people' [21] and he was elected leader in a 'stunning first-round victory that dwarfed even the mandate for Tony Blair in 1994.' [22] In spite of this *democratic mandate,* Corbyn's leadership was never accepted by the PLP and Labour *Centrists* who eventually found their moment to challenge his leadership following the result of the referendum on membership of the European Union (Brexit). Owen Smith was the sole challenger, and Corbyn was once again elected as leader – this time with an increased mandate (61.8%) and a 'majority over Smith in every category – members (59%), registered supporters (70%) and trades union affiliates (60%). The winner pointed out that he had secured his second mandate in a year and urged his colleagues to accept what had been a democratic decision.' [23] Len McCluskey said 'We urge Labour MPs to heed the signal sent by the members, twice now in one year, about the direction they want for the party. This includes respecting and supporting the elected leader and his team; no more sniping, plotting and corridor coups.' [24]

Corbyn and his team were at all times working against a hostile PLP and party machinery, and it was only in August 2017 that they finally won a slim 18-17 majority on the party's ruling NEC. With growing concerns from the membership that Labour MPs were actively working against their democratic wishes, some on the left advocated for *mandatory reselection* [25] in a move that would make MPs accountable to their local party. In spite of popular support from the membership and campaign group Momentum, the new Left-dominated party leadership and trades unions did not give the move their backing. This anti-democratic decision, presumably made on the basis of defending *Left MPs* from the risk of deselection, represents a missed opportunity to radically democratise the Labour Party. The lasting impact of this can be seen in the period following the general election defeat of 2019 and the subsequent election of Keir Starmer as party leader: the near complete disenfranchisement of party members and a dwindling membership, the unilateral decision by Starmer to suspend the whip from Jeremy Corbyn, the routine use of allegation and suspensions against left members and candidates etc. The critical point is this: even under the leadership of Jeremy Corbyn, who sought to democratise the Labour Party and had the support of organised grassroots membership groups like Momentum and a majority on the party's ruling NEC, when facing a hostile and unaccountable PLP who could have been subject to the democratic will of their members, the risk of losing *their own Left MPs* was deemed too great.

With the election of Sharon Graham, the *fault line* lay exposed: an *outsider* had stolen the crown; anything was/is possible! For many union members this outsider status is seen as a strength; Graham was perceived as the democratic candidate. The labour movement – the unions and the Labour Party – was founded upon the democratic principle of one member one vote at regular election intervals of two to three years, not the anti-democratic entitlement of a *job for life*. Tony Benn argued that *Five Essential Questions of Democracy* should be asked of all those in positions of economic, social, and political power: "What power have you got?", "Where did you get it from?", "In whose interests do you use it?", "To whom are you accountable?", "How do we get rid of you?". [26] Will the new general secretary now challenge the sinecure positions of regional secretaries, national officers, full-time officials and impose democratic accountability throughout the union? Will the Labour Party re-establish the democratic principle of open selection for all elected representatives?

# 87
# Conclusion

*'All the early Roman kings in the early early morn, coming down the mountain distributing the corn.*
*They're peddlers and they're meddlers, they buy and they sell.*
*They destroyed your city; they'll destroy you as well.'* ~ *Bob Dylan**

Blame for the betrayal of the Liverpool dockers should certainly not be attributed to one local dock official, who was subject to the authority of other more senior local and national officials of the union. The *Broad Left* failed to support the Liverpool dockers. They failed to use their significant influence with the union's regional barons and paid officials that they promoted to positions of power and influence. No one, other than the Irish comrades, marched and declared their support for the Liverpool dockers from September 1995 to the present day. The *Broad Left* were complicit in the union's General Executive Council betrayal of the dockers through their inaction and inability to exercise their primary purpose of representing the interests of members who were in dispute. Their GEC statement, *not to support the Liverpool dockers*, was placed before the union's Biennial Delegates Conference in Brighton in 1997. It was rejected by the membership, who voted overwhelmingly to support the Liverpool dockers' campaign for reinstatement. [1] This democratic vote was ignored by the GEC, whose members sat on their hands and listened as the general secretary told them that, effectively, the Liverpool dock dispute was over. The failure of the union to use its financial leverage and political influence with organisations such as the TUC, the ITF and the New Labour Party was a scandal.

It is to the senior architects of the TGWU's 1995 strategy towards the Liverpool dockers that we must look, as they received affirmation of their trade unionist principles, not by fighting for the Liverpool dockers' rights, but by *dressing-up in the Queen's ermine*. In the opening lines of their 1998 song, *One by One*, Chumbawamba wrote of the inevitability of Bill Morris realising his sense of *entitlement* to a seat in the House of Lords:

---

* Bob Dylan, 'Early Roman Kings' (song), Album: Tempest (2012)

*'Pontius Pilot came to our town up to the dockyards to see the picket line,*
*We asked him to help, but he just turned around,*
*He's the leader of the union now, leader of the union now.*
*All our questions he ignored, he washed his hands.*
*And he dreamt of his reward, a seat in the House of Lords.' [2]*

Bill Morris was granted a life peerage, taking his seat in the House of Lords on 13 June 2006 after assuming the title of the Honourable Lord Morris of Handsworth, OJ, DL. [3] In 2011, Ray Collins, Morris' former administrative officer, before his appointment to one of the numerous deputy general secretary roles in the TGWU, became Baron Collins of Highbury [4], having spent the previous three years as general secretary of New Labour. Yet another deputy general secretary of the TGWU, Margaret Prosser, was a given an OBE in the Queen's Birthday Honours' List in June 1997; by this time, the Liverpool dockers had stood on their picket lines for one year and nine months. Margaret Prosser OBE was also president of the Trade Union Congress in 1996; from 1996 to 2001 she was treasurer of New Labour. On 11 June 2004, Margaret Prosser was created Baroness Prosser of Battersea in the Borough of Wandsworth. [5] The betrayal of the Liverpool dockers was completed.

After a year of watching the dockers, their wives and their children fight for justice, Bill Morris felt the need to respond to a letter from the dockers by telling the union's General Executive Council that the letter meant: 'Thanks, you're doing nothing; you betrayed us.' [6] As general secretary, he was speaking for the TGWU who, by his actions and statements, had little or no interest in the lives of those working-class men and women who sacrificed everything to honour the primary trade union principle: you never cross a picket line.

The Liverpool dockers' leader, Jimmy Nolan, is proud of his Irish heritage. He is a man of few possessions other than books and a council house in Kirkby. Jimmy Nolan spoke for many of his comrades when he told local historian Brian Marren: 'Growing up working-class in Liverpool means you're taught two things in life: always help your friends and neighbours when they're in need, and never cross a picket line.' [7] Unlike their trade union leaders, these Liverpool dockers and their families had no sense of *entitlement* nor access to money, privilege or high office; instead, they sought election to represent the working-class and expected only that the trade union they created would have supported them.

The betrayal of the Liverpool dockers is a contemporary example of the labour movement's systemic failure to perform its critical function and represent those it was founded to support. The *fault lines* have existed since the formation of the unions and have been exploited as the oligarchic tendencies identified by Robert Michels ensured the centralisation of power and the removal of democratic accountability, serving the interests instead of a powerful cabal who have more in common with *the early Roman kings* than the working class they purport to represent.

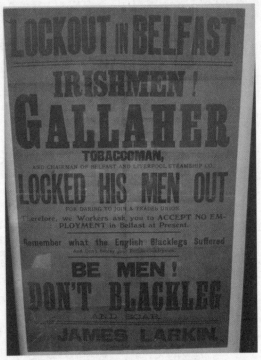

Joe Carden (Mike Carden's dad) on the Liverpool docks, standing on a piece of wood, c. 1950s.

James Larkin poster: "Be men! Don't blackleg and scab." Strikes going on in Ireland at the same time.

Mike Carden's dad Joe Carden (centre) and a gang of Liverpool dockers.

The end of the National Dock Strike outside TGWU Transport House, London, Tuesday 1st August 1989. From left to right: Mike Carden, Joe Baxter, Tony Nelson, Nick Silvano.

TGWU 'Ammo' publication featuring useful statistics and facts for use by members. Cover image features author Mike Carden with Tony Nelson, Mike Carr, Brian Roberts on an anti-Thatcher march, early 1980s.

Mike and shop stewards on union course, Cirencester, 1982. From left to right: Mike Carr, Tony Corrigan, Kevin Robinson, Mike Carden, and Terry Teague.

Mike Carden in discussion on a march during the international conference of Ford convenors in Liverpool around January 1985. The Ford Halewood TGWU banner is visible in the background.

Documentary film flyer about action taken in Liverpool to stop the illegal movement of uranium from Namibia through the port of Liverpool, c. 1986.

Tony Nelson and Mike Carden at an early morning picket.

'Brownie' on the picket line.
© Dave Sinclair

Left:
George Preston with his bicycle © Andrew Testa

Below:
Picket line portraits (from left to right) George Preston, John Farrell, Denis Connolly, and Joe McMullen
© Dave Sinclair

Bill Morris, general secretary of the TGWU, tells dockers he wouldn't be able to face his grandchildren if he couldn't say 'I was there'. A positive sentiment, but history tells a different story. © Dave Sinclair

The dockers vote to continue strike action at a meeting in Transport House, Liverpool. © Dave Sinclair

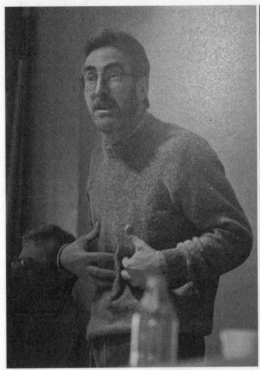

Mike Carden speaking in Transport House, Liverpool © Dave Sinclair

Jimmy Nolan speaking at the TGWU Biennial Delegates Conference in Brighton, 1996. © Dave Sinclair

Terry Teague, Jimmy Nolan, and Mike Carden at an international conference.

Liverpool Unemployed centre shows support for the sacked Liverpool dockers.

Herby Hollerhead, Noam Chomskey, and Irvine Welsh in London, 1996.

Mike Carden with singer/songwriter Billy Bragg.

Liverpool Riverside MP Bob Parry with Mike Carden on the picket line. © Dave Sinclair

Bobby Hagan (pictured) and Peter Wharton were the only Liverpool Boatmen who supported the dockers. © Dave Sinclair

A Liverpool dockers delegation attending a meeting in the Houses of Parliament.

Dockers' demonstration in Liverpool city centre, 1995. © Dave Sinclair

From left to right: Jimmy Davies, Jack Heyman (ILWU), Jimmy Nolan, with Ronnie Bibby holding the banner. © Dave Sinclair

Mike Carden addresses a demonstration from the steps outside St George's Hall. © Dave Sinclair

Demonstration, Sat 29th June 1996. From left to right: Shaun Robinson, Kevin Robinson, Dan Carden, Mike Carden, Tony Benn MP, Frank Lannigan, Jimmy Davies.

Jeremy Corbyn addresses a rally in support of the Liverpool Dockers from St George's Hall steps.

Above: Women of the Waterfront enjoying a night out.

Left: Portrait of Cathy & Rosie Dwyer. © Andrew Testa

The Women of the Waterfront Marching under their banner at a rally in 1996.

Kevin Robinson, Mike Carden, Tony Nelson, and Len McCluskey in the Lord Warden pub.

Jimmy Nolan and Mike Carden at the Edinburgh Park Dockers' club (after the funeral of 'Snowy').
© Dave Sinclair

A night out in the Lord Warden pub (the night the dispute ended). © Dave Sinclair

Mike Carden speaking to dockers at Transport House, Liverpool, with his two sons John and Daniel watching from the front. © Dave Sinclair

Left: Greg Dropkin photographed with a police officer in the background.

Below Left: The Operational Support Division (OSD) at a protest against Argos and their use of scab labour at the port, Liverpool City Centre, 1996. © Dave Sinclair

Below Right: Cathy Dwyer, Colette Melia and Val Bibby with police at the Seaforth picket.

Left:
Mike Carden receives news by telephone that union support for the dispute had officially ended.
© Dave Sinclair

Above:
The CASA entrance on Hope Street Liverpool.

Mike Carden, Andy Green, and delegates at IDC Conference, The Casa, Liverpool.

Tony Nelson, Graham Morris MP, Tony Gardiner, Jimmy Nolan in the CASA, Liverpool.

# References

## Author's Preface

1. D. Aitkenhead 'Thirty Years that shook the world', The Independent on Sunday, 8 December 1996. Available: https://www.independent.co.uk/arts-entertainment/thirty-years-that-shook-the-world-1313556.html

2. Len McCluskey 'Community Spirit will never be defeated', Speech at the Adelphi Hotel 26 September 2015, Unite Live 3 September 2016. Available: http://unitelive.org/community-spirit-will-never-be-defeated/

3. M. Carden Diaries, 'Jack Adams Meeting with Shop Stewards in Transport House Liverpool', 24 September 1997

4. Thomas Flanagan 'The Year of the French (The great rebellion of Ireland 1798)' New York Review Book (1979) p.302

5. James Hinton, 'The Mass Observers: A History 1937-1949', Oxford University Press, 2013 – 'In Liverpool a considerable proportion of dockers are showing very little interest in winning the war or working hard to win it... There is a major industrial conflict from the dockers against the employer class...' p.vii

6. E. Taplin, 'The Dockers' Union: A Study of the National Union of Dock Labourers 1889-1922', Leicester University Press, 1985 (p.22)

7. E.P. Thompson, 'The Making of the English Working Class (1963)', Penguin Modern Classics, 2013 Edition (p.474)

8. ibid. pp.474-475

9. Thomas Carden and Bridget Swift were recorded as passengers on the Register of Vagrants Deported from Liverpool to Ireland between 1821-22. See www.ancestry.co.uk./interactive/6882/4

424286_00441?pid=1057 See also: Virginia Crossman, 'Poverty and the Poor Law in Ireland 1850-1914 (Medicancy and Vagrancy)', Liverpool Scholarship online, 2014. Available: http://liverpool.universitypressscholarship.com/view/10.5949/liverpool/9781846319419.001.0001/upso-9781846319419-chapter-8 See also: Zoe Alker, 'Street Violence in Liverpool', Liverpool John Moores University Phd. Thesis, 2014.

10. Tim Pat Coogan – Wherever Green is Worn: The Story of the Irish Diaspora Arrow Book 2002 p.189 and Edward Rushton letter to the Home Secretary 21 April 1849 quoted also in Frank Neal Sectarian Violence – The Liverpool Experience 1819-1914 Manchester University Press 1988 p.81 See also Henry Mayhew – London Labour and the London Poor -Wordsworth Classics 2008 pp.104-113

11. Tim Pat Coogan, 'The Famine Plot', Palgrave Macmillan, 2012

12. Death Certificate for John Carden, Dock Labourer of 14 Prince Albert Cottages Upper Frederick Street: died 30 May 1933 aged 44 years – five days after being hit by a sling of timber on board a ship berthed in Liverpool docks. Toxteth Park North/County of Liverpool C.B. 30 May 1933 DYE 2571095 See also: Arthur Carden, 'Carden of Mayo & Sligo', Lulu Enterprises, 2018.

13. Eric Taplin, 'The Dockers' Union – A Study of the NUDL 1889-1922', Leicester University Press, 1985 pp.19-20

14. Eric Taplin, 'Irish Leaders and the Liverpool Dockers: Richard McGhee and Edward McHugh', North West Labour History Society (Issue No.9). Available: www.nwlh.org.uk/?=node/140

15. Tony Birtill, 'Brothers in Arms: Ireland and the Spanish Civil War', Irish Post 30 August 1986.

16. Tim Pat Coogan, 'Wherever Green is Worn', 2002, p.190. See also: R.Kee, 'The Green Flag: A History of Irish Nationalism', Penquin Books, 1972 p.491

17. ibid. See also: https://libcom.org/history/liverpool-versus-oswald-mosley-1937

18. Percy Byce Shelley, 'The Masque of Anarchy' is a British political poem written in 1819 following the Peterloo massacre of that year. In his call for freedom, it is perhaps the first modern statement of the principle of nonviolent resistance.

19. M. Carden, 'A Study into the Inadequacy of Trade Unions, irrespective of how well developed they may be, to seriously counter a determined and highly motivated employers.' Master of Arts, University of Warwick, September 1983. See also: M. Carden, 'Union Democracy and Incorporation – A Case Study of the TGWU Merseyside Division with Particular Reference to the Dock Industry', University of Liverpool, Master of Philosophy Thesis, October 1996

## PART ONE: Introduction

## 1 – Liverpool and the 'Liverpool Way'

1. Eric Lynch, 'Liverpool Slavery Trail' Website. Available: http://www.bedand-breakfastliverpool.co.uk/liverpool-slavery-trial.htm

2. R. H. Muir, 'A History of Liverpool 1907' – 'Beyond a doubt it was the slave trade that raised Liverpool from a struggling port to be one of the richest and most prosperous trading centres in the world.' See also: International Slavery Museum http://www.liverpoolmuseums.org.uk/ism/slavery/europe/liverpool.aspx See also: M.G. Simpson, 'Making Representations: Museums in the Post-Colonial Era – Routledge 2012 pp.16-21 (cited in Fryer 1984 p.34) English Heritage, Lawrence Westgraph in 'Built on Slavery' in Context 108 March 2009 p.27 The Institute of Historic Buildings Conservation http://ihbc.org.uk/context_archive/108/slavery/one.html See also: Brian Towers, 'The Rise and Fall of Liverpool's Dockland – Waterfront Blues', Carnegie Publishing, 2011 pp.2-3 and pp.26-26 See also: David Olusoga, 'Black and British: A Forgotten History', Pan McMillan, 2016. See also: www.understandingslavery.com

3. Milton Meltzer, 'Herman Melville – A Biography', Twenty-First Century Books, 1915 p.29. See also: Herman Melville, 'Redburn - His First Voyage', Amazon Books

4. Michael Macilwee, 'The Liverpool Underworld: Crime in the City 1750-1900', Liverpool University Press, 2011 p.1.

5. Giovanni Paolo Panini, 'The Ruins of Rome'. See also: www.the-athenaeum.org. The Steble Street Fountain, known as the 'street urchins seaside'. See also: https://www.youtube.com/watch?v=hIiHaecB2bQ See also: B. Towers, 'Waterfront Blues – The Rise and Fall of Liverpool's Dockland', Carnegie, 2008 pp.140-142

6. A. Carden, 'Carden of Mayo and Sligo', Lulu Enterprises Inc., February 2018, pp.13-25 – Lynn Bateman - ibid. pp.13-25 See also: C.N. Parkinson, 'The Rise of the Port of Liverpool', Liverpool University Press, 1952

7. A. Carden 'Carden of Mayo and Sligo' Lulu Enterprises Inc. February 2018 pp.13-25 Lynn Bateman: 'hence the expression 'Shanghaied' - and upon reaching Liverpool, some had jumped ship and sought sanctuary in the maze of streets hugging the docks.' See also: M. Macilwee 'The Liverpool Underworld – Crime in the City 1750-1900' Liverpool University Press 2011 p.6 See also: http://liverpoolremembrance.weebly.com/chinese-community.html See also: E. Taplin, 'The Dockers' Union – A Study of the National Union of Dock Labourers 1889-1922', Leicester University Press (1985) pp.84-92

8. John Kelly, 'The Graves are Walking – The Great Famine and the Saga of the Irish People, Picador, 2012 pp. 257-258. See also Lynn Bateman - ibid. pp.17-18

9. I.C. Taylor, 'The Court and Cellar Dwelling: The Eighteenth Century Origin of the Liverpool Slum' Available: https://www.hslc.org.uk/wp-content/uploads/2017/05/122-5-Taylor.pdf

10. Robert Kee, 'The Green Flag: A history of Irish Nationalism', Penquin Books, 1972 p.491 See also: Lynn Bateman, 'From Ireland to Liverpool in the 19th.Century' – in A. Carden 'Carden of Mayo and Sligo' Lulu Enterprises Inc. February 2018 p.13

11. The Liverpool Sailor's Home provided important assistance to seafarers in Liverpool, especially during the depression years and the two World Wars. The Liverpool Sailor's Home Trust continues to support seafaring organisations on board ship and retired Liverpool seafarers in their own homes. See: http://www.liverpoolmuseums.org.uk/maritime/archive/info-sheet.aspx?sheetId=5 See

also:
https://en.wikipedia.org/wiki/Liverpool_Sailo
rs%27_Home

12. G. Quirey, 'In Hardship and Hope: A History
of the Liverpool Irish', G&K Publishing, 2017
p.12 See also: F. O'Connor, 'Liverpool: It all
came tumbling down (A photographic survey
and commentary on Liverpool)' Brunswick
Printing and Publishing (1986) See also P.
Aughton, 'Liverpool – A People's History',
Carnegie Publishing, 1993

13. S.G. Checkland, 'Economic Attitudes in
Liverpool 1793-1807', Economic History
Review 2nd Ser V (1952)

14. I.C. Taylor, 'The Court and Cellar Dwelling:
The Eighteenth Century Origin of the
Liverpool Slum' p.80 - £20 million was
required to pay off rich business owners who
owned large plantations overseas. In cities
such as Bristol, it made a lot of rich people
much richer. In 1833, Britain used £20 million,
40% of its national budget, to buy freedom for
all slaves in the Empire. Available:
https://www.hslc.org.uk/wp-
content/uploads/2017/05/122-5-Taylor.pdf
See also: J. Barrie & T. Cork, 'How Taxpayers
were still Paying for British Slave Trade 200
Years Later', Daily Mirror, 13 February 2018.
See also: R. Williamson, 'Liverpool',
Memorandum Books, 1753 in I.C.Taylor ibid.

15. Thomas Burke, 'The Street Trading Children
of Liverpool', Contemporary Review, 1900,
p.726 quoted in M. Macilwee, 'The Liverpool
Underworld – Crime in the City 1750-1900,
Liverpool University Press, 2011, p.6. See also:
Alice Mah, 'Port Cities and Global Legacies –
Urban Identity, Waterfront Work and
Radicalism', Palgrave Macmillan, 2014 pp.181-
182 – 'The hiring of former dockers and
people who were accustomed to the nature of
casual labour had implications for the work
culture at the factory'. See also: A. Miller,
'Poverty Deserved? Relieving the Poor in
Victorian Liverpool', Liver Press, 1988 pp.21-
29. See also G. Philips & N. Whiteside, 'Casual
Labour: The Unemployment Question in the
Port Transport Industry 1880-1970',
Clarendon Press, 1985

16. The Liverpool Domestic Mission, Annual
Report 1859 p.65. See also: the Okhill
Investigation of the Corporate Estate, Lease
Registers 111 and V1 1867-82 1782 -95 &
Okhill's Street Register LIV.R.O. 352
CLE/CON/23/34 quoted in I.C. Taylor, 'The
Court and Cellar Dwelling: The Eighteenth
Century Origin of the Liverpool Slum' p.79 -
https://www.hslc.org.uk/wp-
content/uploads/2017/05/122-5-Taylor.pdf
See also: F. Engels, 'The Condition of the
Working Class in England', Granada, 1981 Ed.

pp.70-74. See also: W.M. Frazer, 'Duncan of
Liverpool: Being an account of the work of
Dr.W.H. Duncan – Medical Doctor of Health
of Liverpool 1847-63', Hamish Hamilton,
1947.

17. W.H. Duncan, 'On the physical causes of the
high rates of mortality in Liverpool: First
Report of the Committee for Inquiring into
the state of large towns and populous districts',
11 (1848) p.124 quoted in I.C. Taylor ibid.
pp.67-68

18. History of Fazakerley Hospital, 1898-1960.
Available:
http://fazakerleyhistory.blogspot.co.uk/

19. Lynn Bateman, 'From Ireland to Liverpool in
the 19th Century' in A. Carden, 'Carden of
Mayo and Sligo', Lulu Enterprises Inc.
February 2018 p.14

20. The Godfrey Edition – Old Ordnance Survey
Maps Toxteth 1906 and also: Gazetteer of
Operating pre-1940 Breweries in England -
https://content.historicengland.org.uk/images
-books/publications/gazetteer-breweries/bhs-
operating-breweries.pdf/
https://www.yelp.co.uk/biz/the-coburg-
liverpool - Time for Tea – Liverpool's longest-
standing love affair. Seven Streets
http://www.sevenstreets.com/time-for-tea-
liverpools-longest-standing-love-affair/

21. Lynn Bateman, 'From Ireland to Liverpool in
the 19th Century' in A. Carden, 'Carden of
Mayo and Sligo', Lulu Enterprises Inc.
February 2018 p.14

22. 'The Three Graces' - Royal Liver Building,
built between 1908 and 1911 and designed by
Walter Aubrey Thomas. It is a grade I listed
building consisting of two clock towers, both
crowned by mythical Liver Birds. The building
is the headquarters of the Royal Liver Friendly
Society. Cunard Building, constructed between
1914 and 1916 and a grade II listed building. It
is the former headquarters of the Cunard Line
shipping company. And the Port of Liverpool
Building, built from 1903 to 1907 and also
grade II listed. It is the former home of the
Mersey Docks and Harbour Board. See:
https://en.wikipedia.org/wiki/Pier_Head The
Pier Head is part of Liverpool's 'Maritime
Mercantile City UNESCO World Heritage
Site, see:
http://www.liverpoolmuseums.org.uk/mariti
me/exhibitions/worldheritagecity/three-
graces.aspx See also: Cunard Yanks, Ritchie
Barton Liverpool Lullabies and Mersey
Memories http://cunardyanks.org/ Liverpool
music fans could often access American vinyl
records brought over the Atlantic on Merchant
Ships.
http://www.liverpoolcityportal.co.uk/beatles/
beatles_influences.html -

https://en.wikipedia.org/wiki/Cammell_Laird - https://www.clbh.co.uk/about-us/history-of-cammell-laird - The History of Cammel Lairds Shipbuiliders – See also Liverpool, Maritime Mercantile City – Nomination of Liverpool for Inscription on the World Heritage Site List – Liverpool City Council January 2003

23. Alice Mah, Port Cities and Global Legacies – Urban Identity, Waterfront Work and Radicalism – Examines the narrative that port cities share as 'cities on the edge'. Palgrave Macmillan 2014 pp.30-50

24. FT Weekend Magazine 'John, Yoko and 'Imagine" 15/16 September 2018 p.36 from 'Imagine John Yoko' – by John Lennon and Yoko Ono – Thames and Hudson 2018

25. Eric Taplin Dock Labour at Liverpool: Occupational Structure and Working Conditions in the Late Nineteenth Century 15 September 1977 pp.142-143 https://www.hslc.org.uk/wp-content/uploads/2017/11/127-8-Taplin.pdf

26. E. Taplin, 'The Dockers Union' 1985, p.39

27. Eric Taplin Dock Labour at Liverpool: Occupational Structure and Working Conditions in the Late Nineteenth Century 15 September 1977 pp.135-137 https://www.hslc.org.uk/wp-content/uploads/2017/11/127-8-Taplin.pdf

28. BBC 4 Timeshift 16:2 Sailors, Ships and Stevedores: The Story of Britain's Docks October 2016. See also: 'A Trip Through Liverpool's Rich Irish History' by Declan McSweeney – The Guardian 15 October 2012

29. BBC 4 Timeshift 16:2 Sailors, Ships and Stevedores: The Story of Britain's Docks October 2016 See also J.T. McKelvey - Dock Labour Disputes in Great Britain Bulletin No.23 March 1953 NY State School of Industrial Relations http://digitalassets.lib.berkeley.edu/irle/ucb/text/lb000195.pdf

30. Tony Lane – Liverpool: The City of the Sea Liverpool - University Press 1997 first published as Liverpool the Gateway to Empire in 1987 by Lawrence and Wishart

31. Radical Liverpool BBC Radio 4 26 September 2016

32. Review of Reviews 12 September 1911 quoted in M. Macilwee The Liverpool Underworld – Crime in the City 1750-1900 Liverpool University Press 2011 p.xiii

33. BBC News 16 August 2011 http://www.bbc.co.uk/news/uk-england-merseyside-14529243 See also 'Send the Gunboats up the Mersey' Liverpool and the 1911 General Strike: B. Benjamin August 7 2014

https://chbenj23.wordpress.com/2014/08/07/send-the-gunboats-up-the-mersey/

34. Liverpool Echo 15 March 2013

35. Liverpool Echo - 7 June 2011

36. Liverpool's Mosque in Brougham Terrace was founded by William Henry Quilliam, a local Liverpool solicitor, members of the 1911 Liverpool strike committee, who embraced Islam in 1887 taking the name Abdullah Quilliam – see Abdullah Quilliam Society www.abdullahquilliam.org

37. Dockers – Their Lives and Legacy on the Liverpool Waterfront – A Trinity Mirror NW2 Publication 2010

38. Ken Loach - Liverpool Echo 15 March 2013.

39. S. Hughes – There She Goes: Liverpool A City On Its Own – The Long Decade 1979-1993 decoubertin 2019 pp.53-55

40. Chris Tobin 'The Liverpool Way: A Noose Around Our Neck' http://www.thedaisycutter.co.uk/2012/03/the-liverpool-way-a-noose-around-our-neck/ The Kirkby Rent Strike began in October 1972 and lasted for over fourteen months see Tom Belger, 'Kirkby Rent Strike Remembered Four Decades on' Liverpool Echo 9th.October 2015 – Toxteth Riots 1981 Background and How it all Began – Liverpool Echo 4th.July 2011 See also Simon Hughes – There She Goes: Liverpool, A City on its Own – decoubertin books 2019 p.176

41. Boris Johnson MP – The Spectator 'Bigley's Fate – We have lost a sense of proportion about what constitutes a tragedy' 16 October 2004 - See also BBC News Channel http://news.bbc.co.uk/1/hi/england/merseyside/3746588.stm

42. ibid.

43. http://www.liverpoolfc.com/hillsborough/inquests see also Hillsborough Disaster: Deadly Mistakes and Lies that Lasted for Decades. By David Conn The Guardian Tuesday 26 April 2016 The Guardian 16 May 2016 http://www.theguardian.com/politics/2016/may/16/orgreave-inquiry-calls-grow-after-damning-hillsborough-verdict-for-south-yorkshire-police see also Orgreave Truth and Justice Campaign https://otjc.org.uk/about/

44. Nicholas Jones 'Thatcher's Promise to fight the enemy within' 3 January 2014 http://www.nicholasjones.org.uk/articles/40-trade-union-reporting/280-thatcher-s-promise-to-fight-the-enemy-within-cabinet-secrets-reveal-her-war-of-attrition-against-scargill see also 'British Ports Hit by New Docks Strike' Reuters 24 August 1984 New York Times

45. The Sun 19 April 1989

## 2 – Historical Overview of the Dispute

# REFERENCES

1. A Captain's Chair is an armchair with a saddle seat and a low curved back with vertical spindles – see https://www.merriam-webster.com/dictionary/captain's%20chair

2. Jim Philips A Karachi Stowage: Docker and the Sea in Twentieth Century Britain https://archives.history.ac.uk/history-in-focus/Sea/articles/phillips.html

3. Frank Deegan – There's No Other Way Toulouse Press 1980 and Bill Hunter – Workers History as Told by Those who Made It - www.billhunterweb.org.uk/interviews/History_as_Told.htm

4. R. Darlington – Syndicalism and the Transition to Communism an International Perspective – Ashgate 2008 pp.220-222

5. The Miners Next Step – Being a Suggested Scheme for the Re-organisation of the Federation – Tonypandy 1912

6. Noah Ablett et al The Miners Next Step – London 1972 p.19 See also Democratic Ideas and the British Labour Movement 1880-1914 L. Barrow & I. Bullock Cambridge University Press 1996 p.291 and G.D.H. Cole Early Pamphlets and Assessment Routledge 2011p.2 and The Miners Next Step – Being a Suggested Scheme for the Re-organisation of the Federation – Tonypandy 1912

7. J.T. Murphy – New Horizons London 1941 p.81 – Also Revisiting the 'Great Labour Unrest' (1911-14) Paris, 15-16 September 2011 University of Paris file:///C:/Users/mikec/Downloads/GLU%20abstracts+cover%20(2).pdf See also: J. Goldstein – The Government of British Trade Unions: A Study of Apathy and the Democratic Process in the TGWU Allen & Unwin 1952

8. Andy Dwyer – Interviewed in, 'The Flickering Flame' Director Ken Loach 1996 Parallax Pictures

9. Mònica Clua Losada, 'The retreat of the union: The Transport and General Workers' Union strategies of renewal in the 1990s.' (contact: mcl500@york.ac.uk) See also: PSA 60th Annual Conference 29 March-1 April 2010 Copyright PSA 2010 pp.14 of 25

10. Geoffrey Goodman. Bill Morris – A Trade Union Miracle Blackamber Inspirations 2010 p.141

11. Mònica Clua Losada, 'The retreat of the union: The Transport and General Workers' Union strategies of renewal in the 1990s.' (contact: mcl500@york.ac.uk) See also: PSA 60th Annual Conference 29 March-1 April 2010 Copyright PSA 2010 pp.14 of 25

12. Jack Jones House Unite see: http://www.unitetheunion.org/uploaded/documents/Jack%20Jones%20House%20PDF11-21815.pdf

13. William Sumner – Militant Within Liverpool City Council 1986-1986: The Impact of and Reaction to a Left-Wing Political Movement in the Labout Party – BA Hons. Dissertation Northumbria University 2016 https://www.northumbria.ac.uk/media/25804383/billy-sumner.pdf See also: Peter Taaffe and Tony Mulhearn – A City that dared to fight – Abebooks 1988 See also: Tony Mulhearn – The Making of a Liverpool Militant – 47books 2019

14. Dave Cotterill - Official History of Sacked Liverpool Dockers 1995 – Unpublished

15. Bill Hunter – Workers' History as told by those who made it - http://www.billhunterweb.org.uk/interviews/History_as_Told.htm

16. Geoffrey Goodman - Bill Morris – A Trade Union Miracle Blackamber Inspirations 2010 p.145 The Bill Morris Website: http://www.billmorris.info/index.htm - Mick O'Reilly - From Lucifer to Lazarus: A Life on the Left Lilliputpress 2019 pp.147

17. http://www.labournet.net/docks2/9608/MORRIS.HTM

18. ibid.

19. ibid.

20. ibid.

21. ibid.

22. South Wales Miners Federation – The Miners Next Step 1912. Available: https://libcom.org/library/miners-next-step-swmf-1912

23. B. Eidlin, Why Unions Are Good – But Not Good Enough. Available: https://www.jacobinmag.com/2020/01/marxism-trade-unions-socialism-revolutionary-organizing See also: V.I. Lenin - Essential Works of Lenin 'What is to be Done' and other works – BN Publishing 2009: See also: The Faces of Economism – Spartacus No.21 1972 https://www.regroupment.org/main/page_economism.html – H. Collins K. Marx The International and the British Trade Union Movement – Science & Society Guildford Press 1962 p.400

24. C. Clynch & Others v TGWU Chronology Case No. LV190318 p.5 See also: Private and Confidential Report Docks Dispute: Dave McCall 14 November 1996 p.14 Also A. Jarvis and K. Smith (eds.) Albert Dock, Trade and Technology – Published by National Museums (1999) pp.119-121

25. C. Clynch & Other v TGWU Chronology Case No. LV190318 p.11 See also TGWU Official Letter from J. Dempsey letter to all Dock Workers 28 July 1995 and Brian Dooley

interviewed by Greg Dropkin February 1998 unpublished extract.

26. Liverpool Echo 18.7.1996 Trevor Furlong quoted, 'Dockers should have been sacked years ago' 18 July 1996 See also The Morning Star 'We should have sacked the lot of them' 18 July 1996

27. Mersey Docks Company Press Release 22 September 1993

28. Hidden Agendas – John Pilger Vintage Books 1999 pp.341-342

29. ibid.

30. ibid.

31. A. Jarvis and K. Smith (eds.) Albert Dock, Trade and Technology – Published by National Museums (1999) pp.119-121

32. The Guardian 23 November 1996 John Pilger. See also 'The Case for the Reinstatement of the Sacked Liverpool Dockers' The Need for a Public Inquiry Merseyside Port Shop Stewards Committee 1st. July 1997

33. The Daily Telegraph 16 March 2005 'Mersey says bid costs have hit £7m profits' Alistair Osbourne See also Liverpool Echo '771m Deal to Buy Out Docks' 9th.June 2005 See also 'Painless Takeover brings dock era to an end. Peel Holdings Now Own MDHC' Larry Neild - The Free Library http://www.thefreelibrary.com/Painless+take over+brings+docks+era+to+an+end%3B+Pe el+Holdings+now+owns...-a0136496435 September 22nd.2005

34. Transport Weekly 6 February 2007

35. Lloyd's List 15 September 1995

36. Patrick Tooher - Foreign Unions rally to support port in a storm –Sunday Independent 21 January 1996 See also Mukal 'Liverpool Dockers Making and Un-Making of a Struggle' in Economic and Political Weekly Vol:33 No.26 June 27- July 23 1998 pp.1612-1614

37. R. Phillips BBC Radio Merseyside Tuesday 27 January 1998 Interview with Tony Benn MP

38. 'Writing the Wrongs' Planet Wild: Directed by Sol Papadopoulos 1999 - Review by John Bohanna http://www.labournet.net/docks2/9907/film. htm

39. The Guardian: Mark Steel, 'Yellow Pages – Yellow Wages in Our Union'; 3 February 1998

40. Liverpool Daily Post 'The Dog that's had its Day' D. Charters, 29 January 1998

41. Guardian, 10 February 2000 'Unions Rise of the Cyber Pickets' - Simon Bowers

42. 'Dockers' Parallax Pictures Director Bill Anderson 1999

43. Len McCluskey, General Secretary of UNITE, Speech at 20th Anniversary of Liverpool Docks' Dispute – Adelphi Hotel, Liverpool, Saturday 26 September 2015

44. Ben Pimlott and Chris Cook Eds. - Trade Unions in British Politics Longman 1982 pp.41-42 See also M. Stephens - Ernest Bevin – Unskilled Labourer and World Statesman A TGWU Publication 1981 p.26 The Great Dock Strike of 1889 See also https://www.ideastore.co.uk/local-history-online-exhibitions-dock-strike

45. TGWU Record 'Setting the Record Straight' Bill Morris February/March 1997

46. TGWU Bulletin January 1998 http://www.labournet.net/docks2/9801/

47. M. Carden Diary of shop stewards meeting with F. Whitty 4 October 1995

48. M. Carden Diary of shop stewards' meeting with F. Whitty 4 October 1995

49. G. Goodman 'Bill Morris: A Trade Union Miracle' Blackamber Inspirations. 2010 p.158

50. G. Goodman 'Bill Morris: A Trade Union Miracle' Blackamber Inspirations. 2010 pp.157-158 See also Ben Pimlott and Chris Cook Eds. Trade Unions in British Politics – Longman 1982 pp.39-41

51. TGWU Record 'Setting the Record Straight' Bill Morris February/March 1997

52. The Trade Union and Labour Relations (Consolidation) Act 1992 pp.10-11

53. John Hendy QC 'In the matter of the 500 dismissed Liverpool Dockworkers and in the matter of an industrial dispute.' Opinion Fax sent by Christian Fisher Wednesday 5th.November 1996 pp.1-3

54. ibid.

55. The fact that no ballot was conducted before the outset of the industrial action or thereafter means that the union is denied by Section 226 of the TULR Act 1992 also pp.12-18 'Even if the union wished to do so (presumably unthinkable) repudiation is no longer an option since the period 'as soon as reasonably practicable after coming to the knowledge of 'the executive committee, president or general secretary, has long passed. The employer was in breach of contract in insisting on a lower rate of overtime pay and Torside may be a shell company controlled by MDHC.'

56. Bill Morris' Speech to the TGWU BDC 1997 http://home.igc.org/~itobr/idm2/lddtue.html

57. Bill Morris' Speech to the TGWU BDC 1997 http://home.igc.org/~itobr/idm2/lddtue.html

58. R. Undy & R. Martin Ballots and Trade Union Democracy Blackwell 1984 pp.85-87

59. New Model Unionism Trade Union Congress - The Union Makes Us Strong http://www.unionhistory.info/timeline/1850_1880.php

60. James Hinton, The Mass Observers: A History, 1937-1949: Oxford University Press (2013) p.204

61. Unite Education publication on the history of, 'The Great Dock Strike of 1889' Unite Education 2015 p.13

62. J. London 'The People of the Abyss' Echo Library Ed. (2007) Robert Tressell 'The Ragged Trousered Philanthropists' First Ed.1914 Grant Richards Ltd.

63. R. Bean - The Liverpool Dock Strike of 1890 In the International Review of Social History Vol:18 Issue 1 April 1973 pp.51-68 https://www.cambridge.org/core/journals/int ernational-review-of-social-history/article/liverpool-dock-strike-of-1890/9DC40C7F0281C88BAE3597FB004EB 599

64. The Great London Dock Strike 1889 by Unite's General Secretary and former Liverpool dock worker, Len McCluskey.

65. M. Carden notes from TGWU GEC Statement 17.9.1996

66. James Larkin January 30 1914 http://www.creativecentenaries.org/rise-labour-movement See also R. Michels Political Parties: A Sociological Study of the Oligarchical Tendencies of Modern Democracy - Collier Books Edition 1962 p.371

## PART TWO: The Origins of Betrayal

## 3 - Life on the Docks

1. Eleanor Marx: A Life. Rachel Holmes Bloomsbury Publishing 2014. See also: 'Australia and the Great London Dock Strike: 1889' by P. F. Donovan Australian Society for the Study of Labour History No.23 November 1972 See also See 'A History of British Trade Unionism' H. Pelling Penguin Books 1967 also 'Up Hill and Down Stream' H. Gosling, Spokesman Books first published 1927 and a History of the TGWU at http://www.unitetheunion.org/growing-our-union/about-us/history/the-history-of-the-tg/

2. Ben Tillett, Memories and Reflections London: John Long, 1931 p.76

3. Hansard Dock Workers' Regulation of Work Bill 12 November 1945 Vol:425 CC1753-822 http://hansard.millbanksystems.com/commo ns/1945/nov/12/dock-workers-registration-of-employment

4. Socialist Worker 14.10.1995

5. The Flickering Flame: Parallax Films Dir. Ken Loach 1996

6. ibid.

7. ibid.

8. Militant 2.2.1996 'No return to the tally or the pen': Speech by Billy Jenkins

9. Frank Lanigan interviewed by Bill Hunter https://www.marxists.org/history/etol/writer s/pennington/1960/xx/dockers.htm

10. E. Taplin – Irish Leaders and the Liverpool Dockers: Richard McGhee and Edward McHugh – North West Labour History Society Issue No.9 And also E. Taplin The Dockers' Union (1985) p.30

11. D.F. Wilson – Dockers Fontana Press 1972 p.228

12. Port Workers' Clarion – Leggett Report Biased No.1 May 1954 – See also D. Critchley - Working Practices and Malpractices in the Ports of Liverpool, London and New York 1945-1972 Liverpool John Moores University Phd. Thesis 1972 p. 25 also Court of Inquiry was held under Lord Shaw in 1919 concluded, 'The system of casualisation must, if possible be torn up by the roots. It is wrong.' W. Hamish Fraser - A history of British Trade Unionism 1700-1998' Palgrave Macmillan (1999) p.145

13. http://hansard.millbanksystems.com/lords/19 54/nov/16/national-dock-labour-scheme National Dock Labour Scheme 16th.November 1954 Ministry of Labour and National Service: Unofficial Stoppages on London Docks Cmnd.8236 (1951) p.29

14. ibid.

15. Bill Hunter 'Harry Constable – In His Own Words' – Living History Library 2017 p.146

16. E. Taplin 'The Dockers Union: A Study of the National Union of Dock Labourers, 1889-1922 Leicester University Press 1985 pp.2-3

17. ibid. p.11 See also: Liverpool Echo 2 May 2015 Memories of Liverpool's Carters – A. Houghton

18. Herman Melville – Autobiographical Novels: Reburn, Typee Omoo and White-Jacket e-artnow 2017 Chapter 32

19. Bill Hunter – They Knew Why They Fought: Unofficial Struggles and Leadership on Liverpool Docks 1945-1989 Index Book 1994 p.6 & p.45

20. G. Taylor – The Dynamics of Labour Relations at the Port of Liverpool 1945-1989 Manchester University Phd Thesis 2012 pp.90-91 See also Mike Cullen – A Liverpool Docker's History – Second Ed. August 2021 p.16

21. ibid. p.143-160 See also 'A Study into the Inadequacy of Trade Unions, irrespective of how well developed they may be, to seriously counter a determined and highly motivated employers.' M. Carden Master of Arts University of Warwick September 1983 - 'Union Democracy and Incorporation – A Case Study of the TGWU Merseyside Division

with Particular Reference to the Dock Industry' Michael Carden University of Liverpool Master of Philosophy October 1996

22. James Hinton, The Mass Observers: A History, 1937-1949: Oxford University Press (2013) p.204

23. ibid.

24. Bill Hunter – They Knew Why They Fought Index Book 1994 p. 5 - Jack London 'The People of the Abyss' (1903)

25. Jim Phillips - The Great Alliance: Economic Recovery and the Problems of Power, 1945-1951: - Pluto Press (1996) pp.47-49

26. Peter Kerrigan's 1958 pamphlet, "What next for Britain's port workers?" http://www.grahamstevenson.me.uk/index.php?option=com_content&view=article&id=328:peter-kerrigan-the-docker-and-actor&catid=11:k&Itemid=112

27. Jimmy McGovern in 'Writing the Wrongs' Channel 4 TV – Planet Wild Films Dir. S. Papadopoulos 1999

28. Christopher Andrew – The Defence of the Realm – The Authorised History of MI5 – Penguin Books 2010. The Guardian 10 October 2009 Kevin Morgan: 'Jack Jones – Not Traitor but Tribune' – The Guardian 1st.January 2001 'Dockers' Leader Passed Strike Tactics to MI5 Agents During National Stoppage' & S. Jeffreys EETPU The Decline of the Narrow Left – International Socialism May 1976 No.88

29. Bill Hunter – They Knew Why They Fought: Unofficial Struggles and Leadership on the Dock 1945-1989 Index Book 1994 p.43

30. Tommy Walsh – Being Irish in Liverpool – St. Michael's Irish Centre 2011

31. Tim Pat Coogan – Wherever Green is Worn – The Story of the Irish Diaspora – Arrow Books 2002 p.192

32. Iain Dale – '27 years Ago Today the Dock Labour Scheme was Abolished – And Here's How I Helped It': See http://www.iaindale.com/posts/2016/04/06/27-years-ago-today-the-dock-labour-scheme-was-abolished-and-here-s-how-i-helped-it-happen 6th.April 2016. See also: Memoirs of a Tory Radical – Nigel Lawson Biteback 2010 and also The Rise and Fall of Liverpool's Dockland – Waterfront Blues: Brian Towers, Carnergie Press 2011 p.284

# 4 - Internal Conflict and TGWU Democracy

1. Eric Taplin 'Near to Revolution: The Liverpool General Transport Strike 1911' Bluecoat Press 1994 - See also Port Cities London – Labour Unrest in the port after 1889 in London http://www.portcities.org.uk/london/server/show/ConNarrative.112/chapterId/2359/Labour-unrest-in-the-port-after-1889.html Eric Taplin in 'The Dockers' Union – A Study of the NUDL 1889 – 1922' Leicester University Press 1985 pp.96-99

2. Anthony Corfield, 'Collective Leadership for the TGWU' Published by R. Brierly, Kent 1968 p.23 and also Some sixty years later, in Joe England's study J. England, Shop Stewards in Transport House: A Comment upon the Incorporation of the Rank and File: Industrial Relations Journal Vol.12.No.5 September 1981. IRRU Warwick University Paper p.24. On rank and file influence on the TGWU GEC see K. Fuller, Radical Aristocrats: Lawrence & Wishart (1985) 1981) See also V.L. Allen, Trade Union Leadership; Longmans:1957 pp.44-48). J. Goldstein, The Government of British Trade Unions: Allen & Unwin (1952) pp.223-227 F. Williams, Ernest Bevin: Hutchinson (1952) p.112)

3. Eric Taplin – The Dockers' Union: A Study of the National Union of Dock Labourers 1889-1922 – Leicester University Press 1985 pp.84-92

4. David Critchley – 'Working Practices and Malpractices in the Ports of Liverpool, London and New York with Special Reference to the Period 1945-1972' LJMU Phd. Thesis October 2003 p.59 Also V.L. Allen 'Trade Union Leadership' Longmans 1957 pp.88-89 and also Bullock, A., The Life and Times of Ernest Bevin: Volume One, Trade Union Leader 1881- 1940 (Heinemann 1960), p. 252.

5. Port Cities London – Labour Unrest in the Port after 1889 – Bevin and the formation of the TGWU see: Royal Museums Greenwich http://www.portcities.org.uk/london/server/show/ConNarrative.112/chapterId/2360/outputFormat/print/Labour-unrest-in-the-port-after-1889.html

6. Jim Phillips - The Great Alliance: Economic Recovery and the Problems of Power, 1945-1951: Pluto Press 1986 p.33 See also Bob Pennington – 'Docks: Breakaway and Unofficial Movements' International Socialism No.2 Autumn 1960 pp.5-11 and also Colin Ross 'Death of the Docks' Authorhouse 2010 pp.36-39

7. Bill Hunter – They Knew why they Fought: Unofficial Struggles & Leadership on the Docks 1945-1989 Index Books 1994 p.31

8. J. Jones Interviewed by M. Carden 4 November 1985 in Transport House, London - See also: Colin Sparks – 'The Bureaucracy in the TGWU' International Socialism No.95 February 1977 pp.7-9

9. G. Goodman 'Bill Morris – A Trade Union Miracle' Arcadia Books Ltd. 2010 p.9

10. Jack Jones, General Secretary of the TGWU 1968-1978: Interviewed by M. Carden 4 November 1985 in Transport House, London
11. ibid.
12. Jack Jones: Union Man – Harper Collins 1986 p.143 see also www.marxist.com/hbtu/chapter_18.htm
13. R. Undy, 'The Devolution of Bargaining Levels in the TGWU 1965-1975': The British Journal of Industrial Relations Vol.9 No.3 (1978) See also H. Clegg, 'The Changing System of Industrial Relations: Blackwell (1979) p.215 and K. Coates & T. Topham, Trade Unions in Britain: Spokesman Books (1980) pp.70-71
14. Daily Telegraph 22.04.2009 See also - Geofrey Goodman: Jack Jones' Obituary printed in The Guardian 22nd.April 2009 See also Tony Birtill, 'Brothers in Arms: Ireland in the Spanish Civil War' Irish Post August 30 1986
15. The Guardian 23rd.November 1996 'They Never Walk Alone' John Pilger
16. R. Undy, 'The Devolution of Bargaining Levels in the TGWU 1965-1975': The British Journal of Industrial Relations Vol.9 No.3 (1978) See also H. Clegg, 'The Changing System of Industrial Relations: Blackwell (1979) p.215 and K. Coates & T. Topham, Trade Unions in Britain: Spokesman Books (1980) pp.70-71 V.L. Allen, Militant Trade Unionism: Merlin Press and International Socialism 1st.Series No.95 February 1997 The Bureaucracy in the TGWU by Colin Sparks
17. Jack Jones, Trade Unionism in the Seventies: TGWU Publications June (1970) and also the TGWU Annual Report and Accounts (1972) p.7
18. Charlie Parker interviewed by the author 23 July 1986 see also TGWU GEC Minute Vol. XLV (1967) Minutes No.59 and No.62 relating to officials wages rates and car allowance. A union officer is entitled to a varied figure of reduced mortgages e.g. in 1989 4.5% on £135,000 mortgage. At this time the salary of a union National Official was in excess of £20,000 (Today Newspaper 7.1.1979. Devlin Final Report Cmnd.2734 August 1965 p.45 - The son of TGWU General Secretary Frank Cousins, John Cousins, was appointed a National Officer of the union prompting talk of a 'Cousin's Dynasty' – G. Goodman (1979) p.570 This was and is still not uncommon amongst the leadership of many unions. See also: T. Lane, 'The Unions Caught on the Ebb Tide': Marxism Today September 1982 – See also J. Kelly, Trade Unions and Socialist Politics: Verso London(1988) p.161 and J. Zeitlin, International Review of Social History: XXXIV (1989) p.60 and also J. Cronin,

19. Industrial Conflict in Modern Britain: Croom Helm (1979) p.82
19. Bill Hunter 'Harry Constable- In His Own Words' Living History Library 2017 p.115
20. ibid. p.116
21. D. F. Wilson Dockers: The Impact of Industrial Change: Fontana (1972) pp.93-133
22. E. Taplin The Dockers Union 1986 pp.110-111

## 5 - Internal Conflict and Breakaways

1. Jim Phillips - The Great Alliance: Economic Recovery and the Problems of Power, 1945-1951: Jim Phillips - Pluto Press (1996) pp.37-44
2. Jim Phillips - The Great Alliance: Economic Recovery and the Problems of Power, 1945-1951: - Pluto Press (1996) pp.37-44
3. Bill Hunter - Harry Constable - In His Own Words: Compiled - Living History Library 2017 pp.100-102
4. H. Hikens, Building the Union – Toulouse Press 1973 p.185
5. Harry Constable - In His Own Words: Compiled by Bill Hunter - Living History Library 2017 pp.120-121
6. ibid. pp.120-122
7. ibid. p.135 See also Colin Ross 'Death of the Docks' Authorhouse 2010
8. H. Hikens: Building the Union - Toulouse Press 1973 p.185 See also the Guardian 1 January 2001 and Harry Constable – In His Own Words: Compiled by Bill Hunter – Living History Library 2017 pp.136-139
9. D.F. Wilson: Dockers Fontana (1972) pp.131-132
10. Bill Hunter – 'They Knew Why They Fought: Unofficial Struggles and Leadership on the Docks 1945-1989' Index Books 1994 p.13
11. Bill Hunter, 'They Knew Why They Fought' Index Books (1994) (Extract taken from Bill Hunter's Website; Hands off the Blue.
12. Bill Hunter, 'They Knew Why They Fought' Index Books (1994) p.32
13. 'Dockers Blues – A Short History of the Blue Union' in Symbols of Solidarity Issue 4 Spring 2011 'For many years the dockers of Hull have resented the way the Transport and General Workers Union has handled our disputes.' https://tubcs.files.wordpress.com/2014/03/symbolsofsolidarity4.pdf
14. Walter Greendale interviewed by Brian Barker 20 July 1981 https://mrc-catalogue.warwick.ac.uk/records/DOC/1/15 Warwick University
15. Harry Constable – In His Own Words: Complied by Bill Hunter – Living History Library 2017 p.145

16. Bill Hunter 'They Knew why they Fought' – Unofficial Struggles and Leadership on the docks 1945-1989 – Index Books 1994 pp.31-45 and also TGWU Region 12 Committee Minutes 6 January 1954

17. F. Lindop, Unofficial Militancy in the Royal Group of Docks 1945-1967: Oral History Group, Vol.12 No.2

18. B. Hunter 'They Knew Why They Fought' Index Books 1994 p.79 http://historicalpassages.blogspot.com/2013/05/how-king-street-kept-eye-on-left-2.html Ian Aitken Tribune 11 November 2014

19. Bill Hunter, Hands Off the Blue Union: Democracy on the Docks: Labour Review Pamphlet February (1958) See also Minutes 12 December 1953 Minute No. TGWU Region 12 Committee 406

20. TGWU Region 12 Committee Minutes 6 January 1954

21. TGWU General Secretary Report 6 December 1954 p.243 See Bill Hunter's Website www.billhunterweb.org.uk – Hands off the Blue Union - See: The Great Alliance: Economic Recovery and the Problems of Power, 1945-1951, Jim Phillips Pluto Press 1996 pp.25-39 see also Office for National Statistics on www.ons.gov.uk

22. T. Lane and K. Roberts, Strike at Pilkingtons - Fontana 1971 p.105

23. E. Taplin - Dock Labour at Liverpool: Occupational Structure and Working Conditions In the Late Nineteenth Century - 15 September 1977 p.143 https://www.hslc.org.uk/wp-content/uploads/2017/11/127-8-Taplin.pdf

24. Professor Fred Lindop 'Unofficial Movements and Trade Unionism in the Major Ports' MSS.371/QD7/DOCKS 2/21 https://mrc-catalogue.warwick.ac.uk/records/DOC/2/21 Harold Marr 1984

25. Liverpool Echo 23August 1972 See also G. Taylor – 'The Dynamics of Labour Relations at the Port of Liverpool 1967-89' Manchester University Phd. Thesis 2012

26. K. Robinson 'We Know Who's Been on Our Side' Interview April 1997 p.73 undertaken by Margaret Jones for her work on 'Contemporary British Activists' From the archive held by K. Robinson – On 'dockers' tallies' see Eric Taplin – The Dockers' Union: A Study of the National Union of Dock Labourers 1889-1922 – Leicester University Press 1985 pp.108-109 See also G. Taylor – 'The Dynamics of Labour Relations at the Port of Liverpool 1967-89' Manchester University Phd. Thesis 2012

27. Lord Devlin Final Report Cmnd.2734 August 1965 p.38 see also Merseyside Port Workers Committee Bulletin 'Defend the Scheme' (undated)

28. TGWU General Secretary Report 6 December 1954 p.243 Retired Liverpool Dock Worker, Phil McSorley, stated that dual membership was so common on the docks that this move to isolate Blue Union members was limited in its affect. Interviewed by the author 15th.July 1986.

29. Denis Anderson interviewed by Professor Fred Lindop for Trade Unionism in British Docks 1980-1982 http://mrc-catalogue.warwick.ac.uk/records/DOC/1

30. F. Deegan (1980) pp.70-71 W. Hunter (1958) Hands Off the Blue Union: Labour Review Pamphlet; See also Bill Hunter, They Knew Why They Fought: (1994) Unofficial Struggles & Leadership on the Docks 1945-1989 – for a detailed study and record of the history of the NAS&D

31. Lord Devlin Final Report Cmnd.2734 August 1965 p.38 TGWU Minutes and Records Vol.5 August 1927 Minutes 745/971

32. F. Deegan, There's No Other Way: Toulouse Press (1980) pp.70-73 and also retired Liverpool Dock Worker, Phil McSorley, stated that dual membership was so common on the docks that this move to isolate Blue Union members was limited in its affect. Interviewed by the author 15th.July 1986. W. Hunter (1958) Hands Off the Blue Union: Labour Review Pamphlet; See also Bill Hunter, They Knew Why They Fought: (1994) Unofficial Struggles & Leadership on the Docks 1945-1989 – for a detailed study and record of the history of the NAS&D

33. M. Allen, Post-War Dock Strikes 1945-1955: Journal of North-West Labour History Group No.15 (1990)

34. F. Deegan, There's No Other Way: Toulouse Press (1980) pp.70-73

35. Liverpool Echo October 1955 and also the Devlin Report (1965) p.80 Para:213 See also - Dock Workers Registration of Employment Bill HC Deb 12 November 1945 vol 415 cc1753-822 –

36. Devlin Report Cmnd.2734(1965) HMSO p.80 para:213 also see Devlin Report Cmnd.2734 August 1965 p.81 C. M. Cunningham, The Dock Industry on Merseyside: Social and Economic Studies: Editor, R. Lawton: Longmans 1970 – Also, F. Deegan (1980) pp.78-83

37. ibid.

38. Peter Kerrigan: Interviewed by Bill Hunter and quoted in W. Hunter, They Knew Why They Fought: Index Books (1994) pp.116-117 http://www.grahamstevenson.me.uk/index.php?option=com_content&view=article&id=32

8:peter-kerrigan-the-docker-and-actor&catid=11:k&Itemid=101

39. Devlin Report Cmnd.2734 (1965) HMSO p.80 para:213 See The Devlin Report, Cmnd.2734 August 1965 p.81 – C.M. Cunningham, The Dock Industry On Merseyside: Social and Economic Studies: Editor, R. Lawton: Longmans 1970 – Also, F. Deegan (1980) pp.78-83 See also Revolutionary History The Trotskyists and the Merseyside Dock Strikes 1954-55
http://revolutionaryhistory.co.uk/index.php/marxist-writers/315-harry-ratner/5474-the-trotskyists-and-the-merseyside-docks-strikes-1954-1955

40. Devlin Report Cmnd.2734 (1965) HMSO p.80 para:213 See The Devlin Report, Cmnd.2734 August 1965 p.81 – C.M. Cunningham, The Dock Industry On Merseyside: Social and Economic Studies: Editor, R. Lawton: Longmans 1970 – Also, F. Deegan (1980) pp.78-83

41. See Graham Stevenson's Web Site 'Peter Kerrigan Docker and Actor'
http://www.grahamstevenson.me.uk/index.php?option=com_content&view=article&id=328:peter-kerrigan-the-docker-and-actor&catid=11:k&Itemid=101

42. Professor Fred Lindop 'Unofficial Movements and Trade Unionism in the Major Ports' MSS.371/QD7/DOCKS 2/21 https://mrc-catalogue.warwick.ac.uk/records/DOC/2/21 Tony Burke 1981

43. F. Deegan 'There's No Other Way' (1980) pp.70-71

44. Colin Ross 'Death of the Docks' Authorhouse 2010 pp.66-67

45. F. Lindop Racism and the Working Class: Strikes in Support of Enoch Powell in 1968 April 2001 Labour History Review (66:1) pp.79-100

46. Docks Breakaways and Unofficial Movements – Bob Pennington International Socialism 1st.Series No.2 Autumn 1960
https://www.marxists.org/history/etol/writers/pennington/1960/xx/dockers.htm See also Seumas Milne & Richard Norton-Taylor 'Racism: Extremists led Powell Marches' The Guardian January 1st.1999
https://www.theguardian.com/uk/1999/jan/01/richardnortontaylor2 - See also http://www.alamy.com/stock-photo-apr-04-1968-dockers-march-on-the-house-of-commons-several-hundred-69433394.html For Danny Brandon see also John McIlroy – 'Dockers' Struggles and Oral History' in Workers Liberty: Reason in Revolt 2 September 2009
https://www.workersliberty.org/story/2009/0

9/02/dockers%E2%80%99-struggles-and-oral-history

47. Satnam Virdee – Racism, Class and the Racialized Outsider – Palgrave Macmillan 2014 pp.115-120

48. Paul Smith – 'Unionisation & Union Leadership: The Road Haulage Section' Continuum 2001 pp.106-111 – See also In Defence of Marxism – Terry McPartlan 17 June 2010 http://www.marxist.com/britain-1974-workers-kick-out-tory-government.htm See also; Roger Thomas '1972 – Dockers Face-Down Tory Government: Britain Came Within Inches of a General Strike' The Socialist Newspaper 25 July 2012: And Lawrence Humphreys – '40 Years Since Pentonville' The National Shop Stewards Network http://shopstewards.net/old-site/news.327.htm

49. Paul Smith 'Unionisation and Union Leadership – The Road Haulage Industry' Routledge 2001 pp.109-110

50. Terry McPartlan - In Defence of Marxism –17 June 2010 http://www.marxist.com/britain-1974-workers-kick-out-tory-government.htm See also; Roger Thomas '1972 – Dockers Face-Down Tory Government: Britain Came Within Inches of a General Strike' The Socialist Newspaper 25 July 2012: And Lawrence Humphreys – '40 Years Since Pentonville' The National Shop Stewards Network http://shopstewards.net/old-site/news.327.htm

51. Rob Sewell – 'In the Cause of Labour' in Socialist Appeal https://www.socialist.net/35-years-ago-britain-on-the-verge-of-revolution66.htm

52. Monica Clua Losada Solidarity, Global Restructuring and De-Regulation: The Liverpool Dockers' Dispute 1995-1998 University of York September 2010 pp.52-53 The retreat of the union: The Transport and General Workers' Union strategies of renewal in the 1990s. Mònica Clua Losada, mcl500@york.ac.uk PSA 60th Annual Conference 29 March-1 April 2010

53. TGWU Broadsheet 'It's Good to be in the TGWU' Published in 1964 - Bill Hunter 'They Knew why they Fought' 1994 Index Books pp.114-117

54. D.F. Wilson, Dockers: The Impact of Industrial Change: Fontana (1972) pp.190-193 see also Merseyside Port Workers Committee Bulletin 'Defend the Scheme' (undated)

# 6 – Incorporation and the Struggle for Control

1. Sean Matgamna – 'Militancy and Solidarity on the Docks in the 1960s - Remembering'

Workers Liberty 3 November 2009
http://www.workersliberty.org/story/2009/1
1/03/militancy-and-solidarity-docks-1960s-
remembering - See also Paul Foot, The Devlin
Report (1966) The Notebook International
Socialism No.24 Spring 1966

2. David Chritchley - Working Practices and
Malpractices in the Ports of Liverpool,
London and New York with Special Reference
to the Period 1945-1972 Phd. Thesis Liverpool
John Moores University October 2003 p.73

3. Vernon Jensen, Hiring of Dock Workers and
Employment Practices in the Ports of New
York, Liverpool, London, Rotterdam, and
Marseilles, Harvard University Press 1964 pp.
156-7

4. David Chritchley Working Practices and
Malpractices in the Ports of Liverpool,
London and New York with Special Reference
to the Period 1945-172 Phd. Thesis LJMU
2003 p.160

5. The Devlin Report on the Docks (1966) p.9:
Vol.273 cc.583-4 Hansard 1803
hansard.millbanksystems.com/lords/.../the-
devlin-report-on-the-docks: See also Paul
Foot, The Devlin Report (1966) The
Notebook International Socialism No.24
Spring 1966

6. The Labour Government V The Dockers 1945
to 1951 - Solidarity Pamphlet Volume 111
No.4 Spring 1964 Available:
https://libcom.org/library/labour-party-
dockers-1945-1951-solidarity

7. ibid.

8. Devlin Report Cmnd.2734 August (1965)
pp.6-11/42-47 See also: Donovan Final Report
June 1968 pp.42-47 on shop steward
organisation.

9. Devlin Report Cmnd.2734 August (1965)
pp.6-11: It is also if interest to note that by
1988 the National Association of Port
Employers considered decasualization had
made the Dock Labour Scheme more
important to the dockers than their individual
employer. See P. Turnbull et al, Cardiff
Business School: The Price of De-Regulating
Britain's Ports. July (1993)

10. Devlin Report. Cmnd:2734 (1965) p.46

11. Devlin Report (1965) p.10 See also M. Falkus
– 'The Blue Funnel Legend: A History of the
Ocean Steam Ship Company 1865-1973'
Macmillan 1990 pp.361-376 and D.F. Wilson -
'Dockers: The Impact of Industrial Change'
Fontana/Collins 1972 and also T. Bunnell -
'From World City to a World in One City'
Wiley/Blackwell 2016

12. ibid.p.10 Labour historian Eric Taplin refers to
the idea of 'preferred or blue-eyed' docker was
never 'guaranteed a job... but was in a much
favoured position compared with the casual
casuals' see The Dockers' Union (1985) p.16
and also pp.108-109

13. ibid.p.10 See also, M. Mellish, The Docks
After Devlin: Heinmann (1972)

14. K. Coates, Editor, Can Workers' Run
Industry? Sphere Books(1968) and Tony
Topham, The Dockers, Sphere
Books(1968)p.170 and Compulsory
Retirement Age for Dockers:
S.I.No.1252(1967) and P. Turnbull and D.
Sapsford, Why Did Devlin Fail?: The British
Journal of Industrial Relations Vol.29 No.1
June 1991.

15. D.F. Wilson, Dockers: The Impact of
Industrial Change (1972) pp.134-171

16. P. Turnbull et al, The Price of Deregulating
Britain's Ports: The Socio Economic Costs of
the Dock Labour Compensation Scheme:
Cardiff Business School, July (1993) D.F.
Wilson, Dockers: The Impact of Industrial
Change (1972) pp.134-171

17. Bill Hunter 'They Knew Why They Fought:
Unofficial Struggles and Leadership on the
Docks 1945-1989' Index Books 1994

18. D.F. Wilson 'Dockers: The Impact of
Industrial Change' Fontana Books (1972)
pp.172-211

19. J. Cruddas The Dignity of Labour politybooks
2021 pp.176-179

20. Marxism Today September 198 Tony Lane -
The Unions Caught on the Ebb Tide

21. Tony Lane, The Union Makes Us Strong:
Arrow Books (1974) p.198 - Tony Lane

22. Len McCluskey, a former shop steward on the
docks and now UNITE General Secretary
would often refer to Bernard Cliff's academic
empathy with concepts of pluralism as
expressed by Lord Donovan. He had studied
Donovan at university.

23. Sunday Times 16th January 1983

24. MDHC Port News Survival Special No.5 July
1981 and No.6 July 1981

25. The Guardian 27 March 2006 Larry Neild

26. Sunday Times 16 January 1983 Roger Elgin -
Jim Fitzpatrick/Liverpool Docks

27. MDHC Port News Survival Bulletin Issue
No.3 May 1981

28. MDHC Port News Revival Special Bulletin
No.1 September 1981

29. MDHC Port Newsbrief 6 July 1982

30. MDHC Port Newsbrief No.12 November
1982 'This is not a dispute over new mannings.
There is no way we can go back; we didn't
negotiate these arrangements for the hell of it.'

31. Marxism Today: The Unions Caught on the
Ebb Tide: Tony Lane September 1982 – See
also See M. Terry, The Emergence of A Lay-
Elite? Some Recent Changes in Shop Stewards
Organisation: Warwick University, Industrial
Relations Research Unit (1978) and R. Hyman,

The Politics of Workplace Trade Unionism: Capital & Class No.8 (1979) pp.54-67 and J. England, Shop Stewards In Transport House: IRJ Vol.12 No.5 (1981)

32. Tony Nelson 6/567 Branch Shop Steward: Interviewed by the author on January 5 1989. 'Quay News' was mainly written by Mike Carden, another 567 Branch Shop Steward. Paul Laverty, a port worker, was one of the primary supporters of Quay News originally at the Consultative Committee. The idea of a Port Wide Rank and File Paper had been brought to the Joint Union Port Committee, the MDHC Central Consultative Committee, who did reluctantly agree to support its publication. This support was soon withdrawn and Quay News, consisting of two-side of A4 paper was effectively financed by 567 Branch being printed and published from the Seaforth Container Terminal.

33. Freight News Weekly March 1983
34. Port of Liverpool Press Release March 1983
35. Taken from Shop Steward, Mike Carden's notebook at one Employers' Association of the Port of Liverpool Meeting held at the Port of Liverpool Building on 30 November 1984
36. The Guardian 27 March 2006 - Larry Neild 'James Fitzpatrick – Dynamic Businessman Whose Vision Helped Save Liverpool Docks'

## 7 - The Liverpool dockers' fightback! Support the Miners!

1. Liverpool Daily Post 13 June 1985 'Ban South African Coal from Docks' - Sid Vincent (NUM) letter to J. Symes (TGWU) 'South African Coal) 13 May 1985 & Peter Heathfield NUM South Yorkshire Miners Secretary to Walton MP Eric Heffer, 6 June 1985 - Shop Stewards Notebooks: M. Carden 28 August 1984 – See also Quay News 1985 'Cole Not Dole'

2. The Guardian 24 August 1984 See also MacGregor, I. *The Enemies Within: The Story of the Miners' Strike, 1984-85* (London: Collins 1986); Winterton, J. & Winterton, R. *Coal, Crisis and Conflict: The 1984-85 Miners' Strike in Yorkshire* (Manchester: Manchester Uni Press 1989); Adeney, M. & Lloyd, J. *The Miners' Strike, 1984-5: Loss Without Limit* (London: Routledge 1988). TGWU circular (number 841273/A), 'Re: M.V. Ostia – Hunterston (Ayeshire), 29 August 1984. TGWU Central Office Inter-Departmental Memo from John Connolly to the General Secretary, 'Re: Hunterston/Ravenscraig – Miners' Dispute', 21 May 1984. See also Sunday Times 4 August 1985 – Andrew Jaspan & Brian Morris 'Miners in Fight to Halt Coal Terminal'.

3. P. Turnbull et al, Dock Strike: Conflict and Restructuring in Britain's Ports: Avebury Business School(1992) pp.84-92. See also Paul Mason: 'The British miners had to be smashed so that we could have facebook… 'Post Capitalism – A Guide to our Future' Allen Lane 2015 p.15

4. Reuters 25.8.1984

5. R. Sewell 'In the Cause of Labour - A History of British Trade Unionism' see Chapter 24: The Enemy Within, available: https://www.marxist.com/cause-labour-history-british-trade-unionism.htm. See also: The Guardian 3.1.2014

6. Miners' Strike @ MinersStrikeOTD -During the #MinersStrike Liverpool dockers raised funds in #solidarity with striking miners pic.twitter.com/jK1hagHulW

7. The Guardian 3 January 2014

8. The Guardian 3 January 2014 'Thatcher Had Secret Plan to Use the Army at the Height of the Miners' Strike' Alan Travis: - Based on the National Archives released in 2014.

9. ibid.

10. MDHC Open Channel Video and Bulletin Vol.3 No.5 June 1984

11. Liverpool Daily Post and Echo News Focus April 1985

12. ibid.

13. M. Carden Shop Stewards Note Book: Notes taken during MDHC Joint Consultative Committee Meeting 4 June 1985.

14. MDHC Port News Vol.7 No.7 September 1985

15. ibid.

16. MDHC Open Channel Vol.4 No.2 October 1985

17. ibid.

18. National Dock Labour Board statistics quoted in correspondence to the Author dated 5 June 1986

19. Aintree Container Base Press Release 29 November 1985

20. MDHC Port Newsbrief No.28 December 1986

21. ibid.

## 8 - The End of the Dock Labour Board Scheme

1. The Times 26 December 1987
2. Liverpool Echo 2 April 1988
3. P. Turnbull et al, Dock Strike: Conflict and Restructuring in Britain's Ports: Avebury(1992) pp.88.97
4. MDHC Port Newsbrief: No.34 March 1988
5. Liverpool Daily Post 30 April 1988
6. Liverpool Daily Post 30 April 1988
7. ibid.

8. Meeting Notes taken at Port Shop Stewards Meeting by the author 30th.September 1988
9. Liverpool Echo 4 October 1988
10. TGWU 6/567 Branch Minute Book 4 October 1988
11. G. Taylor – The Dynamics of Labour Relations at the Port of Liverpool 1967-1989 Manchester Metropolitan University Phd. Thesis August 2012 pp.214-220. See also: Anti-Apartheid Movement: Annual Report October 1987 - September 1988, available: psimg.jstor.org/fsi/img/pdf/t0/1 0.5555/al.sff.document.aamp2b0100066.pdf
12. Liverpool Echo 11 October 1988 See also Sunday Telegraph 20 November 1988
13. International Freight Weekly: 'Wave of Unrest Hits the Mersey' 17 October 1988
14. Liverpool Echo 13 October 1988 Lind McDermott - 'First Shots in the Battle of the Docks'
15. ibid.
16. Liverpool Echo 17 October 1988
17. Port Shop Stewards' Meeting - M. Carden Notebook 19 October 1988
18. Mersey Docks and Harbour Company: Port Newsbrief No.41 November 1989
19. ibid.
20. M. Carden Notebook 29 March 1989
21. ibid.
22. The Flickering Flame Dir. Ken Loach 1996 Parallax Pictures
23. ibid.
24. P. Turnbull et al, Dock Strike: Conflict and Restructuring in Britain's Ports. (1992) pp.157-162
25. The Devlin Report (1965) Cmnd.2734 p.9 and also The Report of the Royal Commission on Trade Unions and Employers' Associations (1968) Cmnd 3623, known as the 'Donovan Report', was an inquiry into the system of collective UK Labour Law. Chaired by Lord Donovan.
26. www.billhunter.org.uk/articles/hands_off_the _blue_union.htm
27. D.F. Wilson, Dockers: The Impact of Industrial Change: Fontana (1972) pp.155-211

# 9 - The Dockers and the TGWU's Broad Left

1. Mike Richardson 'State Intervention and the Abolition of the National Dock Labour Scheme – The Bristol Experience' The Bristol Radical History Group, available: http://www.brh.org.uk/site/articles/abolition -of-the-national-dock-labour-scheme/ See also: John Dempster 'The Rise and Fall of the Dock Labour Scheme' Biteback Publishers 2010
2. Paul Blyton and Peter Turnbull – 'The Dynamics of Employee Relations' Macmillan 1994 p.131
3. Western Daily Press 15 April 1989
4. Bristol Evening Post 21 April 1989
5. Mike Richardson 'State Intervention and the Abolition of the National Dock Labour Scheme – The Bristol Experience' The Bristol Radical History Group, available: http://www.brh.org.uk/site/articles/abolition -of-the-national-dock-labour-scheme/
6. www.libcom.org. Chapter 14: July/August 1989
7. At this time Mike Carden was the secretary to the TGWU Merseyside Co-ordinating Committee and Alan Quinn was the GEC Territorial Representative for Region Six following Stan Pemberton's retirement. The MCC was an unofficial body that met the Saturday after each GEC Meeting in London.
8. Bill Hunter (1994) 'They Knew Why They Fought: Unofficial Struggles and Leadership on the Docks 1945-1989' Index Books, pp.103-113
9. The Financial Times 14 April 1989 C. Leadbetter
10. A. Murray, 'The T&G Story: History of the TGWU 1997-2007' Lawrence & Wishart (2008) pp.176-177
11. A. Murray, 'The T&G Story: History of the TGWU 1997-2007' Lawrence & Wishart (2008) pp.176-177
12. M. Clua Losada – Solidarity, Global Restructuring and De-Regulation: The Liverpool Dockers Dispute 1995-1998 Phd. University of York September 2010
13. Colin Sparks – 'The Bureaucracy in the TGWU' International Socialism No.95 February 1977, available: https://www.marxists.org/history/etol/newsp ape/isj/1977/no095/sparks.htm
14. Charles Leadbetter - The Financial Times 14 April 1989 – See also: John Dempster – The Rise and Fall of the Dock Labour Scheme London – Published by Biteback 2010
15. Rudd and Jones 15/04/1989: The Retreat of the Union: The TGWU Strategies of Renewal in the 1990s, available: www.academia.edu/270266/The_Retreat_of_t he_Union_The_Transport_and_General_Wor kers_Union_Strategies_of_Renewal_In_the_1 990s
16. P. Turnbull et al, Dock Strike: Conflict and Restructuring in Britain's Ports: Avebury(1992) pp.157-173 and also P. Turnbull, The Price of De-Regulating Britain's Ports: The Socio-Economic Cost of the Dock Labour Compensation Scheme; Cardiff Business School July 1993

17. R. Rodgers, Herald Scotland 2 August 1989 'Todd Faces Facts and Orders the Striking Dockers Back to Work';
18. ibid.
19. ibid.
20. LIoyd's List 20 February 1998 - Nigel Lawson: The View from No.11 – Memoirs of a Tory Radical: 1992 - Daily Telegraph 10.4.2009 Iain Dale My part in the Downfall of the NDLS: April 10 2009 Also Iain Dale 'The Blogfather – The best of Iain Dale's Diary' Biteback Publishing 2012
21. The Flickering Flame 1996 Dir. K. Loach Parallax Pictures
22. Great Dock Strike 1889 – The Story of the Labour Movements First Great Victory - Ron Todd, General Secretary of the TGWU p.8.
23. 1989 Strike Leaflet 'Support the Dockers' Issued by the Merseyside Port Shop Stewards
24. Peter Waterman in LabourNet http://www.labournet.net/docks2/9609/ITF DEB4.HTM
25. Peter Waterman, Globalization, Social Movements, and the New Internationalism – Continuum 1998 - ITF News, August 1989:11
26. Peter Waterman, LabourNet http://www.labournet.net/docks2/9609/ITF DEB4.HTM
27. Letter from David Cockroft, ITF, November 13 1990. See also P. Waterman cited on LabourNet http://www.labournet.net/docks2/9609/ITF DEB4.HTM - See also - Resolution for A European Port-Workers Charter 6.8.1989
28. Letter from MDHC T. Furlong to TGWU Docks Official Jimmy Symes 3 August 1989.
29. MDHC Port Operation' Manager Bernard Cliff – Letter to all MDHC Employees 18 August 1989

## 10 - Foundations of Chaos

1. The Flickering Flame Dir. K. Loach 1996 Parallax Pictures
2. ibid.
3. ibid. For Denis Anderson. See also: obituary in Merseyside CND Newsletter Apr/May/June 2017 'Remembering the Fight for Workers' Rights: A Tribute to Union and Campaign Activist Denis Anderson by M. Carden
4. The Flickering Flame Dir. K. Loach 1996 Parallax Pictures
5. Michael Carr (27 May 1947 – 20 July 1990 served as Member of Parliament for Bootle for 57 days in 1990 from his election until his death.
6. The Flickering Flame Dir. K. Loach 1996 Parallax Pictures – See also: 'The dynamics of Labour Relations at the port of Liverpool, 1967-1989' Greig Taylor: Manchester Metropolitan University 2012 Phd. Thesis.
7. M. Clua Losada: 'Solidarity, Global Restructuring and Deregulation: The Liverpool Docks Dispute 1995-98' University of York September 2010 pp.134-35
8. Turnbull et al Turnbull, P. and S. Weston (1991). 'Continuity and Change in the British Port Transport Industry: A Study of the Ports Since Abolition of the National Dock Labour Scheme.' University of Wales, Cardiff Business School. Turnbull, P., C. Woolfson, et al. (1992). Dock Strike: Conflict and Restructuring in Britain's Ports. Aldershot, Avebury.
9. M. Clua Losada: 'Solidarity, Global Restructuring and Deregulation: The Liverpool Docks Dispute 1995-98' University of York September 2010 p.100
10. A. Baldwin et al - Class, Culture and Community: New Perspectives in Nineteenth and Twentieth Century, Cambridge Scholar Publishing 2012 p.105 Some 16,000 Liverpool dockers were registered in the 1960s by 1989 just about 1,000 registered men were left.
11. Liverpool Echo 18 July 1996 and also The Morning Star 18 July 1996 'We should have sacked the lot of them'
12. G. Taylor 'The dynamics of labour relations at the port of Liverpool, 1967-1989' Phd. Thesis Manchester Metropolitan University August 2012 –
13. Terry Southers taped interview with D. Cotterill 17.10.1996
14. ibid.
15. Joe Ladd Senior Interviewed by Dave Cotterill 13.12.1996 Audio Tape DC23
16. M. Carden M. Carden Notebook 27.6.1990
17. M. Carden Notes 3.7.1990
18. M. Carden notes 6.7.1990
19. M. Carden notes 31.7.1990
20. Authors notes 26.9.1990
21. TGWU Docks and Waterways District Committee 10 September 1990 Minute No. 73
22. TGWU Docks and Waterways National Committee, 18 October 1990 Circular No. 900951 See also MDHC Notice, undated, entitled General Cargo – The Future – T. Teague archive
23. M. Carden Diary 24.10.90
24. ibid. 16.11.90
25. Letter from Bernard Cliff, Port Operations Director MDHC, to Jimmy Symes, TGWU Docks' District Secretary – Liverpool Cargo Handling 14 January 1991
26. ibid.
27. Letter from Bernard Cliff, Port Operations Director MDHC, to Jimmy Symes, TGWU Docks' District Secretary – Liverpool Cargo Handling 14 January 1991

28. Peter Turnbull & C. Woolfson et al. 1992, Dock Strike: Conflict and Restructuring in Britain's Ports - Avebury, 1992 p.158Redundancy and Re-Employment in the Docks – UK Data Service available: doc.ukdataservice.ac.uk/doc/3174/mrdoc/pdf /3174userguide.pdf Lavalette, M., & Kennedy, J. - Casual Lives? The social effects of work casualization and the lock out on the Liverpool docks, Critical Social Policy, August 1996 16 (48), 95-107.

29. P. Turnbull & C. Woolfson et al. 1992, Dock Strike: Conflict and Restructuring in Britain's Ports - Avebury, 1992 p.158

30. M. Carden Diaries 22.3.1991

31. M. Carden Diaries 15.4.1991

32. M. Carden Diaries 16.4.1991

33. M. Carden Diaries 19.4.1991

34. ibid.

35. ibid.

36. M. Carden Diaries 19 April 1991

37. M. Carden Notes on Port Shop Stewards Friday 26 April 1991- no disclosure of shop stewards' sons being part of this Torside recruitment process was made at this time.

38. Chris Marsden - Hard Lessons from the Liverpool Docks Lock-Out 14 February 1998 https://www.wsws.org/en/articles/1998/02/l ive-f14.html

39. M. Carden notes of Port Shop Stewards' Meeting Friday 26 April 1991

40. M. Carden Notes Port Shop Stewards 26 April 1991 and also 19 November 1993

41. M. Lavalette and J. Kennedy - Solidarity on the Waterfront-The Liverpool Lock-Out of 1995/96 Liver Press 1996 p.86. See also Bob Ritchie: Undated transcript of interview held with D. Cotterill

42. 'Dockers' 1999 Channel 4 Television – Parallax Pictures/Prism Leisure: Producer Sally Hibbin – Directed by Bill Anderson

43. Monica Clua Losada Solidarity, Global Restructuring and Deregulation: The Liverpool Dockers' Dispute 1995-98 – PhD, University of York Department of Politics September 2010 p.136

44. ibid. p.136

45. Bill Hunter's interview with Frank Lannigan, available: http://www.billhunterweb.org.uk/interviews/ History_as_Told.htm#Frank%20Lannigan

46. The Flickering Flame Dir. K. Loach Parallax Pictures 1996

47. Jimmy Davies Junior interviewed by D. Cotterill October 1996

48. J. Ladd Junior Interviewed by D. Cotterill 13.12.1996

49. M. Carden Meeting Notes Dock Company Stewards Meeting 11.5.1991

50. Meyer et al 'Social Movements: Identity, Culture, and the State' Oxford University Press 2002 pp.147-148

51. Bob Ritchie interview transcript (undated). Held by Dave Cotterill

## 11 - De-recognising Shop Stewards on the Docks

1. M. Carden Diaries 23 May 1991

2. ibid.

3. M. Carden Diaries 23 May 1991

4. M. Carden Diaries 23 May 1991

5. ibid. 27 August 1991

6. ibid. 1 October 1991 and 8 October 1991

7. M. Carden Diaries Liverpool dockers' mass meeting at Transport House 6.11.1991

8. M. Carden Diaries 7 November 1991

9. Undated MDHC Notice 'General Cargo – The Future'

10. M. Carden Meeting Notes Port Stewards 16.11.91 Union official, Jack Dempsey, had met with Bradley, the boss of Torside, and agreed to 'recruit from the union's list of volunteers.'

11. M. Carden Meeting Notes Port Stewards 16.11.91

12. ibid.

13. ibid.

14. ibid.

15. B. Cliff MDHC Port Operations Director Letter to TGWU Official Jack Dempsey 'Torside' 26 November 1991

16. M. Carden Diaries 23 December 1991

17. ibid.

18. M. Carden Meeting Notes Dock Company Shop Stewards 3 March 1992

19. M. Carden Notes Company Stewards 11 March 1992

20. Port of Liverpool MDHC Letter A. Price to J. Dempsey Ref: AP/JK(23) 5 March 1992

21. Port of Liverpool MDHC Letter A. Price to J. Dempsey Ref: AP/JK 16 April 1992

22. M. Carden Diaries 29.4.1992

23. M. Carden Notes Company Stewards 12.5.1992

24. M. Carden Notes Special Port Shop Stewards 6.6.1992

25. ibid.

26. M. Carden Notes Dock Company Stewards 12.6.92

27. M. Carden Notes Company Notes Company Stewards 12.6.92

28. ibid.

29. Letter to Striking Dockers from Bernard Cliff, Port Operations Director, MDHC 22 July 1992

30. Monica Clua Losada Solidarity, Global Restructuring and Deregulation: The Liverpool Dockers' Dispute 1995-98 PhD, University of

York Department of Politics September 2010
p.136-137

31. Ibid

## 12 - Unemployment – a Liverpool Inheritance

1. Helen Grady - 'The English City that wanted to break-away from the UK' The Mersey Militants - BBC News Magazine: 8 November 2014, available: http://www.bbc.co.uk/news/magazine-29953611. See also 'Liverpool – A City that Dared to Fight' Peter Taaffe and Tony Mulhearn: Fortress 1988 See also Marxism Today November 1978 – Tony Lane, Liverpool-City of Harder Times to Come & Merseyside in Crisis (Merseyside Socialist Research Group) See also S. Hughes There She Goes: Liverpool A City on Its Own - decoubertin 2019 pp.90-94

2. Liverpool Echo 27 September 2018 Derek Hatton is back in the Labour Party 33 years after he was kicked out – Liam Thorpe - See also Tony Mulhearn – The Making of a Liverpool Militant – 47books 2019

3. Tony McQuade Interviewed by libcom.org available: libcom.org/library/an-interview-with-tony-mcqade-former-shop-steward

4. The English city that wanted to 'break away' from the UK' By Helen Grady Producer of 'The Mersey Militants' 8 November 2014 available: http://www.bbc.co.uk/news/magazine-29953611

5. Peter Taaffe and Tony Mulhearn 'Liverpool: A City that Dared to fight'– Fortress Books 1988

6. Tony McQuade Interviewed by libcom.org available: libcom.org/library/an-interview-with-tony-mcqade-former-shop steward

7. 'The Failure of Triumph in Speke' – BBC News website, 8 December 2009, available: http://news.bbc.co.uk/local/liverpool/hi/peo ple_and_places/history/newsid_8401000/840 1200.stm See also Tony Lane - 'Liverpool: A City of Harder Times to Come' Marxism Today November 1978 pp.336-343 and also Roger O'Hara – 'Merseyside on the Dole' Merseyside Communist Party 1975

8. Liverpool Echo 14 March 2005 – Larry Neild 'The Wrong Way to Fight A Good Cause' Available: http://www.liverpoolecho.co.uk/news/liverp ool-news/wrong-way-fight-good-cause-3534307

9. 'The Failure of Triumph in Speke' – BBC News website, 8 December 2009, available: http://news.bbc.co.uk/local/liverpool/hi/peo ple_and_places/history/newsid_8401000/840 1200.stm

See also: https://gerryco23.wordpress.com/tag/mersey side-trade-union-community-and-unemployed-resource-centre/ https://en.wikipedia.org/wiki/People's_Marc h_for_Jobs / http://www.liverpoolmuseums.org.uk/mol/vi sit/galleries/peoples/unemployment.aspx https://www.tuc.org.uk/sites/default/files/U WCDirectory.pdf http://blogs.londonmet.ac.uk/tuc-library/2016/05/20/peoples-march-jobs/ http://www.aronline.co.uk/blogs/videos/vide o-speke-closure-on-the-bbc/ See also: Brian Marren 'We shall not be moved: How Liverpool's Working Class fought redundancies, closures and cuts in the age of Thatcher' Manchester University Press 2016. See also 'Class Culture and Community: New Perspectives in 19th. and 20th.Century British Labour History' – Edited by Anne Baldwin et al Cambridge Scholars Publishers 2012 p.98

10. Karl Marx, 1867. Das Kapital. Marx & Engels Collected Works, 35. Chap. XXV

11. Jane Faniel Trade Unions and the Unemployed: Towards a Dialectical Approach – Interface Volume 4(2) 130-157 November 2012 p.151

12. G. Goodman 'Bill Morris a Trade Union Miracle 2012 pp.136-141

13. The Waterboys 1985 song, 'The whole of the moon'

14. Tony Lane - The Unions: Caught on the Ebb Tide - Marxism Today 6 September 1982 p.13

15. As General Executive Member for Region 6 in the 1990s, Mike Carden recalled how he, Ken Brindle and Barry Miller would sit opposite Bill Morris who would always have Ray Collins alongside him. It did appear that it was the Administrative Assistant that was actually running the TGWU on far too many occasions. Bill Morris tended always to await the 'word in his ear' from Ray Collins before he would respond to points or questions raised in the Executive Chamber.

16. M. Clua Losada 'The Retreat of the Union: The TGWU Strategies of Renewal in the 1990' University of York 2010 p.109

17. C. Brady & A.Lorenz – End of the Road – The True Story of the Downfall of Rover Cars – Pearson 2001 p.116

18. M. Clua Losada 'The Retreat of the Union: The TGWU Strategies of Renewal in the 1990' University of York 2010 p.11

19. Geoffrey Goodman 'Bill Morris – A Trade Union Miracle' Blackamber Inspirations 2010 pp.135-138

## 13 - The Local TGWU Alliance with

## the MDHC

1. M. Carden Notes Mass Meeting 22.7.1992 See also: David S. Meyer, Nancy Whittier, Belinda Robnett 'Social Movements: Identity, Culture, and the State': Oxford University Press (2002) p.147
2. M. Carden Notes 22.7.1992 See also: 'Social Movements: Identity, Culture, and the State' David S. Meyer, Nancy Whittier, Belinda Robnett: Oxford University Press (2002) p.147
3. Port of Liverpool MDHC B. Cliff to J. Dempsey Friday 24 July 1992
4. Port of Liverpool MDHC B. Cliff letter to all Liverpool Dockers 31 July 1992
5. Port of Liverpool MDHC B. Cliff letter to J. Dempsey 7 August 1992
6. M. Carden Meeting Notes 11 November 1992 Port Shop Stewards
7. MDHC Letter to Seaforth Dock Workers A. Price 14 January 1993
8. ibid.
9. MDHC Letter to Seaforth Dock Workers: Employee Relations Manager A. Price 17 January 1993 Ref: AP/JK
10. ibid.
11. M. Carden Notes Company Stewards 7.1.93
12. M. Carden meeting notes Wednesday 5 May 1993
13. ibid.
14. M. Carden meeting notes Wednesday 5 May 1993
15. ibid.
16. TGWU Minutes of Docks and Waterways District Committee 10 May 1993
17. TGWU Minutes of Docks and Waterways District Committee 10 May 1993
18. ibid.
19. TGWU Minutes of Docks and Waterways District Committee 10 May 1993
20. M. Carden Diary Records 10.7.1993
21. M. Carden Diary Notes 28 July 1993 and letter confirming this decision of 6/601 signed by Branch Secretary E. Jones
22. ibid
23. Bob Ritchie transcripted but undated interview held by Dave Cotterill 'That casual labour was part of the Torside wage deal which was agreed by the Torside dockers but now he was claiming it to be separate from wage negotiations.'
24. M. Carden Notes Port Shop Stewards 30.7.93
25. ibid.
26. ibid.
27. Bill Morris - A Trade Union Miracle – G. Goodman Black Amber Inspirations 2010 p.136
28. ibid. pp.135-141
29. M. Carden Notes Port Shop Stewards Transport House 6 August 1993
30. M. Carden Notes Port Shop Stewards Transport House 6 August 1993
31. Shop Steward Note of Accreditation Container Terminal MDHC/TGWU
32. Shop Steward Note of Accreditation Container Terminal MDHC/TGWU
33. M. Carden Notes Seaforth Container Terminal on Saturday 28 August 1993, John Simon was crushed to death by a container, it was a tragic accident that only served to highlight the dangers of working on the docks. A container berth has its own unique dangers from straddle carriers to gantry cranes.
34. M. Carden Notes Port Shop Stewards 10.9.93
35. ibid.
36. M. Carden Notes Port Shop Stewards 10.9.93
37. M. Carden Notes Port Stewards 14.10.93 and Seaforth ballot paper.
38. ibid.
39. This policy had been originally decided upon at a meeting of the dockers on 23 September 1993. M. Carden Notebook. See also 22 November 1993. M. Carden Notebook.
40. M. Carden Notes Seaforth Meeting 16.9.93
41. M. Carden Notes 6/601 Branch Meeting 23.9.93
42. M. Carden Notes Seaforth Meeting 6.10.93
43. M. Carden notes from PSS meeting 14.10.93
44. Ibid

## 14 - The Acquisition of the Medway Ports

1. 'The Case for the Reinstatement of the Sacked Liverpool Dockers' The Need for a Public Inquiry Merseyside Port Shop Stewards Committee 1st. July 1997 – See also Paul Blyton, Peter Turnbull The Dynamics of Employee Relations: - Palgrave McMillan: Third Edition 2004 pp.170-174
2. 22 September 1993 Mersey Docks Company Press Release
3. The Independent 20 August 1993 - John Murray 'Mersey may buy Medway: Possible ports sale sparks row over Privatisation'
4. TGWU Record Feb/Mar 1997 LabourNet http://www.labournet.net/docks2/9702/LDR ECORD.HTM
5. David Hellier 'Medway Dockers Set to Sue' The Independent 13 March 1994 See Public Accounts Committee Reports HC Deb 26 October 1994 vol 248 cc899-970 http://hansard.millbanksystems.com/commo ns/1994/oct/26/public-accounts-committee-reports
6. David Hellier 'Medway Chief Under Pressure' The Independent 20 March 1994
7. The Mersey Docks and Harbour Company History – The Funding Universe http://www.fundinguniverse.com/company-

histories/the-mersey-docks-and-harbour-company-history/ See also Mersey Agree Docks Deal with Peel – Financial Times 9th.June 2005

8. David Hellier 'Medway Dockers Set to Sue' The Independent 13 March 1994

9. David Parker The Official History of Privatisation: Popular capitalism, 1987-97 Routledge 2012 p.153 See also Public Accounts Committee Reports HC Deb 26 October 1994 vol 248 cc899-970 http://hansard.millbanksystems.com/commons/1994/oct/26/public-accounts-committee-reports

10. Public Accounts Committee Reports HC Deb 26 October 1994 vol 248 cc899-970 http://hansard.millbanksystems.com/commons/1994/oct/26/public-accounts-committee-reports

11. The Independent 20th.August 1993 - John Murray - Mersey may buy Medway: Possible ports sale sparks row over privatisation –See also The Times 21 August 1993

12. The Financial Times 2 December 1992

13. The Financial Times 5 December 1992

14. Medway Ports 1992 Annual Report and Accounts

15. P.J. Arnold & C. Cooper - A Tale of Two Classes: The Privatisation of Medway Ports in Critical Perspective on Accounting Volume 10 Issue 2 April 1999 pp.127-152 Elsevier http://www.sciencedirect.com/science/article/pii/S1045235498902283

16. Financial Times 2 August 1993

17. Minutes of evidence taken by the Committee of Public Accounts 1994, p. 8

18. Sunday Times 26 September 1993

19. Sunday Times 26 September 1993

20. P.J. Arnold & C. Cooper - A Tale of Two Classes: The Privatisation of Medway Ports in Critical Perspective on Accounting Volume 10 Issue 2 April 1999 pp.127-152 Elsevier - Also Minutes of evidence taken by the Committee of Public Accounts 1994, p. 8 See also TGWU Dock Survey of Membership in British Ports in 1992 http://doc.ukdataservice.ac.uk/doc/3174/mrdoc/pdf/3174userguide.pdf

21. Minutes of evidence taken by the Committee of Public Accounts 1994, p. 8 See also TGWU Dock Survey of Membership in British Ports in 1992 http://doc.ukdataservice.ac.uk/doc/3174/mrdoc/pdf/3174userguide.pdf

22. Financial Times 21 August 1993 -The Times 21 August 1993 - The Guardian 23 September 1993 - See Sunday Times 26th. September 1993 and Lloyds List, 23 December 1993 - In June 1994, the Public Accounts Committee issued a report on its investigation into the Department of Transport's sales of the trust ports. The Sunday Times 3 March 1994 - The Financial Times 14 April 1994 and The Times 5th.July 1996

23. P.J. Arnold & C. Cooper - A Tale of Two Classes: The Privatisation of Medway Ports in Critical Perspective on Accounting Volume 10 Issue 2 April 1999 pp.127-152

24. Elsevier - Alan G. Jamieson 'Not More Ports, But Better Ports: The Development of British Ports since 1945 - The Northern Mariner/Le Marin du nord, VI, No. 1 (January 1996), 29-34.

25. Paul Blyton & Peter Turnbull – The Dynamics of Employee Relations Palgrave McMillan Third Edition 2004 pp.172-176

26. Peter Turnbull - Restructuring and Strategies of Seaports and Port companies: The United Kingdom I. Introduction UK ports have been transformed over - http://www.maritim.uni-bremen.de/ports/global/TURNBUL.pdf See also P.J. Arnold & C. Cooper - A Tale of Two Classes: The Privatisation of Medway Ports in Critical Perspective on Accounting Volume 10 Issue 2 April 1999 pp.127-152 Elsevier

## 15 - The 'Far-Left Militant Tendency' and the General Secretary Share a Platform!

1. M. Carden Notes on Regional Meeting Transport House 6.11.93 This matter was part of the Trade Union Reform and Employment Rights Act (1993) See https://www.legislation.gov.uk/ukpga/1993/19

2. M. Carden Notes on Regional Meeting Transport House 6.11.93 See also 'Bill Morris: A Trade Union Miracle' G. Goodman Blackamber Inspirations 2010 pp.139-145

3. Monica Clua Losada Solidarity, Global Restructuring and Deregulation: The Liverpool Dockers' Dispute 1995-98 PhD University of York Department of Politics September 2010 p.111 G. Stevenson quoted.

4. J. McIlroy (1998). The Enduring Alliance? Trade Unions and the Making of New Labour 1994-1997. British Journal of Industrial Relations 36(4): 537- 564

5. Monica Clua Losada Solidarity, Global Restructuring and Deregulation: The Liverpool Dockers' Dispute 1995-98 PhD University of York Department of Politics September 2010 p.111

6. G. Goodman Bill Morris-A Trade Union Miracle 2010 pp.136-137

7. ibid. p.137

# LIVERPOOL DOCKERS: A HISTORY OF REBELLION AND BETRAYAL

8. Liverpool Daily Post – Ben Scofield 'Union Chief Eddie Roberts Cleared after fourteen-year battle'. 23 May 2008
9. ibid.
10. ibid.
11. Liverpool Daily Post – Ben Scofield 'Union Chief Eddie Roberts Cleared after fourteen-year battle'. 23 May 2008
12. http://www.marxist.com/Europe-old/ireland_tgwu_suspensions.html Peter Black a member of the ATGWU Irish Regional Committee, Belfast: 28/6/2001 see also http://www.socialistparty.org.uk/international/all/International/9160 – See also From Lucifer to Lazarus – M. O'Reilly Lilliput Press 2019
13. Ben Scofield, 'Union Chief Eddie Roberts Cleared after fourteen-year battle', Liverpool Daily Post, 23 May 2008. Text available: https://advance.lexis.com/api/permalink/4ee16a7a-6b6a-4592-ade3-2b82e8f810a7/?context=1519360&federationidp=4HKXSX59158
14. See also: https://www.thefreelibrary.com/%27I%27m+not+here+to+regurgitate+history%27+says+Bill+Morris.-a0179303251TGWU Minutes Regional F&GP 22.11.93
15. ibid.
16. M. Carden Diary 22 November 1993
17. ibid.
18. ibid.
19. M. Carden diary 22 November 1993
20. Correspondence R. Lamb to R. Owens TGWU Regional Secretary Ref: rl/cb 9 January 1993
21. ibid. and Minutes of Regional Finance and General Purposes Committee November 2 1993
22. ibid.
23. TGWU Inter-office Memorandum From E. Roberts, Divisional Organiser to R. Owens, Regional Secretary Copies to R. Lamb and J. Dempsey 2 November 1993
24. ibid.
25. TGWU Inter-office Memorandum From E. Roberts, Divisional Organiser to R. Owens, Regional Secretary Copies to R. Lamb and J. Dempsey 2 November 1993
26. ibid.
27. ibid.
28. Document to Region 6 F&GP – R. Owens, Regional Secretary from R. Morton and K. Robinson 19 November 1993 – See Also Correspondence to Bro. Owens, TGWU Regional Secretary, on 25 May 1993,
29. Minutes of D&W RTG 6.8.93 and 9.8.93 - Minutes Docks and Waterways Regional Trade Group 6 August 1993 & 9 August 1993 - M.

Carden Diary 24 July 1993 - Letter from R. Morton and K. Robinson to R. Owens and the TGWU F&GP 19 November 1993
30. Letter form TGWU Regional Secretary, Bobby Owens to Jack Dempsey 8 December 1993

## 16 - The Seaforth Container Berth Contract (Fire and Re-hire)

1. MDHC Letter: A. Price to J. Dempsey: 'New Working Arrangements - Container Terminal' 16 December 1993 K. Robinson archive
2. MDHC Letter: A. Price to J. Dempsey: 'Changes in Working Arrangements Container Terminal' 17 December 1993 K. Robinson archive
3. TGWU Letter from R. Owens, the Region 6 Secretary to J. Dempsey the Docks Officer, 8 December 1993 Ref: RO/SW
4. M. Carden Notes Officials Meeting with elected members of constitutional committees, Transport House, Liverpool 22.12.93
5. Monica Clua Losada Solidarity, Global Restructuring and Deregulation: The Liverpool Dockers' Dispute 1995-98 PhD University of York Department of Politics September 2010 pp.138-140 The Observer 18 April 2021 T.Wall 'Fire and rehire' tactics rife at workplaces that are in profit…and claiming Covid cash
6. ibid. Losada pp.138-139
7. Monica Clua Losada Solidarity, Global Restructuring and Deregulation: The Liverpool Dockers' Dispute 1995-98 PhD University of York Department of Politics September 2010 pp.138-140
8. Mass Meeting Edinburgh Park Dockers' Club 11 January 1994 Meeting Notes
9. ibid.
10. MDHC Bulletin 2 Appendix No.4 Submission on Behalf of Sacked Liverpool Dockworkers.-House of Commons May 1996
11. TGWU Letter R. Owens RO/SW 8 December 1993
12. M. Carden Notes Seaforth Mass Meeting 13.1.94 'With a £2m loss all dockers could be sacked but suitable alternative employment would be offered with vacancies filled from outside.'
13. M. Carden Notes Seaforth Mass Meeting 13.1.94
14. ibid.
15. M. Carden Notes Port Shop Stewards Meeting Transport House 15.1.94
16. ibid.
17. Letter to J. Dempsey from M. Carden 23 January 1994
18. MDHC RSCT Official Record of Meeting between MDHC and the TGWU Official J.

Dempsey and Shop Stewards M. Cullen, K. McKenna 27 January 1994

19. M. Carden Notes Meeting in Transport House 19 February 1994

20. Meeting with Dempsey, Burrell and Price in Maritime House 23.2.1994

21. Letter from MDHC A. Price to Seaforth Dockers 28 February 1994

22. ibid.

23. M. Carden notes on meeting in Transport House 6.3.94

24. Official TGWU Leaflet for Seaforth Container Terminal Meeting Sunday 6 March 1994 at Transport House

25. MDHC Letter A. Price to Seaforth Container Terminal Dockworkers 'Absenteeism' 9 March 1994

26. Mick Cullen BBC Radio Merseyside 27 January 1998 See also Michael Cullen – A Liverpool Docker's History – Second Ed. August 2021

27. M. Carden notes on disciplinary meeting with MDHC/TGWU 11 March 1994

28. ibid.

29. TGWU Letter E. Roberts to G. Liddy 19 May 1994.

30. Liverpool Echo 21.5.1994

31. Original hand-written letter from Alec Hampton, Terminal Manager RSCT MDHC to A. Gardiner 4 July 1994

32. LabourNet November 1995

33. Liverpool Docker Richie Gerrard Interviewed for the Dockers Charter 20 November 1995

34. 'Me on the Picket Line' Cathy Dwyer 21 November 1995 http://www.labournet.net/docks2/9511/cathy.htm

35. Frank Lannigan in C. Clynch & Others v TGWU Chronology Case No. LV190318

36. MDHC Letter to T. Teague from A. Price 25 May 1994

37. T. Teague Written meeting notes Seaforth Dockers' Meeting Transport House 2 June 1994

38. ibid.

39. MDHC Employee Relations Manager, A. Price letter to Jack Dempsey, Eddie Roberts and Bobby Owens 21 June 1994 Ref:AP/JK

40. ibid.

41. ibid.

42. ibid.

43. ibid.

44. MDHC Employee Relations Manager, A. Price letter to Jack Dempsey, Eddie Roberts and Bobby Owens 21 June 1994 Ref:AP/ - MDHC Letters from Allan Price to Terry Teague and Kevin Robinson Ref:AP/JK 22 June 1994

## 17 - The Bullying and Intimidation Continues

1. TGWU Docks and Waterways National Committee, 25 July 1994 Circular No. 940593

2. TGWU Docks and Waterways National Committee, 27 October 1994 Circular No. 940778

3. M. Clua Losada: The retreat of the union: The Transport and General Workers' Union strategies of renewal in the 1990s Paper to be presented at the 60th Political Studies Association Annual Conference, Edinburgh 29 March – 1 April 2010 pp.17-19 - Fax to Bill Morris 09/04/1994 Department of Politics University of York

4. MDHC Employee Relations Manager, Allan Price, letter to TGWU Official Jack Dempsey 13 September 1994 Ref: AP SMc

5. MDHC Letter to all dockers at the Seaforth Container Terminal from A. Price, Employee Relations Manager, not dated but to be acted upon by Tuesday 20 September 1994.

6. ibid.

7. ibid.

8. MDHC Letter from A. Price to J. Dempsey: 17 November 1994 Ref: AP/SA

9. MDHC Letter to J. Dempsey 18 November 1994

10. MDHC Letter to J. Dempsey 21 November 1994

11. MDHC Letter from A. Price to J. Dempsey Ref:AP.SMc 23 December 1994

12. B. Cliff Port Operations Director 5 January 1995 MDHC Leaflet

13. ibid.

14. Leaflet from T. Teague and K. Robinson 'To All Seaforth Operations Workers' 18 January 1995

15. Handwritten record of 6/601 Branch Meeting 7 January 1995 – K. Robinson archive.

16. Leaflet from T. Teague and K. Robinson 'To All Seaforth Operations Workers' 18 January 1995

17. Royal Seaforth Container Terminal – Manpower Review February 1995

18. ibid.

19. ibid.

20. ibid.

21. ibid.

22. ibid.

23. Kevin Robinson notes of Shop Stewards and Dockers' Mass Meeting 21 February 1995

24. K. Robinson record of MDHC/Union meeting 6 February 1995 and also Terry Teague Mass Meeting 8 February 1995 Handwritten Notes taken from meeting with MDHC 6 February 1995 and Terry Teague Mass Meeting 8 February 1995 Handwritten Notes taken from meeting with MDHC 6 February 1995

25. Terry Teague Mass Meeting 8 February 1995 Handwritten Notes taken from meeting with MDHC 6 February 1995

26. K. Robinson record of mass meeting 8 February 1995

27. ibid.

28. TGWU Letter from Jack Dempsey to Bernard Cliff Director of Port Services MDHC 9 February 1995

29. MDHC Notice to all employees based at the RSCT – Shift Roster April 1995

30. M. Carden Diary and Record of meeting with Jack Dempsey in Transport House, Liverpool on Thursday 2 February 1995

31. M. Carden's Diary 15 February 1995

32. M. Carden's Diary 16 February 1995

33. ibid. Wednesday 22 February 1995

34. Carden would resign from office in February 1999 following discussions with the local Broad Left. Tony Woodhouse, from the Road Transport 6/541 Branch, was elected GEC Representative for Region Six. He would go on to be elected President of the TGWU and later UNITE. Letter of acknowledgement from Bill Morris to M. Carden's letter of resignation. TGWU Ref:WM RC LRD - February 12 1999

## 18 – Torside Ltd and the March of the Yellow Cranes

1. Bob Ritchie interview transcript undated and not accredited – held in dock dispute archive. Also taped interview Dave Cotterill DC29 interview with 14 January 1997

2. ibid.

3. John Ferns interviewed by D. Cotterill in Official History of Sacked Liverpool Dockers 1995 p.17 unpublished and also letter from John Ferns shareholder/docker/ to G. Waddell, Chairman on 30/10/95 calling for a special meeting.

4. Handwritten record of Seaforth Dockers Meeting at Edinburgh Park Saturday 1 July 1995

5. J. McKenzie Chairman 6/601 TGWU Seaforth Branch 3 July 1995

6. Handwritten record of meeting with local TGWU Officers and K. Robinson 7 July 1995 – K. Robinson archive

7. Handwritten record of Seaforth Dockers Meeting at Edinburgh Park Saturday 7 July 1995

8. ibid.

9. T&G North West: Jack Dempsey to members of 6/601, 602,603,605,606 and 6/610 Branches Ref: JD/CY 18 July 1995 'We have, I believe, reached a crisis of confidence position, in that the employer no longer believes that the Union has any control over its members

and therefore, they are questioning why they should recognise the Union. Any unofficial action may well cost you your job, as the employers are adamant that they will sack people who take part in any such action and have stressed this clearly to your Stewards and myself.'

10. Monica Clua Losada - Solidarity, Global Restructuring and Deregulation: The Liverpool Dockers' Dispute 1995-98: PhD University of York Department of Politics September 2010 p.140

11. Quoted in C. Clynch & Other v TGWU Chronology LV190318 p.11

12. Bob Ritchie transcripted undated interview and not accredited – held in dock dispute archive. Also taped interview with Dave Cotterill DC29 14 January 1997

13. Steve Southers interviewed by D. Cotterill 13 December 1996 – audio tape

14. Joe Ladd Junior Interviewed by D. Cotterill 13 December 1996 – audio tape

15. TGWU Official Letter from J. Dempsey letter to all Dock Workers 28 July 1995

16. ibid.

17. J. Dempsey letter to C. McNally 18 August 1995

18. The Liverpool Docker July 1995 Leaflet produced by the dock shop stewards at Seaforth Container Terminal. 'This is the first edition of the Liverpool Docker: Published by UY and FU plc.' The final lines were abbreviations for 'up yours and fuck you Public Limited Company.

19. The Guardian 'Containing Wages on the Waterfront' David Osler 30 August 1995

20. ibid.

21. ibid. See also Peter Turnbull and Victoria Wass 'The Great Dock and Dole Swindle: Accounting for the Costs and Benefits of Port Transport Deregulation and the Dock Labour Compensation Scheme: Public Administration Vol.73 Blackwell Publishers Ltd. 1995 pp.513-534

22. TGWU Letter to Member Employed by Torside Ltd. Jack Dempsey 7 August 1995 Ref.JD/CY

23. TGWU Minutes of the Sefton Geographical Committee, Tuesday 8 August 1995 Bobby Owens, the TGWU Regional Secretary, died on the 8 August 1995 and his funeral took place on Tuesday 15 August 1995.

24. C. Clynch & Other and TGWU Chronology Case No. LV190318 p.2

25. ibid. – Tony Melia also wrote a detailed letter to the Liverpool Daily Post & Echo relating the facts of how the dispute with Torside Ltd. evolved between 11 July 1995 and 25 September 1995 – Letters Page Liverpool Daily Post & Echo 13 October 1995

26. C. Clynch & Other and TGWU Chronology Case No. LV190318 p.2
27. Kevin Robinson Notes of Port Shop Stewards Meeting 5 September 1995
28. Submission on behalf of Sacked Liverpool Dockworkers to the Employment Sub-Committee – House of Commons May 1996 p.8
29. Letters Page Liverpool Daily Post & Echo written by Tony Melia 13 October 1995.

## PART THREE: The 1995 Dispute

## 19 - Monday 25th September 1995: The Dispute Begins

1. Private and Confidential Report: Docks Dispute. Dave McCall, TGWU Regional Secretary. Monday 11 November 1996 p.6
2. ibid.
3. C. Clynch v TGWU Chronology LV190318 p.12
4. John Hendy QC 'C. Clynch and others v TGWU 16 February 2005 p.2
5. Peter Jones Interviewed on BBC Radio Merseyside Docks Audio Tapes Ref: April 1997
6. K. Robinson Interviewed on BBC Radio Merseyside - Audio Tape Ref: Docks April 1997
7. John Pilger, 1998. Hidden Agendas. London: Vintage, pp. 337-8
8. C. Barker and M. Lavelette Leadership and Social Movements Manchester University Press 2001 p.140 See also Monica Clua Losada - Solidarity, Global Restructuring and Deregulation: The Liverpool Dockers' Dispute 1995-98: PhD University of York Department of Politics September 2010 p.145
9. Private and Confidential Report: Docks Dispute. Dave McCall, TGWU Regional Secretary. Monday 11 November 1996 p.11
10. Monica Clua Losada Solidarity, Global Restructuring and Deregulation: The Liverpool Dockers' Dispute 1995-98 PhD University of York Department of Politics September 2010 p.145
11. Tony Melia Email to author 28 September 2018 See also Simon Sloan 'We had Good Days and Bad Days: Triumph and Tragedy in the Oral History Narratives of the Liverpool Dockers. MA Thesis University of Leiden 29 August 2019 pp.9-12
12. Private and Confidential Report: Docks Dispute. Dave McCall, TGWU Regional Secretary. Monday 11 November 1996 p.9
13. ibid.
14. ibid.
15. The Education and Employment Committee 1996 and also Private and Confidential Report: Docks Dispute. Dave McCall, TGWU Regional Secretary. Monday 11 November 1996 p.9-10
16. T. Teague & TGWU Higgins & Co. 23 April 2001 also 2002 p.46
17. David S. Meyer, Nancy Whittier, Belinda Robnett 'Social Movements: Identity, Culture, and the State': Oxford University Press 2002 pp.147-149
18. The Education and Employment Committee 1996; p. 19
19. http://johnpilger.com/articles/what-did-you-do-during-the-dock-strike- and also John Pilger, 'Hidden Agendas' New Press (1998) p.346
20. The Flickering Flame: Ken Loach 1996
21. ibid.
22. C. Clynch and TGWU Case No. LV190318 p.3
23. ibid. Para 3.2 TGWU Report
24. Education and Employment Select Committee May 1996 Paras 37-51 cited in Private and Confidential Report: Docks Dispute. Dave McCall, TGWU Regional Secretary. Monday 11 November 1996 p.12
25. Private and Confidential Report: Docks Dispute. Dave McCall, TGWU Regional Secretary. Monday 11 November 1996 p.13
26. ibid. p.15
27. ibid. p.10-16
28. ibid. p.15
29. ibid. p.15-16
30. ibid. p.6-7
31. Minutes of the Region Six D&W Trade Group Committee held on 6 November 1995 & Docks Dispute Report: Dave McCall, TGWU Regional Secretary. Monday 11 November 1996 p.7
32. C. Clynch & Others: Advice on Tortious Issues: Case No. HQ02X01426 J. Hendy QC 16 February 2002 p.10 and Regional Committee Minutes 6 November 1995
33. ibid. pp. 7-10
34. Docks Dispute Report: Dave McCall, TGWU Regional Secretary. Monday 11 November 1996 p.7 See also M. Carden Diary 6 November 1995

## 20 - Tuesday 26th September 1995: Day Two

1. Private and Confidential Report: Docks Dispute. Dave McCall, TGWU Regional Secretary. Monday 11 November 1996 p.13
2. C. Clynch & TGWU Chronology Case No. LV190318 and also Bradley para 37 Appendices to minutes of evidence

3.  Docks Dispute. Dave McCall, TGWU Regional Secretary. Monday 11 November 1996 pp.10-11

4.  Casual Lives: Critical Social Policy – M. Lavalette and C. Barker in Social Movements: Identity, Culture and the State. David S. Meyer et al, Oxford University Press 2002 pp.140-141 - J. Hendy ibid. See also Lynch & Others v TGWU Royal Courts of Justice 11 December 2002 p.15

5.  Docks Dispute. Dave McCall, TGWU Regional Secretary. Monday 11 November 1996 p.14

6.  ibid. p.14

7.  David S. Meyer, Nancy Whittier, Belinda Robnett: 'Social Movements: Identity, Culture, and the State' Oxford University Press 2002 pp.147-149

8.  TGWU Regional Committee Minutes 6.11.02

9.  Lynch v TGWU 11.1202 p.20

10. Bob Ritchie transcripted interview/undated held by Dave Cotterill and also C. Clynch 7 Others v TGWU Case No. HQ02X01426 16 February 2005 p.43 Torside Stewards response to meeting of 6 November 1995

11. C. Clynch 7 Others v TGWU Case No. HQ02X01426 16 February 2005 p.43

12. ibid.

13. Torside Ltd. Dispute Leaflet Original September 1995

14. Tony Melia Email to author 24 September 2018

15. ibid.

16. Docks Dispute Report. Dave McCall, TGWU Regional Secretary. Monday 11 November 1996 p.14

17. Lynch v TGWU 11 December 2002 p.47

18. C. Clynch & Others v TGWU Chronology Case No. LV190318 p.5 See also Private and Confidential Report Docks Dispute: Dave McCall 14 November 1996 p.14 Jack Dempsey recalls how he 'gave Frank Lannigan a lift home and during the journey he informed me that there was a meeting of the Port Shop Stewards Committee that evening to discuss the Torside problem.'

19. C. Clynch v TGWU Case No. HQ02X01426

20. C. Clynch & Others v TGWU Chronology Case No. LV190318 p.5 See also Private and Confidential Report Docks Dispute: Dave McCall 14 November 1996 p.14 Jack Dempsey recalls how he 'gave Frank Lannigan a lift home and during the journey he informed me that there was a meeting of the Port Shop Stewards Committee that evening to discuss the Torside problem.'

21. Docks Dispute Report: D. McCall 11 November 1996 pp.15-16

22. Joe Ladd Junior Interviewed by D. Cotterill Audio Tape 13.12.1996

23. Interviews by the author with Kevin Robinson and Frank Lannigan September 2018.

## 21 – Wednesday 27th September 1995: Day Three

1.  Docks Dispute Report: D. McCall 11 November 1996 pp.16

2.  ibid. 1996 p.16

3.  ibid. 2002 p.45

4.  Para 1.12 and 5.7 TGWU Report quoted in C. Clynch & Others v TGWU Case No. LV190318 p.7

5.  ibid.p.7 Para 1.12 and 5.7 of TGWU Report

6.  Docks Dispute Report: D. McCall 11 November 1996 pp.16-17 and also transcript held by Dave Cotterill containing statements provided by Bob Ritchie, Joe Morris, Steve Morris and other Torside dockers.

7.  ibid.

8.  Docks Dispute Report: D. McCall 11 November 1996 pp.16-17 and also transcript held by Dave Cotterill containing statements provided by Bob Ritchie, Joe Morris, Steve Morris and other Torside dockers.

9.  ibid.

10. T. Teague & TGWU Higgins & Co. 23 April 2001 and also Bob Ritchie written statement held by Dave Cotterill on the first days of the dispute together with other Torside dockers.

11. C. Clynch & Others: Advice on Tortious Issues: Case No. HQ02X01426 J. Hendy QC 16 February 2002 p.21

12. T. Teague & TGWU Higgins & Co. 23 April 2001 and also Bob Ritchie written statement held by Dave Cotterill on the first days of the dispute together with other Torside dockers.

13. D.Sinclair email to T.Nelson 11.02.2015

14. Bob Ritchie transcribed interview undated but held by Dave Cotterill

15. Docks Dispute Report: D. McCall 11 November 1996 p.17

16. ibid. p.17-18

17. Dave Sinclair email to Tony Nelson 11 February 2015

18. Document Held by T. Teague Torside 1- undated – See also - Brian Towers: The Rise and Fall of Liverpool's Dockland: Waterfront Blues – Carnegie Publishing 2011 pp.293-297

19. M. Carden Diaries 2 April 1996 Negotiations MDHC/TGWU

20. ibid.

## 22 - Thursday 28th September 1995: Day Four

1.  Bob Ritchie statement held by Dave Cotterill on the first days of the dispute.

2. Docks Dispute Report: D. McCall 11 November 1996 p.19
3. T. Teague & TGWU Higgins & Co. 23 April 2001
4. C. Clynch & Others v TGWU Chronology LV190318 p.8 and Para 6.2 TGWU Report: D. McCall 11 November 1996 p.19
5. Handwritten notes by K. Robinson on meeting at Dockers' Club Thursday 28 September 1995 from K. Robinson archive.
6. C. Clynch & Others: Advice on Tortious Issues: Case No. HQ02X01426 J. Hendy QC 16 February 2002 p.8
7. Journal of the North West Labour History Group Issue No.23 -1998/99 'History in the Making: The End of the Liverpool Docks Dispute, 1998' Eric Taplin pp.49-54
8. K. Robinson notes from Transport House Meeting, Thursday 28 September 1995
9. Docks Dispute Report: D. McCall 11 November 1996 p.19
10. K. Robinson notes from Transport House Meeting, Thursday 28 September 1995
11. Docks Dispute Report: D. McCall 11 November 1996 p.19
12. C. Clynch & Others: Advice on Tortious Issues: Case No. HQ02X01426 J. Hendy QC 16 February 2002 p.9
13. ibid. p.9-21 also Dempsey to Adams 6 October 1995 p.7
14. C. Clynch & Others: Advice on Tortious Issues: Case No. HQ02X01426 J. Hendy QC 16 February 2002 p.21
15. T. Teague & TGWU Higgins & Co. 23 April 2001 and also C. Clynch & Others v TGWU Chronology LV190318 p.8 and Para 6.2 TGWU Report: D. McCall 11 November 1996 p.19 and also Bob Ritchie typed statement held by Dave Cotterill.
16. Docks Dispute Report: D. McCall 11 November 1996 p.19
17. ibid. p.19-20
18. ibid. C. Clynch & Others: Advice on Tortious Issues: Case No. HQ02X01426 J. Hendy QC 11 December 2002 p.8 and p.22
19. ibid. p.8 Dempsey to Jack Adams on 6 October 1995
20. C. Clynch & Others: Advice on Tortious Issues: Case No. HQ02X01426 J. Hendy QC 11 December 2002 p.8 and p.22
21. Private and Confidential Letter from A. Price MDHC to T. Teague 28 September 1995 Ref: AP/KN
22. Papers held by T. Teague: Torside 1 Doc.
23. John Pilger Hidden Agendas. London: Vintage 1998, pp. 337-8 quoted in 'How the Liverpool Dockers Launched a Global Movement' Edited by Pauline Bradley and Chris Knight: Published in 2004 by the Radical Anthropology Group in association with Haringey Trades Union Council and the sacked Liverpool dockers.
24. The Guardian 23 November 1996John Pilger 'They Never Walk Alone'
25. Seaforth Container Terminal New Contracts issued by MDHC March 1994 and also Private and Confidential Letter from A. Price MDHC to T. Teague 28 September 1995 Ref: AP/KN
26. Dave Cotterill - Official history of sacked Liverpool Dockers 1995 - p.17
27. The Guardian 23 November 1996 'They Never Walk Alone' John Pilger
28. Lloyd's List 19 September 1995
29. C. Clynch & Others: Advice on Tortious Issues: Case No. HQ02X01426 J. Hendy QC 16 February 2002 p.48
30. J. Davies Junior audio interview with D. Cotterill October 1996

## 23 - The 'Official Record' of the First Four Days

1. Economic Priorities for a Labour Government - Roy Hattersley: Palgrave Macmillan 1987 p.71. See also: https://en.wikipedia.org/wiki/Mersey_Docks _and_Harbour_Company See also Hansard MERSEY DOCKS AND HARBOUR BOARD BILL (By Order) HC Deb 21 June 1971 vol 819 cc1073-141 - House of Commons Guide for giving written or oral evidence to a House of Commons Select Committee p.12, available: https://www.parliament.uk/documents/com mons-committees/witnessguide.pdf
2. House of Commons Education and Employment Select Committee 21 May 1996 p.1 Education and Employment Select Committee: Employment The implications of the industrial dispute in the Port of Liverpool. Education first report with proceedings and appendices. Document type: HOUSE OF COMMONS PAPERS.
3. ibid.p.1
4. House of Commons Education and Employment Select Committee 21 May 1996 p.1 Education and Employment Select Committee: Employment The implications of the industrial dispute in the Port of Liverpool. Education first report with proceedings and appendices. Document type: HOUSE OF COMMONS PAPERS.
5. Letter from Branch 6/610 dated 6 September 1996 to Bill Morris see also resolution from Branch 6/606: 'It is our members' considered view that Brother Dempsey has been totally negligent on this issue resulting in the dismissal of 500 Transport and General Members laying our Union open to possible claims of Non-Representation.'

6. House of Commons Education and Employment Select Committee 21 May 1996 p.1 Education and Employment Select Committee: Employment The implications of the industrial dispute in the Port of Liverpool. Education first report with proceedings and appendices. Document type: HOUSE OF COMMONS PAPERS –pp.17-19

7. Undated letter from Jim Davies, Branch Secretary – Cited in Solidarity, Global Restructuring and Deregulation: The Liverpool Dockers' Dispute 1995-98 Monica Clua Losada PhD University of York Department of Politics September 2010 p.165

8. J. Hendy QC in the High Court of Justice Queen's Bench 16.2.2005 - See also Lynch & Others v TGWU Royal Courts of Justice 11 December 2002 p.15

9. Case No. HQ02X01426 C.C.Lynch & Ors. And the TGWU: 11 December 2002 p.6

10. ibid. 11.12.2002 p.8

11. Geoffrey Goodman, entitled, 'Bill Morris - A Trade Union Miracle' Arcadia Books (2010) p.159

12. D. McCall Report Docks Dispute 11 November 1996 and letter to Bill Morris from D. McCall 14 November 1996

13. D. McCall Report Docks Dispute 11 November 1996 p.1

14. ibid.p.4

15. ibid. p.11 and also Regional Committee Minutes 18 December 1995

16. ibid.

17. T. Teague & TGWU Higgins & Co. 23 April 2001

## 24 - In for the long haul

1. M. Carden Meeting Notes 4 October 1995

2. ibid. See also Tideway: 'Re-instate them says Tribunal' A TGWU Newspaper of Region 1 Number 9 February 1992

3. Letter to MDHC Dock Workers from A. Price, Employee Relations Manager, MDHC Ref: AP/KN 5 October 1995 and also letter from A. Price, Employee Relations Manager, MDHC, to T. Teague, 5 October 1995 Ref:AP/KN

4. Liverpool Daily Post October 6 1995 Port of Liverpool Pickets the Facts

5. ibid.

6. Liverpool Daily Post October 6 1995 Port of Liverpool Pickets the Facts

7. ibid.

8. M. Carden Meeting Notes 6 October 1995

9. Lloyd's List 9.10.1995

10. David S. Meyer, Nancy Whittier, Belinda Robnett: 'Social Movements: Identity, Culture, and the State' Oxford University Press 2002 pp.147-150

11. BBC Radio Four: The World at One 9 October 1995 Mike McKay Northern England Correspondent

12. ibid.

13. ibid.

14. ibid.

15. BBC Radio Merseyside - Morning Merseyside Monday 9 October 1995

16. TGWU Director of Legal Services, Fergus Whitty, to Dave McCall, TGWU Regional Secretary – Ref: FW RC 3348 10 October 1995 See also C. Clynch & Others v TGWU Case No. LV190318 p.9

17. TGWU Director of Legal Services, Fergus Whitty, to Dave McCall, TGWU Regional Secretary – Ref: FW RC 3348 10 October 1995

18. C. Clynch & Others v TGWU Case No. LV190318 p.10

19. TGWU Letter Fergus Whitty to W.Bowley MDHC Director of Legal Services Ref:FW RC3348 22 November 1995

20. M. Carden Meeting Notes 11 October 1995 and Liverpool Echo 11 October 1995 quoted in D. Cotterill 'Official History of the sacked Liverpool Dockers 1995'

21. ibid.

22. ibid.

23. ibid.

24. M. Carden Meeting Notes 11 October 1995 Liverpool Echo 11 October 1995 quoted in D. Cotterill 'Official History of the sacked Liverpool Dockers 1995'

25. ibid.

26. John Williams, S. Hopkins and C. Long 'Passing Rythms: Liverpool FC and the Transformation of Football - Oxford 2001 pp.7-8

27. Early Day Motion 1484 in 1984/5, proposed by Eddie Loyden MP (18.10.95) HC Deb 25 October 1995 vol: 264 cc1119-261119 – Loyden references the guarantees against the use of casual labour given in 1989 following the abolition of the National Dock Labour Scheme as recorded in Hansard Official Report 17th.April 1989 Vol.151 c.45 1121

28. Early Day Motion 1484 in 1984/5, proposed by Eddie Loyden MP (18.10.95) HC Deb 25 October 1995 vol: 264 cc1119-261119

29. ibid.

30. ibid.

31. ibid.

32. ibid.

33. ibid.

34. ibid. See also: Official Report 17th.April 1989 Vol.151 c.45 1121

35. Early Day Motion 1484 in 1984/5, proposed by Eddie Loyden MP (18.10.95) HC Deb 25 October 1995 vol: 264 cc1119-261119

36. ibid.

0# REFERENCES

037. Early Day Motion 1484 in 1984/5, proposed by Eddie Loyden MP (18.10.95) HC Deb 25 October 1995 vol: 264 cc1119-261119Official Report 17th.April 1989 Vol.151 c.45 1121

## 25 -The 'Scabs'

1. Richard Saundry and Peter Turnbull - Melee on the Mersey: Contracts, Competition and Labour Relations on the Docks -: Industrial Relations Journal 27:4 Blackwell Publishers 1996 p.276
2. Education and Employment Committee, HC 413, p.30. See also Solidarity, Global Restructuring and Deregulation: The Liverpool Dockers' Dispute 1995-98 Monica Clua Losada PhD University of York Department of Politics September 2010 p.150 'Drake Port Services was already well known by British dockers. It had established itself as a reliable strike breaking port employment agency based in Kent. In 1993, Southampton dockers had also faced the threat of Drake's, and the Liverpool dockers were familiar with this earlier situation.'
3. TGWU Docks and Waterways National Committee, 29 April 1993 Circular No. 930317
4. ibid.
5. MDHC Annual Report 1997, p. 37
6. ibid.
7. Drake Ports Distribution Services – Extracts from the Port Operatives Agreement 1996 dspd1/96
8. ibid.
9. PDP Services Ltd. Contract of Services for Workers Attention Frank Robotham MDHC Manager – See http://www.abports.co.uk/newsarticle/101/
10. Education and Employment Committee, HC 413, p.30 also Solidarity, Global Restructuring and Deregulation: The Liverpool Dockers' Dispute 1995-98 Monica Clua Losada PhD University of York Department of Politics September 2010 p.150 'Drake Port Services was already well known by British dockers. It had established itself as a reliable strike breaking port employment agency based in Kent. In 1993, Southampton dockers had also faced the threat of Drake's, and the Liverpool dockers were familiar with this earlier situation.'
11. ibid.
12. TGWU Minutes of the Sefton Geographical Committee, Tuesday 8 August 1995
13. ibid.
14. G. Goodman - Bill Morris: A Trade Union Miracle – G. Goodman 2002 pp.136-139
15. ibid.
16. ibid.

17. Monica Clua Losada - Solidarity, Global Restructuring and Deregulation: The Liverpool Dockers' Dispute 1995-98 PhD University of York Department of Politics September 2010 p.114
18. The New Statesman 22 January 1999 Interview – 'Bill Morris; In gentle sorrow rather than anger, he laments that, under Labour, the employers have had all the favours.' P. Wilby: The New Statesman. London http://www.newstatesman.com/new-statesman-interview-bill-morris.
19. Charles Tilly et al, 'Globalization and Labor's Citizen Rights' - Antonia Gentile and Sidney Tarrow: Internationalism - Cambridge University Press 1995 Tilly, C. (1995). Globalization threatens labor's rights. International Labor and Working-Class History, 74247 ,1 –23. 743
20. Charles Tilly et al, 'Globalization and Labor's Citizen Rights' - Antonia Gentile and Sidney Tarrow: Internationalism - Cambridge University Press 1995 Tilly, C. (1995) pp.23-24
21. M. Carden Meeting Notes with Jack Adams DGS, John Connolly National Docks Officer and Dave McCall Region 6 District Official: Transport House 20 October 1995
22. PDP Services Ltd. Contract of Services for Workers Attention Frank Robotham MDHC Manager – See http://www.abports.co.uk/newsarticle/101/
23. Bernard Cliff MDHC Operations Director on 23 October 1995 on BBC 2 - Newsnight
24. Official History of the Sacked Liverpool Dockers 1995 – D. Cotterill
25. ibid.
26. ibid.
27. M. Carden Diary 31.10.1995
28. M. Carden BBC Radio Merseyside Interview Friday 24 October 1997 Audio Tape Ref: Docks April 1997
29. Liverpool Daily Post 2.11.1995 'Labour Plea for Sacked Dockers'
30. Liverpool Echo 'Brigade Bosses Lower Dockers Standard' 3.11.1995
31. Liverpool Echo 'No Pay Bid by Dockers' 7 November 1995
32. ibid.
33. D. Cotterill 'Official History of the Sacked Liverpool Dockers 1995 p.35
34. ibid.
35. ibid.
36. Mass Picket Leaflet February 1997
37. D. Cotterill 'Official History of the Sacked Liverpool Dockers 1995 p.37
38. Socialist Worker quoted in D. Cotterill ibid. p.46
39. Newsline 'Smash Anti-Union Laws' 4.11.1995
40. ibid.

677

41. Liverpool Echo 'Dockers Hold Picket Demo' 6.11.1995
42. D. Cotterill 'Official History of the Sacked Liverpool Dockers 1995 p.37
43. ibid.
44. ibid.
45. ibid.
46. D. Cotterill ibid. Environmental Health Services Report, 24 November 1995
47. ibid.
48. ibid.
49. ibid.
50. ibid.
51. Liverpool Dockers Press Release: Occupation of Drake offices 20 York Place Edinburgh see also A. Lees 'Liverpool – The Hurricane Port Mainstream Publishing 2013 edition p.227
52. Liverpool Echo 30.11.1995 'Iron Curtain shields dockworker from picket'
53. Dockers Charter A Fight for All – November 1995 http://www.labournet.net/docks2/9511/CHARTER.HTM
54. Dr. C. Knight, C. Power and L. Knight - 'The World's First Picket Line – Women and the Origins of Human Morality' MTUCURC 13 November 1996

## 26 - Women of the Waterfront!

1. LabourNet November 1995 http://www.labournet.net/docks2/9511/WOWMTG.HTM
2. ibid.
3. Doreen McNally in a short essay on the Women of the Waterfront emailed to Mike Carden in June 2015.
4. ibid.
5. ibid. See also P. Bradley and C. Knight 'Another World is Possible – How the Liverpool Dockers Launched a Global Movement: Wernham Printers London N17 pp.11-12
6. Doreen McNally in a short essay on the Women of the Waterfront emailed to Mike Carden in June 2015.
7. Andrew Lees, 'Liverpool – The Hurricane Port' Mainstream Publishing 2013 Edition p.227
8. Doreen McNally in a short essay on the Women of the Waterfront emailed to Mike Carden in June 2015.
9. LabourNet November 1995
10. Daniel Sultan Film: 'Words of Liverpool' Artis Diffusion Paris 1996
11. LabourNet November 1995
12. ibid.
13. Peter Kennedy http://www.labournet.net/docks2/other/WOW.HTM) Militant 'Build on the Solidarity 15th.March 1996
14. Bill Hunter 'Workers History as Told by Those Who Made It. Merseyside Dockers, and Women of the Waterfront' Available: http://www.billhunterweb.org.uk/interviews/History_as_Told.htm
15. ibid.
16. ibid.
17. ibid.
18. D. Cotterill History of the Sacked Liverpool Dockers 1995 p.35
19. LabourNet 21st November 1995 and also Dockers Charter November 20 1995
20. Dockers Charter 20 November 1995 Liverpool Docker Ritchie Gerrard
21. A. Lees 'Liverpool – The Hurricane Port' Mainstream Publishing 2013 edition p.227
22. P. Bradley and C. Knight 'Another World is Possible – How the Liverpool Dockers Launched a Global Movement: Wernham Printers London N17 pp.11-12
23. ibid.
24. Cathy Dwyer Interviewed by LabourNet 21 November 1995 http://www.labournet.net/docks2/9511/WOWMTG.HTM
25. ibid.
26. Bill Hunter http://www.billhunterweb.org.uk/interviews/History_as_Told.htm
27. Doreen McNally in a short essay on the Women of the Waterfront emailed to Mike Carden in June 2015.
28. ibid.
29. ibid.
30. ibid.
31. ibid.
32. ibid.
33. ibid.
34. ibid.
35. Docker Charter No.3 January 1996 http://www.labournet.net/docks2/other/CHART3.HTMDoreen McNally in a short essay on the Women of the Waterfront emailed to Mike Carden in June 2015.
36. Doreen McNally in a short essay on the Women of the Waterfront emailed to Mike Carden in June 2015 see also Independent 20 September 1997 'No going back at the Liverpool Docks' Ros Wynne-Jones
37. Daily Mail 'Gaddafi human rights prize for two dock strike wives' Thursday September 4 1997
38. Peter Kennedy: Journal Critique (email 113121.3463@compuserve.com published in LabourNet October 1997
39. ibid.
40. ibid.

41. Michael Lavalette and Jane Kennedy – 'Solidarity of the Waterfront' The Liverpool Lock Out of 1995-96: Liver Press 1996 p.48
42. ibid. 1996 p.51-58
43. Women of the Waterfront Speaking Tour November 1997 Canada http://www.sandelman.ottawa.on.ca/lists/html/opirg-events/1998/msg00039.html
44. ibid.

## 27 - The International Campaign

1. D. Cotterill Official History of the Liverpool Dock Dispute 1995 p.43
2. LabourNet January 1996 http://www.labournet.net/docks2/9601/PETIT.HTM
3. ibid.
4. Financial Times 12 December 1995
5. Liverpool Echo 6.12.1995 'Dockers' Demo'
6. Kevin Robinson's Notes of Shop Stewards meetings 6/7/8 December 1995
7. ibid.
8. ibid.
9. Kevin Robinson's Notes on Dockers Mass Meeting 8 December 1995
10. Kevin Robinson's Notes on 9/10 December 1995
11. Kevin Robinson's Notes on Shop Stewards Meeting 11/12 December 1995
12. ibid.
13. Lloyd's List 13 December 1995 Andrew Guest 'Liverpool threat over jobs', Marine Industries Correspondent
14. LabourNet December 1995 http://www.labournet.net/docks2/9512/UPDATE4.HTM
15. LabourNet December 1995 http://www.labournet.net/docks2/9512/UPDATE3.HTM
16. LabourNet December 1995 http://www.labournet.net/docks2/9601/DIARY.HTM
17. K. Robinson diary 12/13 December 1995
18. ibid.
19. LabourNet 'Diary of an Exceedingly Long-Range Picket' http://www.labournet.net/docks2/9601/DIARY.HTM
20. ibid.
21. LabourNet December 1995 'Diary of an Exceedingly Long-Range Picket' http://www.labournet.net/docks2/9601/DIARY.HTM
22. ibid.
23. ibid.
24. ibid.
25. ibid.
26. Superior Court of New Jersey Chancery Division – ACLU Attorney for Defendents
Morton, Nelson and Billsborow not dated from K. Robinson archive.
27. LabourNet 'The World is our Picket Line' http://www.labournet.net/docks2/9601/FRONT.HTM See also Lloyd's List 29 December 1995 'ACL in threat to pull out of Mersey over docks dispute' Andrew Guest, Marine Industries Correspondent see also The Guardian 'Flying pickets chase ships by plane; Dock workers step up casual labour dispute' Seumas Milne 20 December 1995
28. ibid.
29. See International Dockers' Council http://www.idcdockworkers.org/en/
30. Internationalism is About our Only Hope – Richie Gerrard interviewed by Dave Cotterill http://www.labournet.net/docks2/9511/gerrard.htm
31. The World is Our Picket Line http://www.labournet.net/docks2/other/PICKET.HTM
32. Jim Donovan email to the author 9 September 2019
33. ibid.
34. ibid.
35. ibid.
36. Jim Donovan email to the author 9 September 2019
37. Len McCluskey - Always Red - OR Books 2021 pp.75-81
38. D. Cockcroft and Kees Marges email group discussion Mac Urata forwarded to my email address on 11/10/2021
39. ibid.
40. Jim Donovan email to the author 9 September 2019
41. ibid.
42. ibid.

## 28 - The TGWU Condemns MDHC (for the First and Last Time)

1. LabourNet January 1996 http://www.labournet.net/docks2/9601/TALKS.HTM
2. ibid.
3. Simon Sloan 'We Had Good Days and Bad Day' – Triumph and Tragedy in the Oral History Narratives of Liverpool Dockers MA Thesis University of Leiden 29 August 2019 p.12
4. Kevin Robinson notes from Shop Stewards Meeting Friday 15 December 1995 and mass meeting.
5. ibid.
6. Kevin Robinson notes from Shop Stewards Meeting Friday 18 December 1995 See also the Central Organisation of the Workers of Sweden – SAC https://www.sac.se/ and

https://en.wikipedia.org/wiki/Central_Organi sation_of_the_Workers_of_Sweden

7. Kevin Robinson notes from Shop Stewards Meeting Friday 18 December 1995
8. Kevin Robinson notes from Shop Stewards Meeting 20 December 1995
9. ibid.
10. Greg Dropkin 'Remembering Paco' http://www.labournet.net/docks2/9908/paco 4.htm and also Francisco Ramos Vargos, known to the dockers as Paco was a very respected comrade for dockers worldwide and it seemed right and fitting that the founding meeting of the International Dockers Committee took place in Santa Cruz, Tenerife June 2000 http://www.labournet.net/docks2/0007/idc1. htm
11. Kevin Robinson notes on Mass Meeting Thursday 21 December 1995
12. ibid.
13. ibid.
14. ibid.
15. A songwriter, itinerant laborer, and union organizer, Joe Hill became famous around the world after a Utah court convicted him of murder. Even before the international campaign to have his conviction reversed, however, Joe Hill was well known in hobo jungles, on picket lines and at workers' rallies as the author of popular labor songs and as an Industrial Workers of the World (IWW) agitator. Thanks in large part to his songs and to his stirring, well-publicized call to his fellow workers on the eve of his execution—'Don't waste time mourning, organize!'—Hill became, and he has remained, the best-known IWW martyr and labour folk hero. http://www.aflcio.org/About/Our-History/Key-People-in-Labo r-History/Joe-Hill-1879-1915
16. K. Robinson notes from Mass Meeting 22 December 1995
17. See Tower Colliery http://www.towerregeneration.co.uk/history/
18. Daily Post 'Flying Picket' 24.12.1995
19. Dockers Charter No.2 December 1995 Chris Mooney 'A Really Big Struggle'.

## 29 - Out on the Picket Lines, and 'Who's this ILWU fuck?'

1. A 'caboose' was the name given to a railway wagon with accommodation for the train crew, typically attached to the end of the train – it was also the name given to a kitchen on a ship's deck - See https://en.wikipedia.org/wiki/Caboose -
2. The Observer 5 October 1997
3. K. Robinson Notes 3 January 1996
4. LabourNet January 1996 See also the Dockers Charter September 1996 Edition http://www.labournet.net/docks2/9601/PET IT.HTM
5. Dave Graham Part 2 30.11.95 http://libcom.org/library/dockworkers-disputer-dave-graham-2
6. Greg Dropkin LabourNet 'Mersey Dockers Defy Anti-Union Laws' January 1996 http://www.labournet.net/docks2/9601/PIC KET.HTM
7. ibid.
8. ibid. and also Militant 26 January 1996
9. Dave Cotterill - Official History of Sacked Liverpool Dockers 1995 – p.54 and also Militant 26 January 1996
10. United States District Court for the Northern District of California: ILWU Local 10 v. City of Oakland, et al: November 28 2005
11. See ILWU Local 10 https://ilwulocal10.org/contact-us/ and also http://www.longshoreshippingnews.com/tag/ ilwu-local-10/
12. M. Carden notes of mass meeting Friday 12 January 1996
13. ibid.
14. Issue No.4 of the Dockers Charter January 1996
15. Dave Sinclair - Dockers: The '95 to '98 Liverpool Lockout – Amberley Books 2015 See also http://www.labournet.net/docks2/9601/JAC K.HTM
16. Greg Dropkin LabourNet January 1996 http://www.labournet.net/docks2/9601/JAC K.HTM
17. Dockers Charter: Issue No.4 January 1996
18. ibid.
19. ibid.
20. 'Dockers unanimously reject offer' Friday 26 January 1996 LabourNet http://www.labournet.net/docks2/9601/OFF ER.HTM#ITF
21. Dockers Charter: Issue No.4 January 1996 See also http://www.labournet.net/docks2/9610/HE YMAN.HTM An open letter to Richard Flint, ITF Communications Director ITF Betrayal of the Liverpool dockers' strike. – Dispute Landmarks M. Carden's Archive
22. http://www.labournet.net/docks2/9601/JAC K.HTM
23. Support the Liverpool Dockers – The ITF Supports day of Action 5 December 1996 http://www.labournet.net/docks2/9612/ITF SUP.HTM See also Set to Blow – Greg Dropkin http://www.labournet.net/docks2/9701/BLO W.HTM An Open Letter to Richard Flint by Jack Heyman

http://www.labournet.net/docks2/9610/HE
YMAN.HTM Jack Heyman Edit and
statement to the author 30 July 2015 by email

24. WhatsApp to Terry Teague from K.Marges
October 2021

25. 'Support from Israeli Dockers' LabourNet
January 1996
http://www.labournet.net/docks2/9601/ISR
AEL.HTM

26. Issue No.4 of the Dockers Charter January
1996

27. Liverpool Echo Friday 19 January 1996

28. The Times 21 January 1996 and also Dave
Cotterill 'Official History of the sacked
Liverpool dockers 1995' p.55

29. ibid.

30. ibid.

## 30 - The First Ballot – a 90.3% Rejection of MDHC's First and Final Offer

1. Kevin Robinson notes from mass meeting 26
January 1996

2. ibid.

3. LabourNet January 1996
http://www.labournet.net/docks2/9601/OFF
ER.HTM

4. ibid.

5. Friday 26 January 1996 LabourNet January
1996 http://www.labournet.net/docks2

6. D. Cotterill Official History of the Sacked
Liverpool Dockers 1995 p.32

7. Janet Porter ABC Containerline Collapses
JOC.COM April 9 1996
https://www.joc.com/abc-containerline-
collapses_19960409.html

8. D. Cotterill Official History 1995 p.62

9. ibid.

10. K. Robinson notes of Shop Stewards Meeting
7 February 1996

11. News Line 'Make it official' 7 February 1996

12. ibid.

13. North West Business Insider 14 February 1996

14. Richard Saundry and Peter Turnbull– Labour
Relations Journal 27:4 Melee on the Mersey:
Contract, Competition and Labour Relations
on the Docks Blackwell Publishers 1996 p.276

15. Tape recording of Mass Meeting held 9
February 1996 by D. Cotterill See also
Lavalette and Kennedy 'Solidarity on the
Waterfront – The Liverpool Lock-out of 1995-
96' Liver Press 1996 pp.118-119

16. ibid.

17. M. Carden Diaries 9 February 1996

## 31 - The Liverpool Dockworkers' First International Conference – the

### dispute goes digital!

1. Liverpool Echo 'Dockers to cash in as left
fades away': 6th.February 1996. See also Peter
Taafe and Tony Mulhearn 'Liverpool a City
that Dared to Fight' - Fortress Publishing
1988. See also Tony Mulhearn – The Making
of a Liverpool Militant 47books 2019

2. Bill Hunter 'The Liverpool Seamen's Revolt of
1775' taken from 'Forgotten Hero, The Life
and Times of Edward Rushton', by Bill
Hunter. To read more visit:
www.billhunterweb.org.uk. See also: The
Origins of Working-Class Politics, Liverpool,
by Harold Hikins. Published by the Liverpool
Trades Council to mark 125 years (1973) Page
printed from:
http://www.catalystmedia.org.uk/issues/nerve
9/sailors_revolt.php

3. D. Cotterill - Official History of the Sacked
Liverpool Dockers 1995 p.64

4. Stephen Schwartz Brotherhood of the Sea: A
History of the Sailors' Union of the Pacific –
Now is the time to fight for better conditions
and remedy long-standing grievances – Strike
Call 1934 Published by the Sailors' Union
Transaction Book 1986 pp.143-147

5. Liverpool Daily Post 'Office of Fair Trading to
check MDHC's Irish Sea Monopoly' 28
August 1995

6. LabourNet February 1996
http://www.labournet.net/docks2/9602/legal.
htm

7. LabourNet February 1996
http://www.labournet.net/docks2/9602/resol
ve.htm

8. Liverpool Echo: 'Dockers' Invitation' 20
February 1996

9. M. Carden Diary 21 February 1996

10. www.labournet.net/docks2/9602.

11. Liverpool Echo 22 February 1996

12. LabourNet February 1996
http://www.labournet.net/docks2/9602/great
.htm

13. ibid.
http://www.labournet.net/docks2/9602/great
.htm

14. ibid.

15. See www.labournet.net/docks2/9602

16. LabourNet February 1996
http://www.labournet.net/docks2/9602/great
.htm

17. ibid.

18. ibid.

19. ibid.

20. ibid.

21. ibid.

22. ibid.

23. ibid.

24. ibid.

25. ibid.
26. ibid.
27. ibid.
28. ibid.
29. ibid.
30. ibid.
31. ibid.
32. ibid.
33. Workers Press: 'Plan for World Mersey Docks Boycott' 24 February 1996
34. LabourNet http://www.labournet.net/docks2/9603/CYB ER.HTM
35. The Dockers Charter March 1996'The World is our Picket Line' The Docker Charter March 1996/May 1996
36. Carter, C., S. Clegg, et al. (2003). 'The polyphonic spree: the case of the Liverpool Dockers.' Industrial Relations Journal 34(4): 290.
37. Greg Dropkin http://www.gn.apc.org/labournet/docks/
38. ibid.
39. ibid.
40. 'One for All Dockers' Film
41. ibid.
42. ibid.
43. ibid.
44. Dockers Charter No.5 March 1996 and also http://www.labournet.net/docks2/9602/conf. htm
45. ibid.
46. http://www.labournet.net/docks2/9602/deci ded.htm
47. ibid.
48. ibid.
49. ibid.
50. http://www.labournet.net/docks2/9602/mod erate.htm
51. How government officials worked to sack the Tilbury dockers – LabourNet http://www.labournet.net/docks2/9602/tilbu ry.htm
52. ibid.
53. ibid.
54. Why we were ecstatic when the men refused to cross the picket line http://www.labournet.net/docks2/9602/ecsta tic.htm
55. ibid.
56. Dockers Charter March 1996 Letter sent to International Conference by Alan Fox the son of a Liverpool docker. http://www.labournet.net/docks2/other/CH ART5.HTM
57. What they Decided http://www.labournet.net/docks2/9602/deci ded.htm
58. ibid.
59. ibid.
60. International Conference Supports LabourNet http://www.labournet.net/docks2/9602/intla b.htm
61. LabourNet http://www.labournet.net/docks2/9602/histo ry.htm http://www.labournet.net/sept97/donovan.ht ml
62. Liverpool Echo and Daily Post 22 February 1996
63. John Bowers K. Robinson record of Stewards' meeting Monday 26 February 1996
64. Mersey Docks Sues ILA http://www.labournet.net/docks2/9606/ILA SUE.HTM & http://www.labournet.net/docks2/9606/ILA SUE.HTM
65. http://www.labournet.net/docks2/9606/ILA SUE.HTM
66. K. Robinson record of Stewards' meeting Monday 26 February 1996
67. K. Robinson record of Stewards' meeting Thursday 29 February 1996

## 32 - Bill Morris Makes that Speech

1. Liverpool Echo: 29 February 1996
2. K. Robinson Record of meeting in Transport House, Salford 29 February 1996
3. ibid.
4. ibid.
5. Rational Expectations Theory - An economic idea that the people in the economy make choices based on their rational outlook, available information and past experiences. www.patrickminford.net/book/manual/sectio n3.pdf
6. The Adam Smith Institute is one of the world's leading think tanks. Independent, non-profit and non-partisan, it works to promote libertarian and free market ideas through research, publishing, media commentary, and educational programmes. The Institute was known for its pioneering work on privatization, deregulation, and tax reform, and for its advocacy of internal markets in healthcare and education.
7. Real Face of Professors Minford and Stoney http://www.labournet.net/docks2/9603/MIN FORD.HTM and also the Case for the Re-Instatement of the Sacked Liverpool Dockers 1 July 1997 http://www.labournet.net/docks2/9707/BO OKLET.HTM
8. LabourNet March 1996
9. K. Robinson Record of Shop Stewards' meeting 4 March 1996 and notes of Jack Adams meeting with port workers: 8 March 1996

10. M. Carden Record of First Negotiating Meeting with the MDHC 6 March 1996 Lord Daresbury Hotel in Warrington
11. ibid.
12. ibid.
13. M. Carden Record of First Negotiating Meeting with the MDHC 6 March 1996
14. ibid.
15. ibid.
16. M. Carden Diaries 1 May 1996
17. ibid.
18. Bill Morris' Speech to the Liverpool dockers – 14 March 1996 - LabourNet August 1996 http://www.labournet.net/docks2/9608/MORRIS See also 'Death of the Docks' Colin Ross Author House 2010 p.203
19. Transcript of John Bowers' speech to the Liverpool dockers on 14 March 1996
20. ibid.
21. ibid.
22. Transcript of John Bowers' speech to the Liverpool dockers on 14 March 1996
23. ibid.
24. 'Death on the Waterfront' J.R.Szighethy April 2004 American Mafia.Com http://www.americanmafia.com/Feature_Articles_266.html
25. 'A history of the International Longshoremen's Association at http://www.ilaunion.org/history/ And also see http://www.joc.com/gleason-will-retire-july-president-ila-john-m-bowers-likely-move-post_19870318.html
26. The New York Times 'Thomas Gleason, 92, Who Led Longshoremen's Union, Is Dead' – Dennis Hevesi 27 December 1992
27. Transcript of John Bowers' speech to the Liverpool dockers on 14 March 1996
28. ibid.
29. ibid.
30. ibid.
31. Transcript of Tommy Gleason's speech to the Liverpool dockers on 14 March 1996
32. ibid.
33. ibid.
34. ibid.
35. Jimmy Davies speech at Dockers' Mass Meeting Friday 16 March 1996 – Jane Kennedy Audio Tape 15/3/96 Tape 6
36. ibid.
37. Simon Sloan – 'We Had Good Days and We Had Bad Day' Triumph and Tragedy in the Oral Histories of the Liverpool Dockers – MA Thesis University Leiden 29 August 2019 p.14

## 33 - Economic distortions

1. 'The Real Face of Professors' Minford & Stoney'. Statement by Merseyside Port Shop Stewards' Committee 1996 See

http://www.labournet.net/docks2/9603/ and also Barry Hugill, 'Dockers and Dons unite in wrath against Thatcher's High Priest.' The Guardian 21 April 1996
2. ibid and Liverpool Echo 26 March 1996
3. Liverpool Echo 'Dockers call for talks' 19 March 1996
4. M. Carden Diaries March 1996
5. ibid.
6. LabourNet March 1996
7. Dockers Charter 6th.February 1998 M. Pendleton draft article in K. Robinson archive.
8. Mass Rally 23 March 1996
9. ibid.
10. D. Cotterill 'Official History of the Liverpool Dockers 1995 p.70
11. ibid.
12. ICP Leaflet 'Liverpool dock dispute in danger':19 January 1996
13. ibid.
14. Dave Graham http://www.oocities.org/athens/acropolis/8195/subvert3.htm and also 'The Liverpool Dockers' Dispute – A Summing Up' in the International Library of the Communist Left. http://www.sinistra.net/lib/upt/comlef/cotu/cotugdicee.html
15. M. Carden Diaries 2 April 1996 Lord Daresbury Hotel Warrington MDHC/TGWU
16. ibid.
17. ibid.
18. ibid.
19. ibid.
20. ibid.
21. ibid.
22. ibid.
23. ibid.
24. ibid.
25. ibid.
26. BBC Look North 11.4.1997
27. ibid.
28. Militant – 'Picket Road Chaos' 19 April 1996
29. The Observer 'Dockers and Dons unite in wrath against Thatcherism's High Priest' Barry Hugill 21 April 1996
30. ibid.

## 34 - May Day 1996

1. http://www.labournet.net/docks2/9605/BELFAST.HTM
2. ibid. M. Carden notes on May Day 1996
3. See LabourNet May 1996 and also Militant 'May Day March' 10 May 1996
4. Many Interesting Questions in LabourNet http://www.labournet.net/docks2/9606/DENMARK.HTM
5. ibid.
6. See LabourNet April 1996

7.   Campaign for Human Rights In Turkey
     Report of Delegation to Turkey in K.
     Robinson archive and also Hackney
     Community Law Centre Lord Hylton Letter 13
     February 1997
8.   Turkey: Workers on the March – LabourNet
     http://www.labournet.net/docks2/9606/DE
     NMARK.HTM
9.   ibid.
10.  Emek Gunluk 29 September 1997 p.6
11.  BBC Radio Merseyside 2 May 1996
12.  Michael Lavalette & Jane Kennedy 'Solidarity
     on the Waterfront' Liver Press 1996 p.109
13.  D. Cotterill 'Official History of the Sacked
     Liverpool Dockers 1995' p.77
14.  ibid.
15.  Dockers Charter No.7 June 1996 'Bosnian
     Miners on Liverpool May Day.'
16.  Liverpool Echo 1 May 1996
17.  Newsline 'Union Leaders Under Fire' 3 May
     1996. See also Liverpool Echo: 'Council staff
     back dockers' 30 April 1996
18.  The Guardian 6 May 1996 'Selfless Stand'.
19.  Liverpool Echo: 'Thousands on dockers
     march' and also 'Mayday Madness'1 May 1996
20.  ibid.
21.  D. Cotterill 'Official History of the Sacked
     Liverpool Dockers 1995' p.77
22.  ibid.
23.  ibid.
24.  ibid.

## 35 - Casual Labour and Negotiations Begin Again

1.   Financial Times 21 May 1996
2.   Education and Employment Select
     Committee: Employment implications of the
     industrial dispute in the Port of Liverpool.
     Education and Employment Select Committee
     first report with proceedings and appendices.
     Document1995 HOUSE OF COMMONS
     PAPERS. Education and Employment
     Committee 17 July 1996 p.26
3.   See: http://www.parliament.the-stationery-
     office.co.uk/pa/cm198889/cmhansrd/1989-
     05-24/Debate-11.html Hansard 24 May 1989:
     Column 1022-1023
4.   Education and Employment Select
     Committee: Employment implications of the
     industrial dispute in the Port of Liverpool.
     Education and Employment Select Committee
     first report with proceedings and appendices.
     Document1995 HOUSE OF COMMONS
     PAPERS. Education and Employment
     Committee 17 July 1996 p.26
5.   ibid.
6.   ibid.
7.   ibid.
8.   Education and Employment Select
     Committee: Employment implications of the
     industrial dispute in the Port of Liverpool.
     Education and Employment Select Committee
     first report with proceedings and appendices.
     Document1995 HOUSE OF COMMONS
     PAPERS. Education and Employment
     Committee 17 July 1996 p.26
9.   ibid.
10.  LabourNet 1996
     http://www.labournet.net/docks2/9706/CAS
     UAL.HTM
11.  Liverpool Echo PDP Advert 17 April 1996
12.  LabourNet 1996
     http://www.labournet.net/docks2/9706/CAS
     UAL.HTM
13.  ibid.
14.  'Causal Labour' a Report by Greg Dropkin
     LabourNet 1996
     http://www.labournet.net/docks2/9706/CAS
     UAL.HTM
15.  ibid.
16.  ibid.
17.  M. Carden Diary on negotiations with MDHC
     Wednesday 22 May 1996
18.  M. Carden Record of Shop Stewards' Meeting
     Wednesday 29 May 1996
19.  'Towards a New Future for the Port of
     Liverpool and the People of Merseyside' 31
     May 1996 a press statement identifying their
     overall position at this time.
20.  M. Carden Diary and Record of GEC 3.6.1996
21.  M. Carden Notes on ACAS Meeting 4.6.96
22.  ibid. 4.6.96
23.  ibid. 4.6.96
24.  M. Carden Diary and notes at GEC Meeting
     5.6.1996
25.  ibid.
26.  M. Carden notes on mass meeting at
     Transport House 7.6.1996
27.  ibid.
28.  M. Carden notes on mass meeting at
     Transport House 7.6.1996
29.  ibid.
30.  The News Line 'We have had a ballot we don't
     want another' 6 June 1996: Pat Bennett died in
     May 2015.
31.  ibid.
32.  K.D. Roberts – 'Liverpool Sectarianism – The
     rise and demise' Liverpool University Press
     2017 pp.193-194 also M. Carden's Diary:
     Record of Shop Stewards Meeting held in
     Transport House 10 June 1996 See also S.
     Hughes – There She Goes: Liverpool, a City
     on its own – The Long Decade 1979-1993
     Decoubertin Books 2019 p.49
33.  Liverpool Echo 5 February 1998 See also
     Gordon Hughes & Adam Edwards 'Crime
     Control and Community – The New Politicis
     of Public Safety' Routledge (2002)

34. 'Swedish dockers Come up trumps' LabourNet June 1996 http://www.labournet.net/docks2/9606/SWEDEN.HTM
35. ibid.
36. The Socialist Worker 'How dare Bill Morris push this rotten deal' 8 June 1996
37. ibid.
38. M. Carden Diary: Record of Region 6 F&GP 11 June 1996
39. ibid.
40. ibid.
41. M. Carden's Minutes of Port Shop Stewards' Meeting 12 June 1996
42. LabourNet: Casual Labour Article by Greg Dropkin http://www.labournet.net/docks2/9706/CASUAL.HTM See also: Sarah O'Connor 'Workers have the right to a gig economy that delivers for the 21st.Century – Financial Times 15 September 2018
43. M. Carden's Notes: Shop Stewards Meeting 12 June 1996
44. M. Carden's Notes 12 June 1996
45. M. Carden's Notes from Mass Meeting Friday 14 June 1996
46. M. Carden's Notes 17 June 1996
47. ibid.
48. M. Carden's Notes from Special GEC 19 June 1996
49. ibid. See also, Bill Morris: A Trade Union Miracle; G. Goodman 2010 pp.130-131
50. M. Carden's Notes from Special GEC 19 June 1996
51. ibid.
52. M. Carden Notes from Special GEC 19 June 1996
53. The News Line: 'Reinstate sacked dockers' 14 June 1996
54. ibid.

## 36 - The Cunard Line and the Leaving of Liverpool?

1. M. Carden's Notes Mass Meeting 21 June 1996
2. ibid. See also: Liverpool Echo 21 June 1996
3. LabourNet June 1996
4. ibid.
5. LabourNet June 1996 http://www.labournet.net/docks2/9606/ILASUE.HTM
6. 'Mersey Docks Company in Trouble' Friday 21 June 1996 http://www.labournet.net/docks2/9606/MDHC.HTM
7. ibid. Greg Dropkin http://www.labournet.net/docks2/9606/MDHC.HTM

8. LabourNet June 1996 Mersey docks company in trouble': Report by Greg Dropkin for LabourNet Friday, 21 June
9. M. Carden's Notes Port Shop Stewards 24.6.1996 – this was later found to be a critical moment in which perhaps a 'deal' or settlement could have been reached.
10. M. Carden's Notes from Port Shop Stewards Monday 24 June 1996
11. BBC Radio Merseyside News 24 June 1996
12. 'Mersey Docks Company in Trouble' LabourNet June 1996 http://www.labournet.net/docks2/9606/MDHC.HTM
13. See https://en.wikipedia.org/wiki/Patrick_Minford
14. Liverpool Daily Post 25.6.1996 - 'Minford urges benefit cuts' 25 June 1996 See also S.Hughes There She Goes – Decoubertin Books 2019 pp.29-38
15. Liverpool Daily Post 24 June 1996 see also M. Carden's Notes from Port Shop Stewards Monday 24 June 1996
16. ibid.
17. BBC Radio Merseyside ACL/docks archive interviews tapes 1995-1996: June 1996
18. ibid.
19. ibid.
20. ibid.
21. Lloyd's List 7 August 1996

## 37 - The Dispute Rolls On

1. Harry Bridges: An Oral History about Longshoring – The origins of the ILWU and the 1934 Strike: Edited by Harvey Schwartz Curator, ILWU Oral History Collection. (27 July 2004) Available: https://www.ilwu.org/oral-history-of-harry-bridges/
2. M. Carden's Notes 29 June 1996
3. M. Carden's Notes Taken at Port Shop Stewards Meeting 3 July 1996
4. M. Carden's Notes 1 July 1996
5. Militant 'Solidarity march boosts dockers' 5 July 1996 Docker's Demonstration 29 June 1996
6. The Morning Star 'You have right on your side' 1 July 1996
7. ibid.
8. M. Carden's Notes Taken at Port Shop Stewards Meeting 3 July 1996
9. Liverpool Echo 29 April 2005 – The AC Delco Workers received regular updates from the Liverpool Dockers – In Delco Bulletin No.35 Brian P. Raven, Rainford – Letter An international update was given. Kevin Robinson Archive.
10. M. Carden's Diary 5 July 1996

11. Lloyds List 'Port users criticise dockers' leaders' 6 July 1996
12. M. Carden's Diary 8 July 1996
13. D. Cotterill 'Official History of the Docks Dispute 1995' [unpublished]
14. ibid.
15. M. Carden's Note Book 11 July 1996
16. ibid.
17. ibid.
18. Newsline 24 June 1996
19. ibid.
20. ibid.
21. ibid.
22. Dockers' Summer Festival Programme – Rock the Dock 14 July 1996
23. 'Mersey dockers' occupy Montreal crane' Greg Dropkin LabourNet July 1996 http://www.labournet.net/docks2/9607/MONTREAL.HTM
24. ibid.
25. ibid.
26. Montreal Gazette 16 July 1996
27. ibid.
28. ibid.
29. ibid.
30. Newsline is the paper of the Workers Revolutionary Party - The Hillingdon Hospital Strike began on October 1st, 1995 when 56 domestic and catering workers were sacked See: http://www.wrp.org.uk/news/417
31. Liverpool Echo 'Dockers should have been sacked years ago' 18 July 1996 - The Morning Star 18 July 1996 'We should have sacked the lot of them.'
32. ibid.

## 38 - Splits and Sectarian Interests

1. M. Carden's Notes from Dockers' National Support Group Saturday 20 July 1996
2. ibid.
3. ibid.
4. ibid.
5. ibid.
6. ibid.
7. ibid.
8. ibid.
9. ibid.
10. ibid.
11. ibid. See also: New Internationalist 5 November 1997 'Dancing in the Snow' Anne Marie Sweeney, available: https://newint.org/features/1997/11/05/dancing
12. Dave Graham – LabourNet: 'Those of you who have not seen my earlier reports nor the stuff printed in the Dockers Charter can find it all on the websites www.geocities.com/CapitolHill/3843/dockhome.htm and also June97.htm
13. ibid.
14. ibid.
15. ibid.
16. ibid. and also June97.htm
17. ibid.
18. ibid.
19. Dave Graham – LabourNet:
20. Dave Graham Part 2 30.11.95 http://libcom.org/library/dockworkers-disputer-dave-graham-2
21. ibid.
22. ibid.
23. David S. Meyer, Nancy Whittier, Belinda Robnett: 'Social Movements: Identity, Culture, and the State' Oxford University Press (2002) pp.151-152
24. M. Lavalette & J. Kennedy, Solidarity on the Waterfront – The Liverpool Lock Out of 1995/96: Liver Press 1996 p.99
25. LabourNet, Globalisation, labour internationalism and the Liverpool docks dispute. Available: http://www.labournet.net/docks2/9704/GLOBAL.HTM
26. ibid.
27. ibid.
28. ibid.
29. ibid.
30. ibid.
31. ibid.
32. Email sent to comrades on the death of Bill Hunter from Jerry Spencer 16 July 2015 and also from Martin Ralph - 'This is a message to the many comrades and friends who knew Bill Hunter. The heart of a great fighter stopped on 9 July 2015, he was 95 years old. He had a fall early in the morning and was taken to hospital. They diagnosed a brain haemorrhage which had caused him to go into a coma from which he never recovered. He had recently moved into care accommodation, leaving the flat he had lived in since coming back from Argentina in the early 1990s. Our feelings go to his family Ritchie and Sue and David and his extended family of grand and great-grand daughters and sons... Bill was a great writer, speaker, propagandist and agitator and our memories of the many battles that he waged, that we know about, come flooding back at this moment. We know our embrace and salute of this comrade only has meaning if we continue the fight he gave his entire life to, that is the struggle for working class power and international socialism. And, of course he will continue to live inside our struggles and us. Long live the struggle for socialism. Long live the International Workers League.' See also: Margaret and Martin Ralph email to comrades 15 July 2015
33. ibid.

## 39 - Atlantic Container Line Returns and the death of Mickey Fenn

1. M. Carden Notes Port Shop Stewards Meeting Monday 22 July 1996
2. ibid. Francisco Ramos had a tremendous record in fighting for workers' rights both at home and abroad. He did so much to promote the International Dockworkers' Movement and was widely known and respected by Longshoremen and dockers the world over. Paco died in a tragic accident at Tenerife Docks on 29 July 1999. Greg Dropkin was to write in August 1999 that Francisco Ramos 'was the International Secretary of the Coordinadoro. Paco took the Dockers' 1st International Conference in February 1996 by storm. He sang arias, talked of the scabs who jumped overboard when they saw 800 women heading for their ship, lectured us on the Coordinadora's commitment to rank and file control of the union, and put his finger on the possibilities opening up that week. The night after the international march to the Liverpool Freeport, with 600 crammed into the Dockers Club to celebrate, Paco held court. 'I only want to say one thing… Long Life Dockers! Long Life Dockers! Long Life Dockers!' Then he went back into Spanish. '…I'm proud, not just proud, extremely proud of having been part of your meetings, of your pickets, and even more proud that now here today in Liverpool we have set up the International, and it's not the International for today, it's the International of the future. See: http://www.labournet.net/docks2/9908/paco 4.htm
Writing in 2015 Jack Heyman was to write that after twenty years it will also be a time to remember those class struggle militants who've died tragically like Paco of La Coordinadora, Kenny of the Swedish dockworkers union, amnarbetarforbundet, Ole of the Danish dockworkers union, Gianni of the Italian FILT-CGIL, the dockworker son of Jean Louis Affagard of the Le Havre CGT and others. I will be attending the Liverpool celebration with my wife Carol and look forward to seeing you there to reconnect and to continue the international struggle.
3. Svenka Hamnarbatarforvundet (Swedish Dock Workers' Unon) Goteborg: Yag Annerback & Bosse Johansson 30.7.1996 and M. Carden Notes of Port Stewards Friday 26 July 1996 – In his introduction to the IDC on 8 October 1999 Jimmy Nolan reminded the meeting of the Liverpool dockers' role after the Chilean coup in September 1973 when cargo was blockaded and seafarers were sacked for refusing to sail to Valparaiso. As news filtered through of today's court decision authorising General Pinochet's extradition to Spain, the Chilean exile, Ernesto Arellano, who had turned up to translate for the Spanish comrades told delegates his own story. Ernesto, then a merchant seaman, only managed to remain in Britain after the dockers' found him in Risley Remand Centre awaiting deportation back to Chile in 1977. Dockers like Jimmy Nolan and Jimmy Davies, and seafarers like the last Joe Kenny, made it clear that no ship would sail from Liverpool with Ernesto on board.' Available: http://www.labournet.net/docks2/9910/conf 1.htm
4. M. Carden's Notes Tuesday 30 July 1996
5. M. Carden's Notes from Port Shop Stewards Meeting 1 August 1996
6. ibid.
7. ibid.
8. ibid.
9. M. Carden's Notes from Port Shop Stewards Wednesday 14 August 1996. See also: http://www.labournet.net/docks2/9608/TG WU.HTM
10. LabourNet August 1996 and also Liverpool Daily Post 2 August 1996 'Lets make a fresh start'
11. LabourNet August 1996 http://www.labournet.net/docks2/9608/INT CONF.HTM
12. M. Carden's Notes from Port Shop Stewards Meeting 1 August 1996
13. ibid.
14. ibid.
15. Liverpool Echo 2 August 1996
16. M. Carden's Notes from Mass Meeting 2 August 1996
17. ibid.
18. Liverpool Daily Post 2 August 1996
19. M. Carden Notes from Port Shop Stewards Meeting at TGWU Headquarters in Palace Street, London on Tuesday 6 August 1996.
20. ibid.
21. ibid.
22. ibid.
23. ibid.
24. ibid.
25. The Flickering Flame: Dir. K. Loach 1996 Parallax Pictures
26. ibid.
27. ibid.
28. ibid.
29. ibid.
30. M. Carden Notes Dockers' Mass Meeting Friday 9 August 1996
31. Liverpool Echo: 15 March 2013 'The Big Flame' was writer Jim Allen's second Wednesday Play (BBC, 1964-70), and his first with director Kenneth Loach. After 'The

Lump' (tx. 1/2/1967), about the exploitation of casual labour in the building trade, Allen used his Marxist credentials to depict striking Liverpool dockers' enacting a Communist-style system of workers' control. See BFI Screen online, available: http://www.screenonline.org.uk/tv/id/557251/

## 40 - Reclaim the Streets

1.  M. Carden's Notes Dockers' Mass Meeting Friday 9 August 1996
2.  M. Carden's Notes from Port Shop Stewards' Meeting 12 August 1996
3.  Pauline Bradley & Chris Knight, Another World is Possible: How the Liverpool Dockers Launched a Global Movement Published in 2004 by the Radical Anthropology Group in association with Haringey Trades Union Council and the sacked Liverpool Dockers. Radical Anthropology Group. School of Social Sciences, Media and Cultural Studies, p.17
4.  ibid. p.17
5.  ibid. p.33
6.  ibid. pp.35-36
7.  ibid. pp.35-36
8.  Anonymous author, 'Reclaim the Streets!', Do or Die 6, 1997, available: https://libcom.org/library/do-or-die-6-1997 See also Naomi Klein's interview with John Jordan, RTS Organiser, 10 January 2008 raforum.site/spip.php?article4613
9.  M. Carden's Notes from Port Shop Stewards' Meeting 12 August 1996
10. Peter Kennedy, 'Working Up A Storm in a Port' available: http://www.labournet.net/docks2/other/WOW.HTM
11. Kevin Robinson Notes from Mass Meeting Friday 16 August 1996
12. BBC Radio Merseyside Wednesday 14 August 1996
13. ibid.
14. LabourNet August 1996
15. MDHC Press Release Wednesday 21 August 1996
16. ibid.
17. Regional F&GP Minutes Tuesday 13 August 1996
18. M. Carden's Notes from Port Shop Stewards Wednesday 14 August 1996
19. ibid.
20. ibid.
21. ibid.
22. ibid.
23. Daily Post: 22 August 1996 - 'Five charged after demo'
24. ibid.

25. Chris Bailey http://www.labournet.net/docks2/9608/ITFDEB1.HTM See also, M. Carden Notes on Mass Meeting, held on Friday 23 August 1996
26. M. Carden Notes on TGWU Street Meeting Thursday 29th.August 1996
27. M. Carden's Notes on Palace Street Meeting with Bill Morris and Jack Adams 29 August 1996
28. ibid.
29. ibid.
30. ibid.
31. ibid.
32. ibid.
33. ibid. See also http://www.labournet.net/docks2/9609/ITFDEB3.HTM for copy of ITF Fax on 'support' for the dockers.
34. David Cockcroft, General Secretary ITF, letter to Bill Morris 28 August 1996 Ref:DC/jh from Kevin Robinson's archive documents. See also: http://www.labournet.net/docks2/9609/ITFDEB3.HTM
35. ibid.
36. M. Carden's Notes for Friday 30 August 1996
37. Slump in MDH Profits http://www.labournet.net/docks2/9608/SLUMP.HTM
38. The Flickering Flame - Parallax Pictures Dir. K. Loach 1996
39. ibid.
40. ibid.

## 41 - The Second International Conference of Port Workers and the ITF

1.  Liverpool Echo 'Sacked dockers in legal battle' 31 August 1996
2.  Ken Loach Dir. The Flickering Flame 1996
3.  ibid.
4.  ibid.
5.  ibid.
6.  M. Carden's Notes from 2nd.Dockers' International Conference 31 August 1996
7.  LabourNet September 1996
8.  R. Flint – Communications Dept. Secretary, ITF. See: Greg Dropkin, LabourNet, September 1996 available: http://www.labournet.net/docks2/9609/ITFDEB2.HTM See also: The News Line: 2 September 1996 'Fight for our jobs'
9.  M. Carden's Notes Friday 6 September 1996
10. R. Flint: ITF Press Release London 6 September 1996 See also LabourNet http://www.labournet.net/docks2/9609/ITFDEB3.HTM
11. ibid.

12. Circular 24/D.7/S.10/1996 (23 January 1996) from ITF Dockers Section Secretary, Kees Marges to affiliates reads: (originally the text was in French) available: http://www.labournet.net/docks2/9609/ITF DEB3.HTM
13. Peter Waterman, Institute of Social Studies, The Hague Netherlands available: http://www.labournet.net/docks2/9609/ITF DEB4.HTM
14. ibid.
15. ibid.
16. ibid.

## 42 - The Dispute Continues (Without the TUC)

1. M. Carden Diaries 6.9.1996
2. The Guardian: 10 September 1996 - Stuart Millar 'Smart 'New Unionism' faced with protests of 'betrayed' dockers'
3. ibid.
4. Ken Loach: The Flickering Flame 1996
5. ibid.
6. ibid.
7. ibid.
8. ibid.
9. ibid.
10. Ken Loach: The Flickering Flame 1996
11. ibid.
12. ibid.
13. Kevin Robinson Notes from Meeting with Morris at Blackpool TUC 9 September 1996
14. ibid.
15. ibid.
16. ibid.
17. M. Carden Diaries Friday 13 September 1996
18. TUC Special Edition Dockers' Charter' September 1996
19. M. Carden Notes Friday 13 September 1996
20. http://libcom.org/library/dockworkers-disputer-dave-graham-9
21. ibid.
22. ibid.
23. ibid.
24. The Guardian November 24 1999 Ann Douglas 'Betraying Ignorance of Class Struggle': A Review of the film 'Dockers' The Guardian November 24 1999
25. M. Carden Notes on GEC Tuesday Meeting 17 September 1996
26. ibid.
27. ibid.
28. ibid.
29. ibid.
30. ibid.
31. M. Carden Notes Wednesday 25 September
32. M. Carden's Notes 26.9.96
33. Letter to Bill Morris from Dave McCall Ref: DMcC/SW 14 November 1996 -Confidential
Report Docks Dispute: Dave McCall 14 November 1996
34. TGWU Textile Trade Group Conference: Textile Worker TGWU Publications 'Union Rights Must be Restored Immediately' September 1996

## 43 - The First Anniversary of the Dispute

1. Dockers' Mass Meeting 27 September 1996 Audio Tape 34
2. ibid.
3. Liverpool Echo 27 September 1996 'Billy Bragg'
4. Reuters 28 September 1996 at 10:36 EDT, Copyright 1996, Reuters America Inc.
5. ibid.
6. ibid.
7. The Morning Star 28 September 1996 'Dockers' invite Prime Minister to speak'
8. Pauline Bradley & Chris Knight: Another World is Possible Enter the Dragon by John Davie & Bronwen, Handyside Workers' Press October 1996 pp. 28-30
9. ibid.
10. ibid. pp29-30
11. D. Cotterill: Workers' Press September 28 1996 and also 'Official History of the Liverpool Dock Dispute' D. Cotterill, pp.86-87. See also: http://www.labournet.net/docks2/9610/DE MO.HTM
12. ibid.
13. ibid.
14. ibid.
15. Greg Dropkin: http://digitaljournalist.eu/OnTheRoad/festival-n-travellin-n-party-n-protest-stories-3/
16. http://digitaljournalist.eu/OnTheRoad/festival-n-travellin-n-party-n-protest-stories-3/
17. Daily Post 1.10.96
18. Morning Star 3 October 1996
19. Greg Dropkin 'Lockout 1st. Anniversary Demonstration' www.labournet.net/docks2/9610/DEMO.HTM
20. ibid.
21. Financial Times 1.10.96

## 44 - The TGWU Condemns Solidarity, as the ITF and ILWU Clash

1. The Weekend Guardian (23 November 1996) 'They Never Walk Alone' John Pilger See also: http://www.labournet.net/docks2/9611/PIL GER.HTM
2. ibid.

3. ibid. See also K.D. Roberts – 'Liverpool Sectarianism: The Rise and Demise' Liverpool University Press 2017 pp.193-194
4. Bob Baete letter to Bill Morris 4 October 1996 K. Robinson Archive
5. Bill Morris reply to Bob Baete 9 October 1996 K. Robinson Archive
6. Bill Morris reply to B. McWilliams 9 October 1996
7. B. McWilliams ILWU President to MDHC 2 October 1996
8. M. Carden Notes 2 October 1996
9. M. Carden notes from Shop Stewards Meeting 3 October
10. ibid.
11. LabourNet October 1996 http://www.labournet.net/docks2/9610/HISTORY.HTM
12. M. Carden notes on Shop Stewards Meeting 3 October
13. M. Carden notes 7 October 1996
14. LabourNet 'MP's Intervene in Mersey Dispute' available: http://www.labournet.net/docks2/9610/INTMP.HTM
15. LabourNet, 'An open letter to Richard Flint, ITF Communications Director ITF Betrayal of the Liverpool dockers' strike.' By J. Heyman, ILWU Local 10, October 1996, available: http://www.labournet.net/docks2/9610/HEYMAN.HTM
16. ibid.
17. ibid.
18. ibid.
19. ibid.
20. ibid.
21. ibid.
22. ibid.
23. ibid.

## 45 - Negotiations Begin Again

1. M. Carden Notes Thursday 3 October 1996. See also: record of Mass Meeting 4 October 1996 and M. Carden Notes 7 October 1996.
2. M. Carden Notes 10 October 1996
3. ibid.
4. Mass Meeting Audio Tape: D. Cotterill DC12 11 October 1996
5. Mass Meeting 11 October 1996 D. Cotterill Audio Tape Ref: DC12
6. ibid.
7. ibid.
8. ibid.
9. ibid.
10. M. Carden Notes Monday 14 October 1996
11. M. Carden Notes Tuesday 15 October 1996 - M. Carden Notes Wednesday 16 October 1996
12. Liverpool Echo 26 April 2004 'Ex-dockers' legal fight with union'

13. ibid.
14. M. Carden Notes Wednesday 18 October 1996
15. T. Furlong MDHC Chief Executive letter to unions supporting ITF Circular 21 October 1996.
16. ibid.
17. T. Furlong MDHC Chief Executive letter to the General Secretary of ASLEF, Lew Adams 21 October 1996.
18. ibid.
19. Letter from J. Nolan to Bill Morris 21 October 1996

## 46 - The Paris Conference and the creation of the International Dockworkers' Council

1. LabourNet, 'Spanish Dockers Action for Mersey' available: http://www.labournet.net/docks2/9610/SPAIN.HTM
2. International Dockers' Steering Committee in Paris. See: LabourNet http://www.labournet.net/docks2/9610/PARIS.HTM
3. M. Carden diaries 21 October 1996
4. M. Carden notes of 1st Dockers' International Conference, Paris 26.10.1996
5. ibid.
6. ibid.
7. ibid.
8. ibid.
9. ibid.
10. ibid.
11. ibid.
12. Mumia Abu-Jamal (born Wesley Cook on April 24, 1954) is an American radical convicted for the 1981 murder of Philadelphia police officer Daniel Faulkner. His original sentence of death, handed down at his first trial in July 1982, was commuted to life imprisonment without parole in 2012. Described as "perhaps the world's best known death-row inmate" by The New York Times, supporters and detractors have disagreed on his guilt, whether he received a fair trial, and the appropriateness of the death penalty. See: www.bbc.co.uk/news/world-us-canada-13200859
13. LabourNet, Letter from IDC to Bill Morris, available: http://www.labournet.net/docks2/9610/28OCTLET.HTM See also: M. Carden Notes Wednesday 30 October 1996 - He wrote in his diary that his son Daniel was ten years old on Monday. 'I was not there.'
14. M. Carden Notes Wednesday 30 October 1996. See also: LabourNet, 'Spanish dockers action for Mersey', available:

http://www.labournet.net/docks2/9610/SPA
IN.HTM

15. ibid.
16. M. Carden Notes Wednesday 30 October 1996
17. ibid.
18. ibid.
19. On the Waterfront – Dir.Elia Kazan (1954)
American crime drama film about union
violence and corruption among longshoremen.
On 1 July 2015, Arthur Miller's 'The Hook'
had its opening night at the Everyman Theatre
in Liverpool, a few feet away from the
Liverpool dockers' CASA Community Union
Branch. See 'The Hook' Everyman Theatre
Programme Wednesday 1 July to Saturday 25
July 2015 p.10.
20. M. Carden diaries 30 October 1996
21. M. Carden Notes Wednesday 30 October 1996
22. ibid.
23. M. Carden Notes on Meeting with Bill Morris
in London 30.10.96. See also: Kevin
Robinson's Minutes of the Meeting.
24. ibid.
25. ibid.
26. ibid.
27. ibid.
28. ibid.
29. ibid.
30. ibid.
31. ibid. See also: M. Carden Diaries 1 November
1996
32. Anne-Marie Sweeney director, Greg Dropkin,
Conscious Cinema ('Reclaim the Future'). Port
n a Storm - On-line editing at Oxford Film &
Video and the film was distributed by 'Video
News'. The copies sold for £10 for individuals,
£20 for organisations with all proceeds going
to the dockers' hardship fund.
33. M. Carden Diaries 1 November 1996
34. Liverpool Daily Post 6 November 1996
35. Enigyhet Ger Serger , 'Unity Makes Victory'
LabourNet October 1996, available:
http://www.labournet.net/docks2/9611/WO
WSWED.HTM
36. ibid.
37. ibid.

## 47 - Negotiations Re-open

1. Liverpool Echo 5 November 1996
2. M. Carden diaries 5 November 1996
3. M. Carden Notes 5 November 1996
4. M. Carden Notes 7 November 1996 – Salford
Office Meeting with Adams and McCall
5. M. Carden Notes on Shop
Steward/TGWU/Dock Company negotiations
at ACAS Offices on Thursday 7 November
1996
6. ibid.
7. ibid.

8. ibid.
9. ibid.
10. ibid.
11. ibid.
12. ibid.
13. ibid.
14. ibid.
15. ibid.
16. ibid.
17. M. Carden Notes Friday 8 November 1996
18. ibid.
19. M. Carden Notes Monday 11 November
20. John Hendy QC 'In the matter of the 500
dismissed Liverpool Dockworkers and in the
matter of an industrial dispute.' Opinion Fax
sent by Christian Fisher Wednesday 5
November 1996 pp.1-3 For a wonderful phot-
montage of the the picket that many of these
dockers stood on see Mick Killcullen's
excellent YouTube Video
https://www.youtube.com/watch?v=sDT07ju
Q1V8
21. John Hendy QC 'In the matter of the 500
dismissed Liverpool Dockworkers and in the
matter of an industrial dispute.' Opinion Fax
sent by Christian Fisher Wednesday 5
November 1996 pp.5-7
22. ibid.
23. Port of Liverpool 'Brief on the Current
Situation 18/9/96 Fax from MDHC Central
Executive 4/11/96 from K. Robinson Archive
24. ibid.
25. M. Carden Notes Monday 11 November 1996
26. M. Carden Diary Tuesday 12 November 1996

## 48 - More Negotiations

1. M. Carden Notes 12 November 1996
2. M. Carden Notes on TGWU Region 6 F&GP,
Salford, 13 November 1996
3. M. Carden Notes on Shop Stewards Meeting
14 November 1996
4. ibid.
5. ibid.
6. ibid.
7. Letter from David McCall to Bill Morris: 14
November 1996, ref: DMcC/SW. from D.
McCall 1996 p.21
8. ibid.
9. M. Carden Notes on Shop Stewards Meeting
Thursday 14 November 1996
10. ibid.
11. ibid.
12. ibid.
13. ibid.
14. Lees Lloyd Whitley, 45 Castle Street,
Liverpool, letter to dock workers dated 10/13
September 2001 Ref: AJM RF L250082.1 –
See also the Liverpool Daily Post January 11

2003 - 'Dockers Sue Their Union – T&G accused in Torside walkout'

15. B. Dooley interviewed by G. Dropkin 17 February 1998 LabourNet
16. M. Carden Diary Thursday 14 November 1996
17. M. Carden notes Friday 15 November 1996
18. M. Carden Notes 15 November 1996
19. ibid. See also http://www.parliament.uk/edm/1996-97/275 Primary Sponsor - Eddie Loyden MP – Human Rights in Turkey 28 November 1996 -
20. M. Carden Notes Thursday 21 November 1996
21. The Weekly Worker: 'All out in Liverpool' 22 August 1996
22. LabourNet, 'Dockers welcome continuing crane blockade of Cargill's Gene Beans' available: www.labournet.net/docks2/9611/SOYA.HT M
23. M. Carden Notes Thursday 21 November 1996
24. ibid.
25. ibid.
26. ibid.
27. ibid.
28. ibid.
29. ibid.
30. ibid.
31. ibid.
32. ibid.
33. ibid.
34. ibid.
35. ibid.
36. ibid.
37. M. Carden Notes Friday 22 November 1996
38. R. Morton, Dockers' Mass Meeting 22 November 1996: D. Cotterill Audio Tape
39. Bill Morris' Letter to Mr D. Statham Ref:BM/SAW 15 November 1996: K. Robinson archive.

## 49 - The Human Cost of the Docks Dispute

1. The Guardian 11 April 2014 - Mathew Taylor and Dan Milmo - 'Labour Party Facing Defining Moment'
2. Liverpool Echo 19 September 2005 'The Battle that Left a Bitter City in Despair'
3. 'Employment Rights in the Dock? A Bureau Experience of a Modern Labour Dispute' Citizens Advice Bureau: February 1997
4. ibid.
5. ibid.
6. ibid.
7. ibid.
8. Liverpool Echo 18 October 1995 Letters Page Alison Davies 'Family Devastated by Dock Dispute 'Anfield

9. Liverpool Echo Thursday July 30 1998 'No Going Back – The Bitter Legacy of the Dock Dispute' Jackie Newton
10. ibid.
11. ibid.
12. Liverpool Echo 30 July 1998 'No Going Back – The Bitter Legacy of the Dock Dispute'
13. ibid.
14. Crosby Herald January 15 1998 'Striker's Appeal'
15. The Guardian 24 December 1997 'Turkey and Scouse' Peter Hetherington
16. ibid.
17. The Guardian 'Turkey and Scouse' Peter Hetherington 24 December 1997
18. ibid.
19. ibid.
20. ibid.
21. ibid.
22. ibid.
23. Liverpool Echo 23 October 1997
24. Liverpool Echo 'Why we're still Dock Solid' Monday 29 September 1997
25. ibid.
26. Brian Dooley email 28 September 2015 to M. Carden
27. The Observer: 5 October 1997
28. ibid.
29. ibid.
30. The Observer: Jimmy McGovern 5 October 1997 photograph by Andrew Testa.
31. Letters from dockers' children, LabourNet September 1997, available: http://www.labournet.net/docks2/9709/CHI LDREN.HTM
32. ibid.
33. Jeanette Fox Recalls Docks Rally 28 September 1997 published in News and Views 'Women of the Waterfront' Undated leaflet.
34. Letter to K. Robinson from Michael Schwarz, Bindman & Partners Solicitor 9 October 1996 Ref: Liv/MS/DB
35. Statement of Ruari Martin: Bindman & Partners Solicitor 9 October 1996 Ref: Liv/MS/DB
36. ibid.
37. ibid.
38. ibid.
39. ibid.
40. Merseyside Port Shop Stewards Press Release 2 July 1997
41. Micky Tighe type-written statement 3 July 1996 in K. Robinson archive.
42. Police, Court and legal documents, handwritten notes held by Kevin Robinson.
43. Dockers Charter No.23 February 1998, available: http://www.labournet.net/docks2/9710/FO X.HTM see also the Big Issue 21 April 1997
44. Dockers Charter No.23 February 1998

45. ibid.
46. ibid.
47. Ken Loach, 'The Flickering Flame' Parallax Picture 1996 See also Jean Fox member of Women of the Waterfront: The Rats Weasels the snakes – How can they do it to us? Reprinted in LabourNet October 1997, available: http://www.labournet.net/docks2/9710/FOX.HTM
48. Ken Loach, 'The Flickering Flame' Parallax Picture 1996
49. ibid.
50. Dave Cotterill 'Official History of the Sacked Liverpool Dockers' 1995 p.18

## 50 - John Pilger Writes and Bill Morris Responds

1. John Pilger 'They Never Walk Alone' The Guardian 23 November 1996, available on LabourNet: http://www.labournet.net/docks2/9611/PILGER.HTM
2. TGWU Record Feb/March 1997 Issue 'Setting the Record Straight' text available: http://www.labournet.net/docks2/9702/BMRECORD.HTM
3. ibid.
4. ibid.
5. ibid.
6. David Cockcroft, International Transport Workers Federation general secretary, Bob Baete, Belgian transport workers' national secretary, and Manfred Rosenberg, German dockers' secretary, in the TGWU Record Feb/March 1997 Issue 'Setting the Record Straight' See also http://www.labournet.net/docks2/9702/BMRECORD.HTM
7. Docker Charter February 1997 'Setting the Record Straight' Liverpool dockers respond to Bill Morris first published in the see http://www.labournet.net/docks2/9702/LDRECORD.HTM See also: Michael Lavalette and Jane Kennedy: 'Solidarity on the Waterfront' 1996. p.41
8. Flyer for 'Resistance Fayre Programme'. Sunday 24 November 1996 Transport House Liverpool
9. ibid.
10. Kevin Robinson Written Record of meetings 23/24 November 1996
11. ibid. 25 November 1996
12. 'Dockers welcome continuing crane blockade of Cargill's Gene Beans', LabourNet, available: http://www.labournet.net/docks2/9611/SOYA.HTM
13. ibid.
14. Kevin Robinson Meeting Notes 27 November 1996
15. K. Robinson Notes on Meeting with Merseyside Police 29 November 1996
16. ibid.
17. ibid. See also: M. Carden Notes Thursday 28 November 1996, and Criminal Justice Act (1988) www.legislation.gov.uk/ukpga/1988/33/contents
18. M. Carden Notes 27.11.1996 and also K. Robinson Notes Mass Meeting 29 November 1996
19. Leaflet for London March and Rally Saturday 14 December 1996
20. ibid.
21. M. Carden Notes 27 November 1996
22. ibid.
23. ibid.
24. 'Bernard Cliff dead ', LabourNet, 1 December 1996, available: http://www.labournet.net/docks2/9612/DIED.HTM
25. 'Dockers interview (5 Dec)' LabourNet, 5 December 1996, available: http://www.labournet.net/docks2/9612/5DECMEN.HTM
26. ibid.
27. ibid.
28. ibid.
29. ibid.
30. ibid.
31. ibid.
32. ibid.
33. ibid.
34. ibid.
35. ibid.

## 51 - The December 1996 General Executive Council

1. M. Carden Notes London TGWU GEC Broad Left 1 December 1996
2. ibid.
3. M. Carden Notes GEC Monday 2 December 1996
4. TGWU Letter from Bill Morris to Jimmy Nolan dated 3 December 1996 Ref:WM/RC/LRD
5. TGWU Letter from Bill Morris to Jimmy Nolan date 3 December 1997
6. M. Carden Notes Tuesday 3 December 1996 GEC
7. ibid.
8. ibid.
9. ibid.
10. ibid.
11. ibid.

12. Merseyside Port Shop Stewards Letter from Jimmy Nolan to Bill Morris 10 December 1996 written by M. Carden.
13. M. Carden Notes GEC Wednesday 4 December 1996
14. ibid.
15. ibid.
16. ibid.
17. ibid.
18. ibid.
19. ibid.
20. ibid.
21. M. Carden Notes GEC Friday 6 December 1996 also K. Robinson notes 2 December 1996
22. D. Aitkenhead 'Thirty Years that shook the world' The Independent on Sunday 8 December 1996
23. ibid.
24. ibid.
25. M. Carden Notes Monday 9 December 1996 - The policy was clear in the stewards; minds that 'all delegations were about being self-financing and stopping ships.' In an email on 21 October 2017 to the author Doreen McNally wrote, 'Hi Mike, one more point. When Sue and I needed the fare for France, it was refused for the reasons stated, but they conceded… We returned with £35,000.'
26. Trade Union Certification Officer: Receiving, ensuring compliance with statutory requirements and keeping available for public inspection annual returns from trade unions and employers' … www.certoffice.org/ and also M. Carden Notes 9 December 1996
27. M. Carden Notes 10 December 1996 and also K. Robinson notes on PSS Meeting 10 December 1996
28. ibid.
29. M. Carden Notes 10 December 1996
30. ibid. See also K. Robinson PSS Meeting 10 December 1996
31. ibid.
32. ibid.
33. ibid.
34. ibid. See also K. Robinson PSS Meeting 10 December 1996
35. ibid.
36. K. Robinson PPS/Mass Meeting Notes 13 December 1996
37. Solidarity on the Waterfront 'The Liverpool Lock-Out 1996/96' Michael Lavalette and Jane Kennedy: Liver Press 1996. See also: M. Carden Notes Saturday 14 December 1996 - 'it is really disappointing,' wrote Carden, 'an SWP chronology, no feel or depth considering the access to information…'
38. Tony Russell Mass Meeting Liverpool 13.12.1996 D. Cotterill Audio Tape Ref: DC23
39. ibid.

40. Pauline Bradley and Chris Knight 'Another World is Possible: How the Liverpool Dockers Launched a Global Movement' Ed. p.20 See also: M. Carden Notes Saturday 14 December 1996
41. ibid.
42. The Guardian 14 December 1996 John Pilger: 'Today's Marching Orders'
43. ibid.
44. ibid.
45. TGWU Letter from Bill Morris to Alan Rusbridger 19 December 1996

## 52 - Negotiations Resume

1. M. Carden Notes Monday 16 December 1996 ACAS Office, Manchester
2. ibid.
3. ibid.
4. ibid.
5. ibid.
6. ibid.
7. ibid.
8. ibid.
9. ibid.
10. ibid.
11. ibid.
12. ibid.
13. ibid.
14. M. Carden Notes Monday 16 December 1996 See also K. Robinson Notes on PSS 19 December 1996
15. ibid.
16. ibid.
17. ibid.
18. ibid.
19. ibid.
20. K. Robinson Notes on PSS 17 December 1996

## 53 - The 20th December Mass Meeting and the Third Offer

1. M. Carden Notes Friday 20 December 1996
2. ibid.
3. ibid.
4. Audio Tape by D. Cotterill Mass Meeting 20 December 1996 DC25
5. M. Carden Notes Friday 20 December 1996
6. M. Carden Notes Friday 20 December 1996. See also: Audio Tape Mass Meeting 20.12.96 D. Cotterill DC25
7. ibid.
8. ibid.
9. ibid.
10. Audio Tape Mass Meeting 20.12.96 D. Cotterill DC25
11. ibid.

12. M. Carden Notes Friday 20 December 1996.
See also: Audio Tape Mass Meeting 20.12.96
D. Cotterill DC25

13. Audio Tape Mass Meeting 20.12.96 D.
Cotterill DC25

14. M. Carden Notes 30 December 1996

15. Jack Heyman email to Mike Carden 12
October 2016

16. 'ITF Supports Day of Action' LabourNet
December 1996, available:
http://www.labournet.net/docks2/9612/ITF
SUP.HTM

17. M. Carden Diary 30 December 1996

18. ibid.

19. BBC Radio Merseyside 31 December 1996

20. M. Carden Diary 2 January 1997

21. ibid.

22. M. Carden Diary 3 January 1997 Mass Meeting

23. M. Carden Diary 3 January 1997

24. ibid.

25. M. Carden Diary 6 January 1997

26. ibid. See also: K. Robinson Diary 6 January
1997

27. M. Carden Diary 6 January 1997

28. M. Carden Diary 8 January 1997

29. M. Carden Diary Notes 9 January 1997

30. ibid.

31. M. Carden Notes Mass Meeting10 January
1997

32. ibid.

33. M. Carden Notes National Dockers Support
Group – Saturday 11 January 1997. See also K.
Robinson Notes of Support Group Meeting
11 January 1997

34. ibid.

35. ibid.

36. ibid.

37. K. Robinson Notes on Dockers Support
Meeting 11 January 1997

38. LabourNet January 1997 'Support Group
Meeting' 11 January 1997, available:
http://www.labournet.net/docks2/9701/LIV
SUPP.HTM

## 54 - A Day of World Action

1. M. Carden Notes Port Shop Stewards 14
January 1997 and also K. Robinson Notes on
PSS Meeting Tuesday 14 January 1997.

2. ibid.

3. M. Carden Notes Port Shop Stewards 14
January 1997

4. Greg Dropkin, 'VW Audi Embroiled in
Mersey Docks Dispute Report', LabourNet,
available:
http://www.labournet.net/docks2/9701/AU
DI.HTM See also: M. Carden Notes on visit to
VW in Germany with Tony Woodhouse and
6/541 TGWU Branch

5. LabourNet August 1997 – Blue Monday
Group

6. ibid.

7. San Francisco Chronicle 16 January 1997

8. ibid.

9. ibid.

10. ibid.

11. See LabourNet January 1997 Day of Action –
First Report, available:
http://www.labournet.net/docks2/9701/REP
ORT1.HTM See also: the Balance Sheet
http://www.labournet.net/docks2/9701/BAL
ANCE.HTM

12. LabourNet, 'World Wide Action For
Liverpool', available:
http://www.labournet.net/docks2/other/AC
TION.HTM

13. Mass Picket Leaflet, Monday 20 January 1997.
See also: LabourNet Report by Greg Dropkin
January 1997

14. 'All for One Video' Upnet - Produced by Larry
Duncan January 29 - March 1997

## 55 - Nolan Meets Morris

1. E. Taplin, 'The Dockers' Union – A Study of
the National Union of Dock Labourers 1889-
1922' Leicester University Press 1985 pp.18-22

2. Jack London, 'The Scab' - A speech first given
before the Oakland Socialist Party Local,
5April 1903, available:
https://libraries.ucsd.edu/farmworkermovem
ent/essays/essays/Jack%20London%20-
%20Definition%20of%20Strikebreaker.pdf

3. M. Carden Notes from Port Shop Stewards 14
January 1997

4. ibid.

5. ibid.

6. ibid.

7. ibid.

8. M. Carden Notes TGWU Head Office
London Wednesday 15 January 1997 and also
K. Robinson Notes on Meeting in TGWU
Central Office, Palace Street, London 15
January 1997

9. ibid.

10. ibid.

11. ibid.

12. ibid.

13. M. Carden Notes TGWU Head Office
London Wednesday 15 January 1997

14. ibid.

15. M. Carden Notes TGWU Head Office
London Wednesday 15 January 1997 See also
K. Robinson's detailed notes on this meeting
in London.

16. ibid.

17. ibid.

18. ibid.

19. ibid.

20.   M. Carden Notes Thursday 16 January 1997

## 56 - The Dockers Call for Support from All Workers

1.   J. Nolan 'Letter to support Groups' LabourNet January 1997, available: http://www.labournet.net/docks2/9701/SUPPMEET.HTM
2.   NewsLine, 'Brown promises to 'renew new Labour' 27th September 2005, available: http://www.wrp.org.uk/news/417 See also: Newsline 1 October 2005. See also M. Carden Meeting Notes for Saturday 18 January 1997
3.   M. Carden Meeting Notes for Saturday 18 January 1997
4.   ibid.
5.   ibid.
6.   M. Carden Diary 23 January 1997. See also the Liverpool Daily Post 'Ports join in day of action for dockers'. 21 January 1997
7.   M. Carden Diary 23 January 1997. See also Liverpool Echo 'Dock Protestors in Court' 22 January 1997.
8.   George Johnson interviewed on All for One Video 1997
9.   M. Carden Diary 23 January 1997. See also: 'Bill Morris – A Trade Union Miracle' G. Goodman 2010 pp.128-131
10.  M. Carden Diary 23 January 1997. See also: 'Bill Morris – A Trade Union Miracle' G. Goodman 2010 In this book Morris often refers to racism he had no doubt experienced at various times in his trade union career see p.158 for example
11.  ibid.
12.  G. Goodman 'Bill Morris – A Trade Union Miracle' Blackamber 2010 p.158. See also: Live Union Video of 1997 TGWU BDC in Brighton
13.  Open Eye Gallery – Namibia Nuclear Reactions Open Space BBC2 Thursday 7 September 1989 from the latest documentary video from Open Eye Film, Video & Animation Workshop ACTT franchised for the BBC Community Programme Unit made with the Namibia Support Committee and Liverpool Port Workers.
14.  John Pilger, 'Hidden Agendas' Vintage Book 1998 pp.355-356 and http://www.labournet.net/world/1411/heyman1.html See also: Interview with Ron Todd, former General Secretary of the Transport & General Workers Union and Chair of the TUC International Committee, by Christabel Gurney on 22nd. March 2004, reproduced on the Anti-Apartheid Movement Archives Committee Forward to Freedom project website http://www.aamarchives.org/

15.  The Big Issue 'Danger on the Dockside' Ally Fogg,27 January 1997
16.  Jacobin, 11 September 2021, Owen Dowling – 'When British Workers Stood against the Pinochet Coup' available: https://jacobinmag.com/2021/09/uk-britain-chile-solidarity-campaign-csc-pinochet-regime-trade-unions-allende-labor-fascism
17.  ibid.
18.  M. Carden Notes Friday 24 January 1997
19.  ibid.
20.  ibid.
21.  ibid.
22.  BBC Look North 24 January 1997
23.  Liverpool Daily Post 25 January 1997 and also M. Carden Notes Monday 27 January 1997
24.  LabourNet, 'Comments on New Proposals', available: http://www.labournet.net/docks2/9703/COMMENT.HTM See also: M. Carden Notes Monday 27 January 1997: Howard Keylor - retired member of San Francisco Local 10 ILWU; Björn Borg, Secretary, Swedish Dockworkers' Union; Jack Heyman, San Francisco Local 10 ILWU and Tom Dufresne, President I.L.W.U. Canadian Area.
25.  M. Carden Notes Monday 27 January 1997
26.  ibid.
27.  M. Carden Notes Region Six Committee 29 January 1997
28.  ibid.
29.  ibid.
30.  ibid.
31.  ibid.
32.  ibid.
33.  ibid.
34.  ibid.

## 57 - A Proposal to Supply Labour in the Port of Liverpool

1.   Liverpool Echo 'Sacked Dockers fight on in bid for Co-op' Monday 27 January 1997.
2.   ibid.
3.   M. Carden Notes, 30 January 1997 and also Notes Monday 3 February 1997
4.   Dockers Mass Meeting, 31 January 1997, Audio Recording by D. Cotterill
5.   ibid.
6.   ibid. See: Jimmy Davies speech
7.   ibid. See: Jimmy Davies speech
8.   ibid. See: Mike Carden speech
9.   ibid. See: Mike Carden speech
10.  ibid.
11.  ibid.
12.  Liverpool Echo 3 February 1997. See also M. Carden Notes Friday 7 February 1997
13.  ibid.
14.  John Pilger – 'Hidden Agendas' Vintage Books 1998 p.342

15. Liverpool Daily Post: 'Life in the eye of the storm' 4 February 1997
16. Job Rescue Package: A Proposal to Supply Dock Labour in the Port of Liverpool'. February 1997
17. M. Carden Notes MTUCURC 3 February 1997
18. Greg Dropkin asked 'Is the approach outlined by the TGWU actually similar to hiring halls, whether on the US West Coast or elsewhere? If a L.S.U. was created without the removal of all other employers, what problems would be faced by sacked dockers investing their severance pay or by stewards taking up, or declining to take up, management roles in the new company? What if the L.S.U. is the sole employer? Do the TGWU and Mersey Docks have a mutual interest? Should they?' Available: http://www.labournet.net/docks2/9701/PROPOSAL.HTM
19. M. Carden Notes Tuesday 4 February 1997. See also K. Robinson Notes on PSS Meeting 4 February 1997
20. M. Carden Notes Tuesday 4 February 1997
21. ibid.
22. ibid.
23. ibid.
24. M. Carden Notes Wednesday 5 February 1997
25. ibid.
26. ibid.
27. Tribune, on 31 January 1997. See also M. Carden Notes Wednesday 5 February 1997
28. M. Carden Notes Wednesday 5 February 1997
29. Liverpool Echo 14 February 1997
30. M. Carden notes on Mass Meeting 7 February 1997
31. ibid.
32. 'Stand Up for the Dockers' Flyer: Socialist Party Event at the Flying Picket 8 February 1997
33. A Proposal to supply Dock Labour in the Port of Liverpool – TGWU. See also: M. Carden notes on Meeting 10 February 1997
34. ibid.
35. LabourNet Report by Greg Dropkin February 1997
36. ibid.
37. ibid.
38. ibid.
39. ibid.
40. ibid.
41. M. Carden Diary Wednesday 12 February 1997

## 58 - Support for the Conflict

1. K. Robinson Notes on PSS Meeting 12 February 1997
2. The People's Charter for Social Justice 13 February 1997
3. Draft Article for Dockers' Charter 6 February 1998
4. M. Carden Notes from mass meeting Friday 14 February 1997
5. K. Robinson Notes from Mass meeting Friday 14 February 1997
6. M. Carden diary Tuesday 18 February 1997
7. ITV News 19 February 1997 See also: K. Robinson Notes from Meeting with J. Linden 26 February 1997
8. M. Carden Notes Mass Meeting 21 February 1997
9. M. Carden Notes Mass Meeting 21 February 1997. See also: K. Robinson Notes on Mass Meeting 21 February 1997
10. ibid.
11. ibid. See also: Daily Post, 'Stars plan laugh-in to aid sacked dockers' 19 February 1997 also The Observer 'Comic Relief for Sacked Dockers' 16 February 1997 and also Daily Post 24 February 1997.
12. M. Carden Notes Mass Meeting 21 February 1997. See also: K. Robinson Notes on Mass Meeting 21 February 1997
13. ibid.
14. Doreen McNally email to the author 4 November 2019
15. Thursday 27 February 1997 Kevin Robinson, Mike Carden, Rob Newman and Ken Loach appeared on Roy Greenslade's Granada TV programme, Britain Talks Back.
16. ibid.
17. ibid.
18. ibid.
19. ibid.
20. ibid.
21. ibid.
22. ibid.
23. ibid.
24. ibid.
25. ibid.
26. Liverpool Echo 'Chaos Threat On River: Ship Pilots St for Pay Row Strike' Peter Harvey 28 February 1997. See also: Lloyd's List 'Mersey Docks Accused In Pilotage Row' David Osler. 28 February 1997
27. M. Carden Diary 17 June 1997
28. M. Carden diary Tuesday 18 February 1997
29. ibid.
30. M. Carden Notes Mass Meeting 21 February 1997
31. M. Carden Diary Monday 24 February 1997 See also K. Robinson Notes on PSS Meeting 24 February 1997
32. M. Carden Diary Monday 24 February 1997
33. ibid.
34. ibid.
35. K. Robinson Notes on PSS Meeting Monday 24 February 1997
36. M. Carden Diary Monday 24 February 1997

37. ibid.
38. K. Robinson Notes on PSS 24.2.1997
39. M. Carden Diary Monday 24 February 1997
40. K. Robinson Notes on PSS Meeting 24 February 1997
41. M. Carden Diary Monday 24 February 1997 and K. Robinson Notes on PSS Meeting Monday 24 February 1997
42. K. Robinson Notes on PSS Meeting Monday 24 February 1997
43. M. Carden Diary Monday 24 February 1997 and K. Robinson Notes on PSS Meeting Monday 24 February 1997
44. ibid.
45. ibid.
46. M. Carden Diary Tuesday 25 February 1997
47. The Guardian - Terry Macalister 'Record Profits for Mersey Docks' 16 Feburary 1999
48. Tuesday 25 February 1997 M. Carden Diary
49. ibid.

## 59 - All Docks and Dockers Are the Same – Nearing A Conclusion?

1. LabourNet February 1997, available: http://www.labournet.net/docks2/9702/HISTORY.HTM
2. ibid.
3. M. Carden Notes 27 February 1997: See also K. Robinson's 29 February 1997
4. M. Carden Notes 27 February 1997
5. M. Carden Notes 28 February 1997
6. Greg Dropkin 'Nearing the End Game' February 1997, LabourNet, available: http://www.labournet.net/docks2/9703/7MAR.HTM
7. ibid.
8. M. Carden diary Friday 28 February 1997
9. M. Carden Notes March 2 Sunday 1997 - Mike Carden wrote at the time, 'this motley group, who were likely to oppose being addressed by real trade unionists'.
10. ibid.
11. K. Robinson thought this concert took place on Saturday at the Mean Fiddler and Dodgy raised £7,000 for the dockers' hardship fund. K. Robinson notes 3 March 1997
12. M. Carden Notes TGWU GEC Tuesday 3 March 1997
13. ibid.
14. M. Carden Notes TGWU GEC Tuesday 4 March 1997 See also the TGWU Record April/March 1997
15. ibid.
16. ibid.
17. ibid.
18. K. Robinson Notes on PSS Meeting 4 March 1997 see also M. Carden Notes on TGWU GEC Tuesday 4 March 1997
19. Liverpool Echo 10 March 1997 and also M. Carden Notes TGWU GEC Tuesday 4 March 1997
20. M. Carden Notes 11 March 1997
21. ibid.
22. M. Carden Notes Thursday 13 March 1997
23. ibid.
24. ibid.
25. ibid.
26. Liverpool Echo 'Docks Peace Deal in Sight' 13 March 1997
27. Stuart Cosgrove, Commissioning Editor for Chanel Four television recording held in dockers' archive:
28. ibid.
29. ibid.
30. M. Carden Notes Friday 14 March 1997. See also: 'What's Up Dockers': RDF Television, Televised charity comedy show, OB from The London Palladium Producer Lisa Clark, Director Hamish Hamilton.
31. ibid.
32. M. Carden Notes Friday 14 March 1997
33. M. Carden notes Paris Meeting 15 March 1997
34. M. Carden notes on Shop Stewards' Meeting 17 March 1997
35. MPSS Letter to Bill Morris 4 April 1997
36. J. Spencer letter from Economic Development and European Affairs Office, Liverpool City Council 8 July 1998. See also MDHC Port News Vol.15 Number 3 December 1997 'On top of the World at the Princes Dock': 'KPMG have taken two and a half floors of the state-of-the-art building.'

## 60 - Robbie Fowler and the Liverpool Dockers

1. Observer 4 September 2005, Sarah Edworthy, 'Don't Look Back In Anger'
2. Mike Henson, The Set Pieces, 'I wanted to Contribute to Political Causes Outside of Football – Stig Inge Bjornebye and the Liverpool Dockers Strike', available: https://thesetpieces.com/interviews/i-wanted-to-contribute-to-political-causes-outside-of-football-stig-inge-bjornebye-and-the-liverpool-dockers-strike/ (27 September 2018)
3. ibid.
4. Chris Tobin 'The Liverpool Way: A Noose Around Our Neck' available: http://www.thedaisycutter.co.uk/2012/03/the-liverpool-way-a-noose-around-our-neck/ 18 March 2012. See also: http://www.thisisanfield.com/clubinfo/history/hillsborough/about/
5. J. Kerr; MLSPA. See LabourNet May 1997, available:

http://www.labournet.net/docks2/9705/RO
BBIE.HTM

6.  Marty Size and Billy Barrett - Mersey
    Moments: Robbie Fowler 'Dockers T-Shirt'
    available:
    https://www.youtube.com/watch?v=Lgq-
    KPfLGVI

7.  ibid.

8.  ibid.

9.  ibid.

10. ibid.

11. ibid.

12. Tony Melia interviewed on 'Here and Now'
    ITV Television March 1997

13. N. Klein 'No Space, No Jobs, No Choice, No
    Logo' Published by Flamingo (2000) p.197.
    See also, 'Talkin about a Revolution', C.
    Williams, The Independent on Sunday 4
    October 1998. See also:
    https://en.wikipedia.org/wiki/Liverpool_dock
    ers%27_strike

14. M. Carden Notes Sunday 23 March 1997

15. LabourNet March 1997, 'International
    Dockers' Committee steering group resolution'
    available:
    http://www.labournet.net/docks2/9703/INT
    RES.HTM

16. M. Carden Notes Monday 24 March 1997

17. See: https://en.wikipedia.org/wiki/The_X-
    Files

18. M. Carden Notes Monday 24 March 1997

19. ibid.

20. ibid.

21. ibid.

22. ibid.

23. M. Carden Notes Tuesday 25 March 1997

24. ibid.

25. ibid. See also Daniel Sultan Dir. 'Words of
    Liverpool' Artis Diffusion Paris – 1996 film on
    the Liverpool dock dispute.

26. M. Carden Notes Tuesday 25 March 1997

27. ibid.

28. ibid.

29. Bill Morris - The TGWU and the Liverpool
    Dockers in LabourNet, available:
    http://www.labournet.net/docks2/other/TG
    WU.HTM)

30. ibid.

31. M. Carden Notes Thursday 26 March 1997

32. M. Carden Notes Friday 27 March 1997

33. M. Carden Notes Tuesday 1 April 1997

34. M. Carden Notes Tuesday 1 April 1997 and
    Thursday 3 April 1997

35. Liverpool Echo: BBC Film Crew Liverpool
    Echo Stunt Row 'BBC Crew in Docks Picket'
    3 April 1997

36. M. Carden Notes Thursday 3 April 1997

37. ibid.

38. ibid.

39. M. Carden Notes Friday 4 April 1997

40. ibid.

41. M. Carden Notes Tuesday 8 April 1997

42. M. Carden Notes Friday 4 April 1997

43. The West Australian 'Mersey Men Warn
    Wharfies' Saturday March 29 1997 and also the
    Maritime Workers' Journal March/April 1997
    p.29

44. M. Carden notes 4 April 1997

45. Congressman R. Dellums Letter to Tony Blair
    April 22 1997 available:
    http://www.labournet.net/docks2/9704/DE
    LLUMS.HTM

## 61 - A March for Social Justice – Respect to the Chartists!

1.  BBC Radio Merseyside 12.3.1997

2.  M. Carden Notes Monday 14 April 1997 and
    also Liverpool Daily Post 14.3.1997

3.  ibid. 'I feel I let a lot of people down, but I
    know what I said and how badly it has been
    represented in the Post.' M. Carden

4.  Merseyside Port Shop Stewards Statement
    published on LabourNet April 1997

5.  SchNEWS, Issue 116, printed by 'Justice?'
    available:
    https://schnews.org/archive/pdf/news116.pd
    f

6.  'Merseyside Port Shop Stewards Statement'
    published on LabourNet April 1997, available:
    http://www.labournet.net/docks2/9704/DO
    CKRTS.HTM

7.  'Never Mind The Ballots - Reclaim The
    Streets!' 12th April 1997, available:
    http://www.urban75.org/photos/protest/traf.
    html

8.  'Another World is Possible - How the
    Liverpool Dockers Launched a Global
    Movement' Edited by Pauline Bradley and
    Chris Knight, Published in 2004 by the Radical
    Anthropology Group in association with
    Haringey Trades Union Council and the
    sacked Liverpool dockers. Radical
    Anthropology Group. School of Social
    Sciences, Media and Cultural Studies,
    University of East London, Docklands
    Campus, 4-6 University Way, London E16
    2RD, available:
    http://www.radicalanthropologygroup.org/
    See also: Pauline Bradley's wonderful
    YouTube film -
    https://www.youtube.com/watch?v=r10FJT
    NtCEo

9.  ibid.

10. Russell Brand quoted in Pilkipedea, available:
    http://www.pilkipedia.co.uk/forum/viewtopic
    .php?f=24&t=8248&start=15

11. Simon Hatherstone 'Russell Brand - I want to
    Address the Alienation and Despair' The
    Guardian 11 October 2014

12. Another World is Possible - How the Liverpool Dockers Launched a Global Movement, Edited by Pauline Bradley and Chris Knight - Published in 2004

13. 'Hate Riot Frenzy' by Mark Sully and Christopher Fenot see: http://www.mcspotlight.org/beyond/evading/evst2a.html

14. ibid. See also: M. Carden Notes Tuesday 15 April 1997

15. ibid.

16. 'ILWU Conference support for Liverpool Dockers', LabourNet April 1997, available: http://www.labournet.net/docks2/9704/ILWUCONF.HTM

17. ibid.

18. The Chartists - for example: http://www.parliament.uk/about/living-heritage/transformingsociety/electionsvoting/chartists/overview/chartistmovement/

## 62 - The Liverpool Dockers Fail to Call for UK Solidarity Action?

1. M. Lavalette & J. Kennedy (1996) 'Solidarity on the Waterfront' Liver Press, 1996; see notes from M. Lavalette, LabourNet, available: http://www.labournet.net/docks2/9704/GLOBAL.HTM#ML According to Jimmy Davies' announcement at the dockers' mass meeting, held at Transport House, 'the book is on sale at the back of the hall for £5.95 and people may not have £5.95 but… out of that £5.95, £2 will come back to our hardship fund.' Mass Meeting 13.12.96, D. Cotterill Audio Tape Ref:DC23 See also: https://en.wikipedia.org/wiki/Michael_Lavalette

2. see notes from M. Lavalette, LabourNet, available: http://www.labournet.net/docks2/9704/GLOBAL.HTM#ML

3. Globalisation, labour internationalism and the Liverpool docks dispute http://www.labournet.net/docks2/9704/GLOBAL.HTM

4. 'Social Movements: Identity, Culture, and the State' David S. Meyer, Nancy Whittier, Belinda Robnett: Oxford University Press 2002 pp.151-153

5. 'Lockout 1st Anniversary demonstration', LabourNet, available: http://www.labournet.net/docks2/9610/DEMO.HTM

6. Dockers Charter 'Unshackle the Unions' No.14 April 1997

7. Dockers Charter 'A Fight for All' No.14 April 1997, available: http://www.labournet.net/docks2/9511/CHARTER.HTM

8. Green Left Weekly: 14 May 1997 'Liverpool dockers determined to Win' James Vassilopoulos. See also: Greg Dropkin, LabourNet: Globalisation, Labour Internationalism and the Docks Dispute

9. Dockers Charter No.14 April 1997 p.6

10. D. Gibson: 'Report on Meeting with Merseyside Port Shop Stewards' 26 March 1998

11. ibid.

12. See M. Carden at www.labournet.net/docks2/9704/GLOBAL.HTM

13. Michael Lavalette, LabourNet www.labournet.net/docks2/9704/GLOBAL.HTM#ML

14. Bill Hunter 'They knew why they Fought: Unofficial struggle and Leadership on the Docks, 1945-1989'. Index Books 1994

15. Bill Hunter, LabourNet, www.labournet.net/docks2/9704/GLOBAL.HTM#ML

16. Issue 204 Socialist Review January 1997; Helen Shooter interviews M. Lavelette & J. Kennedy

17. ibid. and Issue 204 Socialist Review January 1997; Helen Shooter interviews M. Lavelette & J. Kennedy. See also: Globalisation, labour internationalism and the Liverpool docks dispute http://www.labournet.net/docks2/9704/GLOBAL.HTM#BH

18. Hugh Rodwell LabourNet www.labournet.net/docks2/9704/GLOBAL.HTM#ML

19. ibid.

20. Bill Hunter LabourNet www.labournet.net/docks2/9704/GLOBAL.HTM#ML

## 63 - Rock the Dock: An Occupation?

1. Brit Awards 24 February 1997 ITV Television

2. NME 4 May 1997

3. ibid.

4. ibid.

5. ibid.

6. M. Carden Notes Friday 25 April 1997

7. M. Carden Notes Monday 28 April 1997

8. ibid.

9. ibid.

10. ibid.

11. ibid.

12. ibid.

13. K. Robinson Diary 1 May 1997

14. M. Carden diary 1 May 1997

15. 'Solidarity With Andrea Stauffacher!' LabourNet May 1997, available: http://www.labournet.net/docks2/9705/ANDREA.HTM

16. 'Message to Andrea Stauffacher from Liverpool dockers' B. Jenkins, LabourNet May 1997, available: http://www.labournet.net/docks2/9705/ANDI.HTM

17. M. Carden diary 1 May 1997

18. K. Robinson Notes on Mass Meeting 2 May 1997

19. K. Robinson Notes on PSS 6 May 1997

20. MDHC Letter to Linden Kenna & Co. T.D. Williams Director of Estates 12 May 1997

21. John Linden letter to MDHC – Linden Kenna & Co. 6 May 1997

22. Liverpool Echo 'New Raid on Dockers' Van Monday 23 June 1997

23. M. Carden diary 13 May 1997

24. ibid.

25. ibid.

26. ibid. - Carden was to write at the time that 'everything seems very dull at the moment as we await outcome of the 'six items' which may end this struggle.'

27. Terry Teague – Report on ITF Dockers' Section Miami Conference 9-10 June 1997 available: http://www.labournet.net/docks2/9706/MIAMI1.HTM

28. K. Robinson Notes on PSS Meeting 8 May 1997

## 64 - The Death of Billy Dunn

1. K. Robinson Notes on Mass Meeting 9 May 1997

2. K. Robinson Notes on Labour History Meeting 10 May 1997 held at Transport House, Liverpool

3. K. Robinson Notes on PSS 13 May 1997

4. M. Carden diary Thursday 15 May 1997

5. ibid.

6. K. Robinson Notes on PSS Meeting Friday 16 May 1997

7. E. Leatherbarrow Communication Director MDHC interviewed by BBC Radio Wales May 1997 Audio Tape Ref:BBC Cymru

8. M. Carden Notes Tuesday 20 May 1997 & 26 June 1997 (A month later Carden was to write that 'this piece of technology [Apple Macintosh Computer] is extraordinary, internet, world-wide web... Dave Cotterill, from the Socialist Party, got this magnificent machine for us. Why did we not pursue this earlier? Greg Dropkin is now on the team permanently and we have much fun with him. He is a great asset to our struggle; his knowledge of the computer; and his political judgement I value deeply'.

9. Liverpool Docker Richie Gerrard Interviewed for the Dockers Charter, 20 November 1995, available:

http://www.labournet.net/docks2/9511/gerrard.htm

10. 'Dockers unanimously reject offer', LabourNet, 26 January 1997, available: http://www.labournet.net/docks2/9601/OFFER.HTM

11. Dockers Charter No.16 June 1997 – M. Carden Diary 23 May 1997

12. BBC TV Here and Now 1997 from dockers' archive video recording – not dated. (June 1997)

13. ibid.

14. ibid.

15. ibid.

16. ibid.

17. ibid.

18. ibid.

19. ibid.

20. M. Carden Notes Tuesday 20 May 1997 & 26 June 1997

21. ibid. See also: Dockers Charter No.16 June 1997

22. Letter from Linden Kenna to Irene Campbell 22 August 1997

23. Letter from Linden Kenna, Ian Dodwell to Kevin Robinson 'Formation of Charity' 17 November 1997

24. Letter from Alan Bleasdale to Kevin Robinson 29 August 1997

25. K. Robinson Notes on Mass Meeting Friday 23 May 1997

26. K. Robinson Diary Saturday 24 May 1997 see also 'Amsterdam Euro March' Report by Bobby Morton, available: http://www.labournet.net/docks2/9706/AMSTDAM.HTM

27. K. Robinson Diary Tuesday 27 May 1997 and also Wednesday 28 May 1997

28. ibid.

## 65 - Internationalism and the Second IDC

1. Bill Hunter LabourNet www.labournet.net/docks2/9704/GLOBAL.HTM#ML

2. IWW Campaign Neptune Jade www.iww.org/history/campaigns/neptunejade/4

3. Jack Heyman, Sunday 22 July 2012: 'Alexander Cockburn: Friend of ILWU Longshoremen Dies' available: www.labournet.net/other/1207/cockburn1.html -

4. 'Stand and Deliver' Greg Dropkin, LabourNet June 1997, available: http://www.labournet.net/docks2/9706/MONTREP.HTM

5. ibid.

6. 'Amsterdam, WOW!' Greg Dropkin, LabourNet June 1997, available: http://www.labournet.net/docks2/9706/WOWAM.HTM
7. ibid.
8. ibid.
9. M. Carden Notes May 25 & 26 May Montreal, Canada
10. ibid.
11. ibid.
12. 2nd. International Dock Workers Conference – Montreal Saturday 25 May 1997. M. Carden Notes
13. ibid.
14. ibid.
15. M. Carden Notes May 25 & 26 May Montreal, Canada
16. Tony Mulhearn – The Making of a Liverpool Militant – 47books 2019 pp.88-91 and M. Carden Notes IDW Conference Montreal Monday 27 May 1997
17. M. Carden Notes IDW Conference Montreal Monday 27 May 1997
18. ibid.
19. ibid.
20. ibid.
21. ibid.
22. ibid.
23. ibid.
24. ibid.
25. M. Carden Notes IDW Conference Tuesday 28 May 1997
26. ibid.
27. ibid.
28. ibid.
29. 'The Empty Seat' by Jack Heyman ILWU Dispatcher June 1997, available: http://www.labournet.net/docks2/9706/SANTOS.HTM
30. ibid.
31. 'Stand and Deliver' LabourNet June 1997, available: http://www.labournet.net/docks2/9706/MONTREP.HTM
32. M. Carden Notes IDW Conference Tuesday 28 May 1997
33. ibid.
34. ibid.
35. ibid.
36. ibid. News reached Mike Carden through the Montreal dockers organising committee, that his wife, Mary, had broken her ankle whilst staying with her mother in Wales. With two young children also to look after he had no alternative but to take the first plane back to London from Montreal and the conference organisors gave every help in this.
37. ibid.
38. M. Carden Diaries 3 June 1997. See also: 'Stand and Deliver' LabourNet June 1997,

available: http://www.labournet.net/docks2/9706/MONTREP.HTM See also: LabourNet June 1997 Message to Liverpool Dockworkers: Montreal May 29 1997 2nd International Conference Des Debardeurs
39. 'T&GWU opposes Liverpool docker addressing ITF dockers' Section Conference', LabourNet, available: http://www.labournet.net/docks2/9706/MIAMI.HTM
40. ibid.
41. 'T&GWU opposes Liverpool docker addressing ITF dockers' Section Conference' LabourNet, available: http://www.labournet.net/docks2/9706/MIAMI.HTM

## 66 - General Executive Council Meeting, June 1997

1. M. Carden Notes Monday 2 June 1997
2. M. Carden Diary 3 June 1997 and also K. Robinson notes on Port Shop Stewards meeting Tuesday 3 June 1997.
3. ibid.
4. ibid. Port Shop Stewards 6 June 1997
5. ibid.
6. TULRA (Consolidation Act 1992) Section 20-21
7. This is a direct reference to Morris' demands that the blockade by Liverpool dockers of Namibian Uranium Hexafloride being used at British Nuclear Fuels before their dismissal. BNF workers were TGWU members involved in fuel manufacture and uranium procurement, as well as recycling used fuel, transporting radioactive materials, engineering, waste management and decommissioning. See: https://fas.org/nuke/guide/uk/corp/bnfl.htm
8. 'Union Need a Global Strategy Says ITF Chief' by David Cockcroft ITF General Secretary, LabourNet, available: http://www.labournet.net/docks2/9706/COCKROFT.HTM See also: M. Carden diary June 1997
9. 'Union Need a Global Strategy Says ITF Chief' by David Cockcroft ITF General Secretary http://www.labournet.net/docks2/9706/COCKROFT.HTM See also: 'TGWU Opposes Liverpool Docker Addressing ITF Dockers' Section Conference', LabourNet, available: http://www.labournet.net/docks2/9706/MIAMI.HTM
10. M. Carden Notes Thursday 5 June 1997, GEC London
11. ibid.
12. ibid.
13. ibid.

14. ibid.
15. ibid.
16. ibid.
17. GEC support notes from M. Carden's diary written in June 1997 prior to the GEC.
18. M. Carden Notes Friday 6 June 1997
19. ibid.

## 67 - The Interview That Established the Liverpool Dockers as a 'Political Movement'

1. The TGWU Record January 1997
2. GEC support notes from M. Carden's diary written in June 1997 prior to the GEC.
3. Peter Kennedy (email 113121.3463@compuserve.com) reprinted from LabourNet October 1997
4. ibid.
5. ibid.
6. ibid.
7. ibid.
8. ibid.
9. ibid.
10. ibid.
11. ibid.
12. ibid.
13. ibid.
14. S. Coulter 'Flexploitation: The Case of the 2012 Spanish Labour Market Reform' LSE 4 June 2014, available: https://blogs.lse.ac.uk/netuf/2014/06/05/flexploitation-the-case-of-the-2012-spanish-labour-market-reform/
15. Peter Kennedy (email 113121.3463@compuserve.com) reprinted from LabourNet October 1997
16. ibid.
17. ibid.
18. ibid.
19. ibid.
20. ibid.
21. ibid.
22. ibid.
23. ibid.
24. ibid.
25. ibid.
26. ibid.
27. ibid.
28. ibid.
29. ibid.
30. ibid.
31. ibid.
32. ibid.

## 68 - LabourNet's Exclusive Report into Casual Labour on Liverpool Docks

1. 'Casual Labour – An Exclusive Report' by Greg Dropkin, LabourNet June 1997, available: http://www.labournet.net/docks2/9706/CASUAL.HTM
2. ibid.
3. ibid.
4. ibid.
5. ibid.
6. ibid.
7. Liverpool Echo 17 January 1984
8. Lloyd's List 9 June 1987
9. 'Casual Labour – An Exclusive Report' by Greg Dropkin, LabourNet June 1997, available: http://www.labournet.net/docks2/9706/CASUAL.HTM
10. ibid.
11. ibid.
12. ibid.
13. ibid.
14. ibid.
15. ibid.
16. M. Carden Notes Friday 6 June 1997
17. M. Carden Notes Tuesday 10 June 1997
18. J. Pilger interviewed at the Dockers' Rally in Liverpool September 1997 - BBC Radio Merseyside Audio Tape Ref: Docks April 1997
19. Colin Freeman and Robert Mendick 'Libya – Tony Blair and Colonel Gaddafi's Secret Meetings' Daily Telegraph 17 September 2011
20. Bobby Morton 'Amsterdam Euro March' on LabourNet, available: http://www.labournet.net/docks2/9706/AMSTDAM.HTM
21. K. Robinson Diary 10 June 1997
22. M. Carden diary Thursday 12 June 1997, K. Robinson Diary 11 June 1997 and also LabourNet June 1997
23. Kevin Robinson's Women of the Waterfront Meeting Notes 18 June 1997
24. Kevin Robinson's record of meeting with Liverpool Dockers' Solicitor, John Linden, 20 June 1997.
25. https://en.wikipedia.org/wiki/Pentonville_Five

## 69 - The ITF

1. M. Carden diary Thursday 12 June 1997
2. 'ITF Miami Report' by T. Teague, LabourNet June 1997, available: http://www.labournet.net/docks2/9706/MIAMI1.HTM
3. ibid.
4. ibid.
5. ibid.
6. ibid.
7. ibid.
8. ibid.

9. ibid.
10. ibid.
11. ibid. Stevenson told the conference that, 'The stumbling block to achieving the right type of settlement was the company refusal to remove the strike breaking agency Drake International from the Container Terminal and other important areas of the port.'
12. 'TTF Miami Report' by T. Teague, LabourNet June 1997, available: http://www.labournet.net/docks2/9706/MIAMI1.HTM
13. ibid.
14. Towards a Labour Supply in the Port of Liverpool – A Document for Discussion 2 February 1998 TGWU Merseyside Port Shop Stewards
15. 'TTF Miami Report' by T. Teague, LabourNet June 1997, available: http://www.labournet.net/docks2/9706/MIAMI1.HTM
16. ibid.
17. ibid.
18. ibid.
19. ibid.
20. ibid.
21. ibid.
22. ibid.

## 70 - Preamble to the Brighton Biennial Delegates Conference

1. M. Carden Diary Port Shop Stewards' Meeting 17 June 1997
2. Leaflet for 'Liverpool Lives – A Celebration of Working-Class Culture' Transport House 21 June 1997
3. M. Carden Diary Monday 23 June 1997
4. ibid.
5. ibid.
6. M. Carden Diary 25 June 1997
7. ibid.
8. M. Carden Notes 27 June 1997. See also: article on the Liverpool Irish Centre which faced closure, 13 June 1997, Anphoblacht - May 2014 Edition, available: http://www.anphoblacht.com/contents/2181
9. Kevin Robinson Notes on Dockers' Mass Meeting 27 June 1997
10. ibid.
11. ibid.
12. M. Carden Notes 1 July 1997
13. 'The Case for the Reinstatement of the Sacked Liverpool Dockers' booklet July 1997, text available on LabourNet: http://www.labournet.net/docks2/9707/BOOKLET.HTM
14. ibid. See also: P. Turnbull and V. Wass - The Great Dock and Dole Swindle: Accounting for the Costs and Benefits of Port Transport De-

Regulation and the Dock Labour Compensation Scheme. Cardiff Business School December 1995, available: https://onlinelibrary.wiley.com/doi/abs/10.1111/j.1467-9299.1995.tb00842.x
15. 'The Case for the Reinstatement of the Sacked Liverpool Dockers' booklet July 1997, text available on LabourNet: http://www.labournet.net/docks2/9707/BOOKLET.HTM
16. ibid.
17. The Times, 26 December 1987. See also: Dockers Charter publication of a lengthy document entitled, 'The Case for the Reinstatement of the Sacked Liverpool Dockers: The need for a Public Inquiry into the Mersey Docks and Harbour Company: Merseyside Port Shop Stewards' Committee, 1 July 1997'
18. PSPRU Public Services Privatisation Research Unit Company Report, January 1997. See also Eric Taplin 'The Dockers Union – A Study of the National Union of Dock Labourers 1889-1922.' Leicester University Press, 1986 p.30. See also: E. Taplin 'Irish Leaders and the Liverpool Dockers: Richard McGhee and Edward McHugh' North West Labour History Society, Issue No.9, available: http://www.nwlh.org.uk/?q=node/140
19. Liverpool Daily Post, November 1996. See also: M. Carden Diary 2 July 1997. See also: http://www.labournet.net/docks2/9707/POLICE.HTM
20. ibid.
21. LabourNet July 1997 http://www.labournet.net/docks2/9707/POLICE.HTM
22. 'Canadian Autoworkers take up campaign against Mersey Police violence' LabourNet, available: http://www.labournet.net/docks2/9707/CAWPOL.HTM
23. M. Carden Diary 2 July 1997
24. ibid.
25. Message of support from Irish Port Workers Liaison Group, LabourNet, July 1997, available: http://www.labournet.net/docks2/9707/IRISH.HTM
26. ibid.
27. ibid.
28. ibid.
29. M. Carden Notes Friday 4 July 1997
30. ibid.
31. ibid.
32. ibid.
33. ibid.
34. ibid.
35. ibid.
36. ibid.

37. ibid.
38. ibid.
39. ibid.
40. ibid.
41. ibid.
42. ibid.
43. ibid.
44. ibid.
45. ibid.
46. ibid.
47. ibid.
48. M. Carden Notes Saturday 5 July Broad Left Meeting held at TGWU BDC
49. M. Carden Notes Tuesday 8 July

## 71 - The 1997 Biennial Delegates Conference

1. P. Bradley & C. Knight, 'Another World is Possible' Published in 2004 by the Radical Anthropology Group in association with Haringey Trades Union Council and the sacked Liverpool dockers. p.17
2. 783 & Union Live Video TGWU BDC Brighton 1997 – The official recording of the 1997 BDC
3. ibid.
4. ibid.
5. ibid.
6. ibid.
7. ibid.
8. ibid.
9. ibid.
10. ibid.
11. ibid.
12. ibid.
13. ibid.
14. ibid.
15. ibid.
16. ibid.
17. ibid.
18. ibid.
19. ibid.
20. ibid.
21. ibid.
22. ibid.
23. ibid.
24. ibid.
25. ibid.
26. ibid.
27. ibid.
28. ibid.
29. ibid.
30. ibid.
31. ibid.
32. Union Live Video TGWU BDC Brighton 1997. See also: 'Dockers defeat TGWU Executive' - A LabourNet Report, 9 July 1997, available:
http://www.labournet.net/docks2/9707/TGCONF2.HTM
33. ibid.
34. ibid.
35. The Regions vote was recorded with the Welsh, Midlands and Scottish Region's 4, 5 and 8 voting against the Liverpool dockers. Region 6, North West, used its entire 59 votes to support their docks members.
36. 'Bill Morris, A Trade Union Miracle' G. Goodman, Black Amber Inspirations, 2010 p.158
37. M. Carden Notes Monday 14 July 1997
38. ibid.
39. ibid.
40. ibid.
41. ibid.
42. ibid.
43. ibid.
44. M. Carden Diary Friday 18 July 1997
45. Ian McCartney MP, Employment Minister response to Bill Morris 20 August 1997
46. M. Carden notes on Mass Meeting Friday 25 July 1997
47. K. Robinson Handwritten notes House of Commons 30 July 1997
48. ibid.
49. ibid.
50. ibid.
51. ibid.
52. ibid.
53. ibid.
54. M. Carden Notes Thursday 31 July 1997
55. ibid.
56. Kevin Robinson's record of Shop Stewards Meeting Thursday 31 July 1997
57. M. Carden Notes Friday 1 August 1997
58. ibid.
59. ibid.
60. ibid.
61. Greg Dropkin LabourNet August 1997
62. M. Carden Notes 7 August 1997
63. ibid.
64. M. Carden Notes 11 August 1997
65. Kevin Robinson 13 August 1997 Notes from Women of the Waterfront Meeting.

## 72 - International Solidarity

1. LIoyd's List, 14 August 1997. See also: 'South African dockers to boycott fruit exports to Sheerness' LabourNet, available: http://www.labournet.net/docks2/9708/SA.HTM
2. ibid.
3. LabourNet September 1997 Correspondence between Jim Nolan and Bill Morris, TG&WU General Secretary 18 August 1997
4. ibid.

5. ILWU International President Brian McWilliam letter to John Monks, President of the TUC 27 August 1997 - LabourNet August 1997, available: http://www.labournet.net/docks2/9708/ILWUITF.HTM

6. ILWU Local 40 letter to J. Monks, General Secretary TUC, 29 August 1997, LabourNet August 1997, available: http://www.labournet.net/docks2/9708/LOCAL40.HTM

7. ibid.

8. M. Carden Notes Friday 22 August 1997

9. ibid.

10. M. Carden Notes Thursday 28 August 1997

11. M. Carden Notes Friday 5 September 1997

12. ibid.

13. M. Carden Notes 28 August 1997

14. 'Robert Taylor US Ports Face Day of Disruption Over the UK Docks Dispute', Financial Times, Thursday 4 September 1997

15. Merseyside Port Shop Stewards; Press Release: for immediate release Monday 8 September 10:00 am - World Wide Dockers Solidarity

16. Steve Zeltzer, San Fransisco Demo at British Consulate 8 September 1997, LabourNet, available: http://www.labournet.net/docks2/9709/SANFRAN.HTM

17. ibid.

18. 'Final Report of actions' LabourNet September 1997, available: http://www.labournet.net/docks2/9709/ROUNDUP.HTM

19. ibid.

20. ibid.

21. ibid.

22. Jack Heyman ILWU Open Letter to Kees Marges, ITF LabourNet September 1997, LabourNet, available: http://www.labournet.net/docks2/9709/MARGES.HTM

23. ibid.

24. ibid.

25. Marges letter to Heyman 22 September 1997, LabourNet, available: http://www.labournet.net/docks2/9709/MARGES2.HTM

26. See ITF Debate on LabourNet, available: http://www.labournet.net/docks2/9709/MARGES3.HTM See also: http://www.labournet.net/docks2/other/ITFDEB.HTM#B

27. It's Never too Late – The Merseyside Port Shop Stewards Comment on Marges – LabourNet September 1997, available: http://www.labournet.net/docks2/9709/LATE.HTM

28. ibid.

29. B. Borg, Swedish Dock Workers' Union, to Merseyside Port Shop Stewards 9th September 1997

## 73 - The Liverpool Dockers Call for Support amidst the fall-out from the BDC

1. LabourNet Report compiled together with Merseyside Port Stewards Press Release Monday 8 September 1997 LabourNet, September 1997, available: http://www.labournet.net/docks2/9709/PREREL.HTM

2. M. Carden Diary Thursday 11 September

3. M. Carden Notes Friday 12 September

4. M. Carden Notes Saturday 13 September 1997

5. ibid.

6. M. Carden Notes on GEC Meeting held in Transport House, London on Monday 15 September 1997.

7. ibid.

8. M. Carden Notes on GEC Meeting held in Transport House, London on Tuesday 16 September 1997.

9. ibid.

10. M. Carden Notes on GEC Meeting held in Transport House, London on Tuesday 16th.September 1997.

11. M. O'Reilly 'From Lucifer to Lazarus – A Life on the Left' Lilliput Publishing 2019 pp.134-135

12. ibid. p.135

13. ibid. pp.134-135. See also: M. Carden Notes GEC Thursday 18 September – Following this session Carden pointed out that this interview with the GEC for his appointment of Irish Regional Secretary was a 'statement of Irish Socialism'.

14. See: http://en.wikipedia.org/wiki/Fuck_the_Millennium 1997 (What The Fuck's Going On?) was performed by 2K as a one-off event at London's Barbican Arts Centre on 17 September 1997. See also: http://www.liquisearch.com/fuck_the_millennium/performance.

15. The Sunday Independent 21st. September 1997 - Ross Wynne-Jones 'No going back at Liverpool docks – Pickets fight on despite two years of TUC and Labour Indifference'.

16. Anne-Marie Sweeney 'Dancing in the Snow' New Internationalist, Issue 296, available: http://newint.org/features/1997/11/05/dancing/

17. M. Carden Notes from Port Shop Stewards 23 September 1997

18. ibid.

19. ibid.

20. ibid.
21. ibid.
22. ibid.
23. ibid.
24. 'Postal Workers and the Liverpool Dockers' Picket Line ' by Greg Dropkin, LabourNet October 1997, available: http://www.labournet.net/docks2/9710/POST.HTM
25. ibid.
26. M. Carden Notes 24 September 1997
27. ibid.
28. K. Robinson Notes on Shop Stewards' Meeting with Jack Adams and Grahame Stevenson 24 September 1997
29. ibid.
30. ibid.
31. ibid.
32. ibid.
33. ibid.
34. M. Carden Notes on Shop Stewards' Meeting 24 September 1997
35. ibid. See also: 'When will the ITF call on its affiliates to support the Liverpool dockers?' letter by Jack Heyman, available: http://www.labournet.net/docks2/9709/MARGES3.HTM 22 September 1997
36. l'Humanite, 25 September 1997. See also: Daphne Liddle 'Liverpool Dockers Unite the Globe' The New Worker No.973, 26 September 1997
37. Press Release Port Shop Stewards 26 September 1997 'The Dart' Issue No.1 - 'The Newsletter of Drakes Workforce', available: http://www.labournet.net/docks2/9709/DRAKE.HTM
38. ibid.
39. ibid.
40. MDHC Port News Vol.15 Number 2 September 1997
41. ibid.
42. ibid.
43. Big Issue: John Pilger 'Docking the Truth' 29 September – 5 October 1997

## 74 - Tension and Pressure Continue to Mount

1. Video of demo held in Dockers Archive Demonstration St. Georges Hall Saturday 27 September 1997
2. ibid.
3. ibid.
4. ibid.
5. M. Carden notes Friday 3 October 1997
6. M. Curran Interviewed on BBC Radio Merseyside 27.9.97 Audio Tape Ref: Docks April 1997
7. Reclaim the Streets on BBC Radio Merseyside - Audio Tape Ref: Docks April 1997

8. ibid.
9. ibid.
10. R. Draper BBC Radio Merseyside Audio Tape Ref: Dock April 1997
11. K. Robinson Record of Mass Meeting Friday 3 October 1997 and Shop Stewards Meeting held on the afternoon of 3 October 1997
12. M. Carden Notes Monday 6 October 1997
13. ibid. See also: Kevin Robinson notes on same meeting.
14. ibid. See also: Kevin Robinson notes on same meeting.
15. Neil Findlay, 'If You Don't Run, They Can't Chase You' Luath Press Ltd. 2021, pp..94-101. See also: M. Carden Notes Tuesday 7 October 1997
16. Daily Mail 'Why the Dockers are putting their Shirts on Blair's Sons' 7 October 1997
17. ibid.
18. M. Carden Notes Wednesday 8 October 1997
19. ibid.
20. M. Carden Diary Monday 13 October 1997
21. ibid.
22. ibid.
23. ibid.
24. Audio Tape BBC Radio Merseyside – Ref: Docks April 1997
25. M. Carden Diary Monday 13 October 1997
26. ibid. See also: K. Robinson Notes from Shop Stewards Meeting 16 October 1997 and also M. Carden Diaries Thursday 16 October 1997

## 75 - The Third Official Ballot

1. M. Carden Notes 18 October 1997
2. ibid.
3. 'Bill Morris imposes ballot on Liverpool dockers' Report by Greg Dropkin, 19 October 1997, LabourNet, available: http://www.labournet.net/docks2/9710/BALLOT.HTM
4. ibid.
5. Sunday Observer 12 October 1997 T&G Policy on the Liverpool Docks - Bill Morris
6. ibid.
7. M. Carden Notes of Port Shop Stewards' Meeting Sunday 12 October 1997
8. ibid.
9. ibid.
10. ibid.
11. BBC Radio Merseyside 20 October 1998 Roger Philips Phone-in Programme Liverpool docker Mick Cullen
12. M. Carden Notes on Regional Committee Tuesday 21 October 1997
13. Bill Morris letter to dockworkers enclosed with ballot papers posted by the Electoral Reform Society 17 October 1997
14. Trevor Furlong, Chief Executive of the MDHC Letter to Bill Morris 13 October 1997

enclosed with ballot papers sent by the Electoral Reform Society

15. MDHC Leaflet with Ballot Paper: 'MDHC Final Offer- It's Time to Decide' October 1997
16. ibid.
17. ibid.
18. ibid.
19. Liverpool Daily Post 'MDHC Appoints Three New Directors' Bill Gleeson 17 October 1997
20. Liverpool Daily Post 'Dock Ultimatum: Take it or Leave it' Jane Haase 20 October 1997
21. Liverpool Echo Editorial 20.10.1997
22. ibid.
23. K. Robinson Notes on Shop Stewards meeting and Mass Meeting 20 October 1997
24. ibid.
25. ibid.
26. ibid.
27. ibid.
28. ibid.
29. ibid.
30. ibid.
31. ibid.
32. ibid.
33. ibid.
34. M. Carden Diary Notes on the TGWU Regional Committee Tuesday 21 October 1997
35. George Orwell Animal Farm Penguin Books 1983 edition p.117
36. ibid. p.120

## 76 - Another Official Ballot – Another Rejection!

1. Jean Fox member of Women of the Waterfront: Reprinted in LabourNet October 1997 http://www.labournet.net/docks2/9710/FOX.HTM
2. ibid.
3. ibid.
4. ibid.
5. ibid.
6. Jimmy Campbell sacked dockworker on Radio Merseyside – Archive Audio Tape April 1997
7. Mike Carden sacked dockworker on Radio Merseyside – Archive Audio Tape April 1997
8. Eric Taplin on Radio Merseyside – Archive Audio Tape April 1997
9. Marty Size Sacked dockworker Radio Merseyside Archive Audio Tape April 1997
10. Thursday 23 October 1997, Andrew Murphy, from the Electoral Reform Society, letter to Bill Morris regarding the result of the MDHC Ballot of TGWU members of the Company Offer.
11. M. Carden Notes Thursday 23 October 1997
12. ibid.
13. TGWU Press Officer, Andrew Murray in 'Former Mersey Employees Reject Company's Offer/The Final Settlement Outvoted by 2 to 1' by Aviva Freudmann, 23 October 1997 in Joc.Com, available: http://www.joc.com/former-mersey-employees-reject-companys-offer-final-settlement-outvoted-2-1_19971023.html
14. ibid.
15. ibid.
16. ibid.
17. MDHC Managing Director Peter Jones in 'Former Mersey Employees Reject Company's Offer/The Final Settlement Outvoted by 2 to 1' by Aviva Freudmann, 23 October 1997 in Joc.Com, available: http://www.joc.com/former-mersey-employees-reject-companys-offer-final-settlement-outvoted-2-1_19971023.html
18. ibid. See also: P. Jones Archive audio tape April 1997 Radio Merseyside
19. 'Liverpool Dockers Refuse to Sell Jobs', World Anarchist News , available: http://www.struggle.ws/ws98/ws53_world.html
20. ibid.
21. BBC Radio Merseyside 23 October 1997 'Pickets Celebrate 69% No Vote' available: http://www.labournet.net/docks2/9710/BALLOT4.HTM
22. Docks Archive Audio Tape Titled: April 1997
23. BBC Radio Merseyside 23 October 1997
24. ibid.
25. 'Pickets Celebrate 69% No Vote' LabourNet, available: http://www.labournet.net/docks2/9710/BALLOT4.HTM M. Carden Notes Friday 24 October 1997 - M. Carden Notes Thursday 23 October 1997
26. Channel Four News 23 October 1997 - The Elm House Pub on Derby Road, near the Gladstone Dock Entrance was a popular pub for dockers managed by a docker, Richie Gerrard, and his wife. He opened the pub for all the pickets in 1995 in the same way that the pub had been a central focal point of the 1989 strike. It was a 'picket centre' throughout the 1995 dispute open from early morning for tea and toast to late morning for beer.
27. 'Government Minister denies TGWU claim over Liverpool dockers'. LabourNet, available: http://www.labournet.net/docks2/9710/GOVMIN.HTM
28. Dockers' Leaflet 'Time to Organise...?' Liverpool Docks Dispute Update
29. ibid.
30. Father Michael De Felice Interview with Roger Phillips: BBC Radio Merseyside, Friday 24 October 1997

31. Peter Jones Interview with Roger Phillips: BBC Radio Merseyside, Friday 24 October 1997
32. ibid.
33. ibid.
34. Roger Phillips: BBC Radio Merseyside, Monday 27 October 1997. See also: Kevin Robinson Notes on Mass Meeting 31 October 1997 and personal papers.
35. ibid.
36. Roger Phillips: BBC Radio Merseyside, Monday 27 October 1997
37. ibid.
38. ibid.
39. J. Freeman, Irish Regional Secretary, Amalgamated T&GWU, Ireland to Mr. W. Morris, General Secretary, T&GWU 27 October 1997, LabourNet, available: http://www.labournet.net/docks2/9710/ITGWU.HTM
40. 'Liverpool Dockers Picket Mersey Docks Vessel in Dublin' by Greg Dropkin, LabourNet, available: http://www.labournet.net/docks2/9710/DUBLIN.HTM
41. ibid.
42. ibid.
43. 'Mick O'Rielly – From Lucifer to Lazarus' Lilliput Press 2019 pp.134-135
44. ibid. 'Liverpool Fights On! 220 – 97 Rejection' October 1997
45. ibid. pp.134
46. ibid. See also: Kevin Robinson Notes on Mass Meeting 31 October 1997.
47. 'Liverpool Dockers Picket Mersey Docks Vessel in Dublin' by Greg Dropkin, LabourNet, available: http://www.labournet.net/docks2/9710/DUBLIN.HTM See also: Mick O'Rielly – From Lucifer to Lazarus Lilliput Press 2019 pp.134-135
48. M. Carden Notes Monday 28 October 1997
49. M. Carden Notes Friday 31 October 1997
50. ibid.
51. 'The Case for the Re-instatement of the Sacked Liverpool Dockers – The Need for a Public Inquiry into the MDHC.' LabourNet, available: http://www.labournet.net/docks2/9707/BOOKLET.HTM See also: M. Carden Notes on Meeting in Parliament 5 November 1997
52. M. Carden Notes on Meeting in Parliament 5 November 1997
53. M. Carden Notes 6 November
54. ibid.
55. ibid.
56. ibid.
57. ibid.
58. K. Robinson Notes on Mass Meeting 7 November 1997
59. M. Carden Notes 7 November
60. 'Liverpool NHS Win Tupe and Face Dole' by G.Dropkin , LabourNet, available: http://www.labournet.net/docks2/9711/NHS.HTM M. Carden Notes Monday 10 November 1997
61. ibid.
62. ibid.
63. M. Carden Notes Friday 15 November 1997
64. 'Liverpool Pickets Shut Cardiff Docks for Two Hours' by Greg Dropkin, LabourNet November 1997, available: http://www.labournet.net/docks2/9711/CARDIFF1.HTM
65. ibid.
66. ibid.
67. ibid.
68. M. Carden Notes Tuesday 18 November 1997
69. Liverpool Echo 'Truce Thanks' Letter Pages 27 November 1997
70. ibid. This office in which 'Hal' lived, was donated to the dockers by TGWU Officer, Mickey Dunne, a respected rank and file union official.
71. ibid.
72. Kevin Robinson Notes of meeting with Sefton Council 20 November 1997

## 77 - The Neptune Jade Picket

1. Medway Ports Handbook 1996, p.11
2. Letter to ILWU, J. Nolan, Reproduced in LabourNet 18 November 1997, available: http://www.labournet.net/docks2/9711/ROBERT.HTM See also: 'The Voyage of the "Neptune Jade"', LabourNet, available: http://www.labournet.net/docks2/other/NEPTUNE.HTM
3. ibid.
4. ILWU Dispatcher November 1997 'The ILWU Fights McCarthyite Witchhunt', LabourNet November 1997, available: http://www.labournet.net/docks2/9711/ILWUJADE.HTM
5. ibid.
6. ibid.
7. ibid.
8. ibid.
9. ibid.
10. ibid.
11. ibid.
12. ibid.
13. ibid.
14. ibid. See also Jack Heyman article by email sent to M. Carden 22 June 2015
15. ibid.
16. ibid.
17. Bay Area Guinness Fleadh June 1998 - Interview by Steve Zeltzer, Labour on the Job. Alice Nutter, vocalist with Chumbawamba

Transcription by Lauri Truitt
http://www.labournet.net/docks2/9809/chumba.htm

18. Neptune Jade Defence Committee Public Announcement November 30 1998 Robert Irminger and Jack Heyman - http://www.labournet.net/docks2/9811/neptune2.htm

19. ibid.

## 78 - The TGWU's new London Office

1. Peter Clee Interviewed for Ken Loach's Film, The Flickering Flame 1996. See also: http://en.labournet.tv/video/6066/flickering-flame and 'Employment Rights in the Dock? A Bureau Experience of a Modern Labour Dispute' Citizens Advice Bureau: February 1997 and also M. Carden Notes Thursday 20 November 1997

2. M. Carden Diary Friday 28 November 1997
3. ibid.
4. Dockers' Leaflet for Lobby of the GEC, 7am Monday 1 December 1997, LabourNet November 1997, available: http://www.labournet.net/docks2/9711/LOBBY.HTM
5. ibid. See also: M. Carden Notes Monday 1 December 1997
6. M. Carden Notes from GEC, London, 1 December 1997
7. ibid.
8. ibid.
9. ibid.
10. ibid.
11. ibid.
12. ibid.
13. ibid.
14. ibid.
15. ibid.
16. ibid.
17. ibid.
18. ibid.
19. ibid.
20. ibid.
21. ibid.
22. ibid.
23. ibid.
24. BBC Radio Merseyside Roger Phillips Phone-in Programme, 1 December 1997
25. M. Carden M. Carden Notes 3 December 1997. See also: Kevin Robinson Notes from Port Shop Stewards' Meeting held in Transport House, Liverpool on Wednesday 3 December 1997
26. M. Carden Notes from GEC, London, 1 December 1997. See also: Kevin Robinson Notes from Port Shop Stewards' Meeting held in Transport House, Liverpool on Wednesday 3 December 1997

27. K. Robinson Notes from Port Shop Stewards' Meeting 3 December 1997
28. M. Carden M. Carden Notes 3 December 1997 and also K. Robinson Notes on Meeting 3 December 1997
29. ibid.
30. ibid.
31. ibid. The 'business as usual' statement was used again by Bobby Morton at the following Shop Stewards Meeting held on Monday 8 December 1997, see: K. Robinson Notes on meeting held in Transport House, Liverpool, 8 December 1997
32. ibid.
33. M. Carden M. Carden Notes 3 December 1997 and also K. Robinson Notes on Meeting 3 December 1997
34. ibid.
35. 'Unexpected Guests at Mersey Docks' by Greg Dropkin, LabourNet December 1997, available: http://www.labournet.net/docks2/9712/UNEXPEC.HTM
36. ibid.
37. ibid.

## 79 - And in the End

1. M. Carden Notes of Port Shop Stewards Committee Meeting, Transport House, Liverpool Monday 3 December 1997 and also K. Robinson Notes on PSS Meeting 8 December 1997
2. ibid.
3. M. Carden Notes of Port Shop Stewards Committee Meeting, Transport House, Liverpool Monday 8 December 1997
4. ibid.
5. ibid.
6. ibid.
7. ibid.
8. ibid.
9. ibid.
10. ibid.
11. ibid.
12. M. Carden Notes on Port Shop Stewards Meeting 9 December 1997 See also K. Robinson Notes on meeting in Transport House 9 December 1997
13. ibid.
14. ibid.
15. ibid.
16. ibid.
17. ibid.
18. M. Carden Diary 12 December 1997
19. ibid.
20. ibid.
21. M. Carden Notes Monday 17 December 1997 and also K. Robinson Notes 17 December 1997

22. Pauline Bradley and Chris Knight 'Another World is Possible: How the Liverpool Docker Launched a Global Movement RAG 2004 pp.24-25

23. M. Carden Notes Wednesday 17 December 1997 - See also M. Carden Notes from 30 December 1997 and K. Robinson Notes on Mass Meeting 19 December 1997

24. M. Carden Notes Wednesday 17 December 1997 - See also M. Carden Notes from 30 December 1997

25. M. Carden Notes Tuesday 30 December 1997

26. ibid.

27. Catholic Pictorial 'Dockers' Hardship Fund only pays £15 a week' Matt Cole 4 January 1998 p.4

28. ibid.

29. ibid.

30. M. Carden's Notes Tuesday 30 December 1998

31. K. Robinson Notes from PSS Meeting 13 January 1998

32. K. Robinson Notes on WOW Meeting 14 January 1998

33. ibid.

34. 'The T&GWU General Secretary's View, and Ours' Interview with Terry Teague, by Greg Dropkin, LabourNet January 1998, available: http://www.labournet.net/docks2/9801/TERRY.HTM

35. ibid.

## 80 - The End of the Liverpool Dock Dispute

1. K. Robinson Notes on Shop Stewards Meeting on Thursday 15 January 1998

2. ibid.

3. M. Carden Notes on Mass Meeting Friday 16 January 1998

4. K. Robinson Notes on Mass Meeting Friday 16 January 1998

5. M. Carden Notes on Mass Meeting Friday 16 January 1998

6. Dockers' Support Group Meeting Minutes Saturday 17 January 1998

7. M. Carden notes on Dockers Support Group Meeting Minutes Saturday 17 January 1998

8. ibid.

9. K. Robinson Notes on Port Shop Stewards Meeting 20 January1998

10. ibid.

11. K. Robinson Notes on Port Shop Stewards Meeting 22 January 1998

12. M. Carden Notes on Port Shop Stewards Meeting 22 January 1998

13. ibid.

14. ibid.

15. ibid. See also: K. Robinson Notes on PSS Thursday 22 January 1998

16. M. Carden Notes from Mass Meeting Thursday 22 January 1998

17. ibid. See also: Port Shop Stewards on the same day.

18. ibid.

19. ibid.

20. K. Robinson Notes on Mass Meeting and PSS held on 22 January 1998

21. M. Carden Notes from Thursday 22 January 1998

22. M. Carden Notes from Mass Meeting Thursday 22 January 1998 and also Port Shop Stewards on the same day.

23. ibid.

24. ibid.

25. M. Carden Notes Friday 23 January 1998

26. K. Robinson Notes of PSS 23 January 1998

27. M. Carden Notes Friday 23 January 1998

28. M. Carden Notes form PSS Meeting and Mass Meeting held on Friday 23 January 1998.

29. M. Carden Notes form PSS Meeting and Mass Meeting held on Monday 26 January 1998.

30. ibid.

31. ibid.

32. M. Carden Notes form PSS Meeting and Mass Meeting held on Monday 26 January 1998.

33. ibid.

34. ibid. See also: MDHC Basis of Agreement with the Port Operations Workers Formerly Employed by the MDHC and Coastal Container Line Issued 26 January 1998: Mike Carden spoke of the extraordinary and unique nature of the Liverpool dock workers' dispute and the need 'to continue with dignity and respect'. See also: K. Robinson Notes on Mass Meeting 26 January 1998.

35. K. Robinson notes on Mass Meeting 26 January 1998

36. ibid.

37. M. Carden Notes on Mass Meeting 26 January 1998 and also K. Robinson Notes on Mass Meeting Monday 26 January 1998.

38. ibid.

39. M. Carden Notes from PSS Meeting and Mass Meeting held on Monday 26 January 1998.

40. ibid.

41. K. Robinson Notes on Mass Meeting 26 January 1998

42. ibid.

43. M. Carden Notes on Mass Meeting 26 January 1998 and also K. Robinson notes on Mass Meeting 26 January 1998.

44. ibid.

45. K. Robinson Notes from Mass Meeting 26 January 1998

46. ibid.

47. ibid.

48. M. Carden Notes from PSS Meeting and Mass Meeting Monday 26 January 1998

49. ibid.

50. ibid.
51. ibid.
52. ibid.
53. ibid.
54. ibid.
55. ibid.
56. ibid.
57. ibid.
58. ibid.
59. ibid.
60. ibid. See also: 'Liverpool dockers dispute is over' LabourNet 26 January 1998, available: http://www.labournet.net/docks2/9801/EN DED.HTM
61. 'The Flame that Lit the World' Statement by the Liverpool Dockers' Victory Defense Committee Oakland San Francisco 28 January 1998, LabourNet, available: http://www.labournet.net/docks2/9801/FLA ME.HTM
62. ibid.
63. ibid.
64. ibid.
65. Jimmy Nolan quoted in Channel 4 Learning, available: http://www.channel4learning.com/support/p rogrammenotes/netnotes/section/printyes/se ctionid100663623_printyes.htm
66. BBC Radio Merseyside, R. Phillips, Monday evening 26 January 1998
67. ibid.
68. ibid.
69. ibid.
70. ibid.
71. BBC Radio Merseyside, R. Phillips, Tuesday 27 January 1998
72. ibid.
73. ibid.
74. ibid.
75. ibid.
76. K. Robinson Notes on PSS Wednesday 28 January 1998
77. ibid.
78. K. Robinson Notes of Women of the Waterfront Meeting Wednesday 28 January 1998
79. ibid.
80. M. Carden Notes Thursday 29 January 1998 see also K. Robinson notes on PSS Meeting 29.1.1998
81. ibid.
82. M. Carden Notes Friday 30 January 1998
83. ibid.
84. ibid. See also: K. Robinson Notes on Mass Meeting 30 January 1998 and also K. Robinson and M. Carden - Notes on PSS Wednesday 28 January 1998

**PART FOUR: The aftermath of the dispute and the legacy of the Liverpool Dockers**

## 81 - Settling Old Scores

1. 'Dockers Betrayed by Morris and Local Leaders', News Line, 28 January 1998
2. ibid.
3. Tony Benn MP 'Free at Last – Diaries 1991-2001' Arrow Books 2003 p.460
4. 'The Dog that's had its Day' by D. Charters, Liverpool Daily Post, 29 January 1998
5. Western Hemisphere Conference—Liverpool Dockers: Defend the ILO Conventions! Available: http://www.hartford-hwp.com/archives/61/070.html
6. 'The working-class history in general of the United Kingdom', available: www.hartford-hwp.com/archives/61/index-dda.html
7. Western Hemisphere Conference—Liverpool Dockers: Defend the ILO Conventions! Available: http://www.hartford-hwp.com/archives/61/070.html
8. The Guardian: Letters Page, 29 January 1998, Bill Morris
9. The Guardian 1 February 1998
10. 'Dockers: They can't live on fresh air', Catholic Pictorial 1 February 1998
11. Mrs. Joan Grocott 'Father Michael's A Giant Among Men' p.21, The Catholic Pictorial: Letters Page, 8 February 1998. See also: Joan Grocott 'Letter to Tony Blair, Prime Minister', 5 October 1997 from Kevin Robinson's Archive.
12. 'Yellow Pages – Yellow Wages in Our Union' by Mark Steel, The Guardian 3 February 1998
13. Letter from Bill Morris, Letters, The Guardian 3 February 1998, text available: http://www.labournet.net/docks2/9802/MO RRIS2.HTM
14. Greg Dropkin – Democracy and the Union: A Reply to Bill Morris LabourNet February 1998 hyttp://www.labournet.net/docks2/9802/GR EG.HTM
15. ibid.
16. Trade Union Review: Issue No.16 April-May 1999 Trade Union Review: J. Barnes
17. Graham Stevenson's website: www.grahamstevenson.me.uk
18. Trade Union Review: Issue No.16 April-May 1999 Trade Union Review: J. Barnes

## 82 - Part of the Union? Scab Labour?

1. LabourNet March 1998 and 'The Dart': Issue No.3 1 February 1998, available: http://www.labournet.net/docks2/9803/TG WU.HTM

2.  'A Question for the TGWU. Are you recruiting Drakes?', LabourNet, available: http://www.labournet.net/docks2/9803/TGWU.HTM

3.  Robert Michels 'Political Parties: A Sociological Study of the Oligarchical Tendencies of Modern Democracy', Collier Books Edition 1962 p.371

4.  The Dart Issue No.3 1 February 1998, available: http://www.labournet.net/docks2/9803/TGWU.HTM

5.  ibid.

6.  ibid.

7.  'Port of Liverpool strike threat averted after deal is struck' Bill Gleeson, Liverpool Echo 3 July 2015

8.  M. Carden Diary Monday 2 February 1998

9.  K. Robinson Notes on PSS 2 February 1998

10. ibid.

11. M. Carden Notes Tuesday 3 February 1998

12. ibid.

13. Dave Sinclair 'Dockers – The '95 to '98 Liverpool Lockout' Amberley Publishing 2015. See also Liverpool in the 1980s, available: www.amberleybooks.com/shop/article_97814 45638157/Liverpool-in-the-1980s.html

14. M. Carden Notes Friday 6 February 1998

15. K. Robinson Notes on PSS 6 February 1998

16. K. Robinson Notes on PSS and Mass Meeting 6 February 1998

17. ibid.

18. M. Carden Notes on PSS and Mass Meeting 6 February 1998

19. M. Carden Notes on Mass Meeting 6 February 1998 and also K. Robinson Notes on Mass Meeting 6 February 1998

20. M. Carden Notes Support Group Meeting Saturday 7 February 1998

21. ibid.

22. ibid.

23. ibid.

24. ibid.

25. ibid.

26. ibid.

27. ibid.

28. ibid.

29. ibid.

30. ibid.

31. ibid.

32. ibid.

33. ibid.

34. ibid.

35. ibid.

36. ibid.

37. ibid.

38. 'Hard lessons from the Liverpool Docks Lock-Out' Chris Marsden – 14.2.98, available: https://www.wsws.org/en/articles/1998/02/live See also: Noel Castree 'Geographic Scale and Grass-Roots Internationalism: The Liverpool Dock Dispute, 1995–1998' School of Geography, Manchester University, available: http://onlinelibrary.wiley.com/doi/10.1111/j.1944-8287.2000.tb00144.x/abstract

39. 'Liverpool Dockers End 28 Month Fight': P. Davies and D. Delange, The Militant Vol.62/No.10, March 16 1998, available: http://www.themilitant.com/1998/6210/6210_6.html

40. Dockers Charter 1997

## 83 - The Initiative Factory and the CASA

1.  M. Carden Notes Monday 9 February 1998 Also K. Robinson Notes on PSS Meeting 9 February 1998

2.  K. Robinson Notes on PSS Meeting 9 February 1998

3.  The Guardian 11 February 1998. See also: http://www.theguardian.com/theguardian/from-the-archive-blog/2014/sep/24/john-prescott-brit-awards-chumbawamba-1988 See also: K. Robinson Notes on Mass Meeting 13 February 1998

4.  ibid. See also https://en.wikipedia.org/wiki/Tubthumping

5.  ibid.

6.  K. Robinson Notes on Mass Meeting 13 February 1998

7.  'Reflecting on Liverpool' by G. Dropkin, LabourNet July 1998, available: http://www.labournet.net/docks2/9807/reflect.htm

8.  'Pension Shortfall Soars at Mersey', Evening Standard 20 August 2002

9.  Liverpool Echo 20 September 2005

10. M. Carden Notes Wednesday 17 February 1998

11. ibid.

12. Tony Mulhearn 'The Making of a Liverpool Militant' 47booksliverpool 2019 pp.158-161. See also: M. Carden Notes Thursday 19 February 1998

13. Email from Doreen McNally to the author 20/10/17: 'In the summing up, at the writer's workshop it wasn't WOW.' See also: D. McNally email to author 2.11.19: 'During the writers workshop for the film Dockers, Jimmy Davies Jnr. and not sure who other one was, either Bob Richie or Tony Melia, said there was a meeting in Ninas bar, and the stewards told Torside to put the picket line up at seaforth... Jimmy Campbell was furious, he started shouting that they had no right and if his and other mens' pension was affected there was going to be murder. The dispute had just ended, 28 months of unity, feelings were

running high. The men had always been told there was no meeting in ninas bar. Fearful of a massive fallout I went to the boardroom and said what had happened. Frank Lannigan went down and told the men that there was no meeting in Ninas bar.'

14. Liverpool Echo 20 September 2005
15. See: 'Dockers' Finalised Shooting Script dated 19 February 1999
16. Liverpool Echo 20 September 2005
17. Des Warren (10 October 1937 – 24 April 2004) was a construction worker, trade union activist and Ricky Tomlinson, one of the Shrewsbury Two imprisoned for conspiracy to intimidate whilst picketing in Shropshire in 1972. His autobiography, 'The Key To My Cell.' In 2013, Ricky Tomlinson continued to campaign for Warren's name to be posthumously cleared
18. The Independent Friday 2 July 1999
19. 'OVERNIGHT RATINGS - Channel 4 strikes out with Dockers drama' Dockers Broadcast Date 16 July 1999, see: www.broadcastnow.co.uk/overnight-ratings-channel-4-strikes-out-with-dockers-drama/1217157.article
20. 'Union Leader is Traitor in dockers' Film' by Fiachra Gibbons, The Guardian 2 July 1999
21. ibid.
22. ibid.
23. ibid.
24. ibid.
25. John Bohanna 'Dockers': 'Five Minutes Experience Is Worth Fifty Years of Reading'. A drama made for British television of a real-life struggle against dismissal and betrayal: A Review 26 July 1999 see: www.labournet.de/internationales/FILM.HTM
26. ibid.
27. ibid.
28. ibid.
29. M. Carden Notes Thursday 19 February 1998
30. See: IF Letter to Members – Re: DfEE Individual Learning Accounts 12 February 2001
31. Professor P. Fowler: letter to Liverpool City Council on 29 Hope Street. June 19 1998) His support for the dockers was also linked to his wish to build Liverpool's first 'Digital Quarter'. (Internal Fax: LJMU Peter Fowler 17 July 1998)
32. M. Carden Notes Thursday 19 February 1998
33. M. Carden Notes on TGWU Region 6 F&GP Monday 23.2.1998
34. M. Carden Notes Tuesday 24 February 1998
35. ibid.
36. ibid.
37. M. Carden Notes Wednesday 25 February 1998

38. ibid.
39. ibid.
40. ibid. and also 'Discussion Document and Information Update: February 1998 LSO/Opportunities in Continuing/Further Education and Information Technology Courses'. K. Robinson archive. See also The Economist, 'The Leaving of Liverpool' August 13 1998 See also LabourNet 'Casualization – Dockers Prove Charges' available: http://www.labournet.net/docks2/9605/CASUAL.HTM
41. ibid.
42. M. Carden Notes General Executive Council, Eastbourne, 2 March 1998
43. K. Robinson Notes from Mass Meeting 2 March 1998
44. ibid. Mike Morris would eventually help establish the Writing on the Wall project which he is still involved with at Toxteth Library see: https://www.writingonthewall.org.uk/wow-publications.html
45. K. Robinson Notes on Turkish and Kurdish Support Group Meeting in Parliament 10 March 1998
46. M. Carden Notes 10 March 1998
47. ibid. When the dockers were at George Knibb's, North Liverpool Regeneration Company at the old site of Bishop Goss School.
48. M. Carden Notes Friday 13 March 1998 A Settlement Agreement is a legally binding agreement between an employer and an employee. Usually, the employee accepts a sum of money in return for agreeing to give up his or her rights to pursue or bring future claims against the employer in return for a payment. You must also receive advice on the terms of the Settlement Agreement and their effect by an independent solicitor or relevant adviser.
49. K. Robinson Notes on Mass Meeting Friday 13 March 1998
50. M. Carden Notes 13 March 1998
51. M. Carden Notes on Mass Meeting 13 March 1998
52. M. Carden Diary Monday 16 March 1998
53. M. Carden Diary 14 May 1998
54. K. Robinson Notes on WOW and Hillsborough Support Group Monday 16th.March 1998 see also M. Carden diary Monday 16 March 1998
55. M. Carden Diary Tuesday 17 March 1998
56. M. Carden Notes Thursday 19 March 1998
57. M. Carden Notes of Merseyside TEC meeting 20 March 1998
58. ibid. M. Carden notes Monday 23 March 1998
59. M. Carden Diary 15 May 1998
60. M. Carden Notes Tuesday 24 March 1998
61. M. Carden Notes 24 March 1998
62. M. Carden Notes 27 March 1998

63. ibid.
64. ibid. Shaping San Francisco – Excavating the City's Lost History http://www.shapingsf.org/found-sf.html
65. M. Carden Notes on PSS 27 March 1998 M. Carden Notes 26 March 1998 and also K. Robinson Notes on Meeting 27 March 1998 - and also Dot Gibson, 'Report on meeting with Merseyside Port Shop Stewards' 26 March 1998
66. ibid.
67. 'Hillsborough Disaster: Deadly Mistakes and Lies that Lasted Decade' David Conn - The Guardian, 26 April 2016, available: https://www.theguardian.com/football/2016/apr/26/hillsborough-disaster-deadly-mistakes-and-lies-that-lasted-decades
68. Jack Hughes – The Tribune 30.3.98 see also http://www.hartford-hwp.com/archives/61/index-dda.html
69. ibid.
70. K. Robinson Notes on Mass Meeting, 17 April 1998
71. At a shop stewards meeting on 29 April 1998 a discussion also took place on Bobby Morton who had now applied for a full-time officer's job with the TGWU. M. Carden M. Carden Notes 17 April 1998 - Bobby became a National Official of UNITE representing workers at national and international level. M. Carden Notes 22.4.1998 K. Robinson Notes on PSS Meeting 29 April 1998
72. Email correspondence from D. Cotterill to M. Carden 27/10/2018 chomsky@MIT.EDU To: davycott@AOL.COM from May 1998
73. Email correspondence from D. Cotterill to M. Carden 27/10/2018 chomsky@MIT.EDU To: davycott@AOL.COM from May 1998
74. Email correspondence between Jack Heyman and Noam Chomsky 22 October 2018 quoted in letter for 'Mumia Abu-Jamal and the Struggle to Defend Jeremy Corbyn'.
75. M. Carden Diary 29.4.1998/ 22 May and 27 May 1999
76. if… is a 1968 British drama film produced and directed by Lindsay Anderson satirising English public school life. See also: J.P. Sartre Being and Nothingness Washington Square Press 1992 p.102 and also M. Carden Notes Wednesday 29 April
77. M. Carden Diary 21.7.99
78. Commissioned in 1998 for Britain's Art Transpennine exhibition, SuperLambBanana is one of the most popular and instantly recognisable pieces of public sculpture in Liverpool. The SuperLambBanana was the work of the Japanese artist Taro Chiezo. Now based in Manhattan, Taro was one of his country's most successful visual artists of the last fifteen years. Through the

SuperLambBanana, Taro aimed to represent both a sense of humour alongside the serious contemporary issue of genetic engineering.
79. AMIP letter from Elisabeth Marliangeas and Xavier Carniaux: Paris 24 February 1996
80. The story of the Casa, available: http://socialcentrestories.wordpress.com/2008/04/29/the-casa-liverpool/

## 84 - The CASA

1. 'Fresh Start – Sacked dockers open night club' The Guardian 21 December 2000
2. http://socialcentrestories.wordpress.com/2008/04/29/the-casa-liverpool/
3. 'Liverpool Dockers New Address' LabourNet, available: http://www.labournet.net/docks2/0003/liver1.htm
4. M. Carden Notes 21 March 2000 and 14/20March 2000 and M. Carden IF Financial Review July 2000
5. See: the Initiative Factory http://www.initiativefactory.org/business See also: https://unitecasacommunitybranch.wordpress.com/tag/bob-crow/
6. Bob Crow – General Secretary of RMT died 11 March 2014
7. http://www.tusc.org.uk/history/ - Jimmy Nolan wrote at the time that he was: 'Convinced that there was a need for such a working-class party.' TUSC was founded by workers, especially some Liverpool dockers - The purpose of the movement was to build a mass party of the working class to establish social justice, democratic rights and public control of the means of production, distribution and exchange, with the aim of establishing a socialist society to end the capitalist system of exploitation, and towards this end to build a united movement of workers at home and internationally.'
8. 'Liverpool Biennial: Misery on the Mersey', by Zoe Pilger, The Independent 6 July 2014 - 'Despite a few wonderful works, the Liverpool Biennial is a dull show that fails to address the impact of the devastating cuts suffered by the city'. See also: 'The Scandalous Decay of a Brilliant Representation of Liverpool's Radical Past' available: https://gerryco23.wordpress.com/2014/10/30/the-scandalous-decay-of-a-brilliant-representation-of-liverpools-radical-past/#more-21539 – The Hardman Street building, which opened its doors in May 1983, served a wide variety of purposes with conference and function rooms for trade unions and other organisations, a Welfare Rights Advice Centre, a small theatre cum

cinema, a basement recording studio, a bar which had a bust of Marx placed (ironically?) next to the till, and the famous Flying Picket music venue, organised by Phil Hayes, developed with funding from artists including Paul McCartney, Elvis Costello, Yoko Ono and Pete Townsend.

9. 'Merseyside Stars Perform for CASA Solidarity Show' Liverpool Echo 17 April 2015

10. https://unitecasacommunitybranch.wordpress.com/ – The Casa Community Branch is the fastest growing Unite Community Branch in the UK. Since its launch in January 2012, we have met at the Casa on Hope Street at 11:00am on the last Saturday of each the month, with many meetings standing room only. At present out of nearly 600 members, 50% are female, 50% are male. See also: 'TUC 150th Anniversary – Dockers Sacked for Refusing to Cross A Picket Line Create Hub to help other workers in Need' by Brian Reade, Daily Mirror 5 September 2018. See also: https://www.msn.com/en-gb/news/world/tuc-150th-anniversary-dockers-sacked-for-refusing-to-cross-picket-line-create-hub-to-help-workers-in-need/ar-BBMSFEc?li=BBoPWjQ&ocid=mailsignout

11. 'DWP Probe into tragic six stone Stephen Smith insists department followed 'followed policy' repeatedly denying him vital benefits.' by Liam Thorpe, Liverpool Echo 19 June 2019

12. Unite the Union – Unite Community Membership, available: https://unitetheunion.org/why-join/membership-types/community-membership/ http://www.unitetheunion.org/growing-our-union/communitymembership/http://www.unitetheunion.org/growing-our-union/communitymembership/communitymembershipbenefits/

13. Sheila Coleman fought the closure and supported the occupation of the Irish Centre in Liverpool and was a prominent Hillsborough campaigner. In one interview she said: 'Over the years I've learned how to speak on behalf of campaigns, and on a personal level I don't like being the focal point, but if you feel you can make a difference you overcome your personal feelings. Plus, I'm a big supporter of Jeremy Corbyn – he has injected humanity back into politics. He's encouraged me by his actions and commitment and encouraged a new generation.' Liverpool Echo 29 September 2016. See also: 'I walked one way the less fortunate walked another' by Kevin Sampson, The Guardian 16 September 2012. Also: The Community Union was formed from the Iron and Steel Trade Confederation, the Power

Loom Carpet Weaver and Textile Workers Union and others see: http://www.community-tu.org/about-community/our-history/ 'Transforming Trade Unionism in the Modern World' http://www.community-tu.org/transforming-trade-unionism-in-the-modern-world/

14. Owen Jones 'Chavs - The Demonization of the Working Class - In modern Britain', Verso 2012

## 85 - A Return to Organised Labour

1. 'Casual Dock Death Boss 'Not Guilty' of Manslaughter' LabourNet, 29 November 2001, available: http://www.labournet.net/docks2/0111/sjones1.htm See also: www.simonjones.org.uk and action@simon.org.uk

2. ibid.

3. ibid. See also: 'Death on the Docks – The Short Life and Violent End of Simon Jones' by Barrie Clement, The Independent 1 March 1999

4. www.simonjones.org.uk

5. A. Gentile and S. Tarrow (2009). 'Charles Tilly, Globalization, and Labour's Citizen Rights.' European Political Science Review, 1, pp 465-493. Available: doi:10.1017/S175577390999018X.

6. A. Lees, 'Liverpool – The Hurricane Port' Mainstream Publishing 2013 edition, pp. 229-230

7. Mersey Docks Shop Stewards Committee. Source: Reclaim The Streets/SCHNews 136 26 September 1997, available: http://www.urban75.com/Action/dockers.html

8. '1907 Dockers and Carters Strike' by Peter Hadden, available: www.marxists.org/history/etol/writers/hadden/2007/05/belfast1907.htm

9. The Dart (5 March 1998) & The Dart (1 February 1998) available: http://www.hartford-hwp.com/archives/61/069.html See also: Merseyside Socialist Organisation 'Drake Employees on Merseyside Suffer Same Conditions as Striking Dockers are Fighting' See also: Liverpool Daily Post 'Powder Keg on the Docks' Tuesday 3 April 2001

10. ibid.

11. 'Powder Keg on the Docks' Liverpool Daily Post, Tuesday 3 April 2001

12. ibid.

13. ibid.

14. BBC Radio Merseyside Roger Phillips Thursday 5 April 2001

15. 'A Last Stand for Dockers' by Barry Turnbull, Liverpool Daily Post, 29 May 2001

16. ibid.

17. ibid.

18. 'Union take dock dispute men' by Barry Turnbull, Liverpool Daily Post 13 July 2001

19. ibid. See also: Liverpool Echo 13 July 2001

20. ibid.

21. ibid.

22. Liverpool Daily Post and Echo 16 July 2001

23. 'Labour Sells Its Shares in MDHC' by Jack Hughes, The Tribune 2 April 1998. See also: http://www.hartford-hwp.com/archives/61/index-dda.html and Dow Schofield Watts 'Takeover Bid for Mersey Docks' 11 November 2004, available: http://www.dswcf.com/takeover-bid-for-mersey-docks/

24. ibid.

25. Street of Walls Private Equity Investment http://www.streetofwalls.com/finance-training-courses/private-equity-training/private-equity-investment-criteria/

26. 'We have to have regard for 900 people still working in the port of Liverpool.' (Bill Morris, Author's Notes from Special GEC 19 June 1996). See also: BBC Radio Merseyside ACL/docks archive interviews tapes 1995-1996: June 1996. See also: M Carden Notes on Shop Steward/TGWU/Dock Company negotiations at ACAS Offices on Thursday 7 November 1996

27. 'The Biggest Company you've never heard of: Lifting the Lid on Peel Group – The Property Firm owned by the Reclusive Tax Exile John Whittaker' The Independent 18 October 2013. See also: 'Peel Holdings Beast Exposed in Salford and Liverpool' in Salford Star 4 April 2013, available: http://www.salfordstar.com/article.asp?id=1761

28. 'The Man Who Built Peel Holdings' Manchester Evening News 30 June 2005

29. 'Mersey says bid costs have hit £7m profits' Alistair Osbourne, The Daily Telegraph 16 March 2005

30. '771m Deal to Buy Out Docks' Liverpool Echo 9 June 2005. See also: 'Painless Takeover brings dock era to an end. Peel Holdings Now Own MDHC' by Larry Neild, The Free Library, available: http://www.thefreelibrary.com/Painless+takeover+brings+docks+era+to+an+end%3B+Peel+Holdings+now+owns...-a0136496435 September 22nd.2005

31. ibid.

32. 'The Biggest Company you've never heard of: Lifting the Lid on Peel Group – The Property Firm owned by the Reclusive Tax Exile John Whittaker' The Independent 18 October 2013.

33. 'Painless Takeover brings dock era to an end. Peel Holdings Now Own MDHC' by Larry

Neild, The Free Library, 22 September 2005 available: http://www.thefreelibrary.com/Painless+takeover+brings+docks+era+to+an+end%3B+Peel+Holdings+now+owns...-a0136496435 See also: https://en.wikipedia.org/wiki/Mersey_Docks_and_Harbour_CompSEEany#History

34. 'The Biggest Company you've never heard of: Lifting the Lid on Peel Group' – Peter Kilfoyle, The Independent 18 October 2013 See also: http://www.liverpoolconfidential.co.uk/news-and-comment/liverpool-more-party-town-than-powerhouse - 'Peel Holdings Beast Exposed in Salford and Liverpool' Salford Star 4 April 2013, available: http://www.salfordstar.com/article.asp?id=1761

35. Karl Marx 'Capital', Vol:1, Chapter Six - The Buying and Selling of Labour Power. See also: https://www.marxists.org/archive/marx/works/1867-c1/ch06.htm

36. This arrangement was positively referenced in confidential correspondence from Peel Ports Group to Len McCluskey dated 11 June 2020

37. 'Port of Liverpool dockers to vote on strike action in pay dispute' Bill Gleeson, Liverpool Echo 11 June 2015

38. ibid.

39. ibid.

40. ibid.

41. ibid. See also: Liverpool Echo 19 October 2014. See also: 'Liverpool Docks Dispute Twenty-Years On – How dockworkers paid with their jobs for refusing to cross a picket line' by Paddy Shennan, Liverpool Echo 20 September 2015 Also: 'British Firm in talks on Liverpool takeover' by Janet Porter, Journal of Commerce 14 October 1987

42. ibid. 'Urgent talks called for Port of Liverpool Workers' Unite the Union 17 October 2014, available: http://www.unitetheunion.org/news/urgent-talks-called-for-as-port-of-liverpool-workers-transferred-to-new-employer/

43. Statement issued by Blue Arrow and Peel Ports in an email to the author from Liverpool dock shop steward, John Lynch. 11 January 2018: 'The Blue Arrow 32 Boatmen will be transferred to Briggs Marine...Blue Arrow will be notified of this decision tomorrow Tuesday 9th January...'

44. Blue Arrow Transition Statement - Peel Ports Brings Agency Staff In-House – Alex Flynn Head of Media & Campaigns Unite 10 January 2018. See also: John Lynch, Liverpool dockers' leader email to supporters along with the press release that accompanied this email on 12

December 2018. UNITE the Union/Peel Ports - Pay and Conditions Package 2018-2021

45. ibid.
46. R. James email to A. Flynn UNITE Head of Media and Campaigns 28 November 2018
47. 'Peel Ports Team Up to Boost Capacity of UK's Liverpool Container Terminal', Seanews International Shipping Magazine 25 September 2019
48. Liverpool Echo 13 August 2021
49. Liverpool Echo 28 October 2021
50. 'Fair Pay for Key Workers – Back the Strikers!' Unite North West, 8 October 2021. See also: 'No to Fire and Re-hire' by R. James, Unite North-West 25 October 2021
51. Patrick Minot was a highly experienced leader of the Le Havre Dockers – a profoundly well-organised rank and file organisation whose history was as radical and revolutionary as many other port workers. Jules Durand 1880-1926 was the radical founder of dockers' trade unionism in Le Havre who was condemned to death by the French State in 1910 for a crime he did not commit see - ttps://fr.wikipedia.org/wiki/Jules_Durand. Mike Carden and John Lynch, current leader of the Liverpool dockers, attended a celebration of the life of Jules Durand at Le Havre University in November 2016. Mike Carden met with Patrick Minot and other retired Le Havre dockers and joked with them about Patrick's modesty in not wanting to be the 'first General Secretary of the IDC'. Available: http://www.labournet.net/docks2/9610/28OCTLET.HTM See also: M. Carden Diary 28.10.1996 and 18.4.2000. See also LabourNet Report: http://www.labournet.net/docks2/0004/idc1.htm
52. ibid.
53. 'IDC Respond to EU Flexibility Plans' 25 October 2000, LabourNet, available: http://www.labournet.net/docks2/0010/idceu1.htm
54. ibid. The IDC had previously decided in Marseilles to take industrial action if the Committee endorsed the Ports Package. The Swedish Dockworkers Union, the Fédération Nationale de Ports et Docks CGT (France) and the Coordinadora (Spain) took the initiative to call for a 24-hour strike. See also: G. Dropkin LabourNet October 2001 IDC European 24hr. Strike, available: http://www.labournet.net/docks2/0110/euidc1.htm
55. ibid.
56. https://www.idcdockworkers.org/

## 86 – The dismantling of democracy

1. The Union Makes us Strong – TUC Online, available: http://www.unionhistory.info/timeline/1880_1914.php
2. Jim Dye 'Defeated but Still Fighting: The Liverpool Docks Dispute – Some Lessons for Socialists' See: http://www.whatnextjournal.org.uk/Pages/Back/Wnext7/Dockers.html
3. ibid.
4. ibid.
5. ibid.
6. J. Goldstein, 'The Government of British Trade Unions', Allen & Unwin 1952. See also: C. Hanson, 'Taming the Trade Unions', Palgrave McMillan 1991. See also: V.L. Allen 'Power in Trade Unions', Longmans 1954. See also: Sidney & Beatrice Webb 'Industrial Democracy', Longmans 1897. See also: P. Devlin 'Port Transport Industry', HM Stationery Office 1956. See also: the Devlin Report 1965, available: https://hansard.parliament.uk/Commons/1965-07-05/debates/322be598-cd16-4e66-ba77-2d417555af4f/DevlinCommittee(Report)
7. 'The Miners Next Step – Being Suggested a Scheme for the Reorganisation of the Federation' Issued by the Unofficial Reform Committee – Written by Noah Ablett, A. Cook and W. Mainwaring 1912. See also: L. Barrow & I. Bullock 'Democratic Ideas and the British Labour Movement 1880-1914', Cambridge University Press 1996. See also: R. Michels 'Political Parties: A Sociological Study of the Oligarchial Tendencies of Modern Democracy' 1911. See also: Tom Mann 'The Industrial Syndicalist', Spokesman Books November 1910. See also: The Industrial Workers of the World (The Wobblies) founded in 1905 Wobblies of the World - Ed. Cole, Struthers & Zimmer Pluto Press 2017
8. J. Goldstein 'The Government of British Trade Unions – A Study of Apathy and the Democratic Process in the TGWU – Forward by Arthur Deakin', Allen & Unwin 1952. See also: C. Hanson 'Taming the Trade Unions – A Guide to the Thatcher Government's Employment Reforms 1980-1990', Macmillan 1991 p.48.
9. Karen Monaghan QC 'Investigation into Sexual Harassment and the Management of Sexual Harassment Complaints within the GMB' 31 August 2020 – Paragraph 40 p.18 & Paragraph 66 pp.29-30
10. Paul Bracchi - Daily Mail 11 September 2020
11. Letter to the Guardian, John Pilger, text available:

http://www.labournet.net/docks2/9801/TRI
BUTES.HTM#anchor36968

12. Letter to the Guardian, Bill Morris, text
available:
http://www.labournet.net/docks2/9802/MO
RRIS.HTM

13. Workers Liberty 'Lessons from the Liverpool
dockers' dispute' 6 February 1998 available:
http://www.workersliberty.org/node/5344

14. 'After McCluskey:Who will win Unite's crown'
by D. Macintyre, New Statesman 17 July 2020

15. The United Left – Who We Are and What We
Do - https://unitedleft.org.uk/more-about-ul/
See also: 'United Left group expels whole
Scottish affiliate section after selection
dispute', Skwawkbox, available:
https://skwawkbox.org/2021/01/09/exclusiv
e-united-left-group-expels-whole-scottish-
affiliate-after-selection-dispute-scottish-
members-call-on-turner-to-condemn/ See
also: Others explained the reason why the
dockers' leadership failed to achieve
reinstatement was because they did not,
'organise the rank-and-file fight within the
TGWU'. See also: Sqwawkbox 9 January 2021
'United Left' group expels whole Scottish
affiliate after selection dispute.

16. 'Walking Through a Dockers' Picket Line 6
July 2009' by Iain Dale, available: iaindale.com
See also: '27 years ago today the Dock Labour
Scheme was abolished – And here's how I
helped it happen' by Ian Dale 6 April 2016

17. BBC Radio 4 Profile: Sharon Graham, 4
September 2021, available BBC iplayer.

18. D. Cockcroft and K. Marges email group
discussion Mac Urata forwarded to my email
address on 11/10/2021

19. 'Why did Labour use this system to elect its
leader?' by Declan McHugh, New Statesman,
available:
https://www.newstatesman.com/politics/201
5/09/why-did-labour-use-system-elect-its-
leader

20. ibid.

21. 'Labour leadership: Jeremy Corbyn elected
with huge mandate' The Guardian, 12
September 2015, available:
https://www.theguardian.com/politics/2015/
sep/12/jeremy-corbyn-wins-labour-party-
leadership-election

22. ibid.

23. 'Labour leadership: Jeremy Corbyn wins
convincing victory over Owen Smith' by
Heather Stewart Political editor and Rowena
Mason, The Guardian 24 September 2016,
available:
https://www.theguardian.com/politics/2016/
sep/24/labour-leadership-jeremy-corbyn-wins-
landslide-victory-party

24. ibid.

25. 'Why the fuss over mandatory reselection of
Labour MPs? Democracy isn't a job creation
scheme.' by Michael Walker, The New
Statesman, available:
https://www.newstatesman.com/politics/the-
staggers/2018/01/why-fuss-over-mandatory-
reselection-labour-mps-democracy-isn-t-job

26. 'Tony Benn and The Five Essential Questions
of Democracy' by J. Nichols, The Nation 14
March 2014

## 87 – Conclusion

1. 'Dockers defeat TGWU Executive' - A
LabourNet Report, 9 July 1997, available:
http://www.labournet.net/docks2/9707/TG
CONF2.HTM

2. Chumbawamba 'One by One' (song) from
'Rock the Dock' Creation Records 1998, see
also: http://www.metrolyrics.com/one-by-
one-lyrics-chumbawamba.html

3. 'New working life peers unveiled' BBC News,
11 April 2006, available:
http://news.bbc.co.uk/1/hi/uk_politics/4896
620.stm

4. House of Lords Minute of Proceedings for 24
January 2011. Available:
https://publications.parliament.uk/pa/ld2010
11/minutes/110125/ldordpap.htm#minproc

5. Baroness Prosser, 'parliamentary career',
available:
https://members.parliament.uk/member/368
4/career

6. Bill Morris GEC/Finance and General
Purposes Committee Statement Tuesday 17
September 1996 Authors Notes

7. Brian Marren 'We Shall Not be Moved – How
Liverpool's Working-Class Fought
Redundancies, Closures and Cuts in the Age of
Thatcher ', Manchester University Press 2016

# Abbreviations

ABP    Associated British Ports
ACAS  Advisory, Conciliation and Arbitration Service
ACL    Atlantic Container Line
ACTSS Association of Clerical Technical and Supervisory Staffs
AFL-CIO American Federation of Labor-Congress of Industrial Organizations
AUEW  Amalgamated Union of Engineering Workers
BDC    Biennial Delegate Conference (TGWU)
BTB    Belgische TransportbeidersBond
CAST  Belgian container line
CCOO  Comisiones Obreras
CGT    Confédération Général du Travail
COSATU Congress of South African Trade Unions
CPGB  Communist Party of Great Britain
DPDS  Drake Ports Distribution Services
DWNC  Docks and Waterways National Committee
FNV    Federatie Nederlandse Vakbeweging
FOCs  Flags of convenience
FPC    Fair Practices Committee
GEC    General Executive Council of the TGWU
GMB    Britain's General Union
ICP    International Communist Party
IDC    International Dockworkers Council
ILA    International Longshoremen's Association

ILWU  International Longshoremen's and Warehousemen's Union
ITF    International Transport Workers' Federation
KPMG  Klynveld Main Goerdeler Peat Maverick
LSO    Labour Supply Organisation
MDHB Mersey Docks and Harbour Board
MDHC Mersey Docks and Harbour Company
MPSS  Merseyside Port Shop Stewards Committee
MRC   Modern Records Centre
MUA   Maritime Union of Australia
NAPE  National Association of Port Employers
NASD  National Association of Stevedores and Dockers
NDLB  National Dock Labour Board
NDLS  National Dock Labour Scheme
NUDL  National Union of Dock Labourers
NUM   National Union of Mineworkers
PLA    Port of London Authority
POWs  Port Operations Workers
RDW   Registered Dock Workers
TEU    Twenty-foot Equivalent Units
TGWU  Transport and General Workers Union
TUC    Trades Union Congress
TUR    Temporary Unattached Register
WFTU  World Federation of Trade Unions
WOW   Women of the Waterfront